Children & Books

Sixth Edition

Children & Books

Sixth Edition

Zena Sutherland
The University of Chicago

Dianne L. Monson
University of Washington

May Hill Arbuthnot

Part Five: Areas and Issues
edited by Dorothy M. Broderick

Cover and part opening illustrations
by Charles Mikolaycak

Scott, Foresman and Company
Glenview, Illinois

Dallas, TX   Oakland, NJ   Palo Alto, CA
Tucker, GA   London, England

Library of Congress Cataloging in Publication Data

Sutherland, Zena.
  Children and books.

  "Part 5: Areas and Issues edited by Dorothy M.
Broderick."
  Bibliography:
  Includes index.
  1. Children's literature—History and criticism.
I. Monson, Dianne L., joint author.   II.   Arbuthnot, May
Hill, 1884–1969, joint author.   III.   Title.
PN1009.A1S879   1981   809'.89282   80-23537
ISBN 0–673–15377–0

Preface
to the Sixth Edition

Children and Books is meant for all adults who are interested in bringing children and books together, but it is designed particularly for classes in children's literature in English and education departments and in library schools, in colleges and universities.

Since the first edition of *Children and Books* over thirty years ago, children's books have achieved a recognition and children's literature is being accorded a respect long overdue. The body of children's literature has grown enormously, courses in the subject have multiplied, and some of the best writers today are devoting all or part of their time to writing children's books. Realization that children's literature both reflects the values of our society and instills those values in children has made increasing numbers of adults aware that children's literature is a part of the mainstream of all literature and that, like adult literature, it is worthy of our respect both for what it is and for what it does.

The title suggests the dual nature of the book's approach. The emphases are on understanding children and their needs, on perspectives and background, on criteria and types of literature, and on artists and authors. In a sense, *Children and Books* has a *major-author* approach. It is impossible to describe all of the good books that have been written for children, but it is possible to introduce readers to the works of most of the major authors and artists of the past and present. The major-author emphasis should spare the reader, particularly the new student, from floundering in a sea of titles.

Children and Books is primarily about books; since the field is so broad, to include other media would mean giving them superficial treatment that would not do them justice. There are, however, some discussions of other media in Parts Four and Five; and the bibliographies for those parts, as well as the Adult References in the appendixes, refer the reader to articles and books on related media.

Organization and Revision

With each edition of *Children and Books*, the authors and the editors have been conscious of the need to reflect changes in our society by new emphases in the text, and to reorganize the text to reflect more accurately the changes in the ways in which children's literature is taught.

In this sixth edition, newly designed, Part One is an overview of children's needs and interests, the range of books for children, types of and criteria for evaluation of children's literature, and history and trends. The first two chapters are new. Chapter 1 describes the state of children's literature today, considering its status, contemporary trends in publishing, and such influences as cultural pressures, economic conditions, censorship, and concepts gained from the knowledge acquired by leaders in the field of child development. Chapter 2, "Understanding Children," examines that knowledge more closely, surveying both the basic needs of children and those aspects of major developmental theories that are most pertinent to children's experiences with literature.

Part Two discusses artists and their illustrations, and includes a chapter on books for the youngest, reflecting a growing area of emphasis in children's literature and education. In Part Three, the types of literature are explored: folk tales, including tall tales; fables, myths, and epics; modern fantasy; poetry; modern fiction and historical fiction; and biography and informational books. In all chapters the text and the bibliographies have been brought up to date, with criteria for each genre discussed at the beginning of the relevant chapter.

Part Four, Bringing Children and Books Together, deals with methodology, discussing the role of the adult and the techniques to be used in introducing children to literature and in evaluating and encouraging their responses to literature.

Part Five, which considers areas and issues relating to children and their books, has been substantially reorganized, with new articles on censorship, research, children and television, and mainstreaming. This section includes bibliographies and suggestions for research.

The Appendixes are Book Selection Aids, Adult References, Publishers and Their Addresses, Children's Book Awards, and Pronunciation Guide. There is a Subject Index in addition to the Author, Illustrator, Title Index.

Special Features

Throughout the discussions of books, authors, and artists, and set off from the text, are "Viewpoints," brief statements from books and articles, not necessarily representing the authors' viewpoint in *Children and Books*, but suggesting some issues to explore.

The bibliographies are extensive, with books pertinent to chapter discussions listed by author and title under Adult References at the end of each chapter, and books for children, separately listed and often divided into subcategories, in all the chapters on types of children's literature. Books mentioned in the text are not annotated; additional entries are. Some out-of-print books are included since they are still available in collections. Each reader undoubtedly will miss one or more favorite books; unfortunately, space limitations necessitate some omissions, even of books the authors would have liked to include. The age levels are suggestions only, as children of the same age often differ markedly in reading skills, interests, and social maturity. Since the text stresses the importance of books about minority groups, symbols are used in many of the bibliographies to denote books that emphasize blacks, Chicanos and Puerto Ricans, Native Americans, and religious minorities, so that such books may be more accessible to readers.

To facilitate the finding of information sources, all adult references and book selection aids are listed, together with annotations and full bibliographic information, in Appendixes A and B at the end of the book. To facilitate the finding of material about authors and artists, all references to major author or artist discussions are singled out in the index by the use of boldface type.

Acknowledgments

For various kinds of assistance in the preparation of this sixth edition, grateful acknowledgments are due to the following people:

for her editing of Part Five: Areas and Issues, Dorothy M. Broderick, University of Alabama;

for the articles in Part Five, Dorothy M. Broderick, Carol A. Emmens, Theodore C. Hines, Alice P. Naylor, Anne Pellowski, and Susan Steinfirst;

for their valuable suggestions as reviewers, Joan W. Blos, University of Michigan; Catherine Bowles, Brigham Young University; Dorothy M. Broderick; Shirley Lukenbill, University of Texas; Bette J. Peltola, University of Wisconsin—Milwaukee; and Steven Yussen, University of Wisconsin—Madison.

for their unflagging patience and guidance, Louise Howe, JoAnn Johnson, and Victoria Stewart, the editors;

for her keen sensitivity to the needs and capabilities of children, Iona Kirk Monson;

for his sage counsel, moral support, and sustaining sense of humor, Alec Sutherland.

Zena Sutherland
The University of Chicago

Dianne L. Monson
University of Washington

Table of Contents

Children *&* Books

Sixth Edition

PART ONE:

Knowing Children and Books

Chapter One: *Children and Books Today*

Book lovers young and old know that there is no pleasure exactly like the moment when book and reader meet and are just right for each other. At the simplest level, that moment is what those of us who work with children and their books are working for. The sense of wonder and satisfaction may be instantaneous, as when a child recognizes, with delight, the familiar excitement of waiting for a visitor and the feeling of Beverly Cleary's Ramona, on the very first page, ". . . twirling around trying to make herself dizzy," or as when a child finds, deeply touched, that he or she cannot forget the poignant ending of *Charlotte's Web,* or even when an informational book is found to contain exactly the facts a child is looking for. The point is that the book has truly affected the reader. Most of us remember such books from our childhood. It isn't a ho-hum-isn't-that-interesting kind of experience; it's exciting, exhilarating.

While the roles of children have changed substantially in this century and the kinds of books published for them have also changed, the moment of enchantment when a child hears or reads for the first time about Ramona, or Charlotte, or Tom Sawyer, isn't very different from the moment of enchantment when children of long ago heard or overheard a grandmother or a tribal storyteller tell the story of the cleverness of Anansi or the magic of Mouse Woman. It is that moment of discovery that we hope to bring to all the children with whom we work. Their delight is our delight.

Adults working in the field of children's literature today find themselves involved with questions of censorship, reading levels, fair representation of ethnic minorities and sex roles, and children's access to materials and services, as well as other serious issues. However, we must not forget that the center of all such concerns is the meeting of a child and a book, an event that we want to make happen over and over again, for as many children as possible, and with as much satisfaction as possible.

That's basically what *Children and Books* is all about: gaining a knowledge of a broad variety of fine children's books, recognizing the diversity of children, and learning both children's changing preferences as they mature, and the ways in which we can bring children and books together—learning to help make the meeting a happy one.

One of the tenets upon which *Children and Books* is based is that love of literature can be a positive and enriching part of everyone's life. Learning to love reading and to enjoy good books in childhood can be the start of a life-long habit that brings pleasure and knowledge. Most children do not have easy access to a wide range of good books, they do not necessarily encounter the best old and new authors, and often they do not know how to seek out books.

Many children learn to read without learning to love reading. The recognition of children's literature may be greater today, and the number of books published may be larger than in 1947 when the first edition of *Children and Books* was published, but a whole new set of problems faces us in getting books into the hands of children, from financing to censorship or to the passive domination of television. Children are not born loving good books; neither are they born hating to read. They can be encouraged and influenced in either direction, and that is where we can hope to make a difference.

As adults who are involved with children and their books, and who are committed to bringing them together, we should ask and try to answer a number of questions:

First, what is children's literature? How can we define it?

Second, what is its present state and where does it seem to be going in the 1980s?

Third, what influences are shaping the books now being published?

What Is Children's Literature?

Consider the pattern of a child's day: Amy reads an ad on the cereal box as she eats breakfast, stops on her way out to read the weather forecast on the TV screen, and asks her mother what a long word in the newspaper headline means. On the school bus she reads a comic. In class she reads her textbook, the instructions on the blackboard, and a note passed by her best friend. Reading is an important part of Amy's life. What part of all this—if any—is children's literature?

Is every book that children read a part of their literature? Their textbooks aren't, save for a language arts anthology here and there. Does children's literature consist, then, of books that children read of their own volition? Not comic books, and not the adult science fiction book borrowed from a parent. Nor is children's literature the same thing as adolescent literature, although the line dividing the two is hazy, and is at times crossed in either direction.

Today, publishing for children has become highly specialized, and there are separate bodies of literature for children and for young adults. Books written for younger adolescents are often popular with readers who have not yet reached their teens. Since those who make

judgments may be swayed by either the popularity or the literary quality of such books, they may be assigned in reviews, book lists, or library collections, to both groups. Publishers usually designate in their catalogues and on book jackets whether a book is intended for children or for young adults, and the decisions of teachers, librarians, or reviewers may be based on the publishers' designations. The lack of sharpness in the dividing line between the two age groups is compounded by the fact that children's reading patterns are highly individual; two children of the same age may differ markedly in their tastes, their ability to comprehend, their reading interests, and their reading responses. One child may read and weep over *Charlotte's Web*, while the other may feel he or she has outgrown it and prefer a contemporary problem novel intended for older readers. In sum, it is easy to say where children's literature begins: with books for preschool children. It is not so easy to say where it ends and adolescent literature begins, although the books themselves may have been published as distinctly-labeled entities or shelved in separate parts of a school or public library.

Is there a way to define children's literature other than specifying what it is not? There are no rigid or absolute definitions and there are differences of opinion among the experts. Some maintain that anything children read and enjoy is a part of their literature. Most authorities in

Viewpoint

Literature gives us an experience that stretches us vertically to the heights and depths of what the human mind can conceive, to what corresponds to the conceptions of heaven and hell in religion. In this perspective what I like or don't like disappears, because there's nothing left of me as a separate person: as a reader of literature I exist only as a representative of humanity as a whole. We'll see in the last talk how important this is.

No matter how much experience we may gather in life, we can never in life get the dimension of experience that the imagination gives us. Only the arts and sciences can do that, and of these, only literature gives us the whole sweep and range of human imagination as it sees itself.—Northrop Frye, *The Educated Imagination*, Indiana University Press, Bloomington, 1964, p. 101.

the field, however, hold that children's literature consists of books that are not only read and enjoyed, but also that have been written for children and that meet high literary and artistic standards. This second position is the one on which this book is based.

When we consider books that have been specifically written for children, it is clear that their literature has had a comparatively short history. Few children of the seventeenth or even the eighteenth century could read, but those who could shared such adult delights as *Aesop's Fables* or Arthurian legends. These books were of course not designed for them; children's appointed reading fare of this period was, save for the rarity like *Mother Goose* or *Little Goody Two Shoes*, primarily educational. There were, therefore, two quite distinct kinds of books read by children: the useful, didactic books that were written to instruct them in manners and morals, and the adult books they read for pleasure. Because they have been loved by generations of children, some of these adult books, like *Robinson Crusoe* and *Gulliver's Travels*, have come to be regarded as a part of the literary heritage of children. Today, as in the past, some children enjoy reading adult books, particularly if the

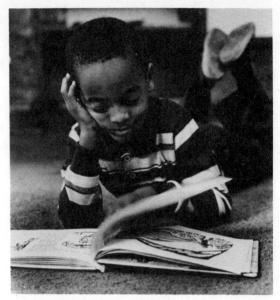

Photograph by Ken Heyman.

books are on a subject in which they have a special interest, or if such books are currently popular and much discussed.

There is today an amazing variety of material in print that is intended for children: picture books, some without text and some designed to clarify concepts or give information, some to tell a story; easy-to-read books, invaluable for the beginning reader and the poor reader; books written with a simple vocabulary but a sophisticated subject or plot, the so-called "high-low" books for the older reluctant reader. There is poetry for children; folk literature that includes tales, myths, fables, epics, and legends, many of which have appeared in handsomely illustrated single-tale editions for use with younger children; modern fantasy that includes imitations of folk tales, science fiction, and original, fanciful tales; historical fiction and biographies; animal stories, sports stories, and mysteries; family stories and problem novels; realistic fiction about people of almost every country or racial or ethnic group. There are informational books on hundreds of topics, and how-to-do-it, or make-it, or play-it books by the dozens. They are in every public and school library, in bookstores and drugstores and airports, on supermarket racks and corner newsstands. There are reading kits, paperbacks and comic books, and children's magazines—and a

Viewpoint

The aim the writer sets himself is the same as that of the magician—to penetrate to the secret, beating heart of life; and by touching it, marvellously to transmute one set of circumstances to another. His method is the same. Instinctually he senses that words are inherently magical, and that by setting one with another he may formulate the language which is his spell. Yet intellectually he is aware that words may be defined only to the extent of ensuring their correct use in context, and all creative writing is an attempt to solve the contradiction this imposes.

In the work of the children's writer, also, there must always be a delicate balance held between the intellectual and the instinctual approach to words—childhood itself being that highly-specialised time when language has as much novelty to emotional and physical experience as to the intellectual. The small child, particularly, relates novel perception so closely to the concept of language that his grasp on the inherent magic of words could also be argued as instinctual.—Mollie Hunter, "The Limits of Language," *Talent Is Not Enough*, Harper & Row, New York, 1976, p. 109.

great deal of print published for adults but read also by children. It is clearly important, therefore, that adults who want to encourage an appreciation of good books be able to discriminate, in this mass of print, between the pedestrian or ephemeral and the distinguished, and know what is going on today in the world of children's literature.

Where Is Children's Literature and Where Is It Going?

It was not until the twentieth century that children's literature was taken seriously enough to warrant a special place in the academic or publishing worlds. There had always been some advocates of its importance, as is evident from the books that were published in the nineteenth century, but it was not until the early 1900s that the first courses designed to train special children's librarians were established at the Carnegie Library School. While books for children had been published by major houses, it was not until 1918 that the first separate children's department was established by Macmillan. Doubleday followed suit nine years later, and other publishers then rather quickly conformed and also set up separate children's sections under the aegis of children's book editors. Today, however, children's literature no longer needs to justify its existence. Although there

Photograph by Marion Bernstein.

are those who refuse to admit that children's literature is a part of the whole body of literature, considering it to be of lesser importance or quality, for most of the literary and educational world the immense importance of children's literature need not be belabored.

Between 1900 and the 1980s, vast changes have taken place in our society and, as in the past, those changes have influenced children's books and are reflected in them. Our culture today has a greater awareness of the variety of children, children who have always been with us but who have not found their counterparts in books as they do today. There is an infinite variety among them: they are bright, average, and dull; they are rural, urban, suburban, migrant, and small-town; they come from happy homes and homes torn by tension. Black, white, Native American, Appalachian, Chicano, Nisei; loved and cherished, unloved and neglected; bookworms and nonreaders—boys and girls whose needs to identify, to develop, to feel pride in race and acceptance in the community are being studied and served. The enormous range of books available today reflects an awareness of the differences among children as well as of the similarities.

Children's literature also reflects much of the conflict and controversy in our society regarding moral standards and life styles. While authors still produce a steady stream of fantasy, humorous stories, poetry, sunny picture books, and informational books, some of the books written today for this diversity of children have been highly controversial. It is clear, especially when we look at the last two decades, that change has become a predominant fact of life, accelerating at such a pace that there has been confusion about traditional values. Many of the enduring values of the past are reflected in books for children, but so are the values of a contemporary society that is less secure and more mobile than earlier generations knew. The children of the 1980s who watch television by the hour are familiar with the mores and the conflicts of the rest of the world, as well as with those of their own country. Television, to a greater extent than any of the other communications media, has made children more sophisticated. Some adults may deplore such sophistication in children and in their books, but the response of authors and publishers to children who are well aware of crime, violence, contemporary sex patterns, and other inescapably evident facets of our society has been to include these facets in books. They are not in all books, and there is a noticeable difference from genre to genre, but there are few kinds of books that do not, today, give evidence of changing times.

While some of the changes have aroused controversy, in many ways children's books, taken as a whole, are better in this century—and even in the last few decades of this century—than they were in the past. They cover more subjects in which children have an interest; the informational books are more accurate and candid. Although every period of the last century produced some outstanding books, the quality of writing in fiction, both realistic and fanciful, is generally much improved. The art in books today includes every medium and every style; while some illustrations are mediocre or awkward, there are also paintings and line drawings of superlative quality. Despite the criticism from some adults, children have welcomed the candor that is evident in trends in contemporary publishing.

One of the subjects that is treated with frankness is death, both the process of dying and the adjustment of those bereaved. In books for younger children the focus tends to be on the death of a pet or on the death of an old person; in books for older children the societal aspects of aging and death are explored: senility, loneliness, the act of dying, and the spectrum of

Viewpoint

One thing that emerges clearly is that most . . . trends are pragmatic phenomena—they derive from market and/or need. So it goes back to the consumer, and you, dear reader, set the trends. Please make them good ones, I beg of you. The thing to keep in mind is that all trends start somewhere—with a prototype that is frequently the brainchild of an author who is lucky enough to have an editor who refuses to think in terms of trends. In my case, the refusal to believe in trends in what I publish comes from my staunch belief in the minority—if *I* really love a book, there's got to be a kid like me somewhere—and even if it develops that the audience and therefore the market for the book is a very select minority indeed, it was still worth publishing.—Ann Durell, "Goodies and Baddies." Reprinted by permission from the December 1969 issue of the *Wilson Library Bulletin.* Copyright © 1969 by the H. W. Wilson Company.

burial practices. In some books there is an emphasis on the range of emotions experienced by those who mourn.

There has also been a veritable flood of books dealing with the handicapped, from such simple stories as Joe Lasker's *He's My Brother*, a sympathetic view of a slow learner, written for the primary grades reader, to *Who Are the Handicapped?*, a sober assessment of the positions of the handicapped in our society by James Haskins. Factual books describe the range of mental, emotional, and physical handicaps, with the greatest number devoted to the latter, and there are novels about children who suffer from these handicaps and who adjust to or overcome them. There are photodocumentaries about real children, many of them expressing the child's desire for acceptance and understanding as well as giving information about a specific handicap. As the movement for mainstreaming (inclusion of the handicapped in the regular classroom) grows, there will probably be more of these books. Not only do they help the handicapped child feel that a disability is not so onerous that it cannot be mentioned in children's books, they also help children who are not handicapped understand that their handicapped classmates are children like themselves, sharing the same needs and pleasures and, above all, able to do many things for themselves.

In response to the feminist movement and a rising protest against sexism in children's books, there have been more biographies of women, more books in which female protagonists play active roles, more girls' sports stories, more reflections of women's careers that realistically parallel today's society, and less depiction of stereotypical sex roles for both males and females, young or old. Third world presses and feminist publishing houses, both proliferating, have contributed to this growing trend in publication.

With increased awareness of, and concern for, the rights of children, those who create and produce children's books have responded with books about children's legal rights, about the social agencies that deal with children, about children as investors, and about children's rights in personal relationships. Some of these books incorporate facts about children's rights into stories about child abuse or the plight of children in foster homes—or, as in Katherine Paterson's touching story of a loving foster

The Changing View of Children in Illustration

1

3

The illustrations of any period reflect the concepts of that time about the role of children and of the family, as well as of what children's books should be. In the first drawing, all attention—even that of the dog—is centered on the father, reflecting the structure of the Victorian family. In Kate Greenaway's picture of children playing, the play is decorous and the children prim; no adult participates in such pastimes. Books of this period were meant to buttress the strong role of the family in society, and to reinforce the idea that children were innocent little creatures easily led astray; they were heavily didactic as well as moralistic. In the third picture, the didacticism is paramount; although sentimentalized like the others, its message is stronger: children who ignore the guidance of adults are in grave danger.

1. Illustration from *British Workingwoman*, 1874.

2. Illustration by Kate Greenaway for "The Village Green" from *Little Ann and Other Poems*, 1883, by Jane and Ann Taylor. Published by George Routledge & Sons. (Original in color)

3. Illustration, "The Dangerous Cliff," from *Furze and Heather for Rainy Weather* in *Birdie's Book*, 1880.

9

5

4

READING for FUN

6

The same static quality is evident in *The Japanese Twins* (1912); although the interest in the foreign and the exotic was strong, the children are just as proper as the little Victorians, and the text is just as didactic. The illustration from *Here, There and Everywhere* (1928), has much of the same quality as the earlier pictures. The children are still from a white, conservative, middle-class background, still prim and obedient. In the 1935 Book Week poster, the four children of a white, well-to-do family are as sedate as ever. The 1944 Book Week poster, however, shows a break in the pattern: World War II was dragging on, people were aware that global understanding might alleviate future conflict and that books could help citizens of the future in such understanding. Although the children's faces have a similar smiling sweetness, the poster presages the end of the all-white world in children's books.

4. Illustration by Marjorie Flack, p. 66. From Dorothy Aldis, *Here, There and Everywhere.* Copyright 1927, 1928, by Dorothy Aldis. Published by Minton, Balch and Company, New York, 1928.

5. Illustration by the author, from *The Japanese Twins*, by Lucy Fitch Perkins. Published by Houghton Mifflin Company. Copyright 1912, and renewed 1940 by Lucy Fitch Perkins. Reproduced by permission of the publisher.

6. Poster by Richard Floethe for 1935 Book Week, sponsored by The Children's Book Council.

7. Poster by Nedda Walker for 1944 Book Week, sponsored by The Children's Book Council.

UNITED THROUGH BOOKS

BOOK WEEK
NOVEMBER 12-18, 1944

7

8

9

Another change in the illustration of children is seen in *Ellen Tebbits* (1951): a more realistic depiction. These children are drawn with humor, they reflect (and even exaggerate) popular conceptions of sex roles, and the interaction between them is apparent. The world of children's books had become big business by this time, and adults were well aware that their audience wanted books that entertained as well as those that taught. The realism and the action of *Chie and the Sports Day* (1965) also reflect such changes; these children far more real than the Japanese twins, and the emphasis is on their similarity to children in other parts of the world rather than their differences. Here's a hint, also, of the breakdown of stereotypical sex roles, as Chie participates in a school sports event. The "Book Power" poster echoes the mood of the 1960's, both in the organized protest and in the awareness of children's rights. The knowledge gained from educational and psychological research had changed society's concept of children; they were no longer seen as malleable puppets to be controlled by adults.

10

8. Illustration by Louis Darling, p. 23. From Beverly Cleary, *Ellen Tebbits*. Copyright 1951 by Beverly Cleary. Published by William Morrow and Company.

9. Illustration by Kazue Mizumura from *Chie and the Sports Day* by Masako Matsuno, reprinted with the permission of Philomel Books. Illustration Copyright © 1965 by Kazue Mizumura. (Original in color)

10. 1969 poster by Emily McCully for the fiftieth anniversary of Book Week, sponsored by The Children's Book Council.

11

12

Hello, Aurora (1966) presents a strong statement of contemporary ideas on sex roles: Aurora's mother is a lawyer, and father, a doctoral student, stays home to study and care for Aurora and her brother. This is a new concept of family life, implying changes in both the roles of parents and the relationships between children and parents. In the next picture, there is a concept of play that differs radically from the restrained scene in the Greenaway book: adults and children play together, and there is a marked freedom in the dancing figures. *One Summer Night* (1977) depicts a multi-ethnic neighborhood; unlike the symbolic mingling of faces in the 1944 poster, these are people who live together, and the urban environment in which they are shown is far from the middle-class milieu of earlier illustrations. In *The Wentletrap Trap* (1978), the members of a Bimini Island family have a natural, casual look that is quite unlike the stiffness of the Victorian family. The emphasis is not on the fact that the characters are black but on the affection and concern felt by each for the others, and both text and pictures show respect for another culture and its customs and values.

13

mother in *The Great Gilly Hopkins*, on the security found in some foster homes.

Certainly the many books by, for, and about black people have constituted one of the most significant of recent trends in children's books. There were comparatively few such books earlier in the twentieth century, but the 1960s and 1970s produced a spate of them, long overdue—books that have faced the problems of black people with candor, fiction in which the characters are drawn with depth, nonfiction in which black history and contemporary issues are explored, poetry in which black pride and black protest are expressed. The fiction in particular is indicative of the growing maturity of the literature for and about black children, for characters are no longer chiefly concerned with winning white approval or acceptance but with facing all the problems of growing up. More and more, these books are being produced by black authors and illustrators.

Books about other minority groups are also growing in number, although demand still exceeds supply. They are to some extent products of the trend in writing and publishing books about blacks that helped raise the consciousness—and perhaps the conscience—of the children's book world, but this movement has also been fed by the growing group consciousness of all minority racial and ethnic segments of the society. There have been increasing numbers of books about Chicanos, Native Americans, Puerto Ricans, and Asian Americans. Today, many more books are being written in, or translated into, Spanish. In a world in which pride in identity is stressed, it is especially important that no child feel that his or her family's customs or belief or language are unworthy of recognition and respect, and such recognition is, belatedly, emerging.

There are two significant trends in nonfiction today. One is the inclusion of subjects that were formerly considered only of adult interest, subjects like pollution, international relations, the stock market, controversy over nuclear power plants, and other topics of concern to the knowledgeable children of our time. A second trend is seen in the care given to producing books that are accurate and authoritative, that provide sources and appendices, and that are written in a straightforward manner. Less often do we see today the book that condescends to young readers; children are treated as a serious audience.

Viewpoint

Our children are black and white, as we ourselves are. We believe that they deserve to have the best books possible, not just mediocre ones, or "will do" or token integration books. We want them to have books that reflect genuine experiences and offer honest explanations. We want them to have books in which they see people like themselves and people whose facial colors and facial profiles are different from theirs. We want them to have books that show the beauty of Blacks and the beauty of Whites, the beauty of Indians and the beauty of Orientals, the beauty of Chicanos and the beauty of Puerto Ricans. The beauty of all. The beauty of people.—From *Starting Out Right* edited by Bettye I. Latimer and funded by the Office of Equal Educational Opportunity, Bulletin No. 2314, 1972, p. viii. Reprinted by permission of the Wisconsin Department of Public Instruction.

Almost all of these trends are combined in contemporary biographies: more representation of minorities, more varied depictions of women in a broad spectrum of careers, more candid portraits of prominent people as human beings with faults and foibles, and more careful documentation and accuracy in writing about all of them.

The United States is not alone in these trends. For example, an increasing number of the books originating in England are also concerned with minority group members and their participation in the society. The same group consciousness and search for identity can be seen in Canada, where increased numbers of books have reflected the Canadian multiethnic heritage and where a national children's book center, the establishment of several new book awards, and the founding of several journals devoted to children's literature all attest to a sense of growing pride in Canadian children's literature.

Designated the International Year of the Child, 1979 was a year of accelerated recognition and observance of the importance of the child throughout the world, but it was a year of focus rather than of beginning. The international cooperation that was emphasized in that year had been going on for some time and had been reflected in the world of children's books, for a growing trend has been the publication, in North America, of books from other countries, many of them in translation. Thus, children are becoming familiar with life as it really is in other countries, getting a quite different view than did the children of earlier generations who read stories in which the children of other countries were a group of stiff little paper dolls in national costumes who ate exotic foods, and had strange customs (i.e., not like ours).

There are, of course, differences among countries in their ideas of government, their philosophies, their customs, and their concepts of how children should be educated and how they should behave, and what should be in their books. We are concerned chiefly, in this book, with our own culture and our own children and their books. To understand what is in our children's literature and why it is there, we must consider some of the factors that play a part in shaping the content of children's books.

Influences on Children's Literature

We have examined some of the trends, the kinds of books that are being published today, and some of the subjects and themes that they contain. The content of children's books is shaped by several factors: by what we know about children and about their needs and expectations, by the economic realities of publishing, and by the culture in which we all live and which, consciously or unconsciously, we reflect as authors, illustrators, editors, reviewers, and educators in the school, the library, and the home.

There are many theories of child development. Some of the ideas of Erik Erikson, Lawrence Kohlberg, Abraham Maslow, and Jean Piaget will be examined in Chapter 2, especially as they relate to children's abilities, preferences, and perceptions in reading. We know that children respond to and identify with characters in the books they read, and that literary experiences may influence their developing sense of values. Children need physical and emotional security; they need beauty and order; and they need both stability and change. They have a sense of justice and an insatiable curiosity. We know that they can bear unpleasant truths, although most children do not live with despair. Most of today's children's books

recognize these needs and capacities, and attempt to respond to them in some manner.

Developmental psychologists and educators tell us that at different stages of childhood, children's reading is influenced by their ability to comprehend language and concepts, and by the interests they develop at succeeding stages of development. Knowledge about what children need, want, and can absorb, obtained through psychological and educational research, has indeed been a factor in guiding those who produce and evaluate children's literature, but decisions on manuscripts are not based solely on such knowledge, for other factors also influence the decision to publish or not publish.

Children's book editors are eager to produce the best books they can, but they are also aware that their books must sell. If they don't sell, the publishing house stops producing children's books—and indeed, the vagaries of financial conditions in the 1970s led to the closing or the takeover of several children's book departments. While most adult books are sold directly to the consumer, the primary market for children's books is the library, either school or public. As federal subsidies for the purchase of books evaporated in the 1970s, publishers could not afford to carry old titles, however good, for which there was a lessening demand, with the result that many long-standing favorites went out of print. As production costs rose along with other costs in our economic system, so did book prices, and the market became increasingly competitive. One result is that editors can no longer afford to take chances on books that don't have a reasonably high profit potential. There are, of course, exceptions; nearly every editor will at times take a chance on a manuscript he or she thinks has unusual qualities even if it doesn't promise material rewards. On the whole, however, manuscripts tend to be chosen for publication because at least moderate success can be predicted—that is, because their authors have already been successful, or because they follow a successful pattern, or because they are on a topic which is of great current interest. This means, to a degree, repetition. There is also a tendency to emphasize, in promoting books, those that are most promising, especially those for which there may be lucrative motion picture or television tie-ins. That means people hear about fewer books. Since most of the tie-ins tend to be for books for older readers, such promotional em-

Viewpoint

To be aware of having been a child—and who am I but the child I was, wounded, scarred and dirtied over, but still essentially that child, for essence cannot change—to be aware of and in touch with this fact is to have the whole long body of one's life at one's disposal, complete and unfragmented. You do not chop off a section of your imaginative substance and make a book specifically for children for—if you are honest—you have, in fact, no idea where childhood ends and maturity begins. It is all endless and all one. And from time to time, without intention or invention, this whole body of stuff, each part constantly cross-fertilizing every other, sends up—what is the right word?—intimations. And the best you can do, if you are lucky, is to be there to jot them down. This being there, this being present, is important, otherwise they are lost. Your role is that of the necessary lunatic who remains attentive and in readiness, unself-conscious, unconcerned, all disbelief suspended, even when frogs turn into princes and when nursemaids, against all gravity, slide up the bannisters. Indeed, on a certain level (not immediately accessible, perhaps, but one which we deride at our peril), the frog is lawfully a prince and the transcending of the laws of gravity—up the bannisters or up the glass mountain, it really makes no difference—is the proper task of the hero. And heroes and their concomitant villains are the stuff of literature.—P. L. Travers, "I Never Wrote for Children," *The New York Times Magazine*, July 2, 1978, p. 19. Copyright © 1978 by the New York Times Company. Reprinted by permission.

phasis is less true of books for younger children. Bookstores, always wary of overstocking, have grown even more cautious. The opinions of reviewers and of compilers of bibliographies and other book selection aids influence what goes into library collections and is, therefore, accessible or not accessible to children. And, because the market is competitive and because critics are scrutinizing books more carefully than they did in the past, editors are turning more frequently to subject-matter experts to check and screen manuscripts. Thus informational books for children are more accurate and authoritative than they have been in the past. In sum, the economic influences at work in our society have had a profound impact on what is published for children as well as what older books stay in print.

Therefore, while the responses of authors and editors to the known needs and interests of children are influences on the content and the quality of books, some of the influences on the authors and editors themselves stem, it is clear, from stresses that are part of the society. Publishing is affected by economic pressure, despite the fact that the total number of children's books published annually has remained fairly constant and that paperback publishing of children's books rose 700 percent in the 1970s.

Economic pressure is, however, only one of the ways in which our culture influences our books. Books are also affected by the socio-political atmosphere, by the causes and protest movements of our time, by the media that pervade our lives and by the society's standards and mores. Children's books are affected, perhaps above all, by the society's concept of the roles of children: what and how they should learn, what their obligations and privileges should be, what rights they have, and what their books should contain. Not least, the content of books may be affected by what adults think they should *not* contain. What is, or is not, or ought to be, in children's books is and will undoubtedly continue to be one of the most controversial aspects of children's literature.

If we examine the whole phenomenon of reflection of the culture in children's books, it is apparent that some of the values or the messages are deliberate, and that some are inherent, for all authors—differ as they may—are themselves products of the culture in which they live.

The influence of a society on books produced for children is nothing new. In colonial times, the sternly pietistic attitude of the culture and its belief that human beings, young as well as old, trembled always at the brink of corruption and damnation was forcefully conveyed in the material that was written for children. In Victorian times, children's books reflected the ornate language patterns of the era, the sanctity of the home and the near-sanctity of the parent, and the prevalent preoccupation with manners and strict morals. There were differences among authors, but taken as a whole, the body of children's literature mirrored the society. And so it does today.

Throughout the last several decades of the twentieth century, there has been a shifting of standards in our society, a loosening of restraints. The Civil Rights movement, protest against the Vietnam War, and Watergate were among the disturbing events that affected the sociopolitical atmosphere. The demands for equality by women, homosexuals, older citizens, ethnic minorities, and the handicapped became stronger and more widely articulated. The divorce rate and the illegitimacy rate, especially among young adolescents, climbed. So did drug addiction. So did adherence to various consciousness-raising groups. Not all of these affected every child directly, but almost every child knew about them. Many children today have seen more violence and more sexual titillation on television dramas and in the news than children of the past knew of; almost every child has heard rough language that earlier generations either never heard or didn't hear until they were adults.

All of these facets of the contemporary culture, deplorable as some may find them, are facts. As facts they first appeared in adult literature and, following a pattern of long standing, after a time lag they began to appear in books for adolescents, then in books for younger children. Through the late 1960s and in the 1970s, one taboo after another was broken in books for children.

Many adults were horrified when, in Louise Fitzhugh's *Harriet the Spy*, a child was left to a servant's care by her preoccupied parents, spied on adults, and was sent to a psychiatrist. They were horrified by the fact that menstruation was discussed in the sequel, *The Long Secret*, by the mention of sex-play between boys in John Donovan's *I'll Get There. It Better Be Worth the Trip*, by the drawings of a naked boy

Viewpoint

A good book is one that, for its time, is wise, sane, and magical, one that clarifies life and tends to improve it. The qualification *for its time* is important: at certain historical moments, wisdom is rage and sanity is madness. At times when reasonableness and goodness are live options, an artist ought to be reasonable and good, speaking calmly, as if from the mountaintop; at other times, as in Jacobean England and some parts of the world at the present time, it may be that one cannot support those same lofty ideals except with dynamite. Either way, true art treats ideals, affirming and clarifying the Good, the True, and the Beautiful. Ideals are art's *ends*; the rest is methodology.—John Gardner, *On Moral Fiction*, Basic Books, New York, 1978, pp. 132–133.

in Maurice Sendak's *In the Night Kitchen*, by a hundred other books that deal with sexual problems or patterns, that included profanity or four-letter words, or that were candid about the delinquency of parents or a case of child abuse. Children, for the most part, took these matters in stride. This was not all that different from what they saw on television, read in newspapers, and saw in films.

No longer is children's literature treated as though it did not exist in the same world as that in which our children's lives are lived. The candor that is in children's books today touches almost every genre. There are picture books that use toilet terms or that are concerned with divorce or death; there are stories about seven-year-olds who worry about father's unemployment. There are poems, some by children, that bitterly protest against racial injustice; there are biographies that tell the whole truth about hitherto-sacrosanct prominent people. There are informational books about rape and alcoholism.

Some adults defend these books on the grounds that children know about these things anyway, that the knowledge will not hurt them, and that we should tell them the truth so that their knowledge will be accurate and because we owe them nothing less than the truth. This, too, is part of our culture, for our society has given children more freedom than those of past generations had, and it has promulgated the recognition of the rights of children. At the same time, there has been a backlash, a current of conservatism, and among the conservative elements in our society there is a strong feeling that it is the responsibility of adults to protect children in their books as in their lives.

Since the standards and the goals of groups and subgroups differ, there is little agreement on where protective lines should be drawn. Most of the criticism of books focuses on language and subjects of which the critics disapprove; some express total disapproval, some feel that it depends on how a subject is handled, and some hold that a subject may be included in books for older children but not in those for younger children. When adults feel such condemnation, it is seldom passive. What they want to do is censor books, although few censors or would-be censors apply the term to themselves.

The problems of censorship are intricate and difficult, and they are not diminishing today.

Because censors want to impose their wishes and because their wishes cover a broad spectrum and may indeed be conflicting, the librarian or teacher may be under pressure by a minority to make a change or decision that affects the majority. The ramifications of the censorship issue are discussed more fully in the article on that subject by Alice Naylor in the Areas and Issues section at the end of this text and are related to Theodore Hines' article on the limitations of children's access to materials. The fear of censorship can engender timidity in teachers and librarians, especially in smaller communities, and can lead to self-censorship as a protective device.

Related to censorship is the back-to-basics movement in education, a backlash reaction to experimental and ancillary programs. It is often the conservative groups who object to what they feel are educational frills who also question or condemn what they consider offensive in the content of children's books, and who challenge the moral and ethical concepts in some contemporary books, while they defend those books that instill values which they approve. Similar concerns, however, may be expressed by those who consider themselves liberal but who also feel sincerely that there are some books that are too sophisticated for children. Adults who oppose censorship are not necessarily lacking in concern for values education; they simply do not consider it their prerogative to insist that books that conflict with their individual ideologies must be kept out of the hands of children, at least not by banning such books from the market or the bookshelves of schools or libraries. Whatever their ideas, it is clear that all adults concerned with children's books feel that what children read is important.

Like adults, children read for many reasons: to dream, to learn, to laugh, to enjoy the familiar and explore the unknown. They read for sheer pleasure and they absorb, in their reading, those facets of books that reflect the developmental values appropriate to their particular stage of growth. Books may help children build a concept of the society in which they live and of their roles in that society; books may help shape and sharpen their concepts about other people and may contribute to their self-understanding. Like adults' books, children's books range from the inaccurate and the mediocre to the reliable, the beautifully written, and the permanently significant. Like adults' books,

Viewpoint

Someday civilization must be simplified and made more just and decent and honest for everyone. Air and water must be cleaned up. Cities that would appall Dante must be made habitable. We must discover how to live together in moderate amity. It will take a good deal of imagination to bring so many opposites into harmony, to create an inwardly desired cohesive order out of so many contradictory compulsions, to design a civilization permitting all decent variables to live together in at least a semblance of understanding.

Perhaps only because they are fresh to experience, children are insatiably curious, wanting to understand everything. Our adult curiosity seldom ranges beyond the small worlds in which we earn our living and relax from our labors. We are not notably addicted to a passionate desire for tolerance. If only we might add a child's fresh eagerness to be friendly to our trove of all recorded knowledge, then our social, economic, and political disorder might begin to assume reasonable clarity.—Harry Behn, *Chrysalis*, Harcourt Brace Jovanovich, 1968, p. 27.

children's books have become more sophisticated and frank in their use of language and their treatment of subjects once considered taboo.

There are books that are timeless in their appeal and books that transcend age barriers. Children's literature in recent years has taken new directions, explored new themes, and opened up possibilities for developing new insight. In the chapters that follow, these changes will be discussed and the criteria for evaluation of individual books will be analyzed. Writers, artists, and editors have joined forces to make many of today's children's books so varied in content, beautiful to look at, and high in quality that adults as well as children enjoy them. The treasures must be sought for, but they are there, a wealth of fine books old and new.

The goals of *Children and Books* include helping concerned adults identify what is good and lasting in the vast array of children's books; describing the criteria by which such books may be evaluated; clarifying the needs, interests, and stages of understanding in children; and suggesting ways in which children and books may be brought together in order to provide children not only with books they will enjoy reading but also with the best in children's literature.

Adult References[1]

ARBUTHNOT, MAY HILL. *Children's Reading in the Home.*

CHILD STUDY ASSOCIATION OF AMERICA. *Insights: A Selection of Creative Literature About Childhood.*

COHEN, MONROE, ed. *Literature with Children.*

COLES, ROBERT. *Children of Crisis.*

COLES, ROBERT, and MARIA PIERS. *Wages of Neglect.*

CROSBY, MURIEL. *An Adventure in Human Relations.*

DUFF, ANNIS. *"Bequest of Wings": A Family's Pleasures with Books.*

———. *"Longer Flight": A Family Grows Up with Books.*

EGOFF, SHEILA, G. T. STUBBS, and L. F. ASHLEY, eds. *Only Connect: Readings on Children's Literature.* Article by Anthony Storr. "The Child and the Book."

FADER, DANIEL N., and ELTON B. McNEIL. *Hooked on Books: Program and Proof.*

FRANK, JOSETTE. *Your Child's Reading Today.*

GERSONI-STAVN, DIANE, ed. *Sexism and Youth.* Part 3, "Books."

HASKINS, JAMES. *Diary of a Harlem Schoolteacher.*

HAVILAND, VIRGINIA, ed. *Children's Literature: Views and Reviews.* Chapter 3, "Children: Their Reading Interests and Needs."

HAZARD, PAUL. *Books, Children and Men.*

HEINS, PAUL, ed. *Crosscurrents of Criticism: Horn Book Essays, 1968–1977.*

HENTOFF, NAT. *Does Anybody Give a Damn?*

———. *Our Children Are Dying.*

HOLT, JOHN. *How Children Fail.*

———. *How Children Learn.*

———. *What Do I Do Monday?*

HYMES, JAMES LEE. *Understanding Your Child.*

JAN, ISABELLE. *On Children's Literature.*

JENKINS, GLADYS G., and HELEN S. SHACTER. *These Are Your Children.*

KUJOTH, JEAN SPEALMAN. *Reading Interests of Children and Young Adults.*

LARRICK, NANCY. *A Parent's Guide to Children's Reading.*

McPHEE, JOHN. *The Headmaster.*

MAYERSON, CHARLOTTE LEON, ed. *Two Blocks Apart: Juan Gonzales and Peter Quinn.*

REID, VIRGINIA M., ed. *Reading Ladders for Human Relations.*

RICHARDSON, ELWYN. *In the Early World.*

ROBINSON, EVELYN ROSE. *Readings About Children's Literature.* Part 1, "The Child and His Reading."

RUDMAN, MASHA KABAKOW. *Children's Literature: An Issues Approach.*

SADKER, MYRA POLLACK and DAVID MILLER. *Now Upon a Time: A Contemporary View of Children's Literature.*

SEBESTA, SAM L., and WILLIAM J. IVERSON. *Literature for Thursday's Child.*

SILBERMAN, CHARLES. *Crisis in the Classroom.*

SMITH, LILLIAN. *The Unreluctant Years.*

TANYZER, HAROLD, and JEAN KARL, eds. *Reading, Children's Books, and Our Pluralistic Society.*

TUCKER, NICHOLAS, ed. *Suitable for Children? Controversies in Children's Literature.*

TUROW, JOSEPH. *Getting Books to Children: An Exploration of Publisher-Market Relations.*

WALSH, FRANCES, ed. *That Eager Zest: First Discoveries in the Magic World of Books.*

WHITE, DOROTHY MARY NEAL. *About Books for Children.*

WHITE, MARIAN, ed. *High Interest—Easy Reading.*

WHITE, VIRGINIA, and EMERITA SCHULTE. *Books About Children's Books: An Annotated Bibliography.*

WINN, MARIE. *The Plug-In Drug: Television, Children, and the Family.*

---

1. Complete bibliographic data are provided in Appendix B.

Chapter

Two: Understanding Children

Children are engaged in a continuous process of learning about themselves and their world. As they mature, that world expands from the home and parents to siblings to peers and, eventually, to people and places they know about but may never actually see. In order to function successfully in society, children must learn to know themselves, to achieve self-identity. They must also learn about social interaction and recognize ways in which they are like as well as different from others. Those are psychosocial ways of thinking. At the same time, children are experiencing tremendous growth in cognitive abilities and in motor skills. Development continually goes on in all three of those areas; thus childhood is a crucial stage of life.

Adults who are responsible for planning educational experiences will find that knowledge of child development is helpful in making literature a meaningful part of children's lives. Developmental psychologists seek to discover what children are like at various stages of maturity. What are their needs? What are their value systems at different ages? What are children's skills and abilities at different ages? What are their reading interests? Some of the questions relate more directly to literary experiences than others. Nevertheless, the research and theory based on these questions have much to tell us that is important to the study and use of children's literature.

An understanding of children's needs, cognitive abilities, psychosocial crises, and moral and social development can help us in selecting the kinds of books and reading-related activities that will be most satisfying to a child of a particular age. In this chapter, we shall briefly survey those aspects of the developmental theories of Abraham Maslow, Erik Erikson, Jean Piaget, Lawrence Kohlberg, and Albert Bandura that are most pertinent to experiences with literature.

Maslow's great concern was for humanistic education and so his thinking focused on the individual's self-actualization as fulfillment of his or her potential. Erikson's psychosocial theories are concerned with the development of individual identity and also with the individual's ability to function in society. Piaget has written most extensively about children's cognitive development, but his work deals with moral growth as well. Kohlberg's work is concentrated primarily on moral development, describing a succession of stages through which an individual moves with increased maturity. Bandura has studied the influence of social models on children's learning. Such theories have implications for the selection of literature because they suggest something about children's interests and needs at various stages of development. They also help to identify cognitive and verbal skills which may influence ability to deal with such literary elements as point of view, flashback, and foreshadowing. Knowledge of child development can be of use both in selecting books and in planning activities to enhance the literary experience.

Maslow's Hierarchy of Needs

Abraham Maslow's views about the education of children were firmly based in a humanistic philosophy of education. He was most concerned with the discovery of identity and humanness, believing that, as we go most deeply into ourselves, seeking individual identity, we also recognize more clearly the whole human species. When we become fully human, we learn not only how we are different from others, but how we are similar to others. Although Maslow worked largely with adults, he had much to say about children as well, applying his ideas to people of all ages. Maslow believed that human needs form a hierarchy, from basic physiological demands to the need for self-actualization. Needs at the lower levels must be reasonably well satisfied before the individual will turn his or her attention to those at the higher levels. For example, a child who is always hungry is not likely to develop much intellectual curiosity.

Maslow identified five levels of basic human needs: physiological, safety, belongingness and love, esteem, and self-actualization, as well as cognitive and aesthetic needs. In the pages that

*Viewpoint*_____

Education must begin, as Dewey concluded his first article of belief, "with a psychological insight into the child's capacities, interests, habits," but a point of departure is not an itinerary. It is just as mistaken to sacrifice the adult to the child as to sacrfice the child to the adult. It is sentimentalism to assume that the teaching of life can be fitted always to the child's interests just as it is empty formalism to force the child to parrot the formulas of adult society. Interests can be created and stimulated. In this sphere it is not far from the truth to say that supply creates demand, that the provocation of what is available creates response. One seeks to equip the child with deeper, more gripping, and subtler ways of knowing the world and himself.—Jerome S. Bruner, *On Knowing*, Belknap Press of Harvard University Press, 1962, pp. 117–118.

follow, we will look at some of the needs children have at various levels. Directly or indirectly, books can help children deal with these needs. This is especially true of books written by sensitive, thoughtful adults who are perceptive observers of children and who remember their own childhoods vividly. Such books not only may help children better understand themselves and others but also should help adults better understand and empathize with their own children and with the children in their classrooms and library centers.

Children's Need for Physical Well-being

A child's sense of physical security ordinarily begins in a mother's or father's arms, includes the routines of eating and sleeping, and comes gradually to encompass everything that gives a sense of comfort and well-being. For both children and adults, material satisfactions may become the chief symbols of security. The old fairy tales were told by people who seldom had enough food to eat or clothing to keep them warm. So their tales are full of brightly burning fires, sumptuous feasts, rich clothes, glittering jewels, and splendid palaces. These are humanity's age-old symbols of physical comfort and security. Undoubtedly some of the appeal of the old *Elsie Dinsmore* stories and of Frances Hodgson Burnett's *Sara Crewe* and *The Secret Garden* lay in this same incredible affluence which the characters enjoyed.

Today, as in earlier times, material security is uncertain, and it continues to be one of people's most pressing needs. So in books as in life, the lack of security and the hunger for it often supply the motive for the action and the theme of the story. In *M. C. Higgins, the Great* by Virginia Hamilton, thirteen-year-old M. C. fears that a sliding spoil heap will destroy his mountain home; he plans ways to get the family to a safer place.[1] In Vera and Bill Cleaver's *Where the Lilies Bloom*, the doughty young heroine struggles fiercely to keep her family together, lying about her father's death to prevent the authorities from separating the children, and out-maneuvering the landlord to keep the house in which they live.

---

1. *M. C. Higgins, the Great*, as well as most of the other books mentioned in this chapter, is discussed elsewhere in the text. See the Index for relevant page references.

In book after book, the search for security will spellbind young readers of the old fairy tales or of the modern realistic books or of the biographies of heroes and heroines, all the way from "Dick Whittington" to *Tom Sawyer* and Harriet Tubman.

Children's Need to Love and Be Loved

Every human being wants to love and to be loved. This need is so pressing that when it is frustrated in one direction it will provide its own substitutes, centering upon almost anything from lap dogs to antiques. Children, too, set up their own substitutes. A child who feels out of favor or rejected may lavish an abnormal amount of affection upon a stray cat, perhaps identifying with the unwanted animal. In John Donovan's *I'll Get There. It Better Be Worth the Trip*, Davy's whole devotion is given, after his grandmother's death, to his dog, Fred.

It is in the family that children learn their first lessons in the laws of affectionate relationships. Books, too, exemplify these relationships. In Ellen Parsons's *Rainy Day Together*, the whole theme is love between parents and children. In Sharon Bell Mathis' *The Hundred Penny Box*, there is a loving relationship between Michael and Aunt Dew. Not only does children's sense of security develop from these family patterns, but also their whole approach to other people and later their search for and treatment of a mate.

Sometimes stories about family life may interpret to fortunate children the significance of their own experiences which they might otherwise take for granted. A child may find traces of his own father in the father of Andy in Joseph Krumgold's *Onion John* or share the longing of the fatherless boy in Charlotte Zolotow's *A Father Like That*. She may recognize her own mother in Mrs. March of *Little Women* or a beloved grandmother in Tomie de Paola's *Nana Upstairs and Nana Downstairs*. Children may share the tender, protective relationship of a girl for a mentally retarded brother in Betsy Byars's *Summer of the Swans*. Through reading books such as these, they may find that their own family will mean more to them. On the other hand, children who have missed these happy experiences may find in family stories vicarious substitutes which will give them some satisfaction and supply them with new insight into what families can be.

From *The Summer of the Swans* by Betsy Byars. Illustration by Ted CoConis. Copyright © 1970 by Betsy Byars. Reprinted by permission of Viking Penguin, Inc.

Another aspect of this need to love and to serve the beloved is the recognition of this same need in other creatures. Stories about wild animals defending their mates or their young or the herd are tremendously appealing. So, too, are stories of pets, steadfast not only in their affection for their own kind but for their human owners as well. Such stories as Sheila Burnford's *The Incredible Journey* have played upon this appeal. *A Heart to the Hawks* by Don Moser is a moving example of a boy's love for a wild creature. Fine animal stories of all kinds will undoubtedly contribute to breaking down the young child's unwitting cruelties toward animals and to building sensitivity to their needs.

Finally, the need to love and to be loved,

which includes family affection, warm friendships, and devotion to pets, leads the child to look toward romance. In children's literature, romance begins early but remains impersonal. The fairy tales, with their long-delayed prince or their princess on a glass hill, are little more than abstract symbols of what is to come.

A flood of novels of romance for teenagers has been produced. While many of them are incredibly stereotyped and predictable, there are growing numbers of competent authors who write well and respect their young readers. They supply realistic pictures of family life, with boys and girls looking away from their families to a serious interest in someone of the opposite sex. And many of these books deal frankly with some of the heartbreaking problems of young people. Zoa Sherburne, for example, in *Too Bad About the Haines Girl,* handles with dignity the problem of the unwed mother. The establishment of a desirable romantic attachment is one of the most important tasks of growing up. A well-written story that shows all the complications of romance, its pitfalls and disappointments as well as its happiness, can provide young people with needed guidance in an approach to one of life's most vital problems.

Out of family affection and trust grows a kind of spiritual strength that enables human beings to surmount dangers, failures, and even stark tragedies. Such books as Louisa May Alcott's *Little Women* and the *Little House* books by Laura Ingalls Wilder leave children with the conviction that decent, kindly people can maintain an inner serenity even as they struggle with and master the problems that threaten them.

Children's Need to Belong

Growing out of the need for security is the need of every human being to belong, to be an accepted member of a group. "*My* mama," or "*My* big brother," the young child says with pride. At first these experiences are merely egocentric extensions of children's self-love, but at least they are beginning to line themselves up with their family, and this acknowledgment of others marks their growing sense of belonging to a group. In time, these same children will identify with friends, school, and later with city and country, and perhaps with a world group.

So children's literature reflects this expanding sense of the group. It begins with stories about the family, the school, and the neighborhood in warm books such as Martha Alexander, Ezra Jack Keats, and Charlotte Zolotow write for the preschool child, Carolyn Haywood for the primary age, and Beverly Cleary for the middle grades. These represent happy group experiences. But there are also stories about children who must struggle anxiously to be liked by the people whose acceptance they long for. Eric in Malcolm Bosse's *The 79 Squares* and Jessica in Marilyn Sachs' *A Secret Friend* are good examples. The story of the child who wins a respected place in groups that once rejected him or her is a satisfying theme from "Cinderella" to *Good-Bye to the Jungle* by John Rowe Townsend.

With the growing consciousness of a world in which all people are brought closer by the developments in communications and transportation, with children's increased awareness of such problems as war, pollution, and racial and social unrest, there is an urgent need for books in which ethnic groups gain not tolerance but respect, books that attack the injustice and discrimination and apathy still prevalent in our society. The young today are aware of social ills. Exposed to the mass media and to the changing mores of the community, they need books that reflect the world in which they live but offer realistic and optimistic solutions. John Tunis, in his sports stories for the preadolescent and teenager, makes his young readers face fully the extra difficulties that beset youngsters of minority groups in winning a place on the team or in the community. This is the general theme also of Eleanor Estes's *The Hundred Dresses.* In Emily Neville's *Berries Goodman* anti-Semitism is candidly portrayed; in Mildred Taylor's *Roll of Thunder. Hear My Cry,* black people face prejudice; and in Laurence Yep's *Sea Glass,* Craig Chin is a child who seems to be rejected by both of the cultures he tries to live with. Sometimes the problem is not one of winning acceptance but of accepting. For example, in Ann Nolan Clark's *Little Navajo Bluebird,* an Indian child passionately rejects white society and its ways and wants to belong only to her own tribal group. Books like these parallel the need of each individual not only to belong with pride to his or her own group, but to identify warmly and sympathetically with ever widening circles of people. When a child from suburbia is stirred by *Listen for the Fig Tree* by Sharon Bell Mathis or wishes she could know Jean George's Julie in *Julie of the Wolves*, her sense of belonging is widening. A good and honest book can strengthen the pride of the minority member and enrich all who read it.

Children's Need to Achieve Competence

The need for competence—the "organism's capacity to interact effectively with its environment"[2]—is a strong motivating force in human behavior. The struggle to achieve competence begins with the infant's visual exploration, with crawling, grasping, and other primitive activities, and grows into the complex physical or intellectual performances of the expert athlete, mathematician, musician, or scientist. Competence is as satisfying as inhibitions and frustrations are disruptive. To be happy or well adjusted, the child or the adult must have a satisfying sense of competence in one area or another.

In Mary J. Collier and Eugene L. Gaier's study "The Hero in the Preferred Childhood Stories of College Men,"[3] the important factor the book heroes had in common was that they performed their unique feats on their own. Whether it was Hansel from the old fairy tale or the realistic Tom Sawyer, the hero's competence was achieved without help from adults, and his independence was the quality that made him memorable and admired. Achieving competence may become the compensation for rejection and a step toward acceptance. This is a frequent theme in stories for children—the lonely child or the shy teenager who develops competence in some field and so wins the admiration and acceptance of the group. Taro Yashima's *Crow Boy*, Eleanor Estes's *The Hundred Dresses*, Nat Hentoff's *Jazz Country*, and Allison Smith's *Reserved for Mark Anthony Crowder* are all built upon this theme.

The young child's first book heroes and heroines are doers, from Edward Ardizzone's Tim, who survived shipwreck and found his lost parents, to David of the Old Testament, who slew the giant Goliath. In later childhood

Illustration by Jerry Pinkney. Copyright © 1976 by The Dial Press. Used by permission of The Dial Press from *Roll of Thunder, Hear My Cry* by Mildred D. Taylor.

and adolescence young readers enjoy the competence of heroes and heroines in adventure, mystery, and career stories and the achievements of famous men and women in biographies. *Carry On, Mr. Bowditch* by Jean Latham is a splendid, true record of competence independently achieved. More and more books are appearing that describe the accomplishments of members of ethnic minority groups: biographies of Benjamin Banneker, Sojourner Truth, Shirley Chisholm, Martin Luther King, Jr., Cesar Chavez, Maria Tallchief, Daniel Inouye, and many other Americans.

There is a stern negative aspect to this hunger for achievement. The struggle for competence may involve failures and complete frustration. Physical handicaps or mental limitations must be faced and accepted.

In Bernard Wolf's *Don't Feel Sorry for Paul*, there is no appeal for sympathy but a sense of

2. Robert H. White, "Motivation Reconsidered: The Concept of Competence." *Psychological Review*. Vol. 66, No. 5, 1959. p. 297.

3. *American Imago*, Vol. 16, No. 2, 1959.

Photograph from *Don't Feel Sorry for Paul*, written and photographed by Bernard Wolf. Copyright © 1974 by Bernard Wolf. By permission of J. B. Lippincott, Publishers.

purpose and a determination to overcome his handicaps on the part of a seven-year-old who requires three prosthetic devices. In this true story, Paul and his family have such common sense and courage that he attends school, takes riding lessons, and achieves competence with vigor and joy. Jamie, in Joe Lasker's *He's My Brother*, is a slow child whose classmates tease him, although the older brother who tells the story makes it clear that Jamie has his respect and love. Emma Sterne's *Blood Brothers* tells the story of Charles Drew, a black ghetto child, who despite discrimination persisted in his pursuit of a medical career and eventually became a distinguished pioneer in blood research. Stories of such persons who refuse to accept defeat help children in the task of growing up.

Children's Need to Know

Parents often complain about the bothersome curiosity of children. But this need to investigate, to know for sure, is a sign of intelligence. In fact, the keener the child is mentally, the wider and more persistent his or her curiosities

will be. The need to know surely and accurately is a basic hunger and one which books help satisfy.

Books about Africa, desert Indians, birds, plants, stones, stars, rockets and jets, DNA, care of pets, do-it-yourself books, and, of course, dictionaries and encyclopedias properly gauged to a child's needs are all available today. Adults need only discover children's particular interests to find books that will answer their questions reliably, stimulate new curiosities, and set them to exploring further to satisfy their need to know and give them, momentarily at least, a certain intellectual security.

Some books not only provide fascinating information but dramatically exemplify the human need to find out, to know for sure. For example, Thor Heyerdahl's *Kon-Tiki* tells the true story of five young men who set out on the flimsy raft Kon-Tiki to prove their theory of the origin and migrations of the Polynesian people. Hans Baumann's *Lion Gate and Labyrinth* tells the story of Heinrich Schliemann, who also needed to know and whose persistent curiosity and zealous investigations led to the discovery of ancient Trojan ruins.

Children's Need for Beauty and Order

There is still another human need that seems curiously at odds with humanity's more utilitarian search for competence and security of various kinds. It is the need for beauty and order.

A wealth of books is available today to satisfy a child's aesthetic needs—authentic poetry, fanciful tales whose content and style are perfectly suited, books that are beautiful in themselves, books that provide various kinds of aesthetically satisfying experiences, and books that help children grow in their appreciation of beauty and order. Shirley Glubok's series about art in various cultures (*The Art of China, The Art of the New American Nation, The Art of the North American Indian, The Art of Ancient Mexico*) are simply written and related to the way people lived. David Macaulay's *Cathedral, City,* and *Pyramid* are remarkable for their beautifully accurate architectural drawing. *Ballet: A Pictorial History* by Walter Terry and *The Wonderful World of Music* by Benjamin Britten and Imogen Holst are fine examples of books about the performing arts written for children by experts in their fields.

Whether in music, dancing, drama, story, painting, or sculpture, the artist seizes upon some aspect of life and re-creates it for us in a new form. We see it whole and understandable; people, events, and places assume a new dimension beyond the mere chronicling of facts.

People are continually seeking aesthetic satisfaction in one form or another and at varying levels of taste. One may find it in the songs of a folk singer. Someone else finds it in a symphony which exalts the sorrows of life to cosmic proportions. Aesthetic satisfaction comes to the small child as well as to the adult, and the development of one's taste depends not only upon one's initial capacities but also upon the material one encounters and upon how it is presented. A child who has chuckled over Miss Muffet and the spider is getting ready to enjoy the poems of A. A. Milne, and to progress to Walter de la Mare's and David McCord's poetry. A child who has been charmed with Beatrix Potter's *The Tale of Peter Rabbit* might be ready to appreciate the humor and beauty of Kenneth Grahame's *The Wind in the Willows*.

Erikson's Theory of Psychosocial Development

Erik Erikson's developmental theory is based on the belief that development consists of a series of psychosocial crises which individuals must successfully resolve as they mature. Those conflicts involve the person's struggle to achieve individuality and, at the same time, to learn to function in society. The different stages of psychosocial development which Erikson has identified are produced by experiences each child has in interaction with his or her world. Of major importance in early life is the interaction between children and the adults who care for them. Play is also important to human development as children work toward reorganizing their inner perceptions to fit the external world in which they must function.

According to Erikson, every individual moves through an orderly sequence of stages, each of which is more complex. Maturation occurs as the individual ascends from one stage to another. At each stage, the individual is faced with a psychosocial conflict which must be resolved before moving on to the next stage of development. These begin in infancy, with the crisis of *trust versus mistrust*. Erikson's stages two through five are of most interest to students of children's literature.

Early Childhood: Achieving Autonomy

Erikson's second stage of development, described as *Autonomy versus Doubt*, generally takes place from about ages 18 months to three years. During this stage, children are involved in a struggle to be an independent self and yet not to cut this self off from others. There is still a need for support from others, particularly from parents. Play is important for these children because it allows them a means for developing autonomy within their own set of rules. As children progress through this stage, they become more aware of adults other than the parents and of older children in the family. In the main, those who serve in the role of parents are the important "others" and law and order is dominant in terms of the social order that prevails. Children of this age seem to like books that deal with relationships between parent and child, like Frank Asch's *Sand Cake*, Robert Kraus's *Whose Mouse are You?* and Beatrix Potter's *Peter Rabbit*. In the latter, there is also an element of law and order which probably reinforces what children are being taught at this stage. That is not to say that we should limit literature for these very young children to family stories that end on an orderly note, but Erikson's concerns about the development of the individual in relationship to society might serve as a guideline in choosing stories to read aloud.

Middle Childhood: Developing Initiative

The next stage, which takes place at about ages three to six, is that of *Initiative versus Guilt.* During these years, children are increasingly expected to be responsible for themselves and for their toys and other possessions. As this new independence develops, so too does the realization that one's behavior may be in opposition to the behavior of others. Whenever there is conflict with another individual, a sense of guilt is likely to arise. Children also grow toward the cultural mores as their consciences take on some of the functions formerly performed by significant adults. During this period, children ask many questions and through the questioning begin to understand things which had previously been mysteries to them. Play takes on two forms: solitary daydreaming and play with other children in which life crises are enacted. Furthermore, imaginative play enables children to think about their future as well as their present roles.

Erikson's description of children at this stage seems to suggest the importance of acquainting them with literature in which story characters,

Stages in Child Development

Stage	Approximate Age Period	Major Features	Psychosocial Crisis (Erikson)	Cognitive Stage (Piaget)	Moral Stage (Kohlberg)
Infancy	Birth to 18 months	Locomotion established; rudimentary language; social attachment	Trust vs. mistrust	Sensorimotor	Premoral (Stage 0)
Early and Middle Childhood	18 months to 6 years	Language well established; sex typing; group play; ends with "readiness" for schooling	Autonomy vs. doubt; Initiative vs. guilt	Preoperational Preconceptual phase Intuitive phase	Obedience and punishment (Stage 1); Reciprocity (Stage 2)
Late Childhood	6 to 13 years	Many cognitive processes become adult except in speed of operation; team play	Industry vs. inferiority	Concrete operational	Good child (Stage 3)
Adolescence	13 to 20 years	Attainment of highest level of cognition; independence from parents; sexual relationships	Identity vs. role diffusion	Formal operational	Law and order (Stage 4)

Adapted from Philip G. Zimbardo and Floyd L. Ruch, *Psychology and Life,* 10th Edition (Scott, Foresman, 1979), p. 223.

too, experience conflict when their actions throw them into opposition with others. Books will give children a chance to experience along with story characters what it is to gradually take more responsibility for their actions. That brings to mind books like Ezra Jack Keats' *Goggles,* Astrid Lindgren's *Of Course Polly Can Do Almost Everything,* and Rebecca Caudill's *Did You Carry the Flag Today, Charley?*

The quality of play is present in many books published for children in the three-to-six-year group. Many are light and humorous but others are serious attempts to show how children play out their concerns. The child's need to play out some ideas through daydreaming suggests a need to be alone at times. A book such as *Evan's Corner* might appeal to some children who find it hard to be left in peace. Other books allow children to play out their fears and dreams, books such as *There's a Nightmare in My Closet, Peter's Chair,* and *Benjie on His Own.* It would seem essential to offer these children a good balance of realistic fiction and fantasy. Folk literature, too, deals inherently with many themes that have to do with the relationship of an individual to others and to society in general and so it, too, should be included in listening experiences.

Late Childhood: Becoming Industrious

Stage four in Erikson's scheme compares roughly to Piaget's concrete operations stage (p. 31) in terms of the ages involved. This stage, which is reached during ages seven to eleven, Erikson terms "late childhood." It is a stage of *Industry versus Inferiority.* Children operating at this stage appear determined to master the tasks that are set for them. They learn to work together with other children toward a common goal and they are almost constantly engaged in activities that allow them to practice skills the culture requires of them. The conflict of industry versus inferiority is related to a sense that they are inferior if they cannot show that they are competent and so these children are constantly measuring themselves against their peers.

Clearly, a good many of the books published for this age group pose situations in which children strive to be as successful as their peers. A number of books, particularly recent ones, have also focused on the way in which children perceive their parents. *Harriet the Spy, Ramona and*

From *Friday Night Is Papa Night,* by Ruth A. Sonneborn. Illustrations by Emily A. McCully. Text copyright © 1970 by Ruth A. Sonneborn. Illustrations copyright © by Emily A. McCully. Reprinted by permission of Viking Penguin, Inc.

Her Father, and books with one-parent families such as *Friday Night Is Papa Night* make parents an important aspect of the story.

The growing determination of children in this group to master new tasks points to the importance of informational books in their lives. Books that show how to identify birds, how to raise hamsters, how to cook, or how to play baseball all have a potential audience among middle- and upper-elementary age children. Some children may work out the conflict of industry versus inferiority vicariously, reading biographies of people who did succeed or realistic fiction about people who overcome hardships. Colin Thiele's *Blue Fin* involves readers with a boy's struggle to prove to his father that he is a competent sailor. It is representative of the kinds of books which appeal to children in this stage.

Adolescence: Establishing Identity

Erikson's stage of adolescence, ages eleven and upwards, is that of *Identity versus Role Diffusion.* As the name suggests, the focal point now is a search for identity. The development of identity is linked with skill mastery. On a broader level, we might say that it includes cultural identity as well as personal identity, identity as a member of a community as well as identity as an individual. Inner demands often run counter to outer demands, leading to diffusion and some instability. Adolescents grapple with the question of who they will become as well as the question of who they are. They often have a close attachment to their parents, yet at the same time are searching for other associations. Inevitably, the question arises of whether the parents still control them and that, of course, creates friction.

Play changes so that it is more likely to be a role playing and experimentation with attitudes and behavior of adults in society. Adolescents babysit, they participate in sports, and they also belong to gangs and to in-groups. Literature for this group includes a range of realistic fiction which can give them a chance to interact with situations in which other teenagers are searching for identity. That means stories in which characterization is worked out with enough depth so that characters' fears and joys are evident throughout as they strive to discover themselves and to experience success. Walter Dean Myers' *The Young Landlords* and Jean McCord's *Turkeylegs Thompson* are two such books.

Piaget's Developmental Levels

Jean Piaget is frequently quoted by educators who relate his developmental studies to curriculum planning. Piaget's early training was in biology and so it is perhaps not surprising that his method of study depends to a large extent on observation and classification of behavior. He views intellect and affect as always together, like two sides of a coin, believing that human emotion, or affect, evolves from the same primary processes as cognitive development.

Much of Piaget's thinking about the child's cognitive development is based on four kinds of operations. They are assimilation and accommodation, conservation, and reversibility. The first two are closely related, for Piaget's stance is that the child develops units of knowledge about the world, called *schemata*. As the child takes note of new information about the environment, that information is *assimilated* into his or her thinking (schemata) and the thinking and behavior are *accommodated* (changed) to re-

flect those new perceptions. In assimilation the person adapts the environment to his or her own use, though that is limited by ability to consolidate the new experiences with previous experience. Accommodation, the reverse of assimilation, occurs when the individual modifies existing thought structures so as to incorporate the new experiences.

Conservation and reversibility are also related, in a sense. Conservation has to do with the child's ability to deal with the difference between appearances and reality, the difference between making judgments on the basis of surface characteristics and being able to make inferences about the real characteristics that underlie appearances. Piaget's classic example is the young child who believes that a taller and thinner glass contains more liquid than a shorter, fatter glass, even though the child has watched as the water was poured from the short to the tall container. The tendency to deal with surface characteristics may extend, also, to social understanding so that the child forms ideas about people and social situations solely on the basis of outward appearance. Reversibility of mental processes is necessary if a child is to accept the fact that the water in the short and tall glasses is the same amount. That comes about when the child realizes that, by pouring the water back into the short glass, the apparent change (taller, thinner equals more) will be undone.

Both temporal and spatial factors are operating in the ability to deal with reversibility. Probably the clearest application to a child's response to literature lies in the ability to process flashbacks so that the child recognizes that the order in which events are described in a story is not necessarily the order in which they really occurred. On a simpler level, it may have to do with the question of whether a wolf in sheep's clothing is really a sheep, as it would appear, or a wolf, as is really so. Both conservation and reversibility of thinking are operating here.

Piaget's observations of children's behavior led him to believe that development proceeds in four major stages and that all children move through those stages in sequence, though not necessarily at the same pace. Although development is viewed as always proceeding forward, there is generally a stage of transition in which the child vacillates between earlier, less mature behavior and the newly gained competence.

The earliest of Piaget's stages is the period of *sensorimotor intelligence* from birth to approximately age two, or until the appearance of language. During this period, the child is particularly concerned with coordinating movement and action. Words come to represent objects and things. The second stage, the *period of preoperational thought*, spans the ages of about two up to eleven or twelve years. Within that stage, Piaget describes the first phase, from about ages two to four, as *preconceptual*. In this phase, most behavior is based on subjective judgment. A second phase, between ages four and seven, he terms *intuitive*. During these ages, children begin to use language successfully to verbalize their mental activities and they are better able to generalize what they experience. From approximately age seven to eleven, children move into what Piaget calls the *period of concrete operations*. Children who have moved into this stage are able to work through a problem so that they combine performance with a verbal explanation or an attempt to reason out the problem. They begin to apply logic to concrete experiences and things. They are able to handle conservation, as it applies to people as well as to objects, they can deal with reversibility, and they develop an understanding of space and time relationships. The period of concrete operations leads, at age eleven or twelve, to Piaget's fourth stage—the *period of formal operations*, in which the young person is able to think beyond immediate experiences and to theorize about a wide variety of things. During this phase of growth, children develop the ability to apply formal logic to abstract constructions and to experiences which represent an ideal and may be contrary to fact. The two phases of *preoperational thought*, the period of *concrete operations*, and the period of *formal operations* are of greatest interest here.

In thinking of the relationship of Piaget's developmental levels to the selection of literature and literary experiences for children, it is important to keep in mind that many of Piaget's observations involve conceptual situations more related to mathematics and science than to the humanities. Much less work has been done in literature. It is important to note the intensely personal nature of responses to literature. Each reader's or listener's response to a story is colored by his or her background and expectations. We need to keep all these things in mind when we consider Piaget's, or any

other, developmental scheme. Finally, it is important to remember that these are stages, not absolute age designations. Some children may enter a new stage earlier than others and there will be some overlap as children are moving from one stage to another. That is, a child may perform at the preoperational level in some situations and at the concrete operational level in others.

The Preconceptual Phase: Discovering the World

During Piaget's preconceptual phase (ages two to four), children are busy discovering the environment. For that reason, concept books (see p. 97) are important. Tana Hoban's *Look Again*, Donald Crews' *Freight Train*, Stephen Lewis's *Zoo City*, and Ezra Jack Keats' *The Snowy Day* are good books for children interested in their surroundings. Children in this stage are basically egocentric. They are inclined to think in the same way as the children in Martha Alexander's *Nobody Asked Me If I Wanted a Baby Sister*, Marjorie Sharmat's *I'm Not Oscar's Friend Anymore*, and Betsy Byars' *Go and Hush the Baby*—the last about a child on the way to play baseball who is asked to take time out to quiet the baby.

The play of two- to four-year-olds centers on *how* and *why*. Activities that may seem fantasy to adults are realistic to these children. There is much imitation of the behavior of others (including the reading behavior of the adults around them). Imitative scenes in books like Robert McCloskey's *Blueberries for Sal* show story characters imitating the activities of their parents and that, in a sense, plays out the fantasy-into-reality.

Children in the preconceptual stage often explain things that happen by giving life to inanimate objects, for example, if they fall, saying that a toy reached out and tripped them. The animism leads quite naturally to a love for nursery rhymes like "Humpty Dumpty" and "Hey, Diddle, Diddle." More common is anthropomorphism, or humanization of animals, found in many folk tales such as "The Three Pigs" and "The Three Bears." This delight in humanizing inanimate objects and animals is also related to a love for fantasy. Many children begin liking fantasy early, and the interest persists into succeeding stages of development.

From *Blueberries for Sal* by Robert
McCloskey. Copyright 1948 by Robert
McCloskey, © renewed 1976 by
Robert McCloskey. Reprinted by
permission of Viking Penguin, Inc.

The Intuitive Phase:
Relating to the World

As children move into the phase of intuitive
thought, roughly ages four to seven, they shift
from the egocentric "it's me" to "I see what's
happening," becoming able to react realistically
to the environment. Their play shows a new,
extended symbolic imagination so that they can
project themselves into other roles and think in
terms of other people. They are moving toward
conservation in terms of recognizing differences between how things *look* and how they
really are.

They are becoming interested in realistic
fiction, particularly fiction that gives them a
chance to relate to one or more of the story
characters. This includes reacting realistically
to the environment. Children have opportunity
for that when they read books like Martha Alexander's *I'll Be the Horse If You'll Play with Me,*
or Alvin Tresselt's *Hide and Seek Fog.* Marjorie
Flack's *Wait for William* suits the new shift from
egocentric behavior to being able to observe
what is happening.

At this stage, too, children become more able
to project themselves into roles. They can relate
to Charley in Rebecca Caudill's *Did You Carry
the Flag Today, Charley* and they can also begin
to appreciate Charley's good and bad points.
When they listen to books like Fassler's *Howie
Helps Himself,* they can begin to develop a sense
of empathy for handicapped children rather
than stereotyping them as "different." They

project themselves into other roles, too, when
they hear Ezra Jack Keats' *Goggles* or Rachel Isadora's *Ben's Trumpet.* For younger children want
to be like the older ones and, in these stories,
they share the feelings of story characters.

These children tend to perceive each attribute of objects (and very likely also story characters) as an absolute—e.g., a character is seen
as brave or foolish, cunning, etc. This tendency
may be dealt with in several ways in the curriculum. One way is to provide plenty of experiences with folk literature and its typically flat
characters.

A second approach, which might be used in
conjunction with folk tale experiences, involves
selecting realistic and fanciful stories that have
more fully developed characters and giving
children experience with discussion and dramatic activities in which they enter into the stories, playing the roles of story characters. The
growing ability to project themselves into other
roles and to think as others think suggests a
need for experiences with realism in literature.
That means selecting books to read to them
and books for beginning readers that might
give opportunity for talking about the feelings
and motives of characters as well as engaging in
role playing and other dramatic activities that
can enhance response. Such books as Marjorie
Sharmat's *I'm Terrific,* Arnold Lobel's *Days with
Frog and Toad,* and George Marshall's *George and
Martha* give experiences with animal characters. Some books of realism for this age with

more fully developed characters are Bernard Waber's *Ira Sleeps Over* and Evaline Ness's *Sam, Bangs and Moonshine.* Those books allow children to assume the role of another person vicariously. Well directed discussion can help them to experience the conflict that is evident within the character's feelings.

Differences between how things *look* and how they *really are* have not been completely worked out by these students. Children in this stage continue to love fantasy and they should be allowed to read and enjoy fantasy without always worrying about whether or not a story is "real." Maurice Sendak's *Where the Wild Things Are* and Ellen Raskin's *Spectacles* can be fun in this view because they contain elements of both reality and fantasy.

The four-to-sevens in this intuitive phase like animal stories. Many of the stories they choose are fantasy, with anthropomorphic representations of animals. Others, however, are realistic. The older children in this group also enjoy nonfiction accounts. Aileen Fisher's *Listen, Rabbit* and Lynd Ward's *The Biggest Bear* are two books of realistic fiction that appeal. Couple them with classic fantasy such as *The Velveteen Rabbit* and *The Story of Babar*, add Berniece Freschet's *The Web in the Grass*, Tana Hoban's *Big Ones, Little Ones*, and Joanna Cole's *A Chick Hatches* to represent informational books and you have an idea of the range of interests these children have. Exposure to many kinds of literature allows these children to test out some of their growing knowledge about the environment and continue to exercise their creative imaginations.

Illustration by the author, from *The Biggest Bear*, by Lynd Ward. Published by Houghton Mifflin Company. Copyright 1952 by Lynd Ward. Reproduced by permission of the publisher.

*Viewpoint*_____

. . . Childhood is the time when the capacity to think that the supernatural may exist touches the point of believing, or actively wishing to believe that it does so. Childhood is the time when we are more sensitive to atmosphere than at any other period in our lives, when our senses are undimmed, when we respond primarily to emotion rather than to thought. It is the time when we rely on ritual, pattern, and order; for a child's world has small bounds, and to feel secure, he must know what these bounds are. To be master in his world he must have a formula which controls all that operates within it.—Mollie Hunter, "The Otherworld," *Talent Is Not Enough*, Harper & Row, New York, 1976, pp. 97–98.

The Period of Concrete Operations: Organizing the World

As children enter the period of concrete operations, approximately ages seven to eleven, they reach a new level of self development that allows them to understand some of the ways they are related to other people. Through play and language, they seek to understand the physical and social world. This seems to imply the importance of realistic fiction which will encourage children to interact with story characters and, through that interaction, to participate in conflict resolution. Books by Beverly Cleary and by Mary Stolz often present day to day situations in which children find that their selves are in conflict with other selves. Books like Paula Fox's *The Stone-faced Boy*, Marilyn Sach's *The Bears' House*, and Katherine Paterson's *The Great Gilly Hopkins* show conflict *within* self as well as conflict with others.

For children in the concrete operational period, concepts of time are more fully developed than at the preceding stage so that ideas about the past, even historical past, become real and important. As children move through this stage of development, they grow in capacity to appreciate historical fiction and the biographies of real-life heroes such as Daniel Boone, Rosa Parks, or Cesar Chavez. Historical fiction set in the U.S., such as Carol Brink's *Caddie Woodlawn*, Jean Fritz's *The Cabin Faced West*, Patricia Gauch's *This Time, Tempe Wick?*, and Ferdinand Monjo's books appeal to children at this stage. Historical fiction set in other countries, such as Katherine Paterson's *The Master Puppeteer* and

Johanna Reiss's *The Upstairs Room,* can appeal to children who are nearing the end of this stage of development.

During the concrete operational period, children also begin to move beyond one-dimensional thinking so that they are able to relate one event to a system of interrelated parts. They are now able to conceive of an event from beginning to end or, vice versa, perceive it backwards from conclusion to beginning. This would seem to suggest the beginning of ability to handle flashbacks in literature. *Mrs. Frisby and the Rats of NIMH* appeals to older children in this group, as does Jean George's *Julie of the Wolves.* If a reader is to process flashback so that it becomes an integral part of the story, it is necessary to hold all of the story segments in a sort of short-term memory and then to rearrange the parts sequentially, as they occurred. Such a procedure calls upon aspects of both conservation and reversibility, as Piaget views the concepts, and requires more sophisticated thinking than children at the early and middle sections of the stage can probably handle.

Just as children who are moving through Piaget's concrete operational period begin to handle events of the past, so they also become able to think in terms of the future. That ability helps to prepare them not only for fantasy which may go back in time, but for science fiction, which generally goes forward in time. *Tom's Midnight Garden,* which moves between past and present, is often read by children at this stage. The more mature readers also enjoy Madeleine L'Engle's *A Wrinkle in Time* and John Christopher's *The White Mountains* trilogy, books which reach into the future.

Piaget says that the seven-to-elevens who are in the concrete operational period internalize moral values. At the later part of the stage (nine to eleven), they are very interested in examining the rules that govern their lives. They seem to have more respect for established standards than for adult authority. In most realistic fiction for this age group, however, a character's personal desires still carry more weight than individual adults or established authority. Henry Huggins' determination to get his dog home on the bus is an example. In fact, *Henry Huggins* and *Ramona the Pest* seem to embody that sense of self. In other genres, the popularity of books such as *The Pushcart War* suggests a willingness of the older children to identify

Illustration by Louis Darling is reproduced by permission of William Morrow & Co., Inc. from *Henry Huggins* by Beverly Cleary. Copyright 1950.

with story characters who question rules and traditional ways of operating. The fantasy of Zilpha Keatley Snyder, Susan Cooper, and Ursula Le Guin also involves readers with situations in which conventional wisdom is brought into question. An examination of rules and what happens when rules and adult authority are rejected might be a logical topic for discussion of literature with children who are moving toward the upper range of this concrete operational stage.

The Period of Formal Operations: Developing New Insights

From approximately age eleven to age fifteen, children progress through what Piaget terms the period of formal operations. As they move from the stage of concrete operations into this new stage, they make great gains in ability to think beyond the present and to formulate theories about physical and social aspects of life. They develop the qualities necessary for true communication so that they are able to take another's point of view and enter into discussion to exchange knowledge. The ability to assume point of view is relevant to both social and intellectual growth. It suggests the importance of encouraging interaction with literary characters and situations. Beyond basic communication, children at the formal operations stage are able to establish whether information is valid by comparing what they see and hear about things (their perceptions) with what they know and deduce about those things. In terms of literature, clearly there is a need to provide experience in contrasting fiction with nonfiction accounts, particularly contrasting historical and biographical fiction with real biography and historical material. There is an increase in ability to link parts and wholes, recognizing a sense of order and the rules that impose that order. This ability might make young people more aware of relationships within the structure of a story, as for example the way that episodes build toward a climax and resolution.

Children at the eleven-plus stage are moving from stereotypical thinking to greater ability to understand and empathize with others and to be more aware of their relationships within the family and within the community. Madeleine L'Engle's *Meet the Austins* gives readers a chance to be involved in situations that call upon their ability to interpret characters' needs and feelings in terms of their relations to one another. A more recent book, *The Great Gilly Hopkins*, does this, too, focusing on the experiences of a foster child. Nicholasa Mohr's *Nilda* shows the life of a barrio child and M. E. Kerr's books, *Is That You, Miss Blue?* and *Love Is a Missing Person*, are compelling stories for children who are ready to interact with the problems and emotions of the teen-age characters. The formal operations stage might be described as a time when readers become more able to suspend disbelief and to enter into a story which is far removed physically from their lives but which embodies the universal concerns and beliefs these children are becoming aware of and able to incorporate into an expanded view of the world.

The Development of Moral Values

Piaget's views of morality are mainly concerned with the individual's respect for the rules of the social order in which he or she lives and with the person's sense of justice. Piaget has suggested that the bases of moral judgment change with the child's age, and he makes a number of predictions about reactions which might be expected at different ages. Intent is an important factor. An older child will believe that it is worse to break a tree branch while stealing apples than to drop a tray of dishes while setting the table, with the emphasis on intent. A younger child would think it worse to break the dishes because more damage was done, being more concerned with the result of the act.

A younger child considers a particular action to be "right" or "wrong" whereas an older child considers the behavior in its context. What is right in one situation may not be right in another. A younger child behaves correctly out of fear of punishment by others while the older child's proper behavior is a result of his or her own decision making. As to the nature of punishment, a more mature individual believes that the punishment should take a form that makes up for harm done or that teaches the person to be better in the future. More mature individuals also take into account the needs and points of view of others when deciding on an action. When misfortunes occur, the more mature person is able to evaluate their causes realistically and does not necessarily view them as retribution for individual behavior.

Viewpoint

I am hoping for characters, perhaps I am *searching* for characters, that children can identify as human, characters they can understand, with whom they can sympathize, or with whom they can themselves identify. Out of this type of shared experience a boy or a girl might catch on to the idea that trying to know your friend is better than judging him. They might come around to the idea that all kinds of people have all kinds of problems, grown-up people even, and other kids, and his or her personal load of guilt or doubt or anxiety might begin to weigh a little less. Yet this is not the primary aim; perhaps it is pompous to have an aim at all; if it is possible to express a *hope* in words, it is simply to continue a shared journey of discovery into the wonderland of human experience.—Ivan Southall, *A Journey of Discovery: On Writing for Children*, Macmillan, New York, 1975, pp. 35–36.

Kohlberg's Stages of Moral Development

Piaget identified a number of developmental trends in morality. Lawrence Kohlberg has systematized Piaget's thinking and developed a hierarchy of moral development.

Although a number of value hierarchies have been developed, Kohlberg's formulation is perhaps the most widely used. At this point, however, it is not clear whether people may function in more than one of his stages at a time and whether they always progress toward a higher stage. There is some reason to think that children (and adults too) may regress to an earlier stage under certain conditions or in special situations. Kohlberg has recently become involved in the development of educational programs designed to facilitate moral growth in terms of this hierarchy, even though some critics have been vocal in pointing out that such education, as Kohlberg structures it, may actually be a means of imposing "middle-class" values on society as a whole.[4]

Value Formation and the Schools

There was a time when teaching and learning moral values was an accepted part of schooling. The McGuffey Readers are good evidence of that. Values were prescribed and taught directly. More recently, however, even though some people have come to believe that the schools have no business dealing with personal values, others in the community cite a lack of values in the young as evidence that moral education is needed. That leads to the question, then, of how moral education is related to the study of literature.

Essentially, all good literature deals with values. Children who read widely and hear stories read and told cannot help but interact with story characters involved in decision making, in formulating personal values, in learning to empathize with the difficulties of people the world over. We can help children to select books that will give them some experience with the valuing process. Even beyond that, we can take note of their responses and can encourage young

4. See Howard Muson, "Moral Thinking: Can It Be Taught?" *Psychology Today* (February 1979), pp. 48ff.

readers to observe the actions of story characters and to think through the motivations for, and consequences of, their actions. Going from there, children can talk about similar situations in their own lives and determine whether the outcome was good or whether they would behave differently if given another chance.

Selecting literature that will play a role in value formation requires attention to characterization and to the kinds of situations that throw story characters into conflict with the values of their society. Such books as Madeleine L'Engle's *A Swiftly Tilting Planet* and Betty Sue Cummings' *Let a River Be* are powerful stories that give readers plenty of opportunity to consider their own values as well as those of the story characters.
and give readers plenty of opportunity to consider their own values as well as those of the story characters.

The advantage of literature as an approach to developing moral values is that the situations in well-chosen literature are realistic. At the same time, they are not as threatening to a reader as they would be if they were part of his or her life. That allows a degree of objectivity in deciding whether the characters acted morally and what alternate forms of behavior would have been more appropriate. The problems with a literature-centered strategy have to do with the selection of material and strategies that members of the community find acceptable. More will be said about potential ways of dealing with moral development in Chapter 15.

Viewpoint

... I became deeply dissatisfied with much of the literature intended to develop the child's mind and personality, because it fails to stimulate and nurture those resources he needs most in order to cope with his difficult inner problems. The pre-p. 'mers and primers from which he is taught to read in school are designed to teach the necessary skills, irrespective of meaning. The overwhelming bulk of the rest of so-called "children's literature" attempts to entertain or to inform, or both. But most of these books are so shallow in substance that little of significance can be gained from them. The acquisition of skills, including the ability to read, becomes devalued when what one has learned to read adds nothing of importance to one's life.—From *The Uses of Enchantment: Meaning and Importance of Fairy Tales* by Bruno Bettelheim, Alfred A. Knopf, New York, 1976, p. 4.

Kohlberg's Stages of Moral Development

Bases of Moral Judgment	Stages of Development
Level I. Moral values reside in external happenings, in bad acts or quasi-physical needs rather than in persons and standards.	*Stage 0.* Premoral. *Stage 1.* Obedience and punishment orientation. The child defers to superior power or prestige, or wants to stay out of trouble. *Stage 2.* The child realizes that right action satisfies its needs and occasionally others'. Self-interest is paramount. "Trade-offs" are valued: "You scratch my back and I'll scratch yours." Loyalty and gratitude don't enter in.
Level II. Moral values reside in performing good or right roles, in maintaining the conventional order and pleasing others.	*Stage 3.* The "good boy–nice girl" orientation. The main thing is to get approval by pleasing and helping others. The child conforms to majority or "natural" behavior. *Stage 4.* The "law and order" orientation. Doing one's duty, respect for authority, and maintaining the social order for its own sake are seen as "moral" actions.
Level III. Moral values reside in principles separate from those who hold and enforce them, and apart from a person's identification with the enforcing group.	*Stage 5.* The legalistic orientation. The rights of others as well as individual rights are recognized. Rules agreed upon by the whole society are accepted as binding, yet looked upon as subject to change. Rights and duties are derived from the social contract. *Stage 6.* The conscience or principle orientation. Universally agreed upon ethical standards rather than "rules" guide moral conduct. The ideas of justice, respect for others, and equality are examples of moral "ideals."

Based on Lawrence Kohlberg, "Moral and Religious Education and the Public Schools: A Developmental View," in *Religion and Public Education* (ed. Theodore R. Sizer). Copyright © 1967 by Houghton Mifflin Company. Used by permission. Courtesy of the National Conference of Christians and Jews.

Bandura's Social Learning Theory

It is not possible, within this chapter, to deal with all of the theories of learning which may be useful background in book selection for children. The study of children's acquisition of social behavior has generated a good deal of interest, however, and warrants some comment even though it cannot be given full coverage.

Traditional learning theory, particularly that of B.F. Skinner, has emphasized the viewpoint that behavioral change is based on principles of operant conditioning—that is, behavior that is reinforced (rewarded) in some way will be learned. Albert J. Bandura and other theorists, however, perceive human learning in a somewhat different way, asserting that children learn vicariously—that is, by observing the behavior of social models. Bandura has shown that learn-ing may occur when a child observes the behavior of others even when the child does not reproduce the responses made by the model and does not receive any reinforcement. According to that theory of social learning, whether or not a child will imitate the behavior of the model depends not only on the behavior but also on the consequences of that behavior—that is, whether the model is rewarded or punished. Therefore, vicarious reinforcement plays a role in the theoretical framework.

It seems evident, too, that the differences between the sex of the child and the sex of a model have some influence on the extent of imitation likely to be seen. The prestige of the model plays a role, too, with high prestige models more likely to be imitated than low prestige models. Furthermore, the behavior of the model is more likely to be imitated when it is reinforced by a high-prestige person than by one with low prestige.

There is a fairly obvious extension of social learning theory to selection of literature and literary experiences for children, for many books have models with whom young readers can identify. If the factors described above are indeed operating, then it would be important to provide books with high prestige role models and books in which the protagonist's behavior is reinforced by a high prestige person. For young children that might suggest books in which the models are parents and other adults in positions of authority. For older children and certainly for adolescents, it would suggest books in which models are peers or cultural heroes such as athletes or people associated with popular culture. Further, it would seem to suggest the importance of characters and situations in the stories which are closely enough related to children's own lives so that they can identify closely with the motivations for behavior and the outcomes of the behavior.

Books to Help Children Grow

In this chapter, we have looked at some information about children's development based on the theories of Abraham Maslow, Erik Erikson, Jean Piaget, Lawrence Kohlberg, and Albert J. Bandura. That information highlighted aspects of social, psychological, and cognitive development, including moral development and social learning. Since children are maturing in so many ways as they progress through the elementary grades, all of these theoretical bases can be of use to people who work with children's reading.

Children's Reading Interests

If we are aware of the changes that occur in children's needs and interests as they mature, we are better able to provide them with books that will help them to grow into each new stage of development. The observations about children's development described in this chapter tell us something about the probable reading interests of children at various stages. Although the ties to reading interests are, in most cases, somewhat subjective, they are nevertheless useful in working with individuals as well as with groups of children who are similar in age.

Research dealing specifically with children's reading interests can confirm or add information to what we can deduce from theories about developmental needs and cognitive and moral development. During the early 1970s, a large number of reading interest studies were reported. Generally, those studies were carried out within a limited geographical area and focused on a fairly narrow age group. Thus we must be cautious about generalizing the results too broadly. Nonetheless, where trends in interests appear across some of the studies, they seem to suggest that children in the early primary grades are more interested in fantasy than in realistic stories. Studies of the interests of second graders suggest that boys like biography and informational books and girls like animal stories.[5] As children move into the upper elementary grades, there is an evident shift toward interest in realistic fiction. One study of the interests of third, fourth and fifth graders indicated that boys were more interested than girls in adventure, tall tales, historical fiction, sports, science, and how-to-do-it books. Girls were more interested in books about animals, fairy tales, modern fantasy, and present-day children living in the United States and in other countries.[6]

A 1971 study by Barchas indicated that fifth graders of four ethnic groups—Anglo, Negro, American Indian, and Mexican-American—were more alike than different in the interests they expressed. The children in ethnic minority groups did express a high degree of interest in titles and topics related to their own ethnic groups and to their immediate environment. However, all groups expressed high interest in mystery-adventure, animal stories, and humor.[7]

Informal information, too, suggests that most small children like stories about animals and machines or vehicles, about playmates and family relationships, and about situations that

5. James Orval Butter, *Expressed Reading Preferences of Children Enrolled in Grade Two in Selected Schools of Colorado.* Unpublished doctoral dissertation, University of Oklahoma, 1964; and Gordon Charles Peterson, *A Study of Library Books Selected by Second Grade Boys and Girls in the Iowa City, Iowa Schools.* Unpublished doctoral dissertation, University of Iowa, 1971.

6. Thomas William Dowan, *Personal Reading Interests as Expressed by Children in Grades Three, Four, and Five in Selected Florida Public Schools.* Unpublished doctoral dissertation, Florida State University, 1971.

7. Sarah Elizabeth Barchas, *Expressed Reading Interests of Children of Differing Ethnic Groups.* Unpublished doctoral dissertation, University of Arizona, 1971.

reflect their own environments. They enjoy rhyme and rhythm and they are pleased by stories that demonstrate the satisfaction of having a wish fulfilled, a problem solved, a new skill learned, or a new situation taken in stride.

The beginning independent reader wants action and variety, appreciates simple or visual humor, and is beginning to be curious about the world. Some younger children enjoy word play. As their world expands, children in the primary grades become interested in children of other lands.

In the middle grades, when children have acquired a better understanding of time and a sense of history, biography begins to appeal. For a time boys tend to scorn stories in which girls are the main characters and girls tend to accept more easily protagonists of both sexes, a

Illustration by Louis Darling, p. 123. From Beverly Cleary, *Ramona the Pest.* Copyright © 1968 by Beverly Cleary. Published by William Morrow and Company, Inc. Published in the United Kingdom by Hamish Hamilton Ltd., London.

situation that may well change as female characters in books are given more active, interesting roles. There is often enthusiastic reaction to fantasy and nonsense humor, an interest in words, and a continuing enjoyment of action, partly seen in a devotion to series fiction, which usually leans heavily on plot. For years adults have deplored and children have relished the stereotyped *Nancy Drew* and *Hardy Boys* books; today the lively adventures of *Ramona the Pest* and *The Great Brain* have devoted followers who eagerly await each new volume.

Many readers of nine, ten, and eleven become addicted to a topic or a genre; subject interests make informational books of growing importance, and children's desire for a clearer understanding of themselves and their relation to others is evident in their interest in fiction about interpersonal relationships, children of other countries and times, sex roles, and family patterns.

Young teenagers today are often concerned about their roles in society and about social problems; they talk about drugs and delinquency, student unrest, the generation gap, the role of women, the manipulations of the stock market, and the struggle for black equality. Many of them read adult books, while some may vary their reading patterns with an occasional book intended for younger children.

Developmental Trends and Book Selection

Generally speaking, the results of interest studies plus information from developmental studies may provide some guidelines for book selection. Caution is important, however, because groups and individuals differ and interest patterns do appear to change somewhat over time. An example is the relatively recent indication that primary children do like informational books in addition to fantasy and realistic stories.

What does all of this information mean, then, to a person who is responsible for bringing children together with books? In book selection, it is as important to know about children as it is to know about literature. Considered from that standpoint, a knowledge of child development becomes a tool for book selection just as familiarity with literature is a tool. Information about developmental levels can help tell us something about children and

Viewpoint_____

I didn't know if I was good or wicked, a heroine or a coward. I don't know that I have found out yet, but I do know that the books I read when I was young helped me towards some sort of understanding. They helped me to place myself, helped me to solve the riddle of why I was here, in this particular place, in this particular body. The books that did this for me were not myths or magic or fantasy but books that seemed to me to be about real people—that is, people I could recognize as real, even if they sometimes had rather unlikely adventures. I don't mean that they were always books about a girl like me, living in a house like mine. They were books that for some reason I could live inside, even if the world they showed me was different from the one I knew.
—Nina Bawden, "Emotional Realism for Young People," *The Horn Book Magazine*, February 1980, pp. 25–26. Copyright © 1980 by Nina Bawden. Reprinted by permission of the author.

also something about the types of literature they are likely to enjoy at a particular age.

A librarian or teacher responsible for guiding children's reading deals with individual children, the real meeting of child and book. The more generalized information about children's development and literature comes into sharper focus when a child appears and asks for a book. Let us say that this is a rather lonely seven-year-old from a home that is neither loving nor particularly stable. Although the child is adequately fed and clothed, clearly there are other needs not satisfied through the family. Now individual reading needs and interests become important. Information from the comments about typical children of the same maturity level can be used to help us second-guess what kinds of literature will have meaning for this child. Perhaps Charlotte Zolotow's *A Father Like That* will help to give a sense of the love that can exist between a father and child or *Ramona the Brave* will engage this child who is entering what Erikson terms the stage of industry versus inferiority. Perhaps she would especially enjoy Arnold Lobel's *Days with Frog and Toad* because of the friendship between the two animals. There is much we do not know about children's reading interests, but we do know enough to make some tentative suggestions of books that might appeal.

Knowledge about characteristics of children at various developmental levels has an obvious value for professionals responsible for book selection. Developmental characteristics can tell us what we need to keep in mind in ordering books for a typical elementary school population, taking into account individual interests and needs as well as group trends. In selecting books for groups of children or individuals, adults should know as much as possible about the particular children they are working with. Chapter 3 discusses in more detail the business of guiding children's book selection. Always the adult should keep in mind the goal: to make reading a pleasurable experience for children so that it will continue to be one of their leisure-time activities.

Adult References[8]

ALMY, MILLIE. *Ways of Studying Children.*

ALMY, MILLIE, E. CHITTENDEN, and PAULA MILLER. *Young Children's Thinking: Studies of Some Aspects of Piaget's Theory.*

AMERICAN COUNCIL ON EDUCATION, COMMISSION ON TEACHER EDUCATION. *Helping Teachers Understand Children.*

APPLEBEE, ARTHUR. *The Child's Concept of Story: Ages Two to Seventeen.*

ASSOCIATION OF HOSPITAL AND INSTITUTION LIBRARIES. *Bibliotherapy: Methods and Materials.*

BANDURA, ALBERT, and RICHARD H. WALTERS. *Social Learning and Personality Development.*

BRUNER, JEROME S. *Toward a Theory of Instruction.*

CHAMBERS, AIDAN. *The Reluctant Reader.*

ERIKSON, ERIK H. *Childhood and Society.*

FAVAT, F. ANDRÉ. *Child and Tale: the Origins of Interest.*

FEITELSON, DINA, ed. *Cross-Cultural Perspectives on Reading and Reading Research.*

FURTH, HANS G. *Piaget for Teachers.*

GESELL, ARNOLD, and FRANCES ILG. *Child Development: An Introduction to the Study of Human Growth.*

ILG, FRANCES L., and LOUISE BATES AMES. *Child Behavior.*

JENKINS, GLADYS GARDNER. *Helping Children Reach Their Potential.*

MAIER, HENRY. *Three Theories of Child Development: The Contributions of Erik H. Erikson, Jean Piaget, and Robert R. Sears, and Their Applications.*

OLLILA, LLOYD O., ed. *The Kindergarten Child and Reading.*

PIAGET, JEAN. *Language and Thought of the Child.*

PIAGET, JEAN, and BARBEL INHELDER. *The Psychology of the Child.*

SARAFINO, EDWARD P., and JAMES W. ARMSTRONG. *Child and Adolescent Development.*

SINGER, DOROTHY G., and TRACEY A. REVENSON. *A Piaget Primer: How a Child Thinks.*

WILKIN, BINNIE TATE. *Survival Themes in Fiction for Children and Young People.*

8. Complete bibliographic data are provided in Appendix B.

Chapter Three: Guiding Children's Book Selection

Books are written for children, but adults buy them. Editors decide on manuscripts, reviewers make judgments, teachers and librarians exhibit books, recommend them, and otherwise guide children's reading. Parents, grandparents, uncles, and aunts select a choice volume for a favorite child. But how can adults know what book a child is going to enjoy?

Actually, they can't know with any degree of certainty. Moreover, they must face the fact that youngsters are skilled at rejecting what is not for them. A book may be judged a juvenile classic by experts in children's literature, but if it is beyond children's understanding or too subtle or sophisticated for their level of appreciation, they can turn it down with a stony indifference which leaves adults baffled and grieved. They need not mourn. Two years later a child may accept that very book with enthusiasm. It is the same with music. A simple melody may appeal to children, while a symphony may confuse them. But if their musical experiences increase as they mature, they hear parts of the symphony, its different movements, over and over, until they understand and enjoy them. Finally, when they hear the whole symphony, they can follow it with pleasure, and its great melodies sing in their memories. So some poems must be heard repeatedly, and some stories must be talked over or listened to while someone who knows and loves them reads aloud.

Through this gradual induction into better and better literature, children catch the theme and savor the beauty or the subtle humor or the meaning that eluded them at first. Sometimes an adult has the privilege of seeing this discovery take place. The children's faces come suddenly alive; their eyes shine. They may be anticipating an amusing conclusion or a heroic triumph. There is a sudden chuckle, or breath is exhaled like a sigh. The book has moved them, perhaps even to laughter or tears, but in any case there is a deep inner satisfaction, and they will turn to books again with anticipation.

This chapter will discuss the elements of literature (setting, viewpoint, characterization, plot, theme, and style), standards for evaluating books, and the range of books for children.

Looking Closely at Books

Adults must know a great deal about books in choosing them for children and in guiding children to them. The chapters in this book will introduce many of the fine authors of the past and present, and will also suggest criteria for judging books in each genre. These chapters are, of course, guides only. In the end, you should choose books for children on the basis of your own first-hand knowledge of the child or groups of children you are working with and of the books themselves.

The best way to know books is to read them. Book selection guides can help and lists of award books are useful, but there is no substitute for reading. Using the lists of book selection aids and prize-winning books included later in this volume is only a first step. Many of the best books are published in paperback, and children can be encouraged to start their own paperback libraries, especially if you can discuss books with knowledgeable enthusiasm. It really isn't enough to feel, "I like it," or "I don't like it." To make wise selections and to stimulate children's interest, one must know why. It is useful to keep records of such data as title, author, publisher, series, illustrator, availability in paperback, and of your opinion of plot, theme, style, characters, etc. You may also want to note passages that would be particularly enticing as baits to reading. Publishers usually suggest the reading level, but this you will want to judge for yourself. (Would a fifth-grade class enjoy this book? Could a slow reader handle it? Will the subject interest a particular child who can read but seldom does?) While you will be careful to avoid the role of censor, you should know the book well enough to judge whether it

Floating away over the roofs of the houses

Illustration by Mary Shepard. Reproduced from *Mary Poppins*, copyright 1934 © 1962, by P.L. Travers, by permission of Harcourt Brace Jovanovich, Inc.

Viewpoint

Those who maintain that criticism ignores the child and has no place in children's literature do children a grave injustice. All of us are concerned about children; all of us want their maximum growth, their greatest pleasure in reading. All of us want children to discover themselves and the world through books. But there is nothing in a poor book that does these things for children. As Smith* and many others have suggested, a poor book sets a child back, a mediocre one leaves children where they are, but a good book moves children on to growth and pleasure, to new understandings and discoveries. To say that criticism has no place in children's literature is to say that literature for children is less important than literature for adults. Few of us would agree. In the words of Walter de la Mare, "Only the rarest kind of best in anything can be good enough for the young."† Children love the best. They always have and they always will.—Rebecca Lukens, "The Child, the Critic, and a Good Book," from *Language Arts*, April 1978. Copyright © 1978 by the National Council of Teachers of English. Reprinted by permission of the publisher and the author.

* Lillian Smith, *The Unreluctant Years* (Viking, 1967).
† Walter de la Mare, *Bells and Grass* (Viking, 1942), p. 11.

should be given to special children or recommended to a class as a whole. If you have kept records of the books you have read, you may have the great satisfaction of being able to recommend another book when a child asks, "Is there any other book just like this one?"

In some classrooms, a teacher will have enthusiastic response to *The Wind in the Willows*; in others, no response at all. In some library story hours *Mary Poppins* may produce hilarity, in others boredom—in the same library. Think how differently you would select, say, for a fourth grade of bright, enthusiastic booklovers and a fourth grade of slow, apathetic readers. Or, in working with individual children, how differently you would choose a book for a child with a sense of humor and a child who is literal.

You can turn to review sources for opinions of books, but in the end you must rely on your own judgment.[1] You should not feel restricted by children's immediate interests in choosing books because these are often narrower than they need to be and because they can change quite quickly. Children's reactions are often immediate and personal, and they often adhere conservatively to a known literary experience such as horse stories or science fiction. Teachers, parents, and librarians should keep children exploring both the best of the old books and the most promising of the new. Since new titles alone number over two thousand a year, you need some criteria to help you select wisely. To develop judgments that are reliable and useful, you need to look closely at a book, not only to appraise its total effect on you but to examine the elements that produce that effect. The traditional literary elements we will be discussing are:

1. *setting*
2. *point of view*
3. *characters*
4. *plot*
5. *theme*
6. *style*

In discussion of these elements, three books will be analyzed as examples, all realistic fiction for better comparison: Rebecca Caudill's *Did You Carry the Flag Today, Charley?* for the youngest children; Laura Ingalls Wilder's *Little House in the Big Woods* for the middle group; and John Rowe Townsend's *The Intruder* for older children.[2]

Setting

Where and when did the story take place?
The setting is the time and the place of the action. Its elements are the geographical location, which may be as broad as a country or city or as narrow as an isolated farm or a single classroom; and the time, which can be a historical period of several decades or more, a season, or

a day. Other aspects of setting may be an occupational pattern or a general milieu or atmosphere, social or emotional. For some readers, or for some books, the setting of a story may be of paramount interest. For others, the action is all-absorbing, and the setting is of minor importance.

The limitations of young children's understanding of time and distance, a sense that expands as they grow older, must be taken into consideration in evaluating books meant for them. There are exceptions, but books for younger children are most comprehensible when their settings are familiar and within the child's limited experience. Fantasy that is set in an imaginary time or place demands careful structuring or it will lack cohesion and credibility. Lloyd Alexander's Prydain books are set in a wholly-conceived world, with its own mores and language and topography; whether books of high fantasy or not, stories that are set in other worlds or invented countries or a future time must be consistent within the parameters of their setting.

The setting of the story should be clear, believable, and, especially in the case of biography or historical fiction, authentic. A book like Irene Hunt's *Across Five Aprils* has strength in part because the author's research enabled her to reveal convincingly the tempo, the ideologies, and the language of the Civil War years—particularly in the conflict that existed in border-state families. Too often, in a mediocre book, the author substitutes for a subtly interwoven, authoritative treatment of a time or a place some laboriously detailed information awkwardly placed and often isolated from the characters and events. On the other hand, an author like Rosemary Sutcliff, who has a vast knowledge of British history, lets her characters give readers necessary details about costumes, for example, or information about military leaders, in dialogue appropriate for the period in which the book is set. A less qualified writer might introduce into the dialogue an unnatural exchange of information that has the synthetic character of a travel brochure. A mediocre story with a hospital setting might have this ridiculous remark by one nurse to another: "Oh, did you know that one must go through decompression to enter a hyperbaric oxygen chamber?" Of course, the other nurse knows it, and the reader knows she knows it. The author simply hasn't been sufficiently skilled to bring in

---

1. Obviously there are various ways to approach a book. Frederick C. Crews in *The Pooh Perplex* (Dutton, 1963) has produced a devastating satire of various literary approaches to criticism. As Orville Prescott remarked in the *New York Times*, "In twelve glittering, brightly malicious essays he has poleaxed and then neatly eviscerated twelve varieties of currently fashionable literary criticism."

2. Rebecca Caudill, *Did You Carry the Flag Today, Charley?* (hardback, 1966; paperback, 1971—Holt, Rinehart & Winston, Inc.). Laura Ingalls Wilder, *Little House in the Big Woods* (hardback, 1932, 1953; paperback, 1971—Harper & Row, Publishers). John Rowe Townsend, *The Intruder* (hardback, 1970—J. B. Lippincott Company).

needed scientific details in a casual, natural way.

"To get to Charley Cornett's house, you turn left off the highway at Main Street, drive to the edge of town, and cross a bridge." So begins *Did You Carry the Flag Today, Charley?* and it goes on to place Charley's home in mountain country: a small house in which Charley lives with his parents, four brothers, and five sisters. Since this is a book for reading aloud to young children, it is quite fitting that there be no specific time, but the "highway" and "drive" make it clear that it is now. No confusion here. It is in the countryside, not the city; Charley is one of a large family. All of these interpretations are within the grasp of small children.

Little House in the Big Woods begins: "Once upon a time, sixty years ago, a little girl lived in the Big Woods of Wisconsin, in a little gray house made of logs." Thus, deftly and simply, Wilder has made it clear not only that (at the time of writing) the story is set sixty years in the past, but that the little girl who was Laura Ingalls lived in pioneer fashion, in a log house. And how much more we learn about the setting because of the capitalization of "Big Woods." It immediately gives an impression of the isolation of the little gray house, and both the pinpointing of a past time and the expectation that readers will understand the locale are appropriate for the level of the readers.

Illustration by Garth Williams from *Little House in the Big Woods* by Laura Ingalls Wilder. Copyright, 1953, as to pictures by Garth Williams. By permission of Harper & Row, Publishers, Inc. and Methuen Children's Books Ltd, London.

In *The Intruder*, Townsend begins with "Sea, sand, stone, slate, sky." Both the staccato introduction and the paragraphs that follow, giving geographical details and historical background, lend emphasis to the importance of the place. The two-page chapter ends, "Sea, sand, stone, slate, sky. That is the landscape," a further emphasis by setting the description apart. Facing the opening lines is a map, another clue to the fact that the setting is important. Townsend assumes that his reading audience will appreciate this, and he creates, in the two pages, an atmosphere that invites an expectation of suspense that depends on the kind of reading experiences older children have had.

Point of View

Who tells the story?
The author may write as an omniscient narrator, who simply describes the characters and gives their thoughts by direct exposition, perhaps at several points in the story. Or the narrator may make no comment and simply let the characters' actions speak for them. If the story is told in first person, the voice may be that of an impartial bystander or of the principal character. In Emily Neville's *It's Like This, Cat*, in which the adolescent protagonist tells the story, we see his parents only through his eyes and must remember that the view of them is therefore limited, so that the author must use other ways of telling the reader what Dave's father is like—through the father's dialogue and actions and through another boy's reaction to him. In Hila Colman's *Claudia, Where Are You?* alternate chapters give the viewpoint of Claudia's mother (in third person) and of the runaway Claudia herself (in first person). If the author uses a diary form or a monologue, as Maia Wojciechowska does in *"Don't Play Dead Before You Have To,"* the point of view is restricted and the only change comes with changing attitudes of the speaker.

Rebecca Caudill's Charley is seen quite objectively, but the author identifies with him by making him the only character whose thoughts are given ("he remembered," "he figured out"), so that the listening or reading audience tends to empathize with him.

In *Little House*, Wilder does the same thing; the story is told in third person (although it is based on her own childhood) and the emphasis is put on Laura as the main character both by

Viewpoint

... A good critic will indeed be aware of theme, plot, style, characterization, and many other considerations, some of them not previously spelled out but arising directly from the work; he will be sensitive; he will have a sense of balance and rightness; he will respond. Being only human he cannot possibly know all that it would be desirable for him to know; but he will have a wide knowledge of literature in general as well as of children and their literature, and probably a respectable acquaintance with cinema, theatre, television, and current affairs. That is asking a lot of him, but not too much. The critic (this is the heart of the matter) counts more than the criteria.

... If the book is for children, he should not let his mind be dominated by the fact, but neither, I believe, should he attempt to ignore it. Just as I feel the author must write for himself yet with awareness of an audience of children, so I feel the critic must write for himself with an awareness that the books he discusses are children's books.

... A book is a communication; if it doesn't communicate, does it not fail? True, it may speak to posterity, if it gets the chance; it may be ahead of its time. But if a children's book is not popular with children here and now, its lack of appeal may tell us something. It is at least a limitation, and it *may* be a sign of some vital deficiency which is very much the critic's concern.—Reprinted by permission of the American Library Association from "Standards of Criticism for Children's Literature," speech by John Rowe Townsend, from *Top of the News*, June 1971, pp. 385–387. Copyright © 1971 by the American Library Association.

introducing her first and by making the first comment on Laura from her viewpoint: "So far as the little girl could see ...."

In *The Intruder*, even more emphasis is given to Arnold as the protagonist, the second chapter beginning, "Arnold saw the boy and girl a few minutes before he saw the stranger," and all of the subsequent actions of the stranger (who claims that *he* is the real Arnold Haithwaite) are seen from Arnold's viewpoint as those of a mysterious intruder.

Characters

Who are the characters? How are they revealed? Do they grow and change?
It is clear from the discussion above that a major character is often distinguished by being the first person in the book to be introduced. Joseph Krumgold, in *... and now Miguel*, opens his story with "I am Miguel." In *The Peterkin Papers*, however, Lucretia Hale sets the lady from Philadelphia apart by introducing her only when the Peterkin family has become so befuddled that she alone can set them straight. In *Charlotte's Web*, E. B. White presents the pig, Wilbur, through a family's discussion of him.

We learn something more from Miguel's very next words: "For most people it does not make so much difference that I am Miguel. But for me, often, it is a very great trouble." The character may thus be revealed by what is said or done, or—as in the case of Wilbur—by what is said about him.

Characterization can be effected by physical description: if we read that a judge in colonial Salem has pursed lips and a frowning brow, that he is dressed in somber black and walks with stiff dignity, we anticipate his stern behavior. What characters say, what they do, how they react to others, how others talk about them are all clues to their personalities. If a major character, he or she must play a dynamic role; if the character changes, the change should be logical for the sort of person the author has drawn. There should be depth of characterization, since to emphasize only one or two traits produces a one-dimensional portrait that is often more caricature than characterization.

Characters must be both believable and consistent. Children soon learn how superficial is the patterned mystery story in which no adult contributes to the solution, while an

Illustration by Jean Charlot from *... And Now Miguel* by Joseph Krumgold. Copyright 1953 by Joseph Krumgold. By permission of Thomas Y. Crowell, Publishers.

Illustration by Ernest H. Shepard from *The Wind in the Willows* by Kenneth Grahame. Illustration copyright 1933 by Charles Scribner's Sons; renewal copyright © 1961 by Ernest H. Shepard. Reprinted by permission of the publisher.

omniscient, persistent, superintelligent child adroitly sees all clues, pursues them, and solves the mystery single-handed.

The characters should develop naturally and behave and talk in ways that are consistent with their age, sex, background, ethnic group, and education.

Whether the story is realistic or fantastic, the characters must be convincing. Although Mary Poppins is in a fanciful story, she is a very convincing character, a severe and crusty individual that no child ever forgets. When Michael asks anxiously, "Mary Poppins, you'll never leave us, will you?" the answer from his new nurse is a stern "One more word from that direction and I'll call the Policeman." Wilbur, the "radiant pig" in *Charlotte's Web*, and Toad of Toad Hall in *The Wind in the Willows* are just as convincing to children as is Harriet the spy. Long after details of plot have been forgotten, children and adults will recall with a chuckle or a warm glow of affection such characters as Jo in *Little Women*, Long John Silver, Henry Huggins, Janey the middle Moffat, Arrietty in *The Borrowers*, and dozens of other salty book characters. It is through depth and perception in characterization that stories become memorable. And it is through such well-drawn individuals that children gain new insight into their own personal problems and into their ever widening relationships with other people.

As is appropriate for small children whose chief interest is the action in a story, Caudill's Charley is revealed more by what he does than by what he says. Cheerfully obstreperous, Charley, who is five and having his first school experiences, *has* to climb an apple tree to see how apples are attached, and when the class is playing at "hoppity" like Christopher Robin, he hops right out the door. It is further revealing that when the teacher tells him to stay out in the rain, he happily pretends he is a rock and enjoys the rain. In all of his brothers' and sisters' daily inquiries about whether or not he has had the honor of being the flag-carrier, it is clear that they know their little brother and hardly expect it—yet they ask "anxiously," making it clear also that Charley is lovable and loved.

The theme of family love is strong in the *Little House* books, and the first thing we learn about Laura, as she lies in a trundle bed listening to a wolf howl, is the security she feels with Pa there to protect her. We also see in Laura's actions that she is a curious child, far less compliant than her sister Mary—and Wilder often uses Mary's behavior as a contrast to define Laura's livelier personality.

Arnold Haithwaite is revealed as an uncommunicative young man by the first passage of dialogue in *The Intruder*, yet when he confronts the intruder he makes no bones about his incredulity that they have the same name. Stalwart, inflexible, and unafraid, Arnold shows his personality in the tenacious way he insists on his identity even when the intruder has usurped his place by convincing others that he is the real Arnold Haithwaite.

Plot

What happens in the story?
Fiction for children usually focuses on what happens, what the action is. In some stream-of-consciousness novels or quiet character studies for adults, very little happens. While there are some children's books of which this is true, most of them are filled with action. Children want characters who have obstacles to overcome, conflicts to settle, difficult goals to win. It is the vigorous action in pursuit of these goals that keeps young readers racing along from page to page to find out how the central character achieves his or her ends. But achieve he or she must, in some way or other.

A plot is basically a series of actions that move in related sequence to a logical outcome;

if there is no sequence or interaction, the book may have a series of episodes (in some books, particularly books of reminiscence, this can be very effective) rather than a plot or story line. Simple as it sounds, a story needs a beginning, a middle, and an end. First the author must set the stage. Then, to have development and momentum, a plot needs conflict, opposition, or a problem. Last, there should be a definitive ending: a climax of action, or even a strong indication of future resolution. A dramatic example of a powerful ending is that of *Helter-Skelter* by Patricia Moyes, in which a young girl hunting a criminal finds that the pleasant young man in whom she has confided is himself the culprit. Alan Garner's *The Owl Service* has an equally powerful conclusion. Here a contemporary setting is the background for a frightening reenactment of a Celtic myth. In the last scene the legend is laid to rest and young Gwyn finally discovers who his father is.

Linked to the development of the plot are the characters, who affect what happens by the sort of people they are and who are, in turn, affected by what happens to them. In stories for the very young, the plot is usually simple, with no subplot, whereas older readers can both understand and enjoy the complexity of a story with many threads.

In *Charley*, the story begins with the fact that a small boy going to school for the first time is told by his brothers and sisters that one child is honored each day by being allowed to carry the flag; as the story develops it becomes evident that Charley is an unlikely candidate. Then an understanding teacher acts—and Charley proudly carries the flag.

Little House is an episodic story; although the book and its sequels show the children growing, the separate incidents of the story might often be interchanged without affecting the outcome.

The plot of *The Intruder* has high dramatic quality. (It was, in fact, filmed for television.) Arnold Haithwaite learns almost immediately that the stranger who establishes himself in Arnold's home is a threat to him—since Arnold is not quite sure of who he really is. He calls the old man with whom he lives "Dad," not having been told that he is the old man's illegitimate grandson. In the struggle for dominance between the boy and the stranger, the plot is given momentum by the fact that the stranger wants not only to take command of the household but also to commercialize the town. The fact that Arnold does not at first know his real identity gives the author an opportunity to unravel threads of past events as well as the immediate action. The conclusion fulfills the promise of the story's opening: a desperate chase on the sands, with the drowning of the criminal in the swift tide and Arnold reaching the safety of an old church, long deserted because it has been for many years cut off from the mainland at high tide.

Theme

What is the main idea of the story?

The theme of the story is its central core, its meaning. For example, the theme of . . . *and now Miguel* is the struggle to attain competence in one's chosen work and so be accepted as a responsible, mature person. The same theme appears in Bianca Bradbury's *The Loner*. In

From *Did You Carry the Flag Today Charley?* by Rebecca Caudill. Illustrated by Nancy Grossman. Copyright © 1966 by Rebecca Caudill. Copyright © 1966 by Nancy Grossman. Reproduced by permission of Holt, Rinehart and Winston, Publishers.

Elizabeth Coatsworth's *Bess and the Sphinx* the theme is overcoming shyness. Often in children's books the theme reflects those developmental values that are inherent in the process of growing up. The theme may be concerned with overcoming jealousy or fear, adjusting to a physical handicap, or accepting a stepparent. Books that have these or other developmental values can help not only the child who shares similar problems but also the child who does not and who needs to learn sympathy and understanding.

Not all books have such themes; some are adventure stories, some written just for fun, and some historical fiction is intended only to highlight a person, a movement, or a period. Indeed, there can be no hard and fast rule about any of the elements of fiction, since there are good books in which almost any aspect may be omitted. The elements discussed here are those which exist in most books.

The theme in *Charley* is that of achieving status and acceptance: Charley has been told that carrying the flag is the signal honor of the school day, and although he is really more excited, by the end of the story, by the fact that he owns his first book, he is well aware that the sign of approval has been carrying the flag. Although the *Little House* books are imbued with family love and pioneer courage, there really is no underlying theme. In *The Intruder*, for all the drama of the action, the theme is the boy's quest for identity.

Viewpoint

... Participation in the continuity of narrative leads to the discovery or recognition of the theme, which *is* the narrative seen as total design. This theme is what, as we say, the story has been all about, the point of telling it. What we reach at the end of participation becomes the center of our critical attention. The elements in the narrative thereupon regroup themselves in a new way. Certain unusually vivid bits of characterization or scenes of exceptional intensity move up near the center of our memory. This reconstructing and regrouping of elements in our critical response to a narrative goes on more or less unconsciously. . . .—Northrop Frye, "The Road of Excess," in *Myth and Symbol; Critical Approaches and Applications*, Northrop Frye, L. C. Knights, and others, edited by Bernice Slote, University of Nebraska Press, Lincoln, 1963, p. 9.

Style

How is the story written? How are the ideas expressed?

Style is very difficult to define. Whole books have been devoted to explaining and exemplifying it. There are many brief definitions—Jonathan Swift's "Proper words in proper places make the true definition of style"; Lord Chesterton's "Style is the dress of thoughts"; Comte de Buffon's "The style is the man." Style involves the author's choice of words, the sentence patterns (simple or involved structure, long or short sentences, arrangement of the words within the sentences), the imagery used, the rhythm of the sentences. There are many styles—as many styles as authors. As Thrall, Hibbard, and Holman say in *A Handbook to Literature*, "The best style, for any given purpose, is that which most nearly approximates a perfect adaptation of one's language to one's ideas."[3] Perhaps the best way to talk about style is simply to look at some passages. Read these excerpts from "The Three Little Pigs" and *Millions of Cats* aloud:

"Little pig, little pig, let me come in."
"No, not by the hair on my chinny-chin-chin."
"Then I'll huff and I'll puff and I'll blow your house in."

"Hundreds of cats, thousands of cats, millions and billions and trillions of cats."

Sorche Nic Leodhas has the true Scottish cadence. The first tale in her *Thistle and Thyme* begins:

An old laird had a young daughter once and she was the pawkiest piece in all the world. Her father petted her and her mother cosseted her till the wonder of it was that she wasn't so spoiled that she couldn't be borne.

How much more convincing that is than a peppering of *hoot-mon*'s and *dinna ken*'s.

Bernard Evslin, in his retelling of the Finn McCool legend, *The Green Hero*, writes of high adventure in prose that has an epic sweep, but when he is describing small events, uses unexpectedly homely and amusing language. In listing the charms of the infant girl with whom the newly born Finn is smitten, he concludes (after rhapsodizing about her eyes and hair), "And teeth—a full set of them—so that she was able to bite Finn quite early."

3. William Thrall, Addison Hibbard, and C. Hugh Holman, *A Handbook to Literature* (Odyssey, 1960), p. 474.

Illustration by Barbara Bascove reprinted by permission of Four Winds Press from *The Green Hero*, © 1975 by Bernard Evslin.

Sid Fleischman's tall tales appeal to children because they are nonsensical, but it is his crisp, casual style that gives such tales as *McBroom's Ear* humor and flavor:

I guess you've heard how amazing rich our farm was. Anything would grow in it quick. Seeds would burst in the ground and crops would shoot up right before your eyes. Why, just yesterday our oldest boy dropped a five-cent piece and before he could find it that nickel had grown to a quarter.

In *Little Calf*, a story of the first year in the life of a whale, Victor Scheffer uses words and word patterns that have a quiet, lyric quality that is admirably suited to the scene he is describing:

On a morning in early October the sea is glass, without a ripple or sound. A feather falls from the breast of an alba-

tross winging its lonely way northwestward to the Leeward Islands and home. The plume drifts lightly to the sea and comes to rest on a mirror image. It is a day when time itself is still.

In style, as in the theme of a book, there should be appropriateness and integrity, the hallmarks of good writing. When they are absent, we often find pedestrian writing: flagrant repetitiveness, stiff dialogue, a gross exaggeration of humor or fantasy, conflict between realism and fantasy, didacticism, superciliousness ("Can YOU see the little duck in the tree?") or a use of language that is poorly chosen for the genre of the book or for the characters in it.

Rebecca Caudill's style in *Did You Carry the Flag Today, Charley?* is brisk and forthright, just as is Charley himself. Small children may not recognize the Appalachian setting, but they can hear the authenticity of the speech patterns and the fact that Charley's comments sound the way a five-year-old's should.

Once inside Miss Amburgey's schoolroom, Charley looked around. Little chairs stood in a circle, with one big chair among them. Behind the big chair was a blackboard, and in a trough underneath lay pieces of chalk. Low tables stood at one side of the room. And there—there, fastened to the wall, was the white washbowl!

Viewpoint

Children defend themselves, I tell you. They manifest at first a degree of inertia that resists the liveliest attacks; finally they take the offensive and expel their false friends from a domain in which they wish to remain the rulers. Nothing is done to create a common opinion among them and yet that opinion exists. They would be wholly incapable of defining the faults that displease them; but they cannot be made to believe that a book which displeases them *should* please them. Whatever their differences may be as to age, sex, or social position, they detest with common accord disguised sermons, hypocritical lessons, irreproachable little boys and girls who behave with more docility than their dolls. It is as though ... they brought into the world with them a spontaneous hatred of the insincere and the false. The adults insist, the children pretend to yield, and do not yield. We overpower them; they rise up again. Thus does the struggle continue, in which the weaker will triumph.—Paul Hazard, *Books, Children and Men* translated by Marguerite Mitchell, The Horn Book, Inc., 1944, p. 49.

Notice how much like an inquisitive child's re-action this is—and how the exclamation point prepares the way for an episode in which Charley squirts water all over himself and several others. In contrast, note the quiet simplicity and the establishment of mood in Wilder's *Little House in the Big Woods*:

She looked at Ma, gently rocking and knitting. She thought to herself, "This is now." She was glad that the cozy house, and Pa and Ma and the firelight and the music, were now. They could not be forgotten, she thought, because now is now. It can never be a long time ago.

And from *The Intruder*, an example of John Rowe Townsend's writing that shows both his gift for brief characterization and the terse dialogue that is typical of Arnold:

Ernest Haithwaite was a small man whose clothes now seemed a size too big for him. His features, always craggy, were sharpening with age. His hair, once plentiful, was thinning and grizzled. He shaved every Sunday, and some-times during the week as well.

The old man was putting his cup down when a tap came on the door that led to the main house. He struggled to get up. Arnold waved him down, handed him his false teeth from the mantelpiece.

"There's a feller staying the night," the old man said.

"I know," said Arnold.

An Analysis of *Blowfish Live in the Sea*

As an example of analysis of the elements of a book (setting, point of view, characterization, plot, theme, and style) and the criteria used in assessing them, let's look at *Blowfish Live in the Sea* by Paula Fox.

It begins: "My brother, Ben, says that blow-fish live in the sea. He says it in many ways. I've found it written on matchbook covers, on brown paper bags from the supermarket, in dust on the windows. That makes Mama mad because you can't get window cleaners to come anymore."[4] On the next page, we learn that this "makes my father mad," and that Ben and his sister do not have the same father. Ben's father is somewhere out west "the last I heard," and the only answer Ben gives, if asked, is "I don't

4. From *Blowfish Live in the Sea* by Paula Fox (Bradbury Press, 1970), pp. 3, 4, 29.

Viewpoint

. . . One of the prime achievements in every good fiction has nothing to do with truth or philosophy or a *Weltanschauung* at all. It is the triumphant adjust-ment of two different kinds of order. On the one hand, the events (the mere plot) have their chrono-logical and causal order, that which they would have in real life. On the other, all the scenes or other divi-sions of the work must be related to each other ac-cording to principles of design, like the masses in a picture or the passages in a symphony. . . . Contrasts (but also premonitions and echoes) between the darker and the lighter, the swifter and the slower, the simpler and the more sophisticated, must have something like a balance, but never a too perfect symmetry, so that the shape of the whole work will be felt as inevitable and satisfying.—C. S. Lewis, *An Experiment in Criticism*, Cambridge University Press, 1961, pp. 81–82.

know, Carrie." Carrie goes on to say that she is twelve and Ben nineteen and that his uncut hair irritates his mother and stepfather.

What a lot to learn in two pages! Carrie has first of all told us that Ben is the most impor-tant character in the story, certainly the most important to her. He prefers not to talk about his father, and Carrie's laconic "the last I heard" makes it clear that he doesn't often hear from him. The viewpoint is Carrie's, but in her comments about her parents' attitude toward one thing—Ben's hair—we suspect conflict. Then we learn Ben has dropped out of school, that after an argument with his stepfather he had stopped bringing his friends home. So the stage is set (and the setting here consists of a comfortable, conventional home and a non-conformist son).

The problem is posed when Ben gets a letter from his father, who is going to be in Boston for the weekend and wants Ben to meet him. "Can't wait," the letter ends, and the reader has been given another clue to the father who has not been heard from for so long. Ben wants Carrie to go with him, which tells us both that he is nervous about meeting his father and that the bond between brother and sister is a strong one. All of the elements of the story have now been established and will be elaborated on, but not until the close of the book is the title ex-plained.

In Boston, Carrie and Ben learn that Ben's father is a raffish but engaging man, a liar, a drifter who has neglected his son save for an occasional boastful letter. In fact, they get to his hotel to find a letter saying that an emergency at the ranch he runs in Arizona has forced him to leave town. "Really, so disappointed for both of us! But soon. Very soon." Ben says bluntly, "He didn't want to see me," and he goes back to the hotel and finds his suspicion verified. Mr. Felix has not left town at all.

He is in his room, not quite sober, and at first puts up a bluff about his lie. Then he admits that he, like Ben, was nervous, and having confessed this, he begins to tell the truth. He owns a motel outside of Boston, not a very profitable venture, and he talks about what a wonderful life he has had. To Carrie it is a record of failure; to Ben the freedom of his father's wanderings sounds enticing. Ben decides to stay with his father and Carrie goes home alone.

Ben's decision is the climax of the plot, and it is made credible by the friction that he has felt at home; the reader has been prepared for it both by the characterization and by the tension and apprehension of Carrie as she reacts to Mr. Felix. And for Carrie, too, the outcome is credible: she misses Ben when she is back home, but she has other interests and is not desolate.

The setting, contemporary and urban, is not a major element of the story except for its underlining of the situation: the contrast between the ordered home in New York and the seedy hotel in Boston, where the young people's expectation of what Felix will be like is shaped by that atmosphere.

The theme is love and the acceptance of frailty that love implies, exemplified both by Carrie, who adores her brother despite his moodiness and rebelliousness, and by Ben, who is old enough to understand his father's ineptitude and irresponsibility and to forgive him for them. Fox is a particularly adept writer in presenting the theme of a story; she lets the characters tell the reader what their concerns are. When Carrie reminisces about an incident earlier in her childhood, she reveals both Ben's sensitivity and her own appreciation of it. And Ben, facing his father with the fact that he has been lied to for years, smiles. We know that Ben is compassionate rather than vengeful. And we know, not because the author *says* people must sometimes make difficult choices but because she *shows* us, that these things happen and that people must adjust to them.

One of the criteria for the evaluation of a book is the interaction between characters and between characters and events. Are the characters firmly enough drawn so that the reader finds their reactions to events believable? And do they, in turn, behave consistently in determining what happens? In *Blowfish Live in the Sea*, Carrie very quickly establishes her own still childlike character by her comments on Ben and her tangential remarks about her friend Abby (an early bloomer), by her reaction to her mother's worries about Ben, and by her conversation with her father. Ben is clearly drawn through Carrie's expressed thoughts as well as by his own dialogue and his stepfather's irritation.

Some of the components of style are comparatively easy to assess: the writing flows smoothly, the dialogue really sounds like people talking, the story has suspense and momentum. Fox's ability to maintain the child's point of view while writing with adult compassion and literary grace is exemplified by Carrie's memory of a family outing years before.

Once when I was standing just behind him, and he was kneeling, I'd suddenly seen how much older he was than I, how much bigger. At that same picnic, a bird had flown right into our windshield just as we parked under some trees. Ben had leaped out of the back seat and run to where the bird had fallen. Then I'd walked over and found him with the bird in his hand, a little mound of smoky feathers.

"It's dead," he said quietly.

Ben had known everything then. I thought about that bird long after winter came, and Ben standing there with it in his hand.

In this tender story of love, Paula Fox never strikes a false note, never inserts a word for effect, never uses a polysyllabic word or a quip when they are out of place. She never comes between the child and the book; it is as though she were a channel between the reader and the characters. Only when Ben is gone does Carrie learn why he wrote "Blowfish live in the sea" everywhere. His father had once sent him a dried blowfish that he had found, he wrote, in the Amazon. It was after Ben learned that blowfish live only in salt water that he inscribed his testimony of resentment against his father's betrayal. How astute of the author not to tell us that at the first, but to let us see how Ben reacts and how his leaving home to join his father indicates the softened judgment and tolerance of maturity.

Standards for Evaluating Books

In the evaluation of children's books there should be neither a casual, uncritical approach nor a rigid adherence to the standards for adult literature. The best in children's literature, as well as the best in adult literature, will meet those standards, but it is incumbent on critics (and this includes parents) to balance each book's strengths and weaknesses and to remember that each kind of book for children has its own requirements. As Lillian Smith points out in *The Unreluctant Years*:

A child's range of choice in his reading will always depend upon what is at hand, and this will largely depend upon his elders. Mistaken ideas among adults about what books a child likes, or should like, must prevent the very object they intend: a love for books and reading. If such misunderstanding is given widespread credence it will eventually affect what books are made generally available to children. (p. 13)[5]

Adults must be wary of pedestrian books, often oversize and profusely illustrated, the kind that bookstore clerks refer to as "grandmother books": slick, busy with detail, often coy, cute, or sentimental. They must try to distinguish between what appeals to some nostalgic adults and what appeals to children. They should guard against bias, preconception, or unevaluated loyalty to a childhood favorite.

Children's literature often reflects the values that adults think are important to encourage, and those who select books for children should be aware of the author's values and assumptions as well as of their own. If an author's attitude toward parent-child relationships, sex mores, civil rights, or any other issue is in agreement with our own, we may tend to approve of the book as a whole, but if the values and assumptions are at variance with our own, we may tend to dismiss it, regardless of its other qualities. For these reasons, it is particularly important for us to analyze books as carefully and objectively as we can. Each book must be judged on its own merits, but it is often illuminating to compare a book with the author's other books and with other authors' books on the same topic or in the same literary genre. The professional—teacher, librarian, reviewer, or editor—should know both the books themselves and the critical literature, since criticism entails making judgments that ought to be both informed and objective.

The special criteria for the various types of children's literature—poetry, folk tales, fables, myths, epics, modern fantasy, modern fiction, historical fiction, biography, and informational books—are discussed in succeeding chapters, and there are also evaluations of individual books, authors, and illustrators. Many different kinds of books can be judged by the criteria we have been discussing for theme, plot, setting, characters, point of view, and style. Biography, for instance, may be so evaluated, but it should also be judged by other equally important criteria (see Chapter 13). One of the essential criteria for judging informational books (see Chapter 14) is accuracy, but style, too, is important. Information can, and should, be presented in an interesting, lively fashion.

The Range of Books for Children

Because childhood should be a time of exploring many kinds of books, adults who work with children should know the different types, both to prevent children from falling into reading ruts and to encourage them to try books of many varieties.

Viewpoint

The . . . argument, 'all taste is relative', must as a matter of simple logic lead also to the conclusion that no one book is inherently better than another. If we accept this, then one of two things is true: either all books are worthless, since if preference is impossible all books are equal and therefore without *value* (for currency depends on varying stages of value); alternatively, if preference is only possible in relative judgments, then discussion is pointless, for everybody is as right as everybody else.

. . . Either some books *can* be dismissed out of hand for reasons which can be precisely given, and which depend on moral and literary principles, or all judgment is purely personal, and there are no grounds for saying that Shakespeare is better than Noël Coward. All our experience and our most valuable traditions uphold the first view: certain books are good, others are bad, and a very large number have something of both. The books are good because they comment on experience with profundity and intelligence, and occasionally with genius; and these qualities lead us to some glimpse of the truth about human experience.—Fred Inglis, *An Essential Discipline*, Methuen Educational Ltd., London, 1968, pp. 3–5.

5. Lillian H. Smith, *The Unreluctant Years* (American Library Association, 1953).

The books discussed in the following chapters are grouped variously—some according to age level or setting (books for the very young, historical fiction), some according to genre (poetry, biography), and so on. This kind of classification, though obviously mixed and inexact, is nonetheless useful, partly because it is based to some extent on the ways that children themselves describe their books.

One means of helping a child out of a reading rut—say, all animal stories or all fairy tales—is first to discover some common elements in the books he or she enjoys and then to use these as a stimulus to change. For example, if a child who reads only animal stories has enjoyed Mehlli Gobhai's *Lakshmi, the Water Buffalo Who Wouldn't*, he or she might be led toward reading other kinds of books with some of the same elements—humor, an Indian setting, or pleasant family relationships.

Picture Books

For prereaders and beginning readers, picture stories are enchanting. Significantly, the older stories which have lasted over the years are, for the most part, built around one or two general themes: love or reassurance, and achievement. *Peter Rabbit*, which is over eighty years old, has both. Peter has a daring adventure but returns

Illustration by Maurice Sendak from *Little Bear* by Else Holmelund Minarik. Pictures copyright © 1957 by Maurice Sendak. An I Can Read Book. By permission of Harper & Row, Publishers, Inc. and The World's Work, Ltd. (Original with color)

Viewpoint

Children, by and large, do not buy their own books. The books they are given are the ones adults think suitable for them, that present the kind of world adults want the children to believe they live in. Sometimes they may be books that the adults themselves have enjoyed, not because they are good books in themselves but because they are easy reading for grownups. That is one explanation, anyway, for the current fashion—almost an obsession it seems to me, sometimes—for teenage or young adult novels, many of which are little more than magazine stories souped up with injections of myth or symbol to make their contents seem weightier. Even real children's books, which I would define as books written for the pre-adolescent, or just-about-to-be-adolescent child, are sometimes judged oddly. A children's book should be judged for the pleasure it gives, for its style and its quality, as any other book is judged. But the way the children's book world has developed in recent years, with its different factions and interests and ideologies, seems to have clouded this simple issue. Conferences have been held, scholarly papers written, earnest and impassioned arguments developed around all sorts of different considerations which really have nothing at all to do with literature or its function and in the course of which (I have sometimes thought) the child himself has been forgotten.—Nina Bawden, "Emotional Realism for Young People," *The Horn Book Magazine*, February 1980, pp. 18–19. Copyright © 1980 by Nina Bawden. Reprinted by permission of the author.

safely to his home where his mother tucks him into bed with a justifiably punishing dose of camomile tea. Love and reassurance make Else Minarik's *Little Bear* books, and many other stories for the youngest, completely satisfying. And then, because the young child is always in an inferior position in relation to older children and adults, he or she yearns for independent achievement or competence. Hence the long life of *Mike Mulligan and His Steam Shovel*, the popularity of the *Madeline* books, and the success of the *Little Tim* stories, in which Tim triumphs gloriously over his many mishaps, such as shipwrecks and mislaying his parents—all books with themes of satisfying achievement.

In evaluating the various editions of the *Mother Goose* books or the many variations on alphabet books, the areas of decision are different. No need to wonder about the appeal of the former, since their rhyme, rhythm, and gay humor are established beyond controversy as appealing to the very young. The areas of decision lie primarily in the format of the book, the choice of rhymes included, and the illustrations (see Chapters 5 and 6). The latter are of paramount importance, too, in ABC books and are, of course, all-important in wordless picture books.

Folk Tales

Challenge and achievement are the heart of the folk-tale themes. The heroes or heroines must perform stern tasks if they are to survive, but the fact that they deal competently with glass hills, giants, witches, wicked machinations, and come through modestly triumphant is both reassuring and encouraging. Stories such as "Cinderella," "The Three Little Pigs," "The Three Billy-Goats Gruff," and "Molly Whuppie" dramatize the stormy conflict of good and evil. And they reiterate the old verities that kindness and goodness will triumph over evil if they are backed by wisdom, wit, and courage. These basic truths are the folk tales' great contribution to the child's social consciousness.

Fables, Myths, and Epics

Older children are the primary audience for the pithy—if sometimes didactic—wisdom of the fables, although many fables have been skillfully used as single versions in picture-story format. All of these forms of literature (fables, myths, and epics) have a quality of universality, and are part of the literary heritage with which all children should become familiar. They may not fully understand the complexity or symbolism of myths and legends, but they can appreciate the drama and beauty of the stories, and the great epics can satisfy a child's reverence for courage and high deeds.

Modern Fantasy

No genre so satisfies the child's boundless imagination as does fantasy, from the adventures of Max in Maurice Sendak's *Where the Wild Things Are* to the intricate depths of Madeleine L'Engle's *A Wrinkle in Time*. It encompasses gay little picture books about friendly ghosts and little-girl witches, low-keyed modern fairy stories like Betty Brock's *No Flying in the House*, blandly told tales like Diana Jones's *The Ogre Downstairs*, the romantic adventure stories by Lloyd Alexander, the picaresque books by Joan Aiken, and the polished

science fiction of Peter Dickinson. All of them can extend the reader's horizons, all of them have the action that appeals to children, many of them provide humor that ranges from daft nonsense to subtle wit, and almost all of them have an ingredient of durable attraction, magic.

Poetry

Poetry, too, extends children's imaginations, although in a different way. Where fantasy opens doors to things beyond belief, poetry gives new inward vision and understanding. The facile appeals of rhyme, rhythm, and repetition in simple verse and the quick humor of nonsense poetry can lead to an appreciation of the beauty of language and the crystallization in poetry of a mood, an emotion, a relationship, or the loveliness of a scene. The storytelling appeal of narrative poetry makes it a good choice for reading aloud as an introduction to the genre, and children may be led from this to lyric poetry and free verse. The increased interest of children and young people in the writing of poetry as well as in reading it is evident in the many collections and anthologies that have appeared and in the numbers of poetry magazines and workshops that have produced new young poets.

Modern Fiction

The themes of love, reassurance, and achievement are prominent in many stories of family life. For the middle years, eight to ten, the pleasant and amusing stories of *Ramona* and *Henry Huggins* take place against a permissive family background of suburbia. So does that great family story for somewhat older readers, *Meet the Austins.* The children in these stories have their problems and difficulties, some funny, some grave; sometimes with the reassurance of family understanding and love and sometimes missing and needing them. This is also true of books about underprivileged migrant workers such as *The Maldonado Miracle* and *Roosevelt Grady.* These books broaden children's social understandings and deepen their sympathies. It is significant that the realistic stories for today's children have gone beyond such books as *The Bobbsey Twins* and *Nancy Drew* stories and present real people confronted with real problems—from earning money for a bike to rebuilding a fairly normal life in a European city in wartime (*Fly Away Home*).

This realistic fiction also acquaints children with a wider world than the city, suburbs, or regional groups of the United States. Books begin to introduce them to family life in other countries. Even in the picture-story stage, French *Madeline* and English *Shirley* are as familiar to American children as are the boys and girls of the United States in American children's books. The tens will enjoy that strange

Illustration by Peter Burchard from *Roosevelt Grady* by Louisa R. Shotwell, reprinted with the permission of Philomel Books and John Farquharson Ltd. Copyright © 1963.

French home-in-the-making described in *Family Under the Bridge,* and the twelves will find out what happens during wartime in Robert Westall's *The Machine Gunners.* Gone are fiesta stereotypes of foreign lands and gone are the stories about a country told by an author who has never seen it or who equates contemporary life with that of a hundred years ago. *Hans Brinker* has been supplemented by Hilda van Stockum's *The Borrowed House.* Today's India is re-created by Shirley Arora in *What Then, Raman?*

There is delightful humorous realism, too, as in Keith Robertson's *Henry Reed, Inc.* From the ingenuous absurdities of Charlotte Zolotow's *When I Have a Son* to the sophisticated humor of James Lincoln Collier's *Rich and Famous,* the young of all ages can find amusing echoes of everyday life. Wherever laughter can be found, it is important that we search for it and relish it.

Historical Fiction

Children may know Paul Revere in story or verse, but do they also know children of Revere's time—eight-year-old Sarah in *The Courage of Sarah Noble* and the twelve- or fourteen-year-old Johnny in *Johnny Tremain?* Historical fiction today is both historically authentic and well written. Indeed, in such books we find some of the best contemporary writing for children and youth. The 1961, 1962, and 1974 Newbery Medals were awarded to books of historical fiction—*Island of the Blue Dolphins, The Bronze Bow,* and *The Slave Dancer,* three books good readers of twelve and over should not miss. In each of the books mentioned in this brief sampling, the theme—from "Keep up your courage, Sarah Noble" to the message that it is only love, not hatred, that can bend a bow of bronze—speaks strongly to children of today.

Biography

Historical fiction and biography may and should be used to reinforce each other. *Johnny Tremain* makes a biography of Paul Revere infinitely more real; Cora Cheney's *The Incredible Deborah* is a stirring example of the valor of a colonial girl; and the homespun frontier boys in William Steele's stories give vivid life to the scene and times of Daniel Boone. Both historical fiction and biography impress children with a sense of the reality of other days. Begin early to introduce children to these "real stories" we call biographies. Even the youngest readers can start with Ferdinand Monjo's simply written biographies and can then move on to many excellent biographies suitable for children of each age level. Books about Paracelsus, Galileo, Joan of Arc, Columbus, Washington, Banneker, Sequoyah, Lincoln, Tubman, Bethune, Robeson, Gandhi, and many others are authentic and as fascinating as fiction.

Informational Books

The category of informational books is so broad and so diverse that almost any need a child has for facts about a subject can be satisfied. There is, however, a need for vigilance on the part of the adult to be familiar with the contents of such books, since many informational books give scant coverage or unbalanced treatment. This is an area in which the author's qualifications are important. The adult working with children should know those authors—and there are many—whose books are accurate, up-to-date, and written at the right level of complexity for their intended audience. Publishers are quick to respond to expressed needs, and the past years have seen an outpouring of books about pollution and ecology, oceanology and space science, and most of the reform and protest movements that stir our society, as well

as books on the arts and sciences, humanity's past record, and our present environment. Handbooks and experiment books, reference books, do-it-yourself books, handsome art books—books by the hundreds—exist to fulfill the child's need to know. The adult can help children choose the best of these books by being aware of the accuracy of the contents, the thoroughness of the indexing (not all informational books need an index), the placement of maps and diagrams, and the organization of the material in a logical sequence.

Children need books to widen their horizons, deepen their understandings, and give them broader social insights. They also need books that minister to their merriment and increase their appreciation of beauty. They need heroism, fantasy, and down-to-earth realism. They need information about themselves and their fast-changing world, and they need books to relieve the tensions of that world. Adults may think in terms of what the child will learn, how the book may improve an attitude, correct a misconception, or ease a fear. If books do this, fine, but the child reads primarily for pleasure. For many children, the right time for a book is fleeting, and gentle guidance may be needed to expand the interests of a child who is in a reading rut so that he or she may not miss a reading experience for which there may never be another time so right.

The analyses in this chapter are meant as guidelines, not as rigid specifications. There are fine books that do not measure up to every standard of good literature but that may have particular values for a particular child, or whose strengths outweigh their weaknesses. Each book should be judged on its own merits. Wide reading at all levels and careful observation of children's reactions to books and of their individual and special interests will also help adults make wise choices in guiding young readers.[6]

Viewpoint

What I have been trying to say expresses my belief that the judgment of children's literature—and all the adult efforts that proceed from that judgment—must be conducted without condescension, without turning one's adult collar in an effort to define and enforce values that are somehow uniquely juvenile. On the contrary, it seems to me that the proper satisfactions of reading, even in the newly literate child—even, indeed, in the non-literate, story-listening child—provide a robust affirmation of our common humanity, our capacity, whether we are young or old, to understand and to be moved by and to gather to ourselves the products of the creative imagination.—Edward W. Rosenheim, Jr., "Children's Reading and Adults' Values." From *A Critical Approach to Children's Literature* edited by Sara Innis Fenwick, University of Chicago Press, 1967, p. 13.

6. For additional help in choosing books for children, see Appendix A.

Adult References[7]

BECHTEL, LOUISE SEAMAN. *Books in Search of Children.*

BLISHEN, EDWARD, ed. *The Thorny Paradise.*

CAMERON, ELEANOR. *The Green and Burning Tree.* Chapter, "Of Style and the Stylist."

CHAMBERS, AIDAN. *Introducing Books to Children.*

———. *Chosen for Children: An Account of the Books Which Have Been Awarded the Library Association Carnegie Medal, 1936–1965.*

COLBY, JEAN POINDEXTER. *Writing, Illustrating and Editing Children's Books.*

COMMIRE, ANNE. *Something About the Author: Facts and Pictures About Contemporary Authors and Illustrators of Books for Young People.*

———. *Yesterday's Authors of Books for Children.*

DE ANGELI, MARGUERITE. *Butter at the Old Price.*

DE MONTREVILLE, DORIS, and DONNA HILL, eds. *Third Book of Junior Authors.*

DONELSON, KENNETH L., and ALLEEN PACE NILSEN. *Literature for Today's Young Adults.*

EGOFF, SHEILA. *The Republic of Childhood: A Critical Guide to Canadian Children's Literature in English.*

EGOFF, SHEILA, G. T. STUBBS, and L. F. ASHLEY, eds. *Only Connect: Readings on Children's Literature.*

FENNER, PHYLLIS. *The Proof of the Pudding.*

———, ed. *Something Shared: Children and Books.*

FENWICK, SARA INNIS, ed. *A Critical Approach to Children's Literature.* Papers by Rosenheim and Nesbitt.

FIELD, CAROLYN W., ed., with VIRGINIA HAVILAND and ELIZABETH NESBITT, consultants. *Subject Collections in Children's Literature.*

FIELD, ELINOR WHITNEY, comp. *Horn Book Reflections: On Children's Books and Reading.*

FISHER, MARGERY. *Intent Upon Reading.*

———. *Who's Who in Children's Books.*

FOX, GEOFF, ed. *Writers, Critics and Children.*

FRYATT, NORMA R., ed. *A Horn Book Sampler.*

FULLER, MURIEL, ed. *More Junior Authors.*

GILLESPIE, JOHN, and DIANA LEMBO. *Introducing Books: A Guide for the Middle Grades.*

———. *Juniorplots: A Book Talk Manual for Teachers and Librarians.*

HAVILAND, VIRGINIA. *Children's Literature: A Guide to Reference Sources.*

———, ed. *Children and Literature: Views and Reviews.* Chapter 11, "Criticism and Reviewing."

HILDICK, WALLACE. *Children and Fiction.* Chapter, "Adult Responsibility: Authors' and Critics'."

HOFFMAN, MIRIAM, and EVA SAMUELS, eds. *Authors and Illustrators of Children's Books.*

HUCK, CHARLOTTE S. *Children's Literature in the Elementary School.*

HUNT, ABBY. *The World of Books for Children.*

HUNTER, MOLLIE. *Talent Is Not Enough.*

KAMM, ANTONY, and BOSWELL TAYLOR. *Books and the Teacher.*

KARL, JEAN. *From Childhood to Childhood: Children's Books and Their Creators.*

KIRKPATRICK, DANIEL, ed. *Twentieth Century Children's Writers.*

KUNITZ, STANLEY J., and HOWARD HAYCRAFT, eds. *The Junior Book of Authors.*

LANES, SELMA G. *Down the Rabbit Hole: Adventures and Misadventures in the Realm of Children's Literature.*

LEPMAN, JELLA. *A Bridge of Children's Books.*

LINES, KATHLEEN, ed. *Walck Monographs.* A series of biographies of authors.

LUKENS, REBECCA J. *A Critical Handbook of Children's Literature.*

MAHONY, BERTHA E., and ELINOR WHITNEY FIELD, eds. *Newbery Medal Books, 1922–1955.*

MEACHAM, MARY. *Information Sources in Children's Literature.*

MEEK, MARGARET, AIDAN WARLOW, and GRISELDA BARTON. *The Cool Web: The Pattern of Children's Reading.*

MEEKER, ALICE M. *Enjoying Literature with Children.*

PILGRIM, GENEVA HANNA, and MARIANNA McALLISTER. *Books, Young People, and Reading Guidance.*

QUIMBY, HARRIET, CLARA JACKSON, and ROSEMARY WEBER. *Building a Children's Literature Collection.*

ROBINSON, EVELYN ROSE. *Readings About Children's Literature.*

ROSENBLATT, LOUISE E. *Literature as Exploration.*

SAYERS, FRANCES CLARKE. *Summoned by Books: Essays and Speeches by Frances Clarke Sayers.*

SCHOOL LIBRARY JOURNAL/LIBRARY JOURNAL. *Issues in Children's Book Selection.*

SMITH, JAMES STEEL. *A Critical Approach to Children's Literature.*

SMITH, LILLIAN. *The Unreluctant Years.*

SOUTHALL, IVAN. *A Journey of Discovery.*

TOWNSEND, JOHN ROWE. *A Sense of Story.*

———. *A Sounding of Storytellers.*

TREASE, GEOFFREY. *Tales Out of School: A Survey of Children's Fiction.* Chapter 1, "How Much Does It Matter?"

VIGUERS, RUTH HILL. *Margin for Surprise: About Books, Children and Librarians.*

WILSON, BARBARA KER. *Writing for Children: An English Editor and Author's Point of View.*

WYNDHAM, LEE. *Writing for Children and Teen-Agers.* Yale French Studies: The Child's Part.

7. Complete bibliographic data are provided in Appendix B.

Chapter Four: Early Children's Books

The flood of children's books being published today is so overpowering that it is important to remind ourselves that there are old books in children's literature as fresh and appealing today as they were a hundred years ago. There are also old books for children which have been discarded, and properly so. Age is no guarantee of a book's excellence, nor recency of its significance. Some of the discards we shall glance at briefly, only to know their kind and to be wary of their reappearance in modern dress—because that is what happens. Pedantic or moralistic stories still appear, although they are neither as frequently published nor as highly praised as they were in the past. The successors to the penny thrillers of decades ago are churned out today in patterned style in series books, such as the *Nancy Drew* stories, and as comic books, where they outdo the penny thrillers in superficiality of characterization and plethora of action. We have not arrived at our wealth of fine modern books for children without considerable trial and error, and the errors are difficult to eradicate. We need perspective in judging children's books. We need to look at the past with modern eyes and view the present with the accumulated wisdom of the past. Where and how did children's literature begin? What has it grown out of and where is it going?

Before children can read, their acquaintance with literature begins, as it began for the race, through listening to the songs and stories of their people. All peoples had their explanations of the beginnings of the world, the coming of their own family or tribe, and the natural phenomena that delighted or terrified them. Mothers of yesterday chanted or sang to their babies. In simpler days, old women told homely tales of the beasts and kept alive legends of strange events. Grandmothers have always been the custodians of traditional tales, both of families and of the larger group, the tribe or the village. The men told stories to the adults of daring exploits and great adventures, and we may be sure the children listened. The professional storytellers, the bards or minstrels, took these tales, embroidered and polished them, and made them into the ballads or the hero tales or the epics of the people. So unwritten folk literature grew and was passed on by word of mouth for centuries before the collectors gathered it together for printing. Much of it was bloody and terrible; some of it was romantic, some coarse and humorous, told by adults to adults. Undoubtedly the children listened and loved many of these tales never intended for their ears and begged for them again and again. We say this with confidence because that is the way they have acquired much of their literature in every generation. Today, children watch adult television programs, take over adult songs, and read the same comics that adults read. They appropriate from adult material those things they understand and enjoy.

The Earliest Books

In the several centuries before the invention of movable type, all books for children were instructional, written by monastic teachers and chiefly intended for the children of wealthy families. These lesson books, often in Latin, began the tradition of didacticism that was to dominate children's books for hundreds of years and to persist as an influence into contemporary times.

Aldhelm (640?–709), abbot of Malmesbury, set the pattern used until the end of the sixteenth century of a text that was either rhymed or in question-and-answer form. In the eleventh century Anselm (1033–1109), archbishop of Canterbury, wrote an encyclopedia that treated such topics as manners and customs, natural science, children's duties, morals, and religious precepts. Such books were meant to instruct and to instill in children edifying principles of belief and conduct; they were not meant to give delight to the young.

It has been argued that the first printed book intended to be read specifically by children, apart from elementary Latin grammars, was a French courtesy book on table manners that was published a few decades after the invention of printing. In about 1487 there appeared *Les Contenances de la Table*, possibly by Jean Du Pré, which contained rhyming quatrains and was apparently very popular, since several fifteenth-century editions survive.

Viewpoint

Illustration for the William Caxton edition of *Aesop's Fables*.

For Adults:
Fables, Romances, Adventures

William Caxton (1422–1491) was England's first printer. He issued a series of books which are still appearing in various versions on our publishers' book lists for children. Caxton's books included, among other titles, Sir Thomas Malory's *Morte d'Arthur*, *The Recuyell of the Historyes of Troye*, *The Boke of Histories of Jason*, *The Historye of Reynart the Foxe*, and *Aesop's Fables*. Tales of King Arthur still give the older child a fine introduction to romance, the story of Odysseus remains a popular adventure story, and the fables are enjoyed by young children even if they do skip the morals. Although Caxton intended his books for adults, children took many of them for themselves, and versions of these same collections continue to delight each generation.

For Children:
Hornbooks and Battledores

While textbooks will not be discussed in detail, no account of children's books is complete without a word about the hornbooks and the battledores. The hornbooks, which first appeared in the 1440s, were not books at all but little wooden paddles on which were pasted lesson sheets of vellum or parchment. These sheets were covered with transparent horn and bound along the edges by strips of brass. Most of the hornbooks were two and three-fourths by five inches. The lesson sheets began with a

From a photograph in *A Little History of the Horn-Book* by Beulah Folmsbee, The Horn Book, Inc., 1942.

cross followed by the alphabet (sometimes in both large and small letters) and by syllables: *ab, eb, ib,* and other vowel and consonant combinations. There would probably be "In the Name of the Father, the Son, and the Holy Ghost" and the Lord's Prayer. The hornbooks differed in content, but in general they were designed to teach the child letters and their combinations and to continue religious instruction. There is still in existence a little hornbook supposedly used by Queen Elizabeth I. We know that these first hornbooks made their way to the New World for the instruction of Puritan children.

The battledore, which was conceived by one of John Newbery's helpers, was in use from about 1746 to 1770. It had three folding cardboard leaves. Unlike the hornbook, it had no religious material but contained alphabets, easy reading, numerals, and woodcut illustrations. Neither the hornbook nor the battledore ever carried anything that was remotely entertaining, so children still sampled adult books.

And a Picture Book

In 1657 a Moravian bishop and educator, John Amos Comenius (1592–1671) put into practice his belief in better education for the young by preparing what is described today as the first picture book—*Orbis Pictus* (The World Illustrated).[1] Comenius's preface indicates the author's sensitivity to children's need for interesting material: "See then here a new help for Schooles, a Picture and Nomenclature of all the chief things in the World, and of mens Actions in their way of Living!" It would serve, he hoped, "To entice Witty Children to it . . . to stir up the Attention . . . by sport, and a merry pastime." (See illustration, p. 130.)

Pedlar's Treasury:
A Tu'penny Treat

Then came the chapmen, the pedlars of the seventeenth and eighteenth centuries, with newssheets, ballads, broadsides, and chapbooks tucked in among their trinkets. Chapbooks were cheap little books that could be bought for as little as a penny. They had from sixteen to thirty-two or sixty-four pages and were often not stitched but merely folded. F. J. H. Darton, in *Children's Books in England*, tells us that surviving copies have been found all carefully sewed with bits of silk or ribbon, perhaps by some young owner. The editors or compilers of these little books took the legends of antiquity, the old tales of the Middle Ages, elements of the fairy tales—any stories they could lay their hands on—and retold them in drastically condensed versions. All literary charm was lost; the grammar was often faulty, but what remained was a heightened sense of action with an adventure on almost every page. The educated upper classes of England may have frowned upon the chapbooks, but the common people of England loved them and bought them continually. Of course the children discovered them and became ardent patrons of the pedlar's treasures, too.

The stories were the kind that children have always liked—adventure stories with heroes who do things. The account of their valiant

1. An edition of *Orbis Pictus*, published in 1887 by C. W. Bardeen, has been reissued by the Singing Tree Press. See Chapter 6 for further discussion of *Orbis Pictus*.

deeds fills a book: *Chapbooks of the Eighteenth Century* by John Ashton. "The History of Valentine and Orson" is the story of twin brothers who were separated in infancy, Orson to be raised by a bear and Valentine to be reared by a king of France. Later, Valentine captured the wild Orson and they performed great deeds together, each winning the hand of a lovely princess. Incidentally, the bear child, Orson, is a forerunner of Mowgli in Kipling's *Jungle Books.*

One favorite, "Tom Hickathrift," is a kind of early English Paul Bunyan. "At ten years old he was six feet high and three in thickness, his hand was like a shoulder of mutton, and every other part proportionable." He pulled up trees, slew giants, and felled four highwaymen at a blow.

In contrast to the colossal Tom Hickathrift, there is Tom Thumb, whose story is told in a chapbook rhymed version of "Tom Thumb His Life and Death." The woodcuts from 1630 show this tiny hero early in his career falling into a bowl of pudding but later riding valiantly into battle atop an enormous war horse.

The attitude of serious-minded adults of the day toward these crude, often vulgar little books was generally scornful. The clergy viewed them with alarm, but at least one man of letters spoke a good word for them. Richard

From the chapbook *Tom Thumb His Life and Death.* Reproduced from an edition (circa 1665) in the John G. White Collection, Cleveland Public Library.

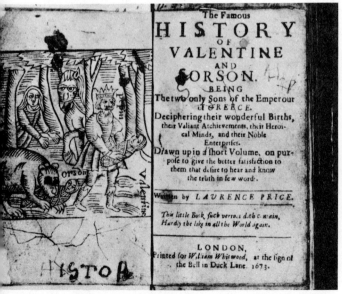

From Laurence Prince's *History of Valentine and Orson.* Reproduced from the d'Alte Welch Collection, The University Library, Department of Special Collections, University of California, Los Angeles.

Steele, in *The Tatler* (No. 95), tells how his young godson was "much turned in his studies" to these histories and adds:

He would tell you the mismanagements of John Hickerthrift, find fault with the passionate temper of Bevis of Southampton and loved St. George for being the champion of England: and by this means had his thoughts insensibly moulded into the notions of discretion, virtue, and honour.

This may be a charitable interpretation of the effects of chapbook reading, but Florence Barry, in *A Century of Children's Books*, adds a cheerful note also. She says:

John Bunyan was the first to reconcile the claims of religion and romance, and he could never have written The Pilgrim's Progress *if he had not been a good customer of the pedlar in his youth.* (pp. 6–7)

Badly written, crudely illustrated, unhonored though they were, the chapbooks preserved and popularized some of the precious elements of literature that children love. But their coarseness probably paved the way for the reaction against tales, stories, and jests—a reaction which produced children's books full of somber warnings and doleful examples.

The Puritans and Perdition

Even while the chapmen were peddling their lurid, lighthearted "Histories," the religious movement was under way that was to affect life on both sides of the Atlantic. Beginning in the late 1500s, about the middle of Queen Elizabeth's reign, the English had become "the people of a book, and that book was the Bible." In London people went daily, in great crowds, to St. Paul's to hear the Bible read aloud, and small Bibles were found in homes everywhere.

A group of deeply religious people whom we know as the Puritans read their Bibles with fervor. They venerated the victims of religious persecution and studied Foxe's *Book of Martyrs* (1563), with its details of death at the stake, and gave the book to their children.

As if this legacy of terror was not enough for small Puritans to endure, a clergyman, James Janeway, wrote in 1671 or 1672 a famous book that was long popular with the heaven-bent adults who ruled over Puritan nurseries. Its full title was:

A Token For Children: *being an Exact Account of the Conversion, Holy and Exemplary Lives, and Joyful Deaths of several young Children. To which is now added, Prayers and Graces, fitted for the use of little Children.*

There were thirteen good little children in this gloomy book, and, considering their lives, it is small wonder that they died young. They spent their time trying to reform, convert, and generally improve everyone they encountered. They brooded on sin and eternal torment and the state of their souls. Morbid and unnatural as this book was with its continual dwelling on death, it grew from the earnest desire of the Puritans to make children happy—not in our modern sense of the word, but in theirs. This meant being secure in the avoidance of Hell and the assurance of Heaven. Unfortunately their method of instilling religious ideas was chiefly through the use of fear—the fear of Hell.

Out of the Puritan world there emerged one great book for children—Bunyan's *Pilgrim's Progress* (Part I, 1678; Part II, 1684). This book was intended for adults and probably reached the children piecemeal as they listened to the adults read it aloud, or discuss it, or tell the more dramatic portions. Reviewing the story, we can easily understand why children enjoyed the book. It is told in the best tradition of the old fairy tales John Bunyan had enjoyed in chapbook form when he was a boy. Bunyan had published, also in 1678, *A Book for Boys and Girls or Country Rhymes for Children.*

John Bunyan (1628–1688), a humble tinker, confessed that one of the sins of his youth was his delight in the "History of the Life and Death of that Noble Knight Sir Bevis of Southampton." As he grew more and more religious, he put away all such light reading and turned to the Bible and to fear-inspiring books such as John Foxe's *Book of Martyrs*. He began to preach such fiery and fearsome sermons that he was locked up for nonconformity to the established Church of England. In jail for years with his Bible and his *Martyrs*, he began to write the

Viewpoint

. . . the evolution of juvenile literature in England has in a very real sense been an account of the gradual and often reluctant realisation that children were meant to enjoy life in their own right, and, to a great extent, on their own terms. The subject, indeed, has a wider reference than its own intrinsic importance, in reflecting a changed and broadening viewpoint towards the upbringing of children.

. . . Harking back to the Puritans and the obstinate vitality of their mental and spiritual approach to the upbringing of children, it is seen to be fundamental to their viewpoint that the only concession permissible of any important difference between children and adults implies not a smaller susceptibility to the temptations of the flesh, but a feebler capacity to withstand them.

For more than one hundred years after the time of the good, godly writers of the Commonwealth period breaks in the cloud of their sombre influence are infrequent and feeble.

. . . The significant fact is that until the eighteen-fifties and even later a carefree attitude unencumbered by moral or instructional preoccupation was strikingly exceptional in writing for children.—Percy Muir, *English Children's Books, 1600–1900*, Batsford, London, 1954, pp. 226–227.

story of a Christian soul on its troublesome pilgrimage through this world to everlasting life. Sir Bevis was not forgotten but was reborn as Christian; the giant Ascapart became the Giant Despair; and so, in good fairy-tale style, Christian fought monsters and enemies with properly symbolic names. But no chapbook tale was ever so somber and so dramatic as this progress of a Christian pilgrim. It begins as a dream:

As I went through the wild waste of this world, I came to a place where there was a den, and I lay down in it to sleep. While I slept, I had a dream, and lo! I saw a man whose clothes were in rags, and he stood with his face from his own house, with a book in his hand, and a great load on his back.

In its original form, with long interludes of theological moralizing, children would have difficulty reading this book, but when the dramatic story is cleared of these obstructions, it is a moving tale. In 1939 an edition abridged and illustrated by Robert Lawson was published.

The *Mayflower* reached our shores in 1620, but the great exodus of Puritans from England to the New World did not take place until around 1630. We can well imagine that those early years of colonization were too difficult for any excursions into book publishing for either children or adults, but the Puritans' passion for education could not long be submerged. The history of their activities in New England is alive with a deep and growing concern for schools and the tools of education, books. As early as 1632, there are references to hornbooks, brought from England with the crosses blotted out—crosses being at that time a religious symbol to which the Puritans objected.

The first book for children to be published in the New World appeared in 1646. It was written by John Cotton and its full title was:

Milk for Babes, Drawn out of the Breasts of Both Testaments, Chiefly for the Spirituall Nourishment of Boston Babes in either England, but may be of like Use for any Children.

Beneath this title it adds *A Catechism in Verse*, and begins:

Who is the Maker of all things?
The Almighty God who reigns on high.
He form'd the earth, He spread the sky.

It continues with all the intricate details of Puritan theology.

24   NEW ENGLAND PRIMER.

Thou shalt not see thy brother s ass or his s fall down by the way, and hide thyself fron. them : thou shalt surely help him to lift then. up again.

THE BURNING OF MR. JOHN ROGERS.

MR. JOHN ROGERS, minister of the gospel in London, was the first martyr in Queen Mary's reign; and was burnt at Smithfield, February the fourteenth, 1554. His wife, with nine small children, and one at her breast, followed him to the stake, with which sorrowful sight he was not in the least daunted, but with wonderful patience died courageously for the gospel of JESUS CHRIST.

From *The New England Primer; or An Easy and Pleasant Guide to the Art of Reading.* Massachusetts Sabbath School Society.

Editions of the *New England Primer* published as early as 1691 have been found, although it is known to have been in print before that. Its famous rhyming alphabet begins:

In Adam's fall
We sinned all.

Thy life to mend
God's Book attend.

In addition, the book contains prayers, poems, the shorter catechism, the Ten Commandments, Bible verses, and pictures. One of these is a quaint woodcut of a Dame's school; another is the picture of a mournful figure contemplating a tombstone; and the prize is a graphic illustration of the burning of Mr. John Rogers, with his wife and ten children looking on, while a jaunty man-at-arms holds them at bay. With tombs and torture, it is difficult to justify the subtitle, "An Easy and Pleasant Guide to the Art of Reading."

As late as 1832, Boston had its own descendant of Janeway's *Token*. It was written by Perkins and Marvin and the title page reads as follows:

> Mary Lothrop
> Who Died In
> Boston
> 1831

The authors add in their preface that their Memoir was prepared "for the purpose of adding another to the bright pictures set before children to allure them into the paths of piety." This was a fairly large book for those days, about three by seven inches, and fully three fourths of it is devoted to the pious Mary's interminable death. The charming little frontispiece shows Mary and her little brother kneeling beside a chair, praying. The boy has struck his sister, and Mary is praying him into a state of repentance. Shortly after that, Mary becomes ill and begins her preparations for death. Gloom descends for the remaining pages. It is to be hoped that Boston children who were given this "bright picture" had recourse to the lusty nonsense of *Mother Goose*. For, despite the Puritans, a pirated edition of this cheerful volume was printed in the New World in 1785.

Fairy Tales and Fables in France

Paul Hazard in his delightful *Books, Children and Men* calls attention to the early portraits of children clad in long velvet skirts, heavily plumed hats, corsets, swords, and ornaments and he remarks, "If, for centuries, grownups did not even think of giving children appropriate clothes, how would it ever have occurred to them to provide children with suitable books?"

Yet around 1697 this miracle occurred in France with the publication of *Histoires ou contes du temps passé avec des moralités* (Histories or Tales of Long Ago with Morals), or, more familiarly, *Contes de ma Mère l'Oye* (Tales of Mother Goose). There is some question today as to whether the tales were written for adults or for children. But whatever the author's intention, they were loved by children. The stories were "La belle au bois dormant" (The Sleeping Beauty); "La petite chaperon rouge" (Little Red Riding Hood); "La Barbe Bleue" (Blue Beard); "Le Maître chat, ou le chat botté" (The Master Cat, or Puss in Boots); "Les fées" (Diamonds and Toads); "Cendrillon, ou la petite pantoufle de verre" (Cinderella, or the Little

Glass Slipper); "Riquet à la houpe" (Riquet with the Tuft); and "Le petit poucet" (Little Thumb).

Did Charles Perrault (1628–1703), member of the French Academy and author of many serious but forgotten works, collect these traditional tales, or was it his eldest son, Pierre Perrault d'Armancour? "Today informed opinion in France . . . favours the son and we may very well leave it at that."[2] Perrault's Fairy Tales, we call them, and their immortality is due as much to the spontaneity and charm of the style as to the traditional content.[3]

Using Aesop and *The Fables of Bidpai* as sources, Jean de la Fontaine (1621–1695) wrote fables to amuse court circles, but they are savored by children today just as they were when they appeared as a series of twelve books in the years 1668–1694. Mme. d'Aulnoy (1650?–1705) turned the old folktale themes into ornate novels for the court. "The Yellow Dwarf" and "Graciosa and Percinet" are sometimes adapted for modern collections but are rarely seen in their original form. Mme. de Beaumont (1711–1780), busy with the education of children, also took time to write some fairy tales for them. Of these, her "Beauty and the Beast" has survived deservedly. Still others took a hand at the fairy tales, but none with the freshness of Perrault.

John Newbery's Books

Meanwhile, in England, it was a happy day for children, steering a perilous course between the pedlar and the Puritan, when in 1729 R. Samber translated Perrault's *Tales of Mother Goose*. No chapbook was ever so thrilling as these eight tales, no "good Godly book" was ever so beloved. At the time, they must have attracted the attention of an English publisher by the name of John Newbery. Not only did his firm later use the title *Mother Goose*, but he may also have discovered through the popularity of the tales the importance of the child as a potential consumer of books.

John Newbery was what we would call today "a character." He dabbled in many things. He

---

2. Percy Muir, *English Children's Books, 1600–1900* (Praeger, 1969), p. 49.

3. For a fascinating account of the "lost manuscript" of 1695, see May Hill Arbuthnot, "Puss, the Perraults and a Lost Manuscript," *Elementary English*, October 1969, pp. 715–721.

wrote; he published; he befriended indigent authors; he did a flourishing business manufacturing and dispensing medicines and a "Medicinal Dictionary." In 1744, along with Dr. James's Fever Powders, Newbery offered for sale his publication:

> A LITTLE PRETTY
> POCKET-BOOK
> Intended for the
> Instruction and Amusement
> of
> Little Master Tommy,
> and
> Pretty Miss Polly.
> With Two Letters from
> Jack the Giant-Killer;
> As also
> A Ball and a Pincushion;
> The Use of which will infallibly make
> Tommy
> a good Boy and Polly a good Girl.
> To which is added,
> A Little Song-Book,
> Being
> A New Attempt to teach Children
> the Use of the English Alphabet,
> by way of Diversion.[4]

For the *"amusement"* of Tommy and Polly, "by way of *diversion"*—here is a new approach to books for children and a momentous one. It marks the beginning of English books for their delight! Of course, Jack the Giant-Killer wrote two exceedingly moral letters to the readers of the *Pretty Pocket-Book*. He had evidently reformed and settled down since the chapbook days, for his lectures are as mild as milk, with no threats anywhere. The letters are followed by a series of games with rhymed directions and morals: marbles, shuttle-cock, blindman's buff, thread the needle, leap frog, and many other old favorites. There are fables, proverbs, and rules of behavior, with a rhyming alphabet and a few poems thrown in for good measure. The morals to the fables are made more romantic and palatable by the signature of Jack the Giant-Killer. The success of the *Pocket-Book* evidently encouraged the publisher because other books for children followed rapidly.

In 1765 *The Renowned History of Little Goody Two Shoes, Otherwise Called Mrs. Margery Two Shoes*, appeared. This is a short juvenile novel, the first of its kind to be written expressly for children. Oliver Goldsmith is supposed to have written *Goody Two Shoes*, which tells the story of a virtuous and clever child, Margery *Meanwell*. At the opening of the book, Margery's father suffers "the wicked persecutions of Sir Timothy *Gripe* and Farmer *Graspall*," who managed to ruin him and turn the whole family out of house and lands. The parents quickly die (evidently no Dr. James's Fever Powders available), leaving Margery and her brother Tommy destitute. Tommy goes to sea and Margery is rescued by charitable Clergyman Smith and his wife. When they buy her two shoes, the child is so overcome with pleasure that she keeps crying out, "Two shoes, Madam, see my two shoes"—hence her name.

This happiness is short-lived, for Gripe forces Smith to turn her out of the house. Back to the hedgerows once more, Margery teaches herself to read with remarkable ease by studying the schoolbooks of more fortunate children. Soon she knows more than any of them and decides to advance their learning. She makes up an alphabet of wooden blocks or "rattle traps" with both small and large letters, puts them into a basket, and goes from house to house helping children to read. Her methods apparently work like a charm, for all her young pupils respond immediately with never a "retarded reader" in the whole countryside.[5]

Goody Two Shoes is full of sociological lessons; its characters are types rather than individuals. Nevertheless, it was entertaining and it was a child's book. Many adults, notably Charles Lamb, recalled the pleasure it gave them when they read it as children.

Between 1760 and 1766, John Newbery, according to many scholars, also published the first edition of *Mother Goose*,[6] but no trace of such a book remains and no contemporary reference to or advertisement of the book has ever been uncovered.[7] On the basis of their research, Jacques Barchilon and Henry Pettit[8] now assert

---

4. No copies of the first English edition (1744) have survived. But in 1944, the two-hundredth anniversary of its first appearance, F. G. Melcher issued a reproduction of the first American edition, which was a reprint by Isaiah Thomas published in 1787 in Worcester, Mass. You can now examine the *Pocket-Book* gaily bedecked with a flowery gilt paper cover after Newbery's custom.

5. *The Renowned History of Little Goody Two Shoes, Otherwise Called Mrs. Margery Two Shoes.* Attributed to Oliver Goldsmith. Edited by Charles Welsh.

6. Even the scholarly Opies give 1765–1766 in their *Oxford Dictionary of Nursery Rhymes* (Oxford, 1951), p. 33.

7. See Chapter 5 for a discussion of *Mother Goose*. Other children's classics mentioned in this chapter are discussed more fully in later chapters. See the Index for relevant page references.

8. *The Authentic Mother Goose Fairy Tales and Nursery Rhymes* (Alan Swallow, Denver, 1960), p. 11.

Mother GOOSE's Melody. 37

JACK and *Gill*
Went up the Hill,
To fetch a Pail of Water;
Jack fell down
And broke his Crown,
And *Gill* came tumbling after.

Maxim.

The more you think of dying, the better
you will live.

ARISTOTLE'S

38 Mother GOOSE's Melody.

ARISTOTLE'S STORY.

THERE were two Birds fat on
a Stone,
   Fa, la, la, la, lal, de;   [one,
One flew away, and then there was
   Fa, la, la, la, lal, de;
The other flew after,
And then there was none,
   Fa, la, la, la, lal, de;
And fo the poor Stone
   Was left all alone,
   Fa, la, la, la, lal, de.

This may ferve as a Chapter of Confequence
in the next new Book of Logick.

From *The Original Mother Goose's Melody*.
Reproduced in facsimile by W.H.
Whitmore (Joel Munsell's Sons, 1899) from
the edition reprinted by Isaiah Thomas of
Worcester, Mass., about 1785.

that there was no such publication during those years. They assume that John Newbery may have planned such a book, but not until 1781 was there an advertisement announcing the first publication by his stepson, T. Carnan, of *Mother Goose's Melody*. John Newbery's firm remained in the family for many years and continued to publish books for children.

The first American edition of *Mother Goose* appeared about 1785 and was probably a pirated reprint of an early Newbery edition. It was published by Isaiah Thomas (1749–1831), of Worcester, Massachusetts, who cheerfully and not quite legally printed his own editions of Newbery's books, possibly for mercenary motives but certainly to the benefit of young Americans. W. H. Whitmore vouched for the fact that two copies of this Isaiah Thomas edition existed in his day, and in 1889 he reproduced the book in full, calling it *The Original Mother Goose's Melody*.[9] The little book is two and one-half by three and three-fourths inches. Preface, fifty-two jingles with maxims, sixteen songs of Shakespeare, and small woodcuts are precisely the same as in the English edition. The maxims are surprising and often amusing, especially the one that follows "Margery Daw," which will surely be applauded by all bewil-

dered readers of footnotes: "It is a mean and scandalous Practice in Authors to put Notes to Things that deserve no Notice."

It is fitting that John Newbery, this first English publisher of books for children, is honored annually when the Newbery Medal is presented for the year's most distinguished book for children written by an American citizen or resident and published in the United States.[10]

Robinson Crusoe

One book emerged from the Puritan world to mark not only the increase of cheerfulness but the beginning of contemporary adventure tales. It was Daniel Defoe's *Robinson Crusoe*, one of the most popular books in all English literature.

Defoe (1659–1731), with a wisdom far in advance of his times, wrote on banks, insurance companies, schools for women, asylums for the insane, and all sorts of social problems. He turned out bitter political and religious satires which landed him in the pillory. He rose to wealth and fame and sank to penury and prison more than once. Writing was his passion, and few men have written more continuously. His most famous book, *The Life and Strange Surprising Adventures of Robinson Crusoe*, appeared in 1719, when Defoe was sixty and nearing the

9. W. H. Whitmore, ed. *The Original Mother Goose's Melody* (Joel Munsell's Sons, 1889). It is reproduced in facsimile from the Isaiah Thomas edition (Worcester, Massachusetts, 1785). Whitmore's introduction gives many interesting facts about the early collections of *Mother Goose*.

10. For the list of books which have been awarded the Newbery Medal see Appendix D.

end of his turbulent career. We are told four editions of it were printed in four months, and for once the old fighter enjoyed fame with no unhappy repercussions of any kind.

Why has this book commended itself to children of each succeeding generation? It was addressed to adults and originally contained masses of moral ruminations that the children must have skipped with their usual agility in the avoidance of boredom. Most children's editions today omit these tiresome reflections and get on with the story.

There was a real-life Alexander Selkirk, marooned for over four years on the island of Juan Fernandez, who not only told his story to Defoe but also gave him his papers. However, it is due to Defoe's skill that Selkirk, as Robinson Crusoe, emerges a favorite world hero. The theme itself is irresistible: man pitted against nature, one man with a whole world to create and control. He must obtain food, provide himself with clothes and shelter, fight off wild animals, reckon time, keep himself civilized and sane.

Here is a book that satisfies children's hunger to achieve competence. Identifying with Robinson Crusoe, they win an ordered, controlled place in the world by their own efforts and foresight. With the coming of Friday, they have the love of a friend whom they in turn nurture and protect. No wonder children read and reread and dramatize this book. All the details are there; every question is answered. It is reasonable and clear—a design for living, complete and satisfying.

The theme of the shipwrecked survivor was used in many books following publication of *Robinson Crusoe*, among them *The Swiss Family Robinson*, written by Johann David Wyss (1743–1818) and published in 1812. Despite its pedantic overtones, this story of a pious, energetic family on a desert island delighted worldwide audiences with its dramatic events.

Gulliver's Travels

Another remarkable book emerged from this period, a political satire not intended for children but read by them and known today as *Gulliver's Travels*. The author, Jonathan Swift (1667–1745), was born in Dublin and died there, Dean of the Cathedral. But between his

Illustration by Louis Rhead from *Gulliver's Travels* by Jonathan Swift. Copyright 1913 by Harper & Row, Publishers, Inc.; copyright 1941 by Bertrand Rhead. Reproduced by permission of Harper & Row, Publishers, Inc.

birth and death, he spent considerable time in London and took an active part in the political life of the times. Recognized today as one of the greatest satirists in English literature, in his own day he was known as a pamphleteer and misanthrope.

Swift wrote his book in Ireland to lampoon the follies of the English court, its parties, its politics, and its statesmen. Worried about the reception of the book, he published it anonymously in 1726 as *Travels into Several Remote Nations of the World*, in four parts, by Lemuel Gulliver. To Swift's surprise and relief, London society, the very society he was making fun of, was highly diverted. In writing these tall tales, Swift seems to have been caught up with the richness of his own invention, and the humor sometimes overshadows the satire.

Children have always loved things in miniature, and they soon discovered the land of the Lilliputians. No one ever forgets Gulliver's waking to find six-inch people walking over him and Lilliputian ropes binding him. All the fascinating details are worked out to scale with logic and precision. Children are untroubled by any double meanings and like the fantasy for itself. The second journey, to the land of giants, Brobdingnag, is the next most popular, but Gulliver in an inferior position, treated like a toy, is not so appealing as the omnipotent Gulliver in Lilliput. The remaining books most children never read. As far as they are concerned, the first adventure makes the book, and it is Lilliput forever!

If Gulliver's travels had not fascinated artists, the book might not have survived in children's reading as long as it has. An early edition illustrated by Charles E. Brock (1894) and later editions illustrated by Arthur Rackham and by Fritz Eichenberg would lure anyone into reading the story.

Poets and Children

About the time *Robinson Crusoe* and *Gulliver's Travels* were published, a gentle nonconformist preacher wrote a book of poetry for children. Isaac Watts (1674–1748) moralized in verse about busy bees and quarrelsome dogs, but he also wrote tender and beautiful hymns, many of which are found today in most hymnals. His *Divine and Moral Songs for Children* (1715) dwelt not on the fearful judgments of God, but on God "our refuge," and many a child must have been comforted by his tender "Cradle Hymn."

Toward the end of the century a major poet, William Blake (1757–1827), published a book of poems for and about children, *Songs of Innocence* (1789), each poem illustrated with Blake's own decorative designs. It is now considered an epoch-making book, but it caused no stir at the time of its publication. A companion volume, *Songs of Experience* (1794), followed. Although most of Blake's unique lyrics are for adults, some of his other poetry appeals to children also.

Ann (1782–1866) and Jane (1783–1824) Taylor's *Original Poems for Infant Minds: By Several Young Persons* (1804) teaches lessons in the manner of Watts's *Moral Songs*, but with a difference. The vigorous, fun-loving Taylors usually tell good stories in their verse and reveal something of the simple, pleasant life of rural England. The book enjoyed immediate popularity and was translated into various languages, but

it is best known today for the familiar "Twinkle, twinkle, little star."

The Butterfly's Ball, published in book form in 1807, was written by William Roscoe (1753–1831), a lawyer and member of Parliament, for the amusement of his little son. There is no story, but there are such fascinating details as a mushroom table with a water dock leaf tablecloth, and there are William Mulready's charming pictures of the insect guests at the ball. However, the verse is tame, and the long popularity of the poem must have been due in part to lack of better verse for children.

Didacticism in France, England, and the United States

In 1762 Jean Jacques Rousseau (1712–1778) proclaimed his theory of a new day for children through his book *Émile*. He believed in the joyous unfolding of a child's powers through a free, happy life. The child Émile was the companion of his tutor; he was free of all books except *Robinson Crusoe;* and he lived vigorously out of doors, learning from experiences and activities. Schools today reflect Rousseau's emphasis on experiences and activities.

In its day *Émile* effected a revolutionary change in people's attitudes toward both children and education. To some people, Rousseau seemed like a breeze blowing away the clouds of Puritan morbidity, and one would naturally expect the ardent Rousseau converts, if they wrote books for children, to write only the happiest ones. Instead, in France, in England, and even in the United States, they began to write painfully didactic stories, sometimes to teach religion, sometimes to inform and educate. The only thing these writers seemed to have carried over from Rousseau was the idea of following and developing the child's natural interests. In practice, they went at the business hammer and tongs. If the poor children picked strawberries, the experience was turned into an arithmetic lesson. If they rolled a snowball, they learned about levers and proceeded from those to wedges. If they took a walk, they had to observe every bird, beast, stone, and human occupation. Day and night these ardent authors stalked their children, allowing them never a moment for play or fancy but instructing and improving on every page. No longer did they

Viewpoint

As the technological achievements of the industrial revolution during the late eighteenth and early nineteenth centuries undermined tradition and quickened social change, children's books became one of the most important instruments in the socialization of the young. In order to shape the productive character structure required by a growing middle-class ethic, book after book offered the child useful facts along with advice on how to behave, stressing the value of utilitarian, rational action and moral behavior, but discouraging imagination and play.

In fashioning their image of the child, didactic writers drew on at least three basic and somewhat contradictory models of child development. They were influenced by Locke's picture of the mind as a "tabula rasa," a blank sheet to be inscribed by the educator with useful information, by Rousseau's idea of the child as naturally good and of education as a process gradually unfolding innate capacities with a minimum of outside interference, and by the older religious concept of human nature according to which the child was originally sinful, and the goal of education was to reshape his wicked impulses. Although each of these models of childhood placed a different emphasis on the polarities of restraint and spontaneity, reason and imagination, work and play, the practice of didactic writers was to juxtapose one model on another, blurring the distinctions between them. Rousseau's principle of allowing the child to learn through the first-hand experience of things (object-lessons), for example, was frequently adopted by didactic writers in order to instill utilitarian knowledge or Christian morality.—Lynne Rosenthal, "*Misunderstood:* a Victorian Children's Book for Adults," *Children's Literature,* Volume 3. Copyright © 1974 by Francelia Butler. Reprinted by permission of Francelia Butler; Children's Literature An International Journal, Inc. Box 370, Windham Center, Connecticut 06280.

threaten children with the fear of Hell, but the pressure of Information hung almost as heavily over their hapless heads.

Here was a revival of didacticism with a vengeance—not the terrifying theological didacticism of the Puritans but the intellectual and moralistic variety. Students who wish to read more about this period should study the works of the French Mme. de Genlis (1746–1830) and Armand Berquin (1749–1791) and those of such English writers as Laetitia Barbauld (1743–1825), Sarah Trimmer (1741–1810), and Hannah More (1745–1833). For most readers, a few examples of this writing will probably suffice.

One of the classic examples of the new didacticism is *The History of Sandford and Merton* (1783–1789) in four volumes by Thomas Day (1748–1789). Tommy Merton was the spoiled, helpless, ignorant son of a rich gentleman, whereas Harry Sandford was the sturdy, industrious, competent child of an honest farmer. Harry was reared out of doors and trained to work and study; there was nothing he did not know and nothing he could not do. Father Merton, handicapped by wealth though he was, saw at once the advantage of having his young darling unspoiled and trained in the ways of the honest Harry. So poor Tommy, little knowing what was in store for him, was put in the charge of the same clerical tutor who had wrought such wonders with Harry. Mr. Barlow trained both boys, but Harry was always used as the perfect example to show up Tommy's ignorance, incompetence, and general orneriness. All day that worthy pair, the omniscient Barlow and the admirable Harry, instructed, disciplined, and uplifted poor Tommy. Through each of the volumes, he was plagued and polished into Rousseau-like simplicity and competence. At the end of four volumes, there he was at last—Tommy Merton remodeled, divested of all his fine apparel, his curls gone, and his life to be given over to study and philosophy forever. Could any reform go further?

Another and perhaps the most gifted exponent of didacticism in children's books was Maria Edgeworth (1767–1849), who told her moral tales with such dramatic realism that they are still remembered. She had an excellent laboratory for developing her stories as she was the second of twenty-two children. She not only helped her father with the education of the younger ones but wrote her stories in their midst, tried them out with the children, and modified them according to their suggestions. Thomas Day himself had a hand in Maria's early education, but her own father seems to have been a greater influence in her writings than anyone else.

Maria Edgeworth wrote many short stories, some deadly dull and unnatural. But at her best, she was a born storyteller. She developed real plots—the first in children's stories since the fairy tales—with well-sustained suspense and surprise endings that took some of the sting out of the inevitable morals. While she told an interesting story, her tales carry such a heavy and obvious burden of moral lessons that her characterizations and excellent plots are sacrificed to didacticism.

Viewpoint

One writer of the period, however, not only deplored the pedantic stories written for children but tried to provide them with more entertaining fare. The best-known contribution to children's literature of Charles Lamb (1775–1835) and his sister Mary (1764–1847) is their *Tales from Shakespeare* (1806), in which they retold the plays from Shakespeare and made them more easily comprehensible and presumably more enjoyable for the young.

It was inevitable that the United States should develop its own brand of didacticism. Samuel G. Goodrich (1793–1860), who wrote under the name of Peter Parley and produced five or six volumes a year, wrote laudatory biographies of famous men and poured out a continuous stream of information in the fields of science, history, and geography. Jacob Abbott (1803–1879) launched a series in which a youth by the name of Rollo was dragged from one city and country to another, bearing up nobly under a steady barrage of travel talks and moralizing. Both men wrote well but pedantically. We shall detect some of their literary descendants in the books of today—information attractively sugared but oppressively informative nevertheless.

Our chief moralist was Martha Farquharson, pseudonym for Martha Finley (1828–1909), whose *Elsie Dinsmore* series began in 1868 and ran to twenty-six volumes. This pious heroine had a way of bursting into tears or fainting with such effect that adult sinners were converted and even Elsie's worldly father was brought to a state of repentance. Most parents developed considerable resistance to Elsie but were baffled by her powers to charm their offspring. Elsie was a spellbinder, for her author had a sense of the dramatic. To this day sensible people remember weeping over Elsie's Sabbath sit-down strike at the piano, when she refused to play secular music for her erring father. She was made to sit on the piano stool until one of her best faints put an end to her martyrdom and Father repented. Elsie was a prig with glamour, and there is no telling how many more of her kind might have developed if certain pioneers had not appeared to clear away the artificiality and to bring laughter, fantasy, and realism to children's books.

Modern Books Begin

Even while Peter Parley was dispensing information, and Maria Edgeworth was teaching her heroines valuable lessons, and Martha Finley's heroine, Elsie Dinsmore, was piously swooning, epoch-making books in both England and the United States were appearing that were to modify the whole approach to children's literature. These children's classics, some as popular today as when they were first published, not only brought laughter, fantasy, and realism into stories for young people, but they began the trend toward better illustrations in children's books. Each of these books will be discussed in greater detail in later chapters; they are reviewed here because they are milestones in the development of children's literature.

Folk and Fairy Tales

Grimms' Popular Stories by Jacob (1785–1863) and Wilhelm (1786–1859) Grimm was translated into English by Edgar Taylor in 1823. Grimms' Fairy Tales, as they were called by the children, became as much a part of the literature of English-speaking children as the *Mother Goose* rhymes. These stories, some of them gathered by the Grimm brothers from the lips of the old storytellers, were occasionally droll but often somber and harrowing.

The *Fairy Tales* of Hans Christian Andersen (1805–1875) appeared in England in 1846,

Illustration by George Cruikshank for *Grimm's Popular Stories.*

translated by Mary Howitt. Many of these stories were Andersen's own adaptations of folk tales which he, too, had heard from the storytellers. But to these he added his own fanciful inventions and immeasurably enriched the child's world of the imagination. Andersen's stories have unusual literary and spiritual values, and they are, for the most part, in a minor key, melancholy and even tragic.

Joseph Jacobs (1854–1916) was the great compiler of English folk tales; and the folklorist Andrew Lang (1844–1912) began, in 1889, with the publication of *The Blue Fairy Book*, a series that is still deservedly popular.

Humor

One of the first notes of gaiety was a long story poem by an American professor, Clement Moore, entitled "A Visit from St. Nicholas" (1822), but known to children as "The Night Before Christmas." This fast-moving, humorous ballad, full of fun, fancy, and excitement, with never a threat or a dire warning to spoil the children's delight, is as beloved now as it was in Moore's day.

Under Queen Victoria, England's industrial age flourished and grew prosperous and pompous. Then suddenly two eminent men produced books that sent the children off into gales of laughter. One, Edward Lear (1812–1888), was an artist who earned his living by making scientific paintings of birds and

reptiles. When he grew too bored with the drawing room, he took refuge with the children. For them he would write absurd limericks which he illustrated on the spot. His *Book of Nonsense* (1846) not only was an unprecedented collection of amusing verses and pictures but perhaps paved the way for another excursion into absurdity.

In 1865 a book appeared that is generally considered the first English masterpiece written for children. It was *Alice's Adventures in Wonderland.* The author was Charles Lutwidge Dodgson (1832–1898), an Oxford don, a lecturer in logic and mathematics, who used the pen name Lewis Carroll. *Alice* still remains a unique combination of fantasy and nonsense that is as logical as an equation. It was first told, and later written, solely for the entertainment of children, and neither it nor its sequel, *Through the Looking Glass,* has the faintest trace of a moral or a scrap of useful information or one improving lesson—only cheerful lunacy, daft and delightful. *Alice* launched the literature of nonsense and fantasy which is told so logically and reasonably that it seems entirely natural.

Two more books brought laughter to children. Written in Germany in 1844 and published the next year, *Struwwelpeter* (Slovenly Peter) by Heinrich Hoffmann (1809–1894) was a collection of merry, prankish rhyming stories intended only to entertain, although the verses are regarded by some people as brutal. It is still in print, having gone into dozens of editions in English. In America, children were captivated by the antics of the Peterkin family. Lucretia Hale (1820–1900) published a series of stories about the Peterkins in magazines, collected them in a book in 1880, and gave the young an unforgettable character: the Lady from Philadelphia.

Illustrations

Both Lear's and Carroll's laughter-provoking books have delightful illustrations—Lear's own outrageous caricatures for his *Book of Nonsense* and Sir John Tenniel's inimitable drawings for Carroll's *Alice.* Deservedly famous, too, are Walter Crane, Randolph Caldecott, and Kate Greenaway,[11] whose charming watercolors

---

11. See Chapter 6 for a fuller account of illustrators of children's books.

From *R. Caldecott's Picture Book* by
R. Caldecott. Reproduced by permission of
Fredrick Warne & Co., Inc., Publishers.

brightened the pages of children's books with decorative designs, appealing landscapes, and figures which hold their own with the best in modern books.

Frederic G. Melcher in 1938 proposed that the American Library Association institute a second award—this one for the most distinguished picture book for children published each year in the United States. At his suggestion, the new medal was named after Randolph Caldecott—a fitting memorial to the man who drew a picture of himself surrounded by children, and who left those children a delightful legacy of storytelling pictures.[12]

Myths: Hawthorne and Kingsley

In the United States Greek myths were introduced to children by a gifted novelist, Nathaniel Hawthorne (1804–1864). Around 1852 *A Wonder-Book for Girls and Boys* was published, followed in 1853 by *Tanglewood Tales for Girls and Boys*. These books contain stories of the Greek gods and heroes, supposedly told to a group of lively New England children by a young college student, Eustace Bright. Eustace talks down to the children; his gods lose much of their grandeur, and his heroes are often child-sized, but the style is delightful.

In England, Charles Kingsley (1819–1875), country parson, Victorian scholar, and poet, also retold the myths for children. His adapta-

12. For a list of the books which have been awarded the Caldecott Medal see Appendix D.

tions not only are closer to the original myths than Hawthorne's romantic versions, but convey the inner significance and grandeur of the myths in a style closer to the classic original. Here are dreams of greatness, presented with the sensitive perception of a poet. Interestingly, in Kingsley's own day these stories were less popular than his original fantasy, *The Water-Babies* (1863), which is marred for us today by its moralizing.

Fantasy

Lewis Carroll's *Alice* was the great masterpiece of fantasy and nonsense, but the nineteenth century saw the publication of several other classics in fantasy for children. In 1841, John Ruskin (1819–1900) wrote *The King of the Golden River*, a long, serious fairy tale, and published it a decade later. In 1867, George Macdonald (1824–1905), Scottish poet and novelist, published a delightfully playful tale, *The Light Princess*, and four years later, his most important children's fairy tale, the imaginative *At the Back of the North Wind*.

Some of the other great British writers of the period tried their hands at fantasy for children. William Makepeace Thackeray (1811–1863) contributed in 1855 *The Rose and the Ring*, a long fairy tale distinguished by its blithe humor; and in 1868, Charles Dickens (1812–1870) wrote, in the best fairy-tale tradition, *The Magic Fishbone*. Dickens's earlier story, *A Christmas Carol* (1843), is firmly ensconced in the list of hardy perennials of both Christmas literature and Victoriana. Rudyard Kipling (1865–1936), storyteller and poet, Nobel Prize winner and advocate of empire, wrote *The Jungle Books* (1894) and *Just So Stories* (1902) with a warmth and affection that make his animal characters part of the permanent heritage of children's lore, along with Beatrix Potter's *The Tale of Peter Rabbit* (1901) and Kenneth Grahame's *The Wind in the Willows* (1908).

From France came the stories of Jules Verne (1828–1905), who wrote for adults but whose books have fascinated children since the first, *From the Earth to the Moon*, was published in 1865. *Twenty Thousand Leagues Under the Sea* (1869) and *Around the World in Eighty Days* (1872) are still popular with both adults and children. In Verne's work, one sees the beginning of the new genre of science fiction.

From Italy came *Pinocchio* by C. Collodi (pseudonym for Carlo Lorenzini, 1826–1890). Published originally in a magazine, as so many books of this period were, the story was translated in 1892 to become an enduring classic.

Edith Nesbit (1858–1924) was one of the first and most skilled writers in combining realism and fantasy. Her first story, *The Story of the Treasure Seekers*, was published in 1899.

Illustration by Arthur Hughes for *At the Back of the North Wind* by George Macdonald.

Realistic Fiction

During the Victorian period there was an increasing awareness of, and response to, children's needs. In England the awareness was most evident in the work of Charlotte Yonge (1823–1901), who wrote family stories based on her own happy childhood, and some school stories, sentimental in tone, moral in intent, and realistic in approach. Her prolific output (well over a hundred books) was read avidly by children of the period.

The epoch-making book in the United States was a modest story of family life. *Little Women*, like Charlotte Yonge's books, was based on the author's own family experiences. The author, Louisa M. Alcott (1832–1888), submitted the manuscript hesitatingly, and her publisher told her as gently as possible how unacceptable it was. Fortunately, he felt some qualms about his judgment and allowed the children of his family to read the manuscript. They convinced him that he was wrong. Those astute little girls loved the book, and it has remained popular with children since its publication in 1868. The story is as genuine a bit of realism as we have ever had. Family life is there—from the kitchen to the sanctuary of the attic, from reading to giving amateur dramatics in which the home-made scenery collapses. But right as all the details are, the reason adults remember the book is the masterly characterizations of the four girls. No longer are people typed to represent Ignorance or Virtue; here are flesh-and-blood girls, as different from each other as they could well be, full of human folly and human courage, never self-righteous, sometimes irritable but never failing in warm affection for each other. This ability to make her characters vividly alive was Louisa M. Alcott's gift to modern realism for children.

L. M. Montgomery's *Anne of Green Gables* (1904), a Canadian story of a lively, independent orphan, was as popular in the United States as it was in Canada.

In his adventure stories for boys, England's George Henty (1832–1902) used his own experiences as a correspondent to furnish the backgrounds; in the same field in the United States, William Taylor Adams (1822–1897) wrote under the fetching pen name of Oliver Optic. That best of all purveyors of rags-to-riches books, Horatio Alger (1834–1899), captivated the young with *Ragged Dick* (1867) and all the succeeding stories that flowed out in the same pattern.

So far, on both sides of the Atlantic, realistic stories for children were primarily about eminently respectable characters. When Samuel Clemens (1835–1910), or Mark Twain as he signed himself, wrote *The Adventures of Tom Sawyer* in 1876, he carried realism across the tracks. In this book Huck Finn and his disreputable father were probably the child's first literary encounters with real people who were not considered respectable but who were likable anyway. Moreover, they were not typed to show the folly of being disreputable. Huckleberry won all hearts and so nearly stole the book from Tom that he had to appear in a book of his own—*The Adventures of Huckleberry Finn* (1884). Mark Twain in these two unsurpassed books not only gave us realism with humor—in itself a new development in literature for children—but also showed warm tolerance in his presentation of people then thought socially unacceptable.

Children's Literature Comes of Age

The Victorian period saw the stream of cheerfulness in children's literature rise steadily. Many of the books written then are still popular and will be considered in detail later. The list of "milestones" is a reminder of these and others that had a major impact on the development of children's literature from 1484 to 1908.

These are individual books that were turning points in children's literature. They not only carry us into the twentieth century with distinction, but their influence is discernible in the writing of today. Laura Richards continued the deft nonsense verses of Lear and Carroll in her *Tirra Lirra* (1932). A. A. Milne's skillful light verse, *When We Were Very Young* (1924), did as much to popularize poetry for young children in schools and homes as Robert Louis Stevenson had done earlier. The small, sweet lyrics of Christina Rossetti were followed by the exquisite poetry of Walter de la Mare and by poetry with the delicacy of Aileen Fisher, the humor of David McCord, the evocative directness of Langston Hughes.

In the field of fairy tales and fantasy, *East o'*

the Sun and West o' the Moon continued the interest in folklore that began with the Grimms. American children could share in the literary heritage of other lands with books like *Tales from a Finnish Tupa* (1936), Indian fables in the several versions of the Jataka stories, and Japanese folk tales in *The Dancing Teakettle* (1949). From the Uncle Remus collections there came a new consciousness of the United States as a repository of regional and racial folklore. *The Jack Tales* (1943), southern variants of European folk tales, stemmed from this interest. If the Italian fairy tale *Pinocchio* (1891) was the lively descendant of Andersen's somber toy stories, so too was the young and equally lighthearted *Winnie-the-Pooh* (1926). Gulliver's Lilliput was not more fascinating than the miniature world of *The Borrowers* (1952). *Rabbit Hill* (1944) continued the great tradition of animal fantasy begun in *The Wind in the Willows*, to be followed by *Charlotte's Web* (1952), *The Cricket in Times Square* (1960), *Animal Family* (1965), and *Watership Down* (1974). And the daft world of *Alice's Adventures in Wonderland* grew perceptibly zanier in the fantastic dreams of Dr. Seuss.

True Americana began with *Little Women* and *Tom Sawyer* and continued to flourish in such descendants as *Little House in the Big Woods* (1932), *Caddie Woodlawn* (1935), the three books about *The Moffats* (1941–1943), and *Across Five Aprils* (1964). It is there, too, in the fine animal story *Smoky* (1926), written in the vernacular of a cowboy, and in an excellent story of the South in the depression era, *The Rock and the Willow* (1963). And it is certainly alive in such regional stories as *Strawberry Girl* (1945), . . . *and now Miguel* (1953), and *Where the Lilies Bloom* (1969).

Illustration by Attilio Mussino. Reprinted with permission of Macmillan Publishing Co., Inc. from *Pinocchio* by Carlo Collodi. First published in 1925. Reissued in 1969. (Original in color)

Milestones in the History of Children's Literature

1484 *Aesop's Fables*, translated and printed by William Caxton.

1646 *Spiritual Milk for Boston Babes*, John Cotton.

1657 or 1658 *Orbis Pictus*, Comenius (original in Latin).

1678 *Pilgrim's Progress*, John Bunyan.

1691 *The New England Primer*.

1697 *Contes de ma Mère l'Oye*, Perrault.

1715 *Divine and Moral Songs for Children*, Isaac Watts.

1719 *Robinson Crusoe*, Daniel Defoe.

1726 *Gulliver's Travels*, Jonathan Swift.

1729 *Tales of Mother Goose*, Perrault (first English translation).

1744 *A Little Pretty Pocket-Book*.

1765 *The Renowned History of Little Goody Two Shoes*.

1781 *Mother Goose's Melody*.

1785 *Mother Goose's Melodies* (Isaiah Thomas edition).

1789 *Songs of Innocence*, William Blake.

1804 *Original Poems for Infant Minds*, Ann and Jane Taylor.

1807 *The Butterfly's Ball*, William Roscoe.

1822 *A Visit from St. Nicholas*, Clement C. Moore.

1823 *Grimms' Popular Stories* (translated into English by Edgar Taylor).

1843 *A Christmas Carol*, Charles Dickens.

1846 *Book of Nonsense*, Edward Lear.

1846 *Fairy Tales*, Hans Christian Andersen (first English translation).

1848 *Struwwelpeter*, Heinrich Hoffmann (first English translation).

1852 *A Wonder-Book for Girls and Boys*, Nathaniel Hawthorne.

1865 *Alice's Adventures in Wonderland*, Lewis Carroll (Charles Lutwidge Dodgson).

1865 *Hans Brinker, or the Silver Skates*, Mary Mapes Dodge.

1867 – 1876 *Sing a Song of Sixpence*, and other toy books, illustrated by Walter Crane.

1868 – 1869 *Little Women*, Louisa M. Alcott.

1871 *At the Back of the North Wind*, George Macdonald.

1872 *Sing-Song*, Christina Rossetti.

1876 *The Adventures of Tom Sawyer*, Mark Twain (Samuel Clemens).

1878 *Under the Window*, Kate Greenaway.

1878 *The House That Jack Built* and *The Diverting History of John Gilpin*, illustrated by Randolph Caldecott.

1880 *The Peterkin Papers*, Lucretia Hale.

1883 *Treasure Island*, Robert Louis Stevenson.

1883 *Nights with Uncle Remus*, Joel Chandler Harris.

1883 *The Merry Adventures of Robin Hood*, Howard Pyle.

1884 *Heidi*, Johanna Spyri (first English translation).

1884 *The Adventures of Huckleberry Finn*, Mark Twain (Samuel Clemens).

1885 *A Child's Garden of Verses*, Robert Louis Stevenson.

1889 *The Blue Fairy Book*, Andrew Lang.

1891 *Pinocchio*, C. Collodi (Carlo Lorenzini). First English translation.

1894 *The Jungle Books*, Rudyard Kipling.

1899 *The Story of the Treasure Seekers*, E. Nesbit.

1901 *The Tale of Peter Rabbit*, Beatrix Potter.

1903 *Johnny Crow's Garden*, L. Leslie Brooke.

1908 *The Wind in the Willows*, Kenneth Grahame.

The picture story so charmingly begun by Beatrix Potter continues in the varied books of Wanda Gág, Maurice Sendak, Russell Hoban, and many others. And if stories of other countries began auspiciously with *Hans Brinker* and *Heidi*, they have grown and strengthened in *The Good Master* (1935), *The Wheel on the School* (1954), *The Happy Orpheline* (1957), *The Silver Sword* (1959), *Wildcat Under Glass* (1968), and *Fly Away Home* (1975). So the types of books that were turning points in children's literature at an earlier period are alive and healthy today, although the kinship between the old and the new may sometimes seem remote.

Of the many good books that have been published in the twentieth century, some stand out. Probably no two people would agree on every one that merits inclusion in a list of landmark books; the older classics have proved themselves, the new ones have yet to do so. Still, those listed here seem milestones either because they are distinguished of their kind or because they have broken new ground, or—as in the past—they are adult books that have been taken by children as their own.

Looking back at the past, it is evident that little today is completely new, but certainly some kinds of books are better written today than ever before and are enjoying such tremendous popularity that they seem to constitute a trend. The trends discussed in Chapter 1 make it clear that many of today's books are

Twentieth-Century Milestones

1921   *The Story of Mankind*, Hendrik Willem Van Loon. A lively and readable history, winner of the first Newbery Medal.

1926   *Winnie-the-Pooh*, A. A. Milne. An enduring fantasy about the lives of a small boy's toy animals.

1928   *Millions of Cats*, Wanda Gág. Dramatic illustrations flow with a story told in the cadence of the oral tradition.

1928   *Abe Lincoln Grows Up*, Carl Sandburg. Authoritative biography written in an easy conversational style.

1932   *Little House in the Big Woods*, Laura Ingalls Wilder. First of a series unmatched for its warm picture of pioneer life.

1934   *Mary Poppins*, P. L. Travers. Highly original fantasy with an unforgettable protagonist.

1937   *The Hobbit*, J. R. R. Tolkien. A classic fantasy for adults and children.

1941   *George Washington's World*, Genevieve Foster. Significant for its broad look at people and events the world over.

1941   *Paddle-to-the-Sea*, Holling C. Holling. A social geography uses a narrative framework for drama and cohesion.

1943   *Homer Price*, Robert McCloskey. Humor with which children can identify, and believable episodes with dramatic appeal.

1943   *Johnny Tremain*, Esther Forbes. Outstanding historical fiction set during the Revolutionary War period. Newbery Award.

1944   *Rabbit Hill*, Robert Lawson. A cozy, engaging story about an animal community. Newbery Award.

1947   *The Twenty-One Balloons*, William Pène du Bois. A fantasy adventure about the inventive people on a volcanic island. Newbery Award.

1952   *Charlotte's Web*, E. B. White. A touching, beautifully written fantasy about animal friendship.

1959   *Tom's Midnight Garden*, Philippa Pearce. Polished style and perceptive characterization give depth to an imaginatively structured time-slip fantasy. Published in England in 1958. Carnegie Award.

1961   *The Incredible Journey*, Sheila Burnford. A deftly sustained tale about three animals who trek through the Canadian wilderness.

1962   *The Snowy Day*, Ezra Jack Keats. Poster-simple composition in a picture book about a black child's imaginative play. Caldecott Award.

1963   *Where the Wild Things Are*, Maurice Sendak. Superb illustrations complement a story in which a child consoles himself with dreams of power. Caldecott Award.

1964   *Harriet the Spy*, Louise Fitzhugh. A boundary-breaking story, candid and perceptive, about an unhappy child.

1964   *The Pushcart War*, Jean Merrill. An adroit mock-history of the struggle against big truckers by the peddlers of New York City.

1964   *The Book of Three*, Lloyd Alexander. First of a five-book cycle of high fantasy in the Welsh tradition.

1969   *Where the Lilies Bloom*, Vera and Bill Cleaver. A trenchant and moving story about an orphaned family in Appalachia.

1970   *Blowfish Live in the Sea*, Paula Fox. Remarkable both for its fine writing style and its perceptive picture of the intricacies of familial relationships.

1974   *M. C. Higgins, the Great*, Virginia Hamilton. One of our great stylists, the author writes with grace and insight about a black family in the Cumberland Mountains. Newbery Award.

1974   *Watership Down*, Richard Adams. A long, intricate, and absorbing fantasy about a rabbit community. First published in England in 1971. Carnegie Award.

---

about serious subjects, deal with contemporary problems, and are designed for children whose sophistication has grown with their exposure to a media-dominated world—a world in which the developmental stages and needs of children are better understood and better reflected in their books than in the past.

How do you spot a trend? Observe a pattern long enough and you are looking backward; to label a current change a trend is to make a judgment about the importance of a development that may prove to be ephemeral. It is within the context of the historic pattern that you must decide. It is against the background of the past—the changed concept of childhood, the establishment of universal education, the growing numbers of libraries for children, the evaluation of literary quality in the elementary school classroom—that publishers have established a broad program of special publishing for children. It is impressive by its sheer weight; it has responded with sensitivity to curricular needs and current interests; it has made reading material more accessible by mass distribution of inexpensively produced books and by a rapidly expanding production of paperback editions of established books—one of the most significant trends in bookmaking. Furthermore, many publishers are broadening their programs to include book-oriented films, film strips, cassettes, and other audio-visual media; and some have established flourishing book clubs. Without any doubt, these are exciting and productive times in the field of children's literature.

Adult References[13]

ASHTON, JOHN. *Chap-Books of the Eighteenth Century.*

BARCHILON, JACQUES, and HENRY PETTIT. *The Authentic Mother Goose Fairy Tales and Nursery Rhymes.*

BARRY, FLORENCE V. *A Century of Children's Books.*

BETT, HENRY. *The Games of Children: Their Origin and History.*

BOSTON, LUCY. *Perverse and Foolish.*

CHAMBERS, ROBERT. *Popular Rhymes of Scotland.*

COMENIUS, JOHANN AMOS. *The Orbis Pictus of John Amos Comenius.*

COMMIRE, ANNE, ed. *Yesterday's Authors of Books for Children.*

CROUCH, MARCUS. *Treasure Seekers and Borrowers: Children's Books in Britain, 1900–1960.*

DARLING, RICHARD L. *The Rise of Children's Book Reviewing in America, 1865–1881.*

DARTON, F. J. H. *Children's Books in England: Five Centuries of Social Life.*

DE VRIES, LEONARD. *Little Wide-Awake: An Anthology from Victorian Children's Books and Periodicals in the Collection of Anne and Fernand G. Renier.*

DOYLE, BRIAN, comp. and ed. *The Who's Who of Children's Literature.*

EDEN, HORATIA K. F. *Juliana Horatia Ewing and Her Books.*

ELLIS, ALEC. *A History of Children's Reading and Literature.*

FIELD, ELINOR WHITNEY, comp. *Horn Book Reflections: On Children's Books and Reading.*

FIELD, LOUISE F. *The Child and His Book: Some Account of the History and Progress of Children's Literature in England.*

FOLMSBEE, BEULAH. *A Little History of the Horn-Book.*

FORD, PAUL LEICESTER, ed. *The New England Primer.*

FRASER, JAMES, ed. *Society and Children's Literature.*

FRYE, BURTON C., ed. *A St. Nicholas Anthology: The Early Years.*

GILLESPIE, MARGARET C. *Literature for Children: History and Trends.*

GOTTLIEB, GERALD. *Early Children's Books and Their Illustration.*

GREEN, ROGER LANCELYN. *Tellers of Tales.*

HALES, JOHN W., and FREDERICK J. FURNIVALL, assisted by FRANCIS J. CHILD. *Bishop Percy's Folio Manuscript.*

HALSEY, ROSALIE V. *Forgotten Books of the American Nursery: A History of the Development of the American Story-Book.*

HAVILAND, VIRGINIA, ed. *Children and Literature: Views and Reviews,* Chapter 1, "Before the Twentieth Century."

HAVILAND, VIRGINIA, and MARGARET COUGHLAN, comps. *Yankee Doodle's Literary Sampler of Prose, Poetry, & Pictures.*

HAZARD, PAUL. *Books, Children and Men.*

HEWINS, CAROLINE M. *A Mid-Century Child and Her Books.*

HÜRLIMANN, BETTINA. *Seven Houses.*

JORDAN, ALICE M. *From Rollo to Tom Sawyer.*

KIEFER, MONICA. *American Children Through Their Books, 1700–1835.*

LANG, ANDREW, ed. *Perrault's Popular Tales.*

LYSTAD, MARY. *From Dr. Mather to Dr. Seuss: 200 Years of American Books for Children.*

McGUFFEY, WILLIAM HOLMES. *Old Favorites from the McGuffey Readers.*

MacLEOD, ANNE SCOTT. *A Moral Tale: Children's Fiction and American Culture 1820–1860.*

MEIGS, CORNELIA, ANNE EATON, ELIZABETH NESBITT, and RUTH HILL VIGUERS. *A Critical History of Children's Literature.*

MOORE, ANNE CARROLL. *My Roads to Childhood.*

MUIR, PERCY. *English Children's Books, 1600 to 1900.*

OPIE, IONA and PETER. *Children's Games in Street and Playground.*

————. *The Lore and Language of Schoolchildren.*

————, eds. *The Oxford Dictionary of Nursery Rhymes.*

The Original Mother Goose's Melody, As First Issued by John Newbery, of London, about A.D. 1760.

PELLOWSKI, ANNE. *The World of Children's Literature.*

QUAYLE, ERIC. *The Collector's Book of Children's Books.*

ROSELLE, DANIEL. *Samuel Griswold Goodrich, Creator of Peter Parley: A Study of His Life and Work.*

ROSENBACH, ABRAHAM S. W. *Early American Children's Books with Bibliographical Descriptions of the Books in His Private Collection.*

ST. JOHN, JUDITH. *The Osborne Collection of Early Children's Books 1566–1910: A Catalogue,* Vols. 1 and 2.

SALWAY, LANCE. *A Peculiar Gift.*

SAXTON, MARTHA. *Louisa May.*

SMITH, DORA V. *Fifty Years of Children's Books.*

SMITH, IRENE. *A History of the Newbery and Caldecott Medals.*

STEWART, CHRISTINA. *The Taylors of Ongar: An Analytical Bio-Bibliography.*

TARG, WILLIAM, ed. *Bibliophile in the Nursery.*

THWAITE, MARY F. *From Primer to Pleasure in Reading.*

TOWNSEND, JOHN ROWE. *Written for Children: An Outline of English Children's Literature.*

TUER, ANDREW W. *Pages and Pictures from Forgotten Children's Books: Brought Together and Introduced to the Reader.*

————. *Stories from Old-Fashioned Children's Books.*

VIGUERS, RUTH HILL, MARCIA DALPHIN, and BERTHA MAHONY MILLER, comps. *Illustrators of Children's Books, 1946–1956.*

WEISS, HARRY B. *A Book About Chapbooks: The People's Literature of Bygone Times.*

WELSH, CHARLES. *A Bookseller of the Last Century. Being some Account of the Life of John Newbery and of the Books he published with a Notice of the later Newberys.*

————, ed. *The Renowned History of Little Goody Two Shoes, Otherwise Called Mrs. Margery Two Shoes.*

---

13. Complete bibliographic data are provided in Appendix B.

PART TWO:

Discovering Books with Children

Chapter Five:
Books for the Very Young

Young children are naturally receptive, responding with enthusiasm to new stimuli and experiences. The preschool years are ones during which it is possible to instill a joy in books, to lead children to the realization that books and reading are sources of pleasure. Through the sharing of our own pleasure in books, we can not only help prepare children for learning to read but can also help them take the first steps toward the habit of reading, a habit that will provide lifelong pleasure.

Since children's first experiences with books and reading usually occur before they go to school, parents and other adults who are responsible for preschool children bear a large responsibility for creating an environment in which children can best develop language skills, formulate attitudes toward reading, and experience pleasure with books.

Studies of home environments of children in nursery schools show clearly how much more advanced in language skills those children are who have been sung to, read to, and talked with. In fact, there is evidence that their greatest response is to language. Infants may enjoy a mother's voice or a father's lap before they appreciate what's being read to them, but the association of books with pleasure can begin in infancy.

Children can make great discoveries about reading before learning to read for themselves. For one thing, seeing adults enjoy their own books can spur a positive attitude toward reading. Moreover, following the story as an adult reads and points out objects on the page, a child learns that the symbols in the book always go from left to right and, just as dependably, from the top to the bottom of the page. That's a big step. And then comes the marvelous realization that an "a" in one word is an "a" in another, that "c-a-t" in one book is exactly the same as "c-a-t" in another book; those are two more big steps, and they are learned most easily in a one-to-one situation when a small child and an adult, or an older child, share a book together.

Interest in very young children and their intellectual development has increased remarkably in recent years. Scientific research suggests that fifty percent of a child's general intelligence is achieved between birth and age four, and an additional thirty percent by age eight. Children's speech and vocabulary development follows a similar pattern, with about thirty-three percent of these skills achieved by the time they are six.

Small wonder, then, that there has been a corresponding flourishing of organizations concerned solely with young children and their education, of books, journals, and articles on myriad aspects of the subject, of special schools for early education, and of books written for this group. This chapter will examine the many kinds of books there are: *Mother Goose* and other books of nursery rhymes, alphabet books and counting books, concept books and picture books without text, picture story books to be read aloud and simply written stories for beginning independent readers.

Books for young children are usually referred to en masse as "picture books." The true picture book is one in which the illustrations are the dominant feature with little or no text. *Brian Wildsmith's ABC* is an excellent example, with large-scale pictures of familiar objects a child can point to and gleefully recognize. An adult may get bored the tenth time a child points and says "dog," but to the child each repetition brings the delight of corroborating a new experience. The picture book affords opportunities for self-discovery experiences, while there is a greater component of sharing in listening to a picture story book being read aloud.

A picture story book has a structured, if minimal, plot; it really tells a story, while a picture book may not. In a picture story the illustrations are so integral a part of the content that the story can be "read" by the child from the pictures (Robert McCloskey's *Make Way for Ducklings,* for example).

Look at picture books, read picture story books aloud, take children to a public library and help them choose their books. Observe their reactions. If a television program is based on a book, follow it up by getting the book if you can; the average preschooler in the United States watches almost thirty-three hours of television each week,[1] and any opportunity for capitalizing on that familiar medium should be seized. Talk about books you have read; tell stories if you possibly can (young children are not very demanding about technique). All of these are pleasurable shared activities, but they also prepare the child (as do street signs, magazines, and box tops) for reading independently. In Chapter 2 we discussed children's needs and the ways in which books can meet those needs, and in Chapter 3 we described some of the criteria by which books can be evaluated. In considering books for young children, we should keep in mind those needs and those criteria as well as the limitations of experience and language of the very young. While this chapter focuses specifically on books for young children,

many other books written for this age, and many of the authors and artists who excel in their creation, are discussed in the following chapter, "Artists and Children's Books," and in the later chapters on modern fantasy, modern and historical fiction, and informational books. You will probably find it useful to look at the following chapter on illustrators along with this chapter, since illustration is an essential element in books for the very young. The emphasis in this chapter is on the content of those books; the emphasis in the following chapter is on the artwork.

Mother Goose

Small children acquire a love for poetry as naturally as did people of early times, through hearing poems spoken or sung and through learning them, almost unconsciously, along with the speaker or singer. Favorite nursery ditties were easily remembered and passed on by word of mouth for generations before they achieved the permanency of print and became known as *Mother Goose.* Old folk rhymes are still important not only because children continue to enjoy them, but because many are skillfully composed, exuberant or dramatic, and lead naturally into modern nonsense verse and narrative poems.

Where did these verses come from? Who was Mother Goose? These are questions that occur to us as we turn over the pages of some beguiling modern editions. Although it is sometimes difficult to distinguish legend from fact, these nursery songs are linked with our historical and literary past.

The name *Mother Goose,* as we saw in Chapter 4, was first associated with the eight folk tales recorded by Perrault. Andrew Lang, in *Perrault's Popular Tales,* tells us that the frontispiece of *Histoires ou contes du temps passé, avec des moralités* (Histories or Tales of Long Ago, with Morals) showed an old woman spinning and telling stories, and that a placard on the same page bore the words "Contes de ma Mère l'Oye" (Tales of Mother Goose). But the name *Mother Goose* has now become so completely associated with the popular verses that most English translations of the Perrault tales omit it from the title of the collection.

Lina Eckenstein, in *Comparative Studies in Nursery Rhymes* (1906), said that the name *Mother*

1. A. C. Nielson and Co. Annual Report (Media Research Group, 1980.)

Viewpoint

... although each new generation of parents, grandfathers, and grandmothers sings and recites to children both the good and the inferior, only that which bests serves the children's needs and tastes remains in their memories. And when he reaches old age, everyone who heard in his childhood these folk chants passes on to his grandchildren, in his turn, the very best, the most vivid and vital. And everything that is out of tune and incongruous with the psychology of the young child is gradually forgotten and becomes extinct; ... In this way an exemplary children's folklore has come into existence—exemplary in its language and rhythm, as well as ideally suited to the intellectual needs of the young child. ...

The great book that is called by the English *Mother Goose* came into being exactly the same way. The rhymes comprised in *Mother Goose*, called nursery rhymes, had been subjected to the same process of collective selection, unconsciously achieved by a long sequence of generations of children. These verses had been sifted through a thousand sieves before this book came into existence.—Kornei Chukovsky, *From Two to Five*, University of California Press, Berkeley and Los Angeles, 1963, p. 94.

Goose was first used in England in connection with Robert Powell's puppet shows, exhibited in London between 1709 and 1711. Powell's plays included, among others, *Robin Hood and Little John*, *The Children in the Wood*, *Whittington and His Cat*, and one called *Mother Goose*. What play did Powell present under the title of *Mother Goose*? It may have been one of Perrault's stories heard from a traveler. At any rate, Perrault's *Contes de ma Mère l'Oye* was translated into English in 1729, and the popularity of the eight tales undoubtedly helped establish still more firmly that delightful nonsense name, *Mother Goose*.

Early Editions of *Mother Goose*

The next mention of the name in England is in connection with John Newbery, whom we discussed in Chapter 4. At one time, Newbery was thought to have published an edition of *Mother Goose's Melody or Sonnets for the Cradle* between 1760 and 1765, but more recent research[2] sug-

gests that he may have planned but did not publish such a book. In 1781 Newbery's stepson, T. Carnan, who continued the Newbery publishing business, advertised in the *London Chronicle* for January 2, "The first publication of *Mother Goose's Melody*."

The first American edition of *Mother Goose* was probably a pirated reprint of an early Newbery edition, published in about 1785 by Isaiah Thomas.[3] Two more notable American editions followed. Between 1824 and 1827, the Boston firm of Munroe and Francis published the *Mother Goose's Quarto, or Melodies Complete*, which contained many rhymes drawn from the Thomas reprint of Newbery's *Melody* but also many apparently old ones printed for the first time. In 1833 this firm made a reprint of the *Quarto* with the title *The Only True Mother Goose Melodies*. Both the *Quarto* and the 1833 edition are important sources for many of the later collections. These editions include, as many of our modern editions do, some poems that are not traditional, such as Walter Scott's "Pibroch of Donnel Dhu" and Shakespeare's "Jog on, jog on, the foot-path way," which are obviously out of place in a collection of folk rhymes.

Origins of the *Mother Goose* Verses

The *Mother Goose* verses underwent many changes during the years when they were passed on by word of mouth, and later when they traveled from one printed edition to another. As with the ballads, variants of the same verses were recited or sung in different places, and which ones were the originals no one can say. Certainly they have led to considerable speculation and to some careful research. Undoubtedly many of the rhymes are mere nonsense jingles, but many others reveal interesting bits of history, old customs, manners, and beliefs. Attempts to find historical characters to fit the people of *Mother Goose* have shown more imagination than documented research. Iona and Peter Opie, scholars of distinction in the field of nursery rhymes, comment in *The Oxford Dictionary of Nursery Rhymes:*

Much ingenuity has been exercised to show that certain nursery rhymes have had greater significance than is now apparent. They have been vested with mystic symbolism, linked with social and political events, and numerous at-

2. Jacques Barchilon and Henry Pettit, eds. *The Authentic Mother Goose Fairy Tales and Nursery Rhymes* (Swallow, 1960).

3. See Chapter 4, p. 64.

tempts have been made to identify the nursery characters with real persons. It should be stated straightway that the bulk of these speculations are worthless. Fortunately the theories are so numerous they tend to cancel each other out. The story of "Sing a song of sixpence," for instance, has been described as alluding to the choirs of Tudor monasteries, the printing of the English Bible, the malpractices of the Romish clergy, and the infinite workings of the solar system. The baby rocked on a tree top has been recognized as the Egyptian child Horus, the Old Pretender, and a New England Red Indian. Even when, by chance, the same conclusions are reached by two writers the reasons given are, as likely as not, antithetical. This game of "interpreting" the nursery rhymes has not been confined to the twentieth century, though it is curious that it has never been so overplayed as in the age which claims to believe in realism. (p. 27)

Qualities That Appeal to Children

Children enjoy the variety of subject matter and mood that continually surprises them in *Mother Goose*. It ranges from the sheer nonsense of:

> Hey! diddle, diddle,
> The cat and the fiddle,
> The cow jumped over the moon.

to the sad and tender ballad of "The babes in the wood":

> My dear, do you know
> How a long time ago
> Two poor little children,
> Whose names I don't know . . .

The following list of examples, to which you can add dozens of others, suggests the variety in these verses:

People (a rich gallery of characters)
    Children—Little Miss Muffet
    Grownups—Old King Cole
    Imaginary—Old Mother Goose when she wanted to wander
    Grotesque—There was a crooked man
Children's pranks—Georgie, Porgie, pudding and pie
Animals—I had a little pony
Birds and fowl—Jenny Wren; Higgledy, piggledy, my black hen
Finger play—Pat-a-cake
Games—Ring a ring o' roses
Riddles—Little Nancy Etticoat
Counting rhymes—One, two, buckle my shoe

HEAR WHAT MA'AM GOOSE SAYS!

My dear little Blossoms, there are now in this world, and always will be, a great many grannies besides myself, both in petticoats and pantaloons, some a deal younger to be sure; but all monstrous wise, and of my own family name. These old women, who never had chick nor child of their own, but who always know how to bring up other people's children, will tell you with very long faces, that my enchanting, quieting, soothing volume, my all-sufficient anodyne for cross, peevish, won't-be-comforted little bairns, ought to be laid aside for more learned books, such as *they* could select and publish. Fudge! I tell you that all their batterings can't deface my beauties, nor their wise pratings equal my wiser prattlings; and all imitators of my refreshing songs might as well write a new Billy Shakespeare as another Mother Goose — we two great poets were born together, and we shall go out of the world together.

No, no, my Melodies will never die,
While nurses sing, or babies cry.

From *The Only True Mother Goose Melodies*, an exact and full-size reproduction of the original edition published and copyrighted in Boston in the year 1833 by Munroe and Francis (Lothrop, Lee and Shepard, 1905).

Counting out—Intery, mintery, cutery-corn
Alphabets—A, is an apple pie
Proverbs—Early to bed, early to rise
Superstitions—See a pin and pick it up
Time verses—Thirty days hath September
Days of the week—Solomon Grundy, born on Monday
Verse stories—The Queen of Hearts, she made some tarts
Dialogue—Who killed Cock Robin?
Songs—A frog he would a-wooing go
Street cries—Hot-cross Buns!
Weather—Rain, rain, go away
Tongue twisters—Peter Piper picked a peck of pickled peppers
Cumulative stories—This is the house that Jack built
Nonsense—Three wise men of Gotham

On the whole, descriptive nature poems, in the modern sense, are conspicuously lacking, as are fairy poems.

Lured on by the variety of these rollicking jingles, children are also captivated by their musical quality. "Sing it again," they insist, when you finish reading or singing one of their favorites. They nod their heads or rock their bodies, marking time to the rhythm. They may suit the words to their own actions.

Saying these verses, children get a happy introduction to rhyme—perfect and imperfect—to alliteration, onomatopoeia, and other sound patterns. Happily they get these without the burden of their labels and so enjoy them light-heartedly. Alliteration, as in "Sing a song of sixpence," tickles their sound sense to a degree that astonishes us. They are also fascinated by the staccato in "Higgledy, piggledy, my black hen" and by the explosive *tle* in "She lays eggs for gen*tle*men." Indeed, the brisk tune of this ditty turns upon its lively use of consonants, the *n* sounds making it ring delightfully. One of the many values of these melodious jingles is that they accustom the ear and the tongue to the musical aspects of the English language. All in all, the verses offer many opportunities for the development of a fine sense of the musical quality of language.

Still another characteristic of these verses that endears them to young children is their action. Jack and Jill fall down, Miss Muffet runs away, Mother Goose rides on her gander, the cow jumps over the moon, Polly puts the kettle on. Here are no meditations, no brooding introspections, no subtle descriptions. In these verses things happen as rapidly and riotously as youngsters would like to see them happening every day.

Some verses contain simple stories. "The Queen of Hearts," for example, is a slight but complete account of the innocent and industrious queen, her tarts stolen, the villain caught, punishment administered, and the villain left in a properly penitent frame of mind. Old Mother Hubbard and her bare cupboard involve considerable suspense before the tale is told out. The brevity of these verse stories makes them acceptable to children as young as two years old and they prepare children to enjoy longer and more involved prose and verse stories.

The sheer fun of *Mother Goose* keeps the verses alive in the hearts of every generation of children. What do children laugh at? It is hard to say; we can only watch and listen. Sometimes they laugh at the sound; often they laugh at the grotesque or the incongruous. Surprise and absurd antics amuse them, and broad horseplay delights them. There are plenty of examples of all these in *Mother Goose*. A man jumps into the bramble bush to scratch his eyes "*in* again"; a pig flies up in the air; Simple Simon goes fishing in his mother's pail; Humpty Dumpty has a fall (falls always bring a laugh).

Finally, children love the pictures that illustrate their favorite book. Whether the edition is so small it can be tucked into a pocket, or so enormous it must be spread out on the floor, the numerous pictures enchant them. Here they share their delight in *Mother Goose* with some of the finest illustrators of each generation, for artists also love the fun and action of these old rhymes and have lavished on them some of their best work. Just as there is endless variety in the stories, the moods, and the characters of these jingles, so there is a like variety in the size, the shape, the color, and the style of pictures that illustrate them. One adult prefers one edition, while a second adult greatly prefers another, but the children simply ask for *Mother Goose*—with colored pictures or black-and-white, simple or elaborate, commonplace or subtle.

Popular Editions

It is impractical to list all the fine editions of *Mother Goose,* but the following choices are popular with parents, teachers, librarians, and children for a variety of reasons.

Mother Goose: or, The Old Nursery Rhymes (1882), illustrated by Kate Greenaway, is a tiny book to fit small hands and pockets and to fill small hearts with delight. It contains forty-four of the brief rhymes, each with its own picture in the quaint Kate Greenaway style. The print is exceedingly small, but for nonreaders this does not matter. The illustrations are gently gay, the colors are soft, and the people exquisitely decorative.

Mother Goose: The Old Nursery Rhymes (1913), illustrated by Arthur Rackham, one of England's great artists, is a splendid edition, brought back into print in 1978. The illustrations are of three types: pen-and-ink sketches, silhouettes, and full-page color. The silhouettes are amazingly effective, for example, the dripping bedraggled cat of "Ding, dong, bell." The color plates are Rackham at his best and in many moods. These are pictures by an artist with imagination and a knowledge of folklore. (See 2, p. 83.)

A good introduction to *Mother Goose* and her

Popular
Mother Goose Books

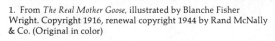

1. From *The Real Mother Goose*, illustrated by Blanche Fisher Wright. Copyright 1916, renewal copyright 1944 by Rand McNally & Co. (Original in color)

2. Illustration by Arthur Rackham. From *Mother Goose.* Copyright © 1926, by Arthur Rackham. Reproduced by permission of Elsevier/ Nelson Books.

3. Illustration by Leonard Leslie Brooke. From *Ring O' Roses.* Reproduced with permission of Frederick Warne & Co., Inc. (Original in color)

4. Illustration from "Little Miss Muffet" from *The Tall Book of Mother Goose*. Illustrated by Feodor Rojankovsky. Copyright 1942, Copyright Renewed 1970 by Western Publishing Company, Inc. Reprinted by permission. (Original in color)

5. From *London Bridge Is Falling Down!* copyright © 1967 by Peter Spier. Reproduced by permission of Doubleday & Company, Inc. (Original in color)

6. From *Mother Goose* by Brian Wildsmith. Copyright © 1964. Reproduced by permission of Franklin Watts, Inc. and Oxford University Press, London. (Original in color)

7. Taken from *Every Child's Book of Nursery Songs* by Donald Mitchell and Carey Blyton. Copyright © 1968 by Donald Mitchell and Carey Blyton. Used by permission of Crown Publishers, Inc.

8. Illustration from *Three Jovial Huntsmen* by Susan Jeffers. Reproduced by permission of Bradbury Press, Inc. (Original in color)

4

5

6

7

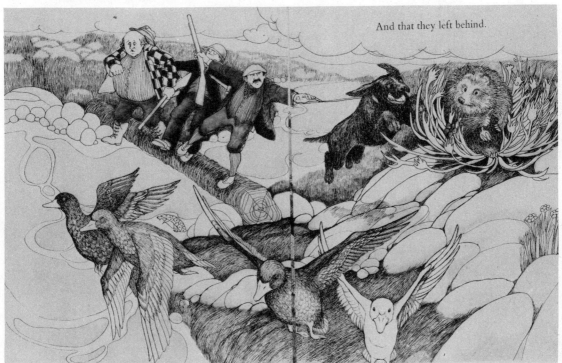

And that they left behind.

8

The fox gives warning,
It's a cold frosty morning.

9

10

11

9. From *Granfa' Grig Had a Pig and Other Rhymes Without Reason from Mother Goose* compiled and illustrated by Wallace Tripp. Illustrations Copyright © 1976 by Wallace Tripp. Reprinted by permission of Little, Brown and Company. (Original in color)

10. From *Cakes and Custard* by Brian Alderson, Illustrated by Helen Oxenbury. Reprinted with permission of William Morrow & Company and William Heinemann, Ltd. (Original in color)

11. Illustration by Arnold Lobel, p. 10. From Arnold Lobel, *Gregory Griggs and Other Nursery Rhyme People.* Copyright © 1978 by Arnold Lobel. Published by Greenwillow Books. (Original in color)

world is the tried and true *The Real Mother Goose* (1965 ed.), illustrated by Blanche Fisher Wright. There are colored pictures on every page; often one picture fills a whole page, or sometimes there are two or three small ones. The characters are dressed in period costumes and can be seen distinctly by a large group of children. The colors are clear washes, sometimes soft and pale but more often bright and lively. It is a big book with a wide selection of traditional verses which the illustrations really illustrate. This is more important than some artists have realized, because small children use pictures as clues to the meaning of the text. (See 1, p. 83.)

In *Ring o' Roses* (1922), Leslie Brooke provides an imaginative and broadly humorous pictorial interpretation of the traditional verses. The characters are in English period costumes and are utterly satisfying interpretations. Simple Simon *is* Simple Simon, daft and delightful. But above all you will remember Leslie Brooke's pigs—after chuckling over them you will never again see pigs as plain pigs. This is, after all, the test of great illustrations: they do more than illustrate—they interpret the text so vividly that they become the embodiment of the words. (See 3, p. 83.)

The Tall Book of Mother Goose (1942), illustrated by Feodor Rojankovsky, is an elongated book, approximately five by twelve inches, which can be easily held. There are delightful picture spreads like the panoramic landscape of "One misty, moisty morning." An equally effective arrangement is the sequence of small pictures like those for "The three little kittens." Rojankovsky was a master of color and realistic texture. His furry kittens, feathery chicks, and woolly mufflers have a depth that almost creates a tactual sensation. His children are husky, everyday youngsters, never beautiful and often very funny. This book, with its 150 rhymes and twice as many pictures, remains popular. (See 4, p. 84.)

Marguerite de Angeli's *Book of Nursery and Mother Goose Rhymes* (1954) contains 376 jingles, 260 enchanting pictures, and innumerable decorations. It is a big book, and it must have been a labor of love for the artist. Children and animals dance and prance across the pages. The book is too big for small children to handle alone, but it is fine for children and adults to look at together. The verses are not arranged in any particular order, so a nursery jingle is often

From *Tom Thumb's Song Book*, J. Lumsden & Son, Glasgow (1815). In *Oxford Nursery Rhyme Book* by Iona and Peter Opie. Reproduced by permission of The Clarendon Press, Oxford.

followed by a ballad of sufficient substance to suit older children. However, the rich offering of verses and illustrations makes this an edition to cherish and to pass on to the next generation.

Lavender's Blue (1954), compiled by Kathleen Lines, is distinguished by Harold Jones's illustrations. Both in color and in black and white, they suggest old engravings. The pages are neatly bordered; the figures are stiffish, not stylized yet not realistic either. Although the colors are muted and there is little humor, the composition of the pictures holds your attention. A cat sits tall, solemn, and mysterious against an interior from which a door opens onto alluring streets. She is framed like a period portrait of a great lady. (See color section, Ch. 6.)

From the rich store of their scholarly study Iona and Peter Opie have compiled *The Oxford Nursery Rhyme Book* (1955), with eight hundred of the verses that have delighted children for generations. The vast collection is skillfully organized. It begins with the simplest ditties and progresses to more mature riddles, songs, and ballads. Almost every verse has a picture— small and black only, but amazingly effective. Many of the illustrations are taken from the old chapbooks and toy books. The work of Thomas and John Bewick is well represented, and the distinguished drawings of contemporary artist Joan Hassall are in keeping with their style. Students of early children's books will find this an invaluable edition, and parents will also enjoy the book. Designed as a companion volume to *The Oxford Nursery Rhyme Book* is the Opies' *A Family Book of Nursery Rhymes* (first published as *The Puffin Book of Nursery Rhymes*). Of its 358

Viewpoint_____

rhymes, 200 are not included in the first book. Precise, delicate drawings by Pauline Baynes grace almost every page, and the notes at the back of the book are as entertaining as they are informative.

Brian Wildsmith's work is distinguished for its magnificent use of rich color, often in a patchwork of vibrant geometric figures. In his *Brian Wildsmith's Mother Goose* (1964) the people are gay in period clothing, and the almost theatrical quality of the pictures gives a sense of milieu as well as of the characters. (See 6, p. 85.)

Another delightful collection is *A Book of Scottish Nursery Rhymes*, edited by Norah and William Montgomerie. Most of the selections are pure Scots, but anyone can recognize and enjoy such favorites as:

> "Pussy, pussy baudrons
> Where have you been?"
> "I've been to London,
> To see the Queen!"
>
> "Pussy, pussy baudrons,
> What got you there?"
> "I got a good fat mousikie,
> Running up a stair!"

One of the impressive collections of the 1960s is *The Mother Goose Treasury* (1966), illustrated by Raymond Briggs. It contains over four hundred verses, most of them from the Opie collection, and each has at least one illustration.

The verses and pictures, many of them small, are scattered over the pages with open-handed abandon. Occasionally there is a full-page or a double-page spread in color. The pictures are greatly varied in mood and treatment: some are bold, some delicate, some restrained, some grotesque, some humorous, but all have charm.

In *Mother Goose Lost* (1971) Trevor Stubley's gay and colorful pictures illustrate a collection of unfamiliar rhymes found by Nicholas Tucker, a British psychologist, while doing research for an article. Another distinguished Englishman in the field of children's literature, Brian Alderson, includes some of his childhood favorites in addition to *Mother Goose* rhymes in *Cakes and Custard* (1975). The best collection since the one by Briggs, this handsomely designed book is illustrated by Helen Oxenbury with pictures that have wit, vigor, and superb draftsmanship. (See 10, p. 86.) Arnold Lobel's *Gregory Griggs and Other Nursery Rhyme People* (1978) is also among the most entertaining new editions. (See 11, p. 86.) Wallace Tripp's *Granfa' Grig Had a Pig and Other Rhymes Without Reason from Mother Goose* (1976) is filled with humorous details that both children and adults will find delightful. (See 9, p. 86.)

A collection of songs, many from *Mother Goose*, has been selected by Donald Mitchell and very simply arranged for piano accompaniment by Carey Blyton in *Every Child's Book of Nursery Songs* (1969). Suggestions for the use of percussion instruments or for vocal participation by children (in rounds or with spoken parts) are included. The black-and-white artwork is amusing. (See 7, p. 85.)

In recent years several very attractive editions of single verses from *Mother Goose* have been published. Margot Zemach's sturdy, raffish figures add humor to the lilt of *Hush, Little Baby* (1976). Both Peter Spier and Ed Emberley illustrated *London Bridge Is Falling Down*—Emberley's fanciful version has an ornate bridge but little period detail; Spier's version has minutely and humorously detailed illustrations and notes on the history of the bridge. (See 5, p. 84.) Barbara Cooney has illustrated with delightful delicacy *Mother Goose in French*, ably translated by Hugh Latham. Maurice Sendak in *Hector Protector* and *As I Went Over the Water* adds a raffish charm to two less familiar verses. For the imaginative and delicately detailed illustrations for *Three Jovial Huntsmen* (1973), Susan Jeffers won the Golden Apple at the Bienniale of Illustrations in Bratislava, an international exhibit. (See 8, p. 85.)

It is clear that no single artistic interpretation is more appropriate than any other. Whether an edition is large in size or small, whether it contains a single verse or many, the illustrations should reflect the mood of the verses, should truly illustrate them rather than being merely decorative, and should be placed on the pages so that they relate to the verses, enabling children to relate words and pictures. The latter is especially important in *Mother Goose* books in which there are several verses and illustrations on a page; the layout of the page should leave no doubt as to which illustration fits each picture. Since such layout is difficult to achieve on a crowded page, adequate spacing is an important criterion in evaluating editions. Whether illustrations are delicate or robust, they should be realistic enough for young children to see the correlation between picture and verse.

Variants of *Mother Goose*

In addition to the many editions of *Mother Goose* there are several collections of nursery rhymes which are fairly close in style and content to the old English jingles.

The American Mother Goose was compiled by Ray Wood and illustrated by Ed Hargis. Children studying frontier life are interested in and amused by this collection. The verses are both rougher and funnier than the English nursery rhymes and are as indigenous to America as a "possum up a gum stump." Here is such familiar doggerel as "I asked my mother for fifteen cents," "How much wood would a woodchuck chuck," and a final section of riddles, games, and finger play. The pen-and-ink sketches are full of hilarious touches that delight adults as much as they do the children.

Maud and Miska Petersham's *The Rooster Crows: A Book of American Rhymes and Jingles* was awarded the Caldecott Medal in 1946. In spite of the inclusion of such American folk rhymes as "A bear went over the mountain" and "Mother, may I go out to swim," the subtitle is difficult to justify because the collection also contains such old-world rhymes as "Sally Waters" and "Oats, peas, beans and barley grows."

A Rocket in My Pocket, compiled by Carl Withers, carries the subtitle *The Rhymes and Chants of Young Americans.* Some four hundred ditties, tongue twisters, derisive chants, and bits of pure nonsense, together with Susanne Suba's line drawings, make this an unusually beguiling book.

Did You Feed My Cow? compiled by Margaret Burroughs, an authority on Afro-American culture, is a book of street games, chants, and rhymes in which traditional folk materials have been adapted by children.

Another collection of rhymes, street chants, games, and songs, *Sally Go Round the Sun*, is based on research by the compiler, Edith Fowke, an expert on Canadian folklore. A collection of Danish nursery rhymes, *It's Raining Said John Twaining,* has been translated and illustrated by N. M. Bodecker with perky, rhythmic verses that have a humorous quality that is echoed in the illustrations. *The Prancing Pony,* translated by Charlotte De Forest, is a compilation of fifty-three favorite nursery song lyrics; the verses reflect Japanese culture but also have a universal appeal. Robert Wyndham's selections of Mandarin verses for *Chinese Mother Goose Rhymes* are beautifully illustrated by Ed Young on pages printed sideways and bordered by columns of Chinese calligraphy.

Lillian Morrison has made a delightful contribution to Americana with her small collections of riddles, auguries, school and playground chants, and amusing autograph album inscriptions. The three books in the last category—*Yours Till Niagara Falls, Remember Me When This You See,* and *Best Wishes, Amen*—are never on library shelves at commencement time.

Tongue Tanglers, compiled by Charles Francis Potter, is popular with both children and speech teachers. There are only forty-four tongue tanglers, but they are gems, and the illustrations in full color add to the hilarity. Potter's selection, chosen from thousands of tongue twisters, ends with that perfect conclusion:

> *Tongue twisters twist tongues twisted*
> *Trying to untangle twisted tangles*
> *My tangs tungled now.*[4]

Alvin Schwartz, in *A Twister of Twists, A Tangle of Tongues,* adds some tongue twisters on modern inventions like pre-shrunk shirts to a collection that includes old favorites.

---

4. From *Tongue Tanglers* by Charles Francis Potter. Copyright 1962 by Charles Francis Potter. Published by The World Publishing Co.

ABC Books

While most alphabet books do help young children learn their ABC's, they also make a contribution to visual literacy, helping the child organize graphic experiences. ABC books are not the only kinds of books that help children in identifying objects, but they do serve as identification books, usually comprising key words that label familiar objects or animals, less often identifying people.

Although early alphabet books like the *New England Primer* served not only to teach children letters but also to give moral instruction, the pictorial ABC books that followed *Mother Goose*'s "A Apple Pie" are all variants on that theme. Edward Lear wrote one of the funniest, all in nonsense phonetics, and it now appears in a delightful illustrated edition. Also working in the nineteenth century, Walter Crane made a charming *Baby's Own Alphabet*, and Kate Greenaway turned *A Apple Pie* into a thing of beauty.

Modern artists have also been intrigued by the austerity of a single letter and the possibilities of making it dramatic. Wanda Gág's *ABC Bunny* has a rhyming text with continuity unusual in such miscellanies. The dark woodcuts are relieved by large scarlet capital letters which suggest the small child's ABC blocks. The pictures (3, p. 91) and story make it a favorite.

Fritz Eichenberg's *Ape in a Cape*, "an alphabet of odd animals," is both funny and phonetic. The "Goat in a boat" looks properly wild-eyed (1, p. 91) like the "Fox in a box." Young children like this book, and it inspires older children to make rhymes of their own.

Roger Duvoisin's *A for the Ark*, shows Noah calling the animals alphabetically. The ducks dawdle because they like the rain. Some bears come with the *B*'s, others with *U* for ursus. On they come, comical or impressive, but all decorative in the artist's most colorful style.

Phyllis McGinley's *All Around the Town* is for older children, an alphabet of city sights and sounds in lively verse, with Helen Stone's pictures as attractive as the text. The witty lyrics combine letter sounds with the maximum rhythm and meaning. For example, one verse begins "V is for the Vendor/ A very vocal man."

In contrast to *All Around the Town, Bruno Munari's ABC* depends for its charm on his masterful use of color and design to build interesting associations around each letter—"A Fly/ a Flower/ a Feather/ and a Fish" with "more Flies" at the top of the page to go buzzing on through the book (2, p. 91). So arresting are his colors and use of space that the visual impact of each page is powerful.

Brian Wildsmith's ABC is a heady experience with color, an ABC book with the simplest of texts and the most glorious rainbow of subtle tints and hues. "cat CAT" says a fuchsia page with letters in three colors, and opposite, against a muted blue, is a green-eyed black cat.

John Burningham's ABC has upper- and lower-case letters and illustrative words on the left-hand pages, facing stunning pictures in bold compositions (5, p. 92). *Celestino Piatti's Animal ABC* is also in rhyme, the illustrations vigorous, richly colored, and poster simple (4, p. 92). Thomas Matthiesen's *ABC* concentrates on familiar objects. Unusually good, simple color photographs face pages that have, in addition to the upper- and lower-case letters and the illustrative words, a few lines of text about the objects—"Shoes keep your feet safe when you walk. They have strings called laces, which often become untied."

Two books are especially useful for environmental awareness. Francine Grossbart's *A Big City* has words which all start with oversize capital letters: Antennas, Buildings, Cars, Doors, Elephant in a zoo, etc., on colored pages with ample blank space. In Marguerite Walters's *City-Country ABC*, half the book has a city setting; turned upside down, the other half has a country setting. The emphasis is alliterative: ". . . and W was everywhere—in the woods, in the whistling wind. There was even a woodpecker."

One of the most graphically outstanding is Dorothy Schmiderer's *The Alphabeast Book*, in which each letter, framed, is reshaped in two other frames to end, in a fourth frame, as an object. This is useful for visual conceptualizing as well as for learning the alphabet. *Still Another Alphabet Book* by Seymour Chwast and Martin Stephen Moskof is an unusual book, too, the pictures varied and inventive, and the entire alphabet used as a frieze on each page. Within the frieze, the letters used in the word for the pictured object are printed in a different color; for example, on the Q page a queenly figure is pictured and within the frieze of the alphabet the letters in "queen" are a different color from the other letters in the alphabet, a technique that intrigues children as a game and fosters reading readiness (6, p. 93).

Popular ABC Books

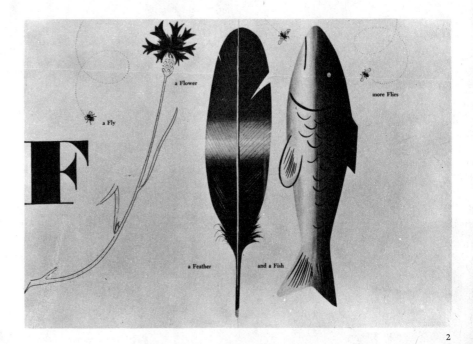

a Fly

a Flower

more Flies

a Feather

and a Fish

G

Goat in a boat

1

1. From *Ape in a Cape.* Copyright 1952 by Fritz Eichenberg.
Reproduced by permission of Harcourt Brace Jovanovich, Inc.
(Original in color)

2. Illustration by Bruno Munari from *Bruno Munari's ABC,* used
with the permission of Philomel Books. Copyright © 1960 by Bruno
Munari. (Original in color)

3. Reprinted by permission of Coward, McCann & Geoghegan, Inc.
from *The ABC Bunny* by Wanda Gag. Copyright 1933 by Wanda
Gag; renewed 1961.

L

for Lizard – look how lazy

3

Z When zebra wears
His stripes at night
The only ones
You see are white

4

5

---

4. Copyright © 1965 by Artemis Verlag, Zurick, Switzerland. First U.S.A. edition 1966 by Atheneum. From Celestino Piatti's *Animal ABC*. Used by permission of Atheneum Publishers. (Original in color)

5. From *John Burningham's ABC*, copyright © 1964, by John Burningham, reproduced by permission of the Bobbs-Merrill Company, Inc., and Jonathan Cape Ltd., London. (Original in color)

---

baby
badger
baker
bear
bird

6

7

---

6. From *Still Another Alphabet Book* by Seymour Chwast and Martin Stephen Mosdof. Copyright © 1969. Used with permission of McGraw-Hill Book Company. (Original in color)

7. Illustrations from Helen Oxenbury's *ABC of Things*. Copyright © 1972 by Helen Oxenbury. Reprinted by permission of Franklin Watts, Inc., and William Heinemann Ltd., Publishers. (Original in color)

8. From *All in the Woodland Early* by Jane Yolen. Illustrations by Jane Breskin Zalben. Text and music copyright © 1979 by Jane Yolen. Illustrations copyright © 1979 by Jane Breskin Zalben. Reprinted by permission of Philomel Books and Curtis Brown, Ltd. (Original in color)

I saw a swift EAGLE,
A FOX in his lair,
I saw a fine GOOSE,
And I saw a young HARE,
    All in the woodland early.
And where are you going this morning in May?
"We're going a-hunting," was all they would say.

8

In *Helen Oxenbury's ABC of Things* the pictures are imaginative and humorous, with letters in bold type and identifying captions on one page for the vigorous drawings on the facing page (7, p. 93). There are two letters combined on each double-page spread of *All Butterflies; An ABC* ("All Butterflies," "Cat Dance," etc.) which Marcia Brown has illustrated with woodcuts in subdued colors. Jane Zalben, in Jane Yolen's *All in the Woodland Early,* combines, in her paintings of forest creatures, a bold use of space with a delicacy of details and color (8, p. 93).

Some of the more sophisticated among the recent ABC books are Leonard Baskin's *Hosie's Alphabet,* which uses difficult words ("Omnivorous swarming locust") and stunning illustrations executed in a variety of techniques; Mitsumasa Anno's *Anno's Alphabet,* with letters shown as pieces of roughly grained wood and with intriguing objects surrounded by a delicate frame that differs on every page; and Muriel Feelings's *Jambo Means Hello,* a Swahili alphabet book illustrated by Tom Feelings with pictures in soft black and white, which gives a vivid impression of East African life as well as words and word definitions for each letter in the Swahili alphabet.

There are many other ABC books and undoubtedly more to come, but these major examples illustrate some of the various types. Since alphabet books provide graphic experience, are used for identifying objects, and often include information and concepts as well as the letters *A–Z,* a primary requisite in choosing them is clarity. Objects should be easily identifiable, and illustrations, whether drawings or photographs, should be consistent with the theme of the book if a specific theme (*A Big City*) is presented. The typeface should be clean rather than ornamented to the point of making the letter of the alphabet difficult to identify. The use of an uncommon word as the key word is inadvisable in alphabet books intended for young children; it may pique the curiosity of some but is liable to frustrate many children who cannot name the object. The illustration should match the key word, and the word itself should use the starting letter in its most commonly pronounced way: it would be unwise, for example, to use the word "children" to illustrate the letter *C.* Words, concepts, and facts are important, but children do need to know the letters of the alphabet.

Counting Books

Like alphabet books, counting books range from those that present numbers, usually numerals from one to ten, in the simplest way, to books that have continuity, tell a story, or are used by an artist as a base for elaborately imaginative shapes or situations. One of the best of such books is Robert Allen's *Numbers: A First Counting Book,* which uses color photographs of

Illustration for the number 10 from *Anno's Counting Book* by Mitsumasa Anno. Copyright © 1975 by Kodansha (Tokyo). By permission of Thomas Y. Crowell, Publishers. Published in the United Kingdom by The Bodley Head, London. (Original in color.)

⑨ **tisa** Men play drums, thumb pianos, bamboo flutes,
(tee·sah) and other instruments.

Excerpted from the book *Moja Means One: Swahili Counting Book* by Muriel Feelings, Illustrated by Tom Feelings. Illustrations Copyright © 1971 by Tom Feelings. Used by permission of THE DIAL PRESS. (Original with color)

familiar objects and also introduces subtly the idea that size and location do not affect components of a numerical unit. After presenting numbers one through ten with facing pictures, the text goes on to show pictures in which there are two groups: apples in a circle, and the same number in a straight line, or pictures of two groups of tomatoes of variant sizes. Young children often confuse mass and numbers, or size and position, so this serves also as a concept book.

Other books that show only groups of objects are Mitsumasa Anno's *Anno's Counting Book,* with handsome illustrations in which objects cumulate, and which incorporates concepts of times, seasons, and sets. Helen Oxenbury's *Numbers of Things,* a tall, narrow book in which the appeal lies chiefly in the deft, humorous illustrations; and Dick Rowan's *Everybody In!* which shows children of various ethnic backgrounds in a series of photographs, each with one more child joining the others in a swimming pool.

Some counting books use rhymes to add interest. Brenda Seymour's *First Counting* has rather sugary pictures, but "1 red engine for my train, 2 new boots for snow and rain," is nicely descriptive and the digits progress from one to twenty. Both John Langstaff and Ezra Jack Keats have used the familiar counting song, *Over in the Meadow,* as the text for books that can help children learn to count while teaching them something about the animals of a meadow

community. Keats's pictures of animals and Feodor Rojankovsky's, in the Langstaff book, are equally appealing in full color. Also in verse, but with more story line, is Emilie McLeod's *One Snail and Me: A Book of Numbers and Animals and a Bathtub;* the gathering of assorted creatures in a huge old tub is an entertaining concept to the young child.

Something similar is *1 One Dancing Drum* by Gail Kredenser, with Stanley Mack's pictures showing a frenetic bandmaster amassing players and instruments in a small, circular bandstand. One dancing drum, two tinkling triangles—they all pile in, but each group is a different color, so it is easy to pick out the nine tootling trombonists, some of whom are perched on top of other musicians. There is a clutter of objects in Russell Hoban's *Ten What?* but as drawn by Sylvie Selig, it's an inspired clutter. The book is also a mystery story, and the baffled detective is surrounded on page 7, where "seven houses were searched," by seven police cars, seven oversize butterflies, seven chairs out on the sidewalk, et cetera.

Muriel Feelings's *Moja Means One* gives numerals from one to ten, the Swahili word for each numeral, phonetic pronunciation, and a sentence in which the names of objects that are to be counted are printed in red. While the geographic references may mean little to young children, the strong, soft pictures by Tom Feelings reinforce the concept of another culture.

Seymour Chwast and Martin Moskof, in *Still*

Another Number Book, do not use cumulation except for a reprise at the close, but use one page for 1, two for 2. Two children are pictured: $1+1=2$. Five dogs? $1+1+1+1+1=5$. The pictures are silly and lighthearted in contemporary, almost pop, style. Another interesting variant is *The One to Fifty Book* by Anne and Alex Wyse, with pictures by Canadian children. It uses a double-page spread for each number, with a numeral, word, and the name of an object on one page, and the appropriate number of drawings of the object on the facing page. The pictures are often awkward but they have vitality and variety, only occasionally becoming confusing as when the left-hand page states "fourteen crayons" and the right-hand page shows fourteen boxes, each labeled "27 crayons." In Harris Petie's *Billions of Bugs,* the text moves from "1 Praying mantis eating a grub," to "10 Walking sticks hide in a shrub," then by tens to 100 and by hundreds to 1,000. It is not a first counting book, but an interesting expansion to use with the child who has become comfortable with numbers.

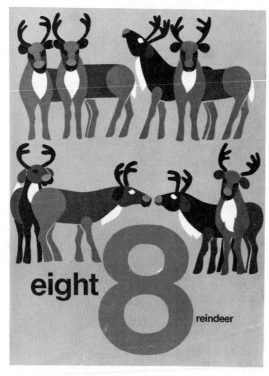

Illustration by John J. Reiss. From *Numbers,* a book by John J. Reiss. Copyright © 1971 by John J. Reiss. Published by Bradbury Press. (Original in color)

Both Ann Kirn's *Nine in a Line* and Benjamin Elkin's *Six Foolish Fishermen* are adapted from folk tales in which counting—or miscounting—is used as a humorous device; the latter especially can afford children the pleasure of seeing characters who are making an obvious mistake. Adults who are evaluating picture counting books should be wary of such pitfalls as the illustration that is out of pattern. In *The Sesame Street Book of Numbers,* for example, four objects follow the numeral 4, five follow 5, and so on—but the picture for 8 shows not eight objects, but an octopus with eight tentacles. This requires a visual sophistication that most young children have not yet achieved, although watchers of the television program on which the book is based may have no problem with it. In the same book, some of the numerals are so over-illustrated as to be difficult to read. Eve Merriam's *Project 1–2–3* is set in a large housing project, an interesting background but one that overshadows the counting function of the book, since the author gives a surfeit of information. For 7, for example, there are many signs on a basement wall: "Check faucets in building 7," "Check 7 incinerator hoppers," and others, and the text reads, "The maintenance men are busy fixing leaks and locks and lots of what gets broken. How many leaking faucets? Drip, drip, drip, drip, drip, drip, drip."

Two final counting books are delightful because of the beauty of the illustrations. Brian Wildsmith's *1,2,3's* has imperfections; when an arrow points to a geometric figure and the text asks "How many?" it isn't clear whether the question means green shapes or triangles. But the composition is handsome abstract art, and the colors are vividly beautiful. John Reiss, in *Numbers,* also uses rich, bright colors but the objects pictured are more familiar ones, the numerals are almost four inches high, colored backgrounds add variety to the pages, and the numbers—after moving from the traditional one to ten—go on, by tens, to 100. The final page shows a shower of a thousand raindrops falling on an umbrella held by a beaming child.

The same sort of clarity needed in ABC books is important in counting books: clear depiction of numerals, close relation of text to pictures, and easily identifiable objects if the objects are intended to be counted. A page crowded with vaguely drawn insects, among which are some intended to represent flies but not easily distinguishable from gnats, will only confuse the child if the text says "7—seven flies." It must be clear *what* is being counted. For very young children just beginning to familiarize themselves with the shapes of numerals and their relation to counting—often learned first by fingers—the best books are those that have plenty of open space to set off numerals and objects, those in which the numerals are large and clear.

Concept Books

In the early years of childhood, when the development of language skills is of paramount importance and when the young child's curiosity creates an interest in all the relationships and categories of a complex world, one of the more difficult areas to master is that of the abstract concept. How big is "big"? How far is "far"? Time, distance, size, mass, color, shape, and the difference between "between" and "through" need to be clarified and amplified in books as well as in conversation. Some concepts have to do with physical matter and can easily be depicted visually; some concepts—time, for example—can be described in words but cannot be shown by illustrations. Concepts like the nature of love or death are abstractions and are more difficult for young children to grasp; they cannot be drawn and they are not easy to explain. Through repeated experiences, explanations, and questions young children can be helped to grasp elusive concepts of their environment.

Small children are often fascinated by their own size and growth. In *The Growing Story* Ruth Krauss explores a child's interest in his own growth, comparing that slow process with the more observable growth of plants and animals. When fall comes and the winter clothes that had been put away for him prove to be too small, the boy triumphantly discovers that he, too, is growing, though he sees no change when he looks in the mirror. Concept books explore differences and similarities in people. Ann McGovern's *Black Is Beautiful* praises the night-black sky, the rich earth, a black butterfly, and black faces; in Barbara Brenner's *Faces* the photographs show not only how features vary but how they are alike in the ways they are used, incidentally presenting concepts about the senses.

Several concepts are combined in Helen Bor-

ten's *Do You Know What I Know?* It explores the senses, presents environmental concepts, and also touches on colors, size differences, and personal preferences, all illustrated with a dazzling variety of styles and techniques. In three books, the versatile Marcia Brown uses stunning full-color photographs and poetic captions to encourage environmental awareness; *Listen to a Shape, Touch Will Tell,* and *Walk with Your Eyes* focus on sharpening children's observation of shapes and textures in nature.

Many concept books have no story line but depend upon accurate description, repetition, and comparison to convey ideas. Books about shapes usually deal with several shapes, as do Miriam Schlein's *Shapes* and John Reiss's *Shapes.* The latter, illustrated in brilliant and effective color, goes past the familiar circle, square, and triangle to include solid forms (showing how squares form a cube) and to more complex ones like oval and rectangle. Examples of each shape are given; for oval, they are musical notes, plums, eggs, and spoons. Tana Hoban uses photographs also in *Shapes and Things* but these are much simpler—silhouettes in white against a black page. The objects are grouped so that children can also perceive the concept of sets: kitchen utensils, tools, objects used at a desk, objects used in sewing. This book has the appeal of a simple game of identification and can be used with very young children. So can Eric Carle's *My Very First Book of Shapes,* with its heavy pages cut in two; the child matches shapes like a half-watermelon, a rectangular kite, an eye, or a worm with the solid black shapes on the second set of pages. Spiral binding makes it easy to flip back and forth.

Photo by Marcia Brown. From Marcia Brown, *Touch Will Tell.* Published by Franklin Watts, New York, London 1979. (Original in color)

Viewpoint

Until children are well into the school years, their attention is caught by objects or scenes that are strong and simple—big bold strokes, bright clear colors, sharp contrasts, and similar overstatements. They need more clues to what they're seeing, hearing, tasting, or touching than adults do. That is, much of a building must be visible if they are going to recognize it—understandably, for they haven't seen many buildings and therefore aren't as able as adults to infer a church from a steeple or a service station from a revolving sign seen through some trees. . . . When children do become aware of details, they tend not to perceive them as parts-of-a-whole but as separate entities—smaller "wholes." This behavior was documented by William A. Miller, who tested the perception of third-graders by asking them to describe the pictures in their own school books. In each picture there were twenty to twenty-six constituent items whose perception was important to an understanding of the pictured scene. The children identified (on the average) fewer than a third of the items.—Muriel Beadle, *A Child's Mind; How Children Learn During the Critical Years from Birth to Age Five* (Garden City, New York: Doubleday & Company, Inc.), 1970, pp. 151–152.

Reiss also has created one of the best of the books on color, with a repetition of examples and—something lacking in some books on the subject—various shades of a color. A frog is in several shades of green, a pale green snake coils through the darker grass, and leaf shapes in a variety of forms are in several shades. While there is no focus on the concept of size, the book also makes it clear that all red strawberries are not the same size, that there are big and small robins with orange breasts. An unusual book on color is *The Adventures of the Three Colors* by Annette Tison and Talus Taylor, which uses transparent overlays to introduce the concept that colors can be mixed to produce another color. A large yellow butterfly on the transparent page, when put over the page with a hot-pink pig produces not just orange but, because of the placement of illustrative detail, an orange snail. The narrative framework about a boy experimenting with color mixture wavers occasionally into irrelevancy, but the book is nonetheless unique in what it achieves.

There are, of course, many books that are not written for the purpose of defining concepts that nevertheless do so, and there are also many books that could be placed as well in one group as another. Some of Tana Hoban's books, for example, that illustrate concepts by making comparisons could be placed with wordless picture books; like *Shapes and Things*, her *Look Again!* has no text but uses pages in which a cut-out square challenges the viewer to identify the portion of the picture shown and then, on a third page, shows the picture in context. Somewhat similar is *What Is It?* by Joan Loss, in which the magnified details in a full-page picture are followed by a small photograph of the whole object, relating the known object to its unfamiliar aspect.

The most effective use of comparisons is probably in those books that deal with elusive concepts: Hoban's *Push-Pull, Empty-Full,* and *Over, Under, & Through* or Peter Spier's *Fast-Slow, High-Low.* Hoban uses one set of pictures for each set of opposite terms, sharp and well-chosen photographs making the comparison very clear. Spier's book has many small drawings on each double-spread and has to be examined more carefully for differences: a couple in tennis shorts and in evening dress, two elephants touching their long trunks to the snouts of two pigs, a long and a short garden hose, the long and short hands on a clock dial, et cetera.

Reprinted with permission of Macmillan Publishing Co., Inc. from *Shapes and Things* by Tana Hoban. Copyright © 1970, Tana Hoban.

Illustration © 1976 by Lois Axeman from *You Go Away* by Dorothy Corey. Reproduced by permission of Albert Whitman & Company, Publishers. (Original in color)

A lesser number of concept books are written with a narrative framework. Location and direction are emphasized in Betsy Maestro's *Where Is My Friend?* in which an elephant searches by going *through* a gate, peering *under* a rock, or looking *behind* her for the mouse which appears, beaming, *in front* of her nose. In *I Wonder What's Under* by Doris Lund, a boy stalls at bedtime by wondering if a monster is under his bed—then wondering what's under the rug that's under the bed, eventually working his way down to the earth beneath the cellar.

The concept of grouping is used in Rodney Peppe's *Odd One OuT*, the title giving a clue to the fact that there's one unit in each set that doesn't belong. A boy goes to school, window-shops, and visits a farm, a park, and a fair, in each case seeing one thing that doesn't belong: a boat on the farm, a cash register in the park, a monkey in the classroom. This does not have a strong story line, but it entertains while encouraging observation and the concept of appropriate placement.

Although there is little action in Walter Myers' *Where Does the Day Go?* it has other strong values in addition to its exploration of the mystery of night and day. The discussion among a group of children shows some of the misconceptions that can arise. The book explains natural phenomena accurately, and it presents an exemplary father who takes an evening walk with his children and their friends, commenting on the fact that people are as different as night and day, and how wonderful that is.

It is, as all parents know, important for young children to learn that parental departure is not synonymous with parental desertion. There are two books that deal nicely, but each in a different way, with the idea that separation need not be traumatic. Dorothy Corey's *You Go Away* shows a baby playing peekaboo, a father tossing his child and catching him, children playing hide-and-seek, and so on. It ends with parents going off with luggage, and with the comforting "You are going far away. . . . you will come back!" In Robert Welber's *Goodbye, Hello*, a series of small creatures leave their mothers happily: "A puppy goes sniffing down the road. Goodbye, Mother . . . (page turn) Hello, toad," and "A child is watching each little creature. Goodbye, Mother . . . (page turn) Hello, teacher."

While concept books cannot be judged by exactly the same criteria as books that have a story line, it is easy to determine the effectiveness of some. The best concept books reinforce ideas by reiterating but not boring readers, and they move from the familiar to the less familiar. They begin with simple ideas and pictures and move on to those that are slightly more complex. Books about shapes or colors can be evaluated for their pictorial success or failure, while books that deal with emotions must be assessed for the effectiveness of the text, and that involves making a subjective judgment. Concept books can help young children see relationships between objects, or see more than one aspect of an idea, or visualize changes, or become aware of similarities or differences.

Books Without Words

While there has been debate over whether wordless books are effective in preparing children for reading, there is little question that prereaders and readers enjoy them. Such books can predispose a young child to the attitude that books are a source of pleasure, can accustom them to the left-to-right pattern of reading, and can introduce them to the concept of sequential action as pages are turned. It must be kept in mind, when evaluating these books, that they are designed to encourage not reading, but reading readiness.

Some of these books are humorous, many are inventive, and a few—like Mitsumasa Anno's *Topsy-Turvies*—are beautifully illustrated. The best wordless books have pictures so clearly drawn that the child can easily follow the plot of the story, if there is a story line. In *Topsy-Turvies*, there is a series of pictures that play with perspective or position, presenting improbabilities to challenge the young imagination. (See color section, Ch. 6.) Some word-

Viewpoint

less books give information, as does Iela and Enzo Mari's *The Apple and the Moth*. The illustrations in this book follow a moth through its egg, caterpillar, cocoon, and adult stages, beginning with the moth's egg in an apple and ending with the next generation's egg in an apple blossom. The child can supply the words, but the science lesson is clear.

Books with no text that are informational are in the minority, but there are several good ones. One is Erich Fuchs' *Journey to the Moon*, which does have two pages of text about the Apollo 11 mission at the beginning of the book but which really tells the story in dramatic and sophisticated pictures. Edward Koren's *Behind the Wheel* shows what you see from the driver's seat in a series of vehicles and machines. Insets show labeled details of the controls, but there's no other text; it's an excellent book for the question and answer approach. *Family* by Ellie Simmons shows a small girl and a very pregnant mother at home; the father arrives, a smiling older woman takes over when the mother leaves for the hospital, and the child happily passes time until her mother comes home with the new baby. The illustrations are a bit sweet, but the story is perfectly clear and the attitude positive.

There are several wordless books that tell a realistic story. In Edward Ardizzone's *The Wrong Side of the Bed* a scowling child has breakfast postponed while he is scrubbed, teases a little sister and is scolded, goes outdoors and can't find anything to do; however, he comes home to a kiss and a cuddle on his mother's lap. In Tomie de Paola's *Pancakes for Breakfast*, the bucolic pictures vividly tell the story of a woman's problems in gathering ingredients to make pancakes. In Nonny Hogrogian's *Apples*, people and animals consume the fruit offered by a pushcart vendor who goes off to replenish his supply from a stand of heavily laden apple trees.

Most of the animal stories are fanciful, but three of the better realistic stories of animals are John Hamberger's *The Lazy Dog*, in which a dog energetically chases a ball and then is so exhausted that a child has to rouse him, and *Pssst! Doggie*—and *Kitten for a Day*, both by Ezra Jack Keats. In the first of these, a cat offers, "Pssst! Doggie—Wanna dance?" and a series of pas de deux follows, with the animals imagining themselves in costumes. The closing, "That was some dance!" is followed by a refreshing

From *The Wrong Side of the Bed* by Edward Ardizzone.
Copyright © 1970 by Edward Ardizzone. Reproduced by
permission of Doubleday & Company, Inc.

vivid picture of children playing in *The Great Cat Chase*, with the story line crystal clear. Dressed in doll clothes, a cat jumps out of a doll carriage and is pursued by his owner, by her police-costumed friend, and by a tricycle rider. After a series of mishaps, all go home for light refreshments. In *Ah-Choo* and *Hiccup*, Mayer bases the humor on the plight of an allergic elephant who sneezes so hard he blows a house down, and on the elephant's aggressive treatment of the hiccups suffered by Ms. Hippo, his lady love. Jose Aruego, in *Look What I Can Do*, gently and indirectly teases children's showoff instincts by having two animals compete in a follow-the-leader orgy; at the end, they are panting with fatigue but rouse themselves to sit on a third animal who says, "Look what I can do."

John Goodall's books use the device of half-pages inserted between each set of full pages, so that the turn of the half-page changes part of each illustration. In *The Ballooning Adventures of Paddy Pork* an adventurous pig rescues a piglet in distress, braves storm and sea monster in his balloon, and returns from his voyage to the plaudits of a porcine crowd. In *The Surprise Picnic* a cat family is startled when the rock on which they're having a picnic proves to be a turtle, and they're in trouble when a storm blows their rowboat away.

An unusual book dealing with fantasy is Lynd Ward's *The Silver Pony*. This is much longer than most wordless books and blends

nap à deux. In the second book, a friendly puppy joins a group of kittens and tries to do whatever they do (he's not very good at meowing), deciding at the end that next time they can all be puppies. There is some text, primarily "Lick, lick, lick," and "Slurp," so this isn't a true wordless book, but it is in the pattern. In *Bobo's Dream* by Martha Alexander, a boy rescues his dog's bone from a larger dog. Napping, the grateful pet dreams of protecting his boy; in the dream he is a large, fierce dog and when he wakes, he is still so confident that he actually does frighten away a large dog. Alexander's pictures differentiate quite clearly between dream and reality.

Of the animal stories in which the creatures behave like animals but within an exaggerated or fanciful framework, the books about a boy and his frog by Mercer Mayer are among the most successful. *Frog Goes to Dinner*, for example, has bubbling humor and plenty of the action children enjoy, as the little stowaway hops out of his boy's pocket at an elegant restaurant and creates havoc. Mayer also creates a

Illustration by Mercer Mayer. From Mercer Mayer, *Hiccup*.
Copyright © 1976 by Mercer Mayer. Used by permission of The
Dial Press.

realism and fantasy in a story about a child who enjoys a series of flights on a magical winged horse, is injured and falls, waking to find he is ill. When he recovers, there's something better than his imaginary horse: a new pony.

In Fernando Krahn's *The Self-Made Snowman*, the plot is not wholly believable but the idea of a gigantic snowman and the Christmas setting appeal to young children. Snow falling from a mountain rolls into a ball and the wind pushes the ball along; in its slide it elongates and picks up branches that become a nose and arms; it slides right into the town square and ends up with a wreath on its head and birds perched on its nose. One of the most ingenious wordless books is *Changes, Changes* by Pat Hutchins. Like *Topsy-Turvies*, it plays with transforming shapes, but it also tells a story as two stiff little wooden dolls shift and adapt the varied shapes of building blocks to make a house, transform it into a fire engine and then into other structures, ending with another house. This has the full-circle action children find satisfying, aesthetic appeal, and the clarity of story line that marks the successful wordless book.

Since the interpretation of books without words depends entirely on the pictures, it is of paramount importance that both the immediate action of each picture and the sequence of action in all the pictures be unequivocally clear. The story line should be distinct if there is a narrative, as in the Goodall books, and the development of any informational sequence should be clear, as in Mari's *The Apple and the*

Moth. These books encourage children to interpret and embellish a story; they are a good catalyst for discussion of the author's (perhaps one should say illustrator's) intent and for the child's creativity, encouraging the language skills that are so integral a part of reading readiness.

Books for Beginning Readers

Many children have learned to read through basal readers which include word repetition but lack a sense of narrative, and this is one of the great assets of many of the fiction books published for first- and second-grade children today, or for those who learn to read before entering school. Since action and humor have strong appeal for young children, some of the contemporary books with these qualities are proving to be as popular as they are effective as reading materials for young children, and many of them have enough narrative flow to read aloud well also.

There have been books in the past that were suitable for the beginning reader, such as Du Bose Heyward's *The Country Bunny and the Little Gold Shoes* or even parts of Kate Greenaway's *Under the Window*, but both of these have more text on the page than would be used today, and the print of Greenaway's book is lamentably small. Two excellent books which appeared in the 1950s are Elizabeth Guilfoile's *Nobody Listens to Andrew* and *The Cat in the Hat* by Dr. Seuss. Nobody believes Andrew has anything important to say until he finally announces loudly and firmly that there is a bear in his bed; pandemonium ensues and is followed by a captured bear and a triumphantly vindicated boy. The story has a mild humor in the writing style, plenty of action, and a situation most children will find familiar: being ignored. It also fulfills all the physical requisites for a beginning reader's book. Seuss, a genre unto himself, uses rhyme, repetition, and nonsense humor in *The Cat in the Hat*. This fast-moving story uses a series of incidents rather than a smooth story line as the irrepressible cat turns a household into a shambles, zooms about on a machine with mechanical arms, and goes off leaving the scene looking as placid as it was before his entry.

Most of these short books have a continuous text, but some authors have divided their texts into short, separate episodes children can handle easily, giving them also the satisfaction of having "chapters" just as older children do. Notable among this group are the books by Else Minarik and by Arnold Lobel. Minarik's *Little Bear* has four stories about an ingenuous cub who makes himself some birthday soup, takes an imaginary trip to the moon, has a bedtime chat about the world's most fascinating topic (himself), and makes an interesting discovery about clothes. The warmth, tenderness, and humor of the story are echoed in Maurice Sendak's pictures. The illustrations for Lobel's books are his own, deft and direct and carefully placed on the pages so that they present no visual barrier to the print. *Mouse Tales* is a series of bedtime stories told by a father mouse to his young; it is simply written and engaging, but it was with *Frog and Toad Are Friends* that Lobel established himself as master of this form. This book was one of the finalists for the National Book Award, and its sequel a Newbery Honor Book; this despite the fact that awards for distinguished literary contributions seldom come to books for beginning readers. What Lobel achieves in *Owl at Home, Mouse Soup, Grasshopper on the Road,* and *Days with Frog and Toad,* is a pervasive feeling of amused affection blended with a wry appreciation of the foibles of the creatures in the stories. The pictures are appealing, but the smoothness of the writing and the establishment of personalities in so limited a space are the strongest aspects of these animal stories.

Humor is a component of a wide variety of stories. There is the single-incident contretemps of Crosby Bonsall's *Mine's the Best,* which develops the situation of two small, hostile boys who have identical balloons. Bonsall's stories have more suspense than most, and usually they concern group activity. *Papa's Lemonade and Other Stories,* by Eve Rice, has five linked, humorous tales about an animal family.

An unusual fusion of fantasy and realism is found in Leonard Kessler's *Kick, Pass, and Run,* which also gives a few facts about a football game, which the animals imitate. There are perhaps too many elements in the book for a smooth blend, but there are all too few sports stories for young children. Kessler's book, like many of Bonsall's, shows black and white children in the illustrations. In Joan Lexau's *The Homework Caper* an interracial friendship is also evident in the pictures as two boys hunt frantically for a lost homework paper, eventually discovering that the little sister of one of them

Illustration from *Frog and Toad Are Friends*, written and illustrated by Arnold Lobel. Copyright © 1970 by Arnold Lobel. By permission of Harper & Row Publishers Inc., and World's Work Limited.

had substituted her "homework" for her brother's. The dialogue is direct and brisk, the solution amicable, and the story given warmth by an understanding teacher and by the boys' realization that they had thought, too, at little Susan's age, that their scribbles were valid communications. Marjorie Sharmat, in *Mitchell Is Moving*, combines a familiar situation, but blandly uses two dinosaurs as the friends who miss each other when one moves away.

Informational books for beginning readers present a challenge to authors, for they entail the arts of writing succinctly and sequentially and of knowing how to abridge material without omitting something of importance. Peggy Parish's *Dinosaur Time* satisfies young children's curiosity on this perennially popular subject by giving the name, its pronunciation, and a few salient facts about eleven kinds of dinosaurs. Except for the dinosaur names, the words are simple; the print is large and the information accurate. *Alligator* by Evelyn Shaw describes a life cycle in narrative form with no anthropomorphism. *Look at Your Eyes* by Paul Showers is a model of simplicity in the description of some basic facts about the human eye. Harlow Rockwell offers a variety of easy projects in *I Did It,* a "how-to" book that incorporates adeptly repeated words. Photographs illustrate Millicent Selsam's *How Puppies Grow,* which follows newly born puppies through stages of development until they are old enough to be played with and become children's pets.

One of the foremost science writers for any age level, Selsam uses a fictional framework in *Tony's Birds,* in which facts about birds are dispersed through a story of a father helping his son learn to become a bird watcher. Other natural science books in narrative form are Nathaniel Benchley's *The Several Tricks of Edgar Dolphin* and Edward Ricciuti's *Donald and the Fish That Walked.* The former injects a playful note by having the dolphin talk to people who don't understand him, and the latter capitalizes on a true event—an invasion in Florida of walking catfish that had escaped from a fish farm. Benchley also achieves, in *George the Drummer Boy,* a comprehensible story about the American Revolution as seen from the viewpoint of a very young British soldier.

While some trade books for beginning independent readers use needed repetition in the unimaginative style of the basal readers, most trade books published today have a limited rather than a rigidly controlled vocabulary. Several publishers (Harper & Row, Crowell, Greenwillow, and Random House, for example) have excellent series designed either for early readers or for readers in the primary grades. Harper & Row has a distinguished series of history books, and Crowell an equally impressive series of science books for beginning readers.

Although standards in series are usually maintained and we may expect a certain level of quality from the better series, still each book should be judged on its own merits and evaluated by the criteria that apply to all books for young readers and particularly to the first books they read alone.

Whatever methods children have learned to read by, they have specific needs in the first books they read independently. The words must be simple enough for them to understand and the sentences brief enough so that the text does not appear formidable. Repetition helps the beginning independent reader, but it should be used with restraint and only when it would occur naturally, if it is used in dialogue. The print should be large and clear, with adequate space between words and between lines, and with not so much text on a page that the print seems discouragingly heavy to a child.

Picture Story Books

While there were illustrated books for young children early in the history of children's books, the picture book really came into its own only when printing techniques made it possible to publish books illustrated in color at a reasonable price. Illustrators like Crane, Greenaway, and Caldecott became well known, and artists who followed them in the early and mid-twentieth century produced varied and intricately developed illustrations. Many artists from other countries came to the United States, and a flourishing exchange was established in translated editions and in copublication programs. The work of many major contributors in the first half of this century, as well as the work of today's illustrators, is discussed in Chapter 6, "Artists and Children's Books."

From Rosemary Wells, *Stanley and Rhoda.* Copyright © 1978 by Rosemary Wells, used by permission of The Dial Press. (Original in color)

Lucky lets children walk around her and under her. She lets them sit on her. Lucky stands very quietly when children are near.

Hold your hand flat when you feed a pony, or the pony may pinch your fingers by mistake.

From *Our Animal Friends at Maple Hill Farm,* by Alice and Martin Provensen. Copyright © 1974 by Alice and Martin Provensen. Reprinted by permission of Random House, Inc. (Original in color)

Most of the discussion here focuses on texts rather than on illustrations. It should be clear, however, that almost every artistic technique and medium have been used successfully in picture story books for young children. In some books the pictures serve as elements of mood, as in Uri Shulevitz's *Dawn,* while in stories like Graham Oakley's adventure tales of the church mice and their friend the church cat, or in the urban vignettes by Eleanor Schick, the illustrations are explicit representations of the setting and the action.

There is seldom enough time in a brief picture story book for full character development, although some may be shown by the illustrations. Many books with memorable characters like Curious George or Ferdinand the Bull or the fractious Rhoda in Rosemary Wells's *Stanley and Rhoda* achieve firm characterization by emphasis on one trait or behavior pattern. George is curious, Ferdinand likes to sit quietly and smell flowers, Rhoda is lazy and messy. Some stories focus on a one-to-one relationship, as do Barbara Borack's *Grandpa* and Charlotte Zolotow's *Do You Know What I'll Do?* in which a child expresses her love for a baby brother. Characterization or individual relationships should be depicted without sentimentality; they should be believable and consistent.

The plot may be as simple as learning to tie a shoe, spending a first day at school or a first night away from home, or making the adjustment to the death of a pet, but it should have a structure: problem and solution, achievement

of a new skill or a new experience, or the presentation of an event or an attitude that effects a change in a character or characters. There are always some books in which structure is lacking but is compensated for by the strength of some other aspect. An example is the Provensens' *Our Animal Friends at Maple Hill Farm,* in which the range of appealing creatures, lively illustrations, and witty captions carry the text along at a good pace.

Whether a picture story is realistic or fanciful, it will appeal to young children if it has humor or action. Again, some books lack these qualities but introduce a provocative concept or establish a mood so well that they appeal to children nevertheless. Although it is the text we are considering here, it should be kept in mind that in many picture story books, as in picture books, the illustrations may be so striking or so humorous as to outweigh the text and make the whole book appealing to children.

Sometimes the appealing element is the information given by the text, by the pictures, or by both. Children are always and actively curious; they are intrigued when they find that another child's family has a pattern that differs from their own or when they learn from a book what it was like in their parents' time, which to them is in a misty past. They are at the same time reassured by similarities in pattern, and they need to identify with others as their circle enlarges, just as they need that first sense of identification with the family group. Children who live in the country find the urban setting

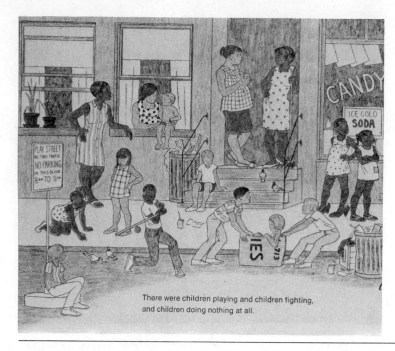

There were children playing and children fighting, and children doing nothing at all.

Illustration by Eleanor Schick reprinted with permission of Macmillan Publishing Co., Inc. from *City in the Summer* by Eleanor Schick. Copyright 1969 by Eleanor Schick. (Original in color)

of books like Eleanor Schick's *City in the Summer* and *Neighborhood Knight* fascinating, just as city children are interested in the details of farm life; each group receives a different kind of pleasure from books that have settings familiar to them. Black children need to see themselves in books, as do members of other ethnic groups, and each group needs to see the others as a part of our society. They must feel both accepted and accepting. Recall Erikson's theory that as the child's ego develops, a major fact of psychosocial growth is his or her persistent need to identify with others, eventually achieving a sense of personal identity built on a firm base of trust and understanding.

This curiosity about people can be satisfied in part by books, as can children's curiosity about themselves, animals, weather, and other aspects of their lives. How does a mother know what to do when the toaster won't work? What is a cousin? What does "dead" mean? How does a dump truck work? Why doesn't the boy next door go to the same church or temple? What is that funny thing hanging around the doctor's neck? Children's questions are endless, their need to know insatiable. They have so much to learn in the early years, and they learn so quickly, that we cannot give them too many books.

Family Life

Young children take pleasure in seeing the familiar relationships of home reflected in their books, whether the characters are human or animals. Children may recognize themselves and their families whether a story is as quiet and realistic as Ellen Parsons's *Rainy Day Together*, which is imbued with the cozy feeling of a day spent with loving parents, or as bouncy as Russell Hoban's *Arthur's New Power*, in which the guitar-playing Arthur learns to get along without electricity.

Very young children are most concerned with parents and their roles in respect to that center of the universe, the child. Books like Charlotte Zolotow's *When I Have a Little Girl* and *When I Have a Son* project quite naturally a child's desire to have a world in which all wishes are granted by obliging parents. A new baby in the family disturbs this world, and picture stories about sibling jealousy may help alleviate a child's feelings of guilt. In Ann Scott's *On Mother's Lap*, it is an Eskimo child who learns to share parental love, but Michael's experience is universal; in Eloise Greenfield's *She Come Bringing Me That Little Baby Girl*, Kevin is black, but his feelings of resentment at the attention paid to the new baby are common to all children. John Steptoe explores similar feelings in *Stevie*, a boldly illustrated book in which a young boy is jealous of a child his mother cares for. The tables are turned in Martha Alexander's *I'll Be the Horse If You'll Play with Me*, as Oliver (who had tried to give away baby Bonnie in *Nobody Asked Me If I Wanted a Baby Sister*) imposes on Bonnie, who learns that she, in turn, can now impose on the younger brother of whom she had been jealous. Rosemary Wells, in *Don't Spill It Again, James*, explores the relationship between two small brothers.

One of the trends in books for children of all ages has been an increasing interest in grandparents. Tomie de Paola's *Nana Upstairs and Nana Downstairs* shows a small child's love for his great-grandmother and his adjustment to her death, which makes it easier to accept his grandmother's death years later. In Charlotte Zolotow's *My Grandson Lew*, the emphasis is not on the grandfather who has died as much as it is on the loving memories a mother and child share and on the comfort such sharing brings. The range of books about grandparents fortunately includes some that are warm or humorous. Children need both the books that will help them adjust to the senility or the death of an older person and those books that depict them as a vital part of the extended family.

Everyday Life Experiences

Closely allied to stories of home and family are books that picture children's experiences as they begin to extend their range of activities: sharing tasks and responsibilities in the home, making small forays into the outside world, becoming acquainted with neighbors. The family is still involved, but the child is growing toward independence and establishing identity, gaining self-confidence through achievement, and satisfying curiosity.

These books about everyday experiences generally deal with the fulfillment of children's needs or their acquisition of new skills or attitudes and the treatment of these subjects ranges from light to serious. There is as much to be gained from a realistic story like Robert Welber's *The Train*, in which Elizabeth's family helps her overcome her fear of crossing a meadow alone, as there is from Lillian Hoban's *Arthur's Honey Bear*. When Arthur sells his old toys, he has to adjust to the fact that he really

still wants the toy bear his little sister buys; this story not only shows a child's logic and a growing ability to compromise, but suggests the way in which even young children can look back and see their own growth.

Small tasks loom large to young children, who take great pride in having their contributions recognized and who often look with envy on older brothers and sisters who go on errands. In Genevieve Gray's *Send Wendell*, the older children evade chores but Wendell—who is six—trots along with good humor when he is sent instead. He earns special recognition, thereby gaining the reward of being considered responsible. The small boy in Lorenz Graham's *Song of the Boat* who finds just the right tree for his father to use in making a canoe takes pride in his father's pleasure and in the fact that he was able to keep up with his father on the long hunt for the perfect tree. The treatment of a child's first night away from home is humorous in Bernard Waber's *Ira Sleeps Over*, but it touches on the child's very real need to have familiar objects about him, as well as on the importance of so sophisticated an event.

Stories about play are important, for children learn by playing. For them it is an important task. In *Morris's Disappearing Bag* by Rosemary Wells, there is a fanciful element, but it doesn't lessen the impact of what Morris and his brothers and sisters learn about sharing gifts. There are rhyme and rhythm in the text of William Cole's *What's Good for a Three-Year-Old?* in which a group of romping children at a birthday party discovers that each of them has a slightly different idea of what is most enjoyable. One of life's harsh lessons is learned in Russell Hoban's *A Bargain for Frances*, as the small badger strikes a disappointing bargain with her friend Thelma. There is no lesson in Petronella Breinburg's *Doctor Shawn*, only a modest, realistic picture of a group of children in imaginative play, as they take roles in the game of "playing hospital." No sex stereotypes here: Shawn and his sister take turns being nurse and doctor. Traditional sex roles are challenged in Charlotte Zolotow's *William's Doll*, in which a small boy is teased because he wants a doll; only his grandmother understands that a boy may want a doll so that he can play at being a father in just the same way that girls pretend to be mothers, that both are preparing for a future task.

School Stories

As more and more children participate in programs at kindergartens, nursery schools, day-care centers, or less formal group programs, the need for books that will prepare them for such experiences becomes clear. One of the simplest presentations is Harlow Rockwell's *My Nursery School*, which has little plot but shows a child taken to school by her father, having a happy morning, and being called for by her mother. The book gently insinuates the ideas of sharing toys and working together on projects. *Did You Carry the Flag Today, Charley?* which is discussed at length in Chapter 3, gives a memorable picture of a free spirit adjusting to the strictures of the classroom. For preschool children whose older brothers and sisters seek attention by decrying school, Miriam Cohen's *Will I Have a Friend?* is a pleasant antidote. Escorted to the first day of kindergarten, a child feels bereft and lonely until the period of leg-waving antics called "rest time" when he meets a kindred spirit. Carol Barkin and Elizabeth James, in *Sometimes I Hate School*, have faced the problem of the child who's unhappy; this is one of a series of books designed to help the young child bridge the gap between home and school.

Friends

Almost every aspect of friendship is explored in the many picture story books about the ups and downs of relationships: learning to share, planning projects, being jealous, having a quarrel, exchanging confidences, and, above all, having fun. One such book, Arnold Lobel's *Frog and Toad Are Friends*, has become a minor classic, with the sequel, *Frog and Toad Together*, not far behind. The stories are short and simple enough for a beginning reader but flow smoothly for reading aloud, and they have a humorous, ingenuous style.

Charlotte Zolotow's writing is notable for the combination of a loving and perceptive eye and a direct, quiet style. In *The Unfriendly Book* she describes the problem of coping with a friend who carps and criticizes other people; the William Pène du Bois illustrations show each friend first as Bertha (the carper) sees them and then as Judy sees them, a valuable lesson in differing viewpoints. *The Hating Book* explores a breakdown in friendship; when there is a con-

Illustration by Harlow Rockwell. From Harlow Rockwell, *My Nursery School*. Copyright © 1976 by Harlow Rockwell. Published in the United Kingdom by A.P. Watt Lt., London.

frontation, there proves to have been a mistake in communications and rapport is reestablished. Zolotow isn't preaching, but two gentle lessons come through: it's better to talk it over than to sulk, and it's wise not to believe the gossip you hear.

The anguish of quarreling is handled with a light touch in Marjorie Sharmat's *I'm Not Oscar's Friend Anymore*, in which a small, brooding boy imagines Oscar moping and desolate. It is in fact the boy himself who is downcast, and when he relents and telephones Oscar, he finds that his friend doesn't even remember the fight they had. There's no cautionary note, but the message is the more effective for its ruefully comic air. The same sort of aura imbues Sharmat's *Gladys Told Me to Meet Her Here*, one of the few books about a boy-girl friendship, which describes the mixed feelings of retribution and loyalty Irving goes through as he waits for Gladys to show up at the zoo.

Humor

While many stories about friendship or families or school are humorous, there are some books in which humor is the most important element. Many of these are fantasies, but some realistic picture stories use exaggeration or nonsense for primary appeal. One such is Winifred Rosen's *Ralph Proves the Pudding*. Approached by a man who says he has just the right face for a television commercial, Ralph is engaged to sample and savor chocolate pudding. He doesn't like it, but enjoys the ice cream the producer provides later. Dismayed by the fact that the finished commercial shows Ralph saying "Wow!" to the pudding, when he'd really been responding to the ice cream,

Ralph (and the reader) learns something about the honesty of advertising.

In Norma Farber's *Where's Gomer?* the humorous appeal is in the florid exaggeration of the rhyming text, as the crew of Noah's Ark bewails the boy who is missing at departure time. "O tempest and flood! O watery ways," his mother wails as she weeps into the stew she's cooking. In *Hamilton Duck's Springtime Story* by Arthur Getz, the humor lies in the obtuseness of the duck who thinks he's in a spring snowstorm, while the pictures show clearly that the "snow" is apple blossoms; it's a good springtime story as well as a funny one.

Tall-tale humor is the appeal in the cheerful story of *The Lady Who Saw the Good Side of Everything* by Pat Tapio. Her house washes away in a rainstorm? She needed a new house anyway. She drifts to sea on a log? She'd always wanted to see the ocean. The cartoon-strip format of *Father Christmas* by Raymond Briggs has details of the kind young children like to point out, as a grumbling Santa fills his pack, loads the sleigh, and catches cold while on his rounds. It is the combination of a realistic situation and one fanciful element that makes Margaret Mahy's *The Boy Who Was Followed Home* diverting, although the illustrative details are often high comedy as well. Robert is pleased when a hippopotamus follows him home but his prob-

lems—and hippopotamuses—multiply until only a witch can solve the problem. In *The Backward Day* by Ruth Krauss, there's a robust, nonsensical humor in the child who puts on his clothes in reverse and comes to breakfast in the morning walking backward and wishing his parents a good night.

Bernard Waber's *I Was All Thumbs* has the double appeal of a situation in which the protagonist makes a series of errors and in which the dialogue plays with words. Children enjoy inventing disasters, and they find it more amusing than adults do if an octopus squirts ink in the wrong direction, as does Legs, the octopus-hero of this story. There's more slapstick in *Farmer Palmer's Wagon Ride* than is found in most of William Steig's books, but that's anything but a deterrent to children's enjoyment of this story, in which a series of minor calamities (always good for a laugh) befalls Farmer Palmer, a pig, as he makes his star-crossed way home from market.

Animals

Almost all children are interested in animal stories, whether they are creatures that behave like human beings, animals that behave like animals but can talk, or animals that behave like animals whether there are people in the story

Illustration by William Steig. Reprinted with the permission of Farrar, Straus and Giroux, Inc. From *Farmer Palmer's Wagon Ride* by William Steig, copyright © 1974 by William Steig. Published in the United Kingdom by Hamish Hamilton Ltd. (Original in color)

Illustration by Lillian Hoban from *Best Friends for Frances* by Russell Hoban. Copyright 1969. Reproduced by permission of Harper & Row, Publishers, Inc. and Faber & Faber, Ltd., London. (Original in color)

or not. Most picture stories featuring animals fall in the first category and some of them (Hoban's Frances, Lobel's Frog and Toad) have already been discussed in this chapter.

Because such stories parody the lives of human beings, it is in their perceptiveness about human foibles and emotions that their importance and appeal lie. It is not that Owl, in Arnold Lobel's *Owl at Home*, acts silly for an owl but that he acts like a silly human being as he tries frantically to be in two places at once, that children laugh at him. Nor is it because Jenny, in Esther Averill's *Jenny and the Cat Club*, is such a charming feline that she's endearing, but because she and the other cats engage in all of the often pompous procedures of formal meetings in human style. Hans Rey's Curious George behaves as young children see themselves behave.

Arthur, in Graham Oakley's *The Church Mouse* and *The Church Mice Adrift*, behaves like a mouse some of the time, like a human other times, and the story is that much funnier by contrast when Arthur practices his crawl stroke in the baptismal font. In sequels like *The Church Mice and the Moon* there is more sophistication as the author pokes fun at people; here he lampoons the scientists who are grooming two mice for a space flight. Marjorie Sharmat takes a few digs at ambitious people in *Walter the Wolf*, in which an almost-perfect little wolf who writes poetry, practices violin without being reminded, and never bites, decides that he really doesn't have to be perfect. In Harry Allard's *It's So Nice to Have a Wolf Around the House*, an

amusing animal story masks a lesson about behavior. The *Little Bear* stories by Else Minarik are for independent readers, but they should also be read aloud to younger children, for they reflect all the familial relations, friendships, and imaginative play of childhood.

Stories in which animals behave as animals except that they talk are usually rather placid, since they offer less opportunity for diversity of behavior or for humor, but they are eminently suitable for the very youngest children. In Mirra Ginsburg's *The Chick and the Duckling*, for example, a newly hatched chick valiantly tries to do everything done by a duckling who was hatched a moment before him. It's a slight tale, but the two baby creatures are on the go every minute, and the painless lesson about species behavior is cheerfully presented. The idea that one is never too old to learn is clear in Leo Lionni's *In the Rabbitgarden*, where two little rabbits disobey an injunction not to eat apples *or else* (or else the fox will get them). Children may take more satisfaction than adult readers-aloud in the inference that adults aren't invariably right. And in Munro Leaf's *The Story of Ferdinand*, a little bull behaves almost entirely like a real bull except for the fact that he prefers to sit under a cork tree and smell flowers, not to

Viewpoint

The child needs somebody in a book with whom he can identify as a child. This accounts for the presence of many animals or children themselves in children's books and the comparative paucity of adults, especially parents—it is striking how parents are always got rid of so quickly. Although a child has parents he doesn't necessarily want to read about them, perhaps because he is experimenting with fantasy, with learning about himself, projecting himself into a book where he is not tied down to the fact that he has to go to bed at half past six and clean his teeth. A widespread mistake about children which is made very often by people who talk about social realism in children's books is to imagine that familiarity breeds content. It is not a question of having details which children can recognize but much more a question of having details which they want to recognize. If we have a picture of a school, children will certainly recognize it but they won't necessarily like it.—Nicholas Tucker, "How Children Respond to Fiction," *Children's Literature in Education 9*, pp. 51–52. Reprinted by permission of Ward Lock Educational Limited.

fight. Bee-stung, he rampages about, is thought
fierce, and is taken to the bull ring. Part of the
humor is in the illustrations, which show the
matador weeping with frustration, and part in
the writing, which uses understatement and refrain ("But not Ferdinand") to achieve its effect
of placidity.

Stories in which animals are seen always behaving strictly like themselves almost always
have some human characters too, as a foil for
the animals or as a viewpoint from which the
animals are seen. *Our Animal Friends at Maple
Hill Farm* by Alice and Martin Provensen has
little story line but has too much text to be
called a picture book, since the long and very
funny captions do tell stories about the highly
distinctive creatures of house and barn: the
greedy, grouchy geese; a coquettish hen; or a
languid Siamese who, in contrast to the other
cats, is beautiful but not interesting. An old favorite is Lynd Ward's *The Biggest Bear*, in which
a boy's pet cub grows older and bigger until the
havoc he creates necessitates his being sent to a
zoo. In Dick Gackenbach's *Do You Love Me?* a
young farm boy who has no playmates accidentally kills the small bird he's found because he
fondles it with such eagerness. The story can
teach a child to be careful with wild creatures
and to handle small ones carefully, and it has a
most satisfying ending as the boy discovers that
his new puppy enjoys cuddling and play as
much as he does.

Adaptations of Folk Tales

In addition to the many contemporary stories
that are told with the cadence and in the pattern of folk literature—stories like Wanda Gág's
Millions of Cats—there are many picture-book
versions of authentic folk tales, stories that
exemplify the mores or morals of their cultures,
that teach a lesson, that explain the natural
phenomena of our world. Some are humorous,
like Dorothy Van Woerkom's version of a German folk tale, *The Queen Who Couldn't Bake Gingerbread*. The monarch who hunts for a perfect
mate is a frequent theme, but here the tables
are turned twice; first, Princess Calliope
demands a husband who can play a slide
trombone, and second, when dreadful burning
smells and squawks pervade the castle, it
proves to be the king cooking and the new
queen practicing the trombone. There's another
kind of humor in Janina Domanska's variant of

From *The Story of Ferdinand the Bull* by Munro Leaf and Robert
Lawson. Copyright 1936 by Robert Lawson (illustrations), renewed
© 1964 by John W. Boyd. Reprinted by permission of The Viking
Press, Inc.

the story of the turtle who falls when he opens
his mouth to speak, forgetting that the stick in
his beak is carried by birds, in *Look, There Is a
Turtle Flying*; here the joke is both a lesson and
that familiar favorite of the young child, a disaster.

Why Mosquitoes Buzz in People's Ears, adapted
by Verna Aardema from a West African folk
tale, is a "why" story, but it also carries a message of justice meted out, and the brilliant illustrations add humor. (See color section, Ch. 6.)
The abstract and symbolic pictures by Gerald
McDermott have been translated from film in
Anansi the Spider, a creation story from the
Ashanti which incorporates a folk-tale device
used in other kinds of stories—the pooling of
talents by a group of people, each of whom is
expert in some way. *Arrow to the Sun* is an adaptation of a Pueblo Indian legend about a boy
who brings the spirit of the Lord of the Sun, his
father, back to the pueblo after he has been
transformed into an arrow.

A favorite tale for storytellers is simply
adapted by Cynthia Jameson in *The Clay Pot
Boy*, the story of a pot that comes to life and vo-

raciously devours everything in its path. Children enjoy the frenzy of the chase in this story and in Paul Galdone's version of *The Gingerbread Boy*. Tomie de Paola's retelling of an Italian folk tale, *Strega Nona*, is imbued with robust peasant humor and stresses the poetic justice of the punishment meted out to a witch's greedy apprentice. Margot Zemach's version of *It Could Always Be Worse* has a simplified telling of the story of a house bursting with people and animals. A picture book version of a tale by the brothers Grimm is illustrated by Maurice Sendak so that the disdainful princess of *King Grisly-Beard*, being taught humility by her husband, takes on the vitriolic mien of Shakespeare's Katherine in *The Taming of the Shrew*. It *does* espouse a traditional view of woman's role, but that is true of much folk literature.

Informational Books

Both in fiction and nonfiction, there have been numbers of books published that satisfy young children's need to know. The best of such books deal with subjects that are within the child's experience, books like Harlow Rockwell's *My Doctor* and *My Dentist*, which de-

scribe and picture instruments and procedures, or Harriet Sobol's *Jeff's Hospital Book*, a photo-documentary about a child's hospital stay for corrective surgery. The latter, particularly, is reassuring, with a patient staff explaining everything that is going on. Alvin Tresselt's *The Dead Tree* gives information about the plants and animals that live in and on a fallen tree until it becomes part of the humus that nurtures the forest. The simple, poetic text is easily comprehended, yet it teaches a valuable lesson in ecology and the life cycle of all living things.

Although written in narrative form, such books as Tomie de Paola's *"Charlie Needs a Cloak"* describe actual procedures of manufacture or craft. The little shepherd in this story shears his sheep, cards and dyes the wool, and spins the cloth for a new red cloak. A book like this is an excellent start for a discussion of where things that we use come from. De Paola uses a humorous story to give information in *The Quicksand Book*.

There are many books about weather, seasons, and other aspects of the environment. The phenomena that are familiar to adults and to older children can amaze, delight, or baffle the very young. The art in writing such books

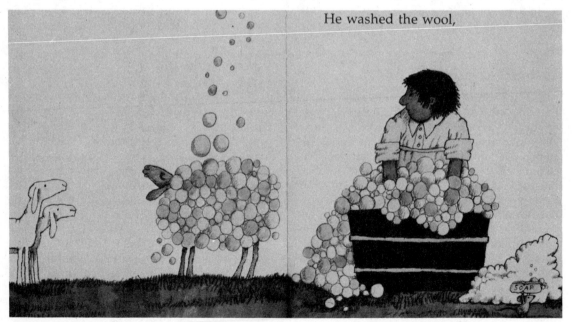

He washed the wool,

From the book "Charlie Needs A Cloak" by Tomie de Paola. © 1973 by Tomie de Paola. Published by Prentice-Hall, Inc., Englewood Cliffs, New Jersey. (Original in color)

involves being accurate, simple, vivid, and knowing what to omit to gain simplicity without sacrificing accuracy. One of the best of the books that present some facet of the natural environment is *Dawn* by Uri Shulevitz. Here the quiet and beautiful pictures, the hushed tone of the text, and the slow, gradual pace of the writing build to a last burst of color as full sunlight fills the scene. *The Snowy Day* by Ezra Jack Keats captures the joy a small child feels when playing in a fresh, full fall of snow. Robert McCloskey's *Time of Wonder* not only portrays vividly the ominous feeling of an approaching hurricane but also the way a family draws together to gain security when danger threatens. In Crescent Dragonwagon's *When Light Turns into Night,* a child goes off to a field at twilight to be alone with the darkening sky and the windblown grass; when she goes home to dinner it is clear that the love and security of the family circle make it possible for her to enjoy the darkening sky, another time of wonder. This is a fine book to read when a child is in a subdued, reflective mood.

The range of picture story books is enormous, but the criteria by which they can be judged are very much the same for all kinds. Whether the story is as simple as Charlotte Zolotow's *May I Visit?* or as profound psychologically as Maurice Sendak's *Where the Wild Things Are,* a story for young children should be brief, it should contain few concepts and none that are beyond comprehension if they are unfamiliar concepts, it should be written in a direct and simple style, and it should have illustrations that complement and extend the text and are never in conflict with it. These same criteria define the admirable and lasting qualities of *Peter Rabbit,* published over eighty years ago, and of *Millions of Cats,* which appeared more than fifty years ago, as well as such treasures of the 1970s as *Frog and Toad Are Friends* or *Why Mosquitoes Buzz in People's Ears.*

The world, for young children, begins at home; they are concerned with small events which to them are of great importance, with the people in their immediate circle, and with what is happening here and now. As they grow older their horizons extend to include neighbors, relatives who are not part of the immediate family, classmates in nursery school or kindergarten, and friends. Their understanding of time, space, distance, and of relative sizes

From *Mothers Can Do Anything* by Joe Lasker. Copyright © 1972 by Joe Lasker. Reproduced by permission of Albert Whitman & Company, Publishers.

grows as they grow. Their books should take such conceptual limitations into account.

These are some of the books for young children. There are many more in the succeeding chapters of this book, stories that are notable as fantasy or realism, poems and folk tales, books of fiction and books of fact that stretch across boundaries of age and sometimes of genre. This chapter is a review of the kinds of books that are appropriate for young children rather than a summary of all that exist. Because many of the picture books in Chapter 6 are also appropriate for this age group, they are listed in the bibliography that follows and are identified by the "6" that precedes them.

Like books for older children, books for the youngest reflect the changes in our society. There are still too few working mothers, although books like Joe Lasker's *Mothers Can Do Anything* and Eve Merriam's *Mommies at Work* show a wide range of working women; still too few active and independent girls; too few protagonists who are members of minority groups; but some change is evident and more will come. It is of the utmost importance that it does come, for the early years are the years in which children learn the most about their world.

Adult References[5]

ANDERSON, ROBERT H., and HAROLD G. SHANE, eds. *As the Twig Is Bent: Readings in Early Childhood Education.*

ANDERSON, VERNA. *Reading and Young Children.*

BARCHILON, JACQUES, and HENRY PETTIT. *The Authentic Mother Goose Fairy Tales and Nursery Rhymes.*

BARING-GOULD, WILLIAM, and CEIL BARING-GOULD. *The Annotated Mother Goose.*

BEADLE, MURIEL. *A Child's Mind: How Children Learn During the Critical Years from Birth to Age Five.*

BETT, HENRY. *The Games of Children: Their Origin and History.*

BUTLER, DOROTHY. *Babies Need Books.*

————. *Cushla and Her Books.*

CHUKOVSKY, KORNEI. *From Two to Five.*

CIANCIOLO, PATRICIA, ed. *Picture Books for Children.*

COODY, BETTY. *Using Literature with Young Children.*

CULLINAN, BERNICE, and CAROLYN CARMICHAEL, eds. *Literature and Young Children.*

DURKIN, DOLORES. *Teaching Young Children to Read.*

ECKENSTEIN, LINA. *Comparative Studies in Nursery Rhymes.*

FORD, ROBERT. *Children's Rhymes, Children's Games, Children's Songs, Children's Stories: A Book for Bairns and Big Folk.*

GESELL, ARNOLD, and others. *The First Five Years of Life: A Guide to the Study of the Preschool Child.*

GREEN, PERCY B. *A History of Nursery Rhymes.*

HALLIWELL-PHILLIPPS, JAMES O. *Popular Rhymes and Nursery Tales: A Sequel to The Nursery Rhymes of England.*

HÜRLIMANN, BETTINA. *Picture-Book World.*

HUTT, S. J., and CORINNE HUTT, eds. *Early Human Development.*

JACOBS, LELAND, ed. *Using Literature with Young Children.*

JOHNSON, FERNE. *Start Early for an Early Start.*

LATIMER, BETTYE I., ed. *Starting Out Right: Choosing Books about Black People for Young Children.*

MacCANN, DONNARAE, and OLGA RICHARD. *The Child's First Books: A Critical Study of Pictures and Texts.*

MILLAR, SUSANNE. *The Psychology of Play.* Chapter entitled "Phantasy, Feeling, and Make-Believe Play."

MOORE, VARDINE. *Pre-School Story Hour.*

OLLILA, LLOYD, ed. *The Kindergarten Child and Reading.*

OPIE, IONA and PETER. *Children's Games in Street and Playground.*

————. *The Lore and Language of Schoolchildren.*

————, eds. *The Oxford Dictionary of Nursery Rhymes.*

The Original Mother Goose's Melody, As First Issued by John Newbery, of London, about A.D. 1760.

PINES, MAYA. *Revolution in Learning: The Years from Birth to Six.* Particularly Chapter 11, "Early Reading."

RICHARD, OLGA. "The Visual Language of the Picture Book."

THOMAS, KATHERINE ELWES. *The Real Personages of Mother Goose.*

WHITE, DOROTHY. *About Books for Children.* Chapter 2, "Picture Books."

————. *Books Before Five.*

YARDLEY, ALICE. *Young Children Thinking.*

Books discussed in Chapter 6 which may also be considered books for early childhood are identified in this bibliography with a "6."

For help in locating books with special purposes or about minorities, see the section "Book Selection Aids" in the Adult References in the Appendixes. In the following bibliography these symbols have been used to identify books about a particular religious or ethnic group:

§ Black
★ Chicano or Puerto Rican
☆ Native American
● Religious minority

5. Complete bibliographic data are provided in Appendix B.

Mother Goose Editions

ADDAMS, CHARLES, ill. *The Chas. Addams Mother Goose.* Harper, 1967.

ALDERSON, BRIAN, comp. *Cakes and Custard: Children's Rhymes Chosen. by Brian Alderson,* ill. by Helen Oxenbury. Morrow, 1975.

6 BRIGGS, RAYMOND, ill. *The Mother Goose Treasury.* Coward, 1966. Greenaway Medal.

BROOKE, L. LESLIE, ill. *Ring o' Roses: A Nursery Rhyme Picture Book.* Warne, 1922.

6 CALDECOTT, RANDOLPH, ill. *Hey Diddle Diddle Picture Book.* Warne, n.d. Some of Caldecott's finest pictures accompany favorite rhymes of the nursery.

CHWAST, SEYMOUR, ill. *The House That Jack Built.* Random, 1973. A clever variation is achieved by having each stiff board page larger than the last.

6 DE ANGELI, MARGUERITE, ill. *Marguerite de Angeli's Book of Nursery and Mother Goose Rhymes.* Doubleday, 1954.

EMBERLEY, ED, ill. *London Bridge Is Falling Down: The Song and Game.* Little, 1967.

6 FRASCONI, ANTONIO, ill. *The House That Jack Built.* Harcourt, 1958.

GREENAWAY, KATE, ill. *Mother Goose: Or, The Old Nursery Rhymes.* Warne, 1882.

GROVER, EULALIE OSGOOD, ed. *Mother Goose: The Volland Edition,* ill. by Frederick Richardson. Hubbard Pr., 1971. A revised version of the 1915 publication with original illustrations.

JEFFERS, SUSAN, ill. *Three Jovial Huntsmen.* Bradbury, 1973.

LINES, KATHLEEN, ed. *Lavender's Blue,* ill. by Harold Jones. Watts, 1954.

LOBEL, ARNOLD, ill. *Gregory Griggs and Other Nursery Rhyme People.* Greenwillow, 1978.

MARTIN, SARAH. *Old Mother Hubbard and Her Dog,* ill. by Ib Spang Olsen. Coward, 1976. Translated from the Swedish (with some variants from the familiar English verses) and delightfully illustrated with ebullient, comic pictures.

MONTGOMERIE, NORAH and WILLIAM, comps. *A Book of Scottish Nursery Rhymes,* ill. by T. Ritchie and Norah Montgomerie. Oxford, 1965.

NESS, EVALINE, ill. *Old Mother Hubbard and Her Dog.* Holt, 1972. A humorous note is added by the dog's clowning.

OPIE, IONA, ed. *Ditties for the Nursery,* ill. by Monica Walker. Walck, 1954.

OPIE, IONA and PETER, comps. *A Family Book of Nursery Rhymes,* ill. by Pauline Baynes. Oxford, 1964.

————, comps. *The Oxford Nursery Rhyme Book,* ill. from old chapbooks, with additional pictures by Joan Hassall. Walck, 1955.

RACKHAM, ARTHUR, ill. *Mother Goose: The Old Nursery Rhymes.* Marathon, 1978.

REED, PHILIP, ill. *Mother Goose and Nursery Rhymes.* Atheneum, 1963. Reissued in 1979 by Regnery, this has quiet woodcut engravings.

ROJANKOVSKY, FEODOR, ill. *The Tall Book of Mother Goose.* Harper, 1942.

SENDAK, MAURICE, ill. *Hector Protector* and *As I Went Over the Water.* Harper, 1965.

SPIER, PETER, ill. *London Bridge Is Falling Down!* Doubleday, 1967.

TRIPP, WALLACE, ill. *Granfa' Grig Had a Pig and Other Rhymes Without Reason from Mother Goose.* Little, 1976.

TUCKER, NICHOLAS, comp. *Mother Goose Lost,* ill. by Trevor Stubley. T. Crowell, 1971.

TUDOR, TASHA, ill. *Mother Goose.* Walck, 1944. Illustrated with scenes of cozy domesticity.

WILDSMITH, BRIAN, ill. *Brian Wildsmith's Mother Goose.* Watts, 1965.

WRIGHT, BLANCHE FISHER, ill. *The Real Mother Goose.* Rand, 1916.

A Few Variants of *Mother Goose*

BODECKER, N. M., comp. *It's Raining Said John Twaining,* tr. and ill. by compiler. Atheneum, 1973.

BURROUGHS, MARGARET TAYLOR, comp. *Did You Feed My Cow? Street Games, Chants, and Rhymes,* ill. by Joe E. DeValasco, rev. ed. Follett, 1969.

DE FOREST, CHARLOTTE B. *The Prancing Pony: Nursery .Rhymes from Japan Adapted into English Verse for Children,* with "Kusa-e" ill. by Keiko Hida. Walker, 1968.

DE KAY, ORMONDE, JR. *Rimes de La Mère Oie: Mother Goose Rhymes Rendered into French.* Little, 1971. More colloquial than Hugh Latham's translation. Illustrations are by Barry Zaid (pedestrian), Seymour Chwast (good), and Milton Glaser (very good).

FOWKE, EDITH, comp. *Sally Go Round the Sun: Three Hundred Children's Songs, Rhymes and Games,* ill. by Carlos Marchiori. Doubleday, 1970.

How Many Strawberries Grow in the Sea? A Songbook of Mother Goose Rhymes, music by Earl Bichel, ill. by George Suyeoka. Follett, 1969.

LANGSTAFF, JOHN. *Ol' Dan Tucker,* ill. by Joe Krush. Harcourt, 1963. Lively picture-book retelling of Ol' Dan Tucker's endless mishaps. Music included.

LATHAM, HUGH, tr. *Mother Goose in French,* ill. by Barbara Cooney. T. Crowell, 1964.

LEACH, MARIA. *Riddle Me, Riddle Me, Ree,* ill. by William Wiesner. Viking, 1970. A collection of over two hundred riddles from folk materials the world over. Sources are given.

LOW, JOSEPH and RUTH. *Mother Goose Riddle Rhymes,* ill. by Joseph Low. Harcourt, 1953. Low has made a modern rebus from nursery rhymes that is beautiful in design and clever in conception—a brain teaser for young and old.

MITCHELL, DONALD, comp. *Every Child's Book of Nursery Songs,* arr. by Carey Blyton, ill. by Alan Howard. Crown, 1968.

MORRISON, LILLIAN, comp. *Black Within and Red Without,* ill. by Jo Spier. T. Crowell, 1953. A scholarly collection of rhymed riddles, wise, witty and often as charming as poetry. Here are traditional puzzlers from ancient Egypt, Greece, the British Isles, the Orient, and the American Ozarks.

———, comp. *Touch Blue,* ill. by Doris Lee. T. Crowell, 1958. "Signs and Spells, Love Charms and Chants, Auguries and Old Beliefs in Rhyme."

PETERSHAM, MAUD and MISKA. *The Rooster Crows: A Book of American Rhymes and Jingles.* Macmillan, 1945. Caldecott Medal.

POTTER, CHARLES FRANCIS, comp. *Tongue Tanglers,* ill. by William Wiesner. World, 1962.

REID, ALASTAIR, and ANTHONY KERRIGAN, trs. *Mother Goose in Spanish,* ill. by Barbara Cooney. T. Crowell, 1968.

SCHWARTZ, ALVIN. *A Twister of Twists, A Tangle of Tongues,* ill. by Glen Rounds. Lippincott, 1972.

WINN, MARIE, comp. and ed. *What Shall We Do and Allee Galloo!* ill. by Karla Kuskin. Harper, 1970. A collection of game and activity songs, each with directions for children's participation. A preface suggests ways to introduce them and appropriate times to use them.

WITHERS, CARL, comp. *A Rocket in My Pocket,* ill. by Susanne Suba. Holt, 1948.

WOOD, RAY. *The American Mother Goose,* ill. by Ed Hargis. Lippincott, 1940.

WYNDHAM, ROBERT, comp. *Chinese Mother Goose Rhymes,* ill. by Ed Young. World, 1968.

6 ZEMACH, HARVE. *Mommy, Buy Me a China Doll,* ill. by Margot Zemach. Follett, 1966.

6 ———, ed. *The Speckled Hen: A Russian Nursery Rhyme,* ill. by Margot Zemach. Holt, 1966.

ZEMACH, MARGOT, ill. *Hush, Little Baby.* Dutton, 1976.

ABC Books

6 ANNO, MITSUMASA, ill. *Anno's Alphabet: An Adventure In Imagination.* T. Crowell, 1975.

BASKIN, LEONARD, ill. *Hosie's Alphabet,* words by Hosea, Tobias and Lisa Baskin. Viking, 1972.

6 BROWN, MARCIA, ill. *All Butterflies: An ABC.* Scribner's, 1974.

6 BURNINGHAM, JOHN, ill. *John Burningham's ABC.* Bobbs, 1967.

CARLE, ERIC, ill. *All about Arthur (an absolutely absurd ape).* Watts, 1974. Arthur left Atlanta because he felt all alone, and his alliterative antics are documented by a combination of photographic and woodcut techniques. Appealingly absurd.

CHWAST, SEYMOUR, and MARTIN STEPHEN MOSKOF, ills. *Still Another Alphabet Book.* McGraw, 1969.

CRANE, WALTER, ill. *Baby's Own Alphabet.* Dodd, n.d.

DUVOISIN, ROGER, ill. *A for the Ark.* Lothrop, 1952.

EICHENBERG, FRITZ, ill. *Ape in a Cape.* Harcourt, 1952.

FARBER, NORMA. *As I Was Crossing Boston Common,* ill. by Arnold Lobel. Dutton, 1975. Too complex for learning the alphabet, but the parade of exotic creatures, from angwantibo to zibet, will fascinate some children.

———. *This Is the Ambulance Leaving the Zoo,* ill. by Tomie de Paola. Dutton, 1975. A lively alphabet book also tells about an Ambulance, Bus, Cars, Drivers in a busy story that has the cumulation young children enjoy.

§6 FEELINGS, MURIEL. *Jambo Means Hello: Swahili Alphabet Book,* ill. by Tom Feelings. Dial, 1974.

6 GÁG, WANDA, ill. *The ABC Bunny.* Coward, 1933.

GREENAWAY, KATE, ill. *A Apple Pie.* Warne, n.d.

GROSSBART, FRANCINE, ill. *A Big City.* Harper, 1966.

LEAR, EDWARD. *ABC,* penned and ill. by author. McGraw, 1965. Facsimile of a manuscript, this edition has the nonsense verses set in type at the back of the book.

McGINLEY, PHYLLIS. *All Around the Town,* ill. by Helen Stone. Lippincott, 1948.

MATTHIESEN, THOMAS. *ABC: An Alphabet Book,* photos by author. Platt, 1966.

MUNARI, BRUNO, ill. *Bruno Munari's ABC.* World, 1960.

§6 MUSGROVE, MARGARET. *Ashanti to Zulu,* ill. by Leo and Diane Dillon. Dial, 1976.

NICHOLSON, WILLIAM, ill. *An Alphabet.* Heinemann/Alan Wofsy, 1975. A handsome reprint of an 1896 Art Nouveau book, with earth-tone woodblocks.

OXENBURY, HELEN, ill. *Helen Oxenbury's ABC of Things.* Watts, 1972.

PIATTI, CELESTINO, ill. *Celestino Piatti's Animal ABC.* English text by Jon Reid. Atheneum, 1966.

PROVENSEN, ALICE and MARTIN, ills. *A Peaceable Kingdom: The Abecedarius.* Viking, 1978. First published in the Shaker Manifesto of 1882, this newly illustrated version adds appropriately quaint, prim people and an enchanting variety of animals to the original lilting rhyme.

ROJANKOVSKY, FEODOR, ill. *Animals in the Zoo.* Knopf, 1962. A handsome zoo alphabet book in color with an animal for every letter.

SCHMIDERER, DOROTHY, ill. *The Alphabeast Book: An Abecedarium.* Holt, 1971.

SENDAK, MAURICE, ill. *Alligators All Around*, in *Nutshell Library.* Harper, 1962.

TUDOR, TASHA, ill. *A Is for Annabelle.* Walck, 1954.

WALTERS, MARGUERITE. *The City-Country ABC: My Alphabet Ride in the City, and My Alphabet Ride in the Country,* ill. by Ib Ohlsson. Doubleday, 1966.

6 WILDSMITH, BRIAN, ill. *Brian Wildsmith's ABC.* Watts, 1963. Kate Greenaway Medal.

YOLEN, JANE. *All in the Woodland Early,* ill. by Jane Breskin Zalben. Collins, 1979.

Counting Books

ALLEN, ROBERT. *Numbers: A First Counting Book,* photos by Mottke Weissman. Platt and Munk, 1968.

ANNO, MITSUMASA, ill. *Anno's Counting Book.* T. Crowell, 1977.

BAYLEY, NICOLA, ill. *One Old Oxford Ox.* Atheneum, 1977. Though the sophisticated text will be lost except on the most unusual child, the framed, lushly intricate illustrations will appeal to all.

CARLE, ERIC, ill. *My Very First Book of Numbers.* T. Crowell, 1974. Board pages, spiral-bound, are cut horizontally so that the child can match top and bottom halves; one has a set of fruits (1 pineapple, 2 bananas) and the other has 1–10 black squares.

CHWAST, SEYMOUR, and MARTIN MOSKOF, ills. *Still Another Number Book.* McGraw, 1971.

ELKIN, BENJAMIN. *Six Foolish Fishermen,* ill. by Katherine Evans. Childrens Pr., 1957.

§ FEELINGS, MURIEL. *Moja Means One: Swahili Counting Book,* ill. by Tom Feelings. Dial. 1971.

HOBAN, RUSSELL. *Ten What? A Mystery Counting Book,* ill. by Sylvie Selig. Scribner's, 1975.

HOBAN, TANA. *Count and See,* photos by author. Macmillan, 1972. Clear, sharp photos for a text that goes from 1–15, by tens to 50, and ends with 100 peas in their pods.

HOBZEK, MILDRED. *We Came A-Marching . . . 1,2,3,* ill. by William Pène du Bois. Parents' Magazine, 1978. The distinctive palette and engaging details of Pène du Bois' paintings add beauty to a rhyming narrative that teaches its young audience how to count 1,2,3 in twelve languages.

IPCAR, DAHLOV, ill. *Ten Big Farms.* Knopf, 1958.

KEATS, EZRA JACK, ill. *Over in the Meadow.* Four Winds, 1972.

KIRN, ANN, ill. *Nine in a Line.* Norton, 1966.

KREDENSER, GAIL. *1 One Dancing Drum,* ill. by Stanley Mack. Phillips, 1971.

6 LANGSTAFF, JOHN. *Over in the Meadow,* ill. by Feodor Rojankovsky. Harcourt, 1957.

LEYDENFROST, ROBERT, ill. *Ten Little Elephants.* Doubleday, 1975. In the "ten little Indians" pattern.

McLEOD, EMILIE. *One Snail and Me: A Book of Numbers and Animals and a Bathtub,* ill. by Walter Lorraine. Little, 1961.

MAESTRO, GIULIO, ill. *One More and One Less.* Crown, 1974. One by one, ten cheerful animals arrive; one by one, they depart.

§ MERRIAM, EVE. *Project 1-2-3,* ill. by Harriet Sherman. McGraw, 1971.

OXENBURY, HELEN, ill. *Numbers of Things.* Watts, 1968.

PETIE, HARRIS, ill. *Billions of Bugs.* Prentice, 1975.

REISS, JOHN, ill. *Numbers.* Bradbury, 1971.

§ ROWAN, DICK. *Everybody In! A Counting Book,* ill. with photos. Bradbury, 1969.

SENDAK, MAURICE, ill. *One Was Johnny: A Counting Book,* in *Nutshell Library.* Harper, 1962. A rhyming text about a small boy's problem of too many visitors who appear one by one.

§ *The Sesame Street Book of Numbers,* by Children's Television Workshop and Preschool Press. Time-Life/Little, Brown, 1970.

SEYMOUR, BRENDA, ill. *First Counting.* Walck, 1969.

WILDSMITH, BRIAN, ill. *1,2,3's.* Watts, 1965.

WYSE, ANNE and ALEX, ill. *The One to Fifty Book.* Univ. of Toronto Pr., 1973.

Concept Books

6 ANNO, MITSUMASA, ill., *The King's Flower.* World, 1979. A foolish king wants everything he possesses to be the biggest in the world—until his huge flowerpot produces an ordinary sized (but beautiful anyway) tulip.

ARUEGO, JOSE, and ARIANE DEWEY. *We Hide, You Seek,* ill. by authors. Greenwillow, 1979.

BATTLES, EDITH. *What Does the Rooster Say, Yoshio?* ill. by Toni Hormann. Whitman, 1978. A nice little story in which two small children visiting a play farm overcome a language barrier by exchanging animal sounds with each other until they find one (moo moo) that is the same in both their languages. Yoshio's words are shown in Japanese and in transliteration.

BORTEN, HELEN. *Do You Go Where I Go?* ill. by author. Abelard, 1972. Objects that can be seen at the park, the barbershop, etc., are grouped so that children may think in terms of clues and sets.

———. *Do You Know What I Know?* ill. by author. Abelard, 1970.

BOSSOM, NAOMI. *A Scale Full of Fish and Other Turnabouts,* ill. by author. Greenwillow, 1979. Paired statements on facing pages play at word "turnabouts": "Box in a ring," for example, becomes "Ring in a box" and "Race for a train" turns to "Train for a race."

§ BRENNER, BARBARA. *Faces,* photos by George Ancona. Dutton, 1970.

BROWN, MARCIA. *Listen to a Shape.*

———. *Touch Will Tell.*

———. *Walk with Your Eyes.* All three are illustrated with photographs by the author. Watts, 1979.

CARLE, ERIC. *My Very First Book of Colors,* ill. by author. T. Crowell, 1974. Spiral-bound, board pages cut in half horizontally so that upper and lower can be matched. Here, each top half has a solid block of color, each bottom has a picture of a familiar object.

———. *My Very First Book of Shapes,* ill. by author. T. Crowell, 1974.

COLE, JOANNA. *A Chick Hatches,* ill. with photos. Morrow, 1976. A simply written account of the development from egg to embryo to fetus to chick is made more meaningful by the accompanying photographs, some in color and almost all enlarged.

§ COREY, DOROTHY. *Tomorrow You Can,* ill. by Lois Axeman. Whitman, 1977. In a multiethnic book, young children are reassured about their potential for accomplishing tasks that are difficult at some stages of growth.

☆ § ———. *You Go Away,* ill. by Lois Axeman. Whitman, 1976.

CREWS, DONALD, ill., *Freight Train.* Greenwillow, 1978. A pared-down description of the cars included in a small freight train also serves to identify black and the primary complementary colors.

———. *Truck.* Greenwillow, 1980. In the same style.

§ FUJIKAWA, GYO. *Let's Play!* ill. by author. Grosset, 1975. Pictures on board pages show everyday life experiences, with some stress on directional concepts.

§ HOBAN, TANA. *Circles, Triangles and Squares.* Macmillan, 1974. Excellent photographs in which the three most familiar geometric forms occur. While a picture that has several different shapes is less explicit as a teaching tool than a page of triangles, there is an alternate value in letting the child discover forms that are not prominent.

——. *Look Again!* Macmillan, 1971.

§ ——. *Over, Under & Through.* Macmillan, 1973.

——. *Push-Pull, Empty-Full.* Macmillan, 1972.

——. *Shapes and Things.* Macmillan, 1970.

HOBERMAN, MARY ANN. *A House Is a House for Me,* ill. by Betty Fraser. Viking, 1978. In an oversize book, Hoberman explores in jaunty rhyme the concept of various kinds of homes as well as the concept that objects are houses (a mirror is a house for reflections, a book is a house for a story).

KRAUSS, RUTH. *The Backward Day,* ill. by Marc Simont. Harper, 1950.

——. *The Growing Story,* ill. by Phyllis Rowand. Harper, 1947.

LOSS, JOAN. *What Is It? A Book of Photographic Puzzles.* Doubleday, 1974.

LUND, DORIS HEROLD. *I Wonder What's Under,* ill. by Janet McCaffery. Parents' Magazine, 1970.

§ McGOVERN, ANN. *Black Is Beautiful,* photos by Hope Wurmfeld. Four Winds, 1969.

MAESTRO, BETSY and GIULIO. *Where Is My Friend?* Crown, 1976.

§ MYERS, WALTER. *Where Does the Day Go?* ill. by Leo Carty. Parents' Magazine, 1969.

PEPPÉ, RODNEY. *Odd One OuT,* ill. by author. Viking, 1974.

PROVENSEN, ALICE. *The Year at Maple Hill Farm,* ill. by Alice and Martin Provensen. Atheneum, 1978. The Provensens go through the year with the animals—wild and domesticated—of the farm. The text is direct and mildly humorous; the illustrations are perky and amusing.

REISS, JOHN J. *Colors,* ill. by author. Bradbury, 1969.

——. *Shapes,* ill. by author. Bradbury, 1974.

RUBEN, PATRICIA. *True or False?* ill. with photos. Lippincott, 1978. These photographs accompanied by true-false questions can be used to reinforce concepts of shape, size, texture, numbers, or simple logic.

——. *What Is New? What Is Missing? What Is Different?* ill. with photos. Lippincott, 1978. A book of photographs encourages observation and moves from simple differences to some that are more complicated.

SCHLEIN, MIRIAM. *Shapes.* W. R. Scott, 1952.

SHOWERS, PAUL. *No Measles, No Mumps for Me,* ill. by Harriett Barton. Crowell, 1980. A simply written explanation of immunization.

SPIER, PETER. *Fast-Slow, High-Low,* ill. by author. Doubleday, 1972.

——. *Gobble, Growl, Grunt,* ill. by author. Doubleday, 1971. Engaging, realistic drawings of animals whose names and sounds are the only text enable children to acquire the concept that each creature makes a distinctive noise.

TISON, ANNETTE, and TALUS TAYLOR. *The Adventures of the Three Colors.* World, 1971.

TRESSELT, ALVIN. *It's Time Now!* ill. by Roger Duvoisin. Lothrop, 1969. Reinforces concepts of seasons by describing seasonal activities. The tone is light, the illustrations bright and vigorous.

——. *What Did You Leave Behind?* ill. by Roger Duvoisin. Lothrop, 1978. In a book encouraging the joy of heightened observation, Tresselt reminds children that one retains more than the physical evidence of beauty or pleasure.

6 ——. *White Snow, Bright Snow,* ill. by Roger Duvoisin. Lothrop, 1947.

UDRY, JANICE MAY. *A Tree Is Nice,* ill. by Marc Simont. Harper, 1956. Designed to give young children awareness of the varied uses and attractions of trees.

WATANABE, SHIGEO. *What a Good Lunch,* ill. by Yasuo Ohtomo. Collins, 1980. A small bear makes a mess of his food but is delighted because he's fed himself.

WELBER, ROBERT. *Goodbye, Hello,* ill. by Cyndy Szekeres. Pantheon, 1974.

6 WELLS, ROSEMARY. *Max's Ride.* Dial, 1979.

WHITE, PAUL. *Janet at School,* ill. with photos. T. Crowell, 1978. Full-color photographs and a straightforward text describe five-year-old Janet (a handicapped victim of spina bifida) at home, at school, on the playground, and on a camping trip.

WINTHROP, ELIZABETH. *That's Mine!* ill. by Emily McCully. Holiday, 1977. A boy and a girl, each building a block castle, discover after some boasting and fighting that they can build bigger and better things if they share and work together.

Wordless Books

§ ALEXANDER, MARTHA. *Bobo's Dream.* Dial, 1970.

6 ANNO, MITSUMASA, ill. *Anno's Journey.* World, 1978.

6 ——. *Topsy-Turvies: Pictures to Stretch the Imagination.* Walker/Weatherhill, 1970.

ARDIZZONE, EDWARD. *The Wrong Side of the Bed.* Doubleday, 1970.

ARUEGO, JOSE. *Look What I Can Do.* Scribner's, 1971.

CARLE, ERIC. *Do You Want to Be My Friend?* T. Crowell, 1971.

CARROLL, RUTH and LATROBE. *The Christmas Kitten.* Walck, 1970. Mother doesn't want the kitten that's been left by a friend, but—to her children's delight—the persistent cat reappears so many times that Mother relents.

DE PAOLA, TOMIE, ill. *Pancakes for Breakfast.* Harcourt, 1978.

FUCHS, ERICH. *Journey to the Moon.* Delacorte, 1969.

GOODALL, JOHN S. *The Ballooning Adventures of Paddy Pork.* Harcourt, 1969.

——. *Paddy Pork's Holiday.* Atheneum, 1976. Like other Goodall books about a lively pig, this has half-pages inserted between each set of full pages. Here Paddy goes off on a hiking trip, has a few adventures, and eventually returns home in fine fettle.

——. *Paddy's Evening Out.* Atheneum, 1973. Paddy Pork's visit to a theater turns into a disruption enjoyed more by the audience than the cast.

——. *The Surprise Picnic.* Atheneum, 1977.

HAMBERGER, JOHN. *The Lazy Dog.* Four Winds, 1971.

HOBAN, TANA. *Big Ones, Little Ones.* Greenwillow, 1976. Pictures of adult animals with their young. See titles also in bibliography for concept books.

HOGROGIAN, NONNY. *Apples.* Macmillan, 1972.

HUTCHINS, PAT. *Changes, Changes.* Macmillan, 1971.

KEATS, EZRA JACK. *Kitten for a Day.* Watts, 1974.

——. *Pssst! Doggie—.* Watts, 1973.

KOREN, EDWARD. *Behind the Wheel.* Holt, 1972.

KRAHN, FERNANDO. *April Fools.* Dutton, 1974. Two young pranksters make a monster, get lost in the woods, and use their creation, atop a long pole, to signal rescuers.

——. *The Self-Made Snowman.* Lippincott, 1974.

MARI, IELA. *The Magic Balloon.* Phillips, 1969.

MARI, IELA and ENZO. *The Apple and the Moth.* Pantheon, 1970.

MAYER, MERCER. *Ah-Choo.* Dial, 1976.

———. *Frog Goes to Dinner.* Dial, 1974.

———. *Frog, Where Are You?* Dial, 1969. Raffish pictures show the troubles of a boy and his dog as they hunt for a pet frog.

———. *The Great Cat Chase.* Four Winds, 1974.

———. *Hiccup.* Dial, 1976.

MAYER, MERCER and MARIANNA. *A Boy, a Dog, a Frog and a Friend,* ill. by Mercer Mayer. Dial, 1971. Playing in a pond, the boy and his pets find a turtle and happily add it to their inner circle.

———. *One Frog Too Many.* Dial, 1975. When a baby frog is added, the older frog is jealous, but he adjusts.

SIMMONS, ELLIE. *Family.* McKay, 1970.

6 WARD, LYND. *The Silver Pony.* Houghton, 1973.

Books for Beginning Readers

☆ BAKER, BETTY. *Partners,* ill. by Emily Arnold McCully. Greenwillow, 1978. Three Native American tales of the Southwest, retold with simplicity and understated humor, describe the trickery of Coyote whose wiles are usually matched by those of his partner Badger.

BENCHLEY, NATHANIEL. *George the Drummer Boy,* ill. by Don Bolognese. Harper, 1977.

6 ———. *Sam the Minute Man,* ill. by Arnold Lobel. Harper, 1969.

———. *The Several Tricks of Edgar Dolphin,* ill. by Mamoru Funai. Harper, 1970.

☆ ———. *Snorri and the Strangers,* ill. by Don Bolognese. Harper, 1976. Set in America over a thousand years ago, this describes, from Snorri's viewpoint, the initial encounters between the people of Snorri's community (immigrant Norwegian descendants) and some native Americans.

BONSALL, CROSBY. *And I Mean It, Stanley,* ill. by author. Harper, 1974. Stanley's identity is kept secret until the end of a running monologue by a small girl who is creating a sort of preschool Watts Tower.

§ ———. *The Case of the Cat's Meow,* ill. by author. Harper, 1965. An amusing mystery story.

§ ———. *The Case of the Scaredy Cats,* ill. by author. Harper, 1971. The staunch crew that coped with the cat's meow finds that girls can hold their own.

———. *Mine's the Best,* ill. by author. Harper, 1973.

———. *Twelve Bells for Santa.* Harper, 1977. Not substantial, but a merry tale, nicely illustrated and including such appealing elements as prizes, presents, reindeer and the real Santa Claus.

———. *Who's Afraid of the Dark?* ill. by author. Harper, 1980. Even the youngest listener should realize that it's the boy who's afraid, not the dog he claims he's protecting.

BRENNER, BARBARA. *Baltimore Orioles,* ill. by J. Winslow Higginbottom. Harper, 1974. Not accurate in color, but reliable in the text that describes one oriole family through a year's life cycle.

BUNTING, EVE. *Winter's Coming,* ill. by Howard Knotts. Harcourt, 1977. A quiet, cozy account of the natural signs of the advent of a hard winter and the preparations made by a family.

CARRICK, MALCOLM. *Mr. Tod's Trap,* ill. by author. Harper, 1980. Mr. Tod, a fox, finally is tricked into staying home with the children while his capable wife goes off to get food, which he's been unable to do.

COVILLE, BRUCE and KATHERINE. *The Foolish Giant.* Lippincott, 1978. Harry the giant (kind, friendly, and brave—but not very bright) is sent away from the village when he becomes a bit of an annoyance. He is reinstated when he saves the villagers (more by chance than wit) from a wicked wizard.

FRESCHET, BERNIECE. *Little Black Bear Goes for a Walk,* ill. by Glen Rounds. Scribner's, 1977. Little Black Bear makes his first solo trip while his mother naps. His actions are authentically bear-like and the underlying message (one learns by experience) will offer encouragement to beginning readers.

GAGE, WILSON. *Down in the Boondocks,* ill. by Glen Rounds. Greenwillow, 1977. The humorous rhyming text concerns a farmer who is deaf to the din surrounding him and a robber who isn't—and is frightened away by the racket.

GREENAWAY, KATE. *Under the Window.* Warne, n.d.

GUILFOILE, ELIZABETH. *Nobody Listens to Andrew,* ill. by Mary Stevens. Follett, 1957.

HEYWARD, DU BOSE. *The Country Bunny and the Little Gold Shoes,* ill. by Marjorie Flack. Houghton, 1939.

HOBAN, LILLIAN. *Arthur's Christmas Cookies,* ill. by author. Harper, 1972. An enterprising monkey bakes cookies for Christmas giving and uses them as tree ornaments when they prove to be rock-hard. Good structure and good humor give a simple story substance.

———. *Arthur's Honey Bear,* ill. by author. Harper, 1974.

———. *Arthur's Pen Pal,* ill. by author. Harper, 1976. Another story about Arthur, the beguiling child in chimpanzee form, in which he wistfully contrasts his sister Violet, who squabbles and teases, with the sibling relationship enjoyed by his pen pal.

———. *Arthur's Prize Reader,* ill. by author. Harper, 1978. A fourth book about the small chimp Arthur who reluctantly comes to accept the fact that his little sister Violet has learned to read.

HOFF, SYD. *The Horse in Harry's Room,* ill. by author. Harper, 1970. Pictures in cartoon style illustrate a story in which a sympathetic teacher handles nicely Harry's belief in his imaginary horse.

HURD, EDITH THACHER. *Johnny Lion's Rubber Boots,* ill. by Clement Hurd. Harper, 1972. One of a series of books about a lion cub who is really just like a small boy, this describes Johnny's indoor play on a rainy day and an equally satisfying puddle-romp. Lots of action, quite a bit of repetition of words.

HUTCHINS, PAT. *The Best Train Set Ever,* ill. by author. Greenwillow, 1978. Three short stories centering around a birthday, Halloween, and Christmas are a bit bland in the telling but imbued with quiet, solid family feeling.

§ KESSLER, LEONARD. *Kick, Pass, and Run,* ill. by author. Harper, 1966.

§ LEXAU, JOAN M. *The Homework Caper,* ill. by Syd Hoff. Harper, 1966.

§ ———. *The Rooftop Mystery,* ill. by Syd Hoff. Harper, 1968. Two boys cope with the traditional male embarrassment about dolls when they carry one to help on moving day. Despite the stereotypical sex role, an amusing story with problem-solution, humor, and an interracial friendship.

LOBEL, ARNOLD. *Days with Frog and Toad,* ill. by author. Harper, 1979.

———. *Frog and Toad All Year,* ill. by author. Harper, 1976. Lobel continues the saga of the devoted friendship of Frog and Toad, this time with five stories that focus on the seasons.

6 _____. *Frog and Toad Are Friends,* ill. by author. Harper, 1970.

6 _____. *Frog and Toad Together,* ill. by author. Harper, 1972. Short, short stories that are funnier than those of the first book and only a little less touching.

_____. *Grasshopper on the Road,* ill. by author. Harper, 1978.

_____. *Mouse Soup,* ill. by author. Harper, 1977.

6 _____. *Owl at Home,* ill. by author. Harper, 1975.

MINARIK, ELSE HOLMELUND. *Father Bear Comes Home,* ill. by Maurice Sendak. Harper, 1959. The illustrations capture to perfection the ingenuous Little Bear and his loving parents in a story that has, for all its brevity, chapter divisions that look impressive to the beginning reader.

_____. *A Kiss for Little Bear,* ill. by Maurice Sendak. Harper, 1968. Grandmothers do often send kisses, but seldom by as amusing a chain of helpers; Skunk breaks the chain when he finds another skunk so attractive he concentrates on kissing her rather than passing the kiss along.

6 _____. *Little Bear,* ill. by Maurice Sendak. Harper, 1957.

6 _____. *Little Bear's Friend,* ill. by Maurice Sendak. Harper, 1960. When a little girl he's become fond of leaves at the end of the summer, Little Bear's parents teach him to write so that he and Emily can communicate.

PARISH, PEGGY. *Dinosaur Time,* ill. by Arnold Lobel. Harper, 1974.

RICCIUTI, EDWARD R. *Donald and the Fish That Walked,* ill. by Syd Hoff. Harper, 1974.

RICE, EVE. *Papa's Lemonade and Other Stories,* ill. by author. Greenwillow, 1976.

§ ROCKWELL, HARLOW. *I Did It,* ill. by author. Macmillan, 1974.

ROSS, PAT. *Meet M and M,* ill. by Marilyn Hafner. Pantheon, 1980. Lightly humorous, a realistic story about friends who quarrel and make up.

SCHULMAN, JANET. *Camp Keewee's Secret Weapon,* ill. by Marilyn Hafner. Greenwillow, 1978. In spite of her pessimistic outlook, Jill finds a friend, a new prowess at sports, and a great enthusiasm for Camp Keewee.

6 SELSAM, MILLICENT. *Benny's Animals and How He Put Them in Order,* ill. by Arnold Lobel. Harper, 1966.

_____. *Greg's Microscope,* ill. by Arnold Lobel. Harper, 1963. Having coaxed his father into buying him a second-hand microscope, Greg learns how to make slides and also learns that he'll have to share the instrument with his fascinated parents.

_____. *How Puppies Grow,* photos by Esther Bubley. Four Winds, 1972.

_____. *Tony's Birds,* ill. by Kurt Werth. Harper, 1961.

SEUSS, DR. *The Cat in the Hat,* ill. by author. Random, 1957.

_____. *The Cat in the Hat Comes Back,* ill. by author. Random, 1958. A sequel to the first book has 26 cats, A–Z, who help the Cat in the Hat in a series of the silly dilemmas he creates.

SHARMAT, MARJORIE. *Mitchell Is Moving,* ill. by Jose Aruego and Ariane Dewey. Macmillan, 1978.

SHAW, EVELYN. *Alligator,* ill. by Frances Zweifel. Harper, 1972.

_____. *Octopus,* ill. by Ralph Carpentier. Harper, 1971. Succinct and accurate, an unfictionalized text about the octopus, written by a scientist, gives facts about feeding, breeding, avoiding predators, and other facets of behavior.

§ SHOWERS, PAUL. *Look at Your Eyes,* ill. by Paul Galdone. T. Crowell, 1962.

THALER, MICHAEL. *Madge's Magic Show,* ill. by Carol Nicklaus. Watts, 1978. Madge puts on a magic show and is embarrassed when her initial attempts to pull a rabbit from a hat produce a chicken, a goat, a turkey, and a horse.

WISEMAN, BERNARD. *Morris Has a Cold,* ill. by author. Dodd, 1978. An amusing story about a literal moose with a head cold and his solicitous but soon exasperated bear friend.

Picture Story Books

6 AARDEMA, VERNA. *Why Mosquitoes Buzz in People's Ears,* ill. by Leo and Diane Dillon. Dial, 1975. Caldecott Medal.

ALLEN, PAMELA. *Mr. Archimedes' Bath,* ill. by author. Lothrop, 1980. A hilarious version of the scientist's discovery about water displacement includes a kangaroo and a wombat; the author-illustrator is Australian.

ALEXANDER, MARTHA. *I'll Be the Horse If You'll Play with Me,* ill. by author. Dial. 1975.

_____. *Nobody Asked Me If I Wanted a Baby Sister,* ill. by author. Dial, 1971.

_____. *We're in Big Trouble, Blackboard Bear,* ill. by author. Dial, 1980. Anthony's imaginary bear eats the neighbors' food and must make reparations.

ALIKI. *At Mary Bloom's,* ill. by author. Greenwillow, 1976. A young child shares the joyous news of the birth of her pet mouse's babies with an older neighbor who has quite a menagerie of her own.

_____. *June 7,* ill. by author. Macmillan, 1972.

_____. *The Two of Them,* ill. by author. Greenwillow, 1979. A quiet, tender story about the love between a child and her grandfather.

ALLARD, HARRY. *It's So Nice To Have a Wolf Around the House,* ill. by James Marshall. Doubleday, 1977.

_____, and James Marshall. *The Stupids Have a Ball,* ill. by James Marshall. Houghton, 1978. The Stupid family (appealing for their joy at being ignorant) decide to celebrate when the children bring home abysmally bad report cards.

6 AMBRUS, VICTOR. *A Country Wedding,* ill. by author. Addison, 1975.

6 ANDERSEN, HANS CHRISTIAN. *The Steadfast Tin Soldier,* ill. by Marcia Brown. Scribner's, 1953.

6 ANDERSON, LONZO. *Two Hundred Rabbits,* ill. by Adrienne Adams. Viking, 1968.

6 ARDIZZONE, EDWARD. *Little Tim and the Brave Sea Captain,* ill. by author. Walck, 1955.

6 _____. *Tim All Alone,* ill. by author. Oxford, 1957. Kate Greenaway Medal.

6 _____. *The Wrong Side of the Bed,* ill. by author. Doubleday, 1970.

ASCH, FRANK. *Sand Cake,* ill. by author. Parents' Magazine, 1979. Bright, solid colors are used to illustrate a story, set on a beach, in which a small bear matches his father's imaginative play.

AVERILL, ESTHER HOLDEN. *Jenny and the Cat Club,* ill. by author. Harper, 1973.

☆ § BARKIN, CAROL, and ELIZABETH JAMES. *Sometimes I Hate School,* photos by Heinz Kluetmeier. Raintree, 1975.

6 BARNHART, PETER. *The Wounded Duck,* ill. by Adrienne Adams. Scribner's, 1979.

BARTOLI, JENNIFER. *Nonna,* ill. by Joan Drescher. Harvey, 1975.

BATE, LUCY. *Little Rabbit's Loose Tooth,* ill. by Diane De Groat. Crown, 1975.

☆ 6 BAYLOR, BYRD. *The Desert Is Theirs,* ill. by Peter Parnall. Scribner's, 1975.

6 _____. *Everybody Needs a Rock,* ill. by Peter Parnall. Scribner's, 1974.

6 BEMELMANS, LUDWIG. *Madeline,* ill. by author. Viking, 1939.

BORNSTEIN, RUTH. *Little Gorilla,* ill. by author. Seabury, 1976. Everybody loved Little Gorilla . . . even after he grew big! The message is clear: love goes on!

BRANDENBERG, FRANZ. *I Wish I Was Sick, Too!* ill. by Aliki. Greenwillow, 1976.

§ BREINBURG, PETRONELLA. *Doctor Shawn,* ill. by Errol Lloyd. T. Crowell, 1975.

6 BRIGGS, RAYMOND. *Father Christmas,* ill. by author. Coward, 1973. Kate Greenaway Medal.

6 ———. *Father Christmas Goes on Holiday,* ill. by author. Coward, 1975.

6 ———. *Jim and the Beanstalk,* ill. by author. Coward, 1970.

6 BROWN, MARCIA. *Dick Whittington and His Cat,* ill. by author. Scribner's, 1950.

6 ———. *Once a Mouse,* ill. by author. Scribner's, 1961. Caldecott Medal.

———. *Stone Soup,* ill. by author. Scribner's, 1947.

6 BROWN, MARGARET WISE. *The Little Island,* ill. by Leonard Weisgard. Doubleday, 1946. Published under pseudonym of Golden MacDonald. Caldecott Medal.

———. *The Runaway Bunny,* ill. by Clement Hurd, rev. ed. Harper, 1962.

BROWN, MYRA BERRY. *First Night Away from Home,* ill. by Dorothy Marino. Watts, 1960.

6 BURNINGHAM, JOHN. *The Baby; The Rabbit; The School; The Snow,* ill. by author. T. Crowell, 1975.

———. *The Blanket; The Cupboard; The Dog; The Friend,* ill. by author. T. Crowell, 1976. Four more titles of the "Little Books" series perfectly scaled by their subjects, their brevity, and their direct simplicity to appeal to the young child.

6 ———. *Borka: The Adventures of a Goose with No Feathers,* ill. by author. Random, 1964. Kate Greenaway Medal.

———. *Come Away from the Water, Shirley.* T. Crowell, 1977. On one page are instructions from parents who've brought their daughter on a beach outing; on the facing page are Shirley's imaginative fantasies of pirates, secret maps, and treasures.

6 ———. *Mr. Gumpy's Motor Car,* ill. by author. Crowell, 1976.

6 ———. *Mr. Gumpy's Outing,* ill. by author. Holt, 1971. Kate Greenaway Medal.

6 BURTON, VIRGINIA. *The Little House,* ill. by author. Houghton, 1942. Caldecott Medal.

6 ———. *Mike Mulligan and His Steam Shovel,* ill. by author. Houghton, 1939.

CALDECOTT, RANDOLPH. *Frog He Would A-Wooing Go,* ill. by author. Warne, n.d.

6 CARIGIET, ALOIS. *Anton and Anne,* tr. by Refna Wilkin, ill. by author. Walck, 1969.

CARLSON, NATALIE SAVAGE. *Marie Louise's Heyday,* ill. by Jose Aruego and Ariane Dewey. Scribner's, 1975.

CAUDILL, REBECCA. *Did You Carry the Flag Today, Charley?* ill. by Nancy Grossman. Holt, 1966.

6 ———. *A Pocketful of Cricket,* ill. by Evaline Ness. Holt, 1964.

§ 6 CLIFTON, LUCILLE. *The Boy Who Didn't Believe in Spring,* ill. by Brinton Turkle. Dutton, 1973.

§ ———. *My Friend Jacob,* ill. by Thomas Digrazia. Dutton, 1980. A touching account of the loving friendship between a small black boy and his retarded adolescent neighbor, who is white.

§ 6 ———. *Some of the Days of Everett Anderson,* ill. by Evaline Ness. Holt, 1970.

§ COHEN, MIRIAM. *Lost in the Museum,* ill. by Lillian Hoban. Greenwillow, 1978. On a visit to the Museum of Natural History, several children follow Danny, who knows where the dinosaur skeleton is. In the process of relocating the class the children learn there are many different ways to be afraid—or brave.

§ ———. *When Will I Read?* ill. by Lillian Hoban. Greenwillow, 1977. A multiethnic classroom, a loving teacher, a child who yearns to read, amusing antics of the children in the class, natural sounding dialogue: who could ask for anything more?

§ ———. *Will I Have a Friend?* ill. by Lillian Hoban. Macmillan, 1967.

COLE, WILLIAM. *What's Good for a Three-Year-Old?* ill. by Lillian Hoban. Holt, 1974.

6 COLMONT, MARIE. *Christmas Bear,* tr. by Constance Hirsch, ill. by Feodor Rojankovsky. Golden Pr., 1966.

6 CRAFT, RUTH. *The Winter Bear,* ill. by Erik Blegvad. Atheneum, 1975.

CROWE, ROBERT L. *Clyde Monster,* ill. by Kay Chorao. Dutton, 1976. A small, awkward, engaging monster is afraid of the dark—people might get him!

6 DAUGHERTY, JAMES. *Andy and the Lion,* ill. by author. Viking, 1938.

DE BRUNHOFF, JEAN. *The Story of Babar, the Little Elephant,* ill. by author. Random, 1937.

DELTON, JUDY. *Two Good Friends,* ill. by Giulio Maestro. Crown, 1974.

DE PAOLA, TOMIE. *Bill and Pete,* ill. by author. Putnam, 1978. What begins as a pleasant if zany home-and-school story ends with a lurid adventure, as a small crocodile is saved from a terrible fate by his toothbrush.

———. *"Charlie Needs a Cloak,"* ill. by author. Prentice, 1974.

———. *Nana Upstairs and Nana Downstairs,* ill. by author. Putnam, 1973.

———. *The Quicksand Book.* Holiday, 1977.

6 ———, ad. *Strega Nona,* ill. by adapter. Prentice, 1975.

6 DE REGNIERS, BEATRICE SCHENK. *A Little House of Your Own,* ill. by Irene Haas. Harcourt, 1955.

6 ———. *May I Bring a Friend?* ill. by Beni Montresor. Atheneum, 1964. Caldecott Medal.

6 ———. *What Can You Do with a Shoe?* ill. by Maurice Sendak. Harper, 1955.

6 DOMANSKA, JANINA. *Din Dan Don It's Christmas,* ill. by author. Greenwillow, 1975.

6 ———. *If All the Seas Were One Sea,* ill. by author. Macmillan, 1971.

———. *Look, There Is a Turtle Flying,* ill. by author. Macmillan, 1968.

DRAGONWAGON, CRESCENT. *When Light Turns into Night,* ill. by Robert Andrew Parker. Harper, 1975.

6 DUVOISIN, ROGER. *Snowy and Woody.* Knopf, 1979.

6 ELKIN, BENJAMIN. *How the Tsar Drinks Tea,* ill. by Anita Lobel. Parents' Magazine, 1971.

6 EMBERLEY, BARBARA, ad. *Drummer Hoff,* ill. by Ed Emberley. Prentice, 1967. Caldecott Medal.

ERICKSON, RUSSELL. *Warton and Morton,* ill. by Lawrence Di Fiore. Lothrop, 1976. Morton (a sedate character) is willing to go along when his brother Warton is stricken by wanderlust. The ensuing adventures lead to a gentle lesson about the need for communication.

★6 ETS, MARIE HALL. *Gilberto and the Wind,* ill. by author. Viking, 1963.

6 ———. *Talking Without Words,* ill. by author. Viking, 1968.

★6 ———, and AURORA LABASTIDA. *Nine Days to Christmas,* ill. by Marie Hall Ets. Viking, 1959. Caldecott Medal.

FARBER, NORMA. *Where's Gomer?* ill. by William Pène du Bois. Dutton, 1974.

6 FATIO, LOUISE. *The Happy Lion,* ill. by Roger Duvoisin. Whittlesey, 1954.

6 FISHER, AILEEN. *Going Barefoot,* ill. by Adrienne Adams. T. Crowell, 1960.

6 ———. *Where Does Everyone Go?* ill. by Adrienne Adams. T. Crowell, 1961.

6 FLACK, MARJORIE. *The Story About Ping,* ill. by Kurt Wiese. Viking, 1933.

FREEMAN, DON. *Will's Quill,* ill. by author. Viking, 1975.

GACKENBACH, DICK. *Do You Love Me?* ill. by author. Seabury, 1975.

6 GÁG, WANDA. *Millions of Cats,* ill. by author. Coward, 1928.

GALDONE, PAUL. *The Gingerbread Boy,* ill. by author. Seabury, 1975.

———. *The Little Red Hen,* ill. by author. Seabury, 1973.

GETZ, ARTHUR. *Hamilton Duck,* ill. by author. Golden Pr., 1972.

———. *Hamilton Duck's Springtime Story,* ill. by author. Golden Pr., 1974.

6 GOUDEY, ALICE E. *The Day We Saw the Sun Come Up,* ill. by Adrienne Adams. Scribner's, 1961.

6 ———. *Houses from the Sea,* ill. by Adrienne Adams. Scribner's, 1959.

§ GRAHAM, LORENZ. *Hongry Catch the Foolish Boy,* ill. by James Brown, Jr. T. Crowell, 1973.

§ ———. *Song of the Boat,* ill. by Leo and Diane Dillon. T. Crowell, 1975.

§ GRAY, GENEVIEVE. *Send Wendell,* ill. by Symeon Shimin. McGraw, 1974.

GREENBERG, BARBARA. *The Bravest Babysitter,* ill. by Diane Paterson. Dial, 1977. In a classic case of role reversal, Lisa sees her frightened babysitter through a thunderstorm by suggesting a series of activities to keep Heather busy.

§ GREENFIELD, ELOISE. *She Come Bringing Me That Little Baby Girl,* ill. by John Steptoe. Lippincott, 1974.

6 GRIMM, JACOB and WILHELM. *King Grisly-Beard,* tr. by Edgar Taylor, ill. by Maurice Sendak. Farrar, 1973.

6 ———. *The Shoemaker and the Elves,* ill. by Adrienne Adams. Scribner's, 1960.

6 HAAS, IRENE. *The Maggie B.,* ill. by author. Atheneum, 1975.

6 HADER, BERTA and ELMER. *The Big Snow,* ill. by authors. Macmillan, 1948. Caldecott Medal.

§6 HALEY, GAIL E., ad. *A Story—A Story: An African Tale,* ill. by adapter. Atheneum, 1970. Caldecott Medal.

6 HALL, DONALD, *Ox-Cart Man,* ill. by Barbara Cooney. Viking, 1979. Caldecott Medal.

6 HANDFORTH, THOMAS. *Mei Li,* ill. by author. Doubleday, 1938.

HAUTZIG, DEBORAH. *The Handsomest Father,* ill. by Muriel Batherman. Greenwillow, 1979. Marsha began having qualms the day before Fathers' Visiting Day. What if her father were somehow different from everyone else's? An ingenuous story expressing a reaction many children share.

HOBAN, RUSSELL. *Arthur's New Power,* ill. by Byron Barton. T. Crowell, 1978.

———. *A Bargain for Frances,* ill. by Lillian Hoban. Harper, 1970.

6 ———. *Bedtime for Frances,* ill. by Garth Williams. Harper, 1960.

———. *Dinner at Alberta's,* ill. by James Marshall. T. Crowell, 1975.

6 HOFFMANN, FELIX, ad. *The Story of Christmas,* ill. by adapter. Atheneum, 1975.

6 HOGROGIAN, NONNY. *One Fine Day,* ill. by author. Macmillan, 1971. Caldecott Medal.

HOLL, ADELAIDE. *The Parade,* ill. by Kjell Ringi. Watts, 1975.

HUGHES, SHIRLEY. *David and Dog,* ill. by author. Prentice, 1978. A child's attachment to a favorite toy, its loss, and its subsequent retrieval form the plot for this engaging tale. Published in England as *Dogger.* Kate Greenaway Medal.

———. *George the Babysitter,* ill. by author. Prentice, 1978. Illustrated with deft, realistic paintings, this simple story describes the vicissitudes of the daily round as George copes with three lively children and a procession of chores.

HURWITZ, JOHANNA. *Busybody Nora,* ill. by Susan Jeschke. Morrow, 1976.

HUTCHINS, PAT. *Rosie's Walk,* ill. by author. Macmillan, 1968.

§ ISADORA, RACHEL. *Ben's Trumpet,* ill. by author. Greenwillow, 1979. A story of a small black boy who plays an imaginary trumpet is set off by black and white illustrations that are startling in their effectiveness.

6 JAMESON, CYNTHIA, ad. *The Clay Pot Boy,* ill. by Arnold Lobel. Coward, 1973.

KAHL, VIRGINIA. *The Duchess Bakes a Cake,* ill. by author. Scribner's, 1955.

★ KEATS, EZRA JACK. *Dreams,* ill. by author. Macmillan, 1974.

§6 ———. *Goggles!* ill. by author. Macmillan, 1969.

§6 ———. *Hi Cat!* ill. by author. Macmillan, 1970.

★§6 ———. *Louie,* ill. by author. Greenwillow, 1975.

§6 ———. *Peter's Chair,* ill. by author. Harper, 1967.

§6 ———. *The Snowy Day,* ill. by author. Viking, 1962. Caldecott Medal.

§6 ———. *Whistle for Willie,* ill. by author. Viking, 1964.

6 KEEPING, CHARLES. *Charley, Charlotte and the Golden Canary,* ill. by author. Watts, 1967. Kate Greenaway Medal.

6 ———. *Joseph's Yard,* ill. by author. Watts, 1970.

KESSELMAN, WENDY ANN. *Time for Jody,* ill. by Gerald Dumas. Harper, 1975.

6 KINGMAN, LEE. *Peter's Long Walk,* ill. by Barbara Cooney. Doubleday, 1953.

6 KIPLING, RUDYARD. *How the Rhinoceros Got His Skin,* ill. by Leonard Weisgard. Walker, 1974.

KRAUS, ROBERT. *Milton the Early Riser,* ill. by Jose and Ariane Aruego. Windmill/Dutton, 1972.

6 ———. *Owliver,* ill. by Jose Aruego and Ariane Dewey. Windmill/Dutton, 1974. An owlet learns to think for himself.

KRAUSS, RUTH. *The Backward Day,* ill. by Marc Simont. Harper, 1950.

6 ———. *A Hole Is to Dig,* ill. by Maurice Sendak. Harper, 1952.

6 KUMIN, MAXINE, and ANNE SEXTON. *Joey and the Birthday Present,* ill. by Evaline Ness. McGraw, 1971.

6 LANGSTAFF, JOHN. *Frog Went a-Courtin',* ill. by Feodor Rojankovsky. Harcourt, 1955. Caldecott Medal.

LAPP, ELEANOR. *In the Morning Mist,* ill. by David Cunningham. Whitman, 1978. Quiet paintings and the monologue of a small boy going fishing with grandfather convey details of the rural setting and the beauty of the early morning stillness before the sun appears.

LAPSLEY, SUSAN. *I Am Adopted,* ill. by Michael Charlton. Bradbury, 1975. A small boy speaks of his adoption casually, he's so secure in the love of his family.

LASKER, JOE. *Mothers Can Do Anything,* ill. by author. Whitman, 1972.

LEAF, MUNRO. *The Story of Ferdinand,* ill. by Robert Lawson, Viking, 1936.

LENT, BLAIR. *John Tabor's Ride,* ill. by author. Atlantic/Little, 1966.

———. *Pistachio,* ill. by author. Atlantic/Little, 1964.

LINDGREN, ASTRID. *Of Course Polly Can Do Almost Everything,* ill. by Ilon Wikland. Follett, 1978. Polly, the youngest of three, takes great satisfaction in the number of skills she's acquired and the responsibility she can carry—even though she does occasionally make mistakes!

LIONNI, LEO. *Geraldine, the Music Mouse*, ill. by author. Pantheon, 1979. Large-scale crayon pictures, handsome in composition and soft in mood, illustrate the story of a mouse who learns to appreciate the higher things in life.

_____. *In the Rabbitgarden*, ill. by author. Pantheon, 1975.

6 _____. *Inch by Inch*, ill. by author. Obolensky, 1960.

6 LIPKIND, WILL. *Chaga*, ill. by Nicolas Mordvinoff. Harcourt, 1955.

6 _____. *Finders Keepers*, ill. by Nicolas Mordvinoff. Harcourt, 1951. Caldecott Medal.

6 LOBEL, ANITA. *King Rooster, Queen Hen*, ill. by author. Greenwillow, 1975.

_____. *The Pancake*, ill. by author. Greenwillow, 1978. In a version of the familiar folk tale aimed at beginning readers, a pancake hears that it is going to be eaten by the cook's seven hungry children and rolls off to escape its fate.

LOBEL, ARNOLD. *A Treeful of Pigs*, ill. by Anita Lobel. Greenwillow, 1978. Framed pictures, wonderfully detailed, combine bucolic charm and humor for this story, in folktale style, of how a farmer's wife outwits her lazy husband.

6 _____. *A Zoo for Mr. Muster*, ill. by author. Harper, 1962.

6 McCLOSKEY, ROBERT. *Blueberries for Sal*, ill. by author. Viking, 1948.

6 _____. *Burt Dow, Deep Water Man*, ill. by author. Viking, 1963.

6 _____. *Make Way for Ducklings*, ill. by author. Viking, 1941. Caldecott Medal.

6 _____. *Time of Wonder*, ill. by author. Viking, 1957. Caldecott Medal.

§6 McDERMOTT, GERALD. *Anansi the Spider*, ill. by author. Holt, 1972.

★6 _____. *Arrow to the Sun*, ill. by author. Viking, 1974. Caldecott Medal.

§6 _____, ad. *The Stonecutter*, ill. by adapter. Viking, 1975.

MAHY, MARGARET. *The Boy Who Was Followed Home*, ill. by Steven Kellogg. Watts, 1975.

MANUSHKIN, FRAN. *Bubblebath!* ill. by Ronald Himler. Harper, 1974.

MARSHALL, JAMES. *George and Martha*, ill. by author. Houghton, 1972.

6 MERRIAM, EVE. *Mommies at Work*, ill. by Beni Montresor. Knopf, 1961.

MILES, MISKA. *Chicken Forgets*, ill. by Jim Arnosky. Atlantic/Little, 1976. Mother Hen instructs Chicken to fill his basket with wild blackberries but each animal he meets advises a better food. Fortunately, his last advisor opts for the berries so Chicken is finally commended for remembering.

6 MILNE, A. A. *When We Were Very Young*, ill. by Ernest H. Shepard. Dutton, 1924.

6 MIZAMURA, KAZUE. *If I Built a Village . . .*, ill. by author. T. Crowell, 1971.

6 MONTRESOR, BENI. *House of Flowers, House of Stars*, ill. by author. Knopf, 1962.

6 _____. *The Witches of Venice*, ill. by author. Knopf, 1963.

6 MOSEL, ARLENE, ad. *The Funny Little Woman*, ill. by Blair Lent. Dutton, 1972. Caldecott Medal.

_____, ad. *Tikki Tikki Tembo*, ill. by Blair Lent. Holt, 1968. A picture book version of a Chinese tale.

NESS, EVALINE. *The Girl and the Goatherd*, ill. by author. Dutton, 1970.

§6 _____. *Josefina February*, ill. by author. Scribner's, 1963.

_____. *Sam, Bangs & Moonshine*, ill. by author. Holt, 1966. Caldecott Medal.

_____. *Tom Tit Tot*, ill. by author. Scribner's, 1965.

NIC LEODHAS, SORCHE. *All in the Morning Early*, ill. by Evaline Ness. Holt, 1963.

_____. *Always Room for One More*, ill. by Nonny Hogrogian. Holt, 1965. Caldecott Medal.

OAKLEY, GRAHAM. *The Church Cat Abroad*, ill. by author. Atheneum, 1973.

_____. *The Church Mice Adrift*, ill. by author. Atheneum, 1977.

_____. *The Church Mice and the Moon*, ill. by author. Atheneum, 1974.

_____. *The Church Mice at Bay*, ill. by author. Atheneum, 1978. In a sixth book about Samson, the church cat, and the mice he has sworn never to harm, their English church is temporarily taken over by a substitute curate, with disastrous and hilarious results.

6 OLSEN, IB SPANG. *Smoke*, ill. by author. Coward, 1972.

OXENBURY, HELEN. *The Queen and Rosie Randall*, ill. by author. Morrow, 1979. The Queen calls on a young child for suggestions about entertaining the visiting King of Wottermazzy.

6 PARNALL, PETER. *The Mountain*, ill. by author. Doubleday, 1971.

PARSONS, ELLEN. *Rainy Day Together*, ill. by Lillian Hoban, Harper, 1971.

PEARSON, SUSAN. *Izzie*, ill. by Robert Andrew Parker. Dial, 1975.

6 PETERSON, HANS. *The Big Snowstorm*, ill. by Harald Wiberg. Coward, 1976.

★6 POLITI, LEO. *Juanita*, ill. by author. Scribner's, 1948.

5 _____. *Moy Moy*, ill. by author. Scribner's, 1960.

6 POTTER, BEATRIX. *The Tale of Peter Rabbit*, ill. by author. Warne, 1901.

PROVENSEN, ALICE and MARTIN. *My Little Hen*, ill. by authors. Random, 1973.

_____. *Our Animal Friends at Maple Hill Farm*, ill. by authors. Random, 1974.

6 RANSOME, ARTHUR. *The Fool of the World and the Flying Ship*, ill. by Uri Shulevitz. Farrar, 1968. Caldecott Medal.

RAYNER, MARY. *Mr. and Mrs. Pig's Evening Out*. Atheneum, 1976. Mrs. Wolf was a fine babysitter for the ten Pig children—until she felt like a snack. Fortunately she is rendered inoperable by her resourceful charges.

REY, HANS. *Curious George*, ill. by author. Houghton, 1941. And its sequels.

ROCKWELL, HARLOW. *My Dentist*, ill. by author. Greenwillow, 1975.

_____. *My Doctor*, ill. by author. Macmillan, 1973.

§ _____. *My Nursery School*, ill. by author. Greenwillow, 1976.

ROSEN, WINIFRED. *Ralph Proves the Pudding*, ill. by Lionel Kalish. Doubleday, 1972.

ROY, RON. *Three Ducks Went Wandering*, ill. by Paul Galdone. Seabury, 1979. Three ducklings scurry about oblivious to, but somehow one step ahead of, a string of predatory animals at their heels.

RUSS, LAVINIA. *Alec's Sand Castle*, ill. by James Stevenson. Harper, 1972.

6 RYAN, CHELI DURAN. *Hildilid's Night*, ill. by Arnold Lobel. Macmillan, 1971.

SCHICK, ELEANOR. *City in the Summer*, ill. by author. Macmillan, 1969.

6 _____. *Neighborhood Knight*, ill. by author. Greenwillow, 1976.

SCOTT, ANN. *On Mother's Lap,* ill. by Glo Coalson. McGraw, 1972.

6 SENDAK, MAURICE. *In the Night Kitchen,* ill. by author. Harper, 1970.

6 ———. *The Nutshell Library,* ill. by author. Harper, 1962.

6 ———. *Where the Wild Things Are,* ill. by author. Harper, 1963. Caldecott Medal.

SHARMAT, MARJORIE WEINMAN. *Gladys Told Me to Meet Her Here,* ill. by Edward Frascino. Harper, 1970.

———. *I'm Not Oscar's Friend Anymore,* ill. by Tony De-Luna. Dutton, 1975.

———. *I'm Terrific,* ill. by Kay Chorao. Holiday, 1977. Sharmat and Chorao are both at their best in this story of a small bear who thinks he's marvelous and is not averse to telling the other young bears so.

———. *Mr. Jameson & Mr. Phillips,* ill. by Bruce Degen. Harper, 1979. Mr. Jameson and Mr. Phillips are animal friends who sail off and find an isolated and beautiful tropical island. When it, too, becomes overpopulated, they take up residence aboard their boat.

———. *Taking Care of Melvin,* ill. by Victoria Chess. Holiday, 1980. Nicely structured, the story of a dog who learned to choose a middle path between being too kind and too brash.

———. *Walter the Wolf,* ill. by Kelly Oechsli. Holiday, 1975.

———. *What Are We Going to Do About Andrew?* ill. by Ray Cruz. Macmillan, 1980. A blithe fantasy about a boy whose family adjusts to the fact that he can fly.

6 SHULEVITZ, URI. *Dawn,* ill. by author. Farrar, 1974.

6 ———. *One Monday Morning,* ill. by author. Scribner's, 1967.

6 ———. *Rain Rain Rivers,* ill. by author. Scribner's, 1967.

SIVULICH, SANDRA STRONER. *I'm Going on a Bear Hunt,* ill. by Glen Rounds. Dutton, 1973.

SKORPEN, LIESEL MOAK. *Mandy's Grandmother,* ill. by Martha Alexander. Dial, 1975.

6 SLEATOR, WILLIAM, ad. *The Angry Moon,* ill. by Blair Lent. Little, 1970.

SOBOL, HARRIET LANGSAM. *Jeff's Hospital Book,* photos by Patricia Agre. Walck, 1975.

★ SONNEBORN, RUTH. *Friday Night Is Papa Night,* ill. by Emily McNully. Viking, 1970. A story that reflects the love and warmth in a Puerto Rican family.

STEIG, WILLIAM. *Farmer Palmer's Wagon Ride,* ill. by author. Farrar, 1974.

———. *Sylvester and the Magic Pebble,* ill. by author. Windmill/Simon, 1969. Caldecott Medal.

§ 6 STEPTOE, JOHN. *Stevie,* ill. by author. Harper, 1969.

STEVENSON, JAMES. *Howard,* ill. by author. Greenwillow, 1980. A duck misses his group's take-off for the south; his landing on a New York rooftop in a snowstorm leads to a series of winter adventures with some new friends.

———. *The Sea View Hotel,* ill. by author. Greenwillow, 1978. Illustrated with cartoon strips, this is the story of a family of three animals who vacation at a resort hotel.

6 SWIFT, HILDEGARDE. *The Little Red Lighthouse and the Great Gray Bridge,* ill. by Lynd Ward. Harcourt, 1942.

TAPIO, PAT DECKER. *The Lady Who Saw the Good Side of Everything,* ill. by Paul Galdone. Seabury, 1975.

TITUS, EVE. *Anatole and the Pied Piper,* ill. by Paul Galdone. McGraw, 1979. In this newest Anatole tale, the mouse-hero's wife takes an active part in planning the rescue of two dozen schoolmice captured by a flute player/composer out to win a music contest.

———. *Anatole in Italy,* ill. by Paul Galdone. McGraw, 1973.

TRESSELT, ALVIN. *The Dead Tree,* ill. by Charles Robinson. Parents' Magazine, 1972.

UCHIDA, YOSHIKO. *The Birthday Visitor,* ill. by Charles Robinson, Scribner's, 1975.

6 UDRY, JANICE MAY. *The Moon Jumpers,* ill. by Maurice Sendak. Harper, 1959.

§ ———. *What Mary Jo Shared,* ill. by Eleanor Mill. Whitman, 1966.

UNGERER, TOMI. *Émile,* ill. by author. Harper, 1960.

VAN WOERKOM, DOROTHY. *The Queen Who Couldn't Bake Gingerbread,* ill. by Paul Galdone. Knopf, 1975.

6 VIPONT, ELFRIDA. *The Elephant and the Bad Baby,* ill. by Raymond Briggs. Coward, 1970.

WABER, BERNARD. *I Was All Thumbs,* ill. by author. Houghton, 1975.

———. *Ira Sleeps Over,* ill. by author. Houghton, 1972.

———. *Lyle Finds His Mother.* Houghton, 1974.

WAGNER, JENNY. *The Bunyip of Berkeley's Creek,* ill. by Ron Brooks. Bradbury, 1977. A familiar figure in Australian folklore, the bunyip plaintively seeks his identity in a story illustrated with beautifully detailed pictures.

6 WAHL, JAN. *Mulberry Tree,* ill. by Feodor Rojankovsky. Grosset, 1970.

WARD, LYND. *The Biggest Bear,* ill. by author. Houghton, 1952. Caldecott Medal.

§ WELBER, ROBERT. *The Train,* ill. by Deborah Ray. Pantheon, 1972.

WELLS, ROSEMARY. *Abdul,* ill. by author. Dial, 1975.

———. *Benjamin and Tulip,* ill. by author. Dial, 1973. Adults think Tulip's sweet, but Benjamin knows she's a bully.

6 ———. *Don't Spill It Again, James,* ill. by author. Dial, 1977.

6 ———. *Max's First Word,* ill. by author. Dial, 1979.

6 ———. *Morris's Disappearing Bag,* ill. by author. Dial, 1975.

———. *Stanley & Rhoda,* ill. by author. Dial, 1978.

6 WILDSMITH, BRIAN. *Brian Wildsmith's Circus,* ill. by author. Watts, 1970.

6 ———. *Brian Wildsmith's Fishes,* ill. by author. Watts, 1968.

6 ———. *Brian Wildsmith's Puzzles,* ill. by author. Watts, 1971.

6 ———. *The Little Wood Duck,* ill. by author. Watts, 1973.

WOLDE, GUNILLA. *Betsy's First Day at Nursery School.* Random, 1976. A soft sell for the young child who is apprehensive about nursery school, this has lively cartoonish drawings.

6 YASHIMA, TARO. *Umbrella,* ill. by author. Viking, 1958.

6 ZEMACH, HARVE. *Duffy and the Devil,* ill. by Margot Zemach. Farrar, 1973. Caldecott Medal.

6 ———. *The Judge: An Untrue Tale,* ill. by Margot Zemach. Farrar, 1969.

6 ———. *Small Boy Is Listening,* ill. by Margot Zemach. Houghton, 1959.

6 ZEMACH, MARGOT, ad. *It Could Always Be Worse: A Yiddish Folk Tale,* ill. by author. Farrar, 1976.

ZOLOTOW, CHARLOTTE. *Do You Know What I'll Do?* ill. by Garth Williams. Harper, 1958.

———. *The Hating Book,* ill. by Ben Shecter. Harper, 1969.

6 ———. *May I Visit?* ill. by Erik Blegvad. Harper, 1976.

6 ———. *Mr. Rabbit and the Lovely Present,* ill. by Maurice Sendak. Harper, 1962.

6 ———. *My Grandson Lew,* ill. by William Pène du Bois. Harper, 1974.

———. *The Unfriendly Book,* ill. by William Pène du Bois. Harper, 1975.

———. *When I Have a Little Girl,* ill. by Hilary Knight. Harper, 1965.

———. *When I Have a Son,* ill. by Hilary Knight. Harper, 1967.

———. *William's Doll,* ill. by William Pène du Bois. Harper, 1972.

Chapter Six:
Artists and Children's Books

Browsing through the shelves of children's books in a bookstore or a library, one is always impressed by the beauty of design and the beauty and variety of illustration in old books and new. Although young children take pleasure in hearing a book read, it is the illustrations they look at, and when they look they are learning to appreciate line, color, pattern, humor, and to see the storytelling quality of a picture. While the visual appeal is especially important for young children, the way a book looks (illustration, layout, and typography) is of importance to readers of all ages.

To study or discuss children's literature and not to include an examination of children's book illustration would be to ignore a significant element in the value and the appeal of these books. Just as a body of writing for children developed slowly, with youngsters at first simply appropriating those adult books that had some interest for them, so has the illustration of children's books developed slowly, bursting finally into the wealth and variety of art we have in twentieth-century books for children.

What is the explanation for today's marvelous richness in children's book illustration? The answer derives in part from the fact that the first books published for children included illustrations either to instruct, as did the courtesy books and alphabet books, or to support and extend the author's text. From the begin-

ning, then, illustrations have served these functions. Certainly the prevalence of illustration in books for children in the past and in the present reflects an adult decision that pictures will attract and hold children's interest or will help them to learn about a subject.

Then and now, artwork in children's books served several functions: to clarify the text or to add information that is not in the text, in the case of nonfiction particularly; to enlarge or interpret the author's meaning, to evoke an appropriate mood, to establish setting or portray character in fiction; or simply to be decorative.

Art is communication, whether it is in a museum or in a book, and to judge the success of artwork in children's books we must evaluate it in terms of whether it speaks to the child. It must also be judged by how well it fits the story (or the informational text) and adapts to the confinements of page space and layout and color reproduction. And certainly we must evaluate the quality of the artwork itself, the artist's use of media and techniques.

Questions we can ask in judging the appropriateness of illustrations to text are:

—Do the pictures reflect the mood of the story (as Uri Shulevitz's do in *Dawn*)? Or do they conflict with it?

—Do the pictures have any details that conflict with a textual statement? If the story describes five children, or a boy carrying a book, or a flower that is blue, the illustrations should have the right number of children, the right object under the boy's arm, the right color in the flower.

—Do the illustrations extend the text without distracting from it? If a page that shows musculature of the human body is so crowded with details that the printed information is obscured, the illustration is artistically inappropriate for the purpose of the text.

The question of whether the artwork speaks to the child is discussed under the heading "Children's Preferences" later in this chapter, but it should be kept in mind that children, especially young children, are not likely to have visual prejudices and preconceptions, and that they are a more eager audience for the artist's creative message than most adults. Certainly one way in which today's artists speak to children is to include in their illustrations youngsters of all ethnic backgrounds, drawn with no stereotypical details, and children and adults in unstereotyped sex roles. While there are no age barriers in the appreciation of art as art, illustrations must be considered in respect to the complexity of the concepts they contain and the relationship of those concepts to children's ability to understand at different ages. Most small children, for example, would find it difficult to understand the intricate details of David Macaulay's architectural drawings in *Pyramid*, drawings that speak eloquently to older children.

Finally, book illustration can be judged as art. Although individual reaction to an artist's work is subjective, all illustrations can be evaluated by artistic standards. Some of the questions we can ask in evaluating the elements in the illustration and its overall effect are:

—How does the artist use color? If the colors are bold and brilliant, do they suit the text they accompany? Or have they simply been splashed about, as colors often are in mass market books, on the premise that the brighter the page, the more it will attract children? Is color an essential element in the layout of the page? Does the color obscure or complement the lines of the drawings? Is the color reproduction of good quality?

—Does the artist use line effectively? A delicate line is appropriate for some stories, a bold one for others. Edward Ardizzone is a master of the economical line; Peter Parnall's line is spare and elegant; the light, broken line used by Robin Jacques is eminently suitable for the fairy tales he so often illustrates. Does the line express movement or is it static? Does the line give strength to the depiction of a person or object by being heavy or crosshatched? Is the line varied?

—Is the artist successful in handling shape? Whether the shape is distinct or vaguely suggested, simple or ornamented, free-flowing or rigid, the shape must suit the mood and intent of the story. How do shapes relate to each other on the page? If the drawing is realistic, is the perspective correct? Do the shapes fill the page or do they clutter it? If they represent characters, do they suggest qualities with which the author has invested them?

—Does the artist give texture to the illustrations? Arnold Lobel, in Cynthia Jameson's *The Clay Pot Boy*, gives the clay pot an unmistakable roundness and solidity; Feodor Rojankovsky's animals have an almost tactile furriness. Many artists use collage, alone or in combination with another medium, to obtain a textural difference. Barbara Cooney achieves the texture of

Viewpoint

Evidence pointing to the aesthetic sensitivity of children can be gathered on all sides. They instinctively respond to balance, order, rhythm, originality—the artist's endless arrangements of color, line, shape, texture, and the writer's ingenious inventions and euphonies. But there are many exposures which can dwarf the natural growth of these responses. When the child is faced with a preponderance of inferior visual and literary impressions, a negative effect upon the development of taste and aesthetic enjoyment can be expected, as surely as a good effect can be predicted (all else remaining equal) when the child is surrounded by an artistic environment. He is not, after all, living in a vacuum.

Creating a beneficial environment for children is one of the most common objectives in education. Teachers and parents scrutinize the child and his surroundings with great care, trying to identify the activities which rouse curiosity and interest, which have strong and lasting effects and to which the child repeatedly returns. Yet they often overlook the arts or give them little emphasis, even when it is clear that few areas of experience involve children so completely and at such an instinctively high level.—Donnarae MacCann and Olga Richard, *The Child's First Books; A Critical Study of Pictures and Texts*, The H. W. Wilson Company, New York, 1973, p. 7.

diaphanous fabric with a thin wash of color, a representational treatment, while other artists use stylized patterns and ornamentation. A vaporous look may suggest fog, while blobs of white out of which objects emerge may fail to do so.

—How are the elements of each page or of facing pages arranged? Even when all other aspects of the illustration are effective, it may fail in its intent if the composition is awkward or if there is not enough space to set off the various parts of the picture or if the illustration does not balance well in relation to the type area. The parts should have balance and direction so that the illustration has both unity and focus. Peter Parnall uses white space to give his pictures a clean, bare look and to focus the eye on elements he wishes to stress. Composition can be used to accentuate a mood or setting; Tomie de Paola, in *Strega Nona*, fills each drawing with sturdy figures in harmony with the robust and humorous folk tale and frames the drawings to suggest an onstage performance.

In evaluating the visual impact of a book, the primary concern is the illustration, but one must also consider the effect and effectiveness of the book jacket, the endpapers, the typeface used, and the way print is used on the page, particularly when it is placed in such a way that print and illustration together make a pattern. Heavy block letters do not suit a delicate fairy tale while they may be both effective and appropriate for a book of modern poetry. A clear, clean type can be lost if it is printed on a dark background or is obscured by illustrative details.

Beautiful pictures can help sell a trivial book, and sometimes poor illustrations can cause a first-rate story to be overlooked. With today's offset printing and remarkable color reproduction, the eye appeal of books is of tremendous importance, and the artist therefore plays a significant role in books for children, whether they are picture books for younger children which have little or no text, picture story books in which the illustrations are an integral part of the whole, or illustrated books in which the pictures are few and play a comparatively minor role.

From what they see in comics and slick magazines as well as in books from supermarket shelves, children know many kinds of pictures. They "read" many parts of their environment, and often have great visual sophistication and experience before they become aware of printed matter, whether in books or on box tops. Due in large part to television, children today probably have a higher degree

From the book *Strega Nona* by Tomie de Paola. © 1975 by Tomie de Paola. Published by Prentice-Hall, Inc., Englewood Cliffs, New Jersey. (Original in color)

of visual experience than children of earlier generations. Building on such experience, we can begin to lead them into an awareness of finer examples of graphic art, old and new. For, as Bertha Mahony says in *Illustrators of Children's Books,* ". . . art in children's books is a part of all art, not an isolated special field. In every period the greatest artists have shared in it."[1] But in the evaluation of illustrations as in the evaluation of stories, the children themselves must be the starting point if we are to meet their needs and extend the range of art they appreciate.

Children's Preferences

Children begin as stern literalists, demanding a truthful interpretation of the text. If a character is described as redheaded, no child is going to accept brown hair without protest. When Ludwig Bemelmans says that there are twelve little girls who go walking from Madeline's school, the child counts to see that the artist has put them all in.

Even young children observe and enjoy all the cozy details of Randolph Caldecott's *Frog He Would A-Wooing Go* or of Eleanor Schick's *Neighborhood Knight* as readily as they follow the everyday drama of weather in Uri Shulevitz's *Rain Rain Rivers.* If the illustrations interpret the story, the child will accept such varied techniques as the splashy colors of Nicolas Mordvinoff's *Finders Keepers,* Robert Lawson's finely detailed pen-and-ink sketches of landscapes and small animals, and Leo and Diane Dillon's bold patterns for *Why Mosquitoes Buzz in People's Ears.*

Being literal, the young child also wants a picture synchronized precisely with the text. When *Make Way for Ducklings* has the mother duck leading her offspring across a busy Boston thoroughfare, the child is glad that Robert McCloskey placed his unforgettable picture with the description and not a page or two later. Older children as well are irked by illustrations that appear before or after the episode they are supposed to represent.

Children are as fond of action in pictures as in stories. They love Ernest Shepard's lively drawings of the skipping Christopher Robin and the droll, carefree abandon of Maurice

Illustration by Eleanor Schick is reproduced by permission of Greenwillow Books from *Neighborhood Knight* by Eleanor Schick. Copyright © 1976 by Eleanor Schick.

Sendak's capering children. We know that young children also like bright colors, but not to the exclusion of black and white or the gentle colors in Adrienne Adams's illustrations for Alice Goudey's *Houses from the Sea* and the muted hues in Arnold Lobel's *Frog and Toad Together.* G. LaVerne Freeman and Ruth Sunderlin Freeman, in their evaluation of children's preferences in picture-book illustration,[2] found that children preferred bright, strong colors but that they also seemed to accept black-and-white pictures. The Freemans suggest that this acceptance may be due to familiarity with black-and-white television programs.

On the whole, there is evidence that children do prefer color to black and white in book illustrations. Yet young children delight also in Lynd Ward's powerful monochromes for *The Biggest Bear,* and older children are pleased with

---

1. The Horn Book, Inc., 1947.

2. *The Child and His Picture Book* (Century House, rev. ed. 1967).

the fine, clear minutiae of William Pène du Bois's drawings for his *Twenty-One Balloons* or those of Edwin Tunis in *Shaw's Fortune.*

Adults often assume that small children do not see details in a picture, but they do. Children look for the small figures of the mice in Graham Oakley's *The Church Mice Adrift.* But the same youngster who will gloat over small details in a picture may also enjoy the bold strength of a single object by Leonard Baskin, or the sharp, clear outlines of Artzybasheff's illustrations for *The Fairy Shoemaker and Other Fairy Poems.*

Children, then, respond to a wide variety of book illustrations—even crude or saccharine drawings if they help tell the story. Their visual sensitivity can open their lives to positive early experience with books as well as enlarge their experience with art. The more they are exposed to authentic art of many styles, the greater the possibility that their tastes will diversify.

Reproducing the Work of the Artist

It's a long way from the drawing board to the finished book. We enjoy today a wealth of varied and beautiful books in part because of the technological advances in printing, in part because of the growing awareness of the importance of early childhood education, and in part because good artists, designers, and editors are dedicated to giving children the best. As Jean Karl, a children's book editor, has said:

It is the publisher's responsibility to choose the illustrator for a picture book, but most try to take the author's preferences into consideration, and all try to find the illustrator who will make the manuscript into a unified book. For this, the author's vision of the finished book is important, because it is part of the author's concept of what he has done.[3]

There are many picture books in which the artist's conception of an author's characters and mood are enchanting in their perfection (for example, Garth Williams's illustrations for Natalie Carlson's *The Happy Orpheline* and Maurice Sendak's for Else Holmelund Minarik's *Little Bear* series). Some of the best picture books, however, are those written and illustrated by the same person. Rosemary Wells,

Arnold Lobel, Martha Alexander, Edward Ardizzone, Maurice Sendak, Uri Shulevitz, Evaline Ness, and Marcia Brown are among the contemporary author-artists in whose books the text and illustrations perfectly complement each other. This is true also of books done for older children by such author-illustrators as Leonard Everett Fisher and Edwin Tunis.

The editor and the book designer must, in collaboration with the illustrator, consider all the visual aspects that contribute both to the beauty of a book and to its appropriateness for its intended audience—the size and clarity of the type, the leading (space between lines), the layout of the page, the amount of print on each page, as well as the illustrations. Of course such picture books as John Goodall's *The Surprise Picnic* and Iela and Enzo Mari's *The Apple and the Moth* (the first, a story; the second, the record of a moth's life cycle) have no words at all, but the pictures have been so carefully planned that what happens is crystal clear. In books for older children, too, the arrangement of all visual material (Anthony Ravielli's precise drawings for *Wonders of the Human Body* are fine examples) illuminates and expands the text.

As Edward Ardizzone insists, "drawing is of paramount importance."[4] The artist must be able to draw, to interpret the story, or, in informational books, interpret accurately the given facts, and to understand the printing processes by which original artwork is converted into illustrations for a book.

There are three basic methods of reproduction—relief, intaglio, and surface or planographic printing. Each of these may be direct (done largely by hand) or indirect (done by mechanical procedures).

In *relief* the surface to be printed is raised. The most familiar examples of direct or manual techniques are probably the wood blocks or linoleum blocks on which a picture is drawn, the surrounding areas cut away, and the remaining portion inked to be impressed upon paper. The indirect or mechanical counterpart is the linecut (also called a line engraving or line block). In this process the illustration is photographed, being mechanically reduced to correct size, on a glass plate. When the film is hardened, it is transferred to a sensitized metal plate and is developed and washed. The lines of the draw-

3. Jean Karl, *From Childhood to Childhood* (John Day, 1970).

4. Edward Ardizzone, "Creation of a Picture Book," *Top of the News,* December 1959.

Viewpoint

---

ing are brought into relief by bathing the plate in acid, which eats away the part that has no lines. The plate, nailed to a wooden block so that the drawing is type-high, will print the raised design on paper.

When a drawing has shadings, a halftone engraving is made. To obtain the shadings, tones between black and white, the drawing is photographed through a halftone screen, which is crosshatched at right angles with fine lines. This breaks the pictorial copy into tiny dots: the darker the gray, the larger the dots. The acid etching for the halftone requires much more care than that for the simple linecut and must be done in stages so that the deeper parts can be re-etched. If colors are used, only one color can be printed at a time. A four-color picture with varying strengths requires four halftone blocks (black, yellow, magenta, and cyan blue can reproduce almost any color or shade of color) to reproduce the shading and intensity of the original.

The second method of reproduction is *intaglio*. In this process the part to be printed is below the surface rather than above the surface as in relief. Mezzotint, steel engraving, and etching are some of the direct or hand intaglio techniques. Photogravure is the indirect or mechanical technique. In this process the surface is broken into dots as for the halftone, but here each dot forms a pit—the variation is in depth rather than in size as in the halftone. The surface ink is scraped off with a knife and the remaining ink is picked out from the pits when paper is pressed on the cylinder. To print color photogravure, a separate plate must be made for each color.

The third method of reproduction is *surface* or *planographic* printing. Stencils and silk screens are examples of direct or hand techniques. Indirect or mechanical techniques include collotype (very expensive and seldom used) and lithography. Lithography is based on the principle that water and grease do not mix. The process was discovered accidentally in 1796, when Aloys Senefelder used a crayon to write a list on a slab of limestone, and then wet and inked the stone. The water repelled ink except for the writing, which didn't hold water because of the crayon grease. In today's printing, the stone is replaced by a sheet of emulsion-coated zinc on which the images are printed photographically, much in the way that halftones are produced, except that the dots are on the emulsion and will accept ink. The bare metal around the dots repels ink, and the dots are impressed in the printing process. Most lithographic work today is produced by offset process, using an extra roller to transfer the impression. The use of offset lithography for color work is one of today's most significant advances in the reproduction of illustrations.

Colors in illustrations may be mechanically separated as already mentioned, or the artist may pre-separate them; that is, make a separate drawing for each color, with transparent sheets perfectly aligned one over the other. If only two colors that do not touch each other are used, the artist can use red and black and instruct the printer to use them as keys for any other two colors.

Evidence of the importance of children's book illustration includes the establishment of the Caldecott Medal in the United States, the Greenaway Medal in England, the Howard-Gibbon Medal in Canada, and the international Hans Christian Andersen Medal for illustrators as well as authors. The American Institute of Graphic Arts now includes the names of children's book illustrators and designers in their annual "Fifty Books of the Year" and holds a biennial Children's Book Show which exhibits some one hundred books chosen for artistic and typographic merit. The Children's Book Council's widely circulated posters by children's book illustrators call attention to Children's Book Week and also to the importance of the illustrations in books for young people.

Many of the artists who have contributed to children's books will be discussed here in chronological order, according to their birth dates. Author-artists like Maurice Sendak are discussed also in genre chapters and many creators of picture books are discussed in Chapter 5; in these other chapters, the focus is on their writing.

Flowers.   XV.   Flores.

Amongst the Flowers the most noted,	Inter flores notissimi,
In the beginning of the Spring are the *Violet*, 1. the *Crow-toes*, 2. the *Daffodil*, 3.	Primo vere, *Viola*, 1. *Hyacinthus*, 2. *Narcissus*, 3.
Then the *Lillies*, 4. white and yellow and blew, 5. and the *Rose*, 6. and the *Clove gilliflowers*, 7. &c.	Tum *Lilia*, 4. alba & lutea, & cœrulea, 5. tandem *Rosa*, 6. & *Caryophillum*, 7. &c.
Of these *Garlands*, 8. and *Nosegays*, 9. are tyed round with twigs. There are added also *sweet herbs*, 10. as *Marjoram*, *Flower gentle*, *Rue*, *Lavender*, *Rosemary*.	Ex his *Serta*, 8. & *Serviæ*, 9. vientur. Adduntur etiam *Herbæ odoratæ*, 10. ut *Amaracus*, *Amaranthus*, *Ruta*, *Lavendula*, *Rosmarinus*, (Libanotis).

From Comenius's *Orbis Pictus*.

Woodcuts and Engravings Before 1800

In 1484 William Caxton issued the first English edition of *Aesop's Fables*, illustrated with woodcuts by some unknown artist or artists. This was an adult book, but if children saw the pictures and heard the stories, they undoubtedly took the book as their own. Since Caxton's publication of the fables these little moralities have been continuously reprinted, usually illustrated by outstanding artists who were doubtless attracted by the dramatic situations the stories embody.

Between the Caxton edition of the fables and the epoch-making *Orbis Pictus*, there were hornbooks and battledores for children but with few or no pictures. There were also the popular chapbooks, enlivened with crude woodcuts, which were beloved by the story-hungry children of the sixteenth and seventeenth centuries.

The *Orbis Pictus* of Comenius is assumed to be the first picture book prepared for children. Today, we would say that it more nearly resembles a primer. It was written in Latin in 1657 or 1658 by a Moravian bishop and translated into most European languages, including English in 1658. The pictures and text are stilted but not without charm. The word *Flores* appears above a small woodcut showing flowers in a vase and also in a field; the picture is followed by a pleasant commentary on spring flowers. Whatever the subject, there was a conscious effort to associate words and pictures and to use the latter to lead directly into the text. The *Orbis Pictus* seems tame and wooden today, but for English-speaking children it marked the beginning of picture books planned especially for them.

Even the Newbery publications, important as they are in the history of children's books, did little to advance the art of illustration. It is generally agreed that only for *Little Goody Two Shoes* (1765) did the artist (possibly Thomas Bewick) execute his woodcuts with unusual grace and synchronize them with the text so that they are illustrations in the true sense of the word—interpreting or illuminating the story.

For the most part these earliest producers of crude woodcuts were minor artists, usually unknown. It was not until the advent of Thomas

From *Aesop's Fables* by Boris Artzybasheff. Copyright 1933 by Boris Artzybasheff. All rights reserved. Reprinted by permission of the Viking Press, Inc.

Bewick that children's books were adorned by a major artist.

Thomas Bewick's first book designed for children was *A Pretty Book of Pictures for Little Masters and Misses or Tommy Trip's History of Beasts and Birds* (1779). This book, exceedingly rare today, is an example of the artist's skill in the use of the woodcut. He developed better tools for this work, made effective use of the white line, and carried the woodcut to a new level of beauty. Most of Bewick's finest drawings seem to have been for books originally planned for adults as, for instance his various editions of Aesop's fables, particularly those of 1784 and 1818. These pictures show the artist's knowledge and love of the whole outdoor world—plants, trees, birds, and beasts. Certainly Thomas Bewick, and to a somewhat lesser extent his brother John, raised the woodcut to a high level of artistic achievement.

An interesting by-product of the Bewicks' contribution is that artists of established reputations began to sign their pictures for children's books.

The Nineteenth Century

William Blake had brought delicate colors into his book for children, *Songs of Innocence* (1789), not by color printing but by hand. Color printing, however, was widely used from about 1803 to 1835, though at the beginning of the nineteenth century the most notable illustrators were still working in black and white.

Examine, in the color section, the two early colored illustrations by unknown artists, the first for *The History of the House That Jack Built* and the second for *A Continuation of the Comic Adventures of Old Mother Hubbard and Her Dog*. They are interesting proof that publishers were beginning to recognize the lure of color in books for young children.

William Mulready

The century began propitiously, then, with some color printing for children's books, but it is the work of William Mulready that first brought distinction to those early years of the century.

This illustrator is remembered for his gay, fanciful drawings for *The Butterfly's Ball* (1807) by William Roscoe. This rhymed description of a fairy picnic enjoyed enormous popularity for over fifty years, aided no doubt by Mulready's amusing pictures in black and white. Some of his bees, snails, butterflies, and other guests of the party have human bodies with true-to-the-species creatures atop their heads or else they are well-drawn insects or animals piloted by elfish figures perched on their backs. The mole, for instance, has a fat, blind gnome for a rider. Unfortunately, the children's books this gifted artist adorned do not stand the test of time as his drawings do. This is a fate that threatens the lasting fame of illustrators in each generation.

Illustration by William Mulready. From *The Butterfly's Ball* by William Roscoe. Published by J. Harris, 1807.

George Cruikshank

George Cruikshank, a great artist of this period, was a satirist and a cartoonist for England's famous *Punch*. In contrast to Mulready, Cruikshank had the good fortune to illustrate an English translation of the Grimms' *Collection of German Popular Stories* (1824 and 1826), a classic that is ageless in its appeal. In black and white, his humorous, lively, cleverly drawn pictures are the embodiment of the tales.

Sir John Tenniel

Inseparable from Lewis Carroll's *Alice's Adventures in Wonderland* (1865) and *Through the Looking Glass* (1871) are the illustrations by Sir John Tenniel, cartoonist for *Punch*. Other artists hopefully make pictures for this classic fantasy, but their illustrations usually seem inadequate when compared with Tenniel's beloved figures. Unforgettable are serious, pinafored, long-haired Alice, the smartly dressed, bustling White Rabbit, and all the other mad, topsy-turvy characters of the Wonderland and the Looking Glass worlds. Strong in line and composition, drawn with beautiful clarity and poker-faced drollery, these illustrations enhance the fantasy and give it convincing reality.

Arthur Hughes

The illustrations of Arthur Hughes are as strongly associated with George Macdonald's *At the Back of the North Wind* (1871) and *The Princess and the Goblin* (1872) as are Tenniel's illustrations with *Alice's Adventures in Wonderland*. Hughes worked in black and white and was an interpreter of fantasy, but his pictures are as different from Cruikshank's or Tenniel's as the

Macdonald books are different from the Grimms' fairy tales or Carroll's *Alice*. For Macdonald's two fairy tales the never-never land of the pictures is all mystery, gentleness, and lovely innocence. These qualities carry over to Hughes's more realistic pictures for Christina Rossetti's *Sing-Song* (1872), little masterpieces of tenderness and beauty.

Walter Crane

In *English Children's Books*, Percy Muir points out in the chapter "The Importance of Pictures" that it was ". . . in the sixties that publishers began first to attempt to sell books to children mainly for the interest of the illustrations." What a line of successors that movement launched! Muir then goes on to show how much modern color printing owes to Edmund Evans, a publisher and an artist in his own right. A pioneer in color printing, Evans had long inveighed against the cheap, gaudy illustrations used in books for children. He firmly believed that even an inexpensive paperback book planned for the nursery child could be beautiful in design and color. In Walter Crane, Evans found an artist to carry out his theories.

Trained as a wood engraver, Walter Crane was greatly influenced by the work of the Pre-Raphaelites and also by his study of Japanese prints. Both of these influences are evident in his pictures—in the idealized figures of women and children and in the sparse, decorative landscapes. Between 1867 and 1876 Crane produced over thirty so-called "toy books,"[5] published chiefly by Routledge and generally undated. Crane took these books so seriously that he worked over every page, including the typography, so that it came out a well-composed whole. His *Baby's Opera* and *Baby's Bouquet* were a series of English nursery songs with words, music, and pictures. Later he decorated, also in color, Hawthorne's *Wonder Book* (1892). (See color section.)

Kate Greenaway

Edmund Evans was greatly taken with the delicate colors and decorative borders of Kate Greenaway's pictures for her own rhymes. He printed her book *Under the Window* (1878) by a

Viewpoint

There is no point, for [the picture book illustrator], in trying to be purely representational. The meaning in his picture comes from the way he arranges colors, lines, shapes, and textures into a special synthesis—one that will please the senses and achieve an aesthetic experience for the reader. Object recognition is a criterion based on the commonplace. It is concerned with simple imitation. The arts are the very antithesis of commonplace standards of imitation, recognition, and the sense of familiarity derived from such considerations.—Olga Richard, "The Visual Language of the Picture Book," *The Wilson Library Bulletin*, December 1969, p. 435.

---

5. The term "toy book" is used today to mean books with pop-ups or cut-outs that make them more toys than books. The Crane "toy books" were simply books intended for the nursery prereading child.

1. Freely brushed color softens the engraved line, and the rhythmic pattern of the trees lends animation to an otherwise static composition that has the formal quality of a stage design. From The History of the House That Jack Built. Reproduced from the D'Alte Welch Collection, American Antiquarian Society.

2. The long horizontal and vertical lines of the barn are an effective foil for the animated, comic figures in a clean, simple drawing with evenly washed tints. Illustration by Leonard Leslie Brooke. From Ring o' Roses. Reproduced with permission of Frederick Warne & Co., Inc.

3. The sharp contrast of the slightly crude color makes the comic figures seem pasted on the flat background in this engraving. From A Continuation of the Comic Adventures of Old Mother Hubbard and Her Dog. Reproduced from the D'Alte Welch Collection, The University Library, Department of Special Collections, University of California, Los Angeles.

1.

3.

2.

YES, that's the girl that struts about,
   She's very proud,—so very proud!
Her *bow-wow*'s quite as proud as she:
They both are very wrong to be
   So proud—so very proud.

See, Jane and Willy laugh at her,
   They say she's very proud!
Says Jane, "My stars!—they're very silly;"
"Indeed they are," cries little Willy,
   "To walk so stiff and proud."

4.

5.

4.   There is subtle characterization in the figures of this skillful drawing, and clever use of
background details: the window frames the proud
one's head and the vine creates a fancy border.
From Kate Greenaway's Under the Window.
Reproduced with permission of Frederick Warne
&·Co., Inc.

5.   The subtle use of color distinguishes this
drawing, the gray-green of the sky blending into
the only slightly lighter ground. The flat, subdued color within lines is reminiscent of Japanese
prints. From Walter Crane's Baby's Bouquet.
Reproduced with permission of Frederick Warne
& Co., Inc.

6.   Composed frontally in simple shapes of contrasting light and dark, the melancholy mood is
deepened by the leaden colors of the foreground.
Illustration by Newell Wyeth. From Treasure
Island by Robert Louis Stevenson. Copyright
1911 by Charles Scribner's Sons. Copyright 1939
by N. C. Wyeth. Reproduced with permission of
Charles Scribner's Sons.

6.

7.

7. *This is a controlled composition, the vigorous treatment of thorny trees balancing a motionless foreground, the rosy tones of ground and sky contrasting with the gray dress, the sober face of the girl contrasting with the impish faces in the water. Mysterious and romantic, a Rackham specialty. Reprinted with permission of Macmillan Publishing Co., Inc. and Mrs. Barbara Edwards, from* English Fairy Tales *by Flora Annie Steel, illustrated by Arthur Rackham. Copyright 1918 by Macmillan Publishing Co., Inc., renewed 1946 by Mabel H. Webster.*

8.

9.

10.

8.   Keenly observant, Potter gave animals human characteristics without distortion. The subdued background colors do not distract us from Peter's expression of smug contentment. From Beatrix Potter's The Tale of Peter Rabbit. Reproduced with permission of Frederick Warne & Co., Inc.

9.   Even the perspective, running from left to right, is comic in a picture that exemplifies Caldecott's vigorous and humorous touch. Color is simple but expressive; we can enjoy all details individually and in combination. From Randolph Caldecott's Hey Diddle and Baby Bunting. Reproduced from the D'Alte Welch Collection, Cleveland.

10.   With great economy of line, action is provided in this watercolor by the angled sails, floating objects, and variations in color within sea and sky. From Little Tim and the Brave Sea Captain by Edward Ardizzone. Reprinted by the permission of Henry Z. Walck, Inc.

He had taken
such good care of her
that she could still dig
as much in a day
as a hundred men
could dig in a week;
at least he thought she could
but he wasn't quite sure.
Everywhere they went
the new gas shovels
and the new electric shovels
and the new Diesel motor shovels
had all the jobs.   No one wanted
Mike Mulligan and Mary Anne any more.
Then one day Mike read in a newspaper that the town
of Popperville was going to build a new town hall.
'We are going to dig the cellar of that town hall,'
said Mike to Mary Anne, and off they started.

11.

11.   *The curving block of type suggests a shovel and movement, and the loose, free drawing brings the steam shovel to life. Illustration by the author, from* Mike Mulligan and His Steam Shovel *by Virginia Lee Burton. Published by Houghton Mifflin Company. Copyright 1939, and © renewed 1967 by Virginia Lee Demetrios. Reproduced by permission of the publisher.*

12.   *There is a surrealist quality to the huge cat, the twisting bird, and the empty, timeless street scene. Illustration by Harold Jones. From* Lavender's Blue, *Mother Goose rhymes compiled by Kathleen Lines. Copyright 1954. Reproduced with permission of Franklin Watts, Inc. and Oxford University Press, London.*

12.

13.

13.   *An angular composition conveys a feeling of suspended motion through the lines of ripples and oars as opposed to the boat. The watercolor wash, carefully controlled, defines shapes with no use of hard lines. From* Time of Wonder *by Robert McCloskey. Copyright © 1957 by Robert McCloskey. Reprinted by permission of The Viking Press, Inc.*

14.   *The solidity of the solitary figure is balanced by the delicacy of the streaks of rain in this deceptively simple illustration which is bold in composition but not heavy. The child's face glows in contrast to the cool blues and purples. From* Umbrella *by Taro Yashima. Copyright © 1958 by Taro Yashima. Reprinted by permission of The Viking Press, Inc.*

14.

15. *Only the two figures are in warm tones, setting them apart from the cool stillness of the summer night. Illustration by Maurice Sendak from* Mr. Rabbit and the Lovely Present *by Charlotte Zolotow. Pictures copyright © 1962 by Maurice Sendak. Reproduced by permission of Harper & Row, Publishers, Inc.*

16. *Strong in design and simple in colors, the details of this woodcut focus the eye on the ferocious face of the tiger, with the blades of grass echoing the animal's stripes. From* Once a Mouse *by Marcia Brown. Copyright 1961 by Marcia Brown. Reproduced with permission of Charles Scribner's Sons.*

The tiger felt offended and humiliated. He forgot all the good he had received from the old man.

"No one shall tell me that I was once a mouse. I will kill him!"

17.

18.

17. *In this brush-and-ink painting, the large bird and branch are checked by their quiet colors, while the vivid group on the right is restrained by numbers, so that the central figure stands out. Separate figures are treated in the Chinese tradition, with each color in flat painting or simple gradations. Illustration by Nancy Ekholm Burkert from* The Nightingale, *translated by Eva La Gallienne. Copyright © 1965. Reproduced by permission of Harper & Row, Publishers, Inc.*

18. *The size of the figures in relation to the ship adds a comic note in a picture that resembles fifteenth-century Flemish work. Reproduced with the permission of Farrar, Straus & Giroux, Inc. From* The Fool of the World and the Flying Ship, *a Russian tale retold by Arthur Ransome, illustrated by Uri Shulevitz, pictures copyright © 1968 by Uri Shulevitz. Published in the United Kingdom by Hamish Hamilton Ltd.*

19. *Thick, soft edges in black and deep browns frame luminous colors given a grainy texture by loosely applied pastel. Illustration from* Stevie *by John Steptoe. Copyright © 1969 by John Steptoe. Reprinted by permission of Harper & Row, Publishers, Inc. and Penguin Books Ltd.*

20. *Beyond the bright, jewel-toned colors, opaque and clear, this controlled abstraction has interplay between light and dark areas of the hen's body. Illustration by Brian Wildsmith for* Brian Wildsmith's Puzzles. *Copyright © 1971. Reproduced by permission of Franklin Watts, Inc. and Oxford University Press, London.*

19.

20.

21.

22.

23.

23.   *The elongated forms and the angled posture of the figure are reminiscent of ancient Greek paintings in this delicate and balanced picture. The solid cluster of narcissus is in contrast to the random blossoms on the right, and the rhythm of hair and folds of the translucent garment creates an interplay between foreground and background. Illustration from* Demeter and Persephone, *translated and adapted by Penelope Proddow, illustrated by Barbara Cooney. Illustrations copyright © 1972 by Barbara Cooney Porter. Reproduced by permission of Doubleday and Company, Inc.*

24.

24.   Color and exaggeration are used to
heighten the comic effect in a picture that has
variety in media and techniques. Illustration
from Mr. Gumpy's Motor Car by John
Burningham. Copyright © 1973 by John Burningham. Reproduced by permission of
Thomas Y. Crowell Company, Inc. and Jonathan Cape Ltd.

25.   In the flatly designed style of Pueblo art,
the illustrator achieves a dramatic effect through
brilliant strips of color in sharply opposed
angles around the head and the circular design
on the figure. From Arrow to the Sun
by Gerald McDermott. Copyright © 1974 by
Gerald McDermott. Reprinted by permission
of the Viking Press.

25.

The nightingale sings his song.

26.

26.   A formal composition in the folk-art tradition is relieved and enriched by subtle variations
of the blue sky and by the random distribution of
stars. The scratch technique that allows the black
base of the forms to show up as lines not only
modulates but gives texture to the secne. Illustration by Janina Domanska from Din Dan
Don It's Christmas. Reprinted by permission
of Greenwillow Books, a division of William
Morrow & Company, Inc.

27.   The small figures of the fleeing children
are given dramatic emphasis by the towering
masses of huge tree trunks whose darkness also
highlights the bright flames of the oven. Illustration by Adrienne Adams from Hansel and
Gretel by the Brothers Grimm, reprinted by
permission of Charles Scribner's Sons. Copyright © 1975 Adrienne Adams.

27.

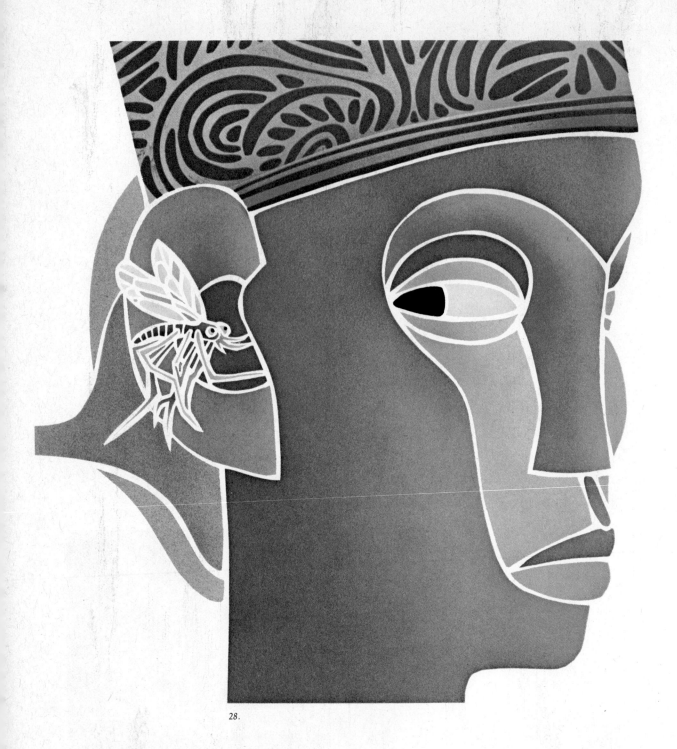

28.

28.   *In a simple and stylized painting, watercolor and pastel are subtly blended, with areas of color separated by a white line of varying depth that also describes detail and becomes an integral part of the design. The cast of the eye adds humor, and the curling pattern of the hat adds elegance while solidifying the composition. Illustration from* Why Mosquitoes Buzz in People's Ears. *Illustrated by Leo and Diane Dillon. Illustrations Copyright © 1975 by Leo and Diane Dillon. Used with the permission of The Dial Press.*

Going by cities

29.

29.   In a frieze effect, the static solidity of an urban skyline is used for effective contrast to the brightness and movement of the freight train, whose speed is emphasized by the thinning trail of black smoke. Illustration from Donald Crews, Freight Train. Copyright © 1978 by Donald Crews. Reprinted by permission of Greenwillow Books, a division of William Morrow & Company, Inc.

30.   By putting the sensuously modelled, strong face and figure of Joseph in the foreground, the artist makes him dominate the painting despite the intricate designs and rich colors of the fabrics. Illustration by Charles Mikolaycak from Barbara Cohen, I Am Joseph. Text copyright © 1980 by Barbara Cohen. Illustration copyright © 1980 by Charles Mikolaycak. Reprinted by permission of Lothrop, Lee & Shepard Books.

30.

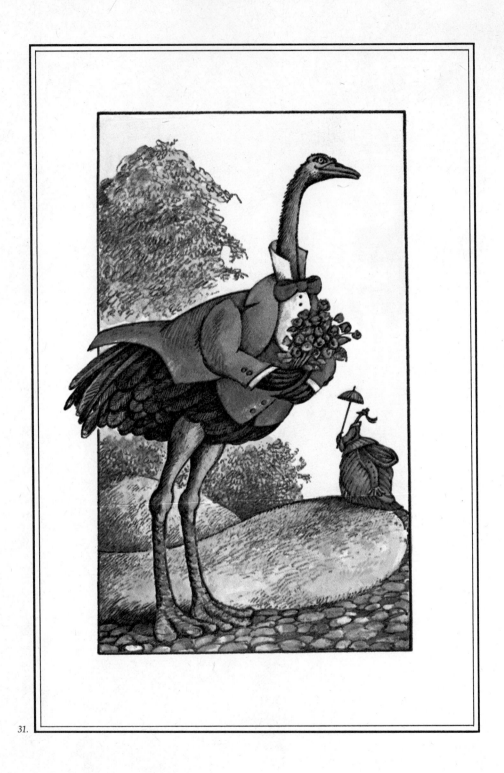

31.

31. *For the fable of "The Ostrich in Love," the decorous frame, the subdued tints, and the rounded lines of the composition function as foils to the prim, awkward ostrich who dominates the picture. Illustration from* Fables *by Arnold Lobel. Copright © 1980 by Arnold Lobel. Reproduced by permission of Harper & Row, Publishers, Inc.*

costly process that reproduced the pictures with remarkable fidelity. To her surprise, the artist found herself famous almost overnight, and she outsold all the other artists of her day, the initial sales of *Under the Window* running to some 70,000 copies. It still sells, and Evans's firm is still printing her books.

Her style was unique—graceful but static figures in quaint old-fashioned clothes, at play, at tea, or otherwise decorously engaged. The pages are gay with garlands of fruits or flowers, mostly in delicate pastel colors. Her pictures often have a gentle humor, and their grace and charm still delight the eye. (See color section.)

Randolph Caldecott

Randolph Caldecott, for whom the Caldecott Medal is named, was the third of Edmund Evans's famous triumvirate and, like the others, owes much to that printer's bold experiments with color printing. Caldecott succeeded and far surpassed Walter Crane in the production of illustrated toy books.

Caldecott grew up in the Shropshire country, familiar with country fairs, the hunt, dogs, horses, and the lovely English landscape, all of which are evident in his pictures. Around 1878

Illustration by Arthur Frost. From *Uncle Remus and His Friends* by Joel Chandler Harris. Published 1892 by Houghton Mifflin.

he began to work on the nursery toy books with which we associate his name and fame. Probably his most famous illustrations (1878) are those for William Cowper's *The Diverting History of John Gilpin* (1785). Caldecott made Cowper's poem into a picture story, funny both to children and adults and a masterpiece of droll action. No one ever drew such humorous horses or such recklessly inept riders. His illustrated *Mother Goose* rhymes in papercovered book form are among his loveliest and most original creations. Caldecott did a number of these toy books, selling at one shilling, and they have seldom been surpassed by our best and most expensive modern picture books. (See color section.)

Arthur Frost

For that classic collection *Nights with Uncle Remus*, Arthur Frost made pen-and-ink pictures as comic and irresistible as that gay rogue, Brer Rabbit himself. Whether he is "sashaying" down the road in his patched and droopy old pants or talking turkey to Tar Baby, he is a picture of rural shrewdness. Frost's whole gallery of animal folk provides as marvelous characterizations as any Caldecott ever made.

Howard Pyle

Howard Pyle was another American artist who worked in black and white. His heroic and romantic pictures for such books as *Robin Hood* (1883), *Otto of the Silver Hand* (1888), and *Men of Iron* (1890) are meticulous in their fidelity to the historical costumes and weapons of the period. Yet his elaborations of robes, courtly trappings, and tournament details are always subordinated to the interpretation of character or mood. The poignancy of young Otto's tragedy moves anyone who looks at those pictures, and, in contrast, the high good humor of Robin Hood is equally evident. Here was an author-artist with a gift for telling stories in words and pictures.

Leslie Brooke

Although some of the work of the English Leslie Brooke was published as late as 1935, he is so much in the Caldecott tradition that he seems to belong to the nineteenth century. In delicate pastel colors he provides glimpses of the English countryside, pictures as charming as any Caldecott produced. His *Mother Goose* characters in *Ring o' Roses* (1922) are delightful, and his pigs are triumphs of whimsical characterization. The *Johnny Crow* books (1903, 1907, and 1935) are his own invention. Johnny Crow is the perfect host for two parties of birds and beasts so adroitly characterized both in verse and pictures that his books are classic examples of what picture books can be in the hands of a creative artist-writer. (See color section.)

The Twentieth Century

Beatrix Potter

Beatrix Potter's *The Tale of Peter Rabbit* (1901), a milestone in children's literature, marks the beginning of the modern picture story—the book in which pictures are so integral a part of the story that the nonreading child can soon "read" the story from the pictures. In Beatrix Potter's books, her clear watercolors show small animals dressed up like human country folk pursuing their activities through fascinating English lanes and meadows or within cozy interiors. The pictures are as beautifully composed as the texts, and in her little books there is a perfect union of the two arts. (See color section.)

Illustration by E.H. Shepard. From *The House at Pooh Corner* by A.A. Milne, 1928. Copyright renewal 1956, by A.A. Milne. Reproduced by permission of the publishers, E. P. Dutton and The Canadian Publishers, McClelland and Stewart Limited, Toronto.

Arthur Rackham

Arthur Rackham, whose distinctive work is easily recognized, illustrated well over fifty books but seemed most at home in the field of folklore. His pictures for *The Fairy Tales of Grimm* (1900) made an immediate impression, and Rackham enthusiasts and collectors began with that publication. There are no fluttering fairies to be found on his pages; instead, there are earthy old gnomes, ogres, and witches, eerie, mysterious, and sometimes menacing. In black and white or full color his pictures are alive with details that the casual observer may miss—small, furry faces or elfin figures peering out from leaves or half hidden in grasses. We are told that Rackham drew his pictures before painting them, a technique that seems to strengthen them, because whether the colors are dark and somber or clear and light they have body and vitality. For *The Wind in the Willows* (1940), his characterizations of Mole, Ratty, Toad, and all the others are inimitable, and the details of picnics and cozy rooms enhance the warmth of that story. Here is an artist with unique gifts which he devoted almost entirely to the illustration of books for children. (See color section.)

Ernest H. Shepard

The deft pen of Ernest Shepard was drawing for *Punch* as early as 1907, but not until the publication of A. A. Milne's *When We Were Very Young* (1924) with the Shepard illustrations were his pen-and-ink sketches widely and affectionately known. Milne's *Winnie-the-Pooh* followed in 1926, *Now We Are Six* in 1927, and *The House at Pooh Corner* in 1928, all illustrated by Shepard. These pen-and-ink sketches of Christopher Robin, Pooh, and their companions show mood, character, and situation. Shepard's interpretative ability is shown again in illustrations for Kenneth Grahame's *The Reluctant Dragon* (1938) and *The Wind in the Willows* (1931). Even Rackham's illustrations for this latter book cannot surpass some of Shepard's sketches. Mole "jumping off all four legs at once, in the joy of living," or Toad picnicking grandly or waddling off disguised as a washerwoman—these pictures and many others are sheer perfection. In 1957 Shepard made eight color plates for *The World of Pooh* and followed, when he was eighty, with eight more for the

Reprinted with permission of Macmillan Publishing Co., Inc. From *The Big Snow* by Berta and Elmer Hader. Copyright 1948 by Berta and Elmer Hader, renewed 1976 by Berta Hader. (Original in color)

Golden Anniversary Edition of *The Wind in the Willows* (1959). His color plates are beautiful but add nothing to the virtuosity of his pen-and-ink sketches.

Kurt Wiese

Sent to China on business, taken prisoner by the Japanese, back to Germany by way of Australia and Africa—somewhere along the line, German-born Kurt Wiese determined to be an artist. This background of travel and of knowledge of many peoples gave color and authenticity to his illustrations for such books as Elizabeth Lewis's *Young Fu of the Upper Yangtze* (1932), Kipling's *Jungle Books* (1932), and Marjorie Flack's *The Story About Ping* (1933).

Perhaps the most outstanding characteristic of Kurt Wiese's work is his amazing versatility. He illustrated over a hundred books, and whether it is Ping, a Chinese duck waddling up the gangplank of his particular junk, or Felix Salten's wild and beautiful *Bambi* (1929), or his own amusing stories *Rabbits' Revenge* (1940) and the Chinese *Fish in the Air* (1948), and whether he is working in black and white or full color, character and situations are illustrated with humor, fidelity to the story, and fine draftsmanship.

To this group of artists, born in the nineteenth century but producing in the early or middle years of the twentieth century, more names could be added. Jessie Willcox Smith used soft, dark colors in her illustrations for Stevenson's *A Child's Garden of Verses* (1905). She was a pu-

pil of Howard Pyle, as was N. C. Wyeth, whose illustrations for *Robin Hood* (1917) and *Robinson Crusoe* (1920) are powerful in composition and rich in color. Thomas Handforth won the Caldecott Medal for *Mei Li* (1938). His black-and-white illustrations are vigorous and full of action, and they make the Chinese heroine seem real and understandable. Another Caldecott winner is the picture book *The Big Snow* (1948) by Berta and Elmer Hader. It is typical of the Haders' work—a slight story, soft colors, and a warm feeling for birds, animals, and kindly people. Marie Hall Ets' sensitive and perceptive watercolors for *Play with Me* (1955), about a little girl learning to be quiet with shy woodland creatures, are quite the loveliest she has ever produced. *Nine Days to Christmas* (1959) won the Caldecott Medal but is, in spite of full, bright colors, less interesting than her earlier books. *Gilberto and the Wind* (1963) and *Talking Without Words* (1970) are among her most effective books.

No book of this size can hope to name and appraise half the talented people who are doing fine and original illustrations for children's books today. Of the sampling of these artists that follows, some were born in the nineteenth century, but most of these began their work in the thirties and some have continued producing in the years following. The exception is Wanda Gág, whose innovative book *Millions of Cats* appeared before the thirties.

Wanda Gág

In 1928, Wanda Gág's picture story *Millions of Cats* ushered in what came to be known as "The Golden Thirties" of picture books. It still outshines in strong story interest many of its successors. It is indeed about as close to perfection as a picture story can be. It is told with all the rhythm and cadence of the old European storytellers and is illustrated with striking black-and-white lithographs that repeat the flowing rhythm of the text. Wanda Gág was steeped in the European folk tales she heard told as a child, and so it is not surprising that her own completely fresh and original stories have a folk flavor. Her illustrations for *ABC Bunny* (1933) and for four small books of *Grimms' Fairy Tales* have the same flowing lines, dramatic black-and-white areas, and homely warmth that are characteristic of everything she did.

Marguerite de Angeli

Whether De Angeli gives us a rebellious young Quaker girl of long ago, kicking her bonnet down the stairs in *Thee Hannah!* (1940), or a too lively young pioneer schoolboy in *Skippack School* (1939), or whether she gives us some two-hundred sixty illustrations for her *Mother Goose* (1954), the people are always lovely to look at, the colors warm and soft, and the details of outdoor scenes or interiors authentic and beautifully composed. Minority groups and historical subjects have held special interest for this artist. The Pennsylvania Dutch in *Henner's Lydia* (1936), the Amish in *Yonie Wondernose* (1944), the Polish children in *Up the Hill* (1942), and the hero of her splendid historical story *Door in the Wall* (1949 Newbery Medal) are most appealing.

James Daugherty

Thomas Handforth's *Mei Li* was awarded the Caldecott Medal in 1938, but another picture story was also worthy of the award that year— *Andy and the Lion* by James Daugherty. Later, this author-artist received the Newbery Medal for his *Daniel Boone* (1939). Both books are as distinguished for their illustrations as for the text. Warm earthiness and a tender appreciation of people mark his pictures. *Andy and the Lion* is entertaining, but the pictures are unforgettable. The rear view of young Andy reaching for a book on high library shelves, or Andy toppling over backward as he extracts the thorn—these have a great gusto. Daugherty's heroic illustrations for *Daniel Boone* (1939) have vigor, and those for *Poor Richard* (1941) reveal his wonderful gift for characterization. James Daugherty's portraits are as distinctive as the heroes they record.

Feodor Rojankovsky

Russian-born Feodor Rojankovsky has done unforgettable illustrations with earthy colors and homely, lovable, old peasant faces for Hans Christian Andersen's *The Old Man Is Always Right* (1940). There is this same earthy quality about all of Rojankovsky's people—the sturdy, unprettified children and the stocky, dumpy grownups with their warm, woolly scarves or mittens. As for his animals, there were never furrier kittens or fluffier feathered fowls. Tex-

ture, rich colors, and good draftsmanship are hallmarks of this artist. It was Rojankovsky's gay, amusing illustrations for *Frog Went a-Courtin'* (1955) by John Langstaff that won him a long deserved Caldecott Medal. He also illustrated *Over in the Meadow* (1966) with John Langstaff and Jan Wahl's *Mulberry Tree* (1970). He was one of the notable colorists among modern artists.

Robert Lawson

If pen-and-ink sketches can be described as witty, Robert Lawson's pictures certainly deserve the description. Who can ever forget the first glimpse of that mild young bull in *The Story of Ferdinand* (1936), peacefully inhaling the fragrance of flowers instead of snorting around the bull ring, or Mr. Popper blandly coping with his penguins in *Mr. Popper's Penguins* (1938), or the scene of the electric shock in *Ben and Me* (1939). In contrasting mood are Lawson's gravely beautiful drawings for *Pilgrim's Progress* (1939) and for *Adam of the Road* (1942), set in thirteenth-century England. Robert Lawson was a master draftsman, and every detail of scenes, costumes, and characterizations is meticulously executed. But not until he wrote as

Illustration by James Daugherty from *Andy and the Lion* by James Daugherty. Copyright 1938, copyright © renewed 1966 by James Daugherty. Reprinted by permission of The Viking Press, Inc. (Original with color)

Now the lion
began to hear the joyous sounds of a military march.
He turned around the next corner,
and there was the town band, marching down the street
between two lines of people.
Ratatatum ratata ratatatum ratatata boom boom.

Before the lion could even nod and say, "*Bonjour*,"
the music became screams and yells.
What a hubbub!
Musicians and spectators tumbled into one another
in their flight toward doorways and sidewalk cafes.
Soon the street was empty and silent.

Illustration by Roger Duvoisin. From *The Happy Lion* by Louise Fatio. Copyright, 1954, by Louise Fatio Duvoisin and Roger Duvoisin. Reprinted by permission of Whittlesey House (McGraw-Hill). (Original in color)

well as illustrated *Ben and Me* did his admirers realize the full scope of his talents and versatility. Text and pictures are equally amusing and full of the wry wisdom that appears again in his own *Mr. Revere and I* (1953), *Rabbit Hill* (1944 Newbery Medal), and its sequel, *The Tough Winter* (1954).

Edwin Tunis

Each book by Edwin Tunis is a product of intensive research and a model of clean draftsmanship and scrupulous accuracy. For his first six books, the line drawings were in pen and ink; to relieve strain on his arm muscles he adopted, on the advice of his physician, crayon-plus-wash both for his work in black and white and for the color drawings for *Chipmunks on the Doorstep* (1971). His books are handsome and vastly informative, *Indians* (1959) being used as a text in American Indian schools and *Weapons* (1954) as a text for the United States Air Force. *Frontier Living* (1961) was a Newbery Medal Honor Book; *The Young United States* (1969), *Colonial Living* (1957), and *Shaw's Fortune* (1966) are, like his other books, evidence that Edwin Tunis was a historian with a drawing board.

Edward Ardizzone

Only a first-rate artist like Edward Ardizzone could bless Tim with such splendid seascapes and glimpses of port towns. Whether the books come in the handsome, outsize edition of the first *Little Tim and the Brave Sea Captain* (1936) or in the small-size edition of *Tim All Alone* (1957), the pictures are watercolors, beautifully reproduced, full of the power of the sea and the jaunty courage of seafaring folk. Master of the economical line, Ardizzone has a droll quality that makes his figures memorable; his illustrations for Cecil Lewis's *The Otterbury Incident* (1969) and for Eleanor Estes's *Miranda the Great* (1967) are as beguiling as those for his own *The Wrong Side of the Bed* (1970). (See color section.)

Roger Duvoisin

Roger Duvoisin uses a variety of techniques and has an unfailing sense of strong composition and design. For Alvin Tresselt's books on weather and seasons, such as *White Snow, Bright Snow* (1947 Caldecott Medal), his colors are flat washes and the pictures simplified to a poster-like effect. For Louise Fatio's series of stories— *The Happy Lion* (1954) and its sequels—and for his own *Snowy and Woody* (1979) his pictures are in soft colors with lively details. Gian-Carlo Menotti's *Amahl and the Night Visitors* (1952) is illustrated in dark, rich colors with a somber, dramatic quality that is at one with this story from the familiar opera. Duvoisin's own books about the hippopotamus Veronica and the series of tales about the goose Petunia have rare humor. Here is a major artist giving his best to children's books.

Ingri and Edgar Parin d'Aulaire

Ingri and Edgar Parin d'Aulaire are the artists who brought the picture biography into its own. It is interesting that Norwegian-born Ingri and Swiss-born and French-educated Edgar should have turned to the heroes of America, their adopted land, for their subjects. After the d'Aulaires make their first sketches, they work directly on the lithograph stone, which gives their pictures unusual strength and depth. These qualities were not so effective in their *George Washington* (1936), in which the pictures have always seemed wooden. But by the time they wrote the text and made the pictures for *Abraham Lincoln* (1939), they were using this difficult medium superbly. The colors in this book are deep and rich, and the pictures are full of authentic factual details. The lines and composition have a sort of primitive simplicity that suggests folk art. *Benjamin Franklin* (1950) is particularly rich in storytelling details, *Leif the Lucky* (1951) and *Columbus* (1955) are the most colorful, *Pocahontas* (1946) and *Buffalo Bill* (1952), the most picturesque. Their large, handsome *The Book of Greek Myths* (1962), *Norse Gods and Giants* (1967), and *Trolls* (1972) are other examples of their versatility.

Lynd Ward

The Biggest Bear (1952) won the Caldecott Medal for Lynd Ward, who was already a well-known illustrator, and that book seems to have overshadowed the lovely pictures he made for Hildegarde Swift's *The Little Red Lighthouse and the Great Gray Bridge* (1942). In spite of its long, awkward title, this is a significant picture story that is made doubly moving by Ward's illustrations. In both books—*The Biggest Bear*, in monochrome, and *The Little Red Lighthouse*, in dark blues and grays with touches of red—it is the artist's sure sense of dramatic contrast that tells

Viewpoint

But it is not safe to identify illustration with the representational and decoration with the abstract elements of art; although this is as true as most generalizations. Both elements may be mingled in one design, and in fact must be if it is to be good. And if it were possible to divide something that is indivisible, we might say that illustration has reference to the meaning of the text and decoration to the appearance of the page . . . .

Midway between the two we have the imaginative type of illustration which rests upon the text but is itself a sort of extension of the text because it says things visually that are not possible to words.

. . . The good illustration must be a good design irrespective of the text it accompanies, and the way it fits the page is of course part of that design.—David Bland, *The Illustration of Books*, Pantheon, New York, 1952, pp. 12, 13.

the stories and grips and holds children's attention. In *The Silver Pony* (1973), the pictures tell the story without a text. Ward has illustrated many books written by his wife, May McNeer, among them *America's Mark Twain* (1962) and *Stranger in the Pines* (1971); he also illustrated Esther Forbes's Newbery Medal book, *Johnny Tremain* (1943).

Adrienne Adams

Houses from the Sea (1959) by Alice Goudey includes some of the loveliest watercolor illustrations Adrienne Adams has made. Since then, her pictures for the Grimms' *Shoemaker and the Elves* (1960) and Andersen's *Thumbelina* (1961) have been exceedingly popular. Her colors are warm and delicate, her pictures full of fascinating details. A most happy collaboration is evident in her delightful pictures for Aileen Fisher's *Going Barefoot* (1960) and *Where Does Everyone Go?* (1961), seasonal poems to which the pictures add lively charm. One of her most engaging conceptions has been the serried ranks of marching rabbits in her husband Lonzo Anderson's story *Two Hundred Rabbits* (1965). In Peter Barnhart's *The Wounded Duck* (1979) and the Grimm brothers' *Hansel and Gretel* (1975), the illustrations are particularly striking for their meticulous detail and dramatic use of color. (See color section.)

Evaline Ness

Evaline Ness uses a variety of techniques ranging from hand-worked tapestry to woodcuts printed on tissue-thin paper, with separate blocks used for each color. Her constant experimentation brings freshness to her handsomely composed illustrations. She used collage with line-and-wash for *Sam, Bangs & Moonshine*, for which she received the Caldecott Medal in 1967. For the three preceding years, the books she illustrated were Honor Books—in 1964 with illustrations for Sorche Nic Leodhas's *All in the Morning Early*; in 1965 for Rebecca Caudill's *A Pocketful of Cricket*; and in 1966 for her version of *Tom Tit Tot*. *Josefina February* (1963) is the first book of her own that she illustrated followed by her own *The Girl and the Goatherd* (1970); *Some of the Days of Everett Anderson* (1970) by Lucille Clifton; *The Truthful Harp* (1967) by Lloyd Alexander; and her own selection of poems about girls, *Amelia Mixed the Mustard* (1975).

From the book *The Girl and the Goatherd*. Text and illustration by Evaline Ness. Copyright © by Evaline Ness. Published by E.P. Dutton and used with their permission. (Original in color)

Garth Williams

Garth Williams has won a formidable number of awards and prizes, including the Prix de Rome for sculpture. His first venture into children's book illustration was for E. B. White's *Stuart Little* (1945). He followed this with White's famous *Charlotte's Web* (1952)—a book that might well have received both the Newbery and the Caldecott medals. For a new edition of Laura Ingalls Wilder's *Little House* books (1953), Garth Williams spent ten years making the pictures, and as a result the pictures and stories are one. Equally successful are his illustrations for Natalie Carlson's books about the French Orphelines, Russell Hoban's *Bedtime for Frances* (1960), Margery Sharp's *Miss Bianca* (1962), and George Selden's *Harry Cat's Pet Puppy* (1974). The artist works both in black and white and full color, and his pictures are always characterized by authenticity of detail. The colors are fresh and soft, the composition vigorous. But whether the story he illustrates is realistic or pure fantasy, historical fiction or modern city life, his superb gift for characterization stands out. No pig could look more foolishly smug than Wilbur, no orphan could flee more desperately from the encircling bicyclists than Josine, no pioneers could look more cozy than the Little House dwellers.

Robert McCloskey

The first artist to be twice winner of the Caldecott Medal is Robert McCloskey, whose big, handsome picture stories are almost as popular with adults as with children. *Make Way for Ducklings* (1941 Caldecott Medal) vies with *Blueberries for Sal* (1948) in popularity. He has also illustrated Keith Robertson's *Henry Reed* stories with great humor. Only in *Time of Wonder* (1958 Caldecott Medal) and *Burt Dow, Deep Water Man* (1963) has this artist used color, but in his powerful black and whites you do not miss the color, so alive they are with realistic details and storytelling power. (See color section.)

William Pène du Bois

Few indeed are the children's book illustrators who can claim both a place in the New York Museum of Modern Art and a Newbery Medal. William Pène du Bois was awarded the Newbery Medal in 1948 for his *Twenty-One Balloons*,

Illustrations by Ezra Jack Keats, pp. 19 & 20. From Ezra Jack Keats, *Louie*. Copyright © 1975 by Ezra Jack Keats. Published by Greenwillow Books. (A Division of William Morrow & Company). Published in the United Kingdom by Hamish Hamilton Ltd., London. (Original in color)

and he has written many distinguished books before and after that year, all with an illogical logic, all illustrated with paintings that are notable for their clean lines and clear colors, as evident, for example, in *Otto and the Magic Potatoes* (1970) and *Call Me Bandicoot* (1970). His boyhood love for the circus is evident in several of his books: *The Great Geppy* (1940) and *The Alligator Case* (1965). Although he has illustrated the books of other writers—George Macdonald's *The Light Princess* (1962), Rebecca Caudill's *A Certain Small Shepherd* (1965), Charlotte Zolotow's *My Grandson Lew* (1974)—the books for which he is both author and illustrator have a felicitous harmony between text and pictures seldom achieved in children's books.

Ezra Jack Keats

In a tough section of Brooklyn, eight-year-old Ezra Jack Keats discovered the beneficial side effects of painting. Some neighborhood boys snatched a painting from him, but when they learned he was the artist, they treated him with respect. The first book he wrote and illustrated, *The Snowy Day* (1963), earned him the Caldecott Medal and later was adapted into a prize-winning film. Keats works as a choreographer does, hanging his illustrations in rows on the walls "to pace the text." Using oils and collage, he achieves a sunny simplicity. His books include *Whistle for Willie* (1963), *Peter's Chair* (1967), *Goggles!* (a 1970 Caldecott Honor Book), *Dreams* (1974), and *Louie* (1975).

Leonard Weisgard

Leonard Weisgard is a major illustrator whose pictures have sold many a second-rate text. He is a great colorist and his paintings are full of exquisite details of small flowers and frolicking animals and decorative birds. His illustrations for Margaret Wise Brown's *Little Island* (1946), painted on pressed wood in tempera and egg white, won him the Caldecott Medal. The seascapes are in deep blues and greens, with the island sometimes lost in mist. The landscapes are in lush yellow-greens and flashing blues. Some of the other books illustrated by this prolific artist are Sesyle Joslin's charming stories about Baby Elephant; Phyllis McGinley's *A Wreath of Christmas Legends* (1967); Charlotte Zolotow's *Wake Up and Good Night* (1971); Rudyard Kipling's *How the Rhinoceros Got His Skin* (1974); and his own *The Beginnings of Cities* (1968).

Barbara Cooney

Children were delighted by Barbara Cooney's black-and-white pictures for those two fine animal stories—Rutherford Montgomery's *Kildee House* (1949) and Barbara Reynolds's *Pepper* (1952). But in color she did not come into her own until she made the pictures for Lee Kingman's *Peter's Long Walk* (1953). They are in muted colors and interpret tenderly a child's sad homecoming which turns out cheerfully. She went on to win the Caldecott Medal for her

Illustration by Antonio Frasconi from *The House That Jack Built*, copyright © 1958 by Antonio Frasconi. Reproduced by permission of Harcourt Brace Jovanovich, Inc. (Original in color)

scratchboard illustrations for *Chanticleer and the Fox* (1958), adapted from Chaucer's "The Nun's Priest's Tale" in *The Canterbury Tales.* Every detail is historically accurate, but what the children love are those pages in bright clear reds, greens, and blues, alive with action. She prefers working in full color, using acrylic paints, but has also used pen and ink for *Cock Robin* (1965), wash for the delicate pictures in Sarah Orne Jewett's *A White Heron* (1963), and charcoal for her pictures in the Grimms' *Snow White and Rose Red* (1966). Her illustrations for *Ox-Cart Man* by Donald Hall (1979 Caldecott Medal) and *When the Sky Is Like Lace* (1975) by Elinor Horwitz exemplify both her artistic diversity and the research that results in authentic detail. (See color section.)

Marcia Brown

No generalizations about the work of Marcia Brown are possible, for she varies her style to suit the content of the story she is illustrating. Her illustrations for *Stone Soup* (1947) are colorful, gay, and earthy, like the rogues who taught the villagers a more generous way of life. *Puss in Boots* (1952) is a gorgeous, flamboyant feline, well adapted to the court life into which he catapults his master. Both *The Steadfast Tin Soldier* (1953) and *Cinderella* (1955 Caldecott Medal) are in misty pinks and blues grayed down to the gentle mood of the tales. The sturdy woodcuts in brown and black for *Dick Whittington and His Cat* (1950) are as substantial as the hero, and in the alphabet book *All But-*

Illustration by Barbara Cooney, From Donald Hall, *Ox-Cart Man.* Text copyright © Donald Hall, 1979. Illustrations copyright © Barbara Cooney Porter, 1979. Published by The Viking Press. (Original in color.)

terflies (1974) the woodcuts are in muted colors. The book that won her second Caldecott Medal, *Once a Mouse* (1961), is completely different from her earlier work. This fable of pride laid low is in jungle colors, and the stylized woodcut pictures have subtle details of expression or posture that tell the story and repay study. Marcia Brown has written and illustrated some charming stories of her own, and has produced several concept books (see Chapter 5) with stunning photographs, but her major contributions to date are her brilliant interpretations of single folk tales. (See color section.)

Antonio Frasconi

Antonio Frasconi is one of the great woodcut artists of our time. His technique has softened the basic, crudely broad areas of the usual woodcut by high artistry in the use of color. He avoids the uncompromising pressure printing of the entire block by printing his woodcuts by hand and, to achieve variations of tone, rubbing a spoon over a paper laid on an inked block. Strong and vivid, his work melds the "dynamics of design and typography" with an imaginative power that pulls the young reader back to his illustrations again and again. A Uruguayan who came to the United States on a scholarship, Frasconi published his first children's book in 1955, the multilingual *See and Say.* Other Frasconi books are *The House That Jack Built* (1958), and *One Little Room, an Everywhere* (1975), a collection of love poems edited by Myra Cohn Livingston and illustrated with small, finely detailed decorations.

Mitsumasa Anno

An outstanding Japanese artist, Mitsumasa Anno has a sense of humor that pervades all of his distinctive books; his love of mathematics is also obvious, especially in *Topsy-Turvies* (1970), an elegant compilation of mathematical impossibilities in space, with drawings that flout deliberately all known rules of perspective. His line and watercolor paintings are beautiful in detail, and his experience as a book designer has contributed to the handsomeness of the page layouts. None of Anno's books has a text, but their language is universal. In *Anno's Alphabet* (1975) the woodgrain letters are beautifully framed by decorative black and white borders;

Illustration by Antonio Frasconi from *The House That Jack Built,* copyright © 1958 by Antonio Frasconi. Reproduced by permission of Harcourt Brace Jovanovich, Inc. (Original in color)

in *Anno's Journey* (1978) the artist records European art and architecture quite seriously but cannot resist a visual joke here and there (a gatehouse is engraved with "Anno 1976"); and in *Anno's Animals* (1979) his love of humor and trompe l'oeil produce a forest full of hidden animals. Anno's draughtsmanship is impeccable, his use of color restrained and sophisticated.

Erik Blegvad

The appeal of Erik Blegvad's illustrations is in the precise detail of his tidy, humorous drawings, the delicate tints of color, and the fidelity to the author's text. For Monica Stirling's *The Cat from Nowhere* (1969), the black-and-white drawings were done in pen and india ink. When he works in full color, he uses a transparent watercolor wash, or a mixture of watercolor and poster colors. His tender feelings for animals are apparent in Lenore Blegvad's *The Great Hamster Hunt* (1969) and in *Mr. Jensen & Cat* (1965), which has enchanting illustrations of Copenhagen. In Ruth Craft's *The Winter Bear* (1975), the full-color pictures capture the beauty of a snow scene, and in Charlotte Zolotow's *May I Visit?* (1976) they reflect both the warmth and humor of the story. The full range of his versatility is most evident in *Self Portrait: Erik Blegvad* (1979).

Charles Keeping

Born in Lambeth, England, Charles Keeping won the Kate Greenaway Medal in 1967 for *Charley, Charlotte and the Golden Canary*. Keeping is noted for his bold approach, his use of vivid colors, and his highly individual style. For *Joseph's Yard* (1969) he used several layers of colored acetate, with drawings in colored ink, which were then shot together as one drawing. His remarkable range shows in the bold black-and-white india-ink drawings for Rosemary Sutcliff's *Heroes and History* (1966), the unexpected perspectives in her *Knight's Fee* (1960), and in the stunning use of line and texture in *The Golden Shadow* (1973) by Leon Garfield and Edward Blishen. Only in their swirling lines is there a resemblance between his black-and-white illustrations and the vibrant color illustrations he uses in his own picture books.

Maurice Sendak

Some of Maurice Sendak's first illustrations were for humorous books like Ruth Krauss's *A Hole Is to Dig* (1952) and Beatrice de Regniers's *What Can You Do with a Shoe?* (1955). They show the tender appeal of children even when

Illustration © 1965 by Erik Blegvad. From *Mr. Jensen & Cat* by Lenore Blegvad. Reproduced by permission of Harcourt Brace Jovanovich, Inc. (Original in color)

Illustration by Mitsumasa Anno from *Anno's Journey*, reprinted by permission of Philomel Books and the Bodley Head. Copyright © 1977 by Fukuinkan-Shoten Publishers, Tokyo. (Original in color)

they are most absurd—round-faced children grinning fiendishly or preternaturally solemn, dressed up in adult clothes or kicking up their heels and cavorting like young colts. This artist with his flair for comic exaggeration is tremendously popular, but in his illustrations for Meindert DeJong's books, *Wheel on the School* (1954), for example, and for his own book *Kenny's Window* (1956), he shows a sensitive perception of the lonely, imaginative, struggling side of childhood, too. One book in full color is a superb example of his versatility. His pictures for Janice Udry's *Moon Jumpers* (1959) are in the green-blues of a moonlit summer's night that suggest the poetry of childhood. The same could be said of his glorious color pictures for Charlotte Zolotow's *Mr. Rabbit and the Lovely Present* (1962).

Sendak moved into further prominence with *Where the Wild Things Are* (1963), which won the Caldecott Medal. Children rejoice over the ferocious, adoring creatures and over the small hero who, sated with adulation, goes home to reality to find his dinner waiting, still hot. Sendak's sensitivity to text and mood are evident in the contrast between his raffish humorous illustrations in the Grimms' story *King Grisly-Beard* (1973) and his gravely beautiful and sophisticated pictures for a collection of Grimm tales, *The Juniper Tree* (1973). The delicacy of the wash drawings for Else Minarik's *Little Bear* (1957), the tenderness of the pictures in Randall Jarrell's *Animal Family* (1965), and the boldness of those in Sendak's own *In the Night Kitchen* (1970) show how completely Maurice Sendak adapts his illustrations to the story and make clear why he received the Hans Christian Andersen Medal in 1970, the first time an American artist was so honored. *Really Rosie* (1975), a paperback based on a television production, incorporates material from several Sendak books. (See color section.)

Blair Lent

Most of Blair Lent's illustrations have been done with cardboard cuts and overlays. The 1965 Caldecott Medal Honor Book recognition was given to his illustrations for Margaret Hodges's *The Wave*, which also received a silver medal at the São Paulo Biennial in Brazil, and in 1973 Lent's pictures of impish, grotesque Japanese spirits in Arlene Mosel's *The Funny Little Woman* were awarded the Caldecott

Illustration by Blair Lent from *The Funny Little Woman* by Arlene Mosel. Illustrations copyright © 1972 by Blair Lent. Reprinted by permission of the publisher, E. P. Dutton. (Original in color)

Medal. His inventive full-color paintings, which heightened the dramatic quality of William Sleator's Tlingit Indian legend, *The Angry Moon* (1970), earned him another Caldecott Honor Book recognition. *John Tabor's Ride* (1966) and *Pistachio* (1964) are examples of Lent's work as author-illustrator.

Brian Wildsmith

Although he says he has "abstract tendencies," Brian Wildsmith's illustrations are brilliant and strongly representational. He sees the pictorial form as being at one with the text, yet each a thing unto itself—complementary—and each able to exist without the other. All of his work is in full color; a Wildsmith trademark is the use of bright contrasting colors in a harlequin pattern. In his technique, gouache is used, moving from impasto down to almost translucent water color effects. The subjects he treats lend themselves to strong visual impact: *Brian Wildsmith's Fishes* (1968), *Brian Wildsmith's Circus* (1970), *Brian Wildsmith's Puzzles* (1971), *The Little Wood Duck* (1973), and *Brian Wildsmith's ABC,* which won the Kate Greenaway Medal for 1962 and was published in the United States in 1963. One of the major British illustrators, Wildsmith has, in addition to his own books, created illustrations for several Jean de la Fontaine fables and for *The Oxford Book of Poetry for Children* (1964), edited by Edward Blishen. (See color section.)

Margot Zemach

Margot Zemach works in ink line and wash, using color to strengthen the drawing rather than obscure it. She uses line in many ways, often boldly in central figures and sketchily in the background, or with careful detail to depict a piece of furniture and with abandon to create frilly ruffles or a curly mop of hair. Most of her earlier books were written by her late husband. Their first was *A Small Boy Is Listening* (1959), and together they adapted and illustrated a Russian folk tale, *Salt* (1965), an Ozark folk song, *Mommy, Buy Me a China Doll* (1966), and a Russian nursery rhyme, *The Speckled Hen* (1966). In her black-and-white pictures for Isaac Bashevis Singer's *When Shlemiel Went to Warsaw* (1968), Margot Zemach demonstrates the essence of her economical use of line and adroitly

Illustration by Margot Zemach. Reprinted with the permission of Farrar, Straus and Giroux, Inc. From *It Could Always Be Worse* by Margot Zemach, copyright © 1976 by Margot Zemach. (Original in color)

echoes the peasant humor of the text. *The Judge: An Untrue Tale* (1969), a Caldecott Honor Book, and *It Could Always Be Worse* (1977) have the same robust and earthy quality. In their *Duffy and the Devil*, the Zemachs adapted a Cornish variant of the Rumpelstiltskin story. It's told with verve, and the illustrations, soft in hues but bold in composition, are humorous and vigorous. In 1974 it was awarded the Caldecott Medal.

Nonny Hogrogian

For the first children's books she illustrated, Nicolete Meredith's *King of the Kerry Fair* (1960), Nonny Hogrogian used woodblocks, as she did for Robert Burns's *Hand in Hand We'll Go* (1965). The illustrations for the 1966 Caldecott Medal book, *Always Room for One More* by Sorche Nic Leodhas, were done in pen and ink, with gray wash and pastels to achieve the quality of mist and heather. Her approach to illustration is that the manuscript comes first, and the pictures grow from it, the mood of the text dictating the technique as much as possible. She used pastels to illustrate the story of the gentle, lovely *Vasilisa the Beautiful* (1970), translated by Thomas Whitney; etchings for an edition of Grimms' tales; and oil paintings for her own *One Fine Day* (1971), which was awarded the Caldecott Medal and in which the illustra-

tions have the full and vigorous quality of the story of a sharp-nosed fox who tries to retrieve his tail. Some of the other books she has illustrated are Barbara Schiller's *The Kitchen Knight* (1965); Isaac Bashevis Singer's *The Fearsome Inn* (1967); and her own *Handmade Secret Hiding Places* (1975) in which she used pencil halftone and line. (See color section.)

Nancy Ekholm Burkert

As might be expected from an artist who sees "absolute perfection" in the compositions of Arthur Rackham, Nancy Burkert's work is full of exquisite detail. In her imaginative treatment of Edward Lear's *The Scroobious Pip* (1968), she is thoroughly at home with the infinite variety of nature, and both the line drawings and the full-color paintings have a firm delicacy. For Natalie Carlson's *Jean-Claude's Island* (1963) she used conté pencil and crayon, and for Eva Le Gallienne's translation of Hans Christian Andersen's *The Nightingale*, she used brush and colored ink to achieve the wonderfully rich color; the authentic detail of her illustrations for this book she provided through her study of ancient Chinese scrolls. Among the other books she has illustrated are John Updike's *A Child's Calendar* (1965), Roald Dahl's *James and the Giant Peach* (1961), and Andersen's *The Fir Tree* (1970), to which she gave pictures that are gravely sweet. (See color section.)

Viewpoint

Many illustrators have tried to write—with varying success—and occasionally authors have tried to draw—with less. One feels that the desire to do a book may be commendable; but without something to say to children and the means to say it, or even the desire to develop the means, one wonders at the arrogance that expects a child to be interested in halfbaked creations, texts or pictures. There is still among laymen a lack of comprehension of the discipline needed to pare a text to a basic line that looks simple. A picture book is as concise as poetry. Text and pictures combine to form an essence that expands in the child's mind.—Marcia Brown, "One Wonders . . . ," in *Illustrators of Children's Books: 1957–1966*, compiled by Lee Kingman, Joanna Foster, and Ruth Giles Lontoft, The Horn Book, Inc., Boston, 1968, p. 24.

Diane and Leo Dillon

Leo and Diane Dillon met while attending the Parsons School of Design and have been working together as one artist since 1957. Although they have separate styles when working individually, they blend these when working on a book together and their work shows great variety of media and techniques. Their illustrations for *Why Mosquitoes Buzz in People's Ears* (1975), a West African tale retold by Verna Aardema, which was awarded the Caldecott Medal, were done with water color and pastels in strong, soft colors and in bold, stylized compositions inspired by the designs of African fabrics. The following year, they again won the medal for their pictures in Margaret Musgrove's *Ashanti to Zulu* (1976). The Dillons adapt the mood and medium of their work to the text it illustrates: in the pictures for Erik Haugaard's *Hakon of Rogen's Saga* (1963), a bleak Viking tale, they use strong black-and-white woodcuts; for Natalia Belting's *Whirlwind Is a Ghost Dancing*

Z Leaping, bending, twisting Zulu (zoo'·loo) dancers salute their new chief. The earth trembles with the thunder of the drums as the dancers thrust their cowhide shields forward and wave their clubs. Their beaded headbands catch the sun. The furry white goatskin bands on their legs and arms move together, as if all the dancers were one person. The Zulus have beautiful and complicated dances for all occasions.

Illustration by Leo and Diane Dillon. From Margaret Musgrove, *Ashanti to Zulu.* Text copyright © 1976 by Margaret Musgrove. Pictures copyright © 1976 by Leo and Diane Dillon. Used by permission of The Dial Press.

(1974), acrylics and pastels are used for stylized, dignified pictures that reflect the grave beauty of Native American poetry and incorporate tribal motifs. The tender story of a small child's love for a very old woman in *The Hundred Penny Box* (1975) by Sharon Bell Mathis has pictures that are framed and slightly blurred in brown and white, giving the effect of an old photograph album. In Lorenz Graham's *Song of the Boat* (1975), an African tale told with the poetic language and cadence of the oral tradition, the Dillons use woodcut style, but the pictures are quite unlike the starkly dramatic illustrations of the Viking tale; the solid masses are lightened by fine lines, patterns, and designs that give variety and movement to the figures. (See color section.)

Arnold Lobel

Arnold Lobel believes that a good illustrator should have a wide repertory of styles at command, and his work shows this whether he uses wash, pencil, or pen and ink, which is his favorite medium. His first book was *A Zoo for Mr. Muster* (1962), but most of his work in the 1960s was illustrating books by other authors. For Millicent Selsam's *Benny's Animals and How He Put Them in Order* (1966), he used a raffish, sketchy line appropriate for the lightness of the story; in Nathaniel Benchley's *Sam the Minuteman* (1969), solid figures in framed drawings. In *Hildilid's Night* (1971) by Cheli Duran Ryan, a noodlehead tale, black-and-white pictures contain finely drawn parallel lines that give a soft solidity to the night scenes. This was a Caldecott Honor Book, as was *Frog and Toad Are Friends* (1971), which is discussed in Chapter 5 and which was also a National Book Award finalist. An unusual book for Lobel is his *On the Day Peter Stuyvesant Sailed into Town* (1971), historical fiction told in rhyme, in which the blue and yellow pictures are based on Dutch tiles. *Owl at Home* (1975) and *Grasshopper on the Road* (1979) use the same format as the Frog books. (See color section.)

Raymond Briggs

Raymond Briggs is best known for illustrations of *The Mother Goose Treasury,* which won him the Kate Greenaway Medal in 1967. To complete that collection of four hundred rhymes, which he selected and illustrated, he worked for two years. Sketching with pencil and working over with pen and ink for the black-and-white pictures and with gouache for those in color, he captured the exuberance and the humor of the rhymes. A prolific worker, Briggs illustrated seven of the Coward-McCann "Champion" series in 1968 and 1969, wrote and illustrated *Jim and the Beanstalk* in 1970, and in the same year illustrated *The Elephant and the Bad Baby* by Elfrida Vipont, *The Christmas Book* compiled by James Reeves, and *The Book of Magical Beasts* edited by Ruth Manning-Sanders. His pictures are deft in composition and are gay with color and movement. For *Father Christmas* (1973) and *Father Christmas Goes on Holiday* (1975), Briggs used a cartoon format.

Uri Shulevitz

Uri Shulevitz, who was born in Poland and spent some of his childhood years in Israel and in France, shares, he says, the belief of the prophet Isaiah—"And a little child shall lead them." He works chiefly in ink, sometimes using it in combination with wash. For the illustrations in *Maximilian's World* (1966), by Mary Stolz, he used a Japanese reed pen. In Dorothy Nathan's *The Month Brothers* (1967) and in Isaac Bashevis Singer's *The Fools of Chelm* (1973), his line drawings have a grave yet comic quality

that befits the folk-tale style. In illustrating Arthur Ransome's *The Fool of the World and the Flying Ship,* for which he won the 1969 Caldecott Medal, his pictures in brilliant color are faithful to the art style of the Russian background of the book. In *Hanukah Money* (1978) his scruffy, cheerful figures echo the humor of a classic story by Sholem Aleichem. He has illustrated with sensitivity the stories of many writers, but has never surpassed the evocative mood and the harmony of pictures and text in his own *One Monday Morning* (1967), *Rain Rain Rivers* (1969), and *Dawn* (1974), which was a Hans Christian Andersen Honor Book. (See color section.)

John Burningham

An English artist, John Burningham made a spectacular entrance into the world of children's books by winning the Kate Greenaway Medal in 1963 with his first book, *Borka, the Adventures of a Goose with No Feathers.* Like most of his work, it was done largely in full color. He uses a wide range of materials: pastels, ink, crayons, montage, charcoal, gouache, and photostats, giving textural variety to his pictures. He varies the style of his work to suit the subject of the book; in *John Burningham's ABC* the composition on pages facing the letters is in

Reprinted by permission of Coward, McCann & Geoghegan, Inc. from *The Elephant & the Bad Baby* by Elfrida Vipont. Illustrations copyright © 1969 by Raymond Briggs. (Original in color)

bold poster style. Humor is a component of most of Burningham's work, even in the bland and dreamy pictures for *Mr. Gumpy's Outing* (1971) for which he also received the Greenaway Medal, the first time an artist had won it twice. A simply written book about a man who takes a crew of animals and children for a glorious boat ride and a high tea, it has flowery pastel pictures with a sunny, bucolic humor quite different from the bold vigor of the alphabet book illustrations. The sequel, *Mr. Gumpy's Motor Car* (1976), is less original but equally amusing; this time the children and animals have to get out and push when an old car stalls in the rain. Four small books that have bright little crayon pictures—*The Baby, The Rabbit, The School,* and *The Snow* (1975)—are nicely done for very young children. (See color section.)

Peter Parnall

Peter Parnall's drawings have a distinctive use of line and space. His work is always uncluttered, his line firm but delicate, often sinuous with movement achieved by parallels that break and flow into each other, and his drawings of flora and fauna are impeccably accurate; many examples have appeared in *Audubon Magazine* and *Scientific American.* He has illustrated books by other authors: Mary Shura's *A Tale of Middle Length* (1966), Miska Miles's *Apricot ABC* (1969), *The Fireside Song Book of Birds and Beasts* (1972) edited by Jane Yolen, and others. Parnall has the ability to draw animals in a comic spirit, as he often does in the song book, but in a book like Alice Schick's *The Peregrine Falcons* (1975) his drawings of birds are meticulously realistic. In the picture books for which Parnall is both author and illustrator, he uses space beautifully, with print and picture placed on the page to the advantage of both. *The Mountain* (1971) is a plea for the preservation of ecological balance, showing the invasion and destruction of a mountain area; color is used with restraint, on many pages only in grass and flowers, while massive tree trunks with intricate veining are drawn in black and white. Parnall's illustrations for Byrd Baylor's *Everybody Needs a Rock* (1974) contributed to its being chosen as a Notable Book by the American Library Association. In 1979 Baylor's *The Way to Start a Day* (1978), illustrated with reverence and dignity by Parnall, was selected as a Caldecott Honor Book.

Charles Mikolaycak

A book designer and illustrator, Charles Mikolaycak feels that children are capable of meeting a challenge, that they have instinctive understanding of art. His paintings are sophisticated and often sensuous, with soft modeling of the human figure combined with bold outlines and strong composition. Although he has illustrated such realistic stories as Vera Cumberlege's *Shipwreck* (1974), he prefers to work with epics and folk tales. Earlier in his career, Mikolaycak tended to use one or two colors, always with modulations, as in the dramatic dun and black pictures for Margaret Hodges' retelling of *The Gorgon's Head* (1972) or the framed black and ash rose illustrations for Mirra Ginsburg's *How Wilka Went to Sea* (1975). His full-color paintings for the Hawaiian legends compiled by Jay Williams, *The Surprising Things Maui Did* (1979) and for Barbara Cohen's Biblical adaptation, *I Am Joseph* (1980) are stunning in composition and in costume detail; they are serious, romantic, and almost voluptuous in use of color. Mikolaycak's sensitivity to the text he is illustrating is, however, equally evident in Ginsburg's *The Three Clever Brothers and Other Fools,* both in the humor of the pictures and in the peasant quality achieved by using a Russian embroidery motif as a running frieze in red, contrasting with the black and white pictures. The drawings on the cover and part opening pages of this edition of *Children and Books* are further examples of Mikolaycak's skill. (See color section.)

Gerald McDermott

Gerald McDermott is primarily a filmmaker, and his first book, *Anansi the Spider* (1972), is based on an animated film version which won the 1970 Blue Ribbon at the American Film Festival. A Caldecott Honor Book, it incorporates the graphics of the Ashanti people in its design montage. Highly stylized forms and brilliant, strident colors are used to illustrate a traditional tale of the spider-hero, Anansi, and his six sons. While the adaptation from film gives McDermott's books a static quality, the illustrations are rich and striking. All of his books are based on folk literature: *The Magic Tree* (1973) on a tale from the Congo; *Arrow to the Sun* (1974 Caldecott Medal) on a Pueblo Indian tale; and *The Stonecutter* (1975) on a Japanese folk tale. (See color section.)

Rosemary Wells

Although she has written several stories for older children, Rosemary Wells is primarily known for the picture books she writes and illustrates. Picture story books like *Morris' Disappearing Bag* (1975) and *Don't Spill It Again, James* (1977) have a sense of wry comedy that pervades the illustrations as well as the text. The stumpy little animal children of her deft drawings appeal both because they capture the essence of children's behavior and because they have marvelously expressive faces. In *Benjamin and Tulip* (1973), for example, much of the humor comes not from what the two do, but from how they look: Benjamin astounded and Tulip smugly victorious when she outwits him yet again. Text and pictures are smoothly complementary, and never more so than in the series of stories about Max; on heavy board pages Wells uses a minimal text, as Max—in *Max's First Word* (1979)—blandly comes out with a polysyllabic answer when his sister is urging him to say a simple word. In *Max's Ride* (1979) the pictures are full of action as Max rides in a baby carriage careening downhill; the book also stresses concepts of direction, as he goes *over* a laundry basket, tumbles *out*, and is bounced *up* in the air, *between* two trees.

David Macaulay

Born in England but now living in the United States, David Macaulay has made a distinctive contribution to children's literature despite the fact that he has published only a few books. The first, *Cathedral: The Story of Its Construction* (1973) was a Caldecott Honor Book and the winner of the Deutscher Jugendbuchpreis for the best nonfiction picture book of 1975, when it was published in the German edition. A student of architecture, Macaulay has, in this and in *City: A Story of Roman Planning and Construction* (1974) and in *Pyramid* (1975), related significant architectural advances to the cultures from which they came. His humor is most evident in the bland spoof *Motel of the Mysteries* (1979), a book that will appeal primarily to older readers. His meticulously detailed drawings show, step by step, the construction procedures for the edifices. Whether the scene is a sweeping panorama of a city, a cutaway drawing that shows the architectural plan, or a small picture of one facet of ornamentation, the il-

lustrations are impressive for the masterful handling of perspective and the consistency with which the artist combines informative drawing with visual beauty.

Other Notable Artists

There are so many creative twentieth-century illustrators of children's books that it is impossible to discuss them all even briefly. Obviously this list of artists should include Dorothy Lathrop, who won the first Caldecott Medal for the pen-and-ink sketches in *Animals of the Bible* (1937); Helen Sewell, whose work is notable for its variation of styles; Theodore Geisel, who, as "Dr. Seuss," uses cartoon art with great flair; and Ludwig Bemelmans, whose first story, *Madeline* (1939), led to other books about her adventures, all sketchily drawn but filled with humor, color, and intriguing scenes of Paris.

Virginia Burton's *Mike Mulligan and His Steam Shovel* (1939) and *The Little House* (1943 Caldecott Medal) have a swirling line and clear, bright colors (see color section); her black-and-white pictures for *Song of Robin Hood* (1947) are strikingly detailed. Nicolas Mordvinoff won the Caldecott Medal for *Finders Keepers* (1951), in which he broke away from prettified art for

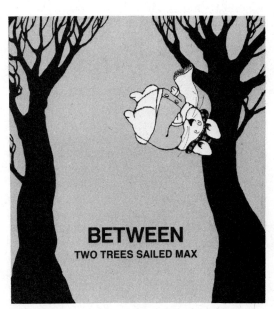

From *Max's Ride* by Rosemary Wells. Text and Illustrations Copyright © 1979 by Rosemary Wells. Reprinted by permission of The Dial Press and Sheldon Fogelman. (Original in color)

children and produced vigorous, humorous drawings with strong line and composition that capture the boldness of William Lipkind's text.

Other notable artists are Nicolas Sidjakov, whose stylized work for *Baboushka and the Three Kings* by Ruth Robbins was awarded the 1960 Caldecott Medal; Beni Montresor, who received the Caldecott Medal in 1965 for Beatrice Schenk de Regniers's *May I Bring a Friend?* in which elaborately decorated pictures give evidence of Montresor's career as a stage designer; and Leonard Everett Fisher, whose stark scratchboard pictures are dramatic in black and white. Victor Ambrus uses ink, watercolor, and oil pastel; his bold composition and humor are evident in *A Country Wedding* (1975). Leo Lionni uses collage as effectively as any artist today, and his rice-paper collage in *Inch by Inch* (1960) made the book a Caldecott Honor Book, as is *Alexander and the Wind-Up Mouse*. Lionni's *Frederick* (1967) and *In the Rabbitgarden* (1975) are animal fables that use collage and paint in handsome compositions. Tasha Tudor works in delicate pastel colors, John Steptoe in harsh, brilliant tones and a style reminiscent of Georges Rouault. (See color section.) Leo Politi's colorful pictures have an awkward but effective simplicity in *Juanita* and *Moy Moy*. Janina Domanska has done striking color etchings, stylized in detail, for *Under the Green Willow* (1971) and *If All the Seas Were One Sea* (1971); her *Din Dan Don It's Christmas* (1975) and *King Krakus and the Dragon* (1979) have the same high sense of design but use richer colors and the motifs of Polish folk art. (See color section.)

Milton Glaser has not illustrated many books for children, but his pictures for Conrad Aiken's *Cats and Bats and Things with Wings* (1965) show amazing virtuosity, each picture in a different mood and technique. Edward Gorey's pen-and-ink illustrations are elegant and distinctive; Brinton Turkle's realistic, simple pictures are as effective in creating an urban setting for Lucille Clifton's *The Boy Who Didn't Believe in Spring* (1973) as for the nineteenth-century town in *Obadiah the Bold* (1965). Ed Emberley won the Caldecott Medal for his illustrations, with a leaded-glass effect from bright colors over woodcut lines, in *Drummer Hoff* (1967), a folk verse adapted by Barbara Emberley. The Caldecott Medal for a 1970 book went to Gail Haley for *A Story, A Story*,

Illustration from *The Maggie B.* by Irene Haas (a Margaret K. Mc Elderry book). Copyright © 1975 by Irene Haas. Used by permission of Atheneum Publishers.

the retelling of an African folk tale with woodcut illustrations that are occasionally crowded but have good design and vitality. Irene Haas combines a romantic mood and humorous details in *The Maggie B.* (1975). Anita Lobel, an adaptable artist, is at her best in Benjamin Elkin's *How the Tsar Drinks Tea* (1971), in which the pictures, appropriately bordered, have a quality of Russian decorative art, or in *King Rooster, Queen Hen* (1975), where she fills the pages with rich textures and patterns. The soft, almost photographic drawings of Symeon Shimin, the distinctive portraiture of Ati Forberg, and the subtle shading of Tom Feelings's pictures in Muriel Feelings's *Jambo Means Hello* (1974) or in his own *Black Pilgrimage* (1972), all have a gentleness that is also strength. A bold freedom is evident in the work of Jose Aruego and Ariane Dewey, whose illustrations for *We Hide, You Seek* (1979) have strength and vigor; and in the work of Tomi Ungerer, whose pictures are the visual equivalent of a comic tall tale. Ed Young and Bernarda Bryson are outstanding for their sense of design and their use of color. John Schoenherr, Irene Brady, Olive Earle, and Hilda Simon are all notable for their scrupulously realistic pictures of animals, and Donald Crews for bold, clean composition and clear colors in poster-simple pictures. (See color section.)

The work of several illustrators is indelibly identified with the characters they have helped bring to life: Beth and Joe Krush for the stories of the Borrowers; Louis Slobodkin for the Moffats; and Paul Galdone for those mice-extraordinary, Anatole and Basil—all of these artists of course have illustrated many other books.

Jean de Brunhoff delighted children with the adventures of that suave French elephant Babar, and Françoise (Seignobosc) has given us a number of books in bright, decorative colors. The Italian artist Bruno Munari provides children with so magnificent a use of color against white space that he could train the color blind to see and rejoice. The illustrations of Swiss Felix Hoffmann for *Sleeping Beauty* (1960) and *The Story of Christmas* (1975) are in the grand style, romantic and grave. The first Hans Christian Andersen Award for illustrations went to Swiss Alois Carigiet, whose *Anton and Anne* (1969) is a good example of the vibrant delicacy of his work. In contrast, another Swiss artist, Celestino Piatti, paints in bold and brilliant modern style. The Danish artist Ib Spang Olsen, who received the Andersen Award in 1972, uses scribbly line and fresh, bright color in contrast to the gloomy smoke of a story about pollution in *Smoke* (1972). Harald Wiberg, in *The Big Snowstorm* (1976) by Hans Peterson, draws beautiful winter scenes of his native Sweden.

Two English illustrators, Margery Gill and Shirley Hughes, do work in color but are better known for their realistic, natural line drawings. C. Walter Hodges won the Kate Greenaway Medal for *Shakespeare's Theatre* (1964), and his fidelity of detail is also seen in sea scenes and the historically based tale of a rescue operation, *The Overland Launch* (1970). Paul Goble, although British, has made a signal contribution to our knowledge of Native Americans with magnificently detailed and historically accurate pictures in books like *Lone Bull's Horse Raid* (1973) and *The Girl Who Loved Wild Horses* (1978). From Japanese-born Taro Yashima have come the sensitive illustrations of children in Japan in *Crow Boy* (1955), and of a Japanese child in America in *Umbrella* (1958), and other works. (See color section.) Kazue Mizumura, who also came to the United States from Japan, has created lively pictures for the stories, set in Japan, of Yoshiko Uchida, as well as for her own *If I Built a Village . . .* (1971).

This is indeed the day of the artist in children's books, and their pictures should afford some protection from the flood of meretricious art that is so readily available. Better one good book with distinguished illustrations than a dozen stereotypes with flashy, poorly executed pictures. For children must have a chance to see truly and subtly. They must have a chance to look and look again at the illustrations in their books. Pictures can help them see the comic

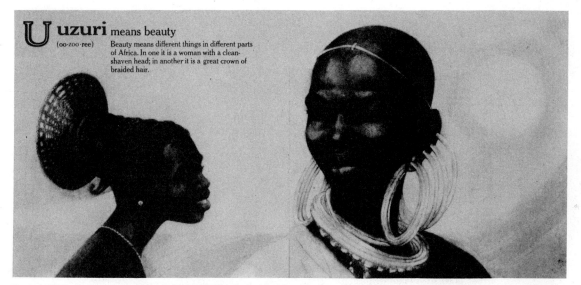

U uzuri means beauty
(oo·zoo·ree)
Beauty means different things in different parts of Africa. In one it is a woman with a clean-shaven head; in another it is a great crown of braided hair.

Excerpted from the book *Jambo Means Hello: Swahili Alphabet Book* by Muriel Feelings, Illustrations by Tom Feelings. Illustrations Copyright © 1974 by Tom Feelings. Used by permission of *The Dial Press.* (Original with color)

From *Lone Bull's Horse Raid* by Paul and Dorothy Goble. Reproduced by permission of Bradbury Press, Inc. and Macmillan London, Ltd. (Original in color)

absurdities of life or its heroic struggles and tragedies. Pictures can give children a sudden breathtaking feeling for the beauty or the wonder of life. Such pictures deepen their perceptiveness and help them to grow.

Many of the children's books mentioned in this chapter appear in the Chapter 5 ("Books for Early Childhood") bibliography, where they are preceded by a "6" to indicate they are discussed here in Chapter 6.

Adult References[6]

ALDERSON, BRIAN. *Looking at Picture Books 1973.*
The Art of Beatrix Potter.
BADER, BARBARA. *American Picturebooks from Noah's Ark to the Beast Within.*
The Bewick Collector.
BILLINGTON, ELIZABETH. *The Randolph Caldecott Treasury.*
BLACKBURN, HENRY. *Randolph Caldecott: A Personal Memoir of His Early Art Career.*
CIANCIOLO, PATRICIA. *Illustrations in Children's Books.*
COLBY, JEAN POINDEXTER. *Writing, Illustrating and Editing Children's Books.* Part II, "Illustrations and Production."

6. Complete bibliographic data are provided in Appendix B.

COMMIRE, ANNE. *Something About the Author: Facts and Pictures About Contemporary Authors and Illustrators of Books for Young People.*
DAVIS, MARY GOULD. *Randolph Caldecott 1846–1886: An Appreciation.*
DOYLE, BRIAN, comp. and ed. *The Who's Who of Children's Literature.*
EGOFF, SHEILA. *The Republic of Childhood: A Critical Guide to Canadian Children's Literature in English.* Chapter 7, "Illustration and Design."
EGOFF, SHEILA, G. T. STUBBS, and L. F. ASHLEY, eds. *Only Connect: Readings on Children's Literature.* Part 5, "Illustration."
ENGEN, RODNEY. *Kate Greenaway.*
———. *Randolph Caldecott: Lord of the Nursery.*
———. *Walter Crane as a Book Illustrator.*
ERNEST, EDWARD. comp., assisted by PATRICIA TRACY LOWE. *The Kate Greenaway Treasury.*
FEAVER, WILLIAM. *When We Were Young: Two Centuries of Children's Book Illustration.*
FREEMAN, G. LAVERNE, and RUTH SUNDERLIN FREEMAN. *The Child and His Picture Book.*
FULLER, MURIEL, ed. *More Junior Authors.*
GOTTLIEB, GERALD R., and others. *Early Children's Books and Their Illustration.*
HOPKINS, LEE BENNETT. *Books Are by People.*
HUDSON, DEREK. *Arthur Rackham: His Life and Work.*
HÜRLIMANN, BETTINA. *Picture-Book World.*
HUTCHINS, MICHAEL, ed. *Yours Pictorially: Illustrated Letters of Randolph Caldecott.*
JOHNSON, DIANA. *Fantastic Illustration and Design in Britain, 1850–1930.*
KINGMAN, LEE, ed. *The Illustrator's Notebook.*
———. *Newbery and Caldecott Medal Books; 1966–1975.*

KINGMAN, LEE, JOANNA FOSTER, and RUTH GILES LONTOFT, comps. *Illustrators of Children's Books, 1957–1966.*

KINGMAN, LEE, GRACE HOGARTH, and HARRIET QUIMBY, eds. and comps. *Illustrators of Children's Books, 1967–1976.*

KLEMIN, DIANA. *The Art of Art for Children's Books.*

———. *The Illustrated Book: Its Art and Craft.*

KUNITZ, STANLEY J., and HOWARD HAYCRAFT, eds. *The Junior Book of Authors.*

LANE, MARGARET. *The Magic Years of Beatrix Potter.*

———. *The Tale of Beatrix Potter: A Biography.*

LARKIN, DAVID, ed. *The Art of Nancy Ekholm Burkert.*

———. *Once Upon a Time: Some Contemporary Illustrators of Fantasy.*

LEAR, EDWARD. *Lear in the Original: 110 Drawings for Limericks and Other Nonsense.*

LINDER, ENID, and LESLIE L. LINDER. *The Art of Beatrix Potter.*

MacCANN, DONNARAE, and OLGA RICHARD. *The Child's First Books: A Critical Study of Pictures and Text.*

MAHONY, BERTHA E., LOUISE P. LATIMER, and BEULAH FOLMSBEE, comps. *Illustrators of Children's Books, 1744–1945.*

MAHONY, BERTHA and ELINOR WHITNEY, comps. *Contemporary Illustrators of Children's Books.*

MILLER, BERTHA MAHONY, and ELINOR WHITNEY FIELD, eds. *Caldecott Medal Books: 1938–1957.*

MOORE, ANNE CARROLL. *A Century of Kate Greenaway.*

MUIR, PERCY. *English Children's Books, 1600 to 1900.*

PITZ, HENRY C. *Howard Pyle: Writer, Illustrator, Founder of the Brandywine School.*

———. *Illustrating Children's Books: History, Technique, Production.*

———. *The Practice of American Book Illustration.*

———, ed. *A Treasury of American Book Illustration.*

QUINNAN, BARBARA, comp. *Fables from Incunabula to Modern Picture Books.*

RICHARD, OLGA. "The Visual Language of the Picture Book."

ROBINSON, EVELYN ROSE. *Readings About Children's Literature.* Part 5, "Illustrations and Children's Books."

VIGUERS, RUTH HILL, MARCIA DALPHIN, and BERTHA MAHONY MILLER, comps. *Illustrators of Children's Books, 1946–1956.*

WARD, MARTHA E., and DOROTHY A. MARQUARDT. *Illustrators of Books for Young People.*

WHALLEY, JOYCE IRENE. *Cobwebs to Catch Flies: Illustrated Books for the Nursery and Schoolroom, 1700–1900.*

PART THREE:

Exploring the Types of Literature

Chapter Seven: Folk Tales

Folklore is sometimes referred to as the "mirror of a people." It reveals their efforts to explain—and perhaps to propitiate—the phenomena of nature which they did not understand, it expresses their interpretation of the relationships among human beings and their fears and desires, it records the mores and the cultural patterns of the society from which it stems, and it gives expression to such deep, universal emotions as joy, grief, fear, jealousy, and awe. Folklore, in the broadest sense of the word, includes all of the great stream of anonymous creation that is the accumulated wisdom and art of simple, everyday people: nursery rhymes, superstitions, games and songs, nursery rhymes and ballads, dance rituals, medicinal arts, old tales, verses and proverbs, fables, myths, legends, hero tales, and epics.

In early times, before universal education brought a widespread reading population, folk literature was meant for people of all ages; in today's more primitive societies where few people can read, this is still true, and the dependence on the oral tradition is still strong. What has changed, in more sophisticated societies, is the primary audience for the folk tale. Today most folk literature is read by children, or read or told to them, even though it was not created for them alone, for the most part. It is natural that children should be the primary audience for folk tales, since the qualities that are universally found in the tales are those to which children respond in any story: the folk tale starts briskly and continues to be filled with action; it often has humor; it appeals to children's sense of justice, since many tales reward good and punish evil; it has little nuance of characterization, so that characters are presented as entirely good, bad, obedient, lazy, and so on; it often includes rhyme or repetition; it is usually pithy; it usually has a satisfying and definite conclusion. In other words, all the things that children, especially small children, like. And if it has magic—and most do—so much the better.

Of the many varieties of folklore, the folk tale is the most familiar and perhaps the most appealing. Interest in folk tales developed in the eighteenth century along with interest in old ballads, but in the nineteenth century a romantic interest in the old tales grew so strong that many thousands were collected all over the globe. Striking similarities were noticed among the folk tales found in different parts of the world, and many theories were advanced to explain these similarities.

Theories of Folk-Tale Origin

Monogenesis

One of the earliest explanations for the similarities among folk tales of different peoples was the Aryan myth theory. The theory asserted that all folk tales came from the Teutonic myths of a single ancestral group. This is sometimes referred to as the theory of *monogenesis* or "single origin." Although the Aryan myth theory has been refuted, it is interesting today because it has been the springboard for some other theories of folk-tale origin.

Polygenesis

One group of scholars believed in the theory of *polygenesis*, or "many origins." They asserted that human beings everywhere in the world are moved by much the same emotions—love and pity, fear and anguish, jealousy and hatred; that all people can observe the results of greed, selfish ambition, or quiet courage and kindliness; that all have seen the ways of cruel stepmothers (Were there no loving ones in the old days, one wonders?); and that all have seen neglected children come into their own. So Andrew Lang and other believers in polygenesis insisted that similar plots could develop in different parts of the world from similar situations common to all humanity. Lang used the widely disseminated

Viewpoint

The fairy tale is a basic form of literature, and of art in general. The ease and calm assurance with which it stylizes, sublimates, and abstracts makes it the quintessence of the poetic process, and art in the twentieth century has again been receptive to it. We no longer view it as mere entertainment for children and those of childlike disposition. The psychologist, the pedagogue, knows that the fairy tale is a fundamental building block and an outstanding aid in development for the child; the art theorist perceives in the fairy tale—in which reality and unreality, freedom and necessity, unite—an archetypal form of literature which helps lay the groundwork for all literature, for all art. We have attempted to show, in addition, that the fairy tale presents an image of man which follows almost automatically from its over-all style. The fairy-tale style isolates and unites: its hero is thus isolated and, for this very reason, capable of entering into universal relationships. The style of the fairy tale and its image of man are of timeless validity and at the same time, of special significance in our age.—Max Lüthi, *Once Upon a Time; On the Nature of Fairy Tales*, translated by Lee Chadeayne and Paul Gottwald with additions by the author, Frederick Ungar Publishing Co., New York, 1970, p. 146.

story of Jason to prove his point. This theory would seem to account for the literally hundreds of variants of "Cinderella" found in Egypt, India, all parts of Europe, and among the North American Indians.

However, modern social anthropologists point out that people are *not* the same the world over. In some cultures, for instance, stepmothers may not be feared at all. The Andaman Islanders apparently are indifferent to whether the children they bring up are their own or other people's—no stepmother problem there! Another objection made to polygenesis is that the same story in all its peculiar details and chains of events could scarcely have grown up quite independently among entirely different groups isolated from each other. But whether there is any validity to the theory of polygenesis, one thing is certain: almost all peoples have produced stories and there are striking similarities among tales of different groups.

Remnants of Myth and Ritual

Some students, convinced that the folk tales preserve the *remnants of nature myths*, continually interpret any traditional story as a nature allegory—whether it is about sleep or forgetfulness, about a hero battling with a dragon, or about a girl being carried off by a polar bear. "Little Red Riding Hood," for instance, has been interpreted as an allegory of sunset and sunrise. The wolf is supposed to symbolize night, and in many versions he succeeds in devouring the little girl, who in her red cape represents the setting sun. This symbolic interpretation is extended in the Grimm version of the story, in which the hunters cut open the wolf and release "Little Red-Cap," the sun, from her imprisonment in the wolf, or night. The Norse "East o' the Sun" with its polar bear and its disappearing Prince was, like the Balder myth (see Chapter 8, p. 198), supposed to explain the disappearance of the sun.

Other folklorists, while not interpreting all the old stories as nature allegories, believed that many of these tales preserved *remnants of other kinds of religious myth and ritual*. For instance, Sir George Webbe Dasent thought that the Norse folk tales contained many of the elements of the Norse myths. He explained that after Christianity came to the Scandinavian countries, the old Norse gods lost their prestige and were gradually changed into the fabulous

As she was coming home
she came to a stile,
and she said:
"Pig, pig, get over the stile,
Or I shan't get home tonight."

"I won't," said the pig.

5

From *The Old Woman and Her Pig* by Paul Galdone. Copyright © 1960. Used with permission of McGraw-Hill Book Company.

creatures of the folk tales. Odin became the Wild Huntsman riding through the sky with his grisly crew. And perhaps the nursery tale of "The Three Billy-Goats Gruff" preserves the memory of Thor's battle with the Frost Giants, for the billy goat was the ancient symbol of Thor, and the huge, stupid trolls could easily be the inglorious descendants of the Frost Giants.

Some scholars believe that cumulative tales like "The House That Jack Built" and "The Old Woman and Her Pig" have ritualistic origins. Other stories too, they think, preserve fragments of spells or incantations. In the Grimms' dramatic "The Goose-Girl," the heroine puts a spell on Conrad's hat:

Blow, blow, thou gentle wind, I say,
Blow Conrad's little hat away. . . .

Ancient superstitions and customs surrounding christenings and marriage ceremonies may also be found in the folk tales. So may propitiations of spirits, witches, the devil, or certain powerful animals (like the bear in the Norse tales).

Origins in Dreams and Unconscious Emotions

Psychoanalytic writers have studied those objects and ideas which appear frequently in fairy tales from all over the world and have asserted that they are *symbols of emotional fantasy* which all people experience. Among such supposedly universal feelings are unconscious sexual love for the parent, hatred of paternal or maternal authority, love or jealousy among brothers and sisters. The ideas and objects representing these feelings are supposed to be the same in folk tales the world over and to explain the similarities among these stories. But social anthropologists object to this theory, too. They maintain that unconscious emotions vary among different peoples and so do the symbols which represent them. The unconscious emotions described, they say, may be the characteristic product of modern urban life rather than expressions that are universal among all peoples, places, and times.

Some authorities think that the stories originated in the *dreams or nightmares* of the storytellers. Stories about a poor girl sent out to find strawberries in the middle of winter (some versions clothe her in a paper dress) might well grow from the bad dreams we have when the night turns cold and we find ourselves with too few blankets. Or consider the story of the poor girl in "East o' the Sun," who kissed the prince and then found herself out on a lonely road—the prince gone, the castle vanished, the little bell that fulfilled her every wish lost forever, and she in rags once more. Is she the embodiment of our anxieties and our reluctance to return from our dreams to a workaday world? So the fatal questions, impossible tasks, and endless discomforts in the folk tales may suggest some of the anxieties that haunt us in our sleep now and then. Perhaps the primitive quality of some of our dreams may also explain the shocking elements in some of the tales. These always seem less horrible in the stories than they actually should seem because they are seldom attended by any realistic details but are indeed vague, dreamlike, and evanescent.

Another phase of the psychological interpretation of folk-tale origin is the idea that the people who created the tales found in fancy the *satisfaction of unconscious frustrations or drives.* These imaginative tales provide *wish fulfillment.* That is, the oppressed peasants who produced some of the tales were "motivated by naive dreams of the success of the despised," and so they told stories about cinder lads going from wretched hovels to fabulous castles, or about a goose girl marrying the prince. It is certain that fairy tales do satisfy deep human needs, particularly the needs for security and competence. In the folk tales, banquets, servants, glittering jewels, and rich clothes are concrete symbols of success. Granting that these tales are primarily

Viewpoint

Having had story built in with childhood, a person is usually in better relation with the pathologized material of obscene, grotesque, or cruel images which appear spontaneously in dream and fantasy. Those who hold to the rationalist and associationist theory of mind, who put reason against and superior to imagination, argue that if we did not put in such grim tales in early impressionable years, we would have less pathology and more rationality in later years. My practice shows me rather that the more attuned and experienced is the imaginative side of personality the less threatening the irrational, the less necessity for repression, and therefore the less actual pathology acted out in literal, daily events. In other words, through story the symbolic quality of pathological images and themes finds a place, so that these images and themes are less likely to be viewed naturalistically, with clinical literalism, as signs of sickness. These images find places in story as legitimate. They *belong* to myths, legends, and fairy tales where, just as in dreams, all sorts of peculiar figures and twisted behaviors appear.—James Hillman, "A Note on Story," *Children's Literature,* vol. 3. Copyright © 1974 by Francelia Butler. Reprinted by permission of Francelia Butler; Children's Literature An International Journal, Inc., Box 370, Windham Center, Connecticut 06280.

for entertainment, there seems to be little doubt that they contain a deeper meaning and an inner significance which the child or adult feels without being conscious of the cause. In discussing Perrault's fairy tales Jacques Barchilon and Henry Pettit say, "Just as the dream expresses innermost wishes in disguised form, the fairy tale masks our real wishes with the appearance of a free fantasy." And again they emphasize the symbolic character of the tales saying, ". . . the veiled symbolism of the fairy tale and its violence fulfill a need in the child's life. The fairy tale is his apprenticeship to life."[1]

Psychoanalysts also hold that "the child, through the comparison between the fantastic and the real, gradually learns to test reality. When children realize that the fairy tale is fictitious, they learn to enjoy it as fiction. This is one giant step not only in the process of rational maturation but in aesthetic development as well."[2]

1. Jacques Barchilon and Henry Pettit, *The Authentic Mother Goose Fairy Tales and Nursery Rhymes* (Swallow, 1960), p. 27.
2. Ibid., p. 26.

Cement of Society

In recent times the science of folklore has merged more and more into the science of social anthropology. To understand the why and wherefore of folk tales, anthropologists have lived intimately with many peoples, visiting their homes, markets, religious ceremonies, and festal celebrations. Of course they cannot visit early peoples who produced the folk tales, but their studies of contemporary societies can cast light on the origin of the old folk tales. Their conclusion may be summed up in one sentence: folk tales have been the *cement of society*. They not only expressed but codified and reinforced the way people thought, felt, believed, and behaved.

Folk tales taught children and reminded their elders of what was proper and moral. They put the stamp of approval upon certain values held by the group, and thus cemented it together with a common code of behavior. They taught kindness, modesty, truthfulness, courage in adversity—and they made virtue seem worthwhile because it was invariably rewarded and evil just as invariably punished. This idea of folk tales as carriers of the moral code helps explain the ethical significance and emotional satisfaction they still hold for us today.

Some of the explanations for the origins of folk tales are dubious, but many of them are reinforced by enough reasonable evidence to make them seem both plausible and probable.

*Viewpoint*_____

The student of fairy tales . . . is aware, of course, if he is experienced, that however ancient the stories may be he must not think of them as if they were archaeological remains, as if they were the actual objects that existed in the past; nor must he regard them (as folklorists used to do) as antiques that have been so scarred by time they have become almost unrecognizable, for this presupposes that they were once whole and perfect, and have ever since been in a state of decay. He knows instead that since they are living things, not fossils, they are subject to mutation. They are as likely to have grown as they became older, as to have shrunk. They are as likely to have acquired significance, or to have acquired fresh significance, as they have passed through sophisticated communities, as to have lost it.—Iona and Peter Opie, *The Classic Fairy Tales*, Oxford University Press, London, 1974, p. 17.

Folklorists now agree that the folk tale is created by most peoples at an early level of civilization. Historically, the tales may contain elements from past religions, rituals, superstitions, or past events. Psychologically, they may serve to satisfy in symbolic form some of humanity's basic emotional needs. Ethically, they may be "the cement of society"—reinforcing our faith in morality and the ultimate triumph of good over evil.

Diffusion of the Folk Tales

Students have found recognizable variants of such tales as "Jason and the Golden Fleece" and "Cinderella" in the manuscripts of ancient India, Egypt, and Greece and on the lips of storytellers in Zulu huts, Navaho hogans, and Samoan villages—from the Russian steppes to African jungles and the mountains of South America. The three tasks, the flight, the pursuit, the lost slipper or sandal, and the undoing of a spell are found in innumerable societies. How were they carried?

First, of course, they were carried orally by the migrations of whole peoples. Later they traveled from one country to another with sailors and soldiers, women stolen from their tribes, slaves and captives of war, traders, minstrels and bards, monks and scholars, and young gentlemen on the grand tour. Some storytellers no doubt polished and improved the tales, while others debased them. If the folk tales traveled by land, they were passed on by many peoples and greatly changed in the process; but if they traveled by sea, they stayed closer to the originals. Sometimes one story theme would combine with others, producing either a variant of the original tale or a relatively new one. So ancient storytellers preserved old stories, produced variants of others, and occasionally dreamed up new ones to pass on. This process is one that continues even today.

The literary (or written) sources of the popular tales did not begin to circulate in Europe until around the twelfth century. Then came the Indian and Irish manuscript collections, vivid and lively importations which were no doubt partly responsible for the flowering of folk art in the thirteenth century. Ballads and stories began to bubble up everywhere, often with the same plots or themes.

During the sixteenth century, popular literature in England made a dignified beginning in print with Caxton's fine English translations of Aesop's fables, the King Arthur stories, the Homeric epics. In England, too, the chapbooks picked up fragments of tales from everywhere and kept them alive in garbled but recognizable versions, dearly beloved by the people.

Predominant Kinds of Folk Tales

No adult can read folk tales without being conscious of the varied groups into which they fall: cumulative tales, talking-beast tales, drolls or humorous tales, realistic tales, religious tales, romances, and, of course, tales of magic. Many classifications have been made, but this one seems to bring in most of the kinds and to emphasize their characteristics.

Illustration by Hans Fischer. Reproduced from *Grimm's Traveling Musicians*, by permission of Harcourt Brace Jovanovich, Inc. (Original in color)

Cumulative Tales

Very young children enjoy the simplest of all stories, the cumulative or repetitional tale. Its charm lies in its minimum plot and maximum rhythm. Its episodes follow each other neatly and logically in a pattern of cadenced repetition. Sometimes, as in "The Old Woman and Her Pig," the action moves upward in a spiral and then retraces the spiral downward to the conclusion. Sometimes, as in the American-English "Johnny-Cake," the Norse "Pancake," and the American "Gingerbread Boy," the action takes the form of a race, and the story comes to an end with the capture of the runaway. Fortunately, the runaway in such stories has forfeited our sympathy by stupidity ("Henny Penny"), or by impudence ("The Pancake"), so that the capture becomes merely the downfall of the foolish or the proud.

Some cumulative stories, like "The House That Jack Built," are mere chants; others, like "The Three Little Pigs" and "The Bremen Town-Musicians," are repetitional and sequential, but have well-rounded plots. Modern examples of the successful use of this pattern are Marjorie Flack's *Ask Mr. Bear*, Wanda Gág's *Millions of Cats*, and Maurice Sendak's *One Was Johnny*.

Talking-Beast Tales

Perhaps young children love best of all folk tales the ones in which animals talk. Sometimes the animals talk with human beings as in "Puss in Boots" but more often with other animals as in "The Cat and the Mouse in Partnership." These creatures talk every bit as wisely as humans, or as foolishly. Possibly their charm lies in the opportunity they give the reader to identify with the cleverest of the three pigs or the most powerful and efficient of "The Three Billy-Goats Gruff." Perhaps the credulity of "Henny Penny" or of the two foolish pigs ministers to the listener's sense of superiority. Certainly children are amused by these old tales for the same reasons that modern children laugh at Snoopy in Charles Schulz's *Peanuts* cartoons. The animals in both the old and the modern creations are exaggerated characterizations of human beings, and in that exaggeration lie their humor and fascination.

These beast tales generally teach a lesson—the folly of credulity and the rewards of courage, ingenuity, and independence—though their didacticism does not stand out so much as in the fables. The stories are so lively and diverting that they are primarily good entertainment. Perhaps the most successful of the modern descendants of the ancient beast tales are Beatrix Potter's *The Tale of Peter Rabbit*, *The Tale of Benjamin Bunny*, and all her other *Tales*. These have joined the ranks of the immortals, along with "The Three Little Pigs."

The Drolls or Humorous Tales

A small body of the folk tales are obviously meant as fun and nonsense. These are the stories about sillies or numskulls, such as the Grimms' "Clever Elsie."

As you may remember, Elsie had a wooer who demanded a really clever bride. On one of his visits, Elsie's family sent her down to the cellar to draw some beer, and there, just over her head, she saw a pick-axe that had been left thrust into the masonry. Immediately she began to weep, thinking to herself,

"If I get Hans, and we have a child, and he grows big, and we send him into the cellar here to draw beer, then the pick-axe will fall on his head and kill him."

She cried so hard and so long that first one member of the household and then another came down to the cellar, listened to her tale, and began to weep, too. Finally, Hans came and, hearing how things were, decided that Elsie was indeed a thoughtful, clever girl and married her. After the marriage Hans, who had evidently taken his bride's measure at last, gave Elsie a task to do in the field and left her there alone. But Elsie, unable to decide whether to work first or sleep first, finally fell asleep in the field and slept until night. Returning home in a great fright, she asked,

"Hans, is Elsie within?" "Yes," answered Hans, "she is within." Hereupon she was terrified, and said: "Ah, heavens! Then it is not I."

And so she ran out of the village and was never seen again.

Like the cumulative tales, the drolls vary in the amount of plot they develop. Some have well-rounded plots; for instance, in "The Husband Who Was to Mind the House" (he does so with disastrous results) and in "Mr. Vinegar" (who trades off his cow as the start of a series of barters which brings him less and less until he has nothing left but a good cudgeling

"And thanks to you for that!" said the wife.

Illustration by Theodor Kittelsen for *Norwegian Folk Tales* collected by Peter Christian Asbjörnsen and Jörgen Moe.

from his wife). The Norse story "Taper Tom" has not only all the droll antics to make the princess laugh but real adventure as well. Finally, the Norse "Squire's Bride" is not only a droll story but also a fine bit of adult satire on elderly wooers of young girls.

Realistic Tales

For the most part, the peoples who created these old tales seem to have had no great taste for using as story material their own "here and now," the stuff of everyday living. Even when they omit all elements of magic, they still tell a fabulous tale: the monster in "Blue Beard," for example, seems to have had some historic basis, but to young readers he is a kind of cross between an ogre and a giant. His English variant, "Mr. Fox," is even less realistic, though strictly speaking there is nothing in either story that could not have happened. Perhaps the prettiest of all realistic stories in our folk-tale collections is the Norse "Gudbrand on the Hillside." This is "Mr. Vinegar," with a loving wife instead of a shrew. Gudbrand's old wife thinks her man can do no wrong; so, sure of his wife's love and understanding, Gudbrand makes a wager with a neighbor that his wife will not blame him no matter what he does. Just as Gudbrand expects, his wife's tender responses to his series of disastrous trades reaches a climax with her heartfelt exclamation:

"Heaven be thanked that I have got you safe back again; you do everything so well that I want neither cock nor goose; neither pigs nor kine."

Then Gudbrand opened the door and said, "Well, what do you say now? Have I won the hundred dollars?" and his neighbour was forced to allow that he had.

Religious Tales

Folk tales using elements of religious beliefs are rarely found in children's collections but are fairly frequent in the complete editions of almost any group. Coming down from the morality plays of the Middle Ages, the devil and St. Peter appear usually in comic roles. The story of the devil who begged to be taken back to hell in order to escape from a shrew of a wife is a popular plot throughout Europe.

The Virgin Mary is usually introduced respectfully and even tenderly. St. Joseph is also introduced as a figure of compassion and as the administrator of poetic justice. The religious folk tales are generally either broadly comic or didactic and are, on the whole, not well adapted to children.

Romances

Romance in the folk tales is usually remote and impersonal, and the characters are often stereotypes. Aucassin and Nicolette are less interesting than their adventures. Enchantments and impossible tasks separate folk-tale lovers, and magic brings them together, whether they be Beauty and the Beast, the Goose Girl and the King, or the girl who traveled east o' the sun and west o' the moon to find her love.

Tales of Magic

Tales of magic are at the heart of folk tales. These are the stories which justify the children's name for the whole group—"fairy tales." Fairy godmothers, giants, water nixies, a noble prince turned into a polar bear, the North Wind giving a poor boy magic gifts to make good the loss of his precious meal, three impossible tasks to be performed, a lad searching for the Water of Life—these are some of the motifs and some of the magical people that give folk tales a quality so unearthly and so beautiful that they come close to poetry. A large proportion of folk tales are based upon magic of many kinds—so it is worthwhile to study these motifs and the fairy folk who flit so mysteriously through the tales.

Fairies and Other Magic Makers

The Little People

The belief in fairies was once astonishingly widespread and persistent among Celtic peoples (particularly in Ireland and Scotland). Even when belief is gone, certain superstitions remain. From these countries comes the idea of trooping fairies, ruled over by a fairy queen, dwelling underground in halls of great richness and beauty. These fairy raths (or forts) are the old subterranean earthworks remaining today in Ireland and Scotland, with the gold and glitter of jewels added by the Celtic imagination. From these hiding places, according to tradition, the fairies emerge at night to carry off men, maidens, or children who have caught their fancy. They may put spells on the cattle or on the work of humans they dislike, or they may come to the assistance of those who win their gratitude. To eat fairy food or to fall asleep in a fairy ring (a ring of especially green grass) or under a thorn tree on May Eve or Halloween is to put yourself in the power of the fairies for a year and a day.

The name by which you refer to these blithe spirits is also a matter of importance in Celtic lore. If you want to play safe, you will never use the word f-a-i-r-y, which reminds them of the unhappy fact that they have no souls. On the Day of Judgment when humans have a chance (however slight) of going up in glory, the wee folk know full well, poor soulless creatures that they are, that they will simply blow away like a puff of down in a strong wind. So address them tactfully as "the good people," "the little people," or "the wee folk," if you would be well treated in return.

Other countries have these little creatures, too. In Cornwall, they are called pixies or piskeys, and they, like their Irish relatives, ride tiny steeds over the moors. In the Arabian tales you meet the jinns, who also live in deserted ruins, often underground, and are respectfully addressed as "the blessed ones." The German dwarfs are usually subterranean in their work and sometimes in their dwelling, too. Although they seem not to insist upon any special form of address, to treat them disrespectfully is to incur sure punishment.

The Norse hill folk live underground also, as do some of the small fairy folk of England and Scotland. There are other resemblances among these three groups. The Norse countries have house spirits, the Tomten, much like the English Lar or Lob-Lie-by-the-Fire and the Scotch Aiken-drum. All these household spirits take up their abode in a house where they are well treated and make themselves useful in many ways. They may be propitiated by bowls of milk or offerings of parsley, chives, and garlic. But woe to the misguided soul who gives them clothes! Such a gift usually offends them and always drives them away, never to return. Oddly enough, the elves in the Grimms' "Shoemaker and the Elves" were delighted by the tiny garments, but they did depart, forever.

Viewpoint

Wise Women, Witches, and Wizards

A few of the fairy folk are consistently evil, but most of them fluctuate in their attitude toward human beings and may be either helpful or ruthless. The wise women, who come to christenings or serve as fairy godmothers, are, on the whole, a grave and serious group. They are not unlike our idea of the Fates, or Norns, who mark off the life span and foretell coming events. One of these wise women aided Cinderella, while a peevish one sent Beauty off to sleep for a hundred years.

Witches and wizards are usually wicked. They lure children into their huts to eat them, or they cast spells on noble youths and turn them into beasts. Russia has a unique witch, Baba Yaga, who lives in a house that walks around on chicken legs. When she wishes to fly, she soars off in a mortar and sweeps her way along with a besom (two objects which may have to be explained to children in advance, by the way). She has some other unique powers that make her quite as fascinating as she is gruesome.

The magicians and sorcerers cast spells but may sometimes be prevailed upon to do a kind deed and help out a worthy youth bent on the impossible. The Celtic "Merlin" is the most romantic of all the sorcerers, but he is seldom mentioned in the folk tales. The English "Childe Rowland," however, enlists Merlin's aid in rescuing Burd Ellen from Elfland.

Occasional imps, like the German "Rumpelstiltskin" and the English "Tom Tit Tot," are hard to classify. They seem to be a kind of hybrid elf and fiend, hoping to get hold of a gay, laughing child to cheer their old age, or of the bride who has to guess their names.

Giants and Ogres

Ogres and ogresses are always bloodthirsty and cruel. Giants, however, are of two kinds: the children call them "bad" and "good." The "bad giants" are a powerful clan using brute force against opponents. They swallow their antagonists whole, as tremendous power seems always to do in any age. They are ruthless and unscrupulous and must be dealt with on their own terms—deceit and trickery. But fortunately they are often thickheaded and rely too much on force, so that clever boys and girls like Jack or "Molly Whuppie" can outwit them and leave them completely befuddled.

The other tribe of giants we meet is the helpful one. They aid the lad who shares his last

Illustration by Blair Lent, from *Baba Yaga* by Ernest Small. Published by Houghton Mifflin Company. Copyright © 1966 by Blair Lent, Jr. Reproduced by permission of the publisher. (Original in color)

crust of bread with them, and of course their aid is magnificent. They can drink up the sea and hold it comfortably until it is convenient to release it again. They feel cold in the midst of fire and suffer from heat in solid ice. They can step lightly from mountain to mountain, break trees like twigs, and shatter rocks with a glance. The lad who lines up these giants on his side is guaranteed to win the princess and half the kingdom into the bargain. But no sluggard, no pompous pretender, no mean soul ever secures this aid. It is freely given only to honest folk about whom shines the grace of goodness.

Fairy Animals

In the world of fairy, domestic animals are as kindly disposed toward human beings as they are in the world of reality. For example, there is that handsome cat of cats, "Puss in Boots"—surely a child given a magic choice of one handy assistant from all the gallery of fairy helpers would choose the witty and formidable Puss. The Norse "Dapplegrim" is a horse of

parts and does fully as well for his master as the Russian Horse of Power in "The Firebird."

Occasionally wild animals take a hand in the magic events of the folk tales. In the Norse story, a gray wolf carries the king's son to the castle of "The Giant Who Had No Heart in His Body," and in the Czech story, old Lishka the fox gives "Budulinek" a ride on her tail, to his sorrow. Wild animals may be for or against human beings. Sometimes they serve merely as transportation, but often they are the real brains of an enterprise.

Magic Objects

In "Herding the King's Hares," Espen Cinderlad receives a remarkable whistle for his kindness to an old hag. With it he can bring order to every runaway bunny in the king's herd, and finally to the royal family as well:

Then the king and queen thought it best to give him the princess and half the kingdom; it just couldn't be helped.
  "That certainly was some whistle," said Espen Cinderlad.

"Molly Whuppie," when pursued by the double-faced giant, runs lightly across the Bridge of One Hair, on which the giant dares take not so much as a single step. That is the kind of power every one of us needs to develop—the power to find a bridge, however slight, on which we can run lightly away from the ogres pursuing us. The folk tales are full of these "Fools of the World," who learn how to use magic tools as the pompous and pretentious never learn to do. Espen Cinderlad, with three impossible tasks to perform, hunts around until he finds the self-propelled axe, the spade, and the trickling water that could be stopped or let loose by him alone. Each of these magic objects told him it had been waiting a long, long time, just for him. The message would seem to be that magic is always waiting for those who know how to use it.

Enchanted People

Being put under a spell is just one of the many complications that beset the heroes and heroines of the fairy tales. Childe Rowland's sister unknowingly courted disaster by running around the church "widdershins"—counterclockwise—and so put herself under the power of the fairies. "Rapunzel," of the long, long hair, was locked up in a tower by a cruel enchantress who was so clever that only a super-prince could worst her. And there are many variants of the folk tale about the royal brothers who are changed into birds, and who can be released from their enchantment only after their little sister has gone speechless for seven long years and spun each of them a shirt of thistledown. The Grimms' touching "The Frog-King" is one of many tales in which either the husband or the wife is a fairy creature or is in the power of some witch or sorcerer. Of these, the Grimms' "The Water-Nixie" is perhaps the most exciting and the Norse "East o' the Sun and West o' the Moon," the most beautiful. In all such stories only love, loyalty, and self-sacrifice can break the enchantment and restore the beloved.

On the whole, the good and evil supernatural forces in the folk tales act according to certain laws. If magic makes wishes come true and points the way to happiness, it does so only with struggles and hardships on the part of the hero or heroine. The true princess suffers pitifully before magic opens the king's eyes and he sees her for what she is—the rightful bride for his son and a gentle, loving girl. These stories are not didactic, but one after another shows that courage and simple goodness work their own magic in this world, that evil must be conquered even if it carries us to the gates of death, and that grace and strength are bestowed upon those who strive mightily and keep honest, kindly hearts.

Distinctive Elements of Folk Tales

For generation after generation, folk tales have continued to be popular with children. Modern youngsters, surrounded by the mechanical gadgets and scientific wonders of our age, are still spellbound by their magic. A brief examination of their form, style, and character portrayal may help explain the charm of the old tales for children. First of all, the form or pattern of the folk tales is curiously satisfying both to children and adults.

The Introduction

The introduction to a folk tale does exactly what its name implies. It *introduces* the reader to the leading characters, the time and place of the story, and the problem to be solved, or the conflict which is the essence of the story.

Viewpoint

The stories often involve the element of *contrast*. Sometimes there is the uneven conflict, which always makes a story more exciting: "Hansel and Gretel" and the wicked witch—two little children pitted against an evil power; Snow White and the cruel Queen. Sometimes the contrast lies within a like group; for example, in "The Three Little Pigs," there are not only pigs and wolf but also a wise pig and foolish pigs. So in "Boots and His Brothers" the humble Boots shows the wisdom his older brothers lack. Contrast heightens the conflict and rouses the reader's sympathy for the weaker or less fortunate or more kindly member of the group.

Folk tales are *objective* and *understandable*, never abstract. They have to do with winning security, earning a living or a place in the world, accomplishing impossible tasks, escaping from powerful enemies, outwitting wicked schemes and schemers, and succeeding with nonchalance. These plots are as vital today as ever and account for the vigor of these old tales.

Time is effectively accounted for by a conventional phrase such as "Once upon a time," "Long ago and far away," "In olden times when wishing still helped one," "A thousand years ago tomorrow," or "Once on a time, and a very good time too." Such folk-tale conventions do more than convey an idea of long age; they carry the reader at once to a dream world where anything is possible.

The *scene* is even more briefly sketched. It is a road, a bridge, a palace, a forest, or a poor man's hut—a place where something is going to happen and soon. No wonder these introductions catch the child's attention. They launch the conflict with no distracting details.

Sometimes the folk tales, like the ballads, get off to such a brisk start that the introduction is almost imperceptible. This one for "The Three Billy-Goats Gruff" is a masterpiece of brevity:

Once on a time there were three Billy-goats, who were to go up to the hill-side to make themselves fat, and the name of all three was "Gruff."

On the way up was a bridge over a burn they had to cross; and under the bridge lived a great ugly Troll, with eyes as big as saucers, and a nose as long as a poker.

There you are! The scene is a bridge with a pleasant stretch of grassy hillside just beyond. The characters are three earnest billy goats of the Gruff family who are desirous of getting fat

on the hillside. Obstacle, Conflict, Problem live under the bridge in the person of an ugly Troll. In the fewest possible words, you have all the makings of a good plot. "The Sleeping Beauty," still a fairly uncomplicated story, must introduce the king, queen, courtiers, the grand christening for the baby princess in the palace, the good fairies for whom plates of gold have been prepared, and the evil fairy who is uninvited and minus a gold plate and therefore thoroughly angry. What will happen? This is the mark of a good introduction: it whets the appetite for more; you "go on" eagerly. For children, brevity of introduction is an important part of the charm of these folk tales. The excitement gets under way with minimum description.

The Development

The development carries forward the note of trouble sounded in the introduction. The quest begins, the tasks are initiated and performed, the flight gets under way, and obstacles of every kind appear, with the hero or heroine reduced to despair or helplessness or plunged

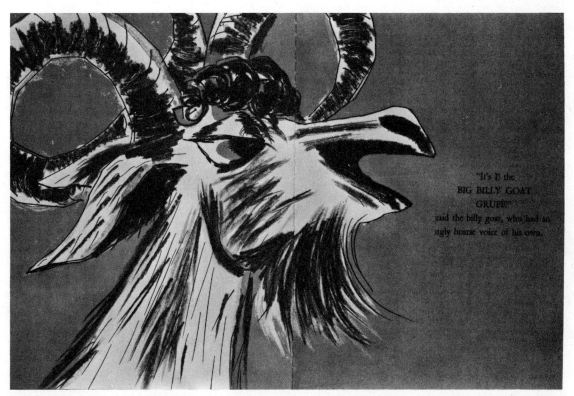

From *The Three Billy Goats Gruff* by Asbjörnsen and Moe, illustrated and copyright 1957 by Marcia Brown. Reproduced by permission of Harcourt Brace Jovanovich, Inc. (Original in color)

into more and more perilous action. This is the heart of the story—action that mounts steadily until it reaches a climax, when the problem or conflict will be resolved one way or the other.

The vigorous plots of the folk tales, full of suspense and action, appeal strongly to young readers. The heroes and heroines *do* things—they ride up glass hills, slay giants who have no hearts in their bodies, outwit wolves, get their rights from the North Wind, or pitch an old witch into an oven she intended for them. Here are no brooding introspectionists but doers of the vigorous sort.

If these tales are to carry conviction, development must be both logical (in terms of the story) and plausible. When in "The Three Little Pigs" one pig is so foolish as to build a house of straw and another to build a house of sticks, you know they are doomed. But when a pig has sufficient acumen to build his house stoutly of bricks, you know perfectly well he will also be smart enough to outwit his adversaries, for such a pig will survive in any society. Another example of a logical, plausible plot development is "Clever Manka," the witty Czech story that is a favorite with older children. Manka by her cleverness wins a fine husband, a judge and burgomaster; but he warns her that she will be banished from his house if she ever uses her cleverness to interfere with his business. Knowing Manka and realizing that one cannot help using what wit the Lord gave one, you feel the conflict approaching. Of course Manka learns of a case where her husband has rendered a flagrantly unfair judgment, and in the interest of justice she interferes. She is found out and banished, but in the face of this ultimate catastrophe, she uses her wit and saves both herself and her husband from permanent unhappiness. Here is a realistic folk tale of clever mind against duller mind, with the clever one saving them both. The ending is surprising but completely logical.

Many of the tales we know preserve unity of interest. Every episode in "The Lad Who Went to the North Wind" concerns the boy's struggles to get his rights for the meal that the North Wind blew away. To achieve unity, a story must preserve a certain economy of incidents. Too many episodes, too long-drawn-out suspense, or too much magic destroys the unity of the tale. The development often contains three tasks or three riddles or three trials. Perhaps there is no particular significance in

Viewpoint

Children are capable, of course, of *literary belief,* when the story-maker's art is good enough to produce it. . . . He makes a Secondary World which your mind can enter. Inside it, what he relates is "true": it accords with the laws of that world. You therefore believe it, while you are, as it were, inside. The moment disbelief arises, the spell is broken; the magic, or rather art, has failed.

. . . at no time can I remember that the enjoyment of a story was dependent on belief that such things could happen, or had happened, in "real life." Fairy stories were plainly not primarily concerned with possibility, but with desirability. If they awakened *desire,* satisfying it while often whetting it unbearably, they succeeded.

. . . The dragon had the trademark *Of Faërie* written plain upon him. . . . Of course, I in my timid body did not wish to have them in the neighbourhood. . . .

This is, naturally, often enough what children mean when they ask: "Is it true?" They mean: "I like this, but is it contemporary? Am I safe in my bed?" The answer: "There is certainly no dragon in England today," is all that they want to hear.—J. R. R. Tolkien, *Tree and Leaf,* Houghton Mifflin, Boston, 1965, pp. 36–37, 40, 41.

the "three" except that the old storyteller, always properly audience-conscious as a good storyteller should be, could see that suspense can be endured just so long before people get impatient. Molly Whuppie can use her bridge of one hair three times and after that she had better finish things off and get home. For it is on suspense that the successful development of folk-tale action depends. Suspense is built up and maintained until it reaches a peak in the climax, after which it declines and the action ends with a flourish.

The Conclusion

The conclusion usually comes swiftly and is as brief as the introduction. In "The Three Billy-Goats Gruff," the ringing challenge of the biggest billy goat announces the climax. The fight ensues, the biggest billy goat is the winner and the Gruff family is now free to eat grass and get fat for the rest of its days. In "The Sleeping Beauty," the kiss breaks the spell for the princess and the whole court, the royal wedding quickly takes place, and in most modern versions that is all, except for the conventional blessing "and they lived happily ever after."

The conclusion ends everything that was started in the introduction. Not only do the heroes and heroines achieve a happy solution for their troubles and a triumphant end to their struggles, but the villains are accounted for and satisfyingly punished. Such conclusions satisfy children's eye-for-an-eye code of ethics and apparently leave their imaginations untroubled—probably because they usually have no harrowing details and are so preposterous that they move cheerfully out of reality.

The folk tale has some conventional endings that are as picturesque as the openings. "The Three Billy-Goats Gruff" concludes

Snip, snap, snout
This tale's told out.

Other endings are: "If they haven't left off their merry-making yet, why, they're still at it"; "A mouse did run, the story's done"; "And no one need ask if they were happy"; "Whosoever does not believe this must pay a taler" (or as we should say, a dollar); "And the mouth of the person who last told this is still warm"; "And now the joy began in earnest. I wish you had been there too." For little children, the chance to vary the name in the last line of the following conclusion makes it one of their favorites.

My tale is done,
Away it has run
To little Augusta's house.

Style

One of the charms of the folk tale is the language and manner of telling the story. For these tales were never read silently; they were told until their form and language patterns were fixed. Consider "Go I know not whither, bring back I know not what," or

"Little pig, little pig, let me come in."
"No, no, by the hair of my chinny chin chin."
"Then I'll huff and I'll puff and I'll blow your house in."

Or read that matchless ending, "As for the Prince and Princess, they . . . flitted away as far as they could from the castle that lay East o' the Sun and West o' the Moon." These are brief examples of folk-tale style—frequently ca-

denced, sometimes humorous, sometimes romantic—with the words suited to the mood and tempo of the tale.

The beginnings and endings of the stories, of course, are particularly good examples of the storyteller's skill in establishing the predominant mood of the story, or breaking off and sending the listeners back to their workaday world. But dialogue in these old stories is also a part of their style—it runs along so naturally that real people seem to be talking. Read aloud the conversation between the old man and his wife in "Gudbrand on the Hill-side." Never once does the swift interchange of news and comments falter for a descriptive phrase such as "said he *uneasily*," or "said she *reassuringly*." Here is just a rapid, natural give-and-take between two people:

"Nay, but I haven't got the goat either," said Gudbrand, "for a little farther on I swopped it away, and got a fine sheep instead."

"You don't say so!" cried his wife; "why, you do everything to please me, just as if I had been with you. What do we want with a goat! . . . Run out child, and put up the sheep."

"But I haven't got the sheep any more than the rest," said Gudbrand; "for when I had gone a bit farther I swopped it away for a goose."

"Thank you! thank you! with all my heart," cried his wife. . . .

So they proceed from disaster to disaster without a single literary interpolation. Notice, too, that the words suffice to establish unmistakably the attitude of each speaker. Words so perfectly chosen make long descriptions unnecessary.

Another characteristic of folk-tale style is the use of rhymes. Indeed, the stories are sometimes part prose and part verse in the old sing-and-say pattern of "Aucassin and Nicolette." Cante-fables, such stories are called—that is, singing stories or verse stories. The frequency of rhymes in some of the old folk tales has caused some speculation about whether the folk tales came from the ballads or the ballads from the tales, since both often have the same subjects. This is a matter for the specialists to settle, but certainly the little rhymes add greatly to the interest of the tales.

"The Well of the World's End" ("The Frog-King") alternates prose and verse, with the frog singing over and over the same words except for the request in the first two lines in which he raises his demands each time:

"Give me some supper, my hinny, my heart,
  Give me some supper, my darling;
Remember the words you and I spake,
  In the meadow, by the Well of the World's End."

Some of the prettiest verses in the folk tales are in the Grimms' "The Goose-Girl" and in the English "The Black Bull of Norroway." The former breaks into rhyme when the faithful horse, Falada, speaks to his mistress. And after he has been killed and his head nailed to the dark gateway, the Goose-Girl, who is really the princess, weeps beneath the gateway saying:

"Alas, Falada, hanging there!"

Then the head answered:

"Alas, young Queen, how ill you fare!
If this your mother knew,
Her heart would break in two."

This piteous dialogue is followed by the song of the Goose-Girl, putting a spell on young Conrad, because he takes too much delight in her golden hair:

"Blow, blow, thou gentle wind, I say,
Blow Conrad's little hat away,
And make him chase it here and there,
Until I have braided all my hair,
And bound it up again."

The Grimms' "Cinderella," "Hansel and Gretel," "The Fisherman and His Wife," "The Juniper Tree," "Little Snow-White," and many others have memorable rhymes which some adults can still recite. The English tales are especially full of them. But many other folk tales are marked by the subtle art of the storyteller who has perfected a fine oral pattern in which rhymes frequently appear.

Character Portrayal

The interest of the modern short story frequently depends far more upon characters than upon plot or action. This is not true of folk tales. Plot is of first importance, and the characters are more or less typed. The good people in these stories are altogether good, and the wicked are so completely wicked that we waste no sympathy on them when, in the end, they are liquidated. So, too, the animals in the folk tales stand for simple traits like loyalty, cleverness, slyness, cruelty.

Reprinted with permission of Macmillan Publishing Co., Inc. From *Grimm's Household Stories* translated by Lucy Crane and illustrated by Johannes Troyer. Copyright 1954 by Macmillan Publishing Co., Inc.

But look for brief flashes of characterization here and there. Cinderella is a teenage girl with her mind on balls and fine clothes. Red Riding Hood is good-hearted but irresponsible. The Lad who went to the North Wind to get his rights for the wasted meal is one of those dogged, stick-to-itive boys who, with right on his side, is going to get his way in the world or know the reason why.

Sometimes the characters are passive, like the Sleeping Beauty, but still sufficiently individual so that each one arouses different reactions. Beauty's doom, hanging over her youth and loveliness like a black cloud, inspires only pity. But the silly, feckless girl in "Tom Tit Tot," with her big appetite and meager wit, is so absurd that you don't particularly mind the hard bargain "that" drives with her.

So while folk-tale people are strongly typed as "good" or "bad" with no subtle distinctions between, they may also be individualized. Sympathy or antagonism is aroused in different degrees by the brief characterizations. A whole portrait gallery of lads and lassies, goose-girls and princes, kings and queens remains in your memory, distinct and convincingly true to human nature.

Why Use Folk Tales with Children Today?

When the poet W. H. Auden reviewed the Pantheon edition of *Grimms' Fairy Tales* for *The New York Times* (November 12, 1944), he made this rather startling statement:

For, among the few indispensable, common-property books upon which Western Culture can be founded—that is, excluding the national genius of specific peoples as exemplified by Shakespeare and Dante—it is hardly too much to say that these tales rank next to the Bible in importance.

Later in the review he added:

It will be a mistake, therefore, if this volume is merely bought as a Christmas present for a child; it should be, first and foremost, an educational "must" for adults, married or single, for the reader who has once come to know and love these tales will never be able again to endure the insipid rubbish of contemporary entertainment.

Ethical Truth

Some people raise a great hue and cry about the ethics of the fairy tales. Of course, the folktale ethics are not always acceptable to the modern moral code. These stories were told by adults to adults in an age when using wits against brute force was often the only means of survival, and therefore admirable.

But folk tales are predominantly constructive, not destructive, in their moral lessons. "The humble and good shall be exalted," say the stories of "Little Snow-White," "Cinderella," "The Bremen Town-Musicians," and dozens of others. "Love suffereth long and is kind" is the lesson of "East o' the Sun" and "One-Eye, Two-Eyes, and Three-Eyes." In "The Frog-King," the royal father of the princess enforces a noble code upon his thoughtless daughter. "That which you have promised must you perform," he says sternly, and again, "He who helped you when you were in trouble ought not afterwards to be despised by you." Indeed, so roundly and soundly do these old tales stand for morality that they leave an indelible impression of virtue invariably rewarded and evil unfailingly punished.

Satisfaction of Needs

Most adults rereading these stories begin to understand Auden's feeling that they are timeless in their appeal. Plumbing, kitchen gadgets, and modes of transportation may change, but human desires and human emotions continue strong and unchanging. These old fairy tales contain in their "picture language" the symbols of some of the deepest human feelings and satisfy in fantasy human desires for security, competence, and love.

Everyone longs for security, the simple physical security of a snug house, warmth, and good food. In the fairy tales, the little hut in the forest is cozy and warm, safe from ravening wolves, and full of the peace of the fireside, with a loaf of bread baking on the hearth and a flavorsome kettle of soup on the hob. And of course there are castles, too; they may be a bit cold and drafty, but Jack or Tattercoats or Espen Cinderlad always seems to settle down very comfortably in the new grandeur. Children identify themselves with either the elegance of the castle or the snug security of the house in the woods. Both are satisfying: the castle speaks of achievement, the little hut of peace and safety.

Human beings are always in search of love. There will never be a time when people do not need loving reinforcement against the hostile world and the thought of death. The old tales are full of loving compensations for fears and hardships. Hansel reassures his little sister and protects her as long as he is able, and Gretel comes to his rescue when he is helpless and in peril. Commoners and royalty alike pursue their lost loves and endure every kind of suffer-

Viewpoint

Beware . . . of the defensive argument now used by "folklore" writers to justify their tampering with sources: "We have the same right as the original storytellers to tell a folktale in our own way." There is no more fundamental fallacy in the presentation of folk materials than this notion. The carrier of oral folk traditions continually alters the tale, song or saying he has heard; such change is at the very heart of oral, unrehearsed narration. But the calculating money-writer, using the very different medium of print in a self-conscious effort to reach readers who already associate "folklore" with froth and fun, is the voice not of the folk but of the mass culture.— Richard M. Dorson, *American Folklore*, The University of Chicago Press, Chicago and London, 1959, p. 4.

Viewpoint_____

. . . nothing in the entire range of "children's literature"—with rare exceptions—can be as enriching and satisfying to child and adult alike as the folk fairy tale. True, fairy tales teach little overtly about the specific conditions of life in modern mass society; these tales were created long before modern society came into being. But from them a child can learn more about the inner problems of man, and about solutions to his own (and our) predicaments in any society, than he can from any other type of story within his comprehension. Since the child is exposed at every moment to the society in which he lives, he will learn to cope with its conditions—provided, that is, that his inner resources permit him to do so. The child must therefore be helped to bring order into the turmoil of his feelings. He needs—and the point hardly requires emphasis at this moment in our history—a moral education that subtly, by implication only, conveys to him the advantages of moral behavior, not through abstract ethical concepts but through that which seems tangibly right and therefore has meaning for him. The child can find meaning through fairy tales.—Bruno Bettelheim, "The Uses of Enchantment," *The New Yorker*, December 8, 1975, p. 50.

ing to free them from enchantments. There is cruelty in these old tales and danger, too, but the real world, like the fairy world, can be cruel and perilous. In reassuring contrast are the symbols of love, lending strength to the weak, offering sanctuary to those in peril, and in the end rewarding their faithfulness or their struggles.

People long not only for love and security but for competence. They are eager to overcome difficulties, to right wrongs, and to stand fast in the face of danger—abilities essential for heroes of any generation. The fairy tales supply unforgettable stories of wicked powers defeated and of gallant souls who in their extremity are granted supernatural strength. Whether or not children are conscious of it, these stories may become sources of moral strength—a strength which is part faith, part courage, and wholly unshakable.

Variety

There is a folk tale for every mood. There are drolls and romances, tales of horror and of beauty. They cover every range of feeling.

Undoubtedly their first appeal to children is *exciting action.* Things happen in these stories with just the hair-raising rapidity that children yearn for in real life and rarely find.

Sometimes there is a strange quiet about these stories. The forest is so still you can hear one bird singing; a little lamb speaks softly to a fish in a brook; the enchanted castle is silent; and the prince falls asleep by the fountain from which gently flows the water of life. Reading some of these strange tales, you feel yourself relaxing. Here there is time for everything.

Children are a natural audience for folk material as is shown in the ways they use rhymes in their play, from the two-year-old murmuring nursery-rhyme refrains to the older child engaging in intricate counting-out games. Most children show a predilection for the cadence and color that are a part of the oral tradition. Children's calm acceptance of magical events and talking beasts in folk tales is not far removed from their own invention of imaginary companions. And in the enjoyment of folk tales children can assimilate a sense of their own cultural identity and an appreciation of others'.

Collections and Collectors

French Fairy Tales

The history of Perrault's unique *Contes de ma Mère l'Oye,* published in 1697 and translated into English in 1729, has already been discussed (p. 62). Perrault's eight stories have rather more polish and sophistication than is usual in the folk tales. In place of dull narrative, they are lively with conversations. Every necessary detail is logically provided for, or its omission underscored as a pivotal point in the plot.

Barbara Leonie Picard's *French Legends, Tales and Fairy Stories* (1955) contains four hero tales, six courtly tales of the Middle Ages, and thirteen legends, or folk tales, with no repetition of Perrault's famous eight. There is more magic in these tales than in Perrault's; the epic tales are full of battles and various complexities, the courtly tales are highly romantic, and the folk tales, though they contain some variants of familiar themes, are more mature in style than the stories they resemble. Good readers will enjoy this collection, and the storyteller will find fresh and exciting material in such stories as "The Grey Palfrey," "The Mouse-Princess," "The Stones of Plouhinec," and "Ripopet-Barabas."

In 1968, Geneviève Massignon's annotated, scholarly collection *Folktales of France* was published by the University of Chicago Press in the Folktales of the World series, a varied and representative selection. A collection long out of print has been made available again with the republication of the Comtesse d'Aulnoy's *The White Cat and Other Old French Fairy Tales* (1967), edited and translated by Rachel Field.

German Folk Tales

The conscientious Grimm brothers (Jacob, 1785–1863; Wilhelm, 1786–1859) began collecting tales with a passionate concern for sources. They were university professors—philologists— and their interest in sagas, ballads, popular tales, and all forms of traditional literature was at first secondary to their interest in the roots and development of the German language. This interest in grammar remained paramount with Jacob, but Wilhelm gradually became more interested in the tales than in any other phase of their work. When they began their collection, it was not with children in mind. They undertook their research as a part of a vast and scholarly study of language origins.

When *Kinder- und Hausmärchen*[3] appeared in

1812 (the second volume in 1815), it caused no particular stir in literary circles. Some critics considered the stories boorish; their publisher friend Brentano thought them slovenly; and yet somehow, in spite of the reviews, the stories were received with an unprecedented enthusiasm. Edition followed edition; translations began, first into Danish, Swedish, and French, then into Dutch, English, Italian, Spanish, Czech, and Polish—in all, some seventeen different languages.

The plots of these tales appeal to all ages from the seven-year-olds to adults, while the style has the peculiarly spellbinding quality of the great storytellers. The Grimms were fortunate in their sources. Besides the "story-wife," Frau Viehmann, there were Wilhelm Grimm's wife, Dortchen Wild, and her five sisters, who had been raised with these old tales and could tell them with effortless fluency. Other relatives, in-laws, and neighbors contributed to the collection.

3. *Nursery and Household Tales* is the usual translation, but for the German *Märchen* we have no precise translation. *Märchen* is legend, fiction, a cock-and-bull story, romance—in short, a fairy tale.

Illustration by Maurice Sendak. Reprinted with the permission of Farrar, Straus and Giroux, Inc. From *The Juniper Tree and Other Tales From Grimm*, selected by Lore Segal and Maurice Sendak, translated by Lore Segal, pictures by Maurice Sendak, copyright © 1973 by Maurice Sendak. Published in the United Kingdom by The Bodley Head, London.

To reread these stories is to find refreshment. Here are somber tales of children turned out to fend for themselves who find love and security after all their hardships. Here are fools, cheerful and irresponsible, and royal youths and maidens, dispossessed, reduced to misery and humiliation, but keeping their innate kindness and tenderness, and so finding love. Here youth responds to the call of great tasks and accomplishes the impossible. These stories color readers' attitudes toward life, toward human relationships, and toward moral standards. They are both fantasy and reality, and they are supremely entertaining. A two-volume edition of the Grimms' tales, *The Juniper Tree and Other Tales from Grimm*, as translated by Randall Jarrell and Lore Segal in a forthright fashion, has been superbly illustrated by Maurice Sendak. Seldom have tales and illustrations been so perfectly matched. Sendak's work is imaginative, tender but terrible, a tour de force. A number of both European and American artists have illustrated individual tales by the Grimm Brothers. Felix Hoffmann is notable for his strong delineation of characters, sturdy and realistic, as in *The Sleeping Beauty*, and in *The*

Bearskinner, one of the last books he illustrated before his death. Nancy Ekholm Burkert has individualized each dwarf in *Snow White and the Seven Dwarfs* with tenderness and delicacy. Trina Schart Hyman has given us another detailed interpretation of the same story as well as a romantic version of *The Sleeping Beauty*. Adrienne Adams's handsome illustrations for tales like *Hansel and Gretel* are deft and darkly colorful. An outstanding contemporary scholar of folklore, Kurt Ranke, has compiled a collection for the Folktales of the World series—*Folktales of Germany*, which includes stories from all German-speaking territories except Switzerland (stories of Switzerland are in a separate volume). Like the other books in the series, this has a wealth of background information about the folklore of the country and a useful section of notes and indexes.

Norwegian Folk Tales

When people talk about the Scandinavian folk tales, they usually mean a particular book, *East o' the Sun and West o' the Moon*, the collection

From *East of the Sun and West of the Moon* by Ingri and Edgar Parin d'Aulaire. Copyright 1938, renewed 1966, © 1969 by Ingri and Edgar Parin d'Aulaire. Reprinted by permission of The Viking Press, Inc.

Illustration by Felix Hoffmann. From Grimm's *The Sleeping Beauty*, copyright 1959, by H. R. Sauerlander & Co., Aarau. Reprinted by permission of Harcourt Brace Jovanovich, Inc., and Oxford University Press. (Original in color)

most people have known and loved, in one edition or another, all their lives. These stories probably rank with *Grimms' Fairy Tales* in their continuous popularity, and for similar reasons. They have the ring of complete sincerity and the oral charm of the storyteller's art at its best. They were recorded by Peter Christian Asbjörnsen (1812–1885) and Jörgen E. Moe (1813–1882), and turned into matchless English by a British scholar, Sir George Webbe Dasent (1817–1896), who was influenced by Jacob Grimm.

Peter C. Asbjörnsen and Jörgen Moe were devoted friends from early boyhood. Both became interested in gathering the popular tales of their native Norway from the lips of old storytellers who were still relating them as they had received them from the lips of preceding generations. When Asbjörnsen, a zoologist, started out on a scientific expedition, he followed his folklore hobby in his spare time. Moe spent his holidays similarly employed, traveling to remote parts of the country and gathering the legends and stories of the district from the storytellers.

While in Stockholm in a diplomatic post, Sir George Webbe Dasent had the great good fortune to meet Jacob Grimm, who urged him to begin a thorough study of the language of the North, especially Icelandic. In the midst of a remarkably strenuous life of study, translations, journalism, and travel, he became interested in

the Norse folk tales and made his masterly translations of the Asbjörnsen-Moe collections, *Popular Tales from the Norse* (1859) and *Tales from the Fjeld* (1874), the two sources for all subsequent English editions.

Folktales of Norway, edited by Reidar Christiansen, is another volume in the Folktales of the World series. In a fascinating foreword, the editor for the series, Richard Dorson, an eminent folklorist of the United States, traces the historical development of the Norwegian tale. As in the other volumes, the provision of a glossary, an index of motifs, and a bibliography make this book of inestimable value to the scholar. Other outstanding collections are *Scandinavian Legends and Folk-Tales,* by Gwyn Jones; *Norwegian Folk Tales,* translated by Pat Shaw Iversen and Carl Norman; two compilations by Mary Hatch, *Danish Tales* and *More Danish Tales;* and Sigrid Undset's adaptations from the Asbjörnsen and Moe collections, *True and Untrue, and Other Norse Tales.*

While the general mood of the Norwegian tales is serious, which is true of most folk tales, there is much more humor, or buoyancy, in the Norse collection than in the German. The people make the best of things with an amusing nonchalance.

There are no fairies in the gauzy-winged tradition, but there is a great deal of magic. Trolls, hill folk, giants, hags, and witch-wives are plentiful. A delightful combination of text and illustrations by Ingri and Edgar d'Aulaire, *Trolls*, is a definitive resource for details. There are magic objects in these tales—fiddles, axes, tablecloths, rams, and sticks. Winds talk and take a hand in the affairs of humans now and then. A polar bear (another symbol of the North) and a great dun bull are both men under enchantments, and there are the colossal horse Dapplegrim, the kindly wolf Gray-legs, and talking beasts of every variety.

For storytelling, "The Pancake" is probably the finest of all cumulative stories because of its humor and rollicking movement. "The Cock and Hen That Went to Dovrefell" has a witty surprise ending that is far more satisfying than its English equivalent, "Henny Penny." These tales, like the Grimms', run the whole gamut from sheer nonsense to the romantic and heroic. They are classics and matchless entertainment which all children should have a chance to hear.

British Folk Tales

When Joseph Jacobs (1854–1916) began compiling the English folk tales, his objective was different from that of the Grimms or of the men who had preceded him in the English field. He intended his collection not for the archives of the folklore society but for the immediate enjoyment of English children. So Jacobs omitted incidents that were unduly coarse or brutal, adapted the language somewhat, especially dialect, and even deleted or changed an occasional episode. He was scrupulous in recording these alterations. At the back of his books, in a section for adult readers called "Notes and References," he gives the sources for each tale and its parallels, and then notes the changes he made.

Jacobs obtained a few of his tales from oral storytellers—some from Australia and one from a gypsy are mentioned. But most of his tales he obtained from printed sources, which he acknowledged. All in all, Joseph Jacobs was a sound enough folklorist. As a matter of fact, he was editor of the British journal *Folk-Lore*. But his greatest contribution is probably in selection and adaptation. Had it not been for his collections, many of these tales might still be gathering dust in antiquarian volumes.

These English tales of Jacobs are remarkable for three things: the giant-killers, the humor, and the large number suitable for the youngest children. From these collections of Jacobs come the favorites, "The Story of the Three Bears," "The Story of the Three Little Pigs," "Henny Penny," "Johnny-Cake," "The Old Woman and Her Pig," and many others.

"Tom Tit Tot," one of the stories which Jacobs rescued from the dusty oblivion of the journal *Folk-Lore*, is undoubtedly the most hilarious of all the variants of "Rumpelstiltskin." This is indeed an admirable example of the cheerfulness in the British stories. The superiority of this version lies in the full and consistent characterization of the silly girl, the impishness of "that," and the amusing hints as to the personality of the king.

Ilustration by Margot Zemach. Reprinted with the permission of Farrar, Straus and Giroux, Inc., and Penguin Books Ltd. From *Duffy and the Devil* by Harve Zemach and Margot Zemach, copyright © 1976 by Margot Zemach. (Original in color)

The tales of giant-killers are another striking feature of the English collections, beginning with the old national hero story "St. George and the Dragon," and continuing through "Tom Hickathrift," "Jack the Giant Killer," and their only feminine rival, the resourceful "Molly Whuppie." These stout characters who make away with monsters were multiplied and perpetuated by the chapbooks, and their adventures have remained popular with British children ever since.

Jacobs remained the chief source of English folk tales until, beginning in 1954, volumes of English, Scottish, and Welsh folk tales were issued in the Oxford Myths and Legends series. Beautifully told, handsome in format and illustrations, these three books have greatly expanded the range of British folk tales.

James Reeves's *English Fables and Fairy Stories* includes many of the old favorites as well as such delightful additions as "The Pedlar's Dream," "The Two Princesses," and "The Fish and the Ring." The style is distinguished, the stories are varied in mood, and they read or tell beautifully.

Flora Annie Steel's *English Fairy Tales* includes most of the familiar stories, smoothly retold and illustrated by Arthur Rackham. One of the tales, "Tattercoats," has been issued as a picture book, with delicate, romantic pictures by Diane Goode.

Folktales of England, edited by Katharine M. Briggs and Ruth L. Tongue (Folktales of the World series), is a collection derived almost exclusively from oral sources. Many of the tales are relics of pagan superstition, many are based on local folk history. The material is divided by types of tales: jocular tales, tall tales, modern legends, wonder tales, etc.

Welsh Legends and Folk Tales by Gwyn Jones includes some of the hero tales of King Arthur and his knights. There are such romances as "Pwyll and Pryderi," "How Trystan Won Esylit," and three about the fairy "Woman of Llyn-Y-Fan." The folk tales are full of magic, incantations, fairy folk, and difficult names.

In *Peter and the Piskies: Cornish Folk and Fairy Tales,* Ruth Manning-Sanders has compiled a lively selection of stories about the small supernatural creatures of Celtic lore. All of her anthologies are excellent.

Harve and Margot Zemach's *Duffy and the Devil* is a highly comic Cornish variant of "Rumpelstiltskin."

From *Heather and Broom* by Sorche Nic Leodhas. Illustrated by Consuelo Joerns. Copyright © 1960 by Leclaire G. Alger. Reproduced by permission of Holt, Rinehart and Winston, Publishers.

The *Scottish Folk Tales and Legends* by Barbara Ker Wilson are largely unfamiliar. There are simple nursery tales for small children, broadly comic stories for older children, a few horrific scare tales, and stories of romantic beauty. Through them all runs the Gaelic fairy lore—spells, enchantments, magic, and many sorts of fairy creatures, sometimes kind, often menacing.

The delightful books by Sorche Nic Leodhas—*Claymore and Kilt, Gaelic Ghosts, Ghosts Go Haunting, Heather and Broom, Sea-Spell and Moor Magic,* and *Thistle and Thyme*—further enrich the Scottish lore with both humor and romance. These stories have been written in such perfect storytelling form that they may be read or told without modification, and their charm is irresistible.

African Folk Tales

Although some books tapped the wealth of African folk material before the 1960s, in that decade began an outpouring of such material. Among the earlier collectors—Harold Courlander, Wilfrid Hambly, Russell Davis, Brent Ashabranner—the most prolific has been Courlander, whose general and regional collections are a rich lode of cultural information as well as a source of pleasure for readers and storytellers. West African tales are retold delightfully by Verna Aardema in *Tales from the Story Hat* and its companion volume, as well as in *Tales for the Third Ear*. East African tales are well represented in three fine collections: Humphrey Harman's *Tales Told Near a Crocodile*, Eleanor Heady's *When the Stones Were Soft*, and W. Moses Serwadda's *Songs and Stories from Uganda*. Folk tales from South Africa are smoothly retold by Aardema in *Behind the Back of the Mountain*. In addition to the many collections of regional and tribal tales, there are distinguished single-tale editions, such as Gerald McDermott's brilliantly illustrated adaptation of a

Reprinted by permission of Coward, McCann & Geoghegan, Inc. from *More Tales from the Story Hat* by Verna Aardema. Illustrations by Elton Fax. Copyright © 1966 by Coward-McCann, Inc.

Congolese tale, *The Magic Tree*, and Aardema's *Why Mosquitoes Buzz in People's Ears* with the Dillons' bold illustrations. Some of the most notable among the steadily growing number of general collections are Joyce Cooper Arkhurst's *The Adventures of Spider*, Hugh Sturton's *Zomo the Rabbit*, Frances Carpenter's *African Wonder Tales*, and Edna Mason Kaula's *African Village Folktales*. An excellent source book is *African Folktales and Sculpture*, second edition, edited by Paul Radin and James Johnson Sweeney.

The stories reflect the fact that the oral tradition is still very strong in Africa, with the tales pertinent to contemporary life and the written language echoing the cadence of speech. Many of the tales are about animal heroes like Anansi, the clever spider; many explain natural phenomena as does the literature of any people who live close to nature; many have a wry and sophisticated humor.

The Arabian Nights

The origin of *The Arabian Nights* is confused and lost in antiquity, partly because these stories belonged to the people and were not considered polite literature. In the Moslem world they circulated only in the coffee houses and the market place. The stories are very old, some

Illustration by Vera Bock. From *Arabian Nights*, edited by Andrew Lang. Copyright, 1898, 1946 by Longmans, Green and Co. Reproduced by permission of David McKay Company.

of them seeming to stem from ancient India, others from North Africa, with an early collection from Persia. A Frenchman, Antoine Galland, made his translation of them in 1704 from a manuscript sent to him from Syria but written in Egypt. The stories were fortunate in that the translator was also a skillful storyteller. These tales of the Orient were given a Gallic touch, so they lack nothing of drama or color. Today, children have turned away from all but a few of these exceedingly long stories.

Russian Folk Tales

A. N. Afanasiev (1826–1871) collected the Russian folk tales as the Grimm brothers collected the German, and there is now an English translation of the complete Afanasiev collection in the Pantheon edition, newly reissued in 1975. These stories are for adult students of folklore, not for children. They are bloody and horrible but full of excitement and color. Certain of

these tales are rather generally familiar to American children—"The Snow Maiden" (sometimes called "Snegourka"), "The Firebird," and "Sadko." All lend themselves to dramatization as well as to storytelling. These and other popular Russian stories are nicely told in Arthur Ransome's *Old Peter's Russian Tales.*

Miriam Morton's impressive anthology, *A Harvest of Russian Children's Literature,* has a sizable section of folk tales, and many tales have been published singly in illustrated editions. Two of Alexander Pushkin's poetic retellings of classic tales, *The Tale of the Czar Sultan* and *The Tale of the Golden Cockerel,* have been opulently illustrated by I. Bilibin.

Spanish Folk Tales

One American storyteller, Ruth Sawyer, thought the Irish stories were matched only by the Spanish, and her own collection seems to bear out her opinion. New and delightful stories for telling can be found in every one of the collections of Spanish tales listed in the bibliography for this chapter. The stories for the youngest children are full of fun, those for the older ones full of grace. *Padre Porko,* for instance, is one of

Illustration by Fritz Eichenberg. From *Padre Porko* by Robert Davis. Copyright 1939 by Robert Davis. Reproduced by permission of Holiday House.

the most enchanting series of talking-beast tales to be found anywhere. The Padre, the gentlemanly pig, is both astute and benignant, and his canny solutions of neighborhood difficulties are made with great elegance.

Excellent collections have come to us in translation from many parts of the world. There are Dorothy Sharp Carter's *The Enchanted Orchard*, tales from the Central American cultures, and her delightful retellings of stories from the West Indies, *Greedy Mariani*.

Virginia Haviland has selected thirty-two stories from around the world for *The Fairy Tale Treasury*, robustly illustrated by Raymond Briggs. *The Classic Fairy Tales*, selected and introduced by scholars Iona and Peter Opie, gives us twenty-four familiar fairy tales as they first appeared in English.

Two subject-oriented collections of note are Maria Leach's *Whistle in the Graveyard*, devoted

Taken from *Kassim's Shoes* adapted and illustrated by Harold Berson. Copyright © 1977 by Harold Berson. Used by permission of Crown Publishers Inc. (Original in color)

to ghost stories, and Rosemary Minard's *Womenfolk and Fairy Tales*, a bringing together of folk tales with women as the main characters.

Many individual folk tales have been published in a picture-book format. Tomie de Paola's *Strega Nona* is a delightful noodlehead tale from Italy, and Harold Berson's *Kassim's Shoes* an amusing Moroccan story with graceful but comic pictures, while Arlene Mosel's *The Funny Little Woman*, with distinctive illustrations by Blair Lent, is from Japan.

It is likely that your librarian can provide native folk tales for practically any country you can name. Some of these have been better translated and adapted than others, but there is scarcely a collection not worth examining.

Folk Tales in the United States

The United States is the fortunate recipient of folklore and folk tales from all over the world. This rich heritage falls into four large categories: (1) tales from black Americans, including the collections known as the Uncle Remus stories; (2) tales from the North American Indians; (3) variants of the European stories; and (4) tall tales. In the general discussion of folk tales few references are made to these American types, for definite reasons. In the first place, the European collections came into print long before American stories developed, and so they

Illustration copyright © 1974 by Atheneum Publishers. Illustration by Trina Schart Hyman from *Greedy Mariani and Other Folk Tales of the Antilles* selected and adapted by Dorothy Sharp Carter (A Margaret K. McElderry Book). Used by permission of Atheneum Publishers.

rather set the standard or pattern of such tales. Moreover, American collected tales differ in so many respects from those of the European groups that they often prove the exception to the very principles discussed as typical. They are, besides, far from a homogeneous group—no generalizations will cover all four varieties. An Uncle Remus tale differs from an American Indian story quite as much as both of them differ from their European relatives or the tall tale differs from all three. In short, each of the four types of American folk tales needs to be considered separately.

Black Folklore

Joel Chandler Harris (1848–1908) became interested in collecting the tales he heard the plantation slaves tell. Born in Georgia and raised on such stories as a child, he knew black dialect, humor, and picturesque turns of speech. Moreover, he had a deep love for the stories and for the people who told them.

The stories, told by Uncle Remus, a plantation slave, are mostly talking-beast tales and the hero is Brer Rabbit, the weakest and most harmless of animals, but far from helpless. Through his quick wit, his pranks, and his mischief, he triumphs over the bear, the wolf, the fox, and the lesser animals. Like the French "Reynard the Fox," he is a trickster, but unlike Reynard, he is never mean or cruel, only a practical joker now and then, a clever fellow who can outwit the big brutes and turn a misfortune into a triumph. No matter what happens to him or what he does, he remains completely lovable.

These stories are, of course, reminiscent of the talking-beast tales of other countries. Some of them may have had their roots in India, but it is generally agreed that most of them originated in Africa or were created in this country. Variants of "The Tar Baby" are found in many lands, but there is a special flavor to the Uncle Remus stories. They show a homely philosophy of life, flashes of poetic imagination, a shrewd appraisal of human nature, a love of mischief, a pattern and style unsurpassed by any other beast tales.

These stories do have their limitations, and the dialect is chief of them. Children in the South may be fortunate enough to hear these tales read by adults who can do justice to the flavorsome dialect. But even when the stories are turned into standard English, they retain their witty folk flavor, just as tales translated from the Norwegian or East Indian or American Indian do. Perhaps translation is the answer here, too. Ennis Rees, in *Brer Rabbit and His Tricks* and *More of Brer Rabbit's Tricks*, has provided such translations with great success. The simplest version for children is Margaret Wise Brown's edition of *Brer Rabbit*.

Other objections to these stories are raised by modern American blacks. In the article en-

Reprinted from *Brer Rabbit and His Tricks*, text © 1967, by Ennis Rees, and illustrations © 1967, by Edward Gorey, a Young Scott Book, by permission of Addison-Wesley Publishing Company, Inc.

titled "Uncle Remus for Today's Children" (*Elementary English*, March 1953), Margaret Taylor Burroughs points out that the tales are full of offensive terms for blacks. She objects to the intrusion of old "Uncle's" personality and point of view. These sometimes add to the wit and wisdom of the stories, but she cites some deplorable examples also. These objections point up the fact that the great body of seven hundred *Uncle Remus Tales* will survive chiefly as source material for gifted storytellers.

The mighty deeds of John Henry, the black folk hero, are described in books by Harold Felton and by Ezra Jack Keats, and Keats has also provided bold, impressive illustrations. An excellent and varied collection of black Americana is Harold Courlander's *Terrapin's Pot of Sense.*

North American Indian Tales

The collecting of North American Indian tales began with the sporadic records of missionaries and explorers, but not until the 1830s was there any serious attempt to bring together the rich body of existing material. Henry Rowe Schoolcraft, a government agent for the Ojibwa Indians, zealously recorded their myths and legends, although not in pure form. Since his time, ethnologists and folklorists in the United States and Canada have collected a voluminous and varied storehouse of Native American folklore. Most of the folklorists have collected tales of one tribe or people, such as Courlander's *People of the Short Blue Corn,* a Hopi anthology, or Sleator's *The Angry Moon,* based on the lore of the Tlingit Indians of Alaska.

While there are recurring themes and variants of specific tales, and even variants of European folk tales, the extant material provides a body of literature that differs distinctly according to region and tribe. Because the American Indian has a reverence for natural things, an affinity for the creatures of the earth and for the earth itself, much of the lore is concerned with nature as a part of religious beliefs and practices. Myths and legends that explain the origins of natural phenomena or the attributes of wild creatures are common to all the Native American cultures, since all of them invested living things with magical powers.

The major types of tales are creation myths; trickster tales, often humorous, in which the hero is either in human or in animal form, as in Eleanor Heady's *Tales of the Nimipoo,* which con-

Illustration by Peter Parnell, p. 9. From Margaret Hodges, *The Fire Bringer.* Text Copyright © 1972 by Margaret Hodges. Illustration Copyright © 1972 by Peter Parnell. Published by Little, Brown and Company. (Original in color)

tains twenty "why" stories with Coyote as the hero; journeys to another world, a story type that often reflects mores and taboos of a tribe; hero tales, often including tests for maturity or courage, like Margaret Hodges' *The Fire Bringer,* in which a Paiute boy, with Coyote's help, seizes fire from the Fire Spirits to ease the winter suffering of his tribe; and marriages between human beings and animals. Each region usually had its own cycle of traditional tales, and as with folklore diffusion everywhere, there are themes and patterns that occur in different regions.

Native Variants of European Tales

The Southern "The Gingerbread Boy," printed in *St. Nicholas* in 1875, "Johnny-Cake" in Jacobs's *English Fairy Tales,* and Ruth Sawyer's story, "Journey Cake, Ho!" are all variants of the Scotch "The Wee Bannock" or the Norse "The Pancake." There are undoubtedly dozens of other European folk tales extant in this country in characteristically modified form, but so far the most amusing and significant collections are *The Jack Tales* and *Grandfather Tales* by Richard Chase, collected from American mountain people. Chase's account of these light-hearted people makes you wish there were more of the stories. He has recorded them in the vernacular of the mountain people who have modified them to local speech and customs. The god Wotan or Woden appears, ancient, mysterious, but as helpful to Jack as he was to Sigurd or Siegfried. Jack is a country boy, unassuming but resourceful, and never nonplussed by the most fantastic adventures. The language is ungrammatical and sometimes rough, but it is humorously effective when handled by as gifted a storyteller as Richard Chase. The mood is decidedly comic, the setting rural. City children may not know "The Old Sow and the Three Little Shoats," but they'll recognize it as "The Three Little Pigs." Many of the tales have been found elsewhere in this country.

Tall Tales

The characteristic of the tall tale that distinguishes it from other humorous stories is its blatant exaggeration. Our older tall tales—with their swaggering heroes who do the impossible with nonchalance—embody delusions of power: dreams of riding a cyclone or mowing down forests, or, in short, blithely surmounting any and every obstacle. They are such flagrant lies

*Viewpoint*_____

that the lyingest yarn of all is the best one, provided it is told with a straight face and every appearance of truth. Babe, Paul Bunyan's blue ox, measures "forty-two axhandles between the eyes—and a tobacco box—you could easily fit in a Star tobacco box after the last axhandle." Pecos Bill, after riding the cyclone successfully, must figure a convenient way of getting down. In short, one characteristic of tall-tale humor is that there must be a great show of reasonableness and precise detail in the midst of the most hilarious lunacy.

There are no complete or satisfying answers to the questions about where all these tales came from or who started them. Some of the older stories are classified as folk tales, but many are probably best described as "fake lore."[4] But regardless of their origins, they are almost invariably humorous. The New England coast produced Captain Stormalong. Paul Bunyan and his blue ox came from the lumber camps. The Western plains started Pecos Bill and his horse the Widow Maker on their careers. Mike Fink was a keelboatman on the Mississippi, while Davy Crockett, Tony Beaver, and John Henry all belong to the South. One artist has covered a map of the United States with these heroes,[5] and it is the most astonishing array of rip-roaring he-men imaginable. Walter Blair has contributed to the tall tale in *Tall Tale America* as has Adrien Stoutenburg in *American Tall Tales* and *American Tall-Tale Animals.* Moritz Jagendorf has compiled several volumes of regional material: *New England Bean Pot*, a book of tales from the middle Atlantic region, and *Folk Stories of the South.* Of the several collections by Maria Leach, an outstanding one is *The Rainbow Book of American Folk Tales and Legends*, which includes tall tales.

The multiplicity of folk-tale collections does not mean necessarily that we should use more of them. Most teachers and librarians are probably using them less than they once did because other types of fiction for children have improved in quality. But we should know that there are now available many national collections of these old tales, and we should select from them a moderate number of suitable variety and use them in balanced proportion to other reading material.

4. See particularly Richard M. Dorson, "Twentieth-Century Comic Demigods," *American Folklore* (University of Chicago Press, 1959), pp. 214–226.

5. See Glen Rounds's end pages for Walter Blair's *Tall Tale America*, an amusing group of fabulous stories.

Adult References[6]

AFANASIEV, ALEXANDER N., comp. *Russian Fairy Tales.*

ASBJÖRNSEN, PETER C., and JÖRGEN MOE. *Norwegian Folk Tales.*

———. *Popular Tales from the Norse.*

BAUGHMAN, ERNEST. *A Type and Motif Index of the Folktales of England and North America.*

BETTELHEIM, BRUNO. *The Uses of Enchantment: Meaning and Importance of Fairy Tales.*

BRIGGS, KATHARINE M. *A Dictionary of British Folk-Tales in the English Language.*

———. *An Encyclopedia of Fairies: Hobgoblins, Brownies, Bogies, and Other Supernatural Creatures.*

———. *The Personnel of Fairyland: A Short Account of the Fairy People of Great Britain for Those Who Tell Stories to Children.*

BRUNVAND, JAN H. *The Study of American Folklore, an Introduction.*

CARLSON, ATELIA, and GILBERT B. CROFF. *World Folk-Tales: A Scribner Resource Collection.*

COLUM, PADRAIC, ed. *A Treasury of Irish Folklore.*

COOK, ELIZABETH. *The Ordinary and the Fabulous: An Introduction to Myths, Legends, and Fairy Tales for Teachers and Storytellers.*

COUGHLAN, MARGARET, comp. *Folklore from Africa to the United States.*

DORSON, RICHARD M. *American Folklore.*

———. *Buying the Wind: Regional Folklore in the United States.*

———, ed. *Folktales of the World series.*

———, ed. *Folktales Told Around the World.*

EASTMAN, MARY HUSE. *Index to Fairy Tales, Myths and Legends.*

FAVAT, F. ANDRÉ. *Child and Tale: The Origins of Interest.*

Funk and Wagnalls Standard Dictionary of Folklore, Mythology and Legend.

GRIMM, JACOB and WILHELM. *The Complete Grimm's Fairy Tales.*

IRELAND, NORMA. *Index to Fairy Tales, 1949–1972: Including Folklore, Legends and Myths in Collections.*

JACOBS, JOSEPH. See listings of his collections of English, Celtic, and Indian folk tales in the following bibliography. They contain significant introductions, and the notes in each appendix are treasures of folklore information.

KRAPPE, ALEXANDER HAGGERTY. *The Science of Folk-Lore.*

LÜTHI, MAX. *Once Upon a Time: On the Nature of Fairy Tales.*

PERRAULT, CHARLES. *Perrault's Complete Fairy Tales.*

RAMSEY, ELOISE, comp. *Folklore for Children and Young People: A Critical and Descriptive Bibliography for Use in the Elementary and Intermediate School.*

SALE, ROGER. *Fairy Tales and After: From Snow White to E. B. White.*

THOMPSON, STITH. *The Folktale.*

———, comp. *One Hundred Favorite Folktales.*

TRAVERS, PAMELA L. *About the Sleeping Beauty.*

ULLOM, JUDITH C., comp. *Folklore of the American Indians: An Annotated Bibliography.*

ZIEGLER, ELSIE. *Folklore: Annotated Bibliography and Index to Single Editions.*

General Collections

AIKEN, JOAN. *The Kingdom Under the Sea and Other Stories,* ill. by Jan Pienkowski. Jonathan Cape, 1979. Eleven folk tales from eastern Europe, strikingly illustrated and retold in graceful, witty style.   10–12

BAKER, AUGUSTA, comp. *The Golden Lynx and Other Tales,* ill. by Johannes Troyer. Lippincott, 1960.

———. *The Talking Tree and Other Stories,* ill. by Johannes Troyer. Lippincott, 1955. Two fine selections by a noted storyteller.   8–11

BROOKE, L. LESLIE, ed. *The Golden Goose Book,* ill. by ed. Warne, 1906. "The Golden Goose," "Tom Thumb," "Three Little Pigs," and "Three Bears" are delightfully illustrated.   5–10

CHILD STUDY ASSOCIATION OF AMERICA. *Castles and Dragons: Read-to-Yourself Fairytales for Boys and Girls,* ill. by William Pène du Bois. T. Crowell, 1958.   9–12

CLARKSON, ATELIA, and GILBERT CROSS, comp. *World Folktales.* Scribner's, 1980. Notes, comments, and lists of parallel stories follow each selection.   11 up

DE LA MARE, WALTER. *Tales Told Again,* ill. by Alan Howard. Knopf, 1959. Graceful versions of familiar tales.   9–12

HAVILAND, VIRGINIA, ed. *The Fairy Tale Treasury,* ill. by Raymond Briggs. Coward, 1972.   9–11

JACOBS, JOSEPH. *The Pied Piper and Other Tales,* ill. by James Hill. Macmillan, 1963. An attractively illustrated edition.   10–12

LEACH, MARIA. *The Rainbow Book of American Folk Tales and Legends,* ill. by Marc Simont. World, 1958. Regional lore, proverbs, riddles, tall tales, and folk tales of North and South America.   9–12

OPIE, IONA and PETER. *The Classic Fairy Tales.* Oxford, 1974.   9 up

PROVENSEN, ALICE and MARTIN, comps. *The Provensen Book of Fairy Tales,* ill. by comps. Random, 1971. A dozen modern fairy stories illustrated with colorful pictures.   9–11

RACKHAM, ARTHUR, comp. *Arthur Rackham Fairy Book,* ill. by comp. Lippincott, 1950. A choice of Rackham's favorite tales.   8–10

———, ill. *Fairy Tales from Many Lands.* Viking, 1974. A reissue of a 1916 title with beautiful, color plates.   10–11

ROSS, EULALIE, comp. *The Buried Treasure and Other Picture Tales,* ill. by Joseph Cellini. Lippincott, 1958. Tales from the Picture Tales series.   7–10

———. *The Lost Half-Hour,* ill. by Enrico Arno. Harcourt, 1963. Good storytelling material.   9–11

UNITED NATIONS WOMEN'S GUILD. *Ride with the Sun: Anthology of Folk Tales and Stories from the United Nations,* ed. by Harold Courlander, ill. by Roger Duvoisin. McGraw, 1955. Each story has been approved by the U.N. representative of the country from which it comes.   10–12

WIGGIN, KATE DOUGLAS, and NORA A. SMITH, eds. *The Fairy Ring,* rev. by Ethna Sheehan, ill. by Warren Chappell. Doubleday, 1967. A good new edition of an old favorite.   9–11

WITHERS, CARL. *A World of Nonsense, Strange and Humorous Tales from Many Lands,* ill. by John E. Johnson. Holt, 1968. Fifty examples of the universal appeal of nonsense and exaggeration.   9–11

Subject Collections

BELTING, NATALIA. *Calendar Moon,* ill. by Bernarda Bryson. Holt, 1964. The text, composed of folklore and myth from varied peoples, moves through the calendar year in this distinctive, strikingly illustrated book.   10–13

———. *The Earth Is on a Fish's Back: Tales of Beginnings,* ill. by Esta Nesbitt. Holt, 1965.

———. *Elves and Ellefolk: Tales of the Little People,* ill. by Gordon Laite. Holt, 1961.   8–12

6. Complete bibliographic data are provided in Appendix B.

GARNER, ALAN, ed. *A Cavalcade of Goblins*, ill. by Krystyna Turska. Walck, 1969. An excellent anthology of excerpts poems, and stories from worldwide sources. A treasure for storytellers. 9–12

HARDENDORFF, JEANNE B., comp. *Tricky Peik and Other Picture Tales*, ill. by Tomie de Paola. Lippincott, 1967. A collection of trickster tales. 9–11

LEACH, MARIA, ed. *How the People Sang the Mountains Up: How and Why Stories*, ill. by Glen Rounds. Viking, 1967. Legends about natural phenomena from many lands. 10–12

———. *The Lion Sneezed: Folktales and Myths of the Cat*, ill. by Helen Siegl. T. Crowell, 1977. A varied collection of poems, tales, and sayings about cats including notes for adults, sources and information about each selection, and a bibliography. 9–11

LURIE, ALISON, ad. *Clever Gretchen and Other Forgotten Folktales*, ill. by Margot Tomes. Crowell, 1980. A selection of tales about women, told with grace and humor. 9–11

———. *Whistle in the Graveyard: Folktales to Chill Your Bones*, ill. by Ken Rinciari. Viking, 1974. 9–11

MANNING-SANDERS, RUTH. *A Book of Charms and Changelings*, ill. by Robin Jacques. Dutton, 1972.

———. *A Book of Devils and Demons*, ill. by Robin Jacques. Dutton, 1970.

———. *A Book of Dragons*, ill. by Robin Jacques. Dutton, 1965.

———. *A Book of Magic Animals*, ill. by Robin Jacques. Dutton, 1975.

———. *A Book of Mermaids*, ill. by Robin Jacques. Dutton, 1968.

———. *The Red King and the Witch: Gypsy Folk and Fairy Tales*, ill. by Victor Ambrus. Roy, 1965. Each has a delightful style and well-chosen tales. 9–11

———. *Tortoise Tales*, ill. by Donald Chaffin. Nelson, 1974. 5–8

MINARD, ROSEMARY, ed. *Womenfolk and Fairy Tales*, ill. by Suzanna Klein. Houghton, 1975. 9–11

SAWYER, RUTH. *Joy to the World: Christmas Legends*, ill. by Trina Schart Hyman. Little, 1966.

———. *The Long Christmas*, ill. by Valenti Angelo. Viking, 1941. Tales by a great storyteller. 8–12

SPICER, DOROTHY. *13 Dragons*, ill. by Sofia. Coward, 1974. Varied and sprightly. 9–11

Collections and Single Tales

African and Ethiopian

AARDEMA, VERNA. *Half-A-Ball-Of-Kenki: An Ashanti Tale*, ill. by Diane Stanley Zuromskis. Warne, 1979. Illustrated with colorful blocked pictures, this double why-story explains why a leopard has spots and why flies always sit on leaves in which kenki has been wrapped. 5–7

———. *More Tales from the Story Hat*, ill. by Elton Fax. Coward, 1966. 7–10

———. *Tales for the Third Ear: From Equatorial Africa*, ill. by Ib Ohlsson. Dutton, 1969. Nine folk tales retold from original sources that give verbatim versions of African storytellers. Full of action and humor and an excellent source for storytelling. 8–10

———. *Tales from the Story Hat*, ill. by Elton Fax. Coward, 1960. 8–12

———, ad. *Behind the Back of the Mountain: Black Folktales from Southern Africa*, ill. by Leo and Diane Dillon. Dial, 1973. 9–11

———, ad. *Who's in Rabbit's House? A Masai Tale*, ill. by Leo and Diane Dillon. Dial, 1977. When Rabbit is threatened by a voice coming from inside her house, the other animals offer to help rout out the intruder. Their helpful suggestions are rather destructive until Frog resorts to scare tactics and frightens the culprit (a harmless caterpillar) out of hiding. 4–7

———, ad. *Why Mosquitoes Buzz in People's Ears: A West African Folk Tale*, ill. by Leo and Diane Dillon. Dial, 1975. A "why" tale retold with verve and magnificently illustrated. Caldecott Medal. 5–8

ARKHURST, JOYCE COOPER. *The Adventures of Spider*, ill. by Jerry Pinkney, Little, 1964. 8–10

ARNOTT, KATHLEEN. *African Myths and Legends*, ill. by Joan Kiddell-Monroe. Walck, 1963. Tales from south of the Sahara tell of "animals, humans and superhumans." 11 up

BRYAN, ASHLEY, ad. *The Adventures of Aku: Or How It Came About That We Shall Always See Okra the Cat Lying on a Velvet Cushion, While Okraman the Dog Sleeps Among the Ashes*, ill. by author. Atheneum, 1976. 9–11

BURTON, W. F. P. *The Magic Drum: Tales from Central Africa*, ill. by Ralph Thompson. Criterion, 1962. Short tales with a fablelike quality that are favorites in the Congo. Illustrated with humor and imagination. 9–12

COURLANDER, HAROLD. *The King's Drum and Other Stories*, ill. by Enrico Arno. Harcourt, 1962. Almost thirty stories from Africa identified by tribal sources. Excellent notes are appended on the origins or interpretations of these folk tales. 9–13

COURLANDER, HAROLD, and GEORGE HERZOG. *The Cow-Tail Switch, and Other West African Stories*, ill. by Madye Lee Chastain. Holt, 1947. Seventeen tales, told in lively style reveal much about the customs of the people. 10–12

COURLANDER, HAROLD, and WOLF LESLAU. *The Fire on the Mountain and Other Ethiopian Stories*, ill. by Robert W. Kane. Holt, 1950. Outstanding in style, illustrations, and content. 10–14

COURLANDER, HAROLD, and ALBERT PREMPEH. *The Hat-Shaking Dance, and Other Tales from the Gold Coast*, ill. by Enrico Arno. Harcourt, 1957. Humorous, droll, or wise are these twenty-one tales of Anansi. 9–12

DAYRELL, ELPHINSTONE. *Why the Sun and the Moon Live in the Sky: An African Folktale*, ill. by Blair Lent. Houghton, 1968. A story about the beginnings of time from the Efik-Ibibio peoples. Beautifully stylized artwork is based on African sources. 5–7

FUJA, ABAYOMI. *Fourteen Hundred Cowries and Other African Tales*, ill. by Ademola Olugebefola. Lothrop, 1971. Unusual stories recorded many years ago by a Yoruba scholar. 9–12

GILSTRAP, ROBERT, and IRENE ESTABROOK. *The Sultan's Fool and Other North African Tales*, ill. by Robert Greco. Holt, 1958. Eleven wise and witty tales, excellent for reading aloud and storytelling. 9–12

GUIRMA, FREDERIC. *Tales of Mogo: African Stories from the Upper Volta*, ill. by author. Macmillan, 1971. Eight stories of the Mossi people which tell of animals, magic, and folk wisdom. 9–11

HALEY, GAIL E., ad. *A Story, A Story: An African Tale*, ill. by adapter. Atheneum, 1970. The story explains the origin of that favorite African folk material, the spider tale. Caldecott Medal. 5–7

HARMAN, HUMPHREY. *Tales Told Near a Crocodile: Stories from Nyanza*, ill. by George Ford. Viking, 1967. 10–11

HEADY, ELEANOR. *When the Stones Were Soft: East African Fireside Tales*, ill. by Tom Feelings. Funk, 1968. 9–11

HOLLADAY, VIRGINIA, comp. *Bantu Tales,* ed. by Louise Crane, ill. by Rocco Negri. Viking, 1970. Nineteen short, well-told tales. 9–11

KAULA, EDNA MASON. *African Village Folktales,* ill. by author. World, 1968. 9–11

SERWADDA, W. MOSES. *Songs and Stories from Uganda,* transcribed and ed. by Hewitt Pantaleoni, ill. by Leo and Diane Dillon. T. Crowell, 1974. 8–10

Arabian

BROWN, MARCIA. *The Flying Carpet,* ill. by author. Scribner's, 1956. This story, so much a part of our language and so difficult to find, is beautifully retold and illustrated. 6–10

COLUM, PADRAIC, ed. *The Arabian Nights: Tales of Wonder and Magnificence,* ill. by Lynd Ward. Macmillan, 1964. Republished after thirty years this outstanding collection will appeal to younger readers. 10–14

DAWOOD, N. J., ad. *Tales from the Arabian Nights,* ill. by Ed Young. Doubleday, 1978. An easier to read version than that of Williams-Ellis, this collection of familiar tales is rendered in modern but flavorful language. 10–13

LANG, ANDREW, ed. *Arabian Nights,* ill. by Vera Bock. McKay, 1946. Fine black-and-white drawings and large print make this a favorite edition for children's reading. 10–14

WIGGIN, KATE DOUGLAS, and NORA SMITH, eds. *Arabian Nights, Their Best Known Tales,* ill. by Maxfield Parrish. Scribner's, 1909. Here are the favorite stories—"Aladdin," "Ali Baba," "The Voyage of Sinbad the Sailor"—gorgeously illustrated in color and well told. 10–14

Canadian

BARBEAU, MARIUS. *The Golden Phoenix: And Other French-Canadian Fairy Tales,* retold by Michael Hornyansky, ill. by Arthur Price. Walck, 1958. Notes as to their origin give these eight tales a special interest. Told with humor and zest. 10–13

CARLSON, NATALIE SAVAGE. *The Talking Cat and Other Stories of French Canada,* ill. by Roger Duvoisin. Harper, 1952. Tales told with vitality and humor and excellent for reading aloud. 8–11

Chinese

BIRCH, CYRIL. *Chinese Myths and Fantasies,* ill. by Joan Kiddell-Monroe. Walck, 1961. Ghosts and magicians and plain folk, too, are characters in this absorbing collection of tales. 11 up

KNIGHT, MARY. *The Fox That Wanted Nine Golden Tails,* ill. by Brigitte Bryan. Macmillan, 1969. A fox learns that transformations bring no happiness. An imaginative, elegant treatment of a familiar theme. 8–9

MOSEL, ARLENE, ed. *Tikki Tikki Tembo,* ill. by Blair Lent. Holt, 1968. An amusing picture book to read aloud. The wash illustrations have an appropriately Oriental beauty. 5–7

RITCHIE, ALICE. *The Treasure of Li-Po,* ill. by T. Ritchie. Harcourt, 1949. These six original fairy tales are told with all the sincerity and dignity of the folk tales which they resemble. 10–14

WOLKSTEIN, DIANE. *8,000 Stones: A Chinese Folktale,* ill. by Ed Young. Doubleday, 1972. A small boy ingeniously contrives a solution to his ruler's problem: how to weigh an elephant. 8–9

———. *White Wave: A Chinese Tale,* ill. by Ed Young. T. Crowell, 1979. A poor farm lad discovers that his cherished moon snail is the goddess White Wave. 8–11

YOLEN, JANE H. *The Emperor and the Kite,* ill. by Ed Young. World, 1967. A tale of ancient China about Djeow Seow, who was so tiny her father the Emperor never noticed her until she saved his life. 5–8

Czechoslovakian

FILLMORE, PARKER. *Shepherd's Nosegay,* ed. by Katherine Love, ill. by Enrico Arno. Harcourt, 1958. Eighteen tales of Finland and Czechoslovakia compiled from Fillmore's out-of-print collections. Excellent for telling and reading aloud. 9–12

HAVILAND, VIRGINIA, ad. *Favorite Fairy Tales Told in Czechoslovakia,* ill. by Trina S. Hyman. Little, 1966. 8–10

Danish

BASON, LILLIAN. *Those Foolish Molboes!* ill. by Margot Tomes. Coward, 1977. These simple, humorous tales are peopled by the Molboes, a blandly and cheerfully stupid bunch whose dilemmas will delight the young audience for whom they were written. 7–9

HATCH, MARY COTTAM. *13 Danish Tales, Retold,* ill. by Edgun (pseud.). Harcourt, 1947. These stories are excellent for reading or storytelling, and are carefully adapted from the Bay translation. 9–13

———. *More Danish Tales, Retold,* ill. by Edgun (pseud.). Harcourt, 1949. 9–13

HAVILAND, VIRGINIA, ad. *Favorite Fairy Tales Told in Denmark,* ill. by Margot Zemach. Little, 1971. Six tales are retold with directness and simplicity. Useful as a source for storytelling as well as for independent reading. 9–11

JONES, GWYN. *Scandinavian Legends and Folk Tales* (see Norwegian tales).

English, Scottish, and Welsh

BRIGGS, KATHARINE, and RUTH TONGUE, eds. *Folktales of England.* Univ. of Chicago Pr., 1965. (Folktales of the World series). 10 up

BROWN, MARCIA. *Dick Whittington and His Cat,* ill. by author. Scribner's, 1950. A lively, readable adaptation of this classic hero tale with strong linoleum cuts in two colors. 4–8

CARRICK, MALCOLM, ad. *The Wise Men of Gotham,* ill. by adapter. Viking, 1975. Blithe and bouncy noodlehead tales. 9–11

COLWELL, EILEEN. *Round About and Long Ago: Tales from the English Counties,* ill. by Anthony Colbert. Houghton, 1974. Brisk, straightforward retellings of twenty-eight tales. 9–12

GALDONE, PAUL, ill. *The Old Woman and Her Pig.* McGraw, 1960. The old nursery favorite is reintroduced as a lively picture book. Another nursery classic made into a picture book by the artist is *Old Mother Hubbard and Her Dog* (1960). 4–7

JACOBS, JOSEPH, ed. *English Fairy Tales,* ill. by John D. Batten. Putnam, n.d.

———. *More English Fairy Tales,* ill. by John D. Batten. Putnam, n.d. These not only are reliable sources for the favorite English tales but also are appealing to children in format and illustrations. 9–12

_____. *King of the Cats,* ill. by Paul Galdone. Houghton/Clarion, 1980. Galdone's version follows the original closely; his pictures are bold, dramatic, and humorous.   5–8

JONES, GWYN. *Welsh Legends and Folk Tales,* ill. by Joan Kiddell-Monroe. Walck, 1955. Retellings of ancient sagas as well as folk and fairy tales are included. Illustrations in color are particularly outstanding.   11–14

MANNING-SANDERS, RUTH. *Peter and the Piskies: Cornish Folk and Fairy Tales,* ill. by Raymond Briggs. Roy, 1966.   10–12

NESS, EVALINE. *Tom Tit Tot,* ill. by author. Scribner's, 1965. A very attractive picture-book variation of the Rumpel-stiltskin story, good for storytelling or for reading aloud.
                                                                5–8

NIC LEODHAS, SORCHE (pseud.). *Always Room for One More,* ill. by Nonny Hogrogian. Holt, 1965. A picture-book version of an old Scottish song. Handsome illustrations. Caldecott Medal.   5–8

_____. *By Loch and by Lin,* ill. by Vera Bock. Holt, 1969.
                                                                9–12

_____. *Claymore and Kilt,* ill. by Leo and Diane Dillon. Holt, 1967.   12–14

_____. *Gaelic Ghosts,* ill. by Nonny Hogrogian. Holt, 1964.
                                                              10–12

_____. *Ghosts Go Haunting,* ill. by Nonny Hogrogian. Holt, 1965.   10–12

_____. *Heather and Broom,* ill. by Consuelo Joerns. Holt, 1960.   10–12

_____. *Sea-Spell and Moor-Magic: Tales of the Western Isles,* ill. by Vera Bock. Holt, 1968.   9–11

_____. *Thistle and Thyme,* ill. by Evaline Ness. Holt, 1962.
                                                              10–12

REEVES, JAMES. *English Fables and Fairy Stories,* ill. by Joan Kiddell-Monroe. Walck, 1954. An attractive collection of nineteen tales illustrated in two colors.   10–14

STEEL, FLORA ANNIE. *English Fairy Tales,* ill. by Arthur Rackham. Macmillan, 1962.   8–12

_____. *Tattercoats: An Old English Tale,* ill. by Diane Goode. Bradbury, 1976.   5–8

WILSON, BARBARA KER. *Scottish Folk Tales and Legends,* ill. by Joan Kiddell-Monroe. Walck, 1954. In addition to the folk tales, a section of stories on the legendary exploits of the Fians is included. Attractive format and illustrations.
                                                              11–14

ZEMACH, HARVE. *Duffy and the Devil: A Cornish Tale Retold,* ill. by Margot Zemach. Farrar, 1973. Caldecott Medal.   5–8

Finnish

BOWMAN, JAMES CLOYD, and MARGERY BIANCO. *Tales from a Finnish Tupa,* from a tr. by Aili Kolehmainen, ill. by Laura Bannon. Whitman, 1936. Here are the everyday folk tales of the Finnish people, not the epic stories. Beautifully told, with effective illustrations.   10–14

FILLMORE, PARKER. *Shepherd's Nosegay* (see Czechoslovakian tales).

French

D'AULNOY, MARIE C. *The White Cat and Other Old French Fairy Tales* by Mme. La Comtesse d'Aulnoy, tr. by Rachel Field, ill. by Elizabeth MacKinstry. Macmillan, 1928, 1967.   8–11

MASSIGNON, GENEVIEVE, ed. *Folktales of France,* tr. by Jacqueline Hyland. Univ. of Chicago Pr., 1968. (Folktales of the World series).   10 up

PERRAULT, CHARLES. *Cinderella: Or The Little Glass Slipper,* ill. by Marcia Brown. Scribner's, 1954. Attractive pastel illustrations. Caldecott Medal.   5–9

_____. *Puss in Boots,* ill. by Marcia Brown. Scribner's, 1952. Wonderful pictures enliven this story of the faithful cat who helps to make a lord of his poor young master.   6–9

_____. *Puss in Boots,* ill. by Paul Galdone. Seabury, 1976. The ebullience and humor of Galdone's pictures are perfectly suited to the tale of the clever cat.   5–8

PICARD, BARBARA LEONIE. *French Legends, Tales and Fairy Stories,* ill. by Joan Kiddell-Monroe. Walck, 1955. A rich and varied source of folklore ranging from epic literature to medieval tales; from legends to fairy tales.   10–14

German

GRIMM, JACOB and WILHELM. *About Wise Men and Simpletons: Twelve Tales from Grimm,* tr. by Elizabeth Shub, ill. by Nonny Hogrogian. Macmillan, 1971. Newly translated from the less familiar first edition, pithy versions of familiar tales.   9–11

_____. *The Bearskinner,* ill. by Felix Hoffmann. Atheneum, 1978.   5–8

_____. *The Donkey Prince,* ill. by Barbara Cooney. Doubleday, 1977. A donkey born to a childless royal couple wanders to a castle where a princess learns to love him, restoring him, of course, to his princely human form. Illustrated with delectable paintings in full color.   7–8

_____. *The Fisherman and His Wife,* tr. by Randall Jarrell, ill. by Margot Zemach. Farrar, 1980. A story of greed and justice, illustrated by handsome pictures, delicate but comic.   5–8

_____. *Grimm's Fairy Tales,* tr. by Mrs. E. V. Lucas and others, ill. by Fritz Kredel. Grosset, 1945. An edition that is thoroughly satisfactory to children. The excellent translation is supplemented by bright, appealing pictures. 9–12

_____. *Grimm's Fairy Tales: Twenty Stories,* ill. by Arthur Rackham. Viking, 1973. Selections from an edition long out of print, illustrated with beauty and vigor.   9–11

_____. *Grimm's Tales for Young and Old.* Doubleday, 1977. A good standard edition.   9–11

_____. *Hansel and Gretel,* tr. by Elizabeth Crawford, ill. by Lisbeth Zwerger. Morrow, 1980. A new and excellent translation.   5–8

_____. *Hansel and Gretel,* tr. by Charles Scribner, ill. by Adrienne Adams. Scribner's, 1975.   8–10

_____. *The Juniper Tree and Other Tales from Grimm,* 2 vols., selected by Lore Segal and Maurice Sendak, tr. by Lore Segal with four tales tr. by Randall Jarrell, ill. by Maurice Sendak. Farrar, 1973.   9 up

_____. *The Shoemaker and the Elves,* ill. by Adrienne Adams. Scribner's, 1960. Colorful illustrations add new beauty to one of the Grimms' best-loved tales for little children. 3–6

_____. *The Sleeping Beauty,* ill. by Felix Hoffmann. Harcourt, 1960. Richly toned pictures. Other Grimm tales illustrated by this artist include *The Wolf and the Seven Little Kids* (1959), *The Seven Ravens* (1963), and *Hans in Luck* (1975).   5–9

_____. *The Sleeping Beauty, from the Brothers Grimm,* ill. by Trina Schart Hyman. Little, 1977.   9–11

_____. *Snow White,* tr. by Paul Heins, ill. by Trina Schart Hyman. Little, 1974.   9–11

_____. *Snow White and the Seven Dwarfs,* freely tr. and ill. by Wanda Gág. Coward, 1938.

_____. *Snow-White and the Seven Dwarfs: A Tale from the Brothers Grimm,* tr. by Randall Jarrell, ill. by Nancy Ekholm Burkert. Farrar, 1972.   9–11

_____. *Tales from Grimm,* freely tr. and ill. by Wanda Gág. Coward, 1936.

_____. *The Traveling Musicians,* ill. by Hans Fischer. Harcourt, 1955. Distinctive illustrations in color make this an outstanding folk-tale picture book.   5–8

_____. *The Twelve Dancing Princesses,* ill. by Errol LeCain. Viking, 1978.   9–11

HAUFF, WILHELM. *Dwarf Long-Nose,* tr. by Doris Orgel, ill. by Maurice Sendak. Random, 1960. Poor Jacob displeases a witch and spends years as an ugly dwarf before regaining his true form and a handsome bride as well. An excellent translation, appealingly illustrated.   9–11

PICARD, BARBARA LEONIE. *German Hero-Sagas and Folk-Tales,* ill. by Joan Kiddell-Monroe. Walck, 1958. *Siegfried* and other sagas, as well as such folk tales as *Ratcatcher of Hamelin,* give children a broader background of German lore than the more familiar Grimm tales.   11–14

RANKE, KURT, ed. *Folktales of Germany,* tr. by Lotte Baumann. Univ. of Chicago Pr., 1966. (Folktales of the World series).   10 up

Indian and Pakistani

BROWN, MARCIA. *Once a Mouse,* ill. by author. Scribner's, 1961. The timid mouse was changed by a kindly hermit into a cat, a dog, and then a tiger who became so cruel he had to be punished. Caldecott Medal.   5–8

GRAY, JOHN E. B. *India's Tales and Legends,* ill. by Joan Kiddell-Monroe. Walck, 1961. Distinguished retellings of India's rich lore, will appeal to older children.   11 up

HITCHCOCK, PATRICIA. *The King Who Rides a Tiger and Other Folk Tales from Nepal,* ill. by Lillian Sader. Parnassus, 1966. A dozen colorful, varied tales, retold in a light and graceful style.   9–11

JACOBS, JOSEPH, ed. *Indian Fairy Tales,* ill. by J. D. Batten. Putnam, 1969. Like Jacobs's other collections, these stories are selected from manuscript sources. They also throw light on fable and folk-tale origins.   9–12

Irish

COLUM, PADRAIC. *The King of Ireland's Son,* ill. by Willy Pogány. Macmillan, 1921, 1967. Seven Irish folk tales about a brave young royal lad.   10–12

DANAHER, KEVIN. *Folktales of the Irish Countryside,* ill. by Harold Berson. White, 1970. Fourteen tales heard by the author from six storytellers. Delightful to read alone or aloud, and a good source for storytellers.   10–12

HAVILAND, VIRGINIA, ad. *Favorite Fairy Tales Told in Ireland,* ill. by Arthur Marokvia. Little, 1961. "Old Hag's Long Leather Bag" and "Billy Beg and the Bull" are among the tales in this attractive, large-print collection.   8–11

JACOBS, JOSEPH. *Munachar and Manachar: An Irish Story,* ill. by Anne Rockwell. T. Crowell, 1970. The cumulation and the nonsense humor are appealing. Good for storytelling or reading aloud.   5–7

_____, ed. *Celtic Fairy Tales,* ill. by John D. Batten. Putnam, 1892.

_____, ed. *More Celtic Fairy Tales,* ill. by John D. Batten. Putnam, n.d. Jacobs includes Welsh, Scotch, Cornish, and Irish in his two Celtic collections. His copious notes are of great value.   9–12

MACMANUS, SEUMAS. *Hibernian Nights,* ill. by Paul Kennedy. Macmillan, 1963. The "last of the great Irish storytellers" compiled this rich collection of twenty-two of his favorite tales chosen from his earlier books.   11 up

O'FAOLAIN, EILEEN. *Irish Sagas and Folk-Tales,* ill. by Joan Kiddell-Monroe. Walck, 1954. This distinguished collection contains epic tales and folk tales to delight both reader and storyteller.   10–14

SHUB, ELIZABETH. *Seeing Is Believing,* ill. by Rachel Isadora. Greenwillow, 1979. Simple, flavorful retellings of an Irish and a Cornish folk tale.   6–8

Italian

CHAFETZ, HENRY. *The Legend of Befana,* ill. by Ronni Solbert. Houghton, 1958. The old Italian Christmas legend beautifully retold and illustrated.   5–9

DE PAOLA, TOMIE, ad. *Strega Nona: An Old Tale Retold,* ill. by adapter. Prentice, 1975.   7–8

HAVILAND, VIRGINIA, ad. *Favorite Fairy Tales Told in Italy,* ill. by Evaline Ness. Little, 1965.   8–10

JAGENDORF, M. A. *The Priceless Cats and Other Italian Folk Stories,* ill. by Gioia Fiamenghi. Vanguard, 1956. An attractive and gay collection for the children's own reading.   10–13

Japanese

BARUCH, DOROTHY. *Kappa's Tug-of-War with Big Brown Horse,* ill. by Sanryo Sakai. Tuttle, 1962. Retelling of an old legend of a little water-imp who steals what he wants, and is at last outwitted by Farmer Shiba.   6–8

GARRISON, CHRISTIAN. *The Dream Eater,* ill. by Diane Goode. Bradbury, 1978. Both small Yukio and the adults he approaches with his problem suffer from nightmares—until the boy finds a baku (an eater of bad dreams) and brings him back to the village. Nicely told, beautifully illustrated.   5–7

McALPINE, HELEN and WILLIAM, comps. *Japanese Tales and Legends,* retold by the McAlpines, ill. by Joan Kiddell-Monroe. Walck, 1959. A choice selection of folklore, legends, and epic tales.   10–14

McDERMOTT, GERALD, ad. *The Stonecutter: A Japanese Folk Tale,* ill. by adapter. Viking, 1975. Brilliant, monolithic art effectively presents the tale of a stonecutter who craves power.   5–8

MOSEL, ARLENE, ad. *The Funny Little Woman,* ill. by Blair Lent. Dutton, 1972. Caldecott Medal.   5–8

STAMM, CLAUS, ed. *Three Strong Women: A Tall Tale from Japan,* ill. by Kazue Mizumura. Viking, 1962. A sturdy girl, her mother, and her grandmother train a cocky young wrestler to new heights of strength for a court performance. A humorous read-aloud, color illustrated.   8–11

_____. *The Very Special Badgers: A Tale of Magic from Japan,* ill. by Kazue Mizumura. Viking, 1960. An amusing and humorous tale of how two badger clans settle a dispute.   8–10

UCHIDA, YOSHIKO. *The Dancing Kettle and Other Japanese Folk Tales,* retold, ill. by Richard C. Jones. Harcourt, 1949. Fourteen folk tales, some of them familiar, many of them new, make this a welcome addition to folklore collections.

_____. *The Magic Listening Cap: More Folk Tales from Japan,* ill. by author. Harcourt, 1955. This second collection is illustrated with the distinctive simplicity characteristic of Japanese art.   9–12

WINTHROP, ELIZABETH. *Journey to the Bright Kingdom,* ill. by Charles Mikolaycak. Holiday, 1979. The blind wife of a ferryman is granted a visit to the legendary kingdom of Kakure-sato where she is able to gaze on her daughter for the first time.   8–10

Mexican and South American

AARDEMA, VERNA, tr. *The Riddle of the Drum: A Tale from Tizapan, Mexico,* ill. by Tony Chen. Four Winds, 1979. A traditional Mexican folk tale, illustrated with bright paintings, about the quest of a prince.   5–8

CARTER, DOROTHY SHARP, ad. *The Enchanted Orchard: And Other Folktales of Central America,* ill. by W. T. Mars. Harcourt, 1973.   10–12

FINGER, CHARLES J. *Tales from Silver Lands.* Doubleday, 1924. The author gathered these outstanding folk tales from the Indians during his South American travels. Newbery Medal.   10–14

JAGENDORF, M. A., and R. S. BOGGS. *The King of the Mountains: A Treasury of Latin American Folk Stories,* ill. by Carybé. Vanguard, 1960. More than fifty tales, listed by country of origin.   10–14

Norwegian

ASBJÖRNSEN, PETER C., and JÖRGEN MOE. *East o' the Sun and West o' the Moon,* ill. by Hedvig Collin. Macmillan, 1953. An attractive edition of a title which first appeared twenty-five years earlier. Based on the Dasent translation.   10–14

———. *East o' the Sun and West o' the Moon,* ill. by Kay Nielsen. Doubleday, 1922. Fifteen favorite stories with highly imaginative illustrations.   10–14

———. *Norwegian Folk Tales* (see Adult References, this chapter).   10–13

———. *The Squire's Bride,* ill. by Marcia Sewall. Atheneum, 1975. A hilarious tale enhanced by comic black-and-white pencil drawings.   8–10

———. *The Three Billy Goats Gruff,* ill. by Marcia Brown. Harcourt, 1957. A favorite folk tale appears in brightly colored picture-book format.   4–7

CHRISTIANSEN, REIDAR T., ed. *Folktales of Norway,* tr. by Pat Shaw Iversen. Univ. of Chicago Pr., 1964. (Folktales of the World series)   10 up

D'AULAIRE, INGRI and EDGAR. *Trolls,* ill. by authors. Doubleday, 1972.   8–10

HAVILAND, VIRGINIA, ad. *Favorite Fairy Tales Told in Norway,* ill. by Leonard Weisgard. Little, 1961. Seven familiar tales, handsomely illustrated in three colors. Includes "Why the Sea Is Salt," "Taper Tom," and "Princess on the Glass Hill."   8–11

JONES, GWYN. *Scandinavian Legends and Folk Tales,* ill. by Joan Kiddell-Monroe. Walck, 1956. Another Oxford contribution to folk-tale collections, this contains several of the familiar stories. Others are hero tales and unusual examples of folklore told with humor and impressive art. 8–12

Polish

BORSKI, LUCIA M., and KATE B. MILLER. *The Jolly Tailor, and Other Fairy Tales,* ill. by Kazimir Klephacki. McKay, 1957. Reissued after many years, this collection translated from the Polish offers fine material for reading and storytelling.   9–12

DOMANSKA, JANINA. *King Krakus and the Dragon,* ill. by author. Greenwillow, 1979. A traditional tale about a humble shoemaker's apprentice who finds a way to slay a dragon is illustrated with stylized, geometric paintings in lavish colors.   5–8

HAVILAND, VIRGINIA, ad. *Favorite Fairy Tales Told in Poland,* ill. by Felix Hoffmann. Little, 1963. Six tales are retold and illustrated here. Large-print format appeals to younger readers.   8–10

SINGER, ISAAC BASHEVIS. *When Shlemiel Went to Warsaw: And Other Stories,* tr. by author and Elizabeth Shub, ill. by Margot Zemach. Farrar, 1968. Eight stories, some based on traditional Jewish tales. The cadence of the writing is especially evident when read aloud. Good for storytelling.   10 up

———. *Zlateh the Goat,* tr. by author and Elizabeth Shub, ill. by Maurice Sendak. Harper, 1966. Seven tales based on middle-European Jewish folk material, told and illustrated with distinction.   10–12

ZAJDLER, ZOE, comp. *Polish Fairy Tales,* ill. by Hazel Cook. Follett, 1968. A more extensive collection than the Borski or Haviland collections. Good for storytelling or independent reading.   9–11

Russian

AFANASYEV, ALEXANDER. *Soldier and Tsar in the Forest: A Russian Tale,* tr. by Richard Lourie, ill. by Uri Shulevitz. Farrar, 1972. A younger, virtuous brother ousts an older one. Illustrations are brilliant and Slavic in feeling.   5–8

DANIELS, GUY, tr. *Foma the Terrible: A Russian Folktale,* ill. by Imero Gobbato. Delacorte, 1970. A funnier Russian noodlehead there never was. Adapted from the Afanasiev collection.   5–8

DE REGNIERS, BEATRICE, ad. *Everyone Is Good for Something,* ill. by Margot Tomes. Houghton/Clarion, 1980. Retold with zest, a Slavic tale about a boy who is rewarded for his kindness.   5–8

DOWNING, CHARLES. *Russian Tales and Legends,* ill. by Joan Kiddell-Monroe. Walck, 1957. Epic, folk, and fairy tales gathered from many areas of Russia.   11 up

DURHAM, MAE. *Tit for Tat and Other Latvian Folk Tales,* ill. by Harriet Pincus. Harcourt, 1967. Mischievous tales told in a direct, colloquial style echoed in the pictures.   9–11

GINSBURG, MIRRA, tr. *How Wilka Went to Sea,* ed. by the translator, ill. by Charles Mikolaycak. Crown, 1975. Finno-Ugric and Turkic tales abounding in witches, giants, and wizards.   9–11

———, tr. *The Kaha Bird: Tales from the Steppes of Central Asia,* ill. by Richard Cuffari. Crown, 1971. Nineteen stories from a dozen cultures, many with a robust, sly humor.   9–11

———, tr. *The Lazies: Tales of the Peoples of Russia,* ed. by translator, ill. by Marian Parry. Macmillan, 1973. Fifteen humorous tales.   8–10

MORTON, MIRIAM, ed. *A Harvest of Russian Children's Literature.* Univ. of Calif. Pr., 1967.   All ages

PROKOFIEFF, SERGE. *Peter and the Wolf,* ill. by Warren Chappell. Knopf, 1940. Delightful picture-book story about young Peter, who outwitted the wolf to rescue the duck. Excerpts from the musical score accompany the text.   7–10

PUSHKIN, ALEXANDER. *The Tale of the Czar Sultan,* tr. by Patricia Lowe, ill. by I. Bilibin. T. Crowell, 1975.   8–10

———. *The Tale of the Golden Cockerel,* tr. by Alessandra Pellizone, ill. by I. Bilibin. T. Crowell, 1975.   8–10

RANSOME, ARTHUR. *Old Peter's Russian Tales,* ill. by Dmitri Mitrokhim. Nelson, 1917, 1976. This is the teacher's most practical source for the Russian tales—in admirable style for telling, reading aloud, or dramatizing.   8–12

———, ad. *The Fool of the World and the Flying Ship: A Russian Tale,* ill. by Uri Shulevitz. Farrar, 1968. A retelling of a Russian tale is brought to life with these vigorous and colorful illustrations. Caldecott Medal.   5–8

RIORDAN, JAMES, ad. *Tales from Central Russia,* ill. by Krystyna Turska. Viking, 1979. Adapted from Afanasiev's collection, these preserve the oral tradition.   9–11

———, ad. *Tales from Tartary*, ill. by Krystyna Turska. Viking, 1979. Warmth and humor distinguish these regional stories from the U.S.S.R. 9–11

ROBBINS, RUTH. *Baboushka and the Three Kings*, ill. by Nicolas Sidjakov, 1960. The familiar Russian folk tale of the selfish old woman and the Wise Men is enhanced by striking modern illustrations. Caldecott Medal. 5–10

TITIEV, ESTELLE, tr. *How the Moolah Was Taught a Lesson and Other Tales from Russia*, ill. by Ray Cruz. Dial, 1976. Four tales, each from a different part of the U.S.S.R. 8–10

WHITNEY, THOMAS P., tr. *The Story of Prince Ivan, the Firebird, and the Gray Wolf*, ill. by Nonny Hogrogian. Scribner's, 1968. A classic Russian fairy tale with a melodramatic plot. 8–10

WYNDHAM, LEE, comp. *Tales the People Tell in Russia*, ill. by Andrew Antal. Messner, 1970. Ten tales, told with gusto, for which sources are cited in an appended note. Also contains three fables and a short list of proverbs. 8–10

ZEMACH, HARVE, ad. *Salt: A Russian Tale*, from a literal translation by Benjamin Zemach of the Russian of Alexei Afansev, ill. by Margot Zemach. Follett, 1965. A picturebook version of a Russian story, with the familiar pattern of the youngest brother surmounting all difficulties and winning a princess. Attractively illustrated. 5–8

Spanish

BOGGS, RALPH STEELE, and MARY GOULD DAVIS. *The Three Golden Oranges and Other Spanish Folk Tales*, ill. by Emma Brock. McKay, 1936. Stories for older children, romantic and exciting. One remarkable ghost story. 10–12

DAVIS, ROBERT. *Padre Porko*, ill. by Fritz Eichenberg. Holiday, 1958. Padre Porko, the gentlemanly pig, has all the benignancy of the Buddha animals, and a certain mannerly elegance besides. Amusing tales, enhanced by good pen-and-ink sketches. 8–12

EELLS, ELSIE SPICER. *Tales of Enchantment from Spain*, ill. by Maud and Miska Petersham. Dodd, 1956. These are romantic tales, rich in magic. 10–14

HAVILAND, VIRGINIA, ad. *Favorite Fairy Tales Told in Spain*, ill. by Barbara Cooney. Little, 1963. Six delightful Spanish tales retold. 8–10

JIMENEZ-LANDI, ANTONIO. *The Treasure of the Muleteer and Other Spanish Tales*, tr. by Paul Blackburn, ill. by Floyd Sowell. Doubleday, 1974. Regional tales which reflect Moorish and Christian traditions. 10–13

Swiss

DUVOISIN, ROGER. *The Three Sneezes and Other Swiss Tales*, ill. by author. Knopf, 1941. Humorous tales, many of which are based on the theme of the stupid fellow who succeeds. 9–12

MÜLLER-GUGGENBÜHL, FRITZ. *Swiss-Alpine Folk-Tales*, tr. by Katharine Potts, ill. by Joan Kiddell-Monroe. Walck, 1958. These tales are a distinguished collection of national folklore in the Oxford series of Myths and Legends. 10–14

United States and Canada: Indian and Eskimo Tales

BAYLOR, BYRD, comp. *And It Is Still That Way: Legends Told by Arizona Indian Children*. Scribner's, 1976. Stories from several Native American tribes, some told with childlike directness, others with a true sense of the storyteller's cadence. 7–9

BELTING, NATALIA M. *The Long Tailed Bear and Other Indian Legends*, ill. by Louis F. Cary. Bobbs, 1961. Animal legends of 22 tribes make this a valuable source. Storytellers will welcome the tribal identification preceding each story. 8–10

COURLANDER, HAROLD. *People of the Short Blue Corn: Tales and Legends of the Hopi Indians*, ill. by Enrico Arno. Harcourt, 1970. 9–11

CURTIS, EDWARD S., comp. *The Girl Who Married a Ghost and Other Tales from the North American Indian*, ill. with photos. Four Winds, 1978. Nine folk tales handsomely complemented by Curtis' posed, romantic photographs. 10 up

DE WIT, DOROTHY, ed. *The Talking Stone: An Anthology of Native American Tales and Legends*. Greenwillow, 1979. Tales arranged by region, with tribal sources given, form a varied selection. 10–12

ERDOES, RICHARD, ed. *The Sound of Flutes and Other Indian Legends*, ill. by Paul Goble. Pantheon, 1976. A fine collection of Plains Indian tales, the result of Erdoes' 25 years listening to Native American storytellers. 10–12

FIELD, EDWARD, comp. *Eskimo Songs and Stories*, tr. by the compiler, collected by Knud Rasmussen, ill. by Kiakshuk and Pudlo. Delacorte, 1973. Rhythmic and vigorous, this collection reflects the cultural patterns of the tribes of the Hudson Bay area. 9–12

FISHER, ANNE B. *Stories California Indians Told*, ill. by Ruth Robbins. Parnassus, 1957. A dozen Indian myths told with zest and ranging from creation myths to humorous tales. 9–12

GILLHAM, CHARLES EDWARD. *Beyond the Clapping Mountains: Eskimo Stories from Alaska*, ill. by Chanimum. Macmillan, 1943. Illustrated by an Eskimo girl, these are unusual and highly imaginative tales. 10–12

HARRIS, CHRISTIE. *Mouse Woman and the Mischief-Makers*, ill. by Douglas Tait. Atheneum, 1977. A companion volume to *Mouse Woman and the Vanished Princesses*. 9–11

———. *Mouse Woman and the Vanished Princesses*, ill. by Douglas Tait. Atheneum, 1976. Six legends of the Northwest Coast Indians about princesses who vanish and are rescued by the Mouse Woman are each slightly over-extended but together form an excellent source for the storyteller. 9–11

———. *Once Upon a Totem*, ill. by John Frazer Mills. Atheneum, 1963. Five superb tales of the Indians of the North Pacific. 9–12

———. *Once More Upon a Totem*, ill. by Douglas Tait. Atheneum, 1973. Three tales based on legends of the Northwest Coast Indians. 9–12

———. *The Trouble with Princesses*, ill. by Douglas Tate. Atheneum, 1980. Each of seven tales is prefaced by a comparison between a New World princess and her Old World counterpart. 10–12

HEADY, ELEANOR B. *Tales of the Nimipoo: From the Land of the Nez Percé Indians*, ill. by Eric Carle. World, 1970. Twenty "why" tales with coyote as the hero. 8–10

HODGES, MARGARET, ad. *The Fire Bringer: A Paiute Indian Legend*, ill. by Peter Parnall. Little, 1972. 8–10

HOUSTON, JAMES. *Kiviok's Magic Journey: An Eskimo Legend*, ill. by author. Atheneum, 1973. A vigorous and dramatic retelling of one of the most popular legends of the Eskimo folk hero. 8–10

McDERMOTT, GERALD, ad. *Arrow to the Sun: A Pueblo Indian Tale*, ill. by adapter. Viking, 1974. Stylized designs and stunning color effectively complement the story of the Boy who brings the spirit of the Lord of the Sun to his pueblo. Caldecott Medal. 5–8

MACMILLAN, CYRUS. *Glooskap's Country, and Other Indian Tales*, ill. by John A. Hall. Walck, 1956. First published in 1918 as *Canadian Wonder Tales*, this is one of the finest collections of Indian stories available. They range from simple "how" stories to complex and mystical tales of magic, superbly told and illustrated. 8–12

MARTIN, FRAN. *Nine Tales of Coyote*, ill. by Dorothy McEntee. Harper, 1950. Authentic tales of Coyote, the Indian animal god. The stories are lively and have a quality of suspense. Illustrations are in color.

————. *Raven-Who-Sets-Things-Right: Indian Tales of the Northwest Coast*, ill. by Dorothy McEntee. Harper, 1975. Tales of a trickster-creator, smoothly told. 9–10

REID, DOROTHY N. *Tales of Nanabozho*, ill. by Donald Grant. Walck, 1963. Stories of the mythical Ojibwa hero to whom Longfellow gave the Iroquois name of Hiawatha. 9–12

SLEATOR, WILLIAM, ad. *The Angry Moon*, ill. by Blair Lent. Little, 1970. 5–7

TOYE, WILLIAM, ad. *The Fire Stealers*, ill. by Elizabeth Cleaver. Oxford, 1980. Bright collages by a Canadian artist make a Nanbosho story vivid. 5–7

United States: Afro-American Tales

BROWN, MARGARET WISE. *Brer Rabbit: Stories from Uncle Remus*, ill. by A. B. Frost. Harper, 1941. 8–10

CHESNUTT, CHARLES W. *Conjure Tales*, retold by Ray Anthony Shepard, ill. by John Ross and Clare Romano. Dutton, 1973. These stories by a black author, first published in 1899, are vigorous and humorous. 10–14

COURLANDER, HAROLD. *Terrapin's Pot of Sense*, ill. by Elton Fax. Holt, 1957. Americana collected in rural regions from black storytellers. 8–11

FAULKNER, WILLIAM J. *The Days When the Animals Talked: Black American Folktales and How They Came to Be*, ill. by Troy Howell. Follett, 1977. Dramatic and compellingly-told animal tales (the chief character is Brer Rabbit) as well as a series of anecdotes about his days of slavery told by Simon Brown to Faulkner. 10 up

FELTON, HAROLD. *John Henry and His Hammer*, ill. by Aldren Watson. Knopf, 1950. 10–12

HARRIS, JOEL CHANDLER. *Brer Rabbit*, ill. by A. B. Frost. Harper, 1941.

————. *Complete Tales of Uncle Remus*, ed. by Richard Chase. Houghton, 1955.

————. *The Favorite Uncle Remus*, ed. by George Van Santvoord and Archibald C. Coolidge, ill. by A. B. Frost. Houghton, 1948. 10 up

KEATS, EZRA JACK. *John Henry: An American Legend*, ill. by author. Pantheon, 1965. 5–8

REES, ENNIS. *Brer Rabbit and His Tricks*, ill. by Edward Gorey. W. R. Scott, 1967. 5–8

————. *More of Brer Rabbit's Tricks*, ill. by Edward Gorey. W. R. Scott, 1968. 5–8

United States: Variants of European Tales

CHASE, RICHARD, ed. *Grandfather Tales*, ill. by Berkeley Williams, Jr. Houghton, 1948. 9–12

————. *Jack and the Three Sillies*, ill. by Joshua Tolford. Houghton, 1950. 8–10

————. *The Jack Tales*, ill. by Berkeley Williams, Jr. Houghton, 1943. American versions of old-world tales from the Cumberlands and the Smokies. 9–12

JAGENDORF, MORITZ. *New England Bean Pot: American Folk Stories to Read and Tell*, ill. by Donald McKay. Vanguard, 1948. Folk tales of six New England states told with zest and humor. Other titles in this regional series are: *Sand in*

the Bag and Other Folk Stories of Ohio, Indiana and Illinois, ill. by John Moment. Vanguard, 1952; *Upstate, Downstate: Folk Stories of the Middle Atlantic States*, ill. by Howard Simon. Vanguard, 1949; and *Folk Stories of the South*, ill. by Michael Parks. Vanguard, 1973. 10–14

SAWYER, RUTH. *Journey Cake, Ho!* ill. by Robert McCloskey. Viking, 1953. Mountain folk-tale version of *The Pancake*. Lively illustrations make this an attractive picture book. 6–10

United States: Tall Tales

BLAIR, WALTER. *Tall Tale America: A Legendary History of Our Humorous Heroes*, ill. by Glen Rounds. Coward, 1944. 10–14

BOWMAN, JAMES CLOYD. *Mike Fink*, ill. by Leonard Everett Fisher. Little, 1957. Mike Fink was one of the greatest legendary riverboatmen, and his adventures are related in tall-tale tradition. 11 up

————. *Pecos Bill*, ill. by Laura Bannon. Whitman, 1937. Pecos Bill is the gayest of our heroes and the closest to the child's sense of humor. The illustrations add to the book's appeal. 9–12

CREDLE, ELLIS. *Tall Tales from the High Hills*, ill. by author. Nelson, 1957. Lively folk tales from the North Carolina Blue Ridge country, fine for reading and telling. 9–12

FELTON, HAROLD W. *Bowleg Bill, Seagoing Cowpuncher*, ill. by William Moyers. Prentice, 1957. Tall-tale nonsense about a cowboy who solves his problems in his own cowboy way. 10 up

LENT, BLAIR. *John Tabor's Ride*, ill. by author. Atlantic, 1966. A tall tale based on a New England legend about a shipwrecked sailor. The appeal of the telling is in the exaggeration, the fantastic situations, and the abundance of salty marine terms. 5–8

McCLOSKEY, ROBERT. *Burt Dow, Deep-Water Man: A Tale of the Sea in the Classic Tradition*, ill. by author. Viking, 1963. Jonah's story pales by comparison with this exuberant tall tale. 5–8

MALCOLMSON, ANNE. *Yankee Doodle's Cousins*, ill. by Robert McCloskey. Houghton, 1941. This is one of the finest collections of real and mythical heroes of the United States. 10–14

ROUNDS, GLEN. *Mr. Yowder and the Steamboat*, ill. by author. Holiday, 1977. A steamboat gets stuck under an elevated track in Manhattan. 8–11

————. *Ol' Paul, the Mighty Logger*, ill. by author. Holiday, 1949. These Paul Bunyan stories are retold with an earthy, exuberant zest. 10 up

SCHWARTZ, ALVIN, comp. *Kickle Snifters and Other Fearsome Critters Collected from American Folklore*, ill. by Glen Rounds. Lippincott, 1976. All of the "fearsome critters" are imaginary beasts of the tall-tale variety, and this is a list of illustrated definitions, with notes on sources included at the back of the book. 8–10

————, comp. *Whoppers: Tall Tales and Other Lies*, ill. by Glen Rounds. Lippincott, 1975. Notes and sources are given for over a hundred whoppers, from one-liners to longer tales. 9–12

SHAPIRO, IRWIN. *Heroes in American Folklore*, ill. by Donald McKay and James Daugherty. Messner, 1962. Five tall-tale heroes include Casey Jones, Joe Magarac, John Henry, Steamboat Bill, and Old Stormalong.

————. *Yankee Thunder, the Legendary Life of Davy Crockett*, ill. by James Daugherty. Messner, 1944. The author is torn between writing about the real Davy and the mythical Davy, but chooses the latter. 10–14

SHEPHARD, ESTHER. *Paul Bunyan*, ill. by Rockwell Kent. Harcourt, 1941. The most complete edition of these tales, this book also has Rockwell Kent's superb pictures.   10–14

STOUTENBURG, ADRIEN. *American Tall Tales*, ill. by Richard M. Powers. Viking, 1966. Eight stories, each about a tall-tale hero.   9–11

United States: Tales in Picture-book Form and General Collections

EMBERLEY, BARBARA, ad. *Drummer Hoff*, ill. by Ed Emberley. Prentice, 1967. An adaptation of a folk verse, with bouncy rhythm and the twin appeals of rhyme and repetition for the very young. Delightful illustrations. Caldecott Medal.   5–7

JAGENDORF, MORITZ, ed. *The Ghost of Peg-leg Peter and Other Stories of Old New York*, ill. by Lino S. Lipinsky. Vanguard, 1966. Tales range from ghost stories of early settlers to a tale about Fiorello La Guardia.   10–13

SPIER, PETER. *The Erie Canal*, ill. by author. Doubleday, 1970. The words of the rollicking song are the text. The illustrations have fascinating details and are faithful to the time and locale.   9–11

Other Countries

AIKEN, JOAN. *The Kingdom Under the Sea and Other Stories*, ill. by Jan Pienkowski. Jonathan Cape, 1979. Eleven folktales from eastern Europe retold with vigor and wit.   10–12

BATES, DAISY, comp. *Tales Told to Kabbarli*, retold by Barbara Ker Wilson, ill. by Harold Thomas. Crown, 1972. Daisy Bates devoted many years to recording aboriginal lore in Australia.   10 up

BELPRÉ, PURA. *Once in Puerto Rico*, ill. by Christine Price. Warne, 1973.

_____. *The Tiger and the Rabbit and Other Tales*, ill. by Tomie de Paola. Lippincott, 1965.

_____. *Perez and Martina*, ill. by Carlos Sanchez. Warne, 1961. Tales of Puerto Rico.   9–11

BERSON, HAROLD, ad. *Kassim's Shoes*, ill. by author. Crown, 1977.   5–8

BRYAN, ASHLEY, ad. *The Dancing Granny*, ill. by author. Atheneum, 1977. Based on a folk tale from the Antilles, this pits Granny Anika (who feels compelled to dance when she hears music) against Spider Ananse (who sings and steals her vegetables as she dances).   5–8

CARPENTER, FRANCES. *The Elephant's Bathtub: Wonder Tales from the Far East*, ill. by Hans Guggenheim. Doubleday, 1962. Burma, Cambodia, Malaya, Vietnam, and other lands of the Far East are represented here.   11–14

CARTER, DOROTHY SHARP, ad. *Greedy Mariani: And Other Folktales of the Antilles*, ill. by Trina Schart Hyman. Atheneum, 1974.   9–11

COURLANDER, HAROLD. *The Tiger's Whisker and Other Tales and Legends from Asia and the Pacific*, ill. by Enrico Arno. Harcourt, 1959. More humorous and philosophic tales gathered by a folklorist who has made a significant contribution to the lore of faraway lands.   9–13

CURCIJA-PRODANOVIC, NADA. *Yugoslav Folk-Tales*, ill. by Joan Kiddell-Monroe. Walck, 1957.   10–14

DEUTSCH, BABETTE, and AVRAHM YARMOLINSKY. *Tales of Faraway Folk*, ill. by Irena Lorentowicz. Harper, 1952. A unique collection of tales from Baltic, Russian, and Asiatic lands.   9–12

_____. *More Tales of Faraway Folk*, ill. by Janina Domanska. Harper, 1963. Fifteen more tales, many from the U.S.S.R.   7–11

EL-SHAMY, HASAN, ed. and tr. *Folktales of Egypt*. Univ. of Chicago Pr., 1980. An erudite forward is followed by a varied selection and extensive roles.   11 up

GRAHAM, GAIL B., ad. *The Beggar in the Blanket: And Other Vietnamese Tales*, ill. by Brigitte Bryan. Dial, 1970. Eight folk tales translated from French sources in Vietnam.   9–11

JEWETT, ELEANORE MYERS. *Which Was Witch? Tales of Ghosts and Magic from Korea*, ill. by Taro Yashima (pseud. for Jun Iwamatsu). Viking, 1953. Fourteen stories with sparkle and suspense, excellent for storytelling.   9–13

JUNNE, I. K. *Floating Clouds, Floating Dreams: Favorite Asia Folk Tales*. Doubleday, 1974. Tales of eleven Asian countries, told in a very readable style.   9–11

KEELY, H. H., and CHRISTINE PRICE, ads. *The City of the Dagger: And Other Tales from Burma*, ill. by Christine Price. Warne, 1971. Folklore and legends are mingled in intricate tales, many of which concern hero-kings of the past.   10–12

KELSEY, ALICE GEER. *Once the Hodja*, ill. by Frank Dobias. McKay, 1943. Twenty-four tales from Turkey filled with humor and simple wisdom.

_____. *Once the Mullah*, ill. by Kurt Werth. McKay, 1954. Stories told by Mullah give insight into Persian life and folklore.   9–12

OLENIUS, ELSA, comp. *Great Swedish Fairy Tales*, tr. by Holger Lundbergh, ill. by John Bauer. Delacorte, 1973. Illustrated by a major Swedish illustrator in a romantic, turn-of-the-century style which suits the gentle magic in the tales.   9–11

PARKER, K. LANGLOH. *Australian Legendary Tales*, selected and ed. by H. Drake-Brockman, ill. by Elizabeth Durack. Viking, 1966. A selection of Australian aboriginal tales first published at the turn of the century.   11–14

SHERLOCK, PHILIP M. *Anansi, the Spider Man: Jamaican Folk Tales*, ill. by Marcia Brown. T. Crowell, 1954. These stories are told by Jamaicans with simplicity and charm.   9–12

SHERLOCK, PHILIP and HILARY. *Ears and Tails and Common Sense*. T. Crowell, 1974. Stories from the Caribbean told with verve and humor.   9–11

SHULEVITZ, URI. *The Magician*, ad. from the Yiddish of I. L. Peretz. Macmillan, 1973. A Passover story about the prophet Elijah, nicely retold and handsomely illustrated.

TASHJIAN, VIRGINIA A., ed. *Once There Was and Was Not*, based on stories by H. Toumanian, ill. by Nonny Hogrogian. Little, 1966. Seven Armenian folk tales, many with familiar elements, beautifully illustrated. A pleasure to read aloud and a good source for storytelling.   9–11

_____, ed. *Three Apples Fell from Heaven: Armenian Tales Retold*, ill. by Nonny Hogrogian. Little, 1971.   9–11

VAN WOERKOM, DOROTHY O., ad. *Abu Ali: Three Tales of the Middle East*, ill. by Harold Berson. Macmillan, 1976. Three short tales for the primary grades reader; in two Abu Ali is outwitted, in a third, he outwits the friends who think they've outwitted him.   7–8

_____, ad. *The Friends of Abu Ali: Three More Tales of the Middle East*, ill. by Harold Berson. Macmillan, 1978. Three humorous noodlehead stories especially adapted for beginning independent readers.   6–8

VO-DINH, ad. *The Toad Is the Emperor's Uncle: Animal Folktales from Viet-Nam*, ill. by adapter. Doubleday, 1970. Stories that reflect humor as well as ethical principle.   9–11

WOLKSTEIN, DIANE, comp. *The Magic Orange Tree and Other Haitian Folktales*, ill. by Elsa Henriquez. Knopf, 1978. A collection distinguished for its humor and variety.   10 up

Chapter Eight: Fables, Myths, and Epics

Fables, myths, and epics, like the ballads and folk tales, are a part of the great stream of folk-lore. While they are not generally so popular with children as the folk tales, they have made an equally important contribution to our literary heritage. The fables have colored our attitudes toward moral and ethical problems. The myths and the epics have become a part of our everyday symbols in both writing and speech. Rarely, in today's literature, can one find heroes like Robin Hood or Finn MacCool or King Arthur to stir young people's imaginations. All these three types of literature, while fundamentally different from each other, have in common their strong moral flavor.

Fables, Parables, Proverbs

Fables are brief narratives which take abstract ideas of good or bad, wise or foolish behavior and attempt to make them concrete and striking enough to be understood and remembered. The chief actor in most fables is an animal or inanimate object which behaves like a human being and has one dominant trait. Whether the characters are humans or beasts, they remain coldly impersonal and engage in a single significant act which teaches a moral lesson. These are the essential elements of the true fable.

Fables have a teasing likeness to proverbs and parables. All three embody universal truths in brief, striking form; and all three are highly intellectual exercises, as exact as an equation. Of the three, the *proverb* is the most highly condensed commentary on human folly or wisdom. It tells no story but presents a bit of wisdom succinctly:

A soft answer turneth away wrath: but grievous words stir up anger. (Proverbs 15:1)

Better is a dry morsel and quietness therewith, than a house full of feasting with strife. (Proverbs 17:1)

It is interesting to find many examples in *Japanese Proverbs* by Rokuo Okada that are amazingly like Biblical proverbs in their implications:

He who wants to shoot the general must first shoot his horse.

A cornered mouse bites the cat.[1]

Perhaps the fable grew out of the proverb, to dramatize its pithy wisdom in story form.

The *parable* is like the fable in that it tells a brief story from which a moral or spiritual truth may be inferred. But its characters, unlike the personified animals or objects of most fables, are generally human beings, like the Wise and Foolish Virgins, or the Prodigal Son, or the

---

1. From *Japanese Proverbs* by Rokuo Okada. Copyright by the Japan Travel Bureau. In *Japan Times Weekly*, December 1, 1962.

Good Samaritan. If the story is told in terms of animals or objects, they are never personified but remain strictly themselves. That is, the seed that falls upon rocky ground has nothing to say for itself, and the house that was built upon sand goes down in the flood strictly a house. The parables use people or things as object lessons.

There are obvious differences among the stories discussed in the following pages under *Fable Collections.* Some are typical fables, some are parables, others resemble folk tales, and many contain maxims or proverbs. All of them, however, embody moral or spiritual wisdom.

Fable Collections

If you say "fables" to an English-speaking child, he thinks at once of *Aesop's Fables.* To a French child, La Fontaine and "fables" are inseparably associated, and so in the Orient it is *The Panchatantra, The Fables of Bidpai,* or the *Ja-tākas.* These major collections of fables, while resembling each other, also show striking differences.

Aesop's Fables

Some modern scholars doubt whether Aesop really existed. G. K. Chesterton suggests that he may be as completely fictitious a character as that other slave, Uncle Remus, who also told

From *Aesop's Fables* by Boris Artzybasheff. Copyright 1933 by Boris Artzybasheff. All rights reserved. Reprinted by permission of the Viking Press, Inc.

beast tales. But his name and fame persist through one edition of the fables after another. Aesop is said to have lived in Greece between 620 and 560 B.C. and is thought to have been a Samian slave. Because free speech under the Tyrants was risky business, Aesop is supposed to have used the fables for political purposes, protecting himself and veiling his opinions behind the innuendos of these little stories. All we know is that the picturesque legends about Aesop have survived with his name.

Translated into Latin in the first and third centuries, the Aesop fables became the textbooks of the medieval schools. In Latin they found their way into England, France, and Germany, were translated into several languages, and were among the first books to be printed by Caxton when he started his famous press in England. Evidently there was infiltration from other sources. Joseph Jacobs said he could mention at least seven hundred fables ascribed to Aesop, although the first known collection of them, made by Demetrius of Phalerum about 320 B.C., contained only about two hundred. Since India, like Greece, had long used the beast tale for teaching purposes, undoubtedly some of the Indian fables gravitated, in the course of time, to the Aesop collection. From whatever source they came, once included in

Viewpoint _____

In every age [*Aesop's Fables*] has had the distinction of being approved of and adapted for the young reader. In style the Aesopian fable is akin to the folk-tale, but, unlike most other traditional lore, it had the good fortune in the ancient world to be moulded into an acceptable form. Often made into a schoolbook and burdened with added moralities, it never lost those pristine characteristics which endeared it to young or unsophisticated minds. Brevity in telling, clarity of style, animal characters with human attributes, pithy lessons about human conduct; these were all features to give life to the fables in every generation. There is little of high ethical purpose in the episodes: they are more like a fascinating looking-glass reflecting the follies of mankind.— M. F. Thwaite, *From Primer to Pleasure,* The Library Association, London, 1963, p. 7.

Aesop they assumed the Aesop form, which is now regarded as the pure fable type. It is a brief story with inanimate objects or animals most frequently serving as the leading characters, and with the single action of the narrative pointing to an obvious moral lesson. James Reeves in his *Fables from Aesop* points out that the virtues which Aesop praises are not the heroic ones but rather "the peasant virtues of discretion, prudence, moderation and forethought. . . . That is why Aesop . . . has always had the affection and regard of ordinary people."

The Panchatantra

The Panchatantra, meaning "five books," was composed in Kashmir about 200 B.C.,[2] and is the oldest known collection of Indian fables. *The Hitopadesa*, or Book of Good Counsel, is considered only another version of *The Panchatantra*,[3] and still another is called *The Fables of Bidpai*. These collections were translated into Persian, Arabic, Latin, and many other languages. In the Latin version the tales became popular throughout medieval Europe.

After the extreme condensation of Aesop, the stories of *The Panchatantra* seem long and involved. They are a textbook on "the wise conduct of life," intricate stories-within-stories, and are interrupted with philosophical verses so numerous that the thread of the story is almost forgotten. Some of these poems are sixteen or twenty verses long, but the quatrain is the more usual type.

> *A friend in need is a friend indeed,*
> *Although of different caste;*
> *The whole world is your eager friend*
> *So long as riches last.*
>
> *Make friends, make friends, however strong*
> *Or weak they be;*
> *Recall the captive elephants*
> *That mice set free.*[4]

These verses are summaries of the stories which seem more like folk tales than fables. On the whole, *The Panchatantra* is for adults rather than children.

From *The Fables of India* by Joseph Gaer, by permission of Little, Brown and Co. Copyright 1955 by Joseph Gaer.

The *Jatakas*

Another collection of ancient Indian fables is the group called the *Jatakas*. The time of their origin is not definitely known. They were in existence in the fifth century A.D., but carvings illustrating Jataka stories have been found which were made as early as the second or third centuries B.C.

Jatakas is a Buddhist name for stories concerning the rebirths of Gautama Buddha, who, according to tradition, was reincarnated many times in the forms of different animals until he became at last Buddha, the Enlightened One. These beast tales, then, are really about a man living briefly as an animal, consorting with other animals, and deriving from these experiences certain ethical lessons.

Joseph Gaer tells us that there are two or three thousand of these stories. Generally, the introduction and body of the tale are in prose, but the conclusions are often verses. Comparatively few of them are suitable for children and then only with considerable adaptation; one such is Nancy De Roin's *Jataka Tales*, a se-

---

2. *The Panchatantra*, translated by Arthur W. Ryder (University of Chicago Press, 1925), p. 3.

3. Joseph Gaer, *The Fables of India* (Little, Brown, 1955), p. 53.

4. *The Panchatantra*, op. cit., pp. 5, 273.

Illustrations by Margot Zemach from *The Frogs Who Wanted A King* and other songs from La Fontaine, collected by Edward Smith. Illustration Copyright © 1977 by Margot Zemach. Published by Four Winds Press, a division of Scholastic Magazines, Inc. Reprinted by permission.

lective edition of simplified fables. Joseph Gaer's versions, in *The Fables of India*, keep close to the original form. Some Jatakas resemble parables from the Bible. Still others are like short folk tales with self-evident morals.

The Fables of La Fontaine

In the twelfth century, Marie de France introduced and popularized the fable in France. Others followed her lead, but Jean de La Fontaine (1621–1695), a contemporary of Charles Perrault, made the fable so completely and gracefully his own that the French coined a word for him, *le fablier*, "the fable-teller." Adapted from an eighteenth century music book for children, *The Frogs Who Wanted a King and Other Songs from La Fontaine* contains Edward Smith's choices of fables; the songs are illustrated with brisk, humorous line drawings and handsome watercolors by Margot Zemach.

La Fontaine was a skilled poet and wrote his fables in graceful verses which are delightful to read and easy to memorize. There are charming descriptions of birds and beasts and of the beautiful Champagne countryside where La Fontaine grew up. The courtier and the man of the world show themselves in the shrewd appraisals of character and the worldly philosophy that permeate the fables:

Now, as everyone knows, white paws do not grow on wolves.

My dear Mr. Crow, learn from this how every flatterer lives at the expense of anybody who will listen to him. This lesson is well worth the loss of a cheese to you.[5]

5. From *The Fables of La Fontaine*, translated by Margaret W. Brown (Harper, 1940), pp. 6, 8, and 19.

La Fontaine used for his sources the Latin versions of Aesop and *The Fables of Bidpai*, and the versions of his predecessor, Marie de France. In spite of the verse form and the characteristic bits of philosophy, these fables of La Fontaine are closer to the Aesop pattern than to the tales from India. They maintain the brevity, the predominant use of animal characters, and, above all, the single striking episode which points up the moral.

Modern Editions of Fables

The fables are both didactic and universal, with their universality making their didacticism bearable if not enjoyable. Children are made uncomfortable by a story that preaches directly, but if they see that the lessons of the fables apply to everyone, they can better appreciate their wisdom and humor.

Excellent collections available today are *Aesop's Fables*, edited and illustrated by Boris Artzybasheff; a newly illustrated edition of *The Fables of Aesop*, edited by Joseph Jacobs; James Reeves's *Fables from Aesop*; and Anne Terry White's *Aesop's Fables*. Reeves has varied the concise narrative form by introducing conversation among the animals, and Anne Terry White has retold the stories in an easy, simple style appropriate for younger children. Louis Untermeyer, in his *Aesop's Fables*, gaily illustrated by Alice and Martin Provensen, has provided an edition of stories humorous and colorful enough to read aloud to children as young as six or seven.

The trend to present the fables in a form appropriate for younger children is most obvious in the publication of single-fable editions, such as Mary Calhoun's *Old Man Whickutt's Donkey*; Jean Showalter's *The Donkey Ride*; and Brian Wildsmith's *The Miller, the Boy, and the Donkey*. Wildsmith has retold and illustrated several other La Fontaine fables in addition to this favorite. In *John J. Plenty and Fiddler Dan*, John Ciardi has told the story of the improvident grasshopper and the industrious ant in an amusing verse version. There are also some attractive adaptations of fables from India for young children. Notable among them are Marcia Brown's Caldecott Medal book, *Once a Mouse*, an animal fable illustrated by color woodcuts; and Paul Galdone's *The Monkey and the Crocodile*, an adaptation of a Jataka tale.

From *Chanticleer and the Fox,* adapted by Barbara Cooney from Chaucer's *Canterbury Tales,* Copyright © 1956 by Harper & Row, Publishers, Inc. by permission of Thomas Y. Crowell, Publisher.

Another collection that has both fables and folk tales is Mirra Ginsburg's *Three Rolls and One Doughnut: Fables from Russia,* which has a vivacious style. A source of Russian fables is Ivan Krylov's *Fifteen Fables of Krylov,* in a colloquial translation by Guy Daniels. A delightful single-fable edition is Barbara Cooney's Caldecott Medal book *Chanticleer and the Fox,* which is based on Geoffrey Chaucer's "The Nun's Priest's Tale" from *The Canterbury Tales.* There are a number of fables in modern dress—a particularly good one is Jean Merrill's *The Black Sheep,* which is far longer than the usual compressed fable form but, in the true spirit of the fable, teaches a lesson about blind conformity.

Myths

The fables are simple, highly condensed lessons in morality. The myth is far more complicated. It attempts to explain—in complex symbolism—the vital outlines of existence:

(1) cosmic phenomena (e.g., how the earth and sky came to be separated); (2) peculiarities of natural history (e.g., why rain follows the cries or activities of certain birds); (3) the origins of human civilization (e.g., through the beneficent action of a culture-hero like Prometheus); or (4) the origin of social or religious custom or the nature and history of objects of worship.[6]

It also attempts to make more acceptable the painful realities of existence—danger, disease, misfortune, and death—by explaining them as part of a sacred order in the universe.

The explanations may seem irrational and inconsistent to the science-minded modern. This is because they are not scientific hypotheses but were created by and appeal to the imagination. The truth of the myth was unquestioned by primitive peoples because it was so closely associated with their sacred beliefs. For them, both nature and society were areas of reverent acceptance—not of objective study, as they are in this age of scientific inquiry.

Evolution of Myths

A number of writers have called attention to the various levels of myth development, their evolution from primitive to highly complex symbolic stories. These developmental stages are important to us because they throw light upon the various types of stories (for example, the *pourquoi* tales) included in myths and help to explain their suitability, or lack of it, as story material for children.

The early part of this evolution is, of course, shrouded in the darkness of prehistoric times. Much research has been devoted to it, but the outlines are still only dimly understood. For one thing, the evolution of myth and religion differs from people to people. Suffice it to say that the Greeks, like many other peoples, passed through a primary stage in which they worshiped an impersonal force believed to pervade all aspects of the universe: sun, moon, crops, rivers. The early Greeks performed rites to propitiate these bodiless forces so that they would grant to the world fertility and life. Later these nature forces were personified in the myths.

Myths, then, did give body—both animal and human—to the mystic forces that early people

6. William Reginald Halliday, "Folklore," in an earlier edition of the *Encyclopaedia Britannica.*

Viewpoint_____

felt in the universe. As these ideas developed, the tendency was to give complex human form to these impersonal forces. These bright sky-dwellers were created in humankind's own image but surpassed humanity in beauty, wisdom, and power.

Imagining these supernatural beings in their own likeness, the people interpreted a flood to mean that the river god was angry with them and intended to punish them. Drouths, earthquakes, good crops and bad crops were all dependent on how humanity stood in the graces of these nature gods. These primitive beginnings of myth were polytheistic; that is, they gave rise to many gods.

Presently these beings developed relationships among each other, assumed certain powers, and suffered limitations of power. Thus in the Greek mythology the first gods were all brothers and sisters—Hestia, Demeter, Hera, Poseidon, Hades, and Zeus. Because Zeus saved them from destruction, he was chosen the supreme ruler, the sky god, while Poseidon ruled the waters and Hades, who dwelt below the earth, ruled the dominion of the dead. From their matings, their children, and the powers and limitations of each of these three powerful brothers arose endless squabbles that bear a melancholy resemblance to the earthly rows of humans.

Each god or goddess came to assume certain powers although every one except Zeus knew distinct limitations to power and was vulnerable to misfortunes in certain respects, even as humans are. Balder, the Norse sun god, whose mother, Frigga, made everything except the mistletoe promise not to harm him, was slain by the insignificant shrub which Frigga had thought too harmless to bother about. Balder the Beautiful died; he went out to sea in his fiery ship, burning like the autumn foliage; the earth wept for him, and cold and darkness followed—a picture of the coming of autumn and winter in the north country. So these deities developed relationships and powers but were subject to certain limitations from other powers.

The extension of a god's powers soon turned him or her into a symbolic figure, standing for certain abstract virtues. So Zeus, from being at first merely a sky god, became the symbol of power and law. Apollo began as the sun god, a beautiful young man with a fiery chariot to drive across the sky daily. Then he became also the god of health and healing, the patron god of physicians. Finally this idea of healing was expanded to include the related but less physical concept of purification, and Apollo then stood for the abstract idea of purity. In some such way as this, many of the gods evolved from mere nature personifications to become symbols of abstract moral attributes.

In some mythologies less sophisticated than the Greeks' the deities have never signified anything more than spirits of earth, sky, sun, moon, or even animals. The American Indian "Old Man Coyote" is such a deity. On the other hand, the Navaho "Turquoise Woman" is not merely a sky goddess but seems to be also a symbol of beauty in the highest sense, meaning harmony and goodness.

Finally, when the gods had come to stand for moral attributes and powers, the next and last stage of myth-making was the development of a priesthood, temples, and a ritual of worship. Then the myth was an organized religion. Apollo had a great temple at Delphi with priests, an oracle, vestal virgins, and elaborate ceremonies and rituals. The Apollo cult represents the last and most complex stage of myth-making, which the mythologies of only highly civilized people attain.

Types of Myths

Among the simplest of myth stories are the why stories, or *pourquoi* tales. Why the woodpecker has a red head and how the arbutus came to be are from the North American Indians. In both Greek and Norse myths these *why* stories become more complex than in the woodpecker and arbutus examples. Take, for instance, the Greek explanation of summer and winter; the story goes that Demeter (the earth mother) has been deprived of her beautiful child Persephone (the grain), who has been carried off by Hades to his realm below the ground. Demeter seeks her child, weeping, but Persephone must remain in Hades' underworld for six months of each year, leaving earth to darkness and cold. Such a story is neither simple nor fully explanatory for children. In much the same vein, the North American Indians of the Southwest have their desert seasonal story of little Burnt-Face, the scorched earth, who sees the invisible chief, the spring rains, and is made beautiful by him and becomes his bride. To children, these are just good fairy tales, as interesting as "Cinderella." However, if in the study of Greeks or Desert Indians you explain to the children the possible meaning of these stories for the people who created them, they are surprised and charmed with the secondary meaning.

From *Persephone and the Springtime* by Margaret Hodges, by permission of Little, Brown and Co. Illustrations Copyright © 1973 by Arvis Stewart. (Original in color)

Many of the myths are, on the whole, too adult in content and significance to be appropriate story material for children. But the simpler tales among them are accepted by the children exactly as they accept any folk tale. One of their favorites is "King Midas," who wished that everything he touched would turn into gold and soon found himself starving in the midst of plenty. Well-told versions of such stories are suitable for children and may be used with or without the background of the people and their mythology.

The ways of the gods with humans are the subject of another group of stories which includes "King Midas." One of the most delightful is "Bellerophon and Pegasus." Bellerophon, a handsome youth, is sent by his host, Iobates, to kill the chimera, which is devastating Lycia. Although Iobates is sure the mission will mean the boy's death, the gods take pity upon Bellerophon and send him the winged Pegasus. That Pegasus, the winged horse of the gods, means "poetry" does not enter children's heads, but that Bellerophon could not kill the terrible chimera until he had first captured and tamed Pegasus makes a good adventure story of unusual beauty. Such stories are really hero tales with a background of myth and they comprise a particularly good group of stories for children. Some of them, like those in the *Odyssey*, later developed into national epics. Stories of the gods' amatory adventures among humans are legion and are not often adapted for children.

Some of the myths warn against particular sins. Pride seems to be especially offensive to the gods. Arachne was turned into a spider because she boasted of her weaving. Bellerophon, after he captured the winged horse, Pegasus, became so sure of himself that he attempted to ride into Zeus's dwelling and was promptly struck blind for his presumption. Some of these myths are almost like fables, and, like the fables, they could be summarized with a maxim or proverb.

Finally, the ways of the gods with other gods furnish us with another body of myth stories, often complex in their significance and adult in content. Here we encounter nature myths which even the folklorists interpret differently and which leave the reader baffled and a bit weary with all the things which aren't what they seem. Frazer's *Golden Bough* is a repository for these tales. In the Greek stories we find involved accounts of creation whose interpretation is decidedly speculative. And throughout the accounts of the gods and their escapades are endless double meanings which may start simply with Gaea, a personification of the Earth, who is touched by Eros (Love) and bears Uranus (Heaven). In *The Golden God: Apollo*, Doris Gates depicts an Olympian who could be cruel or compassionate to other gods or to human beings. Moving and profound is the story of Prometheus, the Titan, who dared the wrath of the gods to bring fire to humanity and suffered endless tortures as a result. Prometheus is so noble a symbol of sacrifice that poets and painters have repeatedly used his story as a subject. But these myths, with their symbolism and inner meanings, are both complex and abstract, and some people feel that they have no place in children's literature.

Sources of Mythologies

Greek Myths

Most of the Greek myths came to us by way of the poet Hesiod, who is supposed to have lived during the eighth century B.C. While he was guarding his father's flocks, so the story goes, the Muses themselves commissioned him to be their poet. So a poet he became, winning a contest and gratefully dedicating a tripod to the Muses, who had shown him the way.

His first famous poem, *Works and Days*, contains the earliest known fable in Greek, "The Hawk and the Nightingale."

Theogony, another poem attributed to Hesiod, contains the Greek myths of the creation and the history of Zeus and Cronus, including Zeus's great battle with the Titans. Hesiod's picture of the defeated Titans, confined and guarded by giants and by Day and Night, is a convincing one.

Hesiod is credited with bringing together in organized form the major portion of Greek mythology. The English translation, although in prose, is good reading.

Roman Myths

The Roman versions of the Greek myths are available to us in the more familiar *Metamorphoses* of the Latin poet Ovid. Born in 43 B.C., Ovid belonged to a wealthy and privileged family. He was educated under famous Roman teachers and became a poet against his father's wishes.

Illustration by Constantinos CoConis, p. 27. From Doris Gates, *The Golden God Apollo*. Copyright © 1973 by Doris Gates. Published by The Viking Press, Inc.

The *Metamorphoses* consists of fifteen books recounting tales of miraculous transformations, hence the title. It begins with the metamorphosis of Chaos to order, follows the Greek development of gods and humans, recounts innumerable *why* stories of flowers, rivers, rocks, and the like. It concludes, appropriately enough, with Julius Caesar turned into a star, and Ovid himself on his way to some form of immortality. These stories, even in our English prose translations, are amazingly dramatic. It is interesting to check modern versions with these stirring tales of Ovid, which are the source of most adaptations.

Norse Myths

Whether the Norse myths began in Norway, Greenland, Ireland, Iceland, or England, it was in Iceland that they were preserved orally and first written down. Iceland, remote from the rest of the world and settled largely by Norwegians, held to the old language, once the speech of all Northern peoples, and so kept the stories alive in their original form. The two collections are the *Elder* or *Poetic Edda*, and the *Younger* or *Prose Edda*.

The *Poetic* and the *Prose Eddas* follow the sing-and-say style, with the difference that the *Poetic Edda* is mostly verse with brief prose passages, and the *Prose Edda* is mostly prose with interspersed poetic passages. Both are difficult books, but there are several adaptations to use with children.

The word *Edda* was orginally the name or title for a great-grandmother. In time it came to stand for the Norwegian court-meter or the art of poetry. In both senses it seems to imply something traditional. The *Elder* or *Poetic Edda* (thirty-four poems) contains the Prophecy, which tells how the world was created, how the gods came to be, and how they fell. There is a book of proverbs, and finally there is the Norse epic, the saga of Sigurd the Volsung. These heroic lays were supposedly collected from oral tradition by Saemund the Learned and committed to writing about the eleventh or twelfth century. By then they must have been exposed to Christian ideas and to other cultures, but they remain, nevertheless, primitive and vigorous.

The *Younger* or *Prose Edda* was not collected until the thirteenth century. The first book, "The Beguiling of Gylfi," contains the bulk of the Norse myths. It was the work of Snorri Sturluson, an Icelander who combined a greedy and traitorous character with a real reverence for the traditional literature he recorded so faithfully.

Why Use the Myths with Children?

It is the rare child who is not enchanted with the stories of mythology. The sky-dwellers of the Greeks and Romans not only left a mark on our language, but they continue to spellbind each succeeding generation of children. Bellerophon taming the winged horse, Icarus plummeting through the sky into the sea, Hermes stepping cloudward on his winged sandals—these somehow catch the imagination with their dramatic beauty. It is not an accident that most of the examples of myths in the preceding pages have been from the Greek. If children can sample only one mythology, it should be the Greek or its Roman adaptation. Our lan-

Viewpoint

guage and our thinking are full of words and ideas derived from these sources.[7] For example, *titanic* comes from the powerful Titans; *erotic* from Eros, the god of love; *panic* from the god Pan; and *cereal* from Ceres, the grain goddess. Minerva with her owl gazes down on us in our libraries. Venus, rising from her sea shell, advertises bath salts or cosmetics. There is a dramatic quality about the myths which has so captured the imaginations of poets that poetry, and English poetry in particular, is filled with classical allusions. Not to know Greco-Roman mythology is to grope more or less blindly through the arts, particularly literature.

But the Norse myths too should be part of the experience of English-speaking children. The people who composed them were a vital source of our customs, laws, and speech. Yet the myths which are their finest expression and the clearest mirror of their life are not nearly so familiar to most of us as the myths of the ancient civilizations of Greece and Rome. The Norse gods do not have the beauty and grace of the classic deities, but they are cast in heroic mold, and there is a grandeur about the tales that is hard to match. Such stories as "How Thor Found His Hammer," "The Apples of Iduna," "Thor's Visit to the Giants," and "The Death of Balder" are fascinating with or without a study of the people.

Both Greek and Norse mythologies, moreover, furnish the background for the great national epics of those countries. Children must

---

7. There is a book devoted to such sources: Isaac Asimov, *Words from the Myths* (Houghton, 1961).

know Greek mythology in order to understand the *Iliad* or the *Odyssey,* and they must know Norse mythology in order to understand the ideals and motives of the heroic characters in the Norse epic *Sigurd the Volsung,* or in Wagner's opera cycle *The Ring of the Nibelungs,* the Teutonic form of the Sigurd epic.

These are a few of the reasons that myths should be used with older children, but the chief reasons are, after all, the beauty and the imaginative quality of the tales themselves.

What Versions of the Myths to Use

The chief difficulty in using mythology with children is to select satisfactory versions of the stories. Nathaniel Hawthorne, artist though he was, did not scruple to turn the gods into petulant children. He told an entrancing story, but he lost almost completely the dignity of the gods, and sometimes he even lost the significance of the story.

Good versions of the myths for children have been made and new ones are still appearing. General standards should help us in selecting the best of these.

Although some adaptation may be necessary, myths should not be written down to children. When this is done, the author is usually trying

to retell myths to children who are too young for them. Six- and seven-year-old children can take only the bare bones of these stories, but children from nine or ten years old to fourteen can enjoy rich versions of some of the originals. For example, Krystyna Turska's adaptation of *Pegasus* makes the myth of the winged horse and his bold rider vividly real with its beautiful illustrations. At home, some children may read myths earlier, but in the mixed groups of the average classroom, the appeal of myths is distinctly to older children.

Finally, adaptations should be simple enough to be thoroughly comprehensible to children without sacrificing either the spirit or the richness of the originals. Too often, in order to simplify these stories, an adapter reduces the colorful details of the original to drab outlines, devoid of charm. Simplification of some of the words is permissible and even essential. But reject an adaptation that omits the rich, descriptive details of Ovid's tale. In the tale of Pegasus, for example, it would be a pity to miss the pictures of the palace, the chariot, and the horses of the Sun, the account of Apollo's love and anxiety for the reckless youth, the portrayal of the boy's terror of the lonely heavens, and the descriptions of the rushing speed, the earth aflame, and finally the Jovian bolt.

According to these standards, what versions of the myths are best to use with children? There has been a flood of new adaptations and

Illustration by William Stobbs. Reproduced from *The Gorgon's Head.* © 1961 by Ian Serraillier. By permission of Henry Z. Walck, Inc.

some new editions of old versions. Of the latter, one of the best is *The Heroes* by Charles Kingsley, Victorian scholar and poet. His stories of Perseus, Theseus, and Jason have a nobility that should prove a wholesome antidote to the banality of much of our mass entertainment. Padraic Colum's *The Golden Fleece* and *The Children's Homer* are superb storytelling for good readers, and the d'Aulaires' big, handsome *Book of Greek Myths* represents years of preparation. The stories are brief but have continuity; the copious and colorful illustrations are uneven in quality but imaginative. This is a splendid book for classroom use. It is also interesting to see how the myths appeal to poets, beginning with Kingsley and Colum. In 1960, British poet Robert Graves brought out his version, *Greek Gods and Heroes,* a lively text that makes clear what is often confusing. And Ian Serraillier, another poet, has told the stories of Perseus, in *The Gorgon's Head,* and Theseus, in *The Way of Danger,* with dramatic beauty. Both can be read by children or may serve as sources for storytelling. The illustrations suggest figures on Greek vases. Other tales by Serraillier include *Heracles the Strong,* illustrated with woodcuts that echo the vigor of the story; *The Clashing Rocks,* the story of Jason; and *A Fall from the Sky,* the story of Daedalus.

The eleven stories from Greek mythology adapted by Katherine Miller in *Apollo* are told in competent but not impressive brief versions. Olivia Coolidge's twenty-seven myths in *Greek Myths,* on the other hand, are mature in approach and are well told. Leon Garfield and Edward Blishen's *The God Beneath the Sea,* a flowing narrative version that clarifies the complexities of Olympian relationships, won the 1970 Carnegie Medal. Their later book, *The Golden Shadow,* takes the life of Heracles as its central theme. *Strangers Dark and Gold* by Norma Johnston is a stirring synthesis of three early versions of Jason's quest for the Golden Fleece. Two very good source books are Edith Hamilton's *Mythology,* which gives excellent background, provides a sense of the sequence of the myths, and is written in polished prose, and Roger Lancelyn Green's *A Book of Myths,* which gives variants of myths from many of the ancient lands. Examine these editions and choose the one or two that best suit your needs as sources for storytelling or references for the children to read themselves.

When you want to use Norse myths and

From *Norse Gods and Giants* by Ingri and Edgar Parin d'Aulaire. Copyright © 1967 by Ingri and Edgar Parin d'Aulaire. Reproduced by permission of Doubleday & Company, Inc.

hero tales, turn again to Padraic Colum, to his *Children of Odin,* a stirring and understandable version of those complex tales. Less difficult for younger readers are Catharine Sellew's *Adventures with the Giants* and *Adventures with the Heroes* and Ingri and Edgar Parin d'Aulaire's *Norse Gods and Giants.* In this last book, the author-artists have illustrated with big, bold pictures and have retold Norse myths in a straightforward style with occasional passages in which the oral tradition is evident. Although *Legends of the North* by Olivia Coolidge has a contemporary tone and lacks the lyric quality of the Colum tales, it has a special quality of vigorous spontaneity. An early adaptation that still serves well is Abbie F. Brown's *In the Days of Giants,* while Dorothy Hosford's *Sons of the Volsungs* and *Thunder of the Gods* cover the myths and the hero cycles in superb style, either for storytelling or reading by the children themselves. These are, however, the most difficult of all stories to tell.

Epic and Hero Tales

In the source collections of myths, both Greek and Norse, there are (in addition to the stories of the gods) tales of human heroes buffeted violently by gods and humanity but daring greatly, suffering uncomplainingly, and enduring staunchly to the end. Such tales, having a human hero as the focus of the action and embodying the ideals of a culture, are called epics.

Characteristics of the Epic

Epics are sometimes written in verse, as in the *Iliad* or the *Sigurd Saga,* and sometimes in prose, as in Malory's *Morte d'Arthur.* The adventures of the legendary hero Robin Hood were preserved by the ballads. The term *epic* is often used quite flexibly to include such dissimilar materials as the great philosophical poem from the Hebrew, the Book of Job, the slight and romantic *Aucassin and Nicolette* from the medieval French, and the comparatively modern *Paradise Lost* by the English poet John Milton.

Most of us, however, think of epics as a cycle of tales, such as the *Odyssey* or the *Iliad,* gathered around one hero. These two heroic narratives have come to typify this particular field of literature. In them, legendary heroes pursue legendary adventures, aided or hindered by

*Viewpoint*_____

[The heroic ideal] had risen into the consciousness of the authors of the Sagas; it was not far from definite expression in abstract terms. In this lay the danger. An ideal, defined or described in set terms, is an ideal without any responsibility and without any privilege. It may be picked up and traded on by any fool or hypocrite. Undefined and undivulged, it belongs only to those who have some original strength of imagination or will, and with them it cannot go wrong.

All is well, however, so long as this heroic ideal is kept in its right relation, as one element in a complex work, not permitted to walk about by itself as a personage. This right subordination is observed in the Sagas, whereby both the heroic characters are kept out of extravagance . . . and the less noble or the more complex characters are rightly estimated. [The Sagas] are imaginative, dealing in actions and characters; they are not ethical or sentimental treatises, or mirrors of chivalry.—W. P. Ker, *Epic and Romance,* Macmillan, London, 1931, pp. 202–203, 206.

partisan gods who apparently leave Olympus for the express purpose of meddling in human affairs. In short, myth may still be with us in the epic, but the dramatic center of interest has shifted from the gods to a human hero. We have moved from Olympus to earth, transferring our sympathies from gods to humans, from divine adventures to human endeavors.

The epic is strongly national in its presentation of human character. Odysseus may never have lived, but he is the embodiment of the Greek ideals of manly courage, sagacity, beauty, and endurance. Sigurd is the personification of Norse heroism; King Arthur is the code of chivalry in the flesh; and Robin Hood is the mouthpiece for England's passionate love of freedom and justice, as he is the ideal of hardy, jovial English manhood. Study the epic hero of a nation and you discover the moral code of that nation and era—all its heroic ideals embodied in one character.

The *Iliad* and the *Odyssey*

The *Iliad* and the *Odyssey* are attributed to Homer, a legendary Greek poet. Songs about the seige of Troy are known to have been sung shortly after the events took place, although the first written forms of the epics did not appear until some six hundred years later. What Homer composed and what he compiled cannot be established, but the great epics known by his name were studied and recited by educated Greeks and there were apparently texts or arrangements of them from around 560 to 527 B.C. Authentic texts are established by 150 B.C. The date of Homer's birth has been variously estimated as from 1159 B.C. to 685 B.C., but by the time stories of Homer's life began to appear, nothing was authentically known about him. George Gilbert Aimé Murray sums up this disputable evidence in the following fashion:

The man "Homer" cannot have lived in six different centuries nor been born in seven different cities; but Homeric poetry may well have done so. The man cannot have spoken this strange composite epic language, but the poetry could and did.[8]

The *Iliad* is certainly complex and long, but the adventures in the *Odyssey,* or *Ulysses,* are exciting and understandable to children. A combined edition, *The Iliad and the Odyssey of Homer*

8. George Gilbert Aimé Murray, "Homer," in an earlier edition of the *Encyclopaedia Britannica.*

adapted by Alfred J. Church, has versions that are well suited to the nine- to eleven-year-old reader, as are the versions in the handsomely illustrated *The Iliad and the Odyssey* adapted by Jane Werner Watson. For a slightly older reader, Padraic Colum's *The Children's Homer* is a distinguished retelling. But for readers of twelve or older, Barbara Leonie Picard's *The Odyssey of Homer* gives more depth in its perceptive portrayal of character.

In this epic the Greek ideals of cool intelligence, patience, and resourcefulness are found in both Penelope and Odysseus. They exhibit these qualities and hold tenaciously to their goals even when humans and gods are arrayed against them. Over "the misty sea," "the wine-dark sea," Odysseus sailed for twenty years and none could stay him. This is a story of fortitude which every generation of children should know.

Sigurd the Volsung

The Norse epic *Sigurd the Volsung* is not so well known as it deserves to be. There is a rugged nobility about the saga stories which some children especially appreciate. Because these tales reflect a simpler social order, many people consider them better suited to children than the Greek epics. This is a debatable point, since anyone who has ever tried to tell the saga of Sigurd knows all too well its difficulties. Obscurities in the text, difficult names much alike, and unpalatable social relationships upon which the main action of the story depends make this epic call for expert handling.

Certainly the saga has some elements of violence in common with those crime stories which the modern child may be reading in the newspapers or seeing in the movies or on television. But their differences are important. In the latter, the tales of blood and murder are often sordid, ignobly motivated, and horrifying. In the Sigmund-Sigurd stories, there is the nobility of great heroism, of keeping your word even though it costs you your life, of self-sacrifice for a great cause, of death rather than dishonor, of ideals of race and family, of intrepid courage and perseverance.

Robin Hood

Of all the hero cycles, *Robin Hood* is unquestionably the children's favorite. It may not be the loftiest epic, and Robin Hood may not be

From *The Merry Adventures of Robin Hood* by Howard Pyle. Copyright 1946 by Charles Scribner's Sons. Reproduced by permission of the publisher.

the noblest hero, but his mad escapades, his lusty fights, his unfailing good humor when beaten, his sense of fair play, and, above all, his roguish tricks and gaiety practically define "hero" for children. Children should read *Robin Hood*, see it in a movie or television version, and read it again. Indeed, no other hero lends himself so readily to dramatization on screen or in classroom as does this gallant outlaw leader.

Children enjoy hearing some of the ballads of Robin Hood read aloud, but the prose version by Howard Pyle, with his spirited illustrations, is the text they should know. It is hard reading for most children, and if they can't read it for themselves, they should hear it. For the lucky superior readers, it remains for generation after generation of children one of the most exciting narratives in all literature. Other rewarding versions of the story are Geoffrey Trease's *Bows Against the Baron* and J. Walker McSpadden's *Robin Hood and His Merry Outlaws*, which is told in a simple but lively style and illustrated with the jaunty drawings of Louis Slobodkin.

King Arthur and the Knights of the Round Table

Opinions differ as to the appropriateness of the King Arthur stories for young children. Certainly they are more mature in content and significance than either the *Odyssey* or *Robin Hood.* The individual adventures of some of the knights are as understandable as those of the Sherwood Forest band, but the ideals of chivalry are far subtler than the moral code of Robin Hood and his men. Often brave deeds are performed for the love of a fair lady, and many feel the cycle is better for the adolescent period when romance is uppermost and codes of conduct are taken seriously.

On the other hand, there are unusually good juvenile editions of the Arthur tales for children which, simplified though they are, satisfy the child's love of knights and knightly adventures. Two of the older editions of the stories of King Arthur and his court remain deservedly popular: Sidney Lanier's *The Boy's King Arthur* and Howard Pyle's *The Story of King Arthur and His Knights,* which Pyle both told and romantically illustrated. Barbara Leonie Picard's *Stories of King Arthur and His Knights* uses lucid language and evokes a feeling of the period, as does Mary MacLeod's *The Book of King Arthur and His Noble Knights,* but MacLeod's book does not achieve the stylistic level of Picard's. Several books tell separate episodes from the Arthurian legend: Barbara Schiller's *The Kitchen Knight;* the collection of four Arthurian tales in T. H. White's *The Once and Future King* that begins with *The Sword in the Stone,* Ian Serraillier's poetic *The Challenge of the Green Knight,* the story of Sir Gawain's battle against the knight who had issued a challenge to the company at Camelot; and Constance Hieatt's scholarly version of the same story, *Sir Gawain and the Green Knight.* Hieatt's *The Joy of the Court* tells the romantic story of Erec and Enid, as does Barbara Schiller's *Erec and Enid.* Teachers who love the Arthur stories will have listeners who enjoy them. Certainly a saturation with any of these hero cycles is an enriching experience.

It is the gentleness and beauty of these stories and the idealistic character of King Arthur and his knights which sometimes furnish children with their first idea of strength in gentleness, of the power that comes through disciplined restraint. Not that children can put these qualities into words, but the qualities are there, embodied in the strong, gentle men who are the heroes of these tales.

Reprinted from *The Ramayana,* text © 1969, by Elizabeth Seeger, and illustrations © 1969 by Gordon Laite, a Young Scott Book by permission of Addison-Wesley Publishing Company, Inc. (Original in color)

The *Ramayana* and the Mahabharata

There was no English version of the *Ramayana* for children until Joseph Gaer's *The Adventures of Rama* was published. This myth-epic of India tells how the god Vishnu came down to earth as Prince Rama, a mortal, to save humanity from the evil powers of Ravan. Once on earth, Rama behaves much like other epic heroes. He fights innumerable battles, marries the beautiful Sita, suffers banishment, gives way to suspicion and jealousy, and is put to shame by the gentle Sita's trial by fire. After that, all goes well, and throughout the ten thousand years of Rama's reign

Unknown were want, disease and crime,
So calm, so happy was the time.

The individual stories resemble Greek myths rather more than the usual epic does. The illustrations suggest dance, in which form the adventures of Rama are often shown in India. A splendid edition of the *Ramayana* has been adapted by Elizabeth Seeger, who has also retold one of India's great hero tales in *The Five Sons of King Pandu*, the story of the Mahabharata. Both books are beautifully illustrated in the Indian tradition, and both have the rolling prose that is so suitable to the intricacies of the stories and to their lofty themes.

Other Epics and Hero Tales

The length and complexity of the epic form may seem a deterrent to young readers, but it allows time for real characterization and for a continual iteration of the moral code. Although the great national epics and hero tales are of particular interest to students of literature and to folklorists, they can be enjoyed by the adolescent reader; and many of the single episodes, especially those of the hero tales, can be appreciated by the preadolescent.

An excellent introduction to the genre is *Hero Tales from Many Lands*, edited by Alice Hazeltine. Her selection of retellings is discriminating, and the book includes sources, background notes, and a glossary. Barbara Leonie Picard's *Hero Tales of the British Isles* also has notes that give historical information.

From the book *Beowulf: Dragon Slayer* by Rosemary Sutcliff. Illustration by Charles Keeping. Illustration copyright © 1962 by The Bodley Head, Ltd. Published by E. P. Dutton & Co., Inc. and used with their permission.

Viewpoint

There is another door that can be opened by reading legends and fairy tales, and for some children, at the present time, there may be no other key to it. *Religio,* in one Latin sense of the word, implies a sense of the strange, the numinous, the totally Other, of what lies quite beyond human personality and cannot be found in any human relationships. This kind of "religion" is an indestructible part of the experience of many human minds, even though the temper of a secular society does not encourage it, and the whole movement of modern theology runs counter to it. In Christian "religious instruction" there is likely to be less and less *religio*: it may very well be in reading about a vision of the flashing-eyed Athene or the rosy-fingered Aphrodite that children first find a satisfying formulation of those queer prickings of delight, excitement and terror that they feel when they first walk by moonlight, or when it snows in May, or when, like the young Wordsworth, they have to touch a wall to make sure that it is really there. Magic is not the same as mysticism, but it may lead towards it; it is mystery "told to the children."—Elizabeth Cook, *The Ordinary and the Fabulous*, Cambridge University Press, London, 1969, p. 5.

Beowulf, the oldest epic in English, has been retold in several editions for the young reader. Two versions that can be enjoyed by ten- to twelve-year-olds are Dorothy Hosford's *By His Own Might, The Battles of Beowulf* and Robert Nye's *Beowulf, A New Telling*, a quite simple prose interpretation of the epic poem. For older children, an outstanding prose version is Rosemary Sutcliff's *Beowulf*, which has a poetic grandeur of style. Ian Serraillier's *Beowulf, the Warrior* is in sonorous and stately verse.

The Babylonian story of Gilgamesh has been retold in several editions; the most notable both in style and illustration is that of Bernarda Bryson. A version that is easier to read is edited by Anita Feagles: *He Who Saw Everything, The Epic of Gilgamesh*. The ornate, mythic style of Jennifer Westwood's *Gilgamesh, and Other Babylonian Tales*, has flavor but limits the book to older readers.

The deeds of Cuchulain, the Irish warrior-hero who was the descendant of a god, are combined in a continuous story in Rosemary

Illustration by Charles Mikolaycak from *The Surprising Things Maui Did,* by Jay Williams. Illustration Copyright © 1979 by Charles Mikolaycak. Published by Four Winds Press, a division of Scholastic Magazines, Inc. Reprinted by permission. (Original in color)

Sutcliff's *The Hound of Ulster.* Another Irish hero, Finn MacCool, leader of the Fenians, is described by Sutcliff in *The High Deeds of Finn MacCool,* a vigorous account of the Fenian legends. These legends are related in vivid style in *The Tangle-Coated Horse and Other Tales* by Ella Young and given a sophisticated, witty retelling in *The Green Hero* by Bernard Evslin.

From continental Europe come other tales of heroes: stories of the legendary Spanish hero, the Cid; the story of Roland from France; in romantic tales from the Kiev cycle, *The Knights of the Golden Table* by E. M. Almedingen; *The Nibelungenlied* from Germany.

Tales from other parts of the world, too, are becoming available for children. Marcia Brown, in *Backbone of the King,* retells the Hawaiian epic of the courtier Pakaa and his son Ku, and in *The Surprising Things Maui Did,* Jay Williams incorporates many of the deeds of a popular Polynesian deity. Dale Carlson's *Warlord of the Gengi* recounts the valorous deeds of a Japanese folk hero. Roland Bertol's *Sundiata, The Epic of The Lion King,* tells of the hero-king who founded the African empire of Mali.

Fable, myth, and epic are different from each other in many ways, yet all three are a part of the great stream of folk literature and are also embodiments of moral truths in story form.

The *fable* teaches briefly and frankly and provides children with their first excursion into the realm of abstract ideas and intellectual speculations about conduct.

The *myth* teaches through symbols which grow more and more complex. The symbolism soon ceases to have the simple, obvious moral of a fable and becomes as complicated as life, and it is then proportionately difficult for a child to understand. Fortunately, the myth stories possess a beauty that is satisfying in itself.

The *epics* have a triple value. They contribute to an appreciation of world literature, to an understanding of national ideals of behavior, and to a comprehension of the dimensions of the valor and nobility of heroism for all humanity.

Adult References[9]

ASIMOV, ISAAC. *Words from the Myths.*
AUSLANDER, JOSEPH, and FRANK ERNEST HILL. *The Winged Horse: the Story of Poets and Their Poetry.*
BARBER, RICHARD. *A Companion to World Mythology.*
BULFINCH, THOMAS. *Age of Fable: Or, Stories of Gods and Heroes.*
EASTMAN, MARY HUSE. *Index to Fairy Tales, Myths and Legends.*
FRAZER, SIR JAMES GEORGE. *The Golden Bough.*
Funk and Wagnalls Standard Dictionary of Folklore, Mythology and Legend.
GUERBER, HELENE A. *Myths of Greece and Rome.*
IRELAND, NORMA. *Index to Fairy Tales, 1949–1972: Including Folklore, Legends and Myths in Collections.*
KIRK, G. S. *Myth.*
MOORMAN, CHARLES. *Kings and Captains: Variations on a Heroic Theme.*
MUNCH, PETER A. *Norse Mythology, Legends of Gods and Heroes.*
OVID. *The Metamorphoses.*
RANK, OTTO. *The Myth of the Birth of the Hero: A Psychological Interpretation of Mythology.*
SCHWAB, GUSTAV. *Gods and Heroes.*
SMITH, RUTH. ed. *The Tree of Life.*
TATLOCK, JESSIE M. *Greek and Roman Mythology.*
Volsunga Saga: The Story of the Volsungs and Niblungs, with Certain Songs from the Elder Edda.

Aesop's Fables

Aesop's Fables, tr. by V. S. Vernon Jones, ill. by Arthur Rackham. Watts, 1967. This is one of the most satisfactory editions both for children and adults. Chesterton's introduction should not be missed. The illustrations appeal to older children. 10–14
Aesop's Fables, ill. by Fritz Kredel. Grosset, 1947. An attractive, readable edition which contains over 150 fables. 10–14

9. Complete bibliographic data are provided in Appendix B.

Aesop's Fables, ill. by Jacob Lawrence. Windmill, 1970. Stark, sophisticated illustrations for a compilation of eighteen fables, moderately well told.   9–11

ARTZYBASHEFF, BORIS, ed. *Aesop's Fables,* ill. by ed. Viking, 1933.   12–14

EVANS, KATHERINE. *A Bundle of Sticks,* ill. by author. Whitman, 1962. An amusing modern picture-book adaptation of the Aesop fable for younger readers. Other adaptations by this author include *The Boy Who Cried Wolf* (1960) and *A Camel in the Tent* (1961).   5–8

The Hare and the Tortoise, ill. by Paul Galdone. McGraw, 1962. Action-filled color illustrations for this Aesop fable heighten suspense for the youngest.   4–7

JACOBS, JOSEPH, ed. *The Fables of Aesop,* ill. by David Levine. Macmillan, 1964.   9–11

KENT, JACK, reteller. *Fables of Aesop,* ill. by reteller. Parents' Magazine, 1972.   7–9

———, reteller. *More Fables of Aesop,* ill. by reteller. Parents' Magazine, 1974. Free adaptations from the Vernon-Jones version, with simple language and comic pictures.   5–7

REES, ENNIS, ad. *Lions and Lobsters and Foxes and Frogs,* ill. by Edward Gorey. Scott/Addison, 1971. Seventeen selections taken from *Fables from Aesop* (Oxford, 1966) by Rees are here illustrated with Gorey's amiable, wild-eyed beasts.   8–10

REEVES, JAMES, ad. *Fables from Aesop,* ill. by Maurice Wilson. Walck, 1962. In his selection of fifty fables, the narrator has introduced brief dialogue and descriptive phrases, while keeping to the spirit of the original. Illustrations, many in color, are exceptional in quality.   9–13

RICE, EVE, ad. *Once in a Wood: Ten Tales from Aesop,* ill. by author. Greenwillow, 1979. Nicely adapted for young readers, these Aesop stories are simple, direct, and pithy, concluding in most cases with a rhyming moral.   6–8

SHOWALTER, JEAN B., ad. *The Donkey Ride,* ill. by Tomi Ungerer. Doubleday, 1967.   5–9

SPRIGGS, RUTH, ed. *The Fables of Aesop: 143 Moral Tales Retold,* ill. by Frank Baber. Rand, 1976. An oversize book, lavishly illustrated. The writing style is direct and colloquial, with a simply phrased moral in italics following the fables.   8–11

Three Aesop Fox Fables, ill. by Paul Galdone. Seabury, 1971. Large figures, with humor and movement, make this good for group showing.   4–7

UNTERMEYER, LOUIS, ed. *Aesop's Fables,* ill. by Alice and Martin Provensen. Golden Pr., 1965.   6–9

WHITE, ANNE TERRY, ed. *Aesop's Fables,* ill. by Helen Siegl. Random, 1964.   8–10

La Fontaine's Fables

CALHOUN, MARY. *Old Man Whickutt's Donkey,* ill. by Tomie de Paola. Parents' Magazine, 1975.

LA FONTAINE, JEAN DE. *The Fables of La Fontaine,* tr. by Marianne Moore. Viking, 1954. These fables retain their original verse form in this translation. A scholarly edition which includes La Fontaine's twelve books of fables and his own original preface. Chiefly an adult source.

———. *The Frogs Who Wanted a King,* ill. by Margot Zemach. Four Winds, 1977.   10–14

———. *The Hare and the Tortoise,* ill. by Brian Wildsmith. Watts, 1967.

———. *The Miller, the Boy and the Donkey,* ill. by Brian Wildsmith. Watts, 1969. Big pages, big print, and jewel-tone colors make these and other single-title editions by Wildsmith attractive.   5–8

Other Fables

ANDERSEN, HANS CHRISTIAN. *The Ugly Duckling, The Emperor's New Clothes,* and others (see Bibliography, Chapter 9).

BRENNER, ANITA. *A Hero by Mistake,* ill. by Jean Charlot. W. R. Scott, 1953. Afraid of his own shadow, this little man accidentally captures some bandits, is hailed as a hero, and learns to behave like one.   6–8

BROWN, MARCIA. *Once a Mouse* (see Bibliography, Chapter 7).

CHAUCER, GEOFFREY. *Chanticleer and the Fox,* ad. and ill. by Barbara Cooney. T. Crowell, 1958. Pictures of colorful beauty and design add delight to the old fable of the crafty fox and the vain cock. Caldecott Medal.   6–9

CIARDI, JOHN. *John J. Plenty and Fiddler Dan,* ill. by Madeleine Gekiere. Lippincott, 1963.   4–9

DAUGHERTY, JAMES. *Andy and the Lion* (see Bibliography, Chapter 5).

DE ROIN, NANCY, ed. *Jataka Tales;* ill. by Ellen Lanyon. Houghton, 1975.   8–9

GAER, JOSEPH. *The Fables of India,* ill. by Randy Monk. Little, 1955. Beast tales from three outstanding collections of Indian fables: The *Panchatantra,* the *Hitopadesa,* and the *Jatakas.* The stories are entertainingly presented, and there is excellent background material on the known history of fable literature for the student.   12–16

GALDONE, PAUL. *The Monkey and the Crocodile,* ill. by author. Seabury, 1969.   5–7

GINSBURG, MIRRA. *Three Rolls and One Doughnut: Fables from Russia,* ill. by Anita Lobel. Dial, 1970.   6–10

KRYLOV, IVAN. *Fifteen Fables of Krylov,* tr. by Guy Daniels, ill. by David Pascal. Macmillan, 1965.   12 up

LOBEL, ARNOLD. *Fables,* ill. by author. Harper, 1980. A pithy and often surprising moral is added, Aesop style, to single-paged fabular anecdotes that face handsome full-page paintings.   8–10

MERRILL, JEAN. *The Black Sheep,* ill, by Ronni Solbert. Pantheon, 1969.   9–11

Greek and Roman Myths and Epics

ANDERSON, LONZO. *Arion and the Dolphins,* ill. by Adrienne Adams. Scribner's, 1978. In a graceful retelling of a Greek legend, young Arion is robbed of the gold he's won in a musical contest. He's rescued from harm by some dolphins while the king of Corinth deals with his assailants.   7–8

BARTH, EDNA, ad. *Cupid and Psyche: A Love Story,* ill. by Ati Forberg. Seabury, 1976. Beautifully illustrated with wash drawings, this is a moving version of the mythical tale of Cupid's love for the mortal, Psyche, and the vengeful jealousy of his mother Venus.   9–11

CHURCH, ALFRED JOHN, ad. *The Aeneid.* Macmillan, 1962. A simplified and dignified version.   10–14

———, ad. *The Iliad and the Odyssey of Homer,* ill. by Eugene Karlin, Macmillan, 1964.   10–14

———, ad. *The Odyssey of Homer,* ill. by John Flaxman. Macmillan, 1951. First published in 1906, this attractively done edition is an excellent source for children to read or adults to tell. Stories are arranged in chronological order.   10–14

COLUM, PADRAIC. *The Children's Homer,* ill. by Willy Pogany. Macmillan, 1925, 1962. A distinguished version in cadenced prose, simple but in the spirit of the original. Vigorous illustrations.

————. *The Golden Fleece*, ill. by Willy Pogany. Macmillan, 1921, 1962. A companion edition to *The Children's Homer*, and equally fine.   10–14

COOLIDGE, OLIVIA E. *Greek Myths*, ill. by Edouard Sandoz. Houghton, 1949. Twenty-seven of the best known Greek myths. Here the gods are not idealized, but the stories have authenticity.   10–16

D'AULAIRE, INGRI and EDGAR PARIN. *Ingri and Edgar Parin d'Aulaire's Book of Greek Myths*, ill. by authors. Doubleday, 1962.   8–11

DE SELINCOURT, AUBREY. *Odysseus the Wanderer*, ill. by Norman Meredith. Criterion, 1956. A lusty, modern retelling of the Odyssey that should lure many young readers into an acquaintance with this epic before high-school days.   11 up

EVSLIN, BERNARD. *Greeks Bearing Gifts; The Epics of Achilles and Ulysses*, ill. by Lucy Martin Bitzer. Four Winds, 1976. Evslin gives fresh life to old legends here; his versions of the *Iliad* and the *Odyssey* use a fluent, witty style that can be as delightfully irreverent as it is sonorous.   12 up

GARFIELD, LEON, and EDWARD BLISHEN. *The God Beneath the Sea*, ill. by Zevi Blum. Pantheon, 1971.   11–14

————. *The Golden Shadow*, ill. by Charles Keeping. Pantheon, 1973.   12–16

GATES, DORIS. *The Golden God: Apollo*, ill. by Constantinos Co-Conis. Viking, 1973. The Apollo myths brought together into a coherent whole. Gates has done the same thing for the myths concerning Zeus in *Lord of the Sky: Zeus* (Viking, 1972); for the Athena myths in *The Warrior Goddess: Athena* (Viking, 1973); and for the Heracles myths in *Mightiest of Mortals: Heracles* (Viking, 1975).   10–11

GRAVES, ROBERT. *Greek Gods and Heroes*, ill. by Dimitris Davis. Doubleday, 1960.   12–15

————. *The Siege and Fall of Troy*, ill. by C. Walter Hodges. Doubleday, 1963. An easy-to-follow narrative history of the Trojan War.   12–16

GREEN, ROGER LANCELYN. *Heroes of Greece and Troy: Retold from the Ancient Authors*, ill. by Heather Copley and Christopher Chamberlain. Walck, 1961. The tales of the Heroic Age have been woven into a unified whole, from the coming of the immortals to Odysseus, the last of the heroes. Beautifully written, and with an introduction that will give insight into the great variety of classic sources used in this fine version.   12 up

————, ed. *A Book of Myths*, ill. by Joan Kiddell-Monroe. Dutton, 1965.   10–12

HAMILTON, EDITH. *Mythology*, ill. by Steele Savage. Little, 1942.   12 up

HAWTHORNE, NATHANIEL. *The Golden Touch*, ill. by Paul Galdone. McGraw, 1959. The old tale of King Midas is imaginatively illustrated with gold-toned pictures.   6–9

JOHNSTON, NORMA. *Strangers Dark and Gold*. Atheneum, 1975.   12–16

KINGSLEY, CHARLES. *The Heroes*, ill. by Vera Bock. Macmillan, 1954. Beautifully retold tales which make a fine cycle for the storyteller.   10–14

————. *The Heroes*, ill. by Joan Kiddell-Monroe. Dutton, 1963.   9–12

LANG, ANDREW. *The Adventures of Odysseus*, ill. by Joan Kiddell-Monroe. Dutton, 1962. Andrew Lang's distinguished retellings of Homer's *Iliad* and the *Odyssey* are reissued in handsome new format. Originally published in his *Tales of Greece and Troy* (1907).   12 up

MACPHERSON, JAY. *Four Ages of Man*, ill. St. Martin's, 1962. Beautifully narrated stories from the Greek myths organized around four periods: "creation and the coming of the gods; pastoral life and the ordering of the seasons; the adventures and the labors of the heroes; war, tragic tales, and decline into history."   13 up

MILLER, KATHERINE. *Apollo*, Houghton, 1970.   9–11

PICARD, BARBARA LEONIE. *The Iliad of Homer*, ill. by Joan Kiddell-Monroe. Walck, 1960. A truly distinguished retelling of the *Iliad*, with characters sympathetically portrayed. *The Odyssey of Homer* (1952) is an equally fine companion volume.   12–15

REEVES, JAMES. *The Trojan Horse*, ill. by Krystyna Turska. Watts, 1969. A Trojan boy describes the invasion of his city.   9–10

SELLEW, CATHARINE. *Adventures with the Gods*, ill. by George and Doris Hauman. Little, 1945. An introduction to the more familiar myths, simply written for younger children.   9–12

SERRAILLIER, IAN. *The Clashing Rocks: The Story of Jason*, ill. by William Stobbs. Walck, 1964.   10–13

————. *A Fall from the Sky: The Story of Daedalus*, ill. by William Stobbs. Walck, 1966.   10–13

————. *The Gorgon's Head: The Story of Perseus*, ill. by William Stobbs. Walck, 1962.   12–14

————. *Heracles the Strong*, ill. by Rocco Negri. Walck, 1970.   10–13

————. *The Way of Danger: The Story of Theseus*, ill. by William Stobbs. Walck, 1963.   12–14

SEWELL, HELEN. *A Book of Myths*, sel. from Bulfinch's *Age of Fable*, ill. by Helen Sewell. Macmillan, 1942, 1964. Some people dislike, others are enthusiastic about the stylized illustrations in black and white, or sharp blue, black, and white. They are undeniably authentic in spirit and detail.   10–14

TOMAINO, SARAH F., ad. *Persephone: Bringer of Spring*, ill. by Ati Forberg. T. Crowell, 1971. A graceful retelling of the Greek legend with delicate and dramatic illustrations.   8–10

TURSKA, KRYSTYNA. *Pegasus*, ill. by author. Watts, 1970. 9–11

WATSON, JANE WERNER. *The Iliad and the Odyssey*, ill. by Alice and Martin Provensen. Golden Pr., 1964.   11–13

Norse Myths and Epics

BROWN, ABBIE FARWELL. *In the Days of Giants*, ill. by E. B. Smith. Houghton, 1902. This is a sterling adaptation of the Norse myths.   10–14

COLUM, PADRAIC. *Children of Odin*, ill. by Willy Pogany. Macmillan, 1920, 1962. Norse myths and hero tales retold in a continuous narrative ending with the death of Sigurd. Our best source for children. In fine modern format.   10–14

COOLIDGE, OLIVIA. *Legends of the North*, ill. by Edouard Sandoz. Houghton, 1951. A wide variety of stories includes tales of the northern gods and heroes, the Volsungs, and other sagas.   12–14

D'AULAIRE, INGRI and EDGAR PARIN. *Norse Gods and Giants*, ill. by authors. Doubleday, 1967.   8–11

HOSFORD, DOROTHY G. *Sons of the Volsungs*, ill. by Frank Dobias. Holt, 1949. A splendid version of the Sigurd tales adapted from William Morris's *The Story of Sigurd the Volsung and the Fall of the Niblungs*.   11–14

————. *Thunder of the Gods*, ill. by George and Claire Louden. Holt, 1952. Distinguished retellings of the Norse myths: stories of Odin, Thor, Balder, Loki, and other familiar tales. Excellent for storytelling or reading aloud.   11–14

KOENIG, ALMA. *Gudrun*, tr. by Anthea Bell. Lothrop, 1979. A heroic romance based on the thirteenth century poem, retold in prose smoothly translated from Middle High German.   11–13

SCHILLER, BARBARA, ad. *Hrafkel's Saga: An Icelandic Story*, ill. by Carol Iselin. Seabury, 1972. A family saga about one of the ancient Icelandic chieftains, told directly in heroic style.   11–13

SELLEW, CATHARINE. *Adventures with the Giants*, ill. by Steele Savage. Little, 1950.   8–11

_____. *Adventures with the Heroes*, ill. by Steele Savage. Little, 1954. Retold in simple language are the stories of the Volsungs and Nibelungs.   9–12

English Epics and Hero Tales

HIEATT, CONSTANCE. *The Castle of Ladies*, ill. by Norman Laliberte. T. Crowell, 1973. One of Gawain's romantic quests, adroitly retold.   10–12

_____. *The Joy of the Court*, ill. by Pauline Baynes. T. Crowell, 1970.   9–11

_____. *Sir Gawain and the Green Knight*, ill. by Walter Lorraine. T. Crowell, 1967.   10–12

HOSFORD, DOROTHY G. *By His Own Might: The Battles of Beowulf*, ill. by Laszlo Matulay. Holt, 1947.   11–16

LANIER, SIDNEY. *The Boy's King Arthur*, ill. by N. C. Wyeth, ad. from Sir Thomas Malory's *History of King Arthur and His Knights of the Round Table*. Scribner's, 1942. An authoritative and popular version of this hero cycle; the best one to use for reading or telling.   10–14

MacLEOD, MARY. *Book of King Arthur and His Noble Knights*, ill. by Henry C. Pitz. Lippincott, 1949.   9–13

McSPADDEN, J. WALKER. *Robin Hood and His Merry Outlaws*, ill. by Louis Slobodkin. World, 1946.   9–12

MALORY, SIR THOMAS. *Le Morte d'Arthur*, ill. by W. Russell Flint. London: Warner, publisher to the Medici Society [1921]. 2 vols. Children who are superior readers are fascinated with this source of the Arthur stories.   12–16

NYE, ROBERT. *Beowulf: A New Telling*, ill. by Allan E. Cober. Hill, 1968.   10–12

PICARD, BARBARA L. *Hero Tales of the British Isles*, ill. by Eric Fraser. Criterion, 1963.   10–13

_____. *Stories of King Arthur and His Knights*, ill. by Roy Morgan. Walck, 1955.   10–13

PYLE, HOWARD. *The Merry Adventures of Robin Hood of Great Renown in Nottinghamshire*, ill. by author. Scribner's, 1946. This is the great prose edition of the Robin Hood tales, the best source for reading and telling.   12–14

_____. *Some Merry Adventures of Robin Hood*, rev. ed., ill. by author. Scribner's, 1954. This book contains a dozen stories adapted from the longer book, and would serve as an introduction for younger readers.   10–13

_____. *The Story of King Arthur and His Knights*, ill. by author. Scribner's, 1933. Any Pyle edition is written with grace and distinction. This is no exception.   12–14

ROBBINS, RUTH. *Taliesin and King Arthur*, ill. by author. Parnassus, 1970. The young poet Taliesin entertains King Arthur's court with his storytelling. The book mingles fact and fiction and the style is poetic.   9–11

SCHILLER, BARBARA. *Erec and Enid*, ill. by Ati Forberg. Dutton, 1970.   9–11

_____. *The Kitchen Knight*, ill. by Nonny Hogrogian. Holt, 1965.   9–11

_____, ad. *The Wandering Knight*, ill. by Herschel Levit.

Dutton, 1971. A retelling of the deeds of the young Lancelot.   9–11

SERRAILLIER, IAN. *Beowulf, the Warrior*, ill. by Severin. Walck, 1961.   12 up

_____. *The Challenge of the Green Knight*, ill. by Victor Ambrus. Walck, 1967.   12–14

Song of Robin Hood, ed. by Anne Malcolmson, music arr. by Grace Castagnetta, ill. by Virginia Lee Burton. Houghton, 1947. Eighteen ballads illustrated with distinguished black-and-white drawings. Traditional music for many of the ballads is included. The book is the result of careful research in art and music.   10–14

SUTCLIFF, ROSEMARY. *Beowulf*, ill. by Charles Keeping. Dutton, 1962.   11 up

_____. *Tristan and Iseult*. Dutton, 1971. A tender retelling of a great love story.   11–14

TREASE, GEOFFREY. *Bows Against the Barons*, ill. by C. Walter Hodges. Hawthorne, 1967.   10–12

Other National Epics and Hero Tales

ALMEDINGEN, E. M. *The Knights of the Golden Table*, ill. by Charles Keeping. Lippincott, 1964.   12–15

_____. *The Story of Gudrun*, based on the third part of the Epic of Gudrun, ill. by Enrico Arno. Norton, 1967. A German tale retold with a dignity appropriate to the romantic sweep of a medieval epic.   12–15

BERTOL, ROLAND. *Sundiata: The Epic of the Lion King*, ill. by Gregorio Prestopino. T. Crowell, 1970.   9–12

☆ BIERHORST, JOHN, ed. *Black Rainbow: Legends of the Incas and Myths of Ancient Peru*. Farrar, 1976. These stories, selected with discrimination and retold with skill, are prefaced by an informative introduction, chronologically arranged, and followed by notes on sources, a reading list, a glossary of terms, and a pronunciation guide.   13 up

BOSLEY, KENNETH, reteller. *The Devil's Horse: Tales from the Kalevala*. Pantheon, 1971. Robust, colloquial retelling of the Finnish heroic ballads.   10 up

BROWN, MARCIA. *Backbone of the King*, ill. by author. Scribner's, 1966.   10–12

BRYSON, BERNARDA. *Gilgamesh*, ill. by author. Holt, 1967.11–14

CARLSON, DALE. *Warlord of the Gengi*, ill. by John Gretzer. Atheneum, 1970.   11–14

DAVIS, RUSSELL, and BRENT K. ASHABRANNER. *Ten Thousand Desert Swords: The Epic Story of a Great Bedouin Tribe*, ill. by Leonard Everett Fisher. Little, 1960. The Bani Hilal were a great and ancient warrior tribe, and their legends are superbly retold for the discriminating reader.   12 up

DEUTSCH, BABETTE. *Heroes of the Kalevala*, ill. by Fritz Eichenberg. Messner, 1940. This version has not only literary distinction but continuity. Text and illustrations bring out the lusty humor of the tales.   10–14

EVSLIN, BERNARD. *The Green Hero: Early Adventures of Finn McCool*, ill. by Barbara Bascove. Four Winds, 1975. A sophisticated, witty retelling in a sequential narrative. 11–14

FEAGLES, ANITA. *He Who Saw Everything: The Epic of Gilgamesh*. Scott/Addison, 1966.   9–11

GAER, JOSEPH. *The Adventures of Rama*, ill. by Randy Monk. Little, 1954. One of the best-loved epics of India is the story of Prince Rama and of his wife Sita, stolen from him by a demon king. The careful selection of incidents makes this an absorbing and unified tale.   12–14

GOLDSTON, ROBERT. *The Legend of the Cid*, ill. by Stephane. Bobbs, 1963. A simple version of the adventures of the Spanish hero. 10–13

HALEY, GAIL. *The Green Man*, ill. by author. Scribner's, 1980. Richly colored illustrations that have the look of medieval tapestries are combined with a straightforward text that incorporates many of the legends of the Green Man, protector of forest creatures. 8–10

HAZELTINE, ALICE, ed. *Hero Tales from Many Lands*, ill. by Gordon Laite. Abingdon, 1961. 11–15

HODGES, ELIZABETH JAMISON. *A Song for Gilgamesh*, ill. by David Omar White. Atheneum, 1971. The story of a young potter of Sumer is woven around the journey of Gilgamesh to the Land of the Living. 11–13

HODGES, MARGARET. *Myths of the Celts*, ill. by Eros Keith. Farrar, 1973. Short tales, well told. 9–11

MARALNGURA, N. and others. *Tales from the Spirit Time*, rev. ed. Indiana Univ. Pr., 1976. A compilation of myths and legends, many of them "pourquoi" tales about animals, collected by Aborigine students in a teacher training program. 8–10

PICARD, BARBARA LEONIE. *Tales of Ancient Persia*. Walck, 1973. Based on a portion of the epic poem *Shah-Nama*, a retelling in flowing narrative style. 12–14

SEEGER, ELIZABETH. *The Five Sons of King Pandu*, ill. by Gordon Laite. Scott/Addison, 1969. 12 up

———. *The Ramayana*, ill. by Gordon Laite. Scott/Addison, 1969. 12 up

SEREDY, KATE. *The White Stag*, ill. by author. Viking, 1937. Based on the legend of the founding of Hungary, a tale of the hero Bendeguz and his son Attila. Newbery Medal. 10–14

The Song of Roland, tr. by Merriam Sherwood, ill. by Edith Emerson. McKay, 1938. This is one of the finest translations of the story of Roland for younger readers, and is illustrated with distinctive line drawings. 12–16

SUTCLIFF, ROSEMARY. *The High Deeds of Finn MacCool*, ill. by Michael Charlton. Dutton, 1967. 11–14

———. *The Hound of Ulster*, ill. by Victor Ambrus. Dutton, 1964. 11–14

———. *The Light Beyond the Forest: The Quest for the Holy Grail*. Dutton, 1980. Tied by their participation in the quest, each of King Arthur's knights who sought the sacred cup is described in a separate chapter. A fine and fluent retelling. 10–12

SYNGE, URSULA, ad. *Land of Heroes: A Retelling of the Kalevala*. Atheneum, 1978. A splendid adaptation of the great Finnish epic draws the separate tales of three magician-heroes together into a smooth whole. 12 up

UDEN, GRANT, ad. *Hero Tales from the Age of Chivalry; Retold from the Froissart Chronicles*, ill. by Doreen Roberts. World, 1969. Twelve tales by the great poet-historian of the fourteenth century. Historically interesting, romantic in approach. 11–13

WESTWOOD, JENNIFER. *Gilgamesh and Other Babylonian Tales*. Coward, 1970. 12 up

WILLIAMS, JAY. *The Surprising Things Maui Did*, ill. by Charles Mikolaycak. Four Winds, 1979. 5–8

YOUNG, ELLA. *The Tangle-Coated Horse and Other Tales: Episodes from the Fionn Saga*, ill. by Vera Bock. McKay, 1968. 12–14

Chapter Nine:
Modern Fantasy

The younger child who has explored *Mother Goose* and the simpler folk tales and the older child who has gone beyond these to myths and epics are both ready for wider reading experiences. While folk literature is full of the truths that generations have deemed worthy of remembering and passing on to their children, and modern realistic fiction presents the facts of present-day life, fantasy is the art form that many modern writers have chosen to present another kind of truth, to lay out for children the realities of life—not in a physical or social sense, but in a psychological sense.

The folk tale often was a realistic story of daily events, but just as often a magical element was injected by means of supernatural beings such as fairies, elves, magicians, ogres, or dragons, or supernatural objects: a pot that skipped, a ship that flew. Folk tales with these magical elements were at times characterized as fairy tales, and we have continued to use this term for tales by modern writers which echo the folk-tale pattern.

Although the distinction between the old folk tale and the modern literary fairy tale is useful to adults, it is of no importance to children. Magic is magic to them whether they find it in Grimm, Andersen, or Dr. Seuss. Children do not think of their stories in the conventional categories of literature or of libraries but describe their favorites broadly as animal stories or funny stories or true stories or fairy tales, by which they mean any tale of magic, old or modern. Eleanor Cameron, in *The Green and Burning Tree*, says,

If we do not quibble over fineness of categories, we then avoid the danger of becoming one of that company of scholars (some of the folklorists among them) who seem to care less about experiencing the truth and beauty of a tale than in being "correct" in putting it into this compartment or that.[1]

The characteristics of the folk and fairy tales that make them particularly appealing to children are the same ones which make fantasy attractive. In fact, interesting story patterns, distinctive style, and memorable characterizations are essential to any good story for children. The special quality of fantasy is that it concerns things that cannot really happen or that it is about people or creatures who do not exist, yet within the framework of each story there is a self-contained logic, a wholeness of conception that has its own reality. If it does not, it fails. Some modern fantasies err because they are over-whimsical or unduly sophisticated or, worse still, because they talk down to children. As we select from the new fantasy being published each year, let's keep in mind (along with good story patterns, style, and characterizations) sincerity, directness, and imagination as essential characteristics.

1. Eleanor Cameron, *The Green and Burning Tree* (Atlantic-Little, Brown, 1969), p. 12.

From the single, short fairy tale modeled after the folk tale by such early writers as Perrault, writers of fantasy moved into the longer book-length tale, where they had more room to present the ambiguities and problems of humanity trying to live up to its best sense of self. J. R. R. Tolkien, Lloyd Alexander, Susan Cooper, Ursula Le Guin, and C. S. Lewis all found that more than one volume was needed to explore the implications of the basic struggle between good and evil. All but one of these, Susan Cooper, found it necessary to create different worlds for their characters.

Besides the use of other-worldly settings and supernatural beings, human or animal, writers of fantasy may manipulate time, create talking animals and toys, give life to inanimate objects, and endow children with extraordinary abilities. A writer of fantasy may combine many of these elements in a tale, as C. S. Lewis does in his Narnia series. We find that events which take many days in Narnia have taken no time in the children's usual world. Lewis also uses talking animals—Aslan, the great lion; Reepicheep, the mouse—and the children's bravery and ability to reason lead to the rescue of sev-

eral enchanted or imprisoned Narnians. Sometimes writers use only one element which is fantastic and tell an otherwise perfectly realistic story, as L. M. Boston does in *The Children of Green Knowe.* Here the happenings are realistic, except that Tolly sees and plays with children who lived three hundred years before him.

While any work of imagination may be serious or humorous according to the intent of the author, playfulness and humor seem to have a particular place in fantasy. The exaggeration which is often found in this type of writing can be a rich source of humor, and children can also find humor in stories with one or two fantastic elements which contrast satisfyingly with ordinary, everyday events.

Whatever the imaginative work the writer of fantasy produces, and whatever elements of magic and the supernatural enter into it, the whole must be acceptable to us as readers, must have consistency and logic, so that we say to ourselves, "I never thought of it that way. But why not?"

The development of modern fantasy has been so astonishing and varied that it merits detailed examination. Because there are so many of these tales, this chapter can consider only a few—stories which have remained favorites over the years, recent ones which have attained great popularity, and certain ones which illustrate trends.

Early Writers —Lasting Influences

Many early writers of fantasy began by using their imaginations to embellish folk and fairy tales. Indeed, in the seventeenth century at the time of Louis XIV, much of the French court was engaged in this pastime. The cult continued for some fifty years and produced the memorable fairy tales of Perrault, Comtesse d'Aulnoy, and Madame Le Prince de Beaumont. These tales are adorned with fairy godmothers, fabulous footwear, and talking beasts. Both "The White Cat" by d'Aulnoy and "Beauty and the Beast" by Le Prince de Beaumont feature a human-turned-animal whose bewitchment is broken by the love and constancy of a human. An intriguing modern variant is Robin McKinley's *Beauty*, written for older readers.

Hans Christian Andersen's first stories for children were likewise elaborations of familiar

Illustration by Fritz Kredel, from *The King of the Golden River*, by John Ruskin, reprinted with the permission of Philomel Books. (Original in color)

Illustration by Erik Blegvad. Reproduced from Hans Christian Andersen's *The Swineherd,* © 1958 by Erik Blegvad, by permission of Harcourt Brace Jovanovich, Inc. (Original in color)

folk and fairy tales, but he soon began to allow his imagination full rein in the invention of plot, the shaping of character, and the illumination of the human condition. These later creations, solely from Andersen's fertile imagination, are called literary fairy tales, to distinguish them from the fairy tales of unknown origin, those created by common folk. Andersen's work served as inspiration for other writers.

John Ruskin, influential British literary critic, wrote "The King of the Golden River" (1841), in which the younger, kinder brother wins the inheritance. Howard Pyle, American illustrator par excellence of Robin Hood and King Arthur, wrote and illustrated his own fairy tales at the end of the last century. Oscar Wilde's allegories "The Happy Prince" and "The Selfish Giant" were sophisticated morality tales. Wilde's literary fairy tales, while having supernatural beings as characters, were concerned with good and evil rather than with magic for its own sake. The point of the tale was the human, not the marvelous, element.

The early writers of fantasy—Perrault, Ruskin, Pyle, Wilde, and especially Andersen—had a lasting influence on the form. They were all authors of highly regarded literature for adults; they had proven their ability to write well, and, in Pyle's case, to illustrate successfully. These men were not unknowns, seeking to carve out a career, but well-known writers, adding a new area to an already established reputation. Except for Oscar Wilde, most of what these writers produced for adults is not read so often today as their works for children. They set high standards for those who followed.

Hans Christian Andersen

Hans Christian Andersen (1805–1875) was born in Odense, Denmark, of a peasant family. His cobbler father owned a few books which his son also cherished, while his uneducated mother worked hard to support her unusual, artistic son in the years between his father's death and Andersen's move to Copenhagen at age fourteen.

Andersen's first book, a travel diary of a walking trip, appeared in 1829, published by himself. His first volume of *Fairy Tales, Told for Children* appeared in 1835, and included "The Tinderbox," "Little Claus and Big Claus," "The Princess and the Pea," and "Little Ida's Flowers." He was no supporter of organized religion, but he did have an abiding faith in God, often expressed in his tales. Andersen poured himself into his writing; it became the vehicle for expressing his emotions, flashes of humor, commentaries on life, and the follies of humankind. Some of his stories are retelling of folk tales: "Little Claus and Big Claus," "The Princess and the Pea," "The Emperor's New Clothes," "The Wild Swans," "The Swineherd," "Clod Hans," and "What Father Does Is Always Right." In these, Andersen took the traditional story and added to it his own inter-

Viewpoint

Fantasy is probably the most sophisticated form of fiction being written today. Not only must it conform to and meet all the standards of good novel writing; it must also use the fantastic, wholly or partially, directly or indirectly, to express what cannot be expressed in any other way. Fantasy carries the reader into a universe beyond everyday reality, where the restraints of time, gravity, and mortality no longer operate. But the strange world projected by fantasy is not a disorderly one. Its conditions are as practical and as consistent as our own. . . .

The purpose of fantasy is not to escape reality but to illuminate it: to transport us to a world different from the real world, yet to demonstrate certain immutable truths that persist even there—and in every possible world.—Sheila Egoff, *The Republic of Childhood,* Oxford University Press, Toronto, 1967, pp. 133, 134.

pretation of character, providing motivation for the action in the tale. The heroes and heroines are not stereotypes; they live and breathe and become individuals, named or not. The princess who can feel a pea under twenty mattresses can never be confused in our thinking with any other princess, sensitive though she may be. Andersen imparted such life to these characters that we feel empathy for the emperor and his courtiers, none of whom naturally wish to admit they are stupid or unfit for office.

But it is in Andersen's own creations, his literary fairy tales, that his genius for characterization is shown. As we read "The Little Mermaid," we shudder at the pain the mermaid must feel as she puts foot to ground, and yet, so persuasive is Andersen's art that, in spite of the physical agony, we still agree with her that the prince is worth dying for.

"The Ugly Duckling" is, rightly or wrongly, seen as symbolic of Andersen's own life. The animosity of the neighbors to the "different" one seems so natural that we wonder if we ourselves would have seen the promise implicit in the awkward creature. The conversations in the poultry-yard ring true both to human nature and the human ear. What mother would not say, "He is my own child and, when you look closely at him, he's quite handsome..."? Because of Andersen, every "ugly duckling" promises a swan.

Andersen's ability to draw character does not rest on extensive description. In a few carefully chosen words he establishes important qual-

ities, leaving our imaginations so stimulated that we supply the rest of the picture. Of the hero of "The Steadfast Tin Soldier" Andersen says, ". . . he stood as firm and steadfast on his one leg as the others did on their two."[2] Later, when the soldier has been attracted to the paper ballerina, Andersen says, "She stood as steadfast on the toes of her one leg as the soldier did on his. His eyes never left her, not even for a moment did he blink or turn away." The only description that Andersen has given us of the soldier is that he has a red and blue uniform, and a rifle. The outward description is not important; what Andersen is emphasizing is the constancy of this character.

Along with his ability to write with the directness of colloquial speech, Andersen was a master of bringing to light the incongruity which underlies humor. In describing the feast to be set before the guests in "The Hill of the Elves," he tells of salads made of toadstool seeds, garnished with moist snouts of mice and dressed with hemlock juice, and pronounces it a "festive—though a bit conservative—menu."

Andersen's fantasies do not lack supernatural beings or things, and many of them have other-worldly settings, talking animals, and personifications of inanimate objects. But his main contribution was to make us look more sharply at daily life through the window of his imagination.

Fantasy with Folk-Tale Elements

Writers of fantasy since the time of Andersen and the French court writers before him have used folk-tale elements in their creations. Especially in the realm of the picture book, their works are often considered so authentic as to be classified as folk tales themselves. One such is *Millions of Cats* (1928) by Wanda Gág. The old man and the woman in the tale who want a cat find themselves forced to choose among "hundreds of cats, thousands of cats, millions and billions and trillions of cats." Told with the simplest of language, the barest of characterization, but with a consummate style which has omitted all but the essential words, illustrated with Gág's own flowing, childlike black-and-white drawings, this story truly seems to be a long-forgotten folk tale, the only fantasy being

2. From "The Steadfast Tin Soldier" in *The Complete Fairy Tales* by Hans Christian Andersen, translated by Erik Christian Haugaard, forward by Virginia Haviland. Copyright © 1974 by Erik Christian Haugaard. Reprinted by permission of Doubleday & Company, Inc. and Victor Gollancz, Ltd.

They came to a pond.
"Mew, mew! We are thirsty!" cried the
Hundreds of cats,
Thousands of cats,
Millions and billions and trillions of cats.

Reprinted by permission of Coward, McCann & Geoghegan, Inc. from *Millions of Cats* by Wanda Gág. Copyright 1928 by Coward-McCann, Inc.; renewed © 1956 by Wanda Gág.

---

the number of cats and the method of reducing them to one.

The Five Chinese Brothers (1938), written by Claire Huchet Bishop and illustrated by Kurt Wiese, falls into the same category. The story of each identical brother coming home to say goodbye to his mother before his execution and being replaced by a brother talented enough to escape the new form of death, with the final escape of the brothers from execution, mirrors the old belief that if you're clever enough to keep from being killed, you're good enough to live. The use of wit to escape evil is a familiar plot in folk tales. Here again the economy of words and the use of only essential line in the illustrations suggest the folk tale.

James Thurber
The Great Quillow
Many Moons

The humor James Thurber showed as a cartoonist and as the author of delightfully satiric fables is evident in his fairy tales for children. *The Great Quillow* (1944) is about a toymaker who is the only person in his village clever enough to think of a way to rid the town of a voracious giant who is depleting the communal larder. Quillow's attendance at meetings of the town council enables Thurber to poke sly fun at the prim requirements of parliamentary procedure.

In *Many Moons* (1943), for which Louis Slobodkin's illustrations won the Caldecott Medal, the Little Princess Lenore lies ill, saying that only if she can have the moon will she recover. The King consults his assorted wise men, who

are equally long-winded, opinionated, and useless. Only the jester has the wisdom to consult the Princess, who makes it clear that to her the moon is golden and small, since she can obscure it by holding up her thumb. She is delighted with the small golden globe the jester brings.

Thurber's light, seemingly effortless tales with their subtle wit have a surface simplicity that many children can enjoy, while those of wider experience can appreciate his perceptive delineation of human nature. Thurber's stories are certainly in Andersen's fairy-tale tradition.

J. R. R. Tolkien
The Hobbit

No other fantasy of our time has appealed to as broad an age range of readers as has *The Hobbit* (1937); children are enthralled by it, and adults probe and discuss the inner meanings of the book and of its companion tale, *The Lord of the Rings*, a complex three-volume sequel. Professor Tolkien was an eminent philologist and an

The Hill: Hobbiton across the Water.

Illustration from *The Hobbit* by J. R. R. Tolkien. Copyright © 1937, 1951, 1966 by J. R. R. Tolkien. Reproduced by permission of the publishers, Houghton Mifflin Company, Boston, and George Allen & Unwin Ltd., London.

authority on myth and saga, and his knowledge provided so firm a base for the mood and style of his writing that there is no need for scholarly demonstration. Middle-earth *is*. Tolkien wrote of it as easily as one writes about one's own home, and the familiarity of approach lends credence to the world he created.

The hero of *The Hobbit* is Bilbo Baggins, a little creature who is neat and quiet, who loves his material comforts, and who has no desire to do great deeds. When he is tricked into going along on a quest, however, the little hobbit rises to the occasion to show that the common person (or hobbit) is capable of heroism.

There are several qualities that contribute to the stature of *The Hobbit*. The adventures are exciting, the characters are differentiated and distinctive, and the book bubbles with humor. One of the amusing qualities is the aptness of the invented personal and place names. Bilbo's mother's unmarried name was Belladonna Took, perfectly in accord with her reputation as a hobbit who had had a few adventures before she settled down as Mrs. Baggins. And what an admirable name for a dragon—Smaug, and what an equally appropriate name for his lair—the Desolation of Smaug. Perhaps a special appeal lies in the very fact that Bilbo Baggins is a quiet little creature, and that his achievements are due to a stout heart, tenacity, and loyalty to his friends rather than to great strength or brilliance. He puts heroism within the grasp of each reader. Many folk-tale elements are present—the human-beast, elves, the enchanted artifact—all woven naturally into the tale.

C. S. Lewis

The Chronicles of Narnia

Well known as a poet and author, C. S. Lewis created for children the strange new world of Narnia, which they first enter through an old wardrobe. *The Lion, the Witch, and the Wardrobe* (1950), about the adventures of four children, is the first of a series of seven books. Narnia is no Utopia. In fact, once the children have become kings and queens of Narnia, they find themselves engaged in the endless conflict between good and evil, symbolized by the benignant Lion Aslan and the malicious Witch. After reigning for many years, the children return to their own world only to find that they have not even been missed, the time scheme in Narnia having differed so from their own.

Viewpoint

Melancholy men, they say, are the most incisive humorists; by the same token, writers of fantasy must be, within their own frame of work, hardheaded realists. What appears gossamer is, underneath, solid as prestressed concrete. . . .

Once committed to his imaginary kingdom, the writer is not a monarch but a subject. Characters must appear plausible in their own setting, and the writer must go along with their inner logic. Happenings should have logical implications. Details should be tested for consistency. Shall animals speak? If so, do *all* animals speak? If not, then which—and how? Above all, why? Is it essential to the story, or lamely cute? Are there enchantments? How powerful? If an enchanter can perform such-and-such, can he not also do so-and-so?

. . . And, as in all literature, characters are what ultimately count. . . . Fantasy . . . goes right to the core of a character, to extract the essence, the very taste of an individual personality. This may be one of the things that makes good fantasy so convincing.—Lloyd Alexander, "The Flat-heeled Muse," *The Horn Book,* April 1965, pp. 142, 143–144, 145.

Prince Caspian carries the children back to Narnia for further adventures. *The Magician's Nephew* goes back to the creation of Narnia by the Lion. When the Lion sings into existence the world, the stars, the land, and then the creatures, the sheer goodness of creation is too much for the Witch. She flees, but the reader knows she will return. *The Last Battle* concludes the series, and brings the world of Narnia to an end. Lewis's stories are so clearly based on Christian theology and the Bible that we sometimes do not recognize the folkloric elements in the tales—the sacrifice of a king for the good of his people, the talking animals and trees, the healing apple.

While Lewis's style verges on the avuncular at times, it is perfectly suited to these Chronicles, where the children are definitely children and not expected to display qualities more appropriate for adults. The children are, on the whole, honest, steadfast, persevering, and able to resist temptation; the larger tasks are always accomplished with the aid of an adult, or a supernatural helper. It is taken for granted that the children do not have to *prove* their inherent goodness; rather there is sorrow that at times one or another of them may fall short of the best of which a child is known to be capable.

Patricia Wrightson

An Older Kind of Magic
The Nargun and the Stars
The Ice Is Coming

Recipient of Australia's Children's Book Award for her first book, *The Crooked Snake,* which was not published in the United States, and again for *The Nargun and the Stars* (1974), Patricia Wrightson has been a channel through which children of her own and other countries have learned the beauty and dignity of the legendary creatures of Aborigine mythology. In *An Older Kind of Magic* (1972) the theme is conservation, as some of the little people use their magic to foil a plan to destroy the botanical garden where they play. Here, and in *The Nargun and the Stars,* the lives of human children and of ancient spirits are credibly intermeshed in a story that is structured with craft and affection for the mighty and mysterious spirits of an ancient world.

Some of the creatures of the earlier books appear in *The Ice Is Coming* (1977) as Wirrun, a young Aborigine, calls on the amoral spirits of rocks and water to help him find and stop the creeping ice. In a sequel, *The Dark Bright Water* (1979) Wirrun again goes into the countryside on a mission; this time he gains love when a ceremonial fire changes a capricious water-spirit into a woman. Unlike *Down to Earth* (1965), a humorous story of a visitor from Mars, these stories are serious in tone, cadenced and stately in style, yet filled with suspense and action.

Lloyd Alexander

The Prydain Books
The Marvelous Misadventures of Sebastian

Lloyd Alexander had planned, in writing about Prydain, only to adapt the Welsh legends he loved, but he became so engrossed in the project that, as he said in his Newbery Medal acceptance speech, "it grew into something much more ambitious."

The first of the five-book Prydain cycle is *The Book of Three* (1964), in which Taran, the hero, is introduced. Taran, Assistant Pig-Keeper, does not have great status, but of course few pig-keepers are responsible for such a pig as Hen Wen, who utters prophecies by using letter sticks. In this book, Taran goes forth with the great warrior Gwydion to fight against the evil Horned King, who has sworn allegiance to Arawn, Lord of the Land of Death. On the quest, Taran and Gwydion are joined by the capricious Princess Eilonwy, the Caliban-like creature Gurgi, and the boastful harpist, Fflewddur Fflam.

Each of the characters is strongly drawn. Unforgettable is the crafty, toadying, whimpering but loyal Gurgi, whose rhymed speech delights readers. The histrionics of Fflewddur have a touch of Mr. Micawber as he pontificates and prevaricates, but his harp, given him by Taliesin, is a rein on his fancy, for whenever he lies, a string breaks.

In the second book, *The Black Cauldron,* Taran again goes on a quest, this time to the Land of Death, where Arawn creates his Cauldron-Born creatures who live on after death. In *The Castle of Llyr,* the Princess Eilonwy is kidnaped, and it is then that Taran first realizes his love for the saucy girl. In *Taran Wanderer* the hero goes forth to seek his true identity and learns that his worth, whatever it is, is dependent on his ability and his accomplishments rather than on his position. The final book in the Prydain cycle, *The High King* (1968), was awarded the Newbery Medal. It tells of the last conflict between Taran and the Death Lord.

Alexander's fantasy is based firmly upon legend, with a multitude of natural and supernatural characters, and some halfway between. Indeed, we learn at the end that all of the major characters except Taran himself are from the Summer Land, where they live forever. Alexander creates distinctive characters, and he is a true master of the light, sophisticated style, preferring discussion to action, although there are great goings and comings in these books. There is much humor as well, but it is the wry shrug of the adult and not the slapstick antic of the child.

Alexander uses many elements of folk literature in his tales—the magic bauble or light that Eilonwy carries, the ability of the pig to prophesy, the magic cauldron and sword, the inexhaustible knapsack of food. Throughout the books runs the muted theme of the hero, the champion of good against the forces of evil—not just the external manifestations of it, but the evil within oneself—the hero who emerges triumphant at the end.

Another intricate tale by Alexander, *The Marvelous Misadventures of Sebastian* (1970), received the National Book Award. A young eighteenth-century musician goes off on a series of romantic adventures. The fantasy is slight here, being a matter of the exaggeration of reality rather than the creation of a new world or supernatural beings. In *The Town Cats and Other Tales* (1978) perceptive insight lies beneath the surface of polished humor. Alexander's later books, *The Wizard in the Tree* (1975), *The Cat Who Wished to Be a Man* (1973), and *The First Two Lives of Lukas-Kasha* (1978) have one or two magical characters or devices, but portray human nature quite realistically.

Ursula Le Guin

A Wizard of Earthsea
The Tombs of Atuan
The Farthest Shore

Ursula Le Guin, like Tolkien, has created a world of her own, Earthsea. It is a place of wizards and mages, spells and charms. *A Wizard of Earthsea* (1968) introduces us to Ged, or Sparrowhawk, seventh son of a seventh son, and tells of his education as a wizard. At one point in his training, Ged cannot resist the temptation to show off his powers, and lets loose a nameless evil to roam the world. He struggles first to escape it, and finally realizes that he cannot avoid it and must meet it head on. *The Tombs of Atuan* (1971) introduces us to Arha, trained from early childhood to be the high priestess of the Kargad Lands, a part of Earthsea. Ged comes to the sacred precincts, searching for half of a magic amulet. He not only finds it, but frees Arha from her servitude to the dark gods. *The Farthest Shore* (1972) shows us Ged as the Archmage, setting out to discover the reason for the decline in potency of the wizards throughout Earthsea. With him goes Arren, destined to be the king of all the lands of Earthsea.

Le Guin is adept at creation of character, concentrating her efforts on her protagonists, defining minor characters in relationship to them. Ged's nature is built up gradually, through action and reaction, and because we learn to know him in this way, we accept him fully. There are marvels and mysteries aplenty—the ability to raise a favorable wind, to talk to dragons—but these are of minor importance to the tale of Ged as a person. Part of Le Guin's power as a storyteller lies in her style—serious, spare, precise. Not for her the earthy humor of Tol-

From *The Town Cats and Other Tales* by Lloyd Alexander, illustrated by Laszlo Kubinyi. Text copyright © 1977 by Lloyd Alexander. Illustrations copyright © 1977 by Laszlo Kubinyi. Reprinted by permission of the publisher, E. P. Dutton.

kien or the sophisticated wit of Alexander. The measured cadence of the language seems to be a retelling in a more modern idiom of an old, old tale.

Susan Cooper

Over Sea, Under Stone
The Dark Is Rising
Greenwitch
The Grey King
Silver on the Tree

A British writer now resident in the United States has written a series of books about the eternal battle between good and evil. In *Over Sea, Under Stone* (1965) Simon, Jane, and Barnaby go to Cornwall on vacation with their parents and an old, white-haired professor friend of the family, Merriman Lyon. There they discover a chalice, believed to be the Grail, but lose in the sea an ancient map and key to the runes on the Grail.

In *The Dark Is Rising* (1973) we meet Will

Stanton, seventh son of a seventh son, and youngest of the Old Ones, an ageless people whose destiny is to fight against evil until the end. In this tale Will learns he is one of them. His education in his heritage is undertaken in part by Merriman Lyon, another of the Old Ones.

Jane is the heroine of *Greenwitch* (1974). The Grail has been stolen, and the children go to Cornwall with Uncle Merry and Will Stanton to recover it. Because Jane has wished for the happiness of the Greenwitch, a time-honored offering fashioned by the women of the village and given to the sea, instead of wishing for herself, Greenwitch gives Jane the map and rune-key from the depths of the ocean. It has lain protected in its lead case since its loss in the first book. The Grail is also recovered.

Will Stanton is the major character in *The Grey King* (1975), a Newbery Medal book. He is sent to Wales to recover from a severe illness, and meets King Arthur's son, Bran, sent for-

ward in time as a baby to protect him from the forces of evil. Bran realizes his heritage, and the sleepers, horsemen from Arthur's time, are awakened to ride against evil in the crucial battle. In the last book, *Silver on the Tree* (1977), Will, Bran, and other defenders of the Light triumph over evil.

Cooper has made increasing use of legend and folklore with each book in the series. Since we have accepted these elements in the stories previously, we are willing to immerse ourselves more deeply as the tale progresses. Setting is important in all of these stories, providing an atmosphere in which old tales naturally come true. Characterization is vivid, especially of the three children and Will Stanton, and there is much action, described in rich, meaning-laden language.

Cooper moves into another level of fantasy in *Jethro and the Jumbie,* a humorous contemporary story for younger readers, in which an indomitable child on a Caribbean island outwits the local ghost.

Other Fantasy with Folk-Tale Elements

Alan Garner has drawn heavily on the legends of Cheshire to tell *The Weirdstone of Brisingamen* and its sequel, *The Moon of Gomrath.* Garner's earlier stories are filled with action at the expense of character development, but in *The Owl Service,* which won a Carnegie Medal, we come to know the young people well as they mysteriously reenact a Welsh legend, their actions inhibited and dictated by the English class structure which circumscribes their lives.

William Mayne has written a few stories including folkloric elements, most notably *Earthfasts,* in which two boys are the means by which a soldier comes alive out of the past. In *A Game of Dark,* a boy escapes the pain of not loving his dying father through retreating into the medieval world. *A Year and a Day* is about a fairy child who stays with two Cornish children; quiet and perceptive, the story is distinctive for its rich use of language.

Barbara Leonie Picard's fairy tales have the true cadence and spirit of folk material. Her *The Faun and the Woodcutter's Daughter, The Goldfinch Garden, The Lady of the Linden Tree,* and *The Mermaid and the Simpleton* have many familiar folk-tale themes, but they are freshly conceived, and the stories are written with a grave simplicity that makes them particularly enjoyable when read aloud.

Text copyright © 1972 by Ursula Le Guin. Illustrated by Gail Garraty from *The Farthest Shore.* Used by permission of Atheneum Publishers.

Scottish folklore provides background and atmosphere in Mollie Hunter's *The Kelpie's Pearls, The Walking Stones,* and *A Stranger Came Ashore.* The rhythm of her writing lends credence to these tales of supernatural beings and happenings.

Rosemary Harris, a Carnegie Medal winner for *The Moon in the Cloud,* has used the ancient story of Noah and the flood and built a sophisticated, amusing tale. *The Seal-Singing* is based on the Celtic belief in seals as supernatural beings.

Tales of Pure Imagination

While many writers of fantasy have chosen to use motifs from folklore in their work, others have created magical and unusual characters and happenings which seem unlike anything that has gone before.

Lewis Carroll, Charles Kingsley, and George Macdonald all wrote fantasies in the late nineteenth century. Kingsley's *The Water-Babies* (1863) and Macdonald's *At the Back of the North Wind* (1871) and his Princess and Curdie stories are still enjoyed by a few children, but these tales seem overly long and very moralistic to modern readers. Lewis Carroll's tales, on the other hand, are full of pure nonsense and rare humor.

Lewis Carroll

*Alice's Adventures in Wonderland
Through the Looking Glass*

The "Alice" books cannot be accounted for on the basis of anything that had preceded them. Charles Lutwidge Dodgson was a sober, sedate cleric who lectured in mathematics at Christ Church, Oxford. Dr. Liddell, a colleague, had three little girls of whom Alice was evidently Dodgson's favorite. Picnicking on a riverbank on a summer afternoon, Dodgson entertained his young friends with the tale of "Alice's Adventures Under Ground." Alice hoped there'd be nonsense in it, and no hopes ever materialized more gloriously. The next Christmas, Dodgson wrote his story as a gift for "a dear child in memory of a Summer day."

Three years after the famous picnic, the story appeared in book form, somewhat enlarged, with the new title *Alice's Adventures in Wonderland* and with Sir John Tenniel's matchless il-

Illustration by Sir John Tenniel. From *Alice's Adventures in Wonderland,* by Lewis Carroll.

lustrations. That was 1865, and six years later the companion volume appeared, both books under the pseudonym Lewis Carroll.

Does anyone who has read the *Adventures in Wonderland* ever forget those opening paragraphs, with the child's comment on books?

Alice was beginning to get very tired of sitting by her sister on the bank, and of having nothing to do: once or twice she had peeped into the book her sister was reading, but it had no pictures or conversations in it, "and what is the use of a book," thought Alice, "without pictures or conversations?"

Then plop! Right into the third short paragraph comes the White Rabbit, with waistcoat and watch. Down he goes into the rabbit hole, murmuring "Oh dear! Oh dear! I shall be too late!" And down the rabbit hole after him goes Alice, "never once considering how in the world she was to get out again." From then on madness takes over.

The best example is "A Mad Tea-Party," where the conversation reminds you uncomfortably of some of the disjointed small talk which you have not only heard but perhaps, horrid thought, even contributed to. The characters appear and disappear, behave with a kind of wild logic, and burst into verses which sing in your head in place of the serious poetry you might prefer to recall. Carroll's characters are masterpieces; it's not so much what they do but what they are that we remember—Alice's matter-of-fact acceptance of all events, puzzling out the sense (surely there must be some!) in this world that others have organized; the Red Queen's determination to have the last (and only) word.

When do children enjoy *Alice*? Needless to say, it should never be required reading. Some children heartily dislike fantasy and to make them read *Alice* would be to turn reading into a penalty instead of a delight. When college students are asked what books they remember enjoying as children, there is often more disagreement over *Alice* than over any other book. Some disliked it heartily or were bored by it; some say *Alice* was one of their favorite books, not as children but at the high-school age. This is perhaps where it really belongs. Most of those who liked *Alice* as children, ten or under, had heard it read aloud by adults who enjoyed it. Those who had to read the book for themselves rarely found it funny until they were older.

Sir John Tenniel in his illustrations for *Alice* has fixed forever the face, figure, and dress of this beloved little girl. Long, straight hair, a grave, prim face, a neat, perky dress covered with a pinafore, and the straight, slim legs clad in horizontally striped stockings make an appealing figure which no one ever forgets. The Tenniel White Rabbit is an equally unforgettable figure with his sporty tweed coat, his massive gold watch and chain, his swagger walking stick—just the kind of fellow who *would* keep the Duchess waiting. The drawings are so alive, so profoundly interpretative, so right, that it's almost impossible to think of these characters except as Tenniel pictured them.

James Barrie

Peter Pan

Of all Sir James Barrie's delightful plays, none has been so popular as *Peter Pan* (1904). Exquisitely performed by Maude Adams at the beginning of the century and later by Mary Martin and Sandy Duncan, it has been as popular with adults as with children. The book *Peter and Wendy* was made from the play. Barrie has, like Carroll, created memorable characters: Peter Pan, the boy who will not grow up; Tinker Bell, the guardian fairy; and the three children—Wendy, John, and Michael—who go off with Peter Pan to Never Never Land. Their adventures with pirates, Indians, and a ticking crocodile are exciting, but in the end they return to their parents to begin the serious business of growing up. When at one point Tink's life is in danger (she drinks some poison intended for Peter Pan by the evil Captain Hook), only one

thing will save her, and so Peter calls through the dusk to all children, "Do you believe in fairies?" And of course, Barrie has made her real to all of us. *Peter and Wendy* is not the masterpiece that *Alice in Wonderland* is, but the names of some of the characters have become household words.

William Pène du Bois

The Twenty-One Balloons

The fantasies of William Pène du Bois are as orderly and logical as mathematics, and his illustrations have the same graceful balance. He himself credits his passion for order to his regimented school life at Lycée Hoche, for which he is as grateful as he is for glorious weekly excursions to the French circus. These and other lifelong interests are reflected in his books—his love of France, the circus, all forms of mechanized transportation, islands, Utopias, and explosions! Look at some of his most notable books: *Bear Party* is a reasonable fable of some quarrelsome bears who grow genuinely fond of each other when they have a fancy dress party. A bear Utopia results. *The Giant* is a logical story of an eight-year-old giant, already seven stories tall but wistfully amiable. He can disrupt a whole city and send the people into a panic by picking up streetcars or automobiles or people for a better look. It is all drawn to scale as precisely as an architect's plan. In *Lazy Tommy Pumpkinhead* the author takes a healthy poke at the electronic age and what can happen when machines fail, and in *The Forbidden Forest* (1979) he burlesques the heroic war story by having a kangaroo, Lady Adelaide, stop World War I.

And best of all there is his Newbery Medal book, *The Twenty-One Balloons* (1947). When its

Viewpoint

hero, Professor William Waterman Sherman, tires of teaching little boys arithmetic, he sets off in a balloon to see the world and be alone. He tells his story of landing on the island of Krakatoa (a real island, by the way) and finding its inhabitants inventors of the most amazing super-gadgets. These are described in detail and drawn meticulously. Since the island is volcanic, the people have planned a machine for escape should the volcano erupt, and of course it does. And off they go in their airy-go-round. Related with the utmost simplicity, the story piles up suspense until the explosion is a relief.

Du Bois's characters are amiable, but he is more interested in machinery than in personality. He handles the practical details with a deft agility that we can only admire.

Mary Norton

The Borrowers

As British as tea for breakfast, but with action, suspense, and characters of universal appeal, *The Borrowers* (1953) by Mary Norton was immediately popular in the United States as well as in Great Britain.

Borrowers are not fairies but small creatures who live in old houses and take their names from the places they inhabit—the Overmantels, for instance, the Harpsichords, and the Clocks, who live under a huge old grandfather's clock in the hall. Homily, Pod, and their daughter Arrietty Clock are the only surviving family of Borrowers in the old house. When a Borrower is seen, there is nothing for him to do but emigrate. Only Pod, climbing curtains with the aid of his trusty hatpin, borrowing a useful spoon now and then or a bit of tea or a portrait stamp of the Queen, only Pod has escaped detection. Arrietty is the problem now. Arrietty wants to see the world and she goes exploring, happily and trustingly even after the boy sees her. They become fast friends, but even the boy cannot prevent the disastrous ending. It is so catastrophic that young readers could not accept it as final. There had to be a sequel, and so we follow the fortunes of these fascinating characters in *The Borrowers Afield, The Borrowers Afloat,* and *The Borrowers Aloft,* with which the series ends, although Homily reminisces about a past event in *Poor Stainless.*

No briefing of these stories can give any conception of their quality. Every character is un-

Illustration by Beth and Joe Krush. Reproduced from *The Borrowers,* copyright, 1952, 1953, by Mary Norton, by permission of Harcourt Brace Jovanovich, Inc.

forgettably portrayed. There is poor Homily with her hair forever awry, loving but a chronic worrier, "taking on" first and then going capably to work. Pod is the sober realist, a philosopher and a brave one. Arrietty is youth and adventure, springtime and hope, too much in love with life to be afraid even of those mammoth "human beans." To read these books aloud is to taste their full richness.

Lucy M. Boston

The *Green Knowe* books

Another distinguished English fantasy, beautifully written and completely absorbing, is *The Children of Green Knowe* (1955) by Lucy M. Boston. It goes back in time from the present and a boy named Tolly to the seventeenth century and three children of his family who died in the great plague.

A lonely child, Tolly is sent to live with his great-grandmother, Mrs. Oldknow, at the family's ancient manor house, Green Knowe. He is soon aware of the presence of other children who come and go. He hears them but cannot see them although he knows his grandmother sees them. She shows him the portrait of the three and tells him the story of each child and their great horse Feste, and presently Tolly sees them also, but he can never touch them. Playing with these children from the past involves Tolly in a terrifying situation. He is saved by St. Christopher, and the story ends serenely.

There are more books in this setting—*Treasure of Green Knowe*, in which Tolly and his great-grandmother again appear; *An Enemy at Green Knowe*, in which Tolly meets a practitioner of black magic; and *The River at Green Knowe*, in which a new set of characters appears. *A Stranger at Green Knowe*, one of the most moving boy and animal tales ever written, brings an escaped zoo gorilla to sanctuary at Green Knowe. Although published two decades after the first book, *The Stones of Green Knowe* goes back to the

Illustrations by Susan Einzig for *Tom's Midnight Garden* by A. Philippa Pearce. Copyright 1958 Oxford University Press. Reproduced by permission.

twelfth century, when the house was built. In all of these stories real life and fantasy are successfully mingled.

Boston's stories are never commonplace. They grow naturally out of the characters of Mrs. Oldknow and Tolly, interacting with the past which is still present in the old house, a subtle juxtaposition of present and past time.

A. Philippa Pearce

Tom's Midnight Garden

Philippa Pearce won the Carnegie Medal for *Tom's Midnight Garden* (1959), an engrossing fantasy with time as a theme. Young Tom, much bored by life in his aunt and uncle's apartment, hears an ancient clock strike thirteen. Immediately he slips into an enchanting garden where he plays with Hatty, a child from the past. Their play is imaginative but made credible because of the logic of "Time no longer," the motto on the clock. These strange midnight adventures of Tom's are later explained somewhat by what adults might call thought-transference. However, they seem quite clear and uncomplicated to readers once they accept Tom's timeless midnight garden. Pearce's style is serene, unhurried, reflective—giving us time to absorb the experience as Tom lives it.

As in all of these tales of pure imagination, it is character that counts. We think at first that it is the action in the tale that delights us. Then we realize that any adventure would be exciting, providing that it happened to Alice, or Arrietty, or Tolly, or Tom.

Penelope Farmer

Charlotte Sometimes
The Summer Birds
A Castle of Bone

Charlotte Sometimes (1969) also has the timeshift theme that is a familiar one in fantasy, but it has seldom been used more dramatically, perhaps because Charlotte alternates between two worlds. Somehow, while in boarding school, Charlotte finds that she is back in the days of World War I and that her name is Clare. Slowly she begins to realize that Clare is her double and that whenever she is in Clare's world, her own place is taken by her doppelgänger. The mystery and suspense are maintained to the end.

In *Emma in Winter* (1966) Charlotte's sister finds that she shares the same dreams as a boy she dislikes, a boy she and Charlotte met in *The Summer Birds*, the most moving of these books. In *The Summer Birds* (1962), a strange boy teaches the sisters to fly, and then all the children in their school enjoy the soaring bliss and freedom of flight. When the summer ends, they learn the boy's identity and the magic is lost. They are again earthbound. The book has an almost palpable aura of magic and an ending with all the inevitability of Greek drama.

In *A Castle of Bone* (1972) four children discover that what seems to be an ordinary cupboard reduces anything put into it to an earlier state of being. A pigskin wallet becomes a squealing piglet; a boy becomes a baby. The problem is: how does one restore the diminished object or person? The psychic sharing of twins is explored in a story for mature readers; *Year King* (1978) is a sophisticated book with deep psychological implications.

Although Farmer's style is smooth, and her characterizations perceptive, we remember the moods and settings of her stories rather than the people in them. We admire her ingenuity but we don't agonize over her characters' problems as we do over those of the Borrowers. The actual workings of the fantastic elements are a little too obvious.

Maurice Sendak

Where the Wild Things Are
Higglety Pigglety Pop!
In the Night Kitchen
Nutshell Library

Maurice Sendak's versatility and craftsmanship as an artist are discussed in Chapter 6. They are qualities that contribute both to the books he has illustrated for other authors and to those he has written himself. The integrity of his conception and the respect he has for children are nowhere more evident than in his own books of fantasy. Best known of his books is the 1964 Caldecott winner, *Where the Wild Things Are*, a picture book that was greeted with delight by many and apprehension by some. Max is a small boy whose noisy ebullience causes his mother to call him a Wild Thing. "I'll eat you up!" he retorts, and is sent to his room, where he solaces himself by imagining a kingdom of wild things, fanged and clawed, all bowing respectfully to their beloved ruler, Max, king of all the wild things. "Let the wild rumpus start," he proclaims, and a mammoth frolic takes place. When Max leaves, his creatures plead with him to stay because they love him so. But he goes back to his room, to real life, and to his supper waiting for him, "and it was still hot." The psychological implications are sound. Children see the reassurance in Max's return home from his fantasy land when he "wanted to be where someone loved him best of all."

The subtitle of *Higglety Pigglety Pop!* (1967) is *There Must Be More to Life*. Its heroine is Jenny, who has everything a dog could want and leaves home because she is not content. She wants something she does not have, and feels "there must be more to life" than having everything. Jenny was drawn from life, immortalizing a dearly loved household pet in soft and amusing black-and-white pictures that are quite different from the bold exaggeration and flamboyance of the wild things. Jenny eventually becomes the leading lady of the World Mother Goose Theater starring as The Dog (typical Sendak humor) in a production of "Higglety Pigglety Pop!" Written with bland directness that belies the nonsensical situation, the story ends with a poignant note from Jenny to her old master in which she says that she cannot tell him how to get to Castle Yonder, because she doesn't know where it is. "But if you ever come this way, look for me."

Maurice Sendak's childhood memories are the basis for much of the setting for *In the Night Kitchen* (1970). The delicious smells of baking coming from the room below, the buildings, seen against a night sky, and the "Mickey Oven" label all contribute to the story of a small boy who, in his dream, falls down into the night kitchen where three identical bakers (all Oliver Hardy) try to stir him into the batter. Sendak's draftsmanship is particularly impressive in these illustrations, and both the pictures and the story are remarkable in their identification with a child's vision.

The four irresistible books that make up Maurice Sendak's tiny *Nutshell Library* (1962) are illustrated with impish, round-faced boys. The text of the four little books is as original as the pictures. *One Was Johnny* is a counting book, which winds up and down in fine, cumulative style. *Pierre,* subtitled "a cautionary tale," describes the horrible fate of a boy who keeps saying "I don't care." But the ending is droll. *Alligators All Around* is one of the funniest alphabet books yet, and *Chicken Soup with Rice* is hilarious nonsense about the months of the year. These are funny books, original and beguiling, in miniature form.

Natalie Babbitt

Tuck Everlasting

Natalie Babbitt shows a high sense of comedy in most of her writing, and a facility for combining ridiculous postures or plights with a bland, ingenuous writing style. Yet these are not the qualities that distinguish what is undoubtedly her most impressive book, *Tuck Everlasting* (1975). It is a story about immortality and death, so smoothly crafted that the deeper implications permeate but do not obscure the action: a girl of ten is befriended by a family that has drunk at a spring that has given them eternal life—and eternal life proves a burden. The pace and drama of the family's attempt to escape observation end on a poignant note, as the protagonist helps their flight but weighs the possibility of herself drinking from the spring.

In *Knee-Knock Rise* (1970) a whole village is terrified by the terrible Megrimum, a creature that doesn't exist; the more poetic *The Search for Delicious* (1969) is based on the fact that a definition of the word "delicious" is needed by the compiler of a dictionary, and a boy courier's quest results in a series of magical adventures. The humor of these books is echoed in The

Illustration by Natalie Babbitt. Reprinted with the permission of Farrar, Straus and Giroux, Inc., and Curtis Brown, Ltd. From *Knee-Knock Rise* by Natalie Babbitt, copyright © 1970 by Natalie Babbitt.

Devil's Storybook (1974) in which an arrogant devil is outwitted in ten lively short stories. Babbitt's ingenious plots are often amusingly farfetched, and she delights in word play as much as does Carl Sandburg in his *Rootabaga Stories* with their garrulous humor.

Penelope Lively

The Ghost of Thomas Kempe
The House in Norham Gardens
The Voyage of QV 66

Although her first novel was published as recently as 1970, Penelope Lively has established herself as one of England's most interesting and versatile writers. She won the Carnegie Medal for *The Ghost of Thomas Kempe* (1973), the story of a boy who moves into an old house and is plagued by the mischievous pranks of a dissatisfied ghost, a sorcerer for whose behavior the boy is blamed. The writing style is matter-of-fact, a good foil for the humorous concept of a Jacobean ghost puzzled by a saran-wrapped world.

In *The House in Norham Gardens* (1974) the heroine dreams at night of her grandfather's expedition to New Guinea, while in the day she copes with a meagre existence with two elderly aunts. Her travels into another time are beautifully meshed with her real life, a rich integration of two cultures. In *The Voyage of QV 66* (1979) a group of animals travels to London in a future, massively flooded England; this is Lively's most warm and amusing story, the animal characters used wittily to point out the foibles of humankind. There are suspense and momentum in *A Stitch in Time* (1976) as a shy and lonely child hears echoes of the past in a rented vacation home.

Helen Cresswell

The Winter of the Birds
A Game of Catch

Writing with equal facility and polish whether the stories are realistic or fantastic, Helen Cresswell is almost as well known in the United States as she is in England. In *The Winter of the Birds* (1976) the concept of terrifying steel birds who come at night, borne by wires, to strike and slash, is deftly merged with a realistic story told from the viewpoints of two people and the author. She creates a true hero in the person of cheerful, generous Finn who helps the lonely old man who is frightened by the birds, and she vividly evokes the atmosphere of the shabby neighborhood in which they live.

In *A Game of Catch* (1977) two children play ball with Kate—but they are children who have stepped from a museum painting, and when Kate sees the picture a second time, the ball has changed from one hand to another. Nicely structured, convincingly meshing the real and the fanciful, the story is just the right length and complexity for readers in the middle grades.

Among Cresswell's other stories of pure imagination are *The Piemakers* (1968) in which there is a pride in craftsmanship which is a recurrent theme in her writing; *Up the Pier* (1972), in which a deserted resort in winter is the setting for the story of a time-trapped family longing to return to their familiar past; and *The Bongleweed* (1973) in which a mysterious plant goes on a rampaging spurt of growth and takes

over a garden. In this book there is some of the humor that is so evident in Cresswell's realistic Bagthorpe series (see Chapter 11) and the structural craftsmanship that is seen in all her writing.

Other Tales of Pure Imagination

The field of fantasy has attracted a number of excellent writers. Anne McCaffrey has created a whole world in *Dragonsong* (1976) and *Dragonsinger* (1977). Her writing style is fluent and vigorous, and her characterization vivid in recounting the adventures of a girl whose longing to become a harper is aided by her skill at training a band of flying fire-lizards to sing.

Jane Langton has taken the Concord, New Hampshire, terrain as her own, sages and all, and has constructed ingenious adventures for Eddy and Eleanor in *The Diamond in the Window, The Swing in the Summerhouse,* and *The Astonishing Stereoscope.* The window, the swing, and the stereoscope project the children into magical times and places.

Antoine de Saint-Exupéry's *The Little Prince* is a poetic, practically plotless fairy tale, whimsical and sophisticated in its concern with the inconsistencies of human behavior. The prince, who comes to earth from another planet, tells much of the story in dialogue form. The lack of action and the allusiveness of the dialogue limit

Viewpoint

... deeper meaning is essential in fantasy. For the characters involved, there is no need for very deep thought. They can enjoy the pleasure of realizing their dearest wishes, only occasionally speculating about their origin. Sometimes (as in E. Nesbit's stories) they can be changed a little, can learn a little from their adventures, as they miraculously travel the world, change their shape, or exploit the power of a button, a lamp-post or a pencil. But the reader who vicariously enjoys these delights should expect something more. The fantasy should exercise his imagination. For the characters in the story there is little time for Why and How. Questions are blown away as they rush from one adventure to another. But the reader can and should ask How and Why. He should be left with a sense of expansion, as if he himself had been flying on a magic carpet and breathing an air more rarefied than his accustomed oxygen....—Margery Fisher, *Intent Upon Reading,* Watts, 1961, pp. 149–150.

the book's appeal to those readers who appreciate style and theme above all else.

The Animal Family by Randall Jarrell also has a poetic quality but is more cohesive in plot and is more smoothly written than *The Little Prince*. Alone in his home near the sea, a hunter falls in love with a mermaid, who comes to live with him. Their family is increased by a shipwrecked boy, a bear, and a lynx, and together they live in love and peace. The writing has a subtle simplicity and ingenuous humor that succeed both in making the element of fantasy believable and in avoiding any semblance of sentimentality.

Distinctive for its witty and polished style, Walter Wangerin's *The Book of the Dun Cow* (1978) creates a complex world of animal heroes, led by Chauntecleer the Rooster, who fight against the huge, evil Wyrm and his invading serpents.

In Elizabeth Coatsworth's *Cricket and the Emperor's Son*, Cricket, a small apprentice, tells a tale each night to the little Prince who cannot sleep, the stories coming from a magic paper that never comes to an end. Coatsworth's Newbery Medal book, *The Cat Who Went to Heaven*, which also has a Japanese setting, is about a struggling young artist who is commissioned to paint a picture for the temple. The temple priest refuses to accept the picture because it shows a cat in the procession of animals approaching Buddha. The little household cat that had been a model for the picture dies, and a miracle occurs; the painted cat now appears at the head of the procession, under the hand of Buddha, which is stretched out in blessing. Coatsworth's tales are well written, whatever the genre.

Modern Stories of Talking Beasts

The talking beasts in the folk tales were, on the whole, a cheerful lot. Silly creatures were liquidated, but the wise pig survived, and smart billy goats gained the grassy hillside in spite of the troll. There was no brooding and no melancholy until Andersen's *Fairy Tales*, whose Ugly Duckling not only was mistreated by others but suffered spiritually. In the two English talking-beast masterpieces, *The Tale of Peter Rabbit* and *The Wind in the Willows*, there are animals with

limitations who make mistakes and commit follies which they shake off with blithe determination. It is the tone and pattern of these lively tales rather than "The Ugly Duckling" which are dominant in animal fantasy. In many of these stories the only fantasy is the animal as near-human, living in human-type surroundings. The humor of these tales generally has the slapstick element that children enjoy.

Beatrix Potter
The Tale of Peter Rabbit

Beatrix Potter, English novelist of the nursery and cheerful interpreter of small animals to small children, has left her own account of how she happened to write her classic, *The Tale of Peter Rabbit*. In a letter to *The Horn Book*, May 1929, she said:

> . . . About 1893 I was interested in a little invalid child. . . . I used to write letters with pen and ink scribbles, and one of the letters was Peter Rabbit.
>
> Noel has got them yet; he grew up and became a hardworking clergyman in a London poor parish. After a time there began to be a vogue for small books, and I thought "Peter" might do as well as some that were being published. But I did not find any publisher who agreed with me. The manuscript—nearly word for word the same, but with only outline illustrations—was returned with or without thanks by at least six firms. Then I drew my savings out of the post office savings bank, and got an edition of 450 copies printed. I think the engraving and printing cost me about £11. It caused a good deal of amusement amongst my relations and friends. I made about £12 or £14 by selling copies to obliging aunts. I showed this privately printed black and white book to Messers. F. Warne & Co., and the following year, 1901, they brought out the first coloured edition.[3]

Children quickly learn by heart these apparently simple little stories[4] of Beatrix Potter's, and how they relish the names of her characters: Flopsy, Mopsy, and Cottontail, Jemima Puddle-Duck, Pigling Bland, Mrs. Tiggy-Winkle, Benjamin Bunny, Peter Rabbit. The stories are plotted carefully, with plenty of suspense to bring sighs of relief when the conclusion is finally reached. Children chuckle

---

3. Beatrix Potter. From a letter to *The Horn Book Magazine*, May 1929. Copyright 1929 by The Horn Book, Inc.

4. Among the companion volumes to *Peter Rabbit* are *The Tale of Benjamin Bunny*, *The Tailor of Gloucester*, *The Tale of Squirrel Nutkin*, *The Tale of Jemima Puddle-Duck*, *The Tale of Mrs. Tiggy-Winkle*, and *The Tale of Tom Kitten*.

over the funny characters, the absurd predicaments, and the narrow escapes. They pore over the clear watercolor illustrations, which are full of action, and absorb delightedly the lovely details of landscapes, old houses, fine old furniture and china.

Children can soon "read" Peter's adventures for themselves, they know them so well; but the charms of that humorous and exciting plot never grow stale—disobedient Peter in Mr. MacGregor's cabbage patch, very complacent at first, then pursued and thoroughly frightened but still keeping his wits about him; next, Peter at home, properly repentant, chastened by his mother, but snug in bed at last and secure. Here is a cheerful Prodigal Son, child-size.

Rudyard Kipling

Just So Stories

Living in India for many years and thus familiar with the Indian Jatakas and the usual pattern of a "why" story, Rudyard Kipling wrote the *Just So Stories* (1902), his own collection of explanatory tales, in amusing imitation of the old form. "How the Whale Got His Throat" and "How the Leopard Got His Spots" begin seriously and end with a logical kind of nonsense that reminds us of *Alice*.

The children's favorite is "The Elephant's Child." This story explains how the elephant's "blackish, bulgy nose, as big as a boot" grew to the long trunk we see today. It was all because of the "'satiable curiosity" of the Elephant's Child who, after innumerable spankings, ran away to seek knowledge by the banks of "the great grey-green, greasy Limpopo River."

These are stories to be read aloud. They are cadenced, rhythmic, and full of handsome, high-sounding words which are both mouth-filling and ear-delighting. Children soon catch on to the grandiloquent style and absurd meanings. The mock-serious tone of these pseudo-folk tales adds to their humor.

In contrast to the *Just So Stories,* Kipling's *Jungle Books* (1894) stand the test of time due in part to his scrupulous avoidance of the temptation to humanize the animals. They may talk but they remain true to their natures. Children get from these stories about the boy Mowgli and the animals who raise him an insight into that wild-animal nature, into the curious likeness of animals and humans, and into the still more curious lines of demarcation.

Kenneth Grahame

The Wind in the Willows

Kenneth Grahame was a lovable, literary, out-of-doorish sort of Englishman with a gift for storytelling. For his small son, nicknamed "Mouse," he used to spin continuous tales at bedtime. Once Mouse refused to go to the seaside because his trip would interrupt the adventures of Toad, to which he was listening. In order to persuade the child to go, his father promised to send him a chapter in the mail daily, and this he did. Sensing their value, the

Illustration from "The Elephant's Child" from *Just So Stories* by Rudyard Kipling, Illustrated by Nicolas Copyright 1952 by Western Publishing Company, Inc. Used by permission. (Original in color)

nursery governess who read the chapters to Mouse mailed them back to his mother for safekeeping. From these letters and bedtime stories grew *The Wind in the Willows* (1908).

Each chapter tells a complete adventure of the four friends—reflective Mole, kindly old Water Rat, shy Badger, and rich, conceited, troublesome Toad. The friends "mess about in boats," have picnics, dine elegantly at Toad Hall, get lost in the Wild Wood, rescue Toad from his life of folly, and even encounter once "The Piper at the Gates of Dawn." But how to explain the appeal of this book?

In the first place, the sensory experiences make the reader one with Mole or Ratty. You can feel the sunshine hot on your fur; you, too, waggle your toes from sheer happiness or stretch out on some cool dock leaves or explore the silent silver kingdom of the moonlit river. Earth and water, a green world of woods and meadows speak to you from every page.

The humor of *The Wind in the Willows,* particularly the humor of the conversations, is subtle, but Toad's antics, his bemused pursuit of his latest fad, his ridiculous conceit, the scrapes he gets into, and the efforts of his friends to reform him furnish enough broad comedy to satisfy everyone. The dialogue is that of the born storyteller, used to children's predilection for talk, improvising dialogue in his own fluent, individual vein. What talk it is—funniest when it is most grave, revealing more of the speaker than any explanatory paragraph. These conversations are as much a part of the style as the descriptions which make the book one of the masterpieces of English literature.

None of these things—sensory appeal, humor, dialogue, or descriptions—accounts for the hold this book takes upon the heart and the imagination. As in Andersen's *Fairy Tales,* it is the inner significance of the story that counts. First of all, there is the warm friendliness of the animals. Each one makes mistakes, has his limitations, but no one ever rejects a friend. The three put up with Toad's escapades as long as they can; then they join together and reform him in spite of himself. Together they endure perils and pitfalls and come safely through only because they help each other. This continual kindliness, the overlooking of other people's mistakes, and the sympathetic understanding which pervade every page warm the reader's heart. There are no hidden meanings or didacticism here, just reassurance and comfort.

New Folks co-ming, Oh my! New Folks co-ming, Oh my! New Folks co-ming, Oh my! Oh my! Oh my!

From *Rabbit Hill* by Robert Lawson. Copyright 1944 by Robert Lawson. Reprinted by permission of The Viking Press, Inc.

Robert Lawson
Ben and Me
Rabbit Hill

Robert Lawson, with his easy storytelling style and beautiful illustrations, added much to the glory of the talking-beast tale. Children consider *Ben and Me* (1939) one of the genuinely funny books. These biographical memoirs of Benjamin Franklin are supposedly written by Amos, a cheeky mouse who modestly admits that he supplied Ben with most of his ideas. The two were almost frozen and Ben had a case of sniffles when Amos thought of the idea of a stove. Ben was a little slow at catching on but finally worked out a very satisfactory contraption. Amos admits that he thoroughly disapproved of Ben's experiments with electricity, but he stuck by his friend in spite of many a shock and some novel results caused by Amos's interference. A series of these fantastic biographies followed.

Good as his humorous biographies are, Lawson really came into his own as a creative writer with *Rabbit Hill* (1944), a Newbery Medal winner. This is the story of Father and Mother Rabbit, their high-leaping son, Little Georgie, aged Uncle Analdas, and a host of other animals. The story begins with the pleasant rumor that new folks are moving into the big house. The question is, what kind of folks will they turn out to be—mean and pinching, or planting folks with a thought for the small creatures who have always lived on the hill? The new folks begin well with a sign "Please Drive Carefully on Account of Small Animals." They plant gardens without fences, sow fields without traps, provide generous "garbidge," and permit no poison. They rescue Willie Fieldmouse from drowning and Little Georgie from an automobile accident. Their crowning beneficence is a beautiful pool and feeding station for the animals.

The Tough Winter (1954), the sequel to *Rabbit Hill*, tells a moving story of what happens to small beasts when snow and ice last too long and there are no kindhearted humans to help.

These books may not have the superlative literary qualities of *The Wind in the Willows*, but they are exceedingly well written and marvelously illustrated. All of the animals, from suspicious Uncle Analdas to worrying Mother Rabbit, are delightfully individualized.

E. B. White

Charlotte's Web

E. B. White, essayist and editorial writer for *The New Yorker*, noted for his lucid, effortless prose, wrote *Stuart Little* (1945), the story of a baby who resembled a mouse, "in fact he was a mouse." Some children liked Stuart's adventures, but many adults were disturbed by the biology of this mouse child of a human family. *The Trumpet of the Swan* (1970), the story of a mute swan who learned to play an instrument so that he could woo his beloved, is a fascinating blend of fantasy and realistic details. But White's masterpiece is *Charlotte's Web* (1952).

Fern, a farmer's child, persuades her father to give her a runt pig he is about to butcher. Fern names her pet "Wilbur," and raises him with a doll's nursing bottle for a feeder. But when Wilbur gains girth, he is firmly banished to the barnyard, and here the fantasy begins. Fern spends long periods of time watching Wilbur daily and discovers that she understands what the animals are saying to each other. Wilbur has learned about the fall butchering and he doesn't want to die. Charlotte, the aloof, intelligent spider, feels sorry for the silly little pig and promises to save him. Her devices for doing this are unique and exceedingly funny. The progress of Wilbur, the "radiant pig," involves all the people on two farms and most of the barnyard creatures, including Templeton, the selfish rat. In the end, Wilbur is saved but Charlotte dies, true to her kind, leaving hundreds of eggs. Birth and death and life go on in their strange and moving cycles.

Illustration by Garth Williams from *Charlotte's Web* by E. B. White. Copyright, 1952, by E. B. White. By permission of Harper & Row, Publishers, Inc. and Hamish Hamilton Children's Books Ltd.

Charlotte's Web is a fantasy universally acclaimed by adults and universally loved by children. Wilbur is a true pig—he relishes slops and good soft muck. But he also is a child, lonesome, without a friend, turning to Charlotte for understanding, reassurance, entertainment, love, and finally a solution to his most urgent problem. Wilbur is no hero: he weeps at the thought of death. But he is obedient and tries his best to live up to all the good things Charlotte weaves about him in her web.

White's writing style is confidential and intimate; he's telling a story just for you, and readers and listeners respond openly to the humor and pathos of these adventures.

George Selden

The Cricket in Times Square
Tucker's Countryside
Harry Cat's Pet Puppy

The Garth Williams illustrations add immeasurably to the charm of Selden's books, as they do for *Charlotte's Web*. In *The Cricket in Times Square* (1960) the New York setting provides a solid base of realism—the animal characters live in the Times Square subway station. Tucker is a tough, slangy city mouse, a pure Damon Runyon character, and his friend Harry Cat is a sage creature who joins him in welcoming the cricket Chester, who has been brought into town in somebody's picnic basket. Chester is also befriended and given publicity by Mario, the boy whose parents run the station newspaper stand. The cricket makes a name for himself when it is discovered that he has perfect pitch and is a concert-grade chirper. The style is breezy, the dialogue entertaining, the whole situation fresh and imaginative.

In *Tucker's Countryside* (1969) Chester, who has gone back to Connecticut, appeals to his old friends to help save the meadow in which he and his country friends live. The stratagem that saves the day is amusingly all too possible.

In *Harry Cat's Pet Puppy* (1974), Harry adopts a dog and experiences all the problems of an anxious parent, compounded by the large size of the pup.

Like E. B. White, Selden brings his animal characters so vividly to life that they are unforgettable personalities, and the books pay tribute to the tenderness and loyalty of friendship.

Other Examples of Talking Beasts

People have observed and lived with animals for a long time, frequently identifying closely with them. It is no wonder that authors have chosen to make beasts talk and that their readers accept these tales so readily. Two books in this category have been awarded prizes: *Mrs. Frisby and the Rats of NIMH* by Robert O'Brien and *Watership Down* by Richard Adams. O'Brien's Newbery Medal tale has some science-fiction aspects, as he tells the story of the rats who have been used as experimental subjects to see how certain injected substances affect their ability to learn, and who escape the National Institute of Mental Health and set up their own society. O'Brien's tale is rich in circumstantial detail, fact piled upon fact, yet compactly and reasonably told. The rabbits in Richard Adams's Carnegie Medal book also seek a new home and, urged forward by a foreboding vision, find it on Watership Down. Adams creates not only a series of adventures, but a folklore for his migrating rabbits. Theirs is an epic struggle, serious, believable, although carried out by what we're accustomed to think of as small, rather helpless animals. Another small creature, an artistic and articulate prairie dog, is the hero of Betty Baker's *Dupper*, and in Nathaniel Benchley's *Kilroy and the Gull* a philosophical killer whale succeeds in his attempt to communicate with people.

In *The Bat-Poet*, Randall Jarrell wrote a story of grave sweetness, a quality echoed in the Maurice Sendak illustrations. This is a small homily on the writing of poetry. His creatures speak and think, and the poetry written by the bat gives marvelously vivid pictures of the owl, the mockingbird, the chipmunk, and the bat.

Most of the fantasy tales about animals are humorous, as are Margery Sharp's *Miss Bianca* stories. Miss Bianca is the most genteel of mice, but her courage is unbounded. With her faithful (but quite ordinary) admirer, Bernard, she embarks on adventures as lurid and melodramatic as those of any detective story, but she is always calm, always completely in charge of the situation.

Another popular talking animal is the enterprising young mouse, Ralph, who makes friends with a boy in Beverly Cleary's *The Mouse and the Motorcycle* and continues his ad-

Copyright © 1971 by Robert C. O'Brien. Illustration by Zena Bernstein. From *Mrs. Frisby and the Rats of NIMH*. Used by permission of Atheneum Publishers.

Illustration by Louis Darling is reproduced by permission of William Morrow & Co., Inc. from *Runaway Ralph* by Beverly Cleary. Copyright 1970. Published in the United Kingdom by Hamish Hamilton Ltd.

ventures in *Runaway Ralph*. The husband-and-wife team of Louise Fatio and Roger Duvoisin has produced the series of *Happy Lion* books. Not only are these stories well told with good plots, sly humor, and surprise endings, but the pictures are rich in details that children pore over. A series of tales about *A Bear Called Paddington* by Michael Bond disarmingly describes life in a middle-class English family; the Browns adopt a small bear from Peru found wandering about in a railway station with a tag that pleads, "Please look after this bear." William Steig, well known as a creator of adult cartoons, has given us droll, sophisticatedly simple animal characters in *Dominic* and in *The Amazing Bone*. For the younger child, an engaging young donkey is the central character in his Caldecott Medal book, *Sylvester and the Magic Pebble*. In *Abel's Island*, a mouse lives in cultured comfort until a flood maroons him on an island; the Robinson Crusoe appeal here is for readers in the middle grades who can appreciate the nuance of the writing.

Talking-beast stories are perhaps the first kind of fantasy that younger children encounter, and there have been an enormous number published, especially in the last several decades. All sorts of creatures, from pandas to goldfish, are talking and adventuring. Two favorites are Margaret Wise Brown's *Goodnight Moon* and Marjorie Flack's *Ask Mr. Bear*, both of which have humor and warm, reassuring family relationships.

Over thirty years old but still appealing are the *Curious George* stories by H. A. Rey. Children easily identify with a monkey who can't help getting into trouble just because he wants to *know* about things.

Modern talking-beast tales should be chosen with discrimination. We can do no better than to reread Beatrix Potter and *The Wind in the Willows* when we are in doubt about the qualities that should distinguish the best new animal fantasies.

Personified Toys and Inanimate Objects

Although the fanciful story about the secret life of toys and other inanimate objects was Andersen's invention, it took the writers of the twentieth century to use this form at the child's level, with an inventiveness and charm that already have made some of these stories children's classics. Andersen's tales of the little china shepherdess and the chimney sweep or the steadfast tin soldier are faintly sad and decidedly adult. Later writers have avoided both these pitfalls. Their dolls, trains, and airplanes are usually cheerful and lively.

Illustration by William Steig. Reprinted with the permission of Farrar, Straus and Giroux, Inc. From *Abel's Island* by William Steig, copyright © 1976 by William Steig. Published in the United Kingdom by Hamish Hamilton Ltd.

Carlo Lorenzini

The Adventures of Pinocchio

The Italian classic *Pinocchio*, written in 1880 by a witty Tuscan, Carlo Lorenzini (pseudonym Collodi), was apparently first translated into English and published in the United States in 1892. From then on, it has held a place in the affections of American children and has undoubtedly influenced American writers.

The story concerns a rogue of a puppet which old Geppetto painstakingly carves out of wood. Hardly has the poor wood-carver finished when the saucy creature makes off in pursuit of his own sweet way. Although full of good resolutions, Pinocchio wastes his money, lies about it, plays hooky from school, and chooses bad companions. Every time he lies to his friend the Blue Fairy, his nose grows longer, until soon he can't turn around in a room without colliding with the walls. The climax is his journey to the Land of Toys, where he finds that he has grown a fine pair of donkey ears and a body to match. Saved again and again by the good Blue Fairy, he learns that she is ill and starving. He is roused at last, earns money to feed and care for both Geppetto and the Fairy, and wakes in the morning to find himself no longer a puppet but a real boy, living with Geppetto in a well-kept home.

This is the children's own epic, presenting young readers with themselves in wood, full of good resolutions, given to folly, sliding through somehow, but with one difference—Pinocchio always comes out on top and never quite loses face. But he does learn his lesson, and readers never doubt it.

A. A. Milne

Winnie-the-Pooh
The House at Pooh Corner

A. A. Milne's *Winnie-the-Pooh* (1926) and *The House at Pooh Corner* (1928) are different from anything that preceded them. They seem to have grown naturally out of poems about Christopher Robin and Pooh, and they also developed from his small son's demands to hear a story for Pooh. The accommodating Milne began to spin a series of tales about Pooh, when he lived in the forest "under the name of Sanders." He calls on Rabbit and eats so much that

he sticks in the door and can't get out. He flies up in a balloon to get some honey out of a tree, tries to imitate a cloud in order to distract the suspicious bees, and finally has to have the balloon shot in order to get down. There are adventures with Piglet, Eeyore the old donkey, Kanga, and Little Roo. *The House at Pooh Corner* introduces Tigger, a new and amusing character, but the tales go on in much the same vein.

Ernest Shepard's illustrations make it clear that most of the animals are really toys like Winnie-the-Pooh. The pictures are full of fascinating details both children and adults enjoy. For instance, Owl's house has two signs at the door. One, under the knocker, says

> PLES RING
> IF AN RNSER
> IS REQIRD

The other, under the bell rope, reads

> PLEZ CNOKE
> IF AN RNSR
> IS NOT REQID

The stories are unusual in that Christopher Robin goes in and out of them on a familiar forest-dwelling level with the animals, but in the end he brings everything back to reality when he sets off up the stairs of his own house, headed for a bath, dragging Pooh by one leg. The stories are finished, Christopher Robin is himself, and Pooh is Pooh.

Christopher Robin is omnipotent in these tales, surely a heady experience for children subject to the whims and demands of their elders. Milne's facility with words delights both children and adults, making this an excellent choice for parent-child sharing. His tone is childlike, innocent, uncondescending, allowing children to laugh at themselves without the necessity of looking to adults for cues.

Virginia Burton

Mike Mulligan and His Steam Shovel
The Little House

Virginia Burton used her brush and words in the happiest possible combination. *Mike Mulligan and His Steam Shovel* (1939) tells the story of Mike, who owns a fine steam shovel with which he does important jobs of excavation until his machine, Mary Anne, is outmoded by new and more powerful models. Then Mike reads about a town which wishes to have a cellar dug for its townhall. Mike and Mary Anne hasten to the scene and offer to dig it in one day or no pay. The city fathers agree, seeing a chance to get their excavation done for nothing, since such a feat seems obviously impossible. The next morning Mary Anne and Mike go to work. Dirt flies in all directions, the watching crowds grow to a mob, and at last, exactly on the hour, the excavation is finished, deep and well squared-off at the corners. The only trouble is that Mike, in his excitement, has dug himself in, and there is no way of getting Mary Anne out. So Mary Anne becomes the furnace of the new town hall and Mike her attendant. Both live a warm, prosperous, and respected life ever after.

Burton's machine stories have certain marked characteristics which help to explain their popularity. The plot always involves a staggering task or action and has considerable suspense. The illustrations heighten the feeling of action by swirling, circular lines that rush across the page and stem from or center on the cause of it all.

But *The Little House,* the winner of the Caldecott Medal for 1943, is Virginia Burton's finest and most distinguished book. A house in the country presently finds itself in the center of a

Illustration by the author, from *The Little House* by Virginia Lee Burton. Published by Houghton Mifflin Company. Copyright © renewed 1969 by George Demetrios. Reproduced by permission of the publisher.

village, and then in the midst of a great city where it is an insignificant obstruction between skyscrapers, with elevated trains overhead, subways beneath, and swarms of people everywhere. Rescued by the descendants of its builder, the little house is taken back to the country where it can once more watch the cycle of the four seasons revolving in ordered beauty.

There is a significance to this book that should make it permanently valuable as literature and art. The evolution of cities in all their complexity and the resultant loss of some of the sweetness of earth and sky are implied in text and picture. The pattern of every picture is the same—rhythmical curving lines which in the country are gracious and gentle but in the city become more and more violent and confused. The house has only a delicately suggested face, and the personification is subordinate to the pattern of these illustrations, something for children and adults to study with growing astonishment and delight.

Burton's personification is much more evident in art than in text, but no one doubts that Mike speaks Mary Anne's thoughts or that the story discloses the Little House's thoughts, though it doesn't speak aloud.

Rumer Godden

The Dolls' House
Impunity Jane
Miss Happiness and Miss Flower

The most common type of personification for younger children is found in doll stories. The novelist Rumer Godden has written a series of them unsurpassed in variety and charm, for her dolls have distinct personalities and in her books they talk and act in character. Only in one respect are they alike. In the hands of their owners they are often misunderstood and badly treated, and always helpless, except for the sheer force of their unique personalities. The first of the series, *The Dolls' House* (1947, 1962), is one of the most dramatic. An exquisite old Victorian doll house is inhabited by proper, genteel dolls. When a strange, haughty doll is added to the group, a doll-sized tragedy takes place, but this ending is as gentle as the spirit of the old house.

Then there is *Impunity Jane* (1954), so called because the clerk tells the buyers that this fin-

Illustration by Adriene Adams. From *Impunity Jane* by Rumer Godden. Copyright 1954 by Rumer Godden. By permission of The Viking Press, Inc. (Original with color)

ger-sized doll can be dropped "with impunity." But her owner does not think much of Jane, so she relegates her to a stuffy old doll house where she sits for years, bored and pining for adventure. When a small boy named Gideon carries her off in his pocket, life begins for Jane. What that boy thinks up for Jane to do! She sails his boat, flies his airplanes, rides on his bicycle, dwells in igloos and wigwams, and generally enjoys life. When Gideon's conscience forces him to own up to his kidnaping, the solution is a joyous one, and he and Jane return happily to a life of exploration and adventure.

In contrast to the intrepid Jane, *Miss Happiness and Miss Flower* (1961) are two exquisite Japanese dolls, almost too gentle to enjoy any adventures. Yet they are the promoters of a long series of activities which help a homesick, timid little girl and quell a jealous one. These dolls give rise to another series of adventures in a book called *Little Plum*. In this story the interest centers less on the dolls and more on their owner Belinda's naughty curiosity and behavior in relation to a new child next door. However, the culmination of the amusing action is a most felicitous Feast of the Dolls in Japanese style. Other doll stories by Godden are *Candy Floss, The Fairy Doll, Home Is the Sailor,* and *The Story of Holly and Ivy.*

Other Stories about Inanimate Objects

Two doll stories have won the Newbery Medal, *Hitty: Her First Hundred Years* by Rachel Field and *Miss Hickory* by Carolyn Sherwin Bailey. Hitty is carved from mountain ash and travels around the world, while Miss Hickory is an apple tree twig with a hickory nut head who lives all her life on the same farm. Both dolls live through adversity bravely and boast definite personalities, many cuts above today's mass-produced dolls.

In *The Dollhouse Caper* Jean O'Connell has written a satisfying story about a family of dolls who come to life when no people are about and who worry about being discarded by their owners, three brothers who are growing up. This book has good characterization, sturdy plot, and smooth writing style.

One of the most touching stories about a toy is Russell Hoban's *The Mouse and His Child.* They are a single unit, a wind-up tin toy that has been discarded. Repaired by a tramp, they go on a quest for love and security. The story has humor and tenderness, and an adventurous plot with general appeal. While the sophistication of its latent meaning and social comment and the difficulty of the vocabulary put special demands on readers, it is well worth the effort.

The Return of the Twelves by Pauline Clarke is an ingenious story about some wooden soldiers

Viewpoint

that had once belonged to the children of the famous Brontë family. Years after the Brontë times, eight-year-old Max Morley finds the Twelves and learns that they "freeze" when they are observed. He wins their confidence and they talk of the past. Max and his sister decide that the soldiers belong in their old home, Haworth, and let them march off rather than offend their dignity by carrying them. Winner of the Carnegie Medal, the book has a polished style, delightful individual characterizations of the soldiers, and enough literary references to intrigue adults as well as young readers.

Humorous Fantasy

While a number of the fantasies mentioned so far in this chapter, such as those by Thurber, Alexander, Carroll, Kipling, Lawson, White, Selden, and Milne, have a great deal of humor, it is the humor of word play or sly remarks on the foibles of animals or humans, a sophisticated humor which demands a certain level of maturity for fullest enjoyment.

Other fantasies have an open, slapstick-style of humor, the kind that is obvious at all levels of understanding and causes us to laugh aloud. Lucretia Hale's *The Peterkin Papers,* stories of a family who cannot solve the most obvious problems without the advice of "the lady from Philadelphia," is a nineteenth-century example.

P. L. Travers
Mary Poppins
Mary Poppins Comes Back

P. L. Travers grew up in Australia, where high, wild winds blow everyone into a dither and make almost anything possible. So an east wind blows *Mary Poppins* (1934) straight into the nursery of the Banks family, and a west wind carries her off. The children first see her coming up the walk, bag in hand, and the next thing she strikes the house with a bang. Once their mother has engaged her as a nurse, Mary slides lightly *up* the banisters as neatly as the children slide down. When she opens her bag, they see it is quite empty, but out of it she takes everything from a folding cot to a bottle of medicine from which she doses the children with incredibly delicious liquid, tasting of strawberry ice or lime-juice cordial or whatever you prefer.

The Poppins books are extremely British, with cooks, gardeners, maids, nannies, nurseries, and teas. The humor is sometimes adult and sometimes whimsical, but children who like these books like them enormously and wear them to shreds with rereadings; others dislike them with hearty scorn. The character of Mary Poppins herself has a flavor all its own. Vain, stern, crotchety, continually overtaken by magic but never admitting it, she is adored by the children she disciplines and enchants.

Theodor Seuss Geisel
And to Think That I Saw It on Mulberry Street
The 500 Hats of Bartholomew Cubbins

Theodor Seuss Geisel chose his middle name for a pen name and then added the "Dr." as a purely honorary touch. His first book for children was *And to Think That I Saw It on Mulberry Street* (1937). A small boy sees only a horse and a wagon on Mulberry Street but begins working up a bigger and bigger yarn to tell his father. Each succeeding page pictures the next addition to his tale until finally two pages across are necessary to get everything in. Then his father fixes him with a cold stare and his tale diminishes suddenly, leaving only the horse and wagon on Mulberry Street.

This rhymed narrative was only a sample of more and better nonsense to come. Of all the Seuss Books *The 500 Hats of Bartholomew Cubbins* (1938) is certainly one of the best. Bartholomew Cubbins takes off his hat to the King only to find the royal coach stopping, and the King commanding him to take off his hat. Puzzled, he puts his hand to his head and finds a hat there. He jerks it off hastily only to find another in its place, and another, and another, and another. He is seized and threatened with death, but still the hats continue to crown his bewildered head. Finally the King sees upon the boy's head the most gloriously regal hat he has ever beheld. In exchange for this elegant hat, he spares Bartholomew's life, and, as the befeathered hat goes on the King's head, Bartholomew finds his own head bare at last. The outline of this story gives no idea of the humor of both pictures and text. This story has a lively sequel, *Bartholomew and the Oobleck* (1949).

Dr. Seuss has the cartoonist's gift for expressing a great deal of humor in a single line or word, and he has maintained the ability to create in uncluttered pictures and text the kind of humor the younger child best enjoys—endless word play, incongruous situations, much action, sure punishment for the truly wicked. His heroes win out not because of brute strength but because the usual cycle of life, gamely lived through, comes round to their side once again.

Seuss has written numerous zany stories, nonsense with basic sense and, at times, basic vocabulary. Children enjoy them all, and will surely feel that Seuss deserves the Wilder Award, which he received in 1980.

Astrid Lindgren
Pippi Longstocking

A Swedish writer is responsible for creating a superchild, the heroine of *Pippi Longstocking* (1950). Pippi is an outrageous and delightful child who lives competently with her monkey and horse and, in this book and its sequels, takes control of any situation in which she finds herself. She curbs some bullying boys, disrupts a school session, and outwrestles two policemen when they try to take her to an orphanage. Indeed, after carrying one in each hand, she sets them down so hard that it is some time before they can get up. Then they report she is not a fit child for the orphanage!

Pippi's antics are exceedingly funny to children. She is a child in charge of her own world, with a sea-captain father conveniently away on the high seas, a chest of gold for sundries, and the warmest of hearts, except for interfering adults.

Jean Merrill
The Pushcart War

Certainly one of the most original fantasies of our time, *The Pushcart War* (1964), has all the ingredients of good fiction. The characters are unusual and distinctively drawn, the setting is colorful, the plot has a tight structure, the style is light and polished, and the theme is significant. Add humor, pace, and the element of fantasy made wholly believable, and the result is sheer delight. The place is New York City, and the problem is that there are so many huge trucks that traffic on Manhattan Island is in a constant snarl. The three big men in trucking

Reprinted from *The Pushcart War*, text © 1964, by Jean Merrill, and illustrations © 1964 by Ronni Solbert, a Young Scott Book, by permission of Addison-Wesley Publishing Company, Inc. Published in the United Kingdom by Hamish Hamilton Ltd., London.

decide that the first step in their campaign to eliminate other vehicles is to attack the pushcart owners. But the little people won't be put down; they fight with pins, and the ensuing number of flat tires puts such a strain on repair facilities that trucks are left stranded all over the island. Led by General Anna, the brave little army of pushcart owners outwits the big business sharks, to say nothing of the mayor whose attitude has been swayed by making him a stockholder. In the most ingenuous fashion, Jean Merrill attacks both corruption in political office and monopoly in business, and she does it with a bland humor that avoids any note of bitterness. The characters and the situation are given validity by an introduction that cites invented sources and by a foreword that is written by an invented historian. The concept is original and the development of the story line amusing, but it is the dialogue that gives the book flavor. In the pushcart owners' strategy session, Old Anna says, "Of course, we have got to fight." "Fight the trucks?" a colleague asks. "How can the pushcarts fight the trucks?" Anna's reply is a clincher: "Maybe you'd rather be dead?"

Other Humorous Fantasy

At the outset, *Mr. Popper's Penguins* by Richard and Florence Atwater gives every indication of being a simple, realistic story about a paperhanger with a passion for the Antarctic. The narration is grave and dignified, skidding suddenly into understated nonsense with the addition of a penguin, Captain Cook, to the family.

Oliver Butterworth's *The Enormous Egg* blandly injects the hatching of a dinosaur into the modern scene, and Scott Corbett's *Ever Ride a Dinosaur?* tells of a brontosaurus (who can make himself invisible) sneaking in to have a look at a dinosaur exhibit. Butterworth's *The Trouble with Jenny's Ear* is the hilarious tale of a small girl whose extrasensory perception is used to advantage in television appearances. In *The Downtown Fairy Godmother*, Charlotte Pomerantz creates a brisk and bustling godmother, assigned the territory of Lower Manhattan, who is working for a promotion.

Joan Aiken's humor tends toward sophistication and language play, but her ability to exaggerate gives her work the slapstick surprise that children appreciate. Her Gothic tale, *The Wolves of Willoughby Chase*, drips with Victorian sentimentality and drama. In *Nightbirds on Nantucket* and *Black Hearts in Battersea* Aiken displays a Dickensian relish for names that indicate character, and a sense of the ludicrous that results in such situations as a pink whale obligingly towing a transatlantic cannon. *Smoke from Cromwell's Time and Other Stories* is a good collection of short stories on fanciful themes, and *The Whispering Mountain* is a broad burlesque of the fanciful adventure story. It has a rollicking plot that incorporates a spurned grandchild, a magic harp, a foreign potentate, and a breed of little men who live in a mountain; and it has a spectrum of dialects overdone to the point of absurdity.

Sid Fleischman's stories are also large-canvas affairs. In *The Ghost in the Noonday Sun*, a pirate kidnaps a boy who can, he thinks, lead him to the treasure of the man he murdered. A tropic isle, plank-walking, buried treasure, and mu-

Reprinted from *The Downtown Fairy Godmother*, Text Copyright © 1978 by Charlotte Pomerantz, Illustrations Copyright © 1978 by Susanna Natti, by permission of Addison-Wesley Publishing Company, Inc.

tinous pirates are just a few of the standard ploys at which the author pokes fun. In *Chancy and the Grand Rascal* the young hero (so skinny he has to stand twice to cast a shadow) goes off to find his little sister Indiana, meets a rogue and shyster, Colonel Plugg, and then finds his uncle, whose ability to lie magnificently routs even the lying Plugg. *By the Great Horn Spoon* is a picaresque tale about the California Gold Rush, in which Young Jack and the family butler, Mr. Praiseworthy, go off to recoup their losses. In the McBroom stories, Fleischman has used the tall-tale style of humor to excellent advantage.

What's humorous in one culture is not necessarily funny in another, but Tove Jansson, whose work received the Hans Christian Andersen Award, is popular internationally. Her books about those engaging imaginary creatures the *Finn Family Moomintroll* have a daft logic all their own.

From *Nightbirds on Nantucket* by Joan Aiken, illustrated by Robin Jacques. Copyright © 1966 by Joan Aiken. Reproduced by permission of Doubleday & Company, Inc.

Science Fiction

Science fiction and fantasy are closely related genres, and they are sometimes difficult to distinguish clearly from one another. At one time science fiction was clearly an extrapolation from known scientific facts. That is, the events of a story were possible, given the advances promised by fact or theory, though perhaps many years in the future. Fantasy, on the other hand, was clearly unreality in the physical sense—talking animals, supernatural beings, a parallel world. Some novels of the future contain unreal elements and may be called science fantasy, but contemporary science fiction often becomes a vehicle for commentary on what social scientists and physical scientists are telling us are facts. What kinds of new governments might we evolve? What stresses will crowding

bring? How will we handle the social problems brought on by an ever lengthening life span? Today's science fiction brings our judgment into play. We ask ourselves: what is right? what is wrong? and find ourselves not far from those fantasies that address the eternal battle between good and evil.

Children of today have seen the fulfillment of many prophecies of science fiction of the past. They seem readier at times than adults to welcome the future. Usually science fiction for children is less bleak than that written for adults, emphasizing the adventure of exploring the unknown, and the fascination of seeing another world and its inhabitants.

Robert Heinlein
Tunnel in the Sky
Podkayne of Mars

The fun and danger of *Tunnel in the Sky* (1955) and Robert Heinlein's many other books about interspace travel is that they seem completely reasonable and factual. No "airy-go-rounds" in these tales. Instead we have to pinch ourselves to remember that we are not pioneering on Mars, sending colonies to Ganymede, or commuting to Hespera. The stories are so well told they carry the reader along in a state of almost unbearable suspense. Although many science-fiction stories include girls, few of them have a girl as the central character. In *Podkayne of Mars* (1963) a sixteen-year-old girl goes on her first trip to Earth and is kidnaped on a Venus stopover. Children just beginning to read science fiction enjoy Heinlein because he is technically accurate without being difficult.

Madeleine L'Engle
A Wrinkle in Time
A Swiftly Tilting Planet

Madeleine L'Engle's notable book *Meet the Austins* is a fine realistic family story. The opening of *A Wrinkle in Time* (1963 Newbery Medal) suggests that it will be a similar kind of story. A storm is raging outside, but within the cozy kitchen Meg Murry and her brother, precocious five-year-old Charles Wallace Murry, are having hot cocoa with their mother. Into this family group comes a strange old woman,

Mrs. Whatsit. She explains that she was "caught in a down draft and blown off course." But having finished her cocoa, she departs with one final word to the mother, ". . . there *is* such a thing as a tesseract." That is what the children's scientist father had been working on for the government when he disappeared. The next day, Meg, Charles Wallace, and Calvin O'Keefe, a friend, meet Mrs. Whatsit and two other strange old women, who warn the children that their father is in grave danger and that only they can save him and only if they are willing to tesser. This involves the "fact" that the shortest distance between two points is not a straight line, but a fold or wrinkle. The children prove to be only too willing to try it. There follows in the complex course of the rest

Viewpoint

of the book a battle between good and evil, love and hate. In the end Meg's love triumphs and her father is saved. All of them tesser back to earth where their lives pick up as they were except for their new-found knowledge of good and evil.

This space story is written in terms of the modern world in which children know about brainwashing and the insidious, creeping corruption of evil.

A second story about the Murrys is *A Wind in the Door* (1973) in which Charles Wallace, the youngest, seems near death. With the help of other-worldly teachers, Meg learns to extend her love even to those who do not seem to deserve it in order to save her brother. In the third title, *A Swiftly Tilting Planet* (1978), Charles Wallace goes back in time to avert a looming tragedy.

L'Engle's books are complicated in their blend of science, philosophy, religion, satire, and allegory, but her ability to draw character and concoct adventurous situations attracts readers.

John Christopher
The White Mountains trilogy

Christopher's stories of the future are written with a breadth of conception and a fidelity of detail that lend conviction. He succeeds admirably in *The White Mountains* (1967) in establishing the believability of his twenty-first-century world. In this world, machine creatures called Tripods control the earth and perpetuate their mastery over human beings by inserting steel caps in the skulls of all children when they reach the age of fourteen, an operation that renders them forever subservient. Three boys—Will, Henry, and Beanpole—have heard that there is a haven in a land the ancients called "Switzerland," and having learned from a Vagrant that free people live in the White Mountains, they decide to escape before they are capped. They have a hazardous but successful journey to a small colony of free humans who live secluded in a mountain. In the second volume, *The City of Gold and Lead* (1967), Will takes part in an athletic contest, the winners of which are to have the privilege of serving the Masters, the Tripods. The other boys go in a spirit of sacrifice; Will goes as a spy. In *The Pool of Fire* (1968) Will describes the intricate sabotage by which the Tripods are defeated, and the new freedom of humankind to set up its own government. As has happened before, there is quarreling and competition, so Will gives up his own plans to work with a small group of people whose goals are world unity and peace. The ending is sober and realistic, a reminder that vigilance against tyranny must be constant. The whole concept of the trilogy is developed with pace and skill—the pitting of good against evil, in a world where few can see the evil, adding suspense to the well-structured action.

The Guardians is science fiction without a fantasy element. It is set in the year 2052, when England is divided into two societies: the megalopolis, huge and sprawling, sharply divided by a frontier from the rest of England, a world occupied by the landed gentry and their servants.

In his later books for children, *The Lotus Caves, Empty World,* and *The Prince in Waiting* trilogy, Christopher has used new settings and time periods, but has not succeeded in creating characters as credible as Will. All of Christopher's books are concerned with serious human problems and humanity's environment; his gift as a science-fiction writer is his ability to treat these problems seriously without making a tract out of an absorbing adventure story.

Peter Dickinson

The Weathermonger
Heartsease
The Devil's Children

An editor of the English humor magazine *Punch* and the author of adult mystery stories, Peter Dickinson was immediately successful as a writer for children. His first book, *The Weathermonger* (1969), is a vigorous and well-written fantasy about an England of the near future, a time in which the British Isles have become mysteriously subject to a state of feudalism in which any mechanical object is taboo, and in which the weather is controlled by magic. Geoffrey, a young weathermonger, escapes to France and comes back secretly with his younger sister on a mission, seeking the cause of the enchantment. The plot is inventive, the characterization vivid, and the very contemporary dialogue, often lightly humorous, a good contrast to the mystic elements of the story.

From *Heartsease* by Peter Dickinson. Illustrated by Nathan Goldstein. Copyright © 1969 by Peter Dickinson. By permission of Little, Brown and Co.

The second book in this trilogy about England in the time of the Changes is *Heartsease* (1969). Only a few people are unmarked by the hatred of machines, the fear of strangers, the belief in witches. Margaret and her cousin Jonathan find a "witch," buried beneath a pile of stones but still alive. He is an American, and he can hardly believe the hysteria and bigotry of the villagers who attacked him. The children plan to help him escape, and they eventually get the man on board the tugboat *Heartsease* and take off, pursued by angry villagers. The book is, as are its companion volumes, an indictment of prejudice. It is also the most dramatic of the three, with a taut suspense in the escape and chase sequences.

In *The Devil's Children* (1970) a small girl who has been left alone in London joins a group of Sikhs, who are unaffected by the prevailing thrall that grips the native population. She is used by them to prevent their making innocent blunders, and she clings to them at first for security despite the fact that they are reviled as the Devil's Children by the villagers in the area where they settled. But she comes to respect them for their intelligence and good will, as the village people eventually do also. Logical plot development, strong characterization, and a sprightly writing style add to the appeal of a cracking good tale. These are superb examples of one facet that is common to many science-fiction stories: the expressed belief in brotherhood and love as necessary ingredients in a shrunken world.

Other Examples of Science Fiction

There are several writers whose science-fiction stories for older readers are good if not distinguished and whose audience greets each new volume avidly.

Andre Norton's earlier stories were concerned with voyages to other worlds through space or time and with problems in dealing with different types of intelligent life. She has made a specialty of the possibilities of communication between humans and animals in such tales as *Moon of Three Rings* and *The Zero Stone*. Her stories have moved into the realm of fantasy, but she continues to create credible, interesting characters and to spin breathtaking adventures, as she does in *Wraiths of Time* (1976), in which a young, black archeologist finds herself time-shifted to an ancient Nubian Kingdom. Most of Alice M. Lightner's books have a medical theme, like that of *Doctor to the Galaxy*, in which a problem of medical research is pursued on a mythical planet. In her *The Galactic Troubadours*, however, the theme is the revival of musical performance in a society that frowns on young people who aren't satisfied with perfectly good taped music. Also realistic rather than fantastic is Sylvia Engdahl's *Journey Between Worlds*, which explores the theme of prejudice of Terrans against Martian colonists. In *Enchantress from the Stars* and *The Far Side of Evil*, she explores the possibilities of control of physical phenomena by mental means. Suzanne Martel's *The City Under Ground* is on a theme that has often been used by writers of adult science fiction: the emergence of a new civilization, conscious of ethical values, from the ruins of the old.

Children enjoy stories about robots, such as Lester Del Rey's *The Runaway Robot* and Carol

Illustration by Ruth Sanderson from *Into the Dream* by William Sleator. Text copyright © 1979 by William Sleator. Illustrations copyright © 1979 by Ruth Sanderson. Reprinted by permission of the publisher, E. P. Dutton.

Ryrie Brink's *Andy Buckram's Tin Men. The Runaway Robot* is set in the future when robots are common, but it is an uncommon robot that becomes so close a friend of his human companion that the two run away together. Andy in *Andy Buckram's Tin Men* is a twelve-year-old who builds four robots out of tin cans, but not until they are struck by lightning during a storm do the four come alive and save Andy's life during the flood caused by the storm.

For younger children, anywhere from eight to eleven, there are numerous fantasies. In William Sleator's *Into the Dream*, two children avert disaster by their telepathic communication. Among the amusing space fantasies are Ruthven Todd's *Space Cat*, Patricia Wrightson's *Down to Earth*, Jerome Beatty's *Matthew Looney* stories, Jay Williams and Raymond Abrashkin's *Danny Dunn* books, Louis Slobodkin's *Space Ship Under the Apple Tree*, and Eleanor Cameron's *Wonderful Flight to the Mushroom Planet*, together with their sequels, make absorbing reading and good introductions to this popular type of literature.

Books That Stir Controversy

Since we must be persuaded by writers of fantasy and science fiction to suspend the rules of the everyday world that we all have known from childhood, it is no wonder that books of this type may stir controversy.

It is hardly necessary to say that a book is not likely to excite discussion if it does not have some excellent qualities. Books that are patterned in plot and pedestrian in style fall by the wayside; books that have a few minor flaws outweighed by their strengths can be enjoyed by successive waves of young readers; and books that are the best of their kind live on to become classics.

Some of the controversial books of the past can be seen, in retrospect, to have been breakers of barriers and small classics of their time. Sometimes it is the content, sometimes the treatment, sometimes only a small facet of the story that causes disagreement about a book.

Certainly one perennial bone of contention has been the Oz books of L. Frank Baum. *The Wizard of Oz* and, to a lesser degree, its sequels have remained favorites of many children despite the fact that many authorities in the field of children's literature feel that the style is flat and dull, and that the inventiveness of the first book was followed by mediocrity and repetition in subsequent volumes. Another book that has been condemned for other reasons by some adults is Helen Bannerman's *The Story of Little Black Sambo,* which is set in India. It is offensive because of the illustrations and because the names "Sambo," "Mumbo," and "Jumbo" have derogatory connotations.

Also attacked, with considerable justification it would seem, as casting aspersion on black people, are the *Dr. Dolittle* books by Hugh Lofting, one of which *(The Voyages of Dr. Dolittle)* won the Newbery Medal in 1923. Children have enjoyed the humorous reversal of roles in the series, with animals guiding and taking care of helpless human beings, and the gravity with which preposterous events are treated. Although the stories have action and humor, they also have disturbing racial epithets, illustrations, and incidents, and some adults have suggested that the offending sections be deleted in new editions of the books.

Quite another sort of difference of opinion has been generated by the books of Julia Cunningham, some of which are fantasy (*Viollet,* in

which a bird, a fox, and a man unite to save the life of a gentle old man) and others (like *Dorp Dead*) which can be taken as fantasy or as realism. Indeed, some of the controversy has been on this very point. Some adults dislike the books because they are sophisticated, complex, and heavy with symbolism and psychological import; others defend the books on the grounds that the symbolism and the author's concern with the struggle between good and evil in our society entitle the stories to be classed among the significant books of our time. Most agree that the writing style is polished and distinctive.

The characters and plots developed by Roald Dahl, primarily an adult author, have also generated sharp debate. In *Charlie and the Chocolate Factory* five children win a contest to enter a wonderfully ingenious manufacturing plant invented by Willy Wonka and operated by pygmies—a device that has been criticized as antiblack. Criticism has also been directed at Dahl's stereotyping of character as a means of discoursing on social behavior. *The Magic Finger* is simpler in structure and stronger in its message: shooting animals for sport is deplorable. An indignant eight-year-old girl points her magic finger at her neighbors who are hunters. The father and sons shrink to tiny winged creatures and the ducks grow enormous, sprout arms that can hold guns, and move into the family's house. Able to understand the animal point of view, the hunters make a pact with the ducks. Less humorous than *Charlie,* this has better construction and a light, easy style. *James and the Giant Peach,* which tells of a boy's flight in a peach made gigantic by magic, shows Dahl's ingenuity in constructing a novel type of spaceship.

Ian Fleming's *Chitty-Chitty-Bang-Bang* is a burlesque of detective stories by a popular writer of adult detective fiction. The marvelous car Chitty-Chitty can rise to an occasion both literally and figuratively, since she takes to air and can (and does) take charge of events when the going gets rough in her family's encounter with a gang of French smugglers. The sophisticated style and zany story line have amused children, and the book has been used as the script for a film, but the sophistication of the parody and the style are felt by many adults to be inappropriate for the audience most interested in stories of animated machines.

Edward Eager's stories (*Magic or Not? The*

Illustration by William Pene du Bois for *The Magic Finger* by Roald Dahl. Copyright © 1966. Reproduced by permission of Harper & Row, Publishers, Inc.

sion of allusions makes the book seem heavily burdened with references that will daunt many readers.

Under each category of modern fantasy many more authors and books could be listed. Most of the examples discussed in this chapter are outstanding because they pointed the way or were exceptions or became classics or seem likely to attain that distinction. Even with innumerable omissions, the list is a long one, and the numbers of these books are increasing yearly. Authors discussed here are generally outstanding in craftsmanship, inventiveness, and creation of character. They have something to say and they say it well.

Most children enjoy fantasy as a change from the here and now, as a breathing space in the serious process of growing up. It is a rare child who does not like some fantasies, and most children enjoy many of them. Adults sometimes wonder why. The probable reason is that they provide children with a flight into other worlds, incredible, exciting, satisfying. Fantasy frees children's own imaginations and helps them to face reality with more creativity and spontaneity of thought. Hans Christian Andersen, Kenneth Grahame, Beatrix Potter, Mary Norton, E. B. White, C. S. Lewis, Lucy Boston, and others have shown children that much of the joy of life depends upon your willingness to take different points of view.

Adult References[5]

ALDISS, BRIAN. *The True History of Science Fiction.*

ARNOTT, ANN. *The Secret Country of C. S. Lewis.*

BLOUNT, MARGARET. *Animal Land: The Creatures of Children's Fiction.*

BOVA, BEN. *Through Eyes of Wonder: Science Fiction and Science.*

BREDSDORFF, ELIAS. *Hans Christian Andersen: The Story of His Life and Work.*

CAMERON, ELEANOR. *The Green and Burning Tree: On the Writing and Enjoyment of Children's Books.* Part 1, "Fantasy."

CARROLL, LEWIS [pseud.]. *The Annotated Alice: Alice's Adventures in Wonderland & Through the Looking Glass.*

COLLINGWOOD, STUART DODGSON. *The Life and Letters of Lewis Carroll (Rev. C. L. Dodgson).*

DEL REY, LESTER. *The World of Science Fiction 1926–1976: The History of a Subculture.*

EGOFF, SHEILA, G. T. STUBBS, and L. F. ASHLEY, eds. *Only Connect: Readings on Children's Literature.* Part 2, "Fairy Tales, Fantasy, Animals."

FIELD, ELINOR WHITNEY, comp. *Horn Book Reflections.* Part 5, "Fantasy, Yesterday and Today."

5. Complete bibliographic data are provided in Appendix B.

Well Wishers, Half Magic, Seven-Day Magic, and others) have intriguing plots and a good style, save for those books in which segments are purportedly but unconvincingly told by the child characters. The author has been criticized by those who feel his material is derivative and his children precocious.

The writing of Norton Juster in *The Phantom Tollbooth* delights many readers, young and old, who are intrigued by words and word play (a light meal consists of lights; a bee is a Spelling Bee) and by the Bunyan-like place names (for example, the Mountain of Ignorance and the Foothills of Confusion). To others the dependence on latent meanings and on comprehen-

GODDEN, RUMER. *Hans Christian Andersen: A Great Life in Brief.*

GREEN, PETER. *Kenneth Grahame.*

HAZARD, PAUL. *Books, Children and Men.*

HEARN, MICHAEL. *The Annotated Wizard of Oz.*

HELMS, RANDEL. *Tolkien's World.*

HIGGINS, JAMES E. *Beyond Words; Mystical Fancy in Children's Literature.*

LANE, MARGARET. *The Tale of Beatrix Potter: A Biography.*

LENNON, FLORENCE BECKER. *Victoria Through the Looking Glass.*

LEWIS, C. S. *Of Other Worlds: Essays and Stories.*

LYNN, RUTH NADELMAN. *Fantasy for Children: An Annotated Checklist.*

SALE, ROGER. *Fairy Tales and After: From Snow White to E. B. White.*

SCHOLES, ROBERT, and ERIC S. RABKIN. *Science Fiction: History, Science, Vision.*

STIRLING, MONICA. *The Wild Swan: The Life and Times of Hans Christian Andersen.*

TOWNSEND, JOHN ROWE. *Written for Children.* Chapter 13, "Fantasy Between the Wars."

TYMN, MARSHALL B., KENNETH J. ZAHORSKI, and ROBERT H. BOYER. *Fantasy Literature: A Core Collection and Reference Guide.*

WAGGONER, DIANA. *The Hills of Faraway: A Guide to Fantasy.*

WILLIAMS, SIDNEY H., and FALCONER MADAN. *The Lewis Carroll Handbook.*

Children's Books

ADAMS, RICHARD. *Watership Down.* Macmillan, 1974. Carnegie Medal.   12 up

AIKEN, JOAN. *Black Hearts in Battersea,* ill. by Robin Jacques. Doubleday, 1964.   9-12

————. *The Faithless Lollybird,* ill. by Eros Keith. Doubleday, 1978. A diverting collection of stories ranging from the realistic to the fanciful; the style is polished, the humor sophisticated.   11-14

————. *The Kingdom and the Cave,* ill. by Victor Ambrus. Doubleday, 1974.   9-11

————. *Nightbirds on Nantucket,* ill. by Robin Jacques. Doubleday, 1966.   10-12

————. *Not What You Expected.* Doubleday, 1974. A collection of short stories.   10 up

————. *Smoke from Cromwell's Time: And Other Stories.* Doubleday, 1970.   10-12

————. *The Whispering Mountain,* ill. by Frank Bozzo. Doubleday, 1969.   10-14

————. *The Wolves of Willoughby Chase,* ill. by Pat Marriott. Doubleday, 1963.   11-13

ALEXANDER, LLOYD. *The Black Cauldron,* Holt, 1965.   11-13

————. *The Book of Three.* Holt, 1964.   11-13

————. *The Castle of Llyr.* Holt, 1966.   10-13

————. *The Cat Who Wished to Be a Man.* Dutton, 1973.
                                                        10-12

————. *The First Two Lives of Lukas-Kasha.* Dutton, 1978.
                                                        10-12

————. *The Foundling and Other Tales of Prydain,* ill. by Margot Zemach. Holt, 1973. Six stories written with grace and humor.   9-11

————. *The High King.* Holt, 1968. Newbery Medal.   11-13

————. *The Marvelous Misadventures of Sebastian.* Dutton, 1970. National Book Award.   9-11

————. *Taran Wanderer.* Holt, 1967.   11-13

————. *The Town Cats and Other Tales,* ill. by Laszlo Kubinyi. Dutton, 1977.   9-11

————. *The Wizard in the Tree,* ill. by Laszlo Kubinyi. Dutton, 1975.   9-11

ALLAN, TED. *Willie the Squowse,* ill. by Quentin Blake. Hastings, 1978. A squowse (the son of a mouse and a squirrel) lives in the wall that joins two houses.   8-10

ANDERSEN, HANS CHRISTIAN. *The Complete Andersen,* tr. by Jean Hersholt, ill. by Fritz Kredel. Heritage, 1952. Jean Hersholt captures both the spirit and fine literary style of Andersen in this translation of 168 tales.   12 up

————. *The Complete Fairy Tales and Stories,* tr. by Erik Christian Haugaard. Doubleday, 1974. Translated in a flowing style, in the cadence of the oral tradition.   9 up

————. *Seven Tales,* tr. by Eva Le Gallienne, ill. by Maurice Sendak. Harper, 1959. Favorite stories chosen for their appeal to younger readers.   7-12

————. Some single-story editions:

The Emperor and the Nightingale, ill. by Bill Sokol. Pantheon, 1959.   9-10

The Fir Tree, ill. by Nancy Burkert. Harper, 1970.   9-11

The Little Match Girl, ill. by Blair Lent. Houghton, 1968.
                                                          9-11

The Nightingale, tr. by Eva Le Gallienne, ill. by Nancy Burkert. Harper, 1965.   9-11

The Steadfast Tin Soldier, tr. by M. R. James, ill. by Marcia Brown. Scribner's, 1953.   6-10

The Swineherd, tr. and ill. by Erik Blegvad. Harcourt, 1958.
                                                          5-9

Thumbelina, tr. by R. P. Keigwin, ill. by Adrienne Adams. Scribner's, 1961.   6-9

The Ugly Duckling, tr. by R. P. Keigwin, ill. by Johannes Larsen. Macmillan, 1967.   6-9

The Wild Swans, ill. by Marcia Brown. Scribner's, 1963.
                                                          6-10

ANNETT, CORA. *How the Witch Got Alf,* ill. by Steven Kellogg. Watts, 1975. A little donkey tries everything, even singing, to get attention.   8-9

ATWATER, RICHARD and FLORENCE. *Mr. Popper's Penguins,* ill. by Robert Lawson. Little, 1938.   8-12

BABBITT, NATALIE. *The Devil's Storybook,* ill. by author. Farrar, 1974.   9-11

————. *Knee-Knock Rise,* ill. by author. Farrar, 1970.   9-11

————. *The Search for Delicious.* Farrar, 1969.   9-11

————. *The Something,* ill. by author. Farrar, 1970. A pithy and funny story about Milo, a hairy little cave dweller, who is afraid of Something in the night. It turns out to be a modern girl. When they meet in dreams, both stoutly declare they are not afraid of each other.   4-6

————. *Tuck Everlasting,* ill. by author. Farrar, 1975.   9-11

BACON, MARTHA. *Moth Manor: A Gothic Tale,* ill. by Gail Burroughs. Little, 1978. In a deft blend of realism and fantasy, the story of a dolls' house and its occupants is carried over three generations.   9-11

BAILEY, CAROLYN. *Miss Hickory,* ill. by Ruth Gannett. Viking, 1968. Newbery Medal.   10-13

BAKER, BETTY. *Dupper,* ill. by Chuck Eckart. Greenwillow, 1976.   9-11

————. *Save Sirrushany! (Also Agotha, Princess Gwyn and All the Fearsome Beasts).* Macmillan, 1978. In a nice spoof of the traditional fairy tale, Agotha, visiting the rather seedy palace of Sirrushany, arranges a trade agreement that will benefit both the royal family and a threatening dragon.
                                                         10-11

BANNERMAN, HELEN. *The Story of Little Black Sambo,* ill. by author. Lippincott, 1923 (first pub. in 1900). Historically interesting but unacceptable.   4-7

BARRIE, SIR JAMES. *Peter Pan,* ill. by Nora Unwin. Scribner's, 1950. Peter Pan and all his delightful companions are visualized for the children by Nora Unwin's illustrations for this edition.   9–12

BAUM, L. FRANK. *The Wizard of Oz,* ill. by W. W. Denslow. Reilly, 1956 (first pub. in 1900). This edition has many of the original illustrations.   8–11

BEATTY, JEROME, JR. *Matthew Looney in the Outback,* ill. by Gahan Wilson. Scott/Addison, 1969. One of a popular series.   9–12

BELLAIRS, JOHN. *A Figure in the Shadows,* ill. by Mercer Mayer. Dial, 1975. More adventures in a sequel to the title below.
———. *The House with a Clock in Its Walls,* ill. by Edward Gorey. Dial, 1973. An orphaned boy discovers the excitement of living with an uncle who has magical powers.   10–12

BENCHLEY, NATHANIEL. *Kilroy and the Gull,* ill. by John Schoenherr. Harper, 1977.   10–12

BIANCO, MARGERY WILLIAMS. *The Velveteen Rabbit,* ill. by William Nicholson. Doubleday, 1926, 1958. How a very old toy rabbit becomes real and goes off into the real world.   4–7

BISHOP, CLAIRE. *The Five Chinese Brothers,* ill. by Kurt Wiese. Coward, 1938.   5–10

BOMANS, GODFRIED. *The Wily Witch and All the Other Fairy Tales and Fables,* ill. by Wouter Hoogendijk. Stemmer, 1977. A brilliant translation of the collected tales of a popular Dutch author.   9–12

BOND, MICHAEL. *A Bear Called Paddington,* ill. by Peggy Fortnum. Houghton, 1960.   8–10
———. *Olga Carries On,* ill. by Hans Helweg. Hastings, 1977. More humorous anecdotes about the engaging guinea pig in which she lets her high esteem for guinea pigs in general, and herself in particular, have full sway.   8–10
———. *Paddington on Top,* ill. by Peggy Fortnum. Houghton, 1975. One in a series of amusing sequels.   8–10
———. *The Tales of Olga da Polga,* ill. by Hans Helweg. Macmillan, 1973. Episodic chapters about a complacent, mendacious guinea pig.   8–10

BOND, NANCY. *A String in the Harp.* Atheneum, 1976. The story of an American family moved to Wales for a year provides a successful setting for the fanciful element (based on Welsh legend) of a lost tuning key from the past that must be returned to its owner.   11–14

BONTEMPS, ARNA, and JACK CONROY. *The Fast Sooner Hound,* ill. by Virginia Lee Burton. Houghton, 1942. How this tall-tale hound could outrun any train, even the Cannon Ball, is gravely related and hilariously pictured.   8–12

BOSTON, LUCY M. *The Castle of Yew,* ill. by Margery Gill. Harcourt, 1965. An imaginative adventure which takes place in a topiary garden.
———. *The Children of Green Knowe,* ill. by Peter Boston. Harcourt, 1955.
———. *An Enemy at Green Knowe,* ill. by Peter Boston. Harcourt, 1964.
———. *Nothing Said,* ill. by Peter Boston. Harcourt, 1971. In this blend of realism and fantasy, a child meets a dryad.
———. *The River at Green Knowe,* ill. by Peter Boston. Harcourt, 1959.
———. *The Sea Egg,* ill. by Peter Boston. Harcourt, 1967. Two small boys find a stone that hatches into a water creature through whom they learn the magical secrets of the sea.
———. *The Stones of Green Knowe,* ill. by Peter Boston. Atheneum, 1976.
———. *A Stranger at Green Knowe,* ill. by Peter Boston. Harcourt, 1961. Carnegie Medal.
———. *Treasure of Green Knowe,* ill. by Peter Boston. Harcourt, 1958.   9–11

BOVA, BENJAMIN. *End of Exile.* Dutton, 1975.
———. *Exiled from Earth.* Dutton, 1971.
———. *Flight of Exiles.* Dutton, 1972. Exiled from earth because they will upset the political equilibrium, a group of scientists sets out aboard a space ship to find a new home. Suspense, drama, and a satisfying ending in this trilogy.   11–13

BRINK, CAROL RYRIE. *Andy Buckram's Tin Men,* ill. by W. T. Mars. Viking, 1966.   10–11

BROOKS, WALTER. *Freddy and the Men from Mars.* Knopf, 1954.
———. *Freddy Goes to Florida.* Knopf, 1949. Between these two books lies a long series of Freddy stories that enjoy great popularity.   9–12

BROWN, MARGARET WISE. *Goodnight Moon,* ill. by Clement Hurd. Harper, 1947.   4–6

BURTON, VIRGINIA LEE. *The Little House,* ill. by author. Houghton, 1942. Caldecott Medal.   5–8
———. *Mike Mulligan and His Steam Shovel,* ill. by author. Houghton, 1939.   6–8

BUTTERWORTH, OLIVER. *The Enormous Egg,* ill. by Louis Darling. Little, 1956.   9–13
———. *The Trouble with Jenny's Ear,* ill. by Julian de Miskey. Little, 1960.   9–11

CAMERON, ELEANOR. *The Court of the Stone Children.* Dutton, 1973. Visiting a museum, Nina meets a ghost-girl from the Napoleonic period. National Book Award.   10–12
———. *Stowaway to the Mushroom Planet,* ill. by Robert Henneberger. Little, 1956.
———. *The Wonderful Flight to the Mushroom Planet,* ill. by Robert Henneberger. Little, 1954.   9–11

CARROLL, LEWIS [pseud. for Charles Lutwidge Dodgson]. *Alice's Adventures in Wonderland* and *Through the Looking Glass,* ill. by John Tenniel. Heritage, 1944 (first pub. in 1865 and 1871). One of the best-loved and most quoted fantasies for children.
Ill. by John Tenniel. Grosset, 1963.
Ill. by John Tenniel. Macmillan, 1963.
Ill. by John Tenniel. World, 1946.
Ill. by Arthur Rackham. Watts, 1966.   10 up

CHRISMAN, ARTHUR BOWIE. *Shen of the Sea: Chinese Stories for Children,* ill. by Else Hasselriis. Dutton, 1925; redesigned 1968. Brisk and humorous fairy tales that were awarded the 1926 Newbery Medal.   10–12

CHRISTOPHER, JOHN. *Beyond the Burning Lands.* Macmillan, 1971. A sequel to *The Prince in Waiting.*
———. *The City of Gold and Lead.* Macmillan, 1967.
———. *Empty World.* Dutton, 1978.
———. *The Guardians.* Macmillan, 1970.
———. *The Lotus Caves.* Macmillan, 1969.
———. *The Pool of Fire.* Macmillan, 1968.
———. *The Prince in Waiting.* Macmillan, 1970.
———. *The White Mountains.* Macmillan, 1967.   11–14

CLARKE, ARTHUR C. *Dolphin Island.* Holt, 1963. A fine science-fiction tale of teenage Johnny Clinton, who becomes interested in dolphins when they rescue him from drowning.   12–15

CLARKE, PAULINE. *The Return of the Twelves,* ill. by Bernarda Bryson. Coward, 1964. British title is *The Twelve and the Genii.* Carnegie Medal.   10–12

CLEARY, BEVERLY. *The Mouse and the Motorcycle,* ill. by Louis Darling. Morrow, 1965.   9–11
———. *Runaway Ralph,* ill. by Louis Darling. Morrow, 1970.   8–10

COATSWORTH, ELIZABETH. *The Cat Who Went to Heaven,* ill. by Lynd Ward. Macmillan, 1930 and 1959. Newbery Medal.   10–14
———. *Cricket and the Emperor's Son,* ill. by Juliette Palmer. Norton, 1965.   10–11
———. *Marra's World,* ill. by Krystyna Turska. Green-

willow, 1975. A lonely, motherless girl finds affection, in an eerie, haunting story. 9–11

COBALT, MARTIN [pseud. for William Mayne]. *Pool of Swallows*. Nelson, 1974. Humor, mystery, and ghosts are combined in a sophisticated story from England. 11–15

COHEN, BARBARA. *Unicorns in the Rain*. Atheneum, 1980. In a variant of the Noah's Ark story, set in a future time, a girl keeps two unicorns from boarding the Ark. 11–14

COLLODI, CARLO [pseud. for Carlo Lorenzini]. *The Adventures of Pinocchio*, tr. by Carol Della Chiesa.
Ill. by Attilio Mussino. Macmillan, 1963.
Ill. by Charles Mozley, large type ed. Watts, 1967. 9–12

COOPER, SUSAN. *The Dark Is Rising*, ill. by Alan E. Cober. Atheneum, 1973.
———. *Greenwitch*. Atheneum, 1974.
———. *The Grey King*, ill. by Michael Heslop. Atheneum, 1975. Newbery Medal.
§ ———. *Jethro and the Jumbie*, ill. by Ashley Bryan. Atheneum, 1979. 8–9
———. *Over Sea, Under Stone*, ill. by Margery Gill. Harcourt, 1965. 10–12
———. *Silver on the Tree*. Atheneum, 1977. 10–12

CORBETT, SCOTT. *Ever Ride a Dinosaur?* ill. by Mircea Vasiliu. Holt, 1969. 9–11

CRESSWELL, HELEN. *The Bongleweed*. Macmillan, 1973. 9–11
———. *A Game of Catch*, ill. by Ati Forberg. Macmillan, 1977. 8–10
———. *The Piemakers*, ill. by W. T. Mars. Lippincott, 1968. 9–11
———. *Up the Pier*, ill. by Gareth Floyd. Macmillan, 1972. 10–11
———. *The Winter Birds*. Macmillan, 1976. 11 up

CUNNINGHAM, JULIA. *Dorp Dead*, ill. by James Spanfeller. Pantheon, 1965. 12 up
———. *Viollet*, ill. by Alan E. Cober. Pantheon, 1966. 10–11

CURRY, JANE LOUISE. *Mindy's Mysterious Miniature*, ill. by Charles Robinson. Harcourt, 1970. Mindy and her neighbor, Mrs. Bright, are captured by a Mr. Putt who has inherited a magic contraption that miniaturizes houses and the people in them. The concept is entertaining and the writing has suspense and pace. 9–11

DAHL, ROALD. *Charlie and the Chocolate Factory*, ill. by Joseph Schindelman. Knopf, 1964. 10–11
———. *James and the Giant Peach*, ill. by Nancy E. Burkert. Knopf, 1961. 10–11
———. *The Magic Finger*, ill. by William Pène du Bois. Harper, 1966. 10–11

DE BRUNHOFF, JEAN. *The Story of Babar, the Little Elephant*, ill. by author. Random, 1937. A series of these books follows and has been continued since the author's death by his son Laurent. 5–8

DE LA MARE, WALTER. *A Penny a Day*, ill. by Paul Kennedy. Knopf, 1960. Walter de la Mare brings poetic beauty to his prose style in six tales of fantasy which offer choice reading aloud. Followed by a companion volume, *The Magic Jacket* (1962). 10–13
———. *The Three Royal Monkeys*, ill. by Mildred Eldridge. Knopf, 1948. Originally published as *The Three Mulla-Mulgars*, this distinguished fantasy is a long story of the adventures of three young monkeys who go in search of their father, a prince from the valley of Tishner. 12–15

DE PAOLA, TOMIE. *The Knight and the Dragon*, ill. by author. Putnam, 1980. The castle librarian provides a solution for the dilemma of a knight and a dragon who are, in a diverting story, total failures in battle. 5–8

DEL REY, LESTER. *The Runaway Robot*. Westminster, 1965. 11–14

DICKINSON, PETER. *The Devil's Children*. Little, 1970. 10–14
———. *Emma Tupper's Diary*, ill. by David Omar White. Atlantic/Little, 1971. A hoax involving sea monsters is at the center of this lively story set in the Scottish highlands. 10–13
———. *The Gift*. Atlantic/Little, 1974. Davy's ability to read minds leads to a frightening adventure. 10–14
———. *Heartsease*. Little, 1969. 10–14
———. *The Weathermonger*. Little, 1969. 10–14

DONOVAN, JOHN. *Family*. Harper, 1976. A touching story about a group of laboratory apes is told by one of their number. 11 up

DRURY, ROGER. *The Finches' Fabulous Furnace*, ill. by Erik Blegvad. Little, 1971. The fabulous furnace, it turns out, is a small volcano in the Finches' cellar. 9–11

DU BOIS, WILLIAM PÈNE. *The Alligator Case*, ill. by author. Harper, 1965. An unusually alert boy detective starts working on the case before the crime is committed. 9–11
———. *Bear Party*, ill. by author. Viking, 1951 and 1963. 5–8
———. *The Forbidden Forest*, ill. by author. Harper, 1978. 8–10
———. *The Giant*, ill. by author. Viking, 1954. 9–12
———. *The Horse in the Camel Suit*, ill. by author. Harper, 1967. The boy detective who solved the *Alligator Case* pits his skill against a troupe of entertainers who turn out to be horse thieves in disguise. 9–11
———. *Lazy Tommy Pumpkinhead*, ill. by author. Harper, 1966. 7–9
———. *Otto and the Magic Potatoes*, ill. by author. Viking, 1970. The broadly nonsensical story of Otto the giant dog and his master who are kidnaped. 9–11
———. *The Twenty-One Balloons*, ill. by author. Viking, 1947. Newbery Medal. 10–12

DUNLOP, EILEEN. *Elizabeth Elizabeth*, ill. by Peter Farmer. Holt, 1977. In an excellent time-shift story set in Scotland, Elizabeth, twelve, finds a mirror that takes her into the eighteenth century. 10–12
———. *The House on Mayferry Street*, ill. by Phillida Gili. Holt, 1977. Eleven-year-old Colin and his invalid sister Marion become intrigued by scraps of evidence that indicate there is a hidden treasure somewhere in the house. 12–15

EAGER, EDWARD M. *Half Magic*, ill. by N. W. Bodecker. Harcourt, 1954.
———. *Magic or Not?* ill. by N. M. Bodecker. Harcourt, 1959.
———. *Seven-Day Magic*, ill. by N. M. Bodecker. Harcourt, 1962.
———. *The Well-Wishers*, ill. by N. M. Bodecker. Harcourt, 1960. 9–11

ENGDAHL, SYLVIA. *Beyond the Tomorrow Mountains*, ill. by Richard Cuffari. Atheneum, 1973. The story of a young man's maturing in a world that is rebuilding after earth is doomed. 11–14
———. *Enchantress from the Stars*, ill. by Rodney Shackell. Atheneum, 1970. 11–14
———. *The Far Side of Evil*, ill. by Richard Cuffari. Atheneum, 1971. 11–14
———. *Journey Between Worlds*, ill. by James and Ruth McCrea. Atheneum, 1970. 11–14

ENRIGHT, ELIZABETH. *Tatsinda*, ill. by Irene Haas. Harcourt, 1963. This original fairy tale offers children penetrating social comment, coupled with the suspense of a well-told story. 9–12
———. *Zeee*, ill. by Irene Haas. Harcourt, 1965. A small, grumpy fairy is befriended by a Person. 9–11

ESTES, ELEANOR. *The Witch Family*, ill. by Edward Ardizzone. Harcourt, 1960. Their pleasant game of drawing witches leads two small girls into incredible adventures when their witches come alive! 10–12

ETS, MARIE HALL. *Mister Penny,* ill. by author. Viking, 1935. Mister Penny's good-for-nothing animals reform and help him in an amusing book. 6–8

FAIRSTAR, MRS. [pseud. for Richard Horne]. *Memoirs of a London Doll,* ill. by Emma L. Brock. Macmillan, 1968 (first pub. in 1846). 9–12

FARMER, PENELOPE. *A Castle of Bone.* Atheneum, 1972. 10–12

———. *Charlotte Sometimes,* ill. by Chris Connor. Harcourt, 1969.

———. *Emma in Winter,* ill. by James J. Spanfeller. Harcourt, 1966. 10–12

———. *The Summer Birds,* ill. by James J. Spanfeller. Harcourt, 1962.

———. *William and Mary.* Atheneum, 1974. Two children come to grips with their separate family problems while being transported to other times and places. 10–12

———. *Year King.* Atheneum, 1977. 13 up

FATIO, LOUISE. *The Happy Lion,* ill. by Roger Duvoisin. Whittlesey, 1954. The first in a consistently popular series. 5–7

FIELD, RACHEL. *Hitty: Her First Hundred Years,* ill. by Dorothy P. Lathrop. Macmillan, 1929. Newbery Medal. 11–14

FLACK, MARJORIE. *Ask Mr. Bear,* ill. by author. Macmillan, 1932, 1958. 3–7

FLEISCHMAN, SID. *By the Great Horn Spoon!* ill. by Eric von Schmidt. Little, 1963. 10–12

———. *Chancy and the Grand Rascal,* ill. by Eric von Schmidt. Little, 1966. 10–12

———. *The Ghost in the Noonday Sun,* ill. by Warren Chappell. Little, 1965. 10–12

———. *Humbug Mountain,* ill. by Eric von Schmidt. Atlantic/Little, 1978. Another hilarious tall-tale adventure, full of salty characters and quirks of fate, concerning a roving newspaper publisher of frontier times. 9–11

———. *McBroom and the Beanstalk,* ill. by Walter Lorraine. Atlantic/Little, 1978. When McBroom's family urges him to enter a contest for liars (he's duly horrified of course) the result is another yeasty tall tale in true Fleischman style. 8–10

———. *McBroom Tells a Lie,* ill. by Walter Lorraine. Atlantic/Little, 1976. More whoppers. 8–10

———. *McBroom's Ear,* ill. by Kurt Werth. Norton, 1969. Another blithe tall tale about the marvelous McBroom farm which produces magnificent crops of food and stories. Enjoyable for reading aloud or storytelling. 8–11

FLEMING, IAN. *Chitty-Chitty-Bang-Bang: The Magical Car,* ill. by John Burningham. Random, 1964. 9–11

FRESCHET, BERNIECE. *Bernard Sees the World,* ill. by Gina Freschet. Scribner's, 1976. Inspired by his extensive reading, Bernard (a mouse) travels as a stowaway via a skateboard, a bicycle, a rowing shell, a ship, and a rocket. 5–8

GÁG, WANDA. *Millions of Cats,* ill. by author. Coward, 1928. 5–8

———. *Nothing at All,* ill. by author. Coward, 1941. Through the use of a magic phrase, a lonesome little invisible puppy becomes "see-able," and finds a happy home. 5–7

GARD, JOYCE. *Talargain.* Holt, 1965. Talargain, the hero, was a foundling in seventh-century England. He had learned to swim with the seals who saved his life when he came home to save his king. 11–14

GARFIELD, LEON. *The Restless Ghost: Three Stories,* ill. by Saul Lambert. Pantheon, 1969. Three splendid ghost stories, all set in the past and all with an authentic ring. 12–15

GARNER, ALAN. *The Moon of Gomrath.* Walck, 1967. 10–12

———. *The Owl Service.* Walck, 1968. Carnegie Medal. 10–12

———. *The Weirdstone of Brisingamen.* Walck, 1969. 10–13

☆ GOBLE, PAUL. *The Girl Who Loved Wild Horses,* ill. by author. Bradbury, 1978. A story in folk tradition of a young Indian girl who becomes so close to the wild horses she loves that she finally becomes one of them. Caldecott Medal. 5–7

GODDEN, RUMER. *Candy Floss,* ill. by Adrienne Adams. Viking, 1960. 8–10

———. *The Dolls' House,* ill. by Tasha Tudor. Viking, 1962. 8–10

———. *The Fairy Doll,* ill. by Adrienne Adams. Viking, 1956. 7–10

———. *Home Is the Sailor,* ill. by Jean Primrose. Viking, 1964. 10–11

———. *Impunity Jane,* ill. by Adrienne Adams. Viking, 1954. 8–10

———. *Little Plum,* ill. by Jean Primrose. Viking, 1963. 8–11

———. *Miss Happiness and Miss Flower,* ill. by Jean Primrose. Viking, 1961. 8–11

———. *The Story of Holly and Ivy,* ill. by Adrienne Adams. Viking, 1958. 7–9

GRAHAME, KENNETH. *The Reluctant Dragon,* ill. by Ernest H. Shepard. Holiday, 1953. A subtly amusing tale about a boy who makes friends with a dragon and arranges to have him meet and fight St. George. 9–11

———. *The Wind in the Willows,* ill. by Ernest H. Shepard. Scribner's, 1953 (first pub. in 1908). 10–12

GRIPE, MARIA. *The Glassblower's Children,* ill. by Harald Gripe. Delacorte, 1973. Two children are kidnaped and held in a castle in this tale in a Gothic vein. 9–11

GROCH, JUDITH. *Play the Bach, Dear!* Doubleday, 1978. Eleven-year-old Hilary is helped through a dreaded piano recital by her teacher, Miss Orphio—who disappears into the piano! 9–11

HALE, LUCRETIA P. *Peterkin Papers,* ill. by Harold Brett. Houghton, 1960 (first pub. in 1880). 10–12

HAMILTON, VIRGINIA. *Dustland.* Greenwillow, 1980. In a sequel to *Justice and Her Brothers,* the psychic quartet meets strange creatures on another planet. 11 up

———. *Justice and Her Brothers.* Greenwillow, 1978. Eleven-year-old Justice is aware of the strange telepathic communication which goes on between her twin brothers Thomas (whom she fears) and Levi (who protects her). Only when she unearths her own psychic powers does she learn how to combat Thomas' malevolence. 12 up

HARRIS, ROSEMARY. *The Moon in the Cloud.* Macmillan, 1970. Carnegie Medal. 10–13

———. *The Seal-Singing.* Macmillan, 1971. 11–14

———. *The Shadow on the Sun.* Macmillan, 1970. A sequel to *The Moon in the Cloud.* The vigorous characterization and dialogue make this as diverting as its predecessor. 10–13

HEINLEIN, ROBERT A. *Have Space Suit—Will Travel.* Scribner's, 1958. An improbable but convincing tale of two youngsters who journey through space and save humanity from immediate destruction. 12–16

———. *Podkayne of Mars: Her Life and Times.* Putnam, 1963. 12–15

———. *Tunnel in the Sky.* Scribner's, 1955. 11–13

HOBAN, RUSSELL C. *The Mouse and His Child,* ill. by Lillian Hoban. Harper, 1967. 9–11

———. *A Near Thing for Captain Najork,* ill. by Quentin Blake. Atheneum, 1976. A wild spoof of adventure tales, hilariously larded with Victorian niceties. 8–10

HOWE, DEBORAH and JAMES. *Bunnicula: A Rabbit-Tale of Mystery,* ill. by Alan Daniel. Atheneum, 1979. The Monroe family's pet rabbit, Bunnicula, is suspected by their cat of being a vampire. 9–11

————. *Teddy Bear's Scrapbook*, ill. by David Rose. Atheneum, 1980. Witty writing and a lively pace make Teddy's boastful tales of his prowess engaging.   7–9

HUNTER, MOLLIE. *A Furl of Fairy Wind: Four Stories*, ill. by Stephen Gammell. Harper, 1977. A lonely orphan, a household Brownie, the Queen of the Fairies, and a suddenly greedy peddler are the central characters in these original tales told in felicitous adherence to the oral tradition.   8–10

————. *The Kelpie's Pearls*, ill. by Joseph Cellini. Funk, 1966.   10–13

————. *A Stranger Came Ashore*. Harper, 1975.   11–13

————. *The Walking Stones*, ill. by Trina Schart Hyman. Harper, 1970.   10–12

————. *The Wicked One*. Harper, 1977. When Colin Grant loses his temper and strikes at a supernatural creature, the Grollican, his troubles begin.   10–12

JANEWAY, ELIZABETH. *Ivanov Seven*, ill. by Eros Keith. Harper, 1967. An uproarious spoof about the Russian army discipline upset by an ingenuous peasant.   11–14

JANSSON, TOVE. *Finn Family Moomintroll*, ill. by author. Walck, 1965. One of a successful series.   9–12

JARRELL, RANDALL. *The Animal Family*, ill. by Maurice Sendak. Pantheon, 1965.   10–12

————. *The Bat-Poet*, ill. by Maurice Sendak. Macmillan, 1967.   10 up

JONES, ADRIENNE. *The Hawks of Chelney*, ill. by Stephen Gammell. Harper, 1978. Because he is a nonconformist living in a primitive civilization, Siri is suspected by the villagers of causing the poor fishing they've had.   12–13

JONES, DIANA. *The Magicians of Caprona*. Greenwillow, 1980. In an ingenious and polished tale, two families famous for their casting of spells end their feud when faced by a common enemy.   10–12

————. *The Ogre Downstairs*. Dutton, 1975. Adroit blending of fantasy and realism in a story about stepbrothers who become friends through magic.   10–11

JUSTER, NORTON. *The Phantom Tollbooth*, ill. by Jules Feiffer. Random, 1961.   11–13

KARL, JEAN. *Beloved Benjamin Is Waiting*. Dutton, 1978. Abandoned by her bickering parents and frightened by threats from some bullies, Lucinda's loneliness is relieved when she learns how to communicate with the voice of a being from another galaxy.   9–11

————. *The Turning Place: Stories of a Future Past*. Dutton, 1976. Short stories blend to give a picture of a changed earth.   10–15

KÄSTNER, ERICH. *The Little Man*, tr. by James Kirkup, ill. by Rick Schreiter. Knopf, 1966. The diverting adventures of little Maxie, two inches high, who becomes a circus performer. Written in lively style by a distinguished German author.   10–11

————. *The Little Man and the Big Thief*, ill. by Stan Mack. Knopf, 1970. Tiny Maxie finds a friend his own size. 9–11

KENDALL, CAROL. *The Gammage Cup*, ill. by Erik Blegvad. Harcourt, 1959. Children who enjoy Tolkien's *The Hobbit* will appreciate this tale of mild revolt among the Minnipins, or little people, and its surprising outcome. A protest against conformity.   10–13

————. *The Whisper of Glocken*, ill. by Imero Gobbato. Harcourt, 1965. A continuation of the chronicles of the Minnipins.   10–12

KENNEDY, RICHARD. *Inside My Feet: The Story of a Giant*, ill. by Ronald Himler. Harper, 1979. It is only after a dramatic and moving confrontation with an old, sad giant that a boy is able to find his lost parents.   9–11

KESTEVEN, G. R. *The Awakening Water*. Hastings, 1979. A science-fiction novel set in a future time centers around the concept of a people kept submissive. When the young protagonist learns there are tranquilizers in the water, he awakens to reality and joins a band of runaways.   11–14

KIDD, VIRGINIA, ed. *Millennial Women: Tales for Tomorrow*. Delacorte, 1978. In a science-fiction anthology, six women writers describe women of a future time.   12 up

KINGSLEY, CHARLES. *The Water-Babies*, ill. by Harold Jones. Watts, 1961.   8–12

KIPLING, RUDYARD. *The Elephant's Child*, ill. by Leonard Weisgard. From the *Just So Stories*, 1902. Walker, 1970.   9–11

————. *The Jungle Book*, ill. by Philip Hays. Doubleday, 1964. Stories of India and the jungle life of the boy Mowgli, adopted by a wolf pack.   9–13

————. *Just So Stories*, ill. by author. Doubleday, 1902. Ill. by J. M. Gleeson. Doubleday, 1912, 1946. Ill. by Nicolas [pseud. for Nicolas Mordvinoff]. Doubleday, 1952.   8–12

KOOIKER, LEONIE. *The Magic Stone*, ill. by Carl Hollander. Morrow, 1978. The witch members of the Fine Thread Association are no match for a very ordinary boy who finds their most powerful magic object.   8–10

LANGTON, JANE. *The Astonishing Stereoscope*, ill. by Erik Blegvad. Harper, 1971.   10–12

————. *The Diamond in the Window*, ill. by Erik Blegvad. Harper, 1962.   11–14

————. *The Fledgling*. Harper, 1980. A delicate and deftly-structured story of a child who learns the joy of flight from a Canada goose.   10–12

————. *The Swing in the Summerhouse*, ill. by Erik Blegvad. Harper, 1967.   10–12

LAURENCE, MARGARET. *Jason's Quest*, ill. by Steffan Torell. Knopf, 1970. A quest takes an oddly matched band of small animals to London.   9–11

LAWSON, ROBERT. *Ben and Me*, ill. by author. Little, 1939. 9–12

————. *Mr. Revere and I*, ill. by author. Little, 1953. Revere's ride from his horse's point of view.   11–14

————. *Rabbit Hill*, ill. by author. Viking, 1944, 1968. Newbery Medal.   9–12

————. *The Tough Winter*, ill. by author. Viking, 1970. 9–12

LE GUIN, URSULA K. *The Farthest Shore*, ill. by Gail Garraty. Atheneum, 1972. National Book Award.   11–14

————. *The Tombs of Atuan*, ill. by Gail Garraty. Atheneum, 1971.   11–14

————. *A Wizard of Earthsea*, ill. by Ruth Robbins. Parnassus, 1968.   11–14

L'ENGLE, MADELEINE. *A Ring of Endless Light*. Farrar, 1980. A sequel to *Meet the Austins* reveals that Vicky has telepathic powers and can communicate with dolphins.   11–14

————. *A Swiftly Tilting Planet*. Farrar, 1978.   11–14

————. *A Wind in the Door*. Farrar, 1973.   11–14

————. *A Wrinkle in Time*. Farrar, 1962. Newbery Medal.   11–14

LEWIS, CLIVE STAPLES. *The Lion, the Witch, and the Wardrobe*, ill. by Pauline Baynes. Macmillan, 1950. Other titles in the Narnia series, in order of appearance, are: *Prince Caspian* (1951), *The Voyage of the Dawn Treader* (1952), *The Silver Chair* (1953), *The Horse and His Boy* (1954), *The Magician's Nephew* (1955), and *The Last Battle* (1956).   8–12

☆ LIFTON, BETTY. *Jaguar, My Twin*, ill. by Ann Leggett. Atheneum, 1976. This is the story of Shun, a Zinacantec Indian, who finds his jaguar, the twin animal spirit that comes to lucky ones in dreams.   9–11

LIGHTNER, ALICE. *Doctor to the Galaxy*. Norton, 1965.   11–14

————. *The Galactic Troubadours*. Norton, 1965.   12–14

LINDGREN, ASTRID. *Pippi Longstocking*, tr. by Florence Lamborn, ill. by Louis S. Glanzman. Viking, 1950. Followed by several hilarious sequels.   9–12

———. *The Tomten*, adapted from a poem by Viktor Rydberg, ill. by Harald Wiberg. Coward, 1961. Unforgettably lovely pictures of the wintry Swedish countryside illustrate the story of a kindly little troll. Equally attractive is *The Tomten and the Fox* (Coward, 1966).   5–7

LIVELY, PENELOPE. *The Ghost of Thomas Kempe*, ill. by Antony Maitland. Dutton, 1973. Carnegie Medal.   9–11

———. *The House in Norham Gardens*. Dutton, 1974.   11–14

———. *A Stitch in Time*. Dutton, 1976.   9–11

———. *The Voyage of QV 66*, ill. by Harold Jones. Dutton, 1979.   9–11

LOFTING, HUGH. *The Story of Dr. Dolittle*, ill. by author. Lippincott, 1920.   9–12

———. *The Voyages of Dr. Dolittle*, ill. by author. Lippincott, 1922. Newbery Medal.   9–12

McCAFFREY, ANNE. *Dragondrums*. Atheneum, 1979. The third book in a science fantasy series, the protagonist here is masterharper Menolly's protégé Piemur, who must learn to adjust to two new assignments when his voice changes.   11–14

———. *Dragonsinger*. Atheneum, 1977.   11–13

———. *Dragonsong*. Atheneum, 1976.   11–13

MACDONALD, GEORGE. *At the Back of the North Wind*, ill. by George and Doris Hauman. Macmillan, 1950.

———. *The Light Princess*, ill. by William Pène du Bois. T. Crowell, 1962.

———. *The Light Princess*, ill. by Maurice Sendak. Farrar, 1969.

———. *The Princess and Curdie*, ill. by Nora S. Unwin. Macmillan, 1954.

———. *The Princess and the Goblin*, ill. by Nora S. Unwin. Macmillan, 1964.

Attractive editions of old favorites.   9–12

McGINLEY, PHYLLIS. *The Plain Princess*, ill. by Helen Stone. Lippincott, 1945. In this parody of a fairy tale, the heroine's appearance improves as she becomes less selfish.   7–10

McKILLIP, PATRICIA. *The Forgotten Beasts of Eld*. Atheneum, 1974. Sybel, who's called all the legendary beasts to her side, finds love is more important than power.   12–14

McKINLEY, ROBIN. *Beauty: A Retelling of the Story of Beauty and the Beast*. Harper, 1978.   11–14

MARK, JAN. *Under the Autumn Garden*, ill. by Judith Gwyn Brown. T. Crowell, 1979. Matthew is a quiet, imaginative child of ten whose curiosity is stimulated by his history class assignment: finding out something about the history of his Norfolk village.   10–11

MARTEL, SUZANNE. *The City Under Ground*, tr. by Norah Smaridge, ill. by Don Sibley. Viking, 1964.   11–14

MAYNE, WILLIAM. *Earthfasts*. Dutton, 1967.   11–14

———. *A Game of Dark*. Dutton, 1971.   10–13

———. *It*. Greenwillow, 1978. An English schoolgirl convinces her neighbors to help her exorcise an evil force.   10–11

———. *A Year and a Day*. Dutton, 1976.   8–10

MAZER, NORMA. *Saturday, the Twelfth of October*. Delacorte, 1975. A girl goes back in time and lives with a primitive tribe.   11–13

MERRILL, JEAN. *The Pushcart War*, ill. by Ronni Solbert. Scott/Addison, 1964.   10–12

MILES, PATRICIA. *The Gods in Winter*. Dutton, 1978. A blend of fantasy and reality based on the idea that Demeter still roams the earth.   10–12

MILNE, A. A. *The House at Pooh Corner*, ill. by Ernest Shepard. Dutton, 1928.

———. *Winnie-the-Pooh*, ill. by Ernest Shepard. Dutton, 1926.

These stories were reprinted in 1961, with larger type and more attractive format.

———. *The World of Pooh*, ill. by E. H. Shepard. Dutton, 1957. Distinctive color illustrations give a festive air to this new large-print volume, containing *Winnie-the-Pooh* and *House at Pooh Corner*.   8–10

NORTON, ANDRE. *The Crystal Gryphon*. Atheneum, 1972. Kerovan, who has hoofs instead of feet, proves worthy of his betrothed.   12–14

———. *The Jargoon Pard*. Atheneum, 1974. Set in a medieval world. Companion volume to the preceding title.   12–14

———. *Lavender-green Magic*, ill. by Judith Gwyn Brown. T. Crowell, 1974. A time-travel adventure with a black heroine.   12–14

———. *Moon of Three Rings*. Viking, 1966.   12–14

———. *Wraiths of Time*. Atheneum, 1976.   12–15

———. *The Zero Stone*. Viking, 1968.   12–14

NORTON, MARY. *Bed-Knob and Broomstick*, ill. by Erik Blegvad. Harcourt, 1957. Prim Miss Price was studying how to be a witch when the Wilson children discovered her. The bit of magic she gave them to ensure silence leads to some enchanting adventures.   9–13

———. *The Borrowers*, ill. by Beth and Joe Krush. Harcourt, 1953. Carnegie Medal. This book was followed by *The Borrowers Afield* (1955), *The Borrowers Afloat* (1959), *The Borrowers Aloft* (1961).   9–12

———. *Poor Stainless*, ill. by Beth and Joe Krush. Harcourt, 1971.   8–10

NÖSTLINGER, CHRISTINE. *Konrad*, ill. by Carol Nicklaus. Watts, 1977. The story of a factory-made child of seven who is delivered by mistake to a scatter-brained but delightful woman.   9–11

O'BRIEN, ROBERT C. *Mrs. Frisby and the Rats of NIMH*, ill. by Zena Bernstein. Atheneum, 1971. Newbery Medal.   9–11

———. *Z for Zachariah*. Atheneum, 1975. A taut science-fiction story of the last people left in the world.   11 up

O'CONNELL, JEAN S. *The Dollhouse Caper*, ill. by Erik Blegvad. T. Crowell, 1976.   8–10

ORMONDROYD, EDWARD. *All in Good Time*, ill. by Ruth Robbins. Parnassus, 1975. In a sequel to *Time at the Top*, families from two time periods merge.   10–13

———. *Theodore*, ill. by John M. Larrecq. Parnassus, 1966. When he is caught in a laundromat load, Theodore, an aging toy bear, must arrange a few small capers to return him to his ordinary dirty state. A good read-aloud story.   3–6

———. *Time at the Top*, ill. by Peggie Bach. Parnassus, 1963. The elevator stops at an extra floor and Susan finds an 1890 family and home.   10–13

OTTO, SVEND. *Tim and Trisha*, ill. by author. Pelham, 1978. Trisha tells her parents she's spent the day cavorting with Tim the troll and his friends.   4–6

PEARCE, A. PHILIPPA. *Tom's Midnight Garden*, ill. by Susan Einzig. Lippincott, 1959. Carnegie Medal.   10–13

PECK, RICHARD. *The Ghost Belonged to Me*. Viking, 1975. A boy of 1913 helps a restless ghost in her efforts to be reburied with her family, in a witty and nostalgic fantasy.   11–13

———. *Ghosts I Have Been*. Viking, 1977. In a sequel to *The Ghost Belonged to Me*, Blossom Culp feigns second sight.   11–14

PEYTON, KATHLEEN. *A Pattern of Roses*, ill. by author. T. Crowell, 1973. The lives of a boy of the present and his counterpart in the past are strangely, convincingly linked.   11–14

PICARD, BARBARA LEONIE. *The Faun and the Woodcutter's Daughter*, ill. by Charles Stewart. Criterion, 1964.   10–12

———. *The Goldfinch Garden*, ill. by Anne Linton. Criterion, 1965.   9–12

———. *The Lady of the Linden Tree*, ill. by Charles Stewart. Criterion, 1962.   10–12

———. *The Mermaid and the Simpleton*, ill. by Phillip Gough. Criterion, 1969.   9–11

PINKWATER, D. MANUS. *Fat Men from Space*, ill. by author. Dodd, 1977. When the fat men from space plunder the earth of all junk food and then disappear, William manages to subsist on healthful foods.   8–11

POMERANTZ, CHARLOTTE. *The Downtown Fairy Godmother*, ill. by Susanna Natti. Addison, 1978.   8–10

POTTER, BEATRIX. *The Tale of Peter Rabbit*, ill. by author. Warne, 1903. Between 1903 and 1930, nineteen books were published in the series.   3–8

PREUSSLER, OTFRIED. *The Satanic Mill*, tr. by Anthea Bell. Macmillan, 1973. A prize-winning German book about an evil miller-magician whose apprentices are doomed to die.   11–14

PYLE, HOWARD. *Pepper and Salt*, ill. by author. Harper, 1923 (first pub. in 1885). Eight fairy tales, wittily retold and well illustrated.

———. *Wonder Clock*, ill. by author. Harper, 1943 (first pub. in 1887). Twenty-four delightful tales, a companion volume to the one above.   10–12

REY, HANS A. *Curious George*, ill. by author. Houghton, 1941. And its sequels.   4–8

ROACH, MARILYNNE. *Presto: Or the Adventures of a Turnspit Dog*, ill. by author. Houghton, 1979. A story about a small dog who runs away from an inn to join a puppeteer in London is fraught with danger and adventure.   10–12

RODGERS, MARY. *A Billion for Boris*. Harper, 1974. Annabel and her friend Boris find a television set that gives the news of the next day. Including stock market prices! 9–11

———. *Freaky Friday*. Harper, 1972. What would a girl do if she woke one morning and found she'd turned into her mother? Annabel tells us what.   9–11

RUSKIN, JOHN. *The King of the Golden River*, ill. by Fritz Kredel. World, 1946.   10–14

SAINT-EXUPÉRY, ANTOINE DE. *The Little Prince*, tr. by Katherine Woods, ill. by author. Harcourt, 1943.   12 up

SANDBURG, CARL. *Rootabaga Stories*, ill. by Maud and Miska Petersham. Harcourt, 1922.   8–12

SARGENT, SARAH. *Weird Henry Berg*. Crown, 1980. In an adroit meshing of realism and fantasy, an elderly woman helps a boy find a solution to the problem of saving a pet dragon that appears in contemporary times.   9–11

SELDEN, GEORGE. *The Cricket in Times Square*, ill. by Garth Williams. Farrar, 1960.   9–12

———. *The Genie of Sutton Place*. Farrar, 1973. A genie released from a carpet accomplishes minor and major miracles in a city story.   10–11

———. *Harry Cat's Pet Puppy*, ill. by Garth Williams. Farrar, 1974.   8–11

———. *Tucker's Countryside*, ill. by Garth Williams. Farrar, 1969.   9–11

SENDAK, MAURICE. *Higglety Pigglety Pop! Or There Must Be More to Life*, ill. by author. Harper, 1967.   8–10

———. *In the Night Kitchen*, ill. by author. Harper, 1970. 5–7

———. *Nutshell Library*, ill. by author. Harper, 1962.   4–7

———. *Where the Wild Things Are*, ill. by author. Harper, 1963. Caldecott Medal.   5–7

SEUSS, DR. [pseud. for Theodor Seuss Geisel]. *And to Think That I Saw It on Mulberry Street*, ill. by author. Vanguard, 1937.   5–8

———. *Bartholomew and the Oobleck*, ill. by author. Random, 1949.   5–8

———. *The Cat in the Hat*, ill. by author. Random, 1957. The Cat provides novel entertainment for two housebound children.   5–8

———. *The 500 Hats of Bartholomew Cubbins*, ill. by author. Vanguard, 1938.   6–10

SHARMAT, MARJORIE. *The Trolls of Twelfth Street*, ill. by Ben Shecter. Coward, 1979. Engaging troll's-eye view of life in a big city.   6–8

SHARP, MARGERY. *Bernard into Battle: A Miss Bianca Story*, ill. by Leslie Morrill. Little, 1979. Another mock romantic adventure centering around the beautiful white mouse Miss Bianca and her stalwart admirer Bernard.   11 up

———. *The Rescuers*, ill. by Garth Williams. Little, 1959. Witty fantasy of three brave mice who rescue a Norwegian poet from imprisonment in a deep, dark dungeon. *Miss Bianca* (1962) relates another brave rescue.   10–13

SINGER, ISAAC BASHEVIS. *The Fearsome Inn*, tr. by author and Elizabeth Shub, ill. by Nonny Hogrogian. Scribner's, 1967. A fanciful tale mingling the Polish-Jewish humor and gusto with the fairy tale genre most deftly. The illustrations have a graceful vitality.   10–12

SLEATOR, WILLIAM. *Into the Dream*, ill. by Ruth Sanderson. Dutton, 1979.   10–12

SLEIGH, BARBARA. *Carbonel: The King of the Cats*, ill. by V. H. Drummond. Bobbs, 1957. Humorous magical tale of two children who rescue the king of cats from the spell of an old witch.   9–12

SLOBODKIN, LOUIS. *Space Ship Under the Apple Tree*, ill. by author. Macmillan, 1967. Eddie's farm vacation at Grandmother's proves anything but quiet when he is joined by Marty, the little man from Martinea, complete with his space ship. First in a series.   8–10

SMITH, AGNES. *An Edge of the Forest*, ill. by Roberta Moynihan. Viking, 1959; Westwind Press, 1974. An allegory of peaceful coexistence.   11–14

SNYDER, ZILPHA KEATLEY. *And All Between*, ill. by Alton Raible. Atheneum, 1976. The two factions in *Below the Root* confront each other in a suspenseful story.   10–12

———. *Below the Root*, ill. by Alton Raible. Atheneum, 1975. A science fantasy set in a community of tree-dwellers.   10–12

———. *Eyes in the Fishbowl*, ill. by Alton Raible. Atheneum, 1968. Dion explores a department store at night and finds that odd things happen.   11–14

STEARNS, PAMELA. *The Fool and the Dancing Bear*, ill. by Ann Strugnell. Atlantic/Little, 1979. A cracking good tale spun from a curse a jealous queen has put on a young king who loves her younger sister.   10–12

STEELE, MARY Q. *Journey Outside*, ill. by Rocco Negri. Viking, 1969. The Raft People float down the dark underground river, looking for a Better Place, but the boy Dilar leaves and makes his way to the strange world of grass and sunshine where he encounters several cultures.   10–12

STEELE, WILLIAM O. *Andy Jackson's Water Well*, ill. by Michael Ramus. Harcourt, 1959. Andy Jackson achieves the incredible by bringing back water to drought-ridden Nashville. A hilarious tall tale that is ideal for storytelling. 9–13

STEIG, WILLIAM. *Abel's Island*. Farrar, 1976.   9–11

———. *The Amazing Bone*. Farrar, 1976.   5–7

———. *Dominic*, ill. by author. Farrar, 1972.   9–11

———. *Sylvester and the Magic Pebble*, ill. by author. Simon, 1969. Caldecott Medal.   5–7

STEWART, MARY. *A Walk in Wolf Wood*, ill. by Emanuel Schoengut. Morrow, 1980. Two children step back in time to help a medieval courtier escape the enchantment of a wicked wizard.   10–11

STOCKTON, FRANK RICHARD. *The Bee-Man of Orn*, ill. by Maurice Sendak. Holt, 1964. The Bee-Man is completely content until he is informed that he has been transformed from some other sort of thing. A charming story, republished with Sendak's delightful illustrations.   10–12

STOLZ, MARY S. *Belling the Tiger*, ill. by Beni Montresor. Harper, 1967. A pointed message in this humorous story.   7–10

————. *Cat in the Mirror*. Harper, 1975. The heroine, Erin, escapes her present unhappiness by moving in time to a household in ancient Egypt.   11–13

STORR, CATHERINE. *The Chinese Egg*. McGraw, 1975. Two English children share precognitive visions that solve a kidnaping.   12 up

TERLOUW, JAN. *How To Become King*. Hastings, 1977. An orphaned boy is offered the kingship of Katoren if he can perform seven impossible tasks.   9–12

THURBER, JAMES. *The Great Quillow*, ill. by Doris Lee. Harcourt, 1944.   8–11

————. *Many Moons*, ill. by Louis Slobodkin. Harcourt, 1943. Caldecott Medal.   7–10

————. *The Thirteen Clocks*, ill. by Marc Simont. Simon, 1950. The cold Duke's hold over Princess Saralinda is broken when Prince Zorn brings him 1000 jewels and the Princess's warmth restarts the clocks.   11–12

————. *The Wonderful O*, ill. by Marc Simont. Simon, 1957. Life without "O" goes on, but love, even footnotes, are lost.   10 up

TITUS, EVE. *Basil in Mexico*, ill. by Paul Galdone. McGraw, 1976. Basil, the detecting mouse of Baker Street, is again called upon to deduce who has stolen an art treasure from a Mexican museum and replaced it with a clever forgery.   8–10

TODD, RUTHVEN. *Space Cat*, ill. by Paul Galdone. Scribner's, 1952. Flyball was a daring cat, and when he accompanied his favorite pilot on a trip to the moon, he not only saved his life but made an important scientific discovery. First of a series.   8–10

TOLKIEN, JOHN R. R. *Farmer Giles of Ham*, ill. by Pauline Diana Baynes. Nelson, 1962. Humorous tale of a simple farmer who finds himself rescuing his village from dragons! 9–12

————. *The Father Christmas Letters*. Houghton, 1976. A collection of the annual letters and pictures from Father Christmas to Tolkien's children.   8–10

————. *The Hobbit*, ill. by author. Houghton, 1938.   5–8

TOWNSEND, JOHN ROWE. *The Creatures*. Lippincott, 1980. In a future time, the elite are visitors from another planet. The lowly people of earth are the "creatures."   11–14

————. *The Visitors*. Lippincott, 1977. A science-fiction novel in which some visitors who claim to be ordinary tourists turn out to be an investigative team from the future.   11–14

TRAVERS, P. L. *Mary Poppins*, ill. by Mary Shepard. Harcourt, 1934.

————. *Mary Poppins Comes Back*, ill. by Mary Shepard. Harcourt, 1935.

————. *Mary Poppins in the Park*, ill. by Mary Shepard. Harcourt, 1952.

————. *Mary Poppins Opens the Door*, ill. by Mary Shepard and Agnes Sims. Harcourt, 1943.   8–12

WABER, BERNARD. *You're a Little Kid with a Big Heart*, ill. by author. Houghton, 1980. A girl of seven, given a magic wish, wants to be old enough to be independent; in a breezy story, she learns that being a child of thirty-nine is no fun.   5–8

WANGERIN, WALTER. *The Book of the Dun Cow*. Harper, 1978.   10–12

WESTALL, ROBERT. *The Devil on the Road*. Greenwillow, 1979. In a time-slip fantasy, John, a university student who thrives on taking chances, trips back to the 17th century.   12 up

————. *The Wind Eye*. Greenwillow, 1977. Three children who are struggling to adjust to stepparents discover, on vacation in an isolated part of the English coast, that an old boat will transport them back to medieval time. 10–13

WHITE, E. B. *Charlotte's Web*, ill. by Garth Williams. Harper, 1952.   10 up

————. *Stuart Little*, ill. by Garth Williams. Harper, 1945.   9–11

————. *The Trumpet of the Swan*, ill. by Edward Frascino. Harper, 1970.   9–11

WILDE, OSCAR. *The Happy Prince and Other Stories*, ill. by Peggy Fortnum. Dutton, 1968.   9–11

————. *The Selfish Giant*, ill. by Gertrude and Walter Reiner. Harvey, 1968.   9–11

WILLIAMS, JAY. *The Practical Princess and Other Liberating Fairy Tales*, ill. by Rick Schreiter. Parents' Magazine, 1978. A collection of six previously published stories notable for their robust, sly humor, their doughty heroines, and their irreverent treatment of traditional fairy tale devices.   7–9

————, and RAYMOND ABRASHKIN. *Danny Dunn and the Antigravity Paint*, ill. by Ezra Jack Keats. McGraw, 1956. One of a popular series.   10–12

WILLIAMS, URSULA MORAY. *Bogwoppit*. Nelson, 1978. Orphaned Samantha has trouble adjusting to her wealthy Aunt Daisy who is eventually kept prisoner in a drain by the fantastical, furry bogwoppits.   10–11

————. *Island Mackenzie*, ill. by Edward Ardizzone. Morrow, 1960. The two survivors from a shipwreck—Miss Pettifer and the captain's cat—find themselves on the same island. A fine mixture of humor, fantasy, and suspense.   10–12

————. *The Moonball*, ill. by Jane Paton. Meredith, 1967. A group of resourceful English children appoint themselves protectors of the moonball—a weird, silky-haired, grapefruit-size, living object—which a professor wishes to subject to scientific investigation.   7–9

§ WINTHER, BARBARA. *Plays from Folktales of Africa and Asia*. Plays, 1976. A collection of short, one-act plays most of which are humorous. They're royalty-free, easy to stage and are provided with production notes.   8–10

WRIGHTSON, PATRICIA. *The Dark Bright Water*. Atheneum, 1979.   12–14

————. *Down to Earth*, ill. by Margaret Horder. Harcourt, 1965.   10–12

————. *The Ice Is Coming*. Atheneum, 1977.   11–14

————. *The Nargun and the Stars*. Atheneum, 1974. Friendly spirits help an Australian family battle the Nargun, an ancient creature of living stone.   10–12

————. *An Older Kind of Magic*, ill. by Noela Young. Harcourt, 1972.

YOLEN, JANE H. *The Girl Who Cried Flowers, and Other Tales*, ill. by David Palladini. T. Crowell, 1974. Five tales with a folklore flavor.   8–10

————. *The Magic Three of Solatia*, ill. by Julia Noonan. T. Crowell, 1974. A romantic adventure tale.   10–11

————. *The Seventh Mandarin*, ill. by Ed Young. Seabury, 1970. Beautifully illustrated tale, in legend style, of seven mandarins who guarded their king, long ago in an eastern land. Good style and good storytelling, despite a rather pallid ending.   7–9

Chapter Ten: Poetry

Poetry can bring warmth, reassurance, even laughter; it can stir and arouse or quiet and comfort. Above all it can give significance to everyday experience. To miss poetry would be as much of a deprivation as to miss music. For these reasons it is essential that we know poetry and that we know how to introduce it to children. The experience of poetry should come with so much pure pleasure that the taste for it will grow and become a permanent part of a child's emotional, intellectual, and aesthetic resources.

For some years, there has been a ground swell of interest in poetry, both in producing it for young people and in encouraging them to write it. Not all of the qualities that distinguish poetry from prose are common to all its forms, but basic to the genre are the concentration or crystallization of mood, emotion, or experience; the use of words or sounds that are evocative; and the use of imagery, oblique or vividly clear. Most poetry provides the satisfaction and challenge of pattern and uses words in a way that is more musical or rhythmic than all but the most lyric prose. The alliteration and refrain that can be obtrusive or redundant in prose become, in a good poem, part of its appeal; in a mediocre poem, an abuse of these devices or a rigid adherence to rhyme, especially when it is forced, can result in doggerel. Rhyme and rhythm, particularly attractive to younger children, reinforce aural enjoyment, for poetry must be heard to be fully savored. The essence of po-

etry is revelation: by the way words are put together, by the richly imaginative use of those words, by the condensation of the poet's conviction, we see with sharpened understanding our own experiences or share with quickened empathy the experiences or dreams of others.

Definitions of poetry are, of course, valueless to children, but they are valuable to adults since they throw light on the manner in which to present poetry.

Robert Frost said that "A poem is a momentary stay against confusion. Each poem clarifies something.... A poem is an arrest of disorder."[1] Frost implied that our experiences come pell-mell, but a poem sorts them out, gives them order and meaning—not merely the essence of an experience but its significance.

Others define poetry:

*Absolute poetry is the concrete and artistic expression of the human mind in emotional and rhythmical language.—*Encyclopaedia Britannica

*The essence of poetry is invention; such invention as, by producing something unexpected, surprises and delights.—*Samuel Johnson

*If I read a book and it makes my whole body so cold no fire can ever warm me, I know that is poetry. If I feel physically as if the top of my head were taken off, I know that is poetry. These are the only ways I know it. Is there any other way?—*Emily Dickinson

---

1. John Ciardi, "Robert Frost: Master Conversationalist at Work," *Saturday Review*, March 21, 1959.

If you examine these definitions and others, you will discover certain ideas recurring: poetry surprises and delights; it sings like music; it makes you feel intensely; poetry gives you an arresting thought often in rhythmic words, plus a shiver up your backbone. When poetry means these things to you, you have genuinely enjoyed it: it becomes a part of you. When it leaves you just where you were, neither aroused nor amused, neither enchanted nor solaced, then poetry has not happened to you; it has passed you by. So it is with children.

Elements of Good Poetry

But how about adults who enjoy doggerel, and children who accept anything that rhymes? Does enjoyment make poetry of these jingles they read? Perhaps for them it does temporarily, but doggerel need not remain their top level of appreciation. Good taste in any field—music, interior decoration, clothes, poetry—is largely a matter of experience. As we become familiar with the best in one field, we gain discrimination there, while in another field in which our experience is limited we may show very poor taste. Harry Behn says, "I believe that children's judgment of what books are best for them to expand into is better than *our* judgment if we make the best as easily available as television."[2] Children's taste will improve if they have repeated experiences with good poetry.

The Music of Poetry

One of the most important characteristics of good poetry is its singing quality, its melody and movement. In the nonsense jingles and humorous verse, for example, words and lines trip along with the lightness of children jumping rope. Clumsy doggerel—in contrast to the verses of Lear, Richards, and Milne—is heavy footed, and its words and lines have no sparkle. If, as Lillian Smith says in *The Unreluctant Years*, the verses of Milne and Lear are not true poetry, they are certainly as debonair and as skillfully written as light verse can be. If a poem is in a mysterious or meditative or wistful mood, the lines move slowly and the words fall subtly on the ear. These are clues to reading poetry aloud and emphasizing the musical pattern. On the whole, the poetry small children like is more lively and lilting than poetry for adults.

2. Harry Behn, *Chrysalis* (Harcourt Brace Jovanovich, 1968), p. 16.

The fact that children enjoy marked rhythms and crisp rhymes accounts for their ready acceptance of second-rate verse if it has these characteristics. But if their ears become attuned to the subtleties and varieties of rhythmic patterns found in poems like those by Stevenson, De la Mare, and Behn, they may detect the labored rhythms and forced rhymes which characterize most mediocre verse.

The Words of Poetry

Poetry uses strong, vigorous words or evocative, rich words or delicate, precise words that define with accuracy. Of course, prose may employ the same words, but poetry ordinarily uses them with greater condensation and in more melodious combinations so that their effect is more striking. Think of the amusing "sneezles and freezles" of Christopher Robin, of John Updike's "stripped and shapely Maple" grieving in November for "the ghosts of her departed leaves," or of Blake's "echoing green," which suggests the calls and shouts of children at their play. Read through these poems and notice both the exact, descriptive words and the sensory, connotative words and phrases which distinguish good poetry from the ordinary: "the still dark night," "skipping along alone," "rain in the city" falling "slant-wise where the buildings crowd," "soaked, sweet-smelling lane," "Apple trees are snowing." Words that stir the imagination, that speak to the senses, that provoke laughter, that move us deeply and strongly—such words are part of the secret of good poetry.

Viewpoint

Poetry is essentially a game, with artificial rules, and it takes two—a writer and a reader—to play it. If the reader is reluctant, the game will not work.

. . . Poetry, . . . is a kind of musical word game which we value because of its expressive qualities. Not all poems are equally musical, or equally playful, or equally expressive. Nor are they necessarily musical, playful, or expressive in the same way. But we can consider these three qualities as the basic constituents of poetry. . . . If a piece of writing is neither especially rhythmical nor especially ironic or metaphorical in its language, it is not poetry, regardless of its dramatic situations or the ideas it presents.—Robert Scholes, *Elements of Poetry*, Oxford University Press, New York, Toronto, London, 1969, pp. 1, 7, 60.

The Content of Poetry

While poetry has strong emotional appeals, it is built around subjects or ideas, and appeals to the intellect as well as the emotions. Even a slight verse like "Little Miss Muffet" has a well-defined idea—security, fright, escape. Children's emotional response to poetry depends upon their grasp of the content. Of course poetry may have almost as varied subject matter as prose, but like any of the other arts, it must invest that content with arresting significance. A slippery baby in a bathtub is Carl Sandburg's "fish child," and Marianne Moore's jellyfish is "an amber-tinctured amethyst." John Ciardi's "thin grin-cat" stalking a bird is ominous in its suggestion of hunger and anticipated satisfaction. So poetry takes the strange or everyday facts of life and gives them fresh meaning. We see colors that seem new because poetry has revealed them.

Selecting Poetry for Children

When we chose a poem for children, we may well test it with these questions: First, *does it sing*—with good rhythm, true, unforced rhymes, and a happy compatibility of sound and subject—whether it is nonsense verse or narrative or lyric poetry? Second, *is the diction distinguished*—with words that are rich in sensory and connotative meanings, words that are unhackneyed, precise, and memorable? Third, *does the subject matter of the poem invest the strange or the everyday experiences of life with new importance and richer meaning?* When a poem does these three things, it is good poetry.[3]

3. Many of the poems discussed in this chapter appear in *Time for Poetry*, Third Edition (Scott, Foresman, 1968) and *The Arbuthnot Anthology of Children's Literature*, 4th ed. (Scott, Foresman, 1976).

People who do not like poetry usually have had unpleasant introductions to poems when they were children. Poetry should be chosen and presented to children with care if we wish to make it appealing to them. Following are some suggestions for do's and don't's:

Don't introduce poetry by dissecting it.

Don't read poetry aloud without practicing enough to read it well.

Don't confuse poems that are *about* children with poems that are *for* children.

Don't present poems that are too long, or that have long descriptive passages.

Don't choose poems that have involved figures of speech or obsolete language.

Don't introduce poetry by having children read it silently.

Don't require children to memorize poetry.

Don't use poetry as a reading exercise.

Don't select poems that are pedantic or that are about a subject in which children probably have a minimal interest, such as reflections on growing old.

Don't select poems with obscure meanings or language too difficult for the child's comprehension.

Illustrations on this page by Trina Schart Hyman, © 1972 by Harcourt Brace Jovanovich, Inc. and reproduced with their permission from *Listen, Children, Listen* by Myra Cohn Livingston.

Do read poetry aloud often.

Do provide a variety of poems in records, books, and tapes.

Do make several anthologies available to children.

Do select contemporary poetry as well as older material.

Do help children avoid sing-song reading aloud.

Do choose poems with comprehensible subject matter.

Do encourage the writing of poetry.

Do choose poems that have action or humor.

Do try choral readings.

These are general suggestions, and are not meant to imply that all figures of speech should be shunned, or that all subject matter in poetry should be wholly within the child's experience, but that such aspects of poetry should be given careful consideration before poems are introduced to children.

We would do well to remember how important it is that children still in the process of learning to read should hear most of their poetry before they are asked to cope with it on the printed page; children's reading abilities are behind their listening abilities in the first few years of school, and so the effort of reading poetry may, during those years, be greater than

Illustration by Trina Schart Hyman, © 1972 by Harcourt Brace Jovanovich, Inc. and reproduced with permission from *Listen, Children; Listen* by Myra Cohn Livingston.

the pleasure of reading poetry. It is also important to keep in mind that today's poets are more understandable to today's children than are most of the older poets, whose work may be better understood and more easily introduced when children reach junior or senior high school.

To Help Children Learn to Enjoy Poetry

Know What Children Like About Poetry

This brings us to the delight of using poetry with children. We must know what they like about poetry and how to expose them to it so the liking grows. Research findings indicate that children's poetry preferences have remained stable throughout the years.[4] Students in the upper elementary grades dislike sentimental poems, preferring those that are humorous; they prefer poetry with everyday language and content to poetry with figurative language or to traditional poetry, and they have a strong liking for poems written in narrative form.

Fortunately, poetry's first and strongest appeal is its *singing quality*, the *melody* and *movement* of the word patterns and the lines. Walter de la Mare calls these qualities "tune and runningness," and they make poetry an aural art like music, to be heard and spoken just as music is to be heard and played. Our business as adults is to savor this singing quality of verse and to learn how to maintain it in our reading.

Next, children like the *story* element in poetry, from "Little Miss Muffet" to "The Highwayman." This is so strong an interest that we should search for fine narrative poetry for every age level. Children will accept the feeblest doggerel if it tells a story. Often the surprising and provocative little story suggestions in the poetry of Walter de la Mare account for the children's enjoying subtler and lovelier verse than they would otherwise appreciate.

Nonsense and *humor* in poetry have great appeal to children. They delight in the daft lunacy of cows jumping over the moon and they move happily from the gaiety and nonsense of *Mother*

4. Ann Terry, *Children's Poetry Preferences; A National Survey of Upper Elementary Grades.* National Council of Teachers of English, 1974.

Goose and Edward Lear to the modern hilarity of Shel Silverstein and John Ciardi. They enjoy the sound of nonsense words, alliteration, and the repetition of phrases in a refrain. But on the way, nonsense merges naturally into light verse. Children chuckle over the gay drama of "The King's Breakfast" and a few years later are grinning over the more intellectual humor of "Macavity the Mystery Cat." For humor can be subtle, and well-written humorous verse is an exercise not only in ear training but also in quick associations, double meanings, satire, or witty implications.

The *sensory content* of poetry (the words and images that evoke seeing, hearing, touching, tasting, smelling responses) constitutes one of its strongest appeals, or, in some cases, accounts for its failure with certain children. If the sensory content is familiar or understandable, then they respond to it with zest. Over half the children in the United States are from urban areas while a large proportion of our poetry is distinctly rural in its sensuous imagery. (Of course, this situation is changing as more and more of the recent poetry has an urban setting.) The city child and the country child have certain experiences in common—wind, rain, snow, sun, moon, stars, heat, cold, fog—but how differently these experiences impinge on the consciousness of each of them. Take snow, for instance, which in the crowded areas of the city is soon a blackish, soggy slush. How, then, can the city child, who knows neither down, nor lambs, nor even clean, soft snow (at least for very long), respond to the feeling of stepping upon "white down," of walking upon "silver fleece," as described in Elinor Wylie's "Velvet Shoes," or of seeing such snow-covered, moonlit fields as are pictured in W. G. Vincent's "Moonlight"? By the time these are laboriously explained, there is not much left of the dreamlike quality of that walk

> At a tranquil pace,
> Under veils of white lace.[5]

In the last several years, fortunately, more and more city poems have appeared. In a poem

The photo appears courtesy of the Library of Congress. From *America Is Not All Traffic Lights: Poems of the Midwest,* comp. by Alice Fleming. Little, 1976.

from *I Thought I Heard the City*, Lilian Moore captures the beauty and quiet of snow in an urban setting.

Snowy Morning[6]

> Wake
> gently this morning
> to a different day.
> Listen.
> There is no bray
> of buses,
> no brake growls,
> no siren howls and
> no horns
> blow.
>
> There is only
> the silence
> of a city
> hushed
> by snow.

There are now many anthologies intended particularly for city children: for example, Robert Froman's *Street Poems,* Nancy Larrick's *On City Streets,* Arnold Adoff's *City in All Directions,* and Lee Bennett Hopkin's *City Talk.*

Poetry should be comprehensible to children, but that does not mean they must have experienced everything they read about. Few children have had an opportunity to observe an ostrich closely, yet how enticingly Aileen Fisher leads them to an easy understanding of ostriches by contrasting ostriches with birds that *are* familiar.

5. From "Velvet Shoes" from *Collected Poems of Elinor Wylie.* Copyright 1921, 1932 by Alfred A. Knopf, Inc. Reprinted by permission.

6. "Snowy Morning." Text copyright © 1969 by Lilian Moore. From *I Thought I Heard the City.* Used by permission of Atheneum Publishers.

Most birds surely
Walk quite poorly
Most birds merely
hop around.

They're securest,
swiftest, surest
on their wings
above the ground,
but OSTRICHES . . . .

In this way, with humor, suspense, rhyme, and rhythm, the child is led through enjoyment to comprehension.

Provide Children with Rich Poetry Experiences

Children's encounters with poetry should include three types of response—*enjoyment, exploration,* and *deepening understandings.* These do not occur always as separate steps but simultaneously. Certainly, children must start with enjoyment or their interest in poetry dies. But if from the beginning they find delight in the poems they hear, they are ready and eager to explore further—more books and more poems of different sorts. Even the youngest children can learn to see implications beyond the obvious. To read for veiled meanings is to identify oneself with the poet, to ask the poet's questions. This is reading for deeper understanding, taking a thoughtful look at what lies beneath the surface. Enjoyment, exploration, and deeper understanding must all be part of children's experience with poetry if we are to help them to love it.

Read Poetry to Children

Poetry began as a spoken art; people listened to it and remembered it because rhyme and meter made it easier to recall than prose. So it should begin for children. Poetry should be heard because of its inherent lyric qualities. Adults should read or speak it aloud and encourage children to join in until, without even realizing it, they have memorized effortlessly dozens of poems which they can speak naturally and gaily. (See Part 4 for a discussion of reading poetry aloud.) Speaking or reading poetry to chil-

7. From *But Ostriches . . .* by Aileen Fisher. Published by Thomas Y. Crowell Company, Inc., Publishers. Copyright © 1970 by Aileen Fisher. Reprinted by permission of the author.

dren should continue all through their childhood.

By early adolescence most children have mastered the mechanics of reading and if their childhood experiences with poetry have been happy, they will go on reading it on their own.

Poetry should never be used as a reading exercise. When children have to struggle with a poem as a reading lesson, they are baffled and discouraged. John Erskine, writing for older students, says in *The Kinds of Poetry:* "The office of the teacher of poetry is easily defined; it is to afford a mediation between great poets and their audience." With children, effective oral reading is the surest mediation.

Mother Goose is a natural starting point with children from two to six or seven years old. Her pages are alive with "tune and runningness" and children respond with vigor. They soon discover that "Ride a cock horse" is a gallop and "To market, to market" is an everyday

Viewpoint

walk, quite unlike the military tread of "The grand Old Duke of York." Body movement of young children is a natural response to these nursery rhymes. They don't know that it is meter and rhyme, line and word patterns that produce these contagious rhythms, but they feel the "goingness" of the verses, and the same qualities can be found in such contemporary nursery rhymes as Clyde Watson's *Catch Me & Kiss Me & Say It Again.* This easy, natural introduction can provide a firm foundation for later interest. *Mother Goose* is discussed more fully in Chapter 5, "Books for the Very Young."

The introduction to poetry for older children should begin as painlessly as it begins for the prereaders. That is, they should hear many poems vigorously read aloud for sheer pleasure, with no analysis during this exploratory stage. Some poetry should be slipped in and introduced with a comment like: "A new poem is like new music. Sometimes you have to hear it several times before you know whether or not you like it." Older children may not always respond with body movements, but they may well identify the gallop of Stevenson's "Windy Nights" or the rattling rhythm of McCord's "The Pickety Fence" even though they cannot analyze the mood in words.

Explore Poetry Books with Children

In the process of enjoying poetry, children will encounter many books and different types of verse. Their explorations will include books by a single author and anthologies of poetry by many poets.

Anthologies are invaluable, and there is no reading experience more satisfying, either in a classroom, a library, or at home, than to settle down with your children to explore a new anthology. Needless to say, you will have explored it first to know its range and contents and to have chosen in advance a group of poems that you feel sure the children will understand and enjoy. Modern anthologies usually provide a high quality of poetry selections and convenient subject matter arrangements, and they rescue from oblivion such out-of-print treasures as "The Pirate Don Durk of Dowdee," "Overheard on a Saltmarsh," and the best of Winifred Welles and Mary Austin. Classrooms and homes should own several anthologies. Here are a few criteria for selecting an anthology from among the many excellent ones available:

1. Examine the author index to discover the range and quality of writers represented. Does it lean heavily on poets of the past, Eugene Field, Riley, Stevenson, Longfellow, or are the best of these balanced by many good modern poets?
2. How many poems does the book contain? Oddly enough, one anthology may contain over five hundred poems while another at approximately the same price includes only two to three hundred. If the quality of the two books is equally good, the first is obviously a better choice.
3. Look for indexes and classifications. The indexes should include authors, titles, and, preferably, first lines. Teachers will find classifications by subjects equally important—such groupings as people, animals, nonsense, magic, our country, seasons, and the like. Organization by subjects is far more important than organization by grades. Indeed, grade levels for poems are impossible and undesirable, no matter how teachers yearn for them, because children's tastes and capacities vary as much as the poems themselves and depend on their varied experiences.
4. Format is important. A heavy volume may be useful in the school library as a reference book, but it will not be good for a child to use or an adult to handle with the child. Good paper, clear type, well-spaced pages, all add to the attractiveness of a book.

Some anthologies not only meet these basic criteria, but provide extra dividends in the form of attractive illustrations, brief introductions to or explanations of poems, and suggestions for reading aloud and choral speaking.

Teach children how to explore and use an anthology. A forthcoming holiday, for example, means a search for the best Halloween or Christmas poems. Undoubtedly the greatest value of a fine anthology is the feeling it gives children for the range and variety of poetry. They will look, browse further, and make discoveries.

In the same way, children should become acquainted with the books of single poets, not merely Stevenson's *A Child's Garden of Verses,*

From *For Me to Say* by David McCord. Illustrated by Henry B. Kane. Copyright © 1970 by David McCord. By permission of Little, Brown and Co.

but David McCord's *For Me to Say*, Harry Behn's *Little Hill*, June Jordan's *Who Look at Me*, and others. This exploration of the works of individual poets guarantees that the child will encounter a range of poetry from the imaginative and subtle lyrics of Walter de la Mare to the robust nonsense of Dennis Lee. Such exploration will also help children to grow emotionally, aesthetically, and intellectually with poetry.

Deepen Children's Understanding of Poems

A third phase of poetry experience involves a more intellectual response than either enjoyment or exploration. It is what John Ciardi has called "reading in depth" or reading for a more complete understanding of the poet's meaning. With the youngest children this begins with talking about word meanings and background experiences and with older children it progresses to a fuller consciousness of implica-

tions, double meanings, possible symbols, and even to some analysis of form.

To help younger children understand the meaning of a poem, we often need to evoke or supplement their background of experience. For instance, suppose a child has never seen a snail. Show a picture of a snail or bring one to school. Then Hilda Conkling's "Little Snail" with "his house on his back" will be visually clear. Walter de la Mare never says in his poem "The Huntsmen" that it is about three boys riding their hobbyhorses upstairs, and so unless children understand this, the "clitter clatter" of those wooden sticks on the stair and the whole meaning of the poem will be obscure.

Sometimes the musical pattern of a poem affects its meaning in ways even very young children can sense. For instance, five-year-olds know that the words in Stevenson's "The Swing" really swing and that the words of Milne's "Hoppity" do hop with Christopher Robin to the very last line which hops to a standstill. Hearing poetry read with an emphasis on its musical patterns, young children can be trained to the point where they are aware, consciously or unconsciously, of what the patterns are making them feel or understand.

Or take Elizabeth Coatsworth's beautiful study in contrasts—"Swift things are beautiful," p. 288. Help the children to hear how the words and lines of the first stanza hurry along, with no long, sonorous vowels or words to delay the crisp, brisk movement. But in the second verse, the long vowels in such mouth-filling phrases as "The pause of the wave/That curves downward to spray" and the heavy last lines, "And the ox that moves on/In the quiet of power," compel a slow, deliberate reading. You simply cannot dash off those last lines briskly.

These brief, simple examples of the way poets use the words and patterns of their verse to suggest action, mood, or meaning are obvious enough for children and are the beginnings of a deeper look at the poetry they enjoy. This deeper look will carry them into the below-the-surface meaning or implications or symbols the poet uses.

Undoubtedly, some teacher has already helped students discover the remarkable likeness of themes in Gerald Johnson's *America Is Born* and Robert Frost's poem "The Gift Outright." In his book Johnson says:

At the start nobody intended to become an American, but everybody did if he stayed in this country. They were changed simply by living (here). . . . George Washington still thought of himself as a trueborn Englishman, although it was impossible for him to be anything of the sort.

What made us Americans was not long and careful thinking about it, but simply seeing what had to be done and doing it. What had to be done here was not exactly what had to be done in England; and in doing it we became something different from Englishmen. (p. 140)

Read the children this and then read "The Gift Outright" several times until they see the connection. Because of the concepts involved, this is not a poem for use with younger children.

The Gift Outright [8]

The land was ours before we were the land's.
She was our land more than a hundred years
Before we were her people. She was ours
In Massachusetts, in Virginia,
But we were England's, still colonials,
Possessing what we still were unpossessed by,
Possessed by what we now no more possessed.
Something we were withholding made us weak
Until we found out that it was ourselves
We were withholding from our land of living,
And forthwith found salvation in surrender.
Such as we were we gave ourselves outright
(The deed of gift was many deeds of war)
To the land vaguely realizing westward,
But still unstoried, artless, unenhanced,
Such as she was, such as she would become.

The relation between this poem and the Johnson passage lies, of course, in the lines, "She was our land more than a hundred years/Before we were her people." Why? Because we were "Possessed by what we now no more possessed"—in other words, England. Which is just another way of saying what Gerald Johnson said. Older children can readily fill in the wars involved in "(The deed of gift was many deeds of war)," but it is more important to challenge the children with those enigmatic last lines—"Such as she was, such as she would become." What would they like our country to become, our United States? This is important because the answer may well lie with them, the children of today, the adults of tomorrow. What would they have our country become that it is not today? The children's answers may not be profound—neither would the answers of most

adults—but at least the poem will have made them look beneath the surface of evolving life in their own country and sense the fact that they, too, are going to play a part in its future. This poem is a perfect example of Frost's own pronouncement that "Each poem clarifies something."

The children who are reading and writing poetry today are searching and probing issues and problems of our time. They want, in addition to poetry that is beautiful in its grace and melody, poetry that is beautiful in strength and candor. They need to explore the new forms, to hear the angry voices, for they are, many of them, angry about what is happening in their world. They should read Coatsworth, De la Mare, and Frost, but they should also read Nikki Giovanni, Vanessa Howard, Leonard Cohen, Mari Evans, Karl Shapiro, and the many other poets who are most immediately concerned, as the children are, with the way things are now.

The Range of Poetry for Children

Although some children cling to one genre or subject in their reading, most like variety, and their preferences change with mood and age. Fortunately, there is such variety in poetry as to satisfy any taste: narrative, dramatic, or lyric; bound verse or free; poems about animals, people, nature, fairies, emotions, causes; poems that are thoughtful or stirring, tender or hilarious. Here we shall cross the lines of form and content in discussing both the wide variety of poetry for children and the poetry children are writing today. We shall consider poetry ranging from nonsense verse and the more serious poems about children's everyday experiences to the quiet probings of Langston Hughes's poetry and the patterned intricacies of poems by May Swenson and Myra Cohn Livingston.

A poem may be written in free verse, which has no requirements of rhyme and meter, or in bound verse, which does. It can be narrative, dramatic, or lyric. Dramatic poetry, a form seldom used in children's poems, reveals the personality of a character primarily through his or her speech or through the speech of other characters. Narrative poetry tells a story and is enjoyed by children for that reason, whether the

8. "The Gift Outright." From *The Poetry of Robert Frost* edited by Edward Connery Lathem. Copyright 1936, 1942 by Robert Frost. Copyright © 1969 by Holt, Rinehart and Winston, Inc. Copyright © 1964, 1970 by Lesley Frost Ballantine. Reprinted by permission of Holt, Rinehart and Winston, Publishers; Jonathan Cape Ltd.; the Estate of Robert Frost; and the editor.

poems are long and serious or brief and humorous. Lyric poems, which are usually short, express an emotion of some kind, often highly personal, and may range in content from the expression of a child's delight in "wiggly mud" to a sad farewell to departing summer.

Nonsense Verse

A good way to introduce children to poetry is with nonsense verse. For young children the gay tradition of nonsense verse was given a rousing start by *Mother Goose* rhymes (see Chapter 5). Children enjoy these amusing jingles, and most adults find a lifelong source of fun in humorous limericks and verse.

Not all people and not all ages are amused by the same jokes. Two-year-olds may chuckle over the hissing *s*'s of "sing a song of sixpence." The hilarity of older children is roused by other forms of nonsense. Just listen to seven-year-olds enjoying Laura Richards's "Eletelephony" (see p. 280).

Nonsense verse, if it is skillfully composed, introduces the child to rhyme, rhythm, and meter and to various types of verse patterns. The neatly turned limerick and the patter of humorous couplets or quatrains in exact meter train the ear to enjoy the sound of words and rhythms, a training that should carry over to catching similar sound patterns in poetry of a higher order.

From Nonsense to Humor

Although no hard and fast line divides humor from sheer nonsense, there is, nevertheless, a difference. Nonsense is more daft, more impossible, while humorous verse deals with the amusing things that befall real people, or might conceivably befall them. Edward Lear and Laura E. Richards sometimes wrote humorous verse, but for the most part their verse is hilarious nonsense. In contrast, A. A. Milne wrote occasional nonsense, but on the whole his poems involve people and situations that are amusingly possible, however improbable they may be.

Usually "The King's Breakfast" is the favorite with most Milne addicts. This starts reasonably with the king asking for a little butter on the "Royal slice of bread," and it moves along smoothly until the sleepy Alderney upsets all royal regularity by suggesting "a little marma-

From *Oh, What Nonsense!* by William Cole and Tomi Ungerer. Illustrations copyright © 1966 by Tomi Ungerer. Reprinted by permission of The Viking Press, Inc.

lade instead." From then on the dialogue becomes entirely daft, reaching a joyous climax when the king bounces out of bed and slides down the banisters. This is, of course, the essence of the fun—the incongruity of a king who is so deeply concerned with marmalade that he whimpers, sulks, bounces, and slides down banisters. The verse pattern of each episode reinforces the mood.

Other writers of humorous verse before the 1950s include the once popular James Whitcomb Riley and Eugene Field. Riley's verses have a mild humor, but they rarely bubble or sparkle. Field's "The Duel" is still enjoyed by children of five or six. This mock tragedy about the gingham dog and the calico cat who "ate each other up" has a pleasant swing and a delightful refrain. Another tragicomic verse is Vachel Lindsay's "The Potatoes' Dance," which tells of the blighted romance of a "tiny Irish lady" and a hapless sweet potato.

Humorous Verse Since the Fifties. One of the most outstanding and prolific writers of humorous verse for children since the 1950s is David McCord, who wrote for adults before he began writing for children. McCord's poems are not all humorous, but the best of them have a captivating playfulness and ebullience which infectiously communicate an enjoyment of words and word play.

William Cole's *Oh, What Nonsense!* and *Oh, How Silly!* are anthologies of humorous poems, the first containing many counting rhymes and jump-rope chants, the second song lyrics and folk rhymes. Dennis Lee's *Garbage Delight*, which won the 1978 award given by the Canadian Library Association as the best book of the year, depends on exaggeration, nonsense, and strong rhythm for its appeal.

In each of her collections of poetry, Eve Merriam provides some amusing gems. Like David McCord, she sometimes uses poetic forms to explain the forms themselves, giving six examples of the couplet in "Couplet Countdown" and demonstrating in "Leaning on a Limerick" both the form and the playful use of words at which she excels.

For older readers, Myra Cohn Livingston's *Speak Roughly to Your Little Boy* is both diverting and instructive. It is a collection of parodies and burlesques, each paired with the original material on which it was based. Some of the selections will also be enjoyed by younger children who can recognize little nuggets of burlesque like J. B. Morton's "Now We Are Sick."

Since anthologists have not found all the humorous verse that has been written, it is a rewarding activity for teachers to make a collection of favorites, or to encourage children to make such a collection. Clever, well-written verses which provoke a chuckle are worth having not only because they bring laughter into a world in need of laughter, but because their rollicking jingles cultivate the ear and lead naturally and painlessly to the enjoyment of lyric poetry.

Poetry of the Child's Everyday World

The world of fantastic nonsense and the child's everyday world of people, pets, and the outdoors may seem far apart. Yet many poets move easily from one to the other and, like the child, are at home in both worlds.

Actually, in the years before Edward Lear introduced his madcap world of nonsense, children had been given to understand that life was not only real but decidedly earnest. Poems were written and read to children for the purpose of improving their manners and uplifting their morals. Yet didactic as some of these early efforts seem today, they marked a dawning recognition of the child's everyday world of people and play, both real and imaginative.

Slowly the idea took form and grew, the idea of a child not as a small adult but as an intensely active person, functioning in a world of his or her own.

The poems of Kate Greenaway marked the transition from verse written for children's instruction to verse written for their entertainment, verse which records the play world from the child's point of view. Even though her verses are often wooden and occasionally unchildlike, they reflect a new consciousness of real children and their everyday play.

Other poets caught this new point of view and began to write a new kind of verse for and about children. Their poems reflect both the child's everyday world of active play and the inner world of imaginative play.

Robert Louis Stevenson wrote only one book of poetry for children, *A Child's Garden of Verses*, but with that one book he became one of the great children's poets. His poems are truly childlike in their approach to play and in the manner in which they mirror the small adventures of a child's day. They are rhythmic and musical, and they see both the imagined and the real with a child's clear eye.

Eleanor Farjeon wrote skillful nonsense verse. Her lyrics are tender and beautiful, and her poetry reflects a sure knowledge of the child's world and wonderment. Her first book, for which she wrote her own music, was *Nursery Rhymes of London Town*. Her writing has zest and playfulness, enjoyment of words, and a variety of subjects and patterns with a seeming spontaneity and an unquestionable charm.

Elizabeth Madox Roberts had the ability to see, feel, and think in a childlike manner that strikes the adult as unerringly right and true. Her single book of poetry for children, *Under the Tree,* uses words and phrases that sound like a child speaking, but only an artist could have chosen words so brilliantly descriptive. Her narrative is as direct as prose, with no pretentiousness, no fanciness, no ethereal theme, but the imagery, the sensitivity, and the identification with the concerns of children bring her poems directly into the child's world of poetry.

Arnold Adoff, in *Make a Circle Keep Us In,* writes of the protective love and warmth in family life with fluent simplicity. In *Eats* he writes with gusto about the delights of favorite foods, and in this book he adds humor to the direct approach of the first book.

Excerpted from the book *Make A Circle Keep Us In,* poems for a good day. Illustrated by Ronald Himler. Illustration Copyright © 1975 by Ronald Himler. Used by permission of Delacorte Press.

I Am Learning

to move my chop
sticks
              through
the
vegetables   and
                  meat
and
        through
the
        oriental
                  treat
we
have
tonight
but   in
between
        my
        smiles
        and
              bites
i
write
a
message
              in
              the
sweet
        and
sour
pork

i
need
a
fork[9]

9. "I am Learning" from *Eats* by Arnold Adoff. Copyright © 1979 by Arnold Adoff. By permission of Lothrop, Lee & Shepard Books (A Division of William Morrow & Company) and Curtis Brown, Ltd.

John Updike, distinguished as a writer for adults and as the 1964 winner of the National Book Award for Fiction, has, in *A Child's Calendar,* written with fresh imagery about the familiar phenomena of the child's changing year.

In this chapter is just a sampling of the many poets who have brought their lyric gifts to interpret the everyday world the child sees and wonders about. Of all the poems available for children, however, those that tell a story have a special appeal for poetry lovers as well as for self-proclaimed detesters of poems.

Traditional Ballads

The ancient ballads are often, because of their dialect and archaic language, difficult for children to read or sing. Yet children are universally fond of poems that tell a story, and a more rousing collection of stories would be hard to find. Both the folk ballads and modern story poems have a common appeal; they tell a story in concentrated form, with a maximum of excitement and a minimum of words. Children may make little distinction between the types,

From *A Child's Calendar*, by John Updike, illustrated by Nancy Ekholm Burkert. Copyright © 1965 by Nancy Ekholm Burkert and John Updike. Reprinted by permission of Alfred A. Knopf, Inc. (Original in color)

for what they enjoy is the swift movement of verse or melody enhancing the dramatic appeal of a good story. The search for these story poems carries us back into folk rhymes and forward to present-day narrative poems, ranging from hilarious nonsense to romance and noble tragedy.

Traditional ballads were passed on by word of mouth long before they were printed, and they were so popular and so rapidly carried about by sailors and travelers that it is difficult today to determine whether a ballad is Danish, Scottish, English, or German in origin. The English and Scottish ballads flourished from the thirteenth to the middle of the sixteenth century. However, it was not until 1765, when Bishop Percy collected and published many of

them in his famous *Reliques,* that they became widely known and appreciated; the ballads that this collection contained had been found by chance in an ancient manuscript. They inspired Sir Walter Scott and others after him to search for and preserve other original ballad materials.

Characteristics of the Traditional Ballads. The old ballad was a song story and its singing quality is still evident in the lilting verses and refrains and in the lively tunes that accompany the words. "Bonny Barbara Allan," for example, tells a tragic tale swiftly and movingly, but the opening verse suggests at once that here is a song:

> In Scarlet Town, where I was bound
>   There was a fair maid dwelling.
> Whom I had chosen to be my own,
>   And her name it was Barbara Allan.

The tune of "The Gypsy Laddie," or its more familiar folk-song variant, "The Raggle, Taggle Gypsies," is a compelling one, but the ballad is also dramatic for reading. Even the most tragic

Viewpoint

... Ballads are widely considered to be plotted narratives, rising from relatively trained minds, taken over and fostered by the folk until they become the verses and masterpieces that our collectors uncover.

The word "plotted" is of particular significance. . . . Plotting is honored by the tradition in which the Anglo-American ballad is born, but there is little evidence to support a contention that the folk, in whose oral heritage the ballad lives, care very much at all for unified action. Their myths and their tales lack unified action, except as a vestige. Generally, the folk tend to discard plotting in favor of something one might call "impact" or "emotional core." . . .

A ballad survives among our folk because it embodies a basic human reaction to a dramatic situation. This reaction is reinterpreted by each person who renders the ballad. As an emotional core it dominates the artistic act, and melody, setting, character, and plot are used only as means by which to get it across. This core is more important to the singer and the listeners than the details of the action themselves.—Tristram P. Coffin, "Mary Hamilton and the Anglo-American Ballad as an Art Form," in *The Critics and the Ballad,* readings selected and edited by MacEdward Leach and Tristram P. Coffin, Southern Illinois University Press, Carbondale, 1961, pp. 245, 246, 247.

Illustration by Virginia Lee Burton, from *Song of Robin Hood* by Anne Malcolmson. Published by Houghton Mifflin Company. Copyright 1947 by Anne Burnett Malcolmson and Virginia Lee Demetrios. Reproduced by permission of the publisher.

ballads, like "Edward" or "Lord Randal," have wistful, tender airs that somehow soften the tragedy.

In many ballads this songlike quality is enhanced by refrains which seem made for dancing. It is a good idea to help children respond to the musical character of the ballads by having them sing some or try to suit rhythmic movements to the words of others or even try lively dance steps to the lustier refrains.

Perhaps the most striking characteristic of the ballads is their dramatic and rapidly unfolding plots. In "Edward," for example, you sense immediately that something is wrong; then you learn that Edward has killed his own father, but not till the last stanza do you know that the mother herself planned the crime and persuaded her son to commit it.

There are of course some comic plots, too, but they are distinctly in the minority. "The Crafty Farmer" outwitting the thief is one of the children's favorites, and they like even better the broad slapstick farce of the stubborn old couple in "Get Up and Bar the Door." The folktale plot of trial by riddle with a bright person substituting for a stupid one is amusingly used in "King John and the Abbot of Canterbury" ("King John and the Bishop").

On the whole, ballad plots are more likely to be tragic than humorous. They celebrate bloody and terrible battles, ghosts that return to haunt their true or their false loves, fairy husbands of human maids, infanticide, murder, faithless love punished, faithful love not always rewarded—sad, sad romance and tragedies in every possible combination.

Incremental repetition is an aid to story-telling. This is a ballad convention in which each verse repeats the form of the preceding verse but with a new turn that advances the story. Reading ballads that use incremental repetition, you will find it easy to imagine a leader starting the pattern by asking the question, a crowd of people singing the refrain, and the same leader, or perhaps the next person in the circle, answering the question.

The author always remains anonymous. Reference to the storyteller is comparatively rare, perhaps only in an opening line. The storyteller merely records the facts of the adventure as objectively as possible and remains completely anonymous.

The ballads, as we have observed, run the whole gamut of subjects and emotions. Here are some categories with a few examples:

Farce—"The Crafty Farmer"; "Get Up and Bar the Door"

Comedy—"King John and the Abbot of Canterbury" ("King John and the Bishop"); "A Gest of Robyn Hode" (with the exception of the account of Robin Hood's death)

Crime—"Edward"; "The Bonny Earl of Murray"; "Lord Randal"; "The Twa Sisters"

Noble tragedy—"Sir Patrick Spens"; "The Hunting of the Cheviot"; "The Battle of Harlaw"; "The Battle of Otterburn" (the ballads of the great battles are generally too involved for the elementary school)

Romance—"Lizie Lindsay"; "Bonny Barbara Allan"; "The Raggle, Taggle Gypsies" ("The Gypsy Laddie")

Fairylore—"The Wee Wee Man"; "Tam Lin"; "Hind Etin"

Ghost story—"The Wife of Usher's Well"

Melodrama—"The Daemon Lover" ("James Harris"); "Lord Randal"; "Bonny Barbara Allan"

Folk Ballads in the United States. Early settlers brought the old Scottish and English ballads to this country, and children in states as remote from each other as Pennsylvania and Texas, or Wisconsin and the Carolinas, heard their parents and their grandparents singing the same ballads that *their* grandparents had sung in the mother country. "Bonny Barbara Allan," for example, was carried by the colonists and pioneer families from one end of the United States to the other.

The collection compiled by Francis Child

(1825–1896) of Harvard stimulated such an interest in these old story songs that collectors began to search for and record their American variants. They found, as you might expect, a large number of ballads being sung or recited throughout the country, but especially in the Southern mountains. There the mountaineers, cut off from the mainstream of immigration and changing customs, had preserved the songs their ancestors brought with them. "Lord Randal" might be hailed democratically as "Johnny Randall," or even "Jimmy Randolph," but he was still begging his mother to make his bed soon for he was "sick to the heart and fain wad lie down." Sometimes the verses had been so altered and patched together that they were incoherent. Most of the ballads had, however, come through with less change than you might naturally expect from several hundred years of oral transmission.

Cecil J. Sharp (1859–1924), an English musician, made early and outstanding collections of these descendants of Scottish-English ballads in the Southern mountains of the United States. His books are valuable contributions to the ballad literature of America, and other collectors have followed his lead. Older children will enjoy the ballads in Sharp's first two volumes, while children as young as three and four are charmed with the *Nursery Songs*.[10]

Once the collectors set to work gathering American variants of the old-world ballads, they began to encounter new ballads and folk songs that are as native to the United States as buckwheat cakes and hominy grits. Here was a rich treasure of ballad-making still in the process of creation. These songs achieve a wistful melancholy or a happy-go-lucky philosophy or a sheer braggadocio distinguishing certain groups of hardy settlers or certain workers such as the Western cowboys.

The native ballads of the United States tell, on the whole, fewer coherent and dramatic stories than do the Scottish-English ballads; but they sing with or without the music. The Negro spirituals reach heights of religious fervor never attained in any old-world ballad, but for their full beauty they need their music. The cowboys' ballads have sometimes a philosophic or a wistful air that is more in the mood of a song

than of a story. The language is easier for us, even the dialect or vernacular, but some of it is rather rough.

With the increasing popularity of folk singing in the middle period of the twentieth century, there has been a renaissance of the ballad form. The outstanding performer-composers are the heroes of the young, the guitar the indispensable instrument, the ballad their own song. One of the most pleasant collections is *As I Walked Out One Evening: A Book of Ballads* compiled by Helen Plotz. And, for the younger children, there is an echoing trend in the publication of single songs in illustrated editions.

Once children realize that ballads are still remembered and treasured, they may turn collectors and discover some ballads in their own families or communities. Once they realize that ballads are still being made not merely by professional poets imitating old forms but by isolated peoples celebrating tragic, comic, or dramatic events, the children, too, may wish to try group composition of a ballad. It is fun and less difficult than it sounds. Radio, newspapers, and television make constant use of such events for sketches and dramas. Why not try casting them into ballad form?

Narrative Poems

The story poems and the old ballad form have proved as attractive to poets as they have to readers. The rapid action, the refrains and repetition, and the rhythm all contribute to the interest and impetus of story poems.

For the youngest children, from five to eight or nine, there are two masterpieces—"A Visit from St. Nicholas" by Clement Clarke Moore and "The Pied Piper of Hamelin" by Robert Browning.

It is interesting to recall that Robert Browning wrote "The Pied Piper of Hamelin" for the amusement of a sick child, with the special intention of supplying him with subject matter he could illustrate. Perhaps this accounts, in part, for the visual quality of the poem, which has endeared it to illustrators. The story of "The Pied Piper" is too familiar to need reviewing, but particular qualities of the poem are worth noting. In the first place, the story moves rapidly. Words hurry and trip along, episodes follow each other swiftly, and lines have the racing tempo first of the scurrying rats and later of the skipping children. The dramatic conflict be-

10. C. J. Sharp, compiler, *English Folk Songs from the Southern Appalachians* (Oxford, 1953); *American-English Folk Songs* (Schirmer, 1918); *Nursery Songs from the Appalachian Mountains* (Novello, 1921–1923).

From *Dick Foote and the Shark* by Natalie Babbitt. Copyright © 1967 by Natalie Babbitt. Reprinted by permission of Curtis Brown, Ltd. (Original with color)

tween greed and honor is sufficiently objective for children to understand, and they approve of the Piper's retributive revenge.

For broad comedy Eugene Field's "The Duel" (the tale of "the gingham dog and the calico cat") and Laura Richards's "The Monkeys and the Crocodile" are perennial favorites. William Allingham's "The Fairy Shoemaker" and Laura Richards's "Little John Bottlejohn" are unusual fairy and mermaid poems, the latter simple enough for the five-year-olds. An amusing venture into history is Arnold Lobel's *On the Day Peter Stuyvesant Sailed into Town*. In Natalie Babbitt's *Dick Foote and the Shark*, the poetic hero saves his own life and that of his terrified father by so doggedly spouting poetry from the bow that the befuddled shark swims away.

The story of Noah's Ark, more than slightly adapted, has several verse versions, including

The Cruise of the Aardvark, in which Ogden Nash's pompous hero discovers belatedly that he is not on an ordinary pleasure cruise. Countee Cullen's *The Lost Zoo* is a good choice for reading aloud to younger children. A lasting favorite is "Custard the Dragon" by Ogden Nash. Search your anthologies and books by single poets for more story poems, because even the fives and sevens enjoy the swiftness and suspense which the rhythmic flow of verse gives to a story.

Scott's "Young Lochinvar," a gay, swashbuckling romance with a galloping tempo, is particularly enjoyed by older children; "The Highwayman" by Alfred Noyes is a favorite romance. William Cowper's "John Gilpin" is only one of many humorous ballads they enjoy. May Sarton has written with sensitivity and grace "The Ballad of Ruby," based on an episode described in Robert Coles's *Children of Crisis*. It tells of a small black child's experience of discrimination when she goes to school. And let's not forget that gem of Americana, Ernest L. Thayer's "Casey at the Bat."

For eleven- to fourteen-year-olds there are many story poems about great events in history. Certainly they should hear "The Landing of the Pilgrim Fathers" by Felicia Dorothea Hemans, with its unforgettable picture of that desolate arrival and its significance in our history. Children may also thrill to the galloping hoofbeats of Henry Wadsworth Longfellow's "Paul Revere's Ride" before they meet the more complex and workaday Revere of the biographies. Arthur Guiterman has written a number of fine historical ballads, but especially recommended are his "Daniel Boone" and "The Oregon Trail." These are significant both as poems and as history. In *Independent Voices*, Eve Merriam has written poems that tell, in a variety of rhyming verse patterns and with a vivid sense of the dramatic, the stories of many great American men and women. In Rosemary and Stephen Benét's *A Book of Americans*, there are many poems you will wish to use with history, but the pair, "Nancy Hanks" and "Abraham Lincoln," are the great favorites.

These poems are typical of the fine narrative verse about people and events in United States history. Such poems can be introduced casually as the history chronology unfolds, or the children may become interested in the theme of heroism and start searching for hero poems of their own.

Lyric Poetry

Ask any teacher or parent who reads aloud to children what kind of poems they like best and the answer will be, "Funny ones."

The rhythm and melody of verse are primary sources of satisfaction to children just as are the rhythm and melody of music. But it is a long way from the tumpity-tump skips and gallops of early childhood to Bach and Beethoven and it is just as far from *Mother Goose* and Edward Lear to Walter de la Mare and Robert Frost. If we are to help children grow up successfully in poetry, we should start where the children are.

For instance, children begin as young as two years old to play with words and respond to their sounds. "Pickle-lillie, pickle-lillie," chants one child, savoring the ear-tickling *l*'s with evident enjoyment. Other children are caught by the charm of other words and phrases, and without knowing why, they respond to the mood evoked by the words. In some such accidental way, children's taste for lyric poetry may begin. It is the responsibility of parents, librarians, and teachers to provide poetry experiences for children that will help them grow up happily with poetry.

It is not that lyric poetry is characteristically obscure or that its sound is more important than its meaning. But authentic poetry not only conveys meaning but generally evokes an emotional response. Children who have the good fortune to hear a poem that gives them a shiver up their backbones or a swift upsurging flood of elation or a sense of quiet and peace are discovering some of the joys of poetry.

From the great body of English lyric verse,

Illustration by Arthur Hughes for *Sing Song* by Christina Rossetti (1872 edition).

children will appropriate certain poems that suit them, and when they have spoken them repeatedly until they know them, the verses become truly their own. They will ask about them, too, and through discussions meaning will be enriched. If most children still prefer the lightest of light verse, just remember that most adults do, too.

William Shakespeare is one of those poets who, although writing for adults, has songs that children enjoy. Children hearing the songs of Shakespeare without being forced to analyze or memorize them soon know the poems by heart, and the words sing in their heads like a popular tune. "Jog on, jog on," from *The Winter's Tale*, is a good march for any excursion of children. "Who is Sylvia?" from *The Two Gentlemen of Verona*; "When icicles hang by the wall," *Love's Labour's Lost*; and "Hark, hark! the lark," *Cymbeline*—these poems have a singing quality and a simplicity of content that bring them within the enjoyment range of older children, especially if they hear the poems before they read them.

William Blake's *Songs of Innocence* is a landmark in English literature as well as in children's literature. The average child may not particularly enjoy some of the more difficult poems, but will enjoy many of them if they are read aloud by someone who likes their melodies. For Blake's poems are songs, full of cadences and lovely sounds.

Christina Rossetti provides the young child with an ideal introduction to lyric poetry in the verses of *Sing Song*, published in 1872. Many of the verses have homely, familiar subjects, but they are written with lyric grace and with a subtle simplicity in the choice of words. What gentleness there is in "The Caterpillar":

> *Brown and furry*
> *Caterpillar in a hurry*
> *Take your walk*
> *To the shady leaf or stalk*
> *Or what not,*
> *Which may be the chosen spot.*
> *No toad spy you,*
> *Hovering birds of prey pass by you;*
> *Spin and die,*
> *To live again a butterfly.*

Many poets of the twentieth century have written outstanding lyric poetry, including Walter de la Mare and Eleanor Farjeon, Sara Teasdale and Elizabeth Coatsworth. Eve Merriam, in *It Doesn't Always Have to Rhyme*, and

Harry Behn, in *The Golden Hive*, or Langston Hughes, in "Snail" or "Dream Variations," have written lines as musical as any lyric poets of the past.

Poetry of Nature

Most of the poets discussed in this category are dissimilar in most respects, but they have one characteristic in common: they observe nature with sensitive interpretation and an imaginative turn that kindles a responsive spark in the reader.

The poems of Sara Teasdale are largely descriptive and often too subtle for the child under ten, but their lyric beauty and poignance captivate some children. Elizabeth Coatsworth's poems are less musical but rich with imagery, less complex but lucid and gay with a quick appeal.

Aileen Fisher, many of whose longer poems (*Once We Went on a Picnic* and *Listen, Rabbit*) have been published singly in picture-book form, has been a prolific writer of verses for children. Her writing is pleasant and patterned, and all of her nature poetry reflects both her awareness of the child's interests and her own deep love of the outdoors and of small, wild creatures. An example of her poetic vision is "Sun Prints."

Sun Prints[11]

The lawn is full of footprints,
golden tracks that show
where the sun went walking
a day or two ago.

My father calls them dandelions.
I think they're sun prints, though.

The Danish explorer Knud Rasmussen brought back from his fifth expedition to the Arctic a large collection of Eskimo poems. A selection from these has been made into a beautiful book for children, *Beyond the High Hills*, illustrated with breathtaking color photographs by a missionary priest, Father Guy Mary-Rousselière. The result is sheer beauty pictorially and verbally, with a dramatic re-creation of Eskimo thoughts, feelings, and way of life. These verses are in free form and have great

Text of "Sun Prints" from OUT IN THE DARK AND DAYLIGHT by Aileen Fisher. Text copyright © 1980 by Aileen Fisher. By permission of Harper & Row, Publishers, Inc.

strength and maturity. To read these poems with the loneliness and beauty of the photographs is a moving experience. They will give children more of Eskimo life and thought than many factual books. *The Wind Has Wings*, a varied and handsomely illustrated collection of Canadian poetry compiled by Mary Downie and Barbara Robertson, includes Eskimo and French songs.

Mary Austin's *The Children Sing in the Far West*, published in 1928, is an older collection of children's poems about America's Southwest. Teachers should slip in some of her best and most characteristic poems now and then—"Charms," "Prayers," and "A Song of Greatness," for example—and at least a few of the children will respond. These poems give young readers a new understanding of and respect for Native Americans. At her best, Mary Austin transcends local color and writes with universal significance.

The Trees Stand Shining, a selection of poetry of the North American Indians, has been compiled by Hettie Jones. The poems are, in fact,

Illustration by Jean Primrose. From *The Creatures' Choir* by Carmen Bernos de Gasztold, translated by Rumer Godden, decorations by Jean Primrose. Copyright © 1965 by Rumer Godden. Illustrations reprinted by permission of The Viking Press, Inc.

untitled songs, fragmentary and brief, often with the terse quality of haiku, that show the affinity the Indian feels for the beauty and strength of nature. Humanity's close relationship to nature is also depicted in John Bierhorst's anthology *In the Trail of the Wind: American Indian Poems and Ritual Orations.* This volume includes poems of the Maya, the Aztec, and the Eskimo as well as those of North American Indian tribes. William Brandon's collection, *The Magic World: American Indian Songs and Poems,* is unusual for its inclusion of a large number of Nahuatl ceremonial songs.

In *A Few Flies and I,* some of the poems of the great Japanese poet Issa have been brought together by Jean Merrill and Ronni Solbert. Richard Lewis, in *Of This World,* also chose some of the Issa poems that show an infinite tenderness toward the small creatures of the world.

Of all the books that share this affection for animals, Carmen Bernos de Gasztold's *Prayers from the Ark* and *The Creatures' Choir,* translated from the French by Rumer Godden, are two of the most beguiling, each poem a percipient picture of the animal that speaks.

The Hedgehog[12]

Yes, Lord, I prick!
Life is not easy—
but You know that—
and I have too much on my shoulders!
I speak of my prickles
but thank You for them.
You at least
have understood me,
that is why You made me
such a pinball.
How else can I defend myself?
When people see me,
my anxious nose
searching for the fat slugs
that devastate the garden,
why can't they leave me alone?
Ah! But when I think proper,
I can roll myself up
into my hermit life.

Amen

Other books about animals are *Cats and Bats and Things with Wings* by Conrad Aiken, William Cole's anthology *An Arkful of Animals,* and

Brownjohn's Beasts by the British poet Alan Brownjohn, whose animals, like those of Carmen Bernos de Gasztold, speak for themselves—and with great wit.

Poetry from Around the World

There Are Two Lives, edited by Richard Lewis, is one of the many other books that are bringing poetry of other lands to English-speaking children. Producing such books is a phenomenon not wholly new but noticeably burgeoning. Lewis chose Japanese and Chinese poetry for *Moment of Wonder* and selected haiku for younger readers in *In a Spring Garden.* He selected poems of the haiku poet Issa in *Of This World* and edited the work of another great haiku poet in *The Way of Silence: The Prose and Poetry of Basho.* Japanese poems are also found in Virginia Baron's *The Seasons of Time,* a selection of ancient tanka poetry, and Harry Behn's two collections of haiku, *Cricket Songs* and *More Cricket Songs.* Nursery rhymes of other lands are discussed in Chapter 5.

In William Jay Smith's *Poems from France,* each poem in French has the English translation on the facing page. Undoubtedly the French poetry best known to English-speaking children is that of de Gasztold, mentioned above.

Helen Plotz's *Poems from the German,* which provides the poems in the original and in English translation, is for older children. For younger readers there are several editions of

Illustration by Lynn Munsinger, from *An Arkful of Animals* by William Cole. Published by Houghton Mifflin Company. Copyright © 1978 by William Cole. Reproduced by permission of the publisher.

12. From *The Creatures' Choir* (British Title: *The Beasts' Choir*), by Carmen Bernos de Gasztold, translated by Rumer Godden. Copyright © 1965 by Rumer Godden. Reprinted by permission of The Viking Press, Inc., and Macmillan London and Basingstoke.

Heinrich Hoffmann's *Slovenly Peter*, now a children's classic, one version of which was translated by Mark Twain.

The first section of Miriam Morton's anthology *A Harvest of Russian Children's Literature* has verses for young children, and there are a few other poems in the book, notably a long narrative poem, "The Little Humpbacked Horse," a fairy tale in verse that is also popular in Russia in dramatized form. Ivan Krylov's *The Fifteen Fables of Krylov* has a dry wit.

From India there is the poetry in Gwendolyn Reed's *The Talkative Beasts: Myths, Fables and Poems of India*, and in Rabindranath Tagore's slim volume *Moon, For What Do You Wait?* In *We, the Vietnamese: Voices from Vietnam*, edited by François Sully, there is a representative section of poetry from a portion of "Kim Van Kieu," Vietnam's best-known epic poem, to folk songs of protest and the poetry of today's underground.

The indefatigable Richard Lewis has selected some of the poetry of ancient Greece for *Muse of the Round Sky* and has chosen poems and songs of primitive peoples of the world for *Out of the Earth I Sing*, most of the selections being from African and North American Indian tribes. *A Crocodile Has Me by the Leg*, compiled by Leonard Doob, has African poems that clearly stem from the oral tradition and have folk wisdom and humor.

For *The Singing and the Gold*, an excellent anthology of world literature compiled by Elinor Parker, many poets contributed to the translations of poetry from thirty-four different languages. While the translation of an art form so tied to language as poetry is cannot give readers the full flavor and nuance of the original, it is still valuable to have the work of poets in other countries available. It is probable that this trend toward international diffusion of an art that is, of all types of literature, the one most elemental, perceptive, and universal will increase as our children grow toward a world less partitioned by boundaries than the world of the past.

Poetry by Children

There have always been children who wrote poetry, and there have been some—like Hilda Conkling and Aliki Barnstone—whose writing has been published and extolled. Never before today, however, has there been so much encouragement by adults working with children in small groups and in classrooms, so many young people forming their own groups to read, write, and discuss poetry.

One of the most sympathetic and informed explorations of this activity is in *Somebody Turned on a Tap in These Kids*, edited by Nancy Larrick and containing articles by such poets as June Jordan, Myra Cohn Livingston, and Eve Merriam, and by others who work with children. In *Poetry Is*, Ted Hughes, a British poet, addresses his remarks about technique, acuity of observation and expression, and imagery, to young people. In *Let Them Be Themselves*, author Lee Bennett Hopkins discusses poetry as one of the ways in which the language arts program may be enriched for disadvantaged children.

Not every child is capable of writing poetry, and it is true that some of the work being done with children is directed as much toward therapeutic as esthetic goals, but the amount of fine poetry that has been published is a testament to the emotional and imaginative capacity of the young. The work of one outstanding young black writer, Vanessa Howard, has been included in several anthologies of poetry by children. The untitled following poem is an example of her depth and vision.

> I am frightened that
> the flame of hate
> will burn me
> will scorch my pride
> scar my heart
> it will burn and i
> cannot put it out,
> i cannot call the fire department
> and they cannot put out the flame
>   within my soul
> i am frightened that the flame
> of hate will burn me
> if it does
> I will die[13]

The Voice of the Children, compiled by June Jordan and Terri Bush, comprises some of the best of the poetry written in a creative writing workshop; Virginia Baron's anthology *Here I Am!* contains poems written by young people from diverse minority groups. "Inevitable poets," Arnold Adoff calls the young people whose poems poured in from all parts of the country to be selected for *it is the poem singing into your*

13. "I am frightened that" by Vanessa Howard from *The Voice of the Children* collected by June Jordan and Terri Bush. Copyright © 1968, 1969, 1970 by The Voice of the Children, Inc. Reprinted by permission of Holt, Rinehart and Winston, Publishers and Julian Bach Literary Agency, Inc.

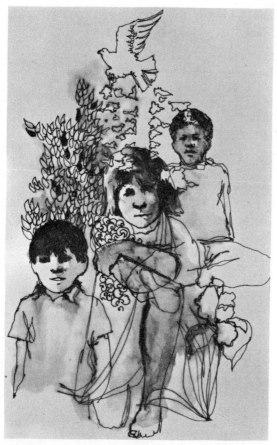

Illustration by Emily Arnold McCully from the book *Here I Am!* edited by Virginia Olsen Baron. Illustrations copyright © 1969 by Emily Arnold McCully. Published by E. P. Dutton and used with their permission.

the use of language is the most marked difference between these poems and those of American children. One of the most touching collections of children's poetry is *I Never Saw Another Butterfly*, poems written by Jewish children in a concentration camp. Many of the poems are remarkable for their courage, vision, and compassion.

Poetry for Now

In the explosive increase of children's interest in reading and writing poetry, there are several striking trends. One is the subject matter with which the young are concerned: they are writing poems about anything and everything they see around them, and although they are still aware of natural beauty and intrigued by the intricacies and mystery of themselves and other people, some of their poetry seethes with anger, sees beauty as well as despair in the urban scene, and faces with candor the afflictions of the world they inherit. In form, too, there is a new freedom: most of the poetry they write and much of the poetry they read is free verse, some of it in shaped patterns, like that of May Swenson's "Redundant Journey," in which the print forms a sinuous pattern on the page, or it

eyes. Kenneth Koch's *Wishes, Lies, and Dreams* contains both the author's description of his work with children in a New York City school and their poetry.

I Heard a Scream in the Streets, edited by Nancy Larrick, is a collection of poems written by young people in the city. Her other anthology of children's poetry, *Green Is Like a Meadow of Grass*, shows the results of children's observation of nature, encouraged by teachers motivated in a poetry workshop.

Miriam Morton has gathered Russian children's poems in *The Moon Is Like a Silver Sickle*, and Richard Lewis has gathered children's poetry in several fine anthologies: *Miracles*, a collection of poetry by children of the English-speaking world; *The Wind and the Rain*, nature poems; and *There Are Two Lives*, poems by Japanese children, a collection in which restraint in

Viewpoint

The search for what is real has led many a poet and his readers to topics once thought of as unpoetic: traffic lights, for example, and escalators, subways and littered sidewalks. On crowded streets and in cluttered hallways man's inhumanity to man shows up dramatically. Adults who have equated poetry with "a host of golden daffodils" may find it difficult to accept this harsh reality for children. Yet this is the children's world, too. . . .

It should not surprise us, then, to find that today's children seek the realistic poetry of bolder voices, speaking in a blunt conversational style. They like poems which debunk the phony and unveil hypocrisy. I think this is one of the reasons why they are held by Eve Merriam's *The Inner City Mother Goose*, which is a biting commentary on the injustices of the American ghetto.

"This is real," explained one fourteen-year-old. "The trouble with poetry at school is it's all covered over with the beautiful."—Nancy Larrick, "Poetry That's Real," *Somebody Turned on a Tap in These Kids*, edited by Nancy Larrick, Delacorte Press, New York, 1971, pp. 4–5.

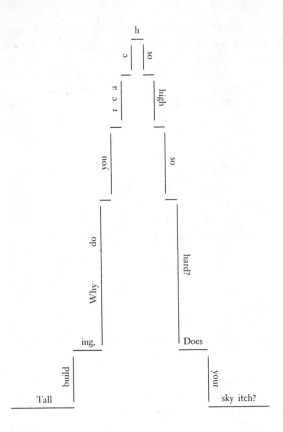

SKYSCRATCHER

From *Street Poems* by Robert Froman. Copyright © 1971 by Robert Froman. Reprinted by permission of the publisher, E. P. Dutton, and Curtis Brown, Ltd.

is the concrete poetry that moves from the oral tradition to appeal to the eye. Free verse, of course, is not new, but it has never been so enthusiastically employed.

Young people are reading avidly the contemporary multi-ethnic voices of protest. There is a marked increase in the numbers of black poets being heard and being represented in anthologies of modern poetry chosen especially for young readers. And—no surprise in a world in which communication has brought peoples closer to each other—there is a growing amount of poetry from other cultures now available in English.

There is no age limit for poetry that is distinguishably, and often distinctively, contemporary. Some of the urban poetry written for very young children is concerned with subjects

and problems that were never mentioned in children's literature before, an acknowledgment of the sophistication of the young. "The City Question" in Robert Froman's *Street Poems* poses the problem of the man lying on the sidewalk. Wino? Junkie? Or ill? Is he dangerous, or should one try to help? Another poem is called "Hail, Polluters." Froman plays with shapes in this intriguing book that manipulates print to accentuate the message of the words; the names of objects in a garbage heap are, for example, actually piled helter-skelter; and in a poem about a dandelion, the print forms a stem and a flower head. Ian Hamilton Finlay's *Poems to Hear and See* are experiments in form by a poet who is a participant in the Concrete Poetry movement, which intends the word to stand for itself as does an ideogram.

In *Mazes* by Muriel Rukeyser, a picture-book format and color photographs are the setting for a poem about a child who explores his surroundings, a lovely lyric but complex enough to make demands on the reader. In Nikki Giovanni's *Ego-Tripping and Other Poems for Young People*, some of the poems are tender, some angry; all are a celebration of being black. May Swenson's poetry has enormous vitality and impact, and is filled with striking images, with patterns in print that she calls Shape Poems, and with the Riddle Poems that require the reader to make a personal contribution toward interpretation. June Jordan's *Who Look at Me* is a long poem that moves, as in a gallery, from one portrait to another of black people. The paintings are by distinguished artists, the poem a passionate statement of the dignity, the pain, the anger, and the pride of the black people.

Who see the block we face
the thousand miles of alabaster space
inscribed keep off keep out don't touch
and Wait Some More for Half as Much?[14]

Robert Hayden, himself a poet, has compiled the work of American black poets in *Kaleidoscope*, an anthology that begins with the poetry of the "Sable Muse" of colonial times, Phillis Wheatley, and proceeds chronologically, with biographical notes, to contemporary writers. Arnold Adoff, in *I Am the Darker Brother*, *Celebrations: A New Anthology of Black Poetry*, and

14. From *Who Look at Me* by June Jordan. Copyright © 1969 by June Jordan. By permission of Thomas Y. Crowell, Publishers, and Joan Daves.

Black Out Loud confines his selections to the work of modern black poets; such established writers as Langston Hughes, LeRoi Jones, Mari Evans, and Arna Bontemps are included, but there are many poems by writers less well known.

There are a dozen or so very good anthologies of modern poetry for young people, and many of them include poems by older poets who have struck a note consonant with today's themes, or poems that are the lyrics of contemporary ballads and protest songs. David Morse's selections in *Grandfather Rock* have been made to show the kinship between such lyrics and poems from Homer's time on: indeed, Morse, in his preface, refers to such poetry as "the rock and roll of the past."

Among the best of the anthologies of modern poetry are *Lean Out of the Window* by Sara Hannum and Gwendolyn Reed; *The Sidewalk Racer and other Poems of Sports and Motion* by Lillian Morrison; *Sounds and Silences: Poetry for Now* by Richard Peck; and *Reflections on a Gift of Watermelon Pickle* by Stephen Dunning, Edward Lueders, and Hugh L. Smith; and *A Poison Tree*, illustrated by Mercer Mayer. Additional anthologies including other collections by these same compilers will be found in the bibliography.

Young poetry lovers do read the poetry of the past, but for most of them the modern poets have a greater appeal, speaking as they do to the issues, and in the language of the present. There has been no lessening of admiration for the poems of Emily Dickinson, Robert Frost, Edna St. Vincent Millay, and W. H.

From *A Poison Tree and Other Poems* illustrated by Mercer Mayer. Copyright © 1977 by Mercer Mayer. Reprinted by permission of Charles Scribner's Sons.

Auden, but there are other poets whose names (in addition to those already mentioned in this chapter) crop up in almost every anthology index: Babette Deutsch, James Dickey, Galway Kinnell, Denise Levertov, Richard Wilbur, Rod McKuen, Howard Nemerov, Pauli Murray. Indeed, almost every contemporary poet is represented and has his or her faction of admirers.

One fact that emerges from a survey of poetry for children is that poets can no more be pigeonholed than light can be captured and boxed. Another fact is that a poem, more than any other kind of literature, has no boundaries and that a suggestion for a reading level is only that—an indication that for many children the poem will probably be most appreciated at a certain age. For children often have a far greater comprehension in listening to a poem than in reading it for themselves, and the poem that awakens a response will produce more attention and understanding on the part of the reader or listener than the poem that can be accepted placidly.

Not every poem is for every child, and some poetry needs intellectual as well as emotional

From *The Sidewalk Racer and Other Poems of Sports and Motion*, comp. by Lillian Morrison. Lothrop, 1977. Photograph by Cathy Cade.

Illustration by Kate Greenaway for "Susan Blue." From *Marigold Garden*, published by Fredrick Warne & Company. (Original in color)

participation. As Agnes Repplier says, in her introduction to a poetry anthology:

In the matter of poetry, a child's imagination outstrips his understanding; his emotions carry him far beyond the narrow reach of his intelligence. He has but one lesson to learn,—the lesson of enjoyment.[15]

The Range of Poets for Children

In contemplating the poetry that children enjoy, it is clear that the range is as varied as the children themselves. Some of the poets who are favorites did not write for children at all; some—like Theodore Roethke and Randall Jarrell—wrote occasionally for them; and others wrote only for them. Those contemporary poets who write in protest or who experiment with form are read as avidly as are the more conventional poets, old and new.

15. From *An Anthology of Modern Verse*, ed. by A. Methuen (Methuen, 1921), p. xiii.

Early Writers—Lasting Influences

Many of the earliest writers of poetry for children wrote a few poems that are still read and loved, but they are revered more for the impetus they gave to writing for children than for the writing itself. Isaac Watts, a preacher who decided that "What is learnt in verse, is longer retained in the memory, and sooner recollected," put his homilies in *Divine and Moral Songs for Children* in 1715. The visionary artist and author William Blake in *Songs of Innocence* (1789) created mood and conveyed ideas through rhythmic verse that speaks to the emotions and to the imagination.

Two sisters, Ann and Jane Taylor, wrote poems as moralistic and didactic as those of Watts, but they wrote wholly for children, and among the *Original Poems for Infant Minds* (1804) there were some that had suspense. They are best remembered for "Twinkle, twinkle, little star." Christina Rossetti's masterpiece is undoubtedly "Goblin Market," which appeared in 1862, a narrative poem that has suspense, vivid imagery, and colorful descriptions. Her *Sing Song* (1872) is a light-hearted nursery classic but it has more complexity than does *Mother Goose*, and it makes subtle and repeated use of vowel and consonant sounds to suggest the feeling or idea described by the words. Emily Dickinson's work has become increasingly beloved by the young. Her poems were revolutionary in their time: short, usually in four-line stanzas, sharply perceptive, often somber but at times playful or witty. There are several editions of her poems that have been chosen for children: *Letter to the World* (1969), edited by Rumer Godden; *Poems* (1964), edited by Helen Plotz; and *Poems for Youth* (1934), edited by Alfred Hampson.

There was an Old Man on
    whose nose
Most birds of the
    air could repose;
But they all flew away at the closing of day,
Which relieved that Old Man and his nose.

From Edward Lear's *The Complete Nonsense Book*.

There was an old man with a beard,
who said, "It is as I feared!

Reprinted with permission of Macmillan Publishing Co., Inc. and Hamish Hamilton Children's Books Ltd. from *Whizz!* by Edward Lear, illustrated by Janina Domanska. Illustration Copyright © 1973 by Janina Domanska. (Original in color)

Lewis Carroll's poetry is much funnier in context, in *Alice's Adventures in Wonderland* (1865) and *Through the Looking-Glass* (1871), than it is when read separately, but his nonsense verses can be enjoyed alone. Ebullient, daft, and rhythmic, poems like "Jabberwocky" have enchanted word-lovers for a century. Carroll's writing is discussed more fully in Chapter 9. Kate Greenaway's verses were undistinguished, but they are simple, childlike, and mildly humorous; without the illustrations upon which her reputation rests, the poems in such books as *Under the Window* (1879) probably would not have survived.

In briefly examining the work of some of the major contributors to children's poetry, who will be discussed in chronological order by their dates of birth, it is possible to see both the diversity and the pattern not only of what children read but of what their society's changing ideas of a child's capabilities and preferences have been.

Edward Lear

The Book of Nonsense
Nonsense Songs and Stories
Whizz!

In England, about 1820, several small books of limericks appeared, the first of which, *Anecdotes and Adventures of Fifteen Gentlemen*, Edward Lear probably read. The limerick form set Lear to writing some of the most famous nonsense in the English language and illustrating it with sketches so amusing that a Lear limerick without the Lear drawing is only half as funny as the two together.

The first collection of Lear's limericks and sketches was published in 1846 as the first *Book of Nonsense*. Writing them must have been great fun for Lear. They were a rest from the painstakingly detailed scientific drawings of birds and animals that were his regular occupation, they were a safe release for his high spirits, and above all they must have been a blessed escape from the illness which pursued but never conquered him.

The second book, *Nonsense Songs and Stories*, published in 1871, includes a variety of humorous verses, among them the pseudoserious narrative poems that seem all the funnier because they are gravely told.

Lear's made-up words are one of the most obvious sources of amusement in these jingles. You find the Pobble who has no toes, the Quangle Wangle with the beaver hat, and the amorous Yonghy-Bonghy Bò. The words in Lear's five sets of alphabet rhymes are mostly of this tongue-twister variety. One begins:

> *A was once an apple-pie,*
> *Pidy,*
> *Widy,*
> *Tidy,*
> *Pidy,*
> *Nice insidy,*
> *Apple-Pie!*

Lear was an excellent craftsman. His meters are exact, his rhymes neat and musical, and his verse has a pleasant sound even at its wildest. Much of it is decidedly melodious. Children linger over the refrains; they also like the ridiculous and eccentric characters in these verses and are especially entertained by the mad troop that populates the limericks, six of which are used as a continuous text illustrated by Janina Domanska in *Whizz!*

Laura E. Richards

Tirra Lirra: Rhymes Old and New

Laura E. Richards's father was Samuel Gridley Howe, who devoted himself to such diverse social causes as the Greek War for Independence, the education of the blind, and the founding of the first school for feebleminded children. Her mother, Julia Ward Howe, was the author of "The Battle Hymn of the Republic." It is not surprising that the children in this family in turn scribbled stories and poetry.

The poems of Laura Richards have a

From *Tirra, Lirra: Rhymes Old and New* by Laura E. Richards. Illustrated by Marguerite Davis. Copyright 1930, 1932, 1934 by Laura E. Richards. Copyright 1955 by Little, Brown and Company. By permission of Little, Brown and Co.

spontaneity and a freshness that are equaled only by their lyric quality. It was her husband who suggested that she send some of her verses to the new magazine for children, *St. Nicholas*, and this she did. From then on, stories and poems came from her pen at an amazing rate. Between stories and biographies, the verses continued to "bubble up" with undiminished charm. But it wasn't until 1932 that a book of her verses called *Tirra Lirra: Rhymes Old and New* was published.

Laura Richards's verses abound in humorous, made-up words. Moreover, no one can play with words with more joyous confusion than she. Children from five to any age have always found much to chuckle over in

Eletelephony[16]

Once there was an elephant,
Who tried to use the telephant—
No! no! I mean an elephone
Who tried to use the telephone—
(Dear me! I am not certain quite
That even now I've got it right.)

Howe'er it was, he got his trunk
Entangled in the telephunk;
The more he tried to get it free,
The louder buzzed the telephee—
(I fear I'd better drop the song
Of elephop and telephong!)

Like "Eletelephony," "Some Fishy Nonsense," "Doggerel," "Sir Ringleby Rose," and many other jingles depend for their fun upon this juggling with words.

But Richards carries her fun beyond mere play with words. She has, in addition to the verse-maker's skill, the dramatic art of a first-rate storyteller. The gentle tale of "Little John Bottlejohn," lured away by a cajoling mermaid, or the gory record of "The Seven Little Tigers and the Aged Cook,"—these and a dozen others depend for their interest upon the skillful storytelling of the author as well as upon her irrepressible sense of the absurd.

Laura Richards has caught in her verses some of the singing quality of words that children enjoy. This lyric quality not only gives distinction to her most extravagant nonsense but makes children more sensitive to the musical qualities of words.

16. "Eletelephony." From *Tirra Lirra: Rhymes Old and New* by Laura E. Richards. Copyright 1935 by Laura E. Richards: Copyright © 1960 by Hamilton Richards. Reprinted by permission of Little, Brown and Co.

Robert Louis Stevenson

A Child's Garden of Verses

The title "poet laureate of childhood" has often been bestowed upon Robert Louis Stevenson, who first captivated adult readers with his essays and fiction, then caught and held the affectionate regard of children with *A Child's Garden of Verses*. This collection appeared in 1885 as *Penny Whistles*, with sixty-three poems and this fond dedication to Stevenson's childhood nurse: "To Alison Cunningham (From Her Boy)." Not all these poems are for children; a few of them are merely about children or are adult reminiscences of childhood. Such poems creep into almost every collection of juvenile poetry but are nevertheless to be avoided; for example, Stevenson's "Whole Duty of Children," or the rarely included "To Any Reader" and "To Willie and Henrietta."

With these exceptions, no careful reading of the poems can fail to leave you impressed with the author's genuine understanding of children. The opening poem, "Bed in Summer," is every child's complaint:

> And does it not seem hard to you,
> When all the sky is clear and blue,
> And I should like so much to play,
> To have to go to bed by day?

His children get up shivering with cold on winter mornings; they yearn to travel; they discover the sea miraculously filling up their holes on the beach; they struggle with table manners; they wonder why they can't see the wind; and they enjoy a world of play and a world of the imagination as well. Here are real children, many-sided and with many interests.

Especially true to child life are the poems involving dramatic play. Imagination transforms a clothes basket into a boat. Climbing up in the cherry tree, the child glimpses not merely the next-door garden but foreign lands and even fairyland. In "A Good Play," the children explain:

> We built a ship upon the stairs
> All made of the back-bedroom chairs.

The poems bristle with the properties and imaginative transformations of that arch magician, the child of about four to seven years old.

Perhaps the largest group of poems under a single general classification is made up of those

concerned with night. What an imaginative group it is, and sometimes scary, too. There are two poems in this night group which are also notable for their rhythm. "Shadow March" is in perfect marching time, but it is an eerie, frightening march of bogies and shadows, not to be used before the children are seven or eight years old and strong enough to stand it. Less scary and still finer is that pounding gallop called

Windy Nights

> Whenever the moon and stars are set,
>   Whenever the wind is high,
> All night long in the dark and wet,
>   A man goes riding by.
> Late in the night when the fires are out,
> Why does he gallop and gallop about?
>
> Whenever the trees are crying aloud,
>   And ships are tossed at sea,
> By, on the highway, low and loud,
>   By at the gallop goes he,
> By at the gallop he goes, and then
> By he comes back at the gallop again.

This example of rhythm illustrates another of the outstanding qualities in Stevenson's *Child's Garden of Verses:* the poems are markedly lyrical.

From *Peacock Pie*, by Walter de la Mare, illustrated by Barbara Cooney. Illustration copyright © 1961 by Barbara Cooney. Reprinted by permission of Alfred A. Knopf, Inc.

Of course, numbers of them have been set to music, but they sing anyway, without benefit of notes. Take the concluding line of "A Good Boy": "And hear the thrushes singing in the lilacs round the lawn." Or listen to the refrain in "The Wind":

> *O wind, a-blowing all day long,*
> *O wind, that sings so loud a song!*

Go through page after page of these poems and you'll find their melody singing in your memory.

Although teachers and parents who were raised on *A Child's Garden of Verses* may feel that the verses are overfamiliar, they must not for-

get that these poems are new to each generation of children. "The Cow," "My Shadow," "The Swing," "Winter-time," and "Time to Rise," in addition to the verses already quoted, are enduring favorites, and children should not miss them. New poets of childhood may make their contributions, but Robert Louis Stevenson has left to young children a legacy of small lyrics.

Walter de la Mare

Rhymes and Verses
Peacock Pie

Adults and children of the English-speaking world lost a great lyric poet when Walter de la Mare died in 1956. For eighteen years he wrote stories and poems and published them under the pseudonym of Walter Ramal. The treasured *Songs of Childhood* was published in 1902 when he was working as a statistician.

All of his poems for young people are now collected in *Rhymes and Verses*. (There is also *Come Hither*, De la Mare's own selection of poems for children.) *Peacock Pie* has been re-issued and is a choice book for the special child to own. Many of his poems are difficult; nevertheless his work contains some poetry that should not be missed. Choose your favorite poems; try them with children; then try certain others that are beautiful but that are not so sure to be enjoyed at first hearing. Who knows what words will catch the imagination of children? When you are using the poetry of a great lyric poet, be adventurous and try a wide selection for the sake of that occasional child who may suddenly be carried away by the magic of poetry.

One characteristic of Walter de la Mare's poems is the use of the unanswered question which leaves the reader wondering. Many of his poems have this enigmatic quality. Of course, too much ambiguity may be discouraging to those children who are literal creatures and like things straight and plain. A little, however, stimulates children's imagination and provokes not only a healthy speculation but the ability to transcend the factual and go over into the world of dreams.

De la Mare could be direct and clear when he wished to, and his children are real flesh-and-blood children. The account of "Poor Henry" swallowing physic is as homely a bit of family life as you can find anywhere. Small children enjoy the matter-of-fact subject matter and the

Viewpoint_____

straightforward treatment of such poems as "Chicken," "The Barber's," and the Elizabeth Ann parts of "A Child's Day." Even these poems for the youngest children, however, are illumined with little touches that invariably lift them above the world of the commonplace.

There are many nature poems in *Rhymes and Verses.* Throughout the poems you find intimate glimpses of flowers, birds, beasts, the sea, and the countryside—all caught and colored with the poet's own peculiar insight. No poetry is more intensely visual than De la Mare's. A "sun-washed drift of seabirds," "rain-sweet lilac on the spray," and, for another sensory experience, those "chuffling" pigs making their "grizzling, gruzzling and greedy" sounds.

Forrest Reid characterizes Walter de la Mare's poetry by saying that it is chiefly "poetry of imagination and *vision* with its hints of loveliness belonging to a world perhaps remembered, perhaps only dreamed, but which at least is not *this* world."[17] The fairy poems, with a great range of mood and style, begin at nonsense level with such delightful absurdities as "Tillie," the old woman who swallowed some magic fern seeds and has been floating around on the wind ever since.

17. *Walter de la Mare: A Critical Study.* Faber and Faber Ltd., 1929.

That De la Mare's work for children has the same beauty found in his books for adults is not surprising when he himself said in his introduction to *Bells and Grass,* "I know well that only the rarest kind of best in anything can be good enough for the young." If anyone has given children "the rarest kind of best" in poetry, it is Walter de la Mare.

Robert Frost

You Come Too

Robert Frost was four times the recipient of the Pulitzer Prize for poetry. In 1950 the United States Senate adopted a "resolution of felicitation" on his seventy-fifth birthday, and in 1961, President-elect John F. Kennedy invited Frost to read one of his poems at the inauguration, the first time a poet had been so honored.

In 1962, the poet's eighty-eighth year, a new book of his poems was published, *In the Clearing,* an arresting title for a last book. Frost died early in 1963. John Ciardi wrote of him, "If he is half radiance he is also half brimstone, and praise be. His best poems will endure precisely

Illustration by Boris Artzybasheff for Walter de la Mare's "Sleepyhead" from *The Fairy Shoemaker and Other Fairy Poems.*

because they are terrible—and holy."[18] In 1979, a picture book version of *Stopping by Woods on a Snowy Evening* was published.

Which of Robert Frost's poems are simple enough for young children? The poet answered this question with the title of his own selections—*You Come Too, Favorite Poems for Young Readers.*

For the nines and tens and older, almost any poem in this collection will carry meaning, more meaning perhaps for the rural than for the urban child. The latter probably has never "out-walked the furthest city light," nor watched "A Hillside Thaw," nor tried "Mending Wall." But fortunately we can all learn by vicarious experiences, and in every poem, the pictures or episodes or ideas are sharply and clearly told with words that have a tonal beauty as captivating as music.

Robert Frost once said, "Every poem is a new metaphor inside or it is nothing"[19]—which implies that the surface meaning of a poem is only the beginning. Frost's poems grow in richness with thoughtful rereading. We may not wish to discuss the various levels of meaning in every poem, but it would be a pity to leave children with nothing more than the obvious scenes the verses report. "A Drumlin Woodchuck" is the amusing soliloquy of a canny old denizen of a hilltop (drumlin) telling how he has managed to evade the hunters. Here is the last verse—

> It will be because, though small
> As measured against the All,
> I have been so instinctively thorough
> About my crevice and burrow.[20]

Here is obviously more than meets the eye. The poet himself referred to it as "my most Vermonty poem." And it is obviously rich, good-humored satire. It might be the poet speaking for himself or anyone who is trying to maintain a little privacy, to protect the right to be one-

self, to live one's own life, to keep one's own secrets. Older boys and girls fighting for a place of their own can appreciate this. "The Road Not Taken" has a different meaning for every human being. Even twelve-year-olds can sense the choices that lie ahead.

Poems such as these from this one small collection of Frost's poetry will help the children move gradually from the purely objective to deeper meanings. Slipped in among the lighter fare, these poems should be read and discussed, paralleled with personal experiences or the experiences of people we know or of people from history, and then they should be read still again for pure enjoyment and enriched meaning. Children should encounter some of Robert Frost's poems so that they can live with the poetry over the years. The poems will grow in significance as the children grow in years and experience.

Carl Sandburg

Early Moon
Wind Song

Carl Sandburg was almost forty years old before he began to be recognized as a writer. He became the author of what is certainly one of the greatest biographies of Abraham Lincoln, *The Prairie Years* and *The War Years*, and he occupies a secure position in American letters.

The publication of his *Chicago Poems* in 1915 created a sensation and brought down upon his head both praise and hostility. Critics seemed to feel either that poetry was going rapidly downhill or that here was another Walt Whitman, a prophet of a new day. His two books of poetry for children are *Early Moon* (1930) and *Wind Song* (1960), both included in *The Sandburg Treasury* along with *Rootabaga Stories, Prairie-Town Boy,* and *Abe Lincoln Grows Up.*

Sandburg's verse is free, the language sturdy and direct, the subjects often indicating his interest in all things American and his sympathy for its little people. Here is an example of his robust simplicity:

Bubbles[21]

> Two bubbles found they had rainbows on their curves.
> They flickered out saying:
> "It was worth being a bubble just to have held
>   that rainbow thirty seconds."

18. "Robert Frost: American Bard," *Saturday Review*, March 24, 1962, p. 15.

19. Charles R. Anderson, "Robert Frost," *Saturday Review*, February 23, 1963, p. 20.

20. "A Drumlin Woodchuck." From *The Poetry of Robert Frost* edited by Edward Connery Lathem. Copyright 1936, 1942 by Robert Frost. Copyright © 1969 by Holt, Rinehart and Winston, Inc. Copyright © 1964, 1970 by Lesley Frost Ballantine. Reprinted by permission of Holt, Rinehart and Winston, publishers; Jonathan Cape Ltd.; the Estate of Robert Frost; and the editor.

21. "Bubbles" © 1960 by Carl Sandburg. Reprinted from his volume, *Wind Song*, by permission of Harcourt Brace Jovanovich, Inc.

Older children can also appreciate the ironical "Southern Pacific." Its biting brevity is exceedingly effective. Easier for them to understand are "Summer Grass" (waiting for rain), "Again?" (about a skyscraper), the poignant "Buffalo Dusk" (good for Western units), "People Who Must" (about a steeple-jack), "Manual System" (about a switchboard operator), and the fine "To Beachey, 1912" (which might be about any aviator of any year).

Sandburg has given some good advice in "Primer Lesson." If you read this to children, let them talk it over.

Primer Lesson[22]

Look out how you use proud words.
When you let proud words go, it is not easy to
*   call them back.*
They wear long boots, hard boots; they walk off
*   proud; they can't hear you calling—*
Look out how you use proud words.

Eleanor Farjeon

Eleanor Farjeon's Poems for Children
The Children's Bells
Kings and Queens

When Eleanor Farjeon began to write, she always took her manuscripts to her father's study, pushed them under the door, and then ran away. "I had a stomach-ache till he came and told me if he liked it," she wrote. "He never kept me waiting. Even if he was writing his own stories, he stopped at once to look at my last poem, and came straight to the Nursery to talk it over with me."

Her first book was the amusing *Nursery Rhymes of London Town*, for which she wrote her own music. This was followed by the lively historical nonsense, *Kings and Queens*, and from then on she wrote prolifically, both prose and poetry.

Kings and Queens, written with her brother Herbert, was republished in 1953 and will delight children wrestling with the solemnity of English history. For instance, "Henry VIII"[23] opens with:

Bluff King Hal was full of beans;
He married half a dozen queens;
For three called Kate they cried the banns,
And one called Jane, and a couple of Annes.

From *You Come Too* by Robert Frost. Wood engravings by Thomas W. Nason. Copyright © 1959 by Holt, Rinehart and Winston. Reproduced by permission of Holt, Rinehart and Winston, Publishers.

And it continues with blithe irreverence to account for the six ladies and their much-marrying spouse.

At their best, Eleanor Farjeon's poems for children, whether nonsense or serious lyrics, are skillfully written. Her rhythms are often as lively as a dance; her meters and rhyme schemes are varied and interesting; and her subject matter has exceptional range.

Unfortunately, the quality of her poems is uneven. She is not, for instance, so adroit at describing the modern child's everyday activities as A. A. Milne, but the moment she turns imaginative, something wonderful happens:

The Night Will Never Stay[24]

The night will never stay,
The night will still go by,
Though with a million stars
You pin it to the sky.
Though you bind it with the blowing wind
And buckle it with the moon,
The night will slip away
Like sorrow or a tune.

22. From *Slabs of the Sunburnt West* by Carl Sandburg, copyright, 1922 by Harcourt Brace Jovanovich, Inc.; renewed, 1950, by Carl Sandburg. Reprinted by permission of the publishers.

23. "Henry VIII" by Herbert and Eleanor Farjeon from *Kings and Queens*. Reprinted by permission of Harold Ober Associates Incorporated. Copyright 1933, 1961 by Eleanor Farjeon.

24. "The Night Will Never Stay" from *Eleanor Farjeon's Poems for Children*. Copyright 1951 by Eleanor Farjeon. Renewed 1979 by Gervase Farjeon. By permission of J. B. Lippincott, Publishers and David Higham Associates, Ltd. for Michael Joseph Ltd.

This curious and lovely poem might well give children their first sense of time, rushing irresistibly along in a pattern of starry nights that will not stand still. In *The Children's Bells*, her "What Is Time?" supplements this poem in a lighter mood. Children like the sound of her companion poems, "Boys' Names" and "Girls' Names," and the surprise endings amuse them.

Eleanor Farjeon was the first writer for children to receive the Hans Christian Andersen Award when it was established in 1956, and each year in her memory the Children's Book Circle in England presents the Eleanor Farjeon Award for "distinguished services to children's books."

A. A. Milne

When We Were Very Young
Now We Are Six

While still a young man, A. A. Milne established himself as a successful writer for adults and as a member of the London literary world. At the time Milne was writing plays and other adult literature, he gave his wife a verse about their son Christopher Robin—"Vespers"—which she sent off to a magazine and which was accepted for publication. Then Rose Fyleman, who was publishing a magazine for children, asked Milne to contribute some children's verses. At first he refused but then changed his mind and sent the poems. When both the editor and the illustrator advised him to write a whole book of verses, he felt it was a foolish thing to do, but again he complied. The result was *When We Were Very Young*, a major sensation in children's books both in England and America. It shares with the second book, *Now We Are Six*, an undiminishing popularity year after year. Milne's plays are amusing, but it is probable that his reputation as a writer will rest more securely upon his two books of verse for children and his two books of stories about Pooh than upon any of his adult stories and dramas.

Milne had a remarkable ability of presenting small children as they are. He gives us their bemused absorption in their private inner world of make-believe, their blithe egotism, their liking for small animals, their toys and games, and the peculiar angle from which they view the odd behavior of those adults who move vaguely on the fringe of their private world.

Viewpoint

. . . I know that a great many children did, and do, like *When We Were Very Young*. I think that such merit as attaches to the verses for this (as distinct from the illustrations to which the book is so obviously indebted) was won by taking pains: more pains, perhaps, than is usual. Whatever else they lack, the verses are technically good. The practice of no form of writing demands such a height of technical perfection as the writing of light verse in the Calverley and *Punch* tradition. *When We Were Very Young* is not the work of a poet becoming playful, nor of a lover of children expressing his love, nor of a prose-writer knocking together a few jingles for the little ones; it is the work of a light-verse writer taking his job seriously even though he is taking it into the nursery. It seems that the nursery, more than any other room in the house, likes to be approached seriously.—A. A. Milne, *Autobiography*, E. P. Dutton and Co., New York, 1939, p. 282.

Christopher Robin speaks for the imaginations of children around four to six years old. His make-believe world is not peopled with the fairies of the eight-year-old but is just the everyday sort of play of the nursery-age child.

The egocentricity of the young child's thought and language has never been recorded more accurately than it was by A. A. Milne. Christopher Robin goes to the market looking for a rabbit and is naively astonished that the market men should be selling mackerel and fresh lavender when *he*, Christopher Robin, wants rabbits. He catalogues his articles of clothing, fascinating because they are his. You can hear the smug emphasis on the personal pronoun. Changing the guard at Buckingham may be very impressive, but the child's only concern is, "Do you think the King knows all about Me?" This is a typical four-year-old, thinking and speaking of everything in terms of himself.

Knowing children's interests, Milne reflects them in his writing. There we find the child's love of small animals and toys. The verses are full of the small child's activities, also. He stalks down the sidewalk missing all the lines. He sits on the stairs and meditates, or he goes hoppity, hoppity, hop. On the whole, he is a busy, active child, immersed in his own affairs and oblivious of any world beyond his own horizon. We can analyze Milne's tripping trochees, his iambs and dactyls, but these academic labels do not seem to convey any idea of the fluid and flashing use he made of words, rhyme, and rhythm to convey character, mood, and action. When Christopher Robin hops through the jingle called "Hoppity," the lines go in exactly the pattern of a child's hop, ending with a big one and a rest, just as hopping always does. But best of all is that juvenile meditation "Halfway Down." Ernest Shepard's sketch, too, has caught the mood of suspended action that is always overtaking small children on stairs. (See the discussion of Shepard's work in Chapter 6.) Why they like to clutter up stairs with their belongings and their persons Milne knew, and he has told us with arresting monosyllables that block the way as effectually as Christopher Robin's small person blocks the stairs. In this first stanza from "Halfway Down"[25] notice "It" and "Stop," which sit as firmly in the middle of the verse as Christopher on the stair.

> *Halfway down the stairs*
> *Is a stair*
> *Where I sit.*
> *There isn't any*
> *Other stair*
> *Quite like*
> *It.*
> *I'm not at the bottom,*
> *I'm not at the top;*
> *So this is the stair*
> *Where*
> *I always*
> *Stop.*

Over and over again, Milne makes a monosyllable or a single word equal three or four words in a preceding line by sheer intensity. It is a device that compels correct reading of the lines, regardless of scansion.

With all of these virtues, it is not surprising that some moderns have come to feel that Milne is the greatest poet for children, certainly their favorite poet. However, delightful as Milne's verses are, they do not cover the full range either of children's interests or of their capacity for enjoying poetry. Many poets achieve greater lyric beauty, more delicate imagery, and deeper feeling for the child's inner world, but certainly we shall never encounter a writer who understood more completely the curious composite of gravity and gaiety, of supreme egotism and occasional whimsy that is the young child.

25. "Halfway Down." From *When We Were Very Young* by A. A. Milne. Decorations by E. H. Shepard. Copyright 1924 by E. P. Dutton & Co., Inc. Renewal, 1952, by A. A. Milne. Reprinted by permission of Elsevier-Dutton Publishing Co., Inc.; the Canadian Publishers, McClelland and Steward Limited, Toronto; E. P. Dutton & Co., Inc., and the British publishers, Methuen Children's Books Ltd.

HALFWAY DOWN

Illustration by E.H. Shepard. From the book *When We Were Very Young* by A.A. Milne. Copyright, 1924, by E.P. Dutton & Co., Inc. Renewal, 1952, by A.A. Milne. Reproduced by permission of the publishers, E.P. Dutton; The Canadian Publishers, McClelland and Stewart Limited, Toronto; and Associated Book Publishers, Ltd., London.

Elizabeth Madox Roberts
Under the Tree

Elizabeth Madox Roberts won several poetry prizes during the period when she was writing the novels for which she is known. The poems that brought a prize while she was in college were later published as *Under the Tree* (1922). A year before her death, a second volume of poems, *Song in the Meadow*, appeared.

Her poems for children have an air of deceptive simplicity that gives the unwary reader no immediate clues to the artistry which makes these poems emotionally satisfying and full of everyday enchantment. Some lines from "The Worm" will serve as an example:

> *Dickie found a broken spade*
> *And said he'd dig himself a well;*
> *And then Charles took a piece of tin,*
> *And I was digging with a shell.*
>
> *Then Will said he would dig one too.*
> *We shaped them out and made them wide,*

And I dug up a piece of clod
That had a little worm inside.

We watched him pucker up himself
And stretch himself to walk away.
He tried to go inside the dirt,
But Dickie made him wait and stay.

His shining skin was soft and wet.
I poked him once to see him squirm.
And then Will said, "I wonder if
He knows that he's a worm."[26]

The children are digging, but notice that they are digging with a broken spade, a piece of tin, and a shell—tools accepted as a matter of course by the child. Then the worm distracts them from their original plan of digging a well, and they experiment with it for a while until a strange idea makes them forget their experiments.

The Roberts child ruminates about things, wonders, and has several scares, but is never fairy-conscious or full of delicate whimsies, having instead a wholesome earthiness and a healthy identification with and delight in nature.

The poems are full of pleasant people and reflect the child's interest not only in other children, but in the grownups at home and abroad. Father fills the little girl's mug at milking time and sings or tells stories to all the children. Mother sends them on picnics and corrects their manners. The townspeople vary from pretty "Miss Kate-Marie," the Sunday school teacher, to Mr. Pennybaker, who makes faces when he sings bass. The intense curious interest that children feel toward the strange antics of grownups is reflected in poem after poem and is summarized in the amusing "People Going By."

Reading these poems, you realize their integrity. No word, no line is dressed up or prettified to sound cute. Cuteness afflicts some modern verse for children and is indeed the curse of juvenile poetry. Here in these poems by Elizabeth Madox Roberts is complete fidelity to child nature. They are grave, simple, and full of the unconscious beauty of children's narratives when they are moved to tell you earnestly of

something they enjoy. You can live with these poems, use them year after year, and never exhaust their richness. No adult can read them without knowing much more about children when finished, and no child can hear them without feeling a kinship with that child who likes to play with wiggle-tails, smell the aromatic herbs of fennel, and eat cherry pie, but who occasionally suffers from every child's all-too-familiar fears.

Elizabeth Coatsworth

Summer Green
Poems
The Sparrow Bush
Down Half the World

Elizabeth Coatsworth's *The Cat Who Went to Heaven* won the Newbery Medal for 1930 but is not as popular with children as her historical tales such as *Away Goes Sally*, *Five Bushel Farm*, and *The Fair American*. Within the pages of these books are some of her best poems, and her poetry is collected in *Summer Green*, *Poems*, *The Sparrow Bush*, and *Down Half the World*.

A certain style in her poetry is well illustrated by the frequently quoted "Swift things are beautiful," from *Away Goes Sally*:

Swift things are beautiful:
Swallows and deer,
And lightning that falls
Bright-veined and clear,
River and meteors,
Wind in the wheat,
The strong-withered horse,
The runner's sure feet.

And slow things are beautiful:
The closing of day,
The pause of the wave
That curves downward to spray,
The ember that crumbles,
The opening flower
And the ox that moves on
In the quiet of power.[27]

Here are the comparisons that the author uses not incidentally but as the theme of the entire poem. You can find other examples of contrasts in all three books. Building a poem around a series of comparisons seems to be a favorite pattern for Elizabeth Coatsworth. It is an exceedingly provocative one for children to study and to try for themselves in their own writing.

26. "The Worm." From *Under the Tree* by Elizabeth Madox Roberts. Copyright 1922 by B. W. Huebsch. Renewed Copyright 1950 by Ivor S. Roberts. Reprinted by permission of Viking Penguin, Inc.

27. "Swift things are beautiful." From *Away Goes Sally* by Elizabeth Coatsworth. Copyright 1934 by Macmillan Publishing Co., Inc., renewed 1962 by Elizabeth Coatsworth Beston. Reprinted with permission of Macmillan Publishing Co., Inc. and Blackie & Son Limited.

Another aspect of her style is the smooth, flowing lines that fall so gently on the ear. Poem after poem has this quietness. The lyric text of *Under the Green Willow*, a picture book, has a subdued, rhythmic quality. Although the lines can frolic now and then, slow-moving calmness predominates. For this reason, reading more than a few of her poems at a time is monotonous.

On the whole these poems are not markedly musical, but they are rich in sensory words; for instance: fallen apples that "smell cidery on the air," sleigh bells that ring "icily sweet," and little buds "no larger than a mouse's ear." You can find examples of her use of words which make you see, smell, taste, touch, and hear.

Her nature poems seem to fall into two classes. Some are straight nature descriptions, and others are brief, lovely descriptions which lead toward, or climax in, a human mood or situation. A fine example of the latter, "How gray the rain," from *Five Bushel Farm*, ends with

> *Serene and bright*
> *The rainbow stands*
> *That was not anywhere before,*
> *And so may joy*
> *Fill empty hands*
> *When someone enters through a door.*[28]

These poems linking together nature and human concerns are notable but they may prove a bit subtle for children and may require discussion before the literal-minded children catch their implications. But the nature descriptions are understandable to all children.

The verses lack the epigrammatic and sparkling quality of similar poems by Christina Rossetti but have instead a straightforward simplicity. In *The Fair American* there is the philosophic

> *To have nothing at all*
> *Is to have much still.*[29]

The poetry of Elizabeth Coatsworth is more ideational than most juvenile verse. It belongs chiefly to older children and will stretch their minds and imaginations.

28. "How gray the rain." From *Five Bushel Farm* by Elizabeth Coatsworth. Copyright 1939 by Macmillan Publishing Co., Inc., renewed 1967 by Elizabeth Coatsworth Beston. Reprinted with permission of Macmillan Publishing Co., Inc. and Blackie & Son Limited.

29. "To have nothing at all." From *The Fair American* by Elizabeth Coatsworth. Copyright 1940 by Macmillan Publishing Co., Inc., renewed 1968 by Elizabeth Coatsworth Beston. Reprinted with permission of Macmillan Publishing Co., Inc. and Blackie & Son Limited.

Rachel Field

Taxis and Toadstools
Poems

Rachel Field's *Six Plays* was published in 1924, and that same year her poems for children, *The Pointed People*, appeared. These attracted favorable attention even though they appeared at the same time that A. A. Milne's *When We Were Very Young* was creating a sensation. Two years later her second book of poems, *Taxis and Toadstools*, was published.

From 1924 to 1942, in a period of only eighteen years, she published some thirty-six books, many of which she herself illustrated. Among her best-known books for children are *Calico Bush*, a historical novel; and the 1930 Newbery Medal book, *Hitty*, the story of a hundred-year-old doll.

Over and over, Rachel Field catches the curious wonderment of children. She shows a child turning back to look at the china dog with the "sad unblinking eye" and wishing for magic words to bring him to life; or wondering if skyscrapers ever want to lie down and never get up! These are authentic child-thoughts, and children respond to their integrity with spontaneous pleasure.

Out of doors, the children of her poems voice that curious kinship with birds, beasts, and growing things that is part of the magic of childhood. Children go to the woods for wild strawberries and forget that there is anything else in the world to do but "fill my hands and eat." They understand the wild creatures, and when they see "The Dancing Bear," they know at once something is wrong, for his eyes look bewildered "like a child's lost in the woods at night."

Field's unique contribution to children's verse is perhaps the three groups of city poems in her *Taxis and Toadstools* called "People," "Taxis and Thoroughfares," and "Stores and Storekeepers."

In the collection of her verses called *Poems*, children like "Good Green Bus," "At the Theater," "The Florist Shop," "The Animal Store," and the favorite "Skyscrapers."

One of the most pleasant poems in this group is "City Rain." The first verse is so clear a picture that children often want to illustrate it. The cozy feeling in the second verse is heightened by the rainy sound of that next-to-the-last line, with its humming *n*'s and *ing*'s:

From *Take Sky* by David McCord. Illustrated by Henry B. Kane. Copyright © 1961, 1962 by David McCord. By permission of Little, Brown and Co.

City Rain[30]

Rain in the city!
  I love to see it fall
Slantwise where the buildings crowd
  Red brick and all.
Streets of shiny wetness
  Where the taxis go,
With people and umbrellas all
  Bobbing to and fro.

Rain in the city!
  I love to hear it drip
When I am cosy in my room
  Snug as any ship,
With toys spread on the table,
  With a picture book or two,
And the rain like a rumbling tune that sings
  Through everything I do.

Rachel Field's poetry never attains the power and sureness of her best prose, but the complete absence of artificiality or juvenile cuteness in these poems commends them to both children and adults.

David McCord

Far and Few
Take Sky
Away and Ago

Speaking at a conference on children's literature, David McCord gave as one of his rules for writing for children:

First, just be a child before you grow up and let nothing interfere with the process. Write it all out of yourself and for yourself. . . . Next, never take the phrase "writing verse for children" seriously. If you write for them you are lost. Ask your brain's computer what you know about a child's mind. The answer is zero.[31]

McCord first began writing verse at fifteen, encouraged, he believes, by two solitary years on an Oregon ranch. *Far and Few*, his first book for children, opens with a poem about "Joe," the greedy squirrel who keeps the birds waiting. It closes with "Fred," an intrepid flying squirrel, the original glider. Children and adults who feed birds will recognize both these characters. Here is

Joe[32]

We feed the birds in winter,
And outside in the snow
We have a tray of many seeds
For many birds of many breeds
And one gray squirrel named Joe.
But Joe comes early,
Joe comes late,
And all the birds
Must stand and wait.
And waiting there for Joe to go
Is pretty cold work in the snow.

Other small beasts are presented—bats, grasshoppers, a snail, starfish, and an especially convincing crowd of crows "spilling from a tree." For sheer nonsense, "Five Chants,"

30. "City Rain" copyright 1926 by Doubleday & Company, Inc. from the book *Taxis and Toadstools* by Rachel Field. Reprinted by permission of Doubleday & Company, Inc. and World's Work Ltd.

31. From David McCord's "Poetry for Children," in *A Critical Approach to Children's Literature*, ed. by Sara Innis Fenwick. University of Chicago Press, 1967, p. 53.

32. "Joe" by David McCord from *One at a Time* (British title: *Mr. Bidery's Spidery Garden*) by David McCord. Copyright 1952 by David McCord. Reprinted by permission of Little, Brown and Company and George G. Harrap & Company Limited.

"Who Wants a Birthday?" and "Isabel Jones & Curabel Lee" are fun. Children under six like to roll the onomatopoetic refrains of "Song of the Train" and "The Pickety Fence" on their tongues. But it takes a perceptive older child to appreciate "The White Ships," "The Shell," "The Starfish," and "The Star in the Pail."

Take Sky, McCord's second book of verse for children, is on the whole more completely humorous than *Far and Few*. His "Write Me a Verse" should appeal to youngsters wrestling with verse forms. In these poems couplets, quatrains, limericks, and triolets are amusingly defined and illustrated. However, there is also much entertainment in this book for the youngest children. In "Sing Song," "Three Signs of Spring," "Sally Lun Lundy," and many other verses, McCord has a wonderful time playing with the sounds of words. He also makes many clever uses of dialogue. The poems in *Away and Ago* are also light and sunny; in this collection he writes about parties, balloons, baseball, and holidays, and in "Like You As It" he plays with words. In 1978, his poems for children were published in a collection entitled *One at a Time*. The poet savors language, but he holds it—like the master craftsman he is—firmly in check.

Harry Behn
The Golden Hive
The Wizard in the Well

Harry Behn has written both prose and poetry for children, and has translated Japanese haiku with precise and delicate sensitivity in *Cricket Songs* and *More Cricket Songs*, both of which are illustrated by reproductions of paintings by Japanese artists.

In his book on poetry, *Chrysalis*, Behn points out that children see a world in every least little thing, and his poems explore with an ever-fresh awareness children's delight in little things about them. *The Golden Hive* is for older readers and includes some fine lyric poems, of which "The Painted Desert" and "Summer" are particularly evocative. His other small books of verse, decorated by the author, speak to young children, five to nine, with lyric charm and unusual variety. There are a few nonsense jingles like "Mr. Pyme," "Dr. Windikin," "Shopping Spree," and the lively "Tea Party."

There are many verses about the child's play world, both real and imaginative. "The New Little Boy" is refreshingly antisocial. "Picnic by the Sea" is a child's view of the queer grownups who sit sunning themselves when there are so many wonders to be explored. "Hallowe'en" is a particularly shivery celebration of that favorite holiday and is delightful for verse choirs to speak for their own pleasure or for an appreciative audience.

Behn's unique contribution is found in those poems where he is helping the child to look at everyday experiences with the eyes of the spirit. Notice the philosophy in

Others[33]

Even though it's raining
I don't wish it wouldn't.
That would be like saying
I think it shouldn't.
I'd rather be out playing
Than sitting hours and hours
Watching rain falling
In drips and drops and showers,
But what about the robins?
What about the flowers?

Read aloud "Early Awake," "Trees," "Spring," "Spring Rain," "The Little Hill," "Lesson," and you will feel the reassurance, the acceptance, and the happy peace that emanate from these and many other poems.

Stephen Vincent Benét
Rosemary Carr Benét
A Book of Americans

Stephen Vincent Benét, a member of a famous family of writers, published his first book of verse while he was a student at Yale University. Twice winner of the Pulitzer Prize for poetry, Benét is probably best known for his epic poem about the Civil War, *John Brown's Body*. With his wife, Rosemary, he wrote *A Book of Americans*, in which popular figures in American history are described in moods ranging from the nonsensical to the deeply serious. "Pilgrims and Puritans," a humorous presentation of the two sides of these colonists, reads in part:

33. "Others." From *The Wizard in the Well*, © copyright 1956 by Harry Behn. Reprinted by permission of Harcourt Brace Jovanovich, Inc.

Pilgrims and Puritans[34]

The Pilgrims and the Puritans
Were English to the bone
But didn't like the English Church
And wished to have their own
And so, at last, they sailed away
To settle Massachusetts Bay.

The stony fields, the cruel sea
They met with resolution
And so developed, finally,
An iron constitution
And, as a punishment for sinners,
Invented boiled New England dinners.

Children like "Captain Kidd," "Peregrine White and Virginia Dare," and the larruping "Theodore Roosevelt." These are genuinely funny. The poem about the Wright brothers is particularly appreciated today by nine- and ten-year-olds for its humorous account of a momentous event in human history.

This is not great poetry, but it gives the reader a series of vivid portraits of some great Americans, written with vigor and simplicity. It can be a delightful addition to the study of the lives of these Americans or of periods in American history.

Langston Hughes

Don't You Turn Back

Langston Hughes began writing verse while he was in high school and later joined the New York group of black writers of the Harlem Renaissance movement. Much of his poetry is in a spirit of racial pride and protest. The poem "I, Too" is in many anthologies, including Lee Bennett Hopkins's selection of Hughes's poems for children, *Don't You Turn Back:*

I, Too, Sing America[35]

I am the darker brother.
They send me to eat in the kitchen
When company comes,
But I laugh,
And eat well,
And grow strong.

Tomorrow,
I'll be at the table
When company comes.
Nobody'll dare
Say to me,

"Eat in the kitchen,"
Then.

Besides,
They'll see how beautiful I am
And be ashamed—

I, too, am America.

Although many of his poems speak for and about black people, Hughes also wrote poetry that speaks for all humankind.

Silence[36]

I catch the pattern
Of your silence
Before you speak.

I do not need
To hear a word.

In your silence
Every tone I seek
Is heard.

These are both serious poems, but there is an ironic humor in much of Hughes's writing, both poetry and prose. Although he wrote several books for children (on jazz, on Africa, on black heroes), his poetry was not created for them. They have, however, overruled him and claimed his poetry for their own. Children enjoy its candor, its humor, and the melodic style that is often reminiscent of ballads and the blues. His last book, published after his death, is *Black Misery*, a series of pithy sentences that are a bitter comment on what a black child faces in our society.

David Littlejohn says of Langston Hughes:

By moulding his verse always on the sounds of Negro talk, the rhythms of Negro music, by retaining his own keen honesty and directness, his poetic sense and ironic intelligence, he has maintained through four decades a readable newness distinctly his own.[37]

34. From *A Book of Americans* by Rosemary and Stephen Vincent Benét. Holt, Rinehart & Winston, Inc. Copyright 1933 by Rosemary and Stephen Vincent Benét. Copyright renewed © 1961 by Rosemary Carr Benét. Reprinted by permission of Brandt & Brandt Literary Agents Inc.

35. "I Too" Copyright 1926 by Alfred A. Knopf, Inc. and renewed 1954 by Langston Hughes. Reprinted from *Selected Poems of Langston Hughes*, by permission of Alfred A. Knopf, Inc.

36. "Silence," from *Fields of Wonder* by Langston Hughes. Copyright 1947 by Langston Hughes. Reprinted by permission of Alfred A. Knopf, Inc.

37. David Littlejohn, *Black on White; A Critical Survey of Writing by American Negroes.* Viking, 1969 (originally published in 1966 by Grossman).

Aileen Fisher

Going Barefoot
Do Bears Have Mothers, Too?
Out in the Dark and Daylight

Aileen Fisher sold her first verses to *Child Life Magazine* while working in Chicago. Yearning to return to the outdoors, she decided to buy a one-way ticket to Colorado, and there she has stayed, writing poetry about the wild creatures she loves. She has also written some excellent biographies and several collections of plays, and has published many books of poetry. Her topics cover the seasons, children's pets, nature as the child encounters it.

With *Going Barefoot* Fisher attained a new freedom of verse patterns, a lighter, gayer touch, and a melodic line that makes this book a delight to read aloud either at one sitting or in parts day by day. It begins with the boy's question—

From *Don't You Turn Back,* by Langston Hughes, illustrated by Ann Grifalconi. Illustration copyright © 1969 by Ann Grifalconi. Reprinted by permission of Alfred A. Knopf, Inc.

How soon
how soon
is a morning in June,
a sunny morning or afternoon
in the wonderful month
of the Barefoot Moon?[38]

Then the young philosopher observes that rabbits go barefoot all year round, so do raccoons, bees, cats, deer, and other creatures, while he must suffer the handicap of socks, shoes, and even galoshes. At last comes the day when he and his mother consult the calendar and the narrative reaches a triumphant conclusion—

June![38]

The day is warm
and a breeze is blowing,
the sky is blue
and its eye is glowing,
and everything's new
and green and growing . . .

My shoes are off
and my socks are showing . . .

My socks are off . . .

Do you know how I'm going?
    BAREFOOT!

This is free and melodic and as full of movement as the restless child waiting for the big day of emancipation from shoes. The poetry about the rabbits, the kangaroos, and other creatures may be read and enjoyed separately or enjoyed as part of the whole. Adrienne Adams' illustrations in full color, with authentic paw prints adorning the end pages, add enchantment to this delightful book.

Out in the Dark and the Daylight is a more varied collection than most of Fisher's books, permeated by imagery and insight, and, as in "The First Day of School," often poignant.

The First Day of School [39]

Peter is often the first one up.
He's always the fastest eater.
But today he toys with his plate and cup . . .
it's the first day of school for Peter.

38. "How soon" and "June." From *Going Barefoot* by Aileen Fisher. Text copyright © 1960 by Aileen Fisher. By permission of Thomas Y. Crowell, Publishers.

39. Text of "The First Day of School" from OUT IN THE DARK AND DAYLIGHT by Aileen Fisher. Text copyright © 1980 by Aileen Fisher. By permission of Harper & Row, Publishers, Inc.

Peter is always the first one dressed.
He's faster than I, and neater.
But today he's certainly second-best . . .
it's the first day of school for Peter.

Peter looks down at his sweater cuff,
and his voice begins to teeter:
"Mom . . . is it hard? Will I know enough?"
It's the first day of school for Peter.

The autumnal *Where Does Everyone Go?* is not quite so exhilarating but exceedingly pleasant to hear and look at. *Up, Up the Mountain* and *In the Middle of the Night* are lyric comments on the beauties of nature; *Feathered Ones and Furry* and *But Ostriches . . .* communicate with humor an affection for animals and an appreciation of the beauty of nature. The poems in *Do Bears Have Mothers, Too?* are addressed to young animals by their mothers; fresh and breezy, they are permeated with fond maternal pride.

Theodore Roethke

I Am! Says the Lamb
Dirty Dinky and Other Creatures

Theodore Roethke received many awards and honors for his poetry, including Guggenheim and Ford Foundation Fellowships, the Pulitzer Prize in 1954, and the National Book Award posthumously in 1965.

Some of his poems are included in anthologies for young people, but *I Am! Says the Lamb* and *Dirty Dinky* are the only collections that can be enjoyed as a whole by children. The rhythm and the sharp imagery appeal to children, who enjoy the poet's wit and his occasional pithy bluntness. Roethke wrote with an ebullience and humor that are especially appealing in such nonsense poems as "The Kitty-Cat Bird." That some of his other poems can be enjoyed by children is obvious on reading

The Bat[40]

By day the bat is cousin to the mouse.
He likes the attic of an aging house.

His fingers make a hat about his head.
His pulse beat is so slow we think him dead.

He loops in crazy figures half the night
Among the trees that face the corner light.

But when he brushes up against a screen
We are afraid of what our eyes have seen:

For something is amiss or out of place
When mice with wings can wear a human face.

It is interesting to compare this poem with "Man and Bat" by D. H. Lawrence and with the poem that begins, "A bat is born . . ." in Randall Jarrell's *The Bat-Poet*.

Lilian Moore

I Thought I Heard the City
See My Lovely Poison Ivy

Lilian Moore decided, in her capacity as an editor, that writers often use too many words. This knowledge and her years of experience as a specialist in reading problems have influenced her poetry, which is simple and direct, yet fluent and witty in a way that younger children can comprehend and appreciate.

Moore has written several stories for children and compiled some poetry anthologies, but it is her own poetry that makes a unique contribution. Children respond to the humor and incongruity of the lighthearted poems in *See My Lovely Poison Ivy*, especially those in which there is a surprising turn, as there is in

Bedtime Stories[41]

"Tell me a story,"
Says Witch's Child.

"About the Beast
So fierce and wild.

About a Ghost
That shrieks and groans.

A Skeleton
That rattles bones.

About a Monster
Crawly-creepy.

Something nice
To make me sleepy."

Hilda Conkling

Poems by a Little Girl
Shoes of the Wind

That a little girl living much in the company of her poet-mother should begin "talking" her own poems is not surprising, but the quality of Hilda Conkling's poems *is*. They are beautiful both in ideas and in expression.

When Hilda was ten years old, *Poems by a Little Girl* was published with a laudatory introduction by the poet Amy Lowell. Hilda's mother said the poems often came when they were walking or just conversing. They stand exactly as the child spoke them. When Hilda was twelve, her second book, *Shoes of the Wind*, was published (selections from the two books have been published under the title *Silverhorn*). After her second book, there were no more poems from Hilda so far as we can discover. Speculations as to why she ceased writing are beside the point. Our concern is with these poems that have important qualities for children.

First of all, their lack of rhyme is sometimes an asset. The time always comes when children are obsessed with rhyming everything and calling it poetry; then it is a good thing to read them some of young Hilda's verses and say, "Here is poetry written by a little girl. It has no rhyme. Why do you suppose it is called poetry?" That question puzzles some children, but eventually they arrive at certain unmistakably poetic qualities in these unrhymed stanzas. "She *sees* things good," one child said after hearing "Moon Song." Another child, hearing "Chickadee" and "Red Rooster," thought the poet remembered how things *sounded*. Eventually, they discover that it is the fresh or different way in which she tells something with just a few words that makes these little verses different from prose. For instance:

Tree-toad is a leaf-gray shadow
That sings.
Tree-toad is never seen
Unless a star squeezes through the leaves,
Or a moth looks sharply at a gray branch.[42]

Hilda Conkling's free style is, then, a salutary antidote for the rhyming passion when it produces only doggerel and seems to handicap the development of original observation and expression. Her limitation for children is that she is predominantly descriptive. She is chiefly concerned with finding the precise words that tell how something looked or felt or appealed to her imagination. While many of her verses contain remarkably fine and discriminating observations, too much of this kind of detailed description overwhelms children.

John Ciardi

I Met a Man
You Read to Me, I'll Read to You
The King Who Saved Himself from Being Saved

John Ciardi has for a number of years been active as a teacher, lecturer, critic, and writer. Much of his poetry for both adults and children has a brisk candor. In his poetry for children, though, the humor and nonsense soften a forthrightness that is sometimes tart. Many of his poems are satirical comments on the reprehensible behavior of children, a vein most appre-

---

41. "Bedtime Stories" from *See My Lovely Poison Ivy* by Lilian Moore. Text copyright © 1975 by Lilian Moore. Used by permission of Atheneum Publishers.

42. From "Tree-Toad" from *Summer-Day Song* by Hilda Conkling. Copyright 1920, renewed 1948 by Hilda Conkling. Reprinted by permission of Random House, Inc.

ciated by the sophisticated reader. However, the topics he develops are usually fresh and original, as, for example, "How to Tell the Top of a Hill," "The River Is a Piece of the Sky," "The Reason for the Pelican." And when he chooses a familiar subject like "Halloween," he treats it freshly, so that it is unlike any other Halloween poem ever written—dramatic and weird, and a brain-tickler for the oldest and best readers.

The omission of words in "Summer Song" makes a good language game.

Summer Song[43]

By the sand between my toes,
By the waves behind my ears,
By the sunburn on my nose,
By the little salty tears
That make rainbows in the sun
When I squeeze my eyes and run,
By the way the seagulls screech,
Guess where I am? At the. . . . .!
By the way the children shout
Guess what happened? School is . . . !
By the way I sing this song
Guess if summer lasts too long?
You must answer Right or. . . . .!

One of Ciardi's interesting experiments in verse for children is *I Met a Man,* written with a controlled vocabulary of some four hundred words. It was planned as a first book for his own child to read and it moves from easy to more difficult in both words and content. "Poetry," the author says, "is especially well designed to lead the child to such recognition [of new words] for rhyme and pattern are always important clues."

Ciardi continued his experiment with a limited vocabulary in *You Read to Me, I'll Read to You,* in which he alternates a poem the child is supposed to read with one for the adult to read, unrestricted by word lists. These, too, are clever verses. In *The King Who Saved Himself from Being Saved,* Ciardi tells an amusing and pointed story that spoofs the stereotypical hero who insists on improving a situation with which everyone

else concerned is perfectly content. This narrative poem is illustrated by Edward Gorey, whose elegant grotesquerie is admirably suited to Ciardi's wit.

Kaye Starbird

A Snail's a Failure Socially
The Pheasant on Route Seven

Kaye Starbird wrote verses as a child and she had poems published in magazines while she was still in college. She has written both satirical verse and serious poetry for adults. In her writing for children she uses a conversational tone and sees everyday experiences from the child's point of view.

Her poems present a child voicing his or her honest opinions or questions about the bugs, beasts, people, and ideas he or she encounters. The poems about the kitten in the mailbox, the toad that needed a baby-sitter, the naughty imaginary sprite who takes over the body of a child who is misbehaving—these and many others are inventive and skillfully composed.

With each book, Kaye Starbird has grown as a poet. Her verse patterns are more deft, her moods more varied. Compare, for example, the humor of the first of the following poems with the nostalgic thoughtfulness with which the second, "One Leaf," begins.

A Snail's a Failure Socially[44]

A snail's a failure socially,
Which means you very seldom see
A crowd of happy, laughing snails
Collected all at once.
The reason's this: when asked to dine
A snail could answer "Yes" or "Fine,"
But if he lived a field away
The trip would take him months.

In short, the most excited snail,
Though pleased to hit the party trail,
Could promptly tidy up and take
A shortcut through the clover;
But asked to Easter luncheon—say—
And getting there Columbus Day,
There'd be at least an even chance
He'd find the party over.

One Leaf[45]

At least a month away from the autumn season
I saw a leaf from the maple break and fall,
Fluttering down for no apparent reason
One windless day when nothing else moved at all.

43. "Summer Song." From the book *The Man Who Sang the Sillies* by John Ciardi. Copyright, ©, 1961, by John Ciardi. Reprinted by permission of J. B. Lippincott Company.

44. "A Snail's a Failure Socially." From the book *A Snail's a Failure Socially* by Kaye Starbird. Copyright © 1966 by Kaye Starbird. Reprinted by permission of Paul R. Reynolds, Inc., 12 East 41st Street, New York, N.Y. 10017.

45. "One Leaf." From the book *The Pheasant on Route Seven* by Kaye Starbird. Copyright, ©, 1968, by Kaye Starbird. Reprinted by permission of J. B. Lippincott Company.

Eve Merriam

Finding a Poem
There Is No Rhyme for Silver
It Doesn't Always Have to Rhyme

Eve Merriam is a teacher of creative writing as well as a writer of prose and poetry for adults and for children. Her first book of poetry for adults, *Family Circle*, won the Yale Series of Younger Poets prize.

Merriam's verse is varied in form, inventive, and often humorous. It usually speaks directly to the child's experience and is especially appealing to the reader who enjoys word-play. Her essay on "Writing a Poem," in *Finding a Poem*, describes the poet's search for the exact word or phrase to express and illuminate her meaning. Both this essay and the chapter entitled " 'I,' Says the Poem" in Nancy Larrick's *Somebody Turned on a Tap in These Kids* are good reading for anyone working with children.

Some notion of the range of her poetry can be seen in two contrasting poems:

Landscape[46]

What will you find at the edge of the world?
A footprint,
a feather,
desert sand swirled?
A tree of ice,
a rain of stars,
or a junkyard of cars?

What will there be at the rim of the world?
A mollusc,
a mammal,
a new creature's birth?
Eternal sunrise,
immortal sleep,
or cars piled up in a rusty heap?

Ping-Pong[46]

Chitchat
wigwag
rickrack
zigzag

knickknack
gewgaw

riffraff
seesaw

crisscross
flip-flop
ding-dong
tiptop

singsong
mishmash
King Kong
*   bong.*

"Landscape" has the provocative imagery and the concern with today's problems that are typical of Eve Merriam's poetry and are qualities that she encourages in the writing of her students. The intensity of her protest against social ills is most clearly seen in *The Inner City Mother Goose*, a collection of angry poems written for adults but relished by many young people.

"Ping-Pong" is a good example of the way she uses words for aural effect; bouncy and rhythmic, the poem evokes the patterned clicking of the game's sound. In *There Is No Rhyme for Silver* and *It Doesn't Always Have to Rhyme*, Merriam—like David McCord—uses poems as illustrations of such literary devices as cliché, homonym, limerick, onomatopoeia, simile, and metaphor.

Gwendolyn Brooks

Bronzeville Boys and Girls

Gwendolyn Brooks's first poem was published when she was thirteen; in 1949 she won the annual prize given by *Poetry* magazine, and in 1950 she received the Pulitzer Prize for Poetry, never before awarded to a black writer.

In all her poetry there is a concern for racial and personal identity. Dan Jaffe says,

The label "Black poetry" ignores Gwen Brooks' ability to speak as a hunchbacked girl, a male preacher, a white spokesman, in varying voices all clearly her own . . . it forgets that though Gwen Brooks learns from Langston Hughes, she also learns from T. S. Eliot; and that she must be more than a replica of either or both.[47]

Her poems for and about children, *Bronzeville Boys and Girls*, speak for any child of any race. Each of the poems is named for a boy or girl. They show a rare sensitivity to the child's inner life—the wonderments, hurts, and sense of make-believe and play. Here are two in contrasting mood.

46. "Landscape" and "Ping-Pong" by Eve Merriam from *Finding a Poem*. Copyright © 1970 by Eve Merriam. Reprinted by permission of Atheneum Publishers, and Eve Merriam c/o International Famous Agency.

47. "Gwendolyn Brooks: An Appreciation from the White Suburbs," by Dan Jaffe. From *The Black American Writer*, v. 2, ed. by Christopher Bigsby (Everett/Edwards, 1969).

Viewpoint

Gwendolyn Brooks has always been committed and lyrical and relevant. Before it was fashionable, she was tone deep in blackness. In the fifties, she was writing poems about Emmett Till and Little Rock and the black boys and girls who came North looking for the Promised Land and found concrete deserts. In fact, she has always written about the sounds and sights and flavors of the black community. Her poems are distinguished by a bittersweet lyricism and an overwhelming concreteness. . . . Her poems celebrate the truth of her life. They celebrate the truth of blackness, which is also the truth of man.—From *To Gwen with Love* edited by Patricia L. Brown, Don L. Lee, and Francis Ward. Johnson Publishing Co., Chicago, 1971, pp. 3, 1.

Cynthia in the Snow[48]

It SUSHES.
It hushes
The loudness in the road.
It flitter-twitters,
And laughs away from me.
It laughs a lovely whiteness,
And whitely whirs away,
To be
Some otherwhere,
Still white as milk or shirts.
So beautiful it hurts.

Vern[48]

When walking in a tiny rain
Across the vacant lot,
A pup's a good companion—
If a pup you've got.

And when you've had a scold,
And no one loves you very,
And you cannot be merry,
A pup will let you look at him,
And even let you hold
His little wiggly warmness—

And let you snuggle down beside.
Nor mock the tears you have to hide.

William Jay Smith

Laughing Time
Boy Blue's Book of Beasts
Mr. Smith and Other Nonsense

William Jay Smith won, among other honors, the Young Poets' Prize of *Poetry* magazine in 1945. He has served as Consultant in Poetry to the Library of Congress, and has written poetry for children as well as poetry and criticism for adults. The verses in *Laughing Time* are not too subtle for very young children and not too simple for the sevens and for the adults who must, perforce, read them aloud.

Children enjoy the idea behind "The Toaster."

> A silver-scaled Dragon with jaws flaming red
> Sits at my elbow and toasts my bread.
> I hand him fat slices, and then, one by one,
> He hands them back when he sees they are done.[49]

Boy Blue's Book of Beasts is equally good nonsense about animals wild and tame—considerably wilder in verse form! There is "a tough Kangaroo named Hopalong Brown/Boxed all the badmen out of town" and "Trim my whis-

Illustration by Ronni Solbert from *Bronzeville Boys and Girls* by Gwendolyn Brooks. Copyright © 1956 by Gwendolyn Brooks Blakely. By permission of Harper & Row, Publishers, Inc.

---

48. "Cynthia in the Snow" and "Vern" from *Bronzeville Boys and Girls* by Gwendolyn Brooks. Copyright © 1956 by Gwendolyn Brooks Blakely. Reprinted by permission of Harper & Row, Publishers.

49. "The Toaster" from *Laughing Time*, published in 1955 by Atlantic-Little, Brown, copyright ©, 1953, 1955 by William Jay Smith. Reprinted by permission of William Jay Smith.

kers! Bless my soul!/Here comes a big brown one-eyed Mole." "A long-haired Yak" in a barber's chair presents a problem and so does a little Raccoon who wants to be something else. All the verses are cleverly written. Smith's *Typewriter Town* is less successful, but it is good to discover a writer of poetry for adults who starts his own children with the musical inventions of nonsense verse. William Jay Smith is also co-editor with Louise Bogan of an excellent anthology, *Golden Journey: Poems for Young People;* and with Virginia Haviland of an annotated bibliography, *Children and Poetry,* which includes a good listing of poetry anthologies.

Myra Cohn Livingston

Whispers and Other Poems
A Crazy Flight and Other Poems

Myra Cohn Livingston was interested in writing and music throughout all her school years, finally abandoning her music study to become a writer and teacher. As a teacher of creative writing, she feels very strongly about the paramount importance of free expression. As she has said in "What the Heart Knows Today":

Happily, we are no longer concerned with those who copy patterns or fill in blanks; the beginning acceptance of blank verse, free verse, haiku has helped somewhat to break the rhyme barrier, but we have a long way to go before we can succeed in recognizing that the tools of poetry are not poetry.[50]

Nevertheless, her own mastery of rhyme and meter makes it clear that she herself is in command of the tools of poetry. Most of her books of verse deal with the sensory experiences, activities, and imaginings of young children.

Whispers[51]

Whispers
  tickle through your ear
  telling things you like to hear.
Whispers
  are as soft as skin
  letting little words curl in.
Whispers
  come so they can blow
  secrets others never know.

Although *A Crazy Flight and Other Poems* is for children eight to eleven, there are no age bar-

Illustration by Jacqueline Chwast. Reproduced from *Wide Awake and Other Poems,* © 1959, by Myra Cohn Livingston, by permission of Harcourt Brace Jovanovich, Inc.

riers to the enjoyment of poetry, and many of Livingston's selections may please both the read-aloud audience and adults. A recognition of changing speech patterns can be observed in "The Sun Is Stuck":[52]

The sun is stuck.
I mean, it won't move.
I mean it's hot, man, and we need a red-hot poker to
  pry it loose,
Give it a good shove and roll it across the sky
And make it go down
So we can be cool,
Man.

Livingston has also edited an anthology for children, *Listen, Children, Listen,* and an excellent anthology for adolescent poetry lovers—*A Tune Beyond Us*—which includes many poems from other languages.

Here, then, are some of the poets who have written joyously and seriously for children. There are of course many other poets whose work is cherished by children, such as Dennis

---

50. "What the Heart Knows Today" by Myra Cohn Livingston. From *Somebody Turned on a Tap in These Kids,* ed. by Nancy Larrick. Delacorte, 1971, p. 11.

51. "Whispers" from *Whispers and Other Poems.* Copyright © 1958 by Myra Cohn Livingston. Reprinted by permission of McIntosh and Otis, Inc.

52. "The Sun Is Stuck" from *A Crazy Flight and Other Poems* by Myra Cohn Livingston. Copyright © 1969 by Myra Cohn Livingston. Reprinted by permission of McIntosh and Otis, Inc.

Lee or Karla Kuskin, whose gay, simple verses appeal to younger children, or Mary O'Neill, whose *Hailstones and Halibut Bones* is a happy experiment with words and colors, associating colors with objects, moods, and feelings, or Valerie Worth, in whose *Small Poems* and *More Small Poems* the free but disciplined verse has both vigor and delicacy. Most anthologies include one or more of the poems of James Tippett, E. V. Rieu, James Reeves, William Allingham, Frances Frost, Vachel Lindsay, Sara Teasdale, and Rose Fyleman. With the flourishing of new black poets, older boys and girls

Viewpoint

Poetry isn't simply a semantic affair, either; it isn't just a matter of words with dictionary meanings. It is made of much more: a complex architecture of semantic and nonsemantic effects, which convert everyday, externally recognizable material into something greater, rather as stone and metal and wood are converted by architecture into Durham Cathedral, the great mosque at Mecca, or the Daibutsu at Kamakura—all different yet all religious statements expressive of multiple and profound meanings. There is a philosophy, a way of thinking, behind the architecture, which gives the buildings a meaning extending beyond anything contained within the material they are built of. The buildings mean more in themselves than they represent or are made of. And we can know this, not only by hearing someone tell us what they mean, but by walking inside and round them and experiencing them. Which means using head, heart, and senses. We can do just the same with poetry.

Children need to be given this idea about poetry (about all literature, actually, but about poetry most of all) as early as possible. Strangely enough, nursery rhymes start to communicate it; and nonsense verse adds another layer by playing about with the possibilities created when conventional rules of language are broken (which is why children laugh at it). But between these two forms and the major work of the poetic heritage lies a puddingy morass of specially composed verse for children which diminishes the idea of poetry into a sort of corrupt telegram: messages couched in rhyme and rumpety-rump rhythm from which has been drained all the challenge of poetic artifice. Children like such stuff for the same reasons that they like candy floss; and if they are never faced with anything else, the real meat of poetry, they grow up with rotten teeth and no stomach for anything that needs chewing.— Aidan Chambers, "Letter from England: Inside Poetry," *Horn Book Magazine*, June 1979. Copyright © 1979 by Aidan Chambers. Reprinted by permission of the author.

read with interest some of the earlier writers like Paul Laurence Dunbar and Countee Cullen. They enjoy the sharp imagery and the patterns that challenge readers in *Poems to Solve* and *More Poems to Solve*, by May Swenson. The bibliography at the end of this chapter reflects children's interest in modern poetry. It includes some excellent general anthologies and a selection of subject anthologies.

Not all of the poets discussed in this chapter and listed in the bibliography have been gifted with lyric genius, but each one has made a contribution which serves to underscore the fact that *children like poetry*. If the lesser of our poets are at first more popular with children than our major poets, it is probably because they are direct and clear; they choose subjects children can understand easily, and they treat the subject briefly and cheerfully. These are standards we must respect in our choice of verse for children. We must remember, too, that they may turn away from obscurity in a poem just as many adults do; that they will endure length usually only in narrative verse that is swift-moving and exciting; and that in general they shun long descriptions. So lyric poets who catch their favor generally do so with poetry that is brief and gay, or markedly melodious. And of course many young people prefer the poetry that speaks to the problems and issues of today.

The poetry in Randall Jarrell's fantasy *The Bat-Poet* is graceful and perceptive, but no more so than the creative musing of the little brown bat who, disappointed at the criticism of his poetry, says, "The trouble isn't making poems, the trouble's finding somebody that will listen to them."[53] Children are listening. They are listening to older poets and younger ones, to poetry of all peoples the world over, to poems that make them laugh and cry and question and see or feel things they have never seen or felt before.

Adult References[54]

ARNSTEIN, FLORA. *Children Write Poetry: A Creative Approach.*
AUSLANDER, JOSEPH, and FRANK ERNEST HILL. *The Winged Horse: The Story of Poets and Their Poetry.*
BEHN, HARRY. *Chrysalis: Concerning Children and Poetry.*
BREWTON, JOHN E. and SARA W., comps. *Index to Children's Poetry.*
CIARDI, JOHN, and MILLER WILLIAMS. *How Does a Poem Mean?*

53. Randall Jarrell, *The Bat-Poet*, Macmillan, 1967, p. 15.
54. Complete bibliographic data are provided in Appendix B.

DREW, ELIZABETH, and GEORGE CONNOR. *Discovering Modern Poetry.*

EASTMAN, MAX. *The Enjoyment of Poetry.*

ESBENSEN, BARBARA JUSTER. *A Celebration of Bees: Helping Children Write Poetry.*

HAVILAND, VIRGINIA, and WILLIAM JAY SMITH, comps. *Children and Poetry: A Selective Annotated Bibliography.*

HILLYER, ROBERT. *In Pursuit of Poetry.*

HOPKINS, LEE BENNETT. *Let Them Be Themselves.*

HUBER, MIRIAM BLANTON. *Story and Verse for Children.*

HUGHES, TED. *Poetry Is.*

KOCH, KENNETH. *Rose, Where Did You Get That Red?*

———. *Wishes, Lies, and Dreams: Teaching Children to Write Poetry.*

LARRICK, NAN Y., ed. *Somebody Turned on a Tap in These Kids.*

LIVINGSTON, MYRA COHN. *When You Are Alone/It Keeps You Capone: An Approach to Creative Writing with Children.*

PAINTER, HELEN. *Poetry and Children.*

RIBNER, IRVING, and HARRY MORRIS. *Poetry: A Critical and Historical Introduction.*

SANDBURG, CARL, ed. *The American Songbag.*

SANDERS, THOMAS E. *The Discovery of Poetry.*

SHAPIRO, JON, ed. *Using Literature & Poetry Affectively.* Part 3, "Using Poetry."

SHAW, JOHN MACKAY. *Childhood in Poetry: A Catalogue.*

SMITH, DOROTHY, and EVA ANDREWS, comps. *Subject Index to Poetry for Children and Young People, 1957–1975.*

TERRY, ANN. *Children's Poetry Preferences: A National Survey of Upper Elementary Grades.*

WITUCKE, VIRGINIA. *Poetry in the Elementary School.*

Children's Books: Anthologies

There are so many good anthologies of poetry for children that it is not possible to list them all here. The following are especially useful for reasons the text or the notes make clear.

In the following bibliography these symbols have been used to identify books about a particular religious or ethnic group:

§ Black
★ Chicano or Puerto Rican
☆ Native American
● Religious minority

§ ABDUL, RAOUL, ed. *The Magic of Black Poetry*, ill. by Dane Burr. Dodd, 1972. Includes poems from many countries. 11 up

ADAMS, ADRIENNE, comp. *Poetry of Earth*, ill. by author. Scribner's, 1972. Discriminating, and good for reading aloud to younger children.   8–10

§ ADOFF, ARNOLD, ed. *Black Out Loud*, ill. by Alvin Hollingsworth. Macmillan, 1970.   11–14

§ ———, ed. *Celebrations: A New Anthology of Black American Poetry.* Follett, 1977.   10 up

———. *City in All Directions*, ill. by Donald Carrick. Macmillan, 1969.   12 up

§ ———. *I Am the Darker Brother*, ill. by Benny Andrews. Macmillan, 1968.   11 up

———. *it is the poem singing into your eyes: anthology of new young poets.* Harper, 1971.   10 up

§ ———, ed. *My Black Me: A Beginning Book on Black Poetry.* Dutton, 1974.   8–11

§ ———, ed. *The Poetry of Black America: An Anthology of the 20th Century.* Harper, 1973.   12 up

ALDAN, DAISY, comp. *Poems from India*, ill. by Joseph Low. T. Crowell, 1969. A collection of poems ranging from ancient times to the present, conservative and idealistic, on the whole.   14 up

§ ALLEN, SAMUEL, ed. *Poems from Africa*, ill. by Romare Bearden. T. Crowell, 1973. Broad in geographical and chronological scope.   12 up

ARBUTHNOT, MAY HILL, and SHELTON L. ROOT, JR., eds. *Time for Poetry*, ill. by Arthur Paul, 3rd gen. ed. Scott, Foresman, 1968. There are more than seven hundred poems in this newest edition of a favorite collection, ranging from *Mother Goose* to T. S. Eliot. The discussion of reading poetry to children and using poetry in verse choirs and the notes throughout the text are invaluable for adults.   4–14

ASSOCIATION FOR CHILDHOOD EDUCATION, LITERATURE COMMITTEE. *Sung Under the Silver Umbrella*, ill. by Dorothy Lathrop. Macmillan, 1935, 1962. A small collection of choice poetry, including selections from the Bible, modern poems, nonsense verse, and Japanese haiku.   4–9

★●§ BARON, VIRGINIA, ed. *Here I Am! An Anthology of Poems Written by Young People in Some of America's Minority Groups*, ill. by Emily Arnold McCully. Dutton, 1969.   8–11

———, ed. *The Seasons of Time: Tanka Poetry of Ancient Japan*, ill. by Yasuhide Kobashi. Dial, 1968.   11 up

BEHN, HARRY, tr. *Cricket Songs: Japanese Haiku*, with pictures selected from Sesshu and other Japanese masters. Harcourt, 1964.   10 up

———, tr. *More Cricket Songs*, ill. with pictures by Japanese masters. Harcourt, 1971.   10 up

☆ BELTING, NATALIA MAREE, comp. *Our Fathers Had Powerful Songs*, ill. by Laszlo Kubinyi. Dutton, 1974. Nine poems from American and Canadian Indian tribes.   9–12

☆ ———, comp. *Whirlwind Is a Ghost Dancing*, ill. by Leo and Diane Dillon. Dutton, 1974. Chiefly poems of creation or natural phenomena from North American Indian tribes.   9 up

☆ BIERHORST, JOHN, ed. *In the Trail of the Wind*, ill. Farrar, 1971.   12 up

BLISHEN, EDWARD, comp. *Oxford Book of Poetry for Children*, ill. by Brian Wildsmith. Watts, 1963. An excellent anthology covering a wide variety of subjects and styles with superb illustrations.   9–12

BOGAN, LOUISE, and WILLIAM JAY SMITH, eds. *The Golden Journey: Poems for Young People*, ill. by Fritz Kredel. Reilly, 1965.   10–14

☆ BRANDON, WILLIAM, ed. *The Magic World: American Indian Songs and Poems.* Morrow, 1971.   11 up

BREWTON, SARA and JOHN, comps. *Birthday Candles Burning Bright: A Treasury of Birthday Poetry*, ill. by Vera Bock. Macmillan, 1960. A delightful anthology of poems arranged by age groups, illustrating the general fun of birthdays and including a choice selection of Christmas poems.   5 up

———, comps. *Laughable Limericks*, ill. by Ingrid Fetz. T. Crowell, 1965.   9 up

———, comps. *Of Quarks, Quasars, and Other Quirks: Quizzical Poems for the Supersonic Age*, ill. by Quentin Blake. T. Crowell, 1977. A diverse selection of poems of our time: pointed, funny, and containing much trenchant commentary.   10 up

———, comps. *Sing a Song of Seasons*, ill. by Vera Bock. Macmillan, 1955. Poems of school days and vacation time.   6–12

☆ CLYMER, THEODORE, ed. *Four Corners of the Sky: Poems, Chants, and Oratory*, ill. by Marc Brown. Little, 1975. Poems of Native American cultures.   10 up

COLE, WILLIAM, comp. *An Arkful of Animals: Poems for the Very Young*, ill. by Lynn Munsinger. Houghton, 1978.   8–10

———, ed. *Beastly Boys and Ghastly Girls*, ill. by Tomi Ungerer. World, 1964. Varied and humorous.   10–12

———, ed. *The Birds and the Beasts Were There*, ill. by Helen Siegl. World, 1963. A choice and lovely collection of verses about animals, birds, and insects, both real and fantastic.   6 up

———, comp. *A Book of Animal Poems*, ill. by Robert Parker. Viking, 1973.   9 up

———, ed. *A Book of Nature Poems*, ill. by Robert Andrew Parker. Viking, 1969.   10–14

———, ed. *Humorous Poetry for Children*, ill. by Ervine Metzl. World, 1955.   8 up

———, ed. *Oh, What Nonsense!* ill. by Tomi Ungerer. Viking, 1966.   9–11

———, comp. *Pick Me Up: A Book of Short Short Poems*. Macmillan, 1972. Two hundred brief poems.   9 up

———, comp. *Poems from Ireland*, ill. by William Stobbs. T. Crowell, 1972. Old and new material.   12 up

———, comp. *Poems from Italy*. T. Crowell, 1972. A bilingual anthology.   12 up

———, ed. *Poems of Magic and Spells*, ill. by Peggy Bacon. World, 1960. Goblins and ghosts, witches and other magical creatures are highlighted in a novel and attractive anthology.   9–13

———, ed. *The Poet's Tales: A New Book of Story Poems*, ill. by Charles Keeping. World, 1971. From folk ballads to sophisticated modern poems.   10–14

COLUM, PADRAIC, ed. *Roofs of Gold: Poems to Read Aloud*. Macmillan, 1964. The editor's favorites from Shakespeare to Dylan Thomas.   11–15

DE FOREST, CHARLOTTE B., ad. *The Prancing Pony: Nursery Rhymes from Japan*, adapted into English verse for children, ill. by Keiko Hida. Walker, 1968.   3–7

DE LA MARE, WALTER, ed. *Come Hither*, 3rd ed., ill. by Warren Chappell. Knopf, 1957.   12 up

———, ed. *Tom Tiddler's Ground*, ill. by Margery Gill. Knopf, 1962. First American edition of a choice compilation of verses for younger children. De la Mare's perceptive notes distinguish his anthologies.   9 up

§ DOOB, LEONARD, ed. *A Crocodile Has Me by the Leg: African Poems*, ill. by Solomon Irein Wangboje. Walker, 1967.   9–14

DOWNIE, MARY, and BARBARA ROBERTSON, comps. *The Wind Has Wings: Poems from Canada*, ill. by Elizabeth Cleaver. Walck, 1968.   9–12

DUNNING, STEPHEN, EDWARD LUEDERS, and HUGH SMITH, comps. *Reflections on a Gift of Watermelon Pickle*. Scott, Foresman, 1967.   11 up

———, comps. *Some Haystacks Don't Even Have Any Needle*, ill. Scott, Foresman, 1969. A splendid collection of poems complemented by reproductions of modern art in full color.   11 up

EATON, ANNE THAXTER, comp. *Welcome Christmas!* ill. by Valenti Angelo. Viking, 1955. A garland of some fifty Christmas poems, chosen with exquisite taste and given decorations of fitting beauty.   all ages

FLEMING, ALICE, comp. *America Is Not All Traffic Lights: Poems of the Midwest*, ill. with photos. Little, 1976.   10 up

———, comp. *Hosannah the Home Run! Poems About Sports*. Little, 1972.   10 up

FOSTER, JOHN, comp. *A First Poetry Book*, ill. by Chris Orr and others. Oxford, 1980. A small but discriminating selection is nicely gauged for primary-grade readers.   7–9

FOWKE, EDITH, comp. *Ring Around the Moon*, ill. by Judith Gwyn Brown. Prentice, 1977. A compilation of riddles, rhymes, rounds, and songs.   8–10

FUJIKAWA, GYO, comp. *A Child's Book of Poems*, ill. by comp. Grosset, 1969. A profusely and attractively illustrated collection of poems, standard fare. Selections are not grouped or arranged.   3–7

GREGORY, HORACE, and MARYA ZATURENSKA, eds. *The Crystal Cabinet*, ill. by Diana Bloomfield. Holt, 1962. A refreshingly original anthology of lyric poetry, wide in range, from Chinese translations to poems by Edith Sitwell.   12 up

HANNUM, SARA, and JOHN TERRY CHASE, comps. *The Wind Is Round*, ill. by Ron Bowen. Atheneum, 1970.   10 up

HANNUM, SARA, and GWENDOLYN REED, comps. *Lean Out of the Window: An Anthology of Modern Poetry*, ill. by Ragna Tischler. Atheneum, 1965.   10–14

§ HAYDEN, ROBERT, ed. *Kaleidoscope: Poems by American Negro Poets*. Harcourt, 1967.   13 up

HILL, HELEN, and AGNES PERKINS, comps. *New Coasts and Strange Harbors: Discovering Poems*, ill. by Clare Romano and John Ross. T. Crowell, 1974. Chiefly mid-twentieth-century poets.   12 up

HOPKINS, LEE BENNETT, comp. *City Talk*, ill. with photos by Roy Aranella. Knopf, 1970.   7–9

———, comp. *Good Morning to You, Valentine*, ill. by Tomie de Paola. Harcourt, 1976. A useful collection of lighthearted poems.   7–10

———, comp. *I Think I Saw a Snail: Young Poems for City Seasons*, ill. by Harold James. Crown, 1969. A selection of poems (four or five for each season) by accepted authors. A few are not particularly city poems.   5–8

☆ HOUSTON, JAMES, ed. *Songs of the Dream People*, ill. by author. Atheneum, 1972. Chants and poems from North American Eskimo and Indian songs.   9 up

HOWARD, CORALIE, comp. *Lyric Poems*, ill. by Mel Fowler. Watts, 1968.   11–14

● *I Never Saw Another Butterfly*. McGraw, 1964.   7–12

JANECZKO, PAUL. *Postcard Poems: A Collection of Poetry for Sharing*. Bradbury, 1979. A very pleasant, very personal choice of poems short enough to be used on a postcard.   10 up

☆ JONES, HETTIE, ed. *The Trees Stand Shining: Poetry of the North American Indians*, ill. by Robert Andrew Parker. Dial, 1971.   8–11

★§ JORDAN, JUNE, and TERRI BUSH, comps. *The Voice of the Children*. Holt, 1970.   10 up

LARRICK, NANCY, comp. *Crazy To Be Alive in Such a Strange World: Poems About People*, ill. with photos. Evans, 1977. Not unusual for the newness of the included poems but for the loving appreciation of the variety and complexity of humankind that permeates it.   10 up

———, ed. *Green Is Like a Meadow of Grass*, ill. by Kelly Oechsli. Garrard, 1968.   5–9

§ ———, ed. *I Heard a Scream in the Streets: Poems by Young People in the City*, ill. with photos by students. Evans, 1970.   10 up

§ ———, ed. *On City Streets*, ill. with photos by David Sagarin. Evans, 1968.   10–14

———, comp. *Room for Me and a Mountain Lion: Poetry of Open Space*. Evans, 1974.   10 up

LEWIS, RICHARD, ed. *I Breathe a New Song: Poems of the Eskimo*, ill. by Oonark. Simon, 1971. Poems that reflect the Eskimo's life and closeness to nature.   9 up

———, ed. *In a Spring Garden*, ill. by Ezra Jack Keats. Dial, 1965.   5–9

———, ed. *Miracles*. Simon, 1966.   all ages

———, ed. *The Moment of Wonder: A Collection of Chinese and Japanese Poetry*, ill. with paintings by Chinese and Japanese masters. Dial, 1964.   all ages

———, ed. *Muse of the Round Sky: Lyric Poetry of Ancient Greece*, tr. by Willis Barnstone and others. Simon, 1969.   8 up

☆ ———, ed. *Out of the Earth I Sing: Poetry and Songs of Primitive Peoples of the World.* Norton, 1968. 8 up

———, ed. *There Are Two Lives: Poems by Children of Japan,* tr. by Haruna Kimura. Simon, 1970. 8–10

———, ed. *The Wind and the Rain,* ill. with photos by Helen Buttfield. Simon, 1968. 8–10

LIVINGSTON, MYRA COHN, ed. *Callooh! Callay! Holiday Poems for Young Readers,* ill. by Janet Stevens. Atheneum, 1978. A fine holiday smorgasbord with a wide range of sources and a high standard in the included selections. 9–11

———, ed. *Listen, Children, Listen,* ill. by Trina Schart Hyman. Atheneum, 1972. 5–8

———. *O Frabjous Day! Poetry for Holidays and Special Occasions.* Atheneum, 1977. 11 up

———, ed. *One Little Room, an Everywhere,* ill. by Antonio Frasconi. Atheneum, 1975. Love poems from a dozen countries, from Biblical times to today. 11 up

———, ed. *Poems of Christmas.* Atheneum, 1980. A broad range of sources has been used for a distinctive anthology with poems grouped under such headings as "The Friendly Beasts" or "Overflowing with Gifts." 10 up

———, ed. *Speak Roughly to Your Little Boy: A Collection of Parodies and Burlesques, Together with the Original Poems, Chosen and Annotated for Young People,* ill. by Joseph Low. Harcourt, 1971. 11 up

———, ed. *A Tune Beyond Us,* ill. by James J. Spanfeller. Harcourt, 1968. 12 up

———. *What a Wonderful Bird the Frog Are: An Assortment of Humorous Poetry and Verse.* Harcourt, 1973. 9 up

LOWER, THELMA, and FREDERICK COGSWELL, comps. *The Enchanted Land: Canadian Poetry for Young Readers.* Gage, 1967. A well-rounded selection. 9–12

McDONALD, GERALD D., comp. *A Way of Knowing: A Collection of Poems for Boys,* ill. by Clare and John Ross. T. Crowell, 1959. A varied and popular collection, representative of modern and traditional poets. Appeals to girls as well as to boys. 10 up

MacKAY, DAVID, comp. *A Flock of Words,* ill. by Margery Gill. Harcourt, 1970. 11 up

METCALF, JOHN, comp. *The Speaking Earth: Canadian Poetry.* Van Nostrand, 1973. 10 up

MOORE, LILIAN, comp. *Go with the Poem.* McGraw, 1979. These selections—most from contemporary poets—are grouped by such subjects as seasons, sports, or the city. 9 up

MOORE, LILIAN, and JUDITH THURMAN, comps. *To See the World Afresh.* Atheneum, 1974. An outstanding anthology. 10 up

MORRISON, LILLIAN, comp. *Best Wishes, Amen: A New Collection of Autograph Verses,* ill. by Loretta Lustig. T. Crowell, 1974. 9–13

———, comp. *The Sidewalk Racer and Other Poems of Sports and Motion.* Lothrop, 1977. 10 up

———, comp. *Touch Blue: Signs and Spells, Love Charms and Chants, Auguries and Old Beliefs, in Rhyme,* ill. by Doris Lee. T. Crowell, 1958. 6–13

———, comp. *Yours till Niagara Falls,* ill. by Marjorie Bauernschmidt. T. Crowell, 1950. 9–13

MORSE, DAVID, ed. *Grandfather Rock.* Delacorte, 1972. 11 up

MORTON, MIRIAM, ed. *A Harvest of Russian Children's Literature.* Univ. of Calif. Pr., 1967. all ages

———, comp. *The Moon Is Like a Silver Sickle: A Celebration of Poetry by Russian Children,* ill. by Eros Keith. Simon, 1972. 9–13

NASH, OGDEN, comp. *I Couldn't Help Laughing.* Lippincott, 1957. 12–14

———, comp. *The Moon Is Shining Bright as Day,* ill. by Rose Shirvanian. Lippincott, 1953. 12–14

NESS, EVALINE, comp. *Amelia Mixed the Mustard and Other Poems,* ill. by comp. Scribner's, 1975. Twenty poems about girls. 8–10

OPIE, IONA and PETER, eds. *The Oxford Book of Children's Verse.* Oxford, 1973. A broad selection, chronologically arranged, also has adult reference use because of the Opies' notes. 5–13

Pandora's Box. Canadian Council of Teachers of English, 1973. Poems written by children for a poetry contest. 8–12

PARKER, ELINOR, comp. *The Singing and the Gold,* ill. by Clare Leighton. T. Crowell, 1962. 12 up

PECK, RICHARD, ed. *Sounds and Silences: Poetry for Now.* Delacorte, 1970. 12 up

PLOTZ, HELEN, comp. *As I Walked Out One Evening: A Book of Ballads.* Greenwillow, 1976. 11 up

———, comp. *The Earth Is the Lord's: Poems of the Spirit.* T. Crowell, 1965. Emphasizes work of contemporary poets. 11 up

☆ ———, comp. *The Gift Outright: America to Her Poets.* Greenwillow, 1977. A judicious balance of traditional favorites and lesser known selections grouped by subject heading. 12 up

———, comp. *Imagination's Other Place: Poems of Science and Mathematics,* ill. by Clare Leighton. T. Crowell, 1955. 12 up

———, comp. *Life Hungers to Abound: Poems of the Family.* Greenwillow, 1978. Another fine anthology representing all aspects of family life, past and present. 12 up

———, comp. *The Marvelous Light; Poets and Poetry.* T. Crowell, 1970. The poets and their work reflect a variety in style and mood. 11 up

———, comp. *Poems from the German,* ill. by Ismar David. T. Crowell, 1967. 11 up

———, comp. *This Powerful Rhyme: A Book of Sonnets.* Greenwillow, 1979. Included selections range from sixteenth-century writing to the work of contemporary poets. Some of the best-known sonnets are omitted to give space to lesser-known poems. 12 up

———, comp. *Untune the Sky: Poems of Music and the Dance.* T. Crowell, 1957. Ranges from reverence to gaiety. 10 up

A Poison Tree and Other Poems, ill. by Mercer Mayer. Scribner's, 1977. 10 up

READ, HERBERT. *This Way, Delight,* ill. by Juliet Kepes. Pantheon, 1956. Includes an excellent essay, "What Is Poetry?" 8–12

REED, GWENDOLYN, comp. *Out of the Ark: An Anthology of Animal Verse,* ill. by Gabriele Margules. Atheneum, 1968. Old favorites and some lesser-known poems representing many centuries. Useful for independent reading or for reading aloud. 10–14

———, comp. *The Talkative Beasts: Myths, Fables and Poems of India,* ill. by Stella Snead. Lothrop, 1969. 8–12

SAUNDERS, DENNIS, comp. *Magic Lights & Streets of Shining Jet,* ill. with photos. Greenwillow, 1978. A pleasant, conservative collection of poems about natural things, some by eminent writers, others by children. 9–12

SCHAEFER, CHARLES, and KATHLEEN MELLOR, comps. *Young Voices: The Poems of Children.* Bruce, 1971. 9–11

SECHRIST, ELIZABETH, comp. *One Thousand Poems for Children,* based on the selections of Roger Ingpen, ill. by Henry C. Pitz. Macrae, 1946. A tremendous collection, excellent for a reference source in school or home. all ages

SEEGER, RUTH CRAWFORD, ed. *Let's Build a Railroad,* ill. by Tom Funk. Dutton, 1954. 4–9

SMITH, WILLIAM JAY, ed. *Poems from France,* ill. by Roger Duvoisin. T. Crowell, 1967. 9 up

SULLY, FRANÇOIS, ed. *We, the Vietnamese: Voices from Vietnam.* Praeger, 1971. Includes poetry. 13 up

SUMMERFIELD, GEOFFREY, ed. *First Voices: The Fourth Book.* Knopf, 1973. In unfortunately small print, this and the three preceding volumes in the series offer a broad range of poems. 10–13

TOWNSEND, JOHN ROWE, comp. *Modern Poetry*, ill. with photos by Barbara Pfeffer. Lippincott, 1974. Poems that reflect the concerns of three decades, 1940s–1960s.   11 up

TRIPP, WALLACE, comp. *A Great Big Ugly Man Came Up and Tied His Horse to Me: A Book of Nonsense Verse*, ill. by comp. Little, 1973.   7–9

UNTERMEYER, LOUIS, ed. *Rainbow in the Sky*, ill. by Reginald Birch. Harcourt, 1935. Untermeyer was one of the first and most indefatigable anthologists for children. This is only one of his many books. They lean heavily on old and familiar poems.   7–12

WALLACE, DAISY, ed. *Fairy Poems*, ill. by Trina Schart Hyman. Holiday, 1980. Several old favorites are among the well-chosen selections in a handsomely-illustrated book.   5–8

———, ed. *Giant Poems*, ill. by Margot Tomes. Holiday, 1978. Fresh, imaginative line drawings add to the humor of a minianthology of poems about ogres and giants.   5–8

———. *Witch Poems*, ill. by Trina Schart Hyman. Holiday, 1976. Eighteen poems illustrated in black and white with a marvelous assortment of witches: comic, ominous, beautiful and gruesome.   8–11

☆ WOOD, NANCY, comp. *Prose and Poetry of the Pueblos*, ill. by Frank Howell. Doubleday, 1974. Thoughts of older members of the Taos.   10 up

☆ ———, comp. *War Cry on a Prayer Feather: Prose and Poetry of the Ute Indians*, ill. with photos. Doubleday, 1979. Poems included here provide an excellent background for understanding the tragic changes that have come to a once-strong people.   12 up

Children's Books:
By Individual Poets

ADOFF, ARNOLD. *Eats*, ill. by Susan Russo. Lothrop, 1979. 9–11

———. *I Am the Running Girl*, ill. by Ronald Himler. Harper, 1979. Evocative and free-flowing, a poem in which a girl speaks of her joy in being a runner.   8–10

———. *Make a Circle Keep Us In*, ill. by Ronald Himler. Delacorte, 1975.   6–8

———. *Tornado!* ill. by Ronald Himler. Delacorte, 1977. A vivid account of a crisis.   8–10

———. *Where Wild Willie*, ill. by Emily Arnold McCully. Harper, 1978. A child is welcomed home after an evening ramble.   5–7

AIKEN, CONRAD. *Cats and Bats and Things with Wings*, ill. by Milton Glaser. Atheneum, 1965.   5–8

ALDIS, DOROTHY. *All Together: A Child's Treasury of Verse*, ill. by Helen D. Jameson. Putnam, 1952. Poems about every-day happenings.   5–9

———. *Quick as a Wink*, ill. by Peggy Westphal. Putnam, 1960. Insect poems.   4–7

ALLINGHAM, WILLIAM. *The Fairy Shoemaker and Other Fairy Poems*, ill. by Boris Artzybasheff. Macmillan, 1928. Poems by Allingham, Walter de la Mare, and Matthew Arnold.   9–12

ARMOUR, RICHARD. *All Sizes and Shapes of Monkeys and Apes*, ill. by Paul Galdone. McGraw, 1970.   5–8

———. *A Dozen Dinosaurs*, ill. by Paul Galdone. McGraw, 1967.   6–9

———. *Odd Old Mammals: Animals After the Dinosaurs*, ill. by Paul Galdone. McGraw, 1968.   9–11

In all his books, Armour's blithe verses give accurate information about animals.

AUSTIN, MARY. *The Children Sing in the Far West*, ill. by Gerald Cassidy. Houghton, 1928.   8–12

BABBITT, NATALIE. *Dick Foote and the Shark*, ill. by author. Farrar, 1967.   9–11

———. *Phoebe's Revolt*, ill. by author. Farrar, 1968.   8–9

BEHN, HARRY. *The Golden Hive*, ill. by author. Harcourt, 1966.   9–12

———. *The Little Hill*, ill. by author. Harcourt, 1949.

———. *Windy Morning*, ill. by author. Harcourt, 1953.

———. *The Wizard in the Well*, ill. by author. Harcourt, 1956.   5–9

BELLOC, HILAIRE. *The Bad Child's Book of Beasts*, ill. by B. T. B. Knopf, 1965. Horrendous nonsense.   6–9

———. *Cautionary Verses*, ill. by B. T. B. and Nicolas Bentley. Knopf, 1959.   9–12

———. *Matilda, Who Told Lies and Was Burned to Death*, ill. by Steven Kellogg. Dial, 1970. A spoof of a Victorian morality tale.   9–12

BENÉT, ROSEMARY, and STEPHEN VINCENT. *A Book of Americans*, rev. ed., ill. by Charles Child. Holt, 1952.   8–14

BLAKE, WILLIAM. *Songs of Innocence*, ill. by Harold Jones. Barnes, 1961. A welcome edition which contains nineteen of Blake's more childlike poems.   6 up

BODECKER, N. M. *Hurry, Hurry, Mary Dear! And Other Nonsense Poems*, ill. by author. Atheneum, 1976. A few of these poems are sheer nonsense, some play with words, all are delightful to read aloud.   7–10

———. *Let's Marry Said the Cherry and Other Nonsense Poems*, ill. by author. Atheneum, 1974. Deft, amusing verses.   9–11

BROOKE, L. LESLIE. *Johnny Crow's Garden*. Warne, 1903.

———. *Johnny Crow's New Garden*. Warne, 1935.

———. *Johnny Crow's Party*. Warne, 1907.   3–7

———. *Leslie Brooke's Children's Books*, 4 vols. Warne, n.d.   5–12

———. *Ring o' Roses* (see Bibliography, Chapter 5).

§ BROOKS, GWENDOLYN. *Bronzeville Boys and Girls*, ill. by Ronni Solbert. Harper, 1956.   7–11

BROWNJOHN, ALAN. *Brownjohn's Beasts*, ill. by Carol Lawson. Scribner's, 1970.   9–11

CARMER, CARL. *The Boy Drummer of Vincennes*, ill. by Seymour Fleishman. Harvey, 1972. A narrative poem about the Illinois frontier in 1779.   8–10

CARROLL, LEWIS. *Alice's Adventures in Wonderland* (see Bibliography, Chapter 9).

———. *The Annotated Snark*, with an introduction and notes by Martin Gardner. Simon, 1962. The full text of Lewis Carroll's great nonsense epic *The Hunting of the Snark* and the original illustrations by Henry Holiday.

———. *Poems of Lewis Carroll*, comp. by Myra Cohn Livingston, ill. by John Tenniel and others. T. Crowell, 1973.   5 up

CAUDILL, REBECCA. *Come Along!* ill. by Ellen Raskin. Holt, 1969. Haiku poems about the year's cycle.   7–9

CAUSLEY, CHARLES. *Figgie Hobbin*, ill. by Trina Schart Hyman. Walker, 1974. Ranges from nonsense verse to poignant or narrative poems.   8–10

CHAUCER, GEOFFREY. *A Taste of Chaucer*, selections from *The Canterbury Tales*, chosen and ed. by Anne Malcolmson, ill. by Enrico Arno. Harcourt, 1964. A careful and discriminating adaptation of—and introduction to—Chaucer. The introduction describes Chaucer and his time.   12 up

CIARDI, JOHN. *The Reason for the Pelican*, ill. by Madeleine Gekiere. Lippincott, 1959.   5–9
Nonsense verses and imaginative poems in this collection launched John Ciardi's books for children. Others are:

———. *I Met a Man*, ill. by Robert Osborn. Houghton, 1961.   4–8

———. *The King Who Saved Himself from Being Saved*, ill. by Edward Gorey. Lippincott, 1965.   9–11

———. *The Man Who Sang the Sillies*, ill. by Edward Gorey. Lippincott, 1961.   4–8

_____. *Scrappy the Pup*, ill. by Jane Miller. Lippincott, 1960.   4–8

_____. *Someone Could Win a Polar Bear*, ill. by Edward Gorey. Lippincott, 1970.   5–8

_____. *You Read to Me, I'll Read to You*, ill. by Edward Gorey. Lippincott, 1962.   5–8

§ CLIFTON, LUCILLE. *Everett Anderson's Nine Month Long*, ill. by Ann Grifalconi. Holt, 1978. Another story poem about the small black boy who is about to be dethroned by a new sibling and is suffering the usual first-child doubts about his mother's love and attention.   5–7

§ _____. *Some of the Days of Everett Anderson*, ill. by Evaline Ness. Holt, 1970.   5–7

COATSWORTH, ELIZABETH. *Away Goes Sally* (see Bibliography, Chapter 12).

_____. *Down Half the World*, ill. by Zena Bernstein. Macmillan, 1968.   12 up

_____. *The Fair American* (see Bibliography, Chapter 12).

_____. *Five Bushel Farm* (see Bibliography, Chapter 12). 11).

_____. *The Sparrow Bush*, ill. by Stefan Martin. Norton, 1966.   9–12

_____. *Summer Green*, ill. by Nora S. Unwin. Macmillan, 1948.   7 up

_____. *Under the Green Willow*, ill. by Janina Domanska. Macmillan, 1971.   5–7

COLE, WILLIAM. *What's Good for a Four-Year-Old?* ill. by Tomi Ungerer. Holt, 1967. One of a series.   3–4

CONKLING, HILDA. *Poems by a Little Girl*. Lippincott, 1920. 6–10

_____. *Shoes of the Wind*. Lippincott, 1922.   6–10

_____. *Silverhorn: The Hilda Conkling Book for Other Children*, ill. by Dorothy P. Lathrop. Stokes, 1924.

CULLEN, COUNTEE. *The Lost Zoo*, ill. by Joseph Low. Follett, 1969.   10 up

DE GASZTOLD, CARMEN BERNOS. *The Creatures' Choir*, tr. by Rumer Godden, ill. by Jean Primrose. Viking, 1965.   11 up

_____. *Prayers from the Ark*, tr. by Rumer Godden. Viking, 1962.   12 up

DE LA MARE, WALTER. *Peacock Pie*, ill. by Barbara Cooney. Knopf, 1961.   6 up

_____. *Rhymes and Verses: Collected Poems for Children*, ill. by Elinore Blaisdell. Holt, 1947.   5 up

DE REGNIERS, BEATRICE SCHENK. *May I Bring a Friend?* ill. by Beni Montresor. Atheneum, 1964. A young child brings his (animal) friends with him when invited to visit the king and queen. Caldecott Medal.   5–7

_____. *Something Special*. ill. by Irene Haas. Harcourt, 1958.   3–6

DICKINSON, EMILY. *Letter to the World*, ed. by Rumer Godden, ill. by Prudence Seward. Macmillan, 1969.

_____. *Poems*, ed. by Helen Plotz, ill. by Robert Kipness. T. Crowell, 1964.

_____. *Poems for Youth*, ed. by Alfred Hampson. Little, 1934.   11 up

FARJEON, ELEANOR. *The Children's Bells*, ill. by Peggy Fortnum. Walck, 1960.

_____. *Eleanor Farjeon's Poems for Children*. Lippincott, 1951.   5–12

_____. *Then There Were Three*, ill. by Isobel and John Morton-Sale. Lippincott, 1965.   4–7

FIELD, EUGENE. *Poems of Childhood*, ill. by Maxfield Parrish. Scribner's, 1904. First published in 1896.   8–12

FIELD, RACHEL. *Poems*, ill. by author. Macmillan, 1957. Favorite selections from this versatile author's earlier books with a few new poems.   6–12

_____. *Taxis and Toadstools*, ill. by author. Doubleday, 1926.   7–12

FINLAY, IAN HAMILTON. *Poems to Hear and See*. Macmillan, 1971.   8–10

FISHER, AILEEN. *But Ostriches . . .*, ill. by Peter Parnall. T. Crowell, 1970.   8–10

_____. *Feathered Ones and Furry*, ill. by Eric Carle. T. Crowell, 1971.   5–8

_____. *Going Barefoot*, ill. by Adrienne Adams. T. Crowell, 1960.   4–8

_____. *In the Middle of the Night*, ill. by Adrienne Adams. T. Crowell, 1965.   5–7

_____. *Listen, Rabbit*, ill. by Symeon Shimin. T. Crowell, 1964.

_____. *Once We Went on a Picnic*, ill. by Tony Chen. T. Crowell, 1975.   4–7

_____. *Out in the Dark and the Daylight*. Harper, 1980.   5–10

_____. *Runny Days, Sunny Days: Merry Verses*, ill. by author. Abelard, 1958.   6–8

_____. *Up, Up the Mountain*, ill. by Gilbert Riswold. T. Crowell, 1968.   8–10

_____. *Where Does Everyone Go?* ill. by Adrienne Adams. T. Crowell, 1961.   4–8

FROMAN, ROBERT. *Street Poems*. McCall, 1971.   8–10

FROST, FRANCES. *The Little Naturalist*, ill. by Kurt Werth. Whittlesey, 1959. Poems of nature.   8–12

_____. *The Little Whistler*, ill. by Roger Duvoisin. Whittlesey, 1949. Poems of the seasons.   8–12

FROST, ROBERT. *Complete Poems of Robert Frost*. Holt, 1949.

_____. *In the Clearing*. Holt, 1962.

_____. *Stopping by Woods on a Snowy Evening*, ill. by Susan Jeffers. Dutton, 1978.   5–9

_____. *You Come Too*, ill. by Thomas W. Nason. Holt, 1959.   11 up

FYLEMAN, ROSE. *Fairies and Chimneys*. Doubleday, 1944. Deftly combines fantasy and reality.   8–10

§ GIOVANNI, NIKKI. *Ego-Tripping and Other Poems for Young People*, ill. by George Ford. Lawrence Hill, 1974. Poems selected by the poet from her published works.   11 up

GREENAWAY, KATE. *Marigold Garden*, ill. by author. Warne, 1910.

_____. *Under the Window*, ill. by author. Warne, 1910.   4–7

HOBERMAN, MARY ANN. *Hello and Good-By*, ill. by Norman Hoberman. Little, 1959.   4–9

HOFFMANN, HEINRICH. *Slovenly Peter, or Pretty Stories and Funny Pictures for Little Children*. Tuttle, 1969.   5–8

HOLMAN, FELICE. *At the Top of My Voice: and Other Poems*, ill. by Edward Gorey. Norton, 1970. Wry, humorous poems.   8–10

_____. *I Hear You Smiling and Other Poems*, ill. by Laszlo Kubinyi. Scribner's, 1973. Free and metric verse; thoughtful and ebullient poems.   8–10

§ HOWARD, VANESSA. *A Screaming Whisper*, photos by J. Pinderhughes. Holt, 1972. One of the most promising young poets writes with depth and insight.   11 up

§ HUGHES, LANGSTON. *Black Misery*, ill. by Arouni. Eriksson, 1969.   10–14

§ _____. *Don't You Turn Back*, selected by Lee Bennett Hopkins, ill. by Ann Grifalconi. Knopf, 1969.   10 up

§ _____. *Fields of Wonder*. Knopf, 1947.   11 up

§ _____. *Selected Poems of Langston Hughes*. Knopf, 1959. 11 up

HUGHES, TED. *Moon-Whales and Other Moon Poems*, ill. by Leonard Baskin. Viking, 1976. In an explosion of fantasy, the eminent British poet envisions a lunatic world; his icy, eerie imagery is echoed by the grotesque, adroit pen and ink drawings of Baskin.   11–14

_____. *Season Songs*, ill. by Leonard Baskin. Viking, 1975. Poems and pictures about the seasons are equally beautiful. A stunning book.   11 up

ISSA. *A Few Flies and I: Haiku by Issa*, ed. by Jean Merrill and Ronni Solbert, from tr. by R. H. Blyth and Nobuyaki Yuasa, ill. by Ronni Solbert. Pantheon, 1969.   8–11

JARRELL, RANDALL. *The Bat-Poet*. Macmillan, 1967. 9–11

§ JOHNSON, JAMES WELDON. *God's Trombones*, ill. by Aaron Douglas. Viking, 1927. Seven verse sermons. Introduction discusses dialect and vernacular. 11 up

§ JORDAN, JUNE. *Who Look at Me*. T. Crowell, 1969. 10 up

KRYLOV, IVAN. *The Fifteen Fables of Krylov*, tr. by Guy Daniels, ill. by David Pascal. Macmillan, 1965. 10–12

KUMIN, MAXINE. *No One Writes a Letter to the Snail*, ill. by Bean Allen. Putnam, 1962. Fresh, bouncy verses. 8–10

KUSKIN, KARLA. *The Bear Who Saw the Spring*, ill. by author. Harper, 1961. A most amiable bear inducts a small dog into the beauties of each of the four seasons. Rhyming text makes this a delightful read-aloud picture book. 5–6

———. *Near the Window Tree*, ill. by author. Harper, 1975. Each poem has a prefatory note, explaining how it came to be written. 7–9

LEAR, EDWARD. *The Complete Nonsense Book*, ed. by Lady Strachey. Dodd, 1942. This volume includes both books referred to in the text: *The Book of Nonsense* and *Nonsense Songs and Stories*. These are available in the original attractive separate volumes from Warne. 8–14

———. *Le Hibou et la Poussiquette*, tr. by Francis Steegmuller, ill. by Barbara Cooney. Little, 1961.

———. *Incidents in the Life of My Uncle Arly*, ill. by Dale Maxey. Follett, 1969.

———. *The Jumblies*, ill. by Edward Gorey. W. R. Scott, 1968.

———. *The Owl and the Pussy Cat*, ill. by William Pène du Bois. Doubleday, 1962.

———. *The Owl and the Pussy-Cat*, ill. by Dale Maxey. Follett, 1970. 5–8

———. *The Quangle-Wangle's Hat*, ill. by Helen Oxenbury. Watts, 1969. 4–8

———. *The Scroobious Pip*, completed by Ogden Nash, ill. by Nancy Ekholm Burkert. Harper, 1968. Stunning, imaginative pictures. 9 up

———. *Whizz!* ill. by Janina Domanska. Macmillan, 1973. 4–6

LEE, DENNIS. *Alligator Pie*, ill. by Frank Newfeld. Houghton, 1975. Bouncy, sunny verse by an eminent Canadian poet. 5–8

———. *Garbage Delight*, ill. by Frank Newfeld. Houghton, 1978. Canadian Book of the Year. 5–9

LENSKI, LOIS. *City Poems*, ill. by author. Walck, 1971. Most of the poems are new; they describe familiar urban sights and activities 5–7

LEWIS, RICHARD, comp. *Of This World: A Poet's Life in Poetry*, ill. with photos by Helen Buttfield. Dial, 1968. 10 up

———. *The Way of Silence: The Prose and Poetry of Basho*. Dial, 1970. 10 up

LINDSAY, VACHEL. *Johnny Appleseed, and Other Poems*, ill. by George Richards. Macmillan, 1928. 10 up

———. *Springfield Town Is Butterfly Town*, ed. by Pierre Dussert, ill. by Vachel Lindsay. Kent State Univ. Pr., 1969. 7–11

LIVINGSTON, MYRA COHN. *A Crazy Flight: And Other Poems*, ill. by James Spanfeller. Harcourt, 1969. 8–11

———. *4-Way Stop and Other Poems*, ill. by James J. Spanfeller. Atheneum, 1976. This collection offers variety, high quality, and handsome illustrations. 10–14

———. *Happy Birthday!* ill. by Erik Blegvad. Harcourt, 1964. 5–7

———. *The Malibu and Other Poems*, ill. by James Spanfeller. Atheneum, 1972. Varied, spontaneous writing. 10–12

———. *O Sliver of Liver and Other Poems*, ill. by Iris Van Rynbach. Atheneum, 1979. A bright variety of verse forms. 10–13

———. *The Way Things Are and Other Poems*, ill. by Jenni Oliver. Atheneum, 1974. Brief poems written from the child's viewpoint. 9–11

———. *Whispers and Other Poems*, ill. by Jacqueline Chwast. Harcourt, 1958. 5–8

———. *Wide Awake and Other Poems*, ill. by Jacqueline Chwast. Harcourt, 1959. 5–8

LOBEL, ARNOLD. *On the Day Peter Stuyvesant Sailed into Town*, ill. by author. Harper, 1971. 5–8

MCCORD, DAVID. *All Day Long: Fifty Rhymes of the Never Was and Always Is*, ill. by Henry B. Kane. Little, 1966. 9–11

———. *Away and Ago*, ill. by Leslie Morrill. Little, 1975. Clever word-play and a sense of fun prevail. 8–11

———. *Every Time I Climb a Tree*, ill. by Marc Simont. Little, 1967. 7–9

———. *Far and Few: Rhymes of the Never Was and Always Is*, ill. by Henry B. Kane. Little, 1952. 5–10

———. *For Me to Say: Rhymes of the Never Was and Always Is*, ill. by Henry B. Kane. Little, 1970. 9–11

———. *One at a Time: His Collected Poems for the Young*, ill. by Henry B. Kane. Little, 1977. 8–13

———. *Take Sky: More Rhymes of the Never Was and Always Is*, ill. by Henry B. Kane. Little, 1962. 8 up

MCGINLEY, PHYLLIS. *All Around the Town* (see Bibliography, Chapter 5).

———. *Mince Pie and Mistletoe*, ill. by Harold Berson. Lippincott, 1961. 6–12

———. *A Wreath of Christmas Legends*, ill. by Leonard Weisgard. Macmillan, 1967. 10–13

☆ MAHER, RAMONA. *Alice Yazzie's Year*, ill. by Stephen Gammell. Coward, 1977. Soft brown and white pictures illustrate a fluid, poetic text that highlights the events of a Navajo girl's eleventh year. 9–12

MERRIAM, EVE. *The Birthday Cow*, ill. by Guy Michel. Knopf, 1978. Brief, brisk word play. 5–8

———. *Catch a Little Rhyme*, ill. by Imero Gobbato. Atheneum, 1966. 5–9

———. *Finding a Poem*, ill. by Seymour Chwast. Atheneum, 1970. 11 up

———. *Independent Voices*, ill. by Arvis Stewart. Atheneum, 1968. 10–12

———. *It Doesn't Always Have to Rhyme*, ill. by Malcolm Spooner. Atheneum, 1964. 10–14

———. *Out Loud*. Atheneum, 1973. Fresh, perceptive, vivid writing. 10–13

———. *There Is No Rhyme for Silver*, ill. by Joseph Schindelman. Atheneum, 1962. Jaunty little verses full of rhythm, nonsense, and child appeal, for the youngest. 5–7

MILNE, A. A. *Now We Are Six*, ill. by Ernest Shepard. Dutton, 1927.

———. *When We Were Very Young*, ill. by Ernest Shepard. Dutton, 1924. These verses were reprinted in 1961, in larger type and more attractive format.

———. *The World of Christopher Robin*, ill. by Ernest Shepard. Dutton, 1958. The complete verses from *Now We Are Six* and *When We Were Very Young* appear in single-volume format with eight new color illustrations. 5–10

MIZUMURA, KAZUE. *I See the Winds*. T. Crowell, 1966. The illustrations vary from attractive to lovely; the poetry ranges from adequate to good. 8–10

MOORE, LILIAN. *I Feel the Same Way*, ill. by Robert Quackenbush. Atheneum, 1967. 6–9

_____. *I Thought I Heard the City*, ill. by Mary J. Dunton. Atheneum, 1969.   8–10

_____. *Sam's Place: Poems from the Country*, ill. by Talivaldis Stubis. Atheneum, 1973.

_____. *See My Lovely Poison Ivy: And Other Verses about Witches, Ghosts and Things*, ill. by Diane Dawson. Atheneum, 1975.   8–10

NASH, OGDEN. *The Cruise of the Aardvark*, ill. by Wendy Watson. Evans, 1967.   7–9

_____. *Custard and Company: Poems by Ogden Nash*, comp. and ill. by Quentin Blake. Little, 1980. Blake's breezy, comic drawings are perfectly appropriate for the inspired lunacy of Nash's wit.   8 up

_____. *Good Intentions*. Little, 1942.   10 up

O'NEILL, MARY. *Hailstones and Halibut Bones*, ill. by Leonard Weisgard. Doubleday, 1961.   6 up

ORGEL, DORIS. *The Good-Byes of Magnus Marmalade*, ill. by Erik Blegvad. Putnam, 1966. Amusing, not-so-fond farewell remarks by a small boy.   8–9

PLATH, SYLVIA. *The Bed Book*, ill. by Emily Arnold McCully. Harper, 1976. No story here, but a happy romp of inventive fancy where beds behave in unexpected ways.   5–7

PRELUTSKY, JACK. *A Gopher in the Garden: And Other Animal Poems*, ill. by Robert Leydenfrost. Macmillan, 1967. 9–10

_____. *Nightmares: Poems To Trouble Your Sleep*, ill. by Arnold Lobel. Greenwillow, 1976. This deliciously awful collection of poems is calculated to evoke simultaneous grins and shudders.   10–14

_____. *Toucans Two*, ill. by José Aruego. Macmillan, 1970. Entertaining light verse.   5–8

RASMUSSEN, KNUD, comp. *Beyond the High Hills: A Book of Eskimo Poems*, ill. by Guy Mary-Rousselière. World, 1961.   7 up

RICHARDS, LAURA E. *Tirra Lirra: Rhymes Old and New*, ill. by Marguerite Davis, foreword by May Hill Arbuthnot. Little, 1955.   5–12

RIEU, E. V. *The Flattered Flying Fish*, ill. by E. H. Shepard. Dutton, 1962. Lovely light verses that savor of Milne and Lewis Carroll and yet have a special quality of their own. There is a tenderness when touching on a child's woes and a happy imaginativeness in the nonsense rhymes.   7–12

RILEY, JAMES WHITCOMB. *The Gobble-uns'll Git You Ef You Don't Watch Out!* ad. from "Little Orphant Annie," ill. by Joel Schick. Lippincott, 1975. The illustrations give new humor to a once-popular poem.   8–9

ROBERTS, ELIZABETH MADOX. *Under the Tree*, ill. by F. D. Bedford. Viking, 1922.   6–10

ROETHKE, THEODORE. *Collected Poems*. Doubleday, 1966. 12 up

_____. *Dirty Dinky and Other Creatures: Poems for Children*, selected by Beatrice Roethke and Stephen Lushington. Doubleday, 1973. Chiefly animal poems, most of them humorous.   8–11

_____. *I Am! Says the Lamb*, ill. by Robert Leydenfrost. Doubleday, 1961.   10 up

ROSSETTI, CHRISTINA. *Goblin Market*, ill. by Arthur Rackham. Watts, 1970.   9 up

_____. *Goblin Market*, ill. by Ellen Raskin. Dutton, 1970.   9 up

_____. *Sing Song*, ill. by Marguerite Davis. Macmillan, 1952.   4–10

RUKEYSER, MURIEL. *Mazes*, ill. with photos by Milton Charles. Simon. 1970.   8–10

SANDBURG, CARL. *Early Moon*, ill. by James Daugherty. Harcourt, 1930.   10–14

_____. *The Sandburg Treasury: Prose and Poetry for Young People*, ill. by Paul Bacon. Harcourt, 1970.   10–14

_____. *Wind Song*, ill. by William A. Smith. Harcourt, 1960. Poems chosen for child appeal cover a wide range of subjects from prayers and people to nature and nonsense.   11–14

SCHWARTZ, DELMORE. *"I Am Cherry Alive," the Little Girl Sang*, ill. by Barbara Cooney. Harper, 1979. Delicate paintings illustrate a poem celebrating the joy of being alive, of being oneself, of being a child.   4–7

SILVERSTEIN, SHEL. *Where the Sidewalk Ends: The Poems and Drawings of Shel Silverstein*. Harper, 1974. Fresh, breezy poetry; much of it has a pointed message for today. 8–11

SMITH, WILLIAM JAY. *Boy Blue's Book of Beasts*, ill. by Juliet Kepes. Little, 1957.   5–9

_____. *Laughing Time*, ill. by Juliet Kepes. Little, 1955. 4 up

_____. *Mr. Smith and Other Nonsense*, ill. by Don Bolognese. Delacorte, 1968.   8–12

_____. *Typewriter Town*. Dutton, 1960.

STARBIRD, KAYE. *The Covered Bridge House*, ill. by Jim Arnosky. Four Winds, 1979. Poems about people, some lyric and some wittily narrative.   9–11

_____. *Don't Ever Cross a Crocodile*, ill. by Kit Dalton. Lippincott, 1963.   5–10

_____. *The Pheasant on Route Seven*, ill. by Victoria de Larrea. Lippincott, 1968.   10–13

_____. *A Snail's a Failure Socially: And Other Poems, Mostly About People*, ill. by Kit Dalton. Lippincott, 1966. 9–11

_____. *Speaking of Cows*, ill. by Rita Fava. Lippincott, 1960.   5–10

STEVENSON, ROBERT LOUIS. *A Child's Garden of Verses*. There are many editions of this classic. These are representative:
Ill. by Jessie Willcox Smith. Scribner's, 1905, 1969. A large book with appealing pictures in soft colors.
Ill. by Tasha Tudor. Walck, 1947. A full edition with pictures in soft pastels using the young Robert Louis himself as the child.
Ill. by Brian Wildsmith. Watts, 1966. The loved and familiar poems are illustrated with the usual Wildsmith riot of color.   5–9

SWENSON, MAY. *More Poems to Solve*. Scribner's, 1971. 10 up

_____. *Poems to Solve*. Scribner's, 1969.   12 up

TAGORE, RABINDRANATH. *Moon, For What Do You Wait?* ed. by Richard Lewis, ill. by Ashley Bryan. Atheneum, 1967.   9 up

TEASDALE, SARA. *Stars To-night*, ill. by Dorothy Lathrop. Macmillan, 1930.   8–12

TIPPETT, JAMES S. *I Live in a City*. Harper, 1924.   5–7

UPDIKE, JOHN. *A Child's Calendar*, ill. by Nancy Ekholm Burkert. Knopf, 1965.   8–10

WATSON, CLYDE. *Catch Me & Kiss Me & Say It Again: Rhymes*, ill. by Wendy Watson. World, 1978.   2–5

_____. *Father Fox's Pennyrhymes*, ill. by Wendy Watson. T. Crowell, 1971.   3–6

WELLES, WINIFRED. *Skipping Along Alone*. Macmillan, 1931. Imaginative poems with a lyric quality.   7–9

WILBUR, RICHARD. *Opposites*, ill. by author. Harcourt, 1973. A series of verses deftly explains opposite terms. 10–12

WORTH, VALERIE. *More Small Poems*, ill. by Natalie Babbitt. Farrar, 1976.   9 up

_____. *Small Poems*, ill. by Natalie Babbitt. Farrar, 1972.   9 up

_____. *Still More Small Poems*, ill. by Natalie Babbitt. Farrar, 1978. Evocative and laser-focused, bringing fresh insights into familiar things.   9 up

Chapter Eleven: Modern Fiction

In the past two decades, realistic fiction has shown more change than any other kind of books for children. Chapter 1 touches on those changes and discusses some of the present-day trends: the increased number of books by and about blacks, native Americans, and Spanish-speaking peoples; the interest in the elderly and the handicapped; the reflections of the feminist movement and other social protest groups. There have been significant changes in the use of frank language and in the treatment of hitherto taboo subjects, and there has been a growing awareness of realistic fiction from other countries, an awareness reflected in the publication of translated books and of United States editions of books published in other English-speaking countries. While some of these books, from our own country or others, cause concern to many adults because of their candid treatment of themes or subjects, many offer excellent writing.

Realistic stories may be just as exciting or humorous or romantic or imaginative as fantasy, but they are always plausible or possible. In a realistic story everything that happens *could* happen. Sometimes the adventures of the hero or heroine may seem rather improbable but still merit the classification of realistic because they are possible. A realistic story is a tale that is convincingly true to life.

Realistic fiction for children includes historical novels (Chapter 12), stories about peoples of other countries, and stories about contemporary life in the United States, the last two categories the major concern of this chapter. Such books help children better understand the problems and issues of their own lives, empathize with other people, and see the complexities of human relationships.

The books discussed in this chapter have been divided into three major groups: books for the youngest children (many of which are also discussed in Chapter 5), books for the middle group, and books for older children. These divisions are not hard and fast, since many children read above their usual reading level when they are interested or may go back to a childhood favorite of their past reading experience. And many adults have found that they can read aloud books intended for children older than those in their audience. The reading levels suggested in the bibliography of this chapter are equally flexible. Besides the three major categories, there are three minor categories: animal stories, sports stories, and mysteries—three of the favorite subject-matter interests of children.

The stories in this chapter are not divided by ethnic or regional groups or by countries. The chapter bibliography, however, is marked so that those who are interested, say, in finding books about black children can do so; and the Subject Matter Index, too, will help readers find such stories.

Criteria for Realistic Stories

How can we evaluate this wealth of realistic fiction for children, when it ranges from picture stories for the youngest to mystery stories and romance for young people? First of all, it may be helpful to review the section in Chapter 3 entitled "Looking Closely at Books," pp. 39–48, and to consider in these books just how effectively setting, point of view, characters, plot, theme, and style are handled. The primary consideration is the power of the story to captivate readers and keep them racing along from page to page, while having sufficient literary distinction to develop children's taste.

Most of this fiction, in addition to telling good stories, satisfies some of children's basic needs. From *One Morning in Maine* to *The Great Gilly Hopkins* there is continual emphasis on winning or holding security. The satisfaction of belonging is very important in *Journey Home* and *Are You There God? It's Me, Margaret*. Loving and being loved is a powerful motive in *The Pinballs* and *Zeely*. Children's love of change and fun is a motivating force in *Henry Huggins* and *Little Eddie*. The need to know is important in *Tom Sawyer, Portrait of Ivan, . . . and now Miguel, Child of the Owl*, and in the mystery tales. The need for competence is a strong motivating force in *Ordinary Jack* and *My Side of the Mountain*, and in many other realistic stories of the past and present.

If these books center on children's basic needs; if they give them increased insight into their own personal problems and social rela-

tionships; if they show that people are more alike than different, more akin to each other than alien; if they convince young readers that they can do something about their lives—have fun and adventures and get things done without any magic other than their own earnest efforts—then they are worthwhile books.

Stories About Minority Groups

No other country in the world has the variety of peoples to be found in the United States. There are such regional groups as the Southern mountain people, the Cajuns, and the migrant groups that follow the crops—picking cotton or beans or strawberries or oranges. Then there are the close-knit communities of immigrants and their descendants making a little Italy or Hungary or Sweden within a larger community. There are groups representing all the major and innumerable minor religious sects, and Americans of every racial background. Since all of these diverse peoples have contributed richly to the life of the nation, it is important that children should meet them vicariously in books in order that they may meet them in person sympathetically and with respect. Children see in books their own images, and if these are distorted or if there is stigma by omission, such self-images are damaged. And it is especially important that the minority group is pictured not as "them" but as "one of us," that the books about children of minority groups show the diversity within the group rather than a stereotype. When there is a need and a response, as there has been for books about black children, there are always the twin specters of the bandwagon book, tailored to fit the need, and of the tract, written with good intent but too burdened by its message to be a good story. Some of these books may be useful temporarily despite their mediocrity, but it is to be hoped that the day will come when there are so many good books for and about every kind of child that we can dismiss those that do not meet all the standards of good literature.

Stories About Children of Other Countries

In early stories about other countries there was a tendency to present the picturesque at the expense of the usual. Readers were given the China of bound feet, the Holland of wooden shoes and lace caps, South America by way of a primitive type of Indian tribe. Some of these faults are still to be found in recently published books (both those written in the United States and those selected for importation from other countries), but such misconceptions are becoming far less common. We must check the information given in such stories against what we know to be true of the present everyday life of people. And we must question any implication that a way of life of people we don't know is queer or quaint rather than simply different. In many of these books the themes are universal, and the stories point up the fact that differences between children of one country and those of another are superficial, based on cultural factors to be valued and preserved rather than on inherent factors.

Books for Younger Children

Our youngest children, anywhere from two years old to seven, seem to have a special need for stories that are as factual and personal as their fingers and toes and the yards and neighborhoods they are beginning to explore.

Forerunners

In the 1920s Lucy Sprague Mitchell called attention to the lack of realistic stories for children under five, and supplied stories centering on the child's own activities, using the child's own language. In 1929 an example of realism for the youngest came from the Swedish. It was a translation of *Pelle's New Suit* (1929), told and illustrated by Elsa Beskow. Text and pictures in color tell how the little boy Pelle needs a new suit. He raises his own lamb and then, for each person who helps him with his suit, he performs some useful service. Finally, for his Sunday best he triumphantly wears his beautiful blue suit.

The most notable of the early followers of Lucy Sprague Mitchell was Margaret Wise Brown, who wrote also under the name of Golden MacDonald. Her *The City Noisy Book* (1939), intended to stimulate the sensory perceptions of young children, was a pioneer and was followed by several more *Noisy* books. Then there was a series contrasting bigness and littleness. The hero of *The Little Fisherman* caught little fish and the big fisherman caught big fish, and so on. Brown's contribution lay chiefly in her sensitive perception of the child's sensory responses to the big, booming confusion of the world.

The books by Margaret Wise Brown launched a torrent of awareness compositions for the young. There were books about night sounds, day smells, wetness, coldness, and colors. By the 1950s it began to look as if we were in for a kind of pernicious anemia of theme and plot, with language experiences in place of sto-

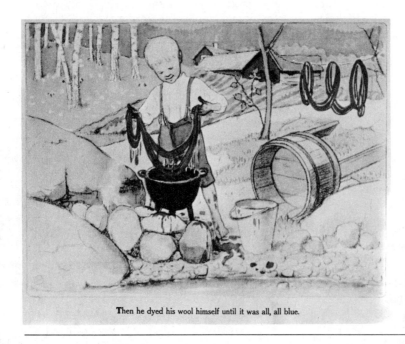

Then he dyed his wool himself until it was all, all blue.

Illustration by Elsa Beskow from *Pelle's New Suit.* Harper & Row, Publishers, 1929. Reprinted by permission of Bonnier Juveniles International, Stockholm. (Original in color) ries and pitter-patter in place of events. These books give children back themselves with little more—no rich entertainment, no additional insight, and no laughter.

Marjorie Flack's *Wait for William* (1935) is a "here and now" story whose whole plot turns on a small boy's struggle to get his shoelaces tied. Any four-year-old can understand and sympathize with William's predicament, and so can adults.

These early examples of realism for the youngest have been followed by a continuing spate of books impressive in their variety, written and illustrated by authors and artists of distinction, and reflecting not only the needs and interests of young children but also the diversity and the changes within our society.

Alvin Tresselt

Hide and Seek Fog
White Snow, Bright Snow

Midway between the awareness and the theme-plot schools of writing for young children lie the picture stories of Alvin Tresselt. Tresselt constructs his stories about weather and nature in simple, rhythmic prose, and with Roger Duvoisin's pictures, they develop a real sense of drama. *Hide and Seek Fog* (1965), for example, describes how the fog affects sea and seaside activities, and *What Did You Leave Behind?* (1978) encourages appreciative observation. These little everyday miracles of the weather are made exciting, something to be watched and enjoyed, never feared. Texts and pictures are full of reassurance and beauty. *White Snow, Bright Snow* won the 1948 Caldecott Medal for Duvoisin.

Edward Ardizzone

The *Little Tim* stories

Even young children need a touch of wildness now and then, which is precisely what the English writer Ardizzone gives them in *Little Tim and the Brave Sea Captain* (1936), his spirited account of Tim's adventures at sea. It all starts with Tim, who plays in and out of boats on the beach. How he becomes a stowaway, learns to be an efficient if reluctant deckhand, and experiences shipwreck makes a thrilling story for the five- to eight-year-olds. Ardizzone's watercolors are as vigorous as his tale. Here is realism for the youngest at its most adventurous

level. Tim's competence and achievements through a series of stories rouse the admiration of his young devotees. Ardizzone's books introduce other heroes, but Tim is the favorite.

Robert McCloskey

Make Way for Ducklings
Time of Wonder

Robert McCloskey was the first artist to win the Caldecott Medal twice, 1942 and 1958. If you look over his picture stories—*Make Way for Ducklings* (1941), *One Morning in Maine* (1952), and *Time of Wonder* (1957)—you discover that they are all built on a theme of reassurance. Children know the ducklings will come safely through their first perilous trip in city traffic because their mother has them in charge. And in that superb book in full color, *Time of Wonder*, the safe, secure world of woods and beach is threatened by the oncoming darkness of a hurricane. How the family prepares for and sur-

Viewpoint

A small child's chief objective intellectually is always to make sense of the immediate world around him. Whilst he might accept some magical fairy story ideas at one stage, these will be rejected later, and the very outsize quality of fairy story imagery makes it easier for the child to recognize that this is a different kind of world, not the same as his at all. But of course there are many other fantasies common to literature at any age that are harder to spot, helping stories to work out so much more conveniently than they generally do in a real life setting, and it is this type of wish-fulfilment that makes adult writers like Alistair MacLean and Ian Fleming so popular. Writing for the young can be full of easy escapism too, and perhaps in some measure should be: children have as much right to fictional flattery and painless, vicarious heroism as any adult. But this should be balanced by other authors more concerned with things as they are. Whilst still being entertained, children can also learn something from these sorts of books that may even help them make better sense of themselves or some of the things they see around them. In doing so, they may also come to realize some of the misperceptions they—or other people—can have about each other.—Nicholas Tucker, "Getting Used to Things as They Are: Nina Bawden as a Children's Novelist." *Children's Literature in Education 13*, 1974, pp. 35–37. Copyright © 1974, APS Publications, Inc. Reprinted by permission of Ward Lock Educational Limited.

He planted himself in the center of the road, raised one hand to stop the traffic, and then beckoned with the other, the way policemen do, for Mrs. Mallard to cross over.

Illustration by Robert McCloskey from *Make Way for Ducklings* by Robert McCloskey. Copyright, 1941, by Robert McCloskey; copyright © renewed 1969 by Robert McCloskey. By permission of the Viking Press, Inc.

vives this menace is so convincingly told and pictured that children feel they too can meet and endure danger. The pictures in the first two books have humor and strength, and some of the paintings in *Time of Wonder* have a breathtaking beauty. (See color section.) McCloskey's books for older children, *Homer Price* (1943) and *Centerburg Tales* (1951), are both written with a humor that has given them enduring popularity.

Carolyn Haywood

"B" is for Betsy
Little Eddie

With the *Betsy* and the *Little Eddie* books of Carolyn Haywood, children progress from the picture story to the illustrated story, with the pictures of secondary importance to the tale. Another mark of increasing maturity is that against a familiar background of family life, the young heroes and heroines move into an ever widening circle of neighborhood and school adventures, camps, and even travel.

"B" Is for Betsy (1939) launched the series of books about the everyday activities of a little girl in suburbia. While the characters in these books remained very close to stereotypes, it was the interpretation of their activities that held the attention of young readers. These gave the child greater self-knowledge, more understanding of other people and experiences, and a greater confidence in approaching their years of growing up. With *Little Eddie* (1947) Carolyn Haywood developed a real boy. Eddie is as earnest as Betsy, but much more alive. *Eddie's Happenings* (1971), *Eddie's Valuable Property* (1975), and *Eddie's Menagerie* (1978) show many signs of Eddie's maturity. These simply written stories have a warmth and a directness that win and hold young readers.

Taro Yashima

Crow Boy

Taro Yashima's striking picture stories are set in his native Japan. *Plenty to Watch* (1954) by Taro and Mitsu Yashima tells of the shops and workers that Japanese children stop to watch as they walk home from school. The stores and the workers may differ from their American counterparts, but the story of children's insatiable curiosity is universal.

Crow Boy (1955), Taro Yashima's third book, was a Caldecott Honor Book and also won the Child Study Award. It has unusual social values as well as pictorial beauty. Crow Boy is a small, silent child who walks to school alone, sits alone, and does not talk. The children call him derisively "Chibi"—tiny boy. But a new schoolmaster discovers that the small outcast walks in from a great distance. He knows where wild potatoes and wild grapes grow, and he knows every call the crows make and can imitate them perfectly. When he does this for the children they call him "Crow Boy" with respect, and he is one of them at last.

Illustration by Taro Yashima from *Crow Boy* by Taro Yashima. Copyright 1955 by Mitsu and Taro Yashima. By permission of the Viking Press, Inc. (Original in color)

Illustration by Gail Owens from *I'll Tell on You* by Joan Lexau. Text Copyright © 1976 by Joan Lexau. Illustrations © 1976 by Gail Owens. Reproduced by permission of the publisher, E.P. Dutton.

Joan Lexau

Olaf Reads
Benjie

Joan Lexau's stories have diversity of style, mood, and subject, but all of them have an understanding of the child's viewpoint, whether they are written for older readers or for children of kindergarten age. Her books for the youngest children are permeated with love and humor.

Olaf Reads (1961) is an amusing tale of a child so enthralled by his new prowess that he takes literally a sign that says "Pull," and finds the whole school responding with a fire drill. In *Benjie* (1964), a very shy black child discovers, when he hunts for his grandmother's lost earring, that it isn't really so hard to talk to people; in *Benjie on His Own* (1970) he learns that he can call on his neighbors for help when his grandmother is ill.

Striped Ice Cream (1968) tells of a child in a working-class family who, tired of hand-me-down dresses from her sisters, is thrilled by a new dress *and* striped ice cream for her birthday. *Me Day* (1971) describes a small boy's joy in seeing his father, who has left home, on his birthday. In *I'll Tell on You* (1976) a girl feels she's not wanted by the coach of her Little League team.

Charlotte Zolotow

Big Sister and Little Sister
The Hating Book
William's Doll

Few writers for small children so empathize with them as does Charlotte Zolotow, whose books—with some exceptions—are really explorations of relationships cast in story form and given vitality by perfected simplicity of style and by the humor and tenderness of the stories. *Big Sister and Little Sister* (1966) is typical of Zolotow's later books, exploring the balances in a one-to-one relationship. *The Hating Book* (1969) describes the ups and downs of friendship. The mother of a fatherless child listens, in *A Father Like That* (1971), to her son's catalog of virtues in his dream-father, who would *never* show off at parent-teacher meetings. *My Grandson Lew* (1974) is a tender story of remembrance, and *Someone New* (1978) a perceptive description of a turning point in childhood. In *William's Doll* (1972), Zolotow shows that little boys as well as little girls may want a doll to play with. Zolotow's understanding of children's emotional needs and problems, and her ability to express them with candor have made her one of the major contemporary writers of realistic books for small children.

Martha Alexander

Out! Out! Out!
The Story Grandmother Told
Sabrina

Tidy, charming little drawings in soft colors add to the appeal of Martha Alexander's realistic stories. In *Out! Out! Out!* (1968) she tells a story without words, the pictures showing the delightful commotion that ensues when a bird flies into the house. In *The Story Grandmother Told* (1969) a bright-faced black child prompts Gramma to tell a favorite tale by telling it herself. *Sabrina* (1971) finds, when she starts nursery school, that other girls like her unusual name. Bonnie, often taken advantage of by her older brother, finds herself on top in *I'll Be the Horse If You'll Play with Me* (1975). In *When the New Baby Comes, I'm Moving Out* (1979) a small boy adjusts to the inevitable. Each story touches on some familiar situation, and the behavior of the children is convincingly natural.

Other Books for Younger Children

The profusion of picture-story books and books for the beginning reader makes it impossible to include every one of the many worthy books that have been published. Lois Lenski, whose regional stories are discussed later in this chapter, pioneered in realism in books for the youngest children. The series that began with *The Little Auto* (1934) and the later series about Debby and Davy are direct and simple, with no wasted words. The engagingly homely children and deft humor of Harriet Pincus's illustrations add immeasurably to the bland text of Lore Segal's *Tell Me a Mitzi*, which has three stories of family life—as it really is. One tale is totally and amusingly improbable, but Mitzi and her little brother Jacob remain sturdily childlike.

Grandparents are a part of life for younger

Illustration by Harriet Pincus. Reprinted with the permission of Farrar, Straus and Giroux, Inc. From *Tell Me a Mitzi* by Lore Segal, pictures by Harriet Pincus, copyright © 1970 by Harriet Pincus. (Original in color)

children. *Kevin's Grandma* (1975) by Barbara Williams shows both a sedate and an adventurous model. *Grandpa's Maria* (1974) by Hans-Eric Hellberg tells of Maria's dependence on Grandpa for stability when her mother goes to a rest home. The locale is Sweden, but the need for security is universal. Max Lundgren, in *Matt's Grandfather* (1972), another story set in Sweden, draws a realistic picture of a small child's acceptance of a senile grandparent.

Death is also a part of life, and an increasing number of books even for younger children show this. In *The Two of Them* (1979) by Aliki, a grandfather is remembered by his granddaughter. Tomie de Paola's *Nana Upstairs and Nana Downstairs* (1973) shows Tommy's adjustment to one death, and, much later, to another. The difficulty of adjusting to the death of a sibling, and particularly of a twin, is honestly portrayed in *My Twin Sister Erika* (1976), a story by Ilse-Margret Vogel, set in Germany.

Another part of life often passed by earlier was the handicapped or mentally retarded child. In *He's My Brother* (1974) by Joe Lasker, a child who is simply slow is the center of interest. *Howie Helps Himself* (1974) by Joan Fassler describes Howie's final triumph of being able to manipulate his wheelchair by himself.

Of the trends observable in contemporary publishing, the increased number of books about black children is a major one. Some of the books are simply affirmations of pride, like Ann McGovern's *Black Is Beautiful* (1969), and some are stories of black children showing competence, as in Janice Udry's *Mary Jo's Grandmother* (1970); overcoming jealousy and learning to love, as Robert does in John Steptoe's beautifully illustrated *Stevie* (1969); or as Johnetta does in Lucille Clifton's *My Brother Fine with Me* (1975). Some books show adjustments to crowded living arrangements, as in June Jordan's *New Life: New Room* (1975) or a child seeking quiet in a crowded home, as in Elizabeth Hill's *Evan's Corner* (1967). In some, the theme is one of problems raised by racial prejudice, such as Billy meets in *A New Home for Billy* (1966) by May Justus. In this story, a black family, anxious to move from a tenement to a house in the country, encounters barriers before they find a community that welcomes them.

Ruth Sonneborn's stories are about Puerto Rican children in the United States; they are stories of universal problems and joys, like the

Illustration by Aliki, p. 20. From Aliki, *The Two of Them.* Copyright © 1979 by Aliki Brandenberg. Published by Greenwillow Books. (A Division of William Morrow & Company) (Original in color)

happiness of having the family all together in *Friday Night Is Papa Night* (1970), rather than of difficulties faced because the children are Puerto Rican. *Magdalena* (1971) by Louisa Shotwell is the story of a lively Puerto Rican child and her beloved grandmother. Leo Politi's picture stories focus on American children of various ethnic backgrounds: Mexican-Americans in *Juanita* (1948) and *Three Stalks of Corn* (1976); Chinese in *Moy-Moy* (1960); and Italian in *Little Leo* (1951). In his Caldecott Medal book, *Song of the Swallows* (1949), Politi describes the coming of spring to the mission of Capistrano. There is still a paucity of books about other minority groups for the youngest readers, but this will surely change.

Almost every trend in realistic fiction for older children seems to be followed by a similar trend in books for younger children. Topics that have been hitherto abjured are emerging, as does divorce in Beth Goff's *Where Is Daddy?* (1969).

Although children in the United States are enjoying more books from other countries than ever before, there are fewer picture stories being written about children of other lands. However, the sprightly stories of Françoise, and Ludwig Bemelmans's *Madeline* (1939) are still read and loved. Marie Hall Ets is one of the few authors who writes about Mexican children; her books are discussed in Chapter 6.

Books for the Middle Group

Before examining present-day realistic stories for the middle and older children, we shall review some of the classic realistic stories that have been landmarks in the history of children's literature and that are popular still: *The Adventures of Tom Sawyer* (1876), *Little Women* (1868), *Hans Brinker, or the Silver Skates* (1865), *Heidi* (1884), and *The Secret Garden* (1909).

Forerunners

A century ago, Samuel Clemens (Mark Twain) introduced children to the seamy side of village life in *Tom Sawyer*. At that time, automobiles, superhighways, airplanes, and television had not tied the small towns so intimately to the large cities that there was little difference between the two. There in *Tom Sawyer* was the isolated country town Samuel Clemens himself had grown up in, with respectable churchgoers on one side and the village ne'er-do-wells on the other. Tom was the link between the two groups. By way of his friendship with Huck, the son of the town drunkard, he knew all the shady characters as well as his Aunt Polly's churchgoing friends. He saw a grave robbery and a murder and had other hair-raising adventures. This book gives children excitement, but it is not lurid or sensational. Along with the excitement and the humor, there is a steady emergence of Tom's code: he keeps his word to a friend; he may be scared to death, but he sees things through; in real peril, he protects a weaker person; he uses his head, keeps cool, and keeps trying. This is as good a code today as it ever was.

Louisa May Alcott's *Little Women* deals with a family of four girls of teen age, but it is to preadolescents that this book makes the greatest appeal, because of their interest in what lies just ahead, their first sense of romance, their dream of being grown up. Many young readers still enjoy *Little Women* as their great-great-grandparents did. Here is the first great juvenile novel of family life—a warm, loving family group, struggling with poverty and with indi-

Viewpoint

The only obligation to which in advance we may hold a novel, without incurring the accusation of being arbitrary, is that it be interesting. . . . The ways in which it is at liberty to accomplish this result (of interesting us) strike me as innumerable, and such as can only suffer from being marked out or fenced in by prescription. They are as various as the temperament of man, and they are successful in proportion as they reveal a particular mind, different from others. A novel is in its broadest definition a personal, a direct impression of life: that, to begin with, constitutes its value, which is greater or less according to the intensity of the impression. But there will be no intensity at all, and therefore no value, unless there is freedom to feel and say. The tracing of a line to be followed, of a tone to be taken, of a form to be filled out, is a limitation of that freedom and a suppression of the very thing that we are most curious about.—Henry James, "The Art of Fiction," in *Makers of Literary Criticism* (vol. II), compiled and edited by A. G. George, Asia Publishing House, London, 1967, p. 352.

vidual problems but sustained by an abiding affection for each other and an innocent kind of gaiety that could make its own fun. Not until the Laura Ingalls Wilder series do we again encounter such a picture of a family, and in no one of the Wilder series is each member of the group more distinctly drawn than are the unforgettable Beth, Jo, Meg, and Amy. Here is characterization that makes each girl a real human being—exasperating, lovable, heroic, absurd, delightful.

Hans Brinker, or the Silver Skates by Mary Mapes Dodge and *Heidi*, written in German by Johanna Spyri, a Swiss, and translated into English in 1884, introduced children in the United States and Canada to daily life in other countries through a strong and engaging story, a tradition that has continued. *Hans Brinker, or the Silver Skates* was immediately successful. It was translated into many languages, and the Dutch people accepted it as the best picture of childhood in Holland that had ever been written up until that time.[1] Dodge had become deeply interested in the history of the Dutch republic and had a twofold purpose: to tell a story about the children of Holland and to weave into that story as much of the history and customs of the people as she could.

Heidi uses the most popular of all themes—a

1. Bertha Mahony and Elinor Whitney, comps., *Realms of Gold in Children's Books.* Garden, 1929, p. 611.

variation of Cinderella, the unwanted, neglected child who comes into her own—but there is a convincing quality about *Heidi* which many modern Cinderellas lack. The child is full of the joy of living. She skips and leaps and she falls in love with an apparently grouchy old grandfather, the goats, and the mountains, all with equal vehemence and loyalty. No child who has read and loved *Heidi* will ever enter Switzerland without a feeling of coming home. This is what books about other lands should do for children—leave them feeling forever a part of that country, forever well disposed toward the people. Such stories of other people create no sense of oddity, no feeling of irreconcilable differences, but a desire to know these people so like themselves.

For a long period after *Tom Sawyer, Little Women, Hans Brinker,* and *Heidi* appeared, there was as little substantial realism for older children as there was for the youngest. Frances Hodgson Burnett's *The Secret Garden* did in some measure span the gap between these early books and those realistic stories which are comparatively recent. It has maintained a

Reprinted with permission of Macmillan Publishing Co., from *Call It Courage* by Armstrong Sperry. Copyright 1940 by Macmillan Publishing Co., Inc. renewed 1968 by Armstrong Sperry. Published in the U.K. by The Bodley Head.

following of devoted readers to this very day, telling a fairy tale of unimaginable riches, of children misunderstood and suffering but conquering all. Burnett enjoys describing great wealth and then showing how it often brings neither a normal nor a happy life—very consoling to those without such wealth. The heroine of *The Secret Garden,* Mary, is plain and bad tempered as well as orphaned and neglected. In the huge estate where she is sent to live, Mary discovers a secret garden, a master with a crooked back, and his ailing son, Colin. Martha, the hearty Yorkshire maid, provides a healthy contrast, and Martha's little brother, Dickon, is the very spirit of the earth as is his wise, kind mother, who has love enough for her own brood of twelve and for the poor little rich children besides. Among them, they get the wretched Colin into the secret garden with Mary. Under Dickon's guidance, the children make the garden grow and bloom once more, without realizing that in the process they, too, will grow and bloom.

Armstrong Sperry

Call It Courage

Call It Courage (1940), a Newbery Medal book, is an exciting story about Mafatu, the son of a Polynesian chief, rejected by his people for his cowardice and marooned on a desert island. This island proves to be the sinister shrine of cannibals. Mafatu maintains life, develops all the necessary arts and skills, makes his own weapons and his own canoe, finally escapes the cannibals, and returns home a hero. This book about the conquest of fear can give young readers the courage to face their own fears with a sense of ultimate triumph.

Eleanor Estes

The *Moffat* stories

Within the United States one of the most captivating book families is unquestionably the Moffats, created by Eleanor Estes. There are three of these books—*The Moffats* (1941), *The Middle Moffat* (1942), and *Rufus M.* (1943).

The stories are set in the 1910s, but the characters and their problems are so real and so universal they seem timeless. There is no general theme, no long suspense, and no exciting climax to these books. Each chapter is a complete episode in the life of one of the Moffats.

The ultimate humor in these situations is provided by the artist, Louis Slobodkin. The Moffat tales and Slobodkin's illustrations represent the perfect union of story and pictures—Rufus M. leaping for a deadly catch in a baseball game; Janey viewing the world amiably from an upside-down angle, looking between her own stout legs, head almost on the ground.

Also illustrated by Slobodkin, Estes's *The Hundred Dresses* (1944) is one of the most effective indictments of prejudice in children's literature, and a poignant story told in an easy, natural style. Wanda Petronski is an outsider, poor and ill-clad, who wears the same dress every day. Taunted, she says she has a hundred dresses at home. She does, and she's drawn them all. Her pictures, exhibited at school, win a medal, but Wanda isn't there. A note from her father says they have moved to a place where "No more holler Polack. No more ask why funny name...." Eleanor Estes was awarded the Newbery Medal for *Ginger Pye* (1951), a story about a family that loses its dog and finds him through the kind offices of three-year-old Uncle Benny. The plot in *The Alley* (1964) revolves around burglary, but the book's appeal is in its picture of a small faculty community. In *The Coat-Hanger Christmas Tree* (1973), a child adjusts to her mother's refusal to have a real tree, and in *The Lost Umbrella of Kim Chu* (1978) a nine-year-old resident of New York's Chinatown solves a mystery.

Estes creates real children wrapped up in their own concerns, playing, interacting, paying scant attention to mere adult problems.

Elizabeth Enright

The Saturdays
Gone-Away Lake

Elizabeth Enright had a gift for realism. *The Saturdays* (1941) introduces the four Melendys, ranging in age from six to thirteen, and deals with their $1.60 Saturdays. These are achieved by pooling all their allowances and by permitting one child to use the whole amount for a Saturday, each in turn. The results are often startling and always amusing. *The Four Story Mistake* (1942) and *Then There Were Five* (1944) continue the family activities in the country and lead to the adoption of a country boy.

The Melendy family has been almost superseded by the popular cousins in *Gone-Away Lake* (1957) and its sequel. In the first book, Portia and her cousin Julian discover an abandoned colony of summer cottages near a swamp that was once a lovely, sparkling lake. In the second book, *Return to Gone-Away* (1961), the family makes the joyous decision to restore one of the old houses and live there the year round. Enright's style is so forthright and lively that this unusual setting becomes completely real and the reader shares the family's joy in that final decision.

The Newbery Medal was given to Enright's *Thimble Summer* (1938), a family story set on a Midwestern farm in the midst of a burning drouth. Just as the drouth is broken by a drenching rain, Garnet finds a silver thimble, which she is convinced will bring her a lucky summer.

Enright's children are, like those created by Estes, very real, although somewhat more venturesome.

Marguerite de Angeli

Bright April
Yonie Wondernose
Thee, Hannah!

Bright April (1946) was one of the earliest books to focus on a black child's problems. The youngest in a prosperous, middle-class family, April finds a happy solution to her difficulties with a prejudiced member of her Brownie troop. There are many books for and about black children now, and books that show urban ghetto life, not just comfortable middle-class surroundings, but this was a rarity when it was published. Marguerite de Angeli was also a pioneer in relating stories about the minority groups around her home in Philadelphia. Her stories are slight, but the warm pictures she paints, both with colors and words, of Amish, Quaker, and Pennsylvania Dutch children are important. *Henner's Lydia* (1936), *Skippack School* (1939), *Yonie Wondernose* (1944), and *Thee, Hannah!* (1940) are all pleasant stories about interesting people.

Yonie Wondernose with his wondering is a favorite, especially when, like the hero of the folk tale, his wondering pays off and he proves his courage as well. Particularly appealing, too, is the little Quaker girl in *Thee, Hannah!* who despises her Quaker garb until she finds herself chosen, because of it, to serve a great cause at

Illustration by Louis Slobodkin. Reproduced from *The Middle Moffat* copyright, 1942, 1970, by Eleanor Estes, by permission of Harcourt Brace Jovanovich, Inc. Published in the U.K. by The Bodley Head, London.

the time of the Civil War. The young girl in *Henner's Lydia* can still be seen on countless Amish farms, learning to be like Mother.

Of first importance are de Angeli's illustrations. These are beautiful in color with springtime freshness and innocence. To be sure, her children—whatever their sex, nationality, or disposition—have always the same little heart-shaped faces and wistful beauty, but they have also a skipping gaiety which is natural to childhood.

Lois Lenski

Strawberry Girl

In 1946, when the Newbery Medal was given to Lois Lenski's *Strawberry Girl,* attention was called to a unique series of books about regional groups from all over the United States.

Lois Lenski began her series with *Bayou Suzette* (1943), a story about the French-speaking people in the bayou section of Louisiana. After *Strawberry Girl* of Florida came *Blue Ridge Billy* (1946), about the North Carolina mountain group, and *Judy's Journey* (1947), which followed the crop pickers from California to Florida and

back to New Jersey. There are many more, including *Project Boy* (1954), which is set in a veterans' housing project and *High-Rise Secret* (1966), in a high-rise housing project.

Strawberry Girl (1945) is typical of these books at their best. It is the story of Birdie Boyer's family, newly moved to Florida's backwoods for the purpose of raising small crops of "sweet 'taters," strawberries, oranges, and the like.

The values of this series are to be found in its objective realism and compassion. Young members of disadvantaged families meet families like their own in these regional stories of Lois Lenski's. And they take heart, because always the ups and downs of these hardpressed, courageous people yield a ray of hope. Things are, or give promise of becoming, better. And to the children of more affluent families, these books give a picture of a kind of family love and loyalty that may be new to them.

Beverly Cleary

Henry Huggins
Ramona the Pest
Mitch and Amy

Beverly Cleary's *Henry Huggins* books are pure Americana, from supermarkets to backyard barbecues, delightfully humorous.

The Huggins family is an average group. The parents are sympathetic to Henry's enterprises but not overly indulgent. All the children in the stories are pursuing their own goals with the frustrations usual to children. The first book begins with Henry's determination to keep and support a stray dog he has acquired and named Ribsy. When the original owner of Ribsy turns up and claims his dog, Henry is in a serious spot. He earnestly wants to do the right thing, but he also wants Ribsy. The solution is a masterly piece of diplomacy.

There are several other books about Henry and even one about *Ribsy* (1964). Each book is built around a real struggle on Henry's part and involves some very funny situations before a hard-won success.

There are four delightful books about Henry's nemesis. Ramona is probably the first kindergarten dropout on record in *Ramona the Pest* (1968), having become convinced that the teacher, whom she adores, doesn't love her any

Illustration by Alan Tiegreen, p. 137. From Beverly Cleary, *Ramona and Her Father*. Copyright © 1975, 1977 by Beverly Cleary. Published by William Morrow & Company, Inc. Published in the United Kingdom by Hamish Hamilton Ltd., London.

more. We follow *Ramona the Brave* (1975) to first grade, where she finds the basics boring, but life still worth living, and to her adjustment to Father's loss of a job and Mother's acquiring one in *Ramona and Her Father* (1977) and *Ramona and Her Mother* (1979). A serious problem for many children is presented in a realistic and encouraging way in *Mitch and Amy* (1967). Mitch and Amy are fourth-grade twins, he a slow reader and she a proficient one. They are, except when under attack, very competitive, yet it is Amy that finds the book that starts Mitch on the path to self-motivated reading.

Cleary's characters are real boys and girls, convincingly alive, and the style of the books is correspondingly plain and everyday, but filled with the type of humor that appeals to her young audience.

Meindert DeJong

The Wheel on the School
Journey from Peppermint Street

The Wheel on the School (1954), a tenderly told story which won the Newbery Medal, gives a remarkably detailed picture of life in a Dutch fishing village and also has unusual social values. The story begins in the tiny village school,

when Lina, the only girl, asks, "Do you know about storks?" This leads to more questions, "Why are there no storks in Shora?" and "How can we bring them back?" These two questions launch a series of activities that begins with the six children and the schoolmaster but presently draws into the circle every person in the village.

Although the book is long for its story, it reads aloud wonderfully and can promote many discussions about the people, the lonely land of sea and sky that is Holland, and the wonder of those great birds that fly home all the way from Africa.

Journey from Peppermint Street (1968), which won the National Book Award for Children's Literature, is set in Holland in the early 1900s. Beautifully written, it is the story of a small boy who goes with his grandfather on a long night walk to visit an "inland aunt." The relationship between the old man and the child, the satisfaction at conquering his nervousness in a strange place, and the confidence gained by little Siebren as he meets new people, have a universality that transcends the setting.

Another story set in Holland is *Far Out the Long Canal* (1964). Because the ice has been bad for several years, and he has had a long illness, nine-year-old Moonta is the only child in town who cannot skate. Any reader can sympathize with his embarrassment, his secret struggles, and the alternate teasing and comfort he gets from friends and family. *The House of Sixty Fathers* (1956) is a vividly realistic story, set in China, of a boy who searches for his lost family.

Although DeJong's style is often repetitious and occasionally ponderous, he has the gift of

Illustration by Maurice Sendak from *The Wheel on the School* by Meindert DeJong. Copyright, 1954, by Meindert DeJong. A Newbery Medal Winner. By permission of Harper & Row, Publishers, Inc. Published in the United Kingdom by Lutterworth Press.

wonder and delight. Whatever the outward action of his tales, it is the inner grace of his children and animals that moves readers, young or old. It is not surprising that in 1962 he won the Hans Christian Andersen International Award for his contribution to the world of children's literature.

Natalie Savage Carlson

The Family Under the Bridge
The Happy Orpheline
The Empty Schoolhouse

Some of the gayest stories about Paris are Natalie Carlson's *The Family Under the Bridge* (1958) and her series about the Orphelines. *The Family Under the Bridge* has to do with the post–World War II period in Paris when housing was difficult to find. The hero is an elderly, jaunty hobo named Armand, completely averse to work, family life, and especially "starlings," as he calls children. Armand has found himself a snug corner under an old bridge. So imagine his horror to return there one night and find it occupied by three children. This is the beginning of the end for carefree, soft-hearted Armand. His series of adventures with the starlings are sometimes very funny and sometimes sad, but in the end he finds himself the adopted grandfather of a family. No pathos here, just a determined struggle for a stable, decent way of life.

The Books about the Orphelines reverse the usual pattern of sad, sad orphans hoping to be adopted. These French orphans love their home to the point where their one fear is adoption. When in *The Happy Orpheline* (1957) poor Brigitte is about to be adopted, she knows she must perform a very wicked deed of some kind to prove she isn't fit for adoption. What she does is hilarious and makes a fitting if confused climax to the adventures of the twenty Orphelines who are still twenty strong at the end. *A Brother for the Orphelines* (1959) and *A Pet for the Orphelines* (1962) are fun, too, and follow the pattern of the others. Each chapter is a complete adventure in the course of which young readers see French life from a child's view.

Emma, who tells the story of *The Empty Schoolhouse* (1965), has dropped out of school but is proud of her bright little sister Lullah. Lullah is black, her friend Oralee white, and they are delighted that there is going to be an integrated school in their Louisiana parish.

Illustration by Garth Williams from *The Family Under The Bridge* by Natalie Savage Carlson. Pictures copyright © 1958 by Garth Williams. By permission of Harper & Row, Publishers, Inc.

There is trouble, though, and parents keep their children away. When Lullah is hurt in a racial incident, the rift between her and Oralee grows—but it is healed, and the episode shocks some parents into a reversal of their decision. The first-person narrative gives consistency and immediacy to an honest and thoughtful story.

Ann Aurelia and Dorothy (1968) is another book about an interracial friendship, and *Marchers for the Dream* (1969) tells about an eleven-year-old girl who goes with her grandmother to Washington to join the Poor People's March. Whatever their settings, Carlson's stories have realistic characters who often display a gentle humor.

Keith Robertson

The *Henry Reed* stories

Children need books also which demonstrate that life is not always earnest, that it can in fact be highly entertaining. *Henry Reed, Inc.* (1958) is such a book. It is Henry's private journal. On a visit to his uncle and aunt who live in the country near Princeton, Henry hears all about the research at that university; so he decides to go into research. He takes over an old barn and paints an enormous sign: HENRY REED, RESEARCH. To the sign, a girl who finds her way into this intellectual domain adds: PURE AND APPLIED. She wants her name added too, but Henry is adamant—she must prove her worth first. Their research activities make this book hilarious reading.

Other Henry Reed stories are direct narrative, equally amusing and often mirroring some new social trend. In *Henry Reed's Big Show* (1970), for example, Henry and Midge put on a rock music festival. These books are highly exaggerated in the pace of their plots, but in every separate episode the activities of the ploymasters Henry and Midge are within the realm of possibility.

Robertson, a versatile author, writes another type of story in *In Search of a Sandhill Crane* (1973). Fifteen-year-old Link spends the summer with an elderly aunt in the Michigan woods, and becomes passionately interested in sandhill cranes. The story is well structured, with a wealth of natural lore, and sympathetic, convincing characters.

Mary Stolz

By the Highway Home
The Noonday Friends
A Wonderful, Terrible Time

Mary Stolz is a prolific author and one of the few authors who write with admirable perception for all ages. In *By the Highway Home* (1971), the death of an older brother, the loss of the father's job, and a subsequent move to a new home create problems of adjustment for a girl of thirteen. A lost job also adds to the tensions in *The Noonday Friends* (1965), in which Franny can see her friend only at lunchtime because Franny must take care of her little brother after school. The story is perceptive in reflecting the way emotions are affected by circumstances and in drawing the relationship between Franny and the small brother who depends on her.

The two friends in *A Wonderful, Terrible Time* (1967) are black girls who go to an interracial summer camp. Sue Ellen is apprehensive; Mady is thrilled and enjoys every moment. Sue Ellen never wants to talk about serious things;

Mady—whose father had been killed in a voter registration drive—does. Integration is not the issue of the book but is one of several problems considered to show the differences in the reactions of the two girls.

The problems a close-knit family faces when one of them—in this case the mother—dies, are honestly and perceptively described in *The Edge of Next Year* (1974). *Lands End* (1973) contrasts life for the only child of staid parents with that of a child from the large, noisy family next door. In *A Dog on Barkham Street* (1960) and *The Bully of Barkham Street* (1963), the same events are considered from different viewpoints.

Stolz brings a special sense of reality to her characters; they are well developed, sympathetically presented, and worth knowing.

Jean Little

Mine for Keeps
Home from Far
Look Through My Window

Born blind, Canadian Jean Little understands the child who is different, and has the ability to spin a good story which makes such differences natural and comprehensible. In *Mine for Keeps* (1962), Sally, who has cerebral palsy, comes home after five years at a school for handicapped children, her apprehension about getting along mixed with self-pity. Through the help of her family and through her own interest in others, Sally gradually overcomes her fears and becomes more independent. The story treats the difficulties of a handicapped child matter-of-factly and emphasizes the point that the family has to adjust to the situation and that each of them makes mistakes. In the sequel, *Spring Begins in March* (1966), Sally smooths the way of her little sister.

In *Home from Far* (1965) Jenny's twin brother Michael is killed, and soon after the accident, Jenny's parents bring two foster children into the home, one named Mike and the same age as Jenny. This is a sensitive study of the attitudes and emotions of children, particularly of Jenny, who at first bitterly resents Mike, and of Mike, who misses his real father.

In *Look Through My Window* (1970) Emily's family takes in four little cousins whose mother is hospitalized. From resentment, Emily moves to love and acceptance, and her horizons are further broadened by a new friend who has one Jewish parent. The discussions between Emily and Kate are candid, those between Emily and her mother tender and sensible, and those between Kate and her father perceptive and honest, as they talk about what it is to be Jewish. In the sequel, *Kate* (1971), the girl moves further to explore her ambivalence and to discover why her father had severed connections with his family. Jean Little has a rare ability to see problems and their ramifications from the viewpoint of the child.

Yoshiko Uchida

The Forever Christmas Tree
The Birthday Visitor

Yoshiko Uchida's versatility is demonstrated by the fact that she has written books for all ages and in several literary styles, from the simplicity of picture story books like *The Forever Christmas Tree* (1963) through the several collections of Japanese folktales cited in the bibliography for Chapter 7, to the historical fiction discussed in Chapter 12. American-born, Uchida was one of the many Nisei who were sent to a relocation center, an experience reflected in several of her books.

The Forever Christmas Tree is set in Japan, where a small boy learns of—and is enthralled by—the Christmas story and the custom of decorating a tree. Since no tree is available, Takashi decorates the pine tree growing at the door of an elderly neighbor's home and finds, to his surprise, that the lonely old man is delighted. The story is tender and reverent but not sentimental, and it demonstrates the traditional reverence for the elderly that is so evident in the Japanese culture.

The Birthday Visitor (1975) has universal qualities, yet is colored by the same traditional quality; here it is the respect due a guest in one's home. Emi, sulking because a minister from Japan is coming as a houseguest and will surely spoil her birthday dinner, is delighted when the guest proves to be both sympathetic and entertaining. Again, the quality of Japanese-American family life is reflected in the firm but gentle discipline Emi gets from her parents.

Also set in the United States is *The Rooster Who Understood Japanese* (1976). Since her mother, a doctor, is busy, Miyo is taken care of by a neighbor after school; she worries about the fact that Mrs. Kitamura's rooster has brought complaints from other neighbors. The solution is credible, the writing gently humorous, and—once more—the relationship between children and adults is depicted with warmth. In such stories as *Hisako's Mysteries* (1969) and *In-between Miya* (1967) both of which are about girls who visit relatives in Tokyo, Uchida explores some of the common problems of pre-adolescence: friendship values, self-image, conflicting goals, and one's relationships with parents.

Marilyn Sachs

The *Amy and Laura* stories
The *Peter and Veronica* stories
Marv

In *Amy Moves In* (1964), Amy's family moves in the 1930s to another section of the Bronx; the pleasant family story about the Sterns ends with Mother going into a hospital. In *Laura's Luck* (1956), Laura and Amy go off to camp, Laura jealous of her younger sister because she adjusts so much more easily. Laura gains confidence and decides she likes camp in a story that is, like the first book, lightly humorous and realistic in dealing with small problems. Not until the third book, *Amy and Laura* (1966), is there a real problem in interpersonal relationships. Laura finds it difficult to accept her invalid mother, away so long, and is relieved at the close of the story when Mama rebels and declares she is going to run her home and be a mother, not a liability.

In *Veronica Ganz* (1968) and *Peter and Veronica* (1969), Marilyn Sachs introduces a perennial bully who becomes friends with the smallest boy in class. Peter, in the second book, is first angry with his mother because she doesn't want his non-Jewish friend to come to his bar mitzvah, then—after he has persuaded his mother—angry at Veronica because she doesn't show up. Both in the candor with which Peter and Veronica discuss their mothers' prejudices and in the new maturity with which they mend their quarrel the story is honest and percipient. In later years, Veronica's daughter is named after a dead aunt who perished in a fire while warning others of the danger. But Mary Rose

Ramirez finally learns *The Truth About Mary Rose* (1973): she was not a paragon.

Marv (1970) tells of a boy who admires his sister Frances more than anyone else in the world, and repeatedly tries to impress her with his accomplishments, always seeking her approval. There are poignant moments and funny ones, but the book's import is the resilience with which youth strives for competence and approval.

A broken home and a mother unable to face reality create a burden impossible for Fletcher and Fran Ellen to shoulder in *The Bears' House* (1971). Fantasies about the dollhouse in her classroom serve as a release for Fran Ellen's emotions. Finally, adults intervene in the situation. In *A Secret Friend* (1978) an interracial friendship is established after a painful, jealous triangle situation ends.

Sachs has a sympathetic understanding of children's concerns and problems, and handles conflicts between generations honestly and realistically. Her dialogue is fresh, breezy, and often very funny.

Louise Fitzhugh

Harriet the Spy
The Long Secret

The very funny and very touching story of *Harriet the Spy* (1964) aroused vigorous controversy for the portraits it drew of prying, quarrelsome Harriet and of her parents, too busy with their social life to pay much attention to their child until she was in real trouble. Eleven-year-old Harriet aspires to be a writer, and, encouraged by her nurse Ole Golly, keeps notes about everything that happens to her and her friends and to the people she studies on her after-school spy route. She keeps notes on her thoughts and observations, too, as when, on the way to see Ole Golly's "family," she writes:

This is incredible. Could Ole Golly have a family? I never thought about it. How could Ole Golly have a mother and father? She's too old for one thing and she's never said one word about them and I've known her since I was born. Also she doesn't get any letters. Think about this. This might be important.

The sequel, *The Long Secret* (1965), is less intense, more sophisticated, and equally funny at times. Harriet, curious as ever but now on very close terms with her parents, is at the beach for the summer. So is the shy Beth of *Harriet the Spy*, now terrified because her mother, a jet set butterfly, has come to disrupt the quiet life Beth and her grandmother lead. The inclusion of an evangelist family, several jaded characters of the jet set, and a wise old man make the book more cluttered and not as effective as *Harriet*, but it has two episodes that are particularly perceptive. In one, Harriet and her mother have a serious discussion of faith and religion, and in the other Harriet and her friends talk about menstruation, a long-standing taboo subject in children's books.

While Harriet has problems many children don't want, she also has a brash courage many children envy. Her honesty makes her an irresistible character.

Illustration from *Harriet the Spy*, written by Louise Fitzhugh. Copyright © 1964 by Louise Fitzhugh. By permission of Harper & Row, Publishers, Inc. and McIntosh and Otis, Inc.

Robert Burch

Queenie Peavy
Simon and the Game of Chance

Queenie Peavy (1966) is a story of the Depression era, set in Georgia, where Queenie, thirteen, has a deserved reputation as a troublemaker and a hoyden. Fiercely loyal to her father, who is in jail, she faces a painful readjustment when he comes home, shows neither affection nor responsibility, breaks his parole, and is returned to jail. Queenie, a staunch little character, realizes that any change in her status must now come from her own changed attitude and behavior. Candid in treatment of the father, this is one of the books that lucidly exemplifies the end of the perfect-parent image in children's literature.

The father in *Simon and the Game of Chance* (1970) is also the harsh character of the story, stern and tyrannical, a man whose rigidity affects the whole life of the family. Simon's immediate problem is his fear that he is in some way responsible for the death of his sister's fiancé, since he had resented the planned marriage. Like Queenie, Simon adjusts in a way consistent with his character and his need to be loved and accepted.

Joey's Cat (1969), a pleasant story for younger children, is about a small black boy who is delighted when his mother changes her mind and lets him bring his cat and her kittens into the house. In *Wilkin's Ghost* (1978) Burch explores the conflict between ethical standards and loyalty to a friend.

Paula Fox

Maurice's Room
A Likely Place
The Stone-Faced Boy
Portrait of Ivan

With the publication of *Maurice's Room* (1966) it became immediately clear that Paula Fox was one of the best new writers in the field of children's literature. Her style is quiet, her vision penetrating, her understanding of children deep and sympathetic. Maurice is an only child whose room is a haven for anything and everything he finds. His parents attempt subtle distractions, but there is no stopping a born collector: when the family moves to the coun-

try, Maurice is bored until he sees the barn, full of Old Things.

A Likely Place (1967) is a testament to the joy of competence. Lewis, tired of the adults who want to help or to improve him, takes great delight in his friendship with an elderly gentleman who treats him as an equal.

In *The Stone-Faced Boy* (1968) a child who is shy and withdrawn in the midst of a boisterous family takes refuge in looking impassive. Only one elderly great-aunt sees what lies behind the stoic facade. This empathetic relationship between a child and someone outside his immediate family is used again in *Portrait of Ivan* (1969), in which lonely Ivan's friendship with the artist who is painting his portrait helps Ivan gain confidence to approach his busy, remote father. The writing is skilled, and the characters are superbly drawn. *Blowfish Live in the Sea* (1970) is discussed at some length in Chapter 3. *How Many Miles to Babylon?* (1967) is the story of a black child persecuted by a gang of older boys. With the historical novel *The Slave Dancer* (1973), Fox won the Newbery Medal, and in 1978 she was given the Hans Christian Andersen Award.

Zilpha Keatley Snyder

The Egypt Game
The Changeling

One of the notable books of 1967 and a Newbery Honor Book, *The Egypt Game* is an absorbing story of sustained, imaginative group play and of interracial friendship. Surprisingly for a child's book, the characters include a murderer who almost captures one of the girls. The children are vividly real, their Egypt Game absorbing, their conversation and personalities distinctive.

In *The Changeling* (1970) a quiet child from a conservative family becomes friends with an unusual girl and only years later realizes how much the disreputable and wildly imaginative Ivy contributed to her own growth and flexibility.

The interest of the young in astrology and the supernatural is reflected in *The Headless Cupid* (1971), in which an unhappy adolescent persuades her newly acquired stepbrothers and stepsisters to become her disciples in the occult. Only when there seems to be evidence of a poltergeist does Amanda lose her pose of superiority. In a sequel, *The Famous Stanley Kidnapping Case* (1979), Amanda's brothers and sister insist—in a very funny story—on going along when she's kidnapped. *The Velvet Room* (1965) is the story of Robin, one of the children in a family of migrant workers, who finds a haven in the Velvet Room, the library of a deserted house. While there are elements of mystery, the book is less a mystery than a story of the need for security and belonging.

These stories are realistic but often involve some supernatural elements which give them an eeriness seldom found in children's books at this level.

Virginia Hamilton

Zeely
M. C. Higgins, the Great
The Time-Ago Tales of Jahdu

A gifted black writer, Virginia Hamilton has shown versatility with each of her books. In *Zeely* (1967) a child visiting in the country is smitten by the beauty of a neighbor who looks like a Watusi queen. The book is impressive both as a picture of a girl's crush on an adult and as a record of a child's growing understanding of racial identity.

The danger posed by the Cumberland Mountain slag heap under whose shadow his family lives makes M. C., thirteen, long to have his family move. But M. C.'s experiences with a folklorist and a girl from "outside," as well as his father's attachment to his ancestral home, make his dreams seem impossible. *M. C. Higgins, the Great* (1974), written in an intricate yet graceful style, won both the Newbery Award and the National Book Award in 1975.

In *The Time-Ago Tales of Jahdu* (1969) and *Time-Ago Lost: More Tales of Jahdu* (1973), Lee Edward stays each day with Mama Luka until his mother is home from work, and each day he hears another story of the legendary Jahdu, crafty and powerful. The tales are beautifully told in the folk tradition, and the small boy learns the joy of being black and proud.

The House of Dies Drear (1968) is a dramatic story set in an old house that had been a station on the Underground Railroad; in *Arilla Sun Down* (1976), Hamilton uses flashbacks to tell the story of a child who knows her black and native American roots, but seeks self-identity. *The Planet of Junior Brown* (1971), a memorable book for older readers, is an imaginative and touching story of a friendship between two boys who are loners, each in a different way.

Hamilton is a skilled writer, one of our great stylists, presenting the black experience with singular distinction of style and viewpoint, and with nuances of meaning for the more mature or culturally aware reader.

Vera and Bill Cleaver

Ellen Grae
Where the Lilies Bloom
I Would Rather Be a Turnip

Although there had been other books about children of divorce before *Ellen Grae* (1967) was published, none had so firmly stated by implication the fact that a parent's love and responsibility are not changed by divorce. Ellen Grae tells her own story, and it becomes instantly apparent that she is an accomplished and artis-

Illustration from *Zeely* by Virginia Hamilton. Illustrations by Symeon Shimin. Illustration © Macmillan, 1967.

From *From the Mixed-Up Files of Mrs. Basil E. Frankweiler* by E.L. Konigsburg. Copyright © 1967 by E.L. Konigsburg. Used by permission of Atheneum Publishers.

with family problems. Another strong character, Fern Drawn in *Dust of the Earth* (1975), works at the difficult job of sheepherding to help her family survive, and has the joy of seeing a disparate group of children and parents become a united family.

In *I Would Rather Be a Turnip* (1971) twelve-year-old Annie Jelks faces a problem that is seldom presented in children's books, the acceptance of an illegitimate child. Annie is aware that everyone in her small town knows that her sister's child was born out of wedlock, and when eight-year-old Calvin comes to live with Annie and her father, she is jealous of her father's love for the boy and apprehensive about the feelings of her friends. The Cleavers deal perceptively with the intricacies of serious problems yet lighten the stories with humor. These books are prime examples of the changes that have occurred in what has been considered appropriate in children's books.

Elaine Konigsburg

From the Mixed-Up Files of
   Mrs. Basil E. Frankweiler
Jennifer, Hecate, Macbeth, William
   McKinley, and Me, Elizabeth
(George)
About the B'nai Bagels

In 1968 Elaine Konigsburg made history in children's books when her *From the Mixed-Up Files of Mrs. Basil E. Frankweiler* was awarded the Newbery Medal and her *Jennifer, Hecate, Macbeth, William McKinley, and Me, Elizabeth* was voted a Newbery Honor Book. They were her first two books. *From the Mixed-Up Files* is an engaging story of two children who leave home and take up residence in the Metropolitan Museum of Art, the details of the expedition capably planned by the older child, Claudia. The unlikely setting is made believable by the bland perfection of details.

Jennifer, Hecate is a story of interracial friendship and sustained imaginative play in which Jennifer, a self-declared witch, permits Elizabeth (who tells the story) to become her apprentice. Both in the relationship between the two protagonists and in their relationships to others there is delightful warmth and humor.

(George) (1970) deals with a serious problem, the schizoid personality, yet the book has high humor, tenderness, and a lively plot. The distinctive achievement of *(George)* is that it

tic teller of tall tales and that she is a child with great sensitivity and loyalty. Despite the seriousness of the problem that faces Ellen Grae and despite its less than satisfactory resolution, the story is permeated with humor. Its sequel, *Lady Ellen Grae*, has less impact but is written with vivacity and sharp characterization. The hero of *Grover* (1970) is Ellen Grae's friend, and his adjustment to his mother's suicide (she has cancer) and to his father's grief is described in a story that shows the sensitivity of the young.

The heroine of *Where the Lilies Bloom* (1969) is one of the strongest characters in children's fiction. Fourteen-year-old Mary Call Luther buries her father herself, and valiantly tries to hold together the family—which includes a mentally retarded older sister—so that the four children will not be sent to a county charity home. This is an excellent example of the need for security as well as of the need to achieve. In the sequel, *Trial Valley* (1977), Mary Call is just as responsible in coping with suitors as she is enables the reader to see that the child with psychological problems is not beyond the pale: Ben is human, intelligent, loving.

About the B'nai Bagels (1969) is a cheerful story, less dramatic than the other Konigsburg books, but enjoyable for the felicity with which Mark describes the awfulness of having his mother manage his Little League team, the nervous pleasure of his first look at a girly magazine, and the indignation aroused by his first encounter with anti-Semitism. *Father's Arcane Daughter* (1976) is a deftly structured story in which the question is whether or not the woman who claims to have been kidnapped seventeen years earlier, is telling the truth. *Altogether, One at a Time* (1971) is a collection of four deftly written short stories, different in plot and mood, alike in their theme of compromise with circumstance. Also in short story form, *Throwing Shadows* (1979) is distinctive for the depth of perception in five young people, each of whom tells his or her own story of a turning point.

Whatever her theme, Konigsburg's stories are amusingly told, with solid substance underneath.

From Betsy Byars, *The TV Kid*. Copyright © 1976 by Betsy Byars. Illustrations copyright © 1976 by Viking Penguin, Inc. Published by the Viking Press. (Original in color)

Betsy Byars

The Midnight Fox
The Summer of the Swans
The Night Swimmers

Although few of her books are humorous, there is in most of Betsy Byar's writing a quiet, understated sense of humor that children quickly recognize and enjoy. More evident, and just as much appreciated, are her compassion and her understanding of the deepest emotions of children. And, as in *The Midnight Fox* (1968) there is an empathy with children's love of animals. Tom, an urban child visiting relatives, has had no interest in animals, but he is so caught by the beauty of a black fox that he becomes absorbed in watching her and her cub; when his uncle pens the cub as bait to trap the mother, Tom releases it, and is delighted when his aunt and uncle prove to be understanding about his deed.

The compassion depicted in Tom appears again in Byars' Newbery Medal book, *The Summer of the Swans* (1970), one of the early books about a retarded child. Charlie's sister Sara is loving and protective, terrified when Charlie

is lost, and glad of the help of a friend, Joe, in finding him. Sara, fourteen and shy, accepts a party invitation from Joe, and comes to a turning point. Like the swans she and Charlie have watched, she knows for the first time that she will move from a first, awkward flight to the confidence of being in her own element. The book has a tender quality and has enough action to balance the quiet unfolding of a situation.

In *The Night Swimmers* (1980) Byars again explores a situation and a turning point in a child's life with insight, again writes with tenderness and grace, again creates a memorable character. Retta is the oldest of three children; motherless, she is a mother to her younger brothers, since their father, a country-western singer, is away at night and asleep for most of the day. Secretly they swim, at night, in a neighbor's pool; it's one of the many ways that Retta tries to keep her brothers busy and happy. She is bereft when they develop other interests, confused by her own reactions of jealousy and resentment. The situation is resolved when a friend of their father's takes over; she's a tough, cheerful woman who's determined to marry Retta's father. Only when she realizes that she can be a child, that somebody else will assume the role of protector, does Retta accept the change in her role, in a story that is touching but never saccharine.

Byars has written some fantasy and some lightly humorous stories, but her strong forte is in depicting troubled children. In both *After the Goat Man* (1974) and *The House of Wings* (1972) she deals perceptively with boys and their relationships with grandfathers who have lived solitary lives; in *The Pinballs* (1977) she depicts the camaraderie of those who are joined in misfortune, in a vivid story about three foster children who gain security from each other and their affectionate foster parents; in *The TV Kid* (1976), a hospitalized child gets over his addiction to television shows; and in *Good-bye, Chicken Little* (1979) a child, appalled by his uncle's death, learns that people have different ways of handling grief. In all her books, Byars affirms a respect for children's resiliency and strength.

Constance Greene

A Girl Called Al
I Know You, Al

There is poignant sympathy for the girl in Constance Greene's *A Girl Called Al* (1969). Plump and caustic, Al is a nonconformist who is won over by the understanding friendship of the building superintendent and who is catapulted into maturity by his death. *I Know You, Al* (1975) tells us more about Al as she faces the problems in her life: being the only girl in the class who hasn't yet begun to menstruate, being too plump, not liking her mother's suitor, and meeting the father she hasn't seen for eight years. Both these stories are entertaining, warm, and perceptive, as is their sequel, *Your Old Pal Al* (1979).

Greene turns to boys and their problems in *The Unmaking of Rabbit* (1972). Paul is shorter than the other boys in his class and has large ears that stick out. He lives with Gran; his mother, even when she remarries, has no place for him. Paul gathers his courage, reads a paper in class about refusing to join a group for break-ins, and is invited to join another group for sleep-outs. He firmly renounces the name Rabbit. *The Ears of Louis* (1974) are also large, but Louis learns to overlook the teasing. Both stories are realistic and written with ease and humor, with sympathetic characters who have believable problems.

Maria Gripe

Hugo and Josephine
The Night Daddy

In her stories about Swedish children, Maria Gripe has shown us that children have similar problems, no matter what their country of origin. *Josephine* (1970), *Hugo* (1970), and *Hugo and Josephine* (1969) describe the problems of the preacher's youngest daughter, who's not sure she's wanted, in and out of school, and her relationship with Hugo, a true individualist. Hugo comes to school when he can spare the time from more important forest pursuits, but he is so gravely sensible and logical that even the teacher accepts his behavior. Josephine learns from Hugo to question other people's conclusions and interpretations, and not to be jealous when Hugo has other friends.

The Night Daddy (1971) and *Julia's House* (1975) tell of the relationship between Julia and Peter, who stays with her when her nurse mother is on night duty. The affection that grows between the two is sympathetically depicted. In the second book we see an older Julia, dividing her loyalties now between Peter and her school friends and teacher. In the meantime, Peter's attention has been caught by a small boy who appears as the main character in *Elvis and His Secret* (1976) and *Elvis and His Friends* (1976). Peter's supportive affection helps Elvis to find his own identity.

Winner of the Hans Christian Andersen Award in 1974, Gripe is distinguished for the depth of her characterizations and the sensitivity with which she portrays relationships. She has the rare ability to be childlike without being childish; she understands the children and so do we. We enter willingly into their joys and sorrows, defeats and triumphs.

Judy Blume

Are You There God? It's Me, Margaret
Then Again, Maybe I Won't

Judy Blume has written a number of frank stories that discuss problems formerly referred to only in veiled terms in books for children. In *Are You There God? It's Me, Margaret* (1970), Margaret and her friends are concerned with physical maturity: when will they begin to menstruate? and when will their breasts develop? Margaret is also confused about religion;

will she be Jewish like her father or Christian like her mother? She doesn't solve all her problems but does decide that her faith is strong, that she can worship in her own way, whatever her formal affiliation.

In *Then Again, Maybe I Won't* (1971), Blume writes with sympathetic insight about an adolescent boy disturbed by his family's changed attitude when they become well-to-do, and by his first sexual stirrings. Karen adjusts to divorce in *It's Not the End of the World* (1972), and in both *Deenie* (1973) and *Blubber* (1974), the protagonists are troubled by adjustment to physical handicaps, concerned not only with their health but also with the effects that their appearance may have on their peer groups.

Blume is astute in her choices of contemporary themes; her dialogue is natural, her characters believable, and her style direct and unaffected. Her stories have a pervasive sense of humor as well as an affectionate understanding of children and young people.

Eleanor Cameron

A Room Made of Windows
To the Green Mountains

Although Canadian-born Eleanor Cameron was first known as a writer of fantasy, and won the National Book Award in 1974 for the fantasy *The Court of the Stone Children*, it is in her realistic writing that her skill at perceptive characterization is most notable.

In *A Room Made of Windows* (1971) the protagonist, Julia, wants to be a writer; self-centered and sensitive, she is distracted by the resentment she feels because her widowed mother plans to marry. The book has a deft meshing of minor plot threads and a smooth, logical development of change in Julia, as she grows more mature and more responsive to the needs of others. It was not until 1977 that a companion volume, *Julia and the Hand of God*, was published; this predates the first book, describing a younger Julia; it is more dramatic, including a fire that sweeps through the city; it is just as deftly written, and concludes with the family's move to a new home where Julia finds her many-windowed room.

In *To the Green Mountains* (1975) there is more depth and maturity in Cameron's writing, and the same adroit integration of subplots. Kath, whose mother manages a small hotel, is devoted to a black man on the staff and disturbed because there is censure of her mother for helping him in his plans to become a lawyer. She's also upset when her mother decides she wants a divorce from her shiftless husband, but pleased by the prospect of returning to the mountains of the title, the green Vermont hills where her grandmother lives and which Kath has always thought of as her haven, and the book ends with Kath and her mother on their way to Vermont. Here, more than in any of her books, Cameron has shown the way in which people affect, and are inevitably affected by, each other.

Katherine Paterson

Bridge to Terabithia
The Great Gilly Hopkins

Katherine Paterson was already well known as the author of two fine historical novels set in feudal Japan, one of which, *The Master Puppeteer*, had won the National Book Award in 1977. It was a surprise and a delight to her readers when she chose another genre and wrote a realistic contemporary story, *Bridge to Terabithia* (1977), which was given the Newbery Medal the following year. Her writing is polished and her characterization strong in describing the depth of friendship between a boy in a rural community and the daughter of a cultured, intellectual pair who have just moved from the city. The two children are enthralled by their sustained imaginative play in a clearing, reached by a rope swing over a ravine, and Jess, the boy, gains security and insight from their relationship. He is desolate when he learns that Leslie, going to their haven alone, has been killed when the rope swing broke—but he realizes later that he has not completely lost Leslie, but has gained from her the ability to share with his sister the warmth and joy he had received from his friend.

Paterson's compassion is again evident in *The Great Gilly Hopkins* (1978), as eloquent a story as the first and as brilliant in characterization. The story of a tough foster child, illegitimate and rejected, is deftly constructed and touching, as Gilly learns to drop her façade of toughness when she meets love. The love comes from a slovenly, cheerful foster mother who teaches Gilly to accept love and to give it. Like *Bridge to Terabithia*, this is economically structured and is written with pace and momentum. *Gilly* won the National Book Award.

Nina Bawden

Rebel on a Rock
The Robbers

Nina Bawden is an English author who has steadily grown in popularity in other English-speaking countries; most of the books she has written for adults and for children have been published in the United States. *Rebel on a Rock* (1978) is the story of one of the children of Carrie, heroine of *Carrie's War*, discussed in the following chapter. Her daughter Jo is one of four children (two are black and adopted) who are vacationing in a small country ruled by a dictator; wanting to help the son of a banished leader, Jo and her family find that they have unwittingly caused his arrest. Bawden creates vividly the atmosphere of the village and its rocky citadel; she writes with pace and momentum, eschewing the temptation of a heroic ending for the more probable and logical one. The book is a good adventure story, but it's also noteworthy for the delicacy with which the author depicts relationships within the family, especially the relationship between Jo and her stepfather.

In *The Robbers* (1979) Bawden shows her understanding of children's loyalties and motivations, for nine-year-old Philip is the most honest and courteous of children, yet he is guilty of attempted robbery, a deed he and his friend Darcy plan because Darcy's brother is in trouble. Philip, who has come to London to live with a cold, bullying father and a new stepmother, had been lonely until he met Darcy's warm and welcoming family. It is then, when Philip is in trouble himself and sees the difference between his father's icy anger and his grandmother's understanding of why sympathy had made him break his own code of behavior, that he decides he will go to live with his grandmother. The characterization is trenchant, the plot beautifully structured, and the writing style polished.

Among other books by Bawden are *A Handful of Thieves* (1967), in which a group of children decides to steal back the money taken from the grandmother of one of them, and *Devil by the Sea* (1976) which was published in England as an adult book. Since this is the story of a man who murders children, it is perhaps indicative of the changing times that it was considered appropriate to publish it, nine years after the original publication, as a book for children.

Other Books for the Middle Group

In books for children, realism in the 1970s tends to mirror the contemporary scene, but there have been fine realistic stories written in the past and so vividly true to life that they, too, are enjoyed by today's children. One of these is Ruth Sawyer's Newbery Medal book, *Roller Skates* (1936), in which ten-year-old Lucinda makes friends as she skates about New York. Other examples are Ursula Nordstrom's *The Secret Language* (1960), in which a homesick child adjusts to the pattern of life at boarding school, and Virginia Sorenson's 1957 Newbery Medal book, *Miracles on Maple Hill*, the story of a family that moves to the country so that Father can regain his health. Louisa Shotwell's *Roosevelt Grady* (1963) concerns a migrant family's desire for a settled life and educational opportunities.

One of the notable developments in the books of the 1970s has been the increasing number of stories about lively, independent girls. Meg is an eleven-year-old who starts a consciousness-raising group in *The Manifesto and Me—Meg* (1974) by Bobbi Katz. Maggie, of Dorothy Crayder's *She, the Adventuress* (1973), proves self-reliant when she travels alone on a

From *The Skates of Uncle Richard*, by Carol Fenner. Illustration copyright © 1978 by Ati Forberg. Reprinted by permission of Random House, Inc.

ship bound for Italy. With brotherly and parental support, Barbara takes over her brother's newspaper route, overturning company rules in *The Real Me* (1974) by Betty Miles.

As is true of books for other age groups, books for the middle group show an increased awareness of children's concern with such situations as death, particularly the death of a family member; adjustment to living with grandparents; and the relationship between children and mentally retarded siblings. In Eth Clifford's *The Rocking Chair Rebellion* (1978), a girl campaigns against discrimination toward old people, and in Richard Parker's *He Is Your Brother* (1976) a boy of eleven convinces his parents that an autistic younger brother can improve. In Kathryn Ewing's *A Private Matter* (1975), a child who lives alone with her mother, and who has accepted an elderly neighbor as substitute father, must adjust to his moving away. Another kind of acceptance is needed in Rose Blue's *Grandma Didn't Wave Back* (1972), wherein a child reluctantly accepts the fact that only a nursing home will provide the constant care Grandma needs. *A Taste of Blackberries* (1973) by Doris Buchanan Smith candidly explores the grief and guilt felt by a boy when his best friend dies of a bee sting.

Among the many books now available about black children in the United States, some have an interracial theme while others are about only black children. Three good examples of the former are Eleanor Clymer's *Luke Was There*

(1973), the tender story of a child's dependence on a black social worker; her story of black pride, *The House on the Mountain* (1971); and Barbara Cohen's *Thank You, Jackie Robinson* (1974), the story of a fatherless white boy whose mother runs an inn and who finds a man-to-man relationship with Davey, the black chef, who likes baseball as much as Sam does. Some of the excellent stories in the latter group are *Sister* (1974) by Eloise Greenfield, Bette Greene's *Philip Hall Likes Me. I Reckon Maybe* (1974), Betty Erwin's *Behind the Magic Line* (1969), and Carol Fenner's *The Skates of Uncle Richard* (1978), in which a small black girl dreams of being a figure skater. In *Sister*, a girl of thirteen is torn between finding her own path to maturity and following that of an older sister whom she's always adored but who now seems to be heading for trouble. In Greene's story about a loving family of rural Arkansas, the protagonist is an eleven-year-old who is torn between admiration for her first love and a stifled conviction that she's as bright as he is—maybe brighter. *Behind the Magic Line* is also a good family story, but more serious in its presentation of the problems of ghetto living.

Eleanor Clymer also has written a sensitive story of a rejected child in *My Brother Stevie* (1967), a story in which a teacher's warm concern offers security; in *The Spider, the Cave, and the Pottery Bowl* (1971) a Native American child learns pride in her heritage.

Children's problems are much alike everywhere in the world despite the fascinating dif-

Viewpoint

ferences of setting and idiomatic language. This is true of Rumer Godden's *The Kitchen Madonna* (1967), a tender story about an aloof child who reaches out to help the homesick Ukrainian maid in his London home, and equally true of E. W. Hildick's *Louie's Snowstorm* (1974), a funny, fast-paced Christmas story in which an American girl plays a lively role. One is an urban story of a single child, told in graceful, polished prose, and the other a rollicking tale of a group of children, but both reflect basic needs. The hero of Patricia Windsor's *Mad Martin* (1976) is a lonely, uncommunicative orphan who learns from a loving, boisterous foster family how to love and laugh. In *What the Neighbors Did and Other Stories* (1973), A. Philippa Pearce tells eight warm, realistic tales about children in a Cambridgeshire village. All British books, each is unique.

The Australian stories of Reginald Ottley and Joan Phipson, too, demonstrate that children are much the same wherever they happen to live, but the most moving story from an Australian author is probably Patricia Wrightson's *A Racecourse for Andy* (1968), its main character a retarded child whose mistaken belief that he owns a race track is treated with great sympathy and understanding by all his friends.

The universality of childhood experience is clear in Hilda Van Stockum's Irish stories about the O'Sullivan family, in Shirley Arora's tale of a boy in India, "What Then, Raman?" (1960), in books from all parts of the world. The mother who works while father studies is a familiar phenomenon in our country, but nobody has been more perceptive about the implications of this life style for children than Anne-Cath. Vestly in her story of a Norwegian family, *Hello, Aurora* (1974). Mary-Joan Gerson, in *Omoteji's Baby Brother* (1974), explores the effect of a baby's advent for a small Nigerian boy. Uganda in the 1940s is the setting for a quiet, serious story of the effects of education for *Mukasa* (1973) by John Nagenda. Through these books children may learn to feel more at home in their expanded world.

Books for Older Children

Although there have been many changes in realistic fiction for younger children and for children in the middle group, the most striking changes have been in realistic fiction for older children. In the most recent books, subjects which were once taboo or elided, such as premarital pregnancy or illegitimate children, are fairly common, and the image of the perfect parent appears in fewer and fewer stories. Problems that confront today's youth are treated with understanding: the generation gap, the drug scene, the dissatisfaction with a materialistic society. And the language used reflects the speech of today, both in the admission of words that were once considered shocking and in the use of black English. Some of the stories are didactic, but the best fiction can win young people because it shows their world and its relationships as they know them to be.

Ann Nolan Clark

Secret of the Andes
Santiago
Medicine Man's Daughter

In My Mother's House (1941) and *Secret of the Andes* (1952) represent something of Clark's range of experience with primitive peoples. Furthermore, she is able to interpret their ways of life so that modern children respect them, and her writing reflects her love for them. *Secret of the Andes*, a Newbery Medal winner, is the story of a dedicated Peruvian Indian boy, the last of a royal line, who has been brought up in the mountains and grows to understand his heritage and his responsibilities. *Santiago* (1955) is about a Guatemalan youth, raised in a Spanish home but determined to find his place in the world as an Indian. Both of these perceptive stories are beautifully written. *Medicine Man's Daughter* (1963) is the story of a girl who, at fifteen, has been chosen by her father as his successor. Stunned when a white man heals a child she cannot help, Tall-Girl rides off to a mission school and in time learns to appreciate the values of both cultures. The story moves slowly, but the information about Navaho life is interesting and the book sustains the mood of Tall-Girl's dedication.

For younger children Clark has written books that give authentic pictures of the life and ideals of the desert Indians. For older and younger children, she writes with a sense of the inner life and ideals of a people. Her cadenced prose is beautiful and unique.

Illustration by John Schoenherr from *Julie of the Wolves* by Jean Craighead George. Illustrations copyright © 1972 by John Schoenherr. By permission of Harper & Row, Publishers, Inc. Published in the U.K. by Hamish Hamilton Ltd., London.

Joseph Krumgold

. . . and now Miguel
Onion John

Joseph Krumgold has given the preadolescent two fine stories of growing up, both winners of the Newbery Medal.

The members of young Miguel's family in *. . . and now Miguel* (1953) have been sheepherders for generations, first in Spain, now in the Southwest country around Santa Fe, New Mexico. Twelve-year-old Miguel is struggling to prove to his father that he is as mature and competent a sheep man as his adored brother Gabriel, who is eighteen. His attempts to prove his maturity and responsibility supply the action of the story. After many disheartening blunders, success comes, but it is tempered with regret. This book, written in the first person, may have to be introduced to children, but it is well worth the time and effort.

Onion John (1959) was not so universally approved as *Miguel* but it too is concerned with problems in family relationships that are part of growing up. Andy is temporarily fascinated by a picturesque old hobo who lives in a shanty at the edge of town. This hero worship causes the first rift between Andy and his father. The story of the whole town trying to uplift and "do good" to the old tramp is an exceedingly funny

and characteristic bit of Americana. But not until Onion John has fled from his do-gooders does Andy realize that he would rather be exactly like his father—the respected owner of the town hardware store—than anyone else.

In *Henry 3* (1967) a boy and his family are in a setting of suburban affluence that seems to encourage conformist behavior. The boy is disturbed by the values of the adults around him and the superficial standards by which many people live.

William Mayne

A Swarm in May
A Grass Rope
The Jersey Shore

William Mayne uses his own experiences as a member of the Canterbury Cathedral Choir School as background for *A Swarm in May* (1957), a deft and humorous account of the ploys and problems of John Owen, ten years old and the youngest "singing boy" in the school. Mayne, in this early and still popular story, showed his ability to create vividly a distinctive atmosphere and to use dialogue in the establishment of character. Unlike many of his later books, this is a humorous story with an affectionate tone.

A Grass Rope (1962), which received the Carnegie Medal, is one of many Mayne stories with a Yorkshire setting; while many of his books have a dark, somber note, this is a sunny tale in which some children investigate traces of an old legend, an interest Mayne explores more fully in some of his fantasy writing. Here one of the charms of the book is the delicacy with which the older children treat the conviction of the youngest that she will find the fairies of the legend; she even weaves a grass rope because she is sure that she will find a unicorn.

The Jersey Shore (1973) is set in the United States, but it is permeated with the English background of the New Jersey grandfather Arthur comes to visit. While this is not Mayne's best writing, it is perhaps his most perceptive book, creating a deep sense of family continuity and the poignancy of an old man's memories. Mayne changed the ending for the American edition, eliminating the fact that Arthur's grandfather is black.

Among the other Mayne titles published in the United States are *The Changeling* (1963), in which three children help an elderly woman retrieve her forgotten past, *The Yellow Airplane* (1974) a story of children who learn, in working together, to forget their past differences, and *Max's Dream* (1978) in which an invalid recovers by following his dream. Many of Mayne's books present stylistic difficulties, especially in his use of dialect and idiom; like other great stylists, he will probably never be one of the most popular children's writers—but he is one of the greatest contemporary writers.

Jean George

My Side of the Mountain
Julie of the Wolves

My Side of the Mountain (1959) is the record of a New York City boy who breaks away from his family to prove that he can maintain life completely on his own in a mountain wilderness for a year. This competent young nonconformist writes, "I am on my mountain in a tree home that people have passed without ever knowing I am here. The house is a hemlock tree six feet in diameter, and must be as old as the mountain itself." How fourteen-year-old Sam perfects his house and how he makes a lamp from deer fat

in a turtle's shell, clothes from deerskins, flour from acorns, and a balanced diet from roots, wild onions, leaves, and livers of animals make absorbing reading. Only the concluding reunion with his family seems mildly contrived.

In *Julie of the Wolves* (1972), George not only tells the story of a girl caught between two cultures—Eskimo and white—but offers fascinating facts about the ways of the wolves. Julie learns to communicate with a small pack of wolves and thus gets food when she is starving on the Arctic tundra. The book won the Newbery Medal and is a good example of George at her best; she is more a naturalist than a narrator, and excels in descriptions of wilderness flora and fauna.

Madeleine L'Engle

Meet the Austins

Meet the Austins (1960), a family-centered book, was one of the first since *Little Women* to handle the death of a loved one so well.

The story begins in a kitchen where mother is preparing a gala dinner for a visiting relative when the telephone rings. It announces the death of a beloved uncle in an airplane crash. The next night, realizing that the two oldest children are not sleeping, the mother gets them up and dressed and they drive up the mountain to talk. The children demand bitterly why God had to take a good man like Uncle Hal, and the mother replies, "Sometimes it's very hard to see the hand of God instead of the blind finger of Chance. That's why I wanted to come out where we could see the stars." They talk it out quietly in between long, healing silences, and then they go home. The children's ups and downs, a serious brother-sister conflict, some funny and some grave situations—all develop against a background of family love. This is a fine family story, as unusual and provocative a book as is the first chapter.

The Moon by Night (1963) is a sequel in which the family goes on a camping trip and Vicky, now fourteen, is concerned with some of the problems of a maturing adolescent: boys, faith, prejudice, and society's values. In *A Ring of Endless Light* (1980), which moves into fantasy, Vicky is sixteen, learning painfully to accept the deaths of some of those she knows, and learning the depths of her strength, love, and faith. (See Ch. 9 Bibliography, p. 251.)

Emily Neville

It's Like This, Cat
Berries Goodman
Garden of Broken Glass

There is no startling drama in *It's Like This, Cat* (1963), a Newbery Medal book, but it is impressive both for its lightly humorous, easy style and the fidelity with which it portrays a fourteen-year-old boy, Dave, who tells the story. Dave has found the first girl with whom he really feels comfortable (her mother is de-

Viewpoint

The official arrival of the new realism was acknowledged in 1964, when the American Library Association awarded the Newbery Medal to Emily Neville for her book, *It's Like This, Cat* (1963). Prior to this time, it was obvious to anyone who thought about it that there were areas of life that young readers could not confront through literature, for example, race relations, premarital sex, pregnancy, and abortion. Divorce and one-parent families, drugs and homosexuality, and the moral issues involved in the making of war were also missing from children's literature.

It is vitally important that young people have such confrontations through literature. It is important because literature can provide deeply involving, vicarious experiences. Literature can offer the reader the chance to know what it is like to become addicted to drugs; what is is like to live in abject and degrading poverty; what it is like to be a member of a different social or cultural group; what it is like to be an unwed and expectant mother.

Through the new realism the reader has the security of being involved without suffering the consequences of involvement. Young readers can test their beliefs and values against those revealed by the author. Within the exclusive privacy of a book, and without the ever-pressing impingement of peer and class values readers can rethink, reassess and, most importantly, refeel their own attitudes about themselves, about others, and about the world in which they live. The result of experience with the new realism can be readers who are more sensitive, more aware of their own humaness and the humaness of others, and more humane.—Shelton L. Root, Jr., "The New Realism—Some Personal Reflections." *Language Arts,* January 1977. Copyright © 1977 by the National Council of Teachers of English. Reprinted by permission of the publisher and the author.

lightfully sketched as an urban intellectual), and he learns, by seeing the relationship between his father and his friend, that his father really is a pretty good guy. The experience of seeing one's parents through a friend's eyes is a common one, usually revelatory and seldom touched on in books for young people.

Berries Goodman (1965) looks back on the two years in which his family lived in a suburb, years in which he had a friend who was Jewish and learned the subtle signs of adult prejudice: the nuances of tone and the light dismissal of subjects with painful implications. He also learns that Sidney's mother is just as biased. The book is an invitation to better understanding, and its serious import is not lessened by a light humor.

Neville understands children and their need to work out relationships and roles. Her style is matter-of-fact but quietly compelling.

Ivan Southall

Hills End
Ash Road
Let the Balloon Go

One of Australia's most notable writers of children's books, Ivan Southall is particularly adept at placing his child characters in a situation of stress or danger, and showing in realistic and exciting fashion how the common sense and courage of the young can prevail over obstacles. In *Hills End* (1963) a group of children who have been exploring a cave with their teacher come back to find their hometown flooded and deserted, and so they organize for survival and rehabilitation. In *Ash Road* (1966), which won the Australian Children's Book of the Year Award, three boys who have been careless while camping start a bush fire. The suspense is built by Southall's use of fragmented incidents fitted together in jigsaw pattern.

Many of Southall's books concern a group, but in *Let the Balloon Go* (1968) the supreme effort of a spastic child, the great achievement of climbing a tree, is as tense and exciting as the flood or the fire of the earlier books. The theme of the story is that all young people want a chance to make their own decisions and take their own risks. Perry of *Benson Boy* (1973) must get his mother, who's having a baby, to the hospital on a wild, stormy night after his father has been knocked unconscious by a fall. This calls not only for physical strength and courage, but for the fortitude to ask help from an estranged neighbor. All of Southall's books combine a faith in the abilities of the young and a dramatic setting in which they demonstrate their capability. *To the Wild Sky* (1967) also won the Book of the Year Award in Australia.

Hila Colman

Classmates by Request
The Girl from Puerto Rico
Claudia, Where Are You?

Carla is one of a group of white high-school students who have asked to transfer to an all-black school in *Classmates by Request* (1964). Her overtures of friendship are rejected by Ellen, who has remained aloof from her family's participation in the campaign for civil rights and who is angry because neither her father nor any other black man was asked to serve on a commission appointed by Carla's father. It is Ellen's father who emerges as the pacifier, stating bluntly that he is not qualified and should not have been asked, and that his friendship with Carla's father is not impaired. The two girls end by marching together in a demonstration. The ending is a bit pat, but the subjects of school integration and race relations are made an integral part of the story rather than a springboard, and the changing attitudes of Ellen and Carla develop naturally out of events.

The Girl from Puerto Rico (1961) has a slight plot but a warm understanding of the situation of the newly arrived Puerto Rican who comes to the United States in happy anticipation and is unprepared for cultural differences, dismayed by housing conditions, and shocked by the discrimination against her people.

A story about the generation gap, *Claudia, Where Are You?* (1969), is Colman's most effectively written book. The chapters tell the story, alternately, from Claudia's point of view and from her mother's. A successful woman who deludes herself into thinking always that everything around her is just what she wants it to be, Claudia's mother cannot understand her daughter's rebellion against her own values. Claudia runs away to the East Village, calling on her parents only when she needs money. Her distraught mother cannot understand

Reprinted with permission of Macmillan Publishing Co., Inc. from *Benson Boy* by Ivan Southall, illustrations by Ingrid Fetz. Illustration Copyright © 1973 by Macmillan Publishing Co., Inc.

Claudia's need for freedom; Claudia cannot live in suburban affluence. The characterization is excellent, the theme universal, the unsweetened ending faithful to the theme. Colman writes easily and prolifically on current themes.

Maia Wojciechowska

Shadow of a Bull
Tuned Out
"Don't Play Dead Before You Have To"

Shadow of a Bull (1964) richly deserved its Newbery Award, for in the conflict of a Spanish boy torn between his inclination and obligation, there are the themes of youth's similar conflict in any time and place, and of the courage of a boy who dares to admit he is afraid. Manolo, whose father had been the greatest bullfighter in Spain, is being trained in his footsteps by the hopeful elders of his Andalusian village. He knows himself a coward, yet he practices and prays—and when he is eleven and has had his first experience in the ring, he decides he is through.

In *Tuned Out* (1968) an adolescent boy's journal describes, in a stark and honest story, the painful experiences of a loved and respected older brother who has become a drug addict. The sober message is particularly effective because it is seen through the younger boy's eyes.

"Don't Play Dead Before You Have To" (1970) explores the sense of commitment and the values of young people in a time of protest. The literary form is unusual, the book being a long monologue by teenager Byron, babysitting a five-year-old genius who immediately accepts all Byron's shallow values. But Byron changes through the course of the book, and—although the form becomes monotonous—there is great impact in his growing concern for others and in his intense yearning for a better world. It is this belief that our only hope is in young people which particularly distinguishes Maia Wojciechowska's writing.

Frank Bonham

Durango Street
The Nitty Gritty
The Vagabundos

Although *Durango Street* (1965) has a black youth as its protagonist, it is less about black delinquents than it is about the slum neighborhood that breeds delinquency. Rufus is a paroled adolescent more suspicious of the social worker assigned to his case than he would be if Alex Robbins were white. While the patient, firm Robbins does have a realistically small effect on Rufus and his gang, the book is more interesting as a fictional study of gang behavior and protocol than as a story.

In *The Nitty Gritty* (1968), another black adolescent is torn between the indolent life of his favorite uncle and the benefits of continuing his education. Again, the story lacks impetus but is perceptive in interpretation of character and motivation, its candor lightened by moments of humor.

In *The Vagabundos* (1969) a white adolescent

follows the trail of his father, who has disappeared from home. By the time he catches up with his father, Eric understands why the simple life of the local fishermen, the vagabundos, holds more satisfaction than do the indolence and boredom of retirement. The book has vivid characterization of the Americans and Mexicans Eric meets, the suspense of the chase, and a perceptive delineation of the relationship between father and son.

Susan Hinton

The Outsiders
That Was Then, This Is Now

The Outsiders (1967) are the members of a tough, lower-class gang who have a running feud with a middle-class gang. Ponyboy is the outsider who tells the story, stark and vivid, of running off to a hideout with a pal who has committed murder. The two give themselves up, and Ponyboy's pal dies in the hospital. Ponyboy faces the fact that the advantage is with those on the inside of society's line, yet knows that if he cannot have help, he must and will help himself and end the vicious circle of hostility and reprisal. Honest and forthright, the story shows the desperation of the need to belong; it has also a bittersweet quality, especially in young Ponyboy's relationship with his older brothers.

The young author's candor and insight that made the book so popular are evident also in her *That Was Then, This Is Now* (1971), which is basically a story of friendship and the choice that teenaged Byron must make when he finds that his best friend is pushing dope. Especially bitter because he has seen drugs ruin a younger boy of whom he is fond, Byron turns Mark in—and hates himself. The characters are vividly real, and no didactic tract on drug abuse could be more convincing than is the story seen from the viewpoint of an adolescent who has himself been a fringe delinquent. *Rumble Fish* (1975) is the tragic story of two brothers—Motorcycle Boy, who has lost his will to live and is killed after committing a senseless robbery, and Rusty-James, the younger, who idolizes his brother and is almost destroyed by his death. The theme of love between brothers is paramount also in *Tex* (1979).

Kristin Hunter

The Soul Brothers and Sister Lou
Guests in the Promised Land

Which side was she on? Lou, at fourteen, wasn't militant, but she didn't trust white policemen, and she warned the gang with whom she sang that a policeman was near and was acting provocative. She knew the gang carried weapons, but she also saw an unarmed boy shot by the police, and found it hard to believe that any white people had good motives. Yet the more she learned of her black heritage, the more proud and confident Lou became, until she made her decision: moderation, not militancy. *The Soul Brothers and Sister Lou* (1968) has too many episodes and a weak ending (sudden success as a vocal group), yet the book is valuable because it gives a vivid and honest picture of one segment of black society and of the dilemma of its young people. In *Guests in the Promised Land* (1973) Hunter's eleven short stories, varied and vigorous, examine facets of the problems of the black child in a white world.

John Rowe Townsend

Trouble in the Jungle
Good Night, Prof, Dear
Noah's Castle

John Rowe Townsend is one of the major writers of realistic fiction for young people in England. His *Trouble in the Jungle* (1969) tells of some slum children who show their mettle when they are temporarily abandoned by adults. To avoid being forced into an institution, the two older children take the younger ones to a refuge in a deserted warehouse and have a dangerous skirmish with criminals who also seek a hideout. The story, which has good characterization and pace, ends on a realistic note: the shiftless father and his mistress return, and the children go back to their home. Although published earlier in the United States (1967), *Good-Bye to the Jungle* is a sequel in which the family moves to a better home and a better life.

Hell's Edge (1969) was a runner up for the Carnegie Medal when it was first published in England. It is the story of a grimy Yorkshire

Illustration by W. T. Mars from *Trouble in the Jungle* by John Rowe Townsend. Illustrations copyright © 1969 by Harper & Row, Publishers, Inc. By permission of J. B. Lippincott, Publishers.

town, Hallersage, in which several young people are interested in an urban renewal project. There is an element of mystery, but this is not a mystery story.

In *Good Night, Prof, Dear* (1971) a shy and overprotected sixteen-year-old falls in love with a waitress he meets when his parents are away on a trip. Although the girl verges on a fallen-woman-with-heart-of-gold type, it is the contrast between her knowledgeable resilience and Graham's diffidence and insecurity that gives the story its real drama. *The Intruder*, another story about a sixteen-year-old, is discussed in Chapter 3.

Noah's Castle (1976) is a compelling, all-too-possible family story. Foreseeing food shortages, Father buys and barricades a huge house, stocks it, and prepares to survive. What his family thinks of all this precipitates more problems.

Townsend has an ear for dialogue, as well as an understanding of adolescent psychology. His books are written with economy of structure and vitality of motive, the style utterly appropriate to the tale.

Theodore Taylor
The Cay

Although the fact that German submarines are attacking islands along the Venezuelan coast during World War II is the occasion for Phillip's departure, this is in no sense a historical novel, since all of the action takes place on a small Caribbean island, *The Cay* (1969), with only two characters. The ship Phillip and his mother are on is torpedoed and the boy finds himself, some hours later, alone on a raft with Timothy, an old man. Infected by his mother's prejudice, Phillip feels only aversion for his black companion at first, but he becomes totally dependent on Timothy when he goes blind as a delayed result of the shipwreck injury. Slowly, patiently, stubbornly, Timothy teaches the boy to fend for himself, refusing to coddle him—and when old Timothy dies, Phillip knows how much he has come to love and respect the wise and charitable man. The bleakness of the setting is a dramatic foil for the action, and there is taut suspense within the economical framework of the plot.

John Donovan
I'll Get There. It Better Be Worth the Trip
Wild in the World

In a compassionate story of childhood's end, John Donovan draws a picture of thirteen-year-old Davy, caught and shaped by his environment in *I'll Get There. It Better Be Worth the Trip* (1969). His beloved grandmother has just died, and Davy comes to New York to live with his mother, a divorced, bitter alcoholic. All he clings to is his beloved dog, and the dog irritates his mother. Sent to a boy's school, Davy meets another pupil adjusting to bereavement, and the two have a brief homosexual relationship. It is handled with great dignity and compassion, not the core of the book but one of the scarring episodes that make Davy know his strength must be in himself.

Wild in the World (1971) is a quite different and an even stronger book, memorable for its stark setting and the dramatic impact of a solitary boy's deep need for love and companionship. John lives alone on a remote mountainside farm until a stray dog—or it may be a wolf, John is not sure—learns to trust him. For the first time, John plays and laughs with the creature he has named "Son." When John dies, still alone, and neighbors find him, his "Son" is chased off but steals back later to sleep and keep his vigil in John's house.

Richard Peck
Don't Look and It Won't Hurt
Representing Super Doll

The second of three daughters, Carol had to take care of her younger sister after their parents' divorce in *Don't Look and It Won't Hurt* (1972). Mom, already bitter, didn't want Carol to have boyfriends and refused to have anything to do with her oldest daughter, Ellen, when she became pregnant. It was Carol who went to Chicago to see Ellen and beg her to come home. A gentle, loving girl, Carol had learned to look away from pain that cannot be alleviated; she has had heavy burdens, but they have made her understanding and mature rather than bitter like her mother.

In *Representing Super Doll* (1974) a beautiful but not very astute girl, Darlene, goes to New York for one round of a teenage beauty contest. Her ambitious mother convinces Verna, Darlene's classmate, to go along as companion. Verna, levelheaded and intelligent, scorns the whole proceeding and goes home—and Darlene does the same. To her mother's fury, she has quit just before the final round. The message is firmly feminist, but Peck does not let the message obscure the story; the plot is solid, the characters strong, and the treatment of adolescent concerns balanced. Dialogue is one of the strong aspects in all Peck's stories, and his books are notable for their fresh viewpoints and their vitality.

Norma Klein

Mom, the Wolf Man, and Me
It's Not What You Expect

While Norma Klein has written for several age levels, her greatest impact is in stories for younger adolescents. The "me" in *Mom, the Wolf Man, and Me* (1972) is Brett, an illegitimate child, who loves living alone with her mother and hopes that life will never change. Then the "wolf man," the owner of an Irish wolfhound, comes along, and the possibility of a change looms. Brett's mother is candid and open, and the suitor as concerned with Brett's feelings as with her mother's.

Many of Klein's stories are about single-parent homes, divorce, remarriage, and the adaptability required of children, as in *It's Not What You Expect* (1973) in which Carla, fourteen, adjusts to her parents' separation, *Taking Sides* (1974), and *Tomboy* (1978). But *Confessions of an Only Child* (1974) tells of eight-year-old Tonia's feelings before the birth and death of a premature baby brother, and her acceptance of the brother born a year later.

Klein is a thoughtful connoisseur of real people and sets down her observations skillfully for us. Her children are not divorced from adult problems and relationships, but live closely, in their urban existences, with real and surrogate parents, who are inevitably frank and open about their emotions. Only occasional older people—grandmothers, baby-sitters—ever suggest that different values might be held by other adults.

M. E. Kerr

Dinky Hocker Shoots Smack
Is That You, Miss Blue?

With *Dinky Hocker Shoots Smack* (1972), a fresh, perceptive advocate for adolescents appeared in the person of M. E. Kerr. Dinky Hocker spends all her money for food and has no dates. Because he wants to take Dinky's visiting cousin to a dance, Tucker finds P. John, a plump square, for Dinky, and instant rapport follows, with Weight Watchers for two. Dinky's parents, who help everyone but their own child, find P. John too reactionary and break up the romance. Dinky's revenge is to inscribe "Dinky Hocker shoots smack" on all the buildings and sidewalks in the neighborhood. Hilariously funny but touching at the same time, this has an excellent style and convincing characterizations.

The problems that come with a parent who is a celebrity are those of Adam in *The Son of Someone Famous* (1974). Alternating chapters by Adam and by Brenda Belle Blossom, his girlfriend, allow Kerr to tell the story from two points of view and yet to keep it intimate and personal. In *I'll Love You When You're More Like Me* (1977), the same alternation of voices creates a vivid picture of the problems of an adolescent television star.

Flanders is sent to a private girls' boarding school in *Is That You, Miss Blue?* (1975). Angry with her mother for leaving home and with her father for apparently deserting her, Flan learns through her school experiences that everyone needs understanding love, even parents and teachers.

Fifteen-year-old Suzy, the narrator of *Love Is a Missing Person* (1975), tells of the problems of her sister, Chicago, and her search for love with someone else's boyfriend. Kerr never offers easy answers to the situations and experiences her characters are involved in, but presents them sympathetically, honestly, and compassionately.

Sharon Bell Mathis

Listen for the Fig Tree
The Hundred Penny Box

An eloquent spokesperson for black culture has created a realistic and moving story of relationships between generations in *Listen for the Fig Tree* (1974). Muffin, who is sixteen and blind, finds that coping with her grief-stricken Momma is a hard task, for Momma, mourning her husband's death, has taken to drink. Muffin's solace lies in her plans to attend her first celebration of the African Kwanza, and she makes a dress for the occasion, a dress in which she looks beautiful—too beautiful. A neighbor attempts rape; other neighbors rescue her, and one makes her a new dress. Muffin has a glorious time at Kwanza, and—although she comes home to find Momma still drinking, still insistent that Daddy's coming home—she faces her problems with new courage, courage gained

From *The Hundred Penny Box* by Sharon Bell Mathis. Text Copyright © 1975 by Sharon Bell Mathis. Illustrations Copyright © 1975 by Leo and Diane Dillon. Reprinted by permission of The Viking Press. (Original with color)

from the feelings of solidarity and strength she had gained at Kwanza.

A story that is primarily for children in the middle grades, *The Hundred Penny Box* (1975) is so tender and delicate that it appeals to many older readers as well. A small boy becomes his great-great-aunt's confidant and protector when his mother wants to get rid of Aunt Dew's big box of pennies. But Michael knows that without her pennies, one for each year of her life, something vital will leave Aunt Dew's life.

Mathis is very successful in delineating characters and establishing setting. Her writing is effectively restrained, her stories convincing and candid.

Other Books for Older Children

In Mildred Lee's *The Skating Rink* (1969) a shy fifteen-year-old boy's life is changed by the skating rink, because the owner teaches Tuck to skate so expertly that he is able to partner an exhibition skater on opening night. Tuck works doggedly to achieve competence and realizes he has won respect, not for his performance but for his application. Lee's *The Rock and the Willow*

(1963) was chosen a Notable Book, and deservedly. It is a powerful and incisive story set in rural Alabama during the Depression years, bleak in its honest portrayal of a hard life, with young Enie bearing the brunt of caring for the family after her mother's death and grudgingly accepting a stepmother. The characters are cameo clear, and Enie's dream of getting away from home and going to college is realistically achieved.

Another story of that period is Mildred Taylor's Newbery Medal book, *Roll of Thunder, Hear My Cry* (1976). A black family encounters persecution and condescension as well as poverty, but is strong in the family's love for each other and for the land they own.

William Armstrong's *Sounder* (1969), a Newbery Medal book, is the grim and moving story of a black sharecropper's family whose father is jailed for stealing food for them.

Spanish Harlem is the setting for *Nilda* (1973) by Nicholasa Mohr, a sharp and candid picture of the life of a barrio child. A new arrival in Harlem, Phyl learns that although Edith is slovenly, her kindness is a bulwark in Rosa Guy's *The Friends* (1973). Alice Childress tells a dramatic, moving story in *a HERO ain't nothin' but a Sandwich* (1973). Thirteen-year-old Benjie insists that he can do without dope any time he wants, but his friends and relatives are more realistic.

The consistent and distinctive first-person style of Scott O'Dell's *Child of Fire* (1974) brings vividly to life an adolescent Chicano boy, seen through the eyes of a parole officer.

Our Eddie (1969) by Sulamith Ish-Kishor is the trenchant story of a tyrannical father so dedicated to helping others that he neglects his own family. The Raphels are English Jews who have moved to New York, where Papa refuses to see that Eddie is truly ill, and only after the boy's death softens his behavior somewhat to his other children.

Florence Crannell Means writes with candor and insight about such problems as the yearning for education felt by a migrant girl, in *Knock at the Door, Emmy* (1956) or the adjustment of a Hopi girl who cannot adjust to her own or the white culture, in *Our Cup Is Broken* (1969). *Shuttered Windows* (1938) was one of the first books to portray blacks realistically. In *Us Maltbys* (1966), Means explores the problems of adjustment within a white family that adds, among other foster children, a black baby boy.

A naturalist in the making, Mike fights futilely against the development of the rural areas near his home, while at the same time remaining a typical young adolescent. Don Moser's *A Heart to the Hawks* (1975) is a convincing character study.

The establishment wins also in *The Chocolate War* (1974) by Robert Cormier. In an all-boy Catholic high school, Jerry's hazing by the Vigils includes an order to refuse to sell chocolates in the school's annual fund-raising event. Jerry obeys, but when the order is rescinded, he stands pat. Retribution inevitably follows in this sobering, dramatic story.

Paula Danziger's *The Cat Ate My Gymsuit* (1974) shows how much an innovative teacher means to bored, self-hating Marcy. When the teacher is fired, Marcy and her friends lead a protest, which her formerly timid mother joins.

The Pigman (1968) was what John and Lorraine called Mr. Pignati, whom they had met when pretending to collect for a charity. The lonely, elderly man is delighted to have the young people as friends, but when he comes back from a hospital stay to find them having a wild party, Mr. Pignati is stunned. Remorseful, they try to make amends, but the old man has had too much excitement and dies of a stroke. Only then do John and Lorraine know that each person's cage is of his own making: "there was no one else to blame any more . . . And there was no place to hide." Told alternately by John and Lorraine, this story by Paul Zindel shows more clearly than a reporter could the restless, pliant amorality that so often marks adolescent behavior, and the deep sensitivity beneath it. In *The Pigman's Legacy* (1980), John and Lorraine atone for their guilt by their kindness to another elderly man.

A dignified, perceptive story of a homosexual relationship, *Trying Hard to Hear You* (1974) by Sandra Scoppettone tells of a crucial summer in the lives of a group of adolescents.

The girl in Barbara Corcoran's *Sam* (1967) has been taught by her father, who keeps her on their island home until she is in high school because he so mistrusts people, but Sam discovers for herself that there are all kinds of people, and that even those like Uncle Everett, a weakling and a gambler, have some good things about them. In *A Dance to Still Music* (1974), Margaret, deaf after an illness, rebels by running away when her mother plans to put her in a special school. In Corcoran's and Bradford Angier's *A Star to the North* (1970) a brother and sister learn to accept each other's inadequacies on a trek through the Canadian wilderness.

Winner of the 1976 Carnegie Medal, Jan Mark's *Thunder and Lightnings* (1979) is rich in Norfolk dialect and idiom; a quiet story, it is given warmth and depth by the strong family relationships and the altruistic friendship between Andrew and the newcomer, Victor, with his passion for Lightnings and any other kind of aircraft.

K. M. Peyton's *Pennington's Heir* (1974), which follows *Pennington's Last Term* (1971) and *The Beethoven Medal* (1972), about a brilliant young pianist with a rebellious temper, is also a story of an early, forced marriage. Pennington appears again in *Marion's Angels* (1979) when he helps save an old church that is slated for destruction. Peyton's ability to create vigorous, believable characters and situations is enhanced by her polished writing style.

A good story which may help readers to understand to some extent the bitterness rampant in Northern Ireland today is Joan Lingard's *The Twelfth Day of July* (1972), the first of several stories about Protestant Sadie and Catholic Kevin.

It is interesting that two prize books from Holland are about children in other countries. Siny van Iterson's *Pulga* (1971) is the story of a Colombian waif who gets a job as a trucker's helper and gains self-confidence from his experience; and Jaap Ter Haar's *Boris* (1970) is a story of brotherhood set in Russia. One of the best of the translations from Russia is Vadim Frolov's *What It's All About* (1968), in which a teenage boy copes with the bitter fact that his mother has left his father to be with another man. Sasha's self-doubt, his budding love affair, and his relationships with classmates give the story balance and depth.

Hesba Fay Brinsmead's *Pastures of the Blue Crane* (1966) is set in Australia, its theme the intrinsic worth of all men. A girl of sixteen who has been living in boarding schools inherits property and finds, in her new home, that her most trustworthy friend is Perry, a quarter-caste. Indignant at the slurs cast on him, Amaryllis is not dismayed when she discovers that she herself is not, as she had always assumed, all white.

Miners in Australia's opal fields work in a harsh, uncompromising setting, which imposes unusual pressures on families. Both Colin Thiele's *Fire in the Stone* (1974) and Mavis Thorpe Clark's *Spark of Opal* (1973) tell of the effects of this life on children, white and aborigine, as they wait for that lucky strike. In Joan Phipson's *When the City Stopped* (1978) the setting is urban for a taut story in which two children cope when a strike paralyzes the city.

One of the best of the stories of conflict and resolution between the old ways and the new is *Sunrise Tomorrow* (1973) by Naomi Mitchison, a story of Botswana. Convincingly drawn characters show the different roles in which young people can contribute to a developing nation.

Animal Stories

Almost all children are interested in animals. Rhymes about "The Three Little Kittens" or the mouse that ran up the clock are early favorites, and *Mother Goose* is supplemented by the more realistic animal picture books. With these, children learn to name all the beasts under the sun from hippopotamuses to anteaters. The folk tales with animal heroes come next; "The Three Little Pigs," "The Little Red Hen," and all the other favorites are heard over and over with endless satisfaction. Children progress from these to the more complex, realistic stories about animals, and for many people the interest lasts a lifetime.

Animal stories can be divided into three groups: those in which animals behave like human beings, those in which they behave like animals save for the fact that they can talk, and those in which they behave like animals. Many of the books in the first two categories can be found in Chapter 5, Books for the Very Young, and in Chapter 9, Modern Fantasy; there are, of course, many animal stories in folk literature as well. The realistic tales range from lighthearted picture books like Nathan Zimelman's *The Lives of My Cat Alfred* (1976) to humorous stories like Phil Stong's *Honk: the Moose* (1935) or the substantial books by Walt Morey.

A primary criterion for realistic fiction about animals is that the animals be objectively portrayed. The author should not interpret behavior or motives through giving the animal powers of speech or thought. Any conjecture about motives of animal protagonists should agree with the interpretation of animal behavior as reliable observers have recorded it. Since tragedy often occurs in the lives of animals, stories about them often are dramatic or melancholy. In evaluating such books, we need to be more than ordinarily alert to what is a true and consistent story, and to what is pure sentimentality or animal melodrama. A little melodrama or a few mediocre books are not going to hurt

From *The Incredible Journey* by Sheila Burnford. Copyright © 1960, 1961 by Sheila Burnford. Reprinted by permission of Little, Brown and Co.—Atlantic Monthly Press and Hodder and Stoughton Limited.

children, but they should not miss the great animal tales in a welter of second-rate ones.

Among the great stories is Sheila Burnford's *The Incredible Journey* (1961), a detailed account of three heroic animals who travel through 250 miles of Canadian wilderness to the place and people that mean home and love to them. Attacked by wild creatures, delayed by well-meaning people, crossing hazardous terrain, a cat and two dogs struggle on to find their family. The animals are never humanized or sentimentalized, and they are described with dignity and restraint in a moving and beautiful story.

Many of the best books about animals are written by authors who specialize in this area. Marguerite Henry, for example, who is probably the most successful writer of horse stories we have ever had, bases each book on thorough research; the stories are well told, the animal heroes are true to their species, and the people are often as memorable as the animals. For *King of the Wind* (1948), which won the Newbery Medal, the author investigated the history of the great Godolphin Arabian, which sired a line of thoroughbreds and changed the physical conformation of racehorses. It is one of the most exciting horse stories ever written. Almost as popular is *Misty of Chincoteague* (1947), a history of the little wild horses on a Virginia island. In *Gaudenzia* (1960) and *White Stallion of Lipizza* (1964), Henry bases her stories on the annual horse race held in Siena and on the Lipizzaners, the precision drilled performing horses of the Spanish Riding School of Vienna.

Other authors who have written prolifically in the field of realistic animal fiction are Walt Morey, Jim Kjelgaard, C. W. Anderson, Jean Doty, and Jean George. All of Morey's books are set in the far North or Northwest, and are imbued with his love for that region and his affection for animals. In *Gentle Ben* (1965) and in *Gloomy Gus* (1970), the protagonists are bears, animal personalities that are as vivid as the perceptively characterized human beings among whom they live. *Kävik the Wolf Dog* (1968) is the dramatic story of a mistreated animal that is being sent to Seattle, escapes, and makes his way back to Alaska and the only person who had been kind to him. In *Year of the Black Pony* (1976) a boy on an Oregon farm tames and trains a spirited pony, a plot that is deftly meshed with a tender family story. Kjelgaard specializes in dog stories, of which the best known is *Big Red* (1956), which was followed by several books about progeny of the lovable and courageous Irish setter. Anderson and Doty specialize in horse stories, Anderson with the "Blaze" series for younger children, splendidly illustrated by the author, and with stories of racehorses for older children, and Doty with simply written stories for the middle grades as well as her more intricate mystery story, *The Crumb* (1976). Jean George wrote many stories on a life-cycle pattern with John George: *Vulpes, the Red Fox* (1948) and *Bubo, the Great Horned Owl* (1954), for example, both make it clear that George is not only an animal lover, but a skilled naturalist. Among her finest books are *The Cry of the Crow* (1980) in which a girl must protect her trained crow from those who, like her father and brothers, will shoot any crow on sight, and *Gull Number 737* (1964), the story of a boy who becomes so interested in his father's research on herring gulls that he develops his own project. In *Coyote in Manhattan* (1968), a wild animal, loose in Central Park, is eventually captured. *The Wounded Wolf* (1978) is the story of a wolf saved by the members of his pack.

One of the most touching and trenchant animal stories is *The Yearling* (1938) by Marjorie Kinnan Rawlings. Although written for adults, it has been discovered by children even as they discover certain adult books and make them their own in every generation. A lonely boy and his pet deer grow up together in the Florida wilderness, but when the growing animal begins to eat the family's scanty crops, the boy's father issues an order: the deer must be shot. Added to the boy's anguish over losing his pet are his own guilt feelings and his anger at his father. This is more tragic than most of the stories in which children give up wild pets, but there are many in which a child feels anguish because a wild creature grows from a baby to a size where it must be returned to live with its own kind.

Some animal stories are factual, based on an author's experience with wildlife. Perhaps the best known of these is Sterling North's *Rascal* (1963), which was so popular that the author wrote a simplified version, *Little Rascal*, two years later—a better adaptation than most books rewritten for children. A description of

From the book *Rascal* by Sterling North. Illustrations by John Schoenherr. Illustration copyright © 1963 by E.P. Dutton & Co., Inc., publishers, and used with their permission.

the engaging ways of a pet raccoon, the first-person account is always objective in observations of animal behavior. Also based on observation is Emil Liers' *An Otter's Story* (1953), a delightful book about one family of playful, affectionate freshwater otters in which the author makes clear their usefulness in the balance of nature both for farmers and for fishermen. While not based on personal experience, Patricia Beatty's *The Staffordshire Terror* (1979) is a well-researched story based on the illegal dogfights held throughout the United States.

The English naturalist Joyce Stranger has, in *Lakeland Vet* (1972), so skillfully woven incidents about animals into the fictional account of a veterinarian's hard life that his love and compassion for all living things are more impressive than the story line. The same sense of compassion is strong in Meindert DeJong's *Along Came a Dog* (1958), illustrated by Maurice Sendak. Gentle but never sentimental, DeJong's stories about animals have a quiet, poignant appeal; here the animals have strong personalities, as a stray dog establishes himself as the protector of a crippled, doughty little hen.

Realistic animal stories for young children are on the whole a cheerful group, often containing excellent illustrations. Although many of Marjorie Flack's books were about dogs, the abiding favorite has been *The Story About Ping* (1933), with Kurt Wiese's pictures catching the spirit of a brisk, homey tale about a rebellious little duck that lives on a boat in the Yangtze River. Lynd Ward's *The Biggest Bear* (1952) is a delectable comedy about a pet bear that grows from a cute baby into a large animal that causes so many problems that the only solution is sending it to a zoo. Liesel Skorpen's *Bird* (1976)

Viewpoint

It is obvious that the naturalist would not indulge in anthropomorphism—the endowment of animals with human traits. It is not so clear that the writers of even the best animal stories should not or do not do so. Some transfer of human intelligence and emotion to the animal character can, in good hands, heighten the emotional impact of a story and strengthen the rapport between writer and reader. . . . But it takes a sure sense of the limits of credibility to keep the realistic animal story from being maudlin or, worse, so confused as to be neither animal story nor outright fantasy.—Sheila Egoff, *The Republic of Childhood*, Oxford University Press, Toronto, 1967, p. 107.

is a diverting story about a boy who is convinced the nestling he's rescued needs his help to fly. Alma Whitney's *Leave Herbert Alone* (1972) is amusing in a wry way, as a small girl is so anxious to show her love for a cat that she frightens him and has to learn a gentler approach.

In Beverly Cleary's *Socks* (1973) the advent of a baby is told from a cat's viewpoint. Socks had been a pampered pet until the intruder came along, and he's resentfully jealous until the baby gets big enough to turn into a playmate. Socks always behaves and thinks like a cat, never a person, yet Cleary invests him with a definite personality in this delightful tale.

The animal stories by Miska Miles have in common a quiet tone, an absence of anthropomorphism, and, in most of them, a consistency in the way they reflect an animal's life from its own viewpoint. In *Nobody's Cat* (1969) a tough, self-sufficient alley cat awakens sympathy by being just what he is: lean, homely, and lonely. There is no sentimentality, no happy ending to his adventures. Other stories are *Mississippi Possum* (1965), *Eddie's Bear* (1970), *Wharf Rat* (1972), and *Otter in the Cove* (1974).

It matters little where an animal story is set, since the interest and affection children feel for creatures, wild or tame, is universal. In *Just a Dog* by Helen Griffiths (1975) the story of a mongrel pup is set in Madrid, but the incidents could be duplicated in any city. Anne de Roo's *Cinnamon and Nutmeg* (1974) takes place in New Zealand, where a farm child, knowing her father won't let her keep the calf and kid she's found, hides them in an abandoned house and gives them loving care. A Scottish farm is the setting for Alec Lea's *Temba Dawn* (1975); when the farm is sold, young Rob succeeds in convincing his father to take a pet calf, Temba Dawn, with them, in an honest and moving story. Most of Lucy Boston's writing is fantasy, but she uses the same setting, an English country house, for *A Stranger at Green Knowe* (1961), a powerful and original story about the understanding and affection between a gorilla that has escaped from a zoo and a young refugee.

There is rarely any need to urge children to read stories about animals. Pet stories bring out children's desire to nurture and protect, and, as they mature, they learn about the piteous vulnerability of animals at the hands of cruel owners or hunters and trappers. Such stories encourage a compassionate sense of kinship with animals. Many of these books teach sex casually in the course of an absorbing story. For children who have little or no knowledge of breeding and the raising of young, these stories are especially valuable. From the stories that center on the proper training of dogs and horses, young readers gain a background for the training of their own pets. There is, of course, a great deal of overlap between such stories and informational books. Much of the fiction gives accurate information, and many informational books about animals have a narrative framework; indeed, it is at times difficult to decide in which class a book belongs.

Since the mere nature of the wild animal's life means chiefly pursuit or being pursued, escape or death; and since the drama of a pet's life turns upon the upsetting of its happy security with a tragic or triumphant outcome, there is bound to be a certain similarity in these tales. Too many of them in a row are monotonous or overly harrowing. Such stories should be read along with other books. But any child is the richer for having had his or her sympathies expanded and tenderness stirred by such great animal books as *Along Came a Dog, Gentle Ben,* and *The Yearling.* Any child is the poorer for having missed the drama of *King of the Wind, The Incredible Journey,* and *A Stranger at Green Knowe.*

Sports Stories

If there is one fault common to most sports stories, it is the formula plot: the beginner, from school playground to professional team, who can't get along with another member of the team or the whole team or the coach because he or she is cocky or wants things his or her own way, eventually rises to heights of glory and acceptance by all by saving the final game in the final minute of play. Another fault common to such stories is the thin plot wrapped around long and often tedious game sequences. Perhaps more than any other kind of realistic fiction, the sports story needs good characterization and good style to give it depth, especially since there is usually little variation in setting and often little opportunity for a meaningful theme.

There are few realistic sports stories for the beginning reader, but Leonard Kessler's *Here Comes the Strikeout* (1965) has simplicity, humor, and an emphasis on perseverance and achievement. Bobby (white) cannot get a hit until he has been coached by his friend Willie (black) and has worked hard to correct his faults. Leon-

ard Shortall, in a good story for seven- to nine-year-olds, describes a boy's first attempts at skiing in *Ben on the Ski Trail* (1965). Beman Lord has written several books for this age group, one of which, *Shrimp's Soccer Goal* (1970), reflects the increasing interest in that sport and is unusual in presenting a woman teacher as the founder and coach of the team. Another good soccer story from Sweden is Kerstin Thorvall's *Gunnar Scores a Goal* (1968).

The popularity of each individual sport is echoed proportionately in children's books, with baseball and football stories far outnumbering all others. One of the most dependable writers for the nine-to-eleven group is Matt Christopher, whose productivity is impressive. *Johnny Long Legs* (1970) and *Tough to Tackle* (1971) are examples of his style: simple, undistinguished plots; good game descriptions; and an emphasis on sportsmanship and team effort. *The Baseball Bargain* (1970) by Scott Corbett has more depth, since the protagonist is tempted to steal a mitt and strikes a bargain with the storekeeper whereby he earns it by working in the store—*if* he can first do three good deeds in a day. Corbett's light, easy style and humor make this a pleasant tale with serious overtones—and good baseball. Alfred Slote's *Stranger on the Ball Club* (1970) also is concerned with ethical values and has good sports writing and deeper characterization than is found in most books at this level; his *Matt Gargan's Boy* (1950) has good game sequences in a story about Danny, son of a major league baseball player, who resents having a girl on his team, especially a girl whose father is courting Danny's divorced mother. William Pène du Bois, in *Porko von Popbutton* (1969), writes a merry tale of ice hockey at a boys' school.

Margaret Potter's *The Touch-and-Go Year* (1969) is flawed by several uses of coincidence in the plot, but is otherwise a fine story about a boy who works to become a professional tennis player—a sport that receives rather scant attention.

The response by publishers to the demand for more books about blacks and other minority groups has included sports fiction, but many of these stories seem obtrusive in their inclusion of such minorities. Indeed, one of the formulas has seemed to be the team in which each player represents a different ethnic background. Stories that approach the particular problems of the black player in sports with honesty and concern are rare, and therefore John Tunis's *All-American* (1942) was all the more exciting when it appeared. It tells the story of a boy who plays high-school football and learns to appreciate each player for his own worth and to fight discrimination. In Jesse Jackson's *Anchor Man* (1947) an influx of black students into a small-town school leads to misunderstanding on both sides, and the author gives a good study of a range of attitudes. Two later books that deal incisively with the special problems of the black player are Robert Lipsyte's *The Contender* (1967), in which a Harlem youth decides, after a successful start in a boxing career, to get an education instead; and Donald Honig's *Johnny Lee* (1971), a story of a black baseball rookie who finds discrimination as well as friendship on the team and in the Virginia town where he plays in a minor league.

In Honig's *Way to Go, Teddy* (1973), a young baseball player is in conflict with the father who wants him to become a lawyer. The details of a rookie's life are lively and authentic; the author was a professional ball player. Another story with rare depth and characterization is *Stubborn Sam* by William Gault. Sam Bogosian goes to college as his father asks—but he still wants to play baseball, and does. In Robert Weaver's *Nice Guy, Go Home* (1968), an Amish boy is drawn into a civil rights conflict in the town where his pro team plays; although he respects the Amish ideals, Johnny cannot remain neutral when he sees injustice.

As in other kinds of fiction, sports stories follow trends and issues. In the past, books about girls' sports have been undistinguished, but more are beginning to appear. *Not Bad for a Girl* by Isabella Taves (1972) is based on a real case of a girl who is put on a Little League team by a sympathetic coach. Sharon plays well, but there is such abuse and persecution by local residents that the coach and Sharon are expelled. The realistic ending gives more impact to the exposure of sexism than any formula happy ending could. Another baseball story, *Something Queer at the Ball Park* by Elizabeth Levy (1975), is a less serious tale with a slightly slapstick mystery element, but it does feature a girl who plays on a team on which the issue of sex roles doesn't even arise. Good at all sports, Zan Hagen moves from football to basketball in R. R. Knudson's *Zanbanger* (1977). In *Rod-and-Reel Trouble* by Bobbi Katz (1974), a girl who has always wanted to enter an annual fishing contest gets a chance when it is, for the first time, open to girls as well as boys; the story has a protagonist who is courageous, sensible, and persistent. The popularity of running and jogging should provide a captive audience for the persevering heroine of Elizabeth Winthrop's *Marathon Miranda* (1979). In Scott Corbett's *The Hockey Girls* (1976), a group of high-school girls are horrified when they discover that an athletic program has been set up for girls, since not any of them are interested in sports. But the field hockey coach, an elderly English teacher, is competent and enthusiastic, and the girls find, once they have attained proficiency, that they enjoy the game.

The interest in the problem of drugs is reflected in William Heumann's *Fastbreak Rebel* (1971), in which the white protagonist on a pro basketball team encourages his coach to sign on a black player who has given up drugs and is especially anxious to show the young people of his deprived neighborhood that there is a better way than the marijuana-to-heroin path.

Although few American readers understand the fine points of cricket, nobody can miss the high-spirited humor of P. G. Wodehouse's *Mike and Psmith* (1969), first published in 1909, but a timeless piece of school humor. Shinty is enough like hockey to be comprehensible to fans, and Margaret MacPherson's *The Shinty Boys* (1963) has a cohesive plot, plenty of action, lively characters, and the flavorful dialogue and atmosphere of the Isle of Skye. Last, for really mature readers, *Today's Game* (1965), by Martin Quigley, is valuable both because of the author's expert knowledge of baseball behind the scene and because of the brisk, professional approach to the problems of a manager, his moves and counter-moves in a crucial game. This is a side of baseball seldom described, and it paves the way for some of the adult baseball classics such as *Bang the Drum Slowly* by Mark Harris and *The Long Season* by Jim Brosnan.

Mystery and Adventure

A classification of children's books which cuts across all groups of realistic fiction in all countries and times is the mystery story. The mystery tale is certainly a striking example of the way in which children's books parallel predominant trends in adult reading interests. With mothers, fathers, and even grandparents all devoted to the "whodunit" school of writing, it is not surprising to find a seven-year-old marching into the children's room of a library and demanding a good mystery story.

Not only do adventure and mystery stories

cut across realistic fiction, but also infringe with impunity on historical fiction, as do many of Mollie Hunter's books: are they historically based tales of adventure or are they historical tales filled with dramatic incidents? Townsend's *The Intruder* and Virginia Hamilton's *The House of Dies Drear*, both mentioned earlier in this chapter, seem primarily realistic stories, yet they may well be considered mystery tales.

The extreme popularity of the mystery tale at present may be a fad as far as children are concerned, artificially stimulated by adult emphasis. An element of mystery has always been a source of interest in a story and always will be. But when innumerable books are written merely for the sake of the mystery, the pattern and mood of such tales are liable to become tiresomely repetitious and the stories are likely to be trash. At their worst, such books are marked by preposterous plots, details left unaccounted for, too many episodes, violence piled upon violence, typed characters, and, finally, poor style.

The virtues of good mystery tales for children are numerous, but first among these is the atmosphere of excitement and suspense which serves as the most tempting of all baits for nonreaders. Comic-strip-addicted and television-fed children demand a highly spiced book fare if they are going to read at all, and these mystery tales are usually adventure stories with plenty of breathtaking action to keep young thrill-seekers absorbed. Another useful feature of such stories is that they help establish a much needed reading skill—rapid silent reading. Children unconsciously speed up their usual reading rate under the stimulus of an agreeable suspense. They will cover pages of a mystery tale at breakneck speed in their desire to find the answers and solve the mystery. This rapid rate of silent reading, together with a little skipping or skimming on the way, is a useful habit for fiction readers to establish—the younger the better.

Finally, if children can be supplied with adventure and mystery stories which are also well written and not too difficult for them to read, unbookish children can be persuaded to read a better type of literature than they might otherwise attempt.

The appeal of suspense often leads children to read above their usual level. Older children will plunge happily into adult mystery stories, and children in the middle grades may have favorite authors whose books are intended for older children. Even the youngest now have

mystery tales: short, easy to read, and wisely laced with humor. Some of these are Joan Lexau's *The Rooftop Mystery* (1968) and *The Homework Caper* (1966); Ben Shecter's *Inspector Rose* (1969), which has a circus setting, Elizabeth Levy's *Something Queer Is Going On* (1973), and Crosby Bonsall's stories—*The Case of the Cat's Meow* (1965) and others with a lively interracial cast.

Popular with the eight-to-ten age group are the tales by Donald Sobol about a boy detective; in *Encyclopedia Brown Saves the Day* (1970) the astute ten-year-old solves a series of short mysteries, with answers at the back of the book. Catherine Storr's *Lucy* (1968) is determined to be a detective, and, much to her surprise, she effects the capture of a gang of thieves.

For the nine- to eleven-year-olds, there's an enticing locked room in Elizabeth Ladd's *A Mystery for Meg (1962). Erich Kästner's Emil and the Detectives* was published in 1930, but the charm of this German author's style is such that the book is still enjoyed.

The series of adventure tales by Alan Coren that begin with *Arthur the Kid* (1978) has elements of mystery, but the author, editor of *Punch* magazine, uses outrageous and very funny exaggeration as ten-year-old Arthur solves all crimes and problems in this and other spoofs of the desperado tale.

It is for the ten- to twelve-year-olds that mystery stories begin to appear in large numbers, although any true fan will read any good mystery—and even some not so good. In Eleanor Cameron's *A Spell Is Cast* (1964), there are logical explanations for all the things that puzzle Cory, and the book has fine characterization. Although the plot of Frank Bonham's *Mystery in Little Tokyo* (1966) is somewhat contrived, Bonham draws a fine picture of the Japanese section of Los Angeles as a solid neighborhood community with rich tradition. Jane Curry's maturity as a writer is evident in *Ghost Lane* (1979), with a tight plot and strong characterization giving substance to a mystery story about an art-theft ring in England, and the American boy who becomes involved in it.

Philippa Pearce's *The Minnow Leads to Treasure* (1958) is notable for its distinctive style and well-paced plot. In *The Minnow*, two boys recover a family treasure that had been lost since the time of the Armada. To the lure of the subject and the suspense of the story are added superbly natural characters, humor, and an evocative atmosphere of long, golden summer days. In Florence Hightower's *The Fayerweather Forecast* (1967), the style is lively and there are some highly entertaining episodes, such as the one in which mother is working for a new school and little Bitsy obligingly quavers out a pitiful tale about the horrors of the decrepit old school. A kidnapping is solved by a doughty girl in Dorothy Crayder's *She and the Dubious Three* (1974), and the heroine is herself kidnaped in Margaret Storey's *Ask Me No Questions* (1975). Local legends permeate *Mystery at the Edge of Two Worlds* (1978) by Christie Harris, whose familiarity with Canada's northwest coast adds color to a fast-paced adventure story.

Catch as Catch Can (1970) by Josephine Poole is an English mystery story in which two children witness an incident on a train and are pursued by criminals, a basic plot often used in adult tales and here executed with finesse. In Keith Robertson's *The Money Machine* (1969), two boys pursue the trail of a counterfeiter, and in Eva-Lis Wuorio's *Save Alice!* (1968) three children have a romping journey through Spain, trying to discover why Alice (a bird) had been shoved into their car and what the dastardly villains who did it are up to. In addition to the fun, the story has delightful dialogue between the British and American contingents of the party.

When we come to the mystery and adventure tales for children of eleven and up, we face an avalanche. One of the great classic tales of adventure is Robert Louis Stevenson's *Treasure Island* (1883), which has been published in many fine editions. The story of Long John Silver and his pirate crew has suspense, masterly characterization, a rousing plot, and an adroit contrast in moral codes. *Crystal Mountain* (1955) by Belle Dorman Rugh was a Newbery Honor book. Set in Lebanon, the story has good intercultural relations as well as an interesting setting and the satisfying solution to a minor mystery. Among Keith Robertson's mysteries for this age group are *Three Stuffed Owls* (1954) and *Ice to India* (1955), a sea story with a wonderfully villainous villain.

Beautifully crafted, written in three strands that are woven together, Robert Cormier's *I Am the Cheese* (1977) begins with a boy's bicycle trip and ends with a dramatic flourish after it becomes clear that the boy is a political hostage. Cormier uses flashbacks and interviews brilliantly to create suspense.

Illustration by Lou Crockett from *Mystery at the Edge of Two Worlds* by Christie Harris. Copyright © 1978 by Christie Harris. Reprinted by permission of Atheneum publishers.

One of the master storytellers of our time in the realm of high adventure is Leon Garfield. His stories are set in the eighteenth century, abound in picturesque language, period details, complicated plots, exaggerated characters (usually of very high or very low estate), and are written so deftly that the wildly implausible is made wholly convincing. In *Black Jack* (1968), for example, a hanged man revives, captures an orphaned boy and holds up a coach from which an insane girl escapes. The boy and girl join a caravan, she regains her sanity, her father is murdered, she goes to an asylum, the repentant highwayman rescues her, and the boy and girl sail off as stowaways in his uncle's ship, presumably to a much quieter life.

In Henry Winterfeld's *Mystery of the Roman Ransom* (1971) the exuberant boys of ancient Rome who solved a puzzler in *Detectives in Togas* (1956), again become involved in a dramatic detective venture when a slave from Gaul tells them he bears a secret message that a senator is doomed to die. The boys are all sons of senators, and they immediately spring into action, lots of it. The story has the pace and suspense that a good mystery story should have, and although it has no historical significance, it gives a modicum of information about ancient Rome; it also has a minor anti-slavery message, vigorous style, and good characterization.

From France come the mystery stories of Paul Berna, whose *A Truckload of Rice* (1970) is a good example of the solid plots, lively chase sequences, and Parisian settings characteristic of most of his books.

The books of Philip Turner are more boys-and-ploys than they are mysteries, though in *Colonel Sheperton's Clock* (1966) the boys, busily investigating an old mystery, find themselves involved with criminals. The first sequel, *The Grange at High Force* (1967), was awarded the Carnegie Medal, and all of the books are distinguished by a vivid picture of an English town and by the sparkling dialogue, which is tossed back and forth from boy to boy like a Ping-Pong ball.

Roderic Jeffries, who writes adult mysteries as Jeffrey Ashford, excels at logical plot construction and authoritative details in police procedure in *Patrol Car* (1967) and *River Patrol* (1969).

Felicity Bell tells her own story in Patricia Moyes's *Helter-Skelter* (1968), an artfully plotted tale of a security leak at a British naval research base, during which the heroine confides in the culprit himself and thereby endangers her life.

Madeleine L'Engle's rather involved adventure story, *The Arm of the Starfish* (1965), revolves around the kidnapping of Poly, the precocious twelve-year-old daughter of Calvin and Meg Murry O'Keefe (of L'Engle's science fiction trilogy). Calvin O'Keefe, now a marine biologist, is working on regeneration of body parts, and there are spies and agents prying about the Portuguese island that is the setting. Despite the complications of plot, the story is strong in appeal because of its theme of the triumph of good over evil, or at least of the humane over the inhumane. This is true also of the sequel, *Dragons in the Waters* (1976).

A fledgling spy almost muffs his first assignment in Christopher Nicole's *Operation Destruct* (1969), a story that has the mad pace of the adult spy stories it mocks, light humor, and refreshing variation in detail, such as the pretty

girl reporter who is far more adept than the hero and who falls for a pop singer. William Mayne, writing under the name of Martin Cobalt, in *Pool of Swallows* (1974) produces a brilliant blend of ghostly happenings, humor, and suspense, as some mysterious pools that suddenly swirl and flood prove to have a logical explanation.

Frank Bonham's *Mystery of the Fat Cat* (1968) is set in a poor neighborhood, Dogtown, where the fate of the Boys' Club is contingent upon a cat. The boys suspect that the cat's caretaker has substituted another animal so that he will not lose his job (he is paid out of an estate which goes to the Boys' Club after the cat's death). The efforts of the boys to prove a fraud has been perpetrated are exciting and believable, and the inclusion of a mentally retarded child as a sympathetic character who contributes to the solution is a bonus.

Of the many mystery anthologies, one that approaches the quality of the best compilations for adults is Joan Kahn's *Some Things Fierce and Fatal* (1971). Other anthologies are included in the bibliography for this chapter.

The books discussed here should suffice to show how mystery cuts across most forms of fiction. Unlike adult "whodunits," the juvenile stories seldom involve murder. Rather, the element of mystery is introduced to heighten interest and suspense. Few of these books have literary distinction, though many are competently written, and mystery tales for children are particularly valuable when, in the course of exciting action, they also emphasize desirable attitudes and social relationships.

The books mentioned in this chapter do not by any means exhaust the list of good realistic fiction for children and young people. To give only the best to children, the adult should be aware of the pedestrian books that are written as "bandwagon" books to satisfy a demand, and should evaluate new books with a critical appraisal of how well they meet the standards discussed in Chapter 3 and fulfill the needs discussed in Chapter 2. The best in this genre will always be those books that depict life honestly and accurately. They are the ones that are interesting in themselves, that present characters who evoke understanding or even self-identification, and that give children new insights into experiences both familiar and unknown.

Adult References[2]

CLARK, ANN NOLAN. *Journey to the People.*

EGOFF, SHEILA. *The Republic of Childhood: A Critical Guide to Canadian Children's Literature in English.* Part 4, "The Realistic Animal Story."

EGOFF, SHEILA, G. T. STUBBS, and L. F. ASHLEY, eds. *Only Connect: Readings on Children's Literature.* Part 6, "The Modern Scene."

ELLIS, ANNE W. *The Family Story in the 1960's.*

FENWICK, SARA INNIS, ed. *A Critical Approach to Children's Literature.* "Literature for Children Without" by Marion Edman.

HILDICK, WALLACE. *Children and Fiction.*

HOPKINS, LEE BENNETT. *Books Are by People.*

LEPMAN, JELLA. *A Bridge of Children's Books.*

REES, DAVID. *The Marble in the Water.*

REID, VIRGINIA M. ed., *Reading Ladders for Human Relations.*

WHITE, DOROTHY, and MARY NEAL. *Books Before Five.*

For additional titles for the youngest children, see the Picture Story Books bibliography, Chapter 5.

For help in locating books with special purposes or about minorities, see the section "Book Selection Aids" in Appendix A. In the following bibliography these symbols have been used to identify books about a particular religious or ethnic group:

§ Black
★ Chicano or Puerto Rican
☆ Native American
● Religious minority

Some Forerunners of Realistic Fiction

ALCOTT, LOUISA M. *Little Women,* ill. by Barbara Cooney. T. Crowell, 1955 (first pub. in 1868–69).

———. *Little Women,* ill. by Jessie W. Smith. Little, 1968. 10–13

BURNETT, FRANCES HODGSON. *The Secret Garden,* ill. by Tasha Tudor. Lippincott, 1962 (first pub. in 1909). 9–11

DODGE, MARY MAPES. *Hans Brinker: or the Silver Skates,* ill. by Hilda Van Stockum. World, 1948 (first pub. in 1865). 10–12

SPYRI, JOHANNA. *Heidi,* ill. by Greta Elgaard. Macmillan, 1962 (first pub. in 1884). 9–11

TWAIN, MARK (pseud. for Samuel Clemens). *The Adventures of Huckleberry Finn,* ill. by John Falter. Macmillan, 1962 (first pub. in 1885). 10 up

———. *The Adventures of Tom Sawyer,* ill. by John Falter. Macmillan, 1962 (first pub. in 1876). 10–14

———. *The Adventures of Tom Sawyer* and *The Adventures of Huckleberry Finn,* ill. by Norman Rockwell, 2 vols. in 1. Heritage, 1952. 10–14

2. Complete bibliographic data are provided in Appendix B.

Realistic Fiction: The United States

§ ADOFF, ARNOLD, ed. *Brothers and Sisters: Modern Stories by Black Americans.* Macmillan, 1970. A discriminating selection of twenty short stories about black youth, varied in period, setting, style, and mood, chosen from a 40-year span. 12 up

§ AGLE, NAN HAYDEN. *Maple Street,* ill. by Leonora E. Prince. Seabury, 1970. A black Baltimore neighborhood is kind to a hostile white family in time of trouble. 8–10

ALBERT, LOUISE. *But I'm Ready To Go.* Bradbury, 1976. A touching story of a fifteen-year-old handicapped girl who suffers from teasing by others, the differences of which she is so keenly aware, and her own feelings of inadequacy and apprehension. 11–14

ALEXANDER, MARTHA G. *I'll Be the Horse If You'll Play with Me,* ill. by author. Dial, 1975. 5–7

———. *Out! Out! Out!* ill. by author. Dial, 1968. 3–5

§ ———. *Sabrina,* ill. by author. Dial, 1971. 3–5

§ ———. *The Story Grandmother Told,* ill. by author. Dial, 1969. 3–6

———. *When the New Baby Comes, I'm Moving Out,* ill. by author. Dial, 1979. 3–5

ALIKI. *The Two of Them,* ill. by author. Greenwillow, 1979. 5–8

§ ARMSTRONG, WILLIAM. *Sounder,* ill. by James Barkley. Harper, 1969. Newbery Medal. 12–15

★●☆ ASSOCIATION FOR CHILDHOOD EDUCATION. *Told Under the Stars and Stripes,* ill. by Nedda Walker. Macmillan, 1945. An interracial collection. 8–12

☆ BAKER, BETTY. *Little Runner of the Longhouse,* ill. by Arnold Lobel. Harper, 1962. Little Runner finally gains his reward of maple sugar in the Iroquois New Year rites. An amusing repetitive Indian tale for beginning readers. 6–7

☆ ———. *The Shaman's Last Raid,* ill. by Leonard Shortall. Harper, 1963. Two Apache children of today learn something of their tribal culture when great-grandfather visits them. 9–11

★ BARTH, EDNA. *The Day Luis Was Lost,* ill. by Lilian Obligado. Little, 1971. Newly arrived in the city, a Puerto Rican child has trouble finding his way to school. 8–10

§ BEIM, LORRAINE and JERROLD. *Two Is a Team,* ill. by Ernest Crichlow. Harcourt, 1945. A black and a white youngster learn to cooperate. 5–8

★ BELPRE, PURA. *Santiago,* ill. by Symeon Shimin. Warne, 1969. Missing his pet, left behind in Puerto Rico, a child finds that his picture of her brings him a new friend. 8–9

§ BERENDS, POLLY BERRIEN. *The Case of the Elevator Duck,* ill. by James K. Washburn. Random, 1973. Gilbert, bright, black, bespectacled, finds a duck in the housing project elevator, where no pets are allowed, and finally finds a home for it. A natural, funny story. 8–10

BLUE, ROSE. *Grandma Didn't Wave Back,* ill. by Ted Lewin. Watts, 1972. 8–10

● BLUME, JUDY. *Are You There God? It's Me, Margaret.* Bradbury, 1970. 10–12

———. *Blubber.* Bradbury, 1974. 9–11

———. *Deenie.* Bradbury, 1973. 10–13

———. *It's Not the End of the World.* Bradbury, 1972. 9–11

———. *Then Again, Maybe I Won't.* Bradbury, 1971. 10–12

§ BONHAM, FRANK. *Durango Street.* Dutton, 1965. 4 up

§ ———. *The Nitty Gritty*, ill. by Alvin Smith. Dutton, 1968. 11–14

★ ———. *Viva Chicano*. Dutton, 1970. A Chicano youth on parole fights to escape from the burdens that have trapped him into delinquency. 13–16

BONSALL, CROSBY. *The Goodbye Summer*. Greenwillow, 1978. Allie, whose widowed mother runs a rooming house, clings with tenacity to those she loves. Only gradually does she realize that farewells are just as much a part of life as loving relationships. 9–11

BRADBURY, BIANCA. *Andy's Mountain*, ill. by Robert MacLean. Houghton, 1969. A warm and lively picture of a cantankerous and determined old man who refuses to give up his farm to the state for a highway and of the love and loyalty between him and his grandson. 10–12

BRIDGERS, SUE ELLEN. *All Together Now*. Knopf, 1979. Twelve-year-old Casey, spending a summer with her grandparents, befriends a retarded man of thirty. 10–12

———. *Home Before Dark*. Knopf, 1977. When her father, a migrant laborer, finally settles down on a tobacco farm, fourteen-year-old Stella anticipates a better life. 11–14

BROOKS, JEROME. *The Testing of Charlie Hammelman*. Dutton, 1977. Charlie, a junior in high school, is faced with a myriad of adolescent problems: he's plump, shy, and terrified of being seen naked and of taking a required swim test. It is unexpectedly the love and encouragement he gets from a girl that makes it all work out. 12–15

———. *Uncle Mike's Boy*. Harper, 1973. A boy adjusting to his parents' divorce and the death of a small sister finds his uncle a source of support and understanding. A warm, sensitive, at times touching, story. 10–12

BROWN, MARGARET WISE. *The City Noisy Book*, ill. by Leonard Weisgard. Harper, 1939. 4–6

———. *The Dead Bird*, ill. by Remy Charlip. W. R. Scott, 1958. A simple story of some children's burial of a bird. 5–7

———. *The Little Fisherman*, ill. by Dahlov Ipcar. W. R. Scott, 1945. 4–6

———. (Golden MacDonald, pseud.). *The Little Island*, ill. by Leonard Weisgard. Doubleday, 1946. Gentle descriptive prose. Caldecott Medal. 4–8

☆ BUFF, MARY. *Dancing Cloud*, ill. by Conrad Buff, rev. ed. Viking, 1957. The Navaho Indians depicted in beautiful prose and pictures. 8–10

☆ BUFF, MARY and CONRAD. *Hah-Nee of the Cliff Dwellers*, ill. by Conrad Buff. Houghton, 1956. A story of the great pueblo cities of the Southwest. 10–12

● ———. *Peter's Pinto*, ill. by Conrad Buff. Viking, 1949. A Utah ranch summer is highlighted for Peter when he acquires a wild pinto pony of his own. Mormon background. 9–11

☆ BULLA, CLYDE. *Eagle Feather*, ill. by Tom Two Arrows. T. Crowell, 1953. Eagle Feather, a young Navaho, loved the outdoor life of a shepherd and had no wish to go to school until changed circumstances made school a longed-for goal. 7–10

☆ ———. *Indian Hill*, ill. by James Spanfeller. T. Crowell, 1963. Adjustment of a Navaho Indian family moved from a reservation to a city apartment. 8–10

———. *Shoeshine Girl*, ill. by Leigh Grant. T. Crowell, 1975. Sarah Ida takes a job shining shoes for spending money, and changes for the better as a result of her relationship with her boss. Quiet but satisfying. 8–10

BURCH, ROBERT. *Ida Early Comes Over the Mountain*. Viking, 1980. Big, awkward, and merry Ida Early wins the love of four motherless children in a Georgia farm family. 9–11

———. *Joey's Cat*, ill. by Don Freeman. Viking, 1969.

§ ———. *Queenie Peavy*, ill. by Jerry Lazare. Viking, 1966. 11–14

———. *Simon and the Game of Chance*, ill. by Fermin Rocker. Viking, 1970. 10–12

———. *Wilkin's Ghost*, ill. by Lloyd Bloom. Viking, 1978. 10–12

BYARS, BETSY C. *After the Goat Man*, ill. by Ronald Himler. Viking, 1974. 10–12

———. *Goodbye, Chicken Little*. Harper, 1979. 9–11

———. *The House of Wings*, ill. by Daniel Schwartz. Viking, 1972. 9–12

———. *The Night Swimmers*, ill. by Troy Howell. Delacorte, 1980. 10–12

———. *The Pinballs*. Harper, 1977. 10–12

———. *The Summer of the Swans*, ill. by Ted CoConis. Viking, 1970. Newbery Medal. 10–12

———. *The TV Kid*, ill. by Richard Cuffari. Viking, 1976. 8–9

§ CAINES, JEANNETTE FRANKLIN. *Abby*, ill. by Steven Kellogg. Harper, 1973. A small black girl learns about her adoption. 3–6

CAMERON, ELEANOR. *Julia and the Hand of God*, ill. by Gail Owens. Dutton, 1977. 9–11

———. *A Room Made of Windows*, ill. by Trina Schart Hyman. Little, 1971. 10–13

§ ———. *To the Green Mountains*. Dutton, 1975. 10–13

CAMPBELL, HOPE. *Why Not Join the Giraffes?* Norton, 1968. Suzie's stuffy boyfriend almost makes her regret her nonconformist parents. 11–14

§ CARLSON, NATALIE SAVAGE. *Ann Aurelia and Dorothy*, ill. by Dale Payson. Harper, 1968. 8–10

§ ———. *The Empty Schoolhouse*, ill. by John Kaufmann. Harper, 1965. 9–11

§ ———. *Marchers for the Dream*, ill. by Alvin Smith. Harper, 1969. 9–11

§ CAUDILL, REBECCA. *A Certain Small Shepherd*, ill. by William Pène du Bois. Holt, 1965. An Appalachian Christmas story, movingly told. 9–11

———. *Did You Carry the Flag Today, Charley?* ill. by Nancy Grossman. Holt, 1966. 5–7

★§ CHILD STUDY ASSOCIATION OF AMERICA. *Families Are Like That!* ill. by Richard Cuffari. T. Crowell, 1975. Ten stories of family life and relationships. 7–9

§ CHILDRESS, ALICE. *A Hero Ain't Nothin' But a Sandwich*. Coward, 1973. 11–14

☆ CLARK, ANN NOLAN. *Along Sandy Trails*, photos by Alfred A. Cohn. Viking, 1969. Not really a story, this book with its beautiful color photos follows an Indian child in the Arizona desert and gives a feeling of the peaceful life and of the color and beauty of the dry land's flowering. 8–10

☆ ———. *In My Mother's House*, ill. by Velino Herrera. Viking, 1941. 8–12

☆ ———. *Little Navajo Bluebird*, ill. by Paul Lantz. Viking, 1943. 8–12

☆ ———. *Medicine Man's Daughter*, ill. by Donald Bolognese. Farrar, 1963. 11–13

CLEARY, BEVERLY. *Ellen Tebbits*, ill. by Louis Darling. Morrow, 1951. The trials and tribulations of being in third grade. 8–12

_____. *Henry Huggins,* ill. by Louis Darling. Morrow, 1950. And other books in the series. 8–10

_____. *Mitch and Amy,* ill. by George Porter. Morrow, 1967. 9–11

_____. *Ramona and Her Father,* ill. by Alan Tiegreen. Morrow, 1977. 8–10

_____. *Ramona and Her Mother,* ill. by Alan Tiegreen. Morrow, 1979. 8–10

_____. *Ramona the Brave,* ill. by Alan Tiegreen. Morrow, 1975. 8–10

_____. *Ramona the Pest,* ill. by Louis Darling. Morrow, 1968. 8–10

_____. *Ribsy,* ill. by Louis Darling. Morrow, 1964. 9–11

CLEAVER, VERA and BILL. *Dust of the Earth.* Lippincott, 1975. 11–14

_____. *Ellen Grae,* ill. by Ellen Raskin. Lippincott, 1967. 9–11

_____. *Grover,* ill. by Frederic Marvin. Lippincott, 1970. 9–11

_____. *I Would Rather Be a Turnip.* Lippincott, 1971. 10–12

_____. *Lady Ellen Grae,* ill. by Ellen Raskin. Lippincott, 1968. 9–11

_____. *Trial Valley.* Lippincott, 1977. 11–14

_____. *Where the Lilies Bloom,* ill. by Jim Spanfeller. Lippincott, 1969. 11–14

CLEMENTS, BRUCE. *Anywhere Else But Here.* Farrar, 1980. Witty and perceptive, the story of a motherless girl of thirteen who accepts and loves a small boy deserted by his mother. 11–14

CLIFFORD, ETH. *The Rocking Chair Rebellion.* Houghton, 1978. 10–12

§ CLIFTON, LUCILLE. *Don't You Remember?* ill. by Evaline Ness. Dutton, 1973. A charming black family story, with a four-year-old who remembers everything. 3–5

§ _____. *The Lucky Stone,* ill. by Dale Payson. Delacorte, 1979. The story that Tee tells serves as a frame for a series of anecdotes from Great-grand's life. 8–10

§ _____. *My Brother Fine with Me,* ill. by Moneta Barnett. Holt, 1975. 7–9

§ _____. *The Times They Used to Be,* ill. by Susan Jeschke. Holt, 1974. 10–11

CLYMER, ELEANOR. *The Get-Away Car.* Dutton, 1978. Maggie and her grandmother prove that grandma isn't ready for an old people's home. 9–11

§ _____. *The House on the Mountain,* ill. by Leo Carty. Dutton, 1971. 8–9

§ _____. *Luke Was There,* ill. by Diane de Groat. Holt, 1973. 9–12

_____. *My Brother Stevie.* Holt, 1971. 9–11

☆ _____. *The Spider, the Cave and the Pottery Bowl,* ill. by Ingrid Fetz. Atheneum, 1971. 8–10

●§ COHEN, BARBARA. *Thank You, Jackie Robinson,* ill. by Richard Cuffari. Lothrop, 1974. 9–11

COLLIER, JAMES LINCOLN. *Rich and Famous: The Further Adventures of George Stable.* Four Winds, 1975. 11–14

_____. *The Teddy Bear Habit, or How I Became a Winner,* ill. by Lee Lorenz. Norton, 1967. Fast pace and fast humor in the TV and recording industry as 13-year-old George's agent tries to make him a star. 10–12

§ COLMAN, HILA. *Classmates by Request.* Morrow, 1964. 12–15

_____. *Claudia, Where Are You?* Morrow, 1969. 12–15

★ _____. *The Girl from Puerto Rico.* Morrow, 1961. 12–15

§ CONE, MOLLY. *The Other Side of the Fence,* ill. by John Gretzer. Houghton, 1967. It's hard to side with the minority when a black family moves into the neighborhood. 8–10

CONFORD, ELLEN. *Felicia the Critic,* ill. by Arvis Stewart. Little, 1973. Why did people get so irritated when Felicia just used common sense and told the truth? Funny, completely natural dialogue. 10–12

CORCORAN, BARBARA. *A Dance to Still Music,* ill. by Charles Robinson. Atheneum, 1974. 11–13

_____. *The Long Journey,* ill. by Charles Robinson. Atheneum, 1970. Laurie, thirteen, is sent on horseback by her grandfather across the state of Montana to find her uncle. The story has pace and suspense, memorable characters, an appealing heroine, and a satisfying ending. 10–12

_____. *Sam,* ill. by Barbara McGee. Atheneum, 1967. 11–14

● CORMIER, ROBERT. *The Chocolate War.* Pantheon, 1974. 12–16

CRAYDER, DOROTHY. *She, the Adventuress,* ill. by Velma Ilsley. Atheneum, 1973. 9–11

CRETAN, GLADYS YESSAYAN. *All Except Sammy,* ill. by Symeon Shimin. Little, 1966. The misfit in a musical Armenian-American family, Sammy finds status and satisfaction in art. 8–10

DANZIGER, PAULA. *The Cat Ate My Gymsuit.* Delacorte, 1974. 11–13

§ DE ANGELI, MARGUERITE. *Bright April,* ill. by author. Doubleday, 1946. 8–11

● _____. *Henner's Lydia,* ill. by author. Doubleday, 1936. 8–10

_____. *The Lion in the Box,* ill. by author. Doubleday, 1975. An old-fashioned Christmas story. 9–11

● _____. *Skippack School,* ill. by author. Doubleday, 1939 and 1961. 9–11

● _____. *Thee, Hannah!* ill. by author. Doubleday, 1940. 9–11

● _____. *Yonie Wondernose,* ill. by author. Doubleday, 1944. 6–9

DE PAOLA, TOMIE. *Nana Upstairs and Nana Downstairs,* ill. by author. Putnam, 1973. 5–8

DE REGNIERS, BEATRICE. *A Little House of Your Own,* ill. by Irene Haas. Harcourt, 1955. A house of your own is important to even the youngest child. 5–7

☆ DISTAD, ANDREE. *Dakota Sons,* ill. by Tony Chen. Harper, 1972. When Tad made friends with an Indian boy, he found out just how pervasive prejudice could be. 9–11

DONOVAN, JOHN. *I'll Get There. It Better Be Worth the Trip.* Harper, 1969. 11–14

_____. *Wild in the World.* Harper, 1971. 11–14

☆ EMBRY, MARGARET. *Shadi.* Holiday, 1971. A story of cultural conflict for an adolescent Navajo girl. 11–14

ENRIGHT, ELIZABETH. *The Four-Story Mistake,* ill. by author. Holt, 1942. 9–11

_____. *Gone-Away Lake,* ill. by Beth and Joe Krush. Harcourt, 1957. 8–10

_____. *Return to Gone-Away,* ill. by Beth and Joe Krush. Harcourt, 1961. 8–10

_____. *The Saturdays,* ill. by author. Holt, 1941. 9–12

_____. *Then There Were Five,* ill. by author. Holt, 1944. 10–13

_____. *Thimble Summer,* ill. by author. Holt, 1938. Newbery Medal. 10–12

§ ERWIN, BETTY. *Behind the Magic Line,* ill. by Julia Iltis. Little, 1969. 9–11

ESTES, ELEANOR. *The Alley,* ill. by Edward Ardizzone. Harcourt, 1964. 9–11

_____. *The Coat-Hanger Christmas Tree,* ill. by Suzanne Suba. Atheneum, 1973. 9–11

_____. *Ginger Pye,* ill. by author. Harcourt, 1951. Newbery Medal. 9–11

_____. *The Hundred Dresses,* ill. by Louis Slobodkin. Harcourt, 1944. 9–11

_____. *The Lost Umbrella of Kim Chu,* ill. by Jacqueline Ayer. Atheneum, 1978. 8–9

_____. *The Middle Moffat,* ill. by Louis Slobodkin. Harcourt, 1942. 9–11

_____. *The Moffats*, ill. by Louis Slobodkin. Harcourt, 1941 and 1968.　　9–11

_____. *Rufus M.*, ill. by Louis Slobodkin. Harcourt, 1943.　　9–11

ETS, MARIE HALL. *Play with Me*, ill. by author. Viking, 1955. An exquisite picture story showing how a little girl makes many animal friends when she learns to be still in the woods.　　3–6

EWING, KATHRYN. *A Private Matter*, ill. by Jean Sandin. Harcourt, 1975.　　9–10

FASSLER, JOAN. *Howie Helps Himself*, ill. by Joe Lasker. Whitman, 1974.　　6–8

§ FAULKNER, GEORGENE, and JOHN BECKER. *Melindy's Medal*, ill. by Elton C. Fax. Messner, 1945. A humorous and tender story of a black girl, Melindy, who is boundlessly happy when the family moves to a new housing project. When a fire breaks out at her school, Melindy proves her bravery.　　8–10

§ FENNER, CAROL. *The Skates of Uncle Richard*, ill. by Ati Forberg. Random, 1978.　　8–9

● FENTON, EDWARD. *Duffy's Rocks*. Dutton, 1974. Timothy, raised by his grandmother, can't rest until he sees his father for himself. An outstanding story of a Roman Catholic family in the Depression years.　　11–13

● FITZGERALD, JOHN DENNIS. *The Great Brain Does It Again*, ill. by Mercer Mayer. Dial, 1975. One of a series about a Roman Catholic family living in a Mormon town. J.D. tells anecdotes about his older brother, who can talk his way out of anything. Lively and funny.　　10–12

FITZHUGH, LOUISE. *Harriet the Spy*, ill. by author. Harper, 1964.　　10–12

_____. *The Long Secret*, ill. by author. Harper, 1965.　　11–13

§ _____. *Nobody's Family Is Going to Change*. Farrar, 1974. A black father scoffs at the daughter who wants to be a lawyer like him, but Emma won't change her mind.　　10–11

FLACK, MARJORIE. *Wait for William*, ill. by author and R. A. Holberg. Houston, 1935.　　4–8

FOX, PAULA. *Blowfish Live in the Sea*. Bradbury, 1970.　　11–14

§ _____. *How Many Miles to Babylon?* ill. by Paul Giovanopoulos. White, 1967.　　9–10

_____. *A Likely Place*, ill. by Edward Ardizzone. Macmillan, 1967.　　9–11

_____. *Maurice's Room*. ill. by Ingrid Fetz. Macmillan, 1966.　　8–10

_____. *Portrait of Ivan*, ill. by Saul Lambert. Bradbury, 1969.　　10–12

_____. *The Stone-Faced Boy*, ill. by Donald A. MacKay. Bradbury, 1968.　　9–11

☆ FREDERICKSEN, HAZEL. *He-Who-Runs-Far*, ill. by John Houser. W. R. Scott, 1970. The book is chiefly devoted to years spent by Pablo, a Papago Indian, in the government school where he learns English and the white man's ways. He becomes convinced he must bring understanding and change to his people but finds that they are not yet ready to accept his ideas.　　10–13

★ GALBRAITH, CLARE K. *Victor*, ill. by Bill Comerford. Knopf, 1971. Victor has a hard time with a new language, and is delighted when Mamacita shows up at school on Parents' Night and airs her secretly learned English.　　8–9

GATES, DORIS. *Blue Willow*, ill. by Paul Lantz. Viking, 1940. A story of migratory farm workers and ten-year-old Janey's longing for a permanent home.　　10–12

GEORGE, JEAN. *My Side of the Mountain*, ill. by author. Dutton, 1959.　　11–14

GOFF, BETH. *Where Is Daddy? The Story of a Divorce*, ill. by Susan Perl. Beacon, 1969.　　3–5

GOFFSTEIN, M. B. *Two Piano Tuners*, ill. by author. Farrar, 1970. Orphaned Debbie lives with her grandfather, an expert piano tuner. He wants Debbie to be a concert pianist; she wants to be a piano tuner as good as Grandpa. The story has humor, affection, and charm.　　8–9

§ GRAHAM, LORENZ. *North Town*. T. Crowell, 1965.

§ _____. *South Town*. Follett, 1958.

§ _____. *Whose Town?* T. Crowell, 1969, In these books the Williams family leaves the South because of discrimination, but finds much discrimination in the North as well. David, a teenager, wavers between militancy and moderation.　　11–14

● GREENE, BETTE. *Morning Is a Long Time Coming*. Dial, 1978. In a sequel to *Summer of My German Soldier*, Patty goes to Europe in search of the mother of her German soldier.11–14

_____. *Philip Hall Likes Me. I Reckon Maybe*, ill. by Charles Lilly. Dial, 1974.　　9–11

● _____. *Summer of My German Soldier*. Dial, 1973. A mistreated Jewish girl living in a small Arkansas town in the 1940s befriends an escaped German prisoner.　　11–14

GREENE, CONSTANCE C. *Beat the Turtle Drum*, ill. by Donna Diamond. Viking, 1976. A moving story of a child's adjustment to her younger sister's death.　　4–6

_____. *The Ears of Louis*, ill. by Nola Langner. Viking, 1974.　　8–10

_____. *A Girl Called Al*, ill. by Byron Barton. Viking, 1969.　　9–11

_____. *I Know You, Al*, ill. by Byron Barton. Viking, 1975.　　8–11

_____. *Leo the Lioness*. Viking, 1970. The theme of the adolescent who grows into a more mature person is handled unusually well here. The writing is convincingly that of a teenager and the dialogue is excellent.　　10–12

_____. *The Unmaking of Rabbit*. Viking, 1972.　　9–11

_____. *Your Old Pal, Al*. Viking, 1979.

§ GREENFIELD, ELOISE. *Sister*, ill. by Moneta Barnett. T. Crowell, 1974.　　10–12

GREENWALD, SHEILA. *The Secret in Miranda's Closet*, ill. by author. Houghton, 1977. Should the daughter of a militant feminist play with dolls?　　8–10

§ GUY, ROSA. *The Friends*. Holt, 1973.　　12–15

☆§ HAMILTON, VIRGINIA. *Arilla Sun Down*. Greenwillow, 1976.　　12–14

_____. *The House of Dies Drear*, ill. by Eros Keith. Macmillan, 1968.　　11–14

§ _____. *M. C. Higgins, the Great*. Macmillan, 1974. Newbery Medal. National Book Award.　　11–13

§ _____. *The Planet of Junior Brown*. Macmillan, 1971.　　12–14

§ _____. *Time-Ago Lost: More Tales of Jahdu*, ill. by Ray Prather. Macmillan, 1973.　　8–10

§ _____. *The Time-Ago Tales of Jahdu*, ill. by Nonny Hogrogian. Macmillan, 1969.　　8–10

§ _____. *Zeely*, ill. by Symeon Shimin. Macmillan, 1967.　　9–11

HAYWOOD, CAROLYN. *"B" Is for Betsy*, ill. by author. Harcourt, 1939, 1968. And other books in the series.　　6–8

_____. *Eddie's Happenings*, ill. by author. Morrow, 1971.　　8–10

_____. *Eddie's Menagerie*, ill. by Ingrid Fetz. Morrow, 1978.　　7–9

_____. *Eddie's Valuable Property*, ill. by author. Morrow, 1975.　　7–9

_____. *Little Eddie*, ill. by author. Morrow, 1947. And other books in the series.　　7–9

HEIDE, FLORENCE PARRY. *Growing Anyway Up*. Lippincott, 1976. The compulsive behavior patterns and self-denigration of a withdrawn, disturbed young girl are depicted with sharp perception.　　10–12

_____. *Secret Dreamer, Secret Dreams.* Lippincott, 1978. Caroline's teacher introduces her in a few pages—after that Caroline (thirteen, a special child who cannot read, write, or speak) tells of her own frustration, anger, and despair.   11–13

HEILBRONER, JOAN. *The Happy Birthday Present,* ill. by Mary Chalmers. Harper, 1962. Peter and Davy, with little money and endless time, shop thoroughly for mother's birthday gift. One of the most delightful of the books for beginning readers.   6–7

§ HENTOFF, NAT. *Jazz Country.* Harper, 1965. A white jazz musician is accepted by a black group.   13 up

_____. *This School Is Driving Me Crazy.* Delacorte, 1975. An interesting story of relationships between students and teachers.   10–13

§ HILL, ELIZABETH. *Evan's Corner,* ill. by Nancy Grossman. Holt, 1967.   5–7

HINTON, S. E. *The Outsiders.* Viking, 1967.   13–15

_____. *Rumble Fish.* Delacorte, 1975.   12–16

_____. *Tex.* Delacorte, 1979.   12–15

_____. *That Was Then, This Is Now.* Viking, 1971.   13–15

HOBAN, RUSSELL C. *Herman the Loser,* ill. by Lillian Hoban. Harper, 1961. A most refreshing picture story of a little boy with a talent for losing who one day becomes a victorious finder.   5–6

_____. *The Sorely Trying Day,* ill. by Lillian Hoban. Harper, 1964. A family finds that hostile or friendly behavior can have a chain effect.   5–7

HOLLAND, ISABELLE. *Alan and the Animal Kingdom.* Lippincott, 1977. Shunted from one relative to another, Alan decides to keep the death of his great-aunt (with whom he's been living) a secret for fear the authorities will dispose of his beloved pets.   10–12

_____. *Amanda's Choice.* Lippincott, 1970. Twelve-year-old Amanda is an *enfant terrible.* When Manuel, a nineteen-year-old musical prodigy from a New York slum, comes to occupy the guest cottage at her family's summer home, Amanda feels he is the first person who understands her. Memorable characterization and good style.   12–14

_____. *The Man Without a Face.* Lippincott, 1972. A boy from an all-female household finds help in an older man's affection. A dignified treatment of a homosexual incident.   12–15

HOLMAN, FELICE. *Slake's Limbo.* Scribner's, 1974. Slake lives in a hideaway in the New York subway for four months, existing like a Crusoe, through resourcefulness. A smooth, novel tale.   10–12

HOPKINS, LEE BENNETT. *Mama.* Knopf, 1977. Mama is tough and so passionately dedicated to seeing that her fatherless sons have everything they need that she easily justifies stealing from them.   8–10

HUNT, IRENE. *Up a Road Slowly.* Follett, 1967. Julie Trelling, left motherless at age seven, is sent to live with an aunt and uncle who provide her with insight into the qualities necessary to become a mature, happy individual. Newbery Medal.   11–14

HUNTER, EVAN. *Me and Mr. Stenner.* Lippincott, 1976. Eleven-year-old Abby reports the story of her adjustment to Mr. Stenner, who moves in when her parents separate and later becomes her stepfather.   10–13

§ HUNTER, KRISTIN. *Guests in the Promised Land.* Scribner's, 1973.   12–15

§ _____. *The Soul Brothers and Sister Lou.* Scribner's, 1968.   12–15

§ HURMENCE, BELINDA. *Tough Tiffany.* Doubleday, 1980. A finely developed account of the redoubtable youngest child in a large black family.   10–12

ISADORA, RACHEL. *Max,* ill. by author. Macmillan, 1976. Max walks his sister to her dancing class and learns that ballet can help him play baseball.   5–7

● ISH-KISHOR, SULAMITH. *Our Eddie.* Pantheon, 1969.   11–14

JACKSON, JACQUELINE. *The Paleface Redskins,* ill. by author. Little, 1958. A family summer is enlivened by imaginative play.   9–11

§ JACKSON, JESSE. *Call Me Charley,* ill. by Doris Spiegel. Harper, 1945.   10–13

§ _____. *Charley Starts from Scratch.* Harper, 1958. Two sensitive stories of a black boy who lives in a white neighborhood. After high school, Charley finds many doors closed to him until he comes in first in Olympic trials.   12 up

§ _____. *Tessie,* ill. by Harold James. Harper, 1968. A black girl wins a scholarship to an all-white private school, and firmly insists on making the best of both worlds.   11–14

§ JORDAN, JUNE. *New Life: New Room,* ill. by Ray Cruz. T. Crowell, 1975.   5–8

● JORDAN, MILDRED. *Proud to Be Amish,* ill. by W. T. Mars. Crown, 1968. Katie has a hard time with guilt feelings when she envies the dress of a child who's not plain.   10–11

§ JUSTUS, MAY. *New Boy in School,* ill. by Joan Balfour Payne. Hastings, 1963. Lennie must adjust to being the only black boy in his class.   7–8

§ _____. *A New Home for Billy,* ill. by Joan Balfour Payne. Hastings, 1966.   5–8

KATZ, BOBBI. *The Manifesto and Me—Meg.* Watts, 1974.   9–12

KERR, M. E. *Dinky Hocker Shoots Smack.* Harper, 1972.   11–14

_____. *Gentlehands.* Harper, 1978. Buddy is impressed by Grandfather Trenker's culture and devotion to stray animals despite the rumors of his atrocious activities while in charge of a Nazi concentration camp.   12–14

_____. *I'll Love You When You're More Like Me.* Harper, 1977.   12–15

_____. *Is That You, Miss Blue?* Harper, 1975.   12–16

_____. *Love Is a Missing Person.* Harper, 1975.   12–15

_____. *The Son of Someone Famous.* Harper, 1974.   12–15

KINGMAN, LEE. *The Year of the Raccoon.* Houghton, 1966. Joey is an ordinary middle child who is helped to overcome feelings of inferiority and inadequacy through his attachment to a pet raccoon.   11–14

KLEIN, NORMA. *Confessions of an Only Child,* ill. by Richard Cuffari. Pantheon, 1974.   9–11

_____. *It's Not What You Expect.* Pantheon, 1973.   11–14

_____. *Mom, the Wolf Man, and Me.* Pantheon, 1972.   10–13

_____. *Taking Sides.* Pantheon, 1974.   11–13

_____. *Tomboy.* Four Winds, 1978.   9–11

§ KONIGSBURG, E. L. *Altogether, One at a Time,* ill. by Gail E. Haley and others. Atheneum, 1971.   9–11

_____. *The Dragon in the Ghetto Caper,* ill. by author. Atheneum, 1974.   10–12

_____. *Father's Arcane Daughter.* Atheneum, 1976.   10–14

_____. *From the Mixed-Up Files of Mrs. Basil E. Frankweiler,* ill. by author. Atheneum, 1967. Newbery Medal.   10–12

_____. *(George),* ill. by author. Atheneum, 1970.   11–14

§ _____. *Jennifer, Hecate, Macbeth, William McKinley, and Me, Elizabeth,* ill. by author. Atheneum, 1967.   9–11

_____. *Throwing Shadows.* Atheneum, 1979.   11–14

★ KRUMGOLD, JOSEPH. *. . . and now Miguel,* ill. by Jean Charlot. T. Crowell, 1953. Newbery Medal.   13–17

_____. *Henry 3,* ill. by Alvin Smith. Atheneum, 1967.   11–14

_____. *Onion John,* ill. by Symeon Shimin. T. Crowell, 1959. Newbery Medal.   11–14

☆ LAMPMAN, EVELYN SIBLEY. *Half-Breed,* ill. by Ann Grifalconi. Doubleday, 1967. A native American boy searches for his white father.   12–15

☆ ———. *Rattlesnake Cave,* ill. by Pamela Johnson. Atheneum, 1974. Jamie learns respect for a Cheyenne tradition.   9–11

LANGNER, NOLA. *Freddy My Grandfather,* ill. by author. Four Winds, 1979. A small girl's thoughts about the grandfather who lives with her and her parents present a clear if slightly static picture of a real person and a real relationship.   7–8

LASKER, JOE. *He's My Brother,* ill. by author. Whitman, 1974.   7–9

———. *Nick Joins In,* ill. by author. Whitman, 1980. In a story about the mainstreaming of exceptional children, Nick adjusts to attending public school.   7–8

☆ LAURITZEN, JONREED. *The Ordeal of the Young Hunter,* ill. by Hoke Denetsosie. Little, 1954. A distinguished story of a twelve-year-old Navaho boy who grows to appreciate what is good in the cultures of the white man and the Indian. Background of the story is Flagstaff, Arizona.   11–14

LEE, MILDRED. *The Rock and the Willow.* Lothrop, 1963.   14–16

———. *The Skating Rink.* Seabury, 1969.   11–13

LE GUIN, URSULA. *Very Far Away from Anywhere Else.* Atheneum, 1976. A story of the problems of a seventeen-year-old intellectual, lacking in surface action but heavy on characterization and the complexity of human relationships.   12–15

L'ENGLE, MADELEINE. *Meet the Austins.* Vanguard, 1960.   10–13

———. *The Moon by Night.* Ariel, 1963.   11–14

LENSKI, LOIS. *Bayou Suzette,* ill. by author. Stokes, 1943.   8–10

———. *Blue Ridge Billy,* ill. by author. Lippincott, 1946.   8–10

———. *High-Rise Secret,* ill. by author. Lippincott, 1966.   8–9

———. *Judy's Journey,* ill. by author. Lippincott, 1947.   8–10

———. *Project Boy,* ill. by author. Lippincott, 1954.   7–9

———. *Strawberry Girl,* ill. by author. Lippincott, 1945. Newbery Medal.   9–12

● LEVOY, MYRON. *Alan and Naomi.* Harper, 1977. Young Naomi, a refugee from Nazi oppression in France, finally begins to forget her fears when she's befriended by Alan only to have all progress negated by a bunch of prejudiced toughs at school.   11–13

★ LEWITON, MINA. *Candita's Choice,* ill. by Howard Simon. Harper, 1959. A warm and understanding story of an eleven-year-old who adjusts slowly to the move from Puerto Rico to New York. When she has a chance to return, Candita decides to stay in New York where she no longer feels an alien.   9–11

§ LEXAU, JOAN. *Benjie,* ill. by Don Bolognese. Dial, 1964.   5–7

§ ———. *Benjie on His Own,* ill. by Don Bolognese. Dial, 1970.   5–8

§ ———. *I'll Tell on You,* ill. by Gail Owens. Dutton, 1976.   5–8

§ ———. *Me Day,* ill. by Robert Weaver. Dial, 1971.   5–8

———. *Olaf Reads,* ill. by Harvey Weiss. Dial, 1961.   6–7

§ ———. *Striped Ice Cream,* ill. by John Wilson. Lippincott, 1968.   7–9

LINDQUIST, JENNIE. *The Golden Name Day,* ill. by Garth Williams. Harper, 1955. A warm story of a Swedish-American Family.   8–10

LIPSYTE, ROBERT. *One Fat Summer.* Harper, 1977. Bobby hates summer when it's more difficult to cover his fat body. But over the course of this particular summer he not only loses weight but learns about the weakness of his hero and the motivations of the bully who persecutes him.   11–15

LOWRY, LOIS. *Anastasia Krupnik.* Houghton, 1979. Anastasia is ten, articulate, precocious, and an only child whose comments are often hilarious.   9–11

———. *Find a Stranger, Say Goodbye.* Houghton, 1978. A well-adjusted college girl who dearly loves her adoptive family sets out to find her natural mother.   11–14

McCLOSKEY, ROBERT. *Blueberries for Sal,* ill. by author. Viking, 1948. Sal gets home safely after following a bear in the blueberry patch.   4–7

———. *Centerburg Tales,* ill. by author. Viking, 1951. Humorous stories.   10–12

———. *Homer Price,* ill. by author. Viking, 1943. Lively, funny stories about an irrepressible boy; one of the first books to spoof comic books.   9–12

———. *Lentil,* ill. by author. Viking, 1940. A boy saves the day in a small town's welcome to a returning citizen by playing the harmonica.   7–9

———. *Make Way for Ducklings,* ill. by author. Viking, 1941. Caldecott Medal.   6–8

———. *One Morning in Maine,* ill. by author. Viking, 1952.   5–7

———. *Time of Wonder,* ill. by author. Viking, 1957. Caldecott Medal.   8–10

§ McGOVERN, ANN. *Black Is Beautiful,* ill. by Hope Wurmfeld. Four Winds, 1969.   5–8

MacLACHLAN, PATRICIA. *Arthur, for the Very First Time.* Harper, 1980. A quiet, timid boy of ten gains confidence while visiting his eccentric elderly relatives, in a gently humorous story.   9–11

§ MATHIS, SHARON BELL. *The Hundred Penny Box,* ill. by Leo and Diane Dillon. Viking, 1975.   8–11

§ ———. *Listen for the Fig Tree.* Viking, 1974.   12–16

MAYNE, WILLIAM. *The Jersey Shore,* Dutton, 1973.   11–12

MAZER, HARRY. *The Dollar Man.* Delacorte, 1974. Marcus longs to know his father, but finds the reality disappointing. Believable and touching.   11–14

MAZER, NORMA FOX. *A Figure of Speech.* Delacorte, 1973. A moving, realistic story of a child's love for her grandfather.   11–14

MEANS, FLORENCE CRANNELL. *Knock at the Door, Emmy,* ill. by Paul Lantz. Houghton, 1956.   12–14

☆ ———. *Our Cup Is Broken.* Houghton, 1969.   12–15

§ ———. *Shuttered Windows,* ill. by Armstrong Sperry. Houghton, 1938.   11–14

★§ ———. *Us Maltbys.* Houghton, 1966.   11–14

MILES, BETTY. *Maudie and Me and the Dirty Book.* Knopf, 1980. A sixth-grade girl is aghast when parents attack her reading of an innocuous book to a first grade.   10–13

———. *The Real Me.* Knopf, 1974.   9–11

MITCHELL, LUCY SPRAGUE. *Here and Now Story Book,* ill. by H. Willem Van Loon and Christine Price, rev. and enlarged ed. Dutton, 1948 (first pub. in 1921). Stories with little plot, but centered on the child's own activities, told in the child's words.   2–7

★ MOHR, NICHOLASA. *El Bronx Remembered: A Novella and Stories.* Harper, 1975. A varied group of stories, atmospheric and told with simplicity of style.   12–14

★ ———. *Nilda,* ill. by author. Harper, 1973.   11–14

MOSER, DON. *A Heart to the Hawks.* Atheneum, 1975.   12–15

§ MURRAY, MICHELE. *Nellie Cameron,* ill. by Leonora E. Prince. Seabury, 1971.   9–11

§ MYERS, WALTER DEAN. *Mojo and the Russians.* Viking, 1977. A small gang of eleven-year-olds, mostly black and living on the upper west side of New York, engage in a series of ploys that are often ridiculous but always funny.   10–12

§ ———. *The Young Landlords.* Viking, 1979. An adolescent gang acquires a slum building by chance and attempts to improve the property.   11–14

NESS, EVALINE. *Sam, Bangs & Moonshine,* ill. by author. Holt, 1966. Sam is a small, mendacious girl and Bangs is her cat and moonshine is the word for all the lies she tells. Attractive illustrations. Caldecott Medal.   5–7

§ NEUFELD, JOHN. *Edgar Allan.* Phillips, 1968. A poignant story of a white family's adoption of a black child, and the pressure that forces them to give him up.   11–14

● NEVILLE, EMILY. *Berries Goodman*. Harper, 1965. 11–14

———. *Fogarty*. Harper, 1969. A fine, thoughtful book about a young college dropout whose plans to be a playwright come to naught but who realizes there is another place in the world for him. 13–15

———. *It's Like This, Cat*, ill. by Emil Weiss. Harper, 1963. Newbery Medal. 11–14

NORDSTROM, URSULA. *The Secret Language*, ill. by Mary Chalmers. Harper, 1960. 7–9

★ O'DELL, SCOTT. *Child of Fire*. Houghton, 1974. 12–15

§ PANETTA, GEORGE. *The Shoeshine Boys*, ill. by Joe Servello. Grosset, 1971. Tony, an Italian-American, becomes a shoeshine boy to help out with the finances when his father loses his job. He joins forces with MacDougal Thompson, a black boy, and the Black and White Shoeshine Company is a great success. 8–10

PARKER, RICHARD. *He Is Your Brother*. Nelson, 1976. 10–11

PATERSON, KATHERINE. *Bridge to Terabithia*, ill. by Donna Diamond. T. Crowell, 1977. Newbery Medal. 10–12

———. *The Great Gilly Hopkins*. T. Crowell, 1978. 10–13

PECK, RICHARD. *Don't Look and It Won't Hurt*. Holt, 1972. 11–14

———. *Representing Super Doll*. Viking, 1974. 11–15

● PECK, ROBERT NEWTON. *A Day No Pigs Would Die*. Knopf, 1972. Anecdotal story of a Shaker boy on a Vermont farm, where families have strong ties. 12–16

PEVSNER, STELLA. *And You Give Me a Pain, Elaine*. Seabury, 1978. Thirteen-year-old Andrea's older sister (sulky and rebellious) is the bane of her existence. 10–12

———. *A Smart Kid Like You*. Seabury, 1975. 10–12

★ POLITI, LEO. *Juanita*, ill. by author. Scribner's, 1948. 5–7

———. *Little Leo*, ill. by author. Scribner's, 1951. 5–8

———. *Moy Moy*, ill. by author. Scribner's, 1960. 5–7

★ ———. *Song of the Swallows*, ill. by author. Scribner's, 1949. Caldecott Medal. 5–7

★ ———. *Three Stalks of Corn*, ill. by author. Scribner's, 1976. 5–8

RABE, BERNIECE. *Naomi*. Nelson, 1975. Life on a Missouri farm during the Depression years, with superstition and religion strong influences on daily life. 11–14

RASKIN, ELLEN. *Spectacles*, ill. by author. Atheneum, 1968. An amusing picture book about the trials and errors of a small girl who myopically sees strange creatures and finally is won over to wearing glasses. 5–7

RICH, LOUISE DICKINSON. *Three of a Kind*, ill. by William M. Hutchinson. Watts, 1970. A foster child forgets her own problems in helping the four-year-old autistic grandson of the couple she lives with. Realistic characters and a warmly portrayed Maine setting. 9–11

ROBERTS, WILLO DAVIS. *Don't Hurt Laurie!* ill. by Ruth Sanderson. Atheneum, 1977. A trenchant story of child abuse ends on a note of hope. 9–11

ROBERTSON, KEITH. *Henry Reed, Inc.*, ill. by Robert McCloskey. Viking, 1958. 11–13

———. *Henry Reed's Big Show*, ill. by Robert McCloskey. Viking, 1970. 10–12

———. *In Search of a Sandhill Crane*, ill. by Richard Cuffari. Viking, 1973. 10–13

RODOWSKY, COLBY. *What About Me?* Watts, 1976. Dorrie, a high school sophomore, has ambivalent feelings about her brother, a mongoloid child. The feelings turn to guilt when he dies suddenly and she realizes how much she really did love him. 11–14

§ ROSE, KAREN. *A Single Trail*. Follett, 1969. Ricky is white and entering a new sixth grade after nine moves. Earl is black and antagonistic in school. Their friendship comes very slowly with help from an understanding teacher. The story has a sturdy honesty. 10–11

● ———. *There Is a Season*. Follett, 1967. Katie Levin dates a

new neighbor, a Roman Catholic boy, but finds that religious pressures interfere. 11–14

● SACHS, MARILYN. *Amy and Laura*, ill. by Tracy Sugarman. Doubleday, 1966. 9–11

● ———. *Amy Moves In*, ill. by Judith G. Brown. Doubleday, 1964. 9–11

———. *The Bears' House*, ill. by Louis Glanzman. Doubleday, 1971. 9–12

● ———. *Laura's Luck*, ill. by Ib Ohlsson. Doubleday, 1965. 9–11

● ———. *Marv*, ill. by Louis Glanzman. Doubleday, 1970. 9–12

● ———. *Peter and Veronica*, ill. by Louis Glanzman. Doubleday, 1969. 9–12

§ ———. *A Secret Friend*. Doubleday, 1978. 9–11

★ ———. *The Truth About Mary Rose*. ill. by Louis Glanzman. Doubleday, 1973. 9–12

● ———. *Veronica Ganz*, ill. by Louis Glanzman. Doubleday, 1968. 10–12

SAWYER, RUTH. *Roller Skates*, ill. by Valenti Angelo. Viking, 1936. Newbery Medal. 12–13

SCHULMAN, JANET. *Jenny and the Tennis Nut*, ill. by Marylin Hafner. Greenwillow, 1978. Daddy encourages his daughter to take up tennis—until her cartwheels down the sidelines convince him she's already found her sport. 7–9

SCOPPETTONE, SANDRA. *Trying Hard to Hear You*. Harper, 1974. 13–18

§ SCOTT, ANN HERBERT. *Sam*, ill. by Symeon Shimin. McGraw, 1967. Although the story is more an expanded situation than a plot, it is a pleasant and realistic picture of Sam and his black, middle-class family. 3–6

SEBESTYEN, OUIDA. *Far from Home*. Atlantic/Little, 1980. A lonely child touches the lives of many adults in a boarding house and finds the father he had never known. 11–13

SEGAL, LORE. *Tell Me a Mitzi*, ill. by Harriet Pincus. Farrar, 1970. 5–7

SHARMAT, MARJORIE WEINMAN. *Goodnight Andrew Goodnight Craig*, ill. by Mary Chalmers. Harper, 1969. Two small boys, who have gone to bed, get noisier and noisier until their father comes in with an ultimatum. The illustrations echo the engaging tone of the story, which is all in dialogue. 4–6

———. *Maggie Marmelstein for President*, ill. by Ben Shecter. Harper, 1975. 9–11

§ SHEARER, JOHN. *I Wish I Had an Afro*, ill. with photos by author. Cowles, 1970. The candor and pathos of the text are uncommon and the quality of the photos is exceptional. 9–11

SHERBURNE, ZOA. *Leslie*. Morrow, 1972. A girl's reluctant first try with marijuana leads to serious consequences. 12–16

———. *Too Bad About the Haines Girl*. Morrow, 1967. Melinda, a teenager, finds that a premarital pregnancy affects others as well as herself. 13–17

§★ SHOTWELL, LOUISA R. *Adam Bookout*, ill. by W. T. Mars. Viking, 1967. An interracial story set in Brooklyn. Adam finds he can't avoid problems by moving from one relative's house to another. 9–11

★ ———. *Magdalena*, ill. by Lilian Obligado. Viking, 1971. 10–12

§ ———. *Roosevelt Grady*, ill. by Peter Burchard. World, 1963. 9–11

SHYER, MARLENE FANTA. *Welcome Home, Jellybean*. Scribner's, 1978. The painful, honest, convincing story of a retarded girl who comes home to live after years in an institution. 10–12

SKOLSKY, MINDY WARSHAW. *Carnival and Kopeck and More about*

Hannah, ill. by Karen Ann Weinhaus. Harper, 1979. This is both a touching and funny story and a shrewdly affectionate exploration of the relationship between a child and her grandmother. 8–10

SKORPEN, LIESEL MOAK. *Elizabeth,* ill. by Martha Alexander. Harper, 1970. Kate was disappointed when she got a rag doll for Christmas instead of the one she wanted. How she came to love the rag doll is told without sentimentality. 5–7

SLEPIAN, JAN. *The Alfred Summer.* Macmillan, 1980. A touching but not mawkish story about the friendship between a boy with cerebral palsy and another who's retarded. 10–12

SMITH, DORIS BUCHANAN. *Kelly's Creek,* ill. by Alan Tiegreen. T. Crowell, 1975. An appealing story of a boy with a learning disability. 9–11

———. *Kick a Stone Home.* T. Crowell, 1974. A fifteen-year-old learns to accept herself, as well as her father's new wife. 11–14

———. *A Taste of Blackberries,* ill. by Charles Robinson. T. Crowell, 1973. 9–11

☆ SMUCKER, BARBARA. *Wigwam in the City,* ill. by Gil Miret. Dutton, 1966. One of the few stories about discrimination against Indians in an urban setting. A Chippewa family in Chicago turns to the American Indian Center for help. 10–12

☆ SNEVE, VIRGINIA DRIVING HAWK. *High Elk's Treasure,* ill. by Oren Lyons. Holiday, 1972. A story of a Sioux Indian family that makes clear the attitudes of contemporary Indians of different generations. 9–12

SNYDER, ZILPHA KEATLEY. *The Changeling,* ill. by Alton Raible. Atheneum, 1970. 10–12

§ ———. *The Egypt Game,* ill. by Alton Raible. Atheneum, 1967. 9–12

———. *The Headless Cupid,* ill. by Alton Raible. Atheneum, 1971. 9–11

———. *The Velvet Room,* ill. by Alton Raible. Atheneum, 1965. 10–12

★ SONNEBORN, RUTH. *Friday Night Is Papa Night,* ill. by Emily A. McCully. Viking, 1970. 6–7

§ SORENSON, VIRGINIA. *Around the Corner,* ill. by Robert Weaver. Harcourt, 1971. A black family welcomes white neighbors. 10–12

———. *Miracles on Maple Hill,* ill. by Beth and Joe Krush. Harcourt, 1956. Newbery Medal. 10–12

● ———. *Plain Girl,* ill. by Charles Geer. Harcourt, 1955. An Amish girl adjusts to public school. 9–11

§ STEPTOE, JOHN. *Stevie,* ill. by author. Harper, 1969. 5–7

§ STERLING, DOROTHY. *Mary Jane,* ill. by Ernest Crichlow. Doubleday, 1959. A story of the beginning of school integration. 10–13

STOLZ, MARY. *The Bully of Barkham Street,* ill. by Leonard Shortall. Harper, 1963. 10–12

———. *By the Highway Home.* Harper, 1971. 11–13

★ ———. *Cider Days.* Harper, 1978. Fifth grader Polly helps a new friend, lonely for Mexico, adjust to Vermont. 9–10

———. *A Dog on Barkham Street,* ill. by Leonard Shortall. Harper, 1960. 10–12

———. *The Edge of Next Year.* Harper, 1974. 10–13

———. *Lands End,* ill. by Dennis Hermanson. Harper, 1973. 10–12

★ ———. *The Noonday Friends,* ill. by Louis S. Glanzman. Harper, 1965. 9–11

§ ———. *A Wonderful, Terrible Time,* ill. by Louis S. Glanzman. Harper, 1967. 9–11

TALBOT, CHARLENE JOY. *A Home with Aunt Florry.* Atheneum, 1974. Orphaned Wendy and Jason are sent to New York City to live with an aunt who lives in a condemned build-

ing and is an inveterate scrounger. Adjustment is not easy. 10–13

★ ———. *Tomas Takes Charge,* ill. by Reisie Lonette. Lothrop, 1966. Two motherless Puerto Rican children, fearing the dreaded Welfare, hide in an abandoned New York building when their father fails to come home. The boy's tender protection of his older, timid sister is beautifully drawn. 9–12

§ TANNER, LOUISE. *Reggie and Nilma.* Farrar, 1971. Nilma, a black woman, and her son, Reggie, enjoy a close relationship with the white family she works for. When Reggie is wrongly suspected of robbing the white family's apartment, the breach is irreparable. Despite the serious problems, the story is not somber. 11–15

§ TAYLOR, MILDRED. *Roll of Thunder, Hear My Cry,* ill. by Jerry Pinkney. Dial, 1976. 12–15

● TAYLOR, SYDNEY. *All-of-a-Kind Family,* ill. by Helen John. Follett, 1951.

● ———. *All-of-a-Kind Family Downtown,* ill. by Beth and Joe Krush. Follett, 1972. Stories about a New York Jewish family of the 1900s, which seems to run only to girls. 9–11

§ TAYLOR, THEODORE. *The Cay.* Doubleday, 1969. 12–15

★ THOMAS, DAWN C. *Mira! Mira!* ill. by Harold L. James. Lippincott, 1970. A Puerto Rican child adjusts to a move to New York not through the usual pattern of recognition in some situation but rather when he sees his first snowfall which he feels "fell from the sky to say 'Welcome.'"

TRESSELT, ALVIN. *Hide and Seek Fog,* ill. by Roger Duvoisin. Lothrop, 1965. 5–8

———. *What Did You Leave Behind?* ill. by Roger Duvoisin. Lothrop, 1978. 5–8

———. *White Snow, Bright Snow,* ill. by Roger Duvoisin. Lothrop, 1947. Caldecott Medal. 5–7

UCHIDA, YOSHIKO. *The Birthday Visitor,* ill. by Charles Robinson. Scribner's, 1975. 7–9

———. *The Promised Year,* ill. by William M. Hutchinson. Harcourt, 1959. A Japanese girl visits the U.S. 9–11

———. *The Rooster Who Understood Japanese,* ill. by Charles Robinson. Scribner's, 1976. 8–9

§ UDRY, JANICE MAY. *Mary Jo's Grandmother,* ill. by Eleanor Mill. Whitman, 1970. 5–7

———. *The Moon Jumpers,* ill. by Maurice Sendak. Harper, 1959. Beautiful color illustrations enhance this mood picture book which describes children frolicking in the moonlight until bedtime interrupts their imaginative play. 5–8

§ WALDRON, ANN. *The Integration of Mary-Larkin Thornhill.* Dutton, 1975. A white minister's daughter is assigned to a black junior high school in the South. 10–13

WALLACE, BARBARA BROOKS. *Victoria.* Follett, 1972. A boarding-school story with a self-centered, complex, and touching heroine. 9–12

§ WEIK, MARY HAYS. *The Jazz Man,* ill. by Ann Grifalconi. Atheneum, 1966. A story that combines harsh realism and brooding lyricism gives a poignant picture of a crippled child in Harlem. This has had high praise for its tender treatment of the child and harsh criticism for the depiction of parental neglect. 9–11

WERSBA, BARBARA. *Tunes for a Small Harmonica.* Harper, 1976. An off-beat teenage student at a private girls' school, J. F. is suddenly smitten by her poetry teacher and decides to play her harmonica on the street to help him earn enough money to go to England to complete his thesis. 12–15

WIER, ESTER. *The Loner,* ill. by Christine Price. McKay, 1963. A boy with no name, no home, no family, is taken in by a woman sheepherder, and he learns what it means to give oneself completely to a job. Vivid characterization, a notable theme.   11–14

§ WILKINSON, BRENDA. *Ludell*. Harper, 1975. Three years in the life of a black girl in a small Georgia town in the 1950s.   11–13

§ ———. *Ludell and Willie*. Harper, 1977. While this is a story about a black adolescent girl, it is also about problems all teenagers share.   11–14

WILL and NICOLAS. *Russet and the Two Reds*, ill. Harcourt, 1962.

———. *The Two Reds*, ill. Harcourt, 1950. Slight but lively stories with the realism of city streets.   5–8

WILLIAMS, BARBARA. *Kevin's Grandma*, ill. by Kay Chorao. Dutton, 1975.   4–6

WINTHROP, ELIZABETH. *Marathon Miranda*. Holiday, 1979. Miranda suffers from asthma but decides to join her new friend, Phoebe, in training for the Central Park marathon anyway.   9–11

WOJCIECHOWSKA, MAIA. *Don't Play Dead Before You Have To*. Harper, 1970.   13–15

———. *Tuned Out*. Harper, 1968.   14–16

WOLITZER, HILMA. *Toby Lived Here*. Farrar, 1978. When Toby's widowed mother has a nervous breakdown and she's sent to stay with an affectionate foster family, she's determined not to like them.   10–12

YASHIMA, TARO. *Umbrella*, ill. by author. Viking, 1958. To small Momo it seemed that rain would never come so that she might use her new blue umbrella and bright red boots. New York background.   4–6

YEP, LAURENCE. *Child of the Owl*. Harper, 1977. The impressive story of a young girl who comes to San Francisco to live with a grandmother she hardly knows, her growing love for this new woman, and her adjustment to her Chinese heritage.   11–14

———. *Sea Glass*. Harper, 1979. Craig, an eighth grader who is short, plump, and awkward at sports, has problems when his family moves from San Francisco's Chinatown to the small coastal town where his father grew up and was a basketball star.   11–13

ZINDEL, PAUL. *The Pigman*. Harper, 1968.   11–14

ZINDEL, PAUL. *The Pigman's Legacy*. Harper, 1980.   11–14

ZOLOTOW, CHARLOTTE, *Big Sister and Little Sister*, ill. by Martha Alexander. Harper, 1966.   5–7

———. *A Father Like That*, ill. by Ben Shecter. Harper, 1971.   5–7

———. *The Hating Book*, ill. by Ben Shecter. Harper, 1969.   5–7

———. *My Grandson Lew*, ill. by William Pène du Bois. Harper, 1974.   3–7

———. *William's Doll*, ill. by William Pène du Bois. Harper, 1972.   5–8

———. *Someone New*, ill. by Erik Blegvad. Harper, 1978.   5–8

Realistic Fiction: Other Countries

Africa

§ BØDKER, CECIL. *The Leopard*, tr. by Gunnar Poulsen. Atheneum, 1975. When a leopard steals a calf, Tibeso sets out to see a wise man and becomes involved with a thief. Set in Ethiopia.   10–12

§ BRADLEY, DUANE. *Meeting with a Stranger*, ill. by E. Harper Johnson. Lippincott, 1964. An American comes to an Ethiopian village to teach sheep-raising and is tested by the boys.   10–12

§ CLIFFORD, MARY LOUISE. *Salah of Sierra Leone*, ill. by Elzia Moon. T. Crowell, 1975. A boy is uncertain which side is right in the political maneuvering surrounding the 1967 elections.   11–13

§ DINNEEN, BETTY. *Lion Yellow*. Walck/McKay, 1975. A Kenyan game park is threatened with closing.   10–12

§ FEELINGS, MURIEL. *Zamani Goes to Market*, ill. by Tom Feelings. Seabury, 1970. Adventures of a small boy in Ghana.   5–8

§ GERSON, MARY-JOAN. *Omoteji's Baby Brother*, ill. by Elzia Moon. Walck, 1974.   8–9

§ ———. *Song of the Boat*, ill. by Leo and Diane Dillon. T. Crowell, 1975.   8–9

§ JONES, TOECKEY. *Go Well, Stay Well*. Harper, 1980. In a story of interracial friendship, two girls find that candor and patience are needed.   11–14

§ MIRSKY, REBA. *Seven Grandmothers*, ill. by W. T. Mars. Follett, 1955. A sequel to the title below.

———. *Thirty-one Brothers and Sisters*, ill. by W. T. Mars. Follett, 1952. Life in a Zulu village.   9–11

§ MITCHISON, NAOMI. *Sunrise Tomorrow: A Story of Botswana*. Farrar, 1973.   12–15

§ NAGENDA, JOHN. *Mukasa*, ill. by Charles Lilly. Macmillan, 1973.   9–11

§ STEVENSON, WILLIAM. *The Bushbabies*, ill. by Victor Ambrus. Houghton, 1965. A most unusual story, both in the setting and in the beautifully built-up relationship between two people different in age, sex, race, and station. The story moves across wild African country.   11–14

§ WELLMAN, ALICE. *Tatu and the Honey Bird*, ill. by Dale Payson. Putnam, 1972. A small boy helps his sister get an education too. Set in Angola.   8–10

Australia and New Zealand

§ BRINSMEAD, HESBA FAY. *Pastures of the Blue Crane*. Coward, 1966.   13–15

CLARK, MAVIS THORPE. *The Sky Is Free*. Macmillan, 1976. A tightly structured story concerning two runaway boys who ultimately gain enough maturity to make a sacrifice for the other.   11–14

———. *Spark of Opal*. Macmillan, 1973.   11–14

OTTLEY, REGINALD. *The Bates Family*. Harcourt, 1969. The Bates family, ten strong, has no home but a wagon as they work as drovers in the outback.   10–13

———. *Boy Alone*, ill. by Clyde Pearson. Harcourt, 1966. The story of a young adolescent in the Australian outback. The atmosphere is wonderfully created; the writing is perceptive. Followed by *Roan Colt* (1967) and *Rain Comes to Yamboorah* (1968).   10–12

PHIPSON, JOAN. *Birkin*, ill. by Margaret Horder. Harcourt, 1966. An engaging story about several children in a small Australian town who care for a calf. Plenty of action and humor.   10–12

———. *The Family Conspiracy*, ill. by Margaret Horder. Harcourt, 1964. The large Barker family lives on an isolated Australian sheep station. A warm, convincing family story with an unsentimental ending.   10–11

———. *Polly's Tiger*, ill. by Erik Blegvad. Dutton, 1974. Polly has problems making friends in a new home.   8–9

———. *When the City Stopped*. Atheneum, 1978.   10–13

SOUTHALL, IVAN. *Ash Road*, ill. by Clem Seale. St. Martin's, 1966.   11–14

———. *Benson Boy*, ill. by Ingrid Fetz. Macmillan, 1973.   10–12

———. *Hills End*. Macmillan, 1963, 1974.   11–14

———. *Let the Balloon Go*, ill. by Ian Ribbons. St. Martin's, 1968.   11–13

———. *To the Wild Sky*, ill. by Jennifer Tuckwell. St. Martin's, 1967.   12–14

SPENCE, ELEANOR. *The Devil Hole.* Lothrop, 1977. This depicts, with great dramatic impact, the effects on a family when the fourth child proves to be autistic.   11–14

————. *The Nothing Place*, ill. by Geraldine Spence. Harper, 1973. Glen has many problems adjusting to deafness, and the sympathy of his new friends seems a hindrance rather than a help.   10–12

SUTHERLAND, MARGARET. *Hello, I'm Karen*, ill. by Jane Paton. Coward, 1976. Karen's life in New Zealand.   7–8

THIELE, COLIN. *Blue Fin.* Harper, 1974. Snook's skipper father is firmly convinced that his son can't do anything right on a tuna boat, but Snook gets an opportunity to prove his worth in this exciting tale.   11–14

————. *February Dragon.* Harper, 1976. Episodic rather than sequential, this story gives a good picture of family and community life in the Australian countryside.   10–12

————. *Fire in the Stone.* Harper, 1974.   11–14

————. *The Hammerhead Light.* Harper, 1977. An old man and a young girl battle together to preserve a condemned lighthouse.   10–12

WRIGHTSON, PATRICIA. *A Racecourse for Andy*, ill. by Margaret Horder. Harcourt, 1968.   10–12

Canada

CORCORAN, BARBARA, and BRADFORD ANGIER. *A Star to the North.* Nelson, 1970.   11–14

HOUSTON, JAMES. *Frozen Fire*, ill. by author. Atheneum, 1977. Set in the far north, this is the suspenseful tale of two young boys who battle snow and cold to rescue a missing father.   9–11

★ ————. *River Runners: A Tale of Hardship and Bravery*, ill. by author. Atheneum, 1979.   12–14

● KAPLAN, BESS. *The Empty Chair.* Harper, 1978. A cozy, realistic story about Jewish family life, this centers around eleven-year-old Becky, her adjustment to her mother's death, and her eventual acceptance of a stepmother.   11–13

LITTLE, JEAN. *Home from Far*, ill. by Jerry Lazare. Little, 1965.   10–13

● ————. *Kate.* Harper, 1971.   10–13

————. *Listen for the Singing.* Dutton, 1977.   10–12

● ————. *Look Through My Window*, ill. by Joan Sandin. Harper, 1970.   9–11

————. *Mine for Keeps*, ill. by Lewis Parker. Little, 1962.   10–12

————. *Spring Begins in March*, ill. by Lewis Parker. Little, 1966.   10–12

————. *Stand in the Wind*, ill. by Emily Arnold McCully. Harper, 1975. Martha and Ellen entertain two American sisters, who at first seem hardly worth knowing.   9–11

MAJOR, KEVIN. *Hold Fast.* Delacorte, 1980. Newly orphaned, a boy of fourteen misses his younger brother and his Newfoundland village; a sympathetic cousin joins him in running away and camping. Canadian Library Association, Best Book of the Year.   12–14

☆ PITSEOLAK, PETER. *Peter Pitseolak's Escape from Death*, ill. by author. Delacorte, 1978. The true account of an Eskimo caught in a swiftly moving ice field with his son.   8–10

Central and South America

BEHN, HARRY. *The Two Uncles of Pablo*, ill. by Mel Silverman. Harcourt, 1959. Small Pablo copes with two antagonistic uncles as well as his own problem of trying to gain an education. An appealing story of Mexico written by a poet very popular with children.   9–11

BONHAM, FRANK. *The Vagabundos.* Dutton, 1969.   12–15

BUFF, MARY and CONRAD. *Magic Maize*, ill. by authors. Houghton, 1953. Guatemalan Indians and their problems.   9–12

BULLA, CLYDE. *Benito*, ill. by Valenti Angelo. T. Crowell, 1961. The encouragement of a successful artist helps orphaned Benito assert his need for time from the endless farm drudgery at Uncle Pedro's to develop his talent.   8–10

CLARK, ANN NOLAN. *Santiago*, ill. by Lynd Ward. Viking, 1955.   12–14

————. *Secret of the Andes*, ill. by Jean Charlot. Viking, 1952. Newbery Medal.   12–14

ETS, MARIE HALL, and AURORA LABASTIDA. *Nine Days to Christmas*, ill. by Marie Hall Ets. Viking, 1959. Ceci, a little girl of Mexico, discovers the fun of Christmas with her first piñata. Caldecott Medal.   5–8

NESS, EVALINE. *Josefina February*, ill. by author. Scribner's, 1963. A warm, quiet read-aloud story set in Haiti.   5–7

O'DELL, SCOTT. *The Black Pearl*, ill. by Milton Johnson. Houghton, 1967. The stark simplicity of the story and the deeper significance it holds in the triumph of good over evil add importance to the book, but even without that it would be enjoyable as a rousing adventure tale with beautifully maintained tempo and suspense as Ramon searches for a giant black pearl in the waters of Baja California.   12–17

RHOADS, DOROTHY M. *The Corn Grows Ripe*, ill. by Jean Charlot. Viking, 1956. Twelve-year-old Tigre, spoiled and lazy, grows up suddenly when his father is injured. Background of the story is Yucatan, among the Mayan Indians.   9–12

SOMMERFELT, AIMÉ. *My Name Is Pablo*, tr. by Patricia Crampton, ill. by Hans Norman Dah. Criterion, 1966. Reflects the problems of the poor in Mexico City.   11–14

STOLZ, MARY. *The Dragons of the Queen*, ill. by Edward Frascino. Harper, 1969. A simply written tale which contrasts new ways of life with the old in Mexico.   10–12

————. *Juan*, ill. by Louis S. Glanzman. Harper, 1970. A story of an orphaned boy, this has fine characterization.   9–11

SURANY, ANICO. *Ride the Cold Wind*, ill. by Leonard Everett Fisher. Putnam, 1964. The story of a small Peruvian boy who wishes to go fishing with his father on Lake Titicaca. He and his sister go boating alone, and when a storm comes up, must be rescued. An appealing theme and setting.   8–10

VAN ITERSON, S. R. *Pulga*, tr. from the Dutch by Alexander and Alison Gode. Morrow, 1971.   11–14

§ ————. *The Spirits of Chocamata.* Morrow, 1977. Set on the Caribbean island of Curacao, this is the story of two boys (a Dutch visitor and a native) who investigate the whereabouts of an escaped prisoner.   11–13

China and Japan

BRO, MARGUERITE. *Su-Mei's Golden Year*, ill. by Kurt Wiese. Doubleday, 1950. It is Su-Mei and her friends of the younger generation who save their Chinese village from famine when the wheat crop is endangered.   11–14

BUCK, PEARL. *The Big Wave*, ill. by Hiroshige and Hokusai. Day, 1948. Jiya leaves the coast after a tidal wave destroys his home and the entire fishing village. When he is grown, he courageously returns to his traditional occupation. There is a heroic quality in the telling which makes this Japanese story a memorable one.   9–13

DeJONG, MEINDERT. *The House of Sixty Fathers*, ill. by Maurice Sendak. Harper, 1956.   11–13

HANDFORTH, THOMAS. *Mei Li*, ill. by author. Doubleday, 1938. The pleasant adventures of a little Chinese girl at the Fair. Caldecott Medal.   5–8

MATSUNO, MASAKO. *A Pair of Red Clogs*, ill. by Kazue Mizumura. World, 1960. A little Japanese girl damages her new red clogs by playing a game with them. Beautifully illustrated in color, with a universal theme.   5–8

SAY, ALLEN. *The Inn-Keeper's Apprentice*. Harper, 1979. Kiyoi becomes an apprentice to Japan's greatest cartoonist at thirteen.   11–14

UCHIDA, YOSHIKO. *The Forever Christmas Tree*, ill. by Kazue Mizumura. Scribner's, 1963.   5–8

———. *In-between Miya*, ill. by Susan Bennett. Scribner's, 1967.   9–12

———. *Sumi and the Goat and the Tokyo Express*, ill. by Kazue Mizumura. Scribner's, 1969. Sumi has a brief but delicious moment in the limelight when she is the only one who can get old Mr. Oda's goat to move from the path of the new Tokyo express. A charming book.   7–9

VINING, ELIZABETH GRAY. *The Cheerful Heart*, ill. by Kazue Mizumura. Viking, 1959. Tomi and her family return to Tokyo after World War II and start life anew.   9–11

YASHIMA, MITSU and TARO. *Plenty to Watch*, ill. by Taro Yashima. Viking, 1954.   8–10

YASHIMA, TARO. *Crow Boy*, ill. by author. Viking, 1955.   8–10

England, Ireland, Scotland, Wales

ARDIZZONE, EDWARD. *Little Tim and the Brave Sea Captain*, ill. by author. Walck, 1955 (first pub. in 1936). First of several books about Tim's adventures at sea.   4–6

———. *Ship's Cook Ginger*, ill. by author. Macmillan, 1978. Tim takes the helm when illness decimates the crew. 7–8

ARUNDEL, HONOR. *The Blanket Word*. Nelson, 1973. Jan realizes that love, the blanket word, can mean something besides entanglement. Typical of Arundel's candid, sympathetic teenage novels.   12–15

ASHLEY, BERNARD. *All My Men*. Phillips, 1978. Having moved from lively London to a small town, Paul is anxious to avoid the dull boys in favor of Billy, a natural leader and bully—even if it means doing things he's ashamed of.   11–13

BAWDEN, NINA. *Devil by the Sea*. Lippincott, 1976.   10–11

———. *A Handful of Thieves*. Lippincott, 1967.   10–12

§ ———. *The Robbers*. Lothrop, 1979.   9–11

BOND, NANCY. *Country of Broken Stone*. Atheneum, 1980. Polished writing distinguishes a story about local resentment against the team conducting an archeological dig.   11–14

CRESSWELL, HELEN. *The Night Watchmen*, ill. by Gareth Floyd. Macmillan, 1970. Josh and Caleb, the most distinctive pair of tramps in contemporary fiction, fascinate young Henry with their enthralling talk and their do-as-you-please life. Not deep characterization, but marvelously vivid characters.   9–11

———. *Ordinary Jack*. Macmillan, 1977. The first in a series based on the Bagthorpe family, each member of which is nutty and endowed with assorted talents . . . except for ordinary Jack. Sequels are *Absolute Zero*, *Bagthorpes Unlimited*, and *Bagthorpes V. the World*.   10–12

———. *The Winter of the Birds*. Macmillan, 1976. A lonely, terrified, recluse, a suicidal man, and a timid young boy are all convincingly rescued from their respective plights by Patrick Finn—loquacious, expansive, radiant, and a true hero.   11 up

DUNCAN, JANE. *Janet Reachfar and the Kelpie*, ill. by Mairi Hedderwich. Seabury, 1976. Small Janet doesn't believe the scary tale the farm hands tell her about a dread creature in the well—until she looks in and is terrified by what turns out to be her own reflection.   9–10

GARDAM, JANE. *Bilgewater*. Greenwillow, 1977. The story of an "ugly" girl's first brush with romance, friendship and haute couture told in touching but humorous style. 12–15

GARNETT, EVE. *The Family from One End Street*, ill. by author. Vanguard, 1960. The story of the big, cheerful Ruggles family who live in a poor neighborhood. Carnegie Medal.   11–13

GODDEN, RUMER. *The Kitchen Madonna*, ill. by Carol Barker. Viking, 1967. Dour Mr. McFadden turns neighborly when ten-year-old Selina becomes his friend.   8 up

———. *Mr. McFadden's Hallowe'en*. Viking, 1975.   8–12

———. *The Rocking-Horse Secret*, ill. by Juliet Stanwell Smith. Viking, 1978. Living alone with her mother, caretaker of old Miss Pomeroy's house, Tibby produces a will that will enable them to remain on the estate after their employer's death.   9–11

HILDICK, E. W. *Louie's Snowstorm*, ill. by Iris Schweitzer. Doubleday, 1974.   10–12

HODGES, CYRIL. *Plain Lane Christmas*, ill. by author. Coward, 1978. Children of a quaint English street threatened by demolition organize a massive Christmas celebration to save it.   9–12

HUNTER, MOLLIE. *The Third Eye*. Harper, 1979. Set in contemporary Scotland, this concerns an earl whose family is under a curse and whose death is being investigated and fourteen-year-old Janet who reluctantly becomes involved.   11–14

KEMP, GENE. *The Turbulent Term of Tyke Tiler*, ill. by Carolyn Dimas. Faber, 1980. The lively, funny tale of a girl who gets into scrapes protecting a mildly handicapped friend. Carnegie Medal.   9–11

KING, CLIVE. *Me and My Million*. T. Crowell, 1979. Ringo is a tough, street-wise London waif whose reading disability propels him into a series of wild and hilarious adventures.   9–11

● LINGARD, JOAN. *Across the Barricades*. Nelson, 1973. Catholic Kevin and Protestant Sadie fall in love in the beleaguered Belfast of today.   11–15

● ———. *Hostages to Fortune*. Nelson, 1977. In a sequel to *A Proper Place* and three earlier books about Sadie and Kevin McCoy, the young Irish couple face continued threats to their Protestant-Catholic marriage both from within and without.   12–15

● ———. *Into Exile*. Nelson, 1973. Kevin and Sadie, now married, find their religious differences cannot be ignored, especially after Kevin's father is killed by a bomb.   12–15

● ———. *A Proper Place*. Nelson, 1975. Kevin and Sadie struggle to make ends meet in Liverpool.   12–15

———. *The Resettling*. Nelson, 1976. In a sequel to *The Clearance*, Maggie McKinley returns to Glasgow to discover that her family has had an eviction notice.   11–14

● ———. *The Twelfth Day of July: A Novel of Modern Ireland*. Nelson, 1972.   11–13

MACKELLAR, WILLIAM. *Wee Joseph*, ill. by Ezra Jack Keats. McGraw, 1957. Young Davie prayed hard, and a small miracle and a great scientific event combine to save Wee Joseph, his runt puppy, from being drowned. A heartwarming story of Scotland.   8–10

McLEAN, ALLAN CAMPBELL. *Storm over Skye*, ill. by Shirley Hughes. Harcourt, 1957. A story rich in Scottish atmosphere tells of two brothers' efforts to solve the sheep stealing that has thrown their community into an uproar. A bit of romance, too.   13–16

McNEILL, JANET. *The Battle of St. George Without*, ill. by Mary Russon. Little, 1968. Urban children in a fight for turf.   10–12

———. *Goodbye, Dove Square*, ill. by Mary Russon. Little, 1969. In this sequel to the above title, all the Dove Square residents have left the area, cleared for renewal. A realistic picture of urban life. 10–13

———. *We Three Kings.* Little, 1974. Estranged cousins are brought together as they salvage a Nativity play almost ruined by a delinquent gang. 9–11

MARK, JAN. *Thunder and Lightnings.* T. Crowell, 1979. Carnegie Medal. 11–14

MAYNE, WILLIAM. *The Changeling,* ill. by Victor Ambrus. Dutton, 1963. 10–12

———. *A Grass Rope,* ill. by Lynton Lamb. Dutton, 1962. 10–12

———. *Max's Dream,* ill. by Laszlo Acs. Greenwillow, 1978. 11–12

———. *A Swarm in May,* ill. by C. Walter Hodges. Bobbs, 1957. 11–13

———. *The Yellow Airplane,* ill. by Trevor Stubley. Nelson, 1974. 8–10

MORGAN, ALISON. *A Boy Called Fish,* ill. by Joan Sandin. Harper, 1973. The story of a boy and his dog, set in rural Wales. 9–11

———. *Pete.* Harper, 1973. Pete, thought by his mother to be on a school trip, runs off from Wales to Scotland to join his father, on a job there, finding both enemies and friends on the way. 10–12

———. *Ruth Crane.* Harper, 1974. Ruth has problems dealing with a younger brother after the death of her father and the hospitalization of her mother and sister after an automobile accident. Set in Wales. 11–14

NESBIT, EDITH. *The Conscience Pudding,* ill. by Erik Blegvad. Coward, 1970. A Christmas story taken from *The New Treasure Seekers,* one of the books about the Bastable children that have become classics. When money is short, the children plan and produce an elaborate Christmas pudding. The period details are charmingly picked up in the illustrations. 9–11

PEARCE, PHILIPPA. *A Dog So Small,* ill. by Antony Maitland. Lippincott, 1963. An unusual story of a gentle, withdrawn young boy's obsessive desire to own a dog. 10–12

———. *What the Neighbors Did and Other Stories,* ill. by Faith Jaques. T. Crowell, 1973. 9–12

PEYTON, K. M. *The Beethoven Medal,* ill. by author. T. Crowell, 1972. 12–15

———. *Marion's Angels.* Oxford, 1979. 12–15

———. *Pennington's Heir.* T. Crowell, 1974. 12–15

———. *Pennington's Last Term,* ill. by author. T. Crowell, 1971. 12–15

RANSOME, ARTHUR. *Swallows and Amazons,* ill. by Helene Carter. Lippincott, 1931. First of a series of stories about four children who live in the Lake District in England. 12–13

ROBINSON, JOAN G. *Charley,* ill. by Prudence Seward. Coward, 1970. Charley, through a misunderstanding, believes she is unwanted by the aunt to whom she is sent and runs away. Good characters, plenty of action, and the perennial appeal of making-it-on-your-own. 9–11

ROBINSON, VERONICA. *David in Silence,* ill. by Victor Ambrus. Lippincott, 1966. The story, set in a small English town, concerns a new boy, David, who has always been deaf. A poignant and interesting story about the isolation and hostility that often are the lot of the deaf. 10–12

STEWART, A. C. *Ossian House.* Phillips, 1976. Obliged to spend eight weeks a year at a home in Scotland bequeathed to him by his grandfather, eleven-year-old John slowly learns to appreciate the people, the land, and the beasts of his heritage. 11–13

STREATFEILD, NOEL. *Ballet Shoes,* ill. by Richard Floethe. Random, 1950. The hard work and unwavering determination that it takes to become a ballet dancer. 11–13

———. *The Children on the Top Floor,* ill. by Jillian Willett. Random, 1965. Life with a television celebrity. 10–12

———. *The Family at Caldicott Place,* ill. by Betty Maxey. Random, 1968. Life is difficult when the father of the family is recovering from a deep neurosis. 9–11

———. *Thursday's Child,* ill. by Peggy Fortnum. Random, 1971. A foundling girl finds her place in life. 9–11

TATE, JOAN. *Wild Boy,* ill. by Susan Jeschke. Harper, 1973. The friendship between two boys, both solitary people. Set in Yorkshire. 10–12

TOWNSEND, JOHN ROWE. *Good-bye to the Jungle.* Lippincott, 1967. 12–14

———. *Good Night, Prof, Dear.* Lippincott, 1970. 12–14

———. *Hell's Edge.* Lothrop, 1969. 11–14

———. *The Intruder.* Lippincott, 1970. 11–14

———. *Noah's Castle.* Lippincott, 1976. 10–14

———. *Trouble in the Jungle,* ill. by W. T. Mars. Lippincott, 1969. 10–12

TURNER, PHILIP. *War on the Darnel,* ill. by W. T. Mars. World, 1969. Three lively English boys engage in a mighty battle with another set of boys who have set up a river barricade. Good characterization and even better dialogue. 10–14

VAN STOCKUM, HILDA. *The Cottage at Bantry Bay,* ill. by author. Viking, 1938.

———. *Francie on the Run,* ill. by author. Viking, 1939.

———. *Pegeen,* ill. by author. Viking, 1941. 10–12

WALSH, JILL PATON. *Goldengrove.* Farrar, 1972. Madge makes a dramatic discovery about her family while visiting her grandmother in Cornwall. 11–13

———. *Unleaving.* Farrar, 1976. A sequel to *Goldengrove.* 11–13

WINDSOR, PATRICIA. *Mad Martin.* Harper, 1976. 10–11

France

BEMELMANS, LUDWIG. *Madeline,* ill. by author. Viking, 1939. Other titles in the series include the Caldecott Medal book *Madeline's Rescue* (1953), *Madeline and the Bad Hat* (1957), *Madeline and the Gypsies* (1959). 5–7

BISHOP, CLAIRE HUCHET. *All Alone,* ill. by Feodor Rojankovsky. Viking, 1953. Villagers in the French Alps learn to work together when two children, herding in the mountains, are isolated by an avalanche. 9–11

———. *Pancakes-Paris,* ill. by Georges Schreiber. Viking, 1947. A half-starved postwar French child receives a miraculous package of American pancake mix. How he meets two American soldiers and gets the recipe makes a heart-warming tale. 8–12

CARLSON, NATALIE SAVAGE. *A Brother for the Orphelines,* ill. by Garth Williams. Harper, 1959.

———. *The Family Under the Bridge,* ill. by Garth Williams. Harper, 1958.

———. *The Happy Orpheline,* ill. by Garth Williams. Harper, 1957.

———. *The Orphelines in the Enchanted Castle,* ill. by Adriana Saviozzi. Harper, 1964. The fourth book about the lively French orphans who live—this time in a small castle—with Madame Flattot. A light and charming story with important (but not obtrusive) overtones about social behavior. 9–11

———. *A Pet for the Orphelines,* ill. by Fermin Rocker. Harper, 1962. 8–10

Germany

BENARY-ISBERT, MARGOT. *The Ark,* tr. by Clara and Richard Winston. Harcourt, 1953. The Lechow family, a mother and four children, are trying to reestablish a somewhat normal life in a bombed-out city. 12–14

_____. *Rowan Farm*, tr. by Richard and Clara Winston. Harcourt, 1954. The family from *The Ark* welcomes home their father. Two superlative stories.   13–17

HÄRTLING, PETER. *Oma*, ill. by Jutta Ash. Harper, 1977. The story of an elderly German woman and her relationship with a small grandson who comes to live with her when his parents are killed.   8–10

PETRIDES, HEIDRUN. *Hans and Peter*, ill. by author. Harcourt, 1963. Two boys have the satisfaction of seeing a hut raised through their own efforts.   7–9

RETTICH, MARGRET. *The Silver Touch and Other Family Christmas Stories*, ill. by Rolf Rettich. Morrow, 1978. A collection of stories, some tender, some humorous, which celebrate the delights and the disasters of the Christmas season.   9–11

VOGEL, ILSE-MARGRET. *My Twin Sister Erika*, ill. by author. Harper, 1976.   6–9

VON GEBHARDT, HERTHA. *The Girl from Nowhere*, tr. by James Kirkup, ill. by Helen Brun. Criterion, 1959. No one believes her father will return, but a little German girl's faith surmounts mockery and pity and is happily rewarded.   10–13

Holland

DeJONG, MEINDERT. *Far Out the Long Canal*, ill. by Nancy Grossman. Harper, 1964.   10–13

_____. *Journey from Peppermint Street*, ill. by Emily Arnold McCully. Harper, 1968. National Book Award.   9–11

_____. *The Wheel on the School*, ill. by Maurice Sendak. Harper, 1954. Newbery Medal.   9–12

DODGE, MARY MAPES. *Hans Brinker: Or the Silver Skates* (see Forerunners).

India

ARORA, SHIRLEY. *The Left-Handed Chank*. Follett, 1966. A village in India accepts modern ideas.   11–14

_____. *"What Then, Raman?"* ill. by Hans Guggenheim. Follett, 1960. A shy, earnest boy, the only person in his village who has learned to read, finds that his accomplishment carries with it the responsibility to help others.   10–12

BOTHWELL, JEAN. *The Little Flute Player*, ill. by Margaret Ayer. Morrow, 1949. Minor disasters stalk Teka, the little village flute player, and grow into tragedy when famine comes. The ten-year-old boy takes his father's place and saves his family from starvation.   9–12

GOBHAI, MEHILL. *Lakshmi: The Water Buffalo Who Wouldn't*, ill. by author. Hawthorn, 1969. A simply written story about a family in India today. The tale has humor as well as an interesting setting, and the theme (mother and son amused at the come-down of father) a broad applicability.   7–9

RANKIN, LOUISE. *Daughter of the Mountains*, ill. by Kurt Wiese. Viking, 1948. Tells of the journey of a little Tibetan village girl to far-off Calcutta in search of her stolen puppy.   10–13

SINGH, REGINALD LAL, and ELOISE LOWNSBERY. *Gift of the Forest*, ill. by Anne Vaughan. McKay, 1942 and 1958. In this distinguished story of rural India, Young Bim, a Hindu boy, finds a tiger cub and cares for it until he is forced to return it to the jungle.   11–14

SOMMERFELT, AIMÉE. *The Road to Agra*, ill. by Ulf Aas. Criterion, 1961. Lalu walks the long road to Agra with his small sister, hoping the doctors there can save her eyesight.   10–11

_____. *The White Bungalow*, ill. by Ulf Aas. Hale, 1963. A sequel to *The Road to Agra*.   10–12

Italy

BETTINA (pseud. for Bettina Ehrlich). *Pantaloni*, ill. by author. Harper, 1957. Colorfully illustrated, this is a warm story of Italian village life and of a little boy's search for his lost dog.   5–8

FLETCHER, DAVID. *Confetti for Cortorelli*, ill. by George Thompson. Pantheon, 1957. To be in the Children's Fancy Dress Parade, Angelo, an orphan of Sicily, needed a costume. How he earned it and gained a home as well makes an original and distinctive story.   6–8

REGGIANI, RENEE. *The Sun Train*, tr. from the Italian by Patrick Creagh. Coward, 1966. A mature story about a family that moves from an almost-feudal society in Sicily to find other problems just as serious in a contemporary Italian urban setting.   11–14

SNYDER, ZILPHA KEATLEY. *The Famous Stanley Kidnapping Case*. Atheneum, 1979.   9–12

Russia

● CORCORAN, BARBARA. *The Clown*. Atheneum, 1975. Liza, a diplomat's daughter who speaks Russian, helps to smuggle a Russian Jewish clown out of the country. Fast-paced adventure.   10–13

FROLOV, VADIM. *What It's All About*, tr. by Joseph Barnes. Doubleday, 1968.   13–15

KASSIL, LEV. *Once in a Lifetime*, tr. by Anne Terry White. Doubleday, 1970. The first-person story of a thirteen-year-old Russian girl's experience as a movie find. The story has a Moscow setting, with good balance of school and family life and excellent characterization.   11–14

KORINETZ, YURI. *There, Far Beyond the River*, tr. by Anthea Bell, ill. by George Armstrong. O'Hara, 1973.   10–12

MAYAKOVSKY, VLADIMIR. *Timothy's Horse*, ad. by Guy Daniels, ill. by Flavio Costantini. Pantheon, 1970. A small boy's wish comes true when he and his father buy a hobby horse. Marvelous illustrations and a rhyming text.   5–7

TER HAAR, JAAP. *Boris*, tr. from the Dutch by Martha Mearns, ill. by Rien Poortvliet. Delacorte, 1970.   10–12

Scandinavia

ANCKARSVÄRD, KARIN. *Aunt Vinnie's Invasion*, tr. by Annabelle MacMillan, ill. by William M. Hutchinson. Harcourt, 1962. The six Hallsenius children live with Aunt Vinnie for a year. An amusing story of modern Sweden.   10–13

_____. *Doctor's Boy*, tr. from the Swedish by Annabelle MacMillan, ill. by Fermin Rocker. Harcourt, 1965. A lively tale set early in the twentieth century.   10–12

BESKOW, ELSA. *Pelle's New Suit*, ill. by author. Harper, 1929.   12–15

FREUCHEN, PETER. *Whaling Boy*, ill. by Leonard Everett Fisher. Putnam, 1958. Per List, not quite twelve, finds life aboard a Danish whaling ship a rugged and adventurous experience. A powerfully written and moving story.   10–13

FRIIS-BAASTAD, BABBIS. *Don't Take Teddy*, tr. from the Norwegian by Lise Sómme McKinnon. Scribner's, 1967. A moving story about a small boy who protects his older retarded brother.   10–13

GRIPE, MARIA. *Elvis and His Friends,* tr. from the Swedish by Sheila LaFarge, ill. by Harald Gripe. Delacorte, 1976. 9–11

——. *Elvis and His Secret,* tr. from the Swedish by Sheila LaFarge, ill. by Harald Gripe. Delacorte, 1976.   9–11

——. *Hugo,* tr. from the Swedish by Paul Britten Austin, ill. by Harold Gripe. Delacorte, 1970.   9–11

——. *Hugo and Josephine,* tr. from the Swedish by Paul Britten Austin, ill. by Harald Gripe. Delacorte, 1969.   7–8

——. *Josephine,* tr. from the Swedish by Paul Britten Austin, ill. by Harald Gripe. Delacorte, 1970.   7–8

——. *Julia's House,* tr. from the Swedish by Gerry Bothmer, ill. by Harald Gripe. Delacorte, 1975.   10–11

——. *The Night Daddy,* tr. from the Swedish by Gerry Bothmer, ill. by Harald Gripe. Delacorte, 1971.   9–11

HELLBERG, HANS-ERIC. *Grandpa's Maria,* tr. from the Swedish by Patricia Crampton, ill. by Joan Sandin. Morrow, 1974.   8–9

JANSSON, TOVE. *The Summer Book,* tr. from the Swedish by Thomas Teal. Pantheon, 1975. Describes the small events of sun-filled days spent by Sophia and her grandmother on an island one summer. For the perceptive reader.   11–13

LINDGREN, ASTRID. *The Children on Troublemaker Street,* tr. by Gerry Bothmer, ill. by Ilon Wiklund. Macmillan, 1964. Swedish children of today and their many activities.   7–9

——. *Rasmus and the Vagabond,* tr. by Gerry Bothmer, ill. by Eric Palmquist. Viking, 1960. Written in a more serious vein than the author's *Pippi Longstocking* series, this is an appealing story of a runaway orphan and the part-time tramp who befriended him.   9–12

LUNDGREN, MAX. *Matt's Grandfather,* tr. by Ann Pyk, ill. by Fibben Hald. Putnam, 1972.   5–7

● SOMMERFELT, AIMÉE. *Miriam,* tr. by Pat Shaw Iversen. Criterion, 1963. The story of a Jewish family during the Nazi occupation of Norway.   12–15

SORENSON, VIRGINIA. *Lotte's Locket,* ill. by Fermin Rocker. Harcourt, 1964.   9–11

UNNERSTAD, EDITH. *The Saucepan Journey,* ill. by Louis Slobodkin. Macmillan, 1951. The Larsson children, all seven of them, spend a wonderful summer in the traveling caravan, helping father sell his saucepans through Sweden.   9–12

VESTLY, ANNE-CATH. *Aurora and Socrates,* ill. by Leonard Kessler. T. Crowell, 1977. In a sequel to *Hello, Aurora,* Vestly explores further the small problems of a child of a nuclear family in an urban setting.   8–10

——. *Hello, Aurora,* tr. from the Norwegian by Eileen Amos, adapted by Jane Fairfax, ill. by Leonard Kessler. T. Crowell, 1974.   8–10

Switzerland

CHÖNZ, SELINA. *A Bell for Ursli,* ill. by Alois Carigiet. Walck, 1953. One of the most beautiful picture stories to come out of Europe, this is also the exciting story of a small Swiss boy determined to have the largest bell to ring in the spring procession.   6–9

RUTGERS VAN DER LOEFF-BASENAU, ANNA. *Avalanche!* tr. by Dora Round, ill. by Gustav Schrotter. Morrow, 1958. Holland's prize-winning children's book for 1955 tells the dramatic story of an avalanche that struck the tiny Swiss village of Urteli and how it affected three young boys.   11–13

SPYRI, JOHANNA. *Heidi* (see Forerunners).

ULLMAN, JAMES RAMSEY. *Banner in the Sky.* Lippincott, 1954. A story of the self-discipline and stern code of ethics that governs the Alpine guides.   12–14

Other countries

AYER, JACQUELINE. *Nu Dang and His Kite,* ill. by author. Harcourt, 1959. A colorful introduction to Siamese life is provided by this story of a small boy's search along the river banks for his lost kite. *The Paper Flower Tree* (1962) is the story of a little girl of Thailand who at last finds her longed-for ornamental tree.   6–8

BALET, JAN B. *Joanjo: A Portuguese Tale,* ill. by author. Delacorte, 1967. The story of Joanjo, a small Portuguese boy, and his acceptance of the independent life of the fisherman after dreams of glory.   5–7

KRUMGOLD, JOSEPH. *The Most Terrible Turk: A Story of Turkey,* ill. by Michael Hampshire. T. Crowell, 1969. Uncle Mustafa and Ali are all that are left of a once-large family. Their relationship is warm and appealing, and the setting, Turkey today, is interesting.   8–10

MERRILL, JEAN. *Shan's Lucky Knife,* ill. by Ronni Solbert. W. R. Scott, 1960. Young Shan outwits the tricky boatman who has taken all his possessions. An excellent read-aloud tale with a Burmese background and folk-tale flavor. 7–10

NÖSTLINGER, CHRISTINE. *Girl Missing.* Watts, 1976. Erika worships her older sister. Her loneliness when Ilse runs away from home turns to chagrin when she learns she's been deceived about Ilse's whereabouts.   11–13

● OFEK, URIEL. *Smoke Over Golan,* ill. by Lloyd Bloom. Harper, 1979. A young boy tells the story of his involvement in the battle on the Golan Heights.   11–13

SEREDY, KATE. *The Good Master,* ill. by author. Viking, 1935. A family who lives on a Hungarian ranch in the early 1900s teaches wild Kate gentler ways.   10–12

——. *The Singing Tree,* ill. by author. Viking, 1939. Another story of Kate, set during World War I.   10–14

SHANNON, MONICA. *Dobry,* ill. by Atanas Katchamakoff. Viking, 1934. Newbery Medal. Dobry, a Bulgarian peasant boy, finds himself longing both to stay at home and to go away to become a sculptor. A rich, multifaceted picture of a culture.   10–13

SPERRY, ARMSTRONG. *Call It Courage,* ill. by author. Macmillan, 1940. Newbery Medal. Published in England as *The Boy Who Was Afraid.*   10–13

● TAYLOR, SYDNEY. *A Papa Like Everyone Else,* ill. by George Porter. Follett, 1966.   9–11

● WATSON, SALLY. *To Build a Land,* ill. by Lili Cassel. Holt, 1957. War-orphaned Leo and his small sister, rescued from the streets of Naples, find a new life in a children's camp in Israel.   11–14

WOJCIECHOWSKA, MAIA. *Shadow of a Bull,* ill. by Alvin Smith. Atheneum, 1964. Newbery Medal.   12–15

WUORIO, EVA-LIS. *The Island of Fish in the Trees,* ill. by Edward Ardizzone. World, 1962. The day-long adventure of two little sisters who trail the doctor around the island to get him to mend their broken doll. The setting is the Balearic Islands, and both story and pictures are exceptionally appealing.   7–9

Animal Stories

AGLE, NAN HAYDEN. *My Animals and Me,* ill. with photos by Emily Hayden. Seabury, 1970. Reminiscences of an animal lover in a book that combines warmth, humor, family anecdotes, and memories of beloved pets in a rural pre-World War I background.   8–10

ANDERSON, CLARENCE. *Billy and Blaze,* ill. by author. Macmillan, 1936, 1962. And its sequels.   5–8

BAUDOUY, MICHEL-AIMÉ. *Old One-Toe*, tr. by Marie Ponsot, ill. by Johannes Troyer. Harcourt, 1959. French children sympathize with a hunted fox. 11–13

BAYLOR, BYRD. *Hawk, I'm Your Brother*, ill. by Peter Parnall. Scribner's, 1976. A boy who yearns to fly captures instead the joy of flight when he frees a young hawk he has caught and tamed. 8–10

BEATTY, PATRICIA. *The Staffordshire Terror*. Morrow, 1979. 10–12

BOSTON, LUCY M. *A Stranger at Green Knowe*, ill. by Peter Boston. Harcourt, 1961. Carnegie Medal. 11–14

BUFF, MARY and CONRAD. *Elf Owl*, ill. by Conrad Buff. Viking, 1958. A story of the desert, beautifully illustrated. 5–8

BURNFORD, SHEILA. *The Incredible Journey*, ill. by Carl Burger. Little, 1961. Canadian Library Association Medal. 11 up

BYARS, BETSY. *The Midnight Fox*, ill. by Ann Grifalconi. Viking, 1968. 9–11

CALLEN, LARRY. *Sorrow's Song*, ill. by Marvin Friedman. Atlantic/Little, 1979. Pinch describes the tribulations he and his mute friend Sorrow have when they discover a small, disabled whooping crane. 10–12

CLARK, BILLY C. *The Mooneyed Hound*, ill. by Nedda Walker. Putnam, 1958. Jeb's handicapped dog proves his mettle as a hunter in the field trials. 9–11

CLEARY, BEVERLY. *Socks*, ill. by Beatrice Darwin. Morrow, 1973. 9–11

DEJONG, MEINDERT. *Along Came a Dog*, ill. by Maurice Sendak. Harper, 1958. 10–12

———. *The Last Little Cat*, ill. by Jim McMullan. Harper, 1961. The timid seventh kitten strays away from his friend, the old blind dog, and encounters many cat enemies before he reaches home and safety. 8–10

DE ROO, ANNE. *Cinnamon and Nutmeg*. Nelson, 1974. 9–11

DOTY, JEAN. *The Crumb*. Greenwillow, 1976. 10–12

DUNLOP, EILEEN. *Fox Farm*. Holt, 1979. Adam had come as a foster child to the Darke family but couldn't get along with their young son Richard until the two joined forces to save a wounded animal. 10–12

FISHER, AILEEN. *Valley of the Smallest: The Life Story of a Shrew*, ill. by Jean Zallinger. T. Crowell, 1966. 11–14

FLACK, MARJORIE. *Angus and the Ducks*, ill. by author. Doubleday, 1930, 1939. First of a series about a frisky, curious Scottish terrier. 4–7

———. *The Story About Ping*, ill. by Kurt Wiese. Viking, 1933. 5–8

GALL, ALICE CREW, and FLEMING CREW. *Splasher*, ill. by Else Bostelmann. Walck, 1945. A flood is a great adventure for a young muskrat and his friends. 8–10

§ GATES, DORIS. *Little Vic*, ill. by Kate Seredy. Viking, 1951. When Pony River, a black boy, sees Little Vic, he believes the colt will be as great as his sire, Man o' War. The boy endures every hardship willingly in his devotion to the colt. 9–12

———. *A Morgan for Melinda*. Viking, 1980. Gates reverses the usual horse story pattern, for it isn't until after her father has bought a horse that Melinda learns to love and ride it. 9–11

GEORGE, JEAN. *Coyote in Manhattan*, ill. by John Kaufman. T. Crowell, 1968. 11–13

———. *The Cry of the Crow*. Harper, 1980. 10–12

———. *Gull Number 737*. T. Crowell, 1964. 12–15

———. *Julie of the Wolves*, ill. by John Schoenherr. Harper, 1972. Newbery Medal. 10–13

———. *The Wounded Wolf*, ill. by John Schoenherr. Harper, 1978. 7–9

GEORGE, JOHN and JEAN. *Bubo, the Great Horned Owl*, ill. by Jean George. Dutton, 1954. 11–14

———. *Vulpes, the Red Fox*, ill. by Jean George. Dutton, 1948, 10–14

GIPSON, FRED. *Old Yeller*, ill. by Carl Burger. Harper, 1956. Travis's mongrel dog is bitten by a rabid wolf while loyally defending his family. He becomes infected and has to be destroyed. This is a moving tale of a boy and his dog, set in pioneer Texas of the 1870s. In a sequel, *Savage Sam* (1962), Travis is aided by Old Yeller's equally gallant son in rescuing two children from Apaches. 11–14

GRIFFITHS, HELEN. *Just a Dog*, ill. by Victor Ambrus. Holiday, 1975. 10–12

HALLARD, PETER. *Puppy Lost in Lapland*, ill. by Wallace Tripp. Watts, 1971. An injured puppy struggles for survival in the wilderness. 10–12

HENRY, MARGUERITE. *Gaudenzia: Pride of the Palio*, ill. by Lynd-Ward. Rand, 1960. 11–14

———. *Justin Morgan Had a Horse*, ill. by Wesley Dennis. Rand, 1954. A story of the development of the Morgan breed of horses. 9–14

———. *King of the Wind*, ill. by Wesley Dennis. Rand, 1948. Newbery Medal. 9–14

———. *Misty of Chincoteague*, ill. by Wesley Dennis. Rand, 1947. 9–14

———. *White Stallion of Lipizza*, ill. by Wesley Dennis. Rand, 1964. 11–13

HOLLING, HOLLING C. *Pagoo*, ill. by author and Lucille W. Holling. Houghton, 1957. A quietly paced, beautifully illustrated life story of a hermit crab. 9–12

JAMES, WILL. *Smoky, the Cowhorse*, ill. by author. Scribner's, 1926. Newbery Medal. The adventures of a range horse. 11–16

KJELGAARD, JIM. *Big Red*, ill. by Bob Kuhn. Holiday, 1956. 12–16

LATHROP, DOROTHY. *Who Goes There?* ill. by author. Macmillan, 1935, 1963. Lovely pictures of small forest creatures. 6–10

LEA, ALEC. *Temba Dawn*. Scribner's, 1975. 10–12

LIERS, EMIL. *An Otter's Story*, ill. by Tony Palazzo. Viking, 1953. 10–13

LINDQUIST, WILLIS. *Burma Boy*, ill. by Nicolas Mordvinoff. Whittlesey, 1953. A thrilling tale of an elephant of the teakwood forests which goes wild, and of young Haji, the elephant boy, who wins his confidence and saves the villagers from disaster. 9–11

McNEER, MAY. *My Friend Mac*, ill. by Lynd Ward. Houghton, 1960. An orphaned and fast-growing moose provides plenty of diversion for lonely little Baptiste of the Canadian woods. 7–9

MAXWELL, GAVIN. *The Otters' Tale*, ill. with photos. Dutton, 1962. A juvenile edition of the author's memorable nature tale of his otter pets, *Ring of Bright Water*. 12–15

MILES, MISKA. *Eddie's Bear*, ill. by John Schoenherr. Little, 1970. 5–8

———. *Mississippi Possum*, ill. by John Schoenherr. Little, 1965. 7–9

———. *Nobody's Cat*, ill. by John Schoenherr. Little, 1969. 8–9

———. *Otter in the Cove*, ill. by John Schoenherr. Little, 1974. 8–10

———. *Wharf Rat*, ill. by John Schoenherr. Little, 1972. 7–9

MONTGOMERY, RUTHERFORD. *Kildee House*, ill. by Barbara Cooney. Doubleday, 1949. Story of an elderly would-be hermit who, building a house in the redwood forest, soon finds it filled with small animals and visited by warring children. The tragicomic episodes make this a nature story of unusual sensitivity and beauty. 10–13

MOREY, WALT. *Gentle Ben*, ill. by John Schoenherr. Dutton, 1965. 11–14

———. *Gloomy Gus*. Dutton, 1970. 10–12

———. *Kävik the Wolf Dog*, ill. by Peter Parnall. Dutton, 1968. 11–14

————. *Year of the Black Pony.* Dutton, 1976.   10–12

MORGENROTH, BARBARA. *Impossible Charlie*, ill. by Velma Ilsley. Atheneum, 1979. Lightly humorous in style, this is the story of a girl who gets her heart's desire, her own horse.   9–11

MOWAT, FARLEY. *Owls in the Family*, ill. by Robert Frankenberg. Little, 1962. A funny and heartwarming story of two owls of Northern Canada, told by their youthful rescuer.   9–12

MUKERJI, DHAN GOPAL. *Gay-Neck*, ill. by Boris Artzybasheff. Dutton, 1927, 1968. Gay-Neck's training as a carrier pigeon in India made him valuable as a messenger in France during World War I. Newbery Medal, 1928. 11–14

NORTH, STERLING. *Little Rascal*, ill. by Carl Burger. Dutton, 1965.   9–11

————. *Rascal: A Memoir of a Better Era*, ill. by John Schoenherr. Dutton, 1963.   12 up

O'HARA, MARY (pseud. for Mary Sture-Vasa). *My Friend Flicka.* Lippincott, 1941. Horsebreeding on a Western ranch.   12 up

PEARCE, ANN PHILIPPA. *The Battle of Bubble and Squeak*, ill. by Alan Baker. Dutton, 1979.   9–11

PHIPSON, JOAN. *Fly Free.* Atheneum, 1979. When Johnny, who loves to trap, is himself caught in an animal trap, he vows he'll give up the sport—if he lives.   12–14

RAWLINGS, MARJORIE KINNAN. *The Yearling*, ill. by N. C. Wyeth. Scribner's, 1938, 1962.   12 up

ROUNDS, GLEN. *The Blind Colt*, ill. by author. Holiday, 1941, 1960.   9–12

SETON, ERNEST T. *Lives of the Hunted*, ill. by author. Schocken, 1967. A favorite realistic saga.   10 up

SHARMAT, MARJORIE WEINMAN. *Morris Brookside, a Dog*, ill. by Ronald Himler. Holiday, 1973.   5–8

————. *Morris Brookside Is Missing*, ill. by Ronald Himler. Holiday, 1974.   5–8

SKORPEN, LIESEL MOAK. *Bird*, ill. by Joan Sandin. Harper, 1976.   5–8

STONG, PHIL. *Honk: the Moose*, ill. by Kurt Wiese. Dodd, 1935.   9–10

STRANGER, JOYCE. *Lakeland Vet.* Viking, 1972.   11 up

WALKER, DAVID E. *Big Ben*, ill. by Victor Ambrus. Houghton, 1969. Fine writing style and characterization in this story about a St. Bernard who is unjustly suspected of being a sheep-killer.   9–11

WARD, LYND. *The Biggest Bear*, ill. by author. Houghton, 1952. Caldecott Medal.   5–8

WHITNEY, ALMA MARSHAK. *Leave Herbert Alone*, ill. by David McPhail. Addison, 1972.   3–6

ZIMELMAN, NATHAN. *The Lives of My Cat Alfred*, ill. by Evaline Ness. Dutton, 1976.   5–8

Sports Stories

BISHOP, CURTIS. *Little League Victory.* Lippincott, 1967. Ed's temper tantrums make it difficult for him to be accepted as a member of the team, but he succeeds in getting over this obstacle.   9–11

CHRISTOPHER, MATT. *Johnny Long Legs*, ill. by Harvey Kidder. Little, 1970.   9–11

————. *Tough to Tackle*, ill. by Harvey Kidder. Little, 1971.   8–10

CORBETT, SCOTT. *The Baseball Bargain*, ill. by Wallace Tripp. Little, 1970.   9–11

————. *The Hockey Girls.* Dutton, 1976. Published simultaneously in Canada by Clarke, Irwin.   9–11

DU BOIS, WILLIAM PÈNE. *Porko von Popbutton*, ill. by author. Harper, 1969.   9–11

GAULT, WILLIAM. *Stubborn Sam.* Dutton, 1969.   11–14

§ GEIBEL, JAMES. *The Blond Brother.* Putnam, 1979. When Rich Gaskins transfers to Marchmont High his life is complicated by being one of the few whites on a black team, a coach who picks him for a favorite, and his affection for a black girl.   12–15

GLANVILLE, BRIAN. *Goalkeepers Are Different.* Crown, 1972. Game descriptions and facts about public relations and international competition are authoritative in a story about a new member of an English pro soccer team.   11–14

§ HEUMANN, WILLIAM. *Fastbreak Rebel.* Dodd, 1971.   11–14

§● HIGDON, HAL. *The Electronic Olympics.* Holt, 1971. A blithe tale of a computerized Olympics and an affable African track star.   11–14

§ HONIG, DONALD. *Johnny Lee.* McCall, 1971.   10–14

————. *Way to Go, Teddy.* Watts, 1973.   11–14

§ JACKSON, JESSE. *Anchor Man*, ill. by Doris Spiegel. Harper, 1947.   12 up

KATZ, BOBBI. *Rod-and-Reel Trouble*, ill. by Janet LaSalle. Whitman, 1974.   8–10

§ KESSLER, LEONARD. *Here Comes the Strikeout*, ill. by author. Harper, 1965.   7–8

KNUDSON, R. R. *Zanballer.* Delacorte, 1972. While the diary form isn't quite convincing, Zan does convey her determination that a girls' football team has a place in school sports.   11–14

————. *Zanbanger.* Harper, 1977.   11–14

● KONIGSBURG, E. L. *About the B'nai Bagels*, ill. by author. Atheneum, 1969.   10–12

LEVY, ELIZABETH. *Something Queer at the Ball Park*, ill. by Mordicai Gerstein. Delacorte, 1975.   7–9

§ LIPSYTE, ROBERT. *The Contender.* Harper, 1967.   12–15

LORD, BEMAN. *Shrimp's Soccer Goal*, ill. by Harold Berson. Walck, 1970. All of Lord's stories about several sports are sound and enjoyable for readers in the middle group.   8–10

MacPHERSON, MARGARET. *The Shinty Boys*, ill. by Shirley Hughes. Harcourt, 1963.   11–13

POTTER, MARGARET. *The Touch-and-Go Year.* Meredith, 1969.   10–12

§ QUIGLEY, MARTIN. *Today's Game.* Viking, 1965.   13 up

RENICK, MARION. *Boy at Bat*, ill. by Paul Galdone. Scribner's, 1961. An amusing story of a boy who gets into one baseball game and demands that his family now call him "Lefty."   7–9

————. *Take a Long Jump*, ill. by Charles Robinson. Scribner's, 1971. A track story that also has good family relationships.   9–11

SHORTALL, LEONARD. *Ben on the Ski Trail*, ill. by author. Morrow, 1965.   7–9

SLOTE, ALFRED. *Hang Tough, Paul Mather.* Lippincott, 1973. A poignant first-person story by a leukemia victim who tries to keep up with his greatest interest, playing Little League ball.   9–12

————. *The Hotshot*, photographs by William LaCrosse. Watts, 1977. A hockey player learns about teamwork, in a story that's also suitable for slow older readers.   9–11

————. *Matt Gargan's Boy.* Lippincott, 1975.   9–11

————. *Stranger on the Ball Club.* Lippincott, 1970.   9–11

§ ————. *Jake.* Lippincott, 1971. A small boy's uncle gives up his free time to coach a baseball team.   9–11

TAVES, ISABELLA. *Not Bad for a Girl.* Evans/Lippincott, 1972.   9–11

THORVALL, KERSTIN. *Gunnar Scores a Goal*, tr. from the Swedish by Anne Parker, ill. by Serge Hollerbach. Harcourt, 1968.   8–10

TOWNE, MARY. *First Serve*, ill. by Ruth Sanderson. Atheneum, 1976. Thirteen-year-old Dulcie is torn between her desire to enter competitive tennis and her fear that her older sister, who also plays, will feel hurt. 11–14

§ TUNIS, JOHN. *All-American,* ill. by Hans Walleen. Harcourt, 1942. 10–14

● _____. *Keystone Kids.* Harcourt, 1943. A fine sports story for the teen age—the happy resolution of anti-Semitic feeling is achieved by the students. 12–16

● WEAVER, ROBERT. *Nice Guy, Go Home.* Harper, 1968. 12–15

WINTHROP, ELIZABETH. *Marathon Miranda.* Holiday, 1979. 9–11

WODEHOUSE, P. G. *Mike and Psmith.* Meredith, 1969. 11 up

Mystery and Adventure

ALEKSIN, ANATOLII GEORGIEVICH. *Alik the Detective.* Morrow, 1977. Six children visiting the cottage of a local author are trapped in the cellar by an inexplicably hostile caretaker. 10–12

ANCKARSVÄRD, KARIN. *The Robber Ghost,* tr. from the Swedish by Annabelle Macmillan, ill. by Paul Galdone. Harcourt, 1961. The disappearance of money from the post office housed in a wing of an old and supposedly haunted Swedish castle arouses the detective instincts of young schoolmates Michael and Cecilia. Good atmosphere and suspense for both boys and girls. 10–12

§ BAWDEN, NINA. *Rebel on a Rock.* Lippincott, 1978. 10–13

BERNA, PAUL. *A Truckload of Rice,* tr. from the French by John Buchanan Brown, ill. by Prudence Seward. Pantheon, 1970. 10–12

BONHAM, FRANK. *Mystery in Little Tokyo,* ill. by Kazue Mizumura. Dutton, 1966. 10–12

§★ _____. *Mystery of the Fat Cat,* ill. by Alvin Smith. Dutton, 1968. 10–14

§ BONSALL, CROSBY. *The Case of the Cat's Meow,* ill. by author. Harper, 1965. All of the Bonsall books are charming and useful. 7–8

BRANFIELD, JOHN. *The Poison Factory.* Harper, 1972. An English girl investigates the possibility that her father's death was caused by nerve gas. 11–14

CAMERON, ELEANOR. *A Spell Is Cast,* ill. by Beth and Joe Krush. Little, 1964. 10–12

_____. *The Terrible Churnadryne,* ill. by Beth and Joe Krush. Little, 1959. Did a strange prehistoric creature really stalk San Lorenzo peak? Tom and Jennifer and the whole town of Redwood Cove are caught up in the strange controversy. A unique, well-written tale of suspense. 9–12

CHANCE, STEPHEN. *Septimus and the Danedyke Mystery.* Nelson, 1973. A former member of the CID investigates the theft of a valuable religious relic. 11 up

COBALT, MARTIN. *Pool of Swallows.* Nelson, 1974. 11–15

★ COREN, ALAN. *Arthur the Kid,* ill. by John Astrop. Little, 1978.

_____. *Klondike Arthur,* ill. by John Astrop. Little, 1979. The indomitable Arthur shows up again, this time to bring grace and culture to a rough Klondike enterprise, the Rotten Old Saloon. Others in the series are *Buffalo Arthur, The Lone Arthur,* and *Railroad Arthur.* 9–11

CORMIER, ROBERT. *After the First Death.* Pantheon, 1979. Different voices tell the story of a man engaged in a secret government project threatened by the hijacking of a bus full of children by terrorists. 12–15

_____. *I Am the Cheese.* Pantheon, 1977. 12–17

CRAYDER, DOROTHY. *She and the Dubious Three,* ill. by Velma Ilsley. Atheneum, 1974. 10–12

CURRY, JANE LOUISE. *The Bassumtyte Treasure.* Atheneum, 1978. A nicely-rendered story turning on the familiar device of a long-lost treasure turning up to save a doomed estate

from passing out of the hands of its owners.

_____. *Ghost Lane.* Atheneum, 1979. 10–12

DEGENS, T. *The Game on Thatcher Island.* Viking, 1977. When subjected to a frightening ordeal at the hands of some bullies, the young victims seize on their opportunity for revenge and put their assailants through the identical punishment they had meted out earlier. 11–13

DILLON, EILIS. *The Singing Cave,* ill. by Stan Campbell. Funk, 1960. Suspense and mystery abound in this outstandingly written tale of the discovery and disappearance of Viking remains from a cave on an Irish isle. 12–15

GARFIELD, LEON. *Black Jack,* ill. by Antony Maitland. Pantheon, 1968. 11–14

_____. *Footsteps.* Delacorte, 1980. A swashbuckling story of the hunt for a lost inheritance, set in eighteenth-century London. 10–13

_____. *The Sound of Coaches,* ill. by John Lawrence. Viking, 1974. A picaresque period tale of a foundling who searches for facts about his real parents. Robust characters, rich dialogue, vigorous style. 12–16

GRIESE, ARNOLD. *The Wind Is Not a River,* ill. by Glo Coalson. T. Crowell, 1978. Two children living on an Aleutian island during World War II must decide whether to treat the wounded Japanese soldier they've found as an enemy or as a human being. 9–11

HARRIS, CHRISTIE. *Mystery at the Edge of Two Worlds,* ill. by Lou Crockett. Atheneum, 1978. 10–12

HIGHTOWER, FLORENCE. *Dark Horse of Woodfield,* ill. by Joshua Tolford. Houghton, 1962. The Woodfield home was a shabby relic, but it housed Buggsie and Maggie Armistead, who trained a horse, solved a mystery, and even bred cocoons to restore the family fortunes. A humorous, substantial family story set in New England. 11–13

_____. *The Fayerweather Forecast,* ill. by Joshua Tolford. Houghton, 1967. 10–13

_____. *Mrs. Wappinger's Secret,* ill. by Beth and Joe Krush. Houghton, 1956. Eccentric Mrs. Wappinger of a Maine resort island is quite sure she has ancestral buried treasure somewhere on her property. Young Charlie Porter, summer visitor, is more than delighted to aid her in a secret treasure-hunting alliance. 11–14

HILDICK, E. W. *Louie's Ransom.* Knopf, 1978. In a fourth book centering around Louie, an English milkman, the protagonist comes to the United States and is kidnapped and held for ransom. 10–12

☆ HOUSTON, JAMES. *River Runners: A Tale of Hardship and Bravery,* ill. by author. Atheneum, 1979. A white and an Indian boy become fast friends on a trek through the Hudson Strait area. 11–13

JEFFRIES, RODERIC. *Patrol Car.* Harper, 1967.

_____. *River Patrol.* Harper, 1969. 11–14

KAHN, JOAN. ed. *Some Things Fierce and Fatal.* Harper, 1971. 11–14

KÄSTNER, ERICH. *Emil and the Detectives,* ill. by Walter Trier. Doubleday, 1930. 9–11

LADD, ELIZABETH. *A Mystery for Meg,* ill. by Mary Stevens. Morrow, 1962. 9–11

L'ENGLE, MADELEINE. *The Arm of the Starfish.* Farrar, 1965. 12–15

_____. *Dragons in the Waters.* Farrar, 1976. 11–15

LEVY, ELIZABETH. *Something Queer Is Going On,* ill. by Mordicai Gerstein. Delacorte, 1973. 7–9

§ LEXAU, JOAN. *The Homework Caper,* ill. by Syd Hoff. Harper, 1966. 6–7

§ _____. *The Rooftop Mystery,* ill. by Syd Hoff. Harper, 1968. 6–8

LINDGREN, ASTRID. *Bill Bergson Lives Dangerously,* tr. by Herbert Antoine, ill. by Don Freeman. Viking, 1954.

_____. *Bill Bergson, Master Detective,* tr. by Herbert Antoine, ill. by Louis Glanzman. Viking, 1952. These two stories from the Swedish are told with considerable humor in spite of their dramatic plots. In *Bill Bergson, Master Detective* Bill and his friends Anders and Eva Lotta track down stolen jewels and restore them to the police. In the other book they identify a murderer.   10–13

McLEAN, ALLAN CAMPBELL. *Master of Morgana.* Harcourt, 1959. Sixteen-year-old Niall solves the mystery of his older brother's injuries in this suspense-filled tale of fishermen and poachers on the Isle of Skye.   13–15

MEADER, STEPHEN. *The Fish Hawk's Nest,* ill. by Edward Shenton. Harcourt, 1952. Exciting tale of smuggling on the New Jersey coast in the 1820s. Good characterizations and background.   11–14

MOYES, PATRICIA. *Helter-Skelter.* Holt, 1968.   12–15

NICOLE, CHRISTOPHER. *Operation Destruct.* Holt, 1969.   12–15

PARKER, RICHARD. *Quarter Boy.* Nelson, 1976. The refurbishing job Charlie does on the quarter boy of an English town clock leads to permanent employment, interest in a girl, and a mystery involving a kidnapped baby.   11–14

PEARCE, PHILLIPA. *The Minnow Leads to Treasure,* ill. by Edward Ardizzone. World, 1958.   10–12

POOLE, JOSEPHINE. *Catch as Catch Can,* ill. by Kiyo Komoda. Harper, 1970.   10–12

RASKIN, ELLEN. *The Tattooed Potato and Other Clues.* Dutton, 1975. A spoof of detective fiction has zany characters and plenty of action.   10–12

_____. *The Westing Game.* Dutton, 1978. Lured by specially prepared ads, six tenant families take residence in Sunset Towers next to the old Westing house where they compete with each other in a devious game to become heir to the major part of the estate. Newbery Medal.   10–13

ROBERTS, WILLO DAVIS. *The View from the Cherry Tree.* Atheneum, 1975. Preparing for a wedding, Rob's family is too busy to listen to his story of a neighbor's fall, which he's seen from a tree. Only the murderer pays attention. 10–13

ROBERTSON, KEITH. *The Crow and the Castle,* ill. by Robert Greiner. Viking, 1957. A superior mystery tale involving two youthful amateur detectives.   11–14

_____. *Ice to India,* ill. by Jack Weaver. Viking, 1955. 12–14

_____. *The Money Machine,* ill. by George Porter. Viking, 1969.   10–12

_____. *Three Stuffed Owls,* ill. by Jack Weaver. Viking, 1954.   12–14

RUGH, BELLE DORMAN. *Crystal Mountain,* ill. by Ernest H. Shepard. Houghton, 1955.   11–13

ST. GEORGE, JUDITH. *Mystery at St. Martin's.* Putnam, 1979. Ruth, twelve, investigates the source of counterfeit bills that have been traced to her father's church.   10–12

SAMPSON, FAY. *The Watch on Patterick Fell.* Greenwillow, 1980. The anger of a mob causes Elspeth's father to send his family away from the English site where radioactive waste is stored, in a story with pace and suspense.   11–14

SHARMAT, MARJORIE WEINMAN. *Nate the Great and the Sticky Case,* ill. by Marc Simont. Coward, 1978. When his friend Claude announces that he's lost his stegosaurus stamp, Nate the great boy detective goes to work.   7–8

SHECTER, BEN. *Inspector Rose,* ill. by author. Harper, 1969.   6–8

SOBOL, DONALD. *Encyclopedia Brown Saves the Day,* ill. by Leonard Shortall. Nelson, 1970.   8–10

STEVENSON, ROBERT LOUIS. *Treasure Island,* ill. by C. B. Falls. World, 1946 (first pub. in 1883).

_____. *Treasure Island,* ill. by N. C. Wyeth. Scribner's, 1945.   11–16

STOREY, MARGARET. *Ask Me No Questions.* Dutton, 1975. 10–12

STORR, CATHERINE. *Lucy,* ill. by Victoria de Larrea. Prentice, 1968.   8–10

TURNER, PHILIP. *Colonel Sheperton's Clock,* ill. by Phillip Gough. World, 1966.

_____. *The Grange at High Force,* ill. by W. T. Mars. World, 1967. Carnegie Medal.   11–14

WHITNEY, PHYLLIS. *Mystery of the Green Cat.* Westminster, 1957. The discovery of a message long hidden in a ceramic cat brings peace to an old neighbor.   11–14

WINTERFELD, HENRY. *Detectives in Togas,* tr. from the German by Richard and Clara Winston, ill. by Charlotte Kleinert. Harcourt, 1956.   10–12

_____. *Mystery of the Roman Ransom,* tr. from the German by Edith McCormick, ill. by Fritz Biermann. Harcourt, 1971.   10–13

WUORIO, EVA-LIS. *Save Alice!* Holt, 1968.   10–12

Chapter Twelve: Historical Fiction

We require that modern fiction for children depict life honestly and accurately. This is also a major requisite for historical fiction. Children can check the experiences described in modern fiction against their own lives and those of their friends or can confirm them through the mass media. But children bring to historical fiction little knowledge of particular periods of history, either through study or reading, and must rely on the author's accuracy in this field.

Generally, the writer of historical fiction aims consciously to tell a story set in a past time, a time about which the majority of the book's readers will have no direct knowledge. In order to tell a story which has the flavor of a chosen time, the author becomes as familiar as possible with the period through reading contemporary accounts in books, newspapers, and magazines, through historical studies, or through the use of interviews or oral history records. The writing of the book then becomes an expression of assimilated knowledge and vicarious experience. Characters may be actual historical personages, or they may be created by the author, people like ourselves inside, although their clothing and habits may be very different. The author shows how these people are directly affected by their environment. Details of daily life—food, clothing, shelter—come naturally into the story as the characters deal with their problems. Emotions grow naturally out of the problems,

and we see how these people were prepared physically and spiritually by their cultural background to meet their daily challenges.

Elizabeth George Speare's *The Witch of Blackbird Pond* is a good example of what we are discussing. Kit, raised in Barbados, comes to live with Puritan relatives in Connecticut in the 1600s and finds a serious, hard way of life, very different from the relaxed and carefree life she had known. Adaptation to her changed environment is not easy for Kit, and her involvement in a witchcraft trial is a logical development in a plot set in New England in the 1600s.

A war story almost always involves battles; still the weapons used, the style of warfare, the support systems, all differ from war to war, from period to period. The Revolutionary War described in Leonard Wibberley's *Treegate* series is very different from World War II, as seen through the eyes of German Hans in James Forman's *The Horses of Anger*. The experiences of the characters reflect the times. In all cases, the plot in a historical novel grows directly out of the period described.

One of the most difficult tasks of the writer of historical fiction is to present natural conversations. If the words and sentence patterns are so archaic as to break the reader's concentration, the author is in difficulty. If the conversations are too contemporary in tone, the mood of the story may be destroyed. For children just mastering their own tongue, language—especially dialect—may be an overwhelming problem in reading historical fiction.

A time sense is also difficult for children to gain; they see their own parents' childhoods as being long ago and World Wars I and II as immeasurably distant in time. Names of historical characters may be difficult, and events taking place outside their own countries have a quality near fantasy for many children. Interest may lag if the author spends too much time building setting; conversely, bewilderment may result if not enough background is presented for full understanding of the plot.

As in any story for children, however, an exciting plot, realistic characters, judicious use of dialogue and dialect, a universal theme, and a strong sense of place and time will help a child over the difficulties created by lack of knowledge.

The successful writer of historical fiction is aware that historical points of view change with time and that treatment of character and fact is

Viewpoint

If writing historical novels has its own special pleasures, it also has its own special difficulties—especially if one knows that one's books are going to be read primarily by children. Children are not less intelligent than grownups. The problem is that they *know* less. In particular, they know less history. The first difficulty, then, is to give the historical setting of one's story and to impart the necessary historical facts without appearing to teach or to preach and—what is more important—without slowing up the pace of the narrative. Both the child and the writer want to hurry on to the action of the story. Yet, if the historical background is not firmly painted in, both child and author come to grief. The characters in the story move in a kind of featureless limbo, and both reader and writer lose interest in them. For this reason, I find the writing of the first chapter of every novel extremely difficult. There is so much to do all at the same moment: there are the characters to describe, the geographical setting to depict, the plot to be introduced, and, on top of all, the problem of history. I know from children themselves that I have not entirely mastered this difficulty, for I sometimes receive letters which begin: "I liked your story except for the beginning which I found boaring [sic]."—Hester Burton, "The Writing of Historical Novels," *The Horn Book,* June, 1969, p. 276.

inevitably affected by the way these things are viewed in the period in which the author is writing. Thus the treatment of women, blacks, and Native Americans in historical fiction changed drastically in the 1970s and the writer should understand this change and see it in its historical perspective.

Occasionally a story is set in a historical period but it could just as well happen today: the social conditions of the times seem to have little impact on the characters' lives and seem to be of minor concern to the author. We can make this another test of historical fiction: Does the author intend to create a vivid picture of another historical period and is that picture vital to the telling of the story? If not, we may have an interesting story, but it is not historical fiction. Tales which were contemporary when written and which are still read by succeeding generations, such as Louisa May Alcott's *Little Women,* have become historical fiction in a sense, but they were not created as historical fiction and they, and others like them, have been considered in this book as realistic fiction.

Where do we draw the line between historical fiction and modern realistic fiction? For the purposes of this chapter we will discuss only those books whose backgrounds are no later than World War II. The books are divided into those for younger readers, the middle group, and older readers, and are arranged within each group by the period or year of the setting for the title discussed, or the first title if there are several titles. All of the books, in varying degrees, comply with the major requirements of good historical fiction for young readers. The research and the authoritative historical milieu are there, but they do not overpower the story. You will note that no single book ever presents all points of view. This need not be a problem if you choose books that present a balance.

What is the value of historical fiction for the children of today? The past is not simply a listing of dates and events, as important and momentous as these may be. The past is people and how people managed to live and love and find joy in accomplishment whatever the times. The historical novel clothes the bare historical facts with trappings of a thousand tiny details, bringing emotion and insight to scholarship. Children learn facts in social studies and history; it is the interpretation of the facts in historical fiction that makes them feel "We were there!"

Early Writers of Historical Fiction

Not all of the early historical fiction written for the children of the United States is still worth reading. A few writers, however, produced books which are as rewarding now as they were when first published.

Howard Pyle was steeped in the traditions and customs of the Middle Ages. He not only wrote fascinating stories about them, but provided powerful illustrations for his own books from a seemingly inexhaustible storehouse of detailed information. His running narrative is always clear, direct, and vigorous. Old speech forms add to the flavor of his tales without unduly impeding the reader.

Otto of the Silver Hand (1888) is a horrifying tale of the robber barons of Germany. One of these had plundered ruthlessly. For revenge, his enemies struck off the hand of his only son, the delicate Otto. Later, because of the silver substitute, the boy was known as Otto of the Silver Hand. The story presents two phases of the life of the period: the turbulent life within the castle strongholds of the robber barons and the peaceful, scholarly pursuits of the monks within their great monasteries. The mutilation of the boy is gently handled, underscoring the infinite pathos of a child in the power of cruel men.

In Pyle's *Men of Iron* (1892), sixteen-year-old Myles Falworth is sent to be a squire to a powerful earl. There he learns that his own father is practically an outlaw, suspected of plotting to take the king's life. In the earl's great castle, Myles is trained in all the intricate feats of knighthood and in the code of chivalry and he is eventually knighted. He frees his father from suspicion and wins the earl's daughter for his wife. Myles has to battle with his own impulsiveness and his too-quick temper as well as with his enemies. This remains an outstanding book about medieval England.

Cornelia Meigs was interested not only in our historical past but also in the beginnings of ideas and their development. Her stories are always something more than historical fiction. Indeed, she manages frequently to illuminate certain problems of the present.

For example, *Clearing Weather* (1928) deals with Nicholas Drury's struggles to keep alive his uncle's shipbuilding business in the discouraging days following the American Revo-

Illustration by Howard Pyle from *Otto of the Silver Hand* by Howard Pyle. Published by Charles Scribner's Sons.

lution. Only through the cooperation of the whole community is the little town able to reestablish itself. The theme of community cooperation is still a good one.

Master Simon's Garden (1929) carries a still more striking theme. In the little Puritan New England settlement called Hopewell, where everything is done for utility and thrift, Master Simon develops his beautiful garden—a riot of colorful flowers and sweet herbs. It is an expression of his philosophy of tolerance and love in complete contrast to the intolerance and suspicion of some of his neighbors.

While Meigs was not a creator of memorable characters, her plots are absorbing and often exciting, stronger because of their genesis in a strong theme. It is the theme which gives unity to the action and significance to the conclusion.

One of the finest books Rachel Field ever wrote is *Calico Bush* (1931), the story of Marguerite Ledoux, a French bound-out girl of thirteen, who travels to the state of Maine with a Massachusetts family in 1743. On the long sail from Marblehead to Mount Desert, Marguerite comes to know the Sargent family and proves to them her grit and resourcefulness. She remains, nevertheless, a servant and an alien in their midst. There are brief days of joy in the new settlement, but there are tragic and frightening days, too—the Sargent baby is burned to death, and an Indian raid is diverted only by Marguerite's courage and ingenuity. At the end of the story, the Sargents gratefully offer Marguerite her freedom, but she will not leave them. The picture of the times and the people is authentic and well balanced. The hardships, the monotony, and the perils of pioneer life are there, unvarnished and frightening. The compensatory rewards may seem slight to modern readers, but there can be no doubt in their minds about the sturdy, undismayed character of these settlers.

Books for Younger Children

For young children who have little understanding of the past, historical fiction should be presented very simply, focusing on a person or just a few people, or on one problem or event. The story needs action and drama, and should avoid any references to events that demand knowledge not provided in the book. Historical fiction for young children is generally about exciting people in history to whom they have frequently been introduced by the mass media—knights, pirates, Vikings, soldiers, pioneers—whether these characters are real or invented.

Clyde Robert Bulla

John Billington, Friend of Squanto
Conquista!

Clyde Bulla's books for children are written in a simple style which does not condescend to young readers. He has the ability to concentrate on one aspect of character, and to describe events which enhance that aspect. In *Squanto* (1954) and *John Billington, Friend of Squanto* (1956), Bulla gives a brief picture of the Pilgrims of Plymouth Colony. *The Sword in the Tree* (1956) tells of treachery punished when a young boy asks King Arthur's help. Other books by Bulla take place during the Viking explorations of America, or—as in the story of Coronado's search for the city of gold in *Conquista!* (1978)—in the early days of the settlement of the Middle and Far West of the United States.

Alice Dalgliesh

The Courage of Sarah Noble
Adam and the Golden Cock

Alice Dalgliesh had the ability to create realistic child characters and to make their concerns important to us without losing sight of the historical elements of her tales.

The Courage of Sarah Noble (1954) is richly historical and, according to Dalgliesh, a real episode of 1707. Eight-year-old Sarah is sent into the wilderness to cook and care for her father because her mother cannot leave or move a sick baby. Before Sarah and her father set off, her mother wraps the little girl in a cloak as warm as her love and says, "Keep up your courage, Sarah Noble." When wolves threaten them in the forest, or they sleep in strange cabins with unfriendly folk, or Sarah is left alone with an Indian family, she wraps her mother's cloak and her words warmly about her and keeps up her courage.

Another tale of colonial times is *The Thanksgiving Story* (1954), a fictional account of the voyage of the *Mayflower* and the first year at Plymouth, culminating in the Thanksgiving feast with the Indians. Centered on the experiences of the Hopkins family, especially the

Illustration by Ronald Himler from *Conquista!* by Clyde Robert Bulla and Michael Syson. Illustrations copyright © 1978 by Harper & Row, Publishers, Inc. By permission of Thomas Y. Crowell, Publishers.

children, it is a remarkably moving story, told with dignity and avoiding stereotyped episodes.

The Fourth of July Story (1956) must have been more difficult to write, with its large gallery of leading characters and the complex theme of independence and restoration of good relationships with England. But again Dalgliesh selected her people and episodes so carefully that the story is dramatic and not too complicated for the understanding and enjoyment of children.

Adam and the Golden Cock (1959) is a Revolutionary War story in which a boy is caught in the conflict between friendship and loyalty, for Adam's friend Paul is from a Tory family. Children of today, aware of conflicting opinions about controversial issues, may see the timeless application of such conflict.

Brinton Turkle

Obadiah the Bold
Rachel and Obadiah

Set in the early nineteenth century, *Obadiah the Bold* (1965) is an engaging tale of the dreams of glory of a small Quaker boy who wants to become a pirate. He decides he will be a sailor like Grandfather after Father very cleverly talks about how brave a man Captain Obadiah Starbuck had been. The text has minimal historical significance, but the illustrations show details of early Nantucket, and both this book and its sequels, *Thy Friend, Obadiah* (1969) and *Rachel and Obadiah* (1978) give children a sense of the period, the Quaker community, and the loving kindness of family life. The soft details of the illustrations are charming in themselves and they are accurately informative in showing costume, architecture, and artifacts of the period.

Ferdinand Monjo

The Drinking Gourd

A fine story about the Underground Railroad is told in *The Drinking Gourd* (1970), in which young Tommy Fuller, sent home from church because of a prank, wanders into the barn and finds a runaway slave family. The explanation given Tommy of the Railroad clarifies it for readers as well as for Tommy, and he understands for the first time the degradation of slavery and the danger runaways face. When a search party comes along, Tommy quickly pretends that he himself is running away from home; the marshal laughs and decides not to search the hay wagon, and so Tommy helps the cause. That night Father explains that he is, he knows, breaking a law but that he must. These are *people.* The story has suspense and action, and in Tommy's participation there is both the joy of achievement and an appreciation of ethical issues.

In later books Monjo has woven stories around historical personages such as Thomas Jefferson (*Grand Papa and Ellen Aroon,* 1974), Abraham Lincoln (*Gettysburg,* 1976), and Nathan Hale (*A Namesake for Nathan,* 1978). Using a child of the family to tell the story, Monjo has effectively presented these men from a child's point of view. Whether these books are classified as historical fiction or biography, there is a sense of history and an emphasis on such qualities as courage, loyalty, and family love.

Other Books for Younger Children

Although *The Apple and the Arrow* (1951) by Mary and Conrad Buff is set in 1292, the story of Switzerland's revolt against Austria has pertinence for young readers today. The tale of the legendary William Tell's leadership is seen from the point of view of the young son from whose head, according to the story, the apple was shot.

Wilma Pitchford Hays has written a number of short, informational books with a historical setting. *May Day for Samoset* (1968), *Christmas on the Mayflower* (1956), and *Yellow Fur and Little Hawk* (1980), a story of the Dakota Sioux, are typical and show the author's knowledge and interest in historical details, which are somewhat purposefully inserted in the tales.

One of the gayest books of historical fiction for young children is Arnold Lobel's *On the Day Peter Stuyvesant Sailed into Town* (1971), delightfully illustrated by the author, a story in rhythmic verse that describes the irascible governor's successful efforts to clean up New Amsterdam.

Lobel's book also is representative of the growing number of books of historical fiction written for beginning readers. Others are Nathaniel Benchley's *Sam the Minuteman* (1969), a lively story of the American Revolution, and Betty Baker's *The Pig War* (1969), based on a

Illustration by Brinton Turkle from *Obadiah the Bold* by Brinton Turkle. Copyright © 1965 by Brinton Turkle. Reprinted by permission of The Viking Press, Inc. (Original in color)

dispute between the United States and Great Britain in 1859 over possession of an island.

Based on a true incident, *Martin and Abraham Lincoln* by Catherine Coblentz was first published in 1947 and reissued twenty years later. The dialogue between the President and the small boy gives information about the American Civil War, and the story not only characterizes Lincoln but poignantly shows how the duress of war affects a child.

Books for the Middle Group

By the time they reach the middle grades, children have acquired some sense of the past and some perspective on its relation to the present. Their lively curiosity leads to conjecture about people of other times, and historical fiction that tells a good story about such people satisfies both their need to know and their appreciation of action. In the books for this group, most of the stories stress courage and problem solving, and the preponderance of historical fiction is set in the comparatively familiar bounds of our own country's past.

Marguerite de Angeli

The Door in the Wall

Marguerite de Angeli's Newbery Medal book, *The Door in the Wall* (1949), is set in thirteenth-century England. Robin's noble father is off to the wars and his mother is with the queen when the plague strikes. Robin falls ill, unable to move his legs, and is deserted by the servants. Brother Luke finds the boy and cares for him. To the despairing Robin he says, "Always remember . . . thou hast only to follow the wall far enough and there will be a door in it." The monks teach the boy to use his hands and his head, "For reading is another door in the wall. . . ." Robin learns to swim and to get around swiftly on crutches, but his back never straightens. However, his spirit is strong, and he plays so heroic a part in saving a beleaguered city that the king honors him, and his parents are moved with joy and pride. This heartwarming story is beautifully illustrated in the author's most colorful style. The characters are less convincing than the situations, but the book is frequently of great interest to children.

Jean Fritz

The Cabin Faced West
Brady

In *The Cabin Faced West* (1958) there isn't much to console Ann. She misses her cousin in Gettysburg and there isn't another child in the pioneer country of Western Pennsylvania for her to play with until she finds a boy her own age. The high point of the story is a surprise visit from George Washington, an eipsode based on historical fact, but the most engaging incident is the one in which Ann's mother stops her work to play tea party with the lonely child.

Brady (1960) is a more mature story, set in the years just before the Civil War. Living in an area where people's feelings are divided, Brady is embarrassed by his father's strong antislavery feelings until events move him to take a position of responsibility. Both books are smoothly written and are convincing in their setting and in period details, but *Brady* also has a depth that stems from strong characterization and a vivid portrayal of the moral issues involved in the Abolitionist position.

Fritz's later novels, *Early Thunder*, set in 1775 Salem, and *I, Adam*, set in nineteenth-century New England, also have strong characters and serious discussions. We appreciate the problems of the characters, but we don't feel close to them. On the other hand, the humor of which Jean Fritz is capable shines forth abundantly in her *Who's That Stepping on Plymouth Rock?* (1975) and *Can't You Make Them Behave, King George?* (1977), representative of the brief, factual tales for younger readers that are no less accurate than her more substantial stories.

Elizabeth Coatsworth

Away Goes Sally
Five Bushel Farm
The Fair American

Elizabeth Coatsworth is an experienced, interesting writer whose works encompass poetry, fantasy, and historical fiction for a range of ages. When writing for older children, she is a strong delineator of character rather than an inventor of exciting episode. *Away Goes Sally* (1934) introduces us to an early nineteenth-century family of three sisters and two brothers who are raising an orphaned niece. The interplay of family relationships is excellent, especially when Uncle Joseph finds a way to move to Maine even when Aunt Nanny has said she will not leave her home. He simply builds her a small house on a sledge and transports everyone in comfort during the snowy winter months. *Five Bushel Farm* (1939) introduces us to Andrew, a sea captain's son who is out of touch with his father through no fault of his own, and who becomes a member of Sally's family in Maine. *The Fair American* (1940) takes the two children on a sea voyage where they help to save a French boy fleeing from the terrorists after the French Revolution.

All the small details of living are interestingly worked into the stories; the children are obedient but resourceful; family cooperation is the normal state of affairs.

Carol Ryrie Brink

Caddie Woodlawn

Caddie Woodlawn (1935) belongs to the Civil War period, but the war plays no part in the story. Caddie and her family live in Wisconsin when Indians are considered a menace, but life on the whole is fairly comfortable. Redheaded Caddie and her two brothers extract every pos-

Reprinted by permission of Coward, McCann & Geoghegan, Inc. from *Can't You Make Them Behave, King George?* by Jean Fritz. Illustrations copyright © 1977 by Tomie de Paola. (Original in color)

sible bit of fun and adventure the frontier settlement can yield. Caddie's long friendship with the Indians and her courageous personal appeal to them helps prevent a threatened uprising.

Laura Ingalls Wilder
The *Little House* Books

As has been noted, children's sense of the past is a confused one at best. Gas lights are more incredible to them than candlelight, and horse-and-buggy travel quite as odd as a trip by canal boat. Indeed, it may be easier for them to underdand and enter into the colonial period of American history than into the more immediate past. The pioneering and settling of the Midwest have fewer picturesque details than has the dramatic first colonization. Frontier life has more humdrum struggle, less romantic adventure. Until Laura Ingalls Wilder undertook the writing of her family's experiences in settling the Midwest, there were no books of this period which really held children's interest.

Children love all the "Little House" books and grow up with the Ingalls girls and the Wilder boys, from *Little House in the Big Woods* (1932) to the romantic *These Happy Golden Years* (1943) when Laura Ingalls and Almanzo Wilder are married. The first book appeals to children of eight or nine; the latter is written for the older reader, who by this time may feel that Laura is an old and dear friend. Few other books give children this sense of continuity and progress.

The saga begins with the Ingalls family in their log cabin in the Wisconsin forests, in *Little House in the Big Woods*. The children are all girls. The oldest is Mary (who later goes blind), then the active Laura, and baby Carrie. Grace eventually displaces Carrie as the baby. In this first book we become acquainted with Ma's skill in cooking wonderful, triumphant meals out of limited resources. Here, too, we first see the little china woman which Ma is to carry with her through all their journeys. She puts it over the fireplace only when the dwelling is worthy, a real house and home. All these things give the children a sense of comfort and security.

Next, the family moves out to the wild Kansas country and begins the adventures described in the *Little House on the Prairie* (1935). *On the Banks of Plum Creek* (1937) finds the In-

galls family in Minnesota; *By the Shores of Silver Lake* (1939) carries them to the Dakota Territory, where they remain either on their lake or in town.

Farmer Boy (1933) begins the account of the Wilder family of boys on their prosperous New York farm. We follow Almanzo Wilder from his first day at school to the proud moment when he is given his own colt to break and train. In this book the modern child is given incidentally a sense of money values in terms of human labor. Almanzo knows fifty cents as so many hours of backbreaking toil over the family potato crop.

The Long Winter (1940) finds the Ingalls family living in town. Of the whole series, this book is one no modern child should miss. One blizzard follows another until the railroads cease to run and the little town is cut off from supplies for months. Finally the wheat begins to give out, and the whole community faces starvation. Then it is Almanzo Wilder, not Pa Ingalls, who rides out into the snow-driven prairie to buy wheat from a farmer who has it. He succeeds, and the conclusion of the book is happy and humorous. *Little Town on the Prairie* (1941) and *These Happy Golden Years* (1943) carry Laura into teaching and then into marriage with Almanzo. *The First Four Years* (1971), a posthumously published book, tells of Laura and Almanzo's first years as struggling farmers. In *These Happy Golden Years*, a title which speaks for the whole series, Laura Ingalls Wilder wrote in her daughter's copy:

> And so farewell to childhood days,
> Their joys, and hopes and fears.
> But Father's voice and his fiddle's song
> Go echoing down the years.[1]

Other Books for the Middle Group

Jane Flory's historical stories are set in and around nineteenth-century Philadelphia. *Faraway Dream* (1968) tells of an orphan apprenticed to a milliner, while *A Tune for the Towpath* (1962) introduces us to a lockkeeper's daughter whose home lies beside a busy Pennsylvania canal.

Carolina's Courage (1964) by Elizabeth Yates is

1. Irene Smith, "Laura Ingalls Wilder and the Little House Books," *The Horn Book*, September–October 1943, p. 306. Delightful account of the author, with family photographs of Ma, Pa, the four girls, and Almanzo.

one of many tales of the wagon trains that crossed the great plains. Lonzo Anderson's *Zeb* (1966) is a taut story of a boy who survives a winter alone in the wilderness when his father and older brother are accidentally killed. In *Trouble River* (1969) by Betsy Byars, Dewey escapes the Indians by rafting himself and his querulous grandmother down river.

Two good Civil War stories for the middle group are F. N. Monjo's *The Vicksburg Veteran* (1971) and Rhoda Bacmeister's *Voices in the Night* (1965). In the Monjo story, General Grant's son participates in the Union victory that gains control of the Mississippi; in the Bacmeister story, a small girl visiting a family that operates a station for the Underground Railroad uses her wits to help one runaway escape. In Anna Gertrude Hall's *Cyrus Holt and the Civil War* (1964), a boy of nine finds the war exciting when it starts but as time goes by becomes increasingly aware of the men wounded and dead, and of the growing burden of deprivation and unwonted responsibilities. Although it is set in the period before the Civil War, *A Gathering of Days: A New England Girl's Journal,*

From *A Pocket Full of Seeds* by Marilyn Sachs. Illustrated by Ben Stahl. Copyright © 1973 by Marilyn Sachs. Reproduced by permission of Doubleday & Company, Inc.

Viewpoint

The historical novelist . . . brings history to people who might otherwise not be exposed to it. He must, first of all, be a story-teller if he is to reach that audience, and this quality is essential to him where it is not to the historian. As a story-teller of history, he is not confined by documentation, as the historian is, but he ought to be acutely conscious of his role as a purveyor of knowledge, as well as information, because it is in this respect that he joins hands with the historian in performing a vital function in our society. . . .

For a great many Americans, a knowledge of the nation's past, and therefore a better chance to understand the present and anticipate the future, depends on what they learn from the historical novel, which informs as it entertains. Clearly, the responsibility of the novelist is great as he maintains the delicate balance between fact and fiction. I believe that the best of the novelists in this field are acutely aware of their responsibility and do their utmost to tell their stories against an accurately researched background. The biographical novelists are even more aware.—John Tebbel, *Fact and Fiction: Problems of the Historical Novelist*, The Burton Lecture, published by the Historical Society of Michigan, Lansing, 1962, pp. 10–12.

1830–32 (1979), for which Joan Blos was awarded the Newbery Medal, is concerned with the issue of whether Catherine (writer of the journal) is justified in helping a runaway slave despite the New Hampshire laws.

The story of the Battle of Little Big Horn is told by fifteen-year-old Red Hawk in *Red Hawk's Account of Custer's Last Battle* (1970) by Paul and Dorothy Goble. Red Hawk, the only fictional character, says sadly, "Once all the earth was ours; now there is only a small piece left which the White Men did not want." He knows that the cause is lost despite the victory won by the Indians. The list of sources indicates the research that gives the book its authenticity of historical detail.

The Peppermint Pig (1975) by Nina Bawden shows an English family temporarily forced to live with relatives as their fortunes fail around the turn of the century, while *Carrie's War* (1973) describes the lives of World War II evacuees in the English countryside. Bawden is skilled in creating credible characters and evoking sympathy for them.

For children who have never experienced the horror of war, books that tell of the plight of children in wartime can evoke some understanding. Alki Zei's *Wildcat Under Glass* (1968, first published in 1963 in Greece) is a story of life under the oppression of dictatorship as experienced by a child, Melia, who lives on a Greek island during the time of prewar German occupation. The story, which begins in August 1936, has drama and momentum, and is particularly effective in showing the reactions of the very young to a rigid regime. In *Petros' War* (1972), Zei describes, from the point of view of a ten-year-old boy, the Italian occupation of Athens during World War II, and in *The Sound of the Dragon's Feet* (1979) she portrays a child's awareness of inequity in pre-revolutionary Russia.

In Susan Cooper's *Dawn of Fear* (1970), a small group of boys, busy with their games and school, are shocked into awareness and fear when one of their number is killed in an air raid.

The effect of the Germans on the lives of European Jews is graphically portrayed in Johanna Reiss's *The Upstairs Room* (1972), where Annie lives hidden away in a farmhouse in wartime Holland, and in its sequel, *The Journey Back* (1976), when Annie goes back to find the poignant, tragic aftermath of war and occupation. In *A Pocket Full of Seeds* (1973) by Marilyn Sachs, French Nicole arrives home for lunch one day to find her family completely gone.

Judith Kerr, in *When Hitler Stole Pink Rabbit* (1971), follows a family as they flee from Germany to Switzerland to France to escape extinction. They come finally to wartime England in *The Other Way Round* (1975), a sequel for older readers.

With *The Stone Book* (1978) Alan Garner, whose books for older readers are stylistically intricate, begins a quartet of linked stories, each a cameo, set in the Cheshire countryside, following four generations of a family. Each is distinctly an entity; each is written with clarity and depth. The others are *Granny Reardon* (1978), *Tom Fobble's Day* (1979), and *The Aimer Gate* (1979).

Books for Older Children

Older readers can range through many time periods, and in their historical fiction there is no need to avoid the complexities of social movements and relationships that existed in the past as they do today. Erik Haugaard's Hakon can move from one cultural pattern to another, Rosemary Sutcliff's Aquila can have a divided allegiance that young people understand. They can enjoy the rich tapestry of a story that has intricate patterns of action in an unfamiliar setting and appreciate the implications that past events have for the present.

Lucile Morrison
The Lost Queen of Egypt

Lucile Morrison's *The Lost Queen of Egypt* (1937) is a thrilling story. It begins about 1580 B.C. in the royal nurseries of Akhenaten, Pharaoh of Egypt, and Nefertiti, his queen. Their six little daughters are being arrayed for the arrival of the Great Royal Mother, who decides that three of the little girls must be betrothed at once to guarantee the succession. Ankhsenpaaten is relieved when the soldierly Tutankhaten is chosen for her, since he alone of the royal blood has shown a reckless courage and vitality equal to her own.

Later, a series of deaths calls this popular young pair to the throne; they become Tutankhamon and Ankhsenamon and seem destined to happiness and a long reign. Instead,

The King and Queen Hunting

Illustration by Franz Geritz from *The Lost Queen of Egypt* by Lucile Morrison. Copyright, 1937, by Harper & Row, Publishers, Inc. Renewed 1965 by Lucile Morrison. By permission of J. B. Lippincott, Publishers.

the young king dies by poisoning and the queen is trapped in the palace to be forced either to marry the traitorous Ay or to die herself. Describing how Kenofer the artist rescues her, and how, in disguise, they turn to the river and live on their boat like hundreds of humble river people, gives the author an opportunity to compare ways of life for queen and commoner.

Eloise Jarvis McGraw

Mara, Daughter of the Nile

Another novel of ancient Egypt is *Mara* (1953), a hair-raising tale of royal intrigue, spies, and true love, in the days when a female Pharaoh, Hatshepsut, has usurped the throne from the rightful king. Mara is a slave who vaguely remembers better days and is determined to escape. She is bought by a mysterious man who offers her luxury if she will serve at court as a spy for the queen. She accepts, and also sells her services as a spy for the king to a young nobleman, Lord Sheftu. Eventually, her love for Sheftu and a deep pity for the wronged king change her from a liar and a cheat to a selfless heroine who endures torture rather than betray her new loyalties. The action is terrifying. Detailed pictures emerge of the daily life of different classes—shopkeepers, rivermen, soldiers, slaves, and royalty.

A second book about ancient Egypt by this writer is *The Golden Goblet* (1961). While it is not quite so powerful a tale as *Mara*, it, too, affords a detailed picture of the times, with a vigorous plot and convincing characters.

Olivia E. Coolidge

Egyptian Adventures

Olivia E. Coolidge is a scholar, and in the course of her entertaining *Egyptian Adventures* (1954) she gives children lively pictures of the Egyptians' superstitions and magic, harvests and hunts, festivals and funerals. The characters emerge fully drawn and colorfully alive. These twelve well-written stories will do much to develop children's feeling for the people and adventures of a far-distant past.

Men of Athens (1962), *Roman People* (1959), and *People in Palestine* (1965) are in the same format, each tale complete in itself and the whole giving a remarkably vivid picture of the diversity of the culture in a historical period. *The King of Men* (1966) is a complex and absorbing novel

based on the Agamemnon legend, and *Marathon Looks on the Sea* (1967) provides a sharp immediacy to the Battle of Marathon. The central character is a boy torn between allegiance to his own Greek people and to the Persian king who has become his friend. *The Maid of Artemis* (1969) tells of a year in the life of an Athenian girl and her choice for the future. In all these books, the combination of scholarly research and a fine writing style re-creates the period so convincingly that the reader has no sense of a disparate culture; each detail of rites and customs, of mores and superstitions, is an integral part of the story.

Henry Treece

Viking's Dawn

An English poet, critic, and teacher, Henry Treece was distinguished both for the sonorous quality of his prose and for his ability to create convincingly the mood and language of the distant past. *Viking's Dawn* (1956) is the first of a trilogy about Harald Sigurdson who, in the eighth century, was the only man on his crew to return from a voyage filled with disasters. In *The Road to Miklagard* (1957) Sigurdson becomes a Moorish slave and travels to Constantinople and then to Russia; and in *Viking's Sunset* (1961) the Vikings come to a new land and live with Eskimos and Indians.

Treece uses ancient Britain as a setting for lively tales like *The Centurion* (1967), a story of a Roman legionnaire. His last book, *The Dream Time* (1967), takes us back to Stone Age Britain. Like Rosemary Sutcliff, Treece was so steeped in history that his stories have a remarkable unity: details of dress and architecture, language, and references to other events have a consistency that makes his books convincing and alive.

Erik Christian Haugaard

Hakon of Rogen's Saga
A Messenger for Parliament

Hakon of Rogen's Saga (1963) is not a traditional saga but a realistic story taking place in the last days of the Vikings. The rocky, mountainous island of Rogen, where Hakon was born, has been handed down in his family from father to son for generations. To Hakon, Rogen Island and his powerful father seem indestructible—but there is a bloody family battle and when it

Viewpoint_____

There is the question of what is acceptable to modern taste, and by that phrase I don't mean anything to do with sexual outspokenness, where indeed the 'modern taste' seems to be for highly spiced dishes. No, I mean quite simply how can the author hold his reader's sympathy, how can the reader identify wholeheartedly with the historical character—all of which is absolutely vital, especially when we are dealing with *young* readers—when so much that is authentic and unavoidable, or at least socially acceptable, in the period of the story repels the reader today?

One's Elizabethan heroine probably had black teeth and anything but a sweet breath. The one atmosphere which was probably authentic in most historical eras was of human bodies too little washed and too heavily clothed. It was not only the villains who smelt. Or take our changed attitude to cruelty. What happens to our readers' sympathy if our debonair Regency hero goes, as well he might, straight from partnering the heroine at an elegant ball to the enjoyment of a public execution at dawn? With the young public I should think that the treatment of animals would be one of the worst stumbling blocks, if we represented it with complete historical accuracy. The old squire dies. He may have included in his last wishes—I believe it was commonly done—that all his dogs should be hanged. It would be a foolhardy author who let his hero carry out that sort of instruction. One can think of countless such difficulties where the author is compelled to present something less than the complete historical picture.—Geoffrey Trease, "The Historical Novelist at Work," *Children's Literature in Education 7*, March 1972, pp. 11–12. Reprinted by permission of Ward Lock Educational Limited.

---

is over, Hakon is an orphan at the mercy of his treacherous uncle, who wants Rogen for his own. How Hakon suffers enslavement and brutal treatment, bides his time, finds a hideout in the mountain caves, mobilizes his few loyal men, and eventually takes Rogen again reads much like an old Norse saga. The author, a Dane familiar with Icelandic sagas, says at the beginning:

"Your dog, your horse, your friend, and you yourself: all shall die. Eternally live only your deeds and man's judgment over them," this was the credo of the Vikings.

In this book the Vikings are of heroic stature and the author clothes their story with nobility.

Its sequel, *A Slave's Tale* (1965), is told by the small slave girl Helga, to whom Hakon is like a

beloved brother. Their affection ripens into love, but this is a minor facet of the story, which is primarily a tale of a voyage to Frankland in a longboat. The writing, in explication and dialogue as well as in the period details, vividly creates the historical milieu and has the sweep and cadence of a Norse epic.

The Rider and His Horse (1968) is set in ancient Israel at the final battle between the Jews and Romans at Masada, while *The Untold Tale* (1971) gives an all-too-clear picture of life for the poor in Denmark in the 1600s. Haugaard's heroes always face horror realistically and unflinchingly, and tragedy is as often the outcome as is triumph. In *A Messenger for Parliament* (1976) a young man named for Oliver Cromwell tells his life story as a camp follower of the Parliamentary Army, in a story that vividly depicts the fierce allegiances of a divided country.

Rosemary Sutcliff

The Lantern Bearers
Dawn Wind

Most critics would say that at the present time the greatest writer of historical fiction for children and young people is unquestionably Rosemary Sutcliff. Her books are superior because they are authentic records of England's earliest history with its bloody raids and its continuous wars for occupation by Norsemen, Romans, Normans, and Saxons, and also because every one of her memorable books is built around a great theme. Her characters live and die for principles they value and that people today still value.

The theme of all her stories, as Margaret Meek[2] points out, is "the light and the dark. The light is what is valued, what is to be saved beyond one's own lifetime. The dark is the threatening destruction that works against it." In *The Lantern Bearers* (1959)[3] the blackness of despair is concentrated in the heart of Aquila, a Roman officer who, when a Saxon raid sweeps down on his father's farm, sees his father slain, and his sister Flavia carried off by the raiders. He himself is left tied to a tree for the wolves and later made a slave by another band. Years later, after he has escaped his thralldom, an old friend says to him:

---

2. *Rosemary Sutcliff.* A Walck Monograph, Walck, 1962.

3. *The Lantern Bearers* is the third book in a trilogy which also includes *The Eagle of the Ninth* and *The Silver Branch*.

It may be that the night will close over us in the end, but I believe that morning will come again. . . . We are the Lantern Bearers, my friend; for us to keep something burning, to carry what light we can forward into the darkness and the wind.

No briefing of these stories can give any conception of their scope and power. They may be difficult, not because of vocabulary, but because of the complexities of the plots in which many peoples are fighting for dominance.

Fortunately, *Dawn Wind* (1962), one of the finest of the books, is also the least complex. Chronologically it follows *The Lantern Bearers,* but it is complete in itself and will undoubtedly send many readers to the trilogy. For the fourteen-year-old hero Owain, the light of the world seems to have been extinguished. He finds himself the sole survivor of a bloody battle between the Saxons and the Britains in which his people, the Britains, are completely destroyed. In the gutted remains of the city from which he had come, the only life the boy finds is a pitiable waif of a girl, lost and half-starved. At first Owain and Regina are bound together in mutual misery, but eventually they are united in respect and affection. So when Regina is gravely ill, Owain carries her to a Saxon settlement, even though he knows what will happen to him. The Saxons care for the girl but sell Owain into slavery. If sometimes despair almost overcomes Owain, his work, in which there is both conflict and triumph, absorbs him. After eleven years, he is freed and sets out at once to find his people and Regina, who has never doubted he would come for her. So life is not snuffed out by the night. A dawn wind blows and two people start all over again with those basic qualities that have always made for survival.

In *Song for a Dark Queen* (1979), Boadicea's story is told by an old harpist, who remembers her as an imperious little girl and as the tragic warrior-queen. Historical details are smoothly integrated into the narrative fabric of the smoothly written story. Whether it is her great trilogy or *The Shield Ring* (1957) or *The Outcast* (1955) or *Warrior Scarlet* (1958) or her later, *The Capricorn Bracelet* (1973), *The Witch's Brat* (1970), or *Blood Feud* (1977), a Viking story, Rosemary Sutcliff gives children and youth historical fiction that builds courage and faith that life will go on and is well worth the struggle.

Cynthia Harnett
Nicholas and the Wool-Pack
Caxton's Challenge

Cynthia Harnett's sketches add to the wealth of informative detail about fifteenth-century England in *Nicholas and the Wool-Pack,* winner of the Carnegie Medal in 1951 under its British title, *The Wool-Pack.* It is not only an exciting story with an element of mystery, but also a colorful picture of the weaving industry and of everyday life of the period. Nicholas, an ap-

Drawing by Richard Cuffari, reprinted by permission of Henry Z. Walck, Inc., from *The Capricorn Bracelet* © 1973 by Rosemary Sutcliff.

prentice to his father, a wool merchant, foils the two Lombardians who are secretly attempting to ruin his father.

Another smoothly written story of the same period is *Caxton's Challenge* (*The Load of Unicorn* [1968] in the British edition), which gives a vivid picture of London at that time, both the text and the maps indicating the careful research that lends authenticity to historical fiction. Again an apprentice is a leading character; Bendy is entranced by the printing machines of his master, William Caxton, and becomes involved in the struggles Caxton has against the resentful scriveners.

The Writing on the Hearth (1971) embroils would-be Oxford scholar Stephen in fifteenth-century English politics. Harnett's stories are solid and sedate, well researched and meticulous in detail.

Elizabeth Janet Gray Vining

Adam of the Road
I Will Adventure

Elizabeth Gray Vining is a born storyteller, although paradoxically her stories are weak in plot construction. Her books develop little excitement; the conflicts are mild, with no breathtaking suspense leading to a climax. Yet she is a careful historian, and her tales have all the authentic minutiae of everyday life long ago which make history convincing. But chiefly she is concerned with people.

In *Adam of the Road* (1943), for which the author won the Newbery Medal, the protagonist happened to have lived in the thirteenth century instead of today. Adam's two loves are his golden cocker spaniel and his minstrel father, but he loses them both for a time. How he seeks the two of them up and down the roads of old England gives children a glimpse into every variety of medieval life—that of jugglers, minstrels, plowmen, and nobles, as real as the people today.

The hero of *I Will Adventure* (1962) is Andrew Talbot, a most beguiling young imp, who takes to himself a line from Shakespeare's *Romeo and Juliet,* "I will adventure." Andrew is journeying to London to be a page to his uncle Sir John Talbot when he has the good luck to hear this play and, by way of a fight with one of the boy players, meets Master Burbage and Shakespeare himself. Andrew is all for signing up with the players, but they won't take him, though Shakespeare, grieving for his own boy

Illustration by Corydon Bell. From *I Will Adventure* by Elizabeth Janet Gray. Reprinted by permission of The Viking Press, Inc.

Hamnet, lets Andrew ride with him for a day's journey. Through Andrew's eyes the reader comes to know intimately many facets of London life in 1596, especially the theater, the plays, and the audiences. Andrew's problems are happily solved, thanks to Shakespeare and a sympathetic uncle.

The Taken Girl (1972) moves us from England to Philadelphia during pre-Civil War days, when Veer, an orphaned servant girl, works with John Greenleaf Whittier in the Abolitionist movement.

Marchette Chute

The Wonderful Winter
The Innocent Wayfaring

Marchette Chute, the author of *Shakespeare of London* and similar studies of Chaucer and Ben Jonson for adult readers, has also written some delightful stories for young people. *The Wonderful Winter* (1954) carries young readers straight into Shakespeare's theater with young Robin, Sir Robert Wakefield, who has escaped from an intolerable home situation. London seems to spell starvation for him until he is befriended by some actors and is taken into the home of the famous John Heminges. Through the warmth and affection of this crowded household, young Robin learns to give and accept love and gaiety. Meanwhile he works and plays small parts in the Burbage Theater, knows the great Shakespeare, and falls in love with *Romeo and Juliet*. When Robin returns to his castle and his duties, he is happy and confident as a result of his wonderful winter.

The Innocent Wayfaring (first published in 1943 and reissued in 1955) is fourteenth-century England brought vividly and authentically to life. Anne is so averse to learning the arts of housewifery that she runs away from her convent school with the prioress's pet monkey for company. The monkey is responsible for her meeting Nick, a poet and a most resourceful young man. He tries to get away from her, but Anne sticks like a burr. Their adventures provide a view of fourteenth-century life, from seamy inns to manor houses. After three days Nick takes Anne back to her family with the agreement that when she has learned housewifery and he his father's business, Nick will come for her. Meanwhile, they have the memory of three enchanting days which led them back to home and responsibility.

Both books are beautifully written by a scholar who can paint a glowing background for her charming stories.

Barbara Willard

The Lark and the Laurel

While several American writers, notably Laura Ingalls Wilder and Leonard Wibberley, have followed a family through the years, Barbara Willard has spanned more than a hundred years of English history, from the early sixteenth century to the mid-seventeenth century, through a family living in Ashdown Forest, in and around a house called Mantlemass. The first of the series, *The Lark and the Laurel* (1970), tells of a child marriage for political ends. The cycle continues with *The Sprig of Broom* (1971), which introduces Richard Plashet, or Plantagenet, unacknowledged son of Richard III, and his son, Medley, who marries into the Mantlemass Manor family. *A Cold Wind Blowing* (1972) shows how the family weathers the Reformation, while in *The Iron Lily* (1973) an unacknowledged Medley woman takes over as

the iron-willed mistress of her husband's forge at his death. Mantlemass is destroyed in the last tale, *Harrow and Harvest* (1974), when civil war erupts. Willard has a strong feeling for place, and it is the locale we remember as much as the events and people.

Patricia Clapp

Constance
I'm Deborah Sampson

With the exception of one character, all of the people described by *Constance* (1968) in her journal existed, and the events are based on the real life of an ancestress of Patricia Clapp's husband. The historical details are smoothly woven into the story, and the description of the early days of the Plymouth Colony is unusually vivid. As she tells of her growing understanding of the Indians, her relationship with her stepmother, her doubts about herself, and her friendship with the young man she will marry, Constance is always a convincing character. The book, which concludes with her marriage in 1626, is particularly valuable because of the graphic depiction of the hardships of the first grim winter and the struggles of the colonists with their English backers.

In writing a novel about the Revolutionary War period, Clapp uses a real person but invents the details of the story told by Deborah in *I'm Deborah Sampson: A Soldier in the War of the Revolution* (1977). The real Deborah did indeed enlist in Washington's army and successfully masquerade as a man. The writing is vividly detailed, and the language and concepts consistent with the period.

Hester Burton

Beyond the Weir Bridge
Time of Trial

Beyond the Weir Bridge (1970) is a vivid piece of historical writing, consistent in language and viewpoint, informative about the period in which it is set, and a truly dramatic story. Richard and Richenda, whose fathers had been killed in 1644 in Cromwell's service, are both fond of shy, bookish Thomas although he is a Royalist. Richenda, indeed, comes to love him when they are grown and with him joins the

Quakers, a denomination then reviled. It is only when Richard, who has become a doctor, sees Thomas's faith bring him to plague-ridden London to help as best he can, that he understands the true humility of the Quaker credo.

Time of Trial, winner of the 1963 Carnegie Medal, also is concerned with the courage of the nonconformist. Seventeen-year-old Margaret Pargeter is the daughter of a London bookseller who is sent to prison for advocating social reform and for printing a book judged inflammatory. *Kate Ryder* (1975) is a compelling tale of England's Civil War, with another strong heroine. Burton's characters always reflect the mores and customs in a time of change, yet are developed as distinctive individuals, and her stories are all the more convincing because her characters' goals are realistically modest.

Mollie Hunter

The Ghosts of Glencoe
The Stronghold

Ensign Robert Stewart, the protagonist of Mollie Hunter's *The Ghosts of Glencoe* (1969), is an officer of the king's army, dedicated to keeping peace in the Highlands. Like many other Scottish officers, Ensign Stewart is torn between loyalty to his king and sympathy for his own people. Shaken by the vengefulness of those who do not share that sympathy, Stewart finally warns the rebels when an attack is planned. The dialogue rings true, and the period details are as meticulously correct as is the historical material.

This careful treatment of fact is a firm base in all of Mollie Hunter's books, although most of them are more highly fictionalized than is *The Ghosts of Glencoe. The Spanish Letters* (1967) is a cloak-and-dagger adventure story, set in Edinburgh in the late sixteenth century, in which two Spanish agents are allied with Scottish traitors planning to abduct King James. *The Lothian Run* (1970) is a tale of spies and smugglers which, like *The Spanish Letters*, is full of plot and counterplot, romantic and sinister. Less dramatic but just as suspenseful is the more somber *A Pistol in Greenyards* (1968), a tale of the Highland evictions of the tenant farmers in the 1850s.

The Thirteenth Member (1971) deals with a coven of witches and part of a plot to kill James

I of Scotland. In *The Stronghold* (1975), winner of a Carnegie Medal, Hunter's ability to construct a convincing tale from historical fragments is very evident. In this book Coll discovers a way to build the multi-storied tower within which his small Scottish tribe can withstand Roman raids during the first century A.D.

Elizabeth George Speare

The Witch of Blackbird Pond
The Bronze Bow

The Witch of Blackbird Pond was the winner of the 1959 Newbery Medal. Orphaned Kit, luxuriously raised in tropical Barbados, comes to live with her Puritan relatives in Connecticut. These cousins try to be kind but they disagree with Kit about almost everything. Her silk dresses and befeathered bonnets scandalize the whole community, and Kit willfully flouts local customs in many ways, most seriously by making friends with an old Quaker woman, Hannah Tupper, the suspected witch of Blackbird Pond. Kit's recklessness climaxes in her arrest, imprisonment, and trial for witchcraft. This terrifying experience brings Kit to realize that no

Viewpoint

"History is people." I have said this often enough to adults as well as to children, and this is the sum of all my research; this is the basis of everything I have learned about the historical novel. History is ordinary people shaped and shaken by the winds of their time, as we in our time are shaped and shaken by the wind of current events. And so, to write about the people of any time, one must know them so well that it would be possible to go back and live undetected among them.

Rather than writing from the outside looking in, then, one will write from the inside looking out. Then also, as when a raised window permits interior and exterior to merge in the air and sunlight flowing into a room, the past will merge with the present. The feelings of past and present will be shared. There will be engagement between reader and characters, irrespective of superficial differences in dress, speech, and habit; and in identifying with these characters, the reader will find his own identity.— Mollie Hunter. From *The Last Lord of Redhouse Castle.* © 1975 by Mollie Hunter. Reprinted by permission of A. M. Heath & Company Ltd.

one of us can live without family or friends. Her stern old uncle defends her even at considerable danger to himself and his family. A forlorn waif Kit had befriended stands by her, and her disapproving, seafaring beau Nat finally manages to extricate Kit. The strength of this book lies in its theme and its well-drawn characters. They are neither wholly good nor wholly bad but a very human mixture of heroism and bigotry, frailty and courage, rebellious recklessness and generous loyalty.

The 1962 Newbery Medal winner, *The Bronze Bow*, is set in Israel during the time Jesus lived. The title comes from II Samuel 22:35—"He trains my hands for war, so that my arms can bend a bow of bronze." This verse fascinates young Daniel, who, along with many Israelites, is looking for the Deliverer to drive the cruel Romans out of their land. Daniel had seen his mother and father wantonly slain by these conquerors. Blinded by his hatred, Daniel kills his sister's hope of love, thereby driving her into mental darkness. Not until he has seen his mute but devoted follower killed and has almost lost his love, Thacia, does Daniel come face to face with the healing love of Jesus. Then at last he understands that it is not hatred and violence, but only love that is strong enough to bend the bow of bronze.

John and Patricia Beatty

At the Seven Stars
Who Comes to King's Mountain?

John and Patricia Beatty's historical novels are based on sound research, and their aim was to entertain rather than to instruct their readers. As Patricia Beatty says, "We hope that our books are more than escape fiction, but we are aware that all fiction offers escape."[4] In *At the Seven Stars* (1967) a fifteen-year-old boy from Philadelphia comes to London in 1752 and meets some of the very real people of that turbulent period. Richard becomes involved in the struggle between the Hanoverian and Stuart supporters, takes refuge in William Hogarth's home, is imprisoned, escapes, enlists the aid of the actor David Garrick, and gets back to America with the help of the Duke of Newcastle.

Who Comes to King's Mountain? (1975) shows the difficulties a Scottish South Carolina boy

has in serving with the rebels rather than the British during the last years of the Revolution. There is never a dearth of action in books by the Beattys or in the books that Patricia Beatty writes alone. In *Hail Columbia* (1970), for example, a suffragette in Oregon in 1893 stirs up the town of Astoria by her vigorous dedication to causes. Since John Beatty's death, Patricia Beatty has focused on the American past in such frontier-heroine stories as *Lacy Makes a Match* (1979), set in California in 1893, or the Texas story, *That's One Ornery Orphan* (1980). Set in 1889, it gives—as do most of Beatty's books—an appended note on sources.

Esther Forbes

Johnny Tremain

Esther Forbes received the 1942 Pulitzer Prize for her adult biography *Paul Revere and the World He Lived In*. Her *Johnny Tremain*, which was an outgrowth of the research expended on *Paul Revere*, received the 1944 Newbery Medal. In her Newbery acceptance speech, she explained that while she was working on the adult biography she had to stifle any tendency toward fiction. But she was continually teased by the story possibilities of Boston's apprentices, who were always getting into scrapes of one kind or another. So she promised herself that as soon as possible she would write some fiction about the apprentices. The resulting book, *Johnny Tremain*, represents a high point in American historical fiction for children and young people.

Johnny Tremain tells the story of a silversmith's apprentice who lived in the exciting days that marked the beginning of the American Revolution. Competent and cocky, a humble artist but an unbearably conceited boy, Johnny is harsh and overbearing with his fellow apprentices and ambitious for himself. Just as he achieves a notable design, the apprentices decide to play a joke on him, with tragic results. Not only is Johnny's design lost but he is left with a burned hand, maimed for life. His career as a silversmith is over.

This is the beginning of a story that carries Johnny and his friend Rab into the thick of Boston's pre-Revolutionary activities. In the first little skirmish of the Revolution, men and boys lined up in the square—some to die. But they knew what they were dying for, Forbes assures us, and they believed it "was worth more than their own lives."

4. Patricia Beatty, "The Two-headed Monster," *The Horn Book*, February 1967, p. 100.

Illustration by Lynd Ward, from *Johnny Tremain* by Esther Forbes. Published by Houghton Mifflin Company. Copyright © renewed 1971 by Linwood M. Erskine, Jr. Reproduced by permission of the publisher.

Johnny Tremain has so many values they are difficult to summarize. Johnny's bitterness over his maimed hand is understandable. This book gives no one-sided account of pre-Revolutionary days but makes the colonists and redcoats come alive as histories never seem to. The British, especially, are amazingly human in their forbearance, while the confusion and uncertainty of the colonists are frighteningly real. All the details of the everyday life of the period are expertly woven into the story, never dragged in for themselves.

Rebecca Caudill

Tree of Freedom

Tree of Freedom (1954), a story about the Revolutionary War period, is sound historical fiction because of its vivid characterizations and homely details of everyday living, which make the past understandable and natural. Each child of a family moving to Kentucky may take one prized possession. Stephanie carries an apple seed, because that is what her grandmother brought from France. When Noel, the eldest son, wants to take his dulcimer, it starts anew the feud between father and son. But the mother intervenes, "Twon't hurt him any. An' a little music won't hurt Kentucky, either. ... He's got his rifle, ain't he, as well as his dulcimore? He'll use it like a man. See if he don't." And he does, but the quarrel is not resolved until the end of the war.

Another fine story is Caudill's *The Far-Off Land* (1964), in which a young girl is taken by flatboat in 1780 from the Moravian settlement in Salem to French Lick. Although she becomes accustomed to the rough ways of the settlers, Ketty cannot accept their hostile behavior toward Indians, since she has been brought up to practice brotherly love. The characterization is strong, the period details convincing and smoothly incorporated into the story.

Leonard Wibberley

The *Treegate* series

Leonard Wibberley paints his stories of Peter Treegate's adventures during the Revolutionary War on a broad canvas. In the first book, *John Treegate's Musket* (1959), John Treegate is a solid, respectable Boston citizen who is loyal to his king, but his son Peter becomes increasingly convinced of the rectitude of the patriot cause and fights against the British at Bunker Hill. In *Peter Treegate's War* (1960), Peter becomes a war prisoner, escapes, crosses the Delaware with Washington, and goes to the southern mountains. *Sea Captain from Salem* (1961) tells the story of Peace of God Manly, who saved Peter's life in the first book, and who is sent on a mission by Benjamin Franklin, in an effort to win French support for the cause. The move to France gives the series variety, and the plot provides some rousing sea battles. In *Treegate's Raiders* (1962), Peter is on a recruiting trip through the mountains, trying to persuade Scottish settlers to forget their clan loyalties and feuds and unite as Americans. The story has vivid martial scenes and ends with the defeat of Cornwallis. All the books give realistic pictures not only of the Revolutionary War but of the significance of that war to the ordinary citizen of the time and to history. In *Leopard's Prey* (1971), *Red Pawns* (1973), and *The Last Battle* (1976), Wibberley moves to the events surrounding the War of 1812; his young protagonists are the two nephews of Peter Treegate.

William O. Steele

Wayah of the Real People
The Perilous Road
The Far Frontier

Few writers re-create wilderness life more vividly and movingly than William Steele. His stories are well written in the vernacular of the times, with good dialogue, plenty of suspense and action, and flesh-and-blood characters—grownups who struggle and survive in a tough pioneer world and expect their children to do the same; frontier boys, ignorant, prejudiced, or wrong-headed, but resourceful and enduring. The significant thing about William Steele's boys is that life changes and develops them, so that the reader sees them grow.

Wayah of the Real People (1964) is an unusual story about a Cherokee boy's year of schooling at Brafferton Hall in mid-eighteenth-century Williamsburg. Wayah suffers all the problems of any child placed in an environment culturally different from his own. Afraid that he has changed, Wayah finds when he has returned to the Real People, that his year away has helped him mature.

In *The Perilous Road* (1958), young Chris Brabson, who hates the Yankees, cannot under-stand how his parents can accept the fact that his older brother has joined the Union Army. After Union soldiers have raided the Brabson livestock, Chris tries a bit of revenge and is surprised, when he gets to know some of the soldiers, that they are people like himself. The story has action and suspense, and, like many of Steele's other books, is set in the Tennessee mountain region.

The Far Frontier (1959) shows another strong-willed boy who is outraged when he finds himself bound out to an absentminded scientist from Philadelphia. But before their long, danger-beset journey through the Tennessee wilderness is over, Tobe has acquired a deep respect for his brave, eccentric companion. Best of all, the boy survives with a lasting hunger for learning and is well on his way with both reading and figuring. Tobe and the naturalist, Mr. Twistletree, are a memorable pair.

Evelyn Lampman

The Tilted Sombrero
Squaw Man's Son

Evelyn Lampman's *The Tilted Sombrero* (1966) takes place at the start of the Mexican War of Independence in 1810, and it includes some real people prominent in that struggle, primarily Father Hidalgo y Costilla, the priest who led the first Indian revolt against Spain. In addition to historical interest, however, the story gives a vivid picture of the stratification of Mexican society. Its protagonist, Nando, is a proud Creole whose family has always been loyal to Spain, and at first he is greatly displeased to learn that his family is not pure Creole, that they have an Indian grandmother. Won over to the patriot cause, Nando changes his attitude. The book has a colorful setting and an action-filled plot, but it is the theme of rebellion against oppression that is its most memorable element. Another historical period (1847) is the setting for a fine pioneer story, *Tree Wagon* (1953), and Lampman's sympathetic identification with Native Americans is evident in both *Squaw Man's Son* (1978), a story of a Modoc-white boy set in Oregon, and *Once Upon the Little Big Horn* (1971), a detailed account of the four-day struggle commonly known as "Custer's Last Stand." *White Captives* (1975) is based on the experience of several children taken from a wagon train by an Apache raiding party in 1851.

Viewpoint

... the historical novelist does not merely acquire information about the past, but absorbs it into his mind. Atmosphere comes out in his books as the overflow of a personality that has made a peculiar appropriation of history. It comes as part of the man himself.

... The virtue and power of the novelist's depiction of men, is not that he observes perpetually and arranges data, but that he enters into the experiences of others, he runs his life into the mould of their lives, he puts himself under the conditioning circumstances of their thinking. He can feel with people unlike himself and look at the world with their eyes and grapple with the issues of life that meet them, because he can put himself in their place, that is to say, because his experience is not entirely and merely his own. It is precisely because personality is not cut off from personality, and a man is not entirely locked up within himself, ... that the novelist can so to speak transpose himself and catch life into a person other than himself.—
H. Butterfield, *The Historical Novel,* Cambridge University Press, London, 1924, pp. 107, 111.

Scott O'Dell

Island of the Blue Dolphins
The King's Fifth
The Captive

There seem to be more good realistic stories about the American Indian set in the past than in the present. Of these stories of the past, one of the most powerful is *Island of the Blue Dolphins* (1961 Newbery Medal).

In the early 1800s off the coast of California, a twelve-year-old Indian girl boards a ship that is to carry the tribe away from their island home where they are being harried and destroyed by Aleutian seal hunters. But when Karana sees that her little brother has accidentally been left behind, she jumps off the moving ship and swims back to him and their island home. A pack of wild dogs kills her brother and begins to stalk the solitary girl. This is the beautifully told story of her survival on the island for eighteen years. She has to prepare her own weapons, build a shelter with a strong fence, maintain a continual search for food, replace her worn-out clothes, all with an eye on the savage pack of dogs. Shining through her struggles and hardships are her quiet resignation, her endurance, her genuine love for her island home, and the great fortitude and serenity she develops. The story of Karana is historically true. Her incredible battles with a bull sea elephant, a devilfish, and the ferocious dogs, and, above all, her years of solitude command the reader's humble admiration for human courage. The sequel, *Zia* (1976) is less impressive, a poignant story of Zia's efforts to find her aunt, Karana.

Also based on history is the story told by Esteban in *The King's Fifth* (1966), his reminiscences of the journey made as a fifteen-year-old cartographer to Coronado. Put ashore to find Coronado's camp, his small group has a dangerous journey searching for the fabled gold of Cibola, and Esteban is later imprisoned on the charge that he has withheld the king's share of the treasure. The transitions between past and present are smoothly bridged, and the historical details are used to enhance rather than obscure an adventurous tale.

The 290 (1976) is an exciting story of naval action during the American Civil War, and in *Carlota* (1977) O'Dell records the efforts of Spanish Californians to maintain their independence after the Mexican-American War. With *The Captive* (1979), O'Dell moves to the sixteenth century and a young Spanish seminarian who is horrified by the slavery he finds in the New World. For *Sarah Bishop* (1980) O'Dell uses a Revolutionary War setting.

Weyman Jones

The Talking Leaf
The Edge of Two Worlds

In two stories about Sequoyah, Weyman Jones brings vividly to life the half-white Cherokee who conceived the idea of giving his people a written alphabet. In *The Talking Leaf* (1965) a young Cherokee, Atsee, had hoped to become a great scout like his father but finds that times have changed, that the Cherokee nation has to change as well. Knowing that his people must become literate, Atsee seeks Sequoyah. Sympathetic, dignified, and beautifully written, the story is moving, its theme apparent in Sequoyah's comment when Atsee asks bitterly if the bolt he is making for a bridge is so that the whites can come into Cherokee country more easily. "Part of growing up," Sequoyah says, "is learning that a bridge goes two ways." In *The Edge of Two Worlds* (1968) a white boy who is the only survivor of an Indian attack on a wagon train travels for mutual protection with Sequoyah, now an old man, but when the time comes that they part, the boy has learned to respect and trust the gentle and dignified Indian. There is no stereotype, no sentimentality in these stories, but a deep understanding and reverence for the man who learned to interpret the written word so that he might help his people.

Christie Harris

Raven's Cry
West with the White Chiefs

Raven's Cry (1966) was given the Canadian Library Association's award as the best children's book of the year in English. The dramatic and impressive story describes the dreadful consequences for the Haida people when white men came in 1775 to hunt sea otter, cheating the poeple and destroying their way of life until only a handful remained. The story is told from the Indian viewpoint, in a vigorous narrative that is complemented by the strong illustrations of Bill Reid, a descendant of the last Haida chief, who duplicates the form of Haida art.

West with the White Chiefs (1965) is based on the journal written by two Englishmen, a story of high adventure in which a small party crosses the Rockies in 1863. The characterization of the whites and Indians, who become friends on the journey, is excellent, and there is some comedy in the pedantic, quarrelsome schoolmaster who foists himself on the party of explorers.

Betty Baker
The Dunderhead War
Walk the World's Rim

The Dunderhead War (1967) is one of the few good books for young people about the Mexican War, which serves as a background for Betty Baker's story of seventeen-year-old Quincy, who is too young to enlist, but travels with his Uncle Fritz and shares some of the adventures of the volunteers. Uncle Fritz has just come to the United States, and his complacent superiority and criticism of that "army of dunderheads" give an outsider's viewpoint and add humor to a lively story.

Many of Baker's books, from stories for beginning readers to serious fiction for adolescents, are about Native Americans. Two of the best are *Walk the World's Rim* (1965), the story of the black slave Esteban who wandered across the country with Cabeza de Vaca and became the hero of the Indian boy Chakoh; and *And One Was a Wooden Indian* (1970), a sensitive novel about a young Apache of the nineteenth century and his first encounter with white people.

Harold Keith
Rifles for Watie

Rifles for Watie, winner of the 1958 Newbery Medal, is substantial historical fiction. The hero of the book is young Jefferson Davis Bussey, who despite his name is a Kansas farm boy and a rabid Unionist. Once in the army, Jeff's name and his stubborn forthrightness get him into trouble with a brutal officer, who persecutes him endlessly. Finally, Jeff is sent as a spy behind the Rebel lines to try to discover where Confederate Stand Watie, full-blooded Cherokee Indian, is getting the new rifles issued for the Union armies. Jeff is captured by the Rebels, but his name, together with a plausible story, allays suspicions. Jeff lives, works, and

Illustration by Bill Reid
From *Raven's Cry* by Christie Harris
Copyright © 1966 by Christie Harris.
Used by permission of Atheneum Publishers.

fights with this Indian regiment for fourteen months. When he finally gets his information and escapes to the Northern side, he leaves his Confederate friends with real regret. He leaves them also with the disturbing realization that heroic, well-intentioned men are fighting and dying on both sides in this horrifying struggle.

Keith has created unforgettable characters and has given us all the hunger, dirt, and weariness of war to balance the heroism of men and boys on both sides.

Peter Burchard
Bimby
Jed

Peter Burchard's approach to the writing of historical fiction is to pinpoint his theme by using a compressed, concise account of an incident or a single day and creating thereby a dramatic impact. In *Bimby* (1968), he follows a young slave through one crucial day in which the boy sees an old friend killed and also learns that his father had died of the punishment he received when he tried to escape. Knowing that she will never see her son again, Bimby's mother gives him information that will enable him to escape, both of them aware that life without freedom is empty. The writing is subdued, so that the poignancy and tension of the story emerge from the events themselves.

In *Jed* (1960), Burchard again avoids didacticism and lets the ethical implications of a boy's conduct make their own impact on the reader. Although he is only sixteen, Jed has already fought at Shiloh, and he is disturbed by the behavior of some of the Yankee soldiers who are his companions at arms. Foraging is stealing, and war is no excuse; war, in fact, is not glamorous. When he finds a small boy who has been hurt, Jed takes the child back to his Confederate family and befriends them. *The Deserter* (1974) is a Civil War spy story, and *Chinwe* (1979) is set in 1838, a story of a brave Ibo woman who is taken by slave traders.

K. M. Peyton
The *Flambards* trilogy

Before K. M. Peyton's *Flambards* trilogy, she produced a series of excellent adventure stories, many of which are set in the past but have little sense of history. With the publication of *Flambards* (1968), Peyton made the Edwardian period an integral part of the book. Flambards is the Russell estate to which Christina Parsons, a young orphan, comes to live with her uncle and his two sons, Mark and Will. World War I is looming, and quiet Will is enthralled by flying. The emphasis on the first frail, experimental planes is a major part of the story, although the plot focuses on Christina's rejection of the

Reprinted by permission of Coward, McCann & Geoghegan, Inc. from *Jed* by Peter Burchard. Copyright © 1960 by Coward-McCann.

powerful bully Mark and her love for Will. One of the ways in which Peyton reflects the changing mores of the period is in Christina's ambivalence about servants: she resents her uncle's treatment of them, yet cannot quite feel that the groom, Dick, is a person.

The book was a runner-up for the Carnegie Medal, which was awarded to Peyton for the second book of the three, *The Edge of the Cloud* (published in the United States in 1970). In this book Will and Christina take refuge with an aunt in Battersea, since Mark and his father were irate because of Christina's choice. For two years they are engaged, Christina always apprehensive because of Will's dangerous vocation. The story ends with their marriage, but it is less a love story than an account of the early days of flying, with its stunt men, and the camaraderie of the still-small group of flyers.

In *Flambards in Summer* (1970) the time is 1916, and Christina is a widow. She finds that Mark has an illegitimate son and brings the boy to Flambards, the neglected estate that she now manages. Eventually she falls in love again. It is significant of the changes in Christina and of the changes in the times that Dick, the former groom, is the man she plans to wed. The characterization is strong and the heroine's development into maturity is a convincing characterization and also a microcosmic picture of the new social structure that came out of World War I.

Elizabeth Foreman Lewis
Young Fu of the Upper Yangtze
To Beat a Tiger

Elizabeth Lewis, who lived in China for many years, wrote *Young Fu of the Upper Yangtze*, winner of the 1933 Newbery Medal. It is the exciting story of a thirteen-year-old Chinese country boy who is brought to the rich city of Chungking in the 1930s and apprenticed to a skillful coppersmith. In time, Young Fu becomes a fine craftsman, but neither easily nor quickly. Meanwhile, he explores the great city and finds everywhere the conflict of old and new ideas. Fu is no idealized hero but exhibits the usual contradictory human traits. He is brave and honest, yet he wastes his master's time and gets into trouble. He works hard, grows skillful, and then gets unbearably cocky. He is frugal one moment and wasteful the next.

Lewis has a later book, *To Beat a Tiger* (1956),

for teenagers and young adults. It is the grim story of sixteen Chinese boys living by their wits on the outskirts of Shanghai. They all know the proverb, "To beat a tiger, one needs a brother's help." Their tiger is starvation and death, and so they lie, steal, and cheat, but share their wretched scraps of food, their hut, filthy rags, and scanty heat. Death strikes one of the gang, and the chance to rise by sheer villainy claims another. Nationalists and Communists are not named, but the two factions are there and the boys are involved. It is a complex story, but once the large gallery of characters is identified, the plot gains momentum and suspense is high.

While Lewis creates many unusual happenings and adventures for her characters, it is in the presentation of the people that she excels. Even minor characters have individuality and presence, and linger in the reader's memory.

Jill (Gillian) Paton Walsh

Fireweed
Children of the Fox

Like Rosemary Sutcliff, the English writer Jill Paton Walsh has so deep a knowledge of the details of historical periods that facts about clothing, or food, or mores of the period are never obtrusive but blend smoothly into the background. This quality is not as evident in *Fireweed* (1970) as it is in some of her later books, not because the details of wartime London are not there or not vivid, but because the focus is on a personal relationship. Two adolescents, both of whom are supposed to have been evacuated from London during the blitz, meet and decide to stay together in an abandoned building; only when it is bombed does Bill realize he has come to love Julie. When he finds her, he knows they will never be together, for her wealthy family has traced her. Sharply etched, the ending is sad, moving, and wholly believable.

In books like *Children of the Fox* (1978) Walsh combines her knowledge of the past and her strong sense of narrative; three young people who lived during the time of the Persian Wars each tell a story of an adventure, and the adventures are linked by the fact that each of them has met the Athenian hero, Themistokles. The stories are given vitality by the enthusiasm of their narrators; each is stirring, and all are based on careful research.

Illustration by Robin Eaton. Reprinted with the permission of Farrar, Straus and Giroux, Inc. From *Children of the Fox* by Jill Paton Walsh, pictures by Robin Eaton, copyright © 1978 by Farrar, Straus and Giroux, Inc.

Among other books by Walsh, *The Emperor's Winding Sheet* (1974) is distinctive for the sweep of events in the siege and fall of Constantinople as seen from the viewpoint of a young British seaman who is first the captive of the Emperor Constantine and later his willing servant and devoted admirer. In *The Huffler* (1975, published in England under the title *The Butty Boy*) Walsh tells the story of a girl who runs away from her very proper Victorian family and poses as a servant in order to fit into the life of a canal-boat family. Here the lore of canal life is an added appeal, but it is always as a storyteller that Jill Paton Walsh gives most delight.

Other Books for Older Children

A story of ancient times is Madeleine Polland's *To Tell My People* (1968). A British girl, taken by Roman invaders, is sent to Rome as a slave. When she escapes and returns to her people, she hopes to share the knowledge she has gained, but they are ignorant and only sneer. She had hoped to bring them peace; they will do nothing but fight. Polland has set several books in this era, telling believable stories with strong characters.

Hans Baumann's stories are always exciting, even though sometimes slowed down by details. In *I Marched with Hannibal* (1962), an old man tells two children about his boyhood experiences, a narrative device that gives the book a sense of immediacy and scope for vivid personal accounts of the marches and battle scenes. Baumann's historical personages are never stock characters but are vividly depicted to add depth to stories with authentic background.

The Namesake (1964) and *The Marsh King* (1967) by Cyril Walter Hodges are sequential tales of King Alfred's struggle against the Danish invaders, stories full of action and fascinating historical details. Another English writer, Geoffrey Trease, moves his hero in *The Red Towers of Granada* (1967) from England in the time of Edward I to Spain. Cast out of his village as a leper, young Robin learns from a Jewish doctor that he has only a minor skin disease. When the doctor leaves England for Spain, Robin goes with him.

Fifteenth-century Poland is the setting for Eric Kelly's 1929 Newbery Medal book, *The Trumpeter of Krakow*, a story based on the oath of the Krakow trumpeters to sound their defiant song every hour. The setting is colorful, the story intriguing both because it has dramatic adventure and because it gives an absorbing picture of the problems of the Polish people.

I, Juan de Pareja (1965), for which Elizabeth Borton de Treviño was awarded the Newbery Medal, is the story of the black slave of the painter Velazquez. Written in autobiographical form, it comes close to biography, but is told as a story. An aspiring artist himself, de Pareja painted secretly until his master realized that here was another artist—and freed him. In de Pareja's descriptions of court affairs and of Velazquez as a person, there is appeal for the reader interested in history and in art, and the story itself moves with pace and dignity.

Another story with a black protagonist is Ann Petry's *Tituba of Salem Village* (1964), a dramatic fictionalization of the inexorable hysteria of the Salem witch-hunt and trials. In Alice Marriott's *Indian Annie: Kiowa Captive* (1965),

Reprinted by permission of Coward, McCann & Geoghegan, Inc. from *The Marsh King* by C. Walter Hodges. Copyright © 1967 by C. Walter Hodges.

Annie comes to love her foster parents and marries into the tribe. The story is set in the antebellum years, and Annie is struck by the fact that a freed slave cannot identify, as she does, with another minority group.

E. M. Almedingen has written many charming historical novels set in Russia, most of them based on family records. *Katia* (1967) is an adaptation of a great-aunt's memoirs, published in Russia in 1874. *Young Mark* (1968) is the true and romantic story of Almedingen's great-great-grandfather, who became a court favorite because of his beautiful singing, grew wealthy, and established the family fortune. The writing is intricate and mature, but the style and the fidelity of the historical background are very appealing.

No group of stories within the genre of historical fiction demonstrates so clearly that literature is an international heritage as do the

Illustration by Victor Ambrus. Reprinted with the permission of Farrar, Straus and Giroux, Inc., and Oxford University Press, London. From *Katia* by E. M. Almedingen, illustrated by Victor Ambrus, copyright © 1966 by E. M. Almedingen.

books about World War II. From Denmark comes Anne Holm's *North to Freedom* (1965), the story of a boy of twelve who escapes from a prison camp in eastern Europe and makes his way to his mother in Copenhagen. Josef Carl Grund's *Never to Be Free* (1970) and Hans Peter Richter's *Friedrich* (1970), both translated from the German, are alike in being told by boys who are at first loyal to Hitler but who change; in Grund's book Gustav is disillusioned by his army experience; in Richter's, the boy who tells the story is disillusioned by what happens to his Jewish friend Friedrich. Both stories are all the more effective for their portrayal of ordinary people. This is also true of a book from France, Colette Vivier's *House of the Four Winds* (1969), for the people who live in the house (an apartment building) are a cross-section of middle-class Parisians, and their valor (or cowardice) during the German occupation has a homeliness that makes the historical period come alive. Margaret Balderson's *When Jays Fly to Barbmo* (1969) moves slowly, but the style fits the bleak setting of a Norwegian island where the German invaders burn the farmhouses.

In Hester Burton's *In Spite of All Terror* (1969), a girl who has been sent out of London for her safety comes back to do her bit on the eve of Dunkirk. One of the most powerful books in this group is Erik Haugaard's *The Little Fishes* (1967), told by a twelve-year-old waif in wartime Italy. Guido lives by stealing because he must to exist. Children compete with adults for survival, yet Guido has faith in humanity. Terrible and true, the story is a testament of hope as much as it is an indictment of war.

Printing a Danish underground paper brings death to Peter's father in *A Kind of Secret Weapon* (1969) by Elliott Arnold. Nathaniel Benchley's *Bright Candles* (1974) shows other facets of the Danish resistance to the Nazi occupation, from sabotage to nationwide support of the Jews. Suspense and vigorous action are hallmarks of books by this versatile writer.

The ravages of war are a recurrent theme in James Forman's books. *Horses of Anger* (1967) concerns a Nazi soldier who begins to doubt the propaganda he has heard and to understand his own prejudice. In Forman's *The Traitors* (1968), a Bavarian pastor suffers because his congregation and his only child espouse the Nazi cause, and he joins the underground rebellion. Forman's books are mature and sophisticated, often profound and provocative, demanding the most of a young reader.

We have only recently begun to see a number of books for children on the Jewish experience during, before, and after World War II, many of them written out of personal knowledge. Perhaps the time lapse was necessary to enable authors to approach the theme with some objectivity. It may also be because we are less inclined in these days of the pervasiveness of the mass media to shelter children from the misdeeds of adults. We are more willing to present life whole, the bad—although not dwelt upon at length—with the good. We are also awaking to the fact that children do not come equipped with a value system, that good citizenship and character must be taught.

The bicentennial celebration in the United States led to an increased publication of historical fact and fiction for young and old to answer demands for information only partially met through the mass media. It seems logical to expect that two hundred years of nationhood and the problems the United States now faces in the ecological and political areas will encourage a continuing interest in the past, an interest in how our ancestors met the many problems of a new environment and a new government.

Adult References[5]

EGOFF, SHEILA. *The Republic of Childhood: A Critical Guide to Canadian Children's Literature in English.* Part 3, "Historical Fiction."

EGOFF, SHEILA, G. T. STUBBS, and L. F. ASHLEY, eds. *Only Connect: Readings on Children's Literature.* Part 3, "Historical Fiction."

FIELD, ELINOR WHITNEY, comp. *Horn Book Reflections.* Part III, "Recreating Other Times."

HOTCHKISS, JEANETTE, comp. *American Historical Fiction and Biography for Children and Young People.*

———, comp. *European Historical Fiction and Biography for Children and Young People.*

HUNTER, MOLLIE. *Talent Is Not Enough.* "Shoulder in the Sky."

IRWIN, LEONARD B., comp. *A Guide to Historical Fiction.*

LOGOSA, HANNAH, comp. *World Culture.*

SUTHERLAND, ZENA. *History in Children's Books.*

Some historical fiction titles may be found in the bibliography for Chapter 11. In the following bibliography these symbols have been used to identify books about a religious or a particular ethnic group:

§ Black
★Chicano or Puerto Rican
☆Native American
● Religious minority

Historical Fiction: The Ancient World

ANDREWS, J. S. *The Man from the Sea.* Dutton, 1971. Their men lost in a storm, the survivors in an early fishing village are aided by a trader from the south. A taut, well-told tale. 11–14

BAUMANN, HANS. *I Marched with Hannibal,* tr. by Katherine Potts, ill. by Ulrik Schramm. Walck, 1962. 12–15

BEHN, HARRY. *The Faraway Lurs.* World, 1963. Tribes of differing cultures meet in early Denmark, with tragic consequences for two young people. 12–15

BULLA, CLYDE ROBERT. *Viking Adventure,* ill. by Douglas Gorsline. T. Crowell, 1963. A Viking's son grows into a man on the long voyage to Wineland and home again. 8–10

CLARKE, PAULINE. *Torolv the Fatherless,* ill. by Cecil Leslie. Faber, 1978. A Viking waif is accidentally stranded when his ship sails without him and is adopted by an elderly earl who later dies fighting Vikings at the Battle of Maldon. 11–14

COOLIDGE, OLIVIA. *Egyptian Adventures,* ill. by Joseph Low. Houghton, 1954. 12–16

———. *King of Men,* ill. by Ellen Raskin. Houghton, 1966. 12 up

———. *The Maid of Artemis,* ill. by Bea Holmes. Houghton, 1969. 10–14

———. *Marathon Looks on the Sea,* ill. by Erwin Schachner. Houghton, 1967. 12–15

———. *Men of Athens.* Houghton, 1962. 12–15

● ———. *People in Palestine.* Houghton, 1965. 12 up

———. *Roman People,* ill. by Lino Lipinsky. Houghton, 1959. 12–15

FYSON, J. G. *The Three Brothers of Ur,* ill. by Victor G. Ambrus. Coward, 1966. Lively tale of a trader's household in the ancient city. 10–14

GARD, JOYCE. *The Mermaid's Daughter.* Holt, 1969. An intricate novel, set in Britain at the time of the Roman occupation, based on the mermaid-goddess cult. 11–14

HAUGAARD, ERIK CHRISTIAN. *The Rider and His Horse,* ill. by Leo and Diane Dillon. Houghton, 1968. 12–17

HAYS, WILMA PITCHFORD. *The Story of Valentine,* ill. by Leonard Weisgard. Coward, 1956. A vivid story of a Christian priest who, when imprisoned, achieved a miracle of faith. 9–12

LAWRENCE, ISABELLE. *The Theft of the Golden Ring,* ill. by Charles V. John. Bobbs, 1948. A complex and exciting story. 11–14

LILLINGTON, KENNETH. *Young Man of Morning.* Faber, 1980. A young Greek sculptor witnesses the battles of Thermopylae and Salamis. 12–14

LINEVSKI, A. *An Old Tale Carved Out of Stone,* tr. by Maria Polushkin. Crown, 1973. The trials of a young, insecure shaman as he tries to lead his tribe wisely in early Siberia. 11–15

McGRAW, ELOISE JARVIS. *The Golden Goblet.* Coward, 1961. 11–15

———. *Mara, Daughter of the Nile.* Coward, 1953. 11–15

MADDOCK, REGINALD. *The Great Bow,* ill. by Victor Ambrus. Rand, 1968. A tightly constructed and convincing story about prehistoric people. Atta is a thoughtful fourteen-year-old who fails his test of manhood because he does not want to kill. 10–12

MORRISON, LUCILE. *The Lost Queen of Egypt,* ill. by Franz Geritz and Winifred Brunton. Lippincott, 1937. 12–14

POLLAND, MADELEINE. *To Tell My People,* ill. by Richard M. Powers. Holt, 1968. 11–13

☆ SCHWEITZER, BYRD BAYLOR. *One Small Blue Bead,* ill. by Symeon Shimin. Macmillan, 1965. Beautifully illustrated, a rhyming text tells a story of primitive people in Arizona. 7–9

SPEARE, ELIZABETH G. *The Bronze Bow.* Houghton, 1961. Newbery Medal. 12 up

SUTCLIFF, ROSEMARY. *Blood Feud.* Dutton, 1977. 12–14

———. *Song for a Dark Queen.* T. Crowell, 1979. 12–15

TREECE, HENRY. *The Centurion,* ill. by Mary Russon. Meredith, 1967. 11–15

WALSH, JILL PATON. *Children of the Fox,* ill. by Robin Eaton. Farrar, 1978. 10–13

European Historical Fiction

ALMEDINGEN, E. M. *Katia,* ill. by Victor G. Ambrus. Farrar, 1967. This has often been classified as a biography. 11–14

———. *Young Mark: The Story of a Venture,* ill. by Victor G. Ambrus. Farrar, 1968. 12–15

ARNOLD, ELLIOTT. *A Kind of Secret Weapon.* Scribner's, 1969. 10–13

BALDERSON, MARGARET. *When Jays Fly to Barbmo,* ill. by Victor G. Ambrus. World, 1969. 11–14

BAWDEN, NINA. *Carrie's War.* Lippincott, 1973. 10–14

———. *The Peppermint Pig.* Lippincott, 1975. 10–14

BEATTY, JOHN and PATRICIA. *At the Seven Stars,* with Hogarth prints and line drawings of Douglas Gorsline. Macmillan, 1963. 12–14

———. *Master Rosalind.* Morrow, 1974. A fascinating and lively picture of Elizabethan theatrical life and the court and criminal circles of the time. 12–14

5. Complete bibliographic data are provided in Appendix B.

BENCHLEY, NATHANIEL. *Beyond the Mists*. Harper, 1975. An old Viking recalls his days with Leif Ericson. 12–15

⬤ ———. *Bright Candles*. Harper, 1974. 12–15

BENTLEY, PHYLLIS. *The Adventures of Tom Leigh*, ill. by Burt Silverman. Doubleday, 1964. 10–14

———. *Forgery*. Doubleday, 1968. 10–14

———. *Oath of Silence*, ill. by Burt Silverman. Doubleday, 1967. Set in England's Yorkshire in the early nineteenth century, these three stories bring the problems of the weavers, facing mechanization, to life. 11–14

BODKER, CECIL. *Silas and Ben-Godik*. Delacorte, 1978. In a sequel to *Silas and the Black Mare*, the two boys (Silas on his mare and the village boy, Ben-Godik, on his horse) encounter a series of adventures. 10–12

———. *Silas and the Black Mare*. Delacorte, 1978. A series of adventures centering around young Silas and the mare he has bargained for culminates in a long and stirring episode involving all the characters from previous incidents. 10–12

———. *Silas and the Runaway Coach*. Delacorte, 1978. A third book in the "Silas" series finds the doughty adolescent again on his own and this time temporarily settled in the home of a wealthy family grateful for his rescue of their runaway coach. 10–12

BUFF, MARY. *The Apple and the Arrow*, ill. by Conrad Buff. Houghton, 1951. 9–12

BULLA, CLYDE. *The Sword in the Tree*, ill. by Paul Galdone. T. Crowell, 1956. 8–10

⬤ BURSTEIN, CHAYA. *Rifka Grows Up*, ill. by author. Hebrew Pub. Co., 1976. A sequel to *Rifka Bangs the Teakettle* set in a small Russian village finds Rifka, now twelve, determined to pass the exam that will permit her to go to high school despite being warned that there is a quota for Jews. 10–12

⬤ BURTON, HESTER. *Beyond the Weir Bridge*, ill. by Victor G. Ambrus. T. Crowell, 1970. 12–15

———. *Castors Away!* ill. by Victor G. Ambrus. World, 1962. A story centering on the great naval battle at Trafalgar. 12–15

———. *The Henchmans at Home*, ill. by Victor G. Ambrus. T. Crowell, 1972. Stories of two generations of a family, during the time of Nelson and the Battle of Trafalgar, and the Victorian era. 12–15

———. *In Spite of All Terror*, ill. by Victor G. Ambrus. World, 1969. 11–14

———. *Kate Ryder*, ill. by Victor G. Ambrus. T. Crowell, 1975. 12–15

———. *Time of Trial*, ill. by Victor G. Ambrus. World, 1964. Carnegie Medal. 12–15

CHUTE, MARCHETTE. *The Innocent Wayfaring*, ill. by author. Dutton, 1955.

———. *The Wonderful Winter*, ill. by Grace Golden. Dutton, 1954. 11–14

CLARKE, JOAN. *Early Rising*. Lippincott, 1976. A lovely period piece, this is set in an English vicarage in the 1880s, where Erica and her brothers and sisters are being brought up by a widowed father and a loving staff. 10–13

COOLIDGE, OLIVIA. *Tales of the Crusades*, ill. adapted from prints by Gustave Doré. Houghton, 1970. Each of the stories that chronicle some facet of the long years of the Crusades is a splendid entity, wonderfully evocative and vividly written. The book does not give a cohesive picture of all those centuries but is impressive both as a literary and a historical work. 13 up

COOPER, GORDON. *An Hour in the Morning*, ill. by Philip Gough. Dutton, 1974. 10–11

COOPER, SUSAN. *Dawn of Fear*, ill. by Margery Gill. Harcourt, 1970. 10–11

DARKE, MARJORIE. *A Question of Courage*. T. Crowell, 1975. A fine story about women's suffrage is set in Birmingham and London before the first world war. 12–14

DE ANGELI, MARGUERITE. *The Door in the Wall*, ill. by author. Doubleday, 1949. Newbery Medal. 8–11

DEGENS, T. *Transport 7-41-R*. Viking, 1974. A grim tale of the aftermath of war as evacuees return to Cologne in 1946. 11–14

FORMAN, JAMES. *Horses of Anger*. Farrar, 1967. 13 up

⬤ ———. *The Traitors*. Farrar, 1968. 13 up

GARFIELD, LEON. *The Night of the Comet: A Comedy of Courtship Featuring Bostock and Harris*. Delacorte, 1979. The path of true love, or even of reasonable facsimiles thereof, runs far from smoothly in the romping, ridiculous tale of three tangled love affairs. 11–13

GARNER, ALAN. *The Stone Book; Granny Reardun*, ill. by Michael Foreman. World, 1978. *The Aimer Gate; Tom Fobble's Day*, ill. by Michael Foreman. World, 1979. 8–10

GARRIGUE, SHEILA. *All the Children Were Sent Away*. Bradbury, 1976. Along with hundreds of other 1940 English evacuees, eight-year-old Sara boarded the H.M.S. Duke of Perth under the stern, dictatorial care of Lady Drume. 8–10

GRUND, JOSEF CARL. *Never to Be Free*, tr. by Lucile Harrington. Little, 1970. 12–15

HARNETT, CYNTHIA. *Caxton's Challenge*, ill. by author. World, 1960. Carnegie Medal. 12–16

———. *Nicholas and the Wool-Pack*, ill. by author. Putnam, 1953. 11–15

———. *The Writing on the Hearth*. Viking, 1973. 12–15

⬤ HAUGAARD, ERIK CHRISTIAN. *Chase Me, Catch Nobody!* Houghton, 1980. Set in 1937, the story of a Danish boy who rescues a Jewish girl while on a visit to Germany. 11–14

———. *Hakon of Rogen's Saga*, ill. by Leo and Diane Dillon. Houghton, 1963. 11–14

———. *The Little Fishes*, ill. by Milton Johnson. Houghton, 1967. 12 up

———. *A Messenger for Parliament*. Houghton, 1976. 12–14

———. *A Slave's Tale*, ill. by Leo and Diane Dillon. Houghton, 1965. 11–14

———. *The Untold Tale*, ill. by Leo and Diane Dillon. Houghton, 1971. 12–15

HODGES, C. WALTER. *Columbus Sails*, ill. by author. Coward, 1950. This well-liked story of Columbus and his voyages is fiction based on facts and is tremendously moving. 11–14

———. *The Marsh King*, ill. by author. Coward, 1967. 12–15

———. *The Namesake*, ill. by author. Coward, 1964. 12–14

HOLM, ANNE. *North to Freedom*, tr. from the Danish by L. W. Kingsland. Harcourt, 1965. 11–13

HUNTER, MOLLIE. *The Ghosts of Glencoe*. Funk, 1969. 11–14

———. *The Lothian Run*. Funk, 1970. 12–15

———. *A Pistol in Greenyards*. Funk, 1968. 11–14

———. *The Spanish Letters*. Funk, 1967. 12–15

———. *The Stronghold*. Harper, 1974. Carnegie Medal. 10–14

———. *The Thirteenth Member*. Harper, 1971. 12–15

⬤ ISH-KISHOR, SULAMITH. *A Boy of Old Prague*, ill. by Ben Shahn. Pantheon, 1963. A graphic story of life in the Jewish ghetto in 1540 Poland. 10–12

JENSEN, NIELS. *Days of Courage*, tr. by Oliver Stallybrass. Harcourt, 1973. A village's lone survivor of the great plague of medieval Europe rebuilds his life. A compelling tale. 12–15

KELLY, ERIC. *The Trumpeter of Krakow*, rev. ed. Macmillan, 1966. Newbery Medal. 12–14

⬤ KERR, JUDITH. *The Other Way Round*. Coward, 1975. 12–15

⬤ ———. *When Hitler Stole Pink Rabbit*. Coward, 1972. 10–12

⬤ KOEHN, ILSE. *Mischling, Second Degree: My Childhood in Nazi*

Germany. Greenwillow, 1977. The author tells how her family, liberals and intellectuals, coped with a government and a philosophy they detested.   12 up

● LEVITON, SONIA. *Journey to America,* ill. by Charles Robinson. Atheneum, 1970. The first-person story of a young Jewish girl and her family from Germany in the late 30s. Dramatic and well written.   10–12

LIVELY, PENELOPE. *Fanny's Sister,* ill. by Anita Lobel. Dutton, 1980. In a tender, amusing story, a Victorian child rebels, then accepts another sister.   9–11

LOVETT, MARGARET, *Jonathan,* Dutton, 1972. The grinding poverty of 1815. England as seen in the struggles of a boy to care for orphaned children.   11–14

MONJO, FERDINAND N. *The Sea Beggar's Son,* ill. by C. Walter Hodges. Coward, 1975. A stirring tale of a Dutch hero of the seventeenth century.   9–12

NÖSTLINGER, CHRISTINE. *Fly Away Home,* tr. by Anthea Bell. Watts, 1975. A gripping survival story set in World War II Vienna.   11–14

OLIVER, JANE [pseud.]. *Faraway Princess,* ill. by Jane Paton. St. Martin's, 1962. Princess Margaret, in flight from England after the Norman Conquest, finds sanctuary in Scotland and later a throne. Excellent historical fiction.   10–13

● ORGEL, DORIS. *The Devil in Vienna.* Dial, 1978. The story of a Jewish girl and her best friend (the daughter of a Nazi officer) who suffer through the tension and agony of the Nazi occupation of Austria.   11–13

PEYTON, K. M. *The Edge of the Cloud,* ill. by Victor G. Ambrus. World, 1970. Carnegie Medal.

———. *Flambards,* ill. by Victor G. Ambrus. World, 1968.

———. *Flambards in Summer,* ill. by Victor G. Ambrus. World, 1970.   12–15

———. *The Right-Hand Man,* ill. by Victor Ambrus. Oxford, 1979. Set in early 19th-century England, this powerful story reflects many of the qualities of the Georgian period from the color and tempo of the time to the callous attitude of the wealthy toward the poor.   12–15

PICARD, BARBARA LEONIE. *Lost John,* ill. by Charles Keeping. Criterion, 1962. John, who has left home to avenge his father's death, is captured by outlaws and becomes one of them. Set in the Middle Ages.   11–14

POLLAND, MADELEINE. *Children of the Red King,* ill. by Annette Macarthur-Onslow. Holt, 1961. Grania and Fergus, children of Ireland's embattled king, are sent as captives to their father's enemy. The events leading to reunion with their father offer a vivid story of the Norman Conquest.   11–13

POPE, ELIZABETH. *The Perilous Gard,* ill. by Richard Cuffari. Houghton, 1974. Set in Elizabethan times. A courageous girl, banished from the then-Princess Elizabeth's side to a remote castle, battles the occult.   11–14

PYLE, HOWARD. *Men of Iron,* ill. by author. Harper, 1891.

———. *Otto of the Silver Hand,* ill. by author. Scribner's, 1888.   10–14

● REISS, JOHANNA. *The Journey Back.* T. Crowell, 1976.   10–13

———. *The Upstairs Room.* T. Crowell, 1972.   9–12

● RICHTER, HANS PETER. *Friedrich,* tr. from the German by Edite Kroll. Holt, 1970.   11–14

● SACHS, MARILYN. *A Pocket Full of Seeds,* ill. by Ben Stahl. Doubleday, 1973.   9–12

SERRAILLIER, IAN. *The Silver Sword,* ill. by C. Walter Hodges. Criterion, 1959. The unforgettable journey of four children who make their way from Warsaw to Switzerland and safety during World War II.   11–14

SKURZYNSKI, GLORIA. *What Happened in Hamelin.* Four Winds, 1979. A story told by a poor orphan boy which offers a plausible explanation of what happened to the children of Hamelin.   5–7

● SLOBODKIN, FLORENCE. *Sarah Somebody,* ill. by Louis Slobodkin. Vanguard, 1970. The warm and sympathetic story of a nine-year-old girl in a Polish village in 1893 who gets a chance to learn to read and write—and to become somebody.   8–10

STREATFEILD, NOEL. *When the Sirens Wailed,* ill. by Judith Gwyn Brown. Random, 1976. A Cockney family is separated during the London blitz.   9–11

SUHL, YURI. *The Merrymaker,* ill. by Thomas di Grazia. Four Winds, 1975. Turn-of-the-century Eastern Europe is the setting for a story of a poor Jewish family.   9–12

● ———. *On the Other Side of the Gate.* Watts, 1975. A young Jewish couple in World War II Poland smuggle their baby to safety in a suspenseful tale.   12–16

SUTCLIFF, ROSEMARY. *The Capricorn Bracelet,* ill. by Richard Cuffari. Walck, 1973.   11–14

———. *Dawn Wind,* ill. by Charles Keeping. Walck, 1962; Walck, 1973.

———. *The Eagle of the Ninth,* ill. by C. Walter Hodges. Walck, 1954. The story of a lost legion in Roman Britain of the second century.

———. *The Lantern Bearers,* ill. by Charles Keeping. Walck, 1959. Carnegie Medal.

———. *The Mark of the Horse Lord.* Walck, 1965. Set in Scotland during the second century, this exciting adventure novel is fast paced with no slackening of suspense up to the last stunning episode.

———. *The Silver Branch.* Walck, 1958. Two young Romans, involved in the bitter intrigue between the ruler of Roman Britain and his rival, play a heroic part in bringing an assassin to justice.

———. *Warrior Scarlet,* ill. by Charles Keeping. Walck, 1958. In a unique tale of Bronze Age England, Drem kills his wolf and regains his tribal status despite a crippled arm.   12–16

———. *The Witch's Brat,* ill. by Richard Lebenson. Walck, 1970. An evocative story of Norman England, based on the actual founding of St. Bartholomew's Hospital. A colorful picture of a historical period, with strong, taut structure and good characterization.   11–14

● TREASE, GEOFFREY. *The Red Towers of Granada,* ill. by Charles Keeping. Vanguard, 1967.   11–14

TREECE, HENRY. *The Dream Time,* ill. by Charles Keeping. Meredith, 1968.   11–14

———. *The Road to Miklagard,* ill. by Christine Price. Criterion, 1957.   11–14

———. *Viking's Dawn,* ill. by Christine Price. Criterion, 1956. First in an absorbing trilogy of eighth-century Viking life, in which youthful Harald Sigurdson acccompanies his father on his first dangerous sea journey. In *The Road to Miklagard* (1957) his voyages are interrupted when he becomes a Moorish slave. In *Viking's Sunset* (1961) Harald, now a chieftain, sails his longboat to the shores of Lake Superior, and death intervenes on this last voyage. Harald's life saga conveys the vast scope of early Viking travels.   11–14

———. *Viking's Sunset,* ill. by Christine Price. Criterion, 1961.   11–14

§ TREVINO, ELIZABETH B. DE. *I, Juan de Pareja.* Farrar, 1965. Newbery Medal.   12–15

VAN STOCKUM, HILDA. *The Winged Watchman,* ill. by author. Farrar, 1962. The Verhagen family, in constant danger from an informer, conceals a British pilot during the occupation.   10–12

VINING, ELIZABETH GRAY. *Adam of the Road,* ill. by Robert Lawson. Viking, 1942. Newbery Medal.   12–14

———. *I Will Adventure,* ill. by Corydon Bell. Viking, 1962.   11–14

● VIVIER, COLLETTE. *The House of the Four Winds,* tr. and ed. by Miriam Morton. Doubleday, 1969.   11–14

WALSH, JILL PATON. *The Huffler,* ill. by Juliette Palmer. Farrar, 1975.   10–12

WATSON, SALLY. *Mistress Malapert.* Holt, 1955. A lively tale of an ancestor of the heroine in *Jade* (1968).   11–14

WELCH, RONALD. *Tank Commander.* Nelson, 1974. A compelling story of an officer's experiences in World War I.   12–15

WESTALL, ROBERT. *The Machine Gunners.* Greenwillow, 1976. Set in England during World War II, this is the story of a group of youngsters who find a machine gun and hide it in an underground shelter which they equip and man. Carnegie Medal.   10–14

WILLARD, BARBARA. *A Cold Wind Blowing.* Dutton, 1973. 11–15

———. *Harrow and Harvest.* Dutton, 1975.   11–15

———. *The Iron Lily.* Dutton, 1974.   11–15

———. *The Lark and the Laurel.* Dutton, 1970.   11–15

———. *The Sprig of Broom.* Dutton, 1972.   10–14

WILLIAMS, URSULA MORAY. *The Earl's Falconer,* ill. by Charles Geer. Morrow, 1961. Training falcons was not the privilege of peasant boys, but young Dickon's rare talent earned him the Earl's favor. A colorful tale of medieval England.   11–14

ZEI, ALKI. *Petros' War,* tr. by Edward Fenton. Dutton, 1972.   10–14

———. *The Sound of the Dragon's Feet.* Dutton, 1979.   9–11

———. *Wildcat Under Glass,* tr. from the Greek by Edward Fenton. Holt, 1968.   10–12

United States Historical Fiction

ANDERSON, LONZO, *Zeb,* ill. by Peter Burchard. Knopf, 1966.   10–14

☆ ARMER, LAURA ADAMS. *Waterless Mountain,* ill. by Sidney Armer and Laura Adams Armer. McKay, 1931. An early Newbery Award book, the story of Dawn Boy, a Navajo boy destined to be a medicine man.   11–15

AVI. *Encounter at Easton.* Pantheon, 1980. Fast-paced, this is a smoothly written account of the escape of two indentured servants, set in 1768.   10–12

§ BACMEISTER, RHODA. *Voices in the Night,* ill. by Ann Grifalconi. Bobbs, 1965.   9–11

§ BACON, MARTHA. *Sophia Scrooby Preserved,* ill. by David Omar White. Atlantic, 1968. A romantic tale of a cultured black girl whose lively adventures are described in the mannered style of early English novelists.   11–13

☆ BAKER, BETTY. *And One Was a Wooden Indian.* Macmillan, 1970.   11–15

———. *The Dunderhead War.* Harper, 1967.   11–14

———. *The Great Desert Race.* Macmillan, 1980. Two adolescent girls drive a steam-powered car in a race from one town to another in 1908.   10–13

———. *The Pig War,* ill. by Robert Lopshire. Harper, 1969.   7–8

☆§ ———. *Walk the World's Rim.* Harper, 1965.   11–14

BALL, ZACHARY [pseud.]. *North to Abilene.* Holiday, 1960. The thousand-mile cattle drive from Texas to Abilene challenges the resourcefulness of orphaned Seth in this fine tale of the early cattle industry.   12–15

BEATTY, JOHN and PATRICIA. *Who Comes to King's Mountain?* Morrow, 1975.   11–15

BEATTY, PATRICIA. *Hail Columbia,* ill. by Liz Dauber. Morrow, 1970.   10–12

———. *Lacy Makes a Match.* Morrow, 1979.   10–12

———. *A Long Way to Whiskey Creek.* Morrow, 1971. Set in

Texas in 1879, a story in which two boys overcome the lingering hostility between Northern and Southern supporters.   10–12

———. *That's One Ornery Orphan.* Morrow, 1980.   10–12

BENCHLEY, NATHANIEL. *Sam the Minuteman,* ill. by Arnold Lobel. Harper, 1969.   7–9

BLOS, JOAN. *A Gathering of Days: A New England Girl's Journal, 1830–32.* Scribner's, 1979. Newbery Medal.   10–12

BOLTON, CAROLE. *Never Jam Today.* Atheneum, 1971. Young Maddy becomes involved, through her Aunt Augusta, in the cause of women's suffrage. A realistic story with a commendable conclusion: Maddy passes up two love interests for the time being in favor of college and a career.   11–14

BRENNER, BARBARA. *On the Frontier with Mr. Audubon.* Coward, 1977. Thirteen-year-old Joseph Mason describes his travels as Audubon's pupil-assistant. The journal is a fictional device but the documented facts it records present a memorable picture of the artist and his work.   10–13

§☆ ———. *Wagon Wheels,* ill. by Don Bolognese. Harper, 1978. A fine frontier story for beginning independent readers describes the experiences of a black family which comes from Kentucky to Kansas in the 1870s.   6–8

☆ BRINK, CAROL RYRIE. *Caddie Woodlawn,* ill. by Kate Seredy. Macmillan, 1935. Newbery Medal.   9–12

● BROOKS, JEROME. *Make Me a Hero.* Dutton, 1980. With three brothers in service, a boy tries, through getting a job and studying for his Bar Mitzvah, to gain status. Set in Chicago during World War II.   10–13

☆ BULLA, CLYDE. *John Billington, Friend of Squanto,* ill. by Peter Burchard. T. Crowell, 1956.   7–9

———. *Riding the Pony Express,* ill. by Grace Paull. T. Crowell, 1948. An easy-to-read but never commonplace story of a boy who carried the mail in an emergency.   8–10

BULLA, CLYDE, and MICHAEL SYSON. *Conquista!* ill. by Ronald Himler. Crowell, 1978.   9–11

§ BURCHARD, PETER. *Bimby,* ill. by author. Coward, 1968.   9–11

———. *Chinwe.* Putnam, 1979.   11–13

———. *The Deserter.* Coward, 1974.   10–12

———. *Jed,* ill. by author. Coward, 1960.   10–13

———. *North by Night,* ill. by author. Coward, 1962. Swift moving escape tale of two Yankee soldiers from a South Carolina Confederate prison.   12 up

BYARS, BETSY. *Trouble River,* ill. by Rocco Negri. Viking, 1969.   9–12

● CAUDILL, REBECCA. *The Far-Off Land,* ill. by Brinton Turkle. Viking, 1964.   12–14

———. *Tree of Freedom,* ill. by Dorothy Bayley Morse. Viking, 1949.   12–14

☆ CLAPP, PATRICIA. *Constance: A Story of Early Plymouth.* Lothrop, 1968.   12–15

———. *I'm Deborah Sampson: A Soldier in the War of the Revolution.* Lothrop, 1977.   10–13

CLARK, ANN NOLAN. *Year Walk.* Viking, 1975. A sixteen-year-old Basque sheepherder comes to Idaho in the early 1900s.   8–11

COATSWORTH, ELIZABETH. *Away Goes Sally,* ill. by Helen Sewell. Macmillan, 1934.

———. *The Fair American,* ill. by Helen Sewell. Macmillan, 1940.

———. *Five Bushel Farm,* ill. by Helen Sewell. Macmillan, 1939.   10–12

COBLENTZ, CATHERINE. *Martin and Abraham Lincoln,* ill. by Trientja. Childrens Pr., 1967.   7–10

☆§ COLLIER, JAMES LINCOLN and CHRISTOPHER. *The Bloody Country.* Four Winds, 1976. This focuses on a Pennsylvania valley community in colonial times whose residents are persecuted by the Pennamites, older residents who attempt to drive the newcomers away.   11–14

———. *My Brother Sam Is Dead.* Four Winds, 1974. Tim Meeker tells of problems in Connecticut in 1775 after his father is imprisoned and his brother joins the rebels.   11–14

———. *The Winter Hero.* Four Winds, 1978. A story based on Shays' Rebellion with an appended note designating the factual from the fictional portions.   11–14

CONSTANT, ALBERTA WILSON. *Those Miller Girls!* ill. by Joe and Beth Krush. T. Crowell, 1965. A period story set in Kansas early in the century. The motherless Miller girls come with their father to his new job at Eastern Kansas Classical College.   10–12

DALGLIESH, ALICE. *Adam and the Golden Cock,* ill. by Leonard Weisgard. Scribner's, 1959.   8–9

☆ ———. *The Courage of Sarah Noble,* ill. by Leonard Weisgard. Scribner's, 1954.

———. *The 4th of July Story,* ill. by Marie Nonnast. Scribner's, 1956.

☆ ———. *The Thanksgiving Story,* ill. by Helen Sewell. Scribner's, 1954.   7–10

EDMONDS, WALTER D. *Bert Breen's Barn,* Little, 1975. Tom Dolan, son and grandson of ne'er-do-wells, steadily works toward his goal of owning an old but sturdy barn. A finely detailed study of country life in the early twentieth century.   12–15

☆ ———. *The Matchlock Gun,* ill. by Paul Lantz. Dodd, 1941. Newbery Medal. Describes an Indian attack on colonial settlers. A book which gives only one side of red-white relations.   10–12

§ FALL, THOMAS. *Canalboat to Freedom,* ill. by Joseph Cellini. Dial, 1966. Orphaned Benja is indentured as a canalboat worker. There he meets Lundius, a freed slave who becomes his friend and teacher. When Lundius is killed working for the Underground Railroad, Ben grieves. The emphasis in the story is on their developing friendship and on Ben's gradual realization of the horrors of slavery.   11–14

☆ FIELD, RACHEL. *Calico Bush,* ill. by Allen Lewis. Macmillan, 1931.   10–14

FINLAYSON, ANN. *Rebecca's War,* ill. by Sherry Streeter. Warne, 1972. A lively tale of the British occupation of Philadelphia.   11–14

FLEISCHMAN, SID. *Mr. Mysterious & Company,* ill. by Eric von Schmidt. Little, 1962. Traveling under their intriguing stage name, the delightful Hackett family give magic shows in small pioneer towns as they work their way west from Texas to a San Diego ranch. A very different and appealing story of the early West.   10–12

FLORY, JANE. *Faraway Dream.* Houghton, 1968.   9–11

———. *The Liberation of Clementine Tipton.* Houghton, 1974.   9–11

———. *A Tune for the Towpath.* Houghton, 1962.   9–11

FORBES, ESTHER. *Johnny Tremain,* ill. by Lynd Ward. Houghton, 1943. Newbery Medal.   12–14

☆ FORMAN, JAMES. *The Life and Death of Yellow Bird.* Farrar, 1973. The story of some of the Indians who did not come to government reservations after the battle at Little Bighorn in 1867.   12–16

§ FOX, PAULA. *The Slave Dancer,* ill. by Eros Keith. Bradbury, 1973. A white boy of 1840 is impressed into work on a slave ship. Newbery Medal.   11–14

§ FRITZ, JEAN. *Brady,* ill. by Lynd Ward. Coward, 1960.   10–13

———. *The Cabin Faced West,* ill. by Feodor Rojankovsky. Coward, 1958.   8–10

———. *Can't You Make Them Behave, King George?* ill. by Tomie de Paola. Coward, 1977.   8–10

———. *Early Thunder,* ill. by Lynd Ward. Coward, 1967. Set in Salem in 1775, the story of a boy whose loyalty moves from King to Patriot cause.   10–14

———. *I, Adam,* ill. by Peter Burchard. Coward, 1963. A good period story, set in New England in the mid-19th century, about a young man who decides that his real goal is an education.   11–14

GAUCH, PATRICIA LEE. *This Time, Tempe Wick?* ill. by Margot Tomes. Coward, 1974. Tempe prevents colonial soldiers from requisitioning her horse.   8–10

☆ GOBLE, PAUL and DOROTHY. *Red Hawk's Account of Custer's Last Battle,* ill. by authors. Pantheon, 1970.   10–12

☆ HAIG-BROWN, RODERICK. *The Whale People,* ill. by Mary Weiler. Morrow, 1963. A dignified picture of the great whale hunters and the training of a young Indian chief.   10–12

HALL, ANNA GERTRUDE. *Cyrus Holt and the Civil War,* ill. by Dorothy Bayley Morse. Viking, 1964.   9–11

HAUGAARD, ERIK CHRISTIAN. *Orphans of the Wind,* ill. by Milton Johnson. Houghton, 1966. A sea story set during the Civil War.   10–12

HAYS, WILMA PITCHFORD. *Christmas on the Mayflower,* ill. by Roger Duvoisin. Coward, 1956.   7–9

☆ ———. *May Day for Samoset,* ill. by Marilyn Miller. Coward, 1968.   7–9

☆ ———. *Pilgrim Thanksgiving,* ill. by Leonard Weisgard. Coward, 1955. The story of the first Thanksgiving.   7–9

———. *Yellow Fur and Little Hawk,* ill. by Anthony Rao. Coward, 1980.   7–9

HUNT, IRENE. *Across Five Aprils.* Follett, 1964. An impressive book both as a historically authenticated Civil War novel and as a beautifully written family story. The realistic treatment of the involved emotional conflicts within a border-state family is superb.   12 up

JOHNSON, ANNABEL and EDGAR. *Torrie.* Harper, 1960. It took the grim realities of a covered-wagon journey to California to jolt rebellious fourteen-year-old Torrie from her self-centered ways. Family relationships are well depicted in this pioneer story of the 1840s.   13–15

☆ JONES, WEYMAN. *The Edge of Two Worlds,* ill. by J. C. Kocsis. Dial, 1968.   10–13

☆ ———. *The Talking Leaf,* ill. by Harper Johnson. Dial, 1965.   10–12

☆ KEITH, HAROLD. *Rifles for Watie.* T. Crowell, 1957. Newbery Medal.   12–16

★ LAMPMAN, EVELYN. *Cayuse Courage.* Harcourt, 1970. A story of the Whitman Massacre told from the viewpoint of a young Indian boy.   10–12

———. *Once Upon the Little Big Horn,* ill. by John Gretzer. T. Crowell, 1971.   10–12

★ ———. *Squaw Man's Son.* Atheneum, 1978.   12–14

☆ ———. *Tree Wagon,* ill. by Robert Frankenberg. Doubleday, 1953.   10–13

☆ ———. *White Captives.* Atheneum, 1975.   11–13

☆ LATHAM, JEAN. *This Dear-Bought Land,* ill. by Jacob Landau. Harper, 1957. An outstanding story of Captain John Smith and the settlement of Jamestown.   11–14

☆ LEECH, JAY, and ZANE SPENCER. *Bright Fawn and Me,* ill. by Glo Coalson. T. Crowell, 1979. Set a century ago, this story is told by a Cheyenne child whose family is participating in an inter-tribal fair, and whose pleasure is dimmed by the fact that she is in charge of her small sister.   5–7

LENSKI, LOIS. *Puritan Adventure,* ill. by author. Lippincott, 1944. Massachusetts is the background of this vivid tale of colonial times. A lighthearted young aunt from England visits a strict Puritan family, bringing gaiety and laughter with her.   11–14

§ LEVY, MIMI COOPER. *Corrie and the Yankee,* ill. by Ernest Crichlow. Viking, 1959. Corrie, a little black girl on a South

Carolina plantation, rescues a wounded Yankee soldier and helps him to safety.   10–13

LOBEL, ARNOLD. *On the Day Peter Stuyvesant Sailed into Town,* ill. by author. Harper, 1971.   5–8

LOWREY, JANETTE. *Six Silver Spoons,* ill. by Robert Quackenbush. Harper, 1971. A British soldier helps two children carry safely the silver spoons made by Paul Revere during the Revolutionary War.   6–8

☆ McGRAW, ELOISE JARVIS. *Moccasin Trail.* Coward, 1952. A white boy attacked by a grizzly is rescued and raised by the Crow Indians. When he meets his family, his conflicts are convincingly portrayed.   11–14

☆ MARRIOTT, ALICE. *Indian Annie: Kiowa Captive.* McKay, 1965.   11–14

MEIGS, CORNELIA. *Clearing Weather,* ill. by Frank Dobias. Little, 1928.   11–14

———. *Master Simon's Garden,* ill. by John Rae. Macmillan, 1929.   11–14

§ MONJO, FERDINAND. *The Drinking Gourd,* ill. by Fred Brenner. Harper, 1970.   7–8

———. *Gettysburg: Tad Lincoln's Story,* ill. by Douglas Gorsline. Windmill/Dutton, 1976.   8–11

———. *Grand Papa and Ellen Aroon,* ill. by Richard Cuffari. Holt, 1974. Thomas Jefferson as seen by his favorite grandchild.   7–9

☆ ———. *Indian Summer,* ill. by Anita Lobel. Harper, 1968. A Kentucky family defends itself against Indian attack while their father is away fighting with George Washington.   7–8

———. *A Namesake for Nathan: Being an Account of Captain Nathan Hale by His Twelve-Year-Old Sister, Joanna,* ill. by Eros Keith. Coward, 1977.   10–13

———. *Poor Richard in France,* ill. by Brinton Turkle. Holt, 1973. Franklin's grandson reports on his exploits in France.   7–9

———. . *The Vicksburg Veteran,* ill. by Douglas Gorsline. Simon, 1971.   7–10

MOORE, S. E. *Secret Island,* ill. by Judith Gwyn Brown. Four Winds, 1977. Set in 1865, Johnny (come from New York City to stay at his aunt's farm) becomes involved with his cousin in spying on Southern sympathizers who are hunting the buried gold from a robbed train.   10–13

☆ O'DELL, SCOTT. *Carlota.* Houghton, 1977.   11–14

☆ ———. *Island of the Blue Dolphins.* Houghton, 1960. Newbery Medal.   11–14

☆ ———. *The King's Fifth,* ill. by Samuel Bryant. Houghton, 1966.   12–15

☆ ———. *Sing Down the Moon.* Houghton, 1970. Bright Morning is a young Navaho girl whose tribe is forced from their homes by white people and driven to Fort Sumner. She persuades her husband to escape and they start their peaceful life anew. The simple, almost terse, style makes more vivid the tragedy and danger.   11–14

———. *Sarah Bishop.* Houghton, 1980.   11–14

§ ———. *The 290.* Houghton, 1976.   11–13

☆ ———. *Zia.* Houghton, 1976.   10–13

§ PETRY, ANN. *Tituba of Salem Village.* T. Crowell, 1964.   12–15

POPE, ELIZABETH MARIE. *The Sherwood Ring,* ill. by Evaline Ness. Houghton, 1958. Beautifully told romances of Revolutionary times and of today are skillfully interwoven in a story rich in suspense and mystery.   12–16

RICHARD, ADRIENNE, *Wings.* Little, 1974. Pip and her brother live in southern California in the 1930s, enthralled by movies and airplanes and their mother's unorthodox friends.   10–14

☆ ROCKWOOD, JOYCE. *Groundhog's Horse,* ill. by Victor Kalin. Holt, 1978. Eleven-year-old Groundhog, a mid-eight-

eenth century Cherokee goes on a solitary quest to rescue his stolen horse and prove her worth to family and friends.   9–11

☆ ———. *To Spoil the Sun.* Holt, 1976. Rain Dove describes her family, her marriages, and the terrible scourges of illness and persecution that came with pale-skinned strangers who are so inexplicably hostile.   11–14

☆ SANDOZ, MARI. *The Story Catcher,* ill. by Elsie J. McCorkell. Westminster, 1963. The dramatic and moving story of Lance, a young Sioux brave who longs to achieve status with his people. The blending of style and subject is impressive.   11–14

SCHAEFER, JACK. *Mavericks,* ill. by Lorence Bjorklund. Houghton, 1967. This is a deeply romantic picture of the old West, written in a strong and flavorful prose, moving back and forth from old Jake Hanlon's past to the present.   12–15

§ SEBESTYEN, OUIDA. *Words by Heart.* Atlantic/Little, 1979. Set in the Reconstruction Era, this is an impressive novel about race relationships and nonviolence centering around a black family strong in their love and pride.   10–12

☆ SHARP, EDITH LAMBERT. *Nkwala,* ill. by William Winter. Little, 1958. Stirringly written historical tale of a young Spokane Indian who at last wins his adult name.   11–13

SNOW, RICHARD. *Freelon Starbird: Being a Narrative of the Extraordinary Hardships Suffered by an Accidental Soldier in a Beaten Army During the Autumn and Winter of 1776,* ill. by Ben F. Stahl. Houghton, 1976. Enlisting in the Continental Army on a lark, Snow's protagonist Freelon presents a tart, funny, vivid picture of life in Washington's army and the surprise attack on Trenton.   12–14

☆ SPEARE, ELIZABETH GEORGE. *Calico Captive,* ill. by W. T. Mars. Houghton, 1957. Stirring junior novel of Miriam Willard, a young Indian captive taken to Canada during the French and Indian Wars.   11–15

● ———. *The Witch of Blackbird Pond.* Houghton, 1958. Newbery Medal.   12–16

STEELE, WILLIAM O. *The Buffalo Knife,* ill. by Paul Galdone. Harcourt, 1952. A thousand-mile flatboat trip is an exciting adventure for a boy of nine.   9–12

———. *The Far Frontier,* ill. by Paul Galdone. Harcourt, 1959.   10–14

———. *The Perilous Road,* ill. by Paul Galdone. Harcourt, 1958.   11–13

☆ ———. *Wayah of the Real People,* ill. by Isa Barnett. Holt, 1964.   11–13

§ TAYLOR, MILDRED. *Roll of Thunder, Hear My Cry,* ill. by Jerry Pinkney. Dial, 1976. Newbery Medal.   12–14

TAYLOR, THEODORE. *The Odyssey of Ben O'Neal,* ill. by Richard Cuffari. Doubleday, 1977. A sequel to *Teetoncey* and *Teetoncey and Ben O'Neal* set aboard ship at the turn of the century continues the adventures of Tee and Ben.   11–13

———. *Teetoncey,* ill. by Richard Cuffari. Doubleday, 1974.

———. *Teetoncey and Ben O'Neal,* ill. by Richard Cuffari. Doubleday, 1975. Teetoncey is the one female survivor of a shipwreck off Cape Hatteras in 1898. The first book tells of her rescue, while the second recounts the struggle to recover valuable cargo aboard the sunken ship.   10–13

● TURKLE, BRINTON. *Obadiah the Bold,* ill. by author. Viking, 1965.   8–9

———. *Rachel and Obadiah,* ill. by author. Dutton, 1978. 8–9

● ———. *Thy Friend, Obadiah,* ill. by author. Viking, 1969. 7–9

UCHIDA, YOSHIKO. *Journey Home,* ill by Charles Robinson. Atheneum, 1978. In a sequel to the title below, the family adjusts to its return home.   10–12

———. *Journey to Topaz,* ill. by Donald Carrick. Scribner's,

1971. A Japanese-American family is sent to a World War II relocation center in Utah.   10–12

———. *Samurai of Gold Hill,* ill. by Ati Forberg. Scribner's, 1972. A well-paced story of a group of Japanese immigrants who come to California in 1869.   10–12

VINING, ELIZABETH GRAY. *The Taken Girl.* Viking, 1972.   11–14

WIBBERLEY, LEONARD. *John Treegate's Musket.* Farrar, 1959. First in an outstanding series. Other titles are: *Peter Treegate's War* (1960), *Sea Captain from Salem* (1961), *Treegate's Raiders* (1962).   12–15

———. *The Last Battle.* Farrar, 1976.   11–14

§ ———. *Leopard's Prey.* Farrar, 1971.   11–14

———. *Red Pawns.* Farrar, 1973.   11–14

WILDER, LAURA INGALLS. *The First Four Years,* ill. by Garth Williams. Harper, 1971. Found among the author's papers after her death, and published without revision, this is the story of her first years as a farmer's wife on a South Dakota homestead. The same charm and virtues as the Little House books.   10–14

———. *Little House in the Big Woods,* ill. by Garth Williams. Harper, 1953. Other titles in the series are: *Little House on the Prairie, On the Banks of Plum Creek, By the Shores of Silver Lake, Farmer Boy, The Long Winter, Little Town on the Prairie, These Happy Golden Years.*   9–14

☆ WILSON, HAZEL. *His Indian Brother,* ill. by Robert Henneberger. Abingdon, 1955. Based on a true incident of the 1800s is this story of Brad Porter, left alone in a Maine pioneer cabin and rescued from starvation by an Indian chief and his son.   10–14

☆§ WOJCIECHOWSKA, MAIA. *Odyssey of Courage: The Story of Alvar Nuñez Cabeza de Vaca,* ill. by Alvin Smith. Atheneum, 1965. Cabeza de Vaca's journey, stressing his affection for the Indians and their regard for him.   12–14

☆§ WORMSER, RICHARD. *The Black Mustanger,* ill. by Don Bolognese. Morrow, 1971. Set in Texas in the period after the Civil War, the story of a white boy whose mentor is a cowboy, half black and half Apache.   10–14

§ WRISTON, HILDRETH. *Susan's Secret,* ill. by W. T. Mars. Farrar, 1957. Suspense-filled story of a little Vermont girl who undertook her absent family's task of guiding fugitive slaves to the next Underground station.   9–12

☆ YATES, ELIZABETH. *Carolina's Courage,* ill. by Nora S. Unwin. Dutton, 1964.   8–10

YEP, LAURENCE. *Dragonwings.* Harper, 1975. A fascinating view of life in the Chinese community of San Francisco in the first years of the twentieth century, including a description of the earthquake.   10–14

Historical Fiction:
Other Countries

BARTOS-HÖPPNER, B. *Hunters of Siberia,* tr. by Anthea Bell. Walck, 1969. A novel set in the early part of the century that is both a plea for conservation of wild life and a remarkable picture of a way of life now ended.   12–15

BAUMANN, HANS. *Sons of the Steppe.* Walck, 1958. Authentic background adds to the story of two of Genghis Khan's grandsons.   12–16

CHAUNCY, NAN. *Hunted in Their Own Land,* ill. by Victor G. Ambrus. Seabury, 1973. The tragic story of the gradual annihilation of the aborigines in Tasmania by the whites.   12–15

DICKINSON, PETER. *Dancing Bear,* ill. by David Smee. Little,

1973. In Byzantium in 558, Silvester, a slave, accompanied by a bear and a holy man, searches for his mistress who was kidnapped by the Huns.   10–14

☆ HARRIS, CHRISTIE. *Raven's Cry,* ill. by Bill Reid. Atheneum, 1966.   10–15

☆ ———. *West with the White Chiefs,* ill. by Walter Ferro. Atheneum, 1965.   11–15

☆ HOUSTON, JAMES. *The White Archer: An Eskimo Legend,* ill. by author. Harcourt, 1967. Kungo is a young Eskimo who vows revenge when his parents are killed and his sister is taken captive by a band of Indians. The description of his years of cold, patient planning is in low key.   10–12

☆ LAMPMAN, EVELYN. *The Tilted Sombrero,* ill. by Ray Cruz. Doubleday, 1966.   11–14

LEWIS, ELIZABETH FOREMAN. *To Beat a Tiger: One Needs a Brother's Help,* ill. by John Heuhnergarth. Holt, 1956.   14–17

———. *Young Fu of the Upper Yangtze,* ill. by Kurt Wiese. Holt, 1932. Newbery Medal. The 1973 edition of this book contains illustrations by Ed Young.   13–15

LITTLE, JEAN. *From Anna,* ill. by Jean Sandin. Harper, 1972. Anna adjusts to Canadian life after her family emigrates from Germany during the Nazi regime.   9–11

———. *Listen for the Singing.* Dutton, 1977. Anna's family encounters prejudice when World War II starts.   10–12

MUHLENWEG, FRITZ. *Big Tiger and Christian,* ill. by Rafaello Busoni. Pantheon, 1952. Long but well-sustained story of the journey of two boys across China and the Gobi Desert in the 1920s.   11–13

NAMIOKA, LENSEY. *The Samurai and the Long-Nosed Devils.* McKay, 1976. Two sixteenth-century Japanese "ronin" (samurai whose liege lords have been ousted and who are available for service) take on the job of protecting a Portuguese missionary and his soldier-companion.   12–14

———. *Valley of the Broken Cherry Trees.* Delacorte, 1980. The two ronin of *The Samurai* investigate the mutilation of the trees and find themselves deeply involved in political conflict.   12–14

O'DELL, SCOTT. *The Captive.* Houghton, 1979. A sixteenth-century story of an idealistic missionary who comes from Spain to the New World, is shipwrecked, and is helped by a Mayan girl.   12–14

PATERSON, KATHERINE. *The Master Puppeteer,* ill. by Haru Wells. T. Crowell, 1976.   11–15

———. *Of Nightingales That Weep,* ill. by Haru Wells. T. Crowell, 1974.   11–15

———. *The Sign of the Chrysanthemum,* ill. by Peter Landa. T. Crowell, 1973.   8–11
Three novels of feudal Japan.

RITCHIE, RITA. *The Golden Hawks of Genghis Khan,* ill. by Lorence F. Bjorklund. Dutton, 1958.

———. *Secret Beyond the Mountains.* Dutton, 1960.

———. *The Year of the Horse,* ill. by Lorence F. Bjorklund. Dutton, 1957. These are outstanding tales of the years of Mongol supremacy.   12–15

● VINEBERG, ETHEL. *Grandmother Came from Dworitz: A Jewish Story,* ill. by Rita Briansky. Tundra, 1969. The first of a series of books on the origins of Canadians (a French edition of each will be published), the story based on the life of the author or illustrator of the book. The text here is sedate but the material is fascinating, giving a vivid picture of the restrictions upon nineteenth-century Russian Jews, their communal life, and their emigration.   9–12

WALSH, JILL PATON. *The Emperor's Winding Sheet.* Farrar, 1974.   11–14

§ WATSON, SALLY. *Jade.* Holt, 1968. A lively tale of an eighteenth-century girl who becomes a pirate.   11–14

Chapter Thirteen: Biography

Biography may be defined as that branch of literature that deals with the history of individual men's and women's lives. Thus the three essential ingredients of good biography are history, the person, and literary artistry. Facts should be authentic and verifiable; the subject should be considered as an individual rather than as a paragon or type; and the writing should be a conscious work of art. This description—with some amplification—not only defines the genre, but suggests the standards by which it can be judged.

Biography As History

Authenticity

If a biography is the history of a person's life, it should be as accurate and authentic as research can make it. That statement is true for all biographies, but its application varies, depending on the nature of the biographee's contributions, and the life the person led. Even today, we know very little about Emily Dickinson's life, and authors wishing to write books about Dickinson are forced to do a great amount of internal analysis of her poems for insights into the kind of person who might have written them. For literary figures, internal analysis of their writings is essential regardless of how much we know about their public and private lives. When they leave detailed diaries or journals, as the writer André Gide did, the biographer is faced with a different problem: the mass of information must be checked against the recorded impressions of the people named by Gide. If these seem contradictory, the biographer must discover what the attitude of Gide's contemporary was—friendly, worshipful, or definitely antagonistic. This may involve consulting the available writings of still other contemporaries who knew both individuals and who in turn left records of their relationships.

When the subject of a biography is a famous public figure, such as George Washington, the search for authenticity takes the biographer to government archives for official papers relating to Washington's life as president. But that is only the beginning, for the same checking and cross-checking with contemporaries' opinions must be pursued. The mass of documents is overwhelming, but rarely definitive, and a good biographer alerts the reader that what is being written is based on known available evidence. A good biographer resembles a good detective, following clues, interviewing people, hearing what the subject has to say, and then—and only then—reaching a tentative conclusion that is presented to readers, who serve as the jury.

Accuracy and authenticity are easier to achieve when writing about people of the past. They are very difficult to achieve when writing of the living or the recently dead. In biography for children, much of what we know is true may be deleted because it is contrary to the image children's authors and publishers wish to convey to young readers. The problem of accuracy can be demonstrated by looking at three biographies of Martin Luther King, Jr., written for children of elementary school age. The easiest of the books, *The Picture Life of Martin Luther King, Jr.* by Margaret B. Young, covers the tumultuous year of the Montgomery, Alabama, bus boycott in one sentence: "After a year the laws were changed." Ed Clayton's *Martin Luther King; The Peaceful Warrior* and James T. De Kay's *Meet Martin Luther King, Jr.* contain more detail about the violence of that year but raise questions about their own authenticity. Is Clayton right when he says that the bomb attempt on King's house found Mrs. King and their daughter in danger ("Coretta grabbed their infant daughter and ran to the rear of the house")? Or is deKay more accurate in telling us that Coretta King was talking to a friend while Yoki (the daughter) slept in a back room? This particular example of discrepancy may seem minor, but it alerts us to the fact that very few biographies for children can be considered accurate or authentic because the authors are simplifying information for young readers, and seldom engage in primary source research.

Objectivity

The *Talmud* says "We see things as we are, not as they are," a statement which reminds us that all data are filtered through human minds. The best biographers are aware of their own biases and take special care to be sure they do not interfere with the search for whatever degree of truth can be found. Good biographers know they are not free to offer personal opinions as fact or to present an interpretation for which there is no evidence. They let deeds speak for themselves. If the behavior of the subject seems ambiguous, the author may speculate about the contradictory evidence, but may not take sides to tell the reader what to think. Was Sam Houston completely honest and disinterested in his dealings with the Indians and with his Cherokee foster father? Marquis James in *The Raven*, a biography of Sam Houston, never tells us how he regards Houston's actions. He presents the evidence and lets us draw our own conclusions. And readers of *The Raven* may

differ in their judgment of Sam, just as Sam's contemporaries themselves differed.

It also follows that the biographer may report only those words and thoughts which were recorded, either by the subject or by those contemporary observers in a position to know. Some biographers have got around this strict limitation by saying, "Perhaps he thought . . ." or "Perhaps he meant what he said, who knows?" Lytton Strachey uses this device repeatedly in his *Queen Victoria*. When the gouty old king whom she was to succeed asked the young Victoria for her favorite tune, she replied without a moment's hesitation, "God Save the King." This, Strachey tells us, "has been praised as an early example of a tact which was afterwards famous." They he adds cryptically, "But she was a very truthful child, and perhaps it was her genuine opinion." He closes his book with a dramatic use of this device. Describing the dying queen, old, blind, and silent, he suggests that she *may perhaps* have recalled her past. Then, as if Victoria were thinking aloud, he briefly and tenderly reviews her life, going back to the little girl in "sprigged muslin, and the trees and the grass at Kensington." Jeanette Eaton also uses it in her account of the dying Washington in *Leader by Destiny*. It is a legitimate device that, overused, may become a not too subtle method of influencing the reader's opinions.

Viewpoint

Biography *is* a craft—like all the other arts—in that it employs techniques which can be learned by anybody, which are outside personal commitment. It can be loosely called a science in that, for part of his labors, the biographer proceeds inductively: he collects facts in order to arrive at conclusions from them. It is an art, however lowly, because the biographer is himself interfused into what he has made, and, like the novelist and the painter, shapes his material in order to create effects.

. . . The novelist's pen is a delicate instrument. If the biographer holds something like that pen in one hand, he has to wield a shovel with the other. His ore is not inner experience, the quicksilver stuff of gland and nerve. It is brute matter, wrested from the earth. . . . To exist at all, it must feed upon the truth of facts, and yet to exist on its highest level, it must pursue the truth of interpretation.—Paul Murray Kendall, *The Art of Biography.* W. W. Norton and Co., New York, 1965, p. xii.

Documentation

For many people, one of the most important tests of a good biography is the accuracy and thoroughness of its documentation. Nicolson in *The Development of English Biography* insists that a biography should be as scrupulously documented as history. Strachey's *Queen Victoria* is a model in this respect, for every incident and every description is conscientiously documented in the footnotes.

In the past, few juvenile biographies were documented by footnotes, although most authors did supply sources in a separate section, a bibliography, or an afterword. Some juvenile biographies, such as *W. E. B. DuBois* by Virginia Hamilton do contain footnotes as well as extensive bibliographies. Others, such as *Fanny Kemble's America* by John Anthony Scott, are written by people whose authority has been established by their adult writings on the subject. Whether children read the footnotes or are impressed by the author's qualifications is not important. What matters is that these changes reflect an increased concern on the part of authors and publishers to give young readers the best biographies possible within the restrictions imposed by age.

Biography As the Individual

All of us are familiar with older biographies which presented Washington the ever truthful, Lincoln the sad, and Benjamin Franklin the thrifty. Franklin seems to have been cast in the role of the thrifty merely because he wrote a number of wise saws on the desirability of this virtue. As a matter of fact, he sent home from England a continual stream of handsome and extravagant presents, such as silver-handled knives, fine china, a whole box of table glass, carpets, even a harpsichord for Sally.[1] Later, in France, his bills for his wine cellar were lavish, and he finally remarked plaintively that frugality was "a virtue I never could acquire in myself."[2] So "perhaps," as the biographers say, his adages on thrift were reminders for his unthrifty self, as well as for the rest of the world.

Franklin is indeed a good example of a figure almost spoiled for young people in the past be-

cause he had been typed as a paragon. Today in the new biographies, such as Thomas Fleming's *Benjamin Franklin*, young people and even children may catch a glimpse of the real Franklin—witty, worldly, urbane, adored by the ladies and adoring them in turn, equally at home in the wilderness and in the court, a scientist, a man of letters, a diplomat, an amateur musician, lazy and prodigiously industrious, in short, a composite of strength and weakness on a grand scale, with a tremendous brain directing the whole. To have made Franklin, of all men, into the image of a stuffy prig was a crime. To rediscover the whole Franklin and reveal him to this generation, as Carl Van Doren has done, is a crowning achievement of modern biography.

Another achievement of current biography for both adults and children is the growing recognition that white males were not the only members of the human race to lead exciting lives and to contribute to civilization, but that women and members of racial and ethnic minorities also have a rich heritage, and have made significant contributions.

The Whole Person

James Boswell's *Life of Samuel Johnson* (1791) is considered one of the greatest biographies in the English language and it is as fully developed a portrait as we could wish for. But, despite Boswell's early demonstration of what a good biography should be, the majority of biographies for both adults and children have treated their subjects as paragons rather than as fallible human beings.

Why this idealization took place is a complex story, but basically biography was treated less as a literary genre than as a political and social tool. In the United States, following the publication of *The Life and Memorable Acts of George Washington* (1800) by the Reverend Mason Weems, the pattern was set for American biographers to depict the country's leaders as paragons. Part of this impetus came from the religious leaders of the nation; part of it came from the historians who were depicting the new nation as fulfilling its "Manifest Destiny." In England, the rise of what we now term Victorian morality dictated that the more human side of people be suppressed, and political factors here, too, influenced whom biographers saw as worthy.

---

1. Carl Van Doren, *Benjamin Franklin*, pp. 176–277.
2. Ibid., p. 637.

From *Benjamin Franklin* by Thomas Fleming. Engraving from the Granger Collection.

possible for an author to think of writing a juvenile biography about Margaret Sanger, the great birth-control pioneer, or about blacks like Malcolm X who had led horrendous childhoods.

This new openness does not mean that anything and everything is acceptable in a juvenile biography. While the definition of what constitutes good taste has changed, the concept itself remains. Authors must always be sure that they are not sensationalizing any events of a person's life. They must be able to point out if a particular fact in their subject's life was very important to the individual being written about, or if it was an idiosyncrasy. Boswell tells us that Samuel Johnson would sneak out after dark to buy oysters for his cat. He did not want the servants to know what he was up to. That was an idiosyncrasy. Had he been sneaking out to visit a mistress, that information would be more important to an understanding of Johnson.

In scholarly biographies, read only by university professors and lay people deeply interested in the person being written about, it has been customary throughout most of the past two centuries to depict the subject as a whole person. Popular biographies, on the other hand, written for the general adult public, have traditionally ignored the personal life if the subject had what were termed "vices." When writing for children the cleansing process was taken a step further and personal tragedies and failures were passed over. In many cases, juvenile biographies did not even depict the person's death.

As society's values have changed and new areas of research have developed, the content acceptable in juvenile biographies has also changed. Divorce is not now seen as a vice, to be suppressed, but as an event to be explained. Describing incidents of failure, rather than lessening a person's worth, shows readers that all people face setbacks at some point in their lives. And we are coming to understand that death is a part of life and cannot be ignored.

By broadening the parameters of what constitutes acceptable content in juvenile biographies, we have also broadened the range of people who can be written about. When the older, rigid standards were in effect, it was im-

Viewpoint

Biography, like fiction, should have its characters so completely realized, its background so true, that everything that happens will seem inevitable. But the characters in the series books are all of a pattern. There is a convention that great men and women invariably started out as normal and likeable youngsters, good mixers, and good sports. There is no inkling of the fact that loneliness and oddity often bear a dark fruit of their own. . . .

In two popular biographies in the Childhood of Famous Americans Series, *Nancy Hanks, Kentucky Girl*, and *Mary Todd Lincoln*, the heroines are so conventional as to be startling to anyone who has read Carl Sandburg's *Abraham Lincoln*. Mary Todd's disastrous disposition, which was to harry the great president so sorely, is passed off as "that terrible Todd temper." She is represented as spunky and lovable, gay, generous, and impulsive, flying off the handle, shaking her curls, and stamping her little foot.

. . . What is gained by telling children that the great of the world have always been well adjusted and genteel?—Fran Martin, "Stop Watering Down Biographies." Reprinted from *Junior Libraries*, December 1959. Published by R. R. Bowker Company. (A Xerox company) Copyright © 1959 by R. R. Bowker Company.

Vivid Details

One of the best methods of assuring that the whole person is presented in a biography is to steep it with rich and arresting details. An adolescent or an adult reading about how Samuel Johnson always had to go through a door on one particular foot finds that information interesting. The reader may already know that certain baseball players always touch third base on their way to the outfield. Few of us, whether children or adults, can easily identify with people who have changed history—whether through politics or breaking Babe Ruth's home-run record—and these human details help us know that great feats in life are accomplished by human beings and not by paragons.

In the past, biographies written for young people failed at precisely this point. They told children about the large affairs in which their subjects played a part but neglected to give any account of the individuals' amusing idiosyncrasies, peculiar bents, and special talents which made them unique. Children delight in Franklin's account of himself as a boy floating in a pond on his back propelled by a kite;[3] or in the story of Davy Crockett crossing an icy river in December, sometimes in and sometimes out of the water, but managing to keep dry his keg of gunpowder, a bundle, and his gun, "Betsy";[4] or of Lincoln holding a child upside down to make tracks on the ceiling as a joke on the stepmother he dearly loved, a joke he righted with a fresh coat of whitewash.[5]

To be told that Penn dressed in sober clothes is dull enough. To learn that even after he turned Quaker he still loved good apparel and went to meet the velvet-clad Lord Baltimore in sober brown but cut by the best London tailor from the finest materials—ah, that is more human.[6] To read that Penn was tried for holding a meeting with other Quakers is dreary, but young people warm immediately to the picture of Penn on trial, shut up in a cage at the back of the courtroom, shouting out his own defense so effectively that he won the jury to his side and later won the right of the jury to have its decisions upheld in the English courts.[7] Little incidents and big ones which reveal spirited human beings who will not be downed and who travel their own unique way bring the individual to life for the reader. Revealing details are the very essence of good biography.

Biography As Literature

If biography is a branch of literature, then it, like any other work of art, should be a consciously planned composition. It has a subject, a theme, unity attained through that theme, style, a pattern of the whole, and a pattern of the parts. These may not be evident to the casual reader, but if the life is written with any skill, they are there.

Theme and Unity

Biography, like history, is based on documented facts. No liberties may be taken with these facts; no flights of fancy are permissible. The biographer begins by assembling all the documents and examining all the evidence. But good biographers feel that they should not give all their accumulated research to the reader in its endless and often trivial details. They recognize that there is a difference between the rich and arresting details discussed earlier and endless presentation of trivia. Each biographer must choose those details which will most truly reveal the subject as the author has come to know him or her. It is in this matter of selection and organization that the biography ceases to be purely history and becomes a work of art. For the author, in reading all the sources and weighing all the evidence, gradually develops a theme. The theme of a biography makes a fundamental statement about the person's life as seen by the biographer. This theme is not, and never can be, the total truth about the person's life, but if it has emerged from the research, it provides readers with a unified view of the man or woman being written about. Biographers fail to write good biography if they approach the research process with a theme in mind, for then, despite all good intentions, they will make the data fit their preconceptions.

Turning to children's or young people's biographies, we often find the theme in the title—*Carry On, Mr. Bowditch* (Nathaniel Bowditch), *Invincible Louisa* (Louisa M. Alcott), and *Susette La Flesche: Voice of the Omaha Indians.*

3. Carl Van Doren, *Benjamin Franklin,* p. 17.

4. Constance Rourke, *Davy Crockett,* pp. 94–97.

5. Ingri and Edgar d'Aulaire, *Abraham Lincoln* (unpaged).

6. Elizabeth Janet Gray Vining, *Penn,* p. 206.

7. Ibid., Chapter 15.

From *Susette La Flesche: Voice of the Omaha Indians* by Margaret Crary. Photograph from the Nebraska State Historical Society.

In *Leader by Destiny*, the life of George Washington, Jeanette Eaton shows how over and over again circumstances and the times interfered with Washington's life and called him to other ways of living. He might have been a homespun frontiersman, playing a gallant part no doubt, but his brother's death gave him Mount Vernon and turned him into a country gentleman. This role was forwarded by his neighbor's wife, the lovely Sally Fairfax (destiny again), who taught him the manners and ways of gentlemen. Then the country squire was called upon for soldiery and more soldiery, and finally he was made the head of the Continental Army. Seven long years of campaigning followed, with his whole heart yearning for the gracious life of Mount Vernon. Then came peace and a chance to realize his desires, but destiny called him once more, this time to the presidency, the gravest responsibility an American had ever faced. Washington played a great part in every role he undertook, but it would seem that these roles were not of his own choosing. He would have been a leader in any situation, but destiny called him to national greatness.

Similar in theme is James Haskins's *Ralph*

Bunche: A Most Reluctant Hero. Bunche's life was filled with "firsts": the first black to earn a Ph.D. in political science; the first black to have a desk in the State Department; and the first American black to win the Nobel Peace Prize. He was a man who seemed always to be in the right place at the right time and his skills were recognized and appreciated by the world's leaders. He would have been content to teach, write, and spend time with his family, but world events called him, like Washington, to greatness.

Not all biographies adhere so closely and obviously to theme and unity as those just cited, certainly not the early examples of biography. But modern biographies, including those for young people, seem to follow this pattern and are organized around a theme which gives a dramatic unity to the book.

Style and Pattern

If biography is to be judged as literature, it must also have a pleasing style. As one authority has said, style is "the auditory effect of prose." The prose must be good to read and it must be appropriate to the subject matter and to the mood of the story.

A fine example of style and pattern in biography is Carl Sandburg's *Abe Lincoln Grows Up*, adapted from his book for adults, *The Prairie Years*, which reads aloud so easily and naturally you just keep reading. Of Tom Lincoln, the father, Sandburg writes:

He wasn't exactly lazy, he was sort of independent, and liked to be where he wasn't interfered with. . . . He was a wild buck at fighting, when men didn't let him alone. A man talked about a woman once in a way Tom Lincoln didn't like. And in the fight that came, Tom bit a piece of the man's nose off. . . . Though he was short spoken, he knew yarns, could crack jokes, and had a reputation as a story-teller when he got started. (pp. 12–13)

A different use of pattern is well illustrated by the opening chapter of Elizabeth Gray Vining's *Penn*, written under her unmarried name, Elizabeth Janet Gray. She describes Penn's father, young Captain Penn, already rising in the English navy, in which eventually he becomes admiral; his wife with her Irish estates; the king with his two sons, James and Charles; a shoemaker named George Fox; an eight-month-old heiress, Gulielma Springett; and the lusty baby, William Penn.

And all these scattered lives were to play their part in the life of the baby who slept and cried and ate and slept again in sight of the steep walls of the old, grim Tower, into which had gone, down the centuries, many prisoners, young and old, frightened and defiant; and from which fewer had come out. The Tower too had its part. (p. 7)

Here, we are told, are all the threads of the story, all the important elements in the life of the baby, who grew to be the man of whom it was said later, "the world has not yet caught up with William Penn." There in that first chapter are the small patterns which will make up the large pattern.

These examples show how biography, although as scrupulously documented as history, may become in the act of composition a branch of literature. Yet good adult biographies are as sound sources for facts as histories. This may also be true of biographies for children and young people but with certain differences.

Biography for Children

Historically, juvenile biographies have differed greatly from adult biographies, but the gap between the two has narrowed as children have become more knowledgeable and adults have become more respectful of children's abilities. While not all current biographies are documented, more and more of them contain footnotes and bibliographic references since the authors know they may be reviewed by people who know the subject as well as by people who are engrossed by the story.

No longer do authors systematically and automatically suppress the human weaknesses of their subjects or avoid relating personal tragedies. As was indicated earlier in the discussion of "The Whole Person," a new level of integrity has been achieved in the writing of juvenile biography.

However, differences remain. Biographies for children will probably never approach the level of documentation that is found in the scholarly adult biographies. Children who can cope with that kind of writing should be introduced to the adult biographies and allowed to find their own levels of understanding.

But if we compare juvenile biography with the popularized adult biographies, we find very few differences, and those that do exist are in favor of the juvenile authors. No biography for children exploits the person being written about to the degree that popularizations for adults do. If personal scandal is introduced into a juvenile biography, it is because it is absolutely vital for understanding the life of the woman or man being written about. In adult biographies, such scenes are often present to titillate the reader rather than to shed light on the subject.

Biographers for young readers usually feel that it is legitimate to cast known facts about an episode into actual dialogue and to interpret the thoughts of their characters; that is, they put words into their subjects' mouths and thoughts into their heads for which there is no documentary evidence. Popularized adult biographies do the same. The authors' excuse, and it is a legitimate one, is that this technique produces a more dramatic narrative.

Undocumented dialogue produces one of two hybrids of genuine biography: first, there is *fictionalized biography*, in which the facts are documented and only a few liberties are taken, such as occasional dialogue for which there is no record; and, second, there is *biographical fiction*, which takes a historical character as a basis for a story semihistorical in nature.

Fictionalized Biography

Most biographies for children are fictionalized. That is, they are based on careful research, but known facts are often presented in dramatic episodes complete with conversation. For instance, Elizabeth Vining, in relating the moving quarrel between Admiral Penn and his young son lately turned Quaker, begins the account with the old Admiral exploding wrathfully, "... three people you may *not* thee and thou—the King, the Duke of York, and myself." This is much more exciting than the plain statement, "The Admiral objected to his son's Quaker use of thee and thou." The quarrel continues the next day, climaxing in the Admiral's terrible threat:

"I am going to kneel down and pray to God that you may not be a Quaker, nor go ever again to any more of their meetings."

and in William's frenzied reply:

"Before I will hear thee pray after any such manner," he cried, "I'll leap out of the window."

It was a high window, too, and, according to Vining, William was saved only by the interruption of one of his father's most elegant friends come to call. Since Vining is a scrupulous research scholar, she probably had some sort of documentary evidence for this quarrel. She does, for instance, give the Admiral's actual letters to William summoning him home for this grim conference. Assuming then that there is a historical basis for the scene, we accept the dialogue, which certainly heightens the drama, the words fairly crackling with suppressed emotion.

Perhaps fictionalized biography is the best pattern of biography for young people. There is no doubt that dialogue based on facts, written by a scholar and an artist, brings history to life and re-creates living, breathing people, who make a deep impression on children.

Biographical Fiction

Jean Lee Latham's Newbery Medal book, *Carry On, Mr. Bowditch,* is sometimes catalogued as fiction, but the reason is not clear. In her acceptance speech the author describes her book as fictionalized biography. She probably makes no more use of imaginary dialogue than does Vining in *Penn,* which is listed as biography. *Mr. Bowditch* does include perhaps a dozen imaginary characters, such as members of ships' crews, but the author adds that "there are about four dozen historical characters . . . handled with accuracy as to time, place, and personality."[8] Certainly this book, based on all the historical documents available, is a magnificent record of a little-known genius. In purpose and in effect on the reader it is biography.

These distinctions among different types of historical literature are not greatly important to the children's use of the books. When young people read biographical fiction, they might be warned, "This is the way it may have happened, but history does not tell us for sure." And when they read biography or even fictionalized biography, they might be told, "Insofar as the author can find historical records, this is the way it *did* happen."

Briefly, the chief distinctions between good biographies for adults and those for children are that, in the latter, sources are less often stated, unsavory episodes are usually omitted, and recorded events are more likely to be enlivened with imaginary dialogue. On the whole, however, modern biographies for children represent scholarly research and conscientious retelling of events in a dramatic style. Such characteristics make these books some of the finest modern contributions to children's literature.

8. *Horn Book,* August 1956.

Work Methods of Biographers

From book-jackets, authors' notes, lists of suggested readings, prefatory remarks, articles by authors on their research methods, and even from those pages in which writers express thanks to those who have helped them, it is clear that the research for biographies for children is taken very seriously indeed. Evidence of careful documentation is found in more and more books for younger and younger children.

Dorothy Sterling, for example, when working on *Captain of the Planter,* a biography of Robert Smalls, went to Beaufort and Charleston, where she talked to people who had known Smalls, and had two visits with his son. She pored over old newspapers and photographs, ransacked library collections and archives, and picked up every lead by correspondence.

Viewpoint

As to the question about the moral obligation of the author to distinguish between fact and fiction in juvenile biography—the author should not pretend to be writing one hundred percent fact if he is introducing invented scenes and dialogue. What I imagine is always based on facts that make the scenes possible and usually even likely. I make the dialogue as plausible as I can, and I always use historical dialogue whenever history obliges me by preserving the words I happen to need.

So much for the line between fact and fiction. Even more important are the needs of the present times. We need to inspire our gifted young people to make an attempt at greatness. We need to make them want to reach out after that splendid, elusive, brass ring known as achievement and make it theirs. Our age is more tawdry than we wish it to be, and we yearn for some heroes and heroines for ourselves and for the future. I have not yet utterly abandoned the Western world. It has produced many men and women who still make my skin prickle. I have not yet abandoned the American experiment, for it has produced large numbers of people whom I wish I might have emulated. That is why I would like my books to arouse young people. To make them understand that all great human beings were once uncertain children, unaware of their powers. I want my books to incite children to dare to do something marvelous. For, if they dare, perhaps they will succeed.—F. N. Monjo. "Great Men, Melodies, Experiments, Plots, Predictability, and Surprises," *The Horn Book Magazine,* October 1975. Copyright © 1975 by The Horn Book, Inc. Reprinted by permission.

Aileen Fisher and Olive Rabe, in "Writing About the Alcotts,"[9] explain how they used the source material collected and published by others and the biographies of men and women who had played a part in the Alcotts' lives, reading whatever could be found about the family and the period. Each worked on the same chapter separately; one welded the two versions and the other edited and revised the resulting chapter. The authors decided to write the story from the viewpoint of a family member so that the book would have an intimate feeling, although they knew it restricted the action to what could be observed.

There are small variations in the ways in which authors patiently dig, sift, compare, record, and revise, but one thing is paramount: a respect for the truth. Marchette Chute says it beautifully:

To put the whole thing into a single sentence: you will never succeed in getting at the truth if you think you know, ahead of time, what the truth ought to be.[10]

The Series

The Bobbs-Merrill Childhood books seem to have launched, in 1932, the biography fever with both children and publishers. As a result, not only is the numerical impact of these books staggering, but the duplication of biographies has reached the point where it is a major feat of memory to recall which George Washington is whose and whose Abraham Lincoln is which.

It would be convenient to be able to make a judgment of each series as a whole, but this is impossible, because within one set of books some are thin or pedestrian and others are of major importance. Although it is difficult to select from a list, it is wasteful for schools or homes or libraries to order every one of any series. It is best to watch for authoritative reviews of individual books. Many of the books discussed in this chapter are from one or another of the series. However, since each series is designed to perform a definite function in the child's reading program, several should be familiar to adults working with children.

Two outstanding series for the beginning reader are the Harper and Row "I Can Read" history books and the Young Crowell Biogra-

phies. The former includes several life stories told from the child's viewpoint; the latter emphasizes minority group members, although it does not focus on them exclusively. The Bobbs-Merrill Childhood of Famous Americans series has high-interest low-vocabulary books, rigidly patterned and often determinedly merry. The Random House Step-Up Books, the Putnam See-and-Read Books, and the Watts Picture Life series are all simply written and variable in quality. The Garrard Discovery Books follow a set format, and although there are exceptions, many of the titles in this extensive series for young children are bland or stilted.

Scribner's Initial Biographies by Genevieve Foster are well written, brief, and useful—but staid in tone. Like the Foster books, the Grosset and Dunlap Signature Books, which the publishers call "life stories," are for the middle grades, but are often highly fictionalized and sometimes of dubious accuracy.

In 1950, Random House launched the Landmark Books, presenting people, movements, and moments in history that have been landmarks in our national life. Some of the contributors are notable, and some of the books are of superior literary quality, but in a series as extensive as this one, it is not surprising that high standards are not always maintained.

The Crowell biographies of women and of poets are outstanding series books for older readers, as are the Harper and Row Breakthrough Books, which emphasize, as the title indicates, a breakthrough in achievements or in human relations. Putnam publishes both a Sports Hero series and an American Hero series, which, like the Houghton Mifflin North Star series, contains lives of heroes in American history. The Horizon Caravel Books and the American Heritage Junior Library are both distinguished for their profuse and beautiful illustrations as well as for their accuracy.

Collective Biographies

Because of the brevity of treatment of each subject in collective biographies, they will not be discussed singly in this chapter. However, many are included in the bibliography, since this form of the genre serves two purposes admirably. The collective biography is an excellent choice for the child whose span of attention is limited, and for the reader who is particularly interested in the career, race, sex, period, or country that is the common denom-

9. Aileen Fisher and Olive Rabe, "Writing About the Alcotts," *Horn Book*, October 1968.

10. Marchette Chute, "Getting at the Truth," *Saturday Review*, September 19, 1953.

inator for the collection. This is an especially popular form for sports biographies—or biographical sketches—but it is also used widely to catch the interest of those children who are infatuated, say, with ballet or medicine (*anything* about ballet or medicine) or with women who broke into new professional fields or with black scientists. Not that collective biographies are catchalls: such books as Isaac Asimov's *Breakthroughs in Science* (1960) or *Leaders of New Nations* (1968) by Leonard Kenworthy and Erma Ferrari are exciting books and an irreplaceable contribution to children's literature.

The following discussions of biographies are grouped under three main divisions: Books for Younger Children, Books for the Middle Group, and Books for Older Children. Within each of these main groups, the discussions are arranged according to the birth date of the subjects of the biographies, so that there is a chronological progression within each section.

The main emphasis throughout is on the authors who are outstanding biographers. However, most of the author-title subsections not only highlight one biography of the author and give some indication of the range of his or her work, but also mention parallel biographies of the principal subject by other authors.

Books for Younger Children

Young children do not have the sense of time necessary to appreciate biography as history. Nor do they have the ability to empathize that makes biography a source of heroes and heroines for older readers. But young children do enjoy a good story and those biographies designed to be read aloud serve that purpose. Young children are also exposed to much more information these days and biographies for them familiarize them with the people behind the names they hear in their everyday lives, such as Washington, Lincoln, and Columbus, who have holidays named after them; and people who have airports, schools, and highways named after them, such as Martin Luther King, Jr., John Kennedy, and others.

There have been some good biographies for young children in the past; they are still valuable, especially for reading aloud. What is flourishing now is the simply written life story or partial biography for the beginning independent reader. The best of this kind are just as accurate as books for older readers, but the

An illustration by Rocco Negri from *The One Bad Thing About Father* by F. N. Monjo. Pictures copyright © 1970 by Rocco Negri. An *I Can Read Book*. By permission of Harper & Row, Publishers, Inc. (Original with color)

person's life is often seen from a child's viewpoint—as in Ferdinand Monjo's *The One Bad Thing About Father*, which gives a son's-eye-view of Theodore Roosevelt. For the young child whose time sense cannot fully encompass the past, this is perhaps the best—but not the only—way to give a biography immediacy and reality.

Alice Dalgliesh

The Columbus Story

The text of the picture biography *The Columbus Story* (1955) is less than thirty pages long. It is vividly alive and re-creates with simple dignity, in a direct writing style, the boyhood of Columbus and the struggles he had in getting support for his first successful voyage. The book carries Columbus through that journey, with none of the tragedy of the later years, and can be read aloud to children as young as five or six. Some second-graders and most third-graders can read it for themselves. Leo Politi's brilliantly colored illustrations complement the dignified tone of the story.

With Dalgliesh's gift for making the past come alive for children (see Chapter 12), it is logical that she should also succeed in writing enjoyable biographies for young children. In her picture biography for readers in the middle grades, *Ride on the Wind* (1956), she describes the dramatic solo flight of Charles Lindbergh across the ocean in "The Spirit of St. Louis."

Clara Ingram Judson's *Christopher Columbus* (1960), written for beginning readers, is a straightforward account in which style is sacrificed to the demands of a controlled vocabulary. An appendix in Ann McGovern's *The Story of Christopher Columbus* (1963) gives information about the way facts were obtained from source materials.

Patricia Miles Martin

Pocahontas

Patricia Miles Martin begins her story of *Pocahontas* (1964) when the Indian girl is eleven years old and sees an English ship arrive. She learns English, becomes friendly with the Jamestown colonists, marries John Rolfe when she is grown, and dies in England, homesick and ready to return to America. Written for beginning independent readers, the book is hampered stylistically by the demands of a limited vocabulary, but it is not dull and not unduly fictionalized. The story of Pocahontas has all the requisites of romantic drama, although there is some question about whether the familiar scene in which she saves the life of John Smith did occur, since Smith did not include it in the first edition of his own book.

Jan Wahl's *Pocahontas in London* (1967) focuses on the Indian girl's experiences in London. However, the writing is stiff and the book notable only for the brilliant color and striking composition of John Alcorn's illustrations. A good choice for reading aloud to young children is *Pocahontas* (1949) by Ingri and Edgar Parin d'Aulaire, with its direct approach, large and colorful pictures, and emphasis on action. (See also Bulla's *Pocahontas and the Strangers*.)

Daniel Boone (1965) is a good example of the many other biographies that Patricia Martin has written for young readers, most of them about famous persons in America's history. *Daniel Boone* tends to be somewhat oversimplified in style, with short sentences and large print, but it gives the major facts about Boone's life at a level comprehensible to the beginning reader. These books are useful but not outstanding, giving young children information rather than an understanding of the biographee's role in history.

Clyde Robert Bulla

Squanto, Friend of the Pilgrims

Children are usually enthralled by the amazing story of Squanto's life. He was taken to England in 1605 and lived there for eight years. Then he returned to this country with John Smith only to be captured and sold to Spain by slave hunters. In Spain he was rescued by the

From the book *A Weed Is a Flower: The Life of George Washington Carver* by Aliki. © 1965 by Aliki Brandenburg. Published by Prentice-Hall, Inc., Englewood Cliffs, New Jersey. (Original in color)

friars and returned once more to his native land. The story is beautifully told by Clyde Bulla, who has a gift for writing easy-to-read books that are never commonplace. His historical tales have a pleasant lilt and swing and substantial content. *Squanto* was published in 1954 with the subtitle *Friend of the White Men*, and in 1969 the title was changed to *Squanto, Friend of the Pilgrims*. The book has the same virtues as Bulla's historical fiction, the genre used in *John Billington, Friend of Squanto* (1956). The other biographies of Squanto written for this age group appear dull and stilted when compared to Bulla's story.

Bulla's *Pocahontas and the Strangers* (1971) is written for eight- to ten-year-olds, but the suspense of the story and the simplicity of style make it appropriate for reading aloud to younger children, especially if read in installments. Other good biographies by Bulla for the beginning independent reader are *Song of St. Francis* (1952), *Lincoln's Birthday* (1966), and *Washington's Birthday* (1967).

Aliki Brandenburg

A Weed Is a Flower

Aliki Brandenburg, who writes as "Aliki," illustrates her own books. In *A Weed Is a Flower* (1965), a biography of George Washington Carver, her pictures show a realistic range of skin tones. The story of the great black naturalist is told in a dry, quiet style with a simple vocabulary. The title is based on a comment attributed to Dr. Carver: "A weed is a flower growing in the wrong place." Born of slave parents, Carver worked his way through school, leaving the college where he had been a student and then a faculty member to join the staff of Tuskegee Institute at the invitation of Booker T. Washington. His distinguished career in agricultural research brought him many honors, and he is probably, along with Martin Luther King, Jr., the most popular black person of note as a subject of biographies for children. Another biography for this group is *George Washington Carver* (1960) by Samuel and Beryl Epstein, a stolid and factual account.

Aliki also has written and illustrated attractive picture biographies: *The Story of Johnny Appleseed* (1963) and *The Story of William Penn* (1964). The latter, like *A Weed is a Flower*, invests its subject with dignity and stature.

From *Abraham Lincoln* by Ingri and Edgar Parin d'Aulaire. Copyright 1939 by Doubleday & Company, Inc. Reproduced by permission of the publisher. (Original in color)

Ingri and Edgar Parin d'Aulaire

Abraham Lincoln

The picture-book biographies of Ingri and Edgar Parin d'Aulaire are a real contribution to the youngest. They are large books, copiously illustrated with full-page lithographs in deep, glowing colors on alternate pages, and with black-and-whites and innumerable small pictures in between. These small pictures fulfill a definite purpose in each book, sometimes adding droll touches to the interpretation of the hero's character, sometimes showing something of his work or progress. In *Benjamin Franklin* (1950), for instance, the decorative borders throughout the book carry a series of Franklin's wise sayings. These are fun for children to discover and read, and they make *Poor Richard's Almanac* more real. Throughout the series, the illustrations are somewhat sylized and occasionally stiff. But this is a minor criticism of pictures that are usually alive with action and full of humor.

Study the details of the pictures in *Abraham*

Lincoln (1939). No need to talk about the door-less dwellings—in one picture a horse has stuck his head into the single room of the cabin and seems to be taking a neighborly interest in the new baby. Notice the little boys' single galluses upon which hang all the responsibility for holding up their scanty pants. No need to say that Mary Todd was something of a termagant, nor that she had a few problems to contend with in Abe. That picture of the wildly dis-ordered parlor, with Abe on the floor in stock-ing feet, and with Mary, arms akimbo, reflected in the elegant mirror, is a demonstration of their fundamental unlikeness. The book is full of the sort of sly humor that characterized Abe.

In the early d'Aulaire books, the texts were simple and the life stories were incomplete. But with *Benjamin Franklin, Pocahontas* (1949, *Buffalo Bill* (1952), and *Columbus* (1955), the content grew richer, with more details. In the case of *Columbus,* the man's whole life is related, even those tragic last voyages.

A weakness in the d'Aulaires' writing is their propensity for using "never" and "always." They tell children in their *George Washington* (1936) that "He learned to be good and honest and never tell a lie." After recounting a delight-ful incident in which young Ben Franklin spent too much money for a whistle, they say "That was the only time Benjamin ever spent a penny unwisely." Children should not take too seriously these overstatements of virtue and should remember the more human aspects of the men being written about.

Viewpoint

Of the many biographies of Abraham Lin-coln, one of the best is Clyde Bulla's *Lincoln's Birthday* (1966). Wilma Hays's *Abe Lincoln's Birthday* (1961), despite the similarity of title, is fiction, based on the events of Lincoln's twelfth birthday. Clara Ingram Judson's *Abraham Lin-coln* (1961) has a rather flat style, but is useful because it is easy to read, factually accurate, and balanced in coverage.

Tobi Tobias
Maria Tallchief

Tobi Tobias has had a lifetime interest in the dance and she writes of Maria Tallchief, world renowned ballerina, with clarity and admira-tion. She conveys to young readers the dedica-tion and hard work that go into making a person a superstar. Tobias handles tastefully Tallchief's divorce from choreographer George Balanchine and, without belaboring the point, informs readers that family life is very difficult to combine with a ballet career.

Another dance biography by Tobias is *Arthur Mitchell* (1975), a book about the man whose determination to dance overcame the bias against black ballet dancers. In *Marian Anderson* (1972), Tobias recounts the story of the woman who made musical history with one of the great voices of the twentieth century. Tobias's inter-est in the arts goes beyond music and dance and is reflected in her biography *Isamu Noguchi; The Life of a Sculptor* (1974).

Other Books for Younger Children

There have been increasing numbers of very simply written biographies to satisfy the curios-ity of children in the primary grades. While the majority of them are about famous men and women in American history, there are also nu-merous biographies of famous sports figures, people in the news, and little known people who have careers of interest to children.

Maggi Scarf's *Meet Benjamin Franklin* (1968) touches on the most familiar events and achievements in Franklin's life. In *The Story of Ben Franklin* (1965), Eve Merriam gives a brief but balanced treatment of Franklin as a family man. Ormonde De Kay's *Meet Andrew Jackson* (1967) is one of the better books in the Random House Step-Up Series.

Martin Luther King, Jr., is a favorite subject, and a favorite book with young readers is Mar-garet B. Young's *The Picture Life of Martin Luther*

King, Jr. (1968). Other figures in the news who have been written about in an easy-to-read style include *Gordon Parks* (1971) by Midge Turk, the story of a versatile and creative black photographer and writer; Ruth Franchere's *Cesar Chavez* (1970), a good picture of the plight of the migrant worker and of the Chicano labor leader; and *Rosa Parks* (1973) by Eloise Greenfield, the story of the woman who precipitated the Montgomery bus strike by refusing to move to the back of the bus.

Marshall and Sue Burchard have developed a satisfactory style and format for their sports hero biographies and have offered young readers the opportunity to read about hockey stars *Bobby Orr* (1973) and *Phil Esposito* (1975), tennis great *Billie Jean King* (1975), and baseball's *Henry Aaron* (1974).

While young children may not be familiar with the writings of Langston Hughes and James Weldon Johnson they can, nevertheless, find much to interest them in Alice Walker's *Langston Hughes, American Poet* (1974) and Ophelia Egypt's *James Weldon Johnson* (1974), both of which reflect the consistently high quality of the Crowell Biography Series. This series is one of the most balanced, containing biographies of women, blacks, Native Americans, and other minorities, as well as biographies about such people as *Eleanor Roosevelt* (1970) by Jane Goodsell and *The Ringling Brothers* (1971) by Molly Cone, which tells of a circus-smitten family who achieved the dream so many children have.

Books for the Middle Group

Children in the middle grades want to know everything there is to know about their special heroes and heroines, the doers—from explorers and scouts of the Old West to today's astronauts and baseball stars. Children are not usually ready for career stories unless they are stories of action, nor are they concerned with character development. Least of all are most children able to appreciate an account of the pursuit of an abstract idea. Penn, with his deep concern for Quakerism and social ideals, is a hero for older children, as is Jefferson, who was so predominantly a man of ideas.

However, through their reading of fairy tales and realistic fiction, children arrive gradually at some broad standards of right and wrong. They may not understand self-abnegation or altruism, but they know all about fair play, kind-

Illustration by Moneta Barnett from *James Weldon Johnson* by Ophelia Settle Egypt. Illustrations copyright © 1974 by Moneta Barnett. By permission of Thomas Y. Crowell, Publishers.

ness, bravery, and justice. These actions they respect, and they admire the heroes and heroines who embody these virtues.

The increasing awareness of the part of authors and editors that young readers like their biographies to be tales of action and achievement rather than stories of the childhood pranks of a great man or woman, straightforward and accurate rather than adulatory, has brought a decided improvement in most of the books for this age group.

Aileen Fisher

Jeanne d'Arc

Aileen Fisher's *Jeanne d'Arc* (1970) is beautifully illustrated with Ati Forberg's quiet, reverent pictures. The story begins with Jeanne at the age of eleven, listening to her father's angry plaints about the English invaders and to his expressed hope that the Dauphin somehow could ascent the throne left vacant by his father's death. When first Jeanne sees a dazzling light and hears a voice tell her that she will be guided by the saints, she is happy and trustful but not, in her piety, surprised. The faith she has in her power to defeat the English and to see the Dauphin crowned, and the tragedy of her imprisonment and death are described with grave simplicity. Aileen Fisher writes in a direct and unembellished prose appropriate to Jeanne's modesty and conviction and she successfully portrays her as a heroine by describing her acts rather than by commenting on them.

In *Joan of Arc; Her Life as Told by Winston Churchill* (1969), reprinted from Churchill's *A History of the English-Speaking Peoples*, comments by the author such as these are frequent: "Unconquerable courage, infinite compassion, the virtue of the simple, the wisdom of the just, shone forth in her." For older readers, Albert Paine's *The Girl in White Armor* (1967; abridged from an earlier version) is well written, historically accurate and detailed, and broad in scope.

Fisher, in collaboration with Olive Rabe, has also written *We Alcotts* (1968), which is for older readers. The biography is told by Mrs. Alcott—in language delightfully stately and appropriate for the period—and focuses on the family's participation in the intellectual ferment of their circle, the abolitionist movement, and new educational theories.

Ronald Syme

Columbus, Finder of the New World

Ronald Syme's series of biographies of explorers began as easy-to-read books for the middle and upper grades—Columbus, Cortes, Champlain, Balboa, Magellan, and others—and broadened to include more detailed biographies of La Salle, John Smith, and Henry Hudson. *Columbus, Finder of the New World* (1952) is typical of the style and approach of all the books. Christopher Columbus is a difficult character to present in a full biography, since the drama of his life rises grandly to the successful conclusion of his first voyage. After that, failure and tragedy take over. It is greatly to Syme's credit that he presents the gloom as well as the glory. In this brief, well-written biography, the Admiral of the Ocean Sea goes down to his death apparently defeated, but his name and his achievements live after him.

Other biographies of Columbus that readers of nine to twelve may enjoy are Armstrong

Illustration by William Stobbs. From *Columbus, Finder of the New World* by Ronald Syme. Copyright 1952 by William Morrow and Company, Inc. Reprinted by permission of the publishers.

Sperry's *Voyages of Christopher Columbus* (1950) and Clara Ingram Judson's *Admiral Christopher Columbus* (1965), not to be confused with her biography of Columbus for younger children. For another slant on the Admiral, children can read Nina Brown Bakers's *Amerigo Vespucci* (1956), which, in discussing why America was named for Amerigo rather than for Columbus and in discussing the relationship between the two explorers, gives a picture of Columbus that helps explain his downfall.

In addition to his books about explorers, Syme has written several biographies of heroes of Latin American countries. For older children, *Bolivar the Liberator* (1968) is a good example of the dramatic pattern of events, set off by a restrained style, that makes Ronald Syme's books as exciting as they are informative. Bolivar became president of the Republic of Great Columbia, which included Venezuela, Colombia, Peru, Ecuador, and Bolivia. Although his fortune and his power were lost, and he died in poverty and isolation, Bolivar's reputation as the most important political figure in South American history has grown with the passing of time. "Few liberators," comments Syme, "have lived long enough to enjoy the benefits derived from their achievement of victory for others." As always, Syme is candid in appraisal and lucid in explaining the complexities of political upheaval. These are characteristics also of *Garibaldi: The Man Who Made a Nation* (1967), of *Toussaint: The Black Liberator* (1971), and of *Zapata, Mexican Rebel* (1971), the latter for readers of nine to twelve, simply written, not as smooth in style as the books for older readers but just as objective.

Harold W. Felton
Mumbet: The Story of Elizabeth Freeman

In our era of consciousness of the exclusion, for many years, of the black contributors to American history, such heroes as Benjamin Banneker and Matthew Henson and such heroines as Sojourner Truth and Mary McLeod Bethune have been described many times. Elizabeth Freeman, though, is one heroine whose true story, dramatic and courageous, is seldom heard. Harold Felton's *Mumbet* (1970) tells how Elizabeth had become "Mumbet" to the Ashleys, the Massachusetts family whose slave she was. When Elizabeth heard of the new Massachusetts constitution which stated that all men were created equal, she called on a lawyer who had visited the Ashley home. He argued her case and in 1781 the black slave won her freedom in the courts of Massachusetts. Uneducated but intelligent, firm in her resolve, Elizabeth Freeman is a fascinating heroine, her triumph given suspense by the obstacles put in her way by the Ashleys, and her later years graced by the indomitable way in which she drove Shays' raiders from the lawyer's home.

Adroitly fictionalized, *Mumbet* is written in a vigorous style, the lengthy introduction making evident the research (with many sources quoted) that provided a firm base for the biography. Felton's careful balance between fact and fiction is again evident in his biography of the woman who donned men's clothing to serve in Washington's army, *Deborah Sampson: Soldier of the Revolution* (1976).

Harold Felton's other books are primarily about the heroes of America's tall tales or about such black heroes of the West as Jim Beckwourth (1966) and *Edward Rose* (1967), all action-filled stories.

Genevieve Foster
The Initial Biographies

The Initial Biographies by Genevieve Foster are brief and add little to our knowledge of the American heroes they describe, but they are written in restrained literary style and provide children with a summary of each person's childhood, youthful struggles, and mature contributions. *George Washington* (1949) has the same accuracy that distinguishes Foster's *George Washington's World*, but is more simplified, yet not written down. Many of the legendary exploits are omitted. In *Abraham Lincoln* (1950) the legends are included and explained—especially the Ann Rutledge affair. Her *Theodore Roosevelt* (1954) makes lively reading as she captures the exuberance of the man.

In *The World of William Penn* (1973), Foster looks at what happened during Penn's lifetime in England, the Continent, the Far East, and colonial America. While not a full biography, it is engrossing reading.

Doris Faber
I Will Be Heard: The Life of William Lloyd Garrison

The subject of Doris Faber's *I Will Be Heard: The Life of William Lloyd Garrison* (1970) is no idealized figure: opinionated, irascible, with no small estimate of his own ability, he was a man whose greatest virtues were a belief in the equality of man and an unwillingness to compromise in any way in the pursuit of that belief. It was a meeting with Benjamin Lundy, whose experiences in the South had caused him to devote his life to speaking against slavery, that started Garrison on the long fight for abolition of that evil. Reviled for many years for the stridency of his views, Garrison did not catch up with the times—the times caught up with him. By the time the Civil War was over, he—who had been threatened, mobbed, and jailed—was lauded and cheered, welcomed by the President, and carried through the streets of Charleston by freed slaves. Through Garrison's biography, the whole pattern of the fight against slavery can be seen. Describing her sources in an afterword, Faber notes that much of the material about abolition is not readily available but was gathered from the files of contemporary journals and from the four-volume biography published by Garrison's sons. Older readers may prefer Jules Archer's *Angry Abolitionist: William Lloyd Garrison* (1969).

Other Faber biographies for the middle group include *Horace Greeley: The People's Editor* (1964), and *Franklin D. Roosevelt* (1974). For older children, Faber has written *Oh, Lizzie: The Life of Elizabeth Cady Stanton* (1972), the famous nineteenth-century feminist.

Clara Ingram Judson

Abraham Lincoln, Friend of the People

Clara Ingram Judson began writing biography in 1939 with a modest little book about Frances Willard called *Pioneer Girl.* That was followed by *Boat Builder: The Story of Robert Fulton* (1940) and others. In 1950, when her *Abraham Lincoln, Friend of the People* appeared, it was evident that this writer, competent in so many fields, had attained new stature as a biographer. It was also evident that Judson's research into source materials was to yield a fresh slant on the man. Her careful studies convinced her, for example, that Abe's childhood was no more "poverty stricken" than that of most of the neighbors. She also brought out the warm family love and loyalty of the Lincoln clan, and Abe himself emerges as a real person.

Many think *Abraham Lincoln, Friend of the People* is the finest book in Judson's biography series. Certainly it can take its place with the Sandburg and Daugherty Lincolns. The illustrations are unique also. In addition to the pen-and-ink drawings, there are colored photographs of the Lincoln dioramas from the Chicago Historical Society. These pictures are eye-catching and vivid.

Clearly, Judson believed the only justification for new biographies of such well-known national figures as George Washington, Thomas Jefferson, Andrew Jackson, and Theodore Roosevelt is that they throw fresh light on, and give children new facts or a new point of view about, the man. Before she wrote a biography, she read the letters, journals, or papers of her hero, searched contemporary magazines and newspapers, and studied the life of the times. As a result, she rescued Washington from the stereotypes that had nearly obliterated him. She even made Jefferson, the man of ideas, intelligible to children. Judson's writing is sometimes stilted, but somehow her deep love of family, her respect for all kinds of people, and her sense of the struggles through which these men came to greatness communicate themselves to children.

Other Books for the Middle Group

Many biographies for the middle grades seem to have been published with more thought for their usefulness as supplementary curricular material than for their literary merit, but they should be used for that purpose and for giving information only if better books are not available. Fortunately, there are now so many good biographies that a reader who enjoys the genre and is not just seeking information about a particular individual has a wide choice.

For Alcott fans, Helen Papashvily's *Louisa May Alcott* (1965) gives a brisk and capable summary of the writer's work and family life. *Nothing Is Impossible; The Story of Beatrix Potter* (1969) by Dorothy Aldis is simply written and uses extracts from Potter's letters and journal to give added color and establish atmosphere. Margaret Davidson's *The Story of Eleanor Roosevelt* (1969) is a good biography of that indomitable woman for this age group. Arnold Dobrin tells the story of another strong woman in *A Life for Israel: The Story of Golda Meir* (1974).

Jean Fritz brings skill and spirit to her biographies and some of the most enjoyable for this age group are *Where Was Patrick Henry on the 29th of May?* (1975), *Why Don't You Get a Horse, Sam Adams?* (1974), and *What's the Big Idea, Ben*

Franklin? (1976). Ferdinand Monjo adds to Lincolniana in *Me and Willie and Pa* (1973), the story of the Lincoln years in the White House as told by Tad. An excellent biography of an explorer is Jean Latham's *Far Voyager: The Story of Captain Cook* (1970).

Arnold Adoff's *Malcolm X* (1970) is very simply written; *The Life of Malcolm X* (1971) by Richard Curtis, for the more mature reader, is candid and comprehensive; and *The Picture Life of Malcolm X* (1975) by James Haskins is simply written but straightforward.

Martin de Porres, Hero (1954) by Claire Huchet Bishop is a moving story of the Peruvian child, half-black, half-Spanish, who devoted his adult life in the sixteenth century to helping the poor and who was beatified in 1837.

Although the writing in Mary Malone's *Actor in Exile: The Life of Ira Aldridge* (1969) is not outstanding, the dramatic story of the black actor makes fascinating reading. With no chance of gaining a place in American theater, Aldridge went to England in 1824. There was prejudice enough there to make his career difficult, but in time he was acclaimed a great tragedian.

With as many biographies as are published today, it is impossible to mention them all. Additional titles are listed in the chapter bibliography, and more are available through sources cited in Appendix A.

Books for Older Children

Children in the middle grades usually demand action, but adolescent readers are also interested in men and women of ideas and ideals. While they enjoy a biography that is dramatic and well told, they may also read biographies for their historical background, their association with causes and movements, or their association with a field in which the reader has a special interest. One reader may consume avidly any biography with a Civil War background; another, any book about a musician; others, books about people whose lives as dancers, chemists, doctors, or teachers satisfy an orientation toward the profession.

Throughout this chapter, parallel biographies have been mentioned, and they exist in profusion for older readers. Adults working with children will want to know such books so that they may help children explore various presentations. Comparing Catherine Owens Peare's

Reprinted by permission of Coward, McCann & Geoghegan, Inc. from *Where Was Patrick Henry on the 29th of May?* by Jean Fritz. Illustrations copyright © 1975 by Margot Tomes.

Mahatma Gandhi: Father of Nonviolence (1969, rev. ed.) and Olivia Coolidge's *Gandhi* (1971), the reader can see that Peare's book with its fictionalized, rather informal narrative style is easier to read and more dramatic, but that Coolidge's is more detailed, dignified, and analytical. Jeanette Eaton's *Gandhi: Fighter Without a Sword* (1950) is notable for the perceptive picture it gives of Gandhi as a man and a spiritual leader. Comparing biographies gives children an opportunity to see how emphasis, style, and viewpoint, the amount of fictionalization or of documentation, and the amount of historical detail can shape a book.

Sidney Rosen
Galileo and the Magic Numbers

From the moment Master Jacopo Borghini introduced the young Galileo to the Pythagorean magic numbers, his life as a physicist and astronomer was determined. Although money was a problem, Galileo acquired an education and, eventually, a teaching position. His annoying habit of asking "Why?" and "How do you know?" made him unpopular with his teachers and colleagues as well as with Roman Catholic authorities. In *Galileo and the Magic Numbers* (1958), Rosen shows clearly the heroism of the man who defied the theological beliefs of his time to make important contributions to human knowledge.

Wizard of the Dome (1969) is an appealing biography for the general reader, since Rosen portrays Buckminster Fuller as a lively, tenacious inventor whose patterns of success and failure as a designer-inventor have a cliffhanger appeal; to the scientifically oriented girl or boy, it has the added attraction of presenting with unusual clarity the theories for which Fuller is now famous. Out of his concepts about the tetrahedron in nature and the application of geodesic structure have come his now-famous geodesic dome construction. The book has a good balance of personal life and of information about Fuller's professional career; it is written in a dignified but informal style, and it makes clear the importance and the innovatory nature of his work. In *Doctor Paracelsus* (1959), Rosen tells the story of Theophrastus Bombastus von Hohenheim, a Swiss doctor who rebelled against superstitions of medical belief and practices of the early sixteenth century.

Elizabeth Yates

Amos Fortune, Free Man

Born an African prince, sold in Boston, well treated by a series of masters, Amos Fortune learned the tanner's trade and eventually bought his freedom. After that, this humble, mighty soul devoted everything he earned to buying freedom for other slaves. Freedom and education were the greatest things in his life. He died a respected member of the little New Hampshire town of Jaffrey, where he had lived so long. When Elizabeth Yates saw the tombstone of Amos, she tells us, she knew she must write his biography. *Amos Fortune, Free Man* (1951 Newbery Medal winner) is written with warmth and compassion. Since most books about slavery deal with the South, it is important to have this picture of slave-running and sales in the North. The details are grim, but Amos Fortune carried suffering lightly because his eyes were on the freedom of the future. It is this characteristic of Fortune's, so clearly depicted by Yates, that causes some modern critics to disparage the book. They disapprove of the quiet way Amos Fortune bore his enslavement with courage and dignity, forgetting the circumstances under which he achieved his own personal integrity and offered the chance to live free to other blacks.

In *Prudence Crandall: Woman of Courage* (1955),

Yates writes of the Quaker schoolmistress who engendered bitter hostility in 1833 when she opened a school for black girls in a Connecticut town.

James Daugherty

Poor Richard

For superior readers with mature interests, Daugherty's *Poor Richard* (1941) has unusual distinction. This book covers Franklin's whole life, his manifold activities, and his amazing talent for friendship among people of all varieties and ages. The chapter called "An American in Paris" opens in this way.

One man alone captured a city. An American had taken Paris single-handed.

All the king's horses and all the king's men could not do what the friendly seventy-year-old journeyman printer was doing in spite of himself. He was surprised and pleased to find himself a hero. He was ready to act the part, knowing all that it might mean for America.

The chapter includes a visit with John Paul Jones, "a one-man navy," and a little later we are treated to the scandalized Abigail Adams's report of a dinner where Mme. Helvétius sat with one arm around Franklin's shoulder and the other on the chair of Abigail's own John. "After dinner," wrote the outraged Mrs. Adams, "she threw herself on a settee where she showed more than her feet." Here, obviously, is a somewhat mature interpretation of the times, written and illustrated with Daugherty's usual gusto and swing.

Daugherty's *Abraham Lincoln* (1943) covers Lincoln's whole life. This book avoids the usual anecdotes found in most of the other juveniles, and with remarkable clarity and power tells the story of Lincoln in relation to the stormy war years. A reviewer summarizing Daugherty's contribution in his three biographies writes:

. . . "Daniel Boone," "Poor Richard" and now "Abraham Lincoln"—are linked together in unity of spirit, an appreciation, in the true sense, of the restless, surging, visionary America which, with all its faults, has borne Titans.[11]

There is something in the spirit which animates Daugherty's pen and brush that seems partic-

11. Ellen Lewis Buell, "The Story of Honest Abe," a review of Daugherty's *Abraham Lincoln* in *The New York Times Book Review*, December 19, 1943.

ularly adapted to the interpretation of titans. His *Abraham Lincoln* illustrations show all the rowdy vigor of his earlier drawings, but predominant in the book is the brooding melancholy of the strangest and perhaps loneliest of our great Presidents. *Abraham Lincoln* is the most serious of Daugherty's three biographies, as we should expect, and is a magnificently clear if tragic picture of this great man.

Daugherty's *Daniel Boone* (1939), for which he won the Newbery Medal, is a spirited biography that has been attacked for bigotry in recent years by some critics. It is true that this book reflects the "Manifest Destiny" theory of the westward movement in American history. It is true that both Indians and blacks are treated in an offhand manner by Daugherty. But that is how Boone would have perceived them and to criticize Daugherty for not making Boone a twentieth-century liberal is overstepping the boundaries of critical analysis.

For a fuller biography of the man at a more mature level, children should read John Mason Brown's *Daniel Boone.*

Leonard Wibberley

Man of Liberty: A Life of Thomas Jefferson

In the years 1963–66, Leonard Wibberley published four volumes about the life of Thomas Jefferson. In 1968, a condensed and slightly revised volume incorporated the volumes into *Man of Liberty: A Life of Thomas Jefferson.*

In his prefatory note for *Man of Liberty*, Wibberley says that he felt his task as a biographer was to round out the picture usually given of Jefferson the statesman by including more information about his personal life. However, the comments he makes about his sources are much more specific and detailed than such notes usually are. Wibberley's choice of material clearly is based on exhaustive as well as discriminating research. He concludes, "I do not think that, however much I had read about Jefferson, I could have written this book about him without having lived in America. It is something that is in the air, and if you press me to say what that something is, I have to answer: Jefferson."[12]

This admiration is not explicit in the text itself. Wisely, Wibberley draws Thomas Jeffer-

12. Leonard Wibberley, *Man of Liberty* (Farrar, 1968), pp. v, vii.

Viewpoint

For how can a book be educational which discourages children from reading? What is educational about a book which is so thin in its characterization, so stilted in its prose, and so contrived in its plotting that the young reader goes to it as to a penance, eyeing his baseball mitt for succor. Unfortunately, there are quite a number of such "educational" books published today. . . . In a large part they consist of the lives of famous men who, judging by the books, could hardly be said to have lived at all. They seem merely to have passed through the Ten Commandments, nodding dutifully to each one of them, never guilty of an error of judgment, let alone a sin, and then died honored by their countrymen, who secretly must have been very glad to get rid of them. . . . But it is a paradox of writing that books which are written for the purpose of being educational (I exlude school books from this discussion) are not. The very emphasis on being educational kills the spirit of the book. While those which are written with a love of a story or of a character or of a time or a place are educational, for something comes to life from between the pages and we stand on Tower Hill in the sixteenth century and hear the executioner cry in anguish, "God pardon me," as he brings down his ax and severs the head of Sir Thomas More from his body. . . .—Leonard Wibberley, "The Land of the Ever Young," *The California Librarian*, January, 1962, pp. 19–20.

son (and the historical figures with whom he lived and worked) so astutely that the man's intellect, ability, and versatility speak for him. The biography is mature in approach, an excellent source of information about the period as well as a fascinating study of Jefferson.

Jeanette Eaton

Leader by Destiny

Washington is undoubtedly one of the most difficult figures to bring alive for children, both because he has been belittled by the trivial anecdotes told about him and because he has the subtle, intangible qualities of a highly civilized human being. Self-discipline and restraint are not easy for children to understand or to appreciate, and for this reason in particular Washington is a better character for adolescents than for children.

The best juvenile biography of Washington, Jeanette Eaton's *Leader by Destiny* (1938), is for the teen age, but it is such an extraordinary book that adults could also profit by reading it. You catch in it, for instance, Washington's lifelong regret for his inadequate education. You also find in this book Washington's single indiscretion, in his relations to his friend's wife, the beautiful Sally Fairfax. He wrote her one letter declaring his love. This letter Sally kept secret until the day of her death, and it remained secret for a hundred years after. In this book you see Washington's affectionate relations with his wife's children, and you see Martha herself as a charming and devoted wife to Washington, who came to appreciate her more and more. This book will help young people and adults know Washington as a very human, often bewildered man with a remarkable gift for inspiring confidence in others.

Elizabeth Ripley
Hokusai

To supplement her background of art education, Elizabeth Ripley studied numerous sources to gain information for her biographies of artists. For *Hokusai* (1968), her story of the Japanese artist (1760–1849), she spent a month in Japan to get background. One of the best in a series of good books, *Hokusai* is particularly charming because of the vivacity and humor of the artist himself. Dismissed by his master from a print design shop because of his unorthodox approach to art, Hokusai lived in poverty until he at long last became famous for the beauty of his prints. A nonconformist, a showman, a cheerful spendthrift, he died at eighty-nine after having changed his name fifty times and having squandered his money. He chose his own tombstone inscription: "Old Man Mad About Painting."

In *Michelangelo* (1953) Ripley shows the artist as almost the victim of his two gifts for painting and for sculpture. Painting with its vision of endless details seemed to enslave him, while sculpture freed his energies and let his creative spirit soar. Each of the books in Elizabeth Ripley's series follows a similar pattern, with a brief coverage of the artist's childhood and youth, and a discussion of his life as it related to his major works.

Another excellent biography of Michelangelo is Robert Coughlan's *The World of Michelangelo 1475–1564* (1966) in the Time-Life Library of Art, written for the mature reader. The text gives full historical background and a dis-

cussion of the artist's work, as well as a perceptive picture of the man. The book is profusely illustrated with photographs of Michelangelo's paintings and sculpture.

Esther M. Douty
Forten the Sailmaker: Pioneer Champion of Negro Rights

James Forten, born ten years before the American Revolution in the Colony of Pennsylvania, was the grandson of a slave and the son of a father both free and proud. When he was eight, he began his schooling with the gentle Quaker Anthony Benezet. At fourteen he signed on a privateer as powder boy, was captured by the British, and gave up his chance to go home as an exchange prisoner to a white friend who was ill. Released later, he shipped to England and worked as a stevedore, returning to Philadelphia to become an apprentice in the sail loft, where his industry and ability so impressed the white owner that he offered to sell the business to James. Thus he became an independent man, *Forten the Sailmaker* (1968), who in time became wealthy and influential in the community.

In 1800, Forten and other free blacks of the city petitioned Congress for a revision of the Fugitive Slave Act, and throughout the rest of his life he gave generously of this time and his fortune helping others, buying the freedom of many slaves, working with the Underground Railroad. Over three thousand people, white and black, attended the funeral of this quiet and respected citizen of Philadelphia.

Carefully written, the book is based on extensive research, both the bibliography and the author's acknowledgments showing Esther Douty's meticulous probing. The book is a good example of how biography shows the valor of a lifetime dedicated to a worthy cause.

The information garnered for this book has also been used in part as background for Douty's *Charlotte Forten: Free Black Teacher* (see p. 425).

Jean Lee Latham
Carry On, Mr. Bowditch

Between the great leaders in the American Revolution and the sturdy frontier people of the push westward is the unique figure of Nathaniel Bowditch. Born in Salem, Massachusetts, in 1773, he never had a day's schooling

Illustration by John O'Hara Cosgrave II, *From Carry On, Mr. Bowditch* by Jean Lee Latham. Copyright, 1955, by Jean Lee Latham and John O'Hara Cosgrave II. Reproduced by permission of the Houghton Mifflin Company.

after he was ten years old. Yet he became an outstanding astronomer, mathematician, and author of *The New American Practical Navigator,* published in 1802 and still a basic text of modern navigation.

When Nathaniel was twelve, his father bound him out for nine years to a ship's chandlery. The boy was near despair, when an old fellow told him, "Only a weakling gives up when he is becalmed! A strong man sails by ash breeze!" That is, he "sails" his boat with ash oars. So Nat sailed. His story is one of continuous toil in the chandlery by day and with books at night. Then came the end of his indenture, and a knowledgeable young man set off on the first of his five adventurous voyages. There is romance in Nat's story, and some tragic as well as some extremely humorous episodes. The climax came when Harvard, a university which he had yearned to attend, bestowed upon this unschooled but brilliant scientist an honorary degree. It is a thrilling story of New England fortitude and love of learning. Jean Latham has told it splendidly, and strong illustrations add to the distinction of this 1956 Newbery Medal book.

Another Latham biography of a great American navigator is *Trail Blazer of the Seas* (1956), the story of Matthew Maury, who worked to establish a naval academy. *Young Man in a Hurry: The Story of Cyrus W. Field* (1958) is a true story but is as exciting as adventure fiction.

Elisabeth Kyle

Girl with a Pen: Charlotte Brontë

Elisabeth Kyle's *Girl with a Pen* (1964) is a story of Charlotte Brontë's life from her seventeenth year to her thirty-first. Competently fictionalized, the biography evokes vividly the bleak parsonage and the beloved moorland country, the affection among the Brontë children and the growing development of their literary interests.

Particularly engaging is the section that describes the reception at the London publishing house of Smith and Elder of a book titled *Jane Eyre* by a writer who called herself Currer Bell. The subsequent acclaim of the book is followed by Charlotte's timid report to her father that she had had a book published and his announcement to her sisters: "Girls, do you know that Charlotte has been writing a book, and it is much better than likely?"

The portraits of Charlotte and her sisters are candid, and the impression of their restricted horizons is so strong that the reader is always conscious of the courage it must have taken the three Brontë sisters as women—and particularly as women from a modest parsonage—to submit their manuscripts.

In her afterword, Kyle refers to this book as a story rather than a biography, but it succeeds in the task of a good biography: it reveals the character of its subject and her achievements, and in stimulating interest in its subject, this captivating biography—or story, as Kyle describes it—is exceptionally successful.

Another of Kyle's lively biographies of writers is *Great Ambitions: A story of the Early Years of Charles Dickens* (1968), covering in great detail Dickens's life between the ages of twelve and twenty-seven, Kyle has also written *Duet: The Story of Clara and Robert Schumann* (1968).

James Playsted Wood

Spunkwater, Spunkwater! A Life of Mark Twain

"The United States has always paid its entertainers extravagantly," says James Wood in *Spunkwater, Spunkwater!* (1968). "Whatever his other excellences, and he had many—and whatever deep, dark mystique ingenious critics have read into his life and work—Mark Twain was first and last an entertainer. It was his celebrity as an entertainer that led to his being enthroned as the American sage. He was the articulate and even voluble symbol of the kind of practical wisdom Americans most admired. He was about as tragic as anyone else, applauded and honored everywhere he went, who was having a wonderful time...." Such candid comment is typical of the fresh and thoughtful approach of James Wood, whose sophisticated style pays readers the compliment of assuming that they will appreciate the nuance of humor and oblique reference.

Mark Twain's life as river pilot, newspaperman, author, lecturer, caustic world traveler, and deeply devoted husband and father is familiar material, included in most of the biographies of Twain. Wood gives an added dimension by his perceptively analytical discussion of Twain's volatile and ebullient personality and by his criticism of Twain's writing. A list of important dates and a bibliography add to the book's general usefulness, and some delightful photographs add to its appeal.

The mature wit and percipience of Wood's analysis of Twain are also evident in his other biographies of writers. In *The Lantern Bearer: A Life of Robert Louis Stevenson* (1965), he is candid in appraisal of Stevenson as a romantic, often illogical man and a superb craftsman. Wood's *The Admirable Cotton Mather* (1971) is particularly interesting because he disputes Mather's reputation as vindictive and bigoted.

Polly Longsworth

I, Charlotte Forten, Black and Free

Polly Longsworth's *I, Charlotte Forten* (1970) is based on Ray Allen Billington's edition of Charlotte's diary, and, according to the author's acknowledgments, is "as close a re-creation of Miss Forten's life and experiences as I am capable of achieving." This explains why the biography begins with Charlotte's sixteenth year, when she came to Salem, Massachusetts, so that she might attend an unsegregated school.

As the granddaughter of the wealthy and respected James Forten, she had been brought up in a home in which good breeding and cultural interests were taken for granted, and in which the leaders of the antislavery movement were accustomed guests. Charlotte continued to meet in Salem such dignitaries as Whittier, Garrison, Douglass, and Phillips, and she decided to devote her life to helping her own people.

Having become a teacher, she volunteered to join the Port Royal Commission that was going to the South Carolina Sea Islands to teach the neglected blacks of Saint Helena. In 1864, she came North to attend her father's funeral, and there the biography ends, although a final chapter describes the Grimké family and her marriage to Francis Grimké, and speaks briefly of their joint years of dedication to helping the black cause through the hard days of postwar disillusionment.

The book is written in first person, in a heavy and rather ornate style appropriate for a nineteenth-century woman of good family. It is nevertheless an exciting book, in part because the pages read like a roll call of all the early crusaders against slavery, in part because the events are intrinsically dramatic, and in part because the picture of a frail and gentle girl so unselfishly devoted to a cause is romantic in the best sense.

Esther Douty's *Charlotte Forten: Free Black Teacher* (1971), a biography for the middle grades, is based on the diary also, but written in third person; it, too, ends with Charlotte Forten's return to the North after her father's death. An afterword briefly describes her subsequent life. More fictionalized than the Longsworth book, this has a few childhood episodes that contribute little to the book and includes some quotations from the diary. Otherwise the books cover most of the same incidents and major events, though there is much more detail and more background in Longsworth's account.

Another outstanding biography by Longsworth is *Emily Dickinson: Her Letter to the World* (1965), written in a quiet style that is a good foil for the romantic subject, and with a balanced attention to the poet's writing and to her personal life.

Dorothy Sterling

Captain of the Planter: The Story of Robert Smalls

Robert Smalls' owner was Henry McKee. Because he could earn more money for McKee by being hired out, Smalls was sent to Charleston, where he worked in a sailing loft and watched the pilots carefully until he became adept at handling boats himself. In 1861, Smalls shipped on the *Planter* as a deckhand. The ship was in the service of the Confederate Navy, and it was the resemblance between its captain and himself that gave Smalls his great idea: an idea that would bring him freedom and put the ship into Union hands. At three A.M. on the morning of May 13, 1862, the black crew quietly maneuvered the ship out of the harbor, stopping to take on some of their wives and children; they were given freedom to pass by the sentinel at Fort Sumter, and the crew proudly hailed a Union ship and turned the *Planter* over.

Disappointed by the fact that the Union Army included no black troops, Smalls visited President Lincoln and persuaded him to change his policy. Dedicated to the causes of freedom and equality, he became a public speaker and a member of Congress.

Dorothy Sterling's story of Robert Smalls, well documented by a list of sources and an extensive bibliography, is dramatic because of its subject matter: Smalls' personal achievement and the events of the years of the Civil War and the Reconstruction. What Sterling had added to the inherent drama of the *Captain of the Planter* (1958) is a powerful picture of the tragedy of the postwar years and a personal portrait of a man whose true greatness lay not in one single courageous act but in the fact that he never compromised his principles for the sake of expediency.

Other biographies by Sterling are *Freedom Train: The Story of Harriet Tubman* (1954), and *The Making of an Afro-American: Martin Robison Delaney 1812–1885* (1971), an extensively documented account of an early exponent of black nationalism. While Dorothy Sterling has written stories, informational books on such diverse topics as caves and caterpillars, and series books, her strongest commitment is clearly to the cause of black equality. Young readers who enjoy her biographies may also want to read her study of events related to the Emancipation Proclamation in *Forever Free* (1963), her history of the American civil rights movement in *Tear Down the Walls!* (1968), and *Speak Out in Thunder Tones* (1973) and *The Trouble They Seen* (1976), both compilations of statements by black people, covering the years 1787–1877.

Shannon Garst

Crazy Horse

Toward the end of the period of westward expansion came the terrible struggles between the advancing hordes of whites and the defending Indians. Several fine biographies of Indian leaders of this period give children the story of these events from the Indians' point of view. *Crazy Horse* (1950) is one of the best of these. It begins with Crazy Horse's training as a boy, shows his bitter experiences with the bad faith and cruelties of the whites and his growing determination to stop their invasion at all costs. The end is sheer tragedy. Crazy Horse is defeated, his people scattered or herded into a reservation, and Crazy Horse, rather than submit, fights to his death. No child who reads this moving record will ever believe the cruelties were all on one side.

Shannon Garst also writes sympathetically of the Sioux way of life in *Sitting Bull, Champion of His People* (1946) and of Sitting Bull's tenacious and courageous fight in a losing battle against white encroachment. Garst's *Kit Carson, Trailblazer and Scout* (1942) is a lively book of frontier life, full of action and the romance of the Old West.

Shirley Graham

Booker T. Washington

Although Shirley Graham's late husband, William E. B. DuBois, had major philosophical differences with Booker T. Washington, Graham writes objectively and sympathetically of the man in her biography *Booker T. Washington* (1955).

Born a slave, Booker was nine when the Emancipation Proclamation brought him freedom and an opportunity to go to West Virginia, where he worked in a salt mine and a coal mine. He took the name "Washington," in fact, from the name of the salt mine and the "Taliaferro" from the name of his father. Bent on getting an education, young Washington worked doggedly to pay his way through Hampton Institute, his academic prowess earning him an appointment as principal of Tuskegee, the new normal school that became Tuskegee Institute.

Although Booker T. Washington became famous for his development of Tuskegee, for bringing George Washington Carver to the faculty, for dining with Presidents, and for being the first black man to get an honorary degree from Harvard University, he has always stirred

*Viewpoint*_____

Certainty of knowledge not only excludes mistake, but fortifies veracity. What we collect by conjecture, and by conjecture only can one man judge of another's motives or sentiments, is easily modified by fancy or by desire; as objects imperfectly discerned take forms from the hope or fear of the beholder. But that which is fully known cannot be falsified but with reluctance of understanding, and alarm of conscience: of understanding, the lover of truth; of conscience, the sentinel of virtue.

He that writes the life of another is either his friend or his enemy, and wishes either to exalt his praise or aggravate his infamy: many temptations to falsehood will occur in the disguise of passions, too specious to fear much resistance. Love of virtue will animate panegyric, and hatred of wickedness embitter censure. The zeal of gratitude, the ardour of patriotism, fondness for an opinion, or fidelity to a party, may easily overpower the vigilance of a mind habitually well disposed, and prevail over unassisted and unfriended veracity.—Samuel Johnson, *The Rambler*, No. 60, Sat., Oct. 13, 1750.

_____

some controversy because of the stand he took on race relations in the famous speech often referred to as the "Atlanta Compromise." In her biography, Shirley Graham has submerged any difference in viewpoint she might have with Washington. Her story is told with an understanding of how Washington's life and experience shaped his ideas. The biography is adroitly fictionalized, many of the incidents based on Washington's autobiography *Up from Slavery*, with anecdotes and dialogue woven smoothly into the narrative. A bibliography gives sources, and a lengthy index makes textual material accessible.

An interesting contrast to Booker T. Washington's story is found in *W. E. B. DuBois* (1972) by Virginia Hamilton, and older children should be encouraged to read this and think about those differences in philosophies between the two men. DuBois was an aristocrat in every sense of the word. He received a doctorate from Harvard, where he studied under such men as William James and George Santayana. He spent two years studying at the University of Berlin. The story of how the scholar became a political activist and one of the most important black leaders in the history of the United States is fascinating.

Shirley Graham has also written *The Story of Phillis Wheatley* (1949), which is well researched but more fictionalized; *Your Most Humble Servant* (1949), the story of Benjamin Banneker; and *His Day Is Marching On* (1971), memoirs of her husband, W. E. B. DuBois.

Mature readers will want to read Booker T. Washington's autobiography *Up from Slavery* and *The Souls of Black Folks* by W. E. B. DuBois.

Catherine Owens Peare

The Louis D. Brandeis Story

Catherine Owens Peare is never adulatory in her attitude toward the men and women whose biographies she writes, but her affection and respect for her subjects are usually clear, as they are in *The Louis D. Brandeis Story* (1970). Coming from a close-knit Austrian-Jewish family that had migrated to Louisville, Brandeis grew up in a circle in which it was taken for granted that cultural, academic, and political interests would be shared and discussed. An ardent student, Louis Brandeis made a distinguished record at Harvard Law School.

With a passion for justice and a concern for the under privileged, Brandeis became a respected figure in the legal hierarchy of Boston, and grew wealthy enough to espouse reform measures and to take cases without a fee to protect the public interest against the depredations of big business monoliths. In his years as an associate justice of the Supreme Court, he won distinction for his idealism, his concern for humanity, and his farseeing understanding of ethical and social implications of the issues involved in cases heard. An ample bibliography of sources is included with Peare's story of his life.

Many of Peare's biographies are concerned with public figures: *The Herbert Hoover Story* (1965) stresses Hoover's role in humanitarian projects, and *The Woodrow Wilson Story* (1963), Wilson's idealism and his influence on world events. In *Mary McLeod Bethune* (1951), she draws an exciting picture of the remarkably energetic black educator.

Iris Noble

Emmeline and Her Daughters: The Pankhurst Suffragettes

Emmeline and Her Daughters (1971), like many of Iris Noble's other biographies, describes with enthusiastic sympathy a pioneer in a reform movement, a champion of a cause. The book's bibliography includes works by Emmeline Pankhurst and by each of her three daughters, clearly the source of many of the intimate details that give the account vitality and authenticity. The tumultuous record of the Pankhursts is seen both as a personal narrative and as the opening salvo in the long battle for equality for women.

Emmeline Pankhurst had been a demure, cultured Victorian wife and mother until the day her husband, who had long fought for feminine liberation, challenged her to take an active part in the struggle. He began her education as a militant participant by taking her to hear debates in Parliament, helping her organize the Women's Franchise League, and encouraging her to run for a minor political office. She was forty when he died, and without his backing her role was even more difficult. It was her daughter Christabel who conceived the idea of a new organization, "*of* women *for* women, one

that will lead all the women of Britain into militant action." So the Women's Social and Political Union was born, the group that was a vigorous spearhead for feminine equality. The actions taken against this dedicated army of women led them to mass demonstrations and acts of violence, but their courage in the face of brutal reprisals eventually won them public admiration, the support of much of the press, and, in 1928, at long last, full suffrage.

Iris Noble deals objectively with dramatic and important events and shows the long struggle as not only a dominating motive in the lives of the four Pankhurst women but the cause of a bitter rupture between Christabel and Sylvia Pankhurst.

Objectivity in reporting and sympathetic understanding of a crusader's ardor are also evident in Noble's *Susan B. Anthony* (1975), the story of the persistent crusader for women's rights. In *Empress of All Russia* (1966), Noble combines broad historical coverage with a vigorous, perceptive characterization of Catherine the Great.

The obstacles that faced women during the nineteenth century are made clear in Patricia Clapp's biography of Elizabeth Blackwell, *Dr. Elizabeth: The Story of the First Woman Doctor* (1974). Written in the first person, this biography is never guilty of over-dramatization.

That the fight begun by the Pankhursts and Anthony is not over can be seen in two very fine biographies of Shirley Chisholm, the first black woman to serve in the United States Congress. Susan Brownmiller's *Shirley Chisholm* (1970) is for slightly younger readers than James Haskins's *Fighting Shirley Chisholm* (1975). Haskins writes here, as in all his books, with a candidness still rare in children's books, a trait also evident in his *Barbara Jordan* (1977).

Howard Greenfeld

Gertrude Stein: A Biography

Of the several biographies of Gertrude Stein that were written for young people in honor of the hundredth year of her birth, Howard Greenfeld's *Gertrude Stein* (1973) is the most sensitive in depicting her personality and the most thorough in analyzing her writing and her role in the turbulent artistic and literary circles of Paris. Greenfeld provides evidence of pains-

From *Gertrude Stein: A Biography* by Howard Greenfeld. Photograph from the Collection of American Literature, Beinecke Rare Book and Manuscript Library, Yale University.

taking research with a lengthy bibliography of sources, and he uses many quotations from Stein's writing or from current articles to corroborate his statements.

The balanced treatment of personal and artistic facets that Greenfeld uses in the Stein biography is also a strong feature of his *Pablo Picasso* (1971) and *Marc Chagall* (1967). In *F. Scott Fitzgerald* (1974), Greenfeld describes the tragedy of Fitzgerald's life with a compassion that never lapses into sentimentality or melodrama. He achieves, in all his biographies, a polished, dignified writing style, and he succeeds in presenting knowledgeable, candid, and vivid pictures of individuals while making clear their roles in artistic or literary history.

Miriam Gurko

Restless Spirit: The Life of Edna St. Vincent Millay

Miriam Gurko's *Restless Spirit* (1962) is a mature and thoughtful biography for adolescent readers. Her sources include published and unpublished material, letters, and interviews. "Curiously, as the mass of notes grew, the more elusive the subject seemed to become," Gurko states in her foreword. And she goes on, "From this assortment of fact and characterization I have had to select those elements which appeared the most credible, and which seemed to have undergone the least alteration as a result

of the passage of time or the presence of certain personal factors."

Brought up by her mother after her parents had separated, Vincent and her sisters had a childhood in which they early became self-reliant. Vincent wrote poetry at the age of five, and many of her childhood poems were published in *The St. Nicholas Magazine.* She had already published "Renascence" and become modestly famous when she entered Vassar at the age of twenty-one. After her graduation, Edna, who no longer used "Vincent" as her name, went to New York to join in the intellectual ferment of Greenwich Village life and in the activities of the newly formed Provincetown Players. After several abortive love affairs, she married Eugen Boissevin, a marriage that was ideal for a poet, since Eugen felt it his role to protect Edna and encourage her work.

The biography includes quotations from Edna St. Vincent Millay's poetry only when they are relevant to the text, and Gurko has integrated smoothly the personal material, the background of the artistic and literary circles in which Edna moved, and the discerning discussion of the poet's work and its place in modern poetry.

Toby Shafter's biography *Edna St. Vincent Millay: America's Best-Loved Poet* (1957) is lighter in style, with much more fictionalization and with approximately half the book devoted to Millay's childhood. However, it is factually reliable and a good introduction for less mature readers.

Other biographies by Miriam Gurko include *Clarence Darrow* (1965), interesting both as an account of the famous Scopes trial and as a study of the nonconformist lawyer who was a defender of unpopular causes. Much of the story also reflects the history of the labor movement. *The Lives and Times of Peter Cooper* (1959), as the title indicates, is concerned with other figures as well as with that of the protagonist, for the inventor and industrialist Cooper was constantly involved in industrial, political, and educational movements.

Theodora Kroeber

Ishi: Last of His Tribe

At the end of the nineteenth century a small band of Yahi Indians lived in solitude and secrecy at the foot of Mount Lassen, their way of life threatened by the white settlers and seekers of gold. *Ishi* (1964) and his people knew that they could survive only if they remained hidden, their ancient villages having been destroyed by the ruthless invaders. As long as they could, the people clung to the sacred ways, the quiet and peaceful pattern of Yahi life. One by one, the others died, and Ishi was alone. "There is nothing to wait for in this empty land, nothing—I am free to go." And so he left, and took the trail to the west, lost his way, and met the saldu, the whites.

To his surprise, they did not kill him; a Stranger was brought, a museum-saldu, who spoke in the tongue of the People, and took Ishi on a train. And so Ishi came to live with the whites in peace, an adviser to the museum people on the ways and the crafts of the Yahi. One of the most striking aspects of *Ishi* is the consistency with which Theodora Kroeber maintains Ishi's viewpoint; even after he comes to live and work with the museum staff, the relationships are seen through Ishi's eyes, and the writing continues to have the beautiful cadence and dignity of Yahi. At the end,

Death came to him as he wished—with his friends in the museum-watgurwa. Majapa and the museum men released his spirit in the old Yahi way. And they saw to it that Ishi had with him those things that a Yahi hunter must take from the World of the Living, for the journey to the west. . . .

The names used are always the Yahi names that Ishi had given.

Alfred Kroeber was Curator of the Museum of Anthropology and Ethnology at the Univer-

Illustration by Ruth Robbins for *Ishi, Last of His Tribe* by T. Kroeber. Copyright 1965. Reproduced by permission of Parnassus Press. Published by Houghton Mifflin Company.

sity of California when Ishi was brought there, and his wife had the benefit of his professional knowledge as well as first-hand information from Ishi. Such familiarity permits a biographer to incorporate cultural details so that they are as intrinsic a part of a life story as they are in *Ishi*, and in Theodora Kroeber's anthropological study for adult readers, *Ishi in Two Worlds*.

Milton Meltzer

Langston Hughes

Perhaps because *Langston Hughes: A Biography* (1968) is about a colleague and friend, it has an immediacy and warmth that Meltzer's other biographies do not have. Perhaps it is that the poet himself sheds light and grace. "Within a few years of his first book," Meltzer says, "he was the poet laureate of his people." Hughes's life and work were a testament to his belief that it was a proud thing to be black, his poetry more bittersweet than bitter.

In Topeka, Kansas, he was the only black child in school; he spent some time on his father's Mexican ranch; he washed dishes in a Paris cafe and worked on a Staten Island truck farm. While working as a waiter in a Washington hotel, he put three of his poems on Vachel Lindsay's table, and that night Lindsay read the poems aloud in public. He went to Spain as a reporter during the Civil War there, and he traveled in Asia and in Russia—in short, he had an exciting and colorful life.

But his travels, his involvement in causes, and his amazingly varied and prolific outpouring of magnificent prose and poetry are almost overshadowed by his passion for truth and justice. That is what Milton Meltzer has succeeded in conveying to the readers of *Langston Hughes*.

The reader will want to explore Hughes's poems, some of which are discussed in the poetry chapters; his short stories, the amusing stories about "Simple," with *The Best of Simple* (1961) comprising selections from earlier books; and his two autobiographical books, *I Wonder as I Wander* (1956, reprinted 1964) and *The Big Sea* (1963).

In an article on the distortions in children's history books, Milton Meltzer says,

Biography is another way to re-create the past. The life of a Tom Paine, a Benjamin Banneker, a Sojourner Truth . . . lets the reader see history from inside, from the mind and heart of an individual struggling to reshape his own time.

In history books, Wendell Phillips and William Lloyd Garrison are only a paragraph or a line, too often dismissed as irresponsible fanatics. Or there is a glancing reference to that other "fanatic," Thaddeus Stevens, painted darkly in the sky of Washington like some vulture hovering over the capital to pick the bones of Southern heroes ennobled in defeat.[13]

Meltzer's *Thaddeus Stevens* (1967) destroys this picture and presents a mature and thoughtful biography of the Pennsylvania lawyer whose tenure in the national Congress was marked by bitter opposition from the South, particularly because of his battle against the fugitive slave laws. Thaddeus Stevens was a champion of public education and racial equality, his efforts on behalf of black people's civil rights continuing after the Civil War and through the years of Reconstruction. Meltzer's description of those years and of Stevens's leadership in the move to impeach President Andrew Johnson is direct and vigorous, one of the most valuable aspects of a fine biography that does, indeed, see history from the viewpoint of "an individual struggling to reshape his own time."

Tongue of Flame: The Life of Lydia Maria Child (1965) and *A Light in the Dark: The Life of Samuel Gridley Howe* (1964) are, like the Stevens biography, imbued with enthusiasm for the causes to which the subjects were dedicated, yet they are not eulogistic in tone. Lydia Child founded the first children's magazine in this country, ran a newspaper, and was a pioneer in the fight against slavery. Howe was a pioneer in work for the blind and for prison reform, in programs to aid the mentally retarded, and provided help to fugitive slaves. Meltzer has let their amazing records speak for them, serving their reputations simply by recording their lives.

Other Books for Older Children

By far the greatest number of biographies are written for readers in the upper grades and high school. Many are, of course, read by younger children. It is not possible to include discussion of all the fine books that are available; fortunately reference books in the field of biography make the material easily accessible to readers seeking information about individ-

uals' lives. Here will be added just a few more outstanding biographies to indicate further the scope of the genre.

Margaret Leighton's *Cleopatra: Sister of the Moon* (1969) gives a good picture of the complicated pattern of Mediterranean countries and depicts Cleopatra not as a siren but as an intelligent woman aware of the transitory nature of her power. In Alice Curtis Desmond's *Cleopatra's Children* (1971) the picture of shifting alliances, feuds, and mounting intrigue is even stronger.

Cornelia Spencer writes objectively and authoritatively of one of China's most important figures in *Sun Yat-sen, Founder of the Chinese Republic* (1967). For insight into the China of today, an excellent title is Jules Archer's *Chou En-lai* (1973).

Among the notable biographies of American historical figures are Esther Forbes's *America's Paul Revere* (1946); Nardi Campion's *Patrick Henry* (1961); Edwin P. Hoyt's *William McKinley* (1967), which stresses McKinley's role as an internationalist ahead of his time; and *Andrew Jackson, Soldier and Statesman* (1963) by Ralph K. Andrist, which is profusely illustrated with material from the time, as is the pattern with other American Heritage books.

Ann Petry has told a well-documented story of another famous American in *Harriet Tubman: Conductor on the Underground Railroad* (1955). The dramatic story of this courageous woman is also told in Hildegarde Swift's *Railroad to Freedom* (1932).

One slave who did not escape was Peter Still, who worked all his life to save enough money to buy his freedom. Still's story is told by Peggy Mann in *The Man Who Bought Himself: The Story of Peter Still* (1975).

Fanny Kemble, the great nineteenth-century Shakespearean actress, cared enough about freeing the slaves that it cost her her marriage to Pierce Butler, Jr., the loss of her children, and divorce at a time when divorce was thoroughly disapproved of. Her story is told with vigor by John Anthony Scott in *Fanny Kemble's America* (1973).

Invincible Louisa: The Story of the Author of Little Women by Cornelia Meigs was first published in 1933 and won the Newbery Medal. It gives a remarkably broad view of the period and of the people in Louisa May Alcott's life as well as a perceptive study of Alcott herself.

The 1969 National Book Award went to Isaac

13. Milton Meltzer, "The Fractured Image," *Library Journal*, Oct. 15, 1968, p. 3923.

Bashevis Singer for *A Day of Pleasure: Stories of a Boy Growing Up in Warsaw*. Illustrated with photographs of the Singer family and of scenes of Warsaw, the nineteen autobiographical stories, told in delightful style, provide a lively picture of the ghetto community and of the author as a child.

Biography, like many other literary forms, reflects contemporary interests, and so there have been increasing numbers of books about minority group representatives in the United States, about leaders of other countries, and about women. One such is James Terzian and Kathryn Cramer's *Mighty Hard Road: The Story of Cesar Chavez* (1970), which is liberally fictionalized but a good study both of Chavez and of the migrant workers' struggle against exploitation. Another is James Haskins's *Adam Clayton Powell: Portrait of a Marching Black* (1974) which presents a very human picture of the flamboyant black leader. In *The Life and Death of Martin Luther King* (1977) Haskins probes thoughtfully into King's philosophy and his convictions.

Virginia Hamilton's *Paul Robeson: The Life and Times of a Free Black Man* (1974) is a moving biography of the great black artist whose political views caused him so much trouble.

Until recently almost all books about Native Americans focused on tribal chiefs, but in recent years authors have begun to give us the stories of lesser known figures. Among the best of these are Margaret Crary's *Susette La Flesche: Voice of the Omaha Indians* (1973), which tells the story of a courageous woman who fought against nineteenth-century injustices perpetrated against the Poncas, and Patrick Des Jarlait's autobiography *Patrick Des Jarlait: The Story of an American Indian Artist* (1975), which is enhanced by examples of Des Jarlait's brilliant watercolors.

At every level of writing for children, but most particularly for those of junior high school age and up, biographers have made great strides in presenting human portraits of the people being written about. Authors, publishers, librarians, teachers, and parents have come to understand that protecting children from knowledge of the human foibles of a person is giving them less than the truth. Children have a right to the truth, the whole truth, in order that they may understand more clearly the men and women about whose lives they are reading.

Adult References[14]

ALTICK, RICHARD D. *Lives and Letters; A History of Literary Biography in England and America.*

BERRY, THOMAS ELLIOTT, ed. *The Biographer's Craft.*

BOWEN, CATHERINE DRINKER. *Biography: The Craft and the Calling.*

CLIFFORD, JAMES L. *From Puzzles to Portraits: Problems of a Literary Biographer.*

———, ed. *Biography as an Art.*

CRAVEN, PAUL R. *Biography.*

FISHER, MARGERY. *Matters of Fact.* Chapter 4, "Biography."

HOTCHKISS, JEANETTE, comp. *American Historical Fiction and Biography for Children and Young People.*

———, comp. *European Historical Fiction and Biography for Children and Young People.*

KULKIN, MARY-ELLEN *Her Way: Biographies of Women for Young People.*

NICHOLSEN, MARGARET. *People in Books: A Selective Guide to Biographical Literature Arranged by Vocations and Other Fields of Reader Interest.*

SILVERMAN, JUDITH. *An Index to Young Readers' Collective Biographies.*

STANIUS, ELLEN, comp. *Index to Short Biographies: For Elementary and Junior High Grades.*

In the following bibliography these symbols have been used to identify books about a religious or a particular ethnic group:

§ Black
★ Chicano or Puerto Rican
☆ Native American
● Religious minority

Collective Biographies

§ ALEXANDER, RAE PACE, comp. *Young and Black in America.* Random, 1970. Well-known black men and women describe the problems they encountered in their youth.   11 up

§ ● ASIMOV, ISAAC. *Breakthroughs in Science*, ill. by Karoly and Szanto. Houghton, 1960.   11 up

BAKELESS, KATHERINE. *Story-Lives of American Composers*, rev. ed. Lippincott, 1962.

———. *Story-Lives of Great Composers*, rev. ed. Lippincott, 1962. For each collection, nineteen composers have been selected.   12–15

● BEARD, ANNIE E. S. *Our Foreign-Born Citizens*, 6th ed. T. Crowell, 1968. Short biographies of Americans of foreign birth or parentage.   10–14

BEARD, CHARLES AUSTIN. *The Presidents in American History*, rev. ed. Messner, 1974. Offers good historical background for each Presidential career.   12–16

BENÉT, LAURA. *Famous American Poets*, ill. with photos. Dodd, 1950. Over twenty poets both recent and past are introduced in brief biographies.   11–14

§ BONTEMPS, ARNA. *Famous Negro Athletes.* Dodd, 1964. Short sketches include personal and career information.   10–12

BOWMAN, KATHLEEN. *New Women in Medicine.* Childrens Pr., 1976. Seven brief biographies, admiring but not adulatory in tone, describe career preparation with emphasis

14. Complete bibliographic data are provided in Appendix B.

on the problems these medical people faced as women. 10–12

§● BUCKMASTER, HENRIETTA. *Women Who Shaped History*. Macmillan, 1966. A fine collective biography of Dorothea Dix, Prudence Crandall, Elizabeth Stanton, Harriet Tubman, and Mary Baker Eddy. 12–15

§● COHEN, TOM. *Three Who Dared*. Doubleday, 1969. Three young men who risked their safety to help bring civil rights to southern black people. 11–14

COY, HAROLD. *The First Book of Presidents*, rev. ed., ill. by Manning Lee. Watts, 1973. A useful ready reference source. 8–10

CRAWFORD, DEBORAH. *Four Women in a Violent Time*. Crown, 1970. Mary Dyer, Anne Hutchinson, Penelope Van Princes, and Deborah Moody fought for personal liberty in colonial times. 11–14

DAUGHERTY, SONIA. *Ten Brave Men*, ill. by James Daugherty. Lippincott, 1951. Good accounts of such national heroes as Roger Williams, Patrick Henry, Thomas Jefferson, and Andrew Jackson.

———. *Ten Brave Women*, ill. by James Daugherty. Lippincott, 1953. 11–15

§ DOBLER, LAVINIA, and WILLIAM A. BROWN. *Great Rulers of the African Past*, ill. by Yvonne Johnson. Doubleday, 1965. Five brief biographies of rulers of African kingdoms during the years 1312–1617. 10–13

DUNSHEATH, PERCY. *Giants of Electricity*. T. Crowell, 1967. Useful both for its biographical and scientific information. 12 up

FANNING, LEONARD M. *Fathers of Industries*. Lippincott, 1962. Emphasis is on men who from industrial revolution days to the present have contributed significantly to inventions having social and economic significance. 12 up

FISHER, AILEEN, and OLIVE RABE. *We Alcotts*, ill. by Ellen Raskin, Atheneum, 1968. 11–14

FREEDMAN, RUSSELL. *Teen-Agers Who Made History*. Holiday, 1961. Stories of eight famous people of the past and present who became eminent in their careers before the age of twenty. 12–14

GUTMAN, BILL. *Modern Women Superstars*. Dodd, 1977. Designed to appeal to the slow reader but not condescending in style, this includes short biographies of Nadia Comaneci, Chris Evert, Dorothy Hamill, Kathy Kusner, Cindy Nelson, and Judy Rankin. 9–12

§ HASKINS, JAMES. *A Piece of the Power: Four Black Mayors*. Dial, 1972. Getting elected is not a guarantee of power or support as these black leaders discovered. 12–15

HIRSHBERG, AL. *The Greatest American Leaguers*. Putnam, 1970. Typical of many such sports biographies, this is breezy and anecdotal. 10–14

JOHNSTON, JOHANNA. *Women Themselves*, ill. by Deanne Hollinger. Dodd, 1973. Brief biographical descriptions of fourteen women. 9–12

§ JONES, HETTIE. *Big Star Fallin' Mama: Five Women in Black Music*. Viking, 1974. Good view of popular music through the lives of Ma Rainey, Bessie Smith, Mahalia Jackson, Billie Holiday, and Aretha Franklin. 12 up

KENNEDY, JOHN. *Profiles in Courage*. Young Readers Memorial ed. abr. Harper, 1964. The Pulitzer Prize was awarded this compilation of stories of men who took courageous stands in some decisive moments in our history. 10–12

§ KENWORTHY, LEONARD, and ERMA FERRARI. *Leaders of New Nations*, ill. by Michael Lowenbein. Doubleday, 1968. Revised edition of 1959 title, with four new leaders added and older material brought up to date. 12 up

LEVY, ELIZABETH. *Lawyers for the People: A New Breed of Defenders and Their Work*. Knopf, 1974. An exciting overview of the lawyers working to defend the public. 11–15

§ McNEER, MAY, and LYND WARD. *Armed with Courage*, ill. by Lynd Ward. Abingdon, 1957. Brief, entertaining biographies of seven dedicated men and women: Florence Nightingale, Father Damien, George W. Carver, Jane Addams, Wilfred Grenfell, Gandhi, and Albert Schweitzer. 9–12

§ MITCHISON, NAOMI. *African Heroes*, ill. by William Stobbs. Farrar, 1969. Eleven tales of great Africans from the sub-Sahara, told in the fluent prose of a storyteller. Much history is included, but the book's impact lies in the richness and dignity of the people and their complex traditions. 12 up

MONTGOMERY, ELIZABETH RIDER. *The Story Behind Great Stories*, ill. by Elinore Blaisdell. Dodd, 1947.

———. *The Story Behind Modern Books*. Dodd, 1949. Short sketches about authors and illustrators of children's books, both classic and recent. 11 up

ORR, FRANK. *Hockey's Greatest Stars*. Putnam, 1970. A Canadian sportswriter gives a lively and informative account of twenty-odd outstanding players. 10–13

§ RICHARDSON, BEN. *Great American Negroes*, rev. by William A. Fahey, ill. by Robert Hallock. T. Crowell, 1956. Vivid accounts of twenty black people who have overcome obstacles and who have contributed to American culture in many fields. 12–16

§ ROLLINS, CHARLEMAE HILL. *They Showed the Way: American Negro Leaders*. T. Crowell, 1964. Each life story is very brief, but the book is valuable for information about black leaders not available elsewhere. Other Rollins biographies are about black poets and black entertainers. 11–14

ROSENBLUM, MORRIS. *Heroes of Mexico*. Fleet, 1970. A survey of emperors, revolutionaries, artists, statesmen, and others who influenced the country's development. 12 up

SABIN, FRANCENE. *Women Who Win*, ill. with photos. Random, 1975. Both amateur and professional athletes are included. 11–14

§ SHOEMAKER, ROBERT H. *The Best in Baseball*, rev. ed. T. Crowell, 1974. From Ty Cobb and Babe Ruth to Cincinnati's Johnny Bench. 10 up

SMITH, ROBERT. *Pioneers of Baseball*, ill. with photos. Little, 1978. A series of brief sketches of some of the men who were baseball "firsts" includes some unexpected names along with the old familiar heroes. 6–9

§ STEVENSON, JANET. *Pioneers in Freedom: Adventures in Courage*. Reilly, 1969. Life histories of men and women, slave and free, who had the courage to fight for the truths stated in the Declaration of Independence. 9–11

STODDARD, HOPE. *Famous American Women*. T. Crowell, 1970. An unusually good collective biography, distinguished by a sprightly style, a variety of fields of endeavor, and the evidence of careful research that makes the book a reference source as well as entertaining reading. 11–15

SULLIVAN, GEORGE. *Queens of the Court*, ill. with photos. Dodd, 1974. Brisk, informal portraits of modern tennis greats. 11–14

§ TERKEL, LOUIS. *Giants of Jazz*, ill with photos. T. Crowell, 1975. A fine overview of jazz musicians and the music they make. 12–16

§ WALKER, GRETA. *Women Today: Ten Profiles*. Hawthorn, 1975. Interesting collection of modern women working in a variety of occupations. 11–14

●§ WEBB, ROBERT. *Heroes of Our Time*. Series 1. Watts, 1964. Followed by companion volumes; Series 4, for example (Watts, 1969), describes influential leaders of their countries and includes Brandt, Davan, Gandhi, Ho Chi Minh, and others. 11–13

WEINBERG, ARTHUR and LILA. *Some Dissenting Voices: The Story of Six American Dissenters*. World, 1970. Life stories of

Steffens, Debs, Darrow, Altgeld, Addams, and Ingersoll, with emphasis on their ideas.   11–15

YOUNG, BOB and JAN. *Liberators of Latin America.* Lothrop, 1970. Eleven biographical sketches are preceded by a chapter giving historical background and a concluding section on the rise of the new republics.   11–14

§ YOUNG, MARGARET B. *Black American Leaders.* Watts, 1969.   10–14

§ ———. *The First Book of American Negroes,* ill. with photos. Watts, 1966.   10–14

Individual Biographies

§ AARON, HENRY LOUIS (1934–   )
Burchard, Marshall and Sue. *Henry Aaron: Sports Hero,* rev. ed., ill. with photos. Putnam, 1974.   8–11
Gutman, Bill. *Hank Aaron.* Grosset, 1973. This book about baseball's superstar is useful for slow older readers as well as young readers.   8–10

ADAMS, SAMUEL (1722–1803)
Chidsey, Donald Barr. *The World of Samuel Adams.* Nelson, 1974. An affectionate but not laudatory biography of the querulous patriot.   12–15
Fritz, Jean. *Why Don't You Get a Horse, Sam Adams?* ill. by Trina Schart Hyman. Coward, 1974.   8–10

ADDAMS, JANE (1860–1935)
Meigs, Cornelia Lynde. *Jane Addams: Pioneer for Social Justice.* Little, 1970. The writing has warmth and cohesion and gives a vivid picture of an era in this excellent biography of an important social reformer.   11–15

ALCOTT, LOUISA MAY (1832–1888)
Meigs, Cornelia. *Invincible Louisa.* Little, 1968 (first pub. in 1933). Newbery Medal.   12–14
Papashvily, Helen. *Louisa May Alcott,* ill. by Bea Holmes. Houghton, 1965.   11–14

§ ALDRIDGE, IRA (1807–1867)
Malone, Mary. *Actor in Exile: The Life of Ira Aldridge,* ill. by Eros Keith. Crowell-Collier, 1969.   9–11

ALLEN, ETHAN (1738–1789)
Holbrook, Stewart. *America's Ethan Allen,* ill. by Lynd Ward. Houghton, 1949. Spirited illustrations in color add to the dramatic story of the "Green Mountain Boys" and their fighting leader.   11–15

§ ANDERSON, MARIAN (1902–   )
Tobias, Tobi. *Marian Anderson,* ill. by Symeon Shimin. T. Crowell, 1972.   7–9

ANTHONY, SUSAN B. (1820–1906)
Noble, Iris. *Susan B. Anthony.* Messner, 1975.   11–14

§ ARMSTRONG, LOUIS (1900–1971)
Eaton, Jeanette. *Trumpeter's Tale: The Story of Young Louis Armstrong,* ill. by Elton Fax. Morrow, 1955. Good biographical writing, and a good history of the development of jazz.   12–14

ASOKA, EMPEROR OF INDIA (3rd century B.C.)
Lengyel, Emil. *Asoka the Great: India's Royal Missionary.* Watts, 1969. The life of the man who spread Buddhism to India, China, and Japan. This is one of a series, "Immortals of Philosophy and Religion," that includes St. Augustine, Confucius, Martin Luther, Moses Maimonides, and St. Francis.   12 up

BACH, JOHANN SEBASTIAN (1685–1750)
Wheeler, Opal, and Sybil Deucher. *Sebastian Bach, the Boy from Thuringia,* ill. by Mary Greenwalt. Dutton, 1937. An easy, popular introduction to this composer.   9–10

BALBOA, VASCO NÚÑEZ DE (1475–1517)
Syme, Ronald. *Balboa, Finder of the Pacific,* ill. by William Stobbs. Morrow, 1956. Other explorer biographies include *Champlain of the St. Lawrence* (1952), *Henry Hudson* (1955), *Magellan, First Around the World* (1953).   10–12

§ BANNEKER, BENJAMIN (1731–1806)
Graham, Shirley. *Your Most Humble Servant: Story of Benjamin Banneker.* Messner, 1949.   14 up

BARTON, CLARA (1821–1912)
Boylston, Helen Dore. *Clara Barton, Founder of the American Red Cross,* ill. by Paula Hutchison. Random, 1955. Emphasizes Barton's work as a Civil War nurse rather than as the founder of the American Red Cross.   9–12

§ BECKWOURTH, JAMES PIERSON (1798–1867)
Felton, Harold. *Jim Beckwourth: Negro Mountain Man,* ill. with photos and prints of the period and maps. Dodd, 1966.   11–14

BEETHOVEN, LUDWIG VAN (1770–1827)
Wheeler, Opal. *Ludwig Beethoven and the Chiming Tower Bells,* ill. by Mary Greenwalt. Dutton, 1942. Not a fully candid biography, but appealing to younger children.   9–10

● BERNSTEIN, LEONARD (1918–   )
Ewen, David. *Leonard Bernstein: A Biography for Young People.* Chilton, 1960. Story of the notable American composer and conductor.   13 up

§ BETHUNE, MARY McLEOD (1875–1955)
Greenfield, Eloise. *Mary McLeod Bethune,* ill. by Jerry Pinkney. T. Crowell, 1977. This biography for younger readers does not have all the fascinating details of the life of the great educator, but it gives salient facts and is nicely balanced in treatment.   7–9
Peare, Catherine Owens. *Mary McLeod Bethune.* Vanguard, 1951.   13–15

BLACKWELL, ELIZABETH (1821–1910)
Clapp, Patricia. *Dr. Elizabeth: The Story of the First Woman Doctor.* Lothrop, 1974.   11–15

BLEGVAD, ERIK (1923–   )
Blegvad, Erik. *Self-Portrait: Erik Blegvad,* ill. by author. Addison, 1979. A brief autobiography marked by the same quirky sense of humor that has contributed to the popularity of Blegvad's children's book illustrations.   10 up

BOLIVAR, SIMON (1783–1830)
Syme, Ronald. *Bolivar the Liberator,* ill. by William Stobbs. Morrow, 1968.   9–12

BOONE, DANIEL (1734–1820)
Brown, John Mason. *Daniel Boone: The Opening of the Wilderness,* ill. by Lee J. Ames. Random, 1952. Fine characterization adds distinction to this biography of the Kentucky pioneer.   12–15
Daugherty, James. *Daniel Boone,* ill. by author. Viking, 1939. Newbery Medal.   12–15
Martin, Patricia Miles. *Daniel Boone,* ill. by Glen Dines. Putnam, 1965.   7–9

BOWDITCH, NATHANIEL (1773–1838)
Latham, Jean Lee. *Carry On, Mr. Bowditch,* ill. by John O'Hara Cosgrave II. Houghton, 1955. Newbery Medal.   11–15

● BRANDEIS, LOUIS (1856–1941)
Peare, Catherine Owens. *The Louis Brandeis Story.* T. Crowell, 1970.   11–13

BRONTË, CHARLOTTE (1816–1855)
Kyle, Elisabeth. *Girl with a Pen: Charlotte Brontë.* Holt, 1964.   12 up
Vipont, Elfrida. *Weaver of Dreams: The Girlhood of Charlotte Brontë.* Walck, 1966. A good biography of Charlotte Brontë, giving a quite absorbing and dramatic picture of the isolated family. Some instances of fairly florid writing and imaginary conversation.   11–14

BUCK, PEARL (1892–1973)

Block, Irving. *The Lives of Pearl Buck: A Tale of China and America.* T. Crowell, 1973. Smoothly written and balanced biography of an amazing woman who was both a talented writer and a compassionate human being.   12 up

§ BUNCHE, RALPH (1904–1971)

Haskins, James. *Ralph Bunche: A Most Reluctant Hero,* ill. with photos. Hawthorn, 1974.   12–16

BUONARROTI, MICHELANGELO (1475–1564)

Coughlan, Robert. *The World of Michelangelo.* Time-Life, 1966. Like other volumes in the magnificent Time-Life Library of Art, this is profusely illustrated with reproductions of the artist's work.   12 up

Ripley, Elizabeth. *Michelangelo.* Walck, 1953.   12–15

CABOT, JOHN (1450–1498)

Hill, Kay. *And Tomorrow the Stars: The Story of John Cabot,* ill. by Laszlo Kubinyi. Dodd, 1968. An excellent biography, convincingly fictionalized and carefully researched, giving vivid pictures of the dream-driven mariner Cabot and of Venice at the zenith of her power. Canadian Library Association Award.   12 up

§ CAMPANELLA, ROY (1921–   )

Schoor, Gene. *Roy Campanella: Man of Courage.* Putnam, 1959. A warm life story of the Dodger catcher who fought against crippling injuries.   9–11

CARSON, CHRISTOPHER (1809–1868)

Bell, Margaret E. *Kit Carson, Mountain Man,* ill. by Harry Daugherty. Morrow, 1952. A short dramatic biography with large print and many illustrations.   8–11

Garst, Shannon. *Kit Carson, Trail Blazer and Scout,* ill. by Harry Daugherty. Messner, 1942.   11 up

CARSON, RACHEL (1907–1964)

Sterling, Philip. *Sea and Earth: The Life of Rachel Carson.* T. Crowell, 1970. A beautifully balanced biography, written with skill and restraint.   12 up

§ CARVER, GEORGE WASHINGTON (1864?–1943)

Aliki. *A Weed Is a Flower: The Life of George Washington Carver,* ill. by author. Prentice, 1965.   5–8

CASSATT, MARY (1845–1926)

Wilson, Ellen. *American Painter in Paris: A Life of Mary Cassatt.* Farrar, 1971. Photographs and reproductions of paintings enliven the story of a distinguished artist. 11 up

CATHER, WILLA SIBERT (1873–1947)

Franchere, Ruth. *Willa,* ill. by Leonard Weisgard. T. Crowell, 1958. Willa Cather's pioneer childhood in Nebraska is vividly portrayed, and younger readers unfamiliar with her novels will enjoy the biography as a good story.   11–14

CATHERINE II, EMPRESS OF RUSSIA (1729–1796)

Noble, Iris. *Empress of All Russia: Catherine the Great.* Messner, 1966.   12–15

● CHAGALL, MARC (1887–   )

Greenfeld, Howard. *Marc Chagall.* Follett, 1967.   12–15

§ CHAMBERLAIN, WILT (1936–   )

Rudeen, Kenneth. *Wilt Chamberlain,* ill. by Frank Mullins. T. Crowell, 1970. The basketball star is described in a simply written and balanced book.   7–9

CHAPLIN, CHARLES (1889–1977)

Jacobs, David. *Chaplin, the Movies, and Charlie,* ill. with photos. Harper, 1975. A total picture of the man who gave pleasure to millions as a comic/commentator on our human frailties.   12 up

CHAPMAN, JOHN (1774–1845)

Aliki. *The Story of Johnny Appleseed,* ill. by author. Prentice, 1963.   7–8

Hunt, Mabel Leigh. *Better Known as Johnny Appleseed,* ill. by James Daugherty. Lippincott, 1950. The life of John Chapman, "American pioneer, missionary, and apple lover," based on old legends and reminiscences gathered by the author.   12–16

★ CHAVEZ, CESAR (1928–   )

Franchere, Ruth. *Cesar Chavez,* ill. by Earl Thollander. T. Crowell, 1970.   7–9

Terzian, James, and Kathryn Cramer. *Mighty Hard Road: The Story of Cesar Chavez.* Doubleday, 1970.   11–14

CHILD, LYDIA MARIA (1802–1880)

Meltzer, Milton. *Tongue of Flame: The Life of Lydia Maria Child.* T. Crowell, 1965.   13–15

§ CHISHOLM, SHIRLEY (1924–   )

Brownmiller, Susan. *Shirley Chisholm,* ill. Doubleday, 1970.   10–14

Haskins, James. *Fighting Shirley Chisholm,* ill. with photos. Dial, 1975.   12–16

CHOU EN-LAI (1898–1976)

Archer, Jules. *Chou En-lai.* Hawthorn, 1973.   12–15

CHUKOVSKY, KORNEI (1882–1969)

Chukovsky, Kornei. *The Silver Crest: My Russian Boyhood,* tr. by Beatrice Stillman. Holt, 1976. A delightful reminiscence by a major Russian writer for children.   11 up

CHURCHILL, SIR WINSTON LEONARD SPENCER (1874–1965)

Coolidge, Olivia. *Winston Churchill and the Story of Two World Wars,* ill. with photos. Houghton, 1960. The twentieth century becomes vividly alive and significant in this story of the great British statesman.   13–16

CLEMENS, SAMUEL LANGHORNE (1835–1910)

Eaton, Jeanette. *America's Own Mark Twain,* ill. by Leonard Everett Fisher. Morrow, 1958. Mississippi riverboat days and life in the West are absorbing highlights of this well-rounded story of one of America's most colorful authors.   12–16

McNeer, May. *America's Mark Twain,* ill. by Lynd Ward. Houghton, 1962. Colorful illustrations and a lively text make this biography attractive to a wide range of readers.   10–14

Wood, James Playsted. *Spunkwater, Spunkwater! A Life of Mark Twain,* ill. with photos. Pantheon, 1968.   11–15

CLEOPATRA, QUEEN OF EGYPT (69–30 B.C.)

Desmond, Alice Curtis. *Cleopatra's Children,* ill. with maps, charts, and photos. Dodd, 1971.   11–14

Leighton, Margaret. *Cleopatra: Sister of the Moon.* Farrar, 1969.   12–15

CODY, WILLIAM (BUFFALO BILL) (1846–1917)

d'Aulaire, Ingri and Edgar Parin. *Buffalo Bill,* ill. by authors. Doubleday, 1952.   7–9

COLUMBUS, CHRISTOPHER (1451–1506)

Dalgliesh, Alice. *The Columbus Story,* ill. by Leo Politi. Scribner's, 1955.   8–10

d'Aulaire, Ingri and Edgar Parin. *Columbus,* ill. by authors. Doubleday, 1955.   7–9

Judson, Clara Ingram. *Admiral Christopher Columbus,* ill. by W. T. Mars. Follett, 1965.   10 up

McGovern, Ann. *The Story of Christopher Columbus.* Random, 1963.   7–10

Sperry, Armstrong. *Voyages of Christopher Columbus,* ill. by author. Random, 1950.   8–10

Syme, Ronald. *Columbus, Finder of the New World,* ill. by William Stobbs. Morrow, 1952.   10–13

COOK, JAMES (1728–1779)

Latham, Jean. *Far Voyager: The Story of James Cook,* maps by Karl W. Stuecklen. Harper, 1970.   10–13

Syme, Ronald. *Captain Cook: Pacific Explorer,* ill. by William Stobbs. Morrow, 1960. The English navigator's eighteenth-century explorations of the South Pacific climax a fast-paced, fully illustrated biography.   10–13

COOPER, PETER (1791–1883)

Gurko, Miriam. *The Lives and Times of Peter Cooper,* ill. by Jerome Snyder, diagrams by Ava Morgan. T. Crowell, 1959.   12 up

CRANDALL, PRUDENCE (1803–1889)

Yates, Elizabeth. *Prudence Crandall: Woman of Courage,* ill. by Nora S. Unwin. Aladdin, 1955.   12–15

☆ CRAZY HORSE, OGLALA CHIEF (1842?–1877)

Garst, Doris Shannon. *Crazy Horse, Great Warrior of the Sioux,* ill. by William Moyers. Houghton, 1950. This biography gives good perspective on why the Indians so bitterly opposed the white men.   12–15

Meadowcroft, Enid. *The Story of Crazy Horse,* ill. by William Reusswig. Grosset, 1954. Biography of the Oglala chief who opposed Custer and who died escaping imprisonment.   9–12

CURIE, MARIE (1867–1934)

Veglahn, Nancy. *The Mysterious Rays: Marie Curie's World,* ill. by Victor Juhasz. Coward, 1977. A quietly dramatic picture of the long years of patient research that led Marie Curie to the tracing and isolation of radium.   8–10

DAMIEN, FATHER (1840–1889)

Roos, Ann. *Man of Molokai: The Life of Father Damien,* ill. by Raymond Lufkin. Lippincott, 1943. Moving story of a great modern saint who spent his life in the service of lepers.   11–14

DARROW, CLARENCE (1857–1938)

Faber, Doris. *Clarence Darrow: Defender of the People,* ill. by Paul Frame. Prentice, 1965. A balanced and objective book.   10–12

Gurko, Miriam. *Clarence Darrow.* T. Crowell, 1965.   13 up

● DAVID, KING OF ISRAEL

Bolliger, Max. *David,* ill. by Edith Schindler. Delacorte, 1967. The life of David up to the point of his becoming King of Israel.   9–12

DA VINCI, LEONARDO (1452–1519)

Noble, Iris. *Leonardo da Vinci: The Universal Genius,* ill. Norton, 1965. Despite a considerable amount of fictionalization, the painter comes alive as a distinctive personality.   11–14

DEBS, EUGENE VICTOR (1855–1926)

Noble, Iris. *Labor's Advocate: Eugene V. Debs.* Messner, 1966. Portrays the movements in which Debs was a pioneer.   11–14

§ DELANY, MARTIN ROBISON (1812–1885)

Sterling, Dorothy. *The Making of an Afro-American: Martin Robison Delany 1812–1885.* Doubleday, 1971.   11 up

☆ DES JARLAIT, PATRICK (1921–1972)

Des Jarlait, Patrick. *Patrick Des Jarlait: The Story of an American Indian Artist,* as told to Neva Williams. Lerner, 1975.   11–14

DICKENS, CHARLES (1812–1870)

Kyle, Elisabeth. *Great Ambitions: A Story of the Early Years of Charles Dickens.* Holt, 1968.   12–15

DICKINSON, EMILY (1830–1886)

Fisher, Aileen, and Olive Rabe. *We Dickinsons: The Life of Emily Dickinson as Seen Through the Eyes of Her Brother Austin,* ill. by Ellen Raskin. Atheneum, 1965.   12–15

Longsworth, Polly. *Emily Dickinson: Her Letter to the World.* T. Crowell, 1965.   13 up

§ DOUGLASS, FREDERICK (1817?–1895)

Douglass, Frederick. *Life and Times of Frederick Douglass,* ad. by Barbara Ritchie. T. Crowell, 1966. First published

in 1842 and last revised by the author in 1892. This is a very good adaptation with no deletion of important material.   11–15

Graham, Shirley. *There Was Once a Slave: The Heroic Story of Frederick Douglass.* Messner, 1947.   12 up

§ DREW, CHARLES RICHARD (1904–1950)

Bertol, Roland. *Charles Drew,* ill. by Jo Polseno. T. Crowell, 1970. First director of the Red Cross Blood Bank, the distinguished black doctor fought prejudice throughout his life.   7–9

§ DuBOIS, W. E. B. (1868–1963)

Hamilton, Virginia. *W. E. B. DuBois: A Biography,* ill. with photos. T. Crowell, 1972.   12–16

Lacy, Leslie Alexander. *Cheer the Lonesome Traveler: The Life of W. E. B. DuBois,* ill. by James Barkley and with photos. Dial, 1970. An excellent biography for young people of one of the most eminent black American leaders. The writing style is brisk, competent, and dispassionate.   12–15

§ DUNBAR, PAUL LAURENCE (1872–1906)

Gayle, Addison. *Oak and Ivy: A Biography of Paul Laurence Dunbar.* Doubleday, 1971. A candid account of the black writer.   11–14

EDISON, THOMAS ALVA (1847–1931)

North, Sterling. *Young Thomas Edison,* ill. by William Barss. Houghton, 1958. Outstanding biography of Edison both as a man and as an inventive genius.   11–15

ELEANOR OF AQUITAINE (1122?–1204)

Konigsburg, Elaine. *A Proud Taste for Scarlet and Miniver,* ill. by author. Atheneum, 1973. Not quite biography, yet more than historical fiction, this is a delightful look at Eleanor, Henry II, and the people around them.   12–16

ELIZABETH I, QUEEN OF ENGLAND (1533–1603)

Hanff, Helene. *Queen of England, The Story of Elizabeth I,* ill. by Ronald Dorgman. Doubleday, 1969.   10–13

§ ELLINGTON, DUKE (1899–1974)

Gutman, Bill. *Duke: The Musical Life of Duke Ellington.* Random, 1977. A musical rather than a personal biography, this is useful as a contribution to musical history in the United States.   12–15

ERICSSON, JOHN (1803–1889)

Burnett, Constance Buel. *Captain John Ericsson: Father of the "Monitor."* Vanguard, 1961. Failure as well as success marked the life of the Swedish-born genius.   12–16

ERIKSSON, LEIF (b. tenth century)

Shippen, Katherine. *Leif Eriksson: First Voyager to America.* Harper, 1951. Well-written, exciting biography of the explorer of Vinland.   11–13

ESPOSITO, PHILLIP (1942–   )

Burchard, Marshall and Sue. *Phil Esposito: Sports Hero,* ill. with photos. Putnam, 1975.   8–11

FIELD, CYRUS (1819–1892)

Latham, Jean Lee. *Young Man in a Hurry: The Story of Cyrus Field,* ill. by Victor Mays. Harper, 1958. An account of the laying of the Atlantic cable and of the unconquerable Cyrus Field.   12 up

FITZGERALD, F. SCOTT (1896–1940)

Greenfeld, Howard. *F. Scott Fitzgerald.* Crown, 1974. 12–15

§ FORTEN, CHARLOTTE (1838–1914)

Douty, Esther M. *Charlotte Forten: Free Black Teacher.* Garrard, 1971.   9–11

Longsworth, Polly. *I, Charlotte Forten, Black and Free.* T. Crowell, 1970.   11–14

§ FORTEN, JAMES (1766–1842)

Douty, Esther M. *Forten the Sailmaker: Pioneer Champion of Negro Rights,* ill. with photos. Rand, 1968.   12–15

§ FORTUNE, AMOS (1709?–1801)

Yates, Elizabeth. *Amos Fortune, Free Man*, ill. by Nora S. Unwin. Dutton, 1950. Newbery Medal.   10–13

FRANCIS OF ASSISI, SAINT (1182–1226)

Bulla, Clyde. *Song of St. Francis*, ill. by Valenti Angelo. T. Crowell, 1952. The appealing story of St. Francis of Assisi presented in simple fashion for younger readers. 8–10

FRANKLIN, BENJAMIN (1706–1790)

Daugherty, Charles Michael. *Benjamin Franklin: Scientist-Diplomat*, ill. by John Falter. Macmillan, 1965. This very simple biography gives a quite adequate biographical outline. Barely fictionalized and not condescending. 8–10

Daugherty, James. *Poor Richard*, ill. by author. Viking, 1941.   12–15

d'Aulaire, Ingri and Edgar Parin. *Benjamin Franklin*, ill. by authors. Doubleday, 1950.   7–9

Eaton, Jeanette. *That Lively Man, Ben Franklin*, ill. by Henry C. Pitz. Morrow, 1948. Franklin's many-sided career, from printer to ambassador.   11–14

Fleming, Thomas J. *Benjamin Franklin*. Four Winds, 1973. Insightful and witty with information not found in most other juvenile biographies.   11–14

Fritz, Jean. *What's the Big Idea, Ben Franklin?* ill. by Margot Tomes. Coward, 1976.   8–10

Merriam, Eve. *The Story of Ben Franklin*, ill. by Brinton Turkle. Four Winds, 1965.   7–9

Scarf, Maggi. *Meet Benjamin Franklin*, ill. by Harry Beckhoff. Random, 1968.   7–11

§ FREEMAN, ELIZABETH (1744?–1829)

Felton, Harold W. *Mumbet: The Story of Elizabeth Freeman*, ill. by Donn Albright. Dodd, 1970.   9–11

FULLER, RICHARD BUCKMINSTER (1895–   )

Rosen, Sidney. *Wizard of the Dome: R. Buckminster Fuller, Designer for the Future*. Little, 1969.   12 up

FULTON, ROBERT (1765–1815)

Judson, Clara Ingram. *Boat Builder: The Story of Robert Fulton*, ill. by Armstrong Sperry. Scribner's, 1940.   9–11

GALILEI, GALILEO (1564–1642)

Cobb, Vicki. *Truth on Trial: The Story of Galileo Galilei*, ill. by George Ulrich. Coward, 1979. Focusing on Galileo's ideas rather than his personal life, this has as its center the conflicting Ptolemaic and Copernican theories of the structure of the universe.   9–10

Rosen, Sidney. *Galileo and the Magic Numbers*, ill. by Harve Stein. Little, 1958.   12 up

GANDHI, MOHANDAS K. (1869–1948)

Coolidge, Olivia. *Gandhi*. Houghton, 1971.   11–14

Eaton, Jeanette. *Gandhi: Fighter Without a Sword*, ill. by Ralph Ray. Morrow, 1950.   13–15

Peare, Catherine Owens, *Mahatma Gandhi: Father of Non-violence*. Hawthorn, 1969.   12 up

GANNETT, DEBORAH (SAMPSON) (1760–1827)

Felton, Harold. *Deborah Sampson: Soldier of the Revolution*. Dodd, 1976.   10–12

McGovern, Ann. *The Secret Soldier: The Story of Deborah Sampson*, ill. by Ann Grifalconi. Four Winds, 1975. A simply written account of the woman who donned men's clothing to serve in the Continental Army.   8–10

GARIBALDI, GIUSEPPE (1807–1882)

Syme, Ronald. *Garibaldi: The Man Who Made a Nation*, ill. by William Stobbs. Morrow, 1967.   11–14

GARRISON, WILLIAM LLOYD (1805–1879)

Archer, Jules. *Angry Abolitionist: William Lloyd Garrison*. Messner, 1969.   12 up

Faber, Doris. *I Will Be Heard: The Life of William Lloyd Garrison*. Lothrop, 1970.   9–12

GAUTIER, FELISA RINCON DE (1897–   )

Gruber, Ruth. *Felisa Rincon de Gautier: The Mayor of San Juan*, ill. with photos. T. Crowell, 1972. A biography that combines Puerto Rican history with the life of an amazing woman.   11–14

☆ GERONIMO, APACHE CHIEF (1829–1909)

Wyatt, Edgar. *Geronimo, the Last Apache War Chief*, ill. by Allan Houser. Whittlesey, 1952. The story of a great Indian hero.   11–14

● GERSHWIN, GEORGE (1898–1937)

Ewen, David. *The Story of George Gershwin*, ill. by Graham Bernbach. Holt, 1943. Memories of an American composer of popular music by a personal friend.   12–16

GOGH, VINCENT VAN (1853–1890)

Dobrin, Arnold. *I Am a Stranger on the Earth: The Story of Vincent Van Gogh*, ill. with reproductions. Warne, 1975. Effectively conveys the essence of Van Gogh's personality and the reproductions convey the essence of his work.   10–12

GRAHAM, MARTHA (1894–   )

Terry, Walter. *Frontiers of Dance: The Life of Martha Graham*, ill. with photos. T. Crowell, 1975. A nice combination of objectivity and affection makes the great dancer real as both artist and person.   11 up

GREELEY, HORACE (1811–1872)

Faber, Doris. *Horace Greeley: The People's Editor*, ill. by Paul Frame. Prentice, 1964.   9–12

GRIEG, EDVARD (1843–1907)

Kyle, Elisabeth. *Song of the Waterfall: The Story of Edvard and Nina Grieg*. Holt, 1970. Also gives a good picture of life in nineteenth-century Norway.   10–12

HAMILTON, ALICE (1869–1970)

Grant, Madeleine P. *Alice Hamilton: Pioneer Doctor in Industrial Medicine*. Abelard, 1968. The inspiring story of a woman whose career encompassed both science and social reform.   12–14

HANCOCK, JOHN (1737–1793)

Fritz, Jean. *Will You Sign Here, John Hancock?* ill. by Trina Schart Hyman. Coward, 1976. An amusing but accurate biography of a signer of the Declaration of Independence, and president of the Continental Congress.   8–10

● HAUTZIG, ESTHER

Hautzig, Esther. *The Endless Steppe: Growing Up in Siberia*. T. Crowell, 1968. The true and harrowing story of five arduous years spent by Esther and her family in forced labor in Siberia, all the more effective because it is told with direct simplicity and no bitterness.   11–15

HAWTHORNE, NATHANIEL (1804–1864)

Gaeddert, Louise. *A New England Love Story*. Dial, 1980. As rich in its depiction of New England intellectualism as it is in describing the lively, devoted Nathaniel and his Sophia.   12–14

HENRY, PATRICK (1736–1799)

Campion, Nardi Reeder. *Patrick Henry: Firebrand of the Revolution*, ill. by Victor Mays. Little, 1961.   12 up

Fritz, Jean. *Where Was Patrick Henry on the 29th of May?* ill. by Margot Tomes. Coward, 1975.   8–10

HERSCHEL, SIR WILLIAM (1738–1822)

Crawford, Deborah. *The King's Astronomer: William Herschel*. Messner, 1968. Although highly fictionalized, the dialogue uses language that seems so right for the period that it is an asset to the book. A good balance of personal and scientific material.   11–14

HITLER, ADOLF (1889–1945)

Shirer, William L. *The Rise and Fall of Adolf Hitler*, ill. with photos. Random, 1961. In this biography of the Nazi dictator, emphasis is on political events, stirringly recorded for younger readers.   11–14

HOKUSAI (1760–1849)

Ripley, Elizabeth. *Hokusai.* Lippincott, 1968.   11–14

● HOOVER, HERBERT CLARK (1874–1964)

Peare, Catherine Owens. *The Herbert Hoover Story.* T. Crowell, 1965.   11–14

HOWE, SAMUEL GRIDLEY (1801–1876)

Meltzer, Milton. *A Light in the Dark: The Life of Samuel Gridley Howe.* T. Crowell, 1964.   12–15

§ HUGHES, JAMES LANGSTON (1902–1967)

Meltzer, Milton. *Langston Hughes: A Biography.* T. Crowell, 1968.   12 up

Walker, Alice. *Langston Hughes, American Poet,* ill. by Don Miller. T. Crowell, 1974.   7–9

HUMBOLDT, ALEXANDER, FREIHERR VON (1769–1859)

Thomas, M. Z. (pseud.). *Alexander von Humboldt,* tr. by Elizabeth Brommer, ill. by Ulrik Schramm. Pantheon, 1960. Von Humboldt's adventures in the South American jungles are vivid and unforgettable in this life story of the explorer-naturalist.   11–15

INOUYE, DANIEL (1924–   )

Goodsell, Jane. *Daniel Inouye,* ill. by Haru Wells. T. Crowell, 1977. This is just short of adulatory in describing Inouye's determination, industry, courage, and altruism.   8–9

☆ ISHI (d. 1916)

Kroeber, Theodora. *Ishi: Last of His Tribe,* ill. by Ruth Robbins. Parnassus, 1964.   12 up

JACKSON, ANDREW (1767–1845)

De Kay, Ormonde. *Meet Andrew Jackson,* ill. by Isa Barnett. Random, 1967.   7–9

Fritz, Jean. *Stonewall,* ill. by Stephen Gammell. Putnam, 1979. Fritz focuses on Jackson's prowess as a military leader, and most of the book is concerned with the years of the Civil War, but the early portion of the text skillfully establishes Jackson's probity, eccentricity, and toughness.   11–14

§ JACKSON, MAHALIA (1911–1972)

Jackson, Jesse. *Make a Joyful Noise Unto the Lord! The Life of Mahalia Jackson, Queen of Gospel Singers,* ill. with photos. T. Crowell, 1974. Excellent biography of a woman of courage, vitality, and integrity.   11–14

JEFFERSON, THOMAS (1743–1826)

Fleming, Thomas J. *Thomas Jefferson.* Grosset, 1971.   11–14

Lisitzky, Gene. *Thomas Jefferson,* ill. by Harrie Wood. Viking, 1933. A well-balanced picture of the many facets of this complex man.   12–15

Wibberley, Leonard. *Man of Liberty: A Life of Thomas Jefferson.* Farrar, 1968.

JOAN OF ARC, SAINT (1412–1431)

Churchill, Winston. *Joan of Arc: Her Life as Told by Winston Churchill,* ill. by Lauren Ford. Dodd, 1969.   8 up

Fisher, Aileen. *Jeanne d'Arc,* ill. by Ati Forberg. T. Crowell, 1970.   8–10

Paine, Albert. *The Girl in White Armor,* ill. by Joe Isom. Macmillan, 1967 (first pub. in 1927).   11–14

§ JOHNSON, JAMES WELDON (1871–1938)

Egypt, Ophelia Settle. *James Weldon Johnson,* ill. by Moneta Barnett. T. Crowell, 1974.   8–10

JONES, JOHN PAUL (1747–1792)

Sperry. Armstrong. *John Paul Jones: Fighting Sailor,* ill. by author. Random, 1953. The life of the naval hero who suffered injustice throughout his career.   10–13

JONES, MARY (1830–1930)

Atkinson, Linda. *Mother Jones: The Most Dangerous Woman in America.* Crown, 1978. A serious, forthright record of Mary Jones, the woman who devoted her life to the labor movement.   12 up

§ JORDAN, BARBARA (1936–   )

Haskins, James. *Barbara Jordan,* ill. with photos. Dial, 1977.   12 up

☆ JOSEPH, NEZ PERCÉ CHIEF (1840–1904)

Davis, Russell, and Brent Ashabranner. *Chief Joseph, War Chief of the Nez Percé.* McGraw, 1962. The tragic story of a peace-loving chief forced into war as his people opposed the westward movement.   12–16

KEMBLE, FRANCES ANN (1809–1893)

Scott, John Anthony. *Fanny Kemble's America.* T. Crowell, 1973.   12–16

KHERDIAN, VERON (1907–   )

Kherdian, David. *The Road from Home: The Story of an Armenian girl.* Greenwillow, 1979. Deported from Turkey in the campaign of persecution against Armenians, Veron reached safety in Syria and came to the U.S. as a sixteen-year-old mail order bride.   11–14

KING, BILLIE JEAN (1943–   )

Burchard, Marshall and Sue. *Sports Hero: Billie Jean King,* rev. ed., ill. with photos. Putnam, 1975.   8–11

§ KING, MARTIN LUTHER, JR. (1929–1968)

Clayton, Ed. *Martin Luther King: The Peaceful Warrior,* ill. by David Hodges. Prentice, 1964.   9–11

De Kay, James T. *Meet Martin Luther King, Jr.,* ill. with photos and drawings by Ted Burwell. Random, 1969.   7–9

Haskins, James. *The Life and Death of Martin Luther King, Jr.,* ill. with photos. Lothrop, 1977.   12 up

Patterson, Lillie. *Martin Luther King, Jr.: Man of Peace,* ill. by Victor Mays. Garrard, 1969.   8–9

Young, Margaret B. *The Picture Life of Martin Luther King, Jr.,* ill. with photos. Watts, 1968.   7–8

LAFAYETTE, MARIE JOSEPH PAUL YVES ROCH GILBERT DU MOTIER, MARQUIS DE (1757–1834)

Eaton, Jeanette. *Young Lafayette,* ill. by David Hendrickson. Houghton, 1932.   12–16

Gottschalk, Fruma. *The Youngest General: A Story of Lafayette,* ill. by Rafaello Busoni. Knopf, 1949. Unusual original sources were used in this biography.   10–14

☆ LA FLESCHE, SUSETTE (1854–1903)

Crary, Margaret. *Susette La Flesche: Voice of the Omaha Indians.* Hawthorn, 1973.   11–14

LAWRENCE, THOMAS EDWARD (1888–1935)

MacLean, Alistair. *Lawrence of Arabia.* Random, 1962. The absorbingly told life story of the great military leader in the Arab-Turkish revolt.   11–14

LAWSON, ROBERT (1892–1957)

Jones, Helen L., ed. *Robert Lawson, Illustrator,* ill. Little, 1972. Lawson's illustrations and his editor's commentary should interest students of children's literature as well as young readers who have enjoyed his books.   10 up

● LEE, ANN (1736–1784)

Campion, Nardi Reeder. *Ann the Word: The Life of Mother Ann Lee, Founder of the Shakers.* Little, 1976. Based on extensive research, Campion's narrative brings a remarkable woman vividly to life.   12 up

LEE, ROBERT EDWARD (1807–1870)

Commager, Henry Steele. *America's Robert E. Lee,* ill. by Lynd Ward. Houghton, 1951. Lee is a hero all America should be proud of, and this biography shows why.   11–15

LILIUOKALANI, QUEEN OF THE HAWAIIAN ISLANDS (1838–1917)

Wilson, Hazel. *The Last Queen of Hawaii: Liliuokalani,* ill. by W. T. Mars. Knopf, 1963. Includes some Hawaiian history.   11–14

LINCOLN, ABRAHAM (1809–1865)

Bulla, Clyde. *Lincoln's Birthday,* ill. by Ernest Crichlow. T. Crowell, 1966. 8–9

Daugherty, James. *Abraham Lincoln,* ill. by author. Viking, 1943. 12–15

d'Aulaire, Ingri and Edgar Parin. *Abraham Lincoln,* ill. by authors. Doubleday, 1939. Caldecott Medal. 12–14

Fisher, Aileen. *My Cousin Abe,* ill. by Leonard Vosburgh. Nelson, 1962. Dennis Hanks tells the story of his younger relative with the warmth and tenderness inspired by the close family relationship. Although introducing a narrator, the author faithfully follows the details of Lincoln's life. 11–15

Foster, Genevieve. *Abraham Lincoln: An Initial Biography,* ill. by author. Scribner's, 1950.

Hays, Wilma P. *Abe Lincoln's Birthday,* ill. by Peter Burchard. Coward, 1961. 7–10

Judson, Clara Ingram. *Abraham Lincoln,* ill. by Polly Jackson. Follett, 1961. 7–9

———. *Abraham Lincoln, Friend of the People,* ill. by Robert Frankenberg and with photos. Follett, 1950. 11–15

Monjo, Ferdinand N. *Me and Willie and Pa,* ill. by Douglas Gorsline. Simon, 1973. 8–10

Sandburg, Carl. *Abe Lincoln Grows Up,* ill. by James Daugherty. Harcourt, 1928. 11–16

LINCOLN, MARY TODD (1818–1882)

Randall, Ruth Painter. *I Mary,* ill. with photos. Little, 1959. A sincere and honest biography of Mary Todd Lincoln which helps to dispel some of the unhappy legends associated with her life. 12–16

LINDBERGH, CHARLES (1902–1974)

Dalgliesh, Alice. *Ride on the Wind,* ill. by Georges Schreiber. Scribner's, 1956. 7–9

☆ LONESOME STAR (c. 1815)

Sobol, Rose. *Woman Chief.* Dial, 1976. A sound biography of Lonesome Star, who lived as husband and wife with another woman and won the name Woman Chief, this also gives a sympathetic and detailed picture of the Plains Indians. 11–13

§ LOVE, NAT (1854?–1921?)

Felton, Harold W. *Nat Love, Negro Cowboy,* ill. by David Hodges. Dodd, 1969. Gives a lively picture of the Old West. 9–10

LUTHER, MARTIN (1483–1546)

McNeer, May. *Martin Luther,* ill. by Lynd Ward. Abingdon, 1953. The fighting spirit of Martin Luther makes his life story both difficult and thrilling. Superb illustrations add distinction to this book. 12–14

McKINLEY, WILLIAM (1843–1901)

Hoyt, Edwin P. *William McKinley.* Reilly, 1967. 13–15

§ MALCOLM X (1925–1965)

Adoff, Arnold. *Malcolm X,* ill. by John Wilson. T. Crowell, 1970. 8–10

Curtis, Richard. *The Life of Malcolm X.* Macrae, 1971. 11–15

Haskins, James. *The Picture Life of Malcolm X,* ill. Watts, 1975. 8–10

§ MARSHALL, THURGOOD (1908–   )

Young, Margaret B. *The Picture Life of Thurgood Marshall.* Watts, 1971. 8–10

§ MARTIN DE PORRES, SAINT (1579–1639)

Bishop, Claire Huchet. *Martin de Porres, Hero,* ill. by Jean Charlot. Houghton, 1954. 12–14

MATHER, COTTON (1663–1728)

Wood, James Playsted. *The Admirable Cotton Mather.* Seabury, 1971. 13 up

MAURY, MATTHEW FONTAINE (1806–1873)

Latham, Jean Lee. *Trail Blazer of the Seas,* ill. by Victor Mays. Houghton, 1956. Absorbing story of the scientific U.S. Naval Lieutenant Matthew Fontaine Maury, who studied winds and currents to reduce ships' sailing time. 11–15

MEAD, MARGARET (1901–1978)

Epstein, Samuel and Beryl. *She Never Looked Back: Margaret Mead in Samoa,* ill. by Victor Juhasz. Coward, 1980. This focuses on one period, but covers all of the anthropologist's life. 9–11

● MEIR, GOLDA (1898–1978)

Dobrin, Arnold. *A Life for Israel: The Story of Golda Meir.* Dial, 1974. 9–12

MICHELANGELO. See BUONARROTI, MICHELANGELO.

MILLAY, EDNA ST. VINCENT (1892–1950)

Gurko, Miriam. *Restless Spirit: The Life of Edna St. Vincent Millay.* T. Crowell, 1962. 13 up

Shafter, Toby. *Edna St. Vincent Millay: America's Best-Loved Poet.* Messner, 1957. 12 up

§ MITCHELL, ARTHUR (1934–   )

Tobias, Tobi. *Arthur Mitchell,* ill. by Carole Byard. T. Crowell, 1975. 8–10

MOZART, JOHANN CHRYSOSTOM WOLFGANG AMADEUS (1756–1791)

Komroff, Manuel. *Mozart,* ill. by Warren Chappell and with photos. Knopf, 1956. Written to commemorate the two-hundredth anniversary of Mozart's birth, this is an outstanding biography. 11–15

Monjo, Ferdinand N. *Letters to Horseface: Being the Story of Wolfgang Amadeus Mozart's Journey to Italy 1769–1770 When He Was a Boy of Fourteen,* ill. by Don Bolognese and Elaine Raphael. Viking, 1975. 10–12

MUIR, JOHN (1838–1914)

Swift, Hildegarde. *From the Eagle's Wing: A Biography of John Muir,* ill. by Lynd Ward. Morrow, 1962. A fascinating biography for budding naturalists. 12 up

MUSIAL, STANLEY FRANK (1920–   )

Robinson, Ray. *Stan Musial: Baseball's Durable "Man."* Putnam, 1963. Comments from Musial's colleagues attest to the popularity of "Stan the Man." 10–12

NIGHTINGALE, FLORENCE (1820–1910)

Nolan, Jeannette Covert. *Florence Nightingale,* ill. by George Avison. Messner, 1946. Florence Nightingale's life story stresses her work rather than her personal life. 11–14

NOGUCHI, ISAMU (1904–   )

Tobias, Tobi. *Isamu Noguchi: The Life of a Sculptor,* ill. T. Crowell, 1974. 8–10

§ NORTHUP, SOLOMON (1808–?)

Knight, Michael, ed. *In Chains to Louisiana.* Dutton, 1971. Adapted from Northup's autobiography in which he told of being kidnapped and sold into slavery. 11–15

ORR, ROBERT (1948–   )

Burchard, Marshall and Sue. *Bobby Orr: Sports Hero,* ill. with photos. Putnam, 1973. 8–10

PAINE, THOMAS (1737–1809)

Coolidge, Olivia E. *Tom Paine, Revolutionary.* Scribner's, 1969. An infinitely detailed and vivid picture of affairs in France, England, and the colonies during Paine's career, and an objective picture of the man. Sophisticated biographical writing. 12 up

PANDIT, VIJAYA LAKSHMI (NEHRU) (1900–   )

Guthrie, Anne. *Madame Ambassador: The Life of Vijaya Lakshmi Pandit,* ill. with photos. Harcourt, 1962. Both an absorbing personal story of India's stateswoman and a unique picture of India's changing history. 13–16

PANKHURST, EMMELINE (1858–1928)

Noble, Iris. *Emmeline and Her Daughters: The Pankhurst Suffragettes.* Messner, 1971.   11–14

PARACELSUS, PHILIPPUS (1493–1541)

Rosen, Sidney. *Doctor Paracelsus,* ill. by Rafaello Busoni. Little, 1959.   12–16

§ PARKS, GORDON (1912–   )

Turk, Midge. *Gordon Parks,* ill. by Herbert Danska. T. Crowell, 1971.   7–8

§ PARKS, ROSA (1913–   )

Greenfield, Eloise. *Rosa Parks,* ill. by Eric Marlow. T. Crowell, 1973.   7–9

Meriwether, Louise. *Don't Ride the Bus on Monday,* ill. by David Scott Brown. Prentice, 1973. A more detailed portrait than the Greenfield title, this conveys the quiet courage and determination Rosa Parks demonstrated when she set off the Montgomery bus boycott.   8–10

● PENN, WILLIAM (1644–1718)

Aliki. *The Story of William Penn,* ill. by author. Prentice, 1964.   8–9

Foster, Genevieve. *The World of William Penn,* ill. by author. Scribner's, 1973.   9–12

Vining, Elizabeth Gray. *Penn,* ill. by George Gillett Whitney. Viking, 1938.   12–16

PICASSO, PABLO (1881–1973)

Greenfeld, Howard. *Pablo Picasso: An Introduction.* Follett, 1971.   12–15

§ PIPPIN, HORACE (1888–1946)

Rodman, Selden, and Carole Cleaver. *Horace Pippin: The Artist As a Black American.* Doubleday, 1972. Full-color paintings by an eminent black artist add to the appeal of the first biography of Pippin for children.   11–13

☆ POCAHONTAS (1595?–1617)

Bulla, Clyde. *Pocahontas and the Strangers.* T. Crowell, 1971.   8–10

d'Aulaire, Ingri and Edgar Parin. *Pocahontas,* ill. by authors. Doubleday, 1949.   7–9

Martin, Patricia Miles. *Pocahontas,* ill. by Portia Takakjian. Putnam, 1964.   7–8

Wahl, Jan. *Pocahontas in London,* ill. by John Alcorn. Delacorte, 1967.   8–9

POLK, JAMES KNOX (1795–1849)

Severn, William. *Frontier President: James K. Polk.* Washburn, 1965. A light tone makes this competent biography especially readable.   12–15

POTTER, BEATRIX (1866–1943)

Aldis, Dorothy. *Nothing Is Impossible: The Story of Beatrix Potter,* ill. by Richard Cuffari. Atheneum, 1969.   9–11

Lane, Margaret. *The Tale of Beatrix Potter: A Biography,* ill. by Beatrix Potter. Warne, 1946. Delightful story of the Victorian artist whose Peter Rabbit tales have delighted young children.   13–16

§ POWELL, ADAM CLAYTON, JR. (1908–1972)

Haskins, James. *Adam Clayton Powell: Portrait of a Marching Black,* ill. with photos. Dial, 1974.   12 up

REVERE, PAUL (1735–1818)

Forbes, Esther. *America's Paul Revere,* ill. by Lynd Ward. Houghton, 1946. Vigorous prose and superb illustrations do much to illumine the history of the Revolutionary period.   11–15

RICHTER, HANS PETER (1925–   )

Richter, Hans Peter. *I Was There,* tr. by Edite Kroll. Holt, 1972. Richter's story begins at age eight when he joined the Hitler youth movement and ends with him and his friends in the Third Reich Army. A dramatic, forceful book.   11–15

RINCON, FELISA DE GAUTIER. See GAUTIER, FELISA RINCON DE.

RINGLING BROTHERS

Cone, Molly. *The Ringling Brothers,* ill. by James and Ruth McCrea. T. Crowell, 1971.   7–9

RIZAL, JOSÉ (1861–1896)

Reines, Bernard. *A People's Hero: Rizal of the Philippines.* Praeger, 1971. A foresighted leader who fought against Spanish tyranny. Rizal was ahead of his time in the battle for equality and civil rights.   7–11

§ ROBESON, PAUL (1898–1976)

Hamilton, Virginia. *Paul Robeson: The Life and Times of a Free Man,* ill. with photos. Harper, 1974.   12 up

§ ROBINSON, JOHN (1919–1972)

Robinson, Jackie, and Alfred Duckett. *Breakthrough to the Big Leagues.* Harper, 1965. Candid about Robinson's problems as the first black player in the major leagues, and very well written.   11–14

Rudeen, Kenneth. *Jackie Robinson,* ill. by Richard Cuffari. T. Crowell, 1971.   7–9

ROGERS, ROBERT (1731–1795)

Gauch, Patricia Lee. *The Impossible Major Rogers,* ill. by Robert Andrew Parker. Putnam, 1977. The story of Robert Rogers, wily leader of a band of rangers in the French and Indian War, written in casual style.   9–11

ROOSEVELT, ELEANOR (1884–1962)

Davidson, Margaret. *The Story of Eleanor Roosevelt.* Four Winds, 1969. One of the better biographies of an indomitable woman.   9–11

Goodsell, Jane. *Eleanor Roosevelt,* ill. by Wendell Minor. T. Crowell, 1970.   8–10

ROOSEVELT, FRANKLIN DELANO (1882–1945)

Faber, Doris. *Franklin D. Roosevelt,* ill. Abelard, 1974. 8–11

Peare, Catherine Owens. *The FDR Story,* ill. T. Crowell, 1962. A remarkably perceptive biography of Roosevelt as an individual and as a political figure.   12–15

ROOSEVELT, THEODORE (1858–1919)

Foster, Genevieve. *Theodore Roosevelt,* ill. by author. Scribner's, 1954.   9–12

Monjo, Ferdinand. *The One Bad Thing About Father,* ill. by Rocco Negri. Harper, 1970.   7–8

§ ROSE, EDWARD (1811–1834)

Felton, Harold W. *Edward Rose, Negro Trail Blazer,* ill. with photos and prints of the period, and maps. Dodd, 1967.   10–14

☆ ROSS, JOHN (1790–1866)

Clark, Electa. *Cherokee Chief: The Life of John Ross,* ill. by John Wagner. Crowell-Collier, 1970. John Ross was a man whose Scottish ancestors had married into the Cherokee Nation and whose integrity earned him the respect of white statesmen as well as the leadership of his tribe. A dramatic and tragic story of the persecution of the Cherokee people.   10–14

§ RUSSWURM, JOHN BROWN (1799–1851)

Sagarin, Mary. *John Brown Russwurm: The Story of Freedom's Journal, Freedom's Journey.* Lothrop, 1970. The subject is interesting both as a little-known figure in antebellum black history in the United States and as an important one in the turbulent early days of Liberian history. 12–15

☆ SACAJAWEA (1786–1884)

Farnsworth, Frances Joyce. *Winged Moccasins: The Story of Sacajawea,* ill. by Lorence Bjorklund. Messner, 1954. An interesting and authentic account of the life of Lewis and Clark's Indian guide.   12–15

SAMPSON, DEBORAH. See GANNETT, DEBORAH (SAMPSON).

SCHLIEMANN, HEINRICH (1822–1890)

Braymer, Marjorie. *The Walls of Windy Troy.* Harcourt,

1960. Distinguished biography of Heinrich Schliemann, who achieved his dream of archeological research on the site of ancient Troy. 12–16

SCHUMANN, CLARA (1819–1896)

SCHUMANN, ROBERT (1810–1856)

Kyle, Elisabeth. *Duet: The Story of Clara and Robert Schumann.* Holt, 1968. 11–14

● SINGER, ISAAC BASHEVIS (1904–   )

Singer, Isaac Bashevis. *A Day of Pleasure: Stories of a Boy Growing Up in Warsaw,* ill. with photos by Roman Vishniac. Farrar, 1969. National Book Award. 11 up

☆ SITTING BULL, SIOUX CHIEF (1831–1890)

Garst, Shannon. *Sitting Bull, Champion of His People,* ill. by Elton C. Fax. Messner, 1946. 11 up

§ SMALLS, ROBERT (1839–1915)

Meriwether, Louise. *The Freedom Ship of Robert Smalls,* ill. by Lee Jack Morton. Prentice, 1971. Simply told, the story of the captain of *The Planter.* 8–10

Sterling, Dorothy. *Captain of the Planter: The Story of Robert Smalls,* ill. by Ernest Crichlow. Doubleday, 1958. 12–15

§ SMITH, BESSIE (1894–1937)

Moore, Carman. *Somebody's Angel Child: The Story of Bessie Smith.* T. Crowell, 1970. The dramatic and sad story of the greatest blues singer of them all. 11–14

☆ SQUANTO, PAWTUXET INDIAN (d. 1622)

Bulla, Clyde. *Squanto: Friend of the Pilgrims,* ill. by Peter Burchard. T. Crowell, 1954. 7–9

STANTON, ELIZABETH CADY (1815–1902)

Faber, Doris. *Oh, Lizzie: The Life of Elizabeth Cady Stanton.* Lothrop, 1972. 12–16

● STEIN, GERTRUDE (1874–1946)

Greenfeld, Howard. *Gertrude Stein: A Biography.* Crown, 1973. 12 up

§ STEVENS, THADDEUS (1792–1868)

Meltzer, Milton. *Thaddeus Stevens and the Fight for Negro Rights.* T. Crowell, 1967. 13 up

STEVENSON, ROBERT LOUIS (1850–1894)

Proudfit, Isabel. *The Treasure Hunter, the Story of Robert Louis Stevenson,* ill. by Hardie Gramatky. Messner, 1939. A full-length biography of a favorite children's author. 10–14

Wood, James Playsted. *The Lantern Bearer: A Life of Robert Louis Stevenson,* ill. by Saul Lambert. Pantheon, 1965. 12 up

§ STILL, PETER (1800–?)

Mann, Peggy. *The Man Who Bought Himself.* Macmillan, 1975. 12–15

STOWE, HARRIET BEECHER (1811–1896)

Johnston, Johanna. *Harriet and the Runaway Book: The Story of Harriet Beecher Stowe and Uncle Tom's Cabin,* ill. by Ronald Himler. Harper, 1977. A smoothly fictionalized biography emphasizing the writing of *Uncle Tom's Cabin* but giving balanced treatment to other aspects of Stowe's life. 8–10

SUN YAT-SEN (1866–1925)

Spencer, Cornelia. *Sun Yat-sen: Founder of the Chinese Republic.* Day, 1967. 12–15

☆ TALLCHIEF, MARIA (1925–   )

Tobias, Tobi. *Maria Tallchief,* ill. by Michael Hampshire. T. Crowell, 1970. 7–9

TERESHKOVA, VALENTINA VLADIMIROVA (1937–   )

Sharpe, Mitchell R. *"It Is I, Sea Gull," Valentina Tereshkova, First Woman in Space,* ill. with photos. T. Crowell, 1975. Excellent view of the woman who made spaceflight history. 11–15

§ TOUSSAINT L'OUVERTURE, PIERRE DOMINIQUE (1746?–1803)

Syme, Ronald. *Toussaint: The Black Liberator,* ill. by William Stobbs. Morrow, 1971. 10–13

§ TUBMAN, HARRIET (1820–1913)

Lawrence, Jacob. *Harriet and the Promised Land,* ill. by author. Windmill, 1968. In this story of Harriet Tubman, the writing is simple, rhythmic, and effective and the pictures are dramatic and vigorous. 7–9

Petry, Ann. *Harriet Tubman: Conductor on the Underground Railroad.* T. Crowell, 1955. A well-documented, thrilling story. 12–16

Sterling, Dorothy. *Freedom Train: The Story of Harriet Tubman,* ill. by Ernest Crichlow. Doubleday, 1954. 10–12

Swift, Hildegarde. *Railroad to Freedom: A Story of the Civil War,* ill. by James Daugherty. Harcourt, 1932. 12–14

VAN GOGH, VINCENT. See GOGH, VINCENT VAN.

VERRAZANO, GIOVANNI DA (c. 1480–1527?)

Syme, Ronald. *Verrazano: Explorer of the Atlantic Coast,* ill. by William Stobbs. Morrow, 1973. Direct, brisk account of the explorer, written with Syme's usual concern for accuracy. 9–11

VESPUCCI, AMERIGO (1451–1512)

Baker, Nina Brown. *Amerigo Vespucci,* ill. by Paul Valentino. Knopf, 1956. 9–12

§ WASHINGTON, BOOKER TALIAFERRO (1859?–1915)

Graham, Shirley. *Booker T. Washington: Educator of Hand, Head and Heart.* Messner, 1955. 10–12

Washington, Booker T. *Up from Slavery.* Houghton, 1917. 12 up

Wise, William. *Booker T. Washington,* ill. by Paul Frame. Putnam, 1968. 7–9

WASHINGTON, GEORGE (1732–1799)

Bulla, Clyde. *Washington's Birthday,* ill. by Don Bolognese. T. Crowell, 1967. 6–8

d'Aulaire, Ingri and Edgar Parin, *George Washington,* ill. by authors. Doubleday, 1936. 7–9

Eaton, Jeanette. *Leader by Destiny,* ill. by Jack Manley Rosé. Harcourt, 1938. 12–15

Foster, Genevieve. *George Washington.* Scribner's, 1949. 9–11

Judson, Clara Ingram. *George Washington, Leader of the People,* ill. by Robert Frankenberg. Follett, 1951. 11–15

McNeer, May. *The Story of George Washington,* ill. by Lynd Ward. Abingdon, 1973. Handsome pictures and simple text. 7–9

WASHINGTON, MARTHA (1731–1802)

Vance, Marguerite. *Martha, Daughter of Virginia: The Story of Martha Washington,* ill. by Nedda Walker. Dutton, 1947. 9–11

WAYNE, KYRA PETROVSKAYA

Wayne, Kyra Petrovskaya. *Shurik: A Story of the Siege of Leningrad,* ill. Grosset, 1970. A dramatic true story of World War II. A nurse in a hospital during the siege of Leningrad adopts Shurik, a homeless orphan. Chilling descriptions of the besieged city and impressive pictures of compassion and courage. 12–15

● WEST, BENJAMIN (1738–1820)

Henry, Marguerite, and Wesley Dennis. *Benjamin West and His Cat Grimalkin,* ill. by Wesley Dennis. Bobbs, 1947. An enchanting biography of one of America's first artists. 9–12

§ WHEATLEY, PHILLIS (1753?–1784)

Graham, Shirley. *The Story of Phillis Wheatley,* ill. by Robert Burns. Messner, 1949. 12–14

WHITMAN, NARCISSA (PRENTISS) (1808–1847)

Eaton, Jeanette. *Narcissa Whitman: Pioneer of Oregon,* ill. by Woodi Ishmael. Harcourt, 1941. This inspiring life of a great pioneer woman is based on early letters and memoirs. 12–16

WHITMAN, WALT (1819–1892)

Deutsch, Babette. *Walt Whitman: Builder for America,* ill.

by Rafaello Busoni. Messner, 1941. A sensitive study of the man, illustrated with copious selections from his poems.   14–16

WILDER, LAURA INGALLS (1867–1957)

Wilder, Laura Ingalls. *West from Home: Letters of Laura Ingalls Wilder, San Francisco, 1915*, ed. by Roger Lea Mac-Bride; historical setting by Margot Patterson Doss. Harper, 1974. For all those who have loved the Wilder "Little House" books.

WILLIAMS, ROGER (1603?–1683)

Eaton, Jeanette. *Lone Journey: The Life of Roger Williams*, ill. by Woodi Ishmael. Harcourt, 1944. Story of the courageous Puritan who left the Massachusetts colony and helped establish Rhode Island.   12–16

Jacobs, William Jay. *Roger Williams*, ill. with authentic prints and documents. Watts, 1975. Authoritative introduction to a genuine free spirit.   10–12

WILSON, WOODROW (1856–1924)

Peare, Catherine Owens. *The Woodrow Wilson Story: An Idealist in Politics*. T. Crowell, 1963.   12–15

§ WONDER, STEVIE (1950–   )

Haskins, James. *The Story of Stevie Wonder*, ill. with photos. Lothrop, 1976. An objective and astute biography of the blind musician.   11–14

WOODHULL, VICTORIA (1838–1927)

Meade, Marian. *Free Woman: The Life and Times of Victoria Woodhull*. Knopf, 1976. Stockbroker, journalist, actress, this colorful woman was the first woman to run for President of the United States.   12–15

§ YOUNG, ANDREW (1932–   )

Haskins, James. *Andrew Young: Man with a Mission*. Lothrop, 1979.   10 up

ZAPATA, EMILIANO (1869?–1919)

Syme, Ronald. *Zapata, Mexican Rebel*, ill. by William Stobbs. Morrow, 1971.   9–11

ZENGER, PETER (1697–1746)

Galt, Tom. *Peter Zenger: Fighter for Freedom*, ill. by Ralph Ray. T. Crowell, 1951. Biography of a famous pre-Revolutionary War printer, who faced trial and prison rather than yield the right of freedom of the press.   12–15

Chapter Fourteen:
Informational Books

If there is one trait that is common to children of all ages, of all backgrounds, of all ethnic groups, it is curiosity. Children read informational books to satisfy that curiosity, whether their books have been chosen to answer questions on a particular subject or to fulfill a desire for broader knowledge. While the criteria (discussed on the following pages) by which all informational books can be judged should serve as a basis for evaluating the thousands of factual children's books in print, additional qualities invest some of them with such distinction that they can be called fine literature. Originality of presentation or concept can contribute to this distinction, but it rests primarily with that least tangible of literary virtues, distinguished style. It is apparent in the clarity and vigor of Isaac Asimov's writing, in the scholarship and wit of Alfred Duggan, in the lyric simplicity of Jean George's *Spring Comes to the Ocean.* Each author uses prose in a way that is individual, each uses phrase and cadence appropriate to the subject, and each achieves distinctive style without sacrificing the basic qualifications for good informational writing.

Evaluating Informational Books

The variety of informational books is vast, ranging from the simplest concept books (which, along with alphabet and counting books, are discussed in Chapter 5, Books for the Very Young) to books for older readers on a variety of complex subjects. The best informational books are written by authors who know their subjects well, and who write about them imaginatively, with an understanding of the needs and limitations of their audience. An expert on a subject may tend toward verbosity or a heavy use of jargon or unnecessarily technical terminology. A practiced writer, on the other hand, may lack the subject knowledge to write with depth. Each book must be judged on its own merits, and those who evaluate books should consider the author's purpose in writing a book and judge not only whether the book meets all criteria for factual writing but also whether the author has written the book so as to fulfill its purpose.

Accuracy

What are the basic criteria by which nonfiction may be judged? Probably the first tenet that would occur to anyone is accuracy. While, clearly, we seek only correct information about a subject, all we can ask of authors is that they be accurate within the boundaries of knowledge at the time a book is written. There is no reason for a book about prehistory to be inaccurate, unless startling new facts have come to light since the book's publication; on the other hand, the author of a survey of the American political system as it functions today must be very guarded about statements on congres-

442

sional control of election procedures, for example, since this is a fluid situation. To avoid inaccuracy, an author must specify that a piece of legislation or a procedure was functioning in a certain way at a certain time.

In writing for young children, who are limited in experience, vocabulary, and knowledge of concepts, authors often find it necessary to omit material; in such cases, their obligation is to omit nothing that is of major importance; that is, the book need not be comprehensive but it must cover major points or it will have the same effect as inaccuracy. We should not substitute simplifed terminology if the correct word is not too difficult for young children; that, too, is a form of inaccuracy. A first book on human anatomy need not, for example, use "clavicle" rather than the more familiar "collarbone," but there is no reason not to use "lymph" even if it is an unfamiliar word, since there is no acceptable substitute.

If we supply children with factual information which is out of date or superficial, we only add to their confusion. Suppose, for instance, we give children purportedly modern books about the Holland of picturesque costumes and quaint, old-fashioned customs or about the old China of rickshaws and queues or about the South America of primitive Indian villages only. Meanwhile, newspapers, magazines, and television newscasts show them pictures of progressive Holland today, China's program of industrialization, and large South American cities. Discerning children can only conclude that books are less reliable references than other sources.

Obviously, accuracy is one of the most important criteria for judging any informational book. There has never been a greater need for accurate information than there is today to help counteract the widely disseminated misinformation to which children are subjected. Adults should encourage them to check so-called facts in reliable sources. This is one way of arming children against credulity and teaching them to weigh arguments, question sources, and search for facts.

Currency

Currency is closely related to accuracy. In many informational books, the date of copyright is especially important. For some subjects, this is of minor importance—David Macaulay's books on architectural landmarks of the past, for example, have been for many years, and are likely to be for many more, some of the best of their type—but even in history or archeology there are new discoveries or new theories. Informational books should represent not only the heritage and the knowledge of the past, but the latest research and contemporary experience as well.

Currency is usually a preeminent factor in choosing the best science books. In many science experiment books, great changes have taken place, and any evaluation of these books would need to consider their currency. Formerly, directions might be given something like this: "Take a teaspoon of this, a teaspoon of that, mix, and . . . will happen." This kind of instruction reflected traditional teaching methods: the teacher demonstrated an experiment, the students tried to duplicate it, and results were expected to be identical. With the discovery method, which emphasizes why things happen, new books give children options as they experiment, and stress observation of scientific method, keeping records, and drawing inferences from conclusions. Conversion to the metric system obviously affects our choices of science experiment books. Changes in educational practices in any area, then, should be reflected in changes in the literature; methods as well as content should be up-to-date.

Organization and Scope

In considering the accuracy and currency and therefore the effectiveness of any informational book, we must decide how successfully the author has simplified material and limited the scope of the subject for the intended audience. One reason the Crowell science books for beginning readers have been successful is that the authors and editors, in limiting the scope of their material, have been careful to select the important facts about a subject and to present them in logical sequence. Too much information, or information that is supplementary, may confuse and mislead a child even though there are no inaccurate statements in the text.

The presentation of material in logical sequence is particularly important. Only in very short books is a continuous text appropriate; in books of substantial length, the text should be broken up with heads and subheads that clarify the relations of the separate parts. A table of contents can also help make clear the organization of the text and the contents of each chapter. Though few books for very young children have an index, even here such aids are found more frequently than before. For most informational books for children in the middle grades and up, an index is a necessity, and the best indexes have cross-references.

The text material should move from the familiar to the unfamiliar, or progress from the simple to the complex, or be in chronological order; arrangement will vary with the nature of the subject. Historical material lends itself to chronological treatment, project books to a simple-to-complex arrangement, and an explanation of an aspect of human physiology, for example, to the familiar-to-unfamiliar sequence.

The Author's Responsibility

Any book that teaches a child how to make something, as in experiment books, should include safety rules and should present lists of materials needed and sources for acquiring them if they are not available in the home. Science experiment books and cookbooks should also make clear when adult supervision or adult participation in a stage of the procedure is needed. Activities suggested should conform with scientific method.

It is also the author's responsibility to ensure the absence of stereotyping by sex, race, age, or religion either in the text or in the illustrations. There are women chemists and business executives; a black doctor may have a white nurse and both may be of either sex; children of all ethnic backgrounds may be interested in a physics experiment and should be so represented in illustrations.

The writing should reflect a scientific attitude, not only in *what* is said, but in *how* it is said: no "Mother Nature" in books about plants and animals, no anthropomorphism in animal characters, although for the very young child some personification of animals is permissible. The facts must not only be current and accurate, but they should be presented so that they build toward concepts and principles. And it is incumbent on the author to keep the intended audience in mind so that the vocabulary, scope, and concepts are close to the child's ability to comprehend.

Authors should carefully distinguish between fact and theory or opinion. To signal an opinion or a theory, they should use such phrases as "In my opinion," "It may be that," or "One group of scientists believes." They should avoid the unsupported generalization and the untenable, all-inclusive generalization, which lets readers assume that the part they have been reading about is the whole. It just isn't true that if you've seen one, you've seen them all, and to imply this is particularly reprehensible in a book about people. Professional men and women often have a bias about theories in their field, and the dependable author informs the reader that he or she holds one idea, but that there are others, or that the text covers only some aspects of a subject. Some of these facts can be learned from the author's background; both the limitation of coverage and the adherence to a theory should be clear.

The Author's Competence

One of the clues to the author's competence is the material considered, that is, the material he or she chooses to include and to omit. John Navarra, for example, includes a chapter on pollution and politics in *The World You Inherit* presumably because, as an expert in the field, he is aware of the urgency of getting enabling legislation for corrective measures.

Authors who have scientific backgrounds should be aware of, and should make explicit, the social implications of their subjects, the effects on people and institutions. An author who is an authority on a subject can write with more originality than the writer who can only reassemble facts provided by others. A true scientist, for example, is not hesitant about showing that—at certain stages—answers must be inconclusive.

Evaluation of the writer's competence is made easier if his or her credentials are given. The book's accuracy may be further confirmed by a list of readers whose specialties qualify them to vouch for the book's information. A list of sources, a bibliography, a glossary, or a chronology add to the value of a book and usually attest to the authoritative knowledge or research involved.

Format

Format should be examined in evaluating an informational book. The child in fifth grade will scorn the book that, because of its size or shape or style of illustration, looks like second-grade fare. The type size and page layout are of more importance in informational books than in other types of books, since confusion may lead to misinterpretation. The reader can be confused by paragraphs irregularly arranged on a page with not enough blank space to make sequence apparent. The chapter heads and subheads should be explicit indicators of content. A photograph or map can lose its value if it is located too far from the discussion to which it pertains. The illustration should always be accurate and should complement and clarify the printed text; it can give too little information or too much. Inadequate labels or captions can lessen or obviate the value of maps, pictures, and diagrams. Photographs that are posed or that are decorative rather than informative can be an irritant. There are some books for which photographs are the best illustrative medium, as they are in *A Life of Their Own* by Aylette Jenness and Lisa Kroeber, and here even the posed pictures of a Guatemalan family *are* informative. The best illustrations reflect some quality of the text, as Leonard Everett Fisher's black-and-white scratchboard drawings reflect the sturdy individuality of the colonial craftsmen in books like *The Tanners*, or as Edwin Tunis's meticulous drawings enhance the reference use of *Frontier Living*.

Style

Finally, informational books must be clearly and interestingly written. Nonfiction can be abysmally dull. The wrong way to combat dullness is to dress it up. Information can and should be written in a straightforward fashion; young readers need no palliative with books on science or geography or nature study. No "Mother Nature knew it was springtime" is admissible in children's nonfiction books, nor does a squirrel need to be referred to as "Little Nutsy." Children don't like to be talked down to. They can take information straight, although they can be bored stiff if the writing is too dry or too heavy. A book may be useful—and there are many that are mediocre in style but useful—but a child will not cherish it unless it is also interesting.

The vocabulary should be geared to the reading ability of the child. Books that are used by young children for identification, or concept books (discussed in Chapter 5), should present ideas simply but with the grouping or repetition that will encourage observation, classification, and deduction. A controlled vocabulary may be helpful for the beginning reader, but most children enjoy writing that has some un-

Viewpoint

In all media, the reviewer of nonfiction most of the time limits himself to asking how much information the book contains. And how accurate or up-to-date it is. Infrequently a reviewer will compare the book with others on the same subject, but only as to factual content. Rarely will he ask what more there is to the book than the mere facts. I would want to ask how well it is organized. What principle of selection animated the writer; what is the writer's point of view; does the writer acknowledge other opinions of value? And then, beyond all this, what literary distinction, if any, does the book have? And here I do not mean the striking choice of word or image but the personal style revealed. I ask whether the writer's personal voice is heard in the book. In the writer who cares, there is a pressure of feeling which emerges in the rhythm of the sentences, in the choice of details, in the color of the language. Style in this sense is not a trick of rhetoric or a decorative daub; it is a quality of vision. It cannot be separated from the author's character because the tone of voice in which the book is written expresses how a human being thinks and feels. If the writer is indifferent, bored, stupid, or mechanical, it will show in the work. The kind of man or woman the writer is—this is what counts. Style in any art is both form and content; they are woven together.—Milton Meltzer. "Where Do All the Prizes Go? The Case For Nonfiction," *The Horn Book Magazine*, February 1976. Copyright © 1976 by The Horn Book, Inc. Reprinted by permission.

familiar words. Older children appreciate the challenge of some new terms that expand their vocabulary and widen their horizons.

With the increasing use of trade books to supplement texts and other curricular materials, the criteria for evaluation seem even more important today than in the past. Even in those books for young children in which a fictional framework is used, the purpose of an informational book is to inform. The best of such books expose a child to differences and lead to questioning and comparing books, to evaluating conflicting theories. The best nonfiction goes beyond the presentation of facts to presentation of principles, concepts, theories, interpretation, and evaluation.

Accuracy, currency, careful organization and presentation, a scientific attitude, responsibility in dealing with fact and opinion, format, and interesting style are some of the criteria by which informational books can be judged. In the rest of this chapter, these criteria will be further examined as they pertain to particular books. The first section presents in alphabetical order twenty-seven outstanding authors of informational books for children and some of the books they have written. The second section discusses briefly a number of other important authors and significant books organized by subject matter (the biological sciences, the physical sciences, the social sciences, religion and the arts, activities and experiments, and reference books). This discussion gives a glimpse of the variety and the riches available in today's informational books.

Irving Adler
The Wonders of Physics

Irving Adler, who has been a teacher of mathematics at the high-school and college levels, is the author of more than fifty books on scientific subjects. His work is notable for the skill and lucidity with which he makes complicated material comprehensible. In *The Wonders of Physics* (1966), for example, written for older children, the clarity of his prose is such that the book can be given even to a seven-year-old child to explain the difference between the Centigrade and Fahrenheit temperature scales.

The Wonders of Physics bears out Jerome Bruner's assertion that "... the foundations of any subject may be taught to anybody at any age in some form."[1] Adler defines the four states of matter (solid, liquid, gaseous, and plasma) succinctly, then discusses them, using subheadings and drawings to make the material easier to understand. In discussing temperature scales, the author carefully identifies each type, along with the scientist after whom it was named, and provides complete descriptions and diagrams. In discussing heat engines, Adler skillfully explains the three laws of thermodynamics. The index includes "see also" references. Page numbers in boldface type refer to a page where there is an illustration of the subject. Throughout the text, cross-references are excellent.

Tools in Your Life (1956) is an account of the development of tools from the primitive ax to atomic energy, tracing the sociological effects of the adoption of new tools or of the clinging to old ones. *Magic House of Numbers* (1957; 1974) describes number systems built on bases other than ten, and includes many intriguing puzzles.

1. Jerome S. Bruner, *The Process of Education* (Harvard Univ. Press, 1966), p. 12.

These books are illustrated by Ruth Adler, who was also coauthor and illustrator of more than thirty titles in "The Reason Why" series. These are short, useful books with descriptive tables of contents but no indexes. Three books for children in the middle grades are *Evolution* (1965), *Sets* (1967), and *Petroleum* (1975), which is written by Irving Adler alone, and for those even younger, *Sets and Numbers for the Very Young* (1969).

Isaac Asimov
Words from History

Biochemist Isaac Asimov has written his own reference book, *Asimov's Biographical Encyclopedia of Science and Technology*, and his writing covers a wide range of subjects, from authoritative discussions of astronomy in books like *Mars, the Red Planet* (1977) and distinctive science fiction to a story for the preschool child, *The Best Thing* (1971).

Words from History (1968) is a good example of Asimov's work in a field outside his own. Like all of his other books, it is distinguished for a witty, informal style and smoothly carries authoritative information. Using one page of text for each word, he gives its etymology and sets it in historical perspective. The following quotation shows how clearly Asimov writes:

Along the Roman roads, the legions tramped, guarding the frontiers and suppressing revolts (and sometimes marching on Rome itself to snatch at the Imperial crown). Distance was important and was measured off by the tireless pacing of the legionaries in convenient units of a thousand paces. In Latin, a thousand paces is "milia Passuum," and this was gradually shortened to the first word alone, in English mile. Our present "mile" is a little longer than the Roman, however, and comes to about 1050 paces or 1760 yards. (p. 141)

Among his other "Word" books are *Words on the Map* (1962) and *Words of Science: and the History Behind Them* (1959). Each of these books follows the same format as *Words from History*, that is, one word and its explanation on one page. *Words from the Exodus* (1963) and *Words in Genesis* (1962) show how much of our everyday speech comes from the Bible.

The Shaping of North America (1973) and its sequel, *The Birth of the United States 1763–1816* (1974), are two of several Asimov books about the formative years of a country; his fresh viewpoint and easy, informal style make history interesting even when he covers familiar information. All of Asimov's history books, despite his tendency to crowd the pages with names and dates, have a breadth and sweep that give readers perspective on events, personalities, and factions.

Building Blocks of the Universe (1957) is an excellent book on chemistry and contains little sidelights which make the scientific words come alive for young people. *How Did We Find Out About Oil?* (1980) gives information on the topic and also shows how individuals contribute to a body of scientific or technological knowledge. *Realm of Numbers* (1959) is a popularizing of arithmetic for those who don't have a knowledge of algebra, geometry, and calculus. A useful series of books on astronomy includes *How Did We Find Out About Atoms?* (1976) and *How Did We Find Out About Black Holes?* (1978). One of the most successful of Asimov's many books about space is *ABC's of Space* (1969), which is illustrated with photographs and drawings from the space program, with short paragraphs for each item. This may be used with very young children, despite the fact that the terminology is sometimes complex.

Jeanne Bendick
Names, Sets and Numbers

The author or illustrator of more than 100 books for children, Jeanne Bendick is probably best known for her lively, humorous illustrations. Her easily recognizable style, which she describes as "relaxed representational" is echoed in the brisk and vigorous writing that skillfully clarifies difficult concepts. Her interest in science developed after she had illustrated a number of science books and had done a lot of reading in order to draw her pictures accurately. She found that she had the ability to present a complex subject in simple terms and in a light, often breezy manner.

Names, Sets and Numbers (1971) is typical of her direct, crisp approach. Although it is recommended by the publisher for grades four to six, the content and style are suitable for younger children:

First, we give names to things.
People have names, like Mike and Karen.
Planets have names, like Earth and Mars.
Every plant we know has a name.
"Buttercup" is a name. So is "pine."
Every animal we know has a name.
"Earthworm" is a name. So is "lion." (p. 8)

Beginning with names as a reference point, the author then moves into sets in a smooth transition. Making small things out of big ones gets across the concept of subsets and classification, another subject to which very young children are being exposed.

Jeanne Bendick has written a number of books, all with the same straightforward tone, in the Watts "First Book" series. *A First Book of Space Travel* (1969, revised several times) is a comprehensive yet simplified look at the subject, from "What Space Is" to "What Space Science Has Done for Earth." *A Place to Live* (1970) is for the read-aloud audience and deals with the interdependence of human, plant, and animal life. Some of Bendick's books deal with weather phenomena. *The Wind* (1964) gives scientific information about how winds are caused and how they travel, preceded by a discussion of myths and superstitions the world over. Some of her books deal with aspects of the physical sciences; *Solids, Liquids and Gases* (1974) uses the process approach to explain the differences between the three states of matter, suggesting basic criteria for comparison and testing, and exemplifying the scientific method. *What Made You You?* (1971) asks

Did you come like a chicken out of an egg? Like a flower out of a bud? Like a rainbow out of raindrops? Like music out of a horn? No, but just as wonderful. YOU were born! (pp. 38, 39)

Blithe as it is, the text gives accurate and explicit information about reproduction and heredity.

Electronics for Young People (1960), *How Much and How Many* (1960), and *The Mystery of the Loch Ness Monster* (1976) are for older children and contain more text than pictures. *Television Works Like This* (1965) and *The Consumer's Catalog of Economy and Ecology* (1974) Bendick wrote in collaboration with her husband, Robert.

Franklyn M. Branley
The Milky Way: Galaxy Number One

Franklyn Branley was, before retirement, an astronomer on the staff of the American Museum-Hayden Planetarium, and Director of Educational Services. Both his professional knowledge and his familiarity with presenting facts to the lay person are reflected in his many books on astronomy and other scientific subjects. He collaborated with Eleanor K. Vaughan

Illustration by Leonard Everett Fisher, p. 39. From Leonard Everett Fisher, *The Blacksmiths*. Copyright © 1976 by Leonard Everett Fisher. Published by Franklin Watts, Inc. Reprinted by permission.

on two interesting books for the very young, *Mickey's Magnet* (1956) and *Timmy and the Tin-Can Telephone* (1959), which present scientific facts in attractive format.

The Milky Way (1969) is one of his books for older readers, using scientific terminology and a scholarly approach. It begins with a history of astronomy, describing early telescopes, the beliefs of early scientists and the ordinary people, and the conflict between Ptolemaic and Copernican theories.

Chapter 4 describes a development of the 1940s, exploring by radio astronomy. With this new device the shape of the Milky Way became more discernible. The last chapter describes the way in which the galaxy may have evolved, and makes conjectures about where it may go from here. The book includes an appendix for finding stellar magnitudes and distances, intended for those who understand logarithms, and a bibliography.

Branley has also written many books for younger children. *The Sun; Our Nearest Star* (1961) is a simple explanation in picture-book format, and *A Book of Mars for You* (1968) speculates about an unmanned landing. These books are in the Crowell "Let's-Read-and-Find-Out Science Books" series. Branley is particularly skilled at selecting salient facts and omitting minor ones, so that his books for readers in lower and middle grades are succinct as well as accurate. In *Eclipse* (1973) he defines

terminology in order to explain clearly the phenomenon of total solar eclipse, and in *Pieces of Another World* (1972) he discusses the collection and analysis of moon rocks, carefully distinguishing between fact and theory, and making clear the interdisciplinary effort of scientists, and in *Color: From Rainbows to Lasers* (1978) he discusses color in relation to light.

None of Franklyn Branley's books has been more popular than *The Christmas Sky* (1966), which is based on the Christmas lecture at the Hayden Planetarium. It discusses the Biblical, historical, and astronomical clues to the true date of the birth of Jesus, and deftly combines scientific facts and a reverent approach.

Leonard Everett Fisher

The Tanners

The Tanners (1966) is one of a series of books by Leonard Everett Fisher on "Colonial Americans and Colonial American Craftsmen." The books are well designed, with a full-page picture on the right facing three-quarters of a page of text on the left, with an occasional double-spread picture. The scratchboard illustrations, drawn with vigor, depict costume details and customs, and there are many small, accurate drawings of the tools of each trade, carefully labeled and described. The first third of *The Tanners* is devoted to history, the last two-thirds to technique, an arrangement used for all books in the series. The author includes a glossary of terms and an index, but provides no bibliography or acknowledgments of any kind. The text is replete, however, with references which are evidence of research. Fisher explains how the tanner played an important part in the economy of the American colonies. The tanner prepared the skins for the parchment-maker, who in turn made vellum, a superior writing surface—on which were written both the Declaration of Independence and the Constitution.

Among his books on Colonial Americans are *The Schoolmasters* (1967) and *The Homemakers* (1973). In the series on Colonial American craftsmen are *The Cabinetmakers* (1966), *The Blacksmiths* (1976), and others. In a series of books about America in the nineteenth century, Fisher comments on the societal changes as well as the institutions he describes in *The Factories* (1979), *The Hospitals* (1980), and *The Railroads* (1979). For younger children he wrote a book about fire engines entitled *Pumpers, Boilers, Hooks and Ladders* (1961). *Two If by Sea* (1970) is a dramatic description of the actions of Paul Revere and three others during two hours of an eventful evening: April 18, 1775.

Genevieve Foster

George Washington's World

Because the subject of history confused her as a schoolgirl, Genevieve Foster, when she decided to write history books for children, thought in terms of what events were going on at the same time all over the world, and what people lived at the same time. By quoting from primary sources, she imparts a sense of nearness to the happenings of long ago.

George Washington's World (1941) is divided into six parts beginning when Washington was a boy and ending with his presidency. The book does an admirable job of presenting a horizontal look at history, a slice of life cross-wise instead of strung out chronologically. When George Washington was a farmer, for instance, James Watt invented the steam engine, James Cook discovered Australia on the other side of the world, and Pompeii was uncovered. California was settled, Japan was a feudal state closed to the world, Marie Antoinette was married in France. All of these events and more were taking place during the period when Boston had a tea party and Paul Revere took his ride.

This book, like its counterparts in the series, is a large volume with interesting illustrations, full index, and separate indexes of places, nations, and events. Although these books are rather formidable, and graded for eleven-to-fourteen-year-olds, the style is so lively and understandable that they are excellent sources for reading aloud to younger children.

The World of Columbus and Sons (1965) and *The World of William Penn* (1973), two other books in the series, are richly documented and have the same original approach to history; the former seems more difficult than *George Washington's World,* and is not so fully illustrated. The Penn book gives a broad view of world events in the years in which Penn was most active as a Quaker and was establishing the Pennsylvania settlements.

The Year of the Pilgrims—1620 (1969), for a younger audience, is more simply written and introduces color in a small volume of 62 pages. In this and in *The Year of the Horseless Carriage—1801* (1975), also for younger children, the text extends beyond the date given in the title.

Jean Craighead George

All Upon a Stone

All of Jean George's books are distinguished for her authoritative treatment of biological subjects and minute knowledge of the habits and the habitat of wild creatures. *All Upon a Stone* (1971) has been singled out not because it is more profound or perceptive than the others, but because of the unusual and explicit way in which it presents ecology to young children.

The book is notable for the harmony between the graceful writing and the handsome pictures by Don Bolognese, who painted a three-foot by four-foot canvas in acrylics first, then used details of the larger work to fill each of the pages of the book. Bolognese chose this technique to reflect the unity of the microcosm of the life on the stone. The whole picture is shown at the end of the book. The opening paragraph draws the analogy:

A stone by a stream in the woods is like a tiny country. It has its own forests, valleys, and pools. It has its own creatures that live out their lives, hunting, sleeping, and working all upon a stone. (p. 1)

In *All Upon a Sidewalk* (1974) a yellow ant explores her small world. George brings into the text, simply written as it is, such aspects as chemical messages and mutually profitable

From *All Upon a Sidewalk* by Jean Craighead George, illustrated by Don Bolognese. Copyright © 1974 by Jean Craighead George and Don Bolognese. Reprinted by permission of the publishers, E.P. Dutton, and Curtis Brown, Ltd. (Original in color)

relationships between species. Again in this book the whole world of the sidewalk is pictured only at the end of the book.

The Hole in the Tree (1957), profusely illustrated by the author, can be enjoyed by very young children. It is the story of various occupants: a bark beetle, a carpenter bee, a black-capped chickadee family, and so on to the family of raccoons that is born there. *The Moon of the Bears* (1967) is one of a series of nature books, "The Thirteen Moons." These books have grown out of George's interest in ecology, especially in the study of the relationship between climate and periodic biological events.

Most of George's books for older readers are fictional, but all of them are concerned with some facet of the natural sciences: wolf behavior in *Julie of the Wolves* (1972), the effects of pollution on wild creatures in *Who Really Killed Cock Robin?* (1971), and the remarkable intelligence of crows in *Cry of the Crow* (1980). None of her fiction for older readers, however, surpasses in writing style *Spring Comes to the Ocean* (1965), in which each chapter describes one form of marine life, beginning with the stirring of the reproductive instinct in the spring. Authoritative, accurate, logically organized, the book is imbued with a sense of wonder and pleasure in the marvelous intricacies of ocean life.

Sonia and Tim Gidal
My Village in Ghana

Sonia and Tim Gidal traveled abroad to acquire facts and photographs for their "My Village" books, and the wealth of detail in that series is evidence of their careful observation. Limiting their subject to one child's friends and family, they give a detailed account of the activities which take place in home, school, and recreation areas during the span of one day, although there may be references to past events.

My Village in Ghana (1969) has a full-color photograph of young James Kodjo Badu on its cover and it is through his first-person, present-tense account that we learn about life in Makranso, which is the center of Ghana. Through Kodjo we learn about the customs, schooling, food, folklore, dress, arts and crafts, and economy of the village as well as the interpersonal relations within his extended family. Kodjo's day begins in his Aunt Lucretia's

household as he helps with the chores, then joins a group of younger children to hear a story about Anansi the spider and why the snake has no legs, told by Nana, the chief. As the day progresses we look into almost every side of village life.

The book has more than eighty black-and-white photographs of many aspects of life in the village. While some are obviously posed, others are candid. In addition, there is a well-drawn map at the end of the book, as well as a sketch of the village in a two-page spread at the beginning. A glossary of foreign words appears (although they are explained the first time they are used in the text). There is also a one-page history of Ghana.

The "My Village" series has had many imitators, but few authors have achieved the natural quality of the Gidals' books, which include *My Village in Germany* (1964), *My Village in Denmark* (1963), and others, numbering over twenty volumes in the series. Two volumes have been written by Sonia Gidal alone: *My Village in Portugal* (1972) and *My Village in Hungary* (1974).

Shirley Glubok
The Art of Ancient Greece

Shirley Glubok majored in art and archeology, received her master's degree in early childhood education, and lectures to children's groups at the Metropolitan Museum of Art. She is well prepared, then, to explain and introduce the arts and crafts of ancient cultures, and her books are impressive because of the combination of authoritative knowledge, simple presentation, dignified format, and a recurrent emphasis on the relationships between an art form and the culture in which it was created.

The Art of Ancient Greece (1963) has clear photographs of sculpture, architecture, pottery, and reliefs in a survey of Greek art. Presented for the middle grades, it is a guided tour in print of art objects gathered from museums all over the world. The book begins with a paragraph describing Greece, and then discusses ancient Greek vases, their beauty, and their various uses. Greek sculpture is discussed, with reproductions of Aphrodite and Apollo and of the Parthenon and its sculpture. Enlarged photographs of the heads are shown so that readers can see the details in the carving. The pages on armor are particularly well designed, with the figures facing each other from opposite pages, both backed by squares of brilliant pink to set off the black-and-white photographs. Glubok has expanded this theme into an entire book, *Knights in Armor* (1969), which is based mostly on the collection of armor in the Metropolitan Museum of Art.

In all of Shirley Glubok's books the page layout and the quality of the reproductions are good; the correlation between the text and the pictures has been careful, and locations in museums are given for all objects pictured.

The Art of Ancient Mexico (1968) is simply written and includes some materials children would be interested in for their familiarity: a pottery figure which appears to be a child in a swing, a man playing a drum and one blowing on a conch shell, and a series of pieces on an ancient ball game, including a player wearing helmet, knee guards, and ankle guards for protection. *The Art of Egypt Under the Pharaohs* (1980) gives a good look at the customs and beliefs of the ancient Egyptian culture through its art, particularly the sculpture and painting in tombs and temples. Another book about ancient times is *The Art of the Vikings* (1978).

While most of the books in the series are about ancient cultures, Glubok has also written many books about art in the United States, including *The Art of Colonial America* (1970), *The Art of the Woodland Indians* (1976), *The Art of the Plains Indians* (1976), and *The Art of America in the Gilded Age* (1974), all of which have supplementary curricular use. This series is unique in its field. It does not give a comprehensive art history of a culture, but it is unexcelled as an introduction for the beginner.

James Haskins

The Consumer Movement

As a teacher at every level from elementary school to university, James Haskins has become familiar with the interests of young readers as well as with their problems, some of which he describes in *Diary of a Harlem Schoolteacher*. He has written many biographies about black men and women as well as nonfiction in the social sciences; his writing is notable for its forthright tone, its casual but dignified style, its objectivity, and the research that is evident in the glossaries, bibliographies, and carefully compiled and cross-referenced indexes.

From *The Art of the Vikings* by Shirley Glubok. Oseberg wagon. Copyright University Museum of National Antiquities, Oslo, Norway.

The Consumer Movement (1975) is, like most of Haskins's books, written for older readers but has minor reference use for children in the middle grades. It is organized by such topics as "The Consumer Movement and the Drug Industry" and "The Consumer Movement and the Toy Industry." Within each section, there is some background material, followed by a history of problems, dangers, consumer action, and legislation; each chapter concludes with a summary statement on ways the consumer may encourage solutions to problems. The subject chapters are preceded by discussions on the consumer movement and consumer needs, and the final chapter emphasizes consumer awareness and the importance of joining the consumer movement.

Street Gangs, Yesterday and Today (1974) is a serious investigation based on newspaper accounts, sociological studies, and interviews. It covers the subject from colonial times to the present, pointing out the fact that there have always been ties of political and criminal elements, and that there are no easy solutions for a social phenomenon that has as some of its causes poverty, loneliness, low status, and class distinctions. Haskins' concern with societal problems is clearly conveyed in *Who Are the Handicapped?* (1978) and *The Quiet Revolution* (1979). He has also written on such diverse topics as *Religions* (1973), a survey of five major faiths, *Witchcraft, Mysticism and Magic in the Black World* (1974), *Jobs in Business and Office* (1974), and *The Creoles of Color of New Orleans* (1975).

From *The Quiet Revolution* by James Haskins. Photograph courtesy of the President's Committee on Employment of the Handicapped.

Holling Clancy Holling

Paddle-to-the-Sea

In a book as imaginative as its title, Holling C. Holling sets down the travels of a little wooden Indian sitting in a canoe carved of wood. Launched in the water in Nipigon country in Canada, the carving floats down through all of the Great Lakes, and finally reaches the sea. During this odyssey of *Paddle-to-the-Sea* (1941), he becomes frozen into the lake water, caught in a forest fire, and picked up by strangers, but always they heed the carving on the bottom of the canoe: "Please put me back in the water. I am Paddle-to-the-Sea," and he is put back in the water to continue his journey.

Fictionalized, this is also a geographical tour de force and a description of the ecology of the land through which Paddle floats. While *Paddle-to-the-Sea* is in truth a demonstration that water from north of Lake Superior makes its way to the Atlantic Ocean, it is much more. It is an imaginative dream of the real-life Indian boy who made the carving, and who later heard that

it had gone far across the ocean to France; it is a picture of the wildlife that surrounds Lake Superior; it is all these things, but because it is the sum rather than the parts, it is a unique work of art. *Paddle-to-the-Sea* was a Caldecott Honor Book in 1942.

Each chapter consists of one page of print alternating with full-page illustrations in full color, so that the story unfolds quickly as Paddle makes his way from the north, through the locks at Sault Ste. Marie, and on down to the ocean. The author shapes each chapter or page around a momentous happening, such as the breaking up of the ice on the river, or going over Niagara Falls. His easy, descriptive style, interspersed with lively conversation, makes the book attractive to children. Just as attractive are the pencil drawings which decorate the margins of the text, intricate accurate diagrams of the locks at the Soo, of a sawmill, or a lake freighter. Labeled well, they describe material which is not covered in the text. Coupled with the full-color paintings, these drawings both complement and enlarge the text, and they show as well as the text does the extensive historical research that Holling did for his books.

Although *Minn of the Mississippi* (1963) is almost identical in format and approach with *Paddle-to-the-Sea*, it is usually classified as a book about a reptile rather than fiction. Minn is a three-legged turtle who travels down the Mississippi from Lake Itasca, Minnesota, to the Gulf of Mexico, which enables Holling to describe the history, geography, climate, and geology of the river's regions.

Holling is also the author of *Pagoo* (1957), which describes in detail the life of a hermit crab, and *Tree in the Trail* (1942), the story of a tree's life over two centuries.

Aylette Jenness

Along the Niger River: An African Way of Life

Living in different parts of the world while on anthropological projects, Aylette Jenness has become interested in the lives of the people she met, and she has recorded them in several excellent photodocumentary volumes. She does not write as an uninvolved observer, but as a sympathetic visitor who hopes to be accepted by those she visits. She writes of peoples who lead lives that are, in varying degrees, primitive, but she does not write with an attitude of

Illustration by the author, from *Paddle-To-The-Sea* by Holling C. Holling. Published by Houghton Mifflin Company. Copyright 1941 and © renewed 1969 by Holling Clancy Holling. Reproduced by permission of the publisher. (Original in color)

(1970), which gives a vivid picture of the same community, Makumiut, and of the impact of white culture on the residents, particularly on the restless adolescents of the village. The writing style is casual and conversational but the tone is serious; Jenness writes with candor and sympathy. The same qualities are in *A Life of Their Own: An Indian Family in Latin America* (1975), written with Lisa Kroeber. The authors spent much time with one family, but also explored the school, the health clinic, the market, and the government of a Guatemalan town, so that the text and photographs together give a well-rounded picture of a community.

Patricia Lauber

Who Discovered America?

In a sharp departure from her earlier works, Patricia Lauber, in *Who Discovered America?* (1970), has written a speculative view of early explorers of America beginning with the people who may have crossed the land bridge between Siberia and Alaska; the Paleo-Indians, who may have inhabited the state of California 17,000 years ago; people who may have come from Southeast Asia to Middle America; the ones who named Vinland; and on through the voyages of Columbus. Lauber has done an excel-

superiority nor does she assume that customs, foods, or clothing are odd or quaint—a weakness in many books about people of other countries.

Along the Niger River (1974) is based on observations made during the three years that Jenness lived in Nigeria. The photographs are excellent, some informative and others merely decorative. The text discusses tribes of the savanna lands that border the Niger in northern Nigeria, and it gives historical background that is a firm base for understanding how modern technology is impinging on traditional living patterns. Comments on customs, mores, and cultural integration are perceptive, and the writing has both objectivity and the warmth that comes only from personal observations and relationships.

Jennes writes, in fact, only about things she has observed. While her first book, *Gussuk Boy* (1967), is fiction, it is based on a year of life in a village on the Bering seacoast. It incorporates many details of Alaskan Eskimo life, but there is far more of interest in *Dwellers of the Tundra*

Photograph from *Along the Niger River: An African Way of Life*, written and photographed by Aylette Jenness. Copyright © 1974 by Aylette Jenness. By permission of Thomas Y. Crowell, Publishers and Harold Matson Company, Inc.

lent job of gathering and synthesizing the often controversial material about this important subject.

Two chapters are particularly interesting: "Visitors from Distant Lands" and "Vinland the Good." In the first, the author presents photographs and documentation of inventions, designs, and motifs that are common to Asia as well as Latin America and asks the question, "Borrowed from the old world or invented in the new?"

This story is not easy to believe. It seems almost impossible that the fishermen could have drifted 8,000 miles and landed in Ecuador, where they taught the Indians to make pottery. Yet archeologists cannot find another way to explain the sudden appearance of this particular pottery in a region where there are no traces of earlier pottery.

About 2,000 years ago, Ecuador seems to have had another visit by voyagers from Asia. The evidence is a collection of pottery objects that were common in Asia but have not been found anywhere else in the New World. They were discovered by archeologists digging near the north coast of Valdivia . . .

These pottery objects found together in one part of Ecuador are nearly impossible to explain, unless they were introduced by people from Asia. They appear suddenly in Ecuador. They seem unrelated to New World pottery objects, but they are like objects that were widely used in the Old World. (p. 64)

In the chapter on Vinland she presents the evidence for the discovery of Vinland as it is outlined in *The Saga of Eric the Red* and *The Greenlander's Saga* and tends to agree with scholars who think that the basic events of these sagas are true. The format of the book is attractive, and the reproductions of photographs, prints, and maps are excellent. The book's nine chapters are well organized and well indexed.

Lauber has written widely in the fields of the sciences and social studies. *All About the Planets* (1960), which includes an introductory chapter on the formation of the solar system, a chapter on the moon, and information on the planets, is a competent work. *Tapping Earth's Heat* (1978) is a lucid discussion of volcanic action and the uses of geothermal energy. Three easy-to-read volumes are: *Your Body and How it Works* (1962), *The Story of Numbers* (1961), and *What's Hatching Out of That Egg?* (1979). Her interest in ecology and conservation is evident in *Everglades Country: A Question of Life or Death* (1973) and *Too Much Garbage* (1974). A quality that makes Lauber's books stimulating is their sense of lively curiosity, a provocative relish that can be shared by the reader and may send one seeking more information.

Robert M. McClung
Thor: Last of the Sperm Whales

In a book with overtones of *Moby Dick*, Robert McClung begins with the story of a sperm whale which destroyed the ships of whalers hunting him 150 years ago. *Thor* (1971) goes on to describe a sperm whale of today that bears the same marking as his ghostly forebear, ramming into the stern of a modern-day catcher boat carrying harpooners. In between there is a detailed description of the birth, feeding, growth, mating, and death of the great sperm whale as it travels the oceans, a great monster of the deep, fifty feet in length and "forty tons of bone and muscle, overlaid by an insulating blanket of blubber nearly a foot thick on his breast." While this is a scientific description of the life of the sperm whale, it is also a story of the relentless slaughter of whales in our century, destruction so great that three species, the great blue whales, the finbacks, and the sei whales, are in danger of extinction.

McClung, a prolific author in his field, has written sympathetically but without sentimentality of all kinds of wildlife. He manages to be thorough, but not dry, and weaves a story without anthropomorphism into his factual approach. Threaded through all of his work is the persistent theme of good conservation practices, and his very early work *Spike: The Story of*

Viewpoint

The difference between the good and bad historian is not so much the difference between a wide, regular, well-ordered and a narrow, irregular, and ill-ordered reading of record. It lies much more in the two qualities of proportion and imagination. Two men, for instance, may sit down to write as historians the events of an ancient battle.

. . . But the space of each is limited, and even if each had an unlimited canvas on which to paint, the truth of the result would still depend upon proportion—upon the discovery of the essential movements and the essential moments in the action; and upon imagination, the power of seeing the thing as it was; landscape, the weather, the gestures and the faces of the men; yes, and their thoughts within.—Hilaire Belloc, *One Thing and Another*, Hollis and Carter, London, 1955, pp. 24, 25.

a Whitetail Deer (1952) is a fine illustration of this. In it, the reader is exposed to the illegal practice of hunters shining a flashlight at night to attract deer. His books for younger children have large type, and clear, simple writing that never descends to oversimplification. In *Shag, Last of the Plains Buffalo* (1960), the author documents the savage slaughter of the buffalo as the white men drove westward with their guns and railroad tracks. *Honker: The Story of a Wild Goose* (1965) and *Hunted Mammals of the Sea* (1978) continue the conservation story.

While McClung's illustrations are not always labeled, they are always accurate and well placed in relation to textual references. His ability to write for different age levels is evident in comparing *Sea Star* (1975), which is written in concise prose, and *Gypsy Moth* (1974), which is detailed enough for adult readers; at both levels the writing is lucid and the information accurate. An excellent book on animal camouflage, *How Animals Hide* (1973) uses color photographs, showing examples of protective adaptation far better than any drawing could.

Illustration by William Downey, p. 31. From Robert M. McClung, *Hunted Mammals of the Sea.* Copyright © 1978 by Robert M. McClung. Published by William Morrow and Company, Inc.

Milton Meltzer
In Their Own Words

The first of the three-volume survey of black history in America, *In Their Own Words*, contains material not previously known to many readers, drawn from letters, diaries, journals, autobiographies, speeches, resolutions, newspapers, and pamphlets of black people in slavery. It traces life on the plantation and conditions in the North in letters from escaped slaves in the free states, and tells of the day of Emancipation. In these excerpts, one can see Milton Meltzer's selectivity in showing the wide range of activity and writings of slaves and freed slaves. The three books are an excellent source of information on what living conditions have been for black people through American history. Volume One is illustrated with black-and-white paintings, drawings, engravings, and photographs, and includes reproductions of a list of slaves belonging to Thomas Jefferson and of posters announcing the sale of slaves. Each excerpt is short, some only two pages; occasionally a document is quoted in full. Each has an introduction by Meltzer and the source is identified at the close. The volumes cover three periods: 1619 to 1865, 1865 to 1916, and 1916 to 1966.

Meltzer's books show his interest in social reform and its effects on the American people. *Time of Trial, Time of Hope* (1966) written with August Meier, describes the many problems and few victories of black people in the United States between the First and Second World Wars. The authors write with authority and from a broad viewpoint that includes political, economic, educational, and cultural problems as well as the role of labor.

Meltzer's book on the labor movement in the United States, *Bread and Roses* (1967), gives a vivid history of the struggles of the laboring class up to 1915. Using comments from contemporary sources, Meltzer documents the grim story of child labor, sweat shops, and defeated attempts to organize. As is true in all his books, the sources cited in *Bound for the Rio Grande; the Mexican Struggle, 1845–1850* (1974) give evidence of the author's meticulous research. Several of Meltzer's books are concerned with the Jewish people: *Never to Forget: The Jews of the Holocaust* (1976) discusses the treatment of Jews in Nazi Germany; Jewish life in Eastern Europe is described in *World of Our Fathers* (1974); and in *Remember the Days* (1974) Meltzer writes a brief history of American Jewry. The last two books were finalists for the now-extinct National Book Award.

Dorothy Hinshaw Patent
Evolution Goes On Every Day

A zoologist, Dorothy Patent has become established as an author whose books are distinguished for their combination of authoritative knowledge, detached and objective attitude, and an ability to write for the lay person with fluency and clarity. Like that exemplary writer for younger children, Millicent Selsam, she communicates a sense of wonder at the complexity and beauty of animal life by her zest for her subject rather than by comments on the marvelous intricacy of the natural order. In *Evolution Goes On Every Day* (1977) she explains some of the evolutionary changes in progress in contemporary species of flora and fauna, analyzing the various factors that effect change or that encourage the emergence of a new species.

Butterflies and Moths: How They Function (1979) is a text that is a model of broad coverage, good organization of material, and clarity in writing style. The book examines almost every aspect of lepidopterans, and discusses the ways in which moths and butterflies, in their various stages, are considered pests or benefactors by people. Patent is a prolific writer; among her other books are *Frogs, Toads, Salamanders, and How They Reproduce* (1975), *How Insects Communicate* (1975), *Plants and Insects Together* (1976), *Animal and Plant Mimicry* (1978), and *Bacteria: How They Affect Other Living Things* (1980). In all her books, Patent carefully distinguishes between fact and conjecture but makes it clear that conjecture and theory, even when erroneous, are part of the scientific method and can be built on to reach truth.

Harvester ants collect seeds and place them in underground storage chambers.

Illustration by Matthew Kalmenoff, with caption, p. 80. From Dorothy Hinshaw Patent, *Plants and Insects Together*. Text copyright © 1976 by Dorothy Hinshaw Patent. Illustrations copyright © 1976 by Holiday House, Inc. Published by Holiday House.

Laurence Pringle
Follow A Fisher

A former science teacher and, for many years, editor of *Nature and Science*, the magazine published by the American Museum of Natural History, Laurence Pringle combines in his books the ability to explain logical relationships and the succinct marshalling of facts that clarify such relationships, especially when they are intricate. In one of his earlier books, *Follow A Fisher* (1973), Pringle demonstrates his understanding of writing for younger children as he describes in crisp, straightforward style the habits and habitat of a member of the weasel family. His concern for conservation of species and for preservation of ecological balance is smoothly incorporated into the simply written, continuous text.

Nuclear Power: From Physics to Politics (1979) is for older readers, an objective approach to the complex dilemma of the nuclear power plant. Although he states that he is "not neutral," Pringle is in fact quite objective in discussing the safety hazards, the violations, the problems of nuclear waste, and the role of the Atomic

Illustration by Tony Chen from *Follow a Fisher* by Laurence Pringle.
Illustrations copyright © 1973 by Tony Chen. By permission of
Thomas Y. Crowell, Publishers.

Energy Commission. The text is as lucid in descriptions of processes as it is in evaluation of moral and ethical questions involved in the provision of energy through nuclear power.

Pringle's interest in ecological balance is manifest in *This Is a River: Exploring an Ecosystem* (1972). In *The Economic Growth Debate: Are There Limits to Growth?* (1978) he considers the impact on the planet and its resources of such aspects of economic growth as dwindling food supplies, pollution, and depletion of natural resources. The breadth of Pringle's interests is indicated by the fact that, although he trained as a wildlife biologist, his books often consider the total environment, sociological factors, and legal or ethical implications of biological problems.

Katharine Savage

The Story of World Religions

A historical as well as descriptive approach, Katharine Savage's *The Story of World Religions* (1967) is a comprehensive, well-written book, useful at both the junior-high and elementary levels, which gives a dispassionate, objective view of religions of the world. The book covers the world's major religions, but it does not include the area south of the Sahara in Africa, or reflect the many changes in the rituals and dress in the Roman Catholic religion, nor does it encompass the unrest in the priesthood of the Roman Catholic Church. It is organized into

fourteen chapters which are roughly chronological, and each treats one religion, sometimes several, of a given area. Well researched, the book has an extensive bibliography, and in her acknowledgments the author cites numerous sources of information as well as sources for the photographs.

Savage's style is dignified but not dry, sympathetic but not sentimental, and her distinction as a writer of informational books is based on comprehensive treatment, reliable research, logical organization of material, and a sense of perspective which sees and emphasizes those aspects of a subject that have real importance. Her other works include *The Story of the United Nations* (1962), in which the first third of the book describes the inception and formation of the U.N., and the last third chronicles crises such as the birth of Israel, the Berlin airlift, and attempts to bring peace to the Congo; and *The Story of Africa: South of the Sahara* (1961), which gives a history of the exploration and exploitation period in Africa.

Millicent E. Selsam

Benny's Animals

Millicent Selsam, one of the most dependably competent authors of science books, writes for all age levels, but she is undoubtedly best known for her books for young readers. Her style is simple and clear, with no extraneous material and no trace of popularization. She defines good science books as "those that show the methods of science at work, that elucidate basic principles of science and are not a mere assembly of facts, that convey something of the beauty and excitement of science, and that interest young people in thinking up good questions for new young scientists to test by experiment."[2]

Benny's Animals (1966) is a particularly good example of the inclusion of methodology and basic principles in a science book for the beginning reader. It is a clear lesson in how animals are classified, with a fictional framework that facilitates the explanation. Benny was a child with a passion for neatness and order, who

2. "Writing About Science for Children," by Millicent E. Selsam. From *A Critical Approach to Children's Literature,* edited by Sara Innis Fenwick. © 1967 by the University of Chicago. Reprinted by permission.

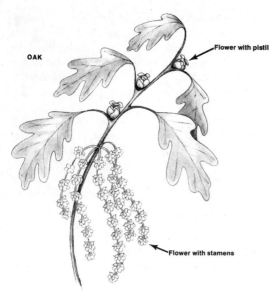

OAK

Flower with pistil

Flower with stamens

From the book, *A First Look at Flowers* by Millicent Selsam and Joyce Hunt. Illustrated by Harriet Springer. Text copyright © 1977 by Millicent E. Selsam and Joyce Hunt. Illustrations copyright © 1977 by Harriet Springer. Used with permission of the publisher, Walker and Company, NY.

wanted to organize his collection of material from the seashore, and this led to questions about the differences between animals. Finally Benny went to the museum to talk with Professor Wood, who suggested that he put the specimens in two piles according to whether or not they had a backbone; then his next step was to divide the animals with backbones into fish, amphibians, reptiles, birds, and mammals. Benny wanted to take classification a step further, but Professor Wood dissuaded him, saying that it would be a lifelong job. The book ends on just the right note, having explained the basic steps in classification and having made the point that there is a rational way of dividing living things. The format is excellent, with continuous text, large print, and plenty of space between the lines. Arnold Lobel's illustrations are appropriate in their earth colors, casually realistic when he portrays the boys and the family, and close enough to reality to be recognizable when he draws the animals, often giving them a little personality. *Greg's Microscope* (1963) and *Let's Get Turtles* (1965) are other titles in this "Science I Can Read" series.

The Amazing Dandelion (1977), *Mimosa, the Sensitive Plant* (1978), and *Bulbs, Corms, and Such* (1974) are for independent readers in lower and middle grades, illustrated with large handsome photographs, some in color, by Jerome Wexler. A group of books which are illustrated by several different artists are *See Through the Jungle* (1957); *See Through the Sea* (1955), a story of underwater life; and *See Along the Shore* (1961), a colorful volume which deals with tides and animals and plants of the seashore.

For still older children are *Land of the Giant Tortoise: the Story of the Galapagos* (1977) and *The Language of Animals* (1962), the latter a fascinating story of communication between animals including sounds, smells, facial expressions, and tail positions. In *Plants That Move* (1962), Selsam tells about the sundew plant, which catches insects, as well as the better-known venus flytrap; and in *Plants That Heal* (1959), she writes an intriguing chapter on plant medicines that are in use today. Introductory texts that stress observation are *A First Look at Flowers* (1977) and *A First Look at Animals with Backbones* (1978). One of Selsam's most interesting books for older readers was written with Jacob Bronowski—*Biography of an Atom* (1963), which traces the history of one carbon atom from its birth in a young star, through the millennia, to a conjectural fate today.

Katherine B. Shippen
Men, Microscopes, and Living Things

Katherine Shippen's books reflect a wide-ranging interest: science, biography, history, music, industry, and other fields. *Men, Microscopes, and Living Things* (1955) exemplifies her careful research and the vitality and grace of a writing style that give her work authority and elegance. In this survey of the work of great biologists, she uses quotations from their writings to enliven the book. Each chapter deals with some aspect of experimental science, concluding with Thomas Hunt Morgan's work in this century, using the fruit fly in studies of heredity. Anthony Ravielli's spidery, delicate line drawings, quite unlike his other work in children's books, give added appeal. It is indexed in full; for example, there are eighteen entries under "Darwin, Charles."

Quotations are used also, as chapter introductions rather than within the text, in *The Great Heritage* (1947), which is still timely because of the wide interest in conservation. *Mir-*

acle in Motion: The Story of American Industry (1955) concisely gives a history of three centuries of industry. In another book for older readers, Shippen collaborated with Anca Seidlova in writing *The Heritage of Music* (1963), a comprehensive and scholarly history of music from its beginning to Edgar Varèse's electronic music. *This Union Cause* (1958) is a history of organized labor in the United States and *The Pool of Knowledge: How the United Nations Share Their Skills* (rev. ed., 1965) is an informative contribution to young people's understanding of many of the peoples of this world as well as of some of the work of the U.N.

Paul and Kay Showers

Before You Were a Baby

Before You Were a Baby (1968), the only book by Paul Showers for which he has a coauthor, is an excellently paced book for readers in the second and third grades, and it is clear enough to be read aloud to younger children. There are repetition and rhythm in sentences like "This new cell grew and grew and grew. And at last it became you." Particularly dramatic are the pictures which show, in color, the increasing size of the baby inside the uterus. On these pages the text is almost nonexistent, and the reader's eye is carried forward by the power of the graphic drawings as they progress from the hunchback figure at six weeks to the completely formed baby of eight months. Using all of the correct terms, such as *testes, sperm,* and *penis,* the book gives an accurate explanation of conception without being either coy or evasive. The book's tone is captured in its opening and closing paragraphs:

Once you were a baby. You were very small. A
     little boy could lift you easily and carry you.
Before you were a baby, you were much smaller.
No one could even see you.

then,

Now the baby is born.
This baby,
     and you,
     and every baby in the world—
came from two tiny cells that nobody could see—
          an ovum
          and a sperm.

The simple style and use of large print, with a minimum of labeled diagrams, is typical of the Crowell series which includes *Before You Were a Baby*. Showers gives accurate information in the very simplest language, chooses important facts, and tells them in logical sequence, so that the child can read the books alone or the adult can use them as a springboard for discussion.

Showers's other books include *Your Skin and Mine* (1965) and *Look at Your Eyes* (1962). The first gives some of the basic facts about skin: sensation, temperature adjustment, hair follicles, and color differences, explaining the latter so that the message about skin color is casual, while the illustrations show children of various colors in connection with the text rather than as an ethnic spectrum for its own sake. In the second, a black child's daily activities are used to show how eyes adjust to light, that eyes are different colors, how the parts of the eye work.

Use Your Brain (1971), *Where Does the Garbage*

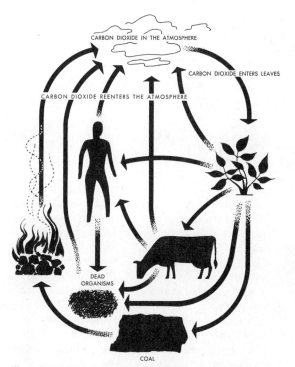

Illustration by Weimer Pursell from *Biography of an Atom* by J. Bronowski and Millicent E. Selsam. Copyright © 1963 by J. Bronowski. Copyright © 1965 by J. Bronowski and Millicent E. Selsam. By permission of Harper & Row, Publishers, Inc.

Go? (1974), and *Me and My Family Tree* (1978) are other concise, informative science books by Paul Showers, and he has also written *Indian Festivals* (1969) and *Columbus Day* (1965) in the same direct and pithy style.

Alvin and Virginia Silverstein

Hamsters: All About Them

Alvin Silverstein is a biology professor and Virginia Silverstein a translator of Russian scientific literature; they have collaborated on over thirty books for young people, from books that deal with a narrow area, such as *Apples: All About Them* (1976) to books on such complex topics as *Sleep and Dreams* (1974). Their work is carefully organized and written in a clear, direct style, and is dependably accurate. The more complicated subjects are not always covered in depth, but they are given balanced treatment, and the Silversteins' writing usually shows their attention to current research and always maintains a scientific attitude.

Hamsters (1974) is one of a series of books for the middle elementary school grades, all subtitled *All About Them*. It is illustrated with photographs that are well placed in relation to textual references, although not all the pictures are informative. Following a brief discussion of the way in which hamsters were introduced into the United States as research animals and became popular as pets, the text gives detailed advice on the care of hamsters, including information on housing and breeding. A concluding chapter describes the importance of the hamster in laboratory studies. Pervading the book is an attitude of respect for the rights and well-being of pets, and there is no trace of fictionalization or anthropomorphism.

The Silversteins have written many books in a series called "Systems of the Body," with books like *The Skeletal System* (1972) and *The Skin* (1972) that have accurate texts, include facts on recent research, and give lucid explanations of intricate physiological functions. In *Exploring the Brain* (1973) the authors give a good overview of what is known on the subject, discussing both the functioning of the brain and the nervous system, and citing laboratory experiments on the effects of drugs and of illness on the human brain. Their emphasis on current research is evident in this book and in *The Sugar Disease: Diabetes* (1980); it is stressed particularly in *The Code of Life* (1972), which explores genetic engineering as well as genetic inheritance and how it functions, and in *The Chemicals We Eat and Drink* (1973), which discusses the benefits or dangers of chemicals in foods, with findings based on testing programs and research studies. The book also considers, as do other Silverstein books, effects on the society, and suggests citizen support of pollution control and of supervisory legislation; a concern for the sociological implications of biological problems is paramount in *Aging* (1979).

Hilda Simon

Living Lanterns: Luminescence in Animals

As a student of art and biology, Hilda Simon is well qualified both as author and artist for the books she has written and illustrated in the field of biology. Her drawings are beautifully detailed and accurate, and the same accuracy is evident in her writing, which is informal and lucid. While there are scientific terms used, the writing is not laden with jargon but can be understood by readers with little background. However, since Simon uses neither anthropomorphism nor condescension and since she treats her subjects in some depth, her books are also appropriate for readers who do have background in biology.

In *Living Lanterns* (1971) Simon begins with a brief survey of what has been known about the phenomenon of luminescence in the past, then describes luminescent creatures according to their habitats (land, air, or sea), and concludes with a discussion of the anatomy of luminescence. Observations are validated by citing research, and the text is explicit in stating the fact that not all the questions about bioluminescence have been answered. Simon's books exemplify the best kind of science writing, authoritative and accurate, illustrated with pictures that are carefully placed and informative, and supplied with indexes, bibliographies, and—in some books—maps that show the ranges of species.

Most of her books are for older readers, but Simon's *The Amazing Book of Birds* (1958) is for the middle grades. Written in a light, informal style, it gives many facts about birds, but the random arrangement makes it less cohesive and therefore less useful than her later work. A study of imitative patterns or adaptations in the insect world, *Insect Masquerades* (1968), is a more typical example of Simon's writing: logically organized, and leading from the discussions of individual creatures to conclusions about the survival potential of insects which have such advantages. The full-color drawings in *Snakes: The Facts and the Folklore* (1973) have crisp, useful captions and can be used for identification. *Snakes* includes a chapter on keeping a snake as a pet, and both books describe the habits and habitats of species in great detail.

Seymour Simon

The Rock-Hound's Book

Seymour Simon's many years as a public school science teacher are reflected in his books both by the knowledgeable ease with which he adapts his style to the comprehension level of the intended audience and by the fact that in many of his books he includes experiments that are clearly explained and that illustrate the principles he is discussing. He moves from the familiar to the less familiar, from the simple to the more complex, in the best tradition of teaching, but his writing has a natural, informal flow that has no didactic tone.

In *The Rock-Hound's Book* (1973) Simon encourages the novice collector, pointing out that rocks are everywhere, that they are composed of minerals, and that rock-collecting is a safe, pleasant, endlessly interesting hobby. He describes qualities that identify mineral components, and supplies advice on where and how to collect with effective zeal. In *The Long View Into Space* (1979) he creates a photographic essay that is handsome, accurate, lucid, and serious: an excellent introduction to astronomical bodies and the phenomena peculiar to each. It is typical of Simon's writing that he carefully explains, in this book, such subjects as novae or spiral galaxies without telling middle-grade readers so much that they are confused or so little that the subjects are not comprehensible.

Among the over fifty other books by Simon are *Life in the Dark: How Animals Survive at Night* (1974), *Meet the Giant Snakes* (1979), *Danger from*

Illustrations by Tony Chen, pp. 20–21. From Seymour Simon, *The Rock-Hounds Book.* Copyright © 1973 by Seymour Simon. Published by The Viking Press, Inc.

Below: Earthquakes, Past, Present, and Future (1979), and *Strange Mysteries* (1980), a potpourri of odd phenomena, reported or documented.

Edwin Tunis

Frontier Living

The immense amount of detail produced in *Frontier Living* (1961) reflects painstaking research; the text contains little conjecture, but only fact upon fact about all aspects of frontier living. Organized generally in an east-to-west pattern, the book, by the author's admission, concentrates mostly east of the Mississippi because, as he said, "Nearly every phase of the far West has been dealt with ... while the forest frontier, with a few notable exceptions, has been bypassed since James Fenimore Cooper stopped romancing about it." And so the book progresses from sections dealing with the Piedmont, in which Indians, forts, and medicine and witchcraft are described, on through the old Northwest Territory, passing then out to Kansas, Colorado, and California. "The Old Northwest" has much excellent material on day-to-day living, and the section on housekeeping is an example of both the author's style and the meticulousness of his research.

The black-and-white line drawings are of uniform excellence and accuracy, whether of a panoramic view of moving half of a canal boat over a mountain, or detailing the intricate works of a small aresenal of early western arms. The author's captions are revealing, too, and often humorous. Of the Bowie knife, he wrote: "The mild and quiet Colonel Bowie didn't design this toadsticker; he gave it his name by way of the mayhem he did with it."

Frontier Living was a Newbery Honor Book, and *Colonial Living* (1957), with a similar format, won the Thomas Alva Edison Foundation's Children's Book Award for special excellence in portraying America's past. *Wheels: A Pictorial History* (1955) and *Indians* (1959) are so comprehensive and profusely illustrated with authoritatively detailed drawings that they have reference use. *Shaw's Fortune* (1966), the picture story of a plantation, differs from earlier books in being chronological, following the growth of the plantation from a cabin in the wilderness clearing to a self-sufficient community in 1752. *The Young United States—1783 to 1830* (1969) is topically organized, covering both daily life and historical events. In *The Tavern at the Ferry* (1973), Tunis follows the changes that occur in the life of a Quaker family and in the building they own; through this, he gives an immediacy to the colonial way of life and to events of the Revolutionary War. Tunis's wit had been evident in his other books, but with the publication of *Chipmunks on the Doorstep* (1971), his first book in the field of natural science, he added a wry humor to the appeals of perceptive observation and beautiful pictures.

The Tea Water pump

Harvey Weiss

Pencil, Pen and Brush: Drawing for Beginners

A major criterion for an activity book is that the instructions tell the reader exactly how to perform the activity. Harvey Weiss's arts and crafts books are clear in explaining procedures, and they encourage readers to use their own initiative.

Pencil, Pen and Brush (1961) has a sophisticated approach for a how-to-do-it book. Using the work of major artists, from Leonardo da Vinci to Maurice Sendak, as well as photographs for models, Weiss presents his instructions in easy steps, never talking down to his readers. Practical advice is given for each step, and readers are given suggestions for striking out on their own; the discussion ends on an encouraging note, with questions and suggestions.

An example of the matter-of-fact procedure used throughout the book is this selection from "Tones":

A tone is a shade of black or a shade of color. When you use a tone combined with a single line, your drawing will look more solid and more interesting. Here is a way to make a figure drawing using tones. Get a small sponge, or a piece of sponge. (If you can't find a sponge a crumpled-up facial tissue will do.) Pour two or three drops of ink onto a plate and add about two tablespoons of water. Mix the ink and water. Dip your sponge lightly into the mixture then press the sponge down lightly on a piece of scrap paper and quickly lift it straight up again. You'll see that the sponge leaves a large and pleasantly textured tone of gray.

Use the sponge to put the main masses of the figure on paper—a few big dabs for the body, some slimmer dabs (with the narrow part of the sponge) for the arms and legs. Then take your pencil, or pen and ink, and draw in the figure with lines. Try using colored ink, instead of black ink, for your tones. Or use water color, which is a transparent paint. (p. 24)

At the end of the book the artist has included a section "About the illustrations" identifying each artist included in the book by the title of his work, and giving the museum in which the original art is located.

Other books deal with three-dimensional materials: *Clay, Wood and Wire* (1956), *Ceramics from Clay to Kiln* (1965), and *Carving* (1976). Again, the artist uses pieces of sculpture, artifacts, woven fabrics, a Buckminster Fuller geodesic dome, masks, and Egyptian pottery as his models. *Paper, Ink and Roller* (1958) is on printmaking for beginners. Although Weiss has reproduced some artists' prints for this book, he uses many examples of his own prints.

Weiss is always clear and explicit, moving from simple projects to more complicated ones; in *Model Cars and Trucks and How to Build Them* (1974), for example, the first model is a solid, one-piece racing car, and the last a large, intricate car that can be ridden. The same careful progression from the familiar and simple to the less familiar and intricate is evident in *How to Run a Railroad* (1978), a book on model trains.

Weiss has also written *Sailing Small Boats* (1967) and *Motors and Engines and How They Work* (1969), an accurate and useful book for the child with a mechanical bent, and one that requires no previous knowledge.

Herbert Zim

Dinosaurs

Among the many books that Herbert Zim has written in various scientific fields, *Dinosaurs* (1954) is a good example of the logical organization, simple and succinct writing, and provision of background information that make his approach admirably suitable for presenting complex information to a reader unfamiliar with the subject. Zim explains the ways in which fossils are formed and the ways in which scientists are able to determine what dinosaurs looked like, and what they ate, by comparing their skeletal structure with those of known creatures. He describes the evolution of dinosaurs, gives details on how the species differed, and provides brief descriptions of some of the better-known kinds. The meticulously drawn black-and-white illustrations parallel the text and are always adequately captioned. The book concludes with a discussion of the ways in which dinosaurs changed during the Age of Reptiles and offers possible reasons for their extinction.

Harold Zim has taught for over thirty years in the fields of science and science education. With his first wife, Sonia Bleeker, he wrote *Life and Death* (1970), one of the best books on this subject for children of elementary school age. The book discusses life expectancy, aging, the clinical definition of death, and the rituals and legal procedures that are followed after death occurs. It concludes with a brief description of death rituals as they are practiced throughout the world.

Zim's lifelong interest in collecting nature specimens is reflected in *Golden Hamsters* (1951)

Illustration by Peter Parnall is reprinted by permission of Charles Scribner's Sons from *Year on Muskrat Marsh* by Bernice Freschet, illustrated by Peter Parnall. Illustration copyright © 1974 by Peter Parnall.

and *Frogs and Toads* (1950), two of a series of small volumes with large print that have proved most attractive to young children. In them, as in *The New Moon* (1980), a text that gives information obtained from lunar probes, the continuous texts are comprehensive. His books on the human body, *Our Senses and How They Work* (1956) and *Your Heart and How It Works* (1959), are for the slightly older child. A professor of science education, Zim exemplifies the objectivity of the scientist's attitude. In *Medicine* (1974), which is a survey of products, not of the profession, he includes information based on research. He has also contributed to the field of informational books as editor and coauthor of a series of Golden Nature Guides, pocket-sized volumes in full color. They are widely circulated in outlets other than libraries and are probably the one most handy tool for quick identification of trees, fish, seashells, fossils, and flowers.

It is obviously impossible to include, in the discussion and the bibliography that follow, all the good informational books or indeed books on every subject. The chapter and the reading lists are meant to give the reader a broad picture of the kinds of material that are available to provide children with pleasure and to satisfy their need for information.

Whenever books are classified as in the following discussion, problems arise, because some of them simply refuse to fit neatly into preordained slots. For example, the early concept books (discussed in Chapter 5) for very young children could be in a separate group here, also: books that present ideas of big and small, books that simply introduce familiar objects, books that familiarize a child with colors. There are books that bridge the physical and biological sciences, books that are about religious holidays but are also activity books, books that describe musical instruments and also tell the reader how to make simple instruments. Books on pollution, for instance, involve weather, natural resources, and chemical change; they involve living things; and they illustrate the problems created by our careless destruction of our environment, problems that have sociological repercussions. Since pollution is a tragedy created by humanity, such books have been placed in the social science list.

The books have been arranged in five broad categories: physical sciences, biological sciences, social sciences, religion and the arts, and activities and experiments. The bibliography for this chapter follows the same pattern.

The Biological Sciences

Partly because of the nationwide concern for more science in the schools, the list of science books has grown phenomenally each year. The list has also grown in breadth of subject. No longer are books in the biological sciences confined to those about familiar plants and animals—today they cover almost every topic from a hen's egg to cryogenics and space medicine. Children's books have abandoned, for the most part, the pseudo-scientific stories and watered-down information of the past and have adopted instead a seriousness and a straightforward approach that children and adults alike can appreciate.

Reports from teachers and librarians show that science rates high in both the types of questions children ask and in the types of books they request. Properly presented, almost any area of scientific knowledge can be made both fascinating and comprehensible to children.

The criteria for informational books discussed earlier in this chapter (see pp. 442–46) of course are applicable in evaluating science books. It is important that the author keeps in mind the child's point of view.

Authors should begin within the framework of the child's limited world. They must expand that world *step by step* at a pace which the child can follow—if they leap, they may leave the child behind. Leading, though, is not enough, for the child will choose to stay behind if the journey becomes uninteresting. What, therefore, is necessary to maintain interest?

Naturally clarity and good organization are of primary importance. Yet no matter how carefully and logically an author develops material, if it sounds like an article for an encyclopedia, the child will often lose interest. Unfortunately many adults look upon science as a cold collection of facts. To them it is devoid of emotion, entirely unrelated to imaginative writing. To the child, however, finding out about science is full of excitement, fascination, joy, and reassurance. What are some more of the books that not only present information clearly and understandably but maintain the reader's interest?

Some books include both the biological and the physical sciences, like Bertha Parker's *Golden Book of Science* (1956), which is designed to introduce the child to a many-faceted field and to encourage pursuing the facets in detail.

Books like Sarah Riedman's *Naming Living Things* (1963) discuss seriously the classification of plants and animals. There is a wide spread between the sophistication of this book and the simple approach of *Benny's Animals* by Millicent Selsam, described earlier, but in terms of accuracy each fulfills its purpose.

With the current stress on ecological balance, many books explore both the plants and the animals of a living community. *The Living Community* (1966) by Carl Hirsch is an introduction to interrelationships among plants and animals; Berniece Freschet's *Year on Muskrat Marsh* (1974) and, Alvin Tresselt's *The Beaver Pond* (1970) give a similar picture of an ecosystem for younger children.

Lucy Kavaler's *The Wonders of Algae* (1961) is an engrossing report on the versatility of one of the simplest of plant forms and of the experiments that have proved its usefulness to people: as a food, as a life-sustaining system for space ships, or as fuel. Kavaler's *Wonders of Fungi* (1964) discusses the myriad uses of some of the 100,000 known species of fungi that are disease producers or that are used as food or medicine. Among the most beautifully illustrated books about plants are Anne Dowden's

This Noble Harvest: A Chronicle of Herbs (1980) and *The Blossom on the Bough* (1975), both of which can be used for identifying plants. The latter can be used as an introduction to botany; it also stresses the importance of plants in the ecology. For younger readers, a good book about the plant kingdom is *Green Is for Growing* (1964) by Winifred and Cecil Lubell. The illustrations are accurate and beautiful; the rhythmic, flowing text describes the characteristics of each group of plants, and it is pervaded with an awareness of the importance of ecological balance.

Both plants and animals are discussed in Glenn Blough's *Soon After September* (1959), the story of what happens in winter to plants, hibernating animals, and migrating birds. *After the Sun Goes Down* (1956) is a story of animals at night, and *Who Lives in This House?* (1957) is about animal families. All of these books are illustrated by Jeanne Bendick and are appealing to younger children; the typeface is large and clear, and the language is simple.

The accurate details of Olive Earle's drawings correspond to the meticulous details of her books about animals. In *Praying Mantis* (1969),

MUGWORT
Artemisia vulgaris

Illustration by Anne Ophelia Dowden from *This Nobel Harvest, a Chronicle of Herbs,* used with the permission of Philomel Books. Copyright © 1979 by Anne Ophelia Dowden.

for example, about half the book describes the life cycle of the female mantis, the other half being notes on the behavior of a single mantis. The tone is often poetic, but the facts are quite accurate. Earle also has written about plant life in *The Rose Family* (1970) and *State Trees* (1973).

Probably the greatest number of books about the animal kingdom are accounts of a single animal. Alice Goudey's stories are authoritative and simply written, giving the life cycle, habits, and habitat in such books as *Here Come the Lions* (1956) and *Here Come the Dolphins* (1961). Another author whose books are dependably accurate and have a direct and dignified style is Dorothy Shuttlesworth, who writes chiefly about insects, although her works include *The Story of Rodents* (1971) and *To Find a Dinosaur* (1973). The evidence here of thorough research is seen also in Shuttlesworth's similar books on ants and on spiders.

Roy Chapman Andrews's *All About Whales* (1954) has the stamp of personal observation, since Andrews worked with these great mammals. Jane Werner Watson's *Whales: Friendly Dolphins and Mighty Giants of the Sea* (1975) is a well-rounded book for the middle grades. Certainly the most beautifully written book on the subject is Victor Scheffer's *Little Calf* (1970), which is for older readers.

Of all the books about dinosaurs, Roy Chapman Andrews's *All About Dinosaurs* (1953) adds another dimension to information, for a large

part of the book is devoted to his own experiences, and he conveys with relish the excitement of locating the first dinosaur eggs found in our time. He also wrote, for younger children, *In the Days of the Dinosaurs* (1959). Basic information on the subject is given clearly and briefly in two quite similar books, *Dinosaurs* (1955) by Marie Bloch, and *Discovering Dinosaurs* (1960) by Glenn Blough.

Louis Darling's most impressive book is *The Gull's Way* (1965). Here there is excellent correlation between Darling's text and his pictures. On a remote coastal island, he observed closely the behavior of two herring gulls as they courted, mated, brooded their eggs, and departed when their offspring became independent. Darling's style changed, in this book, from his competent but conventional description of a bird in *Greenhead* (1954), the study of a mallard duck, to a philosophical, almost tender, outlook on wildlife.

The Bird Watcher's Guide (1961) by Henry Collins is a comprehensive book on all aspects of bird-watching. In addition to books for identifying birds, there are many that describe a single kind of bird. Barbara Brenner's *Baltimore Orioles* (1974) gives accurate information for beginning readers, describing the oriole's life cycle; Berniece Freschet, in *The Flight of the Snow Goose* (1970), uses the life cycle also, but includes ecological aspects, as does Jack Scott in *Canada Geese* (1976).

A good book for identifying seashells is Elizabeth Clemons's *Shells Are Where You Find Them* (1960), which gives advice on collecting and on a separate page describes each shell listed. A good choice for use with very young children is Alice Goudey's *Houses from the Sea* (1959). The slow, easy pace and the delicate illustrations by Adrienne Adams make it a good choice for reading aloud; the fact that two children, wandering along the beach, find fifteen kinds of shells means that there is not too much information for small children to assimilate. The book is prefaced by a note on collecting and closes with a brief account of how shells are formed. *Houses from the Sea* was a Caldecott Honor Book.

In addition to books on animal species, there are excellent ones that explore some special aspect of animal life. Dorothy Shuttlesworth, for example, in *Animal Camouflage* (1966), explains countershading, disruptive coloration, and mimicry. Jack Scott discusses characteristics that have enabled some species to flourish in *The Survivors* (1975) and, in *Return of the Buffalo*

Viewpoint

To write about science for children an author needs to know science, to know children, and to know how to write. . . .

. . . It is not enough to say, "Here is an exciting thing. See the way a caterpillar spins a cocoon." The role of the writer is to write the book so that a child can feel he is *participating* in an observation. . . .

Good science books should communicate some of the excitement of discovery—and the triumph that goes with the solution of scientific problems. They should make a young person understand why Archimedes could jump out of his bath to rush through the streets of Syracuse shouting "Eureka" when he discovered a new physical principle.
—Millicent E. Selsam, "Writing About Science for Children," *A Critical Approach to Children's Literature*, edited by Sara Innis Fenwick. © 1967 by the University of Chicago. Reprinted by permission.

A MATTER OF PROPORTION

elbow — knee
wrist — ankle
hand — foot
two fingers — two toes

Reprinted by permission of Dodd, Mead & Company, Inc. from *Bone for Bone* by Margaret Cosgrove. Copyright © 1970 by Margaret Cosgrove.

(1976) and *Island of Wild Horses* (1978) describes two species that have done so. J. H. Prince describes patterns of courtship and mating in *The Universal Urge* (1973).

All kinds of vertebrate life are considered in Margaret Cosgrove's *Bone for Bone* (1968), a study of comparative anatomy by a medical artist. One of the first drawings in the book, for example, shows skeletons of the mouse and the elephant, divergent outwardly but strikingly alike in their skeletal patterns. Cosgrove discusses, in graceful prose, the relationships between parts of the body, the graduation from simple to complex vertebrates, and the adaptive process by which each animal fits into a way of life. Two beautifully illustrated books by Anthony Ravielli, *Wonders of the Human Body* (1954) and *From Fins to Hands: An Adventure in Evolution* (1968) show body structure and evolutionary changes with great clarity.

Cosgrove's *Eggs—and What Happens Inside Them* (1966) is for a slightly younger audience, and deals with eggs that develop in water or on land, and eggs without shells, concluding with a discussion of the parts of the egg that develop into different parts of the body. A book with remarkable photographs is *Window into an Egg: Seeing Life Begin* (1969) by Geraldine Lux Flanagan. Through a glass window sealed into an eggshell, we see an embryo develop into a chick.

The miracle of reproduction is described in books for every age, from Paul and Kay Showers's *Before You Were a Baby*, discussed earlier in this chapter, and Margaret Sheffield's *Where Do Babies Come From?* (1973), both of which are

clear explanations that use correct terminology yet have a reverent approach toward the miracle of birth, to Eric Johnson's *Love and Sex in Plain Language* (1974), which discusses sexual intercourse and sex mores with frankness and dignity. For the child of eight to ten, Sidonie Matsner Gruenberg's *The Wonderful Story of How You Were Born* (1970) is a direct and simple text, illustrated with tender and dignified drawings by Symeon Shimin. Photographs are used to illustrate the candid, clear text for the same age range in a book translated from the Swedish, Lennart Nilsson's *How Was I Born?* (1975).

The Physical Sciences

Many of today's children know more about science than do some adults. Parents can sympathize with the mother and father who hadn't the remotest idea of the answer when their fourth-grader asked them whether the ionosphere or the troposphere was nearer the earth. Teachers can report numerous situations similar to the one in which a fifth-grader was able to give the class an impromptu lecture in answer to another child's question on how a rocket works. Where are the children getting this information?

Some of it may come from television programs, but science books for children are certainly one of the most important sources of information. In both the extent of subjects covered and in the vocabulary used, children's science books show that there is a new respect for the reader's intelligence and interest.

Many of the concept books for young children, like Eric Carle's *My Very First Book of Shapes* (1974) can stimulate curiosity. Mae Freeman's *Gravity and the Astronauts* (1971) links an important phenomenon in physics to a subject children find alluring, and includes simple home demonstrations.

Isaac Asimov's story about gravity, *The Best New Thing* (1971); books like Illa Podendorf's *Things Are Alike and Different* (1970); and *How Big Is Big? From Stars to Atoms* (1950) by Herman and Nina Schneider all lead young children to curiosity about the world in which they live and about why things happen the way they do. When children begin to ask "how" and "why," then we know that they are ready to explore further in the world of science. It is the primary purpose of all of these books to encourage this desire to know more.

One of the first things a child becomes aware of is the weather. Alvin Tresselt's *Rain Drop Splash* (1946) and *Hide and Seek Fog* (1965) are excellent introductions to aspects of weather for very young children. *The First Book of Weather* (1966) by Rose Wyler is for readers in the middle grades and includes simple experiments. Benjamin Bova's *Man Changes the Weather* (1973) describes the ways in which man has affected the atmosphere, including pollution and a discussion of control agencies, and in John Navarra's *Wide World Weather* (1968), older readers can investigate the scientific, social, and governmental aspects of getting and sharing information, and of weather control and weather satellites.

Walter Buehr's *Water: Our Vital Need* (1967) and Melvin Berger's *The New Water Book* (1973) explain the water cycle and the variation in rainfall in different parts of the earth; the latter also describes the uses of water, water resources, and water pollution. A good first book about the earth is *Your Changing Earth* (1963) by Hy Ruchlis, which describes the beginnings of the earth and the solar system; the development of land, sea, and air; and the ways in which natural forces change the earth's surface. One of the most provocative books about our earth is Melvin Berger's *Jigsaw Continents* (1978), which describes the evidence that has led to acceptance of the theory (not new, but long disputed) of continental drift.

Oceanography is another rapidly expanding frontier; like many other areas of science, it is a subject in which many books bridge the scientific disciplines. Although newer books report some of the more recent knowledge about the sea floor, no book on the subject is more exciting than Rachel Carson's *The Sea Around Us* (1958), which describes the formation of the oceans, tides and currents, marine flora and fauna, and the ocean floor with its volcanic activity. A book that adds immediacy to the information it gives is Peter Briggs's *Science Ship* (1969). Briggs spent three weeks aboard an oceanographic research vessel, *The Discoverer*, and his report gives facts about techniques, equipment, and findings; it also shows how today's scientific investigations demand the skills of scientists from many fields. Melvin Berger's *Oceanography Lab* (1973) is a competent survey of the work of oceanographers that makes clear the way they draw on help from other scientific disciplines.

*Viewpoint*_____

I like books of knowledge; not those that want to encroach upon recreation, upon leisure, pretending to be able to teach anything without drudgery. There is no truth in that. There are things which cannot be learned without great pains; we must be resigned to it. I like books of knowledge when they are not just grammar or geometry poorly disguised; when they have tact and moderation; when, instead of pouring out so much material on a child's soul that it is crushed, they plant in it a seed that will develop from the inside. I like them when they do not deceive themselves about the quality of knowledge, and do not claim that knowledge can take the place of everything else. I like them especially when they distill from all the different kinds of knowledge the most difficult and the most necessary—that of the human heart.—Paul Hazard. *Books, Children and Men* translated by Marguerite Mitchell, The Horn Book, Inc., 1944, p. 43.

Books about the earth and volcanic activity may stimulate a child's interest in the past ages in which the earth as we know it was shaped. *First Days of the World* (1958) by Gerald Ames and Rose Wyler explains the formation of the solar system, the beginnings of oceans, atmosphere, and living things, and goes on to describe the geological changes through the ages. *The First Book of Volcanoes and Earthquakes* (1972) by Rebecca Marcus describes both the causes of these phenomena and the work of seismologists; in Julian May's *Why the Earth Quakes* (1969) the explanations of what causes earthquakes and volcanic eruption is clarified by Leonard Everett Fisher's illustrations.

People have always been fascinated by stars, but never before the space age has there been such general interest and such immediate concern with the far reaches of our universe. Two of the best introductions to astronomy for children of ten to twelve are *The New Golden Book of Astronomy* by Rose Wyler and Gerald Ames (1965), which covers the atmosphere, seasons, and phases of the moon, the members of the solar system, gravity and tides, how stellar measurements are made, and plans for the continuous exploration of space; and Roy Gallant's *Exploring the Universe* (1968), which presents the theories of early astronomers in an easy, informal style. Many of Franklyn Branley's books were discussed earlier in the chapter; no writer in the field of astronomy is more adept at writing simply for young children. For older readers, Robert Richardson's *The Stars and Serendipity* (1971) introduces astronomical discoveries made by scientists who were working on another problem and came across an exciting new find.

Another clever approach, designed for beginners, can be found in *You, Among the Stars* (1951) by Herman and Nina Schneider. As in other books by these same authors, the emphasis is on orienting the young child. Through the theme of an envelope address, the child moves from the family home outward into space step by step until the familiar street address becomes greatly elaborated.

Ask children today what area of science they want to study, and more often than not they will answer "space." In the minds of today's children, studying space often means studying rockets and satellites, not the sun and moon. John Wilford's *We Reach the Moon* (1969) is based on the original adult book and gives the step-by-step development of the NASA program, concluding with some results of the scientific experiments carried out by the astronauts. Bernice Kohn, in *Communications Satellites* (1975), describes the principles by which satellites function, and Ben Bova's *Workshops in Space* (1974) discusses knowledge garnered from satellites. William Wise, in *Monsters from Outer Space* (1979) discusses the observation of UFO's.

To understand the mechanics of the space program, so much of which is based on intricate mathematics, readers must be aware of the mathematical computations on which scientists rely. Lancelot Hogben's *The Wonderful World of Mathematics* (1968) relates the growth of mathematics as a science to changing human needs. With the modern curriculum, in which children are learning new concepts at earlier stages, there have been many books published that use the process approach or deal with one aspect of mathematical concepts. An excellent series, the Crowell "Young Math Books," examines one aspect in each volume. Typical of the series is *Long, Short, High, Low, Thin, Wide* (1971) by James Fey, which discusses measurement and encourages the reader to observe and compare; two of the others are Robert Froman's *Less Than Nothing Is Really Something* (1973) and Jane Srivastava's *Averages* (1975). These books teach something about scientific methods as well as the immediate subject with which they are concerned. *What Do You Mean by "Average"?* (1978)

Illustration by Joel Schick, p. 21. From Elizabeth James & Carol Barkin, *What Do You Mean by "Average"?* Copyright © 1978 by Elizabeth James and Carol Barkin. Published by Lothrop, Lee & Shepard Company. Reprinted by permission.

by Elizabeth James and Carol Barkins discusses such concepts as mean, median, and mode for older readers. Jeanne Bendick's *Take Shapes, Lines, and Letters* (1962), written with Marcia Levin, deals with ideas and relationships rather than with numbers, and the basic principles of computer mathematics are explained in *The New World of Computers* (1965) by Alfred Lewis.

To prepare children for conversion from our traditional system of measurement to the metric system, many authors have discussed its advantages. June Behrens, in *The True Book of Metric Measurement* (1975), gives a clear explanation for readers in the primary grades. For slightly older readers, both Franklyn Branley's *Think Metric!* (1973) and Miriam Schlein's *Metric—The Modern Way to Measure* (1975) discuss both the way in which the metric system works and the reasons it is preferable to the old system of measuring. More background and more details are given in books for readers in the upper elementary grades and in high school. They describe historical development and discuss opposition to the change as well as explaining the need for conversion and the functioning of the metric system.

When we come to physics and chemistry we are entering realms of science which have increasingly enabled humanity to reorder natural existence to suit particular desires or needs. While we want our children to appreciate fully these achievements of applied science, they must also be helped to recognize its limitations if they are to gain a realistic picture of the world in which they live. In this nuclear age, it is perhaps more apparent than ever before that science can bring great good or harm, depending on how we put it to use.

The science of chemistry can be traced back to early times. Roy A. Gallant's *Exploring Chemistry* (1958), for example, begins with the discovery of fire and thereafter tells the absorbing history of efforts to understand and change matter. Ira M. Freeman elaborates upon this story for older children in *All About the Wonders of Chemistry* (1954), describing at greater length such things as molecular structure, the elements, chemical change, and the many ways in which chemistry has contributed to medicine, farming, and industry, for the benefit of modern life. Ira Freeman and A. Rae Patton, in *The Science of Chemistry* (1968), give basic facts about the ways in which atoms and molecules function chemically, and formulas are introduced only in relation to relevant theory. Isaac Asimov, in *Building Blocks of the Universe* (1961), makes clear, in his usual witty and informal style, the chemical elements that are the foundation of all matter. While the complexities of chemistry are seldom explored as a whole for younger children, spects of the subject are discussed in such books as *Millions and Millions of Crystals* (1973) and *Oil: The Buried Treasure* (1975) by Roma Gans, who makes complicated topics very clear in both books by wise selection of facts.

In the purest sense, chemistry is the study of matter only—its composition, its nature, and the changes it constantly undergoes—while physics is the study of matter and energy and the relationship between them. Even at the elementary-school level, more and more books are appearing that cross boundary lines and reveal the strong interrelationship between these sciences. For example, there are now several books which borrow knowledge from chemistry regarding atoms and molecular structure and then go on to apply this knowledge to the recent developments in physics regarding atomic energy and its many uses.

An excellent example for younger children is John Lewellen's *The Mighty Atom* (1955), which very simply, with the aid of familiar analogies and Ida Scheib's clever illustrations, moves from a discussion of the atom with its neutrons, protons, and electrons, to molecular structure and the basic elements and finally to atomic power, the construction and operation of atomic furnaces and engines, and the uses of atomic energy in both war and peace. Margaret

Illustration by Daniel Dorn, Jr. for *The Simple Facts of Simple Machines* by Elizabeth James & Carol Barkin. Reproduced by permission of Lothrop, Lee & Shepard Company.

Hyde's *Atoms Today and Tomorrow* (4th ed., 1970), written with Bruce Hyde, describes the production and uses of atomic energy, and David Woodbury's *The New World of the Atom* (1965) stresses the uses of atomic energy in medicine, in carbon-14 testing, and in nuclear power plants for space exploration.

Mechanics, an area of great interest to children, paves the way for a study of transportation, and is one of the areas in which children can observe and experiment from the first time they are fascinated by the moving parts in their toys. An interesting book for young children is *The True Book of Toys at Work* (1953), in which John Lewellen describes the mechanical principles involved in such things as whistles, electric trains, and balloons. An excellent book for the reader in the middle grades is *The Simple Facts of Simple Machines* (1975) by Elizabeth James and Carol Barkin, a book that discusses principles of physics. Hy Ruchlis' *Orbit: A Picture Story of Force and Motion* (1958) successfully explains Newton's law of universal gravitation as well as his three laws of motion in terms that can be understood by most children above the fourth grade. Action-packed photographs of such things as "flying" cars, acrobatic stunts, and daredevil sports, plus excellent diagrams by Alice Hirsch, help to illustrate these scientific laws, all of which contribute a great deal toward an adequate understanding of transportation vehicles and particularly of space flight.

Naturally the machines which people have built on the principles of mechanics would have limited use indeed without the harnessing of some type of energy other than human power to run them. One of the most comprehensive books on this subject, excitingly illustrated in color by John Teppich, is Lancelot Hogben's *Wonderful World of Energy* (1957). This book constantly reminds the child that, of all the many sources of energy, the greatest is the one which has mastered the others—humanity's own will and drive to go forward. We learn how people have gradually harnessed and put to work energy from wind, water, steam, fire, electricity, and now the atom and the sun. This last source of energy, vast and unlimited, still requires a great deal of study. Its history and future possibilities have been extensively discussed by Franklyn M. Branley in *Solar Energy* (1957). The problems of diminishing sources of energy and the social implications for the future are described in Daniel Halacy's *The Energy Trap* (1975) which discusses possible solutions through new developments and action by individuals and authoritative bodies.

Of all the forms of energy, however, the one with which the child has had the most direct experience is usually electricity. This is not an easy subject for children, and yet it plays such an important role in their everyday lives that we should help them gain at least an appreciation of its great value and some understanding of how it operates. One of the clearest and simplest explanations of this complex subject can be found in *The First Book of Electricity* (1953) by Sam and Beryl Epstein. Since this book is designed for the beginner with no previous knowledge of electricity, new concepts have been fully explained. In addition, there are pages of easy-to-follow instructions for experiments. For older children who already have a basic knowledge of this subject, the greater complexities of electricity are explained in Ira M. Freeman's *All About Electricity* (1957), which introduces a good deal of the history of the development of electrical power and contains whole chapters on various uses of electricity.

Many of the topics we have mentioned are included in *Understanding Science* (1956) by William Crouse. It is a panoramic view in which no subject is treated in depth, but it gives the reader a broad picture of the worlds of pure and applied science. For such background, books like Corinne Jacker's *Window on the Unknown: A History of the Microscope* (1966) and Aaron Klein's *The Electron Microscope* (1974) are most useful.

The Social Sciences

Under the rubric of the social sciences are those subjects that have to do with people in their association with other groups of people: history, political science, anthropology, economics, geography, law, and many others, often—as is true of other sciences—overlapping each other or other disciplines. With so broad a scope, this chapter can only mention some of the good books in areas so extensive yet so finely divided.

Since an understanding of many of these areas is partially dependent on seeing a relationship between past and present, perhaps the best background book for a young child is one that clarifies time concepts. Three such are *The True Book of Time* (1956) by Feenie Ziner and Elizabeth Thompson, which teaches children that there are other ways, in addition to clocks, for measuring time; Miriam Schlein's *It's About Time* (1955), which helps clarify the puzzling relationships implied in "long time, short time"; and Melvin Berger's *Time After Time* (1975), which discusses days, seasons, time measurement, and the inner time-sense of living things in a clear, open-ended text.

Often small children are fascinated by dinosaurs before they understand the earth's time scale, and books about dinosaurs can be used to introduce the beginnings of human prehistory. Julian May's *The First Men* (1968), for the early grades, may be followed in the middle grades by *The First People in the World* (1958) by Gerald Ames and Rose Wyler. For older readers, Eleanor Clymer's *The Case of the Missing Link* (1968), which describes the search for our ancestors and the theories held about them, gives a good account of the way scientists carefully evaluate evidence.

Two reliable books about prehistoric people in North America are William Scheele's *The Earliest Americans* (1963), which investigates the puzzle of when humans first migrated to this continent, and Anne Terry White's *Prehistoric*

America (1951), which describes modern discoveries that have led to a better understanding of prehistoric times. Scheele's *The Mound Builders* (1960) reconstructs what may have happened when a new burial site was created at Hopewell, Ohio.

Sonia Bleeker examined cultural patterns in *The Ibo of Biafra* (1969), *The Maya: Indians of Central America* (1961), and *The Eskimo: Arctic Hunters and Trappers* (1959). An anthropologist, Bleeker wrote vivid accounts based on visits, and was exemplary in her objective approach.

To understand how information about prehistory and early civilizations is acquired, children may turn to a book about archeology as a science. Anne Terry White's *All About Archeology* (1959) or Leonard Cottrell's *Digs and Diggers: A Book of World Archeology* (1964) give information about the development of the science, its methodology, and some of the great discoveries of the past. Dora Hamblin's *Pots and Robbers* (1970) tells some true stories about the dramatic aspects of archeology, many incidents involving thefts and forgeries. In *Behind the Sealed Door* (1977), Irene and Laurence Swinburne describe Howard Carter's methods in investigating the tomb of Tutankhamun.

Viewpoint

Until recently history was taught to the very young as if it were a legend. There were few dates, and those few had a symbolic, almost magical, sound—1492, 1776. . . .

History was recounted as the story of individuals. Plenty of space was left for moralizing so that emphasis could be placed on those virtues which society deemed praiseworthy. Life "before I was born" was presented to the child in such a manner that his moral judgments were inevitable, and children take to morality as ducks to water. These school books resembled the oral history we are beginning to hear so much about. Every event seemed to take place in such bright sunlight that there were no shadows. The causes of war and conflicts were clear. But I wonder whether too much shading will not leave the whole world dark. If good and bad become relative too early, the mark of Cain will be erased; and I think that one should ponder this idea seriously before considering it a fortunate turn.
—Erik Christian Haugaard, "Before I Was Born: History and the Child," *The Horn Book Magazine*, October 1979, pp. 518–519. Copyright © 1979 by Erik C. Haugaard. Reprinted by permission of the author.

There is a wealth of material on ancient civilizations, for many facets of which the art books by Shirley Glubok are good supplementary reading. Victor von Hagen's *Maya, Land of the Turkey and the Deer* (1960) is based on scholarly documents and vividly evokes the people and the period; Ruth Karen's *Kingdom of the Sun* (1975) describes the Inca empire with the same combination of vigorous style and scholarly research. Hans Baumann's *In the Land of Ur* (1969) is written with a sense of excitement, and Joan Joseph's *Black African Empires* (1974), while it lacks such excitement, gives a broad overview of the rich and powerful African empires of the past.

Many of the Columbian biographies include conjecture about the first "discoverers" of America, with honors usually divided between Columbus and the Vikings. Ellen Pugh, in *Brave His Soul* (1970), presents convincing evidence for the theory that a Welsh prince exiled himself and came to North America in 1170. A stunning book that uses source material and binds the excerpts smoothly with the compiler's comments is *The New Land* (1967) by Phillip Viereck.

There is a gratifying abundance of books in world history. One book that exemplifies a fine series about major cultures of the world, published by World, is Thomas Chubb's *The Byzantines* (1959). The learning, the technological skills, and the pride of a prosperous civilization are made excitingly real by the vivid writing. Each volume in the series has a chronological chart that correlates other world events. Alfred Duggan, who was one of the great historical writers of our time, illumined his subject in *Growing Up in 13th Century England* (1962) with authoritative knowledge and sophisticated wit; by portraying five households at different social levels, he was able to show minute details of daily living as well as social customs, recreation, and education.

Often books that are not written as history can illuminate a period. One such book is Joe Lasker's *Merry Ever After: The Story of Two Medieval Weddings* (1976); another is Grant Uden's *A Dictionary of Chivalry* (1968), which won the Greenaway Medal for Pauline Baynes's exquisite illustrations and was a runner-up for the Carnegie Medal, a book as useful as it is handsome.

Books which give children a factual account of the early history of America, its discovery and settlement, include Alice Dalgliesh's *Amer-*

From the book *Kingdom of the Sun* by Ruth Karen, published by Four Winds Press. Photograph courtesy of The American Museum of Natural History.

ica Begins (1958) and Louise Rich's *The First Book of New World Explorers* (1960). And for a record of United States history from 1492 to the present, we have *The First Book of American History* (1957) by the noted historian Henry Steele Commager.

Enid Meadowcroft's *The Land of the Free* (1961) reflects the careful study, shown in her bibliography, which preceded the writing of the book. It is a brief history, but it weaves together the threads of events that form America's history from 1492 to the end of the Second World War. Reading like fiction, *The Land of the Free* points out America's failures as well as triumphs and so places the country's character in true perspective.

The American Revolution and the Declaration of Independence are events of special significance for children, and there are many good books about this period of revolution and confederation. *The First Book of the American Revolution* (1956) by Richard B. Morris will help younger readers understand what these events meant then and what they mean today. Jean Fritz's *Who's That Stepping on Plymouth Rock?* (1975) is as lively as her brief stories of colonial leaders. George Sanderlin's *A Hoop to the Barrel* (1974) discusses the issues and compromises that shaped the writing of the Constitution. Prominent men of the newly formed government are well drawn in *The Great Declaration*

(1958) by Henry Steele Commager. The author uses excerpts from official documents, letters, and diaries in weaving together the story of the Declaration of Independence. The crucial role of women is described in Linda De Pauw's *Founding Mothers* (1975). An unusual viewpoint is given by Clorinda Clarke in *The American Revolution 1775–83: A British View* (1967), a book that has a judicious, long-range outlook and a lively style.

For the very young child interested in American pioneers, Mabel Harmer's *The True Book of Pioneers* (1957) is brief but does an admirable job of covering the subject. Ruth Franchere's *Westward by Canal* (1972) describes the impact of the building of the Erie Canal. William O. Steele's *Westward Adventure* (1962) comprises the true stories of six pioneers and is based on material in diaries and journals.

Charles Flato's *The Golden Book of the Civil War* (1961) is adapted from an American Heritage picture history. Profusely illustrated, it gives a broad and vivid picture of the war years. G. Allen Foster's *Sunday in Centerville* (1971) is as interesting for the discussion of the complex causes of the war, and the preparations for it, as it is for the detailed account of the first Battle of Bull Run.

Daniel J. Boorstin's *The Landmark History of the American People* (2 vols., 1968, 1970) deviates from the usual compilation of facts and dates to discuss the people who influenced patterns of change, and its emphasis is on movements and on regional and national patterns. The approach is stimulating, the style informal, and the analyses acutely perceptive, as might be expected from an eminent historian.

Of the many books on black history in the United States, some of the best are Robert Goldston's *The Negro Revolution* (1968), Dorothy Sterling's *Tear Down the Walls!* (1968) and *The Trouble They Seen: Black People Tell the Story of Reconstruction* (1976), and Johanna Johnston's *Together in America* (1965), all comprehensive and as objective as is consistent with a history of slavery and oppression. Marcella Thum, in *Exploring Black America* (1975), is not chronological but discusses a number of topics in relation to the holdings of specialized museums. Unfortunately, no comparable body of material exists for other minority groups in the United States. Books about Native Americans, however, are growing in number and scope. Richard Erdoes, in *The Native Americans: Navajos* (1979) discusses traditional and modern life styles. Ann

Nolan Clark's *Circle of Seasons* (1970) is a dignified and reverent description of the rites and observances of the Pueblo year. *Red Hawk's Account of Custer's Last Battle* (1970), like other books by Paul and Dorothy Goble, is historically accurate. The story is told dramatically from the viewpoint of a boy who realizes, after the battle at Little Big Horn, that while the Indian victory was definitive, the Indian's fight against white invasion was hopeless. Franklin Folsom's *Red Power on the Rio Grande* (1973) gives the Indian point of view on the Pueblo Revolution of 1680, and Dee Brown has ably adapted *Wounded Knee* (1974) from the moving and powerful *Bury My Heart at Wounded Knee*. There is a wealth of material in Sonia Bleeker's books on individual Indian cultures: *The Sea Hunters: Indians of the Northwest Coast* (1951) and *The Sioux Indians* (1962). Robert Hofsinde, adopted by the Chippewas, wrote with meticulous attention to details in books that dealt with aspects of Native American cultures. *Indian Warriors and Their Weapons* (1965) describes martial weapons and costumes of seven tribes, *Indian Sign Language* (1956) is a glossary of over 500 universal signs of North American tribes, and *Indian Music Makers* (1967) discusses musical instruments. Probably two of the best books available are *The American Indian* (1960) by Oliver La Farge, which has both historical and contemporary material, and May McNeer's *The American Indian Story* (1963), which is more an introduction than a survey, but is distinguished in illustration.

In addition to Milton Meltzer's history of American Jews discussed earlier, other books about minority groups include Harold Coy's *Chicano Roots Go Deep* (1975) and Alberta Eiseman's *The Spanish-Speaking in the United States* (1973), which are candid and sympathetic evaluations of discriminations suffered by Hispanic peoples in the years they have lived in the United States. Edwin Hoyt, in *Asians in the West* (1975), examines with equal candor the record of Caucasian discrimination.

Several books provide information about Canada. Regina Tor, in *Getting to Know Canada*, describes the people of the various provinces, their government, customs, and industries. Lithographs by Lynd Ward help to make May McNeer's *Canadian Story* an exciting account of the history of Canada from the time of the Vikings to the opening of the St. Lawrence Seaway.

Among the books that, in addition to those by Sonia and Tim Gidal, give information about other parts of the world are *The First Book of South America* (1961) by William Carter, which gives an account of the folklore, religions, and history of the continent; John Gunther's books about Africa; the Lippincott series on "Land and People of . . ."; Armstrong Sperry's *All About the Arctic and Antarctic* (1957); and Lois Hobart's *Mexican Mural* (1963). In fact, there are so many that a representative list would be impossible in one chapter on informational books.

Because of the spread of urbanization, the interest in cities is greater today than it has ever been, both from the standpoint of allure and, alas, from the standpoint of the complex problems in urban life. Few are more urgent than pollution. In *Dangerous Air* (1967), Lucy Kavaler cites the causes of air pollution throughout the world and discusses what government, industry, and individual citizens must do to eliminate this danger. John Navarra considers the same problem in *The World You Inherit: A Story of Pollution* (1970) and adds, in a cogent chapter, the legislation and litigation that are involved; in *Our Noisy World* (1969), he discusses the problem of noise pollution. James and Lynn Hahn look to solutions in *Recycling* (1973); and in *The Population Puzzle* (1973) by A. H. Drummond, the associated problem of increasing population density and decreasing resources is examined.

No author has made cities more enticing than Miroslav Sasek. Despite the crime and grime, New York is beautiful in *This Is New York* (1960), with gay, colorful pictures and a lively, humorous text describing the grandeur of a bridge span, the bustle of the garment district, the biggest traffic jams in the world. Of his other books in the series, two of the most attractive are *This Is Edinburgh* (1961) and *This Is Greece* (1966). A sharply different picture emerges in John Holland's *The Way It Is* (1969), a series of photographs, with captions, taken by black and Puerto Rican schoolboys in their home neighborhood.

Alvin Schwartz, in *Old Cities and New Towns* (1968), shows Philadelphia as it is, and as it could be, following renovation and renewal. In a book for young children, *Let's Look Under the City* (1954), Herman and Nina Schneider show the maze of service facilities but emphasize the interdependency of people in making services universally available. Carl Hiller's *Babylon to*

Brasilia (1972) describes the same problems investigated by Alvin Schwartz but adds more recent information, especially about some of the model cities established in various parts of the world.

Children are indefatigably curious about the way other people live and where they live—and why they live there if it's hot (or cold, or rainy, or mountainous . . .). They are curious about differences, open-minded rather than insular. Books can help foster their awareness of the superficiality of differences and the similarity of people everywhere. *Why We Live Where We Live* (1953) by Eva Knox Evans helps them understand the interdependence of people and the geographic limitations upon the choice of homes.

Many of the recent books for children have been written with the objective of making the story of our past and present a "real experience" rather than a superficial one. A stimulating volume to which older children can be guided is *People and Places* (1959) by Margaret Mead. The book is richly informative, springing out of Mead's expert knowledge of people and countries. She begins her first chapter, "Man's Discovery of Man," by stating that human beings are curious about each other and that even the most primitive peoples in the world today wonder about those unlike themselves, and she concludes with discussions about "Man Asks About Man," in which she talks about similarities and differences among peoples of the world. She also offers suggestions as to what steps must be taken to solve humanity's problems so that all may live in a more orderly world. All in all, Mead's book challenges its readers to a deeper understanding not only of themselves but also of other people and places.

Religion and the Arts

Books of religious instruction and prayers are used by devout families in the home, and biographies of religious leaders or stories that present religious diversity can help children understand and respect the beliefs or the nonbelief of others. Books on comparative religion, however, belong in any collection to which children turn for information.

Ruth Smith's *The Tree of Life* (1942) is an anthology consisting of selections from the

*Viewpoint*_____

If his knowledge is to grow through the books a child reads because of his desire to know, it must be the kind of knowledge that grows with his growth. Even a simple, elementary presentation of a subject that has interest for quite young children can awaken curiosity and suggest extensions of knowledge through books beyond the one a child is immediately reading. His interest in the subject may thus become a reading interest developed through childhood into maturity. The satisfactions of such continuous reading interests in the field of knowledge have permanent and rewarding values for children. Their reading of these books is complementary to their pleasure in creative literature, and both are necessary to the mental and imaginative growth of children.—Lillian H. Smith, *The Unreluctant Years,* American Library Association, Chicago, 1953, pp. 180–181.

world's great religions, and is an excellent companion volume to Katharine Savage's *The Story of World Religions,* discussed earlier in this chapter, or the Haskins book, also previously mentioned. In Betsy Smith's *Breakthrough: Women in Religion* (1978) the text examines the experiences and philosophies of five contemporary women who are religious leaders. Edward Rice's *The Five Great Religions* (1973) gives more background than other books that examine major faiths, since Rice believes that the mystical aspects of each are rooted in its beginnings.

The series of books about religious denominations by Kathleen Elgin, of which *The Unitarians* (1971) is an example, describes the history and the beliefs of the denomination, lists some of its famous members of past and present, and gives at length a biography of a leader or prominent member. In *The Vatican* (1970), the managing editor of *Commonweal,* John Deedy, describes the Vatican community's members and its art and history. Howard Greenfeld, in *Passover* (1978) and *Rosh Hashanah* and *Yom Kippur* (1979) describes the origins and the celebration of major Jewish holidays. Elizabeth Seeger describes Buddhism, Confucianism, Hinduism, Shinto, and Taoism in *Eastern Religions* (1973).

Books that encourage the child's interest in music range from such narrow treatments as Larry Kettelkamp's *Flutes, Whistles and Reeds* (1962), which introduces woodwinds and explains how they produce sounds, to the comprehensive treatment in *The Wonderful World of Music* (1958) by Benjamin Britten and Imogen Holst, a history of music, musicians, and instruments that is mature in concept. Much of the book can be appreciated by the reader with no musical background, but the discussions of theory and harmony may present difficulties for the general reader. David Ewen is one of the most prolific and authoritative authors of books about music, writing on musical forms: *Opera* (1971), *Orchestral Music* (1973), *Vocal Music* (1975), and others. Roy Hemming, in *Discovering Music* (1974), gives suggestions for the collector of tapes and records.

There is comparatively little material available about the music of other countries. Betty Warner Deitz and Michael Babatunde Olatunji have written an outstanding book about the way music is used in African cultures south of the Sahara in *Musical Instruments of Africa* (1965); and in *Folk Songs of China, Japan, and Korea* (1964) Dietz collaborated with Thomas Choonbai Park. These books have been compiled with scholarly care, and can help children understand other cultures through their music.

Langston Hughes wrote several books about music: *The First Book of Rhythms* (1954), *Famous Negro Music Makers* (1955), and *The First Book of Jazz* (1955). The latter presents a concise history of the development of jazz in the United States and of its spread to other countries. Hughes discusses the diverse elements that contributed to the complex rhythms of jazz: African, French, and Spanish elements in New Orleans; worksongs and blues; spirituals, ragtime, and minstrel music. James Collier defines jazz and analyzes its forms in *Inside Jazz* (1973). Although not written as an informational book, Nat Hentoff's *Jazz Country* (1965) conveys the essence of the jazz world (see page 356). Another book that gives a history of a popular type of music is Arnold Shaw's *The Rock Revolution* (1969), which includes discussions of performers and comments of critics. In *Gold Guitars* (1971), Irwin Stambler and Grelun Landon tell the story of country-and-western music.

Books about opera, libretti of individual operas, many collections of songs, and books that describe the composition and arrangement of orchestras are listed in the bibliography, as are some of the many song books published for children. There is also a considerable amount of information about music and musicians in the biographies cited in Chapter 13.

A book that bridges the worlds of music and dance is *American Indians Sing* (1967) by Charles Hofmann, in which the information about music, dances, and song-poems includes melodic and dance notation. The relationship of dance to religious observance is emphasized in Lee Warren's *The Dance of Africa* (1972), which discusses also the impact of cultural changes on traditional forms. Perhaps the most comprehensive book on the dance is Arnold Haskell's *The Wonderful World of Dance* (1969). In an impressively authoritative volume, Haskell describes the evolution of the dance and dance forms, with biographical material about famous dancers and choreographers, and with many diagrams of dance notation. There is an especially good section on ritual dances of the Orient; and, throughout the book, dance forms are related to the cultural context in which they evolved. Narrower in scope, *Ballet: A Pictorial History* (1970) by Walter Terry is a good introduction for the reader who is not a balletomane, but it has enough material about outstanding dancers of each historical period to appeal to the lover of ballet. Noel Streatfeild's *A Young Person's Guide to Ballet* (1975) gives a wealth of interesting detail about techniques and ballet history.

Olga Maynard's *American Modern Dancers; The Pioneers* (1965) is an excellent survey of the evolution of modern dance through discussions of the work of great dancers, giving authoritative analyses of techniques, theories, trends, influences, and comparative schools. Maynard gives, in *The Ballet Companion* (1957), a detailed guide to four ballets, and a glossary of ballet terms and techniques. Stunning photographs illustrate Jill Krementz's *A Very Young Dancer* (1976), a photographic essay about a real child who is a ballet student.

Undoubtedly because dancing is a performing art there is comparatively little written about it. When we turn to books about art, however, there is a positive cornucopia of fine books. One of the best general surveys is Janet Moore's *The Many Ways of Seeing* (1968), which discusses the relationship between art and nature, and the relationship between the artist and the world. It analyzes the ways an artist perceives in terms of light, color, composition, and line; it also describes media, materials, and techniques, and suggests ways in which the reader can try some of the ideas discussed and learn to see the elements of an art form. A similar book, with examples ranging from ancient

From *A Very Young Dancer*, by Jill Krementz. Copyright © 1976 by Jill Krementz. Reprinted by permission of Alfred A. Knopf, Inc. Published by A. & C. Black, Ltd. in the British Commonwealth (except Canada), Republic of South Africa and the Irish Republic.

treasures to contemporary works, is *Looking at Sculpture* (1968) by Roberta Paine.

Marion Downer's *The Story of Design* (1964) uses a variety of art objects, shown in photographs, to illustrate the appreciation of design the world over, from primitive times to today. M. J. Gladstone's *A Carrot for a Nose* (1974) and Elinor Horwitz's *Contemporary American Folk Artists* (1975) discuss folk art. In *Looking at Art* (1966) Alice Elizabeth Chase, an art historian, describes the ways in which artists have interpreted their worlds, and the author's explicit and clearly presented views on the nature of art make the book an excellent choice for the reader who is on unfamiliar terrain. Howard Greenfeld writes with authority and zeal in *The Impressionist Revolution* (1972) and *They Came to Paris* (1975).

The Pantheon Story of Art for Young People (1964; 1975) by Ariane Ruskin Batterberry is competently written but slights contemporary work; it has, however, an unusually large number of full-page, full-color illustrations. Some of the series are by Ariane Ruskin under that name, some by Michael Batterberry, some written jointly by the two, as is *Primitive Art* (1973). Ruskin's *Art of the High Renaissance* (1970) emphasizes painters and painting but the comprehensive text covers all art forms. All of the books in this series are profusely and handsomely illustrated.

There are few art books written for adults that cannot be enjoyed by children, if the books are illustrated. The Time-Life Library of Art has magnificently illustrated volumes, each devoted to a single artist. The biographies by Elizabeth Ripley could almost as well be in this chapter as in Chapter 13. Shirley Glubok's books are discussed earlier in this chapter. Books on color for the preschool and primary-age child can encourage aesthetic appreciation as well as teach colors, and some of the first concept books, like Tana Hoban's *Shapes and Things*, can stimulate an awareness of form as well as encourage observation. In other words, information about art can come from many sources other than books about art.

Friedrich von Schlegel called architecture "frozen music," and in Mary Louise King's *A History of Western Architecture* (1967), the illustrations show the patterned precision of Greek temples and the soaring lift of Gothic cathedrals that make this phrase so apt. King emphasizes the new developments of each period, and discusses the factors that influence style. A simpler book that gives architectural history more succinctly is *Understanding Architecture* (1971) by George Sullivan, which explains styles and construction techniques from the rudimentary post-and-lintel buildings to today's skyscrapers and the plans for ecologically oriented homes of tomorrow.

Anne Rockwell's *Glass, Stones and Crown: The Abbe Suger and the Building of St. Denis* (1968) is as interesting for its historical background as it is for the story of Suger, the boyhood friend of Louis Capet, whose life as abbot was devoted to rebuilding St. Denis and incorporating those features that became popular throughout Europe: stained glass windows, flying buttresses and piers, and ribbed vaulting.

The construction of a modern building is described in Ely Jacques Kahn's *A Building Goes*

Up (1969), in which the erection of an office building is detailed from planning to completion. Although David Macaulay's books are discussed in Chapter 6, they also belong here as outstanding books on architecture, save for *Underground* (1976), which has particular application for the social studies.

Activities and Experiments

One of the most popular kinds of activity books is the puzzle book. Martin Gardner's *Perplexing Puzzles and Tantalizing Teasers* (1969) contains riddles, scrambled words, mazes, and puzzles that require logic for solution. It has enough difficult puzzles to tempt the quick child but not so many as to discourage the one who is slow. More difficult is *Math Managerie* (1970) by Robert Kadesch, in which the material is grouped under such headings as probability, binary numerals, and soap-film mathematics. Another kind of brain-teaser is Martin Gardner's *Codes, Ciphers, and Secret Writing* (1972), which describes codes used in history, explains how to concoct or decipher messages, and explains the difference between codes and ciphers. *Egyptian Hieroglyphs for Everyone* (1968) by Joseph and Lenore Scott gives an explanation of how the language developed and makes it easier for the reader to understand hieroglyphic writing.

At the other end of the spectrum are the books that give instruction for physical activities, usually sports. One such is S. H. Freeman's *Basic Baseball Strategy* (1965), which is packed with so much information that it can be used by players older than the middle-grades audience to whom it is addressed, or by coaches for the clear explanations of such fine arts as base stealing, the squeeze play, and when to use the hit-and-run. *Better Softball for Boys and Girls* (1975) by George Sullivan gives advice on play and explains the game clearly. *Bicycling* (1972) by Charles Coombs tells the reader how to choose, use, and take care of a bicycle, and *Roller Skating* (1979) by Ross Olney and Chan Bush, gives the same sort of advice. In Jim Moore's *Football Techniques Illustrated* (1962), there are discussions of offensive and defensive play, advice on running, kicking, passing, and tackling, and the rules of play. Other how-to-do-it sports books can easily be found listed under the names of the sports in such guides as *Children's Catalog*.

A useful group of activity books are those in the fields of arts and crafts: Jan Adkins, in *Toolchest* (1973), gives succinct advice to the amateur carpenter; in *Collage* (1968), Mickey Klar Marks gives instructions for seven different kinds of collage; *The Complete Crayon Book* (1969) by Chester Jay Alkema suggests a variety of projects, from simple to complex, and gives an excellent discussion of media and techniques. *Mask-Making with Pantomime and Stories from American History* (1975) by Laura Ross gives good background history as well as clear instructions. Among the many books on puppetry, two of the best are Eleanor Boylan's *How to Be a Puppeteer* (1970), which gives directions for making and costuming puppets, manipulating them, making sets and scenery, etc., and David Currell's *The Complete Book of Puppetry* (1975), which is comprehensive enough to have reference use. An unusual book in this field is *The Rooster's Horns: A Chinese Puppet Play to Make and Perform* (1978) by Ed Young and Hilary Beckett.

There are general craft books like Susan Purdy's *Festivals for You to Celebrate* (1969), in which the projects are grouped by seasons and suggestions are given for group activities, or Carolyn Meyer's *Christmas Crafts* (1974), which

Illustration by the author, from *City* by David Macaulay. Published by Houghton Mifflin Company. Copyright © 1974 by David Macaulay. Reproduced by permission of the publisher. Published in the United Kingdom by William Collins Sons & Co. Ltd.

From the book *Toolchest: a Primer of Woodcraft* by Jan Adkins. Published by Walker & Company, Inc. New York, N.Y. © 1973 by Jan Adkins. Reprinted by permission.

proposes a project a day through December. Camille Sokol's *The Lucky Sew-It-Yourself Book* (1966) is a hand-sewing book with very simple projects for the seven- to nine-year-old. An example of the specialized book is Jan Beaney's *The Young Embroiderer* (1967), with imaginative suggestions that can stimulate original work; another is Meyer's *Rock Tumbling* (1975). Older children can use almost any cookbook, but *Kids Cooking* (1970) by Aileen Paul and Arthur Hawkins makes cooking easy by listing ingredients and implements on one page, and giving the instructions on the facing page. *The Natural Cook's First Book* (1973) by Carole Getzoff stresses wholesome recipes.

Filmmaking has become tremendously popular, and both Joan Harvath's *Filmmaking for Beginners* (1974) and Robert Ferguson's *How to Make Movies* (1969) give detailed and practical advice on every aspect of the art. Yvonne Andersen gives both the techniques of preparation and the intricacies of filming in *Make Your Own Animated Movies* (1970).

One of the most sensible books on pets is Dorothy Broderick's *Training a Companion Dog* (1965), which is explicit and detailed and gives advice on equipment. Harriet Howard's *If You Had a Pony* (1965) uses photographs to teach the care and training of a pony and to give some information on riding. In *Look What I Found!* (1971), Marshal Case explains how to capture small wild creatures, with suggestions for duplicating the animal's natural habitat and an emphasis on showing kindness and respect for all life forms, and Roger Caras, in *A Zoo in Your Room* (1975) gives sensible advice on pet care. William Weber's *Wild Animal Babies* (1975)

does the same for the care of abandoned or injured small creatures.

In addition to the books that describe specific activities and crafts, there is the comprehensive "doing" book, which presents information about a variety of scientific topics through suggested experiments and activities. And there are books in very specialized areas, like Remy Charlip's *Handtalk: An ABC of Finger Spelling and Sign Language* (1974).

The experiment book has a definite value in that it guides the child toward direct participation in the discovery of knowledge, and, since so many experiences must be gained vicariously, first-hand discovery should be encouraged whenever possible. But experiment books also have a more subtle value. We realize today that education must do more than impart knowledge—it must also teach the child how to use that knowledge in the solution of problems. Glenn Blough once stated:

If pupils are to grow in ability to solve problems they must grow in ability to think of appropriate things to do to discover solutions.[3]

Teaching children how to set up sound experiments and how to interpret the results of these experiments is one way of training them to "think of appropriate things to do."

Good experiment books, for obvious reasons, will suggest only those activities which are safe and those which can be performed with readily available and inexpensive materials; and there are such books today for every age level. Whatever the interest, a child who likes to experiment can benefit from Thomas Moorman's *How to Make Your Science Project Scientific* (1974), which exemplifies the scientific attitudes and methods it describes.

Prove It! (1963) by Rose Wyler and Gerald Ames is for the beginning reader and presents simple experiments performed with ordinary objects. Harlow Rockwell's *I Did It* (1974) has varied, simple experiments and projects for beginning readers to try. Rose Wyler's *What Happens If . . .?* (1974) has safe, easy experiments designed by a teacher of science and science education. Franklyn Branley's *Timmy and the Tin-Can Telephone* is written as a story in which two children learn about the transmission of sound by making a "telephone" out of tin cans, string, and buttons. Harry Milgrom's *Adventures with a Paper Cup* (1968) has an assortment of

3. Glenn O. Blough, "Quality Is What Counts!" *Instructor*, September 1958, p. 6.

From the book *The Chemistry of a Lemon* by A. Harris Stone, illustrated by Peter P. Plasencia. © 1966 by A. Harris Stone, Published by Prentice-Hall, Inc., Englewood Cliffs, New Jersey. Reprinted by permission. (Original in color)

easy experiments in which a cone-shaped cup is used to demonstrate such phenomena as air resistance and sound amplification. This and similar books by Milgrom, or Nancy Larrick's *See for Yourself* (1952), which has simple experiments with air, water, and heat, can stir or encourage an interest in scientific exploration and discovery in young children. A. Harris Stone's *The Chemistry of a Lemon* (1966) was one of the first, and is still one of the best, open-ended experiment books in simple chemistry, a fine example of the scientific method. For the child with a short attention span, Herman Schneider's *Science Fun for You in a Minute or Two* (1975) offers experiments that are brief and require little equipment.

One of the most varied books of experiments, containing material in many of the sciences, is *700 Science Experiments for Everyone*, compiled by UNESCO in 1956. William Moore's *Your Science Fair Project* (1964) has projects grouped by levels from grades three to eight, and is particularly useful for the average student who is required to participate. Alfred Morgan's *Boys' Book of Science and Construction* (1959) has more advanced experiments, and also includes instructions for making such

things as steam turbines, pinhole cameras, and weather vanes.

Elizabeth Cooper's *Science in Your Own Back Yard* (1958) suggests way of observing, collecting, and experimenting in the field of nature study, in a book that can stimulate the individual reader or be used by a group. There is an emphasis on conservation in Ted Pettit's *A Guide to Nature Projects* (1966). Each section of the book deals with a single aspect of the subject and gives background information before discussing experiments.

For the child who has a specific interest, there are such books as Harry Sootin's *Experiments with Magnetism* (1968) or his mineralogy book, *The Young Experimenter's Workbook* (1965), written in collaboration with Laura Sootin. Paul Czaja's *Writing with Light* (1973) shows how one can make pictures without a camera. Both books require only materials that are available in the home or are inexpensive, and the experiments are practical and clearly explained. Rocco Feravolo's *Easy Physics Projects: Air, Water and Heat* (1966) and A. Harris Stone's books are for children of the same age, but they are quite different in approach. Rather than using the open-ended process approach of the Stone experiment books, Feravolo answers the questions raised; little is left to the student's imagination, but the concepts are lucidly presented and the book can be useful to children hesitant about taking initiative.

Reference Books

Although encyclopedias and dictionaries, fact books and almanacs, and indexes and bibliographies are the kinds of books usually meant when reference books are referred to, it should be remembered that many other kinds of books have reference use.

Children's rooms in public libraries often have books that reflect the particular interests of their community, such as foreign language source books, reference materials that give information about local industries, or books about indigenous flora and fauna. School library collections may stress books that fit into curricular units. Both will gather as much as they can about local history, and both will include in their collections some books intended for adult reference use.

There are so many dictionaries and encyclopedias that are valuable, that guides to them are reference books in themselves. Most professional journals include reviews of reference books; *Booklist* and *Wilson Library Bulletin* have special sections devoted to them. Carolyn Sue Peterson's *Reference Books for Elementary and Junior High School Libraries* is a useful annotated bibliography that suggests in its introduction methods of evaluation, most of which require examination of the volumes being considered. Another good source is *General Encyclopedias in Print.* Almost every dictionary and encyclopedia has a coterie of devoted users who feel that their favorite is the best. Each differs, and libraries that can afford to buy all the reference books which meet critical standards usually do so.

In assembling a home reference library, parents would do well to examine carefully the different reference books they are considering. If possible, a home collection for children should include one of the major children's encyclopedias, a reliable dictionary appropriate for the ages of the children in the family, and an atlas. Parents of children with limited vision may want an atlas printed in large type, which is also useful for younger children because the maps are easy to read. In making decisions, parents will want to examine the way material is arranged and to make sure that the type is uncrowded and is large enough to read without strain; they will look for the quality and placement of illustrations and the adequacy of captions or labels, and they will consider aids to pronunciation, glossaries, indexes, and other auxiliary material provided on prefatory or appended pages, including an explanation of symbols used, or other features of the book.

Most adults feel that children should have their own dictionaries, but they are not so sure that children need their own encyclopedias. In homes where books must be carefully budgeted, many families feel that an adult encyclopedia is the better investment. When children are young, parents can help them use the books, and the older children can use them themselves. The best adult encyclopedias last for a lifetime; they may become dated in some respects, but the bulk of the material will carry a child through high school, college, and adult life. If a choice must be made, then decidedly the adult set should be purchased because of its greater richness and long-range value. But when a family can afford both, the children should have their own set. And let's face it—many families cannot afford *any* set. For them, using library copies is an answer.

Many informational series books have reference use, from such erudite books as the Time-Life Library of Art and the American Heritage historical series, to Leonard Everett Fisher's books on colonial crafts. But each book in a series must be evaluated on its own merits. As is true in library collections, a home reference collection will include such books when they are appropriate for the family's particular interests. And if a member of the family is a bird-watcher or a stamp collector, Roger Tory Peterson's *Field Guide to the Birds* or *Scott's Standard Postage Stamp Catalogue* may seem an absolute necessity.

Some families may feel that reference books that reflect their interests are a better investment than an encyclopedia, since it is possible to keep such a subject collection current with less financial outlay than the purchase of an encyclopedia would require. Library-owned encyclopedias are apt to be more current than home sets and are therefore more useful for school assignments.

The library reference collection should include the Bible and other sacred writings and books on comparative religion, whether they are discussions of denominations like Kathleen Elgin's separate treatments or a compendium like Katharine Savage's *The Story of World Religions.* Also useful for information about religion are biographies of religious leaders and such books as Susan Purdy's *Jewish Holidays: Facts, Activities and Crafts.*

Despite the abundance and variety of informational books, they are often given short shrift in discussion of literary quality. To be sure, some are distinguished more for their usefulness than for their style, but many of these books, such as *Chipmunks on the Doorstep* by Edwin Tunis, are as graceful in their prose as are some of the works of fiction that have won awards. And remember that the first Newbery Medal was given to Hendrik Willem Van Loon for *The Story of Mankind,* a history of humanity's origin and evolution that is witty and authoritative, the sort of informational book that amuses, informs, and stimulates readers to further inquiry. What more could one ask?

Adult References[4]

DEASON, HILARY J., comp. *The AAAS Science Booklist.*

FISHER, MARGERY. *Matters of Fact: Aspects of Non-Fiction for Children.*

HUUS, HELEN. *Children's Books to Enrich the Social Studies for the Elementary Grades.*

IRWIN, LEONARD B., comp. *A Guide to Historical Reading: Non-Fiction.*

LOGASA, HANNAH. *Science for Youth.*

PETERSON, CAROLYN SUE. *Reference Books for Elementary and Junior High School Libraries.*

SUTHERLAND, ZENA. *History in Children's Books: An Annotated Bibliography for Schools and Libraries.*

TITOWSKY, BERNARD. *American History.*

VANCE, LUCILLE, and ESTHER TRACEY. *Illustration Index.*

In the following bibliography these symbols have been used to identify books about a religious or a particular ethnic group:

§ Black

★ Chicano or Puerto Rican

☆ Native American

● Religious minority

The Biological Sciences

ADLER, IRVING and RUTH. *Evolution*, ill. by Ruth Adler. Day, 1965. 8–10

ALIKI. *The Long-Lost Coelacanth and Other Living Fossils*, ill. by author. T. Crowell, 1973. A clear explanation of how fossil finds enable scientists to recognize living fossils. 7–9

AMON, ALINE. *Reading, Writing, Chattering Chimps*, ill. by author. Atheneum, 1975. A report on projects in which chimpanzees learn to communicate. 10–12

ANDREWS, ROY CHAPMAN. *All About Dinosaurs*, ill. by Thomas W. Voter. Random, 1953. 9–12

———. *All About Whales*, ill. Random, 1954. 9–11

———. *In the Days of the Dinosaurs*, ill. by Jean Zallinger. Random, 1959. 8–11

ASIMOV, ISAAC. *ABC's of Ecology*. Walker, 1972. 8–11

BENDICK, JEANNE. *How Heredity Works: Why Living Things Are As They Are.* Parents' Magazine, 1975. A good introduction to genetics. 7–9

———. *The Mystery of the Loch Ness Monster*. McGraw, 1976. 11–13

———. *A Place to Live*, ill. by author. Parents Magazine, 1970. 5–8

———. *What Made You You?* ill. by author. McGraw, 1971. 4–7

BLOCH, MARIE H. *Dinosaurs*, ill. by George F. Mason. Coward, 1955. 8–10

BLOUGH, GLENN O. *After the Sun Goes Down*, ill. by Jeanne Bendick. McGraw, 1956. 7–9

———. *Discovering Dinosaurs*, ill. by Gustav Schrotter. Whittlesey, 1960. 8–9

———. *Soon After September: The Story of Living Things in Winter*, ill. by Jeanne Bendick. McGraw, 1959. 7–9

———. *Who Lives in This House? A Story of Animal Families*, ill. by Jeanne Bendick. McGraw, 1957. 7–9

BRADY, IRENE. *Wild Mouse*. Scribner's, 1976. The author traces, in diary form, the development of three mice from blind, helpless newborn nurslings to frisky sixteen-day-olds. 7–9

BRENNER, BARBARA. *Baltimore Orioles*, ill. by J. Winslow Higginbotham. Harper, 1974. 6–7

CLEMONS, ELIZABETH. *Shells Are Where You Find Them*, ill. by Joe Gault. Knopf, 1960. 8–10

COBER, ALAN. *Cober's Choice*, ill. by author. Dutton, 1979. Twenty-three animal drawings accompanied by brief, patternless captions, some giving facts about the species, others a personal comment or reaction. 8 up

COLE, JOANNA. *A Frog's Body*, ill. by Jerome Wexler. Morrow, 1980. Fine color photographs illustrate a clear and comprehensive text. 7–9

COLLINS, HENRY HILL, JR. *The Bird Watcher's Guide*, ill. with photos; line drawings and cover by Richard Harker. Golden Pr., 1961. 10–13

COSGROVE, MARGARET. *Bone for Bone*, ill. by author. Dodd, 1968. 11–15

———. *Eggs—And What Happens Inside Them*, ill. by author. Dodd, 1966. 8–12

CURTIS, ROBERT. *Medical Talk for Beginners*, ill. by William Jaber. Messner, 1976. A dictionary of medical terms with many cross-references, phonetic spellings where the author deems necessary, and adequately labeled illustrations. 9–11

DARLING, LOUIS. *Greenhead*. Morrow, 1954. 10–14

———. *The Gull's Way*, photos and ill. by author. Morrow, 1965. 11–15

DOWDEN, ANNE. *The Blossom on the Bough: A Book of Trees*, ill. by author. T. Crowell, 1975. 11 up

———. *State Flowers*, ill. by author. T. Crowell, 1978. Precise and beautiful paintings are accompanied by a text citing botanical information, the year each flower was adopted and the statutes that each state enacted. 11 up

———. *This Noble Harvest: A Chronicle of Herbs*, ill. by author. Collins, 1980. 10 up

DUNBAR, ROBERT. *Mental Retardation*, ill. with photos. Watts, 1978. This is valuable both as a vehicle for general information and as a platform for the author's purpose of encouraging the acceptance of the mentally handicapped. 9–12

EARLE, OLIVE L. *Paws, Hoofs, and Flippers*, ill. by author. Morrow, 1954. Mammals are classified by their feet. 10–14

———. *Praying Mantis*, ill. by author. Morrow, 1969.

———. *The Rose Family*, ill. by author. Morrow, 1970. 8–10

———. *State Trees*, rev. ed., ill. by author. 1973. 1973. 9–12

EARLE, OLIVE LYDIA, and MICHAEL KANTOR. *Nuts*, ill. by Olive L. Earle. Morrow, 1975. Botanical information that has minor reference use. 8–10

FEGELY, THOMAS D. *Wonders of Wild Ducks*. Dodd, 1975. Good scope in a text that stresses conservation. 10–14

FENNER, CAROL. *Gorilla Gorilla*, ill. by Symeon Shimin. Random, 1973. A narrative framework for a life-cycle book. 8–10

FLANAGAN, GERALDINE LUX. *Window into an Egg: Seeing Life Begin*, ill. with photos. Scott/Addison, 1969. 9–11

FLANAGAN, GERALDINE LUX, and SEAN MORRIS. *Window into a Nest*. Houghton, 1976. A nesting box with open back built against a window enabled the authors to record minute details of the events of chickadee family life. 10 up

FRESCHET, BERNIECE. *The Flight of the Snow Goose*, ill. by Jo Polseno. Crown, 1970. 7–9

———. *The Web in the Grass*, ill. by Roger Duvoisin. Scrib-

---

4. Complete bibliographic data are provided in Appendix B.

ner's, 1972. Handsome illustrations show the spider's world.   4–7

——. *Year on Muskrat Marsh*, ill. by Peter Parnall. Scribner's, 1974.   8–10

GANS, ROMA. *When Birds Change Their Feathers*, ill. by Felicia Bond. Crowell, 1980. Gans moves from the general to the specific, describing how different birds molt, in a lucidly written book.   7–8

GEORGE, JEAN. *All Upon a Sidewalk*, ill. by Don Bolognese. Dutton, 1974.   7–8

——. *All Upon a Stone*, ill. by Don Bolognese. T. Crowell, 1971.   7–8

——. *The Hole in the Tree*, ill. by author. Dutton, 1957.   8–10

——. *The Moon of the Bears*, ill. by Mac Shepard. T. Crowell, 1967. One of a series.   9–11

——. *Spring Comes to the Ocean*, ill. by John Wilson. T. Crowell, 1965.

GORDON, SOL. *Girls Are Girls and Boys Are Boys: So What's the Difference?* ill. by Frank C. Smith. Day, 1974.   8–9

GOUDEY, ALICE E. *Graywings*, ill. by Marie Nonnast. Scribner's, 1964. The life cycle of a herring gull.   6–10

——. *Here Come the Dolphins*, ill. by Garry MacKenzie. Scribner's, 1961.   7–9

——. *Here Come the Lions!* ill. by Garry MacKenzie. Scribner's, 1956.   7–9

——. *Houses from the Sea*, ill. by Adrienne Adams. Scribner's, 1959.   5–7

GROSS, RUTH BELOV. *Snakes*. Four Winds, 1975. An especially competent treatment of habits and habitat; coverage of reproduction is scanty.   8–10

GRUENBERG, SIDONIE MATSNER. *The Wonderful Story of How You Were Born*, rev. ed., ill. by Symeon Shimin. Doubleday, 1970.   8–10

GUILCHER, J. M., and R. H. NOAILLES. *A Fern Is Born*. Sterling, 1971. Clearly detailed photographs and a concise style make this and other books in the series admirable examples of nature writing.   9–12

——. *A Tree Grows Up*, Sterling, 1972. Same format as *A Fern Is Born*.   10–12

HALMI, ROBERT. *Zoos of the World*. Four Winds, 1975. Focuses on the increasing attention paid to the comfort and security of zoo animals.   10–12

HELLMAN, HAL. *Biology in the World of the Future*, ill. Evans, 1971. A knowledgeable and witty foray into the frontiers of biological research, well organized and provocative.   12 up

HIRSCH, S. CARL. *The Living Community: A Venture into Ecology*, ill. by William Steinel. Viking, 1966.   12–14

HOBAN, TANA. *Big Ones, Little Ones*, photos by author. Greenwillow, 1976.   2–5

HOLLING, HOLLING C. *Pagoo*, ill. by L. W. Holling. Houghton, 1957.   8–10

HOPF, ALICE L. *Biography of an Armadillo*, ill. by Jean Zallinger. Putnam, 1976. Within a narrative framework (but without anthropomorphism or undue fictionalization) Hopf describes most of the life cycle of an armadillo.   7–9

——. *Biography of an Ostrich*, ill. by Ben F. Stahl. Putnam, 1975. No anthropomorphism despite a fictional framework.   7–9

HUTCHINS, ROSS E. *The Ant Realm*, ill. with photos by author. Dodd, 1967. The author describes, with his usual zest, the fascinating behavior of various species of ants, both group and individual behavior.   10–14

——. *The Bug Clan*, photos by author. Dodd, 1973. A comprehensive and well-organized survey.   10 up

——. *The Travels of Monarch X*, ill. by Jerome P. Connolly. Rand, 1966. The description of a southward migration of a tagged Monarch butterfly from Toronto to Mexico.   8–10

JOHNSON, ERIC W. *Love and Sex in Plain Language*. rev. ed., ill. by Russ Hoover. Lippincott, 1974.   12–17

JONES, HETTIE. *How to Eat Your ABC's: A Book About Vitamins*, ill. by Judy Glasser. Four Winds, 1976. Each of the major vitamins is discussed separately, followed by a discussion of vitamins in natural foods including charts showing recommended servings for a balanced diet. 9–12

KAMIEN, JANET. *What If You Couldn't? A Book About Special Needs*, ill. by Signe Hanson. Scribner's, 1979. Particular kinds of handicaps are dealt with in separate chapters and some of the causes explained.   10–12

KAVALER, LUCY. *Life Battles Cold*, ill. by Leslie Morrill. Day, 1973. A discussion of the many ways living things adapt to extreme cold.   11–15

——. *The Wonders of Algae*, ill. with photos and with drawings by Barbara Amlick and Richard Ott. Day, 1961.   11–14

——. *The Wonders of Fungi*, ill. with photos and with drawings by Richard Ott. Day, 1974.   11–14

KEVLES, BETTY ANN. *Thinking Gorillas: Testing and Teaching the Greatest Ape*, ill. with photographs. Dutton, 1980. A description of the training and testing of gorillas.   11–14

LAUBER, PATRICIA. *Everglades Country*, photos by Patricia Caulfield. Viking, 1973.   11–14

——. *What's Hatching Out of That Egg?* ill. with photos. Crown, 1979.   7–9

——. *Your Body and How It Works*, ill. by Stephen Rogers Peck, photos by Florence Burns. Random, 1962.   8–10

LAVINE, SIGMUND A. *Wonders of the Eagle World*. Dodd, 1974. Describes physical characteristics, behavior, and the eagle in history and mythology.   9–11

LEEN, NINA. *The Bat*. Holt, 1976. The text (consisting of captions for photographs) corroborates the author's plea that the bat be thought of as useful rather than harmful. 9–12

LERNER, CAROL. *Flowers of a Woodland Spring*, ill. by author. Morrow, 1979. The text, describing the ephemeral flowering plants of early springtime, is coupled with exquisite paintings and drawings.   8–10

LEVINE, EDNA S. *Lisa and Her Soundless World*, ill. by Gloria Kamen. Behavioral Publications, 1974. A discussion of the abilities and limitations of a deaf child.   8–10

LUBELL, WINIFRED and CECIL. *Green Is for Growing*. ill. by Winifred Lubell. Rand, 1964.   8–10

MacCLINTOCK, DORCAS. *A Natural History of Zebras*, ill. by Ugo Mochi. Scribner's, 1976. Every aspect of the zebra species is examined with quiet authority and a relaxed but brisk writing style.   12 up

McCLUNG, ROBERT M. *Gypsy Moth*, ill. by author. Morrow, 1974.   10–14

——. *Honker*, ill. by Bob Hines. Morrow. 1965.   8–10

——. *How Animals Hide*. National Geographic, 1973. 7–10

——. *Hunted Mammals of the Sea*, ill. by William Downey. Morrow, 1978.   10–13

——. *Mice, Moose, and Men: How Their Populations Rise and Fall*. Morrow, 1973. A description of the causes and problems of overpopulation.   9–12

——. *Sea Star*, ill. by author. Morrow, 1975.   7–9

——. *Shag, Last of the Plains Buffalo*, ill. by Louis Darling. Morrow, 1960.   8–10

——. *Spike: The Story of a Whitetail Deer*, ill. by author. Morrow, 1952.   8–9

————. *Thor: Last of the Sperm Whales*, ill. by Bob Hines. Morrow, 1971. 8–10

MARI, IELA and ENZO, ills., *The Apple and the Moth and The Chicken and the Egg*. Pantheon, 1970. First published in Italy, two charming books for the youngest biologists that tell their stories clearly without text. 3–5

MICHEL, ANNA. *The Story of Nim: The Chimp Who Learned Language*, ill. with photographs. Knopf, 1980. An account of an experiment in which a baby chimpanzee learned to communicate in sign language. 9–11

NAPIER, JOHN. *The Origins of Man*, ill. by Maurice Wilson. McGraw, 1969. A fine introductory interpretation of evolution. The author (Director of the Primate Biology Program of the Smithsonian) adds to his professional competence a sense of drama and a simplicity of approach. 9–11

NEWTON, JAMES. *The March of the Lemmings*, ill. by Charles Robinson. T. Crowell, 1976. In direct, simple prose, Newton describes the changes in behavior of lemmings in a community that has become overpopulated leading to the cyclic, suicidal march to the sea. 7–8

NILSSON, LENNART. *How Was I Born? A Photographic Story of Reproduction and Birth for Children*. Delacorte/Seymour Lawrence, 1975. 8–11

NOURSE, ALAN E. *The Body*, by Alan E. Nourse and the Editors of *Life*. Time-Life, 1964. Illustrated with superb photographs. 13 up

OXFORD SCIENTIFIC FILMS. *Bees and Honey*, ill. with photos. Putnam, 1977. A six-page text, divided into brief topics and crisply written, is followed by captioned full-page color photographs, most of which are greatly enlarged.

————. *The Butterfly Cycle*, ill. with photos. Putnam, 1977. Excellent color photographs follow the life of the cabbage white butterfly with only a running line of text at the foot of the page. 8–10

————. *The Stickleback Cycle*, ill. with photos. Putnam, 1979. Superb color photographs illustrate a brief text focusing on the male stickleback. 8–10

PAIGE, DAVID. *Behind the Scenes at the Aquarium*, ill. with photos. Whitman, 1979. Profusely illustrated, this gives readers a fine introduction both to the beauty and interest of aquarium exhibits and to the responsibilities of the staff. 9–11

PARKER, BERTHA MORRIS. *The Golden Book of Science*, ill. by Harry McNaught. Golden Pr., 1956. 8–10

PATENT, DOROTHY HINSHAW. *Animal and Plant Mimicry*, ill. with photos. Holiday, 1978. 11–14

————. *Bacteria: How They Affect Other Living Things*. Holiday, 1980. 11 up

————. *Butterflies and Moths: How They Function*. Holiday, 1979. 12 up

————. *Evolution Goes on Every Day*, ill. by Matthew Kalmenoff. Holiday, 1977. 13 up

————. *Frogs, Toads, Salamanders and How They Reproduce*, ill. by Matthew Kalmenoff. Holiday, 1975. 9–12

————. *How Insects Communicate*. Holiday, 1975. 9–12

————. *Plants and Insects Together*. Holiday, 1976. 9–11

————. *Sizes and Shapes in Nature—What They Mean*. Holiday, 1979. A lucid text, broad in scope, and authoritative. 12–15

PRINCE, J. H. *The Universal Urge: Courtship and Mating Among Animals*. Nelson, 1973. 11 up

PRINGLE, LAURENCE. *Dinosaurs and People: Fossils, Facts, and Fantasies*, ill. with photos. Harcourt, 1978. Describes the work of paleontologists. 11–14

————. *Follow a Fisher*, ill. by Tony Chen. Crowell, 1973. 7–9

————. *The Gentle Desert: Exploring an Ecosystem*. Macmillan, 1977. In an exploration of the North American Desert system, Pringle describes the ecosystems within deserts, discussing the plants and animals of each and how they interrelate. 9–12

————. *The Hidden World: Life Under a Rock*. Macmillan, 1977. Suggesting ways to investigate hidden worlds with least damage to the investigator or the inhabitants, Pringle gives detailed descriptions of some of the most common creatures found under objects on earth or in water. 8–11

————. *This Is a River: Exploring an Ecosystem*. Macmillan, 1972. 9–11

————. *Wild Foods*, ill. with photos. Four Winds, 1978. Following a general discussion are ways to find, recognize, harvest, and prepare about twenty wild plants. 12 up

RAVIELLI, ANTHONY. *From Fins to Hands: An Adventure in Evolution*, ill. by author. Viking, 1968. 9–11

————. *Wonders of the Human Body*, ill. by author. Viking, 1954. 10–12

RIEDMAN, SARAH R. *Naming Living Things: The Grouping of Plants and Animals*, ill. by Jerome P. Connolly. Rand, 1963. 10–12

RUSSELL, SOLVEIG PAULSON. *Like and Unlike: A First Look at Classification*, ill. by Lawrence Di Fiori. Walck, 1973. Authoritative introduction to classification of plants and animals. 8–10

SCHALLER, GEORGE B., and MILLICENT E. SELSAM. *The Tiger: Its Life in the Wild*, ill. with photos, drawings, and maps. Harper, 1969. The author's firsthand experiences add interest to this account of much that is known about tigers. Myths about these animals are also recounted. 10–12

SCHEELE, WILLIAM E. *Prehistoric Animals*, ill. by author. World, 1954. Describes the first five million years of earth's life forms. Cites locations of fossils in museums. 9 up

SCHEFFER, VICTOR. *Little Calf*, ill. by Leonard Everett Fisher. Scribner's, 1970. 12 up

SCHICK, ALICE. *Kongo and Kumba: Two Gorillas*, ill. by Joseph Cellini. Dial, 1974. A comparison of the lives of a gorilla in the wilds and another in a zoo. 8–10

————. *The Siamang Gibbons: An Ape Family*, ill. by Joel Schick. Raintree, 1976. A description of the siamang gibbon is given in narrative form by tracing a particular gibbon from jungle to zoo. 9–11

SCOTT, JACK DENTON. *Canada Geese*, ill. with photos. Putnam, 1976. 10 up

————. *City of Birds and Beasts: Behind the Scenes at the Bronx Zoo*, ill. with photos. Putnam, 1978. Records of one long day show the work of the staff and their deep concern for their charges. 11–14

————. *Island of Wild Horses*, ill. with photos. Putnam, 1978. 10 up

☆ SCOTT, JACK DENTON. *Return of the Buffalo*, ill. with photos. Putnam, 1976. 10 up

————. *The Survivors: Enduring Animals of North America*, ill. by Daphne Gillen. Harcourt, 1975. 10–14

————. *That Wonderful Pelican*, photos by Ozzie Sweet. Putnam, 1975. An authoritative and comprehensive text. 10 up

SELSAM, MILLICENT. *Animals of the Sea*, ill. by John Hamberger. Four Winds, 1976. Simply written, illustrated in full color, and authoritative, this introduction to marine life may also be used for reading aloud to preschool children. 7–8

————. *Bulbs, Corms, and Such,* photos by Jerome Wexler. Morrow, 1974.   8–10

————. *Benny's Animals, and How He Put Them in Order,* ill. by Arnold Lobel. Harper, 1966.   6–8

————. *A First Look at Flowers,* ill. by Harriett Springer. Walker, 1977.   5–8

————. *A First Look at Monkeys and Apes,* ill. by Harriett Springer. Walker, 1979. A simple, accurate text points out the similarities among and differences between New and Old World monkeys and apes.   6–8

————. *Greg's Microscope,* ill. by Arnold Lobel. Harper, 1963.   6–8

————. *Land of the Giant Tortoise: The Story of the Galapagos,* ill. with photos. Four Winds, 1977.   9–12

————. *The Language of Animals,* ill. by Kathleen Elgin. Morrow, 1962.   10–14

————. *Let's Get Turtles,* ill. by Arnold Lobel. Harper, 1965.   7–8

————. *Mimosa, the Sensitive Plant,* ill. with photos. Morrow, 1978.   8–10

————. *Peanut,* ill. with photos by Jerome Wexler. Morrow, 1969.   7–9

————. *Plants That Heal,* ill. by Kathleen Elgin. Morrow, 1959.   11–14

————. *Plants That Move,* ill. by Fred F. Scherer. Morrow, 1962.   8–11

————. *See Along the Shore,* ill. by Leonard Weisgard. Harper, 1961.   7–9

————. *See Through the Jungle,* ill. by Winifred Lubell. Harper, 1957.   7–9

————. *See Through the Sea,* ill. by Winifred Lubell. Harper, 1955.   7–9

————. *Tyrannosaurus Rex,* ill. with photos. Harper, 1978. Gives as much information about the scientific method as it does about dinosaurs.   8–10

SELSAM, MILLICENT, and JEROME WEXLER. *The Amazing Dandelion.* Morrow, 1977.   7–9

————. *Eat the Fruit, Plant the Seed.* Morrow, 1980. Concise and precise advice on starting plants from seed.   8–10

SELSAM, MILLICENT, and JOYCE HUNT. *A First Look at Animals with Backbones,* ill. by Harriet Springer. Walker, 1978.   7–8

SHEFFIELD, MARGARET. *Where Do Babies Come From?* ill. by Sheila Bewley. Knopf, 1973.   5–7

SHIPPEN, KATHERINE B. *Men, Microscopes and Living Things,* ill. by Anthony Ravielli. Viking, 1955.   13–15

SHOWERS, PAUL. *Look at Your Eyes,* ill. by Paul Galdone. T. Crowell, 1962.   6–7

————. *Me and My Family Tree,* ill. by Don Madden. T. Crowell, 1978.   7–8

————. *Use Your Brain,* ill. by Rosalind Fry. T. Crowell, 1971.   5–8

————. *Where Does the Garbage Go?* ill. by Loretta Lustig. T. Crowell, 1974.   7–8

§ ————. *Your Skin and Mine,* ill. by Paul Galdone. T. Crowell, 1965.   6–8

SHOWERS, PAUL and KAY. *Before You Were a Baby,* ill. by Ingrid Fetz. T. Crowell, 1968.   7–8

SHUTTLESWORTH, DOROTHY. *Animal Camouflage,* ill. by Matthew Kalmenoff. Natural History Pr., 1966.   11–14

————. *The Story of Rodents,* ill. by Lydia Rosier. Doubleday, 1971.   9–12

————. *To Find a Dinosaur.* Doubleday, 1973.   9–12

SILVERSTEIN, ALVIN and VIRGINIA B. *Apples: All About Them,* ill. by Shirley Chan. Prentice, 1976.   9–12

————. *Exploring the Brain,* ill. by Patricia De Veau. Prentice, 1975.   10–13

————. *Gerbils: All About Them,* photos by Frederick Breda. Lippincott, 1976.   9–12

————. *Hamsters: All About Them,* photos by Frederick Breda. Lothrop, 1974.   9–12

————. *The Skeletal System: Framework for Life,* ill. by Lee J. Ames. Prentice, 1972.   9–11

————. *The Skin: Coverings and Linings of Living Things,* ill. by Lee J. Ames. Prentice, 1972.   9–11

————. *Sleep and Dreams.* Lippincott, 1974.   12–15

————. *So You're Getting Braces: A Guide to Orthodontics,* ill. by Barbara Remington. Lippincott, 1978. Useful facts and sensible advice about orthodontic care.   10–14

————. *The Sugar Disease: Diabetes.* Lippincott, 1980.   11–14

————. *The World of Bionics.* Methuen, 1980. Focuses on animal research and the way it supplies bionic knowledge.   11–13

SIMON, HILDA. *The Amazing Book of Birds.* Hart, 1958.   9–11

————. *Exploring the World of Social Insects,* ill. by author. Vanguard, 1963. A study of group behavior.   9–13

————. *Insect Masquerades.* Viking, 1968.   11–14

————. *Living Lanterns: Luminescence in Animals,* ill. by author. Viking, 1971.   11 up

————. *Snakes: The Facts and Folklore,* ill. by author. Viking, 1973.   11–15

SIMON, SEYMOUR. *Animal Fact/Animal Fable,* ill. by Diane de Groat. Crown, 1978. Debunks some popular misconceptions.   7–8

————. *Life in the Dark: How Animals Survive at Night,* ill. by Arabelle Wheatley. Watts, 1974.   9–11

————. *Meet the Giant Snakes,* ill. by Harriet Springer. Walker, 1979.   8–10

————. *Strange Mysteries.* Four Winds, 1980.   9–12

STEVENS, CARLA. *The Birth of Sunset's Kittens,* ill. with photos by Leonard Stevens. W. R. Scott, 1969. No cute posed pictures, no saccharine comment, just the miraculous facts of kittens being born.   5–8

STOUTENBURG, ADRIEN. *A Vanishing Thunder: Extinct and Threatened American Birds,* ill. by John Schoenherr. Natural History Pr., 1967. A sobering reminder of human carelessness.   10–12

TRESSELT, ALVIN. *The Beaver Pond,* ill. by Roger Duvoisin. Lothrop, 1970.   5–7

TUNIS, EDWIN. *Chipmunks on the Doorstep,* ill. by author. T. Crowell, 1971.   10 up

WATSON, JANE (WERNER). *Whales: Friendly Dolphins and Mighty Giants of the Sea,* ill. by Richard Amundsen. Western, 1975.   9–12

WEISS, MALCOLM. *What's Happening to Our Climate?* ill. by Paul Plumer. Messner, 1978. A clear and well organized text discusses the long-range changes in the world's climate and all the factors that have contributed to them and will affect the climate of the future.   10–12

ZIM, HERBERT S. *Dinosaurs,* ill. by James G. Irving. Morrow, 1954.   9–11

————. *Frogs and Toads,* ill. by Joy Buba. Morrow, 1950.   8–10

————. *Golden Hamsters,* ill. by Herschel Wartik. Morrow, 1951.   8–10

————. *Medicine,* ill. by Judith Corwin. Morrow, 1974.   9–11

————. *Our Senses and How They Work,* ill. by Herschel Wartik. Morrow, 1956.   9–11

————. *Your Heart and How It Works,* ill. by Gustav Schrotter. Morrow, 1959.   9–11

ZIM, HERBERT S., and SONIA BLEEKER. *Life and Death*, ill. by René Martin. Morrow, 1970.   9–12

ZIM, HERBERT, and LUCRETIA KRANZ. *Crabs*, ill. by René Martin. Morrow, 1974.   8–10

————. *Snails*, ill. by René Martin. Morrow, 1975.   8–10

The Physical Sciences

ADLER, IRVING. *The Changing Tools of Science: From Yardstick to Cyclotron*, ill. by Ruth Adler. Day, 1958; 1973.   12–14

————. *The Giant Golden Book of Mathematics*, ill. by Lowell Hess. Golden Pr., 1960. An explanation of fundamental concepts.   10–14

————. *Magic House of Numbers*, ill. by Ruth Adler. Day, 1957; 1974.   10–14

————. *The New Mathematics*, ill. by Ruth Adler. Day, 1958. An explanation of advanced math.   11–14

————. *Petroleum: Gas, Oil and Asphalt*, ill. by Peggy Adler. Day, 1975.   9–11

————. *Stars: Decoding Their Messages*, rev. ed. Crowell, 1980.   11–14

————. *The Sun and Its Family*, ill. by Ruth Adler. Day, 1958.   12–14

————. *Tools in Your Life*, ill. by Ruth Adler. Day, 1956.   10–14

————. *The Wonders of Physics: An Introduction to the Physical World*, ill. by Cornelius DeWitt. Golden Pr., 1966.   12 up

ADLER, IRVING and RUTH. *Sets*, ill. by Ruth Adler. Day, 1967.   9–11

————. *Sets and Numbers for the Very Young*, ill. by Peggy Adler. Day, 1969.   6–8

AMES, GERALD, and ROSE WYLER. *First Days of the World*, ill. by Leonard Weisgard. Harper, 1958.   8–10

ASIMOV, ISAAC. *ABC's of Space*, ill. Walker, 1969.   8–10

————. *The Best New Thing*, ill. by Symeon Shimin. World, 1971.   5–7

————. *Building Blocks of the Universe*, rev. ed. Abelard, 1961.   14–17

————. *How Did We Find Out About Atoms?* ill. by David Wool. Walker, 1976.   10–12

————. *How Did We Find Out About Black Holes?* ill. by David Wool. Walker, 1978.   10–12

————. *How Did We Find Out About Oil?* ill. by David Wool. Walker, 1980.   10–12

————. *Mars, the Red Planet*, ill. with photos. Lothrop, 1977.   12 up

————. *Realm of Measure*, ill. by R. Belmore. Houghton, 1960. A discussion of measuring systems.   12 up

————. *Realm of Numbers*, diagrams by Robert Belmore. Houghton, 1959.   12 up

————. *Words of Science: and the History Behind Them*, ill. by William Barss. Houghton, 1959.   12–15

BEHRENS, JUNE. *The True Book of Metric Measurement*. Childrens Pr., 1975.   7–9

BENDICK, JEANNE. *All Around You: A First Look at the World*, ill. by author. Whittlesey, 1951.   6–8

————. *The First Book of Space Travel*, rev. ed., ill. by author. Watts, 1969.   8–10

————. *How Much and How Many: The Story of Weights and Measures*, ill. by author. McGraw, 1960.   10–12

————. *Names, Sets and Numbers*, ill. by author. Watts, 1971.   7–10

————. *The Shape of the Earth*, ill. by author. Rand, 1965.   9–11

————. *Solids, Liquids and Gases*, ill. by author. Watts, 1974.   8–10

————. *The Wind*, ill. by author. Rand, 1964.   8–10

BENDICK, JEANNE, and MARCIA LEVIN. *Take Shapes, Lines and Letters*, ill. by Jeanne Bendick. McGraw, 1962.   10–12

BENDICK, JEANNE, and ROBERT BENDICK. *Television Works Like This*, 4th ed., ill. by Jeanne Bendick. McGraw, 1965. 10–12

BERGER, MELVIN. *Jigsaw Continents*, ill. by Bob Totten. Coward, 1978.   8–10

————. *The New Water Book*, ill. by Leonard Kessler. T. Crowell, 1973.   9–11

————. *Oceanography Lab*. Day, 1973.   9–11

BOURNE, MIRIAM. *What Is Papa Up To Now?* ill. by Dick Gackenbach. Coward, 1977. Sally, Benjamin Franklin's small daughter, describes Papa's excitement and pleasure at each discovery he makes while experimenting with electricity.   7–8

BOVA, BENJAMIN. *Man Changes the Weather*. Addision, 1973.   10–13

————. *The Weather Changes Man*. Addision, 1974. A review of man's adjustment to weather, and its influence on his life, from Ice Age to Space Age.   10–12

————. *Workshops in Space*. Dutton, 1974.   11–14

BRANLEY, FRANKLYN M. *A Book of Flying Saucers for You*, ill. by Leonard Kessler. T. Crowell, 1973. A discussion of the phenomena that have been reported as flying saucers. 8–9

————. *A Book of Mars for You*, ill. by Leonard Kessler. T. Crowell, 1968.   6–10

————. *The Christmas Sky*, ill. by Blair Lent. T. Crowell, 1966.   9–11

————. *Color: From Rainbows to Lasers*, ill. by Henry Roth. T. Crowell, 1978.   11–15

————. *Eclipse: Darkness in Daytime*, ill. by Donald Crews. T. Crowell, 1973.   7–9

————. *The Milky Way: Galaxy Number One*, ill. by Helmut K. Wimmer. T. Crowell, 1969.   12 up

————. *Pieces of Another World: The Story of Moon Rocks*, ill. by Herbert Danska. T. Crowell, 1973.   10–13

————. *Shakes, Quakes, and Shifts: Earth Tectonics*, ill. by Daniel Maffia. T. Crowell, 1974. An explanation of the shifting continents distinguishes between known facts and theories.   10–15

————. *Solar Energy*, ill. by John Teppich. T. Crowell, 1957.   11–14

————. *The Sun: Our Nearest Star*, ill. by Helen Borten. T. Crowell, 1961.   5–8

————. *Think Metric!* ill. by Graham Booth. T. Crowell, 1973.   9–11

BRANLEY, FRANKLYN M. and ELEANOR K. VAUGHAN. *Mickey's Magnet*, ill. by Crockett Johnson. T. Crowell, 1956.   5–7

BRIGGS, PETER. *Science Ship: A Voyage Aboard the Discoverer*. Simon, 1969.   11–15

BRONOWSKI, JACOB, and MILLICENT E. SELSAM. *Biography of an Atom*, ill. by Weimar Pursell and with photos. Harper, 1965.   10–14

BUEHR, WALTER. *Water: Our Vital Need*, ill. by author. Norton/Grosset, 1967.   9–11

CARLE, ERIC. *My Very First Book of Shapes*. T. Crowell, 1974.   2–4

CARSON, RACHEL. *The Sea Around Us*, ad. by Anne Terry White, ill. with photos, maps, and drawings. Golden Pr., 1958.   11–14

COOMBS, CHARLES. *Lift-Off: The Story of Rocket Power,* ill. by R. H. Foor. Morrow, 1963. A clear explanation of rocket engines and guidance systems. 9–11

CROUSE, WILLIAM H. *Understanding Science,* rev. ed., ill. by Jeanne Bendick and D. Mahanes. McGraw, 1956. 10–14

DEMING, RICHARD. *Metric Power: Why and How We Are Going Metric.* Nelson, 1974. 11–15

ENGDAHL, SYLVIA, and RICK ROBERTSON. *The Subnuclear Zoo: New Discoveries in High Energy Physics,* ill. with photos. Atheneum, 1977. A survey of old and new knowledge about the structure of matter focuses on particle physics and leads to a description of the ways in which scientists can observe the unobservable. 12 up

EPSTEIN, SAM and BERYL. *The First Book of Electricity,* ill. by Robin King. Watts, 1953. 9–12

§ FEELINGS, MURIEL. *Moja Means One,* ill. by Tom Feelings. Dial, 1971. Soft illustrations add appeal to a counting book that gives numbers 1–10 in Swahili. 5–8

FEY, JAMES T. *Long, Short, High, Low, Thin, Wide,* ill. by Janie Russell. T. Crowell, 1971. 7–9

FREEMAN, IRA M. *All About Electricity,* ill. by Urbanowich. Random, 1957. 10–13

———. *All About the Wonders of Chemistry,* ill. by George Wilde. Random, 1954. 10–13

FREEMAN, IRA M., and A. RAE PATTON. *The Science of Chemistry,* ill. by Zenowij Onyshkewych. Random, 1968. 10–12

FREEMAN, MAE (BLACKER). *Finding Out About Shapes,* ill. by Bill Morrison. McGraw, 1969. A good introduction to spatial conceptualization, with simple definitions. 5–8

———. *Gravity and the Astronauts,* ill. by Beatrice Darwin. Crown, 1971. 10–12

FROMAN, ROBERT. *Less Than Nothing Is Really Something,* ill. by Don Madden. T. Crowell, 1973. 7–9

GALLANT, ROY A. *Exploring Chemistry,* ill. by Lee Ames. Garden City, 1958. 9–13

———. *Exploring the Universe,* ill. by Lowell Hess. Garden City, 1956; rev. ed., 1968. 9–13

GANS, ROMA. *Caves,* ill. by Giulio Maestro. T. Crowell, 1977. A book about the ways in which caves are formed, their size range, and the lure of cave exploration intended for the young independent reader. 7–9

———. *Millions and Millions of Crystals,* ill. by Giulio Maestro. T. Crowell, 1973. 7–8

———. *Oil: The Buried Treasure,* ill. by Giulio Maestro. T. Crowell, 1975. 7–8

GOUDEY, ALICE E. *The Day We Saw the Sun Come Up,* ill. by Adrienne Adams. Scribner's, 1961. Two children rise before dawn, and Mother explains night and day, shadows, and the turning earth. 5–7

HALACY, DANIEL S. *The Energy Trap.* Four Winds, 1975. 12–15

HIRSCH, S. CARL. *Meter Means Measure: The Story of the Metric System.* Viking, 1973. 11–15

HOGBEN, LANCELOT. *Beginnings and Blunders: or Before Science Began.* Grosset, 1970. Primitive man moves toward the earliest civilization, from the first tools to the first cities. 11–14

———. *The Wonderful World of Energy,* ill. by Eileen Aplin and others. Garden City, 1957. 11–14

———. *The Wonderful World of Mathematics,* ill. by Andre. Charles Keeping, Kenneth Symonds. Garden City, 1955; rev. ed., 1968. 10–14

HYDE, MARGARET O., and BRUCE G. HYDE. *Atoms Today and Tomorrow,* rev. ed., ill. by Ed Malsberg. McGraw, 1970. 11–13

JACKER, CORINNE. *Window on the Unknown: A History of the Microscope,* ill. by Mary Linn and with photos. Scribner's, 1966. 13 up

JAMES, ELIZABETH, and CAROL BARKIN. *The Simple Facts of Simple Machines,* photos by Daniel Dorn, diagrams by Susan Stan. Lothrop, 1975. 9–11

———. *What Do You Mean by "Average"?* ill. by Joel Schick. Lothrop, 1978. 10–12

KLEIN, AARON E. *The Electron Microscope: A Tool of Discovery.* McGraw, 1974. 13 up

KOHN, BERNICE. *Communications Satellites: Message Centers in Space,* ill. by Jerome Kuhl. Four Winds, 1975. 9–11

———. *Echoes,* ill. by Dan Connor. Dandelion, 1979. In a direct and simple explanation of a phenomenon that intrigues most children, Kohn explains how sound waves travel to create echoes. 7–9

LAUBER, PATRICIA. *All About the Planets,* ill. by Arthur Renshaw. Random, 1960. 9–11

———. *The Story of Numbers,* ill. by Mircea Vasiliu. Random, 1961. 8–10

———. *Tapping Earth's Heat,* ill. by Edward Malsberg. Garrard, 1978. 8–10

LEWELLEN, JOHN. *The Mighty Atom,* ill. by Ida Scheib. Knopf, 1955. 8–10

———. *The True Book of Toys at Work,* ill. by Karl Murray. Childrens Pr., 1953. 6–8

LEWIS, ALFRED. *The New World of Computers,* ill. with photos. Dodd, 1965. 9–12

MARCUS, REBECCA. *The First Book of Volcanoes and Earthquakes.* Watts, 1972. 9–11

MAY, JULIAN. *Why the Earth Quakes,* ill. by Leonard Everett Fisher. Holiday, 1969. 9–11

NAVARRA, JOHN. *Earthquake.* Chicago Museum of Science and Industry/Doubleday, 1980. A professor of geoscience describes the causes, effects, and measuring of earthquakes. 10–13

———. *Wide World Weather.* Doubleday, 1968. 11 up

NIXON, HERSHELL and JOAN. *Glaciers: Nature's Frozen Rivers.* Dodd, 1980. A comprehensive and accurate text by a geologist and his wife. 9–13

PODENDORF, ILLA. *Things Are Alike and Different,* ill. by John Hawkinson. Childrens Pr., 1970. 7–8

PRINGLE, LAURENCE. *Energy: Power for People.* Macmillan, 1975. 11–13

REED, W. MAXWELL. *The Stars for Sam,* rev. ed., ed. by Paul Brandwein, ill. with photos. Harcourt, 1960. Describes the solar system and the universe and exploration of outer space. Reed's books on the earth and the sea, all durable sources of information, have also been revised. 10–13

RICHARDSON, ROBERT. *The Stars and Serendipity.* Pantheon, 1971. 11–14

RUCHLIS, HY. *Orbit: A Picture Story of Force and Motion,* ill. by Alice Hirsch. Harper, 1958. 10 up

———. *Your Changing Earth,* ill. by Janet and Alex d'Amato. Harvey, 1963. 7–9

SCHLEIN, MIRIAM. *Metric—The Modern Way to Measure.* Harcourt, 1975. 8–10

SCHNEIDER, HERMAN and NINA. *How Big Is Big? From Stars to Atoms,* ill. by Symeon Shimin. W. R. Scott, 1950. 8–11

———. *You, Among the Stars,* ill. by Symeon Shimin. W. R. Scott, 1951. 8–10

SELSAM, MILLICENT E. *Birth of an Island,* ill. by Winifred Lubell. Harper, 1959. The evolution of a volcanic island. 8–10

SHANNON, TERRY, and CHARLES PAYZANT. *Windows in the Sea: New Vehicles That Scan the Ocean Depths.* Childrens Pr., 1973. A description of panoramic-view submersibles and the way they are used in marine exploration.   10–13

SILVERSTEIN, ALVIN and VIRGINIA. *The Chemicals We Eat and Drink.* Follett, 1973.   10–13

SIMON, SEYMOUR. *Danger from Below: Earthquakes: Past, Present, and Future.* Four Winds, 1979.   10–12

———. *The Long View into Space,* ill. with photos. Crown, 1979.   8–10

SRIVASTAVA, JANE JONAS. *Averages,* ill. by Aliki. T. Crowell, 1975.   7–9

———. *Statistics,* ill. by John J. Reiss. T. Crowell, 1973. An excellent introduction explains both the ways statistics are compiled and the ways compilation can affect results.   7–8

TRESSELT, ALVIN R. *Hide and Seek Fog,* ill. by Roger Duvoisin. Lothrop, 1965.   5–8

———. *It's Time Now,* ill. by Roger Duvoisin. Lothrop, 1969.   5–8

———. *Rain Drop Splash,* ill. by Leonard Weisgard. Lothrop, 1946.   4–8

———. *Sun Up,* ill. by Roger Duvoisin. Lothrop, 1949.   5–8

———. *White Snow, Bright Snow,* ill. by Roger Duvoisin. Lothrop, 1947. Caldecott Medal.   5–7

TRIVETT, JOHN V. *Building Tables on Tables,* ill. by Giulio Maestro. T. Crowell, 1975. A lucid presentation of the concepts that are basic to multiplication.   7–9

TUNIS, EDWIN. *Wheels: A Pictorial History,* ill. by author. World, 1955.   11 up

WATSON, CLYDE. *Binary Numbers,* ill. by Wendy Watson. T. Crowell, 1977. One of the simplest descriptions of the binary system yet published for beginners, nicely integrated with helpful illustrations.   7–9

WEISS, HARVEY. *Motors and Engines and How They Work,* ill. by author. T. Crowell, 1969.   10–12

WILFORD, JOHN NOBLE. *We Reach the Moon,* based upon the original book published by *The New York Times* and Bantam Books. Norton/Grosset, 1969.   10–12

WISE, WILLIAM. *Monsters from Outer Space,* ill. by Richard Cuffari. Putnam, 1979.   8–9

WOODBURY, DAVID O. *The New World of the Atom.* Dodd, 1965.   9–11

WYLER, ROSE. *The First Book of Weather,* ill. by Bernice Myers. Watts, 1966.   9–11

WYLER, ROSE, and GERALD AMES. *The New Golden Book of Astronomy,* rev. ed., ill. by John Polgreen. Golden Pr., 1965.   10–12

ZIM, HERBERT. *The New Moon.* Morrow, 1980.   9–11

The Social Sciences

ADAMSON, WENDY WRISTON. *Saving Lake Superior: A Story of Environmental Action.* Dillon, 1974. A citizens' group fights pollution.   11–14

§ ADOFF, ARNOLD, ed. *Black on Black: Commentaries by Negro Americans.* Macmillan, 1968. A collection of material spanning the thinking of black Americans from Frederick Douglass to Dick Gregory. Their viewpoints may differ but they unite in speaking of the problems of a fragmented society.   13 up

ALIKI. *Mummies Made in Egypt,* ill. by author. Crowell, 1979. Gives clear information about the beliefs of the ancient Egyptians that led to mummification and tomb burial.   8–10

AMES, GERALD, and ROSE WYLER. *The First People in the World,* ill. by Leonard Weisgard. Harper, 1958.   8–10

ANCONA, GEORGE. *Growing Older,* ill. with photos. Dutton, 1978. A series of interviews with old people records a diversity of backgrounds to give variety to a book which vitiates any idea that life ends at seventy.   10–11

ASHE, GEOFFREY. *King Arthur in Fact and Legend.* Nelson, 1971. A scholarly, lively investigation of the fictional Arthur and the Arthur of historical and archeological fact.   12 up

ASIMOV, ISAAC. *The Birth of the United States 1763–1816.* Houghton, 1974. A sequel to *The Shaping of North America.*   11–15

———. *The Dark Ages,* ill. Houghton, 1968. From the year 1000 to the advent of chivalry.   12–17

———. *Our Federal Union.* Houghton, 1975. Third in the series on the United States.   13 up

———. *The Shaping of North America: from Earliest Times to 1763.* Houghton, 1973.   13 up

———. *Words from the Exodus,* ill. by William Barss. Houghton, 1963.   11 up

———. *Words from History,* ill. by William Barss. Houghton, 1968.   11 up

———. *Words in Genesis,* ill. by William Barss. Houghton, 1962.   11 up

———. *Words on the Map,* ill. by William Barss. Houghton, 1962.   12 up

BADER, BARBARA. *Trademark Scandinavia.* Greenwillow, 1976. Profusely illustrated with photographs of good quality, this examines the major industries and crafts of Denmark, Finland, Norway, and Sweden.   9–11

☆ BAKER, BETTY. *Settlers and Strangers: Native Americans of the Desert Southwest and History As They Saw It.* Macmillan, 1977. A top-notch historical survey told in narrative style.   9–14

BALES, CAROL ANN. *Chinatown Sunday: The Story of Lilliann Der.* Reilly and Lee, 1973. A photodocumentary examines the life of a Chinese-American family in Chicago.   8–10

☆ ———. *Kevin Cloud: Chippewa Boy in the City.* Reilly, 1972. A photodocumentary that is both candid and dignified.   8–10

BAUMANN, HANS. *In the Land of Ur: The Discovery of Ancient Mesopotamia,* tr. by Stella Humphries, ill. Pantheon, 1969.   13 up

☆ BAYLOR, BYRD. *Before You Came This Way,* ill. by Tom Bahti. Dutton, 1969. Walking in the quiet of a canyon in the southwest, you wonder if you are the first to pass this way and then you see the wall paintings of the past. A handsome, thought-provoking book.   7–9

☆ ———. *The Way to Start a Day,* ill. by Peter Parnall, Scribner's, 1978. A poetic text in picture book format presents some of the ways the sun has been greeted in various times and places.   8–10

BENDICK, JEANNE and ROBERT. *The Consumer's Catalog of Economy & Ecology,* ill. by Karen Watson. McGraw, 1974.   12 up

BERGER, MELVIN. *Time After Time,* ill. by Richard Cuffari. Coward, 1975.   7–9

§ BERNHEIM, MARC and EVELYNE. *African Success Story: The Ivory Coast,* ill. Harcourt, 1970. A lucid and authoritative description of the growth and prosperity of the Ivory Coast since it gained independence.   11–14

§ ———. *In Africa.* Atheneum, 1973. A survey of life styles in a coastal village, a city, a savannah, a forest, and a nomad community.   5–8

BERNSTEIN, JOANNE, and STEPHEN GULLO. *When People Die,* ill. with photos. Dutton, 1977. A discussion of death that is sensible, fairly comprehensive, and tender without being somber or mawkish.   5–8

BLEEKER, SONIA. *The Eskimo: Arctic Hunters and Trappers,* ill. by Patricia Boodell. Morrow, 1959.   9–12

§ ———. *The Ibo of Biafra,* ill. by Edith G. Singer. Morrow, 1969.   10–12

☆ ———. *The Maya, Indians of Central America,* ill. by Kisa N. Sasaki. Morrow, 1961.   9–12

§ BONTEMPS, ARNA. *Story of the Negro,* 3rd ed., ill. by Raymond Lufkin. Knopf, 1958. An authoritative and perceptive black history.   11–14

BOORSTIN, DANIEL J. *The Landmark History of the American People,* 2 vols., ill. Random, 1968 and 1970.   10–14

BRANLEY, FRANKLYN M. *The Mystery of Stonehenge,* ill. by Victor G. Ambrus. T. Crowell, 1969. An exploration of theories about the erection of Stonehenge.   9–11

☆ BROWN, DEE. *Wounded Knee.* Holt, 1974. Adapted by Amy Ehrlich from the adult title, *Bury My Heart at Wounded Knee.*   11–14

CARLSON, DALE BICK. *Girls Are Equal Too: The Women's Movement for Teenagers,* ill. by Carol Nicklaus. Atheneum, 1973. A discussion of the causes and solutions in contemporary sexism.   11–14

CARPENTER, FRANCIS. *The Old China Trade: Americans in Canton 1784–1843,* ill. by Demi. Coward, 1976. An authoritative account of the China trade emphasizing economic and industrial effects and enlivened by descriptions of the doughty sailors and the Chinese with whom they dealt.   11–14

CARTER, WILLIAM E. *The First Book of South America.* Watts, 1961.   9–12

CARTWRIGHT, SALLY. *What's in a Map?* ill. by Dick Gackenbach. Coward, 1976. In a way that small children can easily grasp, Cartwright approaches the concept of what a map is by relating the drawing of things and places to related positions in space.   5–7

CHUBB, THOMAS CALDECOT. *The Byzantines,* ill. by Richard M. Powers. World, 1959. One of a fine series of books about major cultures of the world (Arabs, Aztecs, Slavic peoples, etc.).   11 up

CLARK, ANN NOLAN. *Circle of Seasons,* ill. by W. T. Mars. Farrar, 1970.   10–14

CLARKE, CLORINDA. *The American Revolution 1775–83: A British View,* ill. McGraw, 1967.   10–14

CLYMER, ELEANOR. *The Case of the Missing Link,* rev. ed. Basic, 1968.   15 up

☆§ COHEN, ROBERT. *The Color of Man,* ill. with photos by Ken Heyman. Random, 1968. A fine book on the physical differences among people, and on the nature and dangers of prejudice.   10–13

COLE, SHEILA. *Working Kids on Working.* Lothrop, 1980. Interviews with a wide variety of children, some as young as nine, show the size and diversity of the juvenile labor market.   10–14

COMMAGER, HENRY STEELE. *The First Book of American History,* ill. by Leonard E. Fisher. Watts, 1957.   10–12

———. *The Great Declaration: A Book for Young Americans,* ill. by Donald Bolognese. Bobbs, 1958.   12–14

COOLIDGE, OLIVIA. *Tales of the Crusades,* ill. adapted from prints by Gustave Doré. Houghton, 1970. Each of the stories that chronicle some facet of the long years of the Crusades is a splendid entity, wonderfully evocative, and vividly written. The book is not a cohesive picture but is impressive both as a literary and a historical work.   13 up

COOMBS, CHARLES. *Cleared for Takeoff: Behind the Scenes at an Airport.* Morrow, 1969. An interesting backstage view.   11–15

———. *Spacetrack: Watchdog of the Skies,* ill. with photos and diagrams. Morrow, 1969. Describes the work of the North American Air Defense Command.   10–12

COTTRELL, LEONARD. *Digs and Diggers: A Book of World Archaeology,* ill. with photos. World, 1964.   13 up

★ COY, HAROLD. *Chicano Roots Go Deep.* Dodd, 1975.   11 up

DALGLIESH, ALICE. *America Begins: The Story of the Finding of the New World,* rev. ed., ill. by Lois Maloy. Scribner's, 1958.   8–11

DENNY, NORMAN, and JOSEPHINE FILMER-SANKEY. *The Bayeux Tapestry: The Story of the Norman Conquest: 1066,* ill. Atheneum, 1966. A description of a famous tapestry depiction of the Norman Conquest.   11–15

DE PAUW, LINDA. *Founding Mothers: Women of America in the Revolutionary era.* Houghton, 1975.   12 up

★ DOBRIN, ARNOLD. *The New Life—La Vida Nueva: The Mexican-Americans Today.* Dodd, 1971. A survey of attitudes, problems, and factors that influence the Chicano, using interviews.   10–12

DRUMMOND, A. H. *The Population Puzzle: Overcrowding and Stress Among Animals and Men.* Addison, 1973.   12–15

DUGGAN, ALFRED. *Growing Up in 13th Century England,* ill. by C. Walter Hodges. Pantheon, 1962.   11–14

§ DURHAM, PHILIP, and EVERETT L. JONES. *The Negro Cowboys,* ill. with photos. Dodd, 1965. A great deal of information about the blacks who participated in the westward expansion.   13 up

★ EISEMAN, ALBERTA. *Mañana Is Now: The Spanish-Speaking in the United States.* Atheneum, 1973.   12 up

ELLIOT, SARAH. *Our Dirty Air,* ill. with photos. Messner, 1971. Suggests ways that children can help.   8–10

EPSTEIN, BERYL and SAMUEL. *Who Says You Can't?* Coward, 1969. Instances of causes that seemed lost and the determined people who campaigned for those diverse causes are described in a lively and provocative book.   12 up

☆ ERDOES, RICHARD. *The Native Americans: Navajos,* ill. with photos. Sterling, 1979.   9–11

EVANS, EVA KNOX. *Why We Live Where We Live,* ill. by Ursula Koering. Little, 1953.   9–12

FISHER, LEONARD EVERETT. *The Blacksmiths,* ill. by author. Watts, 1976.   10–12

———. *The Cabinetmakers,* ill. by author. Watts, 1966. 10–12

———. *The Factories,* ill. by author. Holiday, 1979.   10–12

———. *The Homemakers,* ill. by author. Watts, 1973.   9–11

———. *The Hospitals,* ill. by author. Watts, 1980.   10–12

———. *The Peddlers,* ill. by author. Watts, 1968.   10–12

———. *Pumpers, Boilers, Hooks and Ladders,* ill. by author. Dial, 1961.   5–8

☆ ———. *The Railroads,* ill. by author. Holiday, 1979. 10–12

———. *The Schoolmasters,* ill. by author. Watts, 1967. 10–12

———. *The Silversmiths,* ill. by author. Watts, 1964.   10–12

———. *The Tanners,* ill. by author. Watts, 1966.   10–12

———. *Two If by Sea,* ill. by author. Random, 1970.   10–11

§ FLATO, CHARLES. *The Golden Book of the Civil War,* ad. from *The*

American Heritage Picture History of the Civil War. Golden Pr., 1961. 10–12

☆ FOLSOM, FRANKLIN. *Red Power on the Rio Grande: The Native American Revolution of 1680,* ill. by J. D. Roybal. Follett, 1973. 12–15

FOSTER, G. ALLEN. *Sunday in Centerville: The Battle of Bull Run, 1861,* ill. by Harold Berson. White, 1971. 12 up

FOSTER, GENEVIEVE. *George Washington's World,* ill. by author. Scribner's, 1941. 11–14

———. *The World of Columbus and Sons,* ill. by author. Scribner's, 1965. 11–14

———. *The World of William Penn,* ill. by author. Scribner's, 1973. 9–12

———. *The Year of the Horseless Carriage—1801,* ill. by author. Scribner's, 1975. 10–11

———. *The Year of the Pilgrims—1620,* ill. by author. Scribner's, 1969. 8–10

FRANCHERE, RUTH. *Westward by Canal.* Macmillan, 1972. 10–13

FRITZ, JEAN. *Who's That Stepping on Plymouth Rock?* ill. by J. B. Handelsman. Coward, 1975. 8–10

GIDAL, SONIA. *My Village in Hungary.* Pantheon, 1974. 9–11

———. *My Village in Portugal.* Pantheon, 1972. 9–11

§ GIDAL, SONIA and TIM. *My Village in Ghana.* Pantheon, 1970. And other titles in the series. 9–12

☆ GOBLE, PAUL and DOROTHY. *Brave Eagle's Account of the Fetterman Fight: 21 December 1866,* ill. by Paul Goble. Pantheon, 1972. An Oglala Sioux chief describes Indian resistance to white encroachment. 10–12

☆ ———. *Red Hawk's Account of Custer's Last Battle,* ill. by authors. Pantheon, 1970. 10–12

§ GOLDSTON, ROBERT C. *The Negro Revolution,* ill. Macmillan, 1968. 13 up

GORODETZKY, CHARLES W., and SAMUEL T. CHRISTIAN. *What You Should Know About Drugs.* Harcourt, 1970. The dispassionate tone and straightforward style add to the usefulness of this source of information for the young reader. 10 up

GURNEY, GENE and CLARE. *The Launching of Sputnik, October 4, 1957: The Space Age Begins.* Watts, 1975. 10–13

HABENSTREIT, BARBARA. *Men Against War.* Doubleday, 1973. A survey of pacific protest from colonial times to today. 12–15

HAHN, JAMES, and LYNN HAHN. *Recycling; Re-Using Our World's Solid Wastes.* Watts, 1973. 9–12

HALL, ELIZABETH. *Why We Do What We Do; A Look at Psychology.* Houghton, 1973. An authoritative discussion of behavior is based on experimental research. 11–14

HAMBLIN, DORA JANE. *Pots and Robbers.* Simon, 1970. 12 up

HARMER, MABEL. *The True Book of Pioneers,* ill. by Loran Wilford. Childrens Pr., 1957. 7–9

HASKINS, JAMES S. *The Consumer Movement.* Watts, 1975. 12 up

§ ———. *The Creoles of Color of New Orleans,* ill. by Don Miller. T. Crowell, 1975. 11–14

———. *Jobs in Business and Office.* Lothrop, 1974. 10–12

———. *The Quiet Revolution.* T. Crowell, 1979. 11 up

———. *Street Gangs, Yesterday and Today.* Hastings, 1974. 13 up

———. *Who Are the Handicapped?* Doubleday, 1978. 12 up

———. *Witchcraft, Mysticism and Magic in the Black World.* Doubleday, 1974. 11–14

HILLER, CARL E. *Babylon to Brasilia: The Challenge of City Planning.* Little, 1972. 10–13

HIRSCH, CARL. *The Globe for the Space Age,* ill. by Burt Silverman. Viking, 1963. A book that traces the development of globes and stresses their advantage over maps in studying the sphere on which we live. 11–14

HOBART, LOIS. *Mexican Mural: The Story of Mexico, Past and Present.* Harcourt, 1963. 15 up

HODGES, C. WALTER. *Magna Carta,* ill. by author. Coward, 1966. An excellent survey of the conditions leading to the signing of the Magna Carta. 10–14

———. *The Norman Conquest,* ill. by author. Coward, 1966. A companion volume to the above title. The text is crisply informational; the illustrations unusually beautiful and informative. 10–14

———. *Shakespeare's Threatre,* ill. by author. Coward, 1964. The beautiful pictures are filled with informative detail and the text is written with simplicity and authority. The book is a delight. 11 up

☆ HOFSINDE, ROBERT (GRAY-WOLF). *Indian Sign Language,* ill. by author. Morrow, 1956. 9–13

☆ ———. *Indian Warriors and Their Weapons,* ill. by author. Morrow, 1965. 8–13

☆ ———. *Indians at Home,* ill. by author. Morrow, 1964. A discussion of six major types of Indian homes. One of the best of the author's books on the cultures of North American Indians. 9–12

§ HOLLAND, JOHN, ed. *The Way It Is,* ill. with photos. Harcourt, 1969. 8–10

HOLLING, HOLLING C. *The Book of Cowboys,* rev. ed., ill. by author and Lucille Holling. Platt, 1968. 12 up

☆ ———. *The Book of Indians,* rev. ed., ill. by author and Lucille Holling. Platt, 1962. 12 up

———. *Minn of the Mississippi,* ill. by author. Houghton, 1951. 10–12

———. *Paddle-to-the-Sea,* ill. by author. Houghton, 1941. 9–11

———. *Tree in the Trail,* ill. by author. Houghton, 1942. 9–12

HOOPLE, CHERYL, comp. *As I Saw It: Women Who Lived the American Adventure.* Dial, 1978. A series of letters, journal and diary excerpts, and other historical documents gives varied accounts of some of the accomplishments in the lives of women in American history. 11 up

HOYT, EDWIN P. *Asians in the West.* Nelson, 1975. 12 up

———. *Whirlybirds: The Story of Helicopters,* ill. by George J. Zaffo. Doubleday, 1961. Attractive color illustrations. 10–13

§ HUGHES, LANGSTON. *The First Book of Africa,* rev. and rewritten, ill. with photos. Watts, 1964. Explorers, missionaries, the history of ancient Africa, and an evaluation of Africa today are included in this fine introductory book. 10–12

§ ———. *The First Book of Negroes,* ill. by Ursula Koering. Watts, 1952. Not comprehensive, but a competent introduction to black history. 9–11

HYDE, MARGARET. *Hotline!* 2nd ed. McGraw, 1976. Although substantially revised and augmented, this contains as before a general discussion of hotlines followed by separate chapters on hotlines for different needs. 12 up

ITALIANO, CARLO. *Sleighs: The Gentle Transportation,* ill. by author. Tundra, 1978. Meticulously detailed and colorful paintings depict a type of sleigh on every page, with a descriptive text below. 9 up

JANEWAY, ELIZABETH. *The Vikings,* ill. by Henry C. Pitz. Random, 1951. Includes a chapter on Vineland. 9–11

§ JENNESS, AYLETTE. *Along the Niger River: An African Way of Life,* photos by author. T. Crowell, 1974. 10 up

———. *The Bakery Factory: Who Puts the Bread on Your Table,* ill. with photos. T. Crowell, 1978. Text and photographs follow each step of the procedures in a bakery factory. Discussions with some of the workers adds special flavor.   9–12

———. *Dwellers of the Tundra: Life in an Alaskan Eskimo Village*, photos by Jonathan Jenness. Crowell-Collier, 1970.   11–14

JENNESS, AYLETTE, and LISA W. KROEBER. *A Life of Their Own: An Indian Family in Latin America*, photos by authors, drawings by Susan Votaw. T. Crowell, 1975.   10–13

JOHNSON, GERALD W. *America Grows Up: A History for Peter*, ill. by Leonard E. Fisher. Morrow, 1960. One of a series of lively and lucid books on the history and government of the United States.   10–13

———. *America Is Born: A History for Peter*, ill. by Leonard E. Fisher. Morrow, 1959.   10–13

———. *America Moves Forward: A History for Peter*, ill. by Leonard E. Fisher. Morrow, 1960.   10–13

———. *The Congress*, ill. by Leonard E. Fisher. Morrow, 1963.   9–12

———. *The Presidency*, ill. by Leonard E. Fisher. Morrow, 1962.   9–12

———. *The Supreme Court*, ill. by Leonard E. Fisher. Morrow, 1962.   9–12

§ JOHNSTON, JOHANNA. *Together in America: The Story of Two Races and One Nation*, ill. by Mort Künstler. Dodd, 1965.   11–14

§ JOSEPH, JOAN. *Black African Empires*. Watts, 1974.   10–12

☆ KAREN, RUTH. *Kingdom of the Sun: The Inca, Empire Builders of the Americas*, ill. with photos. Four Winds, 1975.   12 up

☆ ———. *Song of the Quail: The Wondrous World of the Maya*. Four Winds, 1973. A vivid account of the impressive achievements of the Mayan civilization.   11 up

KAVALER, LUCY. *Dangerous Air*, ill. by Carl Smith. Day, 1967.   12 up

☆ KIRK, RUTH. *David, Young Chief of the Quileutes: An American Indian Today*, ill. with photos by author. Harcourt, 1967. The true story of a Pacific coast tribe that has moved gracefully into modern life while keeping its respect for Quileute tradition.   9–11

———. *The Oldest Man in America: An Adventure in Archeology*, ill. with photos by Ruth and Louis Kirk. Harcourt, 1970. The story of a search for records of prehistoric man is made more dramatic by the fact that a new dam threatened the project.   10–14

KURELEK, WILLIAM. *Lumberjack*, paintings by author. Houghton, 1974. A depiction of life in a Canadian lumber camp.   10 up

———. *A Prairie Boy's Summer*, ill. by author. Houghton, 1975. This (and the title below) recreates in text and pictures the quality of life on a Manitoba farm.   8–10

———. *A Prairie Boy's Winter*, ill. by author. Houghton, 1973.   8–10

★ KURTIS, ARLENE HARRIS. *Puerto Ricans: From Island to Mainland*. Watts, 1965. A simply written survey, with historical background provided.   9–12

☆ LA FARGE, OLIVER. *The American Indian*. Golden Pr., 1960.   10–12

LASKER, JOE. *Merry Ever After: The Story of Two Medieval Weddings*, ill. by author. Viking, 1976.   8–10

LAUBER, PATRICIA. *Too Much Garbage*. Garrard, 1974.   7–9

———. *Who Discovered America? Settlers and Explorers of the New World Before the Time of Columbus*. Random, 1970.   9–11

LAYCOCK, GEORGE. *Beyond the Arctic Circle*. Four Winds, 1978. An informal and multi-faceted text covers geological, biological, sociological, and historical aspects of the arctic region.   10–14

LeSHAN, EDA. *What's Going to Happen to Me? When Parents Separate or Divorce*, ill. by Richard Cuffari. Four Winds, 1978. The message that feelings of fear, anger, and loss are natural and should not be repressed is presented in a clear, candid style.   9–12

§ LESTER, JULIUS. *To Be a Slave*, ill. by Tom Feelings. Dial, 1968. Excerpts from source material, chronologically arranged, give a moving and explicit picture of slavery.   11–14

LIFTON, BETTY JEAN. *Return to Hiroshima*, ill. with photos by Eikoh Hosoe. Atheneum, 1970. A matter-of-fact, serious, objective assessment of the enduring ramifications of the bombing of Hiroshima. Excellent photos.   10–17

LIPSYTE, ROBERT. *Assignment: Sports*. Harper, 1970. A compilation of articles covering many sports and sports figures. The author, sports columnist for *The New York Times*, writes with authority and a facility for quick and vivid character portrayals.   11–15

LISTON, ROBERT A. *Who Really Runs America?* Doubleday, 1974. An analysis of the power structure in the United States.   12–15

§ LOBSENZ, NORMAN M. *The First Book of Ghana*, ill. with photos. Watts, 1960. A competent historical and cultural overview.   9–11

LONGSTRETH, T. MORRIS. *The Scarlet Force: The Making of the Mounted Police*, ill. by Alan Daniel. Toronto: Macmillan, 1953. First in the "Great Stories of Canada" series.   11 up

MACAULAY, DAVID. *Underground*, ill. by author. Houghton, 1976.   10 up

McHUGH, MARY. *Law and the New Woman*. Watts. 1975. A discussion of the variety of specializations within the legal profession.   12 up

☆ McNEER, MAY. *The American Indian Story*, ill. by Lynd Ward. Farrar, 1963.   9–11

MANNICHE, LISE, tr. *How Djadja-Em-Ankh Saved the Day: A Tale from Ancient Egypt*, ill. by author. T. Crowell, 1977. Available in scroll form or folded accordian style, this ancient Egyptian fantasy reads from right to left and is also told in hieroglyphs.   9–11

MAY, JULIAN. *The First Men*, ill. by Lorence F. Bjorklund. Holiday, 1968.   7–9

MEAD, MARGARET. *Anthropologists and What They Do*. Watts, 1965. The interview is used to introduce some of the specialized fields and techniques of anthropology. A lively and informative career guidance book.   12 up

———. *People and Places*, ill. by W. T. Mars and Jan Fairservis and with photos. World, 1959.   12–14

MEADOWCROFT, ENID LA MONTE. *The Land of the Free*, ill. by Lee J. Ames. T. Crowell, 1961.   8–10

★ MELTZER, MILTON. *Bound for the Rio Grande: The Mexican Struggle 1845–1850*, ill. with prints and photos. Knopf, 1974.   12 up

———. *Bread and Roses: The Struggle of American Labor, 1865–1915*, ill. Knopf, 1967.   12–15

● ———. *Never to Forget: The Jews of the Holocaust*. Harper, 1976.   12 up

● ———. *Remember the Days: A Short History of the Jewish American*, ill. by Harvey Dinnerstein. Doubleday, 1974.   12 up

———. *The Right to Remain Silent*. Harcourt, 1972. A comprehensive survey of man's right to refrain from giving self-incriminating testimony.   12 up

● ———. *World of Our Fathers: The Jews of Eastern Europe.* Farrar, 1974.   12 up

§ ———, ed. *In Their Own Words: A History of the American Negro;* Vol. 1, 1619–1865. T. Crowell, 1964.

§ ———, ed. *In Their Own Words: A History of the American Negro;* Vol. 2, 1865–1916. T. Crowell, 1965.

§ ———, ed. *In Their Own Words: A History of the American Negro;* Vol. 3, 1916–1966. T. Crowell, 1967.   12–15

§ MELTZER, MILTON, and AUGUST MEIER. *Time of Trial, Time of Hope: The Negro in America, 1919–1941,* ill. by Moneta Barnett. Doubleday, 1966.   11–14

● MEYER, CAROLYN. *Amish People: Plain Living in a Complex World,* ill. with photos. Atheneum, 1976. Meyer creates an imaginary but very convincing family to illustrate the roles and problems of various positions in an Amish family and to describe various everyday events.   12 up

☆ ———. *Eskimos: Growing up in a Changing Culture,* ill. with photos. Atheneum, 1977. Meyer postulates a year with an imaginary family and gives a vivid and perceptive picture of the cultural patterns of Eskimos living near the Bering Sea.   12–14

MORGAN, EDMUND S. *So What About History?* Atheneum, 1969. In this stimulating and unorthodox approach to history (this is not a history book), the author stresses the significance of historical interpretation of material objects, from discarded junk to imposing government buildings, as evidence of living patterns.   9–11

MORRIS, RICHARD B. *The First Book of the American Revolution,* ill. by Leonard E. Fisher. Watts, 1956.   9–13

MURPHY, JIM. *Weird & Wacky Inventions.* Crown, 1978. Pictures of each invention with multiple choices for guessing what it is or does are followed by the answer and full explanation. Quite useless and totally fascinating.   9–11

§ MUSGROVE, MARGARET. *Ashanti to Zulu: African Traditions,* ill. by Leo and Diane Dillon. Dial, 1976. A paragraph of text on each page of an oversize book describes some aspect of the cultures of twenty-six African tribes. Caldecott Medal.   8–10

☆ NABOKOV, PETER, ed. *Native American Testimony: An Anthology of Indian and White Relations.* T. Crowell, 1978. A tragic record, eloquently expressed, comprised of statements by native Americans of many tribes over four centuries.
                                                            12 up

NAVARRA, JOHN. *Our Noisy World: The Problem of Noise Pollution.* Doubleday, 1969.   11–14

———. *Supertrains.* Doubleday, 1975. Pollution, energy resources, and traffic problems are factors in planning new transportation systems.   9–12

———. *The World You Inherit: A Story of Pollution.* Natural History Pr., 1970.   12–14

● NAYLOR, PHYLLIS REYNOLDS. *An Amish Family,* ill. by George Armstrong. O'Hara, 1975. A competent survey of Amish society is based on a study of a three-generation family.
                                                            11 up

§ NICKEL, HELMUT. *Arms and Armor in Africa,* ill. Atheneum, 1971. The Curator of Arms and Armor for the Metropolitan Museum of Art describes both contemporary and ancient weapons and armor and relates this information to facts about the cultures of the peoples discussed.   9–14

PACE, MILDRED (MASTIN). *Wrapped for Eternity: The Story of the Egyptian Mummy,* ill. by Tom Huffman. McGraw, 1974. A description of Egyptian death practices includes many facts about the culture of ancient Egypt.   10–14

PARNALL, PETER. *The Mountain,* ill. by author. Doubleday, 1971. Pollution ruins the peace and beauty of a mountainside.   5–7

§ PERKINS, CAROL MORSE, and MARLIN PERKINS. *"I Saw You from Afar": A Visit to the Bushmen of the Kalahari Desert,* ill. with photos. Atheneum, 1965. The daily life of the bushmen in photographs and simple text. The treatment is sympathetic and dignified.   9–11

PERL, LILA. *America Goes to the Fair: All About State and County Fairs in the USA,* ill. with photos. Morrow, 1974. A description of fairs past and present.   10–13

POWELL, ANTON. *The Rise of Islam.* Warwick, 1980. A detailed account of Islamic culture until the sixteenth century.
                                                            10–13

PRICE, CHRISTINE. *Made in Ancient Egypt,* ill. Dutton, 1970. Written in a direct and dignified style, this is a fascinating study of the ancient Egyptians through their tombs, temples, and the many artifacts recovered from burial chambers. A dynastic table and map precede the text, which is profusely illustrated.   11 up

PRINGLE, LAURENCE. *The Economic Growth Debate: Are There Limits to Growth?* Watts, 1978.   12 up

———. *Nuclear Power: From Physics to Politics,* ill. with photos. Macmillan, 1979.   12 up

PUGH, ELLEN, with the assistance of DAVID B. PUGH. *Brave His Soul,* ill. Dodd, 1970.   12–15

RAU, MARGARET. *The People of New China,* ill. with photos. Messner, 1978. The focus here is on such aspects of modern life as education, industry, familial relationships, and the arts.   10–12

———. *The People's Republic of China.* Messner, 1974. Gives both historical background and a full discussion of China today.   10–12

RICH, LOUISE DICKINSON. *The First Book of New World Explorers,* ill. by Cary Dickinson. Watts, 1960.   9–11

SANDERLIN, GEORGE. *A Hoop to the Barrel.* Coward, 1974. 11–15

SASEK, MIROSLÁV. *This Is Edinburgh,* ill. by author. Macmillan, 1961.

———. *This Is Greece,* ill. by author. Macmillan, 1966.

———. *This Is Historic Britain,* ill. by author. Macmillan, 1974.   8–11

———. *This Is New York,* ill. by author. Macmillan, 1960.
                                                            8–11

§ SAVAGE, KATHARINE. *The Story of Africa: South of the Sahara,* ill. with photos and maps. Walck, 1961.   12 up

———. *The Story of the United Nations,* maps by Richard Natkiel. Walck, 1962. rev. ed., 1970.   13 up

☆ SCHEELE, WILLIAM E. *The Earliest Americans,* ill. by author. World, 1963.   10–14

☆ ———. *The Mound Builders,* ill. by author. World, 1960.
                                                            10–14

SCHLEIN, MIRIAM. *I, Tut: The Boy Who Became Pharaoh,* ill. by Erik Hilgerdt. Four Winds, 1978. The six-year-old prince begins his story; his friend Hekenefer takes up the tale after Tutankhamun's mysterious death at age eighteen.
                                                            8–10

———. *It's About Time,* ill. by Leonard Kessler. W. R. Scott, 1955.   6–8

SCHNEIDER, HERMAN and NINA. *Let's Look Under the City,* rev. ed., ill. by Bill Ballantine. Scott/Addison, 1954.   8–10

SCHWARTZ, ALVIN. *The City and Its People: The Story of One City's Government,* ill. with photos by Sy Katzoff. Dutton, 1967. An excellent description of a city of 300,000 people, its administrative structure, problems, and planning.   9–12

————. *The Night Workers*, photos by Ullie Steltzer. Dutton, 1966. Interesting chronological treatment.   7–10

————. *Old Cities and New Towns*, ill. with photos. Dutton, 1968.   11–14

SEED, SUZANNE. *Saturday's Child: 36 Women Talk About Their Jobs*, photos by author. O'Hara, 1973. Interviews with women who describe their jobs and how they prepared for them.   12–17

SHIPPEN, KATHERINE B. *The Great Heritage*, ill. by C. B. Falls. Viking, 1947; rev. ed., 1962.   12–16

————. *Miracle in Motion: The Story of America's Industry.* Harper, 1955.   12–17

————. *The Pool of Knowledge: How the United Nations Share Their Skills*, rev. ed., ill. with photos. Harper, 1965.   11 up

————. *This Union Cause: The Growth of Organized Labor in America*, ill. with photos and drawings. Harper, 1958.   13–15

SHOWERS, PAUL. *Columbus Day*, ill. by Ed Emberley. T. Crowell, 1965.   5–8

☆ ————. *Indian Festivals*, ill. by Lorence Bjorklund. T. Crowell, 1969.   5–8

SILVERSTEIN, ALVIN, VIRGINIA, and GLENN. *Aging.* Watts, 1979.   6 up

★ SINGER, JULIA. *We All Come from Puerto Rico, Too*, ill. with photos. Atheneum, 1977. In commentary mostly by children, this gives a rich and varied picture of Puerto Rican life, achieving an antidote to the "poor emigrant" stereotype presented in most children's stories set in Puerto Rico.   8–10

SPERRY, ARMSTRONG. *All About the Arctic and Antarctic*, ill. by author. Random, 1957.   9–11

SPIER, PETER. *The Legend of New Amsterdam*, ill. by author. Doubleday, 1979. Wonderfully detailed paintings support a text that is mostly descriptive with a bit of narrative interest.   7–9

————. *Of Dikes and Windmills*, ill. by author. Doubleday, 1969. A remarkably interesting book about the long struggle of the Netherlands to claim and hold land from the sea. Written with articulate ease, the book contains a large amount of historical information.   11 up

STEELE, WILLIAM O. *Westward Adventure: The True Stories of Six Pioneers.* Harcourt, 1962.   9–11

§ STERLING, DOROTHY. *Tear Down the Walls! A History of the American Civil Rights Movement*, ill. Doubleday, 1968.   12 up

§ ————, ed. *The Trouble They Seen: Black People Tell the Story of Reconstruction.* Doubleday, 1976.   12 up

STEVENS, LEONARD A. *The Town That Launders Its Water*, ill. with photos. Coward, 1971. A California town has eight man-made lakes for recreation, the water reclaimed from sewage.   11 up

§ STEVENSON, JANET. *The School Segregation Cases: (Brown v. Board of Education of Topeka and others): The United States Supreme Court Rules on Racially Separate Public Education.* Watts, 1973. A comprehensive examination of protest, dissent, and legislation about school integration.   10–14

STOUTENBURG, ADRIEN. *People in Twilight: Vanishing and Changing Cultures*, ill. with photos. Doubleday, 1971. A moving description of the struggle to maintain cultural identity.   11–14

STRAIT, TREVA ADAMS. *The Price of Free Land.* Lippincott, 1979. An autobiographical record of the author's family's start as Nebraska homesteaders is illustrated with photographs from the family album.   10–12

SULLIVAN, GEORGE. *How Do They Package It?* Westminster, 1976. Sullivan describes the various kinds of modern packaging, historical developments in the industry, consumer preferences, and ecological problems.   10–12

SWINBURNE, IRENE and LAURENCE. *Behind the Sealed Door: The Discovery of the Tomb and Treasures of Tutankhamun.* Sniffen Court, 1977.   9–12

§ THUM, MARCELLA. *Exploring Black America: A History and Guide.* Atheneum, 1975.   11 up

TOYE, WILLIAM. *Cartier Discovers the St. Lawrence*, ill. by Laszlo Gal. Toronto: Oxford, 1959. An authoritative account of Cartier's three exploratory voyages.   10–12

TRIPP, ELEANOR B. *To America*, ill. Harcourt, 1969. The author, in an unusual approach, has chosen nine highly localized sources of American newcomers, each demonstrating a different reason for coming to a new land. A vivid picture of the diversity of our forebears.   11–14

TUNIS, EDWIN. *Colonial Craftsmen and the Beginnings of American Industry*, ill. by author. World, 1965. Well-organized and superbly illustrated, the text is comprehensive, lucid, and detailed.   11–14

————. *Colonial Living*, ill. by author. World, 1957.   10–12

————. *Frontier Living*, ill. by author. World, 1961.   10 up

☆ ————. *Indians*, ill. by author. World, 1959.   11 up

————. *Shaw's Fortune: The Picture Story of a Colonial Plantation*, ill. by author. World, 1966.   9–12

● ————. *The Tavern at the Ferry*, ill. by author. T. Crowell, 1973.   9–12

————. *The Young United States—1783–1830*, ill. by author. World, 1969.   10–14

UDEN, GRANT. *A Dictionary of Chivalry*, ill. by Pauline Baynes. T. Crowell, 1968.   11 up

UNSTEAD, R. J. *Living in a Medieval Village*, ill. by Ron Stenberg. Addison, 1973. One of a series of informative books about medieval times stresses the occupations of villagers.   9–11

VAN LOON, HENDRIK WILLEM *The Story of Mankind*, ill. by author. Liveright, 1921, rev. ed., 1951. Newbery Medal.   12–14

VIERECK, PHILLIP, comp. *The New Land: Discovery, Exploration, and Early Settlement of Northeastern United States, from Earliest Voyages to 1621, Told in the Words of the Explorers Themselves*, ill. by Ellen Viereck. Day, 1967.   14 up

☆ VON HAGEN, VICTOR W. *Maya, Land of the Turkey and the Deer*, ill. by Alberto Beltran. World, 1960.   11–14

WALTON, RICHARD J. *America and the Cold War.* Seabury, 1969. An important book, this is a detailed and passionate history of the tangled international situation that followed World War II. The author offers neither verdict nor solution and is careful to so state when comments are conjectural.   12 up

WARREN, RUTH. *Pictorial History of Women in America.* Crown, 1975. A survey of women's contributions from colonial times on.   12 up

WHITE, ANNE TERRY. *All About Archaeology*, ill. by Tom O'Sullivan and with photos. Random, 1959.   10–13

————. *Prehistoric America*, ill. by Aldren Watson. Random, 1951.   9–11

WHITNEY, DAVID. *The First Book of Facts and How to Find Them*, ill. by Edward Mackenzie. Watts, 1966. Author discusses the sorts of questions that can be answered by reference books and describes the major types of reference sources. Not comprehensive, but clear; valuable for the discussion of opinions vs. facts and of discrepancies. 9–11

WINN, MARIE. *The Fisherman Who Needed a Knife: A Story About Why People Use Money*, ill. by John E. Johnson. Simon, 1970. A companion book to the following title, this introduces the concept of money as a common medium of exchange. 4–7

————. *The Man Who Made Fine Tops: A Story About Why People Do Different Kinds of Work*, ill. by John E. Johnson. Simon, 1970. A light fictional framework describing the father who made his son a top is used to explain the division of labor. The ideas are perfectly clear and the author wisely stopped when her point was made. 5–7

★ WOLF, BERNARD. *In This Proud Land: The Story of a Mexican American Family*, ill. with photos. Lippincott, 1978. A photo-documentary, straight-forward, objective, and candid, describing a family of Mexican-Americans living in Texas. 11–14

☆ ————. *Tinker and the Medicine Man: The Story of a Navajo Boy of Monument Valley*, photos by author. Random, 1973. A small boy learns the arts practiced by his father, a medicine man. 9–11

ZINER, FEENIE, and ELIZABETH THOMPSON. *The True Book of Time*, ill. by Katherine Evans. Childrens Pr., 1956. 6–8

Religion and the Arts

BANKS, LYNNE REID. *Sarah and After: Five Women Who Founded a Nation*. Doubleday, 1977. Sarah, Hagar, Rebecca, the sisters Leah and Rachel, and Dinah are the women whose lives are described in a novel based on the Bible but fictionalized enough so that the book is more a continuing story than an adaptation. 12 up

BATTERBERRY, ARIANE (RUSKIN). *The Pantheon Story of Art for Young People*, rev. ed. Pantheon, 1975. 10 up

☆ BATTERBERRY, ARIANE and MICHAEL. *The Pantheon Story of American Art for Young People*. Pantheon, 1976. An impressive work which proceeds chronologically from native Americans to white settlers and on through to the twentieth century. 11 up

BATTERBERRY, MICHAEL. *Art of the Middle Ages*. McGraw, 1972. Well organized and cohesive, a beautifully illustrated book. 12 up

BATTERBERRY, MICHAEL, and ARIANE RUSKIN, ads. *Primitive Art*. McGraw, 1973. 12 up

☆ BIERHORST, JOHN. *A Cry from the Earth: Music of the North American Indians*. Four Winds, 1979. A description of American Indian songs and, to a lesser extent, of the instruments used to accompany singers. 11 up

☆ ————, ad. *Songs of the Chippewa*; ad. from the collections of Frances Densmore and Henry Rowe Schoolcraft, and arranged for piano and guitar by John Bierhorst; ill. by Joe Servello. Farrar, 1974. Simple musical notation is provided; lyrics are in English. 9 up

BONI, MARGARET BRADFORD, ed. *The Fireside Book of Favorite American Songs*, arr. for piano by Norman Lloyd, ill. by Aurelius Battaglia. Simon, 1952. From songs of the Pilgrims to ballads of the Nineties. 8 up

BORTEN, HELEN. *A Picture Has a Special Look*. Abelard, 1961. Describes and illustrates some of the media used by artists. 9–11

BRITTEN, BENJAMIN, and IMOGEN HOLST. *The Wonderful World of Music*, rev. ed. Doubleday, 1968. 8–12

§ BRYAN, ASHLEY. *Walk Together Children: Black American Spirit-*uals, selected and ill. by Ashley Bryan. Atheneum, 1974. Only the melodic line is provided, so no musical training is necessary to pick out the notes. 8–10

BULLA, CLYDE ROBERT. *Stories of Favorite Operas*, ill. by Robert Galster. T. Crowell, 1959. Twenty-three libretti of popular operas. 10–14

CHASE, ALICE ELIZABETH. *Famous Artists of the Past*, ill. with reproductions. Platt, 1964. A very good sampling of the works of some two dozen great artists. There is discussion of the artists and some analysis of most of the pictures in the book. 11–15

————. *Looking at Art*, ill. T. Crowell, 1966. 12 up

COLLIER, JAMES LINCOLN. *Inside Jazz*. Four Winds, 1973. 12–15

COMINS, JEREMY. *Art from Found Objects*. Lothrop, 1974. Directions for using scrap to make objects by collage, assemblage, vacuum forming, and other techniques. 10–12

DEEDY, JOHN *The Vatican*, ill. with photos. Watts, 1970. 10–12

DE MILLE, AGNES. *The Book of the Dance*, ill. by N. M. Bodecker. Golden Pr., 1963. Social, ritual, and theatrical dance history in full, with many color photographs. 11 up

§ DIETZ, BETTY WARNER, and MICHAEL BABATUNDE OLATUNJI. *Musical Instruments of Africa*, ill. by Richard M. Powers and with photos. Day, 1965. 11–12

DIETZ, BETTY WARNER, and THOMAS CHOONBAI PARK. *Folk Songs of China, Japan, and Korea*, ill. by Mamoru Funai. Day, 1964. 9 up

DOWNER, MARION. *Discovering Design*. Lothrop, 1947. An analysis of the elements of design in nature. 11 up

————. *The Story of Design*, ill. with photos. Lothrop, 1964. 11 up

ELGIN, KATHLEEN. *The Unitarians*, ill. by author. McKay, 1971. And others in the series. 9–11

EWEN, DAVID. *Opera: Its Story Told Through the Lives and Works of Its Foremost Composers*. Watts, 1972. 12 up

————. *Orchestral Music: Its Story Told Through the Lives and Works of Its Foremost Composers*. Watts, 1973. 12 up

————. *Solo Instrumental and Chamber Music: Its Story Told Through the Lives and Works of Its Foremost Composers*. Watts, 1974. Discusses instruments, composers, and musical forms. 13 up

————. *Vocal Music: Its Story Told Through the Lives and Works of Its Foremost Composers*. Watts, 1975. 12 up

FAULKNER, MARGARET. *I Skate!* ill. with photos. Little, 1979. Profusely illustrated, the text centers around young skaters and is substantial in both extent and coverage. 10–13

GLADSTONE, J. J. *A Carrot for a Nose: The Form of Folk Sculpture on America's City Streets and Country Roads*. Scribner's, 1974. 10–13

GLAZER, TOM. *Eye Winker, Tom Tinker, Chin Chopper: Fifty Musical Fingerplays*, ill. by Ron Himler. Doubleday, 1973. Fifty songs are included, as are directions for hand movements. 5–11

GLUBOK, SHIRLEY. *The Art of America in the Early Twentieth Century*, ill. with photos. Macmillan, 1974. Reflects, more than do most of Glubok's books, the breadth and variety of art forms within a given period. 10–13

————. *The Art of America in the Gilded Age*, ill. with photos. Macmillan, 1974. 9–12

————. *The Art of Ancient Greece*, ill. with photos. Atheneum, 1963. And other books in this series. 10–13

————. *The Art of China*, ill. with photos. Macmillan, 1973. Not comprehensive, but a fine introduction to an art heritage that spans four millennia. 9–11

_____. *The Art of Colonial America*, ill. with photos. Macmillan, 1970.   9–12

_____. *The Art of the Comic Strip*. Macmillan, 1979. Focuses on artistic style.   9–12

_____. *The Art of Egypt Under the Pharaohs*. Macmillan, 1980.   10–12

☆ _____. *The Art of the Plains Indians*, ill. with photos. Macmillan, 1975.   9–12

★ _____. *The Art of the Spanish in the United States and Puerto Rico*, ill. with photos. Macmillan, 1972. Includes architecture, room interiors, crafts, and religious art objects.   8–10

_____. *The Art of the Vikings*, ill. by Gerard Nook. Macmillan, 1978.   9–12

☆ _____. *The Art of the Woodland Indians*, ill. with photos. Macmillan, 1976.   9–11

_____. *Dolls, Dolls, Dolls*, ill. with photos. Follett, 1975.   8–11

GREENFELD, HOWARD. *Books: From Writer to Reader*. Crown, 1976. Greenfeld discusses the roles of each participant in the book-making process and of the steps in production, literary and physical.   12 up

● _____. *Chanukah*. Holt, 1976. A dignified retelling of the episode in Jewish history that is commemorated by Chanukah.   11 up

_____. *The Impressionist Revolution*. Doubleday, 1972.   12 up

● _____. *Passover*, ill. by Elaine Grove. Holt, 1978.   10–12

● _____. *Rosh Hashanah and Yom Kippur*, ill. by Elaine Grove. Holt, 1979.   10–12

_____. *They Came to Paris*. Crown, 1975.   13 up

GRIGSON, GEOFFREY. *Shapes and Stories: A Book About Pictures*. Vanguard, 1965. Perceptive comments about a selected group of pictures.   10–12

HASKELL, ARNOLD LIONEL. *The Wonderful World of Dance*. Doubleday, 1969.   11–14

HASKINS, JAMES. *Religions*. Lippincott, 1973.   11–14

HEMMING, ROY. *Discovering Music: Where to Start on Records and Tapes, the Great Composers and Their Works, Today's Major Recording Artists*. Four Winds, 1974.   12 up

HIRSCH, S. CARL. *Printing from a Stone: The Story of Lithography*, ill. Viking, 1967. A most interesting book that describes the history of lithography. The writing style is straightforward, lucid, and a bit dry.   12 up

HOBAN, TANA. *Look Again!* ill. Macmillan, 1971. A book of photographs that can pique the young child's curiosity. Blank pages with a square cut out of them expose a portion of a picture behind.   2–4

_____. *Shapes and Things*, ill. Macmillan, 1970. This wordless book is illustrated with white-on-black silhouettes.   2–5

☆ HOFMANN, CHARLES. *American Indians Sing*, ill. by Nicholas Amorosi. Day, 1967.   10–13

☆ HOFSINDE, ROBERT (GRAY-WOLF). *Indian Arts*, ill. by author. Morrow, 1971. An intriguing and decorative book on aspects of North American Indian cultures.   8–11

☆ _____. *Indian Music Makers*, ill. by author. Morrow, 1967.   9–12

HORWITZ, ELINOR. *Contemporary American Folk Artists*. Lippincott, 1975.   11 up

§ HUGHES, LANGSTON. *Famous Negro Music Makers*. Dodd, 1955.   11–14

§ _____. *The First Book of Jazz*, ill. by Cliff Roberts, music selected by David Martin. Watts, 1955.   11 up

_____. *The First Book of Rhythms*, ill. by Robin King. Watts, 1954.   11–14

HURD, MICHAEL. *The Oxford Junior Companion to Music*, 2d. ed. Oxford, 1980. Comprehensive and informative.   11 up

JESSEL, CAMILLA. *Life at the Royal Ballet School*, ill. with photos. Methuen, 1979. A most successful effort to show the slow, arduous, dedicated work that goes into becoming a ballet dancer.   11 up

JOHN, TIMOTHY, ed. *The Great Song Book*, ill. by Tomi Ungerer. Doubleday, 1978. Pleasant arrangements of familiar music illustrated by Ungerer at his comic, dramatic, and colorful best.   all ages

§ JOHNSON, JAMES WELDON, and J. ROSAMOND JOHNSON. *Lift Every Voice and Sing: Words and Music*. Hawthorn, 1970. Simply arranged for piano and guitar chords, a song that has endured as a hymn of black hope since it was written in 1900.   9–11

KAHN, ELY JACQUES. *A Building Goes Up*, ill. by Cal Sacks. Simon, 1969.   10–14

KETTELKAMP, LARRY. *Flutes, Whistles, and Reeds*, ill. by author. Morrow, 1962.   9–11

KING, MARY LOUISE. *A History of Western Architecture*, ill. with photos and diagrams. Walck, 1967.   12–16

KREMENTZ, JILL. *A Very Young Dancer*. Knopf, 1976.   9 up

_____. *A Very Young Gymnast*, ill. with photos. Knopf, 1978. Excellent photographs and a text which has the casual intimacy of a child's conversation portray the lifestyle of a dedicated young gymnast.   9 up

_____. *A Very Young Skater*, ill. with photos. Knopf, 1979. An oversize volume with high quality photographs is based on interviews with the ten-year-old narrator.   9–12

☆ § LANGSTAFF, JOHN M., comp. *The Season for Singing: American Christmas Songs and Carols*, musical settings by Seymour Barab. Doubleday, 1974. Some songs are of European origin; Native American and black music are included.   all ages

LARKIN, DAVID, ed. *The Art of Nancy Ekholm* Burkert. Harper, 1977. A splendid showcase of plates (many in color) introduced by a discussion of the artist's career, theories about art, and the techniques and qualities that made up her style.   12 up

LARRICK, NANCY, comp. *The Wheels of the Bus Go Round and Round: School Bus Songs and Chants*, ill. by Gene Holtan. Golden Gate, 1972. Songs—many of which are old favorites—for singing while riding.   8–10

LUTTRELL, GUY. *The Instruments of Music*. Nelson, 1977. Luttrell describes standard orchestral instruments, American folk instruments, the human voice, and electronic instruments, including in his discussion historical background and how each operates.   11–14

MACAULAY, DAVID. *Castle*, ill. by author. Houghton, 1977. Described here is the planning and building of an imaginary but typical Welsh castle and town of the late thirteenth century.   10 up

_____. *Cathedral: The Story of Its Construction*. Houghton, 1973.

_____. *City: A Story of Roman Planning and Construction*. Houghton, 1974.

_____. *Pyramid*. Houghton, 1975. All of Macaulay's books give almost as much information about the culture as they do about the architectural details of the construction of great edifices. The illustrations are profuse and meticulously detailed.   10 up

MANCHEL, FRANK. *The Talking Clowns: From Laurel and Hardy to the Marx Brothers*. Watts, 1976. While this provides a great deal of information about motion picture history, it is really a collective biography of W. C. Fields, Laurel and Hardy, the Marx brothers, and Mae West. 12 up

———. *When Pictures Began to Move,* ill. by James Caraway. Prentice, 1969. One of the best histories of the motion picture industry for young people, ending with the death of the silent film. Good bibliography. 11–14

MAYNARD, OLGA. *American Modern Dancers: The Pioneers.* Atlantic/Little, 1965. 11 up

———. *The Ballet Companion.* Macrae, 1957. 11–15

MOORE, JANET GAYLORD. *The Many Ways of Seeing: An Introduction to the Pleasures of Art,* ill. World, 1968. 13 up

MYLLER, ROLF. *From Idea into House,* ill. by Henry K. Szwarce. Atheneum, 1974. A detailed explanation of the planning and building of a house. 10–14

§ NAYLOR, PENELOPE. *Black Images: The Art of West Africa,* photos by Lisa Little. Doubleday, 1973. Relates art objects to the cultural beliefs and traditions they reflect. 12 up

PAINE, ROBERTA M. *Looking at Sculpture,* ill. Lothrop, 1968. 9 up

POSTON, ELIZABETH, comp. *The Baby's Song Book,* ill. by William Stobbs. T. Crowell, 1972. Includes songs from other languages as well as English in a collection for young children. 2–5

PRATSON, FREDERICK J. *The Special World of the Artisan.* Houghton, 1974. Stresses the creativity of the artisan in pottery, woodcarving, glassblowing, weaving, and making musical instruments. 11–13

§ PRICE, CHRISTINE. *Made in West Africa,* ill. with photos. Dutton, 1975. Descriptions of art objects are arranged by techniques and media. 11 up

§ ———. *Talking Drums of Africa.* Scribner's, 1973. Discusses the drums, the drumming, and the songs and dances of the Ashanti and Yaruba peoples. 8–10

● PURDY, SUSAN GOLD. *Jewish Holidays: Facts, Activities, and Crafts,* ill. Lippincott, 1969. Each holiday is described and each is followed by directions for some project associated with it. Useful for religious education or for craft groups. 10–12

● RADFORD, RUBY L. *Many Paths to God.* Theosophical, 1970. The basic ideas of twelve living religions and many of their parallel teachings. Each chapter has a list of suggested readings. 10–14

REISS, JOHN. *Colors,* ill. by author. Bradbury, 1969. Not only useful for color identification, but for awakening aesthetic appreciation. 2–5

● RICE, EDWARD. *The Five Great Religions,* photos by author. Four Winds, 1973. 12–15

ROCKWELL, ANNE. *Glass, Stones, and Crown: The Abbe Suger and the Building of St. Denis.* Atheneum, 1968. 11–13

ROGERS, W.G. *What's Up in Architecture: A Look at Modern Building.* Harcourt, 1965. Trends, styles, and architects are discussed in informal, lively writing. 11 up

RUDSTROM, LENNART. *A Family,* ill. by Carl Larsson. Putnam, 1980. Oversize pages accommodate the beautiful paintings of one of Sweden's most eminent artists; the text gives information about Larsson and his work. 10 up

RUSKIN, ARIANE. *Art of the High Renaissance,* ill. McGraw, 1970. 12 up

———. *History in Art.* Watts, 1974. Not history as represented in art, but a history of art, authoritative and comprehensive. 12–15

———. *Nineteenth Century Art.* McGraw, 1968. 13 up

———. *The Pantheon Story of Art for Young People,* ill. Pantheon, 1964. 11–14

———. *17th and 18th Century Art,* ill. McGraw, 1969. Lucid

and informative, a book that serves as an excellent introduction to the art history of two centuries, but is comprehensive and authoritative enough for the knowledgeable reader. 12 up

SAMACHSON, DOROTHY and JOSEPH. *The First Artists,* ill. Doubleday, 1970. A competent survey, with good photographs of cave paintings and engravings, more extensive than the usual treatment of the subject. 10–14

● SAVAGE, KATHARINE. *The Story of World Religions,* ill. with photos and maps. Walck, 1967. 13 up

● SEEGER, ELIZABETH. *Eastern Religions.* T. Crowell, 1973. 12–15

SEGOVIA, ANDRES, and GEORGE MENDOZA. *Segovia: My Book of the Guitar; Guidance for the Beginner,* ill. with photographs by Harold Gscheidle. Collins, 1979. Although this gives instruction and might be included as an activities book, it is also in part autobiographical and describes much of Segovia's ideas about music. 10 up

SHAW, ARNOLD. *The Rock Revolution,* ill. Crowell-Collier, 1969. 12 up

SMITH, BETSY. *Breakthrough: Women in Religion,* ill. with photos. Walker, 1978. 10–12

● ☆ SMITH, RUTH, ed. *The Tree of Life,* ill. by Boris Artzybasheff. Macmillan, 1942, 1946. 13 up

SPIER, PETER, ill. *Noah's Ark.* Doubleday, 1977. Save for a poem, this has no text. The pictures are delightful, showing in precise detail the venerable old story. Caldecott Medal. 5–8

———. ill. *The Star-Spangled Banner.* Doubleday, 1973. Pictures are filled with historic details; text includes a discussion of the War of 1812 and a chart of official flags. 8–11

STAMBLER, IRWIN, and GRELUN LANDON. *Golden Guitars, the Story of Country Music,* ill. with photos. Four Winds, 1971. 12–16

STREATFEILD, NOEL. *A Young Person's Guide to Ballet,* ill. by Georgette Bordier. Warne, 1975. 9–12

SULLIVAN, GEORGE. *Understanding Architecture.* Warne, 1971. 10–14

TERRY, WALTER. *Ballet: A Pictorial History,* ill. Van Nostrand, 1970. 10–12

§ WARREN, FRED and LEE. *The Music of Africa: An Introduction,* ill. with photos and line drawings by Penelope Naylor. Prentice, 1970. Includes lists of books and recordings. 11–14

§ WARREN, LEE. *The Dance of Africa: An Introduction,* ill. by Haris Petie, photos by Vyvian D'Estienne and others. Prentice, 1972. 11 up

§ ———. *The Theater of Africa: An Introduction.* Prentice, 1976. Varied and comprehensive. 11 up

WILDER, ALEC, music by. *Lullabies and Night Songs,* ed. by William Engvick, ill. by Maurice Sendak. Harper, 1965. The choice of songs is very good, the arrangements are simple, the lyrics smooth; the illustrations are delectable. all ages

WINN, MARIE, ed. *The Fireside Book of Fun and Game Songs,* musical arrangements by Allan Miller, ill. by Whitney Darrow. Simon, 1974. Amusing pictures, a wide variety of songs. all ages

WOODWARD, IAN. *Ballet and the Dance,* ill. by Peter Revitt. Chatto, 1979. This brief overview begins with a history of the dance and goes on to discuss the components of ballet, the qualities that contribute to the artistry of a dancer, and the work of choreographers. 10–12

YOLEN, JANE, ed. *Rounds About Rounds,* ill. by Gail Gibbons. Watts, 1977. A very nice collection, from the simple to the more intricate. 9–12

Activities and Experiments

ADKINS, JAN. *The Craft of Sail*, designed and ill. by author. Walker, 1973. The text moves from physical principles and facts about sailboats to techniques of sailing.	11 up
———. *Toolchest*, ill. by author. Walker, 1973.	10 up

ALKEMA, CHESTER JAY. *The Complete Crayon Book*. Sterling, 1969.	10 up

ANDERSEN, YVONNE. *Make Your Own Animated Movies: Yellow Ball Workshop Film Techniques*. Little, 1970.	10–13

§ ARCHER, ELSIE. *Let's Face It: The Guide to Good Grooming for Girls of Color*, rev. ed. Lippincott, 1968. Hair, complexion, makeup, clothes, speech, manners are all covered in this guide.	11–14

ASHE, ARTHUR, and LOUIE ROBINSON. *Getting Started in Tennis*, ill. with photos. Atheneum, 1977. Ashe gives a great deal of sensible advice clearly and sequentially.	10–14

BEANEY, JAN. *The Young Embroiderer*. Warne, 1967.	10–13

BOYLAN, ELEANOR. *How to Be a Puppeteer*, ill. by Tomie de Paola. McCall, 1970. Gives directions for making and costuming puppets, manipulating them, making sets and scenery, etc. Plays for a single puppeteer and a group are included.	8–10

BRANLEY, FRANKLYN M., and ELEANOR K. VAUGHAN. *Timmy and the Tin-Can Telephone*, ill. by Paul Galdone. T. Crowell, 1959.	5–7

BRODERICK, DOROTHY *Training a Companion Dog*, ill. by Harris Petie. Prentice, 1965.	9–12

BUNTING, GLENN and EVE. *Skateboards: How to Make Them, How to Ride Them*. Harvey, 1977. The first section is devoted to making wooden skateboards, the rest to photographs and descriptions of basic and advanced figures.	10–14

CARAS, ROGER. *A Zoo in Your Room*, ill. by Pamela Johnson. Harcourt, 1975.	10–13

CASE, MARSHAL T. *Look What I Found! The Young Conservationist's Guide to the Care and Feeding of Small Wildlife*, ill. with photos by author. Chatham/Viking, 1971.	9–11

CHARLIP, REMY, MARY BETH and GEORGE ANCONA. *Handtalk: An ABC of Finger Spelling & Sign Language*. Parents' Magazine, 1974.	8 up

CHEKI HANEY, ERENE and RUTH RICHARDS. *Yoga for Children*, ill. by Betty Schilling. Bobbs, 1973. Simple instructions and adequate warnings about not overdoing.	8–10

COBB, VICKI, and KATHY DARLING. *Bet You Can't! Science Impossibilities to Fool You*, ill. by Martha Weston. Lothrop, 1980. In a text that offers simple, entertaining experiments, the authors cleverly incorporate and explain principles of gravity, mechanics, fluids, logic, energy, and perception.	9–12

COCHRANE, LOUISE. *Tabletop Theatres*, ill. by Kate Simunek. Plays, 1974. Directions for making stages, puppets, and costumes plus scripts for plays.	10–13

COLMAN, HILA. *Making Movies: Student Films to Features*, ill. by George Guzzi. World, 1969. Explicit and very comprehensive, written in a direct style. The advice is pertinent to career guidance.	12–15

COOMBS, CHARLES IRA. *Bicycling*, ill. with photos and diagrams. Morrow, 1972.	10–13

COOPER, ELIZABETH K. *Science in Your Own Back Yard*, ill. by author. Harcourt, 1958.	10–13

CURRELL, DAVID. *The Complete Book of Puppetry*. Plays, 1975.	11 up

CZAJA, PAUL CLEMENT. *Writing with Light: A Simple Workshop in Basic Photography*. Chatham/Viking, 1973.	11 up

DEVANEY, JOHN. *The Story of Basketball*, ill. with photos. Random, 1976. Profusely illustrated, this focuses on the stars, the games (professional, collegiate, and Olympic) and the contests of the recent past.	10–14

FENTEN, D. X. *Indoor Gardening*, ill. by Howard Berelson. Watts, 1974. Brisk, sensible advice about caring for a wide variety of plants.	9–12
———. *Plants for Pots: Projects for Indoor Gardeners*, ill. by Penelope Naylor. Lippincott, 1969. Informal style and precise drawings give information on the propagation, potting, and care and feeding of house plants.	10–14

FERAVALO, ROCCO V. *Easy Physics Projects: Air, Water and Heat*, ill. by Lewis Zacks. Prentice, 1966.	8–10

FERGUSON, ROBERT. *How to Make Movies: A Practical Guide to Group Filming*. Viking, 1969.	13 up

FREEMAN, S. H. *Basic Baseball Strategy*, ill. by Leonard Kessler. Doubleday, 1965.	10–14

GARDNER, MARTIN. *Codes, Ciphers and Secret Writing*. Simon, 1972.	11 up
———. *Perplexing Puzzles and Tantalizing Teasers*, ill. by Laszlo Kubinyi. Simon, 1969.	8–11

GETZOFF, CAROLE. *The Natural Cook's First Book: A Natural Foods Cookbook for Beginners*, ill. by Jill Pinkwater. Dodd, 1973.	9–11

GLUBOK, SHIRLEY, and ALFRED TAMARIN. *Olympic Games in Ancient Greece*. Harper, 1976. The authors describe an imaginary Olympiad of the 5th century B.C.	10–13

HAWKINSON, JOHN. *Pastels Are Great*. Whitman, 1968. The author explains the basic skills of the technique with enticing examples and explicit instructions.	8–10

HELFMAN, HARRY. *Making Your Own Movies*. Morrow, 1970. Lucid instructions on preparation, equipment, and filming.	10–14

HODGSON, MARY ANNE, and JOSEPHINE RUTH PAINE. *Fast and Easy Needlepoint*. Doubleday, 1978. Instructions for seven simple projects as well as tips on making designs, coping with mistakes, and adding finishing touches.	9–12

HOLZ, LORETTA. *Mobiles You Can Make*, ill. by author, photos by George and Loretta Holz. Lothrop, 1975. Clear, step-by-step instructions for making three kinds of mobiles.	10–14

HORVATH, JOAN. *Filmmaking for Beginners*. Nelson, 1974.	11–15

HOWARD, HARRIET SHRIVER. *If You Had a Pony*, ill. with photos by Susan Rosenthal. Harper, 1965.	9–11

HUDLOW, JEAN. *Eric Plants a Garden*, ill. by author. Whitman, 1971. Clear photographs show a beaming young gardener planning, planting, tending, and harvesting his crop.	7–9

HUSSEY, LOIS J. and CATHERINE PESSINO. *Collecting for the City Naturalist*, ill. by Barbara Neill. T. Crowell, 1975.	9–11

JACKSON, CAARY PAUL. *How to Play Better Soccer*, ill. by Don Madden. T. Crowell, 1978. Simply and clearly written, this includes a history of the game, rules, and techniques.	10–14

KADESCH, ROBERT R. *Math Menagerie*, ill. by Mark A. Binn. Harper, 1970.	11–14

KALB, JONAH. *The Easy Hockey Book*, ill. by Bill Morrison. Houghton, 1977. Not a book intended to teach readers to play hockey but a compilation of advice on individual aspects of the game.	8–10

KIDDER, HARVEY. *Illustrated Chess for Children*, ill. by author. Doubleday, 1970. A really fine book for the beginning chess player. The clear diagrams are very helpful as is the proceeding from basic moves to increasingly complicated ones.	10–13

KUJOTH, JEAN. *The Boys' and Girls' Book of Clubs and Organizations.* Prentice, 1975. Gives sources of information for activities and projects described in the text. 9–12

LARRICK, NANCY. *See for Yourself,* ill. by Frank Jupo. American Bk., 1952. 6–8

LASSON, ROBERT. *If I Had a Hammer: Woodworking with Seven Basic Tools,* photos by Jeff Murphy. Dutton, 1974. Shows incorrect as well as correct procedures in completing simple projects. 10–13

LOPSHIRE, ROBERT. *A Beginner's Guide to Building and Flying Model Airplanes.* Harper, 1967. Step-by-step instructions for assembling planes, and many small tips to ensure good workmanship. 10–12

————. *It's Magic?* ill. by author. Macmillan, 1969. Simple tricks are described within the framework of a humorous story. 7–9

MARA, THALIA, and LEE WYNDHAM. *First Steps in Ballet: Basic Exercises for Home Practice,* ill. by George Bobrizky. Garden City, 1955. Twelve basic barre exercises meant to be used in conjunction with formal training. 8–14

MARKS, MICKEY KLAR. *Collage,* ill. by Edith Alberts and with photos by David Rosenfeld. Dial, 1968. 8 up

————. *Painting Free: Lines, Colors and Shapes,* ill. by Edith Alberts and with photos by David Rosenfeld. Dial, 1965. Step-by-step instructions for the beginner interested in abstract painting. 11 up

MEYER, CAROLYN. *Christmas Crafts: Things to Make the 24 Days Before Christmas,* ill. by Anita Lobel. Harper, 1974. 10 up

————. *Saw, Hammer and Paint: Woodworking and Finishing for Beginners,* ill. by Tony Martignoni. Morrow, 1973. Materials and techniques are described; projects range from simple to difficult. 11 up

MEYER, CAROLYN, and JEROME WEXLER. *Rock Tumbling,* photos by Jerome Wexler. Morrow, 1975. 10–14

MILGROM, HARRY. *Adventures with a Paper Cup,* ill. by Leonard Kessler. Dutton, 1968.

————. *Adventures with a Straw,* ill. by Leonard Kessler. Dutton, 1967. 4–7

————. *First Experiments with Gravity,* ill. by Lewis Zacks. Dutton, 1966. A series of home demonstrations, each prefaced by an explanation of the principle involved. 8–10

MOORE, EVA. *The Seabury Cook Book for Boys and Girls,* ill. by Talivaldis Stubis. Seabury, 1971. A very good first cook book containing nine easy recipes. 7–9

MOORE, JIM. *Football Techniques Illustrated,* rev. ed., ill. by Tyler Micoleau. Ronald, 1962. 10–14

MOORE, WILLIAM. *Your Science Fair Project.* Putnam, 1964. 8–13

MOORMAN, THOMAS. *How to Make Your Science Project Scientific.* Atheneum, 1974. 10–14

MORGAN, ALFRED POWELL. *Boys' Book of Science and Construction,* rev. ed., ill. with plates and diagrams. Lothrop, 1959. 11–14

MOTT, CAROLYN, and LEO B. BAISDEN. *The Children's Book on How to Use Books and Libraries,* ill. Scribner's, 1961. Meets a wide variety of elementary grade needs ranging from writing a book review to using reference books and the library catalog. 9–11

NEUMANN, BILL *Model Car Building,* ill. with photos Putnam, 1971. Full instructions on building, painting tools, materials, and adhesives. Big, clear photographs of equipment and procedures. 10–14

OLNEY, ROSS. *Gymnastics,* ill. by Mary Ann Duganne. Watts, 1976. Olney describes equipment, training, clothing, safety measures, differences between men's and women's events, and judging. 9–11

OLNEY, ROSS, and CHAN BUSH. *Roller Skating,* ill. with photos. Lothrop, 1979. 11 up

PARISH, PEGGY. *Beginning Mobiles,* ill. by Lynn Sweat. Macmillan, 1979. A simple, explicit, nicely illustrated project book in a step-by-step format. 7–9

PAUL, AILEEN. *Kids Outdoor Gardening,* ill. by John DeLulio. Doubleday, 1978. A logically organized book for the beginning young gardener. 9–11

PAUL, AILEEN, and ARTHUR HAWKINS. *Kids Cooking.* Doubleday, 1970. 8–11

PETERSON, JOHN. *How to Write Codes and Secret Messages,* ill. by Bernice Myers. Four Winds, 1966. Lucid explanations of an alluring subject. 9–11

PETTIT, TED S. *A Guide to Nature Projects,* ill. by Walt Wenzel. Norton/Grosset, 1966. 9–12

PURDY, SUSAN. *Festivals for You to Celebrate: Facts, Activities, and Crafts.* Lippincott, 1969. 9–12

ROCKWELL, HARLOW. *I Did It.* Macmillan, 1974. 6–7

————. *Look at This,* ill. by author. Macmillan, 1978. Three very simple projects with instructions written for the beginning independent reader. 6–7

ROSS, LAURA. *Hand Puppets: How to Make and Use Them,* ill. by author. Lothrop, 1969. Includes suggestions for a puppet play. 9–12

————. *Mask-Making with Pantomime and Stories from American History,* ill. by Frank Ross. Lothrop, 1975. 9–11

————. *Puppet Shows Using Poems and Stories,* ill. by Frank Ross, Jr. Lothrop, 1970. Each poem, story, or excerpt from a book is provided with production notes. Simple enough for children to use alone, yet good source material for adults. 9–11

ROTH, ARNOLD. *Pick a Peck of Puzzles,* ill. by author. Norton, 1966. Varied selections: riddles, rebuses, tongue-twisters, pictures with hidden clues, etc. 8–10

SARNOFF, JANE, and REYNOLD RUFFINS. *The Code and Cipher Book.* Scribner's, 1975. Includes such variant puzzlers as pig Latin and cockney slang as well as the usual kinds of codes and ciphers. 9–12

SCHNEIDER, HERMAN, and NINA SCHNEIDER. *Science Fun for You in a Minute or Two: Quick Science Experiments You Can Do,* ill. by Leonard Kessler. McGraw, 1975. 7–10

SCOTT, JOSEPH, and LENORE SCOTT. *Egyptian Hieroglyphs for Everyone: An Introduction to the Writing of Ancient Egypt.* Funk, 1968. 11 up

SEGOVIA, ANDRES, and GEORGE MENDOZA. *Segovia: My Book of the Guitar: Guidance for the Beginner,* ill. with photos. World, 1979. Rudimentary information, a series of short musical studies, and a glossary of musical terms. 10 up

SIMON, SEYMOUR. *The Rock-Hound's Book,* ill. by Tony Chen. Viking, 1973. 9–11

SOKOL, CAMILLE. *The Lucky Sew-It-Yourself Book,* ill. by Bill Sokol, Four Winds, 1966. 7–9

SOOTIN, HARRY. *Experiments with Magnetism,* ill. by Julio Granda. Norton/Grosset, 1968. 9–12

SOOTIN, HARRY and LAURA. *The Young Experimenter's Workbook: Treasures of the Earth,* ill. by Frank Aloise. Norton/Grosset, 1965. 8–11

STONE, A. HARRIS. *The Chemistry of a Lemon,* ill. by Peter P. Plasencia. Prentice, 1966. 8–11

SULLIVAN, GEORGE. *Better Gymnastics for Girls.* Dodd, 1977. The bulk of the text is devoted to step-by-step directions for each movement; also included are a brief history of the sport and an explanation of the four events and the evaluation system.   10–14

———. *Better Soccer for Boys and Girls.* Dodd, 1978. Clear diagrams and photographs complement a comprehensive text that describes the way the game is played, explains the rules, and gives detailed advice on each aspect of play.   9–12

———. *Better Softball for Boys and Girls.* Dodd, 1975.   9–14

———. *This Is Pro Hockey,* ill. with photos. Dodd, 1976. A brief history of the game precedes a description of how it is played.   10 up

SWENINGSON, SALLY. *Indoor Gardening.* Lerner, 1975. Simple, explicit, and adequately illustrated.   8–10

TISON, ANNETTE, and TALUS TAYLOR. *The Adventures of the Three Colors.* World, 1971. Shows color mix by use of transparencies.   5–8

UNESCO. *UNESCO Source Book for Science Teaching: 700 Science Experiments for Everyone,* 2nd ed. UNESCO, 1962.   10–14

UNKELBACH, KURT. *You're a Good Dog, Joe: Knowing and Training Your Puppy,* ill. by Paul Frame. Prentice, 1971. Includes warnings on safety of the puppy and very sensible training procedures.   7–9

WEBER, WILLIAM *Wild Orphan Babies: Mammals and Birds.* Holt, 1975.   10 up

WEISS, HARVEY. *Carving: How to Carve Wood and Stone.* Addison, 1976.   11–14

———. *Ceramics from Clay to Kiln.* W. R. Scott, 1964.   10–14

———. *Clay, Wood and Wire: A How-To-Do-It Book of Sculpture.* W. R. Scott, 1956.   8–17

———. *Collage and Construction,* ill. W. R. Scott, 1970. A good do-it-yourself book in art, simple enough for the younger reader, dignified enough for the older. Discusses not only the materials (easy-to-get) and techniques, but artistic conception.   9–12

———. *How to Make Your Own Books,* ill. with photos. T. Crowell, 1974. Instructions for making different kinds of books follow explanations of procedures like folding, binding, and making covers.   10–14

———. *How To Run a Railroad: Everything You Need To Know About Model Trains.* T. Crowell, 1977.   10 up

———. *Model Cars and Trucks and How to Build Them,* ill. with photos, plans, and drawings. T. Crowell, 1974.   9–12

———. *Paper, Ink and Roller: Print-Making for Beginners.* W. R. Scott, 1958.   9 up

———. *Pencil, Pen and Brush: Drawings for Beginners.* W. R. Scott, 1961.   11 up

———. *Sailing Small Boats,* ill. by Peter Barlow. Scott/Addison, 1967.   10 up

WYLER, ROSE. *What Happens If . . . ? Science Experiments You Can Do by Yourself,* ill. by Daniel Nevins. Walker, 1974.   7–9

WYLER, ROSE, and GERALD AMES. *Prove It!* ill. by Talivaldis Stubis. Harper, 1963.   5–8

YOUNG, ED, and HILARY BECKETT. *The Rooster's Horns: A Chinese Puppet Play to Make and Perform,* ill. by Ed Young. World, 1978.   8–9

YOUNG, RAY. *Bridge for People Who Don't Know One Card from Another,* ill. by Tom Dunnington. Follett, 1964. There's no assumption of previous knowledge, yet the author never talks down. A lucid book for beginners.   11 up

PART FOUR:

Bringing Children and Books Together

Chapter Fifteen: Patterns of Response to Literature

Children who are read to, who later discover books that they love to read, and who are able to respond to what they read should grow into adults who love books. They should, and yet too often the interest in reading fades as children mature. That does not have to happen. Adults who are readers and can show their own excitement about books are the key. A teacher or librarian who perceives literature as a part of the elementary curriculum is most important, for it is through continuing and rewarding experiences with literature that children mature into adults who love to read. Those experiences can—and should—include much good oral reading by adults, opportunity for children to talk about what they read and hear, opportunity at times to participate in activities that can enhance response to and understanding of literature. Experiences with literature may be a separate part of the curriculum or a part of the school library program. They may also be consciously woven into other parts of the curriculum so that they permeate language arts and reading and are present, too, in social studies, science, art, and music. The focus, in any event, should be on the many ways of responding to literature.

From the earliest times, people have waited with anticipation for the wandering storyteller, bard, or minstrel. The old tales such as "The Bremen Town-Musicians" must have brought laughter and a muttered agreement that the poor old animals did, indeed, deserve the comforts they won by their own wits. Other tales, such as "Rumpelstiltskin" or "Tom Tit Tot," may have brought a sense of relief that the imp who would strike such a hard bargain was outwitted at the end of the story. "Cinderella" was a wonderful fantasy for poor people as they entered into the role of the poor cinder girl, seeing the ball through her eyes and experiencing her rise from rags to riches.

A good storyteller saw, in the faces of listeners, response to the story, and shared the audience's reactions to the plight of the characters, feeling their suspenseful interaction with a good plot. Sometimes there was response to the style of the telling. People listening to "The Three Billy-Goats Gruff" came to expect and to repeat, with the storyteller, "Who's that walking over my bridge?" and the favorite ending, "Snip, snap, snout. This tale's told out." This variety of response still is heard and seen when children hear a story well told.

The old tales inspire not only the obvious reactions of laughter or tears, but also the deeper sense of a story linking us to human lives over the ages, a story that has been told time and again in many parts of the world. As Paul Hazard wrote, "Once upon a time, . . . at a period so far removed from us that we are unable to visualize it to ourselves, there was the very same story."[1]

1. Paul Hazard. *Books, Children and Men* translated by Marguerite Mitchell, The Horn Book, Inc., 1944, p. 158.

New tales may bring the same quality of response from readers and listeners. A nine-year-old tells of reading and rereading Laura Ingalls Wilder's *The Long Winter* because the descriptions of the blizzards sent chills up her spine and made her wish that she could be with Laura and Mary beside a roaring fire. A five-year-old nods wisely as Peter, in Ezra Jack Keats's *The Snowy Day,* discovers that the snowball he put in his pocket yesterday has melted.

This chapter and the two chapters that follow are concerned with children's response to literature—the different forms it can take and some ways of encouraging it. We start with the assumption that responding to literature is a positive, enriching experience, one we would like to share with children. Very young children react with instinctual pleasure to stories and rhymes. Yet, too often that joy is lost as they grow older. Our concern is to help children retain their spontaneous love for literature. We hope that by giving children books that meet their needs at different ages, we can encourage a range of appropriate responses and, in the end, see them become adults who read with pleasure and true engagement. But activities to encourage response should never be simply busy work. They should be rooted in the material and should serve the needs and interests of the children. This point bears repeating: Activities to encourage response to literature must grow naturally out of the reading, and different responses—both in variety and quality—must be respected and nurtured.

A giggle over some amusing passage and a tear shed in sympathy for a story character's misfortunes are signs that the reader is interacting with the story. Such interaction is the substance of response. Response to literature need not be overt, as with giggles or tears, but we hope it occurs whenever children become involved with books which have stimulating content and are well written. Reading becomes enjoyable when children experience adventure right along with a story character, find answers to their questions in a book of nonfiction, or remember and repeat favorite poems. Literature becomes enlightening when children begin to interpret incidents and conversations which take place in a story, when they begin to tie fictional events to circumstances in their own lives. Books become intriguing as children gain the sophistication needed to understand the themes that run through them, become aware

of the techniques an author has used to develop interesting characters, or begin to appreciate a certain style of writing. Literature can be challenging if children are encouraged to evaluate content in terms of general quality, interesting ideas, or accuracy of information. All of these experiences involve the response of a reader to a book.

Forms of Response

Response can take many forms. It can be overt and immediate. Then again, it may not be distinguishable at once and, perhaps, not ever. Many responses to literature do not surface until long after the book has been put down. Even then, the response may be a composite of responses to many literary works which have influenced the reader. A composite literary response can emerge, for instance, when we try to deal with a minor misfortune by stating our belief in humanity's ability to succeed through perseverance, an idea we may have encountered in many works of literature, popular as well as classic. A response may surface in an unexpected way, as when children respond to a cartoon character with giggles because the character reminds them of Henry Huggins. More clearly defined is the response of children

Viewpoint

To teach children's literature from the point of view of the reader would seem to be the only defensible way to approach the task whether you are teaching literature to children or to adults. If the purpose for teaching is to introduce readers to books to which they can respond and to encourage self-directed reading, then the responsibility for considering the reader's point of view is clearly evident.

Children's literature is taught to children and to adults; it is taught to adults so that they can be more effective when teaching children. The methods used should reflect the teacher's recognition of the interrelatedness of the two groups of students. College students studying children's literature will try to predict the responses of the child who will read or hear the story or poem, i.e., try to see it from the point of view of the reader.—Norine Odland, "Teaching Children's Literature: From the Point of View of the Reader," in *Elementary English*, November 1972, p. 993.

Photograph by Ken Heyman.

book; from group experience with literature through storytelling, choral speaking, story theater, or some other dramatic activity; or from literature presented and accompanied by discussion.[2] A response need not be active. It does not increase in value because it is overt. It is enough that a child has read or heard a literary selection that inspired interaction with the characters or ideas in the work.

We should not insist or even hope that all response to literature be observable. Nevertheless, response frequently can be seen and it can also be encouraged. As teachers or librarians, we can become aware of the occasions which draw a response, the selections that inspire interaction of readers with books, and the signs of response in faces of readers, listeners, or players. Increasing our awareness, we are better able to nurture response and to make it an important part of a child's reading experience. The key is to watch for and acknowledge response without interfering with it. A response is a very personal thing for a child, and if it is made public by an unthinking adult, the youngster's attitude toward reading may be severely affected. It goes without saying that any response should be treated with the utmost respect and that it should be recognized by adults as a sign that the experience with a story or poem has been strong enough to evoke a reaction.

As you note responses children make to literature, you may also absorb information about the kinds of literary selections particular children enjoy. They may be especially alert to aspects of characterization, plot, or an author's way of creating humor or suspense, or empathic with the predicaments of a story character. Use your observations as a guide to book recommendations for the child or ideas for offering active involvement with other books.

This emphasis on literary response is not new. Writing in 1938, Louise Rosenblatt suggested that the point at which a student meets and interacts with a piece of literature is crucial to response.[3] Her interest was in the way that response may bring a recognition of a value structure in the literature. Response may include an awareness of a universal truth that is passed on from one generation to the next

saying, simply, that the story character has the same problems that they themselves have.

Many responses of children and adolescents involve an emotional interaction with the story or with a story character. Other responses are more complex, sometimes involving the emotional response along with an awareness of the meaning of the story or an evaluation of its quality. Occasionally, a response shows the child's ability to note the author's style or means of developing plot or characterization. It is not likely or even desirable that all of these kinds of responses appear at the same time. If we set a priority, very likely the most important form of response is involvement with a story. Without emotional interaction, young people are not likely to go on to develop a broad range of responses.

Literary response can stem from the experience of an individual child with an individual

2. D. W. Hardy, "Response to Literature; The Report of the Study Group," in *Response to Literature*, ed. J. Squire (Nat. Council of Teachers of English, 1968).

3. Louise Rosenblatt, *Literature as Exploration* (Appleton, 1968; 1938).

through the literary tradition. Such awareness may help a young reader to cope more easily with life's problems.

More recently, the 1966 Dartmouth Conference papers showed a clear focus on the importance of response to the literary experience. Scholars from Great Britain and the United States met to consider the relationship of response to literary experiences at all age levels. Strong recommendations were made for an elementary English curriculum which allows students to respond to aspects of literature which affect them personally—to make an emotional response as well as a response to literary form and style.

A number of researchers in recent years have investigated the nature and form of literary response. Two of them, James Squire and Alan Purves, have made important contributions to our knowledge about responses of older students, and the information has triggered interest in the responses of younger students, as well. The work of those two men will be used here to provide a framework for the discussion of literary response.

The Emotional Reaction

When we become engaged with a story we are reading so that we interact with it, one of the consequences is an emotional response to the work. Test this out by thinking of a piece of fiction you have read and become involved with. Emotional response is shown when a child comments that she could almost feel the cold on the frozen tundra as she read about Julie's experiences with survival (Jean George's *Julie of the Wolves*). When children remark that the bully, Martin, in Mary Stolz's *The Bully of Barkham Street* is like a school bully who terrifies many of them, they are making personal responses to the story. Similarly, children who remark that the house in Elizabeth Hill's *Evan's Corner* looks much like their own are reacting in a personal way. You can also observe nonverbal emotional responses. Emotional reaction can show in children's body movements and in facial expressions when they read or listen to stories. Nonverbal response is evident, too, in dramatization and in pantomime.

Far from being a low-level response to literature, as some English specialists in the past suggested, the emotional response is probably the most important base upon which to build other responses, those involving evaluations of the literary qualities of a work or interpretation of the selection. In fact, Squire, studying the responses of ninth- and tenth-grade students to short stories, found that students who were personally involved with the stories also responded by evaluating the literary qualities of those works.[4] We do not know just how the two forms of response complement each other, but the evidence does at least show the importance of involvement.

In a study of the elements of response present when students write about a work of literature, Alan Purves and Victoria Rippere identified a number of responses termed "engagement-involvement."[5] They range from personal reaction to the work or the author to involvement with characters and relating incidents in the story to the reader's own life. As you begin to bring children actively together with books you will find that many such responses result, though they are more likely physical or oral, than written. The child who expresses pleasure on hearing another story by Robert McCloskey is showing engagement with the work of a particular author. Another youngster who laughs at old Sneep in McCloskey's *Lentil* and comments that he'd like to see the school principal in the same position is making an emotional response to the work. A student responding to Farley Mowat's *Owls in the Family* by describing his own hilarity when his dog chased its tail so hard it tripped and rolled over and over, is showing emotional reaction to the story.

Children who can respond through pantomime may show emotional involvement in their evident relish of a character part or a particularly interesting scene. One child was so engrossed in her characterization of Goldilocks that she forgot to be frightened when Little Bear woke her up. Instead, she greeted him joyfully and took him on home with her to meet her parents! Dramatization opens many doors to active involvement with a story, as does oral interpretation of literature. Emotional response is present, too, when children read or speak character parts with evident enjoyment and good interpretation. Such emotional responses should be valued and encouraged.

4. James R. Squire, *The Responses of Adolescents While Reading Four Short Stories* (Nat. Council of Teachers of English, 1964).

5. Alan C. Purves with Victoria Rippere, *Elements of Writing About a Literary Work; A Study of Response to Literature* (Nat. Council of Teachers of English, 1968).

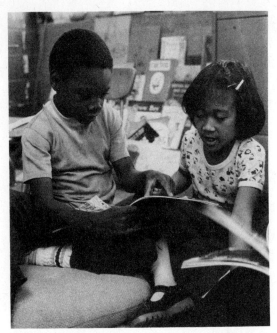

Photograph by Elizabeth Crews.

The Interpretive Reaction

Teachers and librarians responsible for recommending books to children hope that their recommendations will be books that readers can relate to and interpret. Teachers of reading are (or should be) very concerned about developing interpretation skills. Therefore, it is important to look for and recognize interpretive responses that children are capable of making and to provide opportunities for them to gain experience in interpreting literature.

Several types of interpretive response have been identified.[6] Responses made by relatively unsophisticated readers generally have to do with interpretation of stylistic devices such as metaphor, allusion, irony, and symbols; inferences about happenings prior to and following the action of the story, based on information given in the text; and inferences about the nature of a character, about the setting, or about the author's motive.

A child makes an inference or an interpretation when she decides that Russell Hoban's *A Bargain for Frances* was probably written because the writer wanted to show that it is not good to trick your friends. Another inferential response is saying that Sara, in Betsy

6. Ibid., pp. 30–41.

Byars' *Summer of the Swans*, was really a great person but she was kind of hard to get along with because she didn't have much self-confidence. A student may be so inspired by the clear descriptions in Sheila Burnford's *The Incredible Journey* that he asks to illustrate several of the most memorable scenes. His explanation, that he wants to re-create an atmosphere that goes beyond the bare description, suggests that he is making inferences about the setting and is reconstructing scenes from the story.

We cannot emphasize strongly enough that much of what seems essentially interpretation of a story has with it a solid element of personal involvement. If the personal reaction triggers enough interest in a character, setting, bit of action, or underlying idea, the reader will be willing to enter into the spirit of the work and try to interpret it. The obvious need is for us as adults to provide material for response that intrigues, excites, or simply compels the reader to become immersed in the story.

The Critical Reaction

James Squire, in his study of adolescents' responses, defines a category of responses in which the reader judges the general literary quality of the story or reacts specifically to language, style, or characterization. In the Purves classification scheme, some responses to literary elements are included which can be seen in reactions of even young children. They are those responses that show attention to the language and the content of a work. Responses dealing with language include comments a reader makes about writing style, use of rhetorical devices such as personification, use of metaphor and simile, and of imagery. The reaction to language also includes response to the author's use of dialogue and description. The response to content includes reactions to the subject matter or topic, to action in the work, to character description, character relationships, and setting. Other responses identified by Purves as literary perception responses and of interest here are reactions to plot, mood, point of view assumed by the author, and attempts to define the genre of the work.

An example of a child's reaction to literary qualities is a statement that a book was boring because there was not enough action. A child who smiles over a poem because it is a limerick is responding to a literary element. So is a child who expresses pleasure over the perfect little people Mary Norton creates in *The Borrowers.* A reader may laugh at Astrid Lindgren's *Pippi Longstocking* because the author always lets Pippi get the better of adults who try to take advantage of her. Recognizing the author's way of developing humor is a response to a literary element.

Children's responses to literary characteristics may be as specific as: "I didn't get interested in any of the characters because there wasn't enough information about how they looked and felt." Literary judgment may also reflect the specific interest in language, as when a child repeats over and over the line, "I think mice are nice," and pronounces it a favorite line because of the good sound of *mice* and *nice.* On a more general level, children have been known to respond to a book by wondering, aloud, why the author bothered to write it or by excitedly asking whether there are any other books in the library that are like that one.

Responses that reflect some degree of literary judgment often reflect a strong emotional response as well, as is shown by the above examples. We may encourage the literary dimension of a response, if it seems appropriate, by taking a few minutes to talk with the child about the

way an author is developing humor, or what an author might do to make a story character really interesting by use of dialogue as well as description.

The Evaluative Reaction

Although Squire includes judgments about the story in the same category as comments about the literary qualities of the work, he defines another kind of judgment which he calls a "prescriptive judgment." Responses in this category are those in which a reader tells what he or she thinks a character ought to do, based on some absolute standard. Such responses occurred infrequently in the patterns of ninth- and tenth-graders he studied and may not be very common among responses made by young children, either.

Purves, in his scheme for classifying responses, identifies a whole group of responses he terms "elements of evaluation." Among them are responses in which the reader evaluates the emotional appeal of the story. In addition, there are responses which evaluate an author's method: for instance, whether a work is a good or bad example of its genre (as a good or bad poem), or whether the author has used a fresh and interesting approach. Another kind of evaluative response deals with the moral significance of the work and the moral acceptability of lessons taught through the work.

Children are likely to make some kinds of evaluative responses more frequently than others. You should be alert to them so that they can be acknowledged and perhaps discussed further. The prescriptive judgment is easily recognized and can be expanded through discussion. For example, if a reader says emphatically that Harriet, in Louise Fitzhugh's *Harriet the Spy,* ought to throw away her notebook, it would be interesting to ask the child why Harriet might need to keep her notebook about people. What good is it doing her? By helping a reader to explore a response, some reaction to the literary characteristics may also emerge. At the elementary level, however, we are not as interested in instruction as we are in releasing response in children.

We hear fairly often evaluative responses which represent some of the types included in the Purves scheme. Children who say a book is one of the funniest they have ever read are responding with an affective evaluation. A reader

Viewpoint

Our aim, then, should be to refine and develop responses the children are already making—to fairy stories, folk songs, pop songs, television serials, their own game-rhymes, and so on. Development can best be described as an increasing sense of form. In literature, I have suggested this means principally a sense of the pattern of events, and this, however rudimentarily, children certainly feel in the stories that satisfy them. . . . Progress lies in perceiving gradually more complex patterns of events, in picking up clues more widely separated and more diverse in character, and in finding satisfaction in patterns of events less directly related to their expectations and, more particularly, their desires; . . .

But the forms of language itself—its words with their meanings and associations, its syntax, its sounds and rhythms, its images—these contribute to the total form, not as fringe benefits but as inseparable elements of a single effect.—James Britton. "Response to Literature" in *Response to Literature* edited by James R. Squire, National Council of Teachers of English, 1968, pp. 4–5.

who likes this mystery because the plot is different from most is evaluating the author's method of writing as well as evaluating the selection as a good example of its genre. The following response to Robert Lipsyte's *The Contender* shows an evaluation of the moral significance of the book: "It's worth reading because it shows that if you work hard you can get ahead."

Levels of Response

The preceding discussion of responses purposely did not give a value judgment on which kind of response—emotional, interpretive, critical (literary judgment), or evaluative—is most important or sophisticated. All are important and frequently occur in combination with each other. If we were to judge which response mode is most important for elementary school children, the answer would undoubtedly be emotional involvement.

There is a growth factor observable in response, as shown by a study of responses of children in grades three through twelve.[7] The pattern in that study showed that the youngest subjects, the third-graders, made a large number of responses that were literal retellings of the story, as well as some that were evaluative. Fourth-grade students were beginning to add personal involvement responses to the narration and, by fifth grade, children were making fuller retellings of the stories along with evaluations and personal reactions. At the sixth-grade level, interpretive responses began to emerge. The proportion of interpretive responses continued to increase at succeeding grade levels. The interpretive response, then, can be seen as a sign of greater maturity.

Retelling the Story

When we are asked to discuss or react to books we have not really understood, our response is likely to be a retelling of the material we have read. Our response may not include any emotional reaction and we usually do not attempt to interpret the work. Essentially, our response

is literal. It might be considered a less mature or lower-level response than one which involves interpretation or evaluation of the story.

When you discuss books with children, you may find that often your question of "Why did the story end this way?" is met with an answer that is nothing more than a narration of the entire story, without any attempt to interpret events to determine why the author gave it such an ending. It may, at first, seem that the child is avoiding your question. More likely, the child has not reached a level of maturity or experience to be able to respond on a higher level, or perhaps the story was too complex or difficult for the reader. We should recognize if either case is true and offer children opportunities to develop the ability to interpret and evaluate literature and, certainly, to interact with that literature on an emotional level.

Discussing some of his findings concerning the child's response to story, Arthur Applebee notes that at Piaget's preoperational stage of development, up to approximately age seven, the most common verbal response is to retell part or all of the story.[8] Children at this stage are likely to have little sense of the structure of the plot, but are more likely to view it as a succession of separate incidents. As children move into the concrete operations stage, they begin to separate their objective responses from the subjective ones. Although they may not be aware of the distinction, their responses indicate that they recognize a difference between their personal responses and responses that point out some characteristic of the story, such as the genre. Chapter 2 describes other differences in response that may be related to levels of development.

Becoming Involved with Story Characters

Children who express involvement with a story or a character and who make some inferences based on information presented are responding to key story elements. At the elementary school level, the emotional and interpretive responses are probably the most important responses because they allow readers to enter completely into a story and to relate it to their own experiences.

At this level, watch for responses that indicate feeling about the treatment of a story

7. Alan C. Purves, "Research in the Teaching of Literature," *Elementary English*, April 1975, pp. 463–466.

8. Arthur N. Applebee, *The Child's Concept of Story: Ages Two to Seventeen* (University of Chicago Press, 1978).

character or the outcome of a plot. After reading *The Incredible Journey*, a boy remarked with emotion that he suffered along with the old dog but admired him for his persistence and thought it showed that animals, as well as people, will often suffer great hardships if they think the cause is worth it. Another reader commented at the end of a mystery story that it was exciting and the plot ended as she thought it would because one of the clues in the first chapter helped her figure out the solution. A young child responds to Pat Hutchins's *Rosie's Walk* first with squeals of delight at the plight of the fox and then a pronouncement that she guessed the fox deserved it since he was trying to hurt Rosie and he didn't really watch where he was going.

When children interact emotionally with stories, they frequently become involved with characters with whom they can identify. Sometimes readers also meet characters whose lives are very different from their own. The child who reads William Armstrong's *Sounder* and learns from it what it is to be poor and discriminated against may be seeing the problems of ill-treated people for the first time. A youngster, listening to the story of the life of a barrio child, wonders at the problems of daily existence many children face. Discussion and role-playing of story characters' problems can bring children into closer relationship with the characters and help them to begin to develop a sense of empathy.

A scale of empathic behavior, developed on the basis of elementary school children's responses to filmed literature, is shown at right. While these findings are based on response to film, they have a clear application to children's response to literature as well.

The ascending order of behavior begins with simple imitation of behavior and moves to a conscious feeling for or against another person. The level of conscious feeling is superseded by conscious placement of value on both oneself and another which is known as goodwill. At the highest level of response, the person realizes that understanding of self and others is important because each profits from the welfare of the other.

A student responding at the first level on the empathic hierarchy to Jean Little's *From Anna* might simply imitate Anna as a caricature of someone who doesn't see well and bumps into things. At a higher level, the child might observe that Anna was different because she did

A Hierarchy of Empathy

I. **Identification.** A sensory-motor response shown as imitation of self or another. It is carried out purely for its own sake and is seen in facial expressions, body posture, movement, or sounds of a person or animate being that is observed.

II. **Differentiation.** An affective response characterized by conscious awareness of feeling for or against another, *Differentiation* occurs in dramatized or verbalized expression of difference between self and other. At this level, empathy can take the form of *Resistance*, shown through exaggerated imitation in body or speech and physical or verbal withdrawing from a person. It can also emerge as *Re-identification*, shown through behavior such as friendly imitation in body, sound or speech, friendly overtures, gentle teasing, joining another person's plans.

III. **Empathy.** This primarily cognitive response also includes sensory-motor and affective response. It is characterized by active consideration of and placement of value on both self and other to generate goodwill. The highest stage constitutes altruistic goodwill or empathy.

Dorothy Jean Woodbury. "A Hierarchy of Empathy" from *Toward a Theory of Empathy: A Developmental Hierarchy Applied to Response to Filmed Literature*, an unpublished doctoral dissertation. University of Washington, 1975, pp. 57–60.

not have good vision but that she had the same feelings about wanting to do well in school that other people have. At the highest level, a reader might note that a sighted child who got to know Anna and help her could learn about the problems of being partially sighted and could help other people. Role-playing a situation can lead students to identify with and eventually begin to understand the fears and difficulties of others. Such responses can best be described as emotional. At the same time, however, they may also be interpretive since the reader is trying to interpret the motives and behavior of story characters.

You can provide a basis for development of empathy by giving young children time and opportunity to interact with literature. Well-chosen stories can influence the way children view themselves in relation to others. A sensitively written story such as Anne Holm's *North to Freedom* is best read independently so that children can think about the subtle implications for understanding people who are different from them. Other stories, excerpts, or poems may be more effective if interaction is developed through dramatic activities such as role-playing or through discussion. When you read literature that seems to have special significance for value formation, think about ways to encourage interaction with it.

Whenever educating for the development of children's values is suggested, there are concerns that the instruction may become a way of imposing a set of values on them. It is important to keep in mind that value clarification ought to be a means of helping children make moral decisions. The purpose is to give experience in decision making by considering the consequences of an action and weighing the positive points against the negative ones. Children should be encouraged to reflect in those decisions the values inherent in their backgrounds; thus the work with valuing need not be perceived as a means of maintaining the values of the predominant cultural group.

Of the value hierarchies that have been developed, the classification of levels proposed by Lawrence Kohlberg is perhaps the most useful (See page 35). Kohlberg's hierarchy resembles Woodbury's empathy hierarchy in that there is a shift, with maturity, from a self-centered response to one which recognizes mutual respect and universality of application.

A valuing response to literature can come from reading a book like *The Bully of Barkham Street*. Children are able to identify Martin's re-

curring problem—the teasing he gets from classmates because he is fat. When they look at his actions in the first part of the story, as he tries to deal with his problem, they see that he strikes out at children younger than himself whom he can easily out-fight. He also eats more because he dislikes himself for his actions. The consequences are that he sinks deeper into his original problems. Not until his teacher helps him to understand himself is Martin able to change his behavior and to see changes in the consequences of his actions. He becomes, in the end, slimmer and happier. There are many situations in the book which can be used for role-playing or discussion.

Children can experience and respond to characters like Queenie in Robert Burch's *Queenie Peavy*. At the beginning of the story, she acts at the amoral level, doing what she pleases even though she knows she will be punished. As she matures, she progresses at least to the rule-oriented conformist level. Another story character, Kate, in *The Good Master* by Kate Seredy is purely opportunistic at the start but, by the end of the sequel, *The Singing Tree*, she has moved up to a level of valuing which shows some ability to deal on an ethical level. Many stories show a child character who at first cares only about pleasing peers, but who learns to forego peer pressure and to abide by rules which are, presumably, for the good of all. Our main concern is to be sure children see how clearly a good writer can show a character's thoughts and actions so that we can examine the valuing process that is taking place.

We approach value exploration through literature from an emotional response coupled with character interpretation. We can recognize and encourage reader interaction with the values of story characters. Using techniques for discussion, role-playing, and puppetry, it is possible to enhance the process of personal value formation.

Response and Reading Comprehension

The relationship of literary response to reading comprehension is an important idea for teachers and librarians who work with children of elementary school age, for a good literary experience can help to develop the higher-level comprehension skills necessary for effective reading. On the other hand, a good reading

Viewpoint

Identification serves several purposes. First, readers can discover their own problems when they perceive the problems of others. . . .

The fact that the reading process is a private one is an advantage to children with problems. Self-awareness often grows when we are alone. Books fit well into the human need for solitude, for reading is a private experience that allows our inner resources to grow while no one is looking. . . .

If readers wish to rehearse solutions to their dilemmas, they can do it without observation or interference. The identification process often evokes thought about solutions when readers realize that a character has coped with a situation. . . . At times readers then become more amenable to translating their thoughts into action and to making decisions that had formerly been repressed, set aside, postponed, or thought impossible.—Joanne E. Bernstein, *Books to Help Children Cope with Separation and Loss*, R. R. Bowker Company, New York, 1977, p. 25.

program which aims to develop a child's ability to make inferences about, evaluate, and appreciate literature can also enhance children's response to literature.

Writing about the development of reading comprehension abilities, Robert Ruddell describes comprehension as occurring on three levels—*factual, interpretive,* and *applicative.*[9] He notes that the *factual* level involves mostly the information and ideas the reader finds. A child comprehending at the *interpretive* level, however, analyzes the information and infers such relationships as cause and effect, infers main ideas, and predicts the outcome of an event in the story. Also at this level, readers begin to deal with their own values by inferring or interpreting character traits or identifying the author's motive. They bring personal judgment and their own experiences to bear on their interpretations.

At another comprehension level, which Ruddell terms *applicative,* readers apply the knowledge from the story to new situations, make and substantiate value judgments, and engage in problem solving. The comprehension skills at the interpretive and applicative levels can be related to the literary response abilities we have been discussing. At the interpretive level, the ability to infer is closely related to the interpretive response to literature. A child who identifies traits of a key story character by inferring from that character's actions, speech, and unspoken thoughts, is engaging in character trait analysis and also noting, though perhaps not intentionally, the techniques an author uses to develop a character. Thus, a child may describe the protagonist in Beverly Cleary's *Henry Huggins* as a boy who is not especially brave or confident and may judge Henry's actions as inappropriate by suggesting a better way to deal with a problem. In response to the follow-up question, "Why doesn't Henry seem to have much self-confidence?" a child may reply that Henry was not sure he could convince his mother to let him keep the stray dog. The reader may also note that Henry sounds fearful when he calls his mother and that his lack of confidence is also clear when he tries to get on the bus with his dog. Such responses do indicate that the reader is aware of some ways an author can give depth to characterization. Many children would make an emotional as well as a literary

9. Robert B. Ruddell, *Reading-Language Instruction; Innovative Practices* (Prentice-Hall, 1974).

response to a question about Henry Huggins. Some would admit that they sometimes act the way Henry does or that they would be embarrassed—or would laugh—if they had the same predicament on the bus as Henry had when the dog got loose. Children may also suggest that Henry did not use good sense in handling the problem but should have tried some other scheme or given up entirely on the new dog. Value judgments call for a knowledge about the character and the situation. They also require the reader to infer and predict on the basis of what is known. Furthermore, an emotional response gives reason to believe that the child is responding to the story as a piece of literature and that the author has succeeded in drawing captivating characters and situations. The evidence of literary response is even more clear at the applicative level where readers are expected to make value judgments and to substantiate those judgments by referring to the story.

Mature readers understand the material and are able to relate it to their own experiences or to other information that they have. Reading comprehension, then, is the key to literacy. Although literary responses and reading comprehension skills are not specifically the same abilities, there are relationships which can be identified and used so that development of reading skills grows naturally into a mature response to literature. These relationships can be seen in the table on page 512, which juxtaposes the Barrett Taxonomy of Reading Comprehension and the literary responses we have been discussing.

The Barrett Taxonomy includes affective as well as cognitive reading skills. The addition of affective responses to reading, shown in the category termed "Appreciation," draws the classification toward the concerns we have about response to literature—emotional involvement with the story or poem *plus* an at-

Reading Comprehension Skills and Literary Response

Reading
Comprehension* ←——————→ Literary Response

Literal Recall ←——————→ **Narration**

Recall of details, main idea, sequence, comparisons, cause and effect, character traits

Squire's term for a factual retelling of the story**

Inference ←——————→ **Interpretation**

Inferring supporting details, main idea, sequence, comparisons, cause and effect, and character traits; predicting outcomes; inferring literal meanings from figurative language

Making sense of the story; relating the work to what the reader knows about life

Evaluation ←——————→ **Evaluation**

Judgments of reality/ fantasy; fact/opinion; adequacy/appropriateness; worth, desirability, or acceptability

Literary judgment— judgments of the worth of a story or of the quality of writing, depth of characterization, or effectiveness of plot; comments about the appropriateness of a character's behavior

Appreciation ←——————→ **Emotional Involvement**

Emotional response to content, plot or theme; reaction to author's use of language

Comments showing interaction with a story or poem which may reflect joy, excitement, dislike or a range of other emotions

* Adapted from Barrett, Thomas C., "A Taxonomy of Reading Comprehension," *Reading 360 Monograph (1972).* Lexington, Massachusetts, Ginn and Company (Xerox Corporation). Reprinted by permission.

** See James Squire, *The Responses of Adolescents While Reading Four Short Stories* (Nat. Council of Teachers of English, 1964).

tempt to interpret it, evaluate it, and, perhaps, discuss aspects of its literary structure.

When we look at the reading comprehension and response to literature schemes together, the interrelationships are clear. A response to a story or poem which is simply a retelling appears to be similar to and rest upon the comprehension skills identified as literal recall. This

retelling relies mainly on the ability to recall details in sequence.

The details might be important if the reader uses them to infer cause and effect, to figure out the solution to a mystery, to interpret the behavior of a story character, or to form a response to the beautiful setting described by an author. Unless the information that is recalled is extended to other modes of response, the factual retelling is of no great importance when we talk of literary response. Recalling information about character traits can be useful if a child goes on to see how an author develops characterization. Similarly, recall of sequence may be important when a child points out similar plots in two stories. Recognizing character traits and plot structure in these two instances constitutes a response to literary qualities. A number of inferential comprehension skills are important when children respond to literature by trying to interpret it.

Children who have developed skills of inference have background for comparing the clothing of Laura and Mary (the *Little House* books) with current clothing styles (inferring comparisons), talking about why an author included certain characters in the story (inferring cause and effect), or suggesting events that could occur after the story has ended (inferring sequence).

A child who says of *Owls in the Family*, "Wol's bad experience when he first flew came because he didn't have a mother owl to teach him how to fly," shows comprehension of cause and effect. If you look at the statement in terms of literary response, it shows an *interpretation* of a story character's problem.

The difficulties of Ramona (*Ramona the Pest* by Beverly Cleary) were explained by one child as caused by the fact that Ramona wants to do the right thing but usually doesn't succeed. That child cited several instances when Ramona's obedience actually got her into trouble (as when she sat in her seat all morning "for the present"). The character interpretation is built on character trait inference. By asking open-ended questions ("why" rather than "what, who, and where"), you give children experience with inference. Those "why" questions can enrich reading instruction as well as discussion of literature.

Evaluative reading is an important skill which is related directly to evaluation of literature, as was shown in the chart.

This classification of reading skills which in-

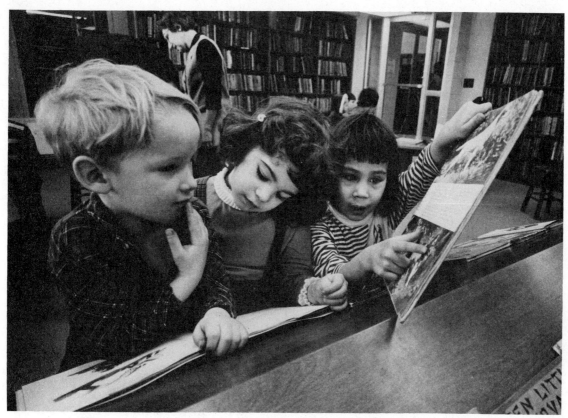

Photograph by Ken Heyman.

cludes affective as well as cognitive abilities also shows the close relationship between reading comprehension and emotional involvement with literature—in this case, appreciation.

Children who are encouraged to respond to characters, content, plot, and theme and to react to the author's use of language are being given experiences that can open the door to a satisfying emotional response to literature. Children who have begun to show involvement with literature may respond with comments like these: "I just hated Martin (*The Bully of Barkham Street*) until he stopped beating up on little kids," "That description of the doughnuts (*Homer Price* by Robert McCloskey) falling all over the floor was really funny," or "If I had been Ramona, I would have pulled that girl's curls, too."

In Barrett's taxonomy, the appreciation skills are based on inference and evaluation. The appreciation level represents ability to react emotionally in addition to grasping the meaning of the story. The emotional reaction can be consciously fostered through the reading program.

Emotional response is a base for other responses which occur at the same time or even at later stages of development and therefore the emotional response must be encouraged and emphasized whenever possible.

When you are aware of the important ties between reading instruction and a literature program, you can strengthen them by building experience with literature into the reading program. You can also extend reading experiences by encouraging children's response to books during library and free reading periods.

Interpreting Pictures

Young children are often taught, as a part of the beginning reading program, to get information from pictures and to interpret them. When they are asked for factual information, they are then often asked to use that information to predict what will happen to characters in the pictures or to interpret what is taking place in the scene.

Picture reading is very likely an important readiness activity for literary response as well as for reading comprehension. A child who is asked to "tell the story" in a book that is completely or almost entirely without text is being asked to respond to the illustrations. John Goodall's *The Ballooning Adventures of Paddy Pork* and Mercer Mayer's *The Great Cat Chase* are examples of wordless books that give children a chance to infer a story from illustrations. Young children of kindergarten age and below may, as often as not, respond with a factual account of what they see in the pictures. Older or more mature "picture readers" are more likely to respond by combining factual observations with their own inferences about what goes on in the story.[10] The younger children are giving a narrational response, the older or more mature ones a response that usually combines emotional involvement with inferences about the pictorial information. Such a story "told" by more mature children may include a considerable number of inferences about the characters and about the plot, including predictions of what may occur as the story progresses. The response, therefore, is a literary response at the same time that it is an exercise in picture comprehension. By providing good experiences with picture books and asking appropriate questions, we can help young children to develop inference skills.

The need for a strong library reading program to complement the skill instruction that goes on in reading class should be evident. Through planned library activities, children can be brought into contact with—and, we hope, interaction with—fine and interesting books. They can have time and opportunity to respond emotionally to the books, to whet their curiosity through reading experiences, and to begin to reorganize some perceptions of the world they live in. They can use vicarious literary experiences as guides to the interpretation of some of life's events.

Evaluating Children's Response

Evaluation of children's learning about literature is seldom done formally. Nevertheless, there are literary behaviors which can be identified and observed throughout a school year. Formal and informal observation can also help you to look at the success of your literature

*Viewpoint*_____

Literature teachers often discuss but seldom define response to literature. They know it is important in the literature classroom and is an assumption in every literature curriculum. Aware that it is not quite the same as what psychologists call response to a stimulus, teachers realize that response to literature is mental, emotional, intellectual, sensory, physical. It encompasses the cognitive, affective, perceptual, and psychomotor activities that the reader of a poem, a story, or a novel performs as he reads or after he has read.—Alan C. Purves with Victoria Rippere. "Elements of Writing About a Literary Work: A Study of Response to Literature," NCTE Research Report No. 9, National Council of Teachers of English, 1968, p. xiii.

program. Evaluation, carried out throughout the course of a program, can give information about these behaviors:

1. knowledge about literature;
2. ability to apply that knowledge in comparing stories or poems or tracing their cultural roots;
3. expressed response—either through oral, dramatic, or artistic form; or through talking or writing about response; and
4. willingness to participate in literary experiences or to respond to literature.[11]

Behaviors (3) and (4) above are closely related to experiences described in the two chapters that follow. You might, for example, evaluate whether oral reading and discussion develops more positive attitudes in your students than role-playing, as shown by children's comments that indicate greater emotional involvement with a story or poem. The best means of assessing response to literature at the elementary level seems to be through adult observation of children's behavior and reactions to literature heard and read. Written responses and objec-

10. Mary Jett Simpson. *Children's Inferential Responses to a Wordless Picture Book; Development and Use of a Classification System for Verbalized Inference* (Unpublished doctoral dissertation. University of Washington, 1976).
11. Alan C. Purves, "Evaluation of Learning in Literature," in *Handbook of Formative and Summative Evaluation of Student Learning.* Benjamin S. Bloom, J. Thomas Hastings, and George Madaus, eds. (McGraw, 1971), pp. 703–710.

tive tests are more useful for evaluating responses of older students.

Willingness to participate in literary experiences and to respond to literature can be assessed by observing children's reading habits, either informally or with a questionnaire, and by noting reactions to literature presented in class. A questionnaire asking children to rank reading according to its importance in their lives might include such other choices as television viewing, participating in sports, or spending time with hobbies. By using such a questionnaire at the beginning and end of a year, it is possible to get some idea of the success of a literature program. Informally noting whether individuals or a group can better interpret literature at the end of the year can add to this evaluation. So, too, can the use of tests of knowledge about literature.

Judgment of the success of an entire program serves its purpose when we make plans for future programs. Evaluation carried out during a program can help us to make changes while the program is still in use. If creative dramatics is not an effective way of involving a certain group of children with literature, frequent observations should make that clear. Another approach, such as discussion, can be substituted and a check made of changes in attitude and/or knowledge as a result of the new strategy. The evaluations need not be more formal than observations of children's reading behavior. How-

ever, conscious evaluation can help to keep a literature program interesting and develop mature responses.

As adults who are involved in bringing children and books together, we would like to make that experience a rewarding one. In this chapter we have discussed a wide range of current theory and research on children's response to literature. Our purpose in this discussion has been to provide a basis for thinking about children's experiences with literature and for organizing activities—the subject of the two chapters that follow.

Adult References[12]

APPLEBEE, ARTHUR N. *The Child's Concept of Story: Ages Two to Seventeen.*

AQUINO, JOHN. *Fantasy in Literature.*

GORSUCH, RICHARD L. "Moral Education from a Psychological View of Man as an Ethical Being."

HAZARD, PAUL. *Books, Children, and Men.*

HOPKINS, LEE BENNETT. *The Best of Book Bonanza.*

PURVES, ALAN C. "Research in the Teaching of Literature." *How Porcupines Make Love: Notes on a Response-Centered Curriculum.*

PURVES, ALAN C., with Victoria Rippere. *Elements of Writing About a Literary Work: A Study of Response to Literature.*

ROSENBLATT, LOUISE M. *Literature as Exploration.*

RUDDELL, ROBERT B. *Reading-Language Instruction: Innovative Practices.*

SQUIRE, JAMES, ed. *Response to Literature.*

———. *The Responses of Adolescents While Reading Four Short Stories.*

Chapter Sixteen: Encouraging Response to Literature

To become mature readers children need opportunities to respond to a variety of reading material. Some children will respond easily to selections that interest them, showing response in their comments as well as in their facial expressions as they read, hear, or recall a story or poem. Other children will need more encouragement and may respond more freely if they are allowed to use physical as well as verbal response, as in a puppet production of a story. Your role is to encourage but never force response, to offer activities that will allow children to actively respond to a selection, to observe and help to extend responses to literature so that they include interpretation and evaluation. At the same time, you should realize that some of the most deeply reflective responses are not observable and that those responses must be honored and not destroyed by too much emphasis on activity. Remind yourself that your goal is not a polished dramatic production but a group of children enjoying an experience with a fine story.

Response-centered activities discussed in this chapter begin with those designed for listening enjoyment—reading aloud to children and storytelling. A third activity, discussion, adds active verbal interchange to listening, and leads to interpretation and evaluation of a selection. The chapter then moves to dramatic activities—role-playing, creative dramatics, story theater, oral interpretation, and puppetry—activities which encourage physical/motor response as an aid to involvement with a story. Writing activities are described last. The act of writing about a literary work requires a certain amount of skill in written expression. Children who have only minimal writing skill will be inhibited in developing response to literature if made to write about what they have read. For that reason, written responses may be fine for some children and some situations but should be used selectively.

Reading Aloud to Children

Parents, teachers, librarians, baby-sitters, all of us who work with children, can enrich our lives as well as those of children when we provide and encourage delight in hearing a good story read aloud well. Pleasurable experiences in listening can create interest in books that carries on through years of adolescence and adulthood. Listening can also provide natural opportunities for development of a listening vocabulary and acquaintance with English syntax. When you read to children, you give them a chance to hear an author's style, to identify with well-developed characters, and sometimes to try to predict the direction the plot will take in tomorrow's installment. Most important of all, you help them to know good books and poems in a relaxed, warm atmosphere.

Oral reading will be most successful when you give the listeners time to get ready to hear a story. For most groups, that readiness involves a few minutes of quiet and a chance to get as comfortable as possible. If the illustrations are important to the story, it also means settling the children close enough to you so that all can see. When you read from a picture book, it is important that you either hold the book so that they can see as you read or pause at the end of a page and take time to show the illustrations.

Selecting Material to Read Aloud

For many people, and certainly for inexperienced readers, the two basic guidelines for selecting materials to read aloud are (1) that you like the selection and (2) that it is well written. As to the first guideline, you are more likely to draw an emotional reaction from listeners if you are involved with the story yourself. You will probably also do a better job of interpreting the characters and developing a sense of mood. However, unless you have chosen a well-written story, you may fail on both counts even though you like the book. A poorly written selection can cause you to feel awkward, to stumble over words, and to fail to make sense of the syntax because the writing lacks grace and polish.

Vivid characterization and a fairly fast-paced story line (a compact, factual account that concentrates more on action and less on description) are also important factors to keep in mind when you select a book to read aloud. Choose characters who will interest listeners and whose dialogue will be interesting and comfortable for you to read. Choose a plot or an organizational scheme that moves at a pace fast enough to keep reader attention, exercising your judgment about what may appeal to the group and keeping in mind age, past experiences, and interests.

The amount of time you can devote to an oral reading session will also influence the way you select material. Never try to read a long selection when you know the attention span of the children is likely to be no more than twenty minutes. You can usually find good stopping points if you have skimmed the material in advance. Sometimes an intriguing question can give the children a chance to wonder about what will happen next. If the story must be

continued for several days, let the children, rather than you, review the story before continuing on with the next reading. Longer selections require special treatment but they are often very appealing to children because they allow fuller appreciation of a good plot and a chance to get well acquainted with the characters. Reading full-length books also gives some children a chance to know certain books they would never read on their own. If you cannot continue a story with the same group of children, consider the many fine poems that they may like. Think, too, of books like Beverly Cleary's *Henry Huggins* and Robert McCloskey's *Homer Price* which have episodic plots, each chapter usually a self-contained experience.

Reading aloud should not be limited to young children. Older children also enjoy being read to and often will read books they have heard previously. Additionally, the oral reading provides a group experience with literature in contrast to the more frequent silent reading activities that older children engage in. Another bonus for children of any age is the opportunity to enjoy the style of a piece. The

Viewpoint

Just So Stories, for example, are far more enjoyable to hear than to read silently. Sensitivity to style is subtle but may be enhanced through good oral reading.

Oral Reading Techniques

When you have chosen a story that is right for you and your children, you are ready to begin preparing to read aloud. Even experienced readers often use some pre-presentation techniques to make a reading more effective. They focus on the literary aspects of a story, qualities such as characterization and author's style, which must be conveyed when you read aloud. That can be done only if you have read, or at least skimmed, the selection to note high points in the plot. The same is true for noting crucial points to be emphasized when you are reading biography or informational material.

Previewing, or studying a selection in advance, will call your attention to the general tone the author uses. Is it serious, cynical, humorous, matter-of-fact? How should the narrator's parts be handled to provide contrast with character parts? Previewing should also show you the personality traits of the story characters so that you can use that information in your interpretation of dialogue. Skimming combined with a more complete reading of some sections of a story can give you an idea of the author's style. Are there long descriptive phrases? Does the author use short, action-packed sentences to instill excitement? Does the writer use unusual words? Are there words or word clusters that must be emphasized as you read? Skimming can help you to prepare quickly to make the most of a character part, a well-written line, or a build-up of conflict within the plot.

If you are a beginner at oral reading, you may want to practice a story aloud several times before reading it to the group. If you are reading from your own copy of a book, you may even want to mark it, underlining words needing emphasis and key punctuation marks so that you will make the most of a phrase or a sentence. If you have trouble keeping a wide enough eye-voice span to read ahead a sentence at a time, try at least to read for phrases so that your oral reading is smooth. The smoothness is the mechanical part of the reading. Beyond that, you must try to give listeners the mood of a selection. Creating mood requires you to bring together all of your knowledge about a work—understanding of theme, plot structure, characterization, and style. Using your voice, you can create a mood that helps listeners into their own interpretation of a story and brings them far enough into a work so that they are able to react intellectually as well as emotionally. Your level of pitch, tone of voice, and the pace of your reading all contribute to mood—a quiet, hushed reading for parts of Robert McCloskey's *Time of Wonder* and a brisk, rapid one for his *Homer Price.*

When you work on characterization, you should consider what you know about the character's personality. How would the person talk? Should you interpret the character as good-natured? domineering and aggressive? frightened or unsure? angry? Would the character generally speak slowly? fast? softly? Would the rate and loudness of speech vary, depending on what was being said? You may find it easier and more rewarding to try to think as the story character thinks and to really put yourself into the role, reading each bit of dialogue as though you were in the shoes of that character. Regardless of the technique you use, you should achieve enough of the spirit of the story so that characters are distinguishable from one another and so that they evoke some emotional response from children who are listening to the story. Needless to say, oral reading should never be overly dramatic or the desired effect will be lost.

Poetry is one of the literary forms most often read aloud. It surely deserves to be. Poetry must be read to children who are not fluent enough readers to appreciate their own poetry reading. Poetry presents a visual barrier to many children reading it—a barrier that doesn't exist when the poetry is heard read aloud.

The question is often asked, "How can a person with little knowledge of poetry and less knowledge of oral interpretation learn to read poetry acceptably?" The answer is to read a poem aloud repeatedly until its tune and its meaning grow. Fortunately, the nonsense ditties of *Mother Goose,* Edward Lear, and Laura Richards, with their crisp or explosive consonants and brisk rhythms, practically force the reader into vigorous, precise speech and give one a sense of tempo and variety. A. A. Milne, too, writes his lines so that they compel a correct interpretation. The subtle lyrics of William

Blake, Christina Rossetti, and Walter de la Mare, and the thought-provoking poetry of Robert Frost, however, require something more than vigor and swing. The works of these poets demand delicate, precise interpretation, and such interpretation must be grown into. So read a poem aloud to yourself first to get the general mood or feeling.

You make many discoveries when you read poetry aloud, because skilled poets write for the ear, and they employ melody and movement consciously for specific ends: (1) sometimes melody and movement are used to suggest the action described in the poem; (2) sometimes they help to establish the mood of the poem; or (3) they may furnish clues to its meaning. When you read a poem aloud, therefore, you catch elements you miss when you read it silently. The second time you try it orally you will interpret it even better because you understand it better.

Photograph by Elizabeth Crews.

Observing Response

Responses to the oral reading of a story or poem are usually spontaneous. Watch for the grin as you show an illustration that captures the humor of a *Homer Price* episode or the sober expressions as listeners enter into the boy's problems in Louisa Shotwell's *Roosevelt Grady*. Many of the responses are likely to reflect emotional involvement with the selection as it is being read.

A pause at the end of a story or poem can give children time to wonder about the selection and try to make some interpretations. A child who comments that he knows how the boy in the story feels because he lost his bike once, too, is making a sort of interpretation by showing empathy for a story character. He is also responding emotionally to the story. Another child may remark that she doesn't like a story character because he often hurts other children and makes them afraid to play outside. She further reflects that this would be a terrible place to live if there were many bullies like that. Value judgment shows up in her response. At the same time, the judgment might reflect interpretation of the theme of a story and an evaluation of a story character's behavior.

Reading aloud may generate many kinds of responses. They should be accepted and encouraged, extended by questions when the oc-

casion is right. Above all, remember that a good book, well read, brings responses from children who could not enjoy and respond to the book on their own because their reading ability would not permit it.

Storytelling

The storyteller's concerns are much like those of the oral reader, with the most apparent difference being that the storyteller does not use a book in presenting material to children. If you want to be a storyteller who re-creates a story so that it captivates your listeners, you might keep these three ideas in mind:

1. Choose a story that you like. If you enjoy the story, you will be able to infuse it with your special insight.
2. Know the story well enough to be comfortable with it and to avoid worry about a lapse of memory.
3. When you tell a story, it is important to establish a relationship with the audience so that they will share the mood of the story with you.

A person with a head full of stories to tell never needs to carry books. When a class goes on a field trip, the bus is often late. A good storyteller can gather the class around and make the time pass quickly. Many a situation which can alarm children unnecessarily or require a restless waiting has been soothed with a story.

The successful storyteller learns how to capture the attention of the audience and hold it. You learn to observe those subtle signs of interest: staring eyes, still hands. You also learn the signs of flagging interest: wiggling, head-turning. By interpreting these signs correctly, the storyteller uses the tricks of the trade to revive interest, to retrieve the child who is on the verge of distraction. With knowledge of your audience, you emphasize those elements of a story that you know will be relished.

Selecting a Story to Tell

The easiest stories to begin with are folk tales. They are easy because they were created orally by storytellers and have perfect form for narration. The form is invariable: a clear, brief introduction that launches the conflict or problem; the development or body of the story with a rising action, increasing suspense, and an exciting climax that marks the turning point in the story and the fortunes of the hero; and, finally, a satisfying conclusion that winds up everything—problems, conflicts, and villains all suitably disposed of. From the simplest cumulative "Pancake" type of story, through "The Bremen Town-Musicians" and "Snow White," to the more subtle "Clever Manka" for the oldest children, these folk tales tell themselves with ease and will help you fall into the storytelling habit and develop your own unique style.

Another good source of stories to tell are the myths. Many of the myths are long and may take two or three story periods to tell; for example, the stories of Perseus and of Theseus. Fortunately, these two tales have been well told by Ian Serraillier in *The Gorgon's Head* and *The Way of Danger*. Reading these books will show you why even the simplest myths demand more imagination in the telling and a more choice vocabulary than the folk tales.

Most stories written these days are for reading, not for telling, but here and there you will find little stories that are as perfect for telling as any folk tale. "Paddy's Three Pets" by Mary Phillips is a good example, also *Torten's Christmas Secret* by Maurice Dolbier, "Peter the Gold-

fish" by Julian Street, and *The Bears on Hemlock Mountain* by Alice Dalgliesh.

If you begin with your favorite folk tales and tell enough of them to get the feel and fun of storytelling in your very bones, then you will be better able to spot a likely candidate for your repertoire, whether it is old or new.

Learning and Telling a Story

Probably no two people learn and re-create stories in quite the same way, but visualizing characters and scenes often helps. In "The Pancake," you might see a snug kitchen with a mother standing close to the stove, her seven hungry children crowding much too near her to watch that fat, sizzling pancake. An old grandfather is sitting over in the corner smoking his pipe. Through the open door—it must be open because the pancake rolls through it—you might see a road winding over the hills and across the country and clear out of sight. You must see the characters, too, some in more detail than others, depending upon how dramatic their words or their roles are in the tale. Visualizing them undoubtedly helps in characterizing them; so if you see the sneering faces of Cinderella's sisters, something of the sneer gets into your interpretation of their words and behavior. Not that you do actually sneer, of course—that is stage business, not storytelling—but still a sneerful suggestion creeps in. And if you are telling a hero tale, something noble and serious comes into your voice, face, and manner.

Choice of words is important in storytelling. As a storyteller, you cannot go far with a meager vocabulary; moreover, you must develop a sensitivity to language, so that you cannot possibly tell an Irish tale with the same vocabulary and cadence you use for a Norwegian story. Read the story aloud first until you get the feel and flavor of its special vocabulary and word patterns. While exact memorizing is usually the wrong approach to the folk tale, the other extreme is much worse—a slipshod telling, a careless use of words.

Such modern colloquialisms as "Boots got real mad," or "The princess looked really great," or "'OK,' said the lad," can ruin the mood and magic of a tale. Words must be chosen with a sensitive perception of the individual style of each tale. The dreamlike romance of "Sadko" calls for a very different choice of words from the rural dialogue of the old man and his good wife in "Gudbrand on the Hillside." Voice, diction, and vocabulary demand the training of your ear. Listen to yourself—to your voice, your speech, and above all, to the words appropriate for your story.

Obviously, if you are going to tell a story you must know it thoroughly. This involves overlearning to such a degree that you cannot possibly forget the tale, but can stand aside and play with the interpretation of the story because you have no worries about the mechanics of recall. Some people feel that memorizing is the only solution. Others consider memorizing the wrong approach to the folk tale for two reasons: First, these naive tales do not have the formal perfection of the literary story; they were always kept fluid and personal by the old tellers. If they are memorized, they are likely to sound stilted and impersonal. Ruth Sawyer, in *The Way of the Storyteller,* pays a tribute to the storytelling of her Irish nurse, who was proud of her art and used it with great dignity. She would close a story with the saying, "Take it, and may the next one who tells it, better it." This is exactly what can happen.

A second reason that exact memorizing is not recommended is that forgetting a single phrase or a connecting sentence may throw you completely off, so that you have to stop or start over or pause awkwardly while you rack your brain for the lost word. This, of course, spoils a story. On the other hand, if the story is thoroughly learned but not memorized it will remain in your memory for years.

The beginnings and endings of your stories, particularly, should be polished until they are smooth and sure. Some storytellers recommend memorizing the beginning and ending of a story and simply writing on a card the key phrases that will help you to recall each section of the story so that you do not omit an important part. The beginning requires special care because it establishes the mood of your tale. You may announce your story informally in any of a dozen ways: "Today we are going to hear about our old friends, 'The Three Billy-Goats Gruff.'" Or, "I've a new story for you today, and it's called 'The Fox and His Travels.'" Or, "You have all heard stories about 'Jack the Giant Killer,' but do you know there was a woman who got the best of a powerful giant? Our story is about her, and her name is 'Molly Whuppie.'"

Then, having announced your story, pause a moment—not too long, not long enough to let the children start squirming again, just long enough for a deep, quiet breath—and then begin.

Observing Response

A storyteller who has established rapport with the group and is able to maintain eye contact with the audience is in a unique position to notice the children's response to the story. The response in a listener's eyes or facial expression that indicates interest, enjoyment, or sadness is the kind of emotional response that is basic to other responses that may follow. That signal, subtle though it may be, indicates a grasp of the story and an ability to interact with characters, with the story line, or with a particular word choice which the listener finds appealing. In a sense, then, a good storyteller monitors the listener's reactions to a story by noticing physical responses and, primarily, facial expressions. You might ask yourself these questions when you have finished telling a story to a group of children:

Photograph by Elizabeth Crews.

1. Which children showed response during the story period?
2. What parts of the story evoked the most response?
3. How did the children show their reactions?
4. Did any child comment about the story at some time after the story hour? If so, did the comment indicate emotional response? interpretation of the story? attention to literary characteristics such as style?
5. Do the reactions give you ideas for future story choices for this group?

Book Discussions

Book discussions can range from a highly structured classroom situation to a simple exchange of opinions between a librarian and a child after a storytelling session has broken up. Discussions can serve many purposes. They give children opportunity to vent their feelings about a story or poem. The give-and-take of discussion may help children interpret the meaning of a selection. Under adult guidance, book discussions can give children insight into an author's purpose and a character's motives and can help them to make reasoned evaluations of the general quality of a book. Discussions can also open children's minds to the many life experiences they meet vicariously through books—the problems of the aged, poor, orphaned, or handicapped, or the way a story character forms values and changes behavior accordingly. Talking about incidents from a story can help children to develop empathy for people they might never know personally. There is a great need to prepare all children to accept and respect the handicapped children who are being mainstreamed in many school districts. Reading and discussing books with handicapped characters who are presented honestly and sensitively may be an important key. Discussions can also point out ways that books help us to know ourselves better.

Book discussions can help you to gain insight into children's values and can permit you to observe children's responses. The material on values-clarification discussion in Chapter 2 suggests some of the ways we might expect children to respond. Sometimes putting problems in terms of book characters makes them easier for children to discuss. For example, a classroom group discussed Kate's outrageous behavior in the first chapter of *The Good Master*. Of course they thoroughly enjoyed her antics, but they came to the conclusion that she behaved that way because she was "mad" at her father for sending her away, and so she took it out on her uncle's family. It was further agreed that most of us are likely to behave foolishly when we think we have been unjustly treated.

Selecting Material for Discussion

Book discussions may be based on selections children have read or on stories they have listened to. A natural opportunity for discussion is following a storytelling or reading aloud session. Stories that are worthy of discussion have clearly developed themes of enough depth to raise questions that will encourage children to draw on their own experiences, interests, and concerns. Select material that allows children to discuss the humorous as well as the serious incidents in literature. Through the humor of Rosemary Wells's *Noisy Nora*, children see a view of life that makes it easier to accept misfortunes and disappointments. Humorous incidents as well as serious ones can lead children to examine their own values.

Fiction, poetry, nonfiction, picture books—all can be effective for stimulating discussion. Children's interests and reading and listening abilities should, of course, be taken into account when selecting material for discussion. The length of time available for the session, too, will influence your decision of how many aspects of a selection, or how complex a work, you will be able to explore. A third guideline should be your own knowledge of the literature you plan to use. In order to conduct a good discussion, you should have a thorough grasp of the themes and literary structure of the work, including an understanding of each character and of the techniques the author has used for character development. Your pre-assessment of a selection influences the depth and quality of a guided discussion because you draw on that assessment as you plan your sequence of questions.

Discussion of wordless picture books is a fine vehicle for encouraging young children to respond to illustrations and to develop a sense of plot structure at the same time. The best wordless picture books interest children enough to evoke emotional involvement with the story told through the pictures. They also have enough plot so that the action carries a child along from one page to the next. Perhaps most important, however, the pictures supply some details necessary to create a good story but they leave enough to the child's imagination to encourage inference about details of characterization and plot. Those inferences are the heart of response to wordless picture books. They can be encouraged by repeated experiences in telling the story from the pictures, especially in a one-to-one situation between an adult and a child. An adult guiding the retelling of a wordless picture-book story can encourage inferences by asking questions such as: What do you think will happen next? Why is she doing that? Where do you think he is going? and others specific to the story.

Formulating Questions

As you prepare for a book discussion, you will need to keep in mind both the qualities of the selection and the abilities of the children. In order to make a pre-assessment of the material, you might ask yourself these questions:

1. What are the important ideas to be gained from the selection?
2. What aspects of the story will require exploration if children are to understand and interpret them?
3. Which story characters are children most likely to identify with?
4. Will they need help in understanding a character's motives?
5. Are there aspects of style or figurative language that should be discussed in order to aid in interpretation?
6. How can this selection be related to children's experiences, interests, and concerns? Using these questions as stepping-stones, you can formulate specific questions that will guide children to interpret and evaluate literature, to note devices an author or poet has used, and, above all, to interact emotionally with the story.

Studies of teachers' questions during reading instruction have indicated that teachers rely too much on factual questions which have only one right answer. Such questions do not lead to a discussion of a work, they simply result in a sort of tennis game between adult and children. (What was the name of the dog? Where did the pirate bury the treasure? etc.) Aside from a few factual questions which may be necessary in order to produce information to serve as a basis for later discussion, most of your questions should ask children to infer, to interpret, to evaluate, and to identify with characters. Their answers of course may vary because each child comes to a literary experience with a different background.

Examples of some open-ended questions based on one chapter of Farley Mowat's *Owls in the Family* follow, with types of possible responses shown in parentheses:

In what ways are the owls, Wol and Weeps, different? (comparing characters and identifying characterization)

Why do you think the author made the two owls so different? (literary judgment, interpretation)

What questions would you like to ask Billy about his owls? (involvement, interpretation)

What was the funniest part of the story? (involvement, evaluation)

What is so funny about the scene where two owls try to learn to fly? (literary judgment, involvement)

How did Wol feel when he fell to the ground the first time he flew? Have you ever felt that way? How did you behave? (involvement, empathy)

Were the owls tame or wild? What information did you get from the story to back your answer? (interpretation, literary judgment regarding character traits)

Many other questions could, of course, also be used. A discussion should be fluid and kept personal in terms of the story and the group, following up on answers so that students can pursue a question to greater depth. As a follow-up to the last question above, you might want to ask: What can happen to a wild animal after it has been tamed? What is the author telling you in this story that might apply to any wild animal?

In general, then, discussion questions focus on characters, on favorite parts of the plot, on the relationship between episodes, on the author's message, and on evaluation of a selection. Some basic question types which can be adapted to many books are:

Which story character did you like best? Why? (evaluation, involvement)

If you had been a character in this story, how would you have acted if _____? (involvement, empathy, interpretation)

Do you think _____ did the right thing when he/she _____? (evaluation, valuing)

How else could _____ have handled the problem about the _____? What would you have done? (involvement, evaluation, valuing, interpretation)

What do you think this author is trying to tell us about the way people learn to have respect for themselves? (interpretation, literary understanding of theme)

What important idea (or theme) did you find throughout this story? (interpretation of main idea, literary understanding of theme)

What was the most interesting or exciting part of the story? (evaluation, involvement)

Did you learn anything from the story that will help you get along better with people and perhaps to understand yourself better? (valuing, empathy)

How is this story like _____ (another story they know)? (literary judgment, interpretation)

How did the author manage to make this so funny that you laughed out loud? What techniques did he/she use? (literary judgment of style, involvement)

What does _____ (figure of speech) mean in this poem? (literary knowledge, interpretation)

In general, the questions beginning with *why, what,* and *which* lead to a more open discussion that the sorts of questions beginning with *when* and *where.*

A questioning technique which can be very effective in helping children to become involved with a story character or situation requires that you preface a question by asking the child to take the point of view of a story character. This technique works not only to create involvement with human characters, but also with animal characters in some stories. In *Owls in the Family*, for instance, some children become so involved with the owls that they are easily able to respond to a question like: "You are Mutt [the family dog]. Why do you defend Weeps from other dogs even though you don't seem to like owls yourself?" Answers may show that children recognize that quality in a family dog that feels responsible to protect all who live under that roof and perhaps senses that the weaknesses of some family members require greater care. Using the character-point-of-view question as a beginning, you can help children to sense the author's point of view by asking questions such as: "How would the story be told if the author were telling it through Wol's eyes?" "Who is the author using as the storyteller here?" "Is it one of the story characters or is the author reporting everything that all characters experience and think?"

Pacing a Discussion

An adult guiding a book discussion has the responsibility of keeping it going by interjecting appropriate questions. Since children are responding to one another's questions as well as to the adults' questions, skill is required to keep the discussion from rambling and to maintain a pace that holds interest. The ability to know *when* to ask another question or to probe an answer more deeply is one of the keys to an effective discussion. Linked to that ability is the sense of how long and when to pause so that students can reflect on the question and synthesize their thoughts to formulate a good answer.

Some work has been reported in science education which relates to pace of questioning.[1] Essentially, the work has involved monitoring the amount of time between questions to see whether the length of time allowed influences the kinds of responses given. Findings suggest that a greater amount of "wait-time" leads to responses showing higher levels of thinking about the problem (above factual reporting, for example). These findings in turn have led to some work in training teachers to increase the amount of time they allow students before going on to another question or giving the answer themselves.

The increase in interpretation and other higher-level responses in science activities may be a guideline to adults who lead book discussions. A factual question, as "Who were the characters in this story?" may not require a very long wait for answers. It simply requires recalling information. A question that requires interpretation or evaluation, however, requires children to relate their own experiences to the story and, in the case of evaluation, to make judgments based on that synthesis.

1. Mary Budd Rowe, "Reflections on Wait-time; Some Methodological Questions," *Journal of Research in Science Teaching* 11 (1974): 263–279.

Viewpoint

Yet the primacy of pleasures as an end in reading is now quite widely accepted, and we have indeed gone further and asked some searching questions about the nature and sources of that pleasure. And because those sources properly lie in only two places—the written work before the reader and the mind of the reader himself—we have been led to concentrate upon that unique, immediate encounter between book and reader, largely and quite deliberately, neglecting such peripheral matters as the biography of the author, the circumstances under which the book was composed, its reputation, or—as I've already suggested—its "lesson." And in consequence we find ourselves driven to think, not primarily about authors and subject matters and "reading" generally, but about specific books and their readers—what goes on in books, what goes on in the people, young and old, who read them.—Edward W. Rosenheim, Jr. "Children's Reading and Adults' Values" in *Only Connect* edited by Sheila Egoff, G. T. Stubbs and L. F. Ashley. Oxford University Press (Canadian Branch), 1969, p. 18.

thesis. If you ask, "Do you think that Max acted wisely in the way he treated the wild things? Why or why not?" children will need a longer time. Questions of this sort require an interaction with the story to formulate an answer and will usually require some reflection. The combination of open-ended questions and enough time for reflective answers should encourage literary responses that show involvement with a story but also some attempt to interpret the story or to make judgments about it.

Organizing for Discussion

Many book discussions are adult-led because they follow the reading or telling of a story to a group. The adult may be a parent, librarian, or a teacher. A large-group discussion requires a leader who is able to maintain a good pace, to encourage many children to participate, and to keep the discussion on the track. Obviously, the open-ended question, especially one which asks for a personal involvement with some aspect of the story or an interpretation based on personal experiences, can permit almost every child to respond if there is time. A leader must be able to accept all responses but to keep children focused on the question. Furthermore, the leader should try to maintain a neutral attitude in conducting discussions and not interject his or her own opinions. If children know that you censure the behavior of a certain story character, they are less likely to give you open, candid answers. On the other hand, you can build on their naive responses in some cases to lead them to a better understanding of a character's behavior and why certain kinds of behavior are not highly valued in our society.

An adult-led small-group discussion is often more enjoyable for children than a large-group discussion. They need to be at ease with the other participants and to feel free to ask as well as answer questions. Small-group discussions can follow oral reading or storytelling by an adult. They can also work well when the children have all read the same story on their own. In working with gifted children, a seminar version of the small-group discussion is effective. In this arrangement, each student either reads the same book or reads a book that represents a particular genre. For example, all may choose one book of modern fantasy. Your questions in the discussion guide the students to see how all of their books are similar in terms of fantasy. Have characters been manipulated so that they are talking animals, small people, superhuman beings? Is the setting on another planet, inside our earth, or in a mythical country? Has the time been manipulated so that the story takes place far in the future? Such a discussion can help children to note literary devices used by an author. It can also lead to evaluation of the books and to interpretation of events in the stories.

Another kind of small-group discussion is that in which one child acts as leader. Though a child must be relatively mature to keep a discussion going, the group's responses can be much freer than when an adult is in the group. Because student leaders will not be adept at keeping a discussion going at a good pace, the amount of time alloted should be fairly short, probably not more than fifteen minutes.

Book discussions can occur in many situations, among them a one-to-one discussion of child and adult or child and child. In these informal discussions, the child can use an adult as a sounding board as was the case when a child asked, "Were you disappointed when Sam (Jean George's *My Side of the Mountain*) had people as visitors?" Children need time to sit quietly and chat with one another about books, too. When you overhear some of those conversations, notice the kinds of information discussed. (Needless to say, you do not intrude.) Some of the most persuasive "book-selling" goes on in those meetings and some good ideas about favorite passages are also exchanged. To facilitate discussions, you can set up a classroom or library corner where children and adults feel free to talk about books in their spare time. By providing the right atmosphere, you can inspire a natural response to literature and a love for many kinds of books.

Dramatic Activities

Dramatic activities provide marvelous opportunities for children to interact with literature. They are especially good for young children who are able to respond physically even though they may not be able to respond verbally with much ease. The activities we will discuss which work well as vehicles for literary response are role-playing, creative dramatics, story theater, oral interpretation (including Readers Theatre), and puppetry. Story theater and puppetry are activities that children who are slow learners can enjoy.

Role-playing

Role-playing is an educational strategy. It sets up a problem situation for children to come to grips with and allows them to "play through" the problem in order to discover alternate solutions and the results of those solutions. The emphases are on decision making and its consequences, and the goal is to promote social values. In the process, personal values may be influenced rather significantly.

Experiences with literature can be enhanced by role-playing. When children are involved with a character and are confronted with that character's problem as they are in role-playing, the way is open to a satisfying literary response. By sharing the challenges and frustrations of a literary character, children may learn to appreciate an author's say of handling plot and characterization and at the same time develop personal and social values.

The material best suited to role-playing is the problem story, so-called because it develops a problem which students can become involved with and try to deal with. Some stories written especially for the role-playing situation are included in *Role-Playing for Social Values* by

Fannie and George Shaftel. A well-written piece of realistic fiction can also provide thought-provoking problem situations. In choosing episodes from literature, be certain that the characters are well developed and the problem situation is clearly defined. Beyond these points, the plot should have a logical stopping place so that students can play out their endings. Books with episodic plot structure, in which each chapter is an almost self-contained story, work well because the length of the selection is easier to handle than a full-length book.

What kinds of problems provide good material for role-playing? First of all, they should be problems that students can identify with. That means well-stated universal fears, concerns, or temptations—difficulties common to people in all kinds of environments. If the setting and story characters are familiar to your students, the problem situation may also be easier for them to deal with. A second basis for judging material is whether the problem it raises will help students to develop a personal value system.

The problem stories included by the Shaftels involve situations dealing with integrity, responsibility for others, being fair, accepting others, and wishing you were bigger or better. Some books with sections that develop these problems are:

Responsibility for Others—*Don't Take Teddy* by Babbis Friis-Baastad

Being Fair—*A Bargain for Frances* by Russell Hoban

Accepting Others—*After the Goat Man* by Betsy Byars, *Take Wing* and *From Anna* by Jean Little, "Inviting Jason" from *Altogether, One at a Time* by Elaine Konigsburg

Accepting Others, Surmounting Prejudice—*The Other Side of the Fence* by Molly Cone, *Berries Goodman* by Emily Neville, and *The Borrowed House* by Hilda van Stockum.

Wishing You Were Bigger or Better—*Wait for William* by Marjorie Flack, *The Ears of Louis* by Constance Greene.

The general procedure for conducting a role-playing session includes these nine steps recommended by the Shaftels:[2]

2. From *Role-Playing for Social Values* by Fannie R. and George Shaftel. Prentice-Hall, Inc., 1967, p. 84. Reprinted by permission of the authors.

1. Warm-up (teacher introduction and reading of the problem story)
2. Selecting role-players
3. Preparing the audience to observe
4. Setting the stage
5. The enactment
6. Discussion and evaluation
7. Further enactments
8. Further discussion
9. Generalizing

In Step 1, the adult encourages children to think about how the story might end. This alerts them and helps them to identify with literary characters. A typical question would be, "What do you think will happen now?" In Step 2, the adult can ask students to describe characters and then ask a student who seems to identify with a character to play that role. Step 3 requires that the audience members be prepared for their part. They may be asked to watch carefully to decide whether the solution is a realistic one. In Step 4, the players decide what they are going to do but do not practice dialogue. The adult can help them get into the

Photograph by Leonard McCombe, *Life Magazine* © Time, Inc.

roles by encouraging them to describe the staging they are using. Step 5 focuses on the role-playing itself with each actor playing the part of the character he or she represents. Acting ability should not be criticized, since the focus is on the problem solution. Step 6 includes the follow-up discussion and evaluation. During that period the observers discuss their opinions of the character portrayals and of the consequences of their actions. Adults should encourage children to think in terms of consequences and alternative behaviors. In Steps 7, 8, and 9, the role-players try new interpretations based on ideas that came from the discussion in Step 6. The final step is important because it encourages students to make some assessment of the outcomes of each portrayal and to determine what they think is the best way to deal with the problem.

Although the approach to role-playing developed by Fannie Shaftel uses an unfinished problem story which children must work with, this procedure can be adapted so that after reading an entire book, as a sort of post-reading or listening experience, children are asked to explore different possible solutions to a problem situation by playing the roles of story characters as they might deal with that problem. For example, this situation might be set up for Vera and Bill Cleaver's book *Where the Lilies Bloom:* You are Mary Call Luther and her family. You have been offered a lot of money to let a motion picture company film your home and tell the story of your lives. How are you going to handle this? What will you decide? In this technique, as with point-of-view questioning, broach the first question as "You are _____ " to help children get into their roles and see the problem through their characters' eyes.

During Steps 5–9 of the Shaftel strategy for conducting role-playing, children's responses should be obvious to the adult observer. Questions such as the following will help you to evaluate the kinds and degrees of responses made:

1. Do students seem able to interpret a character's feelings about the problem?
2. Do students show emotional involvement with characters and with the problems posed? Are they able to put themselves into a character role?
3. In discussion and enactment, do students show empathy for characters?
4. Does the question of values enter into the discussion, either explicitly or implicitly?

In role-playing, response is, of course, the key to success. And as in other activities, some responses show greater depth of interpretation than others. Certainly, a child who is able to speak convincingly in the role of a story character is making an attempt to interpret that character's approach to the problem. If a child is also able to assume some of the emotions of a character, so much the better. In many children, a strong interaction with a character shows in the content of what is spoken, in the tone of voice used, and in nonverbal signals such as facial expression and body movements.

As important as response to characters is, however, the crucial reaction in role-playing is a reasoned response to the problem situation. Children's responses often show them grappling with their own values in order to seek out a solution to the problem. Sometimes a response is complete enough to include reasons for the solution or to show the mental steps the child went through before arriving at the solution. Children who are able to carry out dialogue effectively while staying within the roles of their story characters can arrive at a problem solution through the conversation. This shows a high level of response in terms of interpretation, emotional involvement, and evaluation of a situation. Whether their problem solution achieves a high moral value should be looked at separately.

Creative Dramatics

While role-playing develops responses that show interpretation of a story problem and involvement with characters, creative dramatics develops responses that indicate a child's involvement with characterization and plot structure. In role-playing, you ask children to deal with a "what if" proposition, to extend a plot in order to create their own conclusions. In creative dramatics, you ask children to interpret a story which is structurally complete, using suitable voice and actions. The dramatization centers on interpreting character and plot to draw out the major themes. Dialogue is improvised but is true to the sense of characters and theme.

Children who participate in creative dramatics need certain technical skills, to be sure. They must be able to recall the sequence of episodes in the plot, to interpret an author's characterization so as to create real characters, to use vocal ability and body gestures to produce a dramatization that is believable. With guidance, children grow in ability to handle these literary and dramatic interpretation skills. They become skilled in interpreting a story, learning to infer missing details they need for their re-creation of a character, dialogue, or plot. Children also gain personally from experiences with creative dramatics. In addition to the value of the experience itself, they learn to work together and to express themselves unaffectedly and fluently as the dramatization provides an avenue for release of tension and for enjoyment of a story. Development of personal values and appreciation for good literature can also grow from participation in creative dramatization.

Selecting Material for dramatization. A well-written story, one interesting to the children, with some kind of conflict and a fair amount of action, provides good material for dramatization. Characters should be well enough developed so that children can distinguish different character types in the story. Good dialogue is important for children who are not very adept at improvising dialogue.

Some stories successful with primary-age children are: single chapters from Beverly Cleary's *Ramona* books or *Henry Huggins;* Marjorie Flack's *Ask Mr. Bear;* Pat Hutchins' *Rosie's Walk* and *The Surprise Party;* and folk tales such as "The Three Billy-Goats Gruff," "The Three Little Pigs," or "The Pancake." The repetitious plot structure of folk tales makes them easy for young children to handle and the characters, though not highly developed, contrast well enough so that children can portray them effectively.

Material for older students might include: "The Bremen Town-Musicians" and other more complex folk tales like "Urashima Taro and the Princess of the Sea" and "The Tiger, the Brahman and the Jackal"; Dr. Seuss's *The King's Stilts;* episodes from Mark Twain's *Tom Sawyer* or Kenneth Grahame's *The Wind in the Willows,* or scenes from contemporary stories such as Jean George's *Julie of the Wolves* or Elaine Konigsburg's *From the Mixed-Up Files of Mrs. Basil E. Frankweiler.*

Preparing a Dramatization. The adult who guides a creative dramatization has many things to keep in mind. The adult leader has the responsibility to set the mood for a dramatization and to plan warm-up activities that will prepare children to move freely and speak easily. Creative drama can be initiated with children of any age but the leader must be sure to base the activities on the children's past expe-

riences with drama. A simple warm-up activity is pantomiming favorite animals while classmates try to guess what they are. A similar activity for older students involves pantomiming an awkward or embarrassing experience so that other members of the group can tell what it is. Once a mood for drama has been set, it is time to tell or read (preferably tell) the story or poem you have chosen. This presentation should be made vivid by your use of description and emphasis on important parts of the plot. Above all, the story line must be clear so that the plot is easy for children to grasp.

Following the telling of the story, help children to identify the scenes they will need to dramatize and write them on the board. This requires you to think through the story in advance in order to give help in working through the scenes. Taking one scene at a time, help the children break it down into a sequence of smaller actions, thinking of characters who will be needed and the action that is involved. At this point you may analyze each of the major scenes until all have been discussed, or you may begin by having students dramatize just the first scene before they analyze the others.

The first step of dramatization should include discussion of characters—how they look, how they act, even what they think. You may want to let all the students pantomime the characters before proceeding to the dramatization of the scene. At that point, children should be given a chance to volunteer for the parts they wish to play. Remember that in creative dramatics the cast and the audience both have a part to play. To prepare the cast, after characters have been discussed and progression of the plot has been reviewed, give them some time in a private place to rehearse and work out their dramatization. Encourage them to create dialogue they think is natural for those characters. Prepare the audience members so that they are ready to look for good things in the performance and also for some things that they think could be changed in order to create a better production.

The first playing of a scene should be carefully set up so that the area where the production will be given is cleared except for any necessary furniture. (Most costumes and props can be left to the viewer's imagination.) A signal should be given by the adult leader to show the students when to begin and bring to a close their dramatization, since it is sometimes necessary to limit the amount of time allowed or to stop so that some action can be discussed. You may simply hold up your hand, or you may prefer to dim the lights or to use a soft bell so that you can be heard even though the players are not looking at you.

When children have played a scene (or sequence of scenes), engage the audience in discussion of the performance to help them evaluate the effectiveness of characterization and dialogue. Try to get them also to judge the faithfulness to the plot structure of the original story. Following the discussion, the scene may be replayed by the same group of children or by another group selected from the audience. This procedure of playing, discussing, and replaying continues until the entire story has been enacted. If students have done one scene at a time, they then put together the entire sequence in one performance with the audience watching to see how smoothly they can connect the scenes.

In summary, the steps in guiding a creative dramatics production are:

1. Choose a good story or poem.
2. Tell or read it to the children.
3. Involve them in identifying the characters and the scenes needed for the dramatization.
4. Carry out in-depth discussion of character traits and allow time for pantomiming of characters.
5. Let children decide who will play each character part.
6. Give the players a short time to analyze the first scene and to plan and practice their performances, creating their own dialogue.
7. Prepare the audience to critique the performance.
8. Have the scene played before the audience.
9. Guide audience discussion of the scene.
10. Allow for a replaying of the scene, either with the same cast or with a new group.
11. Work on each scene in the same way, then play through the entire story.
12. Guide audience discussion of the complete enactment.
13. Replay, if there is time.

Observing response. Creative dramatics allows for many forms of response to a selection. Children are challenged to identify and interpret an author's development of characterization and plot. During the dramatization itself and also during the discussion that follows, notice responses related to recognition of literary characteristics of the story and interpretation of the work. Some children are able to talk of plot structure, for example, as the child who said it was important for the big billy goat to walk over the bridge, too, before he butted the troll to pieces because the story should show the same thing happening to all three of the goats. That recognition of plot structure is a literary response, as is the comment by an older child that Georgie's accident, in Robert Lawson's *Rabbit Hill*, is an important part of the plot because it adds to other parts of the story that show the ways people and animals affect each other. Children respond to characterization by pointing out words an author uses to describe a character, by conveying through facial expression something of the character's personality, or by using dialogue which shows a character's feelings. Such responses show a grasp of the literary qualities of a piece. Response to characterization can also emerge as an emotional response when a student shows vividly, through actions, an involvement with a character.

Interpretation of literary qualities adds greatly to effective dramatization. A child who realizes that the boy in Rebecca Caudill's *A Pocketful of Cricket* loves his cricket because he is a farm child and it is his special security in the strange school environment may slip in some dialogue expressing that idea. Another child who recognizes, in a story problem, something he or she has also struggled with may express the similarity of experiences through dialogue. Interpretation is shown by facial expression and bodily gesture as well, though these are more limited to interpretation of a character's feelings.

A spirited dramatization is usually evidence of emotional response to the story. So is a thoughtful discussion after the playing, a discussion that reveals interest of the audience in the story as well as in the quality of the dramatization. When the emotional response is added to an intelligent interpretation of the ideas in the story, a very good dramatization usually is given.

Story Theater

Story theater is a kind of dramatization in which a narrator reads or tells the story while the actors pantomime the action. In story theater, inanimate objects—a rock, for example—as well as animal or human characters may be represented by players in the pantomime.

Directing story theater is not difficult. The emphasis on pantomime rather than more formal acting with dialogue removes some of the demands and complexity of creative dramatics. The important steps in directing are these:

1. Read aloud or tell the story to be dramatized.
2. Help children to identify characters (animate and inanimate).
3. Guide the group pantomiming of each character part and make sure some child will be responsible for that part in the dramatization.
4. Review the story plot with the group so that children will be ready to participate.
5. Allow time for individuals to practice the actions they plan to use for their pantomimes.
6. Arrange the area where the dramatization will take place. As with creative dramatics, no props are needed. Instead, in story theater, children can portray inanimate objects referred to in the story.
7. Read or tell the story as the actors pantomime it. (Note: a child may also serve as narrator, especially if the story is read.)

A description of the preparation for a story theater production of *Anansi the Spider*, illustrated by Gerald McDermott, will illustrate the steps outlined above. With the children sitting comfortably around her, the leader read aloud the story of Anansi, showing McDermott's brilliantly colored illustrations as she went along. At the close of the reading, she asked students to think back through the story to identify the characters they would need if they were to dramatize it. She wrote the names of characters on the board as they were mentioned and again showed the illustration of the globe of light to remind the children that they might also need to include it, as well as the forest in which it was seen. The character list complete, the leader called attention to one character at a time, asking children how they would pantomime that character and giving them a few minutes to try out the characterization. When all the characters had been discussed and dramatized, the leader asked for volunteers to take the character parts in the story theater production. She then reviewed the plot briefly with the group. They arranged themselves in the proper locations for the beginning of the story (some outside of the "stage" area, waiting for entrance) and the leader began reading the

Photograph by Ken Heyman.

story, pacing it so that children had time to carry out their actions and to make entrances. When the story was over, several children expressed a desire to try it again because they weren't quite satisfied with their performances. After a short discussion of the problems they encountered, they practiced for a few minutes and the leader again read the entire story. What evaluation there is must be done by the actors, since everyone is a participant. (If you have a large group, expand the numbers and kinds of inanimate objects portrayed such as trees, doors, flowers, etc.) However, the focus is not on evaluation so much as on freedom to participate and a genuine enjoyment of the experience. That freedom is enhanced because there is no audience. The experience is really one of group cooperation toward a common goal.

When you select material for story theater, bear in mind that the best material for work with children is a folk tale or a myth with distinctive characters and a relatively uncomplicated plot. Since children will interpret the characters through pantomime only, the best selections will provide clear distinctions among characters that can be shown easily through large body movements. In *Anansi the Spider*, for example, the six sons have such names as Roadbuilder, River Drinker, Stone Thrower, Game Skinner, See Trouble, and Cushion. Children find it easy to devise movements that will indicate who the character is.

The cumulative plot commonly found in folk tales works well for story theater, especially with young children who need a fairly simple plot structure. Stories such as "The Three Billy-Goats Gruff" or "The Three Little Pigs" are fun for preschool and primary age children. In "The Three Little Pigs" the cast of characters can be augmented by allowing some children to play the roles of the pig's houses. A more elaborate folk-tale plot, such as "The Bremen Town-Musicians," is great fun for older children. In addition to the four animals, you can have as large a band of robbers as the stage area can accommodate.

As you read folk literature, try to pick out tales and myths that would lend themselves well to pantomime. Keep your own file of good story theater selections. Remember that children (even intermediate-grade children) enjoy playing animal roles as much as they do human roles. Don't overlook tales such as "Gudbrand on the Hill-side" where the husband sets off to sell his cow but trades it stupidly for a whole succession of animals and comes home with only a shilling. That story has enough animal roles and interesting human characters to make it a good choice. *Why Mosquitoes Buzz in People's Ears,* told by Verna Aardema and illustrated by Leo and Diane Dillon, is a fine choice for younger children.

Story theater material need not be limited to folk literature. Picture books such as *Drummer Hoff* by Ed and Barbara Emberley, *Rosie's Walk* by Pat Hutchins, or *Mr. Gumpy's Outing* by John Burningham are good sources for dramatization. So are poems like "Days That The Wind Takes Over" from Karla Kuskin's *Near the Window Tree,* "The Monkeys and the Crocodile" from Laura Richards's *Tirra Lirra,* and any number of *Mother Goose* rhymes like "Hey! diddle, diddle."

Material for use with older students should include some of the more complex folk tales and myths. Many of Aesop's fables are effective in story theater, among them "The Lion and the Mouse" or "Belling the Cat." Good folk tales are "Momotaro; Boy-of-the-Peach," "The Tiger, the Brahman and the Jackal," or "Anansi's Hat-shaking Dance." Myths and epics that make effective productions are "Atalanta's Race," "Cupid and Psyche," and "The Curse of Polyphemus." Selected episodes from *Robin Hood* also provide good material for pantomime as do episodes from *Pippi Longstocking, Homer Price* (especially the doughnut-machine scene with students representing the machine), *The Pushcart War,* and other contemporary books. Once you begin to work with story the-

ater, you will find many poems, tales, and episodes from full-length books which work well.

Response to literature is seen in story theater in creative character portrayal which shows appreciation for the story character in relation to the complete story. Response is also revealed through the smoothness with which a child fits a character interpretation into the ongoing dramatization. When this happens, a child has grasped the plot structure and, in some cases, shows an appreciation for the style of the story by attempting to suit the style and pace of the action to the style of the selection. A young child responding to the rhythm of "Ride a cock horse" by playing the character role in perfect rhythm with the *Mother Goose* rhyme, is acknowledging the style of a piece. As you observe children engaged in story theater, you will notice many other examples of emotional response, interpretation, and response to the literary qualities of a piece.

Oral Interpretation

Another response activity for children to try is to orally interpret a story. By oral interpretation we mean a degree of dramatization with the voice to re-create a story vividly for listeners and to give a sense of the kinds of people the story characters might be. Notice that we said "dramatization with the voice." Oral interpretation does not include physical acting out except for an occasional gesture. Oral interpretation techniques are, of course, necessary for any successful oral reading, and are frequently used by adults who read to children and by children who read aloud, either voluntarily or as part of a classroom assignment. People who read aloud effectively, whether adults or children, have mastered the art of using the voice expressively. Because children need guidance and practice in that skill, oral interpretation work should be part of every classroom literature and reading program. Suggestions given here may be useful for adults, too, who wish to improve their oral reading.

Oral interpretation enriches the literary experience for reader and listener. At its best it grows out of interaction with a story and its characters. It is a re-creation of the original story, not a transformation of it as in creative drama, but a reading in which the reader interprets underlying themes, characters, and plot, and projects the combined image for listeners. The child who reads obviously must understand and appreciate the story. It is also important that the story characters take shape and become almost real for the reader. As to plot, the reader must recognize major scenes and transition passages so that the reading carries on at a pace that highlights important events and contrasts one character with another. Because oral interpretation does not demand the more physical interpretation involved in role-playing, creative drama, and story theater, children who are hesitant about performing may find it a more rewarding and less threatening response activity.

As with all the activities we have been discussing, the first and most important consideration in selecting material is that it should be interesting to the children who will read it. In many cases, that means it should be about experiences they have shared. A fast-paced mystery or action story is another good choice to interest readers and listeners.

In choosing stories for oral interpretation, look for selections that have a number of characters, preferably characters that differ in ages and/or personality so that the reader, or readers, will be challenged to use their voices expressively to differentiate one character from another. The quality of the dialogue is, therefore, of prime importance.

Material for use with younger readers might include Else Minarik's *A Kiss for Little Bear* or any of the other *Little Bear* books. They are easy reading books, yet are well written with dialogue that makes sense and is not stilted. The cumulative folk tales like "Henny Penny" or "The Gingerbread Boy" provide enough dialogue and repetition to keep young readers interested. Pat Hutchins's *The Surprise Party* works well, too. Another book which does not have dialogue but can work for oral interpretation is *Drummer Hoff* by Barbara and Ed Emberley. Stories that are superior in characterization and style of writing and that give children a chance to use their voices to interpret joy, anger, fear, a range of emotions, can be used for a good oral interpretation experience. A book that is weak in style or characterization will not work. You can easily get a sense of an author's style by reading aloud a page or two. A book written by a good stylist practically reads itself and you find yourself making the most of every nuance. Identify and keep a file of books you feel have these qualities.

It is easier to find oral interpretation material for children above third grade. Some authors seem to write dialogue more naturally than others. E. L. Konigsburg, Madeleine L'Engle, and Beverly Cleary are three authors who write character parts that children enjoy interpreting and dialogue that seems natural. *The Wind in the Willows* and *The Hobbit* have chapters which make excellent material for oral interpretation, too. As you find other authors you enjoy reading aloud, add their books to your list of recommended materials. Remember, though, that a book should be scanned for those passages which may be too difficult or less interesting for young readers.

Poetry is a rich source of material for practice of oral interpretation skills. The second stanza of "The Pied Piper of Hamelin" by Robert Browning is a good one to use; so are Carl Sandburg's "Buffalo Dusk" *(Smoke and Steel)*, "Seal" by William Jay Smith *(Boy Blue's Book of Beasts)*, and "Sliding" by Myra Cohn Livingston *(Whispers and Other Poems)*.

> We can slide
>   down
>   the
>   hill
>   or
>   down
>   the
>   stair
>   or
>   down
>   the
>   street
> or anywhere.
>
> Or down the roof
>   where the shingles broke,
>   Or down the trunk
>   of the back-yard oak.
>
> Down
>   the
>   slide
>   or the ice
>   or the slippery street,
>
> We can slide
>   on our sled
>   or our skates
>   or our feet.
>
> Oh, it's lots of fun to go outside
> And slide
>   and slide
>   and slide
>   and slide.[3]

This poem, like some others that are good for oral interpretation, is written in a form that im-

3. "Sliding" from *Whispers and Other Poems*. Copyright © 1958 by Myra Cohn Livingston. Reprinted by permission of McIntosh and Otis, Inc.

mediately gives a young reader some clues about how it should be read. The phrase "down the" is repeated several times and it suggests a feeling which can be conveyed by the voice, a long slur that moves across several pitches.

Another poem that is great fun to read aloud is David McCord's "The Pickety Fence." The form of this poem urges the reader to establish the rhythm of a fence by emphasizing each word that rhymes with "pickety."

> The pickety fence
> The pickety fence
> Give it a lick it's
> The pickety fence
> Give it a lick it's
> A clickety fence
> Give it a lick it's
> A lickety fence
> Give it a lick
> Give it a lick
> Give it a lick
> With a rickety stick
> Pickety
> Pickety
> Pickety
> Pick[4]

These poems not only read aloud exceptionally well, but they sharpen children's sensitivity to the use of language and the creation of mood.

When you guide students in preparation for the oral interpretation of a story or poem, you first need to encourage them to read the passage through carefully in order to note (1) the characters—who they are, what kinds of people they are, and how each might talk, (2) the plot—how it develops, what the climax is, and where it occurs, (3) high points of the plot which should be emphasized in the reading, and (4) specific words or phrases which should be emphasized. In reading poetry, this last point is the crucial one. Obviously such close analysis will require several close readings of the selection. You may want to encourage students to underline (mentally or with a soft pencil) the crucial words, to show where the voice would be raised or lowered, or to mark critical punctuation marks so that important pauses will be observed.

Once this kind of analysis has been completed, children should turn to the vocal inter-

4. "The Pickety Fence" from *One at a Time* (British title: *Mr. Bidery's Spidery Garden*) by David McCord. Copyright 1952 by David McCord. Reprinted by permission of Little, Brown and Company and George G. Harrap & Company Limited.

pretation of what is on the page. And this involves an interpretation of character roles which draws on the reader's ability to interact with the feelings and ideas of those characters. Vocal interpretation also involves manipulation of the voice to produce tone, inflection, and pauses that will create the desired effect and convey the emotional tone of the passage.

If the oral interpretation involves poetry, children should practice the oral reading until the flow of words is appropriate to the rhythm pattern of the poem. When children work with free verse, they may need even more guidance in suiting the pace of reading to the mood of the poem. When they have had time to perfect the reading of poem or story, the finished performance should be taped or presented to an audience.

Readers Theatre. In addition to oral interpretation in which a single reader reads to a group, the form known as Readers Theatre has become popular as a means of staging oral interpretation presentations. Readers Theatre requires not one reader, but a narrator and as many readers as are needed to cover all the character parts. This more formal technique is especially effective for children who are secure enough readers that they can direct their attention to the interpretation of character parts, following the written story only as a sort of script.

When you look for Readers Theatre material, look for good characterization and a style that reads aloud comfortably. You can judge the effectiveness of the style by reading a section aloud and listening for a natural flow of language. Selections for Readers Theatre should have enough characters to make the reading interesting but probably not more than five or six for a smooth production. The narrator provides the description that cannot be handled through dialogue and serves as a bridge between dialogue sections so that the plot moves along clearly. If the narrator's part includes lengthy discussions or descriptions and if the selection is otherwise effective, you might want to consider cutting the length of such passages. Some books that provide good excerpts for Readers Theatre are Robert O'Brien's *Mrs. Frisby and the Rats of NIMH*, Elaine Konigsburg's *From the Mixed-Up Files of Mrs. Basil E. Frankweiler* and *About the B'nai Bagels*, and Else Minarik's *A Kiss for Little Bear*. Although this last book may be read completely, short sections of the other books may be selected on the basis of the criteria we have been discussing.

Guiding Readers Theatre requires a somewhat more elaborate sequence of steps than other forms of interpretation. First, the children who are going to interpret the story must choose the character parts they will play. Generally, the narrator should be a strong reader. In fact, when Readers Theatre is adapted for use with young children, an adult can read the narrator's part, cuing the children if they have trouble following the format.

When character parts have been decided on, Readers Theatre practice proceeds in much the same way as oral interpretation. The readers should be encouraged to become familiar with the whole selection so that they identify the themes to be emphasized and are aware of unique qualities of the author's style. Each reader turns next to an in-depth analysis of his/her part, getting to know the character (in the case of the narrator, getting acquainted with all characters) and trying to decide how that character looks, acts, and talks. Allow time for the children to practice their parts, providing a tape recorder for them to use, if possible. And remind them not to read the "he said's" and "she said's." The production will sound smoother without them.

When individual parts have been rehearsed, it is time to put the production together. This involves, at first, rather informal practice sessions with the readers standing or sitting facing the narrator. Enough time should be allowed for these rehearsals so that students are able to read expressively and coordinate the reading with other parts. The help of an adult at this point can be valuable. If you notice that a reader is having trouble coming in at the right time, help the child to circle the key words that the previous reader will say and to listen for cues.

The final step is to stage the production. Because no props or costumes are used, this is really quite simple. You should try to find enough folders alike so that the readers can use them to hold their copies of the story. If high stools are available, they can be used also. If not, readers may sit on low chairs and rise to read or they can remain standing throughout the reading. Whichever arrangement is used, it is effective to have the readers of character roles facing the narrator and placed in a semicircle so that they can see one another. In that

way, both audience and readers have a feeling of interaction among the characters and a recognition that the narrator is keeping the thread of the plot running smoothly.

The Readers Theatre production is now ready for an audience. Younger children often enjoy watching and listening to this kind of presentation. If the readers have done a good job preparing, they can serve as good models to the younger children, too. An alternative to presentation before an audience is to prepare a videotape or a regular tape recording. If this is done, you can add background music or other sound effects which enhance the performance. A videotape is especially interesting to children later on, as they can notice how well they complemented the vocal interpretation with facial gestures and other bodily motions, limited though they are by staying in one place and holding a script.

The readers' responses to the story are most evident in tone of voice and facial expressions used to convey character interpretation. A lively interpretation or one which is especially moving indicates a high degree of emotional response by the reader. A reader who is able to show a character's feelings clearly has also been successful in interpreting the motives of the character and has probably recognized some fine points of the author's talent for characterization. The reader may also have sensed the author's purpose in including that character in the story. A narrator who successfully keeps the production moving shows awareness of the progression of incidents in the plot, of the importance of each incident, and, often, recognition of the relationships among story characters. Though Readers Theatre is not a discussion technique or a form that utilizes dramatization, it does, nevertheless, give opportunity for in-depth response to literature.

Occasionally, a reader may fail to interpret a role effectively or a narrator may show, by halting voice and stilted presentation, that he or she does not sense where the plot is going. You can seize those opportunities to engage the readers in interpretation of the story by such questions as: How does Jamie feel toward Claudia? How would he show it? What will happen as a result of the conversation? Working from questions that guide the readers in understanding the story more clearly, you can move to questions that require them to re-think their interpretations of character and narrator parts, questions such as: What tone of voice would Jamie use to show that he is a little afraid of Claudia even though he does admire her? How can the narrator effectively lead up to the next happening in the story by changing his or her reading? How can you show, by your voice and face, what Claudia is thinking? By working from story interpretation to character interpretation, you may help the readers to an increased emotional response to the characters and to the story itself.

Choral Speaking. If your class is responsive to poetry, you may want to introduce them to choral speaking to give an added dimension to their enjoyment. Choral speaking is another oral interpretation activity which gives children opportunity to enjoy and experiment with the sound of literature. Although some prose, especially folk literature, adapts well to choral speaking, poetry is the easiest form to use and usually the most effective, since a poet is generally concerned with effects of sound. The rhyme and meter of poetry appeal to children, and rhymes that are pleasant to hear can also be fun to say. The pleasure of interpreting a favorite poem orally is one of the rewards of choral speaking. Another is the sense of group participation toward an artistic effect. When children are accustomed to hearing poetry, when they have discovered how much like music it is in its variety of rhythms, moods, and melodies, and when they like it well enough to explore further, you may tell them something about choral speaking or speaking choirs.

Effective choral speaking requires the same attention to key words and pauses as effective oral interpretation of any kind. Children should probably hear a poem several times in order to sense the mood they will want to convey, whether rollicking, funny, sad, mysterious, or wondering. The next step is to help them identify key words in a line that should be emphasized. That helps to develop a natural flow to the speaking, one that clarifies the sense, and can help to eliminate some of the sing-song quality that often goes with poetry reading. In that regard, you may want to call attention to the punctuation marks which are signals to pause—periods, commas, and dashes. Attention to them can help to keep a group together as well as to increase the effectiveness of the presentation.

Mood is important in choral speaking and

can be enhanced by building contrast between parts of the selection. Grouping voices for effect is a good technique. A mysterious or scary part can be taken by a group of children with lower voices. By contrast, children with high voices can be grouped to speak lines that have a lilt and a happy swing. Another way of achieving contrast in sound is to have the whole group speak most of the lines and assign lines requiring special effects to a single voice. Remind children to keep their voices light and natural. Increase in volume can be achieved by adding more voices rather than forcing the tone.

Choral speaking is much like singing. Careful breath control and attention to rhythm are important. Sometimes, with formal verse choirs, one person acts as a director, using hand movements similar to those used with a singing chorus, but this is rare. For most informal situations, you need not direct the children but just get them started together, letting the rhythm of the piece carry them through.

Familiar lines and phrases in poetry and prose can be a good introduction to choral speaking. If you are reading aloud a folk tale such as "The Three Billy-Goats Gruff," encourage children to join you in "Trip, trap! Trip, trap! Trip, trap! went the bridge," increasing in volume when the middle-sized goat crosses and becoming very loud for the big billy goat's crossing.

For older children, "Overheard on a Saltmarsh" by Harold Monro is a good introduction to choral speaking through unison speaking of lines. This poem is essentially a dialogue between a goblin and a nymph. After several unison readings, you might want to read the goblin part (marked with a G) and let the whole group of children read the nymph part (N). Later, you can divide the children into two groups so that one group takes each part. This same procedure can be useful in introducing other poems, too.

(G) *Nymph, nymph, what are your beads?*
(N) *Green glass, goblin. Why do you stare at them?*
(G) *Give them me.*
(N)   *No.*
(G) *Give them me. Give them me.*
(N)   *No.*
(G) *Then I will howl all night in the reeds,*
   Lie in the mud and howl for them.
(N) *Goblin, why do you love them so?*
(G) *They are better than stars or water,*

Better than voices of winds that sing,
Better than any man's fair daughter,
Your green glass beads on a silver ring.
(N) *Hush, I stole them out of the moon.*
(G) *Give me your beads, I desire them.*
(N)   *No.*
(G) *I will howl in a deep lagoon*
     For your green glass beads, I love them so.
     Give them me. Give them.
(N)   *No.*[5]

A good choral-speaking file of poetry and prose is useful. Anthologies of children's literature such as *The Arbuthnot Anthology*[6] contain many poems and folk tales suitable for choral speaking. Try to find at least ten poems you would like to use plus several folk tales or other short prose pieces. Keep them in a loose-leaf notebook or in a card file so that you can add new selections as you find them.

Puppetry

Puppetry allows children to plan a dramatization, create dialogue, and work for effective use of the voice. In those respects it is similar to creative dramatics. However, since the puppeteer is not in view of the audience, the voice becomes extremely important as the means of creating a story interpretation. Puppetry is less threatening than other forms of dramatic activity for children who do not feel comfortable physically performing before an audience. Creating a puppet that will suit the character part unites puppetry with art in much the same way that drama relies on the artistic sense of set and costume designers. In puppetry, as in other forms of drama, the goal is to produce a unified visual and auditory effect that will effectively show the plot and the characters but, above all, will capture the spirit of the story. If the mood of the story is humorous, the puppet production should reflect that accurately. That is why so much literary response is involved in the planning of any successful dramatic presentation.

Action is an important ingredient in a good story for puppetry. Conflict is also a desired, though not a necessary, attribute. The number of characters is limited by the size of a puppet

Photograph by Marjorie Pickens.

stage (not more than five or six characters, as a rule) and those characters should contrast enough to make the production interesting. Subtle character differences will be lost. The popular Punch and Judy shows are good examples of the effectiveness of action, conflict, and strong characterization.

In creative dramatics and other theater productions, the actors are able to create three-dimensional characters with a range of emotions. The use of puppets tends to make the characters flat, often limiting them to such strong emotions as anger, fear, or joy but rarely showing much depth of feeling. Again, subtle emotions will be lost. For that reason, folk tales with their relatively flat characters are a good choice for puppet presentation.

Although puppet shows can involve a fairly elaborate plot, including several acts and scenes, beginners should choose stories with simple plots. The repetitive plot structure of many folk tales is another good reason for selecting them. If you produce "The Three Billy-Goats Gruff," for example, you have action consisting of three similar conflicts between the goats and the troll. The progression is easy to follow because of the order in which the goats enter the story—small to large—and the ending is easy to remember. The plot structure and the small number of characters make it a good choice.

Bear in mind the kind of setting you might need for a story and think about ways that the characters could be made into puppets. In "The Three Billy-Goats Gruff" the only necessary additions to a bare puppet stage would be the bridge and a hill with green grass. The charac-

5. "Overheard on a Saltmarsh" by Harold Monro from *Children of Love* (London: The Poetry Bookshop, 1913). Reprinted by permission of Lynn McGregor.

6. See *The Arbuthnot Anthology*, Parts One and Two.

ters can easily be constructed as paper-bag puppets, or hand puppets with papier-mâché heads. They can be made distinctive because of the contrasting sizes of the three goats and because the troll is evil and menacing in contrast to the goats. Remember that the puppet production will highlight the plot and the contrast between characters.

"Gudbrand on the Hill-side" is suitable for puppetry because it has a repetitive plot and the cast of characters can be whittled down by having only the animals and their owners appear on stage. "The Pancake" works well because of its repetitive language. Children's voices offstage can be used for several parts. "The Bremen Town-Musicians" can be easily adapted for puppetry by using an open box at one end of the stage for the robber's house. Some other tales which can be adapted for puppetry are "Tom Tit Tot," "Snow White," "Henny Penny," "The Three Little Pigs," and "The Three Bears."

A puppet production can take several forms, depending upon the kind of puppets used and whether a script is read or the dialogue is created by the puppeteers. Those decisions are made on the basis of the story you choose and the age level of children who will participate. Marionettes (puppets moved by strings from overhead) require a good deal of skill to handle but finger puppets, hand puppets, stick puppets, paper-bag puppets, balloon puppets, and adaptations of these are easy for preschool and elementary school children, and even for many handicapped children, to make and handle. With these options in mind, you can easily help children find or create puppets to go with a story.

When you have chosen a story for the production—and you may wish to do this on your own or with the help of the children—read it to the group, asking them to listen first for the characters they will need to represent by puppets. At the close of the reading, involve the children in a discussion so that they identify the characters and talk about the personality of each, whether that character's actions are predictably good or bad, whether the character is happy, sad, angry, funny, and so forth.

When the characters have been listed and discussed, children are ready to begin planning the puppets they will want to use. At this point, you may want to have several different types of puppets to show if you want the children to help with the decision of what kind to make. In preparation, you should think through the story to determine the most suitable kind of puppet for the characters, also keeping in mind the amount of time available to produce the puppets and the abilities of the children.

Although we will not give specific instructions here for making puppets, some possible means of preparing them may be helpful. Hand puppets may be purchased. They may be made from old socks with eyes, ears, noses, and mouths made of felt or some other material. Papier-mâché heads can also be fitted with mittens or socks for use as hand puppets. Finger puppets can be made from toilet-paper rolls or from mittens, in which case each finger can represent a different character. Stick puppets usually have heads made of papier-mâché set onto a dowel rod. A dress or clothing of some sort can be attached to the head, covering the stick and allowing the puppeteer to simulate arm movements of the puppet. Paper-bag puppets, among the simplest to make, require only decoration with eyes, ears, hair, etc. The balloon puppets are decorated with cut paper features and arms and limbs. They can be manipulated by a length of small dowel rod attached to the balloon opening.

When children design the facial features of the puppets, they should keep in mind the most important personality traits of the characters. If a puppet must appear happy as well as sad in the show, what kind of features will be best? The change of mood can be made by manipulating the face of a sock puppet. Can it also be shown by the way the puppet moves on the stage? How should the villain of a play look? the hero? How can a puppet's looks show kindness or helplessness? Such problems must be dealt with by puppeteers, and children will learn about character traits as they work with puppets. Encourage them to refer to the story from time to time to refresh memories about the characters.

When the puppets have been produced, guide the children in a review of the story in preparation for the show. The review should focus on identification of key episodes (later translated to scenes) which can be portrayed by the puppets and sections of the story which can be told by the narrator. You might want to help children make a simple chart showing a breakdown of the story line as this example for "The Three Billy-Goats Gruff" shows:

Narrator
Scene 1: Smallest goat walks over bridge
Narrator
Scene 2: Middle-sized goat walks over bridge
Narrator
Scene 3: Biggest goat walks over bridge and fights with troll
Narrator

When the simple outline has been made, the puppeteers may rehearse their dialogue for each of the scenes. When dialogue is created by the children, only one child is needed to operate the puppet and supply the voice. If you have students read dialogue from a story, they will probably have to work in pairs. one child reading and the other operating the puppet. An option is to have the dialogue recorded in advance of performance. That gives children more freedom to concentrate on maneuvering the puppets. If slow learners are mainstreamed in a regular classroom, they can participate as puppeteers more easily if they do not have to memorize or read dialogue. Background music can also be recorded over the dialogue and at scene changes to fill the pauses.

The puppet show should be rehearsed so that children learn to use a puppet stage to the best effect, especially to show the conflicts between characters clearly. If a puppet stage is not available, a table may be used as a stage by turning it on its side or by leaving it upright and covering it with a sheet, the children crouching out of sight behind it. Children should have opportunities to present their puppet shows to audiences so that they see the effect the characters and voices have on spectators. A videotape of the performance can also let them see the results of their work.

Response to the puppet show should reveal enjoyment as well as some understanding of the literary components of the story. Children who are eager to give their show to another class or to watch a show again reveal emotional involvement. A young child who comments that he likes the witch because she sounds as scary as she looks is responding to the characterization. Children often respond to plot by working hard to get just the right build-up of suspense or by highlighting an ending.

Written Response

If writing about literature is to be truly response, the students should be good enough writers that the act of writing does not interfere with expression of their feelings and ideas about a selection. The writing assignment should be structured for less mature writers so that they are not required to produce lengthy reports or essays about books. Whatever the format used, you should keep in mind the purpose of written response—to encourage children to think about the meaning of a story or poem and to react to its value.

Writing activities can develop awareness of the literary characteristics of prose and poetry. Sometimes a written response will carry a child beyond a response to that single book and inspire a creative effort to write an original story or poem. Through written response, children can experiment with form and style, trying to develop their own stories or poems based on plot structure or poetic form they have enjoyed. They may respond to point of view and characterization by trying to rewrite a story or episode as it might have been seen through the eyes of one of the characters. They can become more aware of the interaction of characters by trying to write a script for a favorite story.

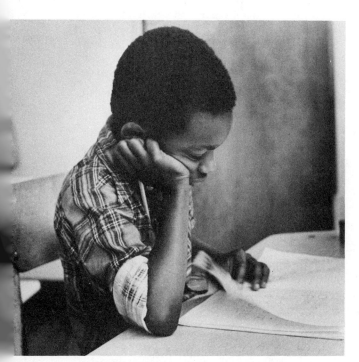
Photograph by Ken Heyman.

For some children, the written response may be the fullest expression of their responses to literature. These may be children who are somewhat shy about entering into a discussion or into dramatic activities. They most certainly are children who have well-developed writing skills. They may also be children who delight in mulling over a selection, thinking it through and pondering its meaning. That takes time and, for some children, it also takes solitude.

Keeping a diary record of books read, including a reaction to each book, is one kind of written assignment that older children can handle. The writing need not be lengthy, but children should be encouraged to record every book they begin even though the reaction may be, "I didn't finish it because it wasn't interesting." You may also want to encourage them to comment about ideas they gained from the book. Children may evaluate the books according to whether they are good enough to recommend to other students. If you sit down with a child after the diary has been kept for a period of time you both will find it interesting to identify favorite types of books and to look at the kinds of reactions to each book. If a diary has been kept for an entire year, children will find changes in their reading interests over that period of time, moving perhaps from an exclusive interest in animal stories to some interest in fantasy, and you will often find an increase in ability to show several different kinds of responses, including interpretation, evaluation, or literary judgment as well as emotional involvement.

Keeping a diary may lead students to illustrate a story in order to express their response to it. Children who are not adept at writing can illustrate key episodes and write a caption of one or two sentences for each. To do this the reader must determine which episodes are important and which can also be illustrated. The written caption should describe what is happening in the picture and should tell how it relates to the rest of the story. The exercise calls for close attention to character description and ability to interpret the descriptions artistically. The illustrations may be kept by a child as a sort of diary of books read or they may be used as part of a bulletin board display about books.

The traditional written book report is generally not the best way to encourage response to a story. It usually becomes an exercise to be read only by the teacher, especially when the writing process is a burden to the child who is required to write the report. A slight change in approach

Viewpoint

Language can be used as a means of feeding the child with facts which he is expected to memorise, or it can be used as a means of helping the child to clarify and express ideas he had formulated himself. By comparison with original thinking, memorising is an impoverished quality of the mind. In any sphere, learning which requires the child to think for himself is far superior to the type of mini-learning which depends basically on memorising. When the child has sufficient personal experience to which the experience of others can be attached, reading and writing become a major means of imparting and articulating knowledge. In the early stages it is highly important for learning to be a thinking, rather than a mere memorising, process, for the use a person makes of knowledge is the reason for acquiring it. How he uses knowledge depends on the quality of thought he brings to the acquisition of it.—Alice Yardley, *Young Children Thinking* (London: Evans Brothers Limited), 1973, pp. 47–48.

can make these reports useful to other students and give some purpose to the project. A card file of book reviews written by the children can be set up and can become an important part of the reference section of a classroom or library. A recommended format for the cards includes title and author, a short plot summary, and some comments indicating what the student felt was good or not good about the book. This written work should encourage an evaluation response and often some reaction to literary qualities as well.

Another variation on the traditional book review is the point-of-view book report. To introduce this format, you might ask a child who has just finished a book to name his or her favorite character from the story. Follow by saying, "You are _____ (name of story character). Tell the story the way you saw it." Once children become accustomed to the idea, you can simply instruct them to choose one story character and retell the story as they think that character would tell it. This approach leads to many opportunities for identifying with story characters, to emotional involvement with the story, and to interpretation of events.

Reports are not the only kinds of useful written responses to books. Creating a script from a favorite book can allow children a good deal of creative interpretation. The script can be designed for a puppet show or for a dramatization of the story. This activity requires that the child select an episode and decide which ideas can be conveyed by means of the dialogue already in the story and what information will have to be supplied by a narrator. Some of the narration can be drawn from the story, but the child will have to write an introduction to the episode, to be read by the narrator. The finished script can be performed before an audience. Seeing his or her script produced, however simply, should encourage the writer.

Creative writing often is inspired by books and poems children read. They may experiment with the plot structures and poetic forms they have enjoyed in their recreational reading. Many stories for young children—Pat Hutchins' *Rosie's Walk* and John Burningham's *Mr. Gumpy's Outing*, for example—follow a simple plot in which the principal character sets out on a journey and returns home at the end of the story. Stories with that structure can be shown on a flannelboard or chalkboard as circle stories, with the beginning and ending scenes at the top of the circle and the others proceeding around clockwise. After reading or hearing several such stories, children can make their own circle stories, drawing the illustrations, placing them on a large piece of chart paper, and writing a caption or short sentence under each picture so that the story can be told by words or by pictures.

A more complex writing activity but a very enjoyable one for many children is the photo essay. As a follow-up to reading an informational book about animals, for example, a child may decide to make a photo essay about how wild animals in the neighborhood spend the winter. If a camera is available, the child might take pictures of the wildlife, developing them and selecting certain ones to use for the essay. If photography is impossible, pictures from magazines and newspapers can be used. The pictures are arranged in the order needed to tell the story and an account is written, telling about the struggles of the animals and birds. The final step is to arrange the pictures and the text artistically on each page so that they complement one another. This may be done on large sheets of construction paper or on half sheets.

When children enjoy reading so much that they want to write their own stories or poems, they are showing a special kind of response. Creative writing is often a much greater effort than children think it will be, but the reward of having someone else read their stories is usually worth the work involved. Children usually need some guidance in thinking through these questions:

1. Who will your characters be and how will you describe each one?
2. Where and when will the story take place?
3. What kind of conflict (or problem) do you plan for the characters?
4. How will the plot lead up to the climax?
5. How will the conflict be solved and the story end?

You might want to ask the children to think about how these questions were treated in a book they recently read. Encourage them to proceed from there to devise their own characterizations and plot. The finished draft may be read by younger children or placed on a "writing corner" table to be read by others in the classroom or library.

The activities described in this chapter are suggested as ways of providing active participation in literature for those children who respond well to an activity-centered literature program. The ideas should also provide means of tempting and drawing out the child who is less enthusiastic about books and reading. Regardless of the approach you use, be ever alert to the hint of a response, whether it is a look of pleasure or concern over a book, poem, or passage; awareness of literary structure, style, or characterization; or interpretation of some aspect of a selection or judgment of the merit of a piece. By fostering that early response, you may lead a child to a depth of response that can produce an avid and sensitive reader.

Adult References[7]

ARTLEY, A. STERL. "Oral Reading as a Communication Process."

BAMMAN, HENRY A., MILDRED A. DAWSON, and ROBERT J. WHITEHEAD. *Oral Interpretation of Children's Literature.*

BRIDGE, ETHEL B. "Hickory Dickory Dock: Prelude to Choral Speaking."

CARLTON, LESLIE, and ROBERT H. MOORE. *Reading, Self-Directive Dramatization and Self-Concept.*

CHAMBERS, DEWEY W. *Literature for Children: Storytelling and Creative Drama.*

COGER, LESLIE IRENE, and MELVIN R. WHITE. *Readers Theatre Handbook: A Dramatic Approach to Literature.*

CURRELL, DAVID. *The Complete Book of Puppetry.*

7. Complete bibliographic data are provided in Appendix B.

FORDYCE, RACHEL. *Children's Theatre and Creative Dramatics: An Annotated Bibliography of Critical Works.*

GILLIES, EMILY. *Creative Dramatics for All Children.*

LAMME, LINDA LEONARD. "Song Picture Books—A Maturing Genre of Children's Literature."

MAY, JILL P. "Encouraging Children's Creative Oral Responses Through Nonnarrative Films."

MONSON, DIANNE, and DAYANN McCLENATHAN, eds. *Developing Active Readers: Ideas for Parents, Teachers, and Librarians.*

MOORE, VARDINE. *The Pre-School Story Hour.*

OMOTOSO, SAM. "Storytelling: A Cherished Cultural Heritage in Nigeria."

POST, ROBERT M. "Children's Readers Theatre."

ROSS, ELINOR P. "Comparing Folk Tale Variants."

ROWE, MARY BUDD. "Reflections on Wait-time: Some Methodological Questions."

SEBESTA, SAM LEATON. "The Neglected Art: Thought Questions."

SHAFTEL, FANNIE R., and GEORGE SHAFTEL. *Role-Playing for Social Values: Decision-Making in the Social Studies.*

SHEDLOCK, MARIE L. *The Art of the Storyteller.*

SIKS, GERALDINE B. *Creative Dramatics: An Art for Children.*

STEWIG, JOHN WARREN, and SAM L. SEBESTA, eds. *Using Literature in the Elementary Classroom.*

TOOZE, RUTH. *Storytelling.*

WAGNER, JOSEPH A. *Children's Literature Through Storytelling.*

WARD, WINIFRED. *Playmaking with Children from Kindergarten Through Junior High School.*

Chapter Seventeen: Introducing Literature to Children

In Chapters 5 through 14 we discussed the various types of writing for children—poetry, fantasy, and biography, for example. Suggestions for introducing children to these specific kinds of books are developed in this chapter. In a sense, this material represents a synthesis and application of ideas discussed in the preceding two chapters, where we considered the patterns of response to literature and methods of encouraging that response. The suggested activities here are based on the question: How can I best present this book to encourage children's responses? These responses may show involvement, interpretation, awareness of literary qualities, and/or evaluation of the story.

The goal of a literature program is to develop reading habits that will stay with children through adulthood. As children grow older, more and more of their reading should be independent reading from books of their own selection. The activities discussed here are designed to open doors to literature and to encourage reaction to books.

Formal study of literature is not usually a part of the elementary school curriculum. Experiences with literature most often come through the library program, the reading program, or the language arts program. A review of Chapter 16 will show the close ties of many of the activities there with what is typically included in language arts. A review of Chapter 15 will suggest relationships between what is considered literary response and the comprehension skill development included in a good reading program. Librarians will recognize that ideas from both chapters are related to sound objectives of a library program. A strong literature program can contribute substantially to the general educational experience and, above all, help children to enjoy reading.

Certain questions underlie any recommendations for literature-related activities: What abilities can children develop at this level? What materials and activities are appropriate for developing those abilities? As we saw in Chapter 2, the answers to such questions are closely tied to developmental characteristics of children. Communication skills continue to grow from infancy but require guidance and practice for fullest development. Listening skills are developed through storytelling and reading aloud to children. They are also fostered through planned book discussions, where children must respond to one another's ideas about a story. Speaking skills come into play in discussion, in role-playing, and in activities related to creative dramatics, puppetry, and oral interpretation. Writing skills are practiced when children respond to a literary selection with a writing activity. Ability to relate to others, to empathize, to appreciate problems common to people everywhere, is encouraged through book discussions and role-playing of problem situations.

Selecting appropriate materials for developing these abilities requires great care. Making a story or poem serve the activity by changing or manipulating a character or plot is generally not a good idea, as it shows a certain lack of respect for literature and for an author's purposes. Sensitive selection of material, on the other hand, can enhance the appeal of literature by showing how it helps us to understand and deal with our uncertainties and fears, how it provides release from tension through laughter, and how it gives us appreciation for the beauty of the language.

The use of media such as films, cassettes, and television productions based on literature can be an interesting addition to the curriculum. Children who have had experience with some of the Miller-Brody cassettes of Newbery Award books may be encouraged to plan what they would include on a cassette for one of their favorite books.[1] Comparison of a book with a film or television production is also a means of creating good discussions about literary characteristics.

Careful matching of activities with books is critical if those activities are to enhance rather than detract from the literary work. The activity should focus on a significant quality of the literature and not distort a poem or story simply for the sake of providing some activity for children. For instance, a story should not be used for puppetry if the literary qualities of plot, characterization, or style would be trivialized by such an adaptation. The same caution holds true for such activities as creative dramatics, story theater, role-playing, and oral interpretation. When activities are carefully selected and developed around appropriate material to generate responses, the combination can take a child into a book so that a memorable experience results. That is the goal of the abbreviated plans in this chapter.

The chart on pages 546–547 suggests how a teacher or librarian could expose children to a wide variety of books and encourage various kinds of responses. The chart lists recommended book activities discussed later in the chapter. Included are books for young children (preschool to age 6), for primary-age children (ages six to eight or nine), and for children in the intermediate grades (ages nine to twelve). Books for the first group are coded with a *(1)*, for the second group with a *(2)*, and for the third group with a *(3)*. If a book is usable with a broad range of ages, this is indicated by more than one number. Not all blocks on the chart are filled in. Some are blank because activities do not seem appropriate for certain types of literature as, for example, storytelling with informational books. Others are open so that you can use ideas from previous chapters in combination with books you select to create your own additions to the chart.

The starred books on the chart are those for which detailed activity plans are included in this chapter. Many books can be used successfully with more than one activity, and suggested alternatives are listed with each title.

You should not, by any means, look upon the books and activities described here as guidelines to be followed to the letter. They are simply included as models with the hope that you will try them and then use the ideas to create your own activities for books and poems you choose. If you follow through with the presentation of stories and poetry suggested here (or with alternate selections of your own choice), a fairly well-balanced, response-centered literature program can result. The program would not be complete, of course, unless children also were involved in a great deal of independent reading of library materials.

Picture Books

Since picture books appeal to primary-age children as well as preschoolers, some of the activities have been developed for primary-grade and could even be used with intermediate-grade children. This is especially true of the story theater presentation. Some of the activities require little time to carry out. Others are best done over a period of several days.

Reading Aloud

May I Bring a Friend? by Beatrice Schenk de Regniers, illustrated by Beni Montresor (choral speaking, role-playing).[2]

This is a fine book to read aloud to preschoolers who are delighted by the imaginative quality of the colorful illustrations. The "reading" of the pictures shares importance with lis-

---

1. Miller-Brody Productions, Inc., offers a Newbery Award Library consisting of recorded dramatizations, cassettes, and sound filmstrips, as well as books and teaching guides.

2. Activities in parentheses would also be suitable for this selection.

tening to the lively text, so children should be seated where they can see the illustrations as the story is read.

Emotional response to the fun of the story can be developed as well as literary response to the amusing illustrations, to the rhythm and rhyme of the verse, and to a recognition of the problems and solutions that make up each episode of the plot.

You can use the cover illustration effectively to introduce the story by asking children whom they see on the cover and who the little boy's friend is. Encourage them to listen and watch the illustrations to see what happens in this story about a queen, a king, and a little boy. As you read, be sure to emphasize the rhythm and rhyme of the lines, as young children generally respond well to those effects.

To encourage greater interaction with the events of the plot, you might want to pause after reading "So I brought my friend . . . ," inviting children to guess at who the friend might be or whom they would take if they were having tea at the palace. The words spoken by the king and queen provide opportunity for use of good oral interpretation techniques and you will probably find children joining you on "Hello" each time the king greets a new guest. Children may also enjoy guessing at the problems that may arise when the latest guest (for example, the hippopotamus) sits down to tea. They might like to guess where the elephant can sit and will be amused at the solution.

Throughout the reading, show the illustrations carefully. You might want to take time following the story to show all of them again, inviting children to look for surprising things in the pictures, such as the king and queen hanging their feet over the dock while they fish and the dismayed look on the king's face when the hippopotamus tries to sit next to him. Children will want to hear the story many times. Encourage them to join you on familiar verses so that they learn to use their voices to interpret rhythm and rhyme.

Discussion

Ox-Cart Man by Donald Hall, illustrated by Barbara Cooney (reading aloud, writing).

These illustrations will very likely evoke an emotional response without the aid of discussion. However, if children are given a chance to talk about the text and illustrations, the importance of the illustrative technique may become more clear. Discussion will be most effective with a small group of children. Ideally, they should be seated so that they can see the illustrations clearly because the illustrations form an important part of the historical perspective.

The discussion ought to arouse the children's curiosity about the details of everyday life more than 150 years ago. Some of the information is in the text, but the details are in the illustrations. The focus is really on the self-sufficiency of these people. It is important, too, for children to recognize that the story and illustrations show activities of the ox-cart man's family across seasons—in fall, winter, and spring.

The cover illustration is a good introduction to discussion of the book. Let the children study it so as to see what the ox-cart man and his ox and cart look like. They may be interested, too, in the details of the barn with wood stored neatly and in the fallen golden leaves that suggest autumn. With that introduction, read the story, emphasizing the poetic quality of language and showing the illustrations as you read along. Ideally, children would also have a chance to study the illustrations at close range.

To initiate discussion, you might ask children to describe some of the things the family made and grew. Where did they get their yarn, linen, wood, sugar, apples, potatoes, and other things? How is that different from our lives? Why did the ox-cart man have to make such a long trip in order to sell the things his family had made? At this point, you might want to ask children to look again at the pictures of his journey. What did he see along the way? What scenes do they like best?

Call attention to the other illustrations in the book, encouraging children to decide which of the activities on the farm they would most enjoy. Which illustrations do they like the best? What feeling does the illustration give them? Why is it so interesting? Finally, show all the illustrations again, asking children to look carefully at the trees. How do they show clearly the time of year in which each scene takes place? What other details has the illustrator included to give us a real sense of how time passes? Through discussion, children may become aware of the importance of illustrations to help give a sense of life in other times.

Genres	Suggested Activities			
	Reading Aloud	Storytelling	Discussion	Role-Playing
Picture Books and Wordless Picture Books	*May I Bring a Friend? (1) Millions of Cats (1)	The Tale of Peter Rabbit (1)	Nothing Ever Happens on My Block (1, 2) Ox-Cart Man (2)	Crow Boy (2, 3)
Folk Literature	*Tikki Tikki Tembo (1)	*"The Fisher-man and His Wife" (2, 3)	Tom Tit Tot (2) "Rumpelstiltskin" (2)	Once a Mouse (2)
Poetry	Far and Few (2, 3) *Where the Sidewalk Ends (2, 3)		*"Low Tide" (3)	
Fantasy	Mr. Rabbit and the Lovely Present (1)	"The Emperor's New Clothes" (2)	*The Borrowers (2) The White Mountains (3)	The Pushcart War (3)
Animal Stories	Nobody's Cat (1, 2) The Incredible Journey (3)		*Owls in the Family (2, 3)	*The Biggest Bear (2) A Bargain for Frances (1, 2)
Realistic Fiction	*A Pocketful of Cricket (1)		The Hundred Penny Box (3) *The Cay (3)	*The Bully of Bark-ham Street (2, 3) *Child of the Owl (3)
Historical Fiction/ Biography	*And Then What Happened, Paul Revere? (2)	*The Story of Johnny Appleseed (1)	Journey to Topaz (3)	Cesar Chavez (2, 3)
Informational Books	*Jambo Means Hello (2, 3)		*How to Turn Lemons into Money (3)	*Handtalk (2, 3)

(1) Preschool (2) Primary (3) Intermediate   *Book is discussed in this chapter.

Suggested Activities

Creative Dramatics	Story Theater	Oral Interpretation	Puppetry	Writing Activities
*Where the Wild Things Are (1, 2)	*Why Mosquitoes Buzz in People's Ears (2, 3) Drummer Hoff (1, 2)	A Kiss for Little Bear (1, 2)	"The Three Billy-Goats Gruff" (1)	*Time of Wonder (2, 3) Miss Nelson is Missing (2)
*The Four Musicians" (2)	"The Hare and the Tortoise" (1) "The King's Drum" (2)		*"The Pancake" (1, 2)	
	"Little Miss Muffet" (1)	"Mice" (2)	*"The Monkeys and the Crocodile" (2)	Hailstones and Halibut Bones (2, 3)
Caps for Sale (1, 2)	*In the Forest (1) The King's Stilts (3)	*Mrs. Frisby and the Rats of NIMH (3)	.	Paul Bunyan (2, 3)
Rabbit Hill (2, 3)	Sylvester and the Magic Pebble (2)	Runaway Ralph (2, 3)		*The Bat-Poet (3)
The Adventures of Tom Sawyer (3)	The Time-Ago Tales of Jahdu (2, 3)	*Ramona the Pest (2, 3)		My Side of the Mountain (3) The Great Gilly Hopkins (3)
The Witch of Blackbird Pond (3)		The Little House Books (2, 3)		North to Freedom (3) *A Gathering of Days (3)
Push-Pull, Empty-Full (1)			How to Be a Puppeteer (2) Puppet Shows Using Poems and Stories (3)	Small Worlds Close Up (3) Zoo City (1, 2)

Creative Dramatics

Where the Wild Things Are by Maurice Sendak (reading aloud, story theater).

This picture book is well known to many children. They are attracted to the vivid illustrations and enter gladly into the wild rumpus, enjoying the humor of the situation and reveling in the rhythm of the ungainly dance. And, at the close of the festivities, they understand Max's desire to go home to where "someone loved him best of all," which expresses the need most humans have for a close relationship with others rather than the adulation of a large number of strangers.

Responses which can be encouraged by means of dramatization include emotional response through enjoyment of story and pictures and empathy for Max's situation. Some children will also recognize and interpret the theme that being with people who love you is the most important thing. Children may also respond to the literary style and artistic qualities of the book. The plot structure really reveals a story within a story and this can be clearly shown through the dramatization. The characterization of Max and the marvelous illustrations add to enjoyment. Children will note Max's changes of mood, shown by his posture and facial expressions, and use that information to develop their own pantomimes.

Introduce this splendid picture book so that all the children in the group can enjoy the pictures. You might introduce it by showing the cover picture as you read the title, then asking the children whether they would like to go to a land inhabited by creatures resembling the one in this illustration. What kinds of adventures might they have? Turn, next, to the first-page illustration of Max in his wolf suit and tell children to listen and watch the pictures to find out what happens to Max in the story. Each picture has a wealth of detail that children will enjoy, so pace your reading to allow time for them to examine each picture before you move on to the next page. Allow time, too, for the spontaneous expressions of delight that are likely to come from the listeners. When the story has been read completely, you can decide whether to continue with the dramatization or to save it for a second session. A good picture book is enjoyed even more at a second reading so it may be better, especially with children below first-grade level, to read the story at two sessions.

Whenever possible, give children a chance to enjoy the pictures on their own between the two readings. Prior to the second reading, you may want to show the pictures to the group and give them time to tell what they especially enjoy in each. You can call attention to changes in Max's facial expression as the story progresses, asking children to try their own expressions of wickedness, shrewdness, delight, and sadness. This is a good activity to prepare for a dramatization of the story. In fact, with young children, a "dramatization" may be no more than your rereading of the story while all children mime the part of Max, or participate in the wild rumpus scene.

During the second reading, older children should listen carefully to notice the order in which the events take place. Ask them also to listen for the sayings that are repeated several times during the story. When you have finished reading, you might ask the children where the story begins and ends (in Max's house) and where the rest of it takes place (the ocean and the kingdom of the wild things). To further establish the setting for older children, you might help them identify scenes of the story: Max's house, Max's room, the ocean, the land of the wild things, the ocean, and Max's room, in that order.

With those scenes in mind, ask children to decide what characters they will need for dramatizing each scene. They may include Max's dog and inanimate objects, such as the vines and the boat, which are important for the action of the story. There can be any number of wild things, so that all children in the group will be involved in the dramatization. The next steps are to let children decide who will play each part and to give them time to practice pantomiming their roles and to improvise dialogue where it is needed. At this point, be sure those who want to are able to look at the illustrations again to notice the movement in each picture.

Prior to the dramatization, the staging should be planned so the children know what areas of the room will be used as Max's room, as the ocean, and as the land of the wild things. You will want to remind the children to listen well so that they come in at the right time. If the children are very inexperienced, you might want to provide the narration by reading from the text and pausing at the speaking parts to let children supply the dialogue. A word of caution: Since Max has a very active part, it might be wise to choose a child who is quite independent and able to remember the story line to play that part.

As a follow-up to the dramatization, you can talk with the children about their performance. What did they especially enjoy about the story? Why did Max go on his journey and why did he return home? Was his behavior similar to anything they have done? If you want to emphasize the literary structure, you might reread the first and last sections which take place in Max's room and ask children whether that part could be a story by itself. Then read the "journey" section, beginning and ending with the boat trips so that children can see the story within a story.

This book has many possibilities for extending enjoyment of literature and, indeed, the arts. If an appropriate record is available, you might want to use that during the wild rumpus scene to help children get into the spirit of the sort of dance that is shown in the illustrations.

Story Theater

Why Mosquitoes Buzz in People's Ears by Verna Aardema, illustrated by Leo and Diane Dillon (choral speaking, storytelling, reading aloud).

Picture books that have illustrations with a strong sense of rhythm and movement are good sources of material for story theater productions. Story theater is closely related to dance. Like dance, it requires an interaction with mood and a depiction of that mood through movement. In a fine picture book, the mood is conveyed directly through the illustrations and also, usually, through the words of the story.

In *Anansi the Spider*, Gerald McDermott's graphics are beautifully designed. The book is a fine vehicle for story theater because the actions of story theater do not have to "use" the book; they develop spontaneously from interaction with it. The same thing is true of *Why Mosquitoes Buzz in People's Ears*, in which the Dillons' illustrations show strong, flowing movement. Indeed, every curve of an animal functions as part of the overall design. The rhythm of the prose and stylistic touches of onomatopoeia elaborate the movements made by the animals. Going through the book, reading the text and looking at the illustrations, you are struck with the strong sense of physical movement. Children who have listened to the story and studied the pictures may interact with them to give a meaningful interpretation. Responses which may be encouraged through the story theater experience are an emotional response to the characters and their common problem; literary response, showing appreciation for style of illustrations and style of writing, especially the onomatopoeia; and interpretation of the theme, telling how the tribal people arrived at the mythical explanation of the mosquito as a nuisance.

The story should be read with much attention to the oral interpretation of character parts and of onomatopoetic words. Pictures should be displayed so that all children can see them. When the reading is completed, you might want to let children review the story, identifying the key characters in the order of their appearance.

At the close of the reading, children will want to talk about the sequence of events that lead up to the mosquito's banishment from the council of the animals. You might explain that this is a folk tale and ask them how such a story might have started. In the discussion, you may want to introduce the myth as one way early people tried to explain happenings they could not really understand, such as earthquakes and volcanic eruptions.

Since the pictures tell the story so beautifully, you would be wise to go through the book once again, just showing the pictures and encouraging children to look at them carefully to notice how the animals look and how they seem to move.

If the story is to be used for story theater dramatization, you probably should plan that activity for a second day, beginning that day with a second reading of the story. Ask children to listen for sounds used to describe each animal and for the sequence of events in the story. When the reading is completed, ask children to repeat the onomatopoetic sounds ("mek, mek," etc.) used in the story to describe each animal. Give them a few minutes to develop their own interpretations of the animal, basing them on illustrations and on the verbal descriptions. They might enjoy trying to show how an iguana might move so as to make a sound like "mek, mek, mek, mek." At this time, children might also want to decide who will play the part of each animal during the story theater production. When they have had time to practice and have decided how to use available space for a stage, you are ready for the reading. Read with the best oral interpretation techniques, pacing the story so that children have time to pantomime the character parts and emphasizing the onomatopoetic words so that your reading inspires the actors.

For follow-up discussion to the story theater

production, you might focus on such questions as:

What strange events in nature are being explained in this story?
How did the storyteller and the illustrators let us know what the characters were like?
Which illustration(s) do you like best? Why?

The format of this plan can be adapted for use with other folk tales, including many of the Anansi stories.

Writing Activity

Time of Wonder by Robert McCloskey (discussion, oral interpretation).

Many kinds of responses may be opened up through *Time of Wonder*. Certainly a good reading of it will stir some children to ask for a repeat because "the words are so nice." After a second reading, you can ask which were their favorite descriptions. Some children will respond emotionally because they, too, have had an experience at the seashore or at a lake in the wilderness. With a few thought-provoking questions from an adult, some children may be able to deal with an underlying theme which emerges in the last paragraph with the question, "Where do hummingbirds go in a hurricane?" With encouragement, children will appreciate the dramatic changes in weather shown in the illustrations. They will notice the contrast between scenes with a great turbulence and those of great serenity, the contrasts in people's moods as well as the contrasts in nature.

When the story has been read once with a sensitive interpretation and plenty of time for children to enjoy the illustrations, you might want to substitute a showing of the Weston Woods film for a second reading. Whichever plan you choose should help children to focus on the effective use of illustrations to re-create the many moods of weather and the out-of-doors. Find time for some discussion of favorite scenes from the story and encourage children to think of the way they felt as they looked at the pictures and listened to the words this author used to describe the coming storm and the clearing afterward.

If children have shown interest in the story, you might suggest that they make their own picture essays, selecting some aspect of nature that they see every day. They should decide for themselves what to describe, draw the illustrations or take photographs, and write the crea-

tive descriptions that will go alongside each picture and create a story. You might remind them of the care with which McCloskey chose words to make the verbal description as vivid as the pictures. When the illustrations and creative writing have been completed, children should have a chance to plan the layout of the work, using a photo-album format made from sheets of construction paper.

Folk Literature

Reading Aloud

Tikki Tikki Tembo, retold by Arlene Mosel, illustrated by Blair Lent (storytelling, story theater).

This retelling of a Chinese folk tale has enough suspense to involve children with the problems and misfortunes of Chang and his brother, Tikki tikki tembo. The illustrations capture the rather easygoing mood of the village but they also describe quite explicitly the dangerous position of being in the bottom of a well!

Responses which may be generated through a reading of the story include emotional involvement with the story as children feel concern for the safety of first one boy and then the other. Children may also respond to literary qualities of the story, particularly the cumulative plot structure and the use of rhythm and rhyme in the long name. And children will love to repeat that with you: "Tikki, tikki, tembo-no sa rembo-chari bari ruchi-pip peri pembo."

You might preface the story by asking children to think of the longest name they have ever heard. Then read the title of the story and tell them that this is just part of the name of one of the boys they will hear about. His whole name was so long that it got him into lots of trouble. They are to listen to see how he got into and out of that trouble.

As you read, use your voice and hand gestures to emphasize the development of plot and the movement of the action from one place to another (from the well to the stream to the old man and again to the well) and try to pause during the second episode, when Tikki tikki tembo falls into the well, so that children have a chance to think ahead and try to decide what will happen next, based on their knowledge of Chang's escapade. Let children join you each time Chang struggles to pronounce Tikki tikki tembo's long name. They will want to hear the story again and again and will enjoy retelling it themselves. In fact, you can show the illustration at the end of the story and let children use it to prompt their retelling of the tale.

Storytelling

"The Fisherman and His Wife" from *Grimm's Household Tales*, translated by Margaret Hunt (story theater, puppetry).

Folk tales are part of the oral tradition and are the single richest source for storytelling. "The Fisherman and His Wife" is a story with a moral children cannot miss. It is a good choice for storytelling because the incidents are repetitious, yet they build in such a way that it is quite easy to keep the plot sequence in mind. The rhyme that is repeated each time the fisherman goes to seek the flounder also provides a kind of structure for the story and children will enjoy repeating it with you as they become familiar with it.

Responses that develop rather naturally to this story are emotional involvement with the woman's greed and her undoing as well as interpretation of the theme of the story and literary response through appreciation for the repeated rhyme. Responses may also show that children are examining their own values.

The story is not difficult. A fisherman catches a flounder that is really an enchanted prince. The fisherman gladly releases the fish when he finds it can talk. But his wife, when she learns of it, is furious that he has not asked the flounder to grant a wish. The upshot of it is that the poor fisherman returns to the sea, calls back the flounder, tells his wife's wish, and the flounder grants it. This process is repeated six times until finally the flounder has had enough and sends the couple back to their original living quarters, a hovel. The secret in memorizing the story is to think of the sequence of the wishes: (1) to live in a cottage, (2) to live in a castle, (3) that the wife should be King, (4) that she should be Emperor, (5) that she should be Pope, and (6) that she should be like God. The last is too much for the flounder and he returns the couple to their condition at the start of the story.

There is certainly a lesson in the story, and when you pause at the end you can give children time to reflect on the outcome of the wife's greedy ways. If children respond spontaneously or with a little encouragement to "think about what that story tells us," the way

is open to a discussion in which they may share their own experiences that bear on the same lesson. If children do not share their ideas quite spontaneously, do not force a discussion. That would put the focus on the "lesson" and perhaps on self-righteous moralizing and not on enjoyment of the story itself.

Children may notice that the same episode is repeated over and over with just a little change each time. If they do, you might encourage them to think about other stories like "The Three Billy-Goats Gruff" that have similar repetitive story patterns.

Discussion

Tom Tit Tot, illustrated by Evaline Ness (storytelling, role-playing, puppetry).

The story can be read aloud with time allowed afterward for a discussion, or it may be paired with "Rumpelstiltskin" to show children how very similar stories can appear in different countries in somewhat different forms.

Responses to *Tom Tit Tot* may include emotional reaction to the girl's predicament and elation when she finds out the strange creature's name. Children may also recognize the language of the tale as unique to another time in history and therefore an important quality of the folk tale. They may respond also to the literary characteristics of the plot, recognizing that the creature appears three times to the girl—the magic number three that they have seen in such other tales as "The Three Billy-Goats Gruff" and "The Three Little Pigs." Literary response may also be encouraged when children have heard and compared "Rumpelstiltskin" and *Tom Tit Tot*. Children will recognize similarities and differences in the characters and plot as well as differences in the language of the two versions.

When you have read *Tom Tit Tot*, you might pause to see what kinds of spontaneous responses children make. You may work from these responses to develop a discussion of aspects of the story that mark it as a folk tale. You might ask children to recall some of the words used to describe the girl. What did her mother call her? What could the word "gatless" mean? Ask them to think of other words used that sound old-fashioned. They should recognize "upped and oped it" and "Noo, t'ain't" as well as others. You might also ask what they especially enjoyed about the story to allow them to express emotional reaction to plot and characters. To develop response to literary characteristics, you can ask how many times the creature returns for the girl to guess its name, encouraging children to recall other tales they know that are built on a repetition of three similar episodes. If the children know "Rumpelstiltskin," questions can help them to note the main character in each and to compare them, to identify the problem and its solution in each story, and to compare the language in the British version with the translation of "Rumpelstiltskin" from the German.

Creative Dramatics

"The Four Musicians" from *The Oak Tree Fairy Book*, ed. by Clifton Johnson (story theater, storytelling).

This tale has enough action and enough surprises to provide good material for creative dramatics. Children will respond with empathy to the plight of the animals and express pleasure at the good turn their lives take. Emotional response may also be evident in laughter as children realize that the robber has misunderstood the rooster's crowing for the cries of a man on the roof shouting, "Chuck him up to me." Children are sure to enjoy the dramatic experience. In addition, they may react to literary structure by recognizing the common folk-tale theme of the poor but good person overcoming the villain.

When the tale has been told or read, ask the children to think about the story characters. Who were the musicians, and what talents did they use to make their journey a success? Before proceeding further with the plot review, you might want to let the whole class pantomime each character, adding sound effects if your walls are thick enough! Be certain to remind them that these are old, unwanted animals, poor in spirit at the beginning, but gaining courage when they are together. They may also want to pantomime the robbers as they are surprised at their meal. With that background, ask children to recall the sequence of events they will need for producing a dramatization. Essentially, there are three major scenes: the first when the four animals meet along the road; the second when they come upon the house, see the robbers inside, frighten them away, and finish the feast; and the third when

the robbers return and are frightened away again by the animals. Once characters have been chosen, the scenes can be practiced one at a time, first pantomimed and then with dialogue created by the children. Finally, all three scenes are played in a continuous dramatization.

Puppetry

"The Pancake" from *Tales from the Fjeld* by Peter Asbjörnsen and Jörgen Moe, translated by Sir George Webbe Dasent (storytelling, choral speaking).

"The Pancake" is one of several versions of this tale. Another well-known one is *Journey Cake, Ho!* by Ruth Sawyer. "The Pancake" can be adapted quite easily for puppetry, using paper bag puppets, finger puppets, or balloon puppets. A balloon puppet attached to a stick is especially effective in creating a sense of movement, for the pancake is, of course, always moving. This idea is adapted from a production of "Henny Penny" by Aurora Valentinetti.[3]

Responses will include emotional reaction as children enjoy the escapades of the pancake and foresee its demise. In terms of literary response, children may notice the use of rhyming names and repeat them along with the storyteller. They will notice the cumulative plot structure, with the pancake repeating the names of all the animals it has outwitted each time a new character appears. You may want to give a chance for evaluation of the story by reading *Journey Cake, Ho!* after children have completed the puppet production of "The Pancake." Ask them to decide which version they most enjoyed.

A number of words and sayings are repeated throughout the story, so the telling of the story should be true to the original to keep the flavor of the language. Unless you can memorize it, a reading will probably be more effective than a telling. When the story has been presented and perhaps repeated, with the children joining in on the familiar parts, they will be ready to assemble the cast of characters needed for a puppet show.

During the show, one child is responsible for each character. Using a table turned on its side

---

3. Alvina Burrows, et al., *New Horizons in the Language Arts* (Harper & Row, 1972), p. 163.

as a stage, the action takes place with the pancake crossing in front of the stage over and over, each time meeting one of the hungry creatures, beginning with Manny Panny and ending with Piggy Wiggy. As Piggy Wiggy swallows the pancake, the puppeteer behind the table can pop the balloon, creating an ending that will satisfy young audiences. In order to keep the story line going well, the adult reader should pay careful attention to pacing.

Poetry

Reading Aloud

Where the Sidewalk Ends, written and illustrated by Shel Silverstein (oral interpretation, writing).

The poems in this collection are most notable for their humor. Related to that is the importance of reading them so that the funniness is enhanced, so that play on words is heightened and the pacing of each poem suits the treatment of theme. Before you read, decide what is funny about each poem. How does the author create the humor? Is it through alliteration, play on words, pacing? How should the poem be read so as to get the best effect?

Children will want to hear the poems more than once. In the case of those such as "Boa Constrictor," encourage them to join in on the second or third reading, adding pantomime as they begin to memorize the poem.

A bit of discussion following some of the poems will help children to recognize why a poem is funny. They can begin to realize that the children in these poems are much like themselves and to wonder who they are really laughing at.

Discussion

"Low Tide" from *The Malibu and Other Poems* by Myra Cohn Livingston (oral interpretation).

*Found. One red starfish
at low tide. One
plump, prickly starfish wrested by arm,
by leg, squirming among
purple, bubbling sea urchins.*

*Plop him in a pail? Scoop up the
salt water? His color will fade.
He will miss his bubbling urchins.*

*Grab him by the arm. Return him
to his rock, his pink anemone.
One red starfish. Lost.*[4]

If a poem is to be discussed, it should have form and content that will inspire discussion. That is essential because a forced discussion will become simply a question-answer period and will very likely lead to a dislike for poetry. "Low Tide" is a poet's description of an experience many children have had. They may never have seen a live starfish or an anemone, but they have probably captured tadpoles or even small water bugs in puddles.

Response may be an emotional reaction, centering on the joy of finding something as fascinating as a starfish. Children may relate to the speaker in the poem, explaining what they would have done if they had found the starfish, perhaps thinking of their values concerning ecology. There may also be a reaction to the literary qualities of the poem, responses that show a listener's attention to description or to form.

The title is a good introduction to the poem. Read it and ask children what they would expect to see on a beach at low tide. If your children are not acquainted with ocean and tidal changes, it may be necessary to explain briefly the way a beach looks when the water sweeps out to sea, leaving hundreds of yards of exposed sand. Read the poem once, not too quickly, emphasizing the first and last words so that children get a sense of the form of this free verse. Let them discuss it informally if they offer comments. Then read it again.

After the second reading, you may want to open up a discussion by asking children whether they have ever had an experience like this poet is describing. Why did the speaker in the poem decide not to keep the starfish? Is the last part of the poem as fast-moving and happy as the first? Why not? How does the pace of the poem reflect the speaker's mood?

To help children think about the use of descriptive words and phrases, ask if they could draw a picture of what they heard. If necessary, reread, asking them to listen for all the ways this poet paints a word picture for us. How is the starfish described? The sea urchins? Chil-

4. From *The Malibu and Other Poems* (A Margaret K. McElderry Book). Copyright © 1972 by Myra Cohn Livingston. Used by permission of Atheneum Publishers and McIntosh and Otis, Inc.

dren may also become aware of form if you show the poem so that they can see the one-word beginning and ending. Ask children how "Found" and "Lost" shape the poem, even though it does not have a regular rhyme scheme.

Puppetry

"The Monkeys and the Crocodile" from *Tirra Lirra* by Laura Richards (choral speaking, story theater).

> Five little monkeys
>   Swinging from a tree;
> Teasing Uncle Crocodile,
>   Merry as can be.
> Swinging high, swinging low,
>   Swinging left and right:
> "Dear Uncle Crocodile,
>   Come and take a bite!"
>
>   Five little monkeys
>   Swinging in the air;
> Heads up, tails up,
>   Little do they care.
> Swinging up, swinging down,
>   Swinging far and near:
> "Poor Uncle Crocodile,
>   Aren't you hungry, dear?"
>
>   Four little monkeys
>   Sitting in the tree;
> Heads down, tails down,
>   Dreary as can be.
> Weeping loud, weeping low,
>   Crying to each other:
> "Wicked Uncle Crocodile,
>   To gobble up our brother!"[5]

This is an example of poetry that can be adapted for use with puppets without ruining the effect of the poem. Indeed, the brief but neatly developed plot presents a strong visual effect. Children will enjoy showing the transition from verse 2 to verse 3 (five teasing monkeys to four sad monkeys) with puppets.

The activity described here can involve children in several different kinds of responses. The foremost response should be enjoyment of the poem, shown through spontaneous reaction to the poem's words and rhythm. Response may also involve interpretation as children realize that too much teasing can indeed lead to sad consequences for children as well as monkeys. They may also grow in literary awareness

5. From *Tirra Lirra* by Laura E. Richards. (Boston: Little, Brown and Company), 1955.

as they develop a sense of the plot structure. This should, however, be developed informally, not through direct instruction.

Actual work with puppets should be preceded by several readings of the poem. On the second or third reading, encourage children to join you on the conversational lines at the end of each stanza. In that way, the whole group can eventually be involved and can experience the rhythm of the poem.

The puppets can be simple finger puppets. In order to create a production that enhances the poetic qualities, the children must hear the poem many times. Emphasize the rhythm of lines like "Swinging high, swinging low" and "Weeping loud, weeping low," encouraging children to repeat them with you. You might also suggest that children move their hands or their bodies in rhythm as the monkeys might move, trying to convey the feeling of happiness or sadness. The final reading, done with puppets, can combine your reading of the poem with children joining in on the last lines of each verse.

Fantasy

Discussion

The Borrowers by Mary Norton (oral interpretation, writing activities).

This book can give children some ideas about the characteristics of fantasy. Most important, it can generate strong emotional response. Children are intrigued with the lives of the tiny people; they share the Borrowers' fear of discovery and they enjoy the clever uses the Borrowers have for items we "lose." The stories are so intriguing that more than one child has remarked that it almost seems possible there could be little people behind the walls. Children can also respond to literary aspects of the story. They begin to appreciate the use of point of view to create an effect and it is rather a surprise when they realize that the "human beans" described by the tiny Borrowers in this story are very much like themselves. With some guidance, children can also see that the author has used manipulation of characters in a clever way to create this fantasy. For in this story it is the characters who make it a fantasy. They are not talking animals as in Russell Hoban's *A Bargain for Frances*, nor are they people from another planet. They are tiny people who look and talk and feel just like us. The setting is realistic; only the characters have been manipulated to produce the fantasy.

There is enough suspense in these episodes to hold attention as you read them aloud. Take advantage of the places where good oral interpretation skills will pay off. At the end of the first chapter, pause and give children a few minutes to react spontaneously to the story if they wish. Some children will enter into the spirit of the story if you ask them what they have lost lately and how the Borrowers might be able to use it. Give them a chance to think about how the Borrowers must feel when they hear the heavy tramp of footsteps entering a room near them. You might try some point-of-view questions such as: You are Pod. Where were you when you first realized the boy had seen you? What were your first thoughts? That information is quite clearly given in the book. To switch point of view, you might then say: You are the boy. What did you think when you saw the tiny creature halfway up the curtain in the nursery?

When the book has been completed, you should give children a chance to think back over the story. Did it seem real to them? What could have happened? What could not be possible? How did the author change the characters so that she made the story a fantasy rather than a realistic story? Interpretation may come into play, too, when children discuss the reasons that some things terrified the Borrowers but seem completely harmless to us.

Story Theater

In the Forest by Marie Hall Ets (reading aloud).

This enjoyable story is simple enough so that young children can dramatize it. There are twelve animal characters in addition to a boy and his father, so it is possible to involve quite a large group. Response to the story will surely be at the emotional level as children interact with the joyousness of the walk. Some children will show involvement with the characters through good pantomime.

Because the pictures are not large, you may want to gather children closely around you for the reading. Following that, let them think over the characters to decide which they enjoyed most. A second look at the pictures may aid them in remembering the cast of characters. As a story character is identified, you might want to let children imitate the character, encouraging them to use bodily motion and good

facial expressions to develop the pantomime. When all characters have been identified and mimed, let children choose their parts and find places in the room. Read the story, pausing so children can play out the character roles, adding appropriate noises when they can.

Oral Interpretation

Mrs. Frisby and the Rats of NIMH by Robert O'Brien (discussion, writing activities).

This story offers children a marvelous opportunity for adventure. Many children also develop a feeling of empathy for the rats as well as for Mrs. Frisby and her family. Underlying it all is the question: Where can the mass of new scientific information take us? This fantasy, through humor and pathos, gives readers a chance to consider that important question. Responses may take the form of emotional reaction to the problems of the story characters and should also include inferences about the events that lead to interpretation of the author's purpose.

Children find it easy to identify with the rats and to interpret their behavior. Readers Theatre is a good way to build on the interpretation. It is particularly effective for this story because there are a number of sections with extended dialogue involving several characters. In order to prepare children for the oral interpretation, agree upon the cast of characters in the section. For example, the episode from page 115 (mid-page) to 119 would need: narrator, Nicodemus, Justin, Dr. Schultz, Julie, and George. Ask the children to think about the personalities of those characters, so far as they know them. What are their motives in this scene? What tone of voice would they assume in speaking to one another? What does each character have to gain from what happens? You might also ask them how this scene relates to the outcome of the story. What significance does it have? The last question is based on the assumption that, in order to do a good Readers Theatre presentation, children have read the entire story so that they understand the interrelationships among characters and events.

When children have some ideas about the role each character plays in the scene, let them choose parts and practice their reading independently. You might want to read the narrational parts or work with the narrator so that the child makes that part a good structure for the dialogue.

If children enjoy this section of the story, they may want to search for other short passages they can adapt for Readers Theatre. One other good section is from page 200 (last paragraph) to page 202 (next to last paragraph).

Animal Stories

Discussion

Owls in the Family by Farley Mowat (oral interpretation, writing activities).

Farley Mowat, a Canadian naturalist, wrote this highly entertaining story about a boy and his two pet owls. Oral reading of part or all of the story followed by discussion gives children a chance to share their enjoyment and to appreciate what the author is telling them about wild creatures. Emotional response should emerge in the form of laughter at amusing incidents and descriptions and, for some children, in an understanding of Billy's friendship with his owls. Feelings of empathy for one or another of the characters may also be expressed. Through discussion, children may become aware of a literary quality of the story as they see how frequently the author injects humor involving a story character's mishaps. Evaluation can be a part of the response pattern if children are asked how the author has succeeded in giving the owls qualities that are both human and animal-like.

The entire book is suitable for reading aloud and is written with an episodic plot structure so that each chapter stands alone. Too much discussion of any book can interfere with enjoyment of the story. Nevertheless, there are times when discussion is important so that children can share their thoughts about a story and, with your guidance, begin to understand why they appreciate the writing. Discussion can be reserved for the end of the story or, as we suggest here, initiated at the end of a chapter or of several chapters.

To set a situation for discussion of the Mowat book, you might want to read the first five chapters aloud, pausing after Chapter 5 to give the children a chance to react. You can begin the discussion by noting parts of the story that brought laughter from the group as you read. Ask why they laughed. What had the author done to create a funny scene? Why did they laugh when Wol falls with a thud as he is learning to fly? Why did they laugh when

Weeps refuses to even try to open his wings and falls like a rock instead? Perhaps they will recognize the ridiculousness of each situation and also the fact that we often laugh at another person's misfortune. (They may recall laughing when a friend got his trousers caught in a bicycle wheel and tumbled off.) Why does that make us feel good?

Children may be interested in talking about the relationship Bill has with his owls. Why does he seem to know what they are thinking? Some children may be able to compare their relationships with pets to the example in the story. A natural extension of this questioning tack leads to student evaluation of the way these animals are presented. You can pursue this by asking children in what ways the owls in the story appear human and in what ways they appear like wild animals. If students are able to make these comparisons, you might ask whether they think the author should have included the wild animal episodes (such as the killing of the cat) as well as the accounts of the owls' almost human behavior. What is he telling us?

Role-Playing

The Biggest Bear by Lynd Ward (discussion, reading aloud).

The fact that this animal story is based on an underlying set of values makes it possible for readers to relate to the situations Johnny finds himself in. Children should be encouraged to respond emotionally to the story—to enjoy the pictures as well as the story line and to identify with Johnny's feelings about his bear. They may also evaluate the story ending by role-playing and then discussing the author's solution to Johnny's problem.

Successful role-playing depends on the degree to which children can interact with a problem and work out their own solutions. The story must set up a problem children understand and care about. *The Biggest Bear* can draw a strong emotional response from children and can also encourage interpretation of the story and sometimes evaluation of the story ending. Responses may also indicate that the story involves children in value formation.

To involve children to the fullest, it is a good idea to read the story aloud to the group, showing the pictures so that all the children can enjoy them. There are several good places to stop for role-playing of a story problem situation. The first is on page 47 when Johnny is told that the bear must go. When the children have looked at that picture, you might pose this point-of-view situation: You are Johnny. Talk the situation over with your father. What will you do? Ask two children to volunteer to play the roles of Johnny and his father and let them carry on a conversation to help Johnny decide what to do about the bear. Several other pairs of children may also want to participate when the first group is finished.

Continue reading the story. You may want to stop again on pages 52, 56, and 60 so that Johnny and his father can try to solve the problem of the bear each time he returns. Or you may prefer an uninterrupted reading of the story, stopping at page 76 where the bear is captured for a zoo. Children will enjoy giving opinions of that problem solution. You may want to invite them to be Johnny and his friends. Ask: Was this a good solution to the problem for Johnny *and* for the bear? What other ending can you think of? Which do you prefer?

Writing Activity

The Bat-Poet by Randall Jarrell (reading aloud, discussion, oral interpretation).

This story, with prose interwoven with poetry, is unusual and beautifully written. Because of its quality, it deserves to be read aloud by an experienced reader. The approach suggested here is a combination of oral reading, discussion, and follow-up writing activities.

Responses to be encouraged are an emotional response to the bat's need to share his experiences with others. Many children will empathize with the bat's frustration at not being able to interest the other bats in the wonderful things he sees during his daytime excursions. Children will respond, also, to the content of the poems as well as to such literary characteristics as the author's choice of words. Certainly they should hear the poems several times so that they are aware of the musical quality combined with superb description.

You might present the book to children by asking whether they have ever thought what the world might look like to an animal, such as a squirrel or a bird. What would they notice? What could be important to such creatures? In this book, they will view life through the eyes of a bat. The story is too long to be read at one sitting, so you may read only certain parts or find good stopping points. It would be a good idea to stop occasionally to let children repeat and enjoy some of the poetry and other especially fine descriptive passages. In order to prepare for later writing activities, you may want to begin a chart titled "Good Descriptions," writing a few phrases from the opening of the story and encouraging children to help you decide what to add to the chart as you go along. Some ideas for the beginning are: "the color of coffee with cream in it," "a fur wave went over them," and "squirrels chattered . . . like two rocks being knocked together."

The follow-up writing activity can be based on children's appreciation of descriptions used in the story. You might simply ask them to choose some animal (or bird) that they are quite familiar with and perhaps can observe frequently. Several options are available for a writing activity based on this story. Some children may want to write a prose and poetry description of the creature, as was done in *The Bat-Poet*. Others may prefer to describe the world as it might be seen by the creature, getting experience in writing from a different point of view. In either case, emphasis should be on producing fresh, descriptive phrases, emphasizing some of the techniques used by the writer of this fine book.

Modern Fiction

Reading Aloud

A Pocketful of Cricket by Rebecca Caudill (discussion, role-playing).

Young children look forward to that magic time when they will go to school. They can also be somewhat fearful about that important event, especially if they have listened to stories told by older children. Caudill's story about the first day at school for a country boy is told with sensitivity, and when it is read aloud well, it can draw young children to the boy so that they, too, experience some of his sadness at trading his free farm existence for a life of school buses and classrooms. Although the story is rather slight, it is a moving description of a teacher's sympathy for a small boy who finds a sort of security in his cricket. The most important responses will be those which show emotional involvement and empathy with the boy and his problem. Children may also interpret the situation as similar to times when they may have wanted a familiar object (such as a doll or a teddy bear) near them in a strange place.

Discussion

The Cay by Theodore Taylor (role-playing, writing activities).

Phillip, a white boy living in Curaçao during World War II, and Timothy, a West Indian, are the central characters in this story. Phillip had grown up with the prejudice that black people were different from whites in many ways. That prejudice sets the stage for a conflict in his feelings when he is shipwrecked and finds himself on a raft, alone with the elderly black man, Timothy. Timothy's kindness, the terrifying experience of the hurricane, and Timothy's death are described from the point of view of the now-blind narrator, Phillip. Use such questions as: You are Phillip. How did you picture the island? What do you remember best about Timothy? How did your "picture" of Timothy change as you lived with him? How would you describe the hurricane, as it felt and sounded to you? How would you describe Timothy during the hurricane, telling how he treated you and what he meant to you? When did you realize that you were no longer prejudiced against Timothy? What do you think caused the change in your feelings?

A movie has been made of the story. It would be interesting to divide students into three groups for discussion of the story: those who have seen the movie, those who have read the book, and those who have read the book and seen the movie. Children who have read the book might be asked to describe the way they visualize the setting and characters. Those who have seen the movie might also be asked to give their impressions of the scenery and the characters, based on what they gained from the film. Those contrasting descriptions could lead to a good discussion about the contrast between the visual presentation in the film and the descriptions in the book. Children who have experienced the story through both book and film might have interesting comments concerning these questions: What is lost in a movie version of a story? Can a movie really let you imagine how a blind person perceives the world? On the other hand, are there parts of the story that seem better told in the film version than in the book?

Role-Playing

Child of the Owl by Laurence Yep (discussion, writing activities).

In order to participate fully in role-playing, children must recognize and relate to the story characters' problems. They must be able to experience situations in the story from the characters' points of view. *Child of the Owl* presents a clear-cut situation for role-playing because the story focuses on Casey's difficult adjustment to life in San Francisco's Chinatown. Caught between two cultures—her grandmother's Chinese way of life and her father's westernized life—Casey is constantly faced with situations which are puzzling to her. To enter into the story completely, children must also be able to understand how Casey's grandmother, Paw-Paw, feels about her life in Chinatown.

To lead children into the role-playing, you might wait until the entire book has been read and then pose situations such as these: You are Casey just after you arrived in Chinatown. Describe Paw-Paw as you saw her then. What does she mean to you? When students have had time to recapture that effect, ask them to shift to a later part of the story. Now Paw-Paw is in the hospital. Describe the thoughts that you have about her. What does she mean to you now? Why have your thoughts about her changed?

For a somewhat more difficult challenge, set up this situation. Read aloud or have children read pages 28–29, where Casey first meets Paw-Paw. Then say: You are Paw-Paw. Your grandchild is coming to stay with you. You don't really know her but you know that her way of life is different from yours. What thoughts are going through your mind as you see her arrive? You might ask them to take Paw-Paw's point of view after she and Casey have come to know each other, say after the two of them have been to Chinese movies (pp. 83–93). Now, as Paw-Paw, how would you describe Casey? Have your feelings about her changed? How?

Whatever the questions used to motivate role-taking, they should help children to understand more fully the concerns that motivate story characters.

Oral Interpretation

Ramona the Pest by Beverly Cleary (discussion, creative dramatics).

This is a delightful book to read aloud. Listeners are amused by Ramona's antics, but they also realize that she is a little person with fears and needs quite like their own. They can respond emotionally by laughing at her but also by feeling compassion and empathy for her. Building on the emotional response, children can begin to interpret the story by inferring that Ramona seems to be a little girl who doesn't mean to be naughty but who sometimes gets into trouble because she thinks she has been badly treated by someone. They may also infer that the author is trying to show us the things that can happen to make kindergarten (or any school experience) difficult for children.

Oral reading of the story should take advantage of the many dialogue parts that help to build Ramona as a character. Numerous sections of the story are appropriate for Readers Theatre work. It is preferable, of course, that children read or hear the entire story before singling out one section for oral interpretation. An effective section is near the beginning, where Ramona goes to school for the first time (pp. 10–17, ending with the amusing "present" misunderstanding). Another good section is the scene where Ramona is stuck in the mud and must be pulled out by Henry Huggins (pp. 114–125). A third choice is the "dawnzer" episode (pp. 171–173). Third- and fourth-graders are far enough advanced to read these sections and they are also enough older than Ramona that they can feel a sort of security in having passed through the difficult kindergarten period.

Historical Fiction and Biography

Reading Aloud

And Then What Happened, Paul Revere? by Jean Fritz (discussion, creative dramatics).

A cleverly illustrated description of old Boston opens this account of some of Paul Revere's adventures. Emotionally, children will respond to the humorous descriptions such as Paul's advertisement of his art in making false teeth, and they will enter into the excitement of his life as a secret agent and an express rider between Boston and Philadelphia. They may make some evaluation of the story if they are able to compare it with other sources.

There are many human touches in this telling of Paul Revere's life as a patriot. Your reading can add greatly to children's interest in the man as a person as well as a patriot. You can pause in strategic places to give children a chance to think about the situation and consider what Paul might do next. A good example of that is the picture of Paul and his friends on the dock when he realizes he has no spurs, with a caption reading, "What could be done?" Children may come up with the same idea as Paul—to send the dog home with a note so that his wife could attach the spurs to the dog's collar and send them back.

An important part of this book is the inclusion of notes from the author. Children should be made aware of them and you may want to read some or all aloud.

Storytelling

The Story of Johnny Appleseed by Aliki (reading aloud, discussion).

Young children are interested in living things. They enjoy planting seeds and watching them sprout. Though they may not be able to imagine a country without carefully tended orchards and fields, they will be interested in this story about a man who cared enough about trees and about people to spend part of his life planting seeds that could eventually produce fine orchards. Children respond emotionally to the character of Johnny Appleseed, especially when the story is told convincingly. The picture book by Aliki provides a basic story line which storytellers can use or adapt. You may want to show the illustrations from the book as you tell the story of Johnny Appleseed's life.

Writing

A Gathering of Days by Joan W. Blos (discussion).

An activity for older children following the reading of either poetry or prose ought to serve to make children more aware of the qualities of the genre. In particular, the activity should help them to realize why the book or poem is a good example of that genre.

A Gathering of Days uses the form of a journal as an avenue to historical fiction. The approach gives a sense of the immediacy of day-to-day concerns in pioneer times. It also encourages an emotional response to the experiences of Catherine Cabot Hall, the narrator. It is that autobiographical quality that makes the book a natural vehicle for inspiring writing activities.

To lead children from the reading to the writing experience, you might ask them to think about Catherine's journal. What kinds of experiences did she choose to include? Why were they important to her? What is there about the writing that causes us to feel that we actually know Catherine and can understand the problems of a girl growing up in the early 1800s? Children should be able to recognize that Catherine includes enough of her own emotions in the journal so that the bridge between contemporary lives and her own is made possible. The person's life makes the history come alive.

As follow-up to the discussion, ask children to think of the day-to-day episodes in their lives that they would include if they were trying to give a good picture of what it is like to be living in the late twentieth century. Ask them to keep a journal for several weeks, making entries nearly every day, as is done in *A Gathering of Days*.

Informational Books

Reading Aloud

Jambo Means Hello by Tom and Muriel Feelings (discussion, role-playing).

This beautifully illustrated picture book is an alphabet book that will interest older children as well as those in the primary grades. Information in the book ranges from an introduction with a map showing countries where Swahili is spoken to definition and pronunciation of twenty-four Swahili words, one for each letter of the Swahili alphabet. Word concepts are elaborated in the double-page illustrations.

Do not neglect the introduction when you read the book aloud, for it presents important information about the people who speak Swahili. You can also use it to acquaint children with the fact that an introduction is an important part of many nonfiction books. As you read the book, show the pictures so that children can see how the pictures help to develop word concepts. You may want to let children

speak some of the words together, pantomiming the concepts as they say the new words. That is an effective procedure for words like *heshima* (respect), *jambo* (hello), *rafiki* (friend), and *Karibu* (welcome).

Responses to be sought and encouraged are, of course, enjoyment of the language and curiosity about word meanings, responses which touch on emotional reaction, interpretation, and attention to literary qualities. Children may show interest in similarities between Swahili and English, evident in words for father, mother, and school. Discussion may lead children to seek other information about how words enter a language.

Discussion

How to Turn Lemons into Money by Louise Armstrong (role-playing, writing).

This guide to economics, described in terms children can understand, is likely to promote lively discussion. A lemonade stand is used as the model for a business. As the business of running the stand is described, the vocabulary of economics is introduced. Discussion could focus on interpretation of the text and illustrations and on application of the ideas to new situations. Appropriate questions to generate discussion might be: If *you* were to go into business, what would you make and sell? How would you decide on the market value of your product? Where might you get a *capital loan* if you needed one? What would you call another person who was selling the same product? Suppose you were ready to liquidate your assets. What would they be? What other kind of business would you like to open next? Write a set of guidelines for someone else who is thinking of starting a business.

Role-Playing

Handtalk by Remy Charlip, Mary Beth and George Ancona (discussion).

Handtalk is a book which builds children's curiosity about ways of communicating without speech. If you introduce the book by describing the world of a deaf person who must rely on eyes alone for communication, you can create sensitivity to the handicap of deafness. Experience with the book should help children to develop empathy with deaf people and admiration for the way they are able to communicate. The illustrations in the book include signing as well as finger spelling. As one example, the letter *L* is introduced with *Love.* A large colored picture shows Mary Beth signing *love* by crossing her hands over her chest. At the bottom of the page, small photos show the correct finger spelling for each letter of the word. The inside book cover shows a large number of other words or ideas which can be signed.

You may want to introduce this informational book by letting children look at each of the pictures, practicing several of the signs. When children have had a chance to study the book, they will be ready for a role-playing situation in which you ask a question and ask them to answer it by signing, as though that were their only means of communication. Examples of questions are:

What is your favorite food?
How do you like to spend your spare time?
How do you feel about animals?

A follow-up discussion might give children a chance to compare the advantages of signing and finger spelling to decide which is the more effective and which might communicate more easily.

Summary

In all the books recommended and activities suggested in this chapter and in all the books and activities you find work well in your own experiences, the key to your success will be building on children's enjoyment. Response to literature can take place only when children have enjoyed a story or poem. This idea may seem obvious on the surface, and yet it can be lost sight of so easily when choosing books and activities for a particular group of children with particular needs and tastes. If you take pleasure or enjoyment as the starting point and as the goal of a literature program, you are likely to have most success measured in terms of enthusiastic readers. Through the enjoyment, a sense of literary structure may develop and children may be encouraged to try to interpret aspects of the work. Occasionally, they will look at the story or poem critically, evaluating it in some fashion. Most important, however, we hope children will enjoy these experiences with literature so much that they will want to read and reread books independently, to take time alone with favorite picture books, and to investigate the books of other authors.

A second hope is that you, the adult, will seek out other books and poems that you would enjoy sharing with children, adapting some of the activities in this chapter to your own material. A further hope is that you can provide plenty of books and a pleasant reading environment. An activity-centered program in combination with a strong program of independent library reading can provide the basis for ever increasing enjoyment of and reliance on reading as a leisure-time pursuit.

Children's Books Mentioned in This Chapter

AARDEMA, VERNA. *Why Mosquitoes Buzz in People's Ears,* ill. by Leo and Diane Dillon. Dial, 1975.

ALIKI. *The Story of Johnny Appleseed,* ill. by author. Prentice, 1963

ALLARD, HARRY. *Miss Nelson Is Missing,* ill. by James Marshall. Houghton, 1977.

ANDERSEN, HANS CHRISTIAN. *The Emperor's New Clothes,* ill. by Virginia Lee Burton. Houghton, 1962.

ARBUTHNOT, MAY HILL, and ZENA SUTHERLAND. *The Arbuthnot Anthology of Children's Literature,* 4th ed. Scott, Foresman, 1976. (See for "The Fisherman and His Wife," "The Bremen Town-Musicians," "The Hare and the Tortoise," "The Pancake," and "Rumpelstiltskin.")

ARMSTRONG, LOUISE. *How to Turn Lemons into Money,* ill. by Bill Basso. Harcourt, 1976.

BLOS, JOAN W. *A Gathering of Days.* Scribner's, 1979.

BOYLAN, ELEANOR. *How to Be a Puppeteer.* McCall, 1970.

BROWN, MARCIA. *Once a Mouse,* ill. by author. Scribner's, 1961.

————, ill. *The Three Billy-Goats Gruff.* Harcourt, 1957.

BURNFORD, SHEILA. *The Incredible Journey,* ill. by Carl Burger. Little, 1961.

CAUDILL, REBECCA. *A Pocketful of Cricket,* ill. by Evaline Ness. Holt, 1964.

CHARLIP, REMY, MARY BETH and GEORGE ANCONA. *Handtalk,* ill. with photos. Parents, 1974.

CHRISTOPHER, JOHN. *The White Mountains.* Macmillan, 1967.

CLEARY, BEVERLY. *Ramona the Pest,* ill. by Louis Darling. Morrow, 1968.

————. *Runaway Ralph,* ill. by Louis Darling. Morrow, 1970.

COURLANDER, HAROLD. *The King's Drum,* ill. by Enrico Arno. Harcourt, 1962.

DE REGNIERS, BEATRICE SCHENK. *May I Bring a Friend?* ill. by Beni Montresor. Atheneum, 1964.

EMBERLEY, BARBARA. *Drummer Hoff,* ill. by Ed Emberley. Prentice, 1967.

ETS, MARIE HALL. *In the Forest,* ill. by author. Viking, 1944.

FEELINGS, MURIEL. *Jambo Means Hello,* ill. by Tom Feelings. Dial, 1974.

FRANCHERE, RUTH. *Cesar Chavez,* ill. by Earl Thollander. T. Crowell, 1970.

FRITZ, JEAN. *And Then What Happened, Paul Revere?* ill. by Margot Tomes. Coward, 1973.

FYLEMAN, ROSE. *Fifty-One Nursery Rhymes.* Doubleday, 1931, 1932.

GÁG, WANDA. *Millions of Cats,* ill. by author. Coward-McCann, 1928.

———. *My Side of the Mountain,* ill. by author. Dutton, 1959.

GRILLONE, LISA, and JOSEPH GENNARO. *Small Worlds Close Up.* Crown, 1978.

HALL, DONALD. *The Ox-Cart Man,* ill. by Barbara Cooney. Viking, 1979.

HAMILTON, VIRGINIA. *The Time-Ago Tales of Jahdu,* ill. by Nonny Hogrogian. Macmillan, 1969.

HOBAN, RUSSELL. *A Bargain for Frances,* ill. by Lillian Hoban. Harper, 1970.

HOBAN, TANA. *Push-Pull, Empty-Full.* Macmillan, 1972.

JARRELL, RANDALL. *The Bat-Poet,* ill. by Maurice Sendak. Macmillan, 1967.

LAWSON, ROBERT. *Rabbit Hill,* ill. by author. Viking, 1944.

LEWIS, STEPHEN. *Zoo City.* Greenwillow, 1976.

LIVINGSTON, MYRA COHN. *The Malibu and Other Poems,* ill. by James Spanfeller. Atheneum, 1972.

MATHIS, SHARON BELL. *The Hundred Penny Box,* ill. by Leo and Diane Dillon. Viking, 1975.

McCLOSKEY, ROBERT. *Time of Wonder,* ill. by author. Viking, 1957.

McCORD, DAVID. *Far and Few,* ill. by Henry B. Kane. Little, 1952.

MERRILL, JEAN. *The Pushcart War,* ill. by Ronni Solbert. Scott/Addison, 1964.

MILES, MISKA. *Nobody's Cat,* ill. by John Schoenherr. Little, 1969.

MINARIK, ELSE. *A Kiss for Little Bear,* ill. by Maurice Sendak. Harper, 1968.

MOSEL, ARLENE. *Tikki Tikki Tembo,* ill. by Blair Lent. Holt, 1968.

MOWAT, FARLEY. *Owls in the Family,* ill. by Robert Frankenberg. Little, 1962.

NESS, EVALINE, ill. *Tom Tit Tot.* Scribner's, 1965.

NORTON, MARY. *The Borrowers,* ill. by Beth and Joe Krush. Harcourt, 1953.

O'BRIEN, ROBERT C. *Mrs. Frisby and the Rats of NIMH,* ill. by Zena Bernstein. Atheneum, 1971.

O'NEILL, MARY. *Hailstones and Halibut Bones,* ill. by Leonard Weisgard. Doubleday, 1971.

PATERSON, KATHERINE. *The Great Gilly Hopkins.* Crowell, 1978.

POTTER, BEATRIX. *The Tale of Peter Rabbit,* ill. by author. Warne, 1903.

RASKIN, ELLEN. *Nothing Ever Happens on My Block,* ill. by author. Atheneum, 1966.

RICHARDS, LAURA E. *Tirra Lirra,* ill. by Marguerite Davis. Little, 1955.

SAWYER, RUTH. *Journey Cake, Ho!* ill. by Robert McCloskey. Viking, 1953.

SENDAK, MAURICE. *Where the Wild Things Are,* ill. by author. Harper, 1963.

SHEPHARD, ESTHER. *Paul Bunyan,* ill. by Rockwell Kent. Harcourt, 1941.

SILVERSTEIN, SHEL. *Where the Sidewalk Ends,* ill. by author. Harper, 1974.

SLOBODKINA, ESPHYR. *Caps for Sale,* ill. by author. W. R. Scott, 1947.

SPEARE, ELIZABETH GEORGE. *The Witch of Blackbird Pond.* Houghton, 1958.

STEIG, WILLIAM. *Sylvester and the Magic Pebble,* ill. by author. Windmill, 1969.

STOLZ, MARY. *The Bully of Barkham Street,* ill. by Leonard Shortall. Harper, 1963.

TAYLOR, THEODORE. *The Cay.* Doubleday, 1969.

UCHIDA, YOSHIKO. *Journey to Topaz.* Scribner's, 1971.

WARD, LYND. *The Biggest Bear,* ill. by author. Houghton, 1952.

WILDER, LAURA INGALLS. *The Little House in the Big Woods,* ill. by Garth Williams. Harper, 1953. (See others in the series also.)

YASHIMA, TARO. *Crow Boy,* ill. by author. Viking, 1955.

YEP, LAURENCE. *Child of the Owl.* Harper, 1977.

ZOLOTOW, CHARLOTTE. *Mr. Rabbit and the Lovely Present,* ill. by Maurice Sendak. Harper, 1962.

PART FIVE:

Areas and Issues

Areas and Issues
———Children and Books

Introduction

*Dorothy M. Broderick, Editor** *

"Areas and Issues—Children and Books" is designed to bring to the attention of teachers, librarians, and all adults interested in children's reading and children's development a few of the concerns that help or hinder us in our attempts to make reading and books an important part of each child's life. The areas change with time, which does not mean that areas covered in previous editions, such as racism and sexism, are not still pressing problems. Rather, in selecting the present topics, we are merely reflecting current emphasis in areas that continue to have great impact on the education system.

Censorship of school materials has mushroomed in recent years. Where once the major problems in the field of censorship focused on mass market publications, in recent years the shift to removing materials from classrooms and school libraries has occurred. When schools and libraries had trouble in the past, the censor was usually an individual who had become upset with a particular book being used in the classroom or circulated from the library. That has changed today and the censor is usually an organized group with long lists of books or subjects objectionable to the group's philosophical view of life. Coping with organized groups requires very different skills than coping with a single person. Moreover, the most notable attacks on schools in the late 1970s were led by members of Boards of Education. These changes require that school personnel be well educated in the issues involved in censorship and in understanding the purpose of the First Amendment.

Research is a key to understanding. When done well, it offers the researcher new insights, verifying or disproving popular conceptions. It is vital that we produce the research studies that help us understand better the impact that print and nonprint materials have on youthful readers and viewers. This is particularly true since the censors assume a direct relationship that noncensors perceive as simplistic.

The one area in which numerous attempts have been made to correlate the effects of a medium upon children is television. While the majority of popular articles on television and children continue to focus on perceived adverse effects, the scholarly research shows more ambivalence in assigning behavioral changes to television viewing. The television industry has countered attacks on its programming by devising ingenious techniques by which teachers can

* Dorothy M. Broderick is Associate Professor in the Graduate School of Library Service at the University of Alabama, Tuscaloosa.

use the medium to further reading competency. Since it is clear that television is not going to disappear, creative teachers have begun to understand that using it wisely is more productive than hoping that children will stop watching.

Mainstreaming of the physically disabled and the Educable Mentally Retarded has become a major priority in American schools. The Independent Education Profiles necessary for each disabled child to receive the education appropriate to his or her needs requires a sound background by classroom teachers. Working with specialized school personnel, the classroom teacher of the future will find it easier to develop I.E.Ps. if she or he has read and viewed widely the materials by and about the disabled in our society.

As we enter the 1980s there is little question that understanding other nations and their cultures is vital to the continued peaceful existence of the United States. The earlier we impart to children an accurate and sympathetic understanding of other peoples of the world, the brighter the future will be for a peaceful world in which all nations can co-exist despite differing—and conflicting—cultural values.

In order for all of the above goals to be achieved, there must be wide access to materials for all children regardless of where they live or how rich or poor their community. Adults whose primary responsibility is serving children's information needs have been extremely reluctant to accept the fact that these needs cannot be met in a self-contained library (school or public). The concept of networking, in which many libraries band together to provide the information and services necessary to satisfy youthful patrons' needs, has yet to be widely accepted by youth-serving librarians. School libraries, at least, have accepted the idea that not all information is best conveyed in print form and have made great strides toward producing truly multi-media resource centers. Few public library children's rooms have reached that point. If children's information needs are to be met in the future, schools and public libraries must learn to share resources.

The bibliographies accompanying the following articles will allow interested adults to gain knowledge of and insight into the importance of the subjects. The articles here are designed to provide an initial introduction to the subjects covered; the bibliographies will allow for true expertise to be acquired.

Censorship

Alice P. Naylor*

Literature has the power to shock and to challenge ideas and feelings. Some readers prefer not to be disturbed or to entertain ideas different from their own. That is a matter of personal choice.

Persons who, on the other hand, take action to block other people's access to books are called *censors*. Hundreds of attempts to prohibit the availability of reading materials and films are reported every year throughout the United States. The prime purpose of dozens of individuals and organizations is to remove materials from library shelves and school classrooms. Other organizations and individuals are equally vigilant in trying to maintain the right of all people—including children—to read and view what they wish. Most of the attempts to censor and the struggle to retain freedom of access to materials are fought at the community level, with the group that can marshall the most public support for its position carrying the day.

When cases reach the courts, they are argued under the First Amendment to the Constitution of the United States:

"Congress shall make no law respecting an establishment of religion, or prohibiting the free exercise thereof; or abridging the freedom of speech, or of the press . . ."

At the start of the 1980s, the United States Supreme Court has rendered decisions under the First Amendment affecting youth rights in only two cases. The first was in 1943, *Barnette v. West Virginia*; it established the right of children not to be forced to salute the flag since their religion (Jehovah's Witnesses) forbade them to do so. The second case was *Tinker v. Des Moines Independent School District* (1969); it declared that students have the right to express political opinions in school. The case involved the wearing of black armbands to protest the Vietnam War, and one of the youths involved was ten years of age.

Since 1969 the Supreme Court has not addressed the question of youth rights in relation to the First Amendment. However, there have been a number of Federal District Circuit Court

* Alice P. Naylor is Chairperson of the Department of Educational Media at Appalachian State University.

rulings on the question of the right of Boards of Education to remove materials from school libraries. Unfortunately the rulings are in conflict, a situation that indicates that shortly the Supreme Court will have to rule and establish "the law of the land."

Decisions in *Minarcini v. Strongsville City School District* (1976), *Chelsea Right to Read Committee v. Chelsea School Governing Committee* (1978), and *Salvail v. Nashua Board of Education* (1979) have denied school boards the right to remove materials from school shelves simply because a majority of the board members find the materials personally offensive. On the other hand, decisions in *Bicknell v. Vergennes Union High School* (1979) and *Pico v. Board of Education, Island Trees* (1979) have ruled that school boards have the right to remove any materials—for whatever reason—the board members wish removed. Teachers and librarians must pay attention to court rulings covering the area in which they work since lower federal court decisions are binding on them. Equally important will be the Supreme Court decision, should one be forthcoming in the near future.

With the exception of the *Barnette* and *Tinker* cases, all of the above cases involved senior high schools and it is unclear whether the judges in the *Strongsville*, *Chelsea*, and *Nashua* cases would write the same decisions if the conflict involved children in elementary schools. While young children's right of free speech has not been argued before the courts yet, censorship of books for younger children is, nevertheless, an everyday occurrence.

Three broad issues evolve from the contest between the censors and advocates of children's intellectual freedom: (1) morality, what it is and how it is learned; (2) community standards in a pluralistic society, and (3) professional prerogative.

Views of Morality

To understand who is a censor and who is not, it is important to understand how different people view the concept of morality. In our pluralistic society there are many views of morality, the differences being too complex and numerous for a full exposition here. Basically, the conflict is between people who perceive morality as a series of "shoulds" and "oughts" that can be taught at home, in the school, and in the church by preaching and modeling, and those who perceive morality as a set of values internalized by the individual through the processes of acquiring knowledge and making and defending decisions.

When one believes that virtuous behavior can be taught by example and preaching, it follows that nonvirtuous behavior can be learned in the same way. This leads to a willingness to suppress materials that demonstrate nonvirtuous behavior, whether such behavior is actually condoned in the materials. An ordinary "fun" book such as Rockwell's *How to Eat Fried Worms* is objected to because it is believed that youthful readers will rush out to collect and fry worms. For years Lindgren's *Pippi Longstocking* was not bought by many librarians who feared that Pippi's disrespectful attitude toward authority figures would lead children to imitate her outrageous behavior.

The most frequent causes for objection are those of language and sex. *My Special Best Words* by John Steptoe is objected to because it contains slang words for bathroom functions. Sendak's *In the Night Kitchen* has sometimes been removed entirely from library shelves or

Viewpoint

Censorship is an old, old problem. As I said before, it runs in the human family throughout history. Probably when the first man said, "I think . . . ," he was confronted by his cave brother or sister, who said, "You can't say that!" And, of course, what makes it all so tricky is that it is not a case of good against evil, where the sides are clearly drawn. It is a question of good versus good, your perceived good as opposed to my perceived good. The Fundamentalist parent has as much right to his view of the world and society as anyone else. And he has the right to forbid his child to read books he considers harmful. In the realm of the abstract, it's all very clear and easy. But when the abstract becomes specific, it's not easy at all. What about the book that ninety-nine percent of the parents and all of the librarians and teachers find harmless and even commendable but that offends one parent? Should that parent's child be required to read it, if it is on a reading list? On the other hand, does the objecting parent have the right to insist that no other child read it? Most of us would say no.—Isabelle Holland, "On Being a Children's Book Writer and Accompanying Dangers," *The Horn Book Magazine*, February 1980, pp. 37–38. Copyright © 1980 by Isabelle Holland. Reprinted by permission of JCA Literary Agency, Inc.

had diapers painted on the nude little boy.

Less traditional censors are objecting to the immorality of bigotry, violence, sexism, and other anti-human values when expressed in literature. Bannerman's *Little Black Sambo* is the most controversial book in terms of perceived racism while feminists object to such books as *The Giving Tree* by Silverstein, which they see as reinforcing sexual stereotypes.

Are any or all of these books immoral? Will they induce immoral behavior in the children who read them? Should children have access to sex information without regard to their parents' wishes or control? Is profanity ever justified in books for children? Can books foster bigotry and anti-human values? How does the advocate of intellectual freedom for children respond to the question of morality?

John Milton wrote in *Areopagitica:*

"It is from out of the rind of one apple tasted that knowledge of good and evil, as two twins cleaving together, leaped forth into the world. And perhaps this is that doom which Adam fell into of knowing good and evil, that is to say, of knowing good by evil."

Most modern developmental psychologists would agree with Milton that it is impossible to know good without knowing evil. Moral development along the stages specified by Kohlberg (see Chapter 2, p. 35) requires stimulation of conflict in the minds of children by their having to choose from among alternatives when faced with a moral dilemma. Values clarification education is based on a similar premise: that one comes to acquire values by learning to make choices. Literature is not only valuable in this respect, it is essential since it allows children to confront choices they might not otherwise experience in their lives.

The better the book, the more choices it offers. Thus, the story of Cinderella can stimulate discussion of the dilemma between choosing to be kind or to be selfish. Or, it can be discussed in terms of whether the ultimate goal in life for women is to marry well, a prince if possible.

What concerns many adults is that books presenting ideas they disapprove of will not be discussed under the leadership of a trained teacher or other responsible adult. These adults worry about the free borrowing of materials from libraries without any subsequent discussion to clear up the child's confusion. The only response to this concern is to point out that teachers, librarians, and parents have the responsibility to project a warm, accepting attitude toward the children's questioning, whatever the topic, thus creating the atmosphere in which they will talk about the ideas books give them.

The importance of allowing—indeed, actively encouraging—discussion is indicated by the research of W. Cody Wilson, a behavioral sciences professor, who reported in the Winter 1978 issue of *Top of the News* that adolescents functioned at lower levels of moral reasoning on Kohlberg's scale in relation to sex than in relation to nonsexual social, political, and economic issues. Wilson concluded that the lower levels of reasoning occur because adolescents have less information on sex and less opportunity to discuss issues related to sexual morality.

Wilson further concluded that many adults prefer adolescents to function at lower levels of moral reasoning in sexual issues. Stages 1 and 2 on the Kohlberg scale (fear of punishment, promise of reward) reflect reasoning encouraged by adults who believe that the best way to assure proper behavior is to lay down a series of edicts: "Don't have sex because you'll become pregnant," "Don't use profanity because people won't like you." Edicts tend to stifle growth whereas discussion can stimulate it. If more adults come to understand the "developmental journey" undertaken to achieve high level moral reasoning, they may also come to understand that children become more moral when they can determine for themselves what is right and what is wrong.

Community Standards in a Pluralistic Society

To define obscenity the Supreme Court at one time relied on something called "community standards." The Court, finding this too elusive for definition on the national level, then looked to the local community to determine standards. In our pluralistic society there are many communities, many local standards: urban and rural, middle class and working class, many religions and ethnic minorities, and so on.

Until the Civil Rights movement of the 1960s and the rise of feminism, it was taken for granted that the "melting pot" theory of United States culture was a desirable goal: all people were to strive to become as much like the dominant white, Anglo-Saxon, Protestant group as possible. As blacks and women demanded the right to define their own identity and values, other groups within society began to press for acceptance of their cultural heritage and ethnic minorities which had once perceived English as the only acceptable language began to take pride in their native language and customs. This new emphasis on pluralism has been referred to as the "tossed salad" theory of culture. Neither is without its critics; in a democracy, the minorities must have their rights respected. On the other hand, for a society to have coherence, there must be some generally agreed upon values accepted by all—or most—groups within the society.

Since society as a whole has not yet been able to resolve this dilemma, it is not surprising that the conflict is reflected in controversies over what is and is not acceptable in children's books. The result is that Bannerman's *Little Black Sambo* is seen by some as a very funny, delightful story, while it is intolerable to others. Eve Merriam's *The Inner City Mother Goose* has been labeled obscene by some and a classic by others.

What is at issue in this conflict is a confusion between the democratic process of voting by which majority decision is the rule and the purpose of the First Amendment, which is to assure freedom of expression to all, not subject to the vote of the majority. As Berninghausen pointed out in "Intellectual Freedom in Librarianship,"

". . . many of the 216 million Americans do not endorse the first ten amendments to the U.S. Constitution. In fact, there is evidence that, to some of us, the Bill of Rights seems subversive and dangerous. The free inquiry and expression seemingly guaranteed by the First Amendment are rejected by the most intransigent of both right and left."

As pointed out earlier, all people have the right to decide for themselves what they will and will not read, what they do and do not find acceptable. The conflict occurs when people want to impose their views on the entire community. Minority groups do have their own communities and their own standards and they have a right to find those standards represented in textbooks and library materials.

The basic question is whether intellectual freedom lies somewhere beyond community standards. Studies have shown that stereotypes and images that denigrate many segments of society abound in children's literature. Is it censorship to ask that all Indians not be portrayed as living one hundred years ago and behaving as "savages"? Should books that show blacks as intellectually inferior be allowed shelf space? The stereotype of women as exclusively wives and mothers is offensive to feminists.

When looking at the total body of children's literature, modern day critics often forget—or neglect to mention—that many of the books being criticized come from another era where the attitudes expressed within them were accepted by society in general. The scene in *Caddie Woodlawn* by Caroline Brink in which Mr. Woodlawn gives Caddie a lecture about it being time for her to stop being a tomboy and become a young lady is often cited by critics of books that restrict the choices of girls in society. There might be less criticism of books in which mothers are shown in aprons, blacks are nonexistent, Indians are on the war path, old people are like children, etc. if it were not for the fact that the sheer number of such books reinforces acceptance of stereotypes.

Many of these books, as representations of widely held social views, can provide the conflict necessary to teach the difference between human and anti-human standards in literature and in life. Teachers, parents and librarians are needed to help children recognize the conflict and to reach some personal resolution to it.

Professional Prerogative

Censorship was defined by Freud as "the psychological force which represses ideas, impulses, and feelings, and prevents them from entering consciousness in their original form." The fact is that we are all censors. We all have the capacity to repress that which makes us uncomfortable. This quite human activity is complicated for librarian-teachers who are trained and made responsible for the selection of materials for children. That training provides librarian-teachers with "selection standards" that ask abstract questions such as, "Are the characters believable?" The answer, obviously, is very dependent on the person doing the answering, which is why we have some people answering yes and others no.

In general, most librarian-teachers working with children exercise a fairly high level of self-censorship in the process of selecting books. This undoubtedly accounts for the comparatively minimal controversy over censorship of young children's books.

Some librarians automatically reject books which have pictures of the nude human body, profane words, references to sex, realism which depicts weaknesses in the fabric of our society, and negative images of adults. What is not clear is how much of this self-censorship is unconscious and how much of it is based on a conscious decision to try and avoid conflict within their communities. We do know from a study conducted by Professor Mary Woodworth of the Wisconsin University Library School that when challenges are made by professionals within a school system to materials owned by the school libraries, 71 percent of those challenges result in the removal of the materials. When the challenges come from outside the system—from parents or other interested adults—the challenges are successful in only 30 percent of the cases. These results would tend to indicate that professionals are more receptive to self-censorship (internal),

Viewpoint

So it is ironic and terribly disconcerting when that ancient figure, the censor, shows up not where we expect him to be, among the fogies on the right, but on the side we always thought of as liberal and progressive, the left. The motive, of course, remains the same: the absolute necessity of bringing up right-thinking children, of protecting them not from four-letter words and sex and what used to be called the baleful influence of atheistic communism but from what a recent set of guidelines has termed racism, sexism, elitism, materialism, individualism, ageism, and other stereotypes, messages, and implications.

It's very easy to make light of this. And I would like to say immediately that, not unlike their predecessors of the right, the censors on the left have a germ of truth in their justifications. If there were not that germ of truth, there would be no problem. Because the total lie is always easy to combat. It stands out a mile and can be knocked down by almost anyone. It is when some degree of truth, however small, is blended into the distortion that people are seduced.—Isabelle Holland, "On Being a Children's Book Writer and Accompanying Dangers." *The Horn Book Magazine*, February 1980, pp. 39–40. Copyright © 1980 by Isabelle Holland. Reprinted by permission of JCA Literary Agency, Inc.

than they are to external attempts at censorship.

The willingness to resist external challenges is based on a very real concern by school professionals for their rights under the concept of academic freedom. In order to function effectively, teachers and school librarians must feel reasonably secure from arbitrary attacks from the community concerning both teaching techniques and the materials selected to help them reach an educational goal.

What Can One Person Do?

While the following suggestions will be most applicable for teacher-librarians, they apply to the classroom as well as the library.

1. Know and apply literary criteria to the books selected. More often than not censors choose quality books to attack, for the very reason that they are the books having the most forceful impact on the reader. Try not to be placed in the position of defending a bad book and know how to defend a good book on the basis of the writer's craft.

2. Share the selection process by requesting that the school board authorize creation of a committee to include teachers, school administrators, librarians, parents, school board members, representatives from the community, and children. A representative committee is less vulnerable than a single person. Moreover, the committee members will become more sensitive to the complexities of selection by participating in the process and will be a knowledgeable base of support should controversy arise.

3. Go outside of the selection committee for expert opinion in areas of competency not represented on the committee. For example, ask a medical doctor for opinions on the accuracy of information on anatomy and physiology.

4. Join organizations which are committed to support of the First Amendment. Read the literature they publish and keep abreast of what is happening in other places. Know where to turn to for help if you become involved in a censorship controversy (see list of organizations, p. 572).

5. Publicize the role of intellectual freedom in a democratic society and the dangers of censorship. Have the selection committee prepare news releases on its decisions, appear on talk shows or before community groups to discuss the selection decision-making process, talk

with the editors of local newspapers. The mistake too many people make is to think that keeping quiet is the best way to keep the censor from the door, but having an informed community is far better support for freedom than silence.

6. Read the article by June Berkley (pp. 180–186) in *Dealing with Censorship* by James E. Davis (see bibliography) and determine if your school can replicate the education of parents achieved by the Fort Frye High School faculty.

7. Request that the school board establish a committee to draw up a written materials selection policy and to develop procedures for handling complaints. Examples are available from the American Library Association and the National Council of Teachers of English. However, keep in mind that such documents will be paper tigers unless you have organized the kind of public support outlined above.

8. Be sure the library owns sufficient copies of the many fine books on First Amendment rights written for children and bring the books to the attention of the appropriate teachers as well as publicizing them through displays.

9. Provide opportunities, both structured and extemporaneous, for children to discuss their reactions to controversial books. If there is a library club, some of its meetings may be used to discuss books that raise controversial issues (sexism, racism, the First Amendment).

10. Research your community so that you are aware of and sensitive to the range of community values existing. Ask candidates for public office to take a position on the freedom to read.

Conclusion

A Gallup Poll taken in late 1979 found that three out of four adults had no idea of what the First Amendment to the Constitution is or what it deals with. The preservation of a democratic way of life depends on more people understanding the concept of free speech willed to us by the framers of the Constitution. The schools are an obvious place to begin such an educational process, not by mere readings from textbooks, but by the example of school personnel as articulate defenders of freedom. Censorship is an evil, and as Edmund Burke pointed out, "The only thing necessary for the triumph of evil is for good men to do nothing." Teachers and librarians cannot afford to be among those who do nothing.

Bibliography

Books

ANDERSON, A. J. *Problems in Intellectual Freedom and Censorship.* Bowker, 1974. Various court cases dealing with pornography as relating to education and the community are presented with analytical comments.

BERNINGHAUSEN, DAVID. *The Flight From Reason: Essays on Intellectual Freedom in the Academy, the Press, and the Library.* ALA, 1975. A collection of essays dealing with censorship, freedom of information and forms of erotica. Famous court cases are analyzed.

BRODERICK, DOROTHY. *Library Work With Children.* Wilson, 1977. Fully half of this text discusses the complex issues facing the selector of books for children. Particularly valuable is the discussion on making choices on human issues such as racism and sexism.

BUSHA, CHARLES, ed. *An Intellectual Freedom Primer.* Libraries Unlimited, 1977. Contains seven essays by various authors on the question of censorship in different settings such as the performing arts, bibliographic control of erotica, and security systems.

DAVIS, JAMES E. *Dealing With Censorship.* NCTE, 1979. This book is a must for anyone working with children and media. It provides background, case studies, legal decisions and analysis. The Gablers are the subject of one article and preventive measures that of another.

DHAVAN, RAJEEV, and CHRISTIE DAVIES, eds. *Censorship and Obscenity.* Rowan, 1978. The authors provide hard-hitting analyses of the arguments of lawmakers who apply the law in order to censor. Although primarily British, the identification of who censors and why can be applied universally.

ERNST, MORRIS, and ALAN SCHWARTZ. *Censorship: The Search for the Obscene.* Macmillan, 1964. Contains listings of obscenity laws of the United States and urbane analysis of various famous court cases dealing with interpretations of obscenity.

FITZGERALD, FRANCES. *America Revised.* Little, 1979. A noted historian suggests that the accepted non-controversial history textbooks used in our schools are not factual or truthful.

GINSBURG, HERBERT, and SYLVIA OPPER. *Piaget's Theory of Intellectual Development.* Prentice, 1979. With particular application to the concerns of educators, the authors provide a lucid introduction to this aspect of Piaget's theory.

HEFLEY, JAMES C. *Textbooks on Trial.* Victor, 1976. Distributed by The Mel Gablers, P.O. Box 7518, Longview, TX 75602. A sympathetic report on the activities of Mel and Norma Gabler to remove objectionable textbooks from schools. Must reading for those involved in public education.

HENTOFF, NAT. *The First Freedom: The Tumultuous History of Free Speech in America.* Delacorte, 1980. The first truly popular history of the First Amendment in which the complexities of the topic are explicated in eloquent prose.

Human (And Anti-Human) Values in Children's Books. Council on Interracial Books for Children, 1976. The contents of all children's trade books of 1974 are analyzed for twelve "isms" by Council representatives. Although leaning toward censorship themselves and prescriptive directions to authors, the Council does provide in this book a worthwhile consciousness-raising experience.

"Intellectual Freedom Manual." *Office for Intellectual Freedom.* American Library Association, 1974. Contains the Library Bill of Rights and interpretations through various court cases. Also discusses what to do before the censor comes and receiving assistance from ALA in dealing with problems of censorship.

JENKINSON, EDWARD B. *Censors in the Classroom.* Southern Illinois Univ. Press, 1979. This is a thorough, readable reporting of censorship battles over trade and text books across the country. Valuable insights are provided by the author into the multi-faceted causes of censorship, and several chapters give directions on what to do about it.

McCLELLAND, DAVID. *Power: The Inner Experience.* Irvington, 1975. The developmental stage theory of feelings of power posited by McClelland is consistent with other theories of human development. His theory was tested partially through analysis of folklore.

MacCANN, DONNARAE, and GLORIA WOODARD. *Cultural Conformity in Books for Children: Further Readings in Racism.* Scarecrow, 1977. For a more complete discussion of the image of minorities in children's books, this book is thorough in its presentation of the issues and mention of titles.

MILL, JOHN STUART. *On Liberty.* Norton, 1975. Mill discusses the nature of liberty in a free society and what responsibilities the individual has towards society as a whole. However, he states that individuals should vigorously fight all attempts of society to interfere in private affairs.

MILTON, JOHN. *Aeropagitica.* British Book Centre, 1975. A treatise by Milton to the Lords and Commons in 1643 in regard to an act licensing all printers by the crown. Milton states that this will hinder man's search for truth and discourage learning.

PINAR, WILLIAM. *Curriculum Theorizing.* McCutchan, 1975. These essays on theories of curriculum show concern for the developmental needs of children, rather than for content, exclusively.

SCHAUER, FREDERICK. *The Law of Obscenity.* Bureau of National Affairs, 1976. Designed primarily for lawyers, this book presents definitions and measurement tests for obscenity in a social context. Contains a section of court cases and analyses.

WILCOX, MARY M. *Developmental Journey: A Guide to the Development of Logical and Moral Reasoning and Social Perspective.* Abingdon, 1979. A very clear and handy guide for leaders of discussion groups. Directions are given on how to tailor the discussion to match the cognitive, moral and social stages of participants. The author clearly presents the theories of Piaget and Kohlberg.

WOOD, L. B. *A Decade of Censorship in America; The Threat to Classrooms and Libraries, 1966–1975.* Scarecrow, 1979. A research study of classroom and library censorship from 1966–1975. Obscenity, politics, sex, and language were causes of 54.7% of all cases.

Articles

"ALA Protests Federal Obscenity Measure." *Newsletter on Intellectual Freedom* (September 1977): 125+. In general terms the ALA rejects anti-obscenity laws as unwarranted intrusions upon the basic freedoms guaranteed in the Constitution. Obscenity laws which are directed at the control of communication rather than at anti-social action represent a form of censorship ultimately aimed at total control of individuals' lives.

BOAZ, MARTHA. "What to Do Before the Censor Comes and After." *Newsletter on Intellectual Freedom* (September 1965): 59–62. The author has prepared a list of recommendations to have on hand before the censor arrives, such as a written book selection policy and complaint policy, and gives a step-by-step checklist for combatting censorship.

BRODERICK, DOROTHY. "Censorship Reevaluated." *Library Journal* (November 1971): 3810–18. Librarians have time and again broken the covenant which has existed between the library and the community. In the name of intellectual freedom, many librarians defend materials that perpetuate attitudes that hinder the growth of individuals. Librarians must fight to affect attitudes rather than reflect existing ones.

———. "Racism, Sexism, Intellectual Freedom, and Youth Librarian." *Top of the News* (1977): 324–26. The author feels that librarians need to become more aware of the problems inherent in dealing with racist/sexist literature. In particular, authors who distort or suppress information to support their views should be screened carefully, and ultimately librarians need to work towards influencing attitudes to overcome traditional biases toward libraries.

BURGER, ROBERT. "Kanawha Textbook Controversy." *Library Quarterly* (April 1978): 143–62. Intellectual rights of children are still in the hands of parents who are reluctant to permit children any degree of freedom. Should children be exposed to material which parents find objectionable? The author discusses professional prerogatives.

"Censorship and the Schools." *Journal of Research and Development in Education* (Spring 1976): 52–59. What is the responsibility of schools toward protecting students from exposure to sensitive material? Schools and librarians should not attempt to replace parents as selection agents and imposing intellectual freedom restraints should be done with care.

"Censorship and the Teaching of English." *Arizona English Bulletin* (February 1975): whole issue. A collection of very useful provocative articles on all phases of the subject. Helpful ideas for both teachers and librarians are included. This is one of the best sources of information.

"Censorship Dateline—Schools." *Newsletter on Intellectual Freedom* (September 1976): 116+. These are a series of articles documenting attempts at censorship of reading materials in various schools across the country and how each school meets the crisis.

FIELDING, K. B. "How to Prevent Censorship: Cultivate Social Politicians." *American Libraries* (November 1976): 623+. As long as libraries are at the mercy of community tax support certain bureaucratic games must be played and a balance achieved to insure continued success. Following populist rather than autocratic methods will get the community involved in library activities and gain support.

FINLEY, PATRICIA. "Advocating Children's Rights." *Newsletter on Intellectual Freedom* (September 1974): 129–131. Children's librarians have a special obligation to pursue intellectual freedom for young students and help them develop their own critical attitudes towards what they read. Parental guidance must play an important role in helping the young reader create personal evaluative criteria for selection.

"Foundation to Appeal Social Standards." *Newsletter on Intellectual Freedom* (May 1976): 56+. The Freedom to Read Committee decided to appeal the obscenity conviction of Jerry Smith. The case hinged on whether Federal jurisdiction or state "community standards" prevailed. The Federal prosecutor argued that use of the mails constituted a federal offense, but Smith's lawyer stated that "community standards" of recipients of "obscene" material had not been clearly established.

"Free Access to Libraries for Minors." *Newsletter on Intellectual Freedom* (September 1972): 125+. In many cases minors are denied use of total library facilities due to restrictive administrative practices which are contrary to the Library Bill of Rights. Regardless of techniques employed (i.e., colored library cards, etc.) all patrons should have full access to the total collection.

"Freedom and Constraint in Children's Literature." *Wilson Library Bulletin* (October 1976): 144–176. Five articles covering various aspects of freedom and constraint, both modern and historical, in children's books.

HARVEY, JAMES. "Intellectual Freedom and School Libraries." *School Media Quarterly* (1973): 111–12. The author cites the Rochester, Michigan censorship case which states that some tailoring of materials in a school is necessary but should not be taken to extremes.

KLEIN, NORMA. "More Realism for Children." *Newsletter on Intellectual Freedom* (September 1974): 131–33. The author responds to a letter objecting to her book, *Mom, The Wolfman and Me,* which states that the book distorts reality and encourages promiscuous behavior on the part of female readers. Klein responds that certain traditional values need to be broken down but this does not result in a breakdown of all values, but merely substitutes more intelligent, rational ones in their place.

KRUG, JUDITH F. "Intellectual Freedom and the Rights of Children." *School Media Quarterly* (Winter 1973): 132–35. "Loco Parentis" is a widespread disease through which parents dominate their children's reading habits and thinking patterns. The Gault decision of 1967 and Tinker vs. Des Moines Independent Community School of 1969 are cited and analyzed in support of children's rights.

"Library Bill of Rights." *Newsletter on Intellectual Freedom* (March 1979): 23. Presented are the text of the current Library Bill of Rights and proposed revisions. These revisions allow a broader service-oriented interpretation for librarians.

MAZER, NORMA. "Comics, Cokes and Censorship." *Top of the News* (January 1976): 162–70. The author raises the question of whether parents should exercise strict control over their children's reading habits, based on her own personal experience of raising four children. What are we risking if we censor our children's reading material?

"NYLA Acts on Rights on Minors." *Newsletter on Intellectual Freedom* (January 1979): 1+. In preparation for a governor's conference, the New York Library Association prepared a statement urging governmental support for the rights of minors to information even above parental rights to deny that information.

PROCUNIAR, PAMELA ELLEN. "The Intellectual Rights of Children." *Wilson Library Bulletin* (1976): 163+. Adults need to be capable of intelligent decision-making in regard to their children's reading. The more parents shelter their children from questionable material, the less they will be able to participate meaningfully in society. Parents must give them intellectual freedom in order for them to grow.

"Schools." *Newsletter on Intellectual Freedom* (September 1976): 116+. This section contains a number of articles describing censorship attempts in schools across the country and how each library deals with the crisis.

SILVER, LINDA. "Judging Books in Our Business." *School Library Journal* (January 1979): 25–35. Selection of books for libraries on the basis of popularity should be served only to a degree. Librarians should be aware of the power of the literature they control, and should not strictly adhere

to the letter of the law in relation to intellectual freedom if it substitutes taste, judgment and common decency.

"Teenage Views on Book Censorship." *Intellect* (March 1975): 354+. The study reported here indicated adolescents are uninformed and confused on the subject of free access to information. In questioning, constitutional guarantees were not supported by adolescents.

"Two Federal Judges Uphold Library Censorship." *Newsletter on Intellectual Freedom* (November 1979): 1294+. The article discusses two important censorship cases. The first is the Island Trees case on Long Island in which *Down These Mean Streets* was removed from junior high school libraries under court order. The second is in Vermont at Vergennes Union High School in which the school board was upheld in its power to remove questionable books from the library.

VAN DEN HAAG, ERNEST. "Free Speech and Censorship." *Newsletter on Intellectual Freedom* (September 1974): 109+. The author discusses the reasons for freedom of speech and ideas, limitations needed, and misuse of the powers of free speech and selection of materials which have occurred and should not be repeated.

"What Teachers Need to Know." *English Education* (May 1979): 237–40. Teachers need to know the law, the potential danger to their position, the issues which books raise, and how to defend their academic freedom.

WILLIAMS, DIANNE MCAFFEE. "Dealing with Censorship." *Wisconsin Library Journal* (March 1978). This article provides helpful hints beginning with a policy statement and followed by procedures to follow if confronted with book protesters.

WOODS, L. B. "Patterns in the Censorship of Children's Materials." *Newsletter on Intellectual Freedom* (March 1979): 25–26. Children's materials are increasingly addressing subjects formerly considered taboo and those new levels of realism will draw increased activity from censors. If parents object to their children being exposed to controversial ideas, then it is their responsibility, not the librarian's, to supervise the reading material of their children.

Organizations

American Civil Liberties Union. 22 E. 40 Street, New York, NY 10016. ACLU is a major source for both information about civil liberty matters and as support for people involved in First Amendment legal cases. State chapters also exist and should be consulted.

American Library Association. Office for Intellectual Freedom. 50 E. Huron Street, Chicago, IL 60611. The Office for Intellectual Freedom will accept collect telephone calls from people in trouble; will provide packets containing information, sample documents, and other support materials.

Freedom to Read Foundation, 50 E. Huron Street, Chicago, IL 60611. This legal support organization contributes financial and legal advice to many different people involved in fighting censorship in the courts.

National Council of Teachers of English. 1111 Kenyon Road, Urbana, IL 61801. The NCTE has endorsed a document entitled "The Student's Right to Read," which is available from that organization, as well as other documents concerned with the problems of teaching in a free atmosphere.

Periodicals

Newsletter on Intellectual Freedom. Published bimonthly by the ALA Intellectual Freedom Committee. Available from: American Library Association, 50 E. Huron Street, Chicago, IL 60611. The *Newsletter* is one of the most valuable resources for locating information concerning censorship activities across the nation. It brings together items that are, of necessity, scattered throughout magazines and newspapers.

Research in Children's Literature

Susan Steinfirst*

Research is a premeditated scholarly or scientific investigation or inquiry which attempts to increase knowledge and yield universal generalizations or laws. This broad definition is straightforward and really not so very difficult if you consider the root of the word "research," which is the French word "rechercher," meaning "to seek out" or "study again."

To pinpoint the definition of research in children's literature poses a problem. The very phrase "children's literature" implies a conflict. It implies that this research is the domain of both child specialists and literature specialists, both of whom approach research from different points of view and with different goals. The child specialist (who could be a psychologist, sociologist, or broadly speaking, a teacher or librarian) is a social scientist who is most interested in generating truths or principles about the relationship between children and their books. The literature specialist (the humanist or English scholar) is not particularly interested in the audience (the child) but is concerned with the literature itself—its content, form, and structural contents, and with bringing children's literature into the "mainstream" of literature for adults.

Although there may be differences among their approaches to research, all researchers—librarians, educators, historians, sociologists, literary critics—agree on the usefulness of research. Most adults would agree that reading is beneficial for children; this is a generalization

* Susan Steinfirst is Assistant Professor in the School of Library and Information Science at the University of North Carolina.

that can be tested. Many adults charge that television is a deterrent to reading; this too is an assumption that can be tested. We have heard claims that sexism and racism are rampant in today's books for children, and these are claims that can be verified or negated by research. Research is needed to accumulate a fund of facts, thereby eliminating assumptions, generalizations, and claims.

For example, in 1958, George Norvell conducted a now-classic reading interest study of 24,000 children in grades 3 to 6 and determined that they did not like to read the same books adults liked them to read. This not only verified an assumption that those who work with children and books had held for some time, it also had implications for writers of children's books, for critics of children's books, and for the compilers of the "best books" lists that crop up every year. Similarly, it has been determined by Judith Noble in a 1971 study of 125 randomly selected books, and by a number of other researchers, that the family most frequently represented in children's books is middle-class and white. Such research should alert teachers, librarians, and writers of children's books to the implications this finding has for non-white, non-middle-class readers in this country. And Janelle Avenell Paris, in a 1977 comparative analysis of occupations presented in 150 works of realistic fiction, showed statistically that children's fiction gives an "extremely limited view of the work world, especially in terms of female careers," places negative values on manual labor, "perpetuates the division of labor by sex," and has not kept pace with economic and social realities in our changing world. This type of research alerts those of us who care about children and books to the social and cultural values that are reflected in children's literature, and to the possible need to supplement what is presented in it by offering other values, either personally or with alternative literature.

Research that tests assumptions, verifies claims, and sorts out generalizations is an especially important tool in helping adults see patterns in children's literature, detect shortcomings in adult attitudes about children and their reading, and relate children's literature to adult cultural, societal, and literary values. In the final analysis, it is hoped that research will help us use books more wisely with children.

Research Methods

As previously stated, there is a lack of consensus on how research should be done. Many practitioners adopt the methodologies of social science research, which can be lumped together into three major groups: the survey method, the statistical method, and the historical method.

Survey, or descriptive research, as it is sometimes called, consists of those techniques which serve to gather contemporary data, either by direct measurement or by solicitation from others. The survey method is used, for example, in reading-interest studies when children are questioned about their reading interests either by means of a questionnaire or in personal interviews.

Statistical research is concerned with the quantitative relationships between objects, events, persons, nations, or institutions. The researcher will manipulate variables, make detailed observations of the process, and record the results or the effects on other variables statistically. This method of research is not often encountered in children's literature studies because it is extremely difficult to control the variables. For example, while sex and age of children are variables, it is almost impossible to prove that they are determinates in children's attitudes or interests because social class, economic level, and other demographic factors about their lives may be more important than either age or sex in determining children's interests or values.

The historical method concerns itself with people, objects (in the case of children's literature, books) and events of the past. Using primarily original sources, the author tries to determine what influenced past events and what, if any, impact that knowledge has for the present. For example, a study of the development of periodicals for children in the United States would be a historical study.

The above methods of research are basically used by social scientists. Literature specialists divide into two categories. The first are those belonging to the "new criticism" school, a popular type which emphasizes the autonomy of the literary work and demands a close analysis of all its aesthetic components: analysis of rhythm and the rhyme of poetry, for example, or the images and symbols utilized in poetry and prose, and analysis of style and composition. For these researchers, the work stands alone without regard to the life of its author and the time of creation.

The second category of literary research involves the researcher in the life and times of the author as well as in the internal content of the book or books being analyzed. The difference between these two schools can best be explained by the researcher who might analyze *Alice's Adventures in Wonderland* by internal examination of the book, and the researcher who would relate it to Lewis Carroll's life and relationship with the original Alice. Neither of these two types of researchers is interested in the child appeal of the material being evaluated, but the researcher analyzing social, political, and cultural values of the time the work was created is interested in the influence environment has on literary creation.

There is less literary research than social science research into children's literature because the literary researcher's colleagues have a definite bias against children's books. The assumption (albeit incorrect) is made that children's literature is "simple" and not worthy of analytic study. This attitude changes only in relation to works deemed classics (e.g., those by Robert Louis Stevenson), and usually does not apply to contemporary children's literature unless the authors (e.g., E. B. White, Tolkein) also write for adults.

Published Research

Most published research is done in the universities as master's theses and doctoral dissertations in graduate departments of education, English, and librarianship. Up-to-date abstracts of these theses and dissertations are printed monthly in *Dissertation Abstracts, Dissertation Abstracts International*, and ERIC and annually in *Research Studies in Education, a Subject and Author Index of Doctoral Dissertations, Reports and Field Studies*, and *Research Methods Bibliography*.

Articles summarizing research in children's literature can be found in the leading education and library journals: *Language Arts* and *English Journal*, published by the National Councils of Teachers of English; *School Library Journal, Top of the News* (published by the Association of Library Service to Children and the Young Adult Services Division of the American Library Association), and *Children's Literature in Education*. *Bookbird*, published in England under the auspices of the International Board on Books for Young People (IBBY) and the International Institute for Children's Literature and Reading Research, lists findings in international research; and *Signal* and *Junior Bookshelf*, two British periodicals, provide articles about children's literature and research. Studies concerned with popular materials, e.g. comic books, may be summarized in the *Journal of Popular Culture*.

Humanities scholars publish their findings in several humanities-oriented journals, but especially in *Children's Literature* (called *Children's Literature: The Great Excluded* through Volume III), which is the annual publication of the Children's Literature Association and the Seminar on Children's Literature of the Modern Language Association. An interdisciplinary journal devoted to research in children's literature has appeared in the last few years. *Phaedrus: An International Journal of Children's Literature Research* lists and synopsizes current dissertations and periodical articles. Several issues have highlighted research from different countries and most issues contain a section in which special children's collections useful for research on a particular country or countries are described.

Although much research done by graduate students, professors, and some practitioners is published annually, there is a large quantity of important research carried on every year by students of children's literature in their undergraduate and graduate courses. Most of this, unfortunately, is not reported at all.

Types of Research

Reading-Interest Studies. A great deal of the research on children's literature done each year consists of reading-interest studies, in which the researcher tries to determine what children read. There are several techniques for this: interviews with children, the use of diaries or logs, records of library books checked out, and requests by children for their favorite story to be read to them. Because children are often inarticulate about their reading tastes and preferences and because we know, for example, that they may very well take a book out of a library to please a helpful librarian and then not read it, reading-interest surveys have been criticized for lacking accurate, dependable methods.

However, because so many have been done

and repeated with nearly the same results, there is much to be learned from them. A good example is the Norvell study cited earlier which showed that children and adults often differ in their choices of books and standards of literature. We also know from these reading-interest studies that boys and girls read the same types of books until about first grade, when sex becomes a determining factor in the selection of books. We know that three- to five-year-olds prefer illustrations with a lot of colors, and ones that have light tints and dark shades rather than bright, saturated pictures. Studies have been done which determine differences in poetry selection by age, by sex, and by type of poem. There are reading-interest studies that provide us with information about what types of books children prefer (animal, fairy tale, adventure, etc.) at different age levels. We have studies that attempt to contrast the reading interests of children in different socioeconomic classes, of children from different ethnic groups, of mentally and physically disabled children with mentally and physically able children. Other studies test the effect of media on reading preferences. Despite the pitfalls of a sometimes overly subjective methodology and the vagaries of children, this is a type of research that can be conducted by students who work with children and books, with a satisfying degree of success.

Content Analysis. Content analysis is a specific research methodology in which a detailed description of the contents of a carefully selected group of books is based on a very systematic, objective study of specific aspects in each book. Its accuracy is based on its being highly quantitative and objective (free from bias). One example of a good content analysis is a doctoral dissertation by Gloria Blatt, done in 1972, on violence in children's literature. She carefully selected books dealing with violence that appeared on the ALA Notable Children's Books lists from 1960 to 1970. She analyzed each book statistically for: (1) the total amount of space devoted to violence; (2) the details and intensity of the violence; (3) the characters involved in the violence; (4) what the violent deeds were; (5) the relationship of the participants in violent actions, and (6) what value judgments were made about the acts of violence by the characters in the books. Her analysis of the data showed that there was no increase in the incidence of violence over the ten-year period, that historical fiction contained more violence than realistic fiction, and that many value judgments *against* violence were made in the books.

Although there is much analysis of content done by graduate students, it would be safe to say that most such research carried on today is not real content analysis. It is theme analysis—descriptive research that analyzes the content of literature in order to investigate certain ideas, attitudes, and patterns in these books. Examples of this type of research abound: realism in fantasy books; elements of fantasy in realistic fiction; racism, sexism, ageism in children's literature; racial and ethnic stereotyping in children's materials; sex roles as revealed by the female characters in Newbery Medal books; divorce and separation themes in children's books, and death in recent fiction. And these are just a few.

The majority of research reported in our periodical literature is theme analysis. It is a valid type of research, but less reliable than content analysis since it does not use the same objective, quantitative, systematic techniques. The task of the researcher who uses this method is to choose a body of books that contain the themes or issues to be studied, and to compare these themes (which tend to reflect contemporary concerns) to determine what social and cultural values are being transmitted to children by books. This type of analysis can be done by students in a reasonable amount of time. Subjects should be chosen with care to avoid repetition of those that have already been studied extensively. Conclusions are based on the prevalence or absence of the theme or attitudes in question.

Bibliographies. Bibliographies are compilations of books, periodical articles, and other media, usually possessing a common subject or theme. Some are simply listings; others include descriptive or critical annotations. If the researcher links the books together in prose form and analyzes them in some way, it is called a bibliographic essay. Several very interesting bibliographies have appeared in the journals and in full length books in recent years. The topics covered include Holocaust literature for children; books about divorce; sports books for boys or girls; books about the dance; science books for the middle-grades, and rites of passage books for pre-adolescents. This is often a

rewarding type of research for the student who will be working with children and will have a need for such a list.

Author and Illustrator Studies. Although there has really not been much biographical research done on contemporary authors and illustrators, this is also a reasonable type of research for students in children's literature courses. Several compilations of author/illustrator biographies are available (see Appendix B) for the student who wants to do an in-depth study of an author or illustrator, relating the life of the author/illustrator to the body of work created, or, perhaps, to compare two or more authors' or illustrators' works. There have also been a few doctoral dissertations and books written about historical figures in the world of children's books.

Genre Studies. This is a study of one type of literature in which the researcher can either look at the genre historically (for example, the nineteenth-century roots of fantasy) or study an author who wrote persistently in that genre (Tolkien, Macdonald, C.S. Lewis, as fantasists), or research the themes that have run through one type of literature over a long period of time (e.g., good versus evil in fantasy). Many anthropologists and psychologists study folklore (tales as well as other forms of oral literature and childlore such as jump-rope rhymes) to determine their meanings and values for children or to ascertain how the genre reflects the culture from which it came. Historical fiction offers a fertile field of study, as the author must attempt to incorporate cultural and social values of the period being written about. Biography might be looked at to see if it is intended to have an effect on the "moral character" of its readers. A comparison of books about the Civil War written thirty years ago with a group written today might show how our attitudes have changed; a study of books written about Civil War by southerners and northerners might reveal differences in attitudes.

Even though it is not really a specific type of children's literature, research on foreign children's books, either in the original language or in translation, gives enormous insight into the history, culture, and social values of another country. Comparing original-language and translated versions is also an exciting project for the researcher fluent in the original language. We can also learn how one country seeks to inculcate nationalistic values through its books, or if any country's children's literature might be (overtly or covertly) propagandistic. A comparison of how two countries handle the same themes in their books for children (for example, how contemporary British and German books treat the theme of nationalism in their historical fiction about World War II, or how contemporary American and Russian books delineate sex roles in their children's books) would make a fascinating and feasible short-term study.

Historical Research. Historical research, which is generally a lengthy process, has been limited mainly to doctoral students and educators. Good historical research might trace the development of one type of material (books on American history, for example), or might just be a study of the literature of a period such as the Victorian domestic novel for children or late-nineteenth-century adventure stories for boys. Such research should always be placed in historical perspective. This means that the historian of children's literature should not only know the history of children's literature, but the history—social, cultural, and economic—of the period and/or country being studied, as well as the history of childhood. The student who wants to do historical research as a semester project would be well advised to limit the study to a familiar country or period and to have taken a course in historical research in the history department.

Others. The foregoing are the main types of research that are open to the student researcher, but several others are available. The study of readers' responses to literature makes a fascinating project. Children's responses are not always verbal. How do we study the emotional responses that we know children have but do not articulate? Does the child's response change with additional hearings of a story? Does the child respond differently if a story is read on a one-to-one basis rather than to a group? These questions require a very sophisticated research instrument in order to be answered and such research is best undertaken by people with a background in psychology and child development.

For students who plan to be reading teachers, readability studies involving the use of readability formulas that have been devised and published by several educators may be a wise choice. Testing and comparing these readability formulas is an interesting study in itself. Another study could compare the readability levels of very popular books with highly praised books with few readers.

Sources and Procedures

Pick a topic that will sustain your interest for the duration of the project. A look at the periodical literature listed in the bibliography might be a help in deciding on a specific project. Volumes 1, 3, 4, and 5 of *Children's Literature* include long and varied lists of research topics that could be handled in a semester. After selecting a topic, the next step is to become familiar with material germane and allied to the topic. The *Reader's Guide to Periodical Literature* or *Library Literature* will lead to periodical articles that have appeared on the subject. *ERIC Abstracts, Psychological Abstracts, Dissertation Abstracts*, and W. Bernard Lukenbill's *Working Bibliography of American Doctoral Dissertations in Children's and Adolescents' Literature, 1930–71*, are a few of the sources which can be consulted to locate information on dissertations and other major research projects on the subject selected. In addition, standard bibliographic tools, the library's card catalogue, and the reference librarian can help track down books and other materials about the subject.

Background readings help a researcher formulate a *hypothesis*. A hypothesis is a statement, or assertion, that is subject, under certain conditions, either to proof or verification, or to disproof. Beginning researchers often feel that disproving a hypothesis invalidates the research, but disproving is as valid as proving an assumption. The purpose of a hypothesis is to provide a framework within which to investigate the chosen topic. The methodology used and the whole research design will depend on the original hypothesis or proposal, so careful formulation is essential.

The role of the researcher, to go back to our original definition of research and its roots, is to study thoroughly, to seek out, to search again. This requires reading thoroughly all the material that has been located on the research topic, using original sources (the books or materials themselves) and secondary sources (books and articles about the subject, such as critical reviews and prior research). From reading, observing, and, if applicable, quantitative data gathering and interviewing, using some predetermined methodology, the researcher makes some evaluation and critical decisions about all the data gathered. The final step is to write up the conclusions arrived at.

Research is a three-pronged activity: gathering data through observation, measurement, or reading; analyzing the data; and deriving conclusions.

Trends and Needs

A survey of current research, especially that done in library schools and education departments and published in the periodical literature, indicates that research today deals primarily with how social and cultural values are reflected in literature for children. There is much literature on different aspects of the family (particularly its dissolution), on the elderly, on sexism and racism, on views about different ethnic and minority groups and cultures in the United States. The issues of death and stereotyping of all kinds are popular issues as we enter the 1980s. We appear to be most interested in studying fantasy as a genre, and to a lesser extent, science fiction and contemporary realistic fiction.

Among the topics that have not been over-researched are: (1) magazine and newspaper reading by children; (2) religious literature for children; (3) the content of informational books of all types; (4) how the elements of format influence the popularity of books with different aged children; (5) the impact of popular materials (comic books, joke books) and mass media on reading; (6) how literature affects the elementary language arts programs; and (7) the usefulness of books in helping children cope with personal problems.

Good research not only builds a fund of knowledge, it tells us what we do not know and what we need to find out. In children's literature there is much to do and much to find out.

Bibliography

About Research and Research Methods

BARZUN, JACQUES, and HENRY GRAFF. *The Modern Researcher.* 3rd ed., revised. Harcourt, 1977. A classic work that suggests ways to do research.

BEKKEDAL, TEKLA K. "Content Analysis of Children's Books." *Library Trends* 22 (1973): 109–26. Discusses content analysis as a tool and reviews several studies done using this technique. Bibliography of studies appended.

BROWN, GEORGE. "Literature in the Elementary School." *Review of Educational Research* 34 (1964): 187–94. Reviews research studies pertaining to reading interests, the relationship of the library to the elementary school literature program, evaluation, and analysis of children's literature and individualized reading.

BUSHA, CHARLES. "Research Methods." In *Encyclopedia of Library and Information Science*, Vol. 25. Dekker, 1978, pp. 254–93. A very clear, concise description of research techniques.

CANTOR, JOANNE R. "Research on Television's Effects on Children." *Phaedrus* 5 (1978): 9–13. Discusses the research of social psychologists, sociologists, and communication researchers on the effect of television on children with special emphasis on "imitation" (of television characters), violence, and "distraction."

HENNE, FRANCES E. "Toward a National Plan to Nourish Research in Children's Literature." *Wilson Library Bulletin* 50 (October 1975): 131–37. A plea for basic collections of children's literature, specialized collections, resource-sharing, and cooperative planning of collection building.

HUNT, PETER. "Children's Book Research in Britain." *Signal* (1978): 12–15. Discusses the author's list of research done in British institutions of higher education up to 1977. The 119 works are divided into five categories: literature, language and linguistics, librarianship, education, and illustration.

HUUS, HELEN. "Interpreting Research in Children's Literature." In *Children, Books, and Reading*, ed. by Mildred Dawson. Perspectives in Reading, No. 3. International Reading Association, 1964, pp. 123–45. Discusses research in children's literature in five major areas: reading preferences, poetry, mass media, reading materials, and effects of reading. Bibliography of studies.

KELLY, R. GORDON. "American Children's Literature: An Historiographical Review." *American Literary Realism, 1870–1910* 6 (1973): 89–107. A critical review of historical research on American children's books.

KERLINGER, FRED N. *Foundations of Behavioral Research: Educational and Psychological Inquiry.* 2nd ed. Holt, 1973. A difficult, but comprehensive approach to all aspects of social science research.

KINNEL, ERIC. "Can Children's Books Change Children's Values?" *Educational Leadership* 28 (1970): 209–14. This review deals with studies on the effects of reading on children and the social content of books that could influence behavior. Includes a bibliography of several studies.

LEHTONEN, MAIJA. "Reflections on Children's Literature." *Bookbird* 11 (1973): (2) 10–15; (3) 22–28. A professor of general and comparative literature discusses the role of the humanist in literary research into children's books.

ÓRVIG, MARY. "One World in Children's Books?" *Top of the News* 28 (1972): 399–422. In this annual Arbuthnot Honor Lecture, this author, the director of the Swedish Institute for Children's Books, makes a passionate plea for more research into "internationalism within the field of children's books."

PURVES, ALAN C., and RICHARD BEACH. *Literature and the Reader: Research in Response to Literature, Reading Interests and the Teaching of Literature.* NCTE, 1972. Analyzes research studies done through 1969 in the areas listed in the title, summarizes findings, and discusses implications for further research. Includes selected bibliography of studies.

ROBINSON, HELEN M., and SAMUEL WEINTRAUB. "Research Related to Children's Interests and to Developmental Values of Reading." *Library Trends* 22 (1973): 81–108. In two parts, reviews studies in reading interests of pre-school and primary and middle grade students, and high school students, and studies of the developmental values of reading. Bibliography.

SILVERMAN, JIM. "A Rack of Journals: Research in Children's Literature." *Children's Literature* 8 (1980): 193–204. A discussion of how eight leading American and British children's literature journals report research.

WELLEK, RENÉ, and AUSTIN WARREN. *Theory of Literature.* 3rd ed. Harcourt, 1956. This classic text on New Criticism stresses the study of the nature, form, function, and contents of literature rather then its relationship to the environment that influenced its creation. Two chapters, "Literature and Psychology," and "Literature and Society," are especially useful for anyone wishing to do literary research with children's materials.

ZIMET, SARA F. "Children's Interest and Story Preferences: A Critical Review of the Literature." *Elementary School Journal* 67 (1966): 122–30. A critical look at some of the pitfalls of reading-interest studies.

Source Guides

Children's Books in the Rare Books Division of the Library of Congress. Rowman and Littlefield, 1975. V. I, Authors; V. II, Chronological. A catalogue description of 15,000 volumes of nineteenth and early twentieth century books in the Library of Congress's Children's Rare Books Division. Preparation by Virginia Haviland, chief of this department.

Children's Literature (titled *Children's Literature: The Great Excluded* through Volume 3), 1972– (annual). Edited by Francelia Butler through the auspices of the Children's Literature Association and the Seminar on Children's Literature division of the Modern Language Association. Published by the University of Connecticut, Temple University, and now Yale University, this annual publication, though heavily humanist in thrust, presents essays on all aspects of children's literature. Of particular interest is a list of suggested research topics in several issues and a listing of current interdisciplinary research.

Children's Literature Abstracts, May 1973– (quarterly). International Federation of Library Associations. This service abstracts material appearing in educational and library science journals from around the world. English, American, and continental sources predominate. Access to material is provided through a broad subject arrangement.

Dissertation Abstracts and *Dissertation Abstracts International.* 1952– (monthly). Includes abstracts of dissertations accepted by participating colleges and universities. Comprehensive subject and author indexes are available.

FIELD, CAROLYN W., ed. *Subject Collections in Children's Literature.* Bowker, 1969. Describes the holdings of collections useful in children's literature research. Books, manuscripts, and other items included. Currently being updated and expanded.

HAVILAND, VIRGINIA, et al. *Children's Literature: A Guide to Reference Sources.* Library of Congress, 1966.

———. *Children's Literature: A Guide to Reference Sources.* First Supplement. Library of Congress, 1972.

———. *Children's Literature: A Guide to Reference Sources.* Second Supplement. Library of Congress, 1977. Extensive guides to various sources of materials relating to children's literature. Subject approach provided.

Library Literature, 1933/35– (quarterly). Contains lists of master's and doctoral theses on children's literature under the heading "Library Schools—Theses."

LUKENBILL, W. BERNARD. *A Working Bibliography of American Doctoral Dissertations in Children's and Adolescents' Literature, 1930–1971.* Occasional Paper, No. 103. Univ. of Illinois, Graduate School of Library Science, 1972. Identifies and describes over a hundred doctoral dissertations

accepted by American colleges and universities. Extensive bibliography included.

MCNAMEE, LAWRENCE F. *Dissertations in English and American Literature: Theses Accepted by American, British and German Universities, 1865–1964.* Bowker, 1968.

———. *Dissertations in English and American Literature. Supplement One: Theses Accepted by American, British and German Universities, 1964–1968.* Bowker, 1969.

———. *Dissertations in English and American Literature. Supplement Two: Theses Accepted by American, British and German Universities, 1969–1973.* Bowker, 1974. Although limited, these works offer access to some foreign dissertations dealing with children's literature.

Osborne Collection of Early Children's Books, 1566–1910. Toronto Public Library. Vol. I, 1958: Vol. II, 1975. A very useful catalogue of early English and American children's books arranged by subject. Prepared by Judith St. John, the Osborne Collection's curator.

Phaedrus: An International Journal of Children's Literature Research. Fall 1973– (biannual). Attractively printed journal, edited by James Fraser, which disseminates information about research in children's and adolescents' literature. The publication covers periodicals, textbooks, comics, song books, boxed games, films, television, and the oral literature of children. Excellent bibliographic features are included which cite material drawn from diverse scholarly fields and languages. Lists dissertations and periodical literature.

Research Studies in Education: A Subject and Author Index of Doctoral Dissertations, Reports and Field Studies, and a Research Methods Bibliography. 1941/51– (annual). Excellent source both for dissertations completed during the preceding year and for proposals accepted. Children's literature topics generally appear under the subject heading "Methods of Teaching; Teaching Aids; Libraries."

U.S. EDUCATIONAL RESEARCH INFORMATION CENTER. *Resources in Education.* 1966– (monthly). Commonly known as ERIC, this is a comprehensive source for all types of material dealing with education, including children's literature. Entries include dissertations, reports, conference proceedings, books, unpublished material, etc.

U.S. LIBRARY OF CONGRESS. *National Union Catalog of Manuscript Collections.* 1959– (annual). Describes the manuscript holdings of participating libraries in the United States. Subject-index approach offers access to a limited amount of material relating to children's literature.

Representative Studies

BLATT, GLORIA. "Violence in Children's Literature: A Content Analysis of a Select Sampling of Children's Literature and a Study of Children's Responses to Literary Episodes Depicting Violence." Unpublished Ph.D. dissertation, 1972. Michigan State University. Her content analysis determined that there has been no substantial increase in violence in children's books.

BRODERICK, DOROTHY. *The Image of the Black in Children's Fiction.* Bowker, 1973. This is a "historical, literary, and critical analysis of the portrait of the black that emerges from children's books published between 1827 and 1967."

BUTLER, FRANCELIA. "Skip Rope Rhymes as Reflections of American Culture." *Children's Literature* 5 (1977): 104–16. A historical and international look at skip rope rhymes as reflections of their periods and cultures.

BUTLER, JAMES. "Expressed Reading Preferences of Children Enrolled in Grade 2 in Selected Schools of Colorado." Unpublished Ph.D. dissertation, 1964. University of Oklahoma. The researcher read 24 books to 165 grade school children and found that sex was the differentiating factor and that intellectual ability, socio-economic environments, and reading competence were not determiners of preference.

CAPPA, DANTE. "Sources of Appeal in Kindergarten Books." *Elementary English* 34 (1957): 259. Based on his 1953 dissertation, "Reactions of Kindergarten Children to Story Books Read by Teachers," University of California at Berkeley. Cappa determined that 2,500 children liked simple, "fanciful" books best but that illustrations ranked first in appeal. Information and humor ranked far below illustrations and story content.

CATA, JUANITA O. "The Portrait of American Indians in Children's Fictional Literature." Unpublished Ph.D. dissertation, 1977. University of Mexico. This analysis of the portrayal of American Indian characters determined that most writers of children's fictional literature need to provide a more accurate portrayal of Indian characters.

COSBY, WILLIAM, JR. "An Integration of the Visual Media Via *Fat Albert and the Cosby Kids* into the Elementary School Curriculum as a Teaching Aid and Vehicle to Achieve Increased Learning." Unpublished Ed.D. dissertation, 1976. University of Massachusetts. Studies the effects of television in general, and *Fat Albert and the Cosby Kids* in particular, as a successful means to eliminate institutional racism.

DIETERICH, DANIEL, and LAUREL LADEVICH. "Medium and the Message: Effects of Television on Children: ERIC/RCS Reports." *Language Arts* 54 (1977): 196–204. An overview of the research on the effects of television on children. Of particular interest is the section on the effect of television on children's language development which found that, in a study involving 153 students in K–6, "exposure to television appears to hinder the child's development of language and that the impact is most negative in the eight- to eleven-year-old range."

DIXON, BOB. *Catching Them Young: Political Ideas in Children's Fiction.* London: Pluto, 1976. An examination of a variety of literature—comics, fantasy, religious books—to show "how ruling ideas are promoted."

GARDNER, HOWARD, and WILLIAM LOHMAN. "Children's Sensitivity to Literary Styles." *Merrill-Palmer Quarterly* 21 (1975): 113–26. A study of 84 males and females at four separate age levels (7, 11, 14, and 19) determined that the pre-adolescents show little explicit awareness of stylistic factors, but the adolescent and college-age subjects can focus on features relevant to style detection.

GAST, DAVID. "Characteristics and Concepts of Minority Americans in Contemporary Children's Fictional Literature." Unpublished Ed.D. dissertation, 1965. Arizona State University. The author studied the treatment of five minority groups and determined that although stereotypes did exist, they were positive stereotypes emphasizing middle class values.

GREEN, MARY LOU JOHNSON. "The Image of Death as Portrayed in Fiction for Children." Unpublished Ph.D. dissertation, 1975. Lehigh University. Analyzes "death imagery," vocabulary, and thematic approach in ninety works of fiction for children and concludes that there is a need for more quality books with death content for young children, there is a more violent portrayal of death in books for children over 9, that the portrayal of the impact of the death of a protagonist's parents is handled in a "fair and responsible way," and that authors treat the death of a parent as having more significant impact on the life of a main character than the death of a friend.

GUÉRON, JACQUELINE. "Linguistic Patterns in Children's Verse." *Children's Literature: The Great Excluded* 2 (1973): 197–208. Details how a recent development in linguistics, the Halle-Keyser theory of prosody, can be applied to the analysis of children's verse.

HAWKINS, KARLA JEAN. "Elementary School Children's Preferences for Selected Elements of Humor in Children's Books as Determined by Sex and Grade Level." Unpublished Ph.D. dissertation, 1977. University of Georgia. Using four types of humor (humor predicament situation, absurdity, incongruity, and verbal humor), the author determined, with a random sample of 150 second, fourth, and sixth grade students, that "humor preference is an individual trait," and that sex was not a significant factor in preferring type of humor and age was only a factor in perceiving verbal humor.

HENNEN, THOMAS J., and VIDA STAUNTON. "Let There Be Peace: An Annotated Bibliography of Anti-War Literature and Realistic Fiction About War." *Language Arts* 54 (1977): 66–70. This "anti-war" bibliography of fifteen books for upper elementary and junior high students is intended to "help them see war from the perspective of the victim."

HILLMAN, JUDITH STEVINSON. "Analysis of Male and Female Roles in Two Periods of Children's Literature." *Journal of Educational Research* 68 (1974): 84–88. A study of 120 books from the 1930s and the mid-1960s to mid-1970s was conducted to identify changes in sexual role standards of males and females. Her conclusions were that children are now finding more females in their books, slightly more occupational diversity for females, and a greater variety of behaviors and emotions expressed by males and females.

HOARE, GEOFFREY. "The Work of David Macaulay." *Children's Literature in Education* 8 (1977): 12–20. An excellent analysis of this illustrator's sophisticated books for children that argues that Macaulay's drawings do have appeal for children.

JACOBS, LELAND. "Democratic Acculturation in American Children's Historical Fiction." Unpublished Ph.D. dissertation, 1946. Ohio State University. An analysis of thirty-nine books in which he found that the literature dealt primarily with periods of settlement and war, that northern locales were emphasized, that town settings were mostly rural and small, that the professional soldier was a predominant figure, and that the family represented was white, middle-class, small, and strongly patriarchal.

KELLY, G. GORDON. *Mother Was a Lady: Self and Society in Selected American Periodicals, 1865–90.* Greenwood, 1974. Using selected American children's periodicals, for the years 1865–90, the author analyzes adult values and attitudes of the nineteenth century that children were supposed to believe in.

KOLMER, ELIZABETH. "The McGuffey Readers: Exponents of American Classical Liberalism." *Journal of General Education* 27 (Winter 1976): 309–16. Shows how the McGuffey Readers mirror the values of nineteenth century America: "patriotism, love of nature, acknowledgement of the God of this creation, sanctity of private property, and the doctrine of self-help and success."

KUJOTH, JEAN SPEALMAN, comp. *Reading Interests of Children and Young Adults.* Scarecrow, 1970. A compilation of reading interest studies.

MacDONALD, RUTH K. "Literature for Children in England, 1659–1774." Unpublished Ph.D. dissertation, 1977. Rutgers University. This study seeks to "determine writers' attitudes toward children and literature for them."

MacLEOD, ANNE. "For the Good of the Country: Cultural Values in American Juvenile Fiction, 1825–1860." *Children's Literature* 5 (1976): 40–51. Based on the author's dissertation, "Children's Fiction and American Culture, 1825–1860." Discusses the literature as a source for the study of cultural history.

MATTERA, GLORIA. "Bibliotherapy in a 6th Grade." Unpublished Ed.D. dissertation, 1961. Pennsylvania State University. Using 6th grade students' oral and written statements about books given to help them face and solve problems as well as the Bloomer Identification Figure Test, the author concluded that bibliotherapy had been effective.

MONSON, DIANNE. "Children's Test Responses to Seven Humorous Stories." *Elementary School Journal* 68 (1968): 334–39. Based on her dissertation, "Children's Responses to Humorous Situations in Literature," University of Minnesota, 1966. Studied 635 fifth grade children to determine (1) what these children find humorous in literature and (2) the influence of the instrument used for eliciting the response made to humorous literature.

NOBLE, JUDITH ANN. "The Home, the Church, and the School Portrayed in American Realistic Fiction for Children, 1965–1969." Unpublished Ph.D. dissertation, 1971. Michigan State University. An analysis of 125 books in which she determined that the family described most was middle class, white; that very little information was included about religion; and that school and education were mentioned in three-quarters of the books, although the treatment was negative.

NORVELL, GEORGE W. *What Boys and Girls Like to Read.* Silver Burdett, 1958. A classic reading-interest study of 24,000 third to sixth graders based on the techniques used in his earlier study of young people in grades 7–12, reported in *The Reading Interests of Young People.* The later work gives special attention to the influence of age, sex, and intelligence on reading preferences of younger children.

PARIS, JANELLE AVENELL. "A Comparative Analysis of Occupations Presented in Children's Realistic Fiction, 1950–54 and 1970–74." Unpublished Ph.D. dissertation, 1977. Texas Women's University. A content analysis of 150 children's realistic books to test the hypothesis that there is "a discernible trend toward increasing honesty and realism relating to career content in children's fiction."

RACHLIN, SUSAN K., and GLENDA VOGT. "Sex Roles as Presented to Children by Coloring Books." *Journal of Popular Culture* 8 (1974): 549–56. Studies thirty coloring books as a form of popular culture that perpetuates existing stereotypes, particularly in regard to occupational opportunity.

STEINFIRST, SUSAN. "The Origins and Development of the ABC Book in English from the Middle Ages through the Nineteenth Century." Unpublished Ph.D. dissertation, 1976. University of Pittsburgh. Analyzes the genre, as it emerged, to reflect the historical, educational, cultural, social, and religious trends of each period.

SUTHERLAND, ZENA. "Biography in the United States." *Children's Literature in Education* 7 (1976): 116–20. Shows how contemporary biography reflects changes in society's attitudes.

TIBBETTS, SYLVIA-LEE. "Research in Children's Literature: A Need for Standardized Procedures." *Elementary English* 52 (1975): 503–4. A criticism of the variety of techniques used in reading interest studies and a call for a standardized procedure of investigation.

VUKELICH, CAROL, et al. "Sex Bias in Children's Books." *Childhood Education* 52 (1976): 220–22. The authors compared the activities, roles, and relative importance assigned to males and females in selected picture books and found that the image of female children was a blatantly subservient one and that women were portrayed as having occupational choices limited to the service occupational roles while males had a wide variety of occupational roles to pick from.

ZACHARIAS, LEE. "Nancy Drew, Ballbuster." *Journal of Popular Culture* 9 (1976): 1027–38. A fascinating analysis of "the information given the reader about the female role in society" through the character of Nancy Drew.

Turning Kids on to Books—Through Television

Carol A. Emmens*

Television is today's all-purpose scapegoat. Many parents and teachers point the finger of blame at TV for youthful problems ranging from vandalism to poor eating habits to low reading scores. But as H. A. Mencken wrote, "All problems have a simple answer—the wrong one."

Millions of parents and teachers assume television is an archenemy of reading; however, we have no proof that unplugging the TV will promote the cause of reading on a long term basis. In fact, evidence is mounting that television, properly exploited, can be a strong ally of reading.

Preschool children are often prepared to learn to read *because* they watch television. Through "Sesame Street" children learn the alphabet and develop reading readiness skills. "Captain Kangaroo" also promotes skills necessary for reading and promotes books when the Captain reads a story.

Commercials, generally maligned for trying to sell children sugar-laden and junk foods, may actually serve a purpose in reading instruction. Dr. Kenneth S. Goodman, Professor of Education at the University of Arizona and a reading consultant for publishers and schools, points out that preschoolers recognize cereal names because the commercials are repeated so often. Making the connection between meaning and written symbols, he states, is the "first big hurdle in learning to read."

* Carol A. Emmens is Project Director for a New Jersey cable television station and an author of books about television.

Still, there are children who experience reading difficulties and TV is often blamed. Yet, even Dorothy G. Singer, who is the Co-Director of the Family Television and Consultation Center at Yale University and a vocal critic of TV, conceded, "Television has been accused of interfering with a child's acquisition of language skills and reading, and of impeding his or her imagination. In actuality, there is a paucity of empirical evidence that can substantiate these claims."

Despite all the "new" reading programs introduced in the 1960s and early 1970s, current projections are that 25 percent of the population will be illiterate by the end of the 1980s. Dr. Rudolph Flesch, author of *Why Johnny Can't Read and What You Can Do About It*, contends, "TV isn't the cause of poor reading. Television is an alibi that some educators have used to explain their own failures."

The Educational Testing Service and surveys of reading teachers have found that the television show "The Electric Company" significantly improves basic reading skills of its target audience and that it has been adopted enthusiastically by schools on a large scale. It appears that children more readily retain what they see and hear on the TV screen than what they learn from their textbooks or the chalkboard. An in-depth study of a school in the Lincoln Heights School District in Ohio revealed that the third grade viewers of "The Electric Company" were six months ahead of the nonviewers in reading comprehension.

Sometimes Johnny and Mary can read and read well but won't. But now a number of innovative programs are designed to capitalize on their tremendous interest in television to stimulate them to read. Television, used in conjunction rather than in competition with the classroom is a powerful tool.

Script Reading

Voice over, pan, superimpose, and *close-up* are terms known to millions of children because TV scripts are as much at home in the classroom as in Norman Lear's office and they do a better job of teaching and motivating reading than standard textbooks.

Through the CBS Television Reading Program and the Capital Cities Communication Reading Program, teachers are provided with scripts and guides to television specials, series, or movies. These scripts involve shows that are fictional in nature or docu-dramas. Students read the scripts before the broadcast, and while watching the program is not mandatory in many classrooms, many students do watch the program with the script in hand, thus reinforcing the value of the printed word. Whether the program is watched or not is irrelevant to the reading of the scripts. Both the CBS and Capital Cities programs are aimed at grades 5–12. Like short stories, plays or novels, scripts provide opportunities for analyzing plots, characters and themes, for developing vocabulary, for studying literary devices and for discussing personal, ethical and social values. Scripts also spur related activities such as writing. And students love them!

The CBS Network office chooses the specials for the reading program, arranges the copyright clearances and develops the guides, but the project is essentially carried out by the local CBS affiliates, which generally work in cooperation with local newspapers that print the scripts.

CBS entered the project slowly, experimenting with selected scripts in cities such as St. Petersburg, Florida. The positive responses from teachers prompted CBS to expand the program in 1978. Scripts of six specials were offered to teachers in 50 cities. Again, the response was positive and CBS again enlarged the program. Now over 90 affiliates, serving four million students, take part. The made-for-TV movies selected for the 1979–80 reading program included "The Shining Season," "All Quiet on the Western Front," "Aunt Mary," and "Mayflower: The Pilgrims' Adventure."

Alvany Wilson, a supervisor of high school English in Hillsborough County (Florida) had this to say about the program: "With all the emphasis on functional literacy in Florida, the remediation and compensatory education, this came along at the right time. All kinds of students are able to use it. We found uses for it in drama classes, as part of language arts, with our average students who are often overlooked and with our special classes as well. It's not often that we have such a valuable directed activity that involves families as well."

Capital Cities Communications offers a similar program once a month. Besides using specials such as "A Woman Called Moses," the Capital Cities program uses such shows as "Happy Days," "Mork and Mindy," and "The White Shadow." These are shows with ongoing youth appeal.

The Capital Cities program proved it motivates students. Teachers using the program testify that teenagers who read the script for the mini-series "Eleanor and Franklin" went on to read the book by Joseph Lash. Librarians in schools and public libraries in cities where the program is used have noted an increased demand for materials related to the television show's topic. The bibliographies provided by Capital Cities in the teachers' guides are at best uninspiring, and at worst outdated, repetitious, and only marginally related to the TV programs. Think what could happen with good reading lists!

The seed for the CBS and Capital Cities script reading programs was planted in Philadelphia in 1971 by Dr. Michael McAndrew. He decided to channel his students' enthusiasm for TV into the reading of scripts of such popular programs at the time as "Ironsides" and "I Love Lucy." McAndrew tirelessly transcribed the scripts from videotapes of the programs. At the beginning of the project, the seniors in his English class read on a sixth grade level; by June they had increased their reading ability an average of one and a half years.

But there was a catch. McAndrew was violating copyright laws. Producers were persuaded to cooperate with McAndrew when they saw the positive results of using scripts in the classroom. There was one condition—McAndrew had to share his script reading program, and share it he did. Today, Capital Cities Communications serves over 65,000 students in 12 cities across the country.

Scholastic Magazines, which has received less publicity, actually pioneered the use of movie and TV scripts or "retellings" in 1964 when *Scope* was launched. *Scope* is directed at students in grades 8–12 with reading levels of grades 4–6. *Senior Scholastic, Junior Scholastic, Voice, Action, Sprint* and *Literary Cavalcade* also publish scripts of programs ranging from sitcoms ("All in the Family") to mini-series ("Roots") to children's specials ("Dinky Hocker") to documentaries ("This Child is Rated X").

The high interest/low reading level scripts from Scholastic fill a void left by traditional texts and the reading levels of the scripts or retellings are as low as grade two. The monthly Scholastic materials provide a variety of reading levels whereas the professional scripts supplied by CBS and Capital Cities are written on one level, generally appropriate for students in grades 5–12. The teacher is free to choose the activities best suited for her or his students.

Sprint magazine is aimed at fourth-, fifth-,

and sixth-grade students who read on the second-grade level. Editor Vicky Chapman utilizes movie and TV scripts to motivate students who have been frustrated by their reading failures: "Our goal is to give youngsters topics that are so interesting that they get carried away, and simply forget they're worried." Amazingly, teachers confirm that students are willing to struggle and to stretch themselves in order to read TV scripts, which leads to improved skills and higher test scores.

Motivating Reading

Often Johnny and Mary can read but won't, sometimes because they watch television night after night. But simultaneously, TV leads children to books. Peggy Charren, President of Action for Children's Television, a group primarily critical of television in relation particularly to commercials directed at children, but also with violence and other anti-human content, admits, "If a show is in any way tied to a book, kids will storm the library for it." It is this very power of television to influence children's behavior that concerns the critics of the medium.

Television tie-in is a phrase reserved for materials connected with a television production and should not be confused with script reading. Tie-ins can be original paperbacks, comic books, and highly illustrated novelizations, or they can be re-issued paperbacks of books that have been adapted for television. On the whole, original materials, whatever the format, tend to be sloppily written with little or no character development. The dialogue is stilted and unrealistic. In short, they suffer from the faults any poor book has. Perhaps the best known series of spin-offs is the "Star Trek" series, which is very uneven in quality, some titles being quite acceptable while others are sheer trash. When the television tie-in is a re-issue of a previously published work, the inside content remains the same, while the publisher replaces the cover with the star or stars of the television program.

Despite their faults, original television tie-ins do enable teachers and parents to achieve their first priority: getting children to read. Whether biographies of television personalities, scripts, novelizations, or trivia, TV and movie tie-ins are never on a library shelf; they are always in circulation. The questions teachers and librarians must answer in relation to the tie-in phenomenon is whether reading *anything* is better than reading nothing.

Television consumes material at a tremendous rate and with the proven popularity of adaptations of books, both fiction and nonfiction, children's and adults', the industry has turned more and more to books as a source for programming. The book industry cooperates in this venture, knowing that readers, whether eight or 80, will hunt for books adapted for television. Perhaps the most dramatic example of this relationship occurred when the day after the first episode of *Roots* by Alex Hailey was aired, 67,000 hardcover copies of the book were sold. When "Little House on the Prairie" premiered on TV, the sales of Laura Ingalls Wilder's books increased three-fold. Between 1953 and 1978, book sales have increased 28 percent proportionally more than the population, indicating that television is not destroying book sales or reading.

In response to the criticism that television was not providing any original quality programming for children, all four major networks have initiated series directed to children. Books and short stories are the basis for many films on the "CBS Library," the "ABC Afterschool Specials," the "NBC Special Treats," and "Once Upon a Classic" on Public Broadcasting Service. The long list of children's books adapted for TV includes: *New York City Too Far from Tampa Blues* by T. Ernesto Betancourt; *The Lion, the Witch and the Wardrobe* by C.S. Lewis; *The Winged Colt* by Betsy Byars; Constance Green's *Beat the Turtle Drum* (aired as "Very Good Friends"); *Soup and Me* by Robert Newton Peck; *The Contest Kid* by Barbara Brooks Wallace, and *The Secret Garden* by Frances Hodgson Burnett. In addition to the specials, "The Wonderful World of Disney" uses a large number of children's books for its programs.

According to Squire D. Rushnell, the vice-president in charge of children's programs for ABC-TV, approximately 50 percent of the "Afterschool Specials" are adaptations of books. He has said, ". . . our preference is to adapt a good book. It is easier. The development period is normally shorter. And, often, the resulting screenplay is better." But ABC develops original scripts because "many of the stories we wish to explore have not been written in book form. Second, adaptable books are hard to find."

Involved in the question of what makes a book adaptable is the cloudy area of censorship, or "taboos" practiced by television. Current social issues, such as youthful alcoholism, have been explored in such films as *The Boy Who Drank Too Much* by Shep Greene and Sandra Scoppettone's *The Late Great Me;* and Richard Peck's novel about rape, *Are You in the House Alone?* was a prime time show. However, Paula Danziger's *The Cat Ate My Gymsuit,* one of the most popular young teen novels, has been rejected by TV because it contains a controversy involving a teacher's refusal to salute the flag. Just what is acceptable content to television moguls is unclear to authors, publishers, and agents.

A different problem arises out of adaptations when the television program is given a different title from the book. When a title change occurs, books can languish on the shelf because children are unaware of the connection between book and TV program, as was the case when Louise Fitzhugh's *Nobody's Family Is Going to Change* was aired as the Emmy Award-winner "The Tap Dance Kid" on NBC. To its credit, NBC now footnotes its presentations; that is, the stars tell the viewers the titles of the books which are the sources for the TV movies.

The biggest problem with the children's specials aired in the after-school hours is that the peak viewing hours for children are the early evening so the specials do not receive as large an audience as possible or desirable. Some parents have a ban on all after-school television viewing, while many children join other family members in watching soap operas. Thus, teachers who want to turn students on to reading must alert them to TV programs based on books.

Teachers can also use the television programs in the classroom since a large percentage of them are available for sale or rental on 16mm or videotape. ABC's educational division, ABC Learning Resources, distributes the "Weekend Specials" and news specials. Learning Corporation of America and Time-Life Multimedia distribute selected titles from the "NBC Special Treats" and the ABC "Afterschool Specials." In addition, producers of educational television programs, such as the Agency for Instructional Television, offer series designed to teach and to motivate reading.

Weston Woods, which produces and distributes audiovisual materials based on picture books, recently announced it will explore ways of adapting books for an educational TV series.

Using books adapted for TV in the classroom makes students both print and electronically literate, and cross-media analysis presents the advantages and disadvantages of each medium. Discussions can center on differences in how the characters are developed in each medium and how television changes or eliminates characters from the book. Other discussion areas include how the theme may be altered, how the plot is simplified or expanded, and how the dialogue is rewritten. Such classroom discussions also help children become better informed viewers and may lead to a future generation that will be unwilling to accept second-rate productions.

The major reason for educators' use of television tie-ins is to lead students to read a wide range of books. Prime Time School Television prepares teachers' guides for specials and made-for-TV movies such as "All Quiet on the Western Front." The guides are printed in educational magazines such as *Media & Methods* and *Learning,* and include bibliographies as well as activities for teaching comprehension and analysis. The Cultural Information Service is a non-profit ecumenical agency which publishes bi-weekly reviews of the arts as well as guides and bibliographies for TV programs and movies.

Teachers Guides to Television, edited by Gloria Kirshner, are exactly what their name implies. They, too, contain bibliographies. However, these bibliographies are designed for generally good readers.

Teachers know they must take their students from where they are to where the teachers want them to be. By talking to students about their television viewing habits, teachers acquire clues as to the students' interests. A "Star Trek" fan may be led to read science fiction works by Isaac Asimov (writing as Paul French) and the juvenile writings of Robert Heinlein and Arthur C. Clarke. Police and private-detective show fans may find the works of Jay Bennett and Lois Duncan to their reading taste, and "Mork and Mindy" fans may delight in David Pinkwater's *Fat Men from Space.*

There is very little on television that cannot lead to reading. Weather reports can lead to reading science books on weather; westerns can lure children to read the really good pioneer stories, and, of course, sports offer unlimited possibilities. Children today are interested in a wide variety of people, places, and events. Teachers and librarians can capitalize on that interest by calling attention to books related to the news and to programs with wide youth appeal and make the books accessible. The TV set is *always* accessible; it's generally the focal point of the living room or den. Books need to be equally accessible if they are to compete.

Suggestions for Term Papers

1. For four Saturday mornings, watch the children's programming on a local station from 9 a.m. to noon. Do a content analysis for *one* of the following: (a) the number of violent acts per half hour show; (b) the ratio of female to male characters and the level of "activeness" of each sex; (c) the number of minority characters and the role assigned them.

2. Select one prime time popular television show and prepare a bibliography of related library materials that should appeal to children viewers of the show.

3. If the FCC has not banned advertising on programs for children (a decision under consideration as this book goes to press), analyze the difference in products advertised on Saturday morning and those advertised in prime time periods.

4. Many children's books have been the topic of television productions as after school specials and prime time shows. If you have access to an Audiovisual Collection containing four or more 16mm films (or videotapes) of these shows, analyze the changes made in the television shows from the content of the original books.

Bibliography

Bibliographies

GORDON, THOMAS F., and MARY ELLEN VERNA. *Mass Communication Effects and Processes, A Comprehensive Bibliography, 1950–1975.* Sage, 1978. A research bibliography of media-effects literature containing 2,703 entries arranged in alphabetical order by author with an extensive cross-referenced subject index and non-primary author index.

Books

BLUEM, A. WILLIAM, and ROGER MANVELL. *Television: The Creative Experience.* Hastings, 1967. A collection of articles dealing with educational TV and its impact on the public.
BRONFENBRENNER, URIE. *The Two Worlds of Childhood: U.S. and U.S.S.R.* Russell Sage, 1970. Chapter 4 of this book gives a cogent analysis of TV and its impact on American children.
BROWN, LES. *Television: The Business Behind the Box.* Harcourt, 1971. A discussion of the politics involved in the TV industry.
CATER, DOUGLAS, and STEPHEN STRICKLAND. *TV Violence and the Child.* Russell Sage, 1975. The book deals successively with television as an object of concern, research findings, response of critics, and TV industry response.
COMSTOCK, GEORGE, STEVEN CHAFEE, NATON KATZMAN, MAXWELL McCOMBS, and DONALD ROBERTS. *Television and Human Behav-*

ior. Columbia Univ. Press, 1978. Interprets research evidence on social and behavioral effects of television viewing. Covers program content, audience make-up, influence of television on American lives and behavior, and recommendations for television policy-making and future research.

FESHBACK, SEYMOUR. *Television and Aggression: An Experimental Field Study.* Jossey-Bass, 1971. The report of a research project conducted with children who watched violent television while in a residential setting.

FRANK, JOSETTE. *Television: How to Use It Wisely with Children.* Rev. ed. Child Study Assn. of America, 1976. A discussion of how much time a child should spend before TV and what content should be selected.

GATTEGNO, CALEB. *Toward a Visual Culture.* Outerbridge and Diestenfrey, 1969. A discussion of the impact and influence of TV and suggestions for dealing with TV.

HALLORAN, J. D., and P. R. ELLIOT. *Television for Children and Young People.* International Publications Service, 1971. A study dealing with English television for children.

HALLORAN, JAMES, R. L. BROWN, and D. C. CHANEY. *Television and Delinquency.* Leicester Univ. Press, 1970. A comprehensive review of English information about TV and its relationship to delinquency.

HARMONAY, MAUREEN, ed. *Promise and Performance: Children with Special Needs.* Ballinger, 1977. An excellent collection of articles dealing with the images of the disabled presented on television and examples of programming that meet special needs. Contains important background information for teachers and others involved with mainstreaming.

HOWE, MICHAEL J. A. *Television and Children.* Linnet, 1977. A psychologist, Howe brings considerable insight into his synthesis of research into the effects of television on children.

JOHNSON, NICHOLAS. *How to Talk Back to Your Television Set.* Little, 1970. The author tells the various important aspects of television, especially the educational value of television, and describes how the public can reform television.

KLAPPER, JOSEPH. *The Effects of Mass Communication.* Free Pr., 1960. This author attempts to integrate research findings and expert conjecture into some tentative generalizations about mass media influences on attitudes and behavior.

LESSER, GERARD. *Children and Television: Lessons from "Sesame Street."* Random, 1974. The history and background of the program. The book discusses the research done about the show, written by the show's research director.

LIEBERT, ROBERT, JOHN NEAL, and EMILY DAVIDSON. *The Early Window: Effects of Television on Children and Youth.* Pergamon, 1973. The history of television and its role in today's world. A good review of research done on this topic and a look at some new research to come. Good resource book.

McLUHAN, MARSHALL, and QUENTIN FIORE. *The Medium is the Message.* Bantam, 1967. An in-depth discussion of media and their effects on society. Gives the reader a background in understanding the medium.

MAYER, MARTIN. *About Television.* Harper, 1972. This book presents television as a most persuasive form of communication.

MELODY, WILLIAM. *Children's Television: The Economics of Exploitation.* Yale Univ. Press, 1973. A study of the economic characteristics of commercial children's television. Focuses on TV's economic forces and trends and evaluates the public's attitude toward commercial children's TV.

NOBLE, GRANT. *Children in Front of the Small Screen.* Russell Sage, 1975. Permeating this analysis of television's effects on children is a fascinating analogy between the "small

screen" and village life in contrast to the large screen of film and urban life.

POTTER, ROSEMARY LEE. *New Season: The Positive Use of Commercial Television with Children.* Merrill, 1976. Filled with very practical suggestions as to how to use commercial television programs to develop language arts skills.

QUINLAN, STERLING. *The Hundred Million Dollar Lunch: The Broadcasting Industry's Own Watergate.* O'Hara, 1974. Presents the case of the deviant side of the broadcasting industry.

SCHWARTZ, TONY. *The Responsive Chord.* Anchor/Doubleday, 1972. An in-depth discussion on communication theory and practice. The author makes the valid point that this medium has not been extended to its fullest potential.

SHERRINGTON, RICHARD. *Television and Language Skills.* London: Oxford Univ. Press, 1973. Outlines the association between the disciplines of television production and language teaching and solicits a change in this relationship in regard to the use of television in the teaching of language skills.

STEIN, ALETHA HUSTON, and LYNETTE KOHN FRIEDRICH. *Impact of Television on Children and Youth.* Univ. of Chicago Press, 1975. Reviews and discusses research dealing with the relation of television violence to aggressive behavior in children and young adults, conditions affecting this relationship, and the influence of television on children's understanding of social roles and stereotypes, cognitive development, and prosocial behavior.

WINN, MARIE. *The Plug-in Drug.* Viking, 1977. Unlike so many books that focus on the content of television, Winn's major concern is with the act of watching itself. Insightful, provocative.

Articles

BANDURA, ALBERT. "Social Learning Through Imitation." In *Nebraska Symposium on Motivation.* Univ. of Nebraska Press, 1962, pp. 211–74. The studies indicate that exposure to human models portraying aggression on film is the most influential method of producing and shaping some aggressive behavior.

———. "Vicarious Processes: A Case of No-Trial Learning." In *Advances in Experimental Social Psychology,* Vol. 2, ed. by Leonard Berkowitz. Academic Press, 1965, pp. 1–55. A review of how children learn by observation, both theory and research findings. A good reference source.

BANDURA, ALBERT, D. ROSS, and SHEILA ROSS. "Imitation of Film-Mediated Aggressive Models." *Journal of Abnormal and Social Psychology* 66 (1963): 3–11. A study of young children's imitation of aggressive behavior when exposed to film aggression.

BUSCH, JACKIE S. "Television's Effects on Reading: A Case Study." *Phi Delta Kappan* 59 (June 1978): 668–71. Report of a research study verifying Schramm's conclusion that television helps preschool and primary grade children, but by ages 10 to 12, knowledge declines among heavy television viewers, even those of high ability. If teachers do not learn to use television, the future is bleak.

"Children's TV Commercials: Policy and Research." *Journal of Communication* 4 (Autumn 1974): 113–44. An interesting view of how TV commercials are bought by programs and the research aspect of their use with the viewers.

COHEN, DOROTHY. "Is TV a Pied Piper?" *Young Children* (November 1974): 4–14. Is the promise of television living up to its expectations or are we dealing with a very different kind of learning? The article deals with this important question.

CULHANE, JOHN. "Report Card on Sesame Street." *New York Times Magazine* (May 24, 1970): 34–35. The article points out that Sesame Street gets high marks in cognitive-skills development, but fails when social science is involved.

FEELEY, JOAN T. "Television and Reading in the Seventies." *Language Arts* 52 (September 1975): 797–801 +. A review of the research done to determine what type of show a child will choose.

GERBNER, GEORGE, and LARRY GROSS. "The Scary World of TV's Heavy Viewer." *Psychology Today* 9 (April 1976): 41–45 +. Adults who watch television four or more hours per day have a warped view of the dangers of the real world based on the violence they see on the screen. This fear is preparing people to play the role of victim and may be contributing to the flight from the cities, and "television may have become our chief instrument of social control."

GOUGH, PAULINE B. "Introducing Children to Books Via Television." *Reading Teacher* 32 (January 1979): 458–62. Summarizes the various Instructional Television (ITV) programs available to help teachers utilize television as an incentive to reading.

HEERMAN, CHARLES E., and PATRICIA R. CALLISON. "Reading Profile of a Small Midwestern School." *Reading Improvement* 15 (Summer 1978): 101–4. There is a discrepancy between the amount of television middle grade students watch and the amount their parents perceive them watching. Enlisting parents is an important move for teachers wishing to counteract the reduction in reading time caused by television viewing.

LARRICK, NANCY. "Children of Television." *Teacher* (September 1975): 75–76. An article which gives emphasis to the role of parents and teachers in dealing with the television child.

LEE, BARBARA. "Prime Time in the Classroom." *Journal of Communication* (Winter, 1980): 175–80. The Senior Project Director of the CBS script reading program details the findings emerging from the project.

LEIFER, AIMEE, NEAL GORDON, and SHERRYL GRAVES. "Children's Television More Than Mere Entertainment." *Harvard Educational Review* 44 (May 1974): 213–19. The authors state that while TV is entertaining to children, it also socializes them. The authors deal with the question of economic factors being more important than children's learning, involving commercial TV.

"Should We Ban TV Advertising to Children?" *National Forum* 69 (Fall 1979): 13–24. Three articles, one saying yes, one saying no, and the third looking at the financial implications of a ban as well as the problems in defining what is a children's program.

SINGER, DOROTHY G. "Reading, Imagination, and Television." *School Library Journal* 26 (December 1979): 31–34. Heavy television viewing among preschoolers limits both their imagination and use of language since both require time and interaction with parents or peers, time usurped by television.

SNOW, C. P. "The Printed Word: Excerpt from Address." *Writer* 90 (December 1977): 24–26. A short article concerned with the positive and negative effects of television upon the printed word.

STRICKLER, DARRYL S., and BEVERLY FARR. "TV as a Tool to Improve Basic Communication Skills?" *Language Arts* (September 1979): 634–40. A summary of some of the instructional television programs developed to enhance communication skills, complete with addresses of developing agencies.

"TV and Kids: What Teachers Are Complaining About." *Learning* (October 1979): 44–49. A mini-series in which Nancy Larrick defines the problem, followed by two very helpful pieces by teachers offering many specific suggestions on how to combat the problems television creates.

"TV as a Teacher's Ally." *Instructor* 87 (March 1978): 82–84. A series of four short pieces on how to use television in teaching and to recognize its value.

"TV's Effects on Children and Adolescents: A Symposium of Eleven Studies." *Journal of Communication* 25 (Autumn 1975). A wealth of information covering all major concerns.

ZUCKERMAN, DIANA M., DOROTHY G. SINGER, and JEROME L. SINGER. "Television Viewing, Children's Reading, and Related Classroom Behavior." *Journal of Communication* (Winter, 1980): 166–74. Reports the results of a study of children in New Haven measuring the relationship between television viewing and attentiveness in the classroom, imaginativeness, and enthusiasm. The latter two qualities related to the type of programs watched, rather than the amount of television viewed.

Periodicals

Better Radio and Television. National Association for Better Broadcasting, 373 N.W. Avenue, Los Angeles, Cal. 90004. One issue each year includes the annual guide to "Television for the Family: A Comprehensive Guide to Family Viewing."

Journal of Advertising Research. Advertising Research Foundation, 3 E. 54th St., New York, N.Y. 10022. Articles about television advertising and other advertising research.

Journal of Broadcasting. Broadcast Education Association, Temple University, Philadelphia, Pa. 19122. This magazine is dedicated to all aspects of the broadcasting industry.

Journal of Communication. Annenberg School of Communications in cooperation with the International Communication Association, P.O. Box 11358, Philadelphia, Pa. 19101. All aspects of communication are reviewed in this magazine.

TV Guide. Box 4000, Radnor, Pa. 19088. Popular and informative; articles involved with television. Lists shows for the week.

Television Quarterly. National Academy of Television Arts and Sciences, 291 South La Cienega Blvd., Beverly Hills, Cal. 90211. Many subjects covered in this magazine including news, art design, TV, radio, and news.

Addresses

ABC Learning Resources. 1330 Avenue of the Americas, New York, NY 10019.

Action for Children's Television. 33 Hancock Avenue, Newton Centre, MA 02159.

Agency for Instructional Television. Box A, Bloomington, IN 47401.

CBS Television Reading Program. 51 W. 52 St., New York, NY 10019.

Capitol Cities Communications, 4100 City Line Ave., Philadelphia, PA 19131.

Cultural Information Service. Box 92, New York, NY 10016.

Learning Corp. of America. 1350 Avenue of the Americas, New York, NY 10019.

National Association for Better Broadcasting. 373 N. Western Ave., Los Angeles, Cal. 90004.

National Association of Broadcasters. 1771 N Street, N.W., Washington, D.C. 20036.

National Association of Educational Broadcasters. 1346 Connecticut Avenue, N.W., Washington, D.C. 20036.

Prime Time School Television. 120 S. LaSalle St., Chicago, IL 60603.

Scholastic Magazines. 50 W. 44 St., New York, NY 10036.

Teachers Guides to Television. 699 Madison Ave., New York, NY 10021.

Television Information Office. 745 Fifth Avenue, New York, NY 10022.

Time-Life Multimedia. Time and Life Building, New York, NY 10020.

Weston Woods. Weston, CT 06880.

Mainstreaming

The Editor

The Education of All Handicapped Children Act (PL 94–142) mandates that all children with special educational needs be provided with the least restrictive environment for learning. Education is responding to that law with what is labelled mainstreaming.

As schools have worked toward implementing the law, four major challenges have been identified as necessary for success: (1) physical changes in the environment; (2) increasing teacher/staff sensitivity; (3) increasing understanding of the disabled by nonhandicapped peers, and (4) providing the appropriate educational materials for the disabled students. Each of these is inseparably intertwined with the others, so it is not possible to discuss them as totally discrete entities.

One very popular method of determining what changes in the physical environment are needed that also increases the understanding of teachers and nondisabled students is to set aside a day on which teachers and students come to school in wheelchairs, on crutches, with blindfolds, or play deaf by ignoring all audio communications (announcements over the P.A. system, bells for changing classes, etc.). Besides helping identify physical obstacles, this technique helps the physically able understand the amount of energy expended by those in wheelchairs or on crutches, and thus become more sympathetic to the pace appropriate to the needs of the disabled.

Before teachers, librarians, and other school staff can develop techniques for increasing the understanding of nondisabled students about their disabled peers, they must increase their own understanding. Unless we have had personal experience with disabled people within our own families or among our close friends, we are likely to have many misconceptions about disabled people. Books can play a large part in helping overcome and change those misconceptions.

Perhaps the strongest misconception held by many people is that physically disabled people are also mentally retarded. Of course, we ought to know better. Helen Keller, whose *The Story of My Life* remains a moving account of a fine intelligence, is a wonderful example of a multiply handicapped person whose achievements exceeded those of most nonhandicapped people. *To Race the Wind* by Harold Krents, the autobiography that inspired the play *Butterflies Are Free,* is another excellent book, written with humor and perspective and, most of all, intelligence.

However important books are in this sensitizing process—and they are important—a good film is an even more meaningful experience since films do not allow us the same degree of imposing our own perceptions on the material as books do. The Academy Award winning *Who Are the DeBolts And Where Did They Get 19 Kids?* shows the great joy severely handicapped children can have from life when they are loved and accepted for what they are.

The second greatest misconception is that all handicapped people are alike. Wide reading and viewing (see bibliography/cinemagraphy) will show how inaccurate this assumption is. There are people who are born with one or more limbs missing (e.g. *A Day in the Life of Bonnie Consolo*) and there are those who are victims of accidents or war (e.g., *Against All Odds* by Tom Helms). The problems faced by the person born with a physical disability are very different from those of one struck down after some years of being among the physically able.

The literature about mainstreaming consistently discusses the importance of school staff developing an I.E.P. for each disabled student. Those initials stand for Individualized Educational Program and serve to reinforce the idea that disabled students are not all alike. The blind student's needs are different from the deaf student's needs. And both are different from the needs of students suffering from progressively degenerative diseases or those who are among the Educable Mentally Retarded.

Since classroom teachers cannot know in advance which kind of handicapped student they are likely to encounter in their classes, it is suggested that they read widely in the general area and know how to locate information on specific disabilities when they have an actual child to work with. Teachers who do not find themselves with a disabled child in the classroom still have a responsibility to sensitize themselves and their nondisabled students to the needs of the handicapped, not only because the school may contain such students in other classrooms, but because society as a whole must become more responsive to the rights of the disabled.

Working with Nondisabled Students

The first rule in working with nondisabled students is to be sure that class discussions of the handicapped occur *in the absence of* the disabled children. This allows for freer discussion and saves the disabled children from feeling in the spotlight.

Before selecting children's books for the students to read and discuss, it is vital that teachers use their knowledge to evaluate the books, not in terms of readability, but in terms of accuracy of presentation of the disability being fictionalized. The major mistake some teachers and librarians make in evaluating fiction is to decide that if it is moving or inspirational or literary, it is also accurate. Using *Notes from a Different Drummer* (Baskin and Harris) and *Books About Handicaps* (Bisshopp) teachers and librarians can determine the books they want to try out with students.

There are some very fine books for the youngest children, who are among the least biased and therefore the most open to understanding if the opportunity is offered them. *Handtalk: An ABC of Finger Spelling & Sign Language* by Remy Charlip and Mary Beth Miller is a beautiful book that introduces signing and finger spelling to children in grades K–3. For the same age group, *Katie's Magic Glasses,* by Jane Goodsell, is a delightful story of a child who has deteriorating vision and who sees things clearly when given glasses. *Rachel,* by Elizabeth Fanshawe, is the story of a young girl who uses a wheelchair, but refuses to be restricted by it. These are just a few of the stories teachers can use with primary grade children to raise their consciousness about physically disabled children. As the age/grade level increases, the supply of books increases accordingly, and there is no reason why elementary school children should not have many positive experiences, albeit vicarious, with the disabled.

Films also play an important part in this increased sensitivity. Even the youngest students love watching Bonnie Consolo use her feet to peel vegetables, open refrigerator doors, and do other household chores. They can admire Moira of *Moira: A Vision of Blindness,* an eleven-year-old, born blind, who lives a very active life.

In trying to reach elementary school children, teachers must be aware that children are no different from adults when it comes to being kind and accepting of others different from ourselves. The portrait Judy Blume paints in *Blubber* of the class tyrant who bullies friends and torments enemies is all too accurate a depiction of unhappy children. Teachers must be aware of such children and help them with their unhappiness. Otherwise, they will be the leaders in persecuting the disabled in the school.

Working with Disabled Students

Physically disabled children who are not mentally retarded have exactly the same needs and interests as nondisabled children. The only differences come from the format in which those needs can be met and the degree of sophistication. The latter occurs because handicapped children often have fewer life experiences than the more mobile children in our society and not because they are less capable of maturation. It is vital to understand that maturation, particularly in relation to psychological development, is dependent upon life experiences. The more restricted these experiences, the slower the maturation process. One sees this demonstrated most vividly in Keyes's *Flowers for Algernon* (the movie version is *Charly*) in which Charly's rapid cognitive development does not help him deal with the problems of relating to women and having an adult relationship.

The importance of understanding the role experiences play in the maturity level of children is the recognition that the disabled children may need books at a less-mature level than their peers, even though their cognitive development is equal to, or above, the other children's. Classroom teachers and librarians who will be recommending materials to the disabled children need to consult closely with the counselor or psychologist assigned to work with them in order to understand the special emotional needs of each child.

Acquiring the correct format for each disabled child is a true challenge for the school librarian whose responsibility is to provide classroom teachers with the materials they need as well as to stock the school library with "something for everyone." Some blind children may read Braille; others may need talking books or cassettes. The partially sighted will need large print books and audio materials. On the other hand, the deaf will need books that are both signed and printed and filmstrips and films that are captioned.

Students with motor-coordination problems will need a wide variety of materials, depending on the severity of their disability. Some may be able to read standard books with the aid of a page-turner; others may need cassettes or overhead projectors.

There is an increasing number of commercial producers of materials for the handicapped, but like all new industries, the end products are not always of high quality or even what is needed. School librarians trained in the production of audiovisual materials can be extremely useful in adapting currently owned materials to the needs of the disabled as well as in creating new materials specifically designed for an individual student.

Throughout the United States and Canada, there are groups of volunteers who have learned to use a Braille typewriter and are willing to transcribe standard print books into Braille upon request. Other groups will record books on cassettes. High school craft classes can be recruited to make plaster of paris maps to accompany books on cassettes, helping blind students to visualize, for example, the route Lewis and Clark took to cross the country.

Perhaps the most important point to keep in mind in selecting materials for use with the disabled is that there is no difference in the standards to be applied. The same high quality materials selected for the nondisabled students are appropriate for the disabled. Shoddiness should be rejected, whoever the prospective clientele.

General Bibliography

Autobiographies

BLEIER, ROCKY, and TERRY O'NEIL. *Fighting Back.* Stein & Day, 1975. Warner pb. After a crippling injury in Vietnam, Rocky Bleier ignored doctors' dire predictions and eventually won a starting position with the 1975 Super Bowl champion Pittsburgh Steelers.

BOURKE-WHITE, MARGARET. *Portrait of Myself.* Simon, 1963. An account of Bourke-White's career in commercial photography, her two unsuccessful marriages, and her fight with Parkinson's disease. She is as unsparing as her camera in describing her illness and treatment.

BROWN, CHRISTY. *My Left Foot.* Simon, 1955. Cerebral palsy caused Christy Brown to be unable to move any of his limbs with the exception of his left foot. That foot gets put through a lot, as Christy relates in his autobiography.

CAMPANELLA, ROY. *It's Good to Be Alive.* Little, 1959. NAL pb.

The story of big league catcher Roy Campanella, whose near fatal auto accident left him paralyzed. His fight for life and partial recovery are recalled in detail, including Campy's homecoming and his return to baseball as coach and advisor.

DeBOTTAZI, ANA MARIA TRENCHI, *To Live Again.* Dodd, Mead, 1978. On the verge of becoming an internationally known pianist, Ana Maria is brain-damaged in an auto accident. Her fight to play again culminates in a Town Hall recital.

EARECKSON, JONI, *Joni.* Zondervan, 1976. Bantam pb. As a result of a diving accident at age 17, Joni is paralyzed from the neck down. We hear of her struggles to accept her condition and trust God again. The illustrations are her own, done holding a pen in her teeth.

————. *A Step Further.* Zondervan, 1978. Joni relates more of what is happening in her life and how she has grown closer to God and her fellow human beings.

HELMS, TOM. *Against All Odds.* Crowell, 1978. Warner pb. After injuring his spine in an accident while hitching home from college, Tom learns to walk again, only to have a recurrent accident even more paralyzing because of a medical disagreement.

HOCKEN, SHEILA. *Emma & I.* Dutton, 1978. NAL pb. After years of blindness, Sheila Hocken acquires Emma as a guide dog, falls in love, and discovers an operation that miraculously restores her sight.

KELLER, HELEN. *The Story of My Life.* Doubleday, 1954. Dell pb. Blind and deaf, Helen Keller grew to be one of America's greatest women with the help of her inspired teacher, Anne Sullivan.

KRENTS, HAROLD. *To Race the Wind.* Putnam, 1972. Bantam pb. Blinded by too much oxygen as an infant, the indomitable Krents "mainstreams" himself all the way to Harvard Law, only to find himself drafted in the 1960s with a 1-A classification.

LEE, LAUREL. *Walking Through the Fire.* Dutton, 1977. Bantam pb. Pregnant with her third child, Lee is diagnosed as having Hodgkins disease. Her hospital journal is more interesting than the TV production, as she relates her decision to avoid radiation to save the baby while her spiritual strength helps her through the crisis.

MIERS, EARL SCHENCK. *The Trouble Bush.* Rand, 1966. Miers tells in detail how he overcame his problems as a victim of cerebral palsy from his childhood through his education at Rutgers University, and ultimately in his career as publisher and writer.

NASAW, JONATHAN LEWIS. *Easy Walking.* Lippincott, 1975. After a paralyzing accident and a six-month ordeal of three operations, many drugs (prescribed as well as recreational), casts, braces, wheelchairs, and crutches, Willie Nasaw returns to the world less mobile but just as irreverent as before.

PUTNAM, PETER. *Keep Your Head Up, Mr. Putnam.* Harper, 1952. After recovering from a shooting accident, Putnam is totally blind and goes to the Seeing Eye in Morristown, N.J. for a dog and some unexpected adventures.

RESNICK, ROSE. *Sun and Shadow.* Atheneum, 1975. Resnick shares funny experiences with a guide dog and some frustrating encounters with impersonal bureaucracies as well as her career as pianist and as a social welfare worker.

ROSENTHAL, TED. *How Could I Not Be Among You?* Persea, 1973. Avon pb. A young Berkeley poet, dying of leukemia, tells of the beauty of life as he reveals his thoughts and feelings about death. Illustrated with stills from the PBS-TV documentary.

RUSSELL, ROBERT. *To Catch an Angel.* Vanguard, 1962. Being accidentally blinded did not stop Russell's pursuit of an education and career as a college English teacher.

SECHEHAYE, MARGUERITE. *The Autobiography of a Schizophrenic Girl.* NAL, 1970. Renee's story of her retreat into the schizophrenic world of fantasy and details of her slow recovery. Renee's psychotherapist, Sechehaye, provides interpretations.

SIZEMORE, CHRIS COSTNER. *I'm Eve.* Doubleday, 1977. Jove pb. The real heroine of *Three Faces of Eve* tells her own story of being twenty-two separate personalities.

SMITHDAS, ROBERT S. *Life at My Fingertips.* Doubleday, 1958. Facing the same handicaps as Helen Keller—without an Anne Sullivan—Smithdas became the first person so disabled to receive a master's degree.

STEINMARK, FREDDIE. *I Play to Win.* Little, 1971. Small for a defensive back, Freddie had what it took to make first string with the Texas Longhorns and he didn't miss a game until he lost a leg to cancer.

SULLIVAN, TOM. *If You Could See What I Hear.* Harper, 1975. NAL pb. The son of a Boston politician tells how it feels to be blind while he attends Harvard, struggles to become a musician, and falls in love.

VALENS, E. G. *A Long Way Up.* Harper, 1966. Warner pb. (Paperback title: The Other Side of the Mountain). A skiing accident in 1955 left Jill Kinmont an 18-year-old quadriplegic who then became as successful a teacher as she had previously been an Olympic skier.

VISCARDI, HENRY. *A Man's Stature.* Erikkson, 1972. Born with stumps for legs, Viscardi describes his struggles to learn to walk on artificial limbs, his teaching amputees to walk during WW II and his years as Executive Director of J.O.B. (Just One Break).

WILLIS, JACK and MARY. *But There Are Always Miracles.* Viking, 1974. After suffering a broken neck in a surfing accident, Jack Willis fights to live while Mary waits in suspended animation to learn if they can be married and what kind of marriage they can have.

ZAHARIAS, BABE DIDRIKSON. *This Life I've Led.* Barnes, 1955. Dell pb. The all-time best American woman athlete tells how she became so good with the help of her loving Norwegian-American family and her Greek-American husband before being struck down with cancer.

Biographies

AXLINE, VIRGINIA M. *Dibs In Search of Self.* Houghton, 1965. Ballantine pb. The perceptive portrait of a disturbed child's successful struggle for identity through therapy, as he changes from a totally withdrawn child to a sensitive, intelligent person.

BARTON, BETSEY. *As Love Is Deep.* Duell, 1957. A journal in which the author tells of her mother's final illness; as a young girl, Barton had experienced a crippling accident and her mother's loving care had been her bulwark; now the daughter had to be strong.

BIGLAND, EILEEN. *Helen Keller.* Phillips, 1967. A moving account of the multiply-handicapped woman who, with her teacher's help, went on to become internationally famous for her work on behalf of the disabled.

BLANK, JOSEPH P. *19 Steps up the Mountain: The Story of the DeBolt Family.* Lippincott, 1976. Jove pb. The DeBolts specialize in salvaging "unadoptable" disabled kids, both U.S. and Asian—and 19 kids can make a very big family!

BLINN, WILLIAM. *Brian's Song.* Bantam, 1972. Tough, tender story of the true friendship between Brian Piccolo and Gale Sayers as they cope together with Brian's cancer and death.

BRADY, MARI. *Please Remember Me.* Doubleday, 1977. Archway pb. Serving as a hospital recreation aide, 22-year-old Mari meets 15-year-old Graham, a mischievous and caring teenager suffering from cancer, and they become special friends.

BREISKY, WILLIAM. *I Think I Can.* Doubleday, 1974. Karen's journalist father recounts her progress—after brain damage and complications from a viral illness—on a professional therapy program executed by family, friends, and neighbors.

BRICKHILL, PAUL. *Reach for the Sky.* Norton, 1954. Bantam pb. Douglas Bader lost both legs in an air crash, and not only learned to walk again, but became a WW II flying ace.

BROWNING, ELIZABETH. *I Can't See What You're Saying.* Coward, 1972. Freddie, the author's son, makes slow progress, despite being aphasic and partially deaf, from a non-speaking child into a 17-year-old blacksmith's apprentice.

BRUCKNER, LEONA S. *Triumph of Love: An Unforgettable Story of the Power of Goodness.* Simon, 1954. The mother of a son who was born without arms describes the sorrows and ultimate triumphs of accepting the small boy into their otherwise normal family.

BUCHANAN, WILLIAM. *A Shining Season.* Coward, 1978. Bantam pb. Stricken with cancer at the height of his track career, John Baker used the time left to coach elementary school children so well that they demanded their school be renamed for him after his death.

CARSON, MARY. *Ginny: A True Story.* Doubleday, 1971. When a six-year-old girl is hit by a truck on her way home from school, her chances of survival are slim at best. The story of her rehabilitation, as told by her mother, conveys the values of youth, innocence and most of all faith when confronted with tragedy.

COPELAND, JAMES. *For the Love of Anne.* Ballantine, 1976. The true story of an autistic child whose sleeping mind is awakened by her parents' determination and love. Based on the diary Anne's father kept.

D'AMBROSIO, RICHARD. *No Language But a Cry.* Doubleday, 1970. Dell pb. After being nearly burned to death by mentally ill parents, Laura did not speak and faced a lifetime in institutions until Dr. D'Ambrosio accidentally discovered her at age twelve.

FOX, RAY and ERROL. *Ambrosia: The Story of a Girl's Winning Fight for Life.* Knopf, 1979. Stricken at thirteen, by sixteen Angela's leukemia was virulent, treatment severe, but her parents prohibited the doctor from telling her the truth. Now in remission and happily married, Angela lives with the knowledge the leukemia can recur any moment.

GAUCHAT, DOROTHY. *All God's Children.* Hawthorne, 1976. Dorothy and Bill Gauchet began their involvement with physically handicapped children in 1947 when they took in a six-month-old child who had already outlived its life expectancy. Over the years, the couple built up their facilities to care for thirty-five children, each of whom has a unique story.

GREENFELD, JOSH. *A Place for Noah.* Holt, 1978. A moving, sometimes bitter, account of life with a mentally retarded child for the mature reader.

GUNTHER, JOHN. *Death Be Not Proud.* Random, 1953. Seventeen-year-old Johnny Gunther's last months of life are told by his father who watched him live bravely and beautifully in the face of an incurable brain tumor.

HASKINS, JAMES. *The Story of Stevie Wonder.* Lothrop, 1976. Dell pb. Stevie Wonder is the sunshine in many people's lives and the story of how the blind black boy from Michigan grew to be a man and mature musician is all here.

IPSWITCH, ELAINE. *Scott Was Here.* Delacorte, 1979. Stricken with Hodgkin's disease, Scott suffers as much from the treatment and cruelty of others as from the disease itself, but his delight in life shines through even as death claims him.

JONES, RON. *Acorn People.* Bantam, 1976. The author, a first-time counselor at a summer camp for multiply handicapped kids, tells how five boys learned to swim, cook, and climb mountains—in defiance of others' expectations of what handicapped kids could do.

JURY, MARK and DAN. *Gramp.* Grossman, 1978. Penguin pb. In this photo-essay of their grandfather's final three years, Mark and Dan Jury show the difficulties and love required to care for an increasingly senile old person who chooses to die at home.

KAUFMAN, BARRY. *Son Rise.* Harper, 1976. Warner pb. Using two local teenagers as part of a homemade treatment team, the Kaufmans bring their son from an autistic stupor at age one to a verbal and active boy by age two and a half.

KILLILEA, MARIE. *Karen.* Prentice, 1962. Dell pb. Inspirational story of Karen, who despite cerebral palsy, misdiagnosis, and advice "to put her away," learns to talk, walk, read, and write thanks to a mother who would not give up.

———. *With Love from Karen.* Dell, 1964. Written in answer to readers who loved *Karen*, this sequel tells about Karen's teenage years. Both titles are available as Talking Book/Cassette/Braille eds.

LEVITT, ROSE. *Ellen: A Short Life Long Remembered.* Chronicle, 1974. Bantam pb. Told by her mother and through her own poems and letters, this is the haunting story of a dying teenager's legacy of love.

LUND, DORIS. *Eric.* Lippincott, 1974. Dell pb. Eric's losing fight for life against leukemia at seventeen is enhanced by the loving and suffering mother who tells his story, and by a love affair with a young nurse.

Mac CRACKEN, MARY. *Circle of Children.* Lippincott, 1973. NAL pb. Talking Book/Cassette/Braille editions. The moving story of a teacher's experiences in a school for emotionally disturbed children.

———. *Lovey.* Lippincott, 1976. NAL pb. A second heart-rending account of MacCracken's work with disturbed children centers around Hannah, a child so withdrawn and unmanageable that everyone but Mary considers her a hopeless case.

MASSIE, ROBERT and SUZANNE. *Journey.* Knopf, 1975. Warner pb. The twenty-year account of Robert and Suzanne Massie's attempts to find help for their hemophilic son Bobby and relief from the exhaustion of the struggle.

MORRIS, JEANNIE. *Brian Piccolo.* Rand, 1971. Dell pb. After telling us how Brian Piccolo made it as a running back for the Chicago Bears, the author takes us into the hospital for those last desperate days until he died of cancer at age twenty-six.

SPRADLEY, THOMAS S. and JAMES P. *Deaf Like Me.* Random, 1978. Seemingly normal at birth, Lynn Spradley was later diagnosed deaf as a result of the mid-1960s rubella epidemic, and was taught sign language by her parents in defiance of the "experts."

THIGPEN, CORBETT, and HERVEY M. CLECKLEY. *Three Faces of Eve.* McGraw, 1957. Popular Lib. pb.; Regent House pb. The first account of a multiple personality as revealed by the doctors who were confronted with and learned to treat "Eve White."

TIDYMAN, ERNEST. *Dummy.* Little, 1974. A young black man who is a deaf-mute is accused of murder and a deaf attorney fights five years for his release.

WESCHLER, JAMES. *In a Darkness.* Norton, 1972. A *New York Post* editor chronicles the ten-year siege of his son with mental illness, eight psychiatrists and five mental hospitals before Michael's suicide in 1969.

WILSON, DOROTHY CLARKE. *Handicap Race: The Inspiring Story of Roger Arnett.* McGraw, 1967. Track star Arnett becomes a paraplegic following an accident, but adopts children and by using ingenious devices becomes mobile and independent.

———. *Hilary.* McGraw, 1972. At twenty, Hilary Pole is stricken with a disease that leaves her without muscular control, but a unique project helps her regain that most valuable of human resources—communication.

———. *Take My Hands: The Remarkable Story of Dr. Mary Verghese.* McGraw, 1963. Shortly after she became a surgeon, an accident made Mary a paraplegic. She continues to perform delicate operations—from a wheelchair!

WILSON, LOUISE. *This Stranger, My Son.* Putnam, 1968. NAL pb. From beautiful baby to difficult child to paranoid schizophrenic teenager, Tony so disrupts family life that they finally have to send him away.

Films

Angela's Island. Films, Inc. 1978. 23 min. Eleven-year-old Angela is a paraplegic fighting to overcome her problems with the help of a counselor who is herself handicapped by polio. 1979 EFLA Blue Ribbon.

David. Phoenix Films. 1977. 10 min. Tragic story of 16-year-old David, gunned down by police when he reaches for the card that identifies him as a deaf-mute. Even knowing it is going to happen doesn't lessen the horror. Great for discussion once you recover from the emotional impact.

A Day in the Life of Bonnie Consolo. Barr Films. 1975. 17 min. Born without arms, Bonnie Consolo drives a car, cooks, does housework, and takes care of her children—all with her feet.

Get It Together. Pyramid. 1977. 20 min. Crippled in an auto accident, Jeff Minnebraker fought back to finish college, marry, and become a recreational therapist.

Happiness Is Loving Your Teacher. Wombat. 1978. 28 min. Unpopular Tony (female) provokes a confrontation with the new wheelchair-bound substitute teacher, Mr. Toderick, who goes back to the rehabilitation center thinking himself a failure until a telephoned apology clears the air. Fictional depiction of two outsiders with marvelous classroom scenes. Janis Ian singing "Seventeen" is the perfect background score.

Helen Keller in Her Story. Phoenix Films. 1973. 48 min. "A simple, honest, tremendously moving film . . ." Academy Award for the Best Feature-Length Documentary. Filled with stars.

Help Wanted. Carousel Films. 1978. 14 min. The *60 Minutes* segment about Lynn Thompson, the severely disabled young woman who got herself a job—and not only lost her government benefits, but was threatened with having to repay $10,000. For Lynn, suicide seemed the only way out and she took it.

I Am Not What You See. Filmmakers Library. 28 min. This interview with psychologist Sondra Diamond, so handicapped by cerebral palsy that she cannot do the simplest tasks for herself, is the most revealing portrait of the richness of the inner life of the handicapped—and of the senseless cruelty of those who would claim for themselves the label "normal." First Prize, International Rehabilitation Film Festival.

James Is Our Brother. Time Life Multimedia. 1979. 22 min. James is a 16-year-old mongoloid and his family tries to let him experience as much of life as possible. 1979 EFLA Red Ribbon.

Leo Beuerman. Centron Corporation. 1969. 14 min. Leo was born with multiple handicaps, protected by his mother; but after her death, he determined to become a self-sufficient person. With the help of many ingenious devices, designed and built by Leo, he is able to get around and support himself. Provides a super model for all of us as to the meaning of courage and zest for life.

Like Other People. Perennial. 1973. 37 min. Margaret and Willy are two spastics, confined to wheelchairs, trying to be independent, loving people. People who turn away, to avoid "seeing" the handicapped in our society, will be unnerved by the power of the film. They, of course, are the ones who need most to see it.

Mainstreaming in Action. Togg Films, Inc. 1979. 25 min. James has cerebral palsy, and struggles to make people see that a crippled body houses a fine mind and that all he wants is the right to a place in the world.

Moira: A Vision of Blindness. DeNonno Pix, Inc. 1979. 23 min. Narrated by 11-year-old Moira, born blind. Shows her at home, school, climbing trees, diving—and viewers realize how many misconceptions we carry about blind people and their capabilities. 1979 EFLA Blue Ribbon.

Who Are the DeBolts and Where Did They Get 19 Kids? Pyramid. 1978. 72 min. The original, uncut for television, version of this thoroughly delightful, moving story of the DeBolts and their family of handicapped—but beautiful and alive—kids. Academy Award for Best Feature-Length Documentary.

Librarians, teachers, counselors and all others interested in the world of the handicapped should ask to be placed on the mailing list to receive *Rehabfilm Newsletter,* 20 W. 40 St., New York, NY 10018. It is quarterly and free. From the same address, for $2.00 you may have a copy of the *Film Review Catalogue.* This group sponsors the International Rehabilitation Film Festival and is active in encouraging the portrait of the disabled in film.

Important Addresses

Council for Exceptional Children, 1920 Association Drive, Reston, VA 22091.

National Audiovisual Center/General Services Administration, Division of National Archives and Records Services, Washington, DC 20409.

Professional Bibliography

Bibliographies

BASKIN, BARBARA, and KAREN H. HARRIS, eds. *Notes from a Different Drummer: A Guide to Juvenile Fiction Portraying the Handicapped.* Bowker, 1977. The authors discuss selecting, evaluating, and using juvenile fiction which focuses on the disabled. Over four hundred titles are annotated and reading levels are indicated. Title and subject indexes included.

BISSHOPP, PATRICIA, comp., *Books About Handicaps for Children and Young Adults.* Meeting Street School, 667 Waterman Avenue, East Providence, RI 02940. This very fine bibliography includes both recommended and not recommended titles. Covers all areas of the physically handicapped as well as emotional dysfunction. Subject and Interest Level indexes.

GILBERT, LAURA-JEAN. "Materials, Program Suggestions for Hearing-Impaired Children." *School Media Quarterly* 4 (Spring 1976): 263–68. The author encourages that special efforts be made to communicate with deaf children and to help them to communicate with their families and friends. Included are listings of books to aid teachers and

parents, for very young and elementary age children, and texts for the study of sign language.

High Interest-Low Vocabulary Reading Materials Including Books and Kits: Intermediate, Junior High, and Senior High School Levels. Texas Area Learning Resource Center, 1975. A listing of series books and audio-visual materials. Bibliographic and descriptive information, including price, is given.

Large Type Books in Print. Bowker, 1976. Lists books for the visually handicapped appearing only in 14-point type or larger. The volume itself is in 18-point type print. General reading and textbooks are the divisions and are arranged alphabetically by title under broad subjects. Title and author indexes included.

Library Services to the Exceptional Child. ALA. This is a packet of twelve items and includes bibliographies.

Special Education. National Audio Visual Center, General Services Administration. This booklet lists selected U.S. government audiovisuals for child use and teaching training. Includes physical descriptions of the materials, control numbers, rental fees, sale prices, annotations, and additional notes on use and production.

Vocational Education Resource Materials: A Bibliography of Free Loan Materials for Handicapped and Special Education. Center for Studies in Vocational and Technical Education, 1975. Provides descriptive notes of materials and includes an annotated list of films.

WRIGHT, LOUISE M. "A Look Behind the Wall of Silence." *Ohio Library Association Bulletin* (April 1977). Briefly discusses suggested readings for young deaf people, books of interest to deaf adults, and books to create an understanding of the deaf by those who can hear.

Books

ANDERSON, ROBERT M., JOHN G. GREER, and SARA J. ODLE, eds. *Individualizing Educational Materials for Special Children in the Mainstream.* University Park Press, 1978. Presents a framework for a sequential program for the acquisition of competencies related to the utilization of instructional materials. Emphasis is placed on procedures for selecting, retrieving, adapting, constructing, assessing, and evaluating materials.

AYRAULT, EVELYN WEST. *Growing Up Handicapped.* Seabury, 1977. This valuable tool introduces parents and professionals to the range of problems that accompany growing up differently. Appendices contain extensive listings of agencies and sources serving the handicapped.

BARNES, ELLEN, CAROL BERRIGAN, and DOUG BIKLEN. *What's the Difference? Teaching Positive Attitudes Toward People with Disabilities.* Human Policy Press, 1978. Written for teachers and children, this book addresses myths about handicapping conditions, discusses teachers' feelings and attitudes and suggests activities which can be used to help develop healthy attitudes toward disabled persons.

BASKIN, BARBARA HOLLAND, and KAREN H. HARRIS, eds. *The Special Child in the Library.* ALA, 1976. A collection of articles discussing aspects of library service to all special children, ranging from mentally retarded to physically disabled to gifted. While the discussion focuses on adult books, the principles apply to all ages and all types of disabilities.

BLECK, EUGENE E., and DONALD A. NAGEL, eds. *Physically Handicapped Children—A Medical Atlas for Teachers.* Grune and Stratton, 1975. A must reference book for all school libraries and special education teachers. This handbook by two medical doctors thoroughly covers fundamental medical facts of disabling conditions and gives practical suggestions for teachers including parent counselling and emergencies.

BORNSTEIN, HARRY, LILLIAN HAMILTON, KAREN SAULNIER, and HOWARD ROY, eds. *The Signed English Dictionary.* Galludet College Press, 1975. This Manual Signed English System dictionary contains over two thousand words which represent the language level of preschool and elementary children. It has good illustrations and is used easily.

BRAMLEY, GERALD. *Outreach: Library Services for the Institutionalised, the Elderly, and the Physically Handicapped.* Linnet, 1978. This British publication provides interesting historical background on services for the blind, deaf, and physically disabled as well as practical advice.

BROWN, SARA L., and MARTHA S. MOERSCH, eds. *Parents on the Team.* Univ. of Michigan Press, 1978. This excellent collection is for parents and teachers. It points out the roles parents can play in and out of the classroom especially as advocates in securing services for their children.

EDGINGTON, DOROTHY. *The Physically Handicapped Child in Your Classroom.* Charles E. Thomas, 1976. This valuable resource tool gives regular classroom teachers knowledge of six major disorders that cause physical handicaps in children and includes a chapter on orthopedic appliances.

FAIRCHILD, THOMAS, ed. *Mainstreaming Series.* Teaching Resources Corporation, 1977. Written for regular classroom teachers needing basic information regarding the various exceptionalities, each book in this helpful series addresses itself to one area of exceptionality.

HARE, BETTY A., and JAMES M. HARE. *Teaching Young Handicapped Children.* Grune and Stratton, 1977. Emphasizing ages three to six, this book is intended to provide teachers with practical direction and strategies of programming for handicapped children. Provides specific teaching suggestions, methods, and materials in detail.

HASAZI, SUSAN E., PAUL RICE, and ROBERT YORK. *Mainstreaming: Merging Regular and Special Education.* Phi Delta Kappa Educational Foundation, 1979. This booklet defines mainstreaming and outlines the implications and implementation of Public Law 94–142. A general overview of the roles of educators and parents is given.

KERNALEGUEN, ANNE. *Clothing Designs for the Handicapped.* Canada: Univ. of Alberta Press, 1978. A collection of easy to follow directions for alterations of ready-to-wear clothing and simple patterns for adults and children with special needs.

KIRK, SAMUEL A. *Educating Exceptional Children.* 2nd ed. Houghton, 1972. This volume is a standard textbook for an introductory course on exceptional children. It presents an integrated and unified concept of exceptional children with each chapter covering a different disability.

LONG, KATE. *Johnny's Such a Bright Boy, What a Shame He's Retarded.* Houghton, 1977. Although written in fictional form, research and factual information is woven into this entertaining book. The story depicts a school system moving toward mainstreaming. It reveals the complexities of labeling and segregation and encourages readers to support constructive efforts for change.

LORING, JAMES, and GRAHAM BURN, eds. *Integration of Handicapped Children in Society.* London: Routledge and Kegen Paul, 1975. The selections in this book address many important and relevant questions, attitudes, and problems concerning mainstreamed handicapped children.

MARQUIS WHO'S WHO, INC. *Yearbook of Special Education.* Marquis Who's Who, 1979. This state of the art compilation provides current information regarding educating persons with special needs. Contributors include educators, government and private sources, and journals and books.

MOORES, DONALD F. *Educating the Deaf.* Houghton, 1978. Designed as a reference or source book for professionals dealing with deaf individuals, this basic text deals with the educational and psychological implications of deafness.

NATIONAL ADVISORY COUNCIL ON EDUCATION PROFESSIONS DEVELOPMENT. *Mainstreaming: Helping Teachers Meet the Challenge.* Washington, D.C., 1976. This report explores the definition, scope, and implications of mainstreaming. It also queries teacher preparation in this area and develops specific recommendations based upon the answers found.

PATTERSON, GEORGE W. *Helping Your Handicapped Child.* Augsburg, 1975. Contains very helpful chapters on the needs of the child and family involvement. It also discusses common concerns voiced when rearing a handicapped child.

PAUL, JAMES, ANN TURNBULL, and WILLIAM CRUICKSHANK. *Mainstreaming, A Practical Guide.* Syracuse Univ. Press, 1977. Designed as a practical guide for principals, teachers, other school professionals and officials, and parents, this book covers preparation for and implementation of mainstreaming in public schools, and preservice and inservice teacher education. The authors emphasize shared responsibility and involvement.

PRESCHOOL SIGNED ENGLISH PROJECT. *Signed English Series.* Galludet College, 1972–75. This series of small books focuses on a very young audience and includes some old favorites. It was designed for the preschool and elementary hearing impaired/deaf children.

SAVAGE, JOHN F., and JEAN F. MOONEY. *Teaching Reading to Children with Special Needs.* Allyn and Bacon, 1979. This book is designed to help regular classroom teachers better understand the unique needs that children have in learning how to read and provides suggestions for meeting special needs. It focuses primarily on beginning grades.

SCHMID, REX E., JUDEE MONEYPENNY, and RONALD JOHNSTON, eds. *Contemporary Issues in Special Education.* McGraw Hill, 1977. This excellent book can be used as a primary text for special education introductory courses, in-service programs or independent study. For each topic covered, there are introductory comments, a group of reading selections, a study guide, and self tests.

SCHULTZ, JAMES G. *Special Education Teaching Games.* T. S. Dennison, 1975. Contains games designed by the author for classroom use with handicapped children. It is printed in large, bold type and can be referred to easily and quickly by teachers and aides. Materials used in the games are practical, readily available and need little or no preparation.

Services and Materials for the Handicapped. Proceedings of an Institute for School Library Media Professionals, August 12–17, 1979. Northern Illinois University, Department of Library Science, DeKalb, IL. Henry C. Dequin, Project Director. These proceedings are an excellent introduction, providing basic information on all aspects of mainstreaming.

SMITH, ROBERT M., and JOHN T. NEISWORTH. *The Exceptional Child: A Functional Approach.* McGraw-Hill, 1975. Intended primarily as an introductory text for students in special education, this book is a valuable tool for regular educators encountering mainstreamed children. Emerging trends and the children involved in them are the concern of this volume.

STROM, MARYALLS G., ed. *Library Services to the Blind and Physically Handicapped.* Scarecrow, 1977. Not all of the articles in this very fine collection are concerned with the needs of children, but all offer valuable insights into the attitudes necessary to provide service and are helpful in building an understanding of the disabled as human beings with the same needs as those without disabilities.

TURNBULL, ANN P., and JANE B. SCHULZ. *Mainstreaming Handicapped Students: A Guide for the Classroom Teacher.* Allyn and Bacon, 1979. Directed to the regular classroom teacher, this practical book provides explanation of the educational characteristics of handicapped children, principles of mainstreaming, and instructional strategies for implementation of the integration of handicapped children.

U.S. DEPARTMENT OF HEALTH, EDUCATION, AND WELFARE, ADMINISTRATION FOR CHILDREN, YOUTH, AND FAMILIES. *Mainstreaming Preschoolers.* DHEW, 1978. This series of eight manuals was prepared to assist Head Start teachers and staff. However, their clear and informative presentations can benefit all who provide learning experiences for preschool handicapped children. Each book covers a specific handicapping condition and contains an annotated bibliography.

VELLEMAN, RUTH A. *Serving Physically Disabled People.* Bowker, 1979. Services and sources for all types of libraries and all ages of the disabled are described by an exemplary school librarian with years of experience in the field.

Articles

"Barrier-Free Rooms for the Disabled." *Better Homes and Gardens* 51 (March 1979): 32–36. Based on research data, the Iowa Easter Seal Society designed and created a model living space for wheelchair-bound persons. The article gives details about furnishings and accessories, buying information, and an address for more information on barrier-free designs.

BYBEE, RODGER W. "Helping the Special Student Fit In." *Science Teacher* 46 (May 1979): 22–24. Suggestions contained in this article will help teachers meet the unique needs of disabled students.

CARPENTER, WILLIAM. "Why Mainstreaming Will Succeed While Some Other Special Education Will Fail." *Education* 99 (Summer 1979): 368–69. Success of the expanding special education programs of the next ten years will depend on mainstreaming of all handicapped children. The author mandates an overall plan, offers valid suggestions for implementation and introduces the child's side of mainstreaming.

COCHRANE, PAMELA V., and DAVID L. WESTLING. "The Principal and Mainstreaming: Ten Suggestions for Success." *Educational Leadership* 34 (April 1977): 506–10. The authors outline ten valuable suggestions for school principals when implementing the integration of handicapped children in their schools.

DALY, MARGARET. "Handicapped Children in the Classroom— What 'Mainstreaming' Is All About." *Better Homes and Gardens* 58 (September 1979): 38–49. Intended mainly for parents, this article defines mainstreaming and the law which authorized it. The author focuses on many important aspects and effects of PL 94-142 and outlines the steps that should be taken by parents of handicapped children. Included are several addresses for more information.

DEQUIN, HENRY C. "Selecting Materials for the Handicapped." *Top of the News* 35 (Fall 1978): 57–66. The author collects in this and the following article many of the difficult to uncover materials selection tools in the field of special education. He thoroughly lists and describes excellent sources of materials and retrieval systems and includes addresses and some prices.

———. "Sources of Information about the Handicapped." *School Library Journal* 26 (November 1979): 38–41. See above annotation.

DRESANG, ELIZA T. "There Are No Other Children." *School Library Journal* (September 1977): 19–23. An informative article offering many useful and concrete ideas for instructional materials centers based on the author's own experience as a media specialist. She focuses upon the needs of the special child and his/her right to be served.

ENIS, CAROL A., and MICHAEL CATARUZOLO. "Sex Education in the Residential School for the Blind." *Education of the Visually Handicapped* 4 (May 1972): 61–64. Discusses the special problems of sex education of blind children in residential schools, where this issue is just becoming apparent.

FLYNN, JAMES R., RICHARD C. GACKA, and DAVID A. SUNDEAN. "Are Classroom Teachers Prepared for Mainstreaming?" *Phi Delta Kappan* 59 (April 1978): 562. Attitudes of regular and special education teachers toward mainstreaming were surveyed. The answers given for "I feel adequately prepared to teach mainstreamed students" are outlined and a table of responses given. Addresses are given for obtaining a more complete report of the study.

FOULKE, EMERSON, and THOMAS UHDE. "Do Blind Children Need Sex Education?" *New Outlook for the Blind* 68 (May 1974): 193–200, 209. Presents a preliminary report of a study conducted to learn the extent and accuracy of blind adolescents' knowledge about human sexuality and their attitudes about sexual behavior. Also described is a recently launched Human Sexuality Opinion Survey intended to gather information about attitudes toward sex education programs for blind children in general and about the methods and content of such programs in particular.

GREEN, KERRY. "Services for the Handicapped: What the AV Professional Can Do." *Media & Methods* 16 (March 1980): 39–40. An excellent article which presents a practical checklist for school media specialists when adapting their programs and materials to fit the needs of handicapped children. A listing of organizations and agencies providing learning aids and information is given.

HENNE, JOHN F. "Serving Visually Handicapped Children." *School Library Journal* 25 (December 1978): 36–37. Information is given on large print books, tapes, recordings, films, and TV to be used in media centers. A lengthy materials suppliers list is included.

HOGGAN, INELLA M. "David Mainstreams Himself." *Teacher* 96 (December 1978): 49–50.

———. "A Sequel to David's Story." *Teacher* 96 (January 1979): 75. These sensitive and informative articles describe David, a quadriplegic, and Mindy, a paraplegic, in their efforts to accomplish the goals they have set for themselves. The author admits her own initial scepticism and effectively points out a key to the success of mainstreaming—attitude.

HOLMES, RUTH V. "The Planning and Implementation of a Sex Education Program for Visually Handicapped Children in a Residential Setting." *New Outlook for the Blind* 68 (May 1974): 219–25. Notes that careful planning is necessary to establish a constructive, comprehensive, and developmental program in sex education for visually handicapped children and youth. The development, characteristics, and success of a program established in 1965 in a residential setting are described.

HOYT, JANE HAUSER. "Feeling Free." *American Education* 14 (November 1978): 24–28. Reviews the PBS film series "Feeling Free" which portrays disabled children as being not all that different in feelings and concerns as non-handicapped children.

JACKSON, ANITA. "A Case for Mainstreaming: First Contact with Handicapped Students." *The American Music Teacher* 29 (September-October 1979): 18. The author supports through experience that teachers of music should have few problems in teaching mainstreamed students. She presents concrete suggestions for a successful experience with handicapped children based on her own contact with them.

KUHN, JUDITH. "A Comparison of Teachers' Attitudes Toward Blindness and Exposure to Blind Children." *New Outlook for the Blind* 65 (December 1971): 337-40. A blindness information scale applied to two groups of teachers established that positive attitudes toward blindness will not come about automatically through exposure to blind persons. It is concluded that inservice training, more information about blindness and blind adults, role playing, and up-dating of college courses are needed.

KUNZWEILER, CHARLES E. "Mainstreaming—Will It Really Work?" *Education* 99 (Spring 1979): 233-35. The author explores the reasons for mainstreaming and its long-term success. He states that until parents and educators deal with their own transformation—human love and acceptance—nothing of lasting value will come of this movement.

"The Language of Disability: Disabled—Yes; Handicapped—No." *The Unabashed Librarian* 26 (1978): 30. (Adapted from Council on Interracial Books for Children *Bulletin* 8 (1978).) Advocates avoidance of handicapist language which dehumanizes, connotes dependence or suggests the inability to participate in the life of the community. Gives examples of the offensive terms followed by the preferred ones.

LIETZ, JEREMY, and JEFFREY KAISER. "The Principal's Role in Administering Programs for Exceptional Children." *Education* 100 (Fall 1979): 31-40. Reports the results of a study which investigated the ideal and real influence of building principals in twenty-seven key operational decision-making tasks identified by the Council for Exceptional Children and pertinent to the delivery of EHC services.

METCALF, MARY JANE. "Helping Hearing Impaired Students." *School Library Journal* 25 (January 1979): 27-29. Although the author is a librarian at a school for the deaf, she related relevant information and many useful suggestions for use in a mainstreamed school media center.

MACGREGOR, KIRK. "First Steps in Mainstreaming." *Media and Methods* 15 (April 1979): 46-48. The author, a physically handicapped teacher, presents and outlines several sensible key first steps for the success of the newly mainstreamed school and classroom.

MCINTOSH, DEAN K. "Mainstreaming: Too Often a Myth, Too Rare a Reality." *Academic Therapy* 15 (September 1979): 53-59. The author predicts the failure of mainstreaming unless an adequate plan of action is taken. He advocates a total commitment on the part of all persons involved, a well-developed plan for teacher-training, and a public relations scheme for informing the public.

MCKALIP, KEITH J. "Developing Acceptance Toward the Handicapped." *School Counsellor* 26 (May 1979): 293-98. Teachers and students need counsellor assistance in learning how to accept and interact with mainstreamed handicapped pupils. The author outlines the three steps necessary in developing this acceptance and improving classroom conditions for all people.

MORI, ALLEN A. "The Handicapped Child in the Mainstream—New Roles for the Regular Educator." *Education* 99 (Spring 1979): 243-49. Mainstreaming will place new demands upon the regular classroom teacher. This article outlines the new roles and describes the accompanying functions. Emphasis also is placed on development of quality continuing professional education programs to prepare regular teachers for their new roles.

POWELL, JACK V. "Mainstreaming Eight Types of Exceptionalities." *Education* 99 (Fall 1978): 55-58. This article offers environmental and program conditions for eight types of exceptionalities in mainstreamed classrooms.

ROGER, VINCENT. "Chris Rogers, Special Teacher." *Phi Delta Kappan* 61 (September 1979): 57. A warm, moving article about an active handicapped elementary school teacher. It portrays her quiet courage which helps her cope with everyday activities which most of us take for granted.

STROUD, MARION B. "Do Students Sink or Swim in the Mainstream?" *Phi Delta Kappan* 60 (December 1978): 316. Summarizes a study done by Ohio's EMR Program Development Project comparing climates of the special education and mainstreamed regular classrooms. The results concluded that the two kinds of classrooms were more alike than different and identified several positive teacher patterns.

VOLKMANN, CHRISTINA SHAMBERGER. "Integrating the Physically Disabled Student into the Elementary School." *Education* 99 (Fall 1979): 25-30. Examines the problems of dealing with various categories of physically disabled elementary children. Specific ideas are presented that encourage the handicapped student to accept responsibility, feel needed, and develop basic skills.

WOODBURN, VICKIE and MARGE SCHUSTER. "Mike Was Our First Deaf Student." *Today's Education* 67 (April 1978): 77-78. An excellent article which outlines the steps taken by the resource teacher and school counselor when Mike, a deaf student, entered a regular junior high school. The authors advise open lines of communication between the student, teachers, counselor, resource teacher, and parents.

Internationalism in Children's Literature

Anne Pellowski*

Internationalism in children's literature has at least three important aspects. One has to do with the development of printed and visual materials for children in areas of the world which have until recently had no such materials and the development as well of opportunities for children to experience these materials, as in libraries and cultural centers. A second involves the exchange of children's books from one country to another, either in original form or in translation. A third, and the one which is perhaps most important for the teacher or librarian working with children, is concerned with the

* Anne Pellowski is Director-Librarian of the Information Center on Children's Cultures, UNICEF.

way different cultures are depicted and represented in the children's books of any given country.

Taking these three aspects in order, the first to be considered is whether there has been improvement in the extent of children's literature published in countries that up until recently had only oral literature, and whether the quality *and* quantity has improved in those countries that had modest amounts of printed and visual literature for children. The improvements within a few individual countries are noticeable, but when viewed from the perspective of total, worldwide production, these books are overwhelmed by the European, North American, and Japanese literature for children. Especially for young children—those that must be read aloud to and those just beginning to read—there is so little indigenous publishing in Africa, Latin America and the Caribbean, and Asia (always excepting Japan), that one can say the majority remain unserved. This is unfortunate, given the evidence that indicates reading motivation and skills are most easily developed at this early stage.

Four of the countries that have improved the quantity, quality, and availability of books for this age in recent years are Brazil, Iran, Turkey, and Venezuela, but their experts are the first to admit they still have a long way to go. Bangladesh, India, Indonesia, Kenya, Pakistan, and the Philippines have increased the amount of children's literature for the middle and upper primary grades, but the quality has not kept pace with the quantity. Ghana, Korea, and Thailand have produced a scattered number of titles, usually in paperback editions, but their availability is sporadic.

The above refers only to trade materials for children, in magazine, book, or visual format. Mass-market materials in all these areas are invariably all imported from the handful of nations that continue to dominate the field: Italy, Japan, Spain, and the United States. Colombia finds itself in the unique position of first-rate printer of such mass market types as trick books with movable parts, but the production is for other countries, and the planning, writing, editing, illustrating, and designing are all done by the large publishing houses in Europe or North America. Needless to say, most of these materials, however colorful and attractive they might be, are not particularly effective in meeting the needs of local children.

With regard to the second aspect, the exchange among countries, one must ask whether this new children's literature from developing countries (or from economically advanced countries which have not had much children's book production) has penetrated and affected the children's literature of European and North American countries and Japan. The answer is: only to a very small degree.

Using the collection of the Information Center on Children's Cultures, it is possible to identify only nine direct translations or adaptations of children's books from developing areas into American English in the period from 1968 to 1979. This includes five books from Iran, three from Greece, and one each from Brazil, Nigeria, and Puerto Rico. Except for translation into English, the U.S. editions were essentially the same as the originals.

It is also possible to identify books of six authors from developing areas whose work was not published in their home countries, but appeared directly in English. They include two each from Jamaica and Vietnam, one from South Africa, and one from Thailand. These figures do *not* include folk tales translated or adapted from an indigenous language, nor do they include mass-market titles.

Only in the use of illustrators coming from developing areas of the world has there been some improvement, and this has occurred chiefly because illustrators continue to come to the United States to work. European artists, who fled to the U.S. between the two World Wars and later, were a major force in the "internationalizing" of the looks of U.S. children's books up to 1960. Since that time, there have been relatively few European artist/illustrators coming to live and work in North America, but there has been a decided increase in the numbers coming from Asia and Latin America. Some of the better-known ones are: Fernando Krahn (Chile), Ed Young (China), Mehlli Gobhai (India), Tony Chen (from Jamaica but of Chinese ancestry), Carlos Antonio Llerena Aguirre (Peru), Jose Aruego (Philippines), Antonio Frasconi (Uruguay), and Vo Dinh (Vietnam).

Japanese illustrators have also been appearing with much greater frequency in U.S. children's books, both in terms of the picture book translations from Japanese texts and of newly commissioned works originating in the U.S. For the most part, these illustrators continue to live in Japan, but some (e.g., Noriko Ueno and Kazue Mizumura) live and work in North America.

Insofar as the translations from Western European languages are concerned, there was an increase in the total number translated from 1976 to 1979, as compared with the period from 1960 to 1965. But the increase can be almost totally accounted for by the increased translations from German-language publishers, which in the earlier period were still recovering from the war. No completely reliable and firm statistics are available, but a rough calculation based on titles listed in *Translated Children's Books* and *Books from Other Countries* and in the card catalog of the Information Center on Children's Cultures produces the results shown in Table 1. On the other hand, the translations from Eastern European countries present a very different picture, as shown in Table 2. Western Europe has roughly two-thirds the child population of Eastern Socialist Europe (as here defined). Its trade publications for children are stronger and probably more numerous in titles. On the other hand the Eastern European socialist countries have stronger and more extensive mass-market publishing for children.

It is easy to see from the above information that the sharing of children's literature via translation is still limited to exchange among the publishing giants.

Table 1   Translations from Western European Countries

Territory or Language of Origin	No. of Titles Translated and Published in U.S.	
	1950–1965	1966–1979
Danish	8	27
Finnish	6	4
Norwegian	22	15
Swedish	86	98
German (including East and West Germany, Austria, Switzerland)	117	154
French	90	83
Dutch	14	24
Spanish	4	4
Italian	14	9
Flemish	–	3
Total	361	421

Table 2   Translations from Eastern European Countries

Territory or Language of Origin	No. of Titles Translated and Published in U.S.	
	1950–1965	1966–1979
Czech and Slovak	0	11
Hungarian	0	2
Polish	0	3
Serbo-Croatian	1	3
U.S.S.R.	10	38
Total	11	57

The third aspect of internationalism relates to materials developed in North America which deal with a wide variety of fictional and factual representations of other peoples and other cultures. Frequently, visitors from small developing countries are surprised to see that their cultures are represented by more materials for children, produced and published in the English language, than exist in their own vernaculars. In most cases, these are by North American or European writers and illustrators who have spent time in the country or area.

The evaluation of these materials is most difficult. In establishing the validity of *fictional and folkloric materials*, the following represent some of the questions we must ask:

1. Was the material created by a participant of the culture or by an observer of it? Is this made clear in the introductory material?
2. Has it been edited to remove all elements which are morally or socially not accepted in our society or have some of these intrinsic values of the society concerned been allowed to remain intact, e.g., polygamy, matter-of-fact acceptance of body functions, early marriage or love relationships?
3. If it is historical, is this clearly indicated?
4. If it is folkloric, is the source clearly identified?

In regard to *illustrations, photographs, or films*, the following questions can be asked:

1. Is there obvious stereotyping, such as *always* depicting Chinese children with pigtails, African children without clothes, Mexican children as barefoot boys with burros, etc.?
2. Are the facial characteristics of any race al-

most *always* the same, without regard for the fact that there are infinite varieties within all races?

3. Is the comparative wealth or poverty of a nation or people illustrated with honesty or is it exaggerated?
4. Is there overemphasis on rural or village life with no proportionate attention to urban life?
5. Are the unusually different customs depicted more for their shock value than as illuminations of parts of the total structure of the culture?

For *factual materials* we can ask:

1. What is the copyright date? Does this limit the usability of the work?
2. If the copyright date is recent, do geographical and political facts truly reflect the latest changes?
3. Whose point of view is represented—the insider or the outsider or both?
4. What kind of sources are given?

To answer some of these questions demands a firsthand knowledge, which many of us do not have and which is not acquired merely through the reading of a few books and the viewing of fewer films. But one can partly test validity without actually knowing all the answers. A condescending tone or an oversimplified explanation of a complex question can warn of bias, even though one might not be able to pinpoint errors.

The popular adage "Every little bit helps" simply cannot apply when one is concerned about introducing children to other cultures. If the material is derogatory instead of objective, or vivid but inaccurate and one-sided, chances are it will hinder rather than help. It would be better not to attempt an introduction to another people if it cannot be done with sensitivity and care.

In preschool years and the early grades, children still have few definitely formed concepts of nationality. They are, however, conscious of racial, religious, social, and cultural differences, especially if these differences are visible. Most research indicates that in these early years children need to see and experience the difference as well as the sameness of things, since this helps to build up the self-image. Care should be taken to show that "different" is not synonymous with "inferior."

Picture books in other languages can be shown, especially if one is working with children who know another language. In this way, children often learn to take pride in their background rather than secretly feeling ashamed of it because it is so different from that of the peer group.

Older children need materials of much more substance, materials which recognize the concepts of nationality and country, region, and continent, as well as social and cultural values. They still prefer to view these issues as they concern individual children, rather than whole societies.

Suggestions for Term Papers

1. Using standard selection lists and some of the specialized bibliographies mentioned below, identify and locate all of the children's materials related to a *small* country or area of the world about which you know very little. There should be no more than 20 items available. Read and view the materials. Then give a short critical analysis of each item, and describe how you would or would not use it with children, in a school or library program. If possible, find a foreign student in your college or university who is from that part of the world and discuss your findings. Report the gist of your discussion in the term paper, and indicate where it helped you in the critical evaluations.

2. Locate and identify a wide variety of children's materials related to a *large* country or area of the world, about which much has been written and produced for children (e.g. Mexico, India, Kenya, the Middle East). Select about ten items of fiction and ten of nonfiction that have received generally favorable reviews. Read and view all of the items, give a brief critical analysis for each one, and then summarize whether the fictional items or the nonfictional have been more effective in giving you a "feel" for the country or area. Describe briefly what you think children will be able to intuit or perceive about family and school life, about different cultural and political values, by being exposed to these materials.

3. If there is a non-English-speaking immigrant group in your area whose language you are able to speak, interview some of the older members of that group and report on the printed, filmed, or oral literature they were exposed to as children. Try to get them to be as specific as possible, in terms of titles of stories or books or films. Interview some of their children or grandchildren presently growing up in

the U.S. or Canada, and find out what they are reading and viewing. Describe and discuss your results in written form.

4. If you are fluent in another language and have access to children's material in other languages, make a bibliographical and critical description of a select group of the books published for children in your second language; contrast and compare that group of books with a similar group of children's books in the English language. Try to select very specific types, such as concept picture books, sex education books, folk tales of African origin, realistic modern stories that center on school life, etc. Be careful to compare books from approximately the same time frame, and for similar age and interest levels.

5. Select a basic theme or subject area such as ecology, food, family life, holidays, World War II, etc. Locate and read or view at least ten items that deal with the subject from a local or national point of view; then do the same for ten items that deal with the same subject from a global or international point of view. They should all be for children of approximately the same age and interest level. Give a short critical analysis of each item and tell how you would or would not use each with children. Try to reach some conclusions as to whether your subject is best approached from a local or national view, a global view, or both.

Suggestions for Practice Teaching or Other In-Service Training

1. Develop a teaching unit in such a way that you can bring in and use with the children a wide array of print and nonprint materials that expand the concepts into global or international ones. For example, a language arts unit could cover other alphabetic systems, a mathematics unit could cover other numerical systems, a social studies unit could cover other social and political systems, etc.

2. When doing practice work with preschool children over six to eight weeks, plan a weekly picture-book story hour that includes materials in translation, materials that are indigenous to the U.S. and Canada in production and content, and original English-language materials that deal with other peoples and cultures. Try to observe any difference in response among the children to the three different types.

3. Include a reading-aloud period weekly, and complete the reading of a classic from another country, such as the original *Pinocchio* or *The Wonderful Adventures of Nils* by Selma Lagerlof. Or read aloud a modern foreign book in translation, of high literary quality, that is not likely to be read by the children themselves because of forbidding length, need for background information, or some other reason.

Bibliography

Bibliographies

AL-QAZZAZ, AYAD, et al. *The Arabs in American Textbooks.* Women Concerned About the Middle East, 1975. After a detailed analysis of textbooks, the authors go on to recommend some trade books that are acceptable.

Books from Other Countries. 1968–1971 comp. by Elana Rabban; 1972–1976 comp. by Anne McConnell. American Assoc. of School Libraries, 1978. Translated books from other countries.

Japanese Children's Books of International Interest. Tokyo: Japan Section of IBBY, c/o Japan Library Association, 1978. An annotated, illustrated list of books in Japanese, some of which have been translated into English.

List of Lists. Information Center on Children's Cultures, U.S. Committee for UNICEF, 331 East 38th St., New York, NY 10016. Revised twice annually. A one page listing of bibliographies available, by country and subject areas. This is sent free upon receipt of a stamped, self-addressed envelope.

MAKINO, YASUKO. *Japan Through Children's Literature: A Critical Bibliography.* Duke Univ. Center for International Studies, Occasional Paper #5, 1978.

Printed for Children: World Children's Book Exhibition. K. G. Saur, 1978. Excellent, short critical essays for each country are followed by lists of children's books that were on exhibit during the Frankfurt Book Fair, 1978, which honored International Year of the Child.

SCHMIDT, NANCY J. *Children's Books on Africa and Their Authors: An Annotated Bibliography.* Africana, 1975. Supplement, 1979. A helpful tool for use in locating English language children's books (regardless of country of origin) that have Africa as their setting or subject.

SCHON, ISABEL. *A Bicultural Heritage: Themes for the Exploration of Mexican and Mexican-American Culture in Books for Children and Adolescents.* Scarecrow, 1978. Annotated comments on many of the standard fictional and nonfictional books related to Mexico are followed by suggestions as to how to use many of the books, even those with some stereotypes, in leading book discussions. This is one of the few guides that shows how even flawed material that is attractive to children can be used to good advantage.

SHORESMAN, MICHELE, and ROBERT GUMPORT. *Shao Nian Gong—A Children's Palace: Ideas for Teaching About China.* Univ. of Illinois, Center for Asian Studies, 1978. Includes a curriculum guide as well as a list of good books and other media on China.

STONE, FRANK A. *Modern Middle Eastern Fiction: An Approach to Studying the Area.* World Education Project, School of Education, Univ. of Connecticut, 1974. An annotated list suited for junior high and up.

WERTHEIMER, LEONARD. *Books in Other Languages: How to Select and Where to Order Them.* Ottawa: Canadian Library Assoc., 1976.

Books

ASSOCIATION FOR LIBRARY SERVICE TO CHILDREN. *The Arbuthnot Lectures, 1970–1979.* American Library Association, 1980. Includes a biographical sketch of May Hill Arbuthnot by Zena Sutherland.

BROOKS, PETER. *The Child's Part.* Beacon, 1969. Historical aspects of children's literature (mainly English and French) but from quite different points of view than those found in the usual histories of children's books.

HAVILAND, VIRGINIA, ed. "The International Scene." In *Children and Literature: Views and Reviews.* Scott, Foresman, 1972, pp. 326–90. Articles by eight international specialists are included in this chapter.

HAWKES, LOUISE R. *Before and After Pinocchio: A Study of Italian Children's Books.* Paris: The Puppet Press, 1933. (Available as a reprint from Singing Tree Press, 1968). A history and criticism of Italian children's literature from classical Roman civilization to 1930. Books are treated as genuine literature, not a sub-genre.

HÜRLIMANN, BETTINA. *Europaische Kinderbücher in drei Jahrhunderten.* 2nd ed. Zurich: Atlantis Verlag, 1963. (Published as *Three Centuries of Children's Books in Europe* by World Publishing, 1969.) A lively, personal history of European highlights of children's literature. A good background book.

JAN, ISABELLE. *Sur la Littérature enfantine.* Paris: Les Éditions Ouvrières, 1969. (Published as *On Children's Literature* by Schocken Books, 1974.) An intriguing and quite different approach to children's literature as a part of world literature.

KLINGBERG, GÖTE, MARY ØRVIG, and STUART AMOR. *Children's Books in Translation: The Situation and the Problems.* Stockholm: Almqvist and Wiksell (for The Swedish Institute for Children's Books), 1978.

LEPMAN, JELLA. *Die Kinderbuchbrücke.* Frankfurt-Main: S. Fischer Verlag, 1964. (Published as *A Bridge of Children's Books* by the ALA, 1969.) A moving, personal account of the author's attempts to build a "bridge of understanding through children's books" in the International Youth Library at Munich and later through the founding of the International Board on Books for Young People.

ØRVIG, MARY. *Children's Books in Sweden, 1945–1970: A Survey.* Stockholm: Swedish Institute for Children's Books, 1973. A succinct summary in English of this important period in the development of Swedish children's literature, including sections on recent trends and studies.

PELLOWSKI, ANNE. *Creating Children's Books in Developing Countries: Problems, Perspectives and Suggestions.* Paris: UNESCO, 1979. (In preparation)
———. *Creative Arts in Relation to Children.* (Discussion Papers on Themes Related to International Year of the Child). United Nations, IYC Secretariat, 1979.

SCHON, ISABEL. *Mexico and Its Literature for Children and Adolescents.* Arizona State University, Center for Latin American Studies, 1977. A study related to the indigenous literature of Mexico.

Articles

Children and International Education: A Portfolio of Articles. Association for Childhood Education International, 1972. Ten short articles that would be helpful to anyone attempting to improve the global content and approach to all types of children's materials, and the techniques of using them.

PELLOWSKI, ANNE. "Children's Library Science." In *Comparative and International Library Science,* ed. by John F. Harvey. Scarecrow, 1977. Discusses the role of the children's library and its effect on the spread of children's literature.
———. "The Changing Role of Children's Library Service." *Wilson Library Bulletin* 54 (October 1979): 94–98. Continues the discussion begun in the chapter above.

For an abundance of articles, see the subject heading "Children's Literature" with various countries as subheadings in the index called *Library Literature.*

Periodicals

Asian Book Development. Newsletter. The Asian Cultural Centre for UNESCO, No. 6 Fukuromachi, Shinjuku-ku, Tokyo 161, Japan. Quarterly.

Bookbird. International Institute for Children's Juvenile and Popular Literature, Mayerhofgasse 6, A-1040 Vienna, Austria. Quarterly (Irregular). 1957– . Covers the international children's book scene; reviews recent materials about the children's literature; lists recommended books for translation; and, on occasion, publishes in-depth articles.

Information Bulletin on Reading Materials. UNESCO Regional Centre for Reading Materials in South Asia, 26/A, P.E.C.H.H.S., Karachi 29, Pakistan. Quarterly, 1959– . Although this publication is concerned with all of the problems of general book writing, publishing and distribution, a major emphasis is on materials for children and new literates. An invaluable aid to the person interested in a study of the newly developing children's literature in South Asian countries.

Such journals as *Phaedrus, Children's Literature* and *Children's Literature in Education* also have frequent issues that are international in scope.

Access, Networking, and Children's Services

*Theodore C. Hines**

In an article for the Fifth Edition of *Children and Books,* I reported a number of factors which placed barriers in the way of children's access to materials through public library children's services and school media centers. I wish I could report now a trend toward lowering those barriers. This does not seem to be the case.

In the interval since that original article, Mary Frances Kennon Johnson and I were asked to prepare a position paper on School Media Programs and Networking for the National Commission on Library Service and In-

* Theodore C. Hines is Professor in the Library Science/Educational Technology Division, School of Education at the University of North Carolina, Greensboro.

formation Science (ERIC Document: ED 175 442). That experience, and my work on establishing the Children's Media Data Bank (see *Top of the News,* Winter 1980, pp. 176–180) and in trying to persuade librarians and media specialists interested in service to children to make use of proven newer computer technology to increase service to children and children's access to materials have left me profoundly pessimistic about substantial improvements in the immediate future.

This is particularly troubling since in the last few years there have been growing pressures and opportunities which have even further enhanced the desirability of networking for children's services: pressures on budgets such as inflation, recession, and taxpayer revolts; opportunities such as the tremendous decrease in computing costs and the growth of microcomputers and of distributed computing. Networking is the banding together in cooperative projects through computers, teletypes, interlibrary loan systems, and other technological and standard procedures to assure all patrons of access to the information and services they need, regardless of their age or financial status.

It has been hard to put a handle on the problems which I observe, except to say that they are occasioned more often by librarians of good will than by anything else. "We have," as Pogo put it, "met the enemy, and they is us." What is particularly disconcerting about the refusal of librarians to band together to provide wide access for children is that most public library children's specialists work in libraries that have joined together in such networks as OCLC (the Ohio College Library Center) to provide librarians with better access to the information they need. Why the concept is not expanded to include youthful patrons remains a mystery.

It has also been hard to find an easy way to express my concerns concisely and in an organized fashion. What I have finally done is to set down a series of *obiter dicta,* in no particular order, and certainly of very unequal importance. Some of these observations naturally group themselves—others do not, so I have left them where they fell.

Basic Assumptions That Need to Be Assumed More Often

—The range of children's interests is almost infinitely broad.
—No one public library children's room or

school media center can afford either to purchase or house enough titles to meet this infinity of interests.
—Failure to obtain a needed or wanted title for the user is, as far as the user is concerned, exactly equivalent in its effects to censorship of that title.

Professionalism

—Librarians express much concern about censorship, little or none about their failure to provide the breadth of materials needed.
—Two successive sets of excellent standards for school media centers have failed to produce any real movement toward effective centralization of services within school districts.
—If only a tiny proportion of librarians interested in children's services would join the major professional association, they would dominate the American Library Association—instead of leaving it, by default, to be dominated by the Association of Research Libraries, and then complaining about its lack of attention to the needs of public and school libraries.
—The majority of librarians working with children have not insisted upon—or provided for themselves—any access to the literature of their own profession as witnessed by the vast difference between library periodicals' subscription figures and the number of librarians in the United States. This, coupled with non-attendance at professional meetings and lack of centralization at system and district levels means that years of experience may tend to bring increasing obsolescence rather than increasing competence.
—For all too many children's services people, Cataloging in Publication and centralized cataloging seem to have offered the opportunity to spend more time than original cataloging would require to second guess and change the decisions made by the experts—mainly for the worse. This preoccupation with where a book is placed in the collection rather than the ability to retrieve it wherever placed, is one of the largest time wasters in librarianship.
—In all too many school or public library systems, the children's services staffs in different buildings have never even met one another, much less joined together to solve common problems.
—We librarians are well aware of the urgent need for both good school media centers and good public library services to children, yet we all too often quarrel and refuse to cooperate. If

we don't learn to cooperate, we may well find ourselves forced into union with a resultant degradation of services. It's coming, it's coming.
—Nobody seems willing to start a new service, however needed, unless someone else, preferably the federal government, pays for it.
—There is a dim feeling among many of us that somewhere someone will come up with some magical cheap turnkey computer system which will solve everything for us without our having to learn anything or do anything. In the words of Josh Billings, 'taint so.
—More research would be helpful, of course. It is always useful to know more. The trouble with librarians, however, as Dr. Charles Bernier said long ago in another context, is basically not a lack of research, but our failure to apply what we already know.

User Services

—If effective information about and interchange of materials to meet children's needs has not been achieved even within most school systems or public library systems, how can we achieve practical networking among systems and across types of libraries?
—Internal networking of this kind is not resisted primarily by such outside forces as superintendents or school or public library boards. It is resisted primarily by librarians.
—In part because librarians in children's services have not cared, library networks have been built mainly for the large library collections, not for large library publics: those of the school and public libraries.
—I don't want to be taught how to use libraries. I want to get the materials or information I came for. It seems not unreasonable to believe that children feel the same way.
—Thanks to the microcomputer revolution more children undoubtedly have access to computers at home (by a factor of, say, 100 or more) than have access to any kind of computer at school. One hesitates to think what the ratio is to computer access in school media centers or computer use for school media center purposes.
—It is fairly readily possible to search for obscure ERIC documents in a computer based system. It is much more difficult to search for children's books with a potential of 50,000 outlets in the United States. ERIC documents of as few as ten pages may receive 11 descriptors (subject headings), while major juvenile titles are given less than three.
—If the major revolution in technology actually

accepted by libraries is the photocopy machine (rather than the computer), the word has not yet reached children's services. The number of elementary school media centers and children's public library rooms in which children have easy access to a photocopy machine is infinitesimal.
—It is difficult to see why there aren't daily deliveries among the school media centers and public libraries in every community.
—If someone sends a lot of children to use the library, the first impulse of many librarians is to complain.
—Multilation and theft problems are more likely to be the result of adult failures in organization than the inherent beastliness of children.
—Service to teachers is one of the most neglected aspects of school media centers and of public libraries. It shares this distinction with lack of service to parents.
—There is much less duplication of titles across school media centers and school media centers and public library services than is generally thought. (This has been shown in a doctoral study of secondary schools; a similar study is now under way at the elementary-school level and one intuitively knows the earlier finding will be replicated.) On the most rudimentary level, the simplest computer base consisting only of LC card numbers and locations for a given area would enormously increase availability of materials. Has anyone done it?

Selection and Acquisition

—If effective (rather than wilful) withholding of words, viewpoints, or information were the definition of censorship, then censorship of electronics has been far more successful than censorship of sex. Parenthetically, high technology electronics is our second leading export—second only to grain, proving once again that man does not live by bread alone.
—Children's libraries and media centers are dangerously bibliographically destitute. Many —nay, the vast majority—do not even own the basic basics: the *Children's Catalog* and the *Elementary School Library Collection*. And many of those that do have these titles do not have the current edition.
—For the most part, children's libraries and media centers tend largely to order only newly published titles. This is not simply to the detriment of their own collections—it has resulted in an increasing number of excellent older titles

going out of print, and becoming unavailable to anybody.

—Big, highly organized systems are no guarantee of quality. Would you believe a major city school system which takes an average of two years from time of publication to get a title on the shelves? You better believe it. One system may be better than another, but none is proof against incompetence.

—Children's collections tend to be weak in such areas as science (except nature study), engineering, mathematics, and computing, presumably because of lack of knowledge of these areas by librarians. The puzzler is that a similar lack of knowledge of geography and history does not seem to prevent the purchasing of books in these fields.

—Nonprint seems to mean nonexistent for all too many public library children's services personnel—who'd kitten at the thought of kits.

—Adult materials in many nonfiction areas, especially those assuming no previous background on the part of the reader, are often as suitable for children as for adults—and often the best or only books on the topic available for children. Why do so many librarians, and for that matter so many of the reviewing media, consider only materials that a publisher has specifically labeled as juvenile?

—Children's services people seem to care too little for their reference function. For example, neither reviewers nor librarians seem to look for quality in indexes. All too often, they get what they deserve.

—Journals (magazines) are frequently the cheapest and most efficient way to provide many types of information. Microform backfiles are cheaper than binding, and solve space problems where space is limited. Judging by the number of micro-readers or reader-printers sold to schools, and by subscriptions to indexing services, children's services have ignored these sources of information.

—Buying materials only once or twice a year is very nearly the stupidest procedure I know. Perhaps the only thing stupider is insisting that annual purchasing is required by school regulations—ask the cafeteria manager if that is the case.

—There are some librarians who have successfully ignored the world about them for so long that they can sincerely believe that nothing is worth reading unless it has literary or esthetic value—they should try my computer manuals sometime.

—There is a small subspecies of public librarians who somehow think that if a topic is in the curriculum there is something wrong with providing materials about it.

—Bibliographic services are all very well, but perhaps the finest basis for wise selection—especially when financing is as shaky as it is today—is the media evaluation center; a prime objective for good networking. There are all too few such centers. They lack support and understanding by those who most need them. Perhaps no wonder—the cataloging and collection of at least one nationally touted center is a disgrace—far worse than the average school library in my area.

The Classifier's Best Friend— His "Other"

—Children's services, according to Robert Leigh years ago, were the classic success story of the public library. The reason he thought so was that no one had tried to measure the success by considering how many of the customers continued to read as adults. By that measure, children's services may be the classic failure.

—The Library of Congress, by policy, does not provide Cataloging in Publication (or any other cataloging) for what are among the most used single titles published in the United States—namely, textbooks below the college level.

—For too many teachers and librarians the word disadvantaged is considered a synonym for stupid. The difference between being ignorant and being dumb escapes many adults working with children and the result is a failure to provide the high quality materials needed to overcome ignorance.

—Perhaps the most neglected group of children in our society are those we label gifted. Proper social concern does not mean ignoring one group in favor of another; it means equal services and materials for all groups according to their abilities.

—It is terribly ironic that many of the things we are doing because we think they are required by mainstreaming are the things we should have been doing for everyone all along—namely providing each child with the most favorable intellectual and physical environment necessary for maximum learning to take place.

Appendix A: Book Selection Aids[1]

The AAAS Science Booklist, comp. by Hilary J. Deason, 3rd ed. Selected and Annotated List of Science and Mathematics Books for Secondary School Students, College Undergraduates, and Nonspecialists. American Assoc. for the Advancement of Science, 1970.

About 100 Books: A Gateway to Better Intergroup Understanding, comp. by Ann G. Wolfe. American Jewish Committee, 1969. A sixth edition, largely comprising books published in 1967, 1968, and 1969, reflecting the trends and unsolved problems in intergroup relations during that period. Arranged by age.

Adventuring with Books: A Book List for Elementary Schools, ed. by Shelton Root and the Committee on the Elementary School Book List of the National Council of Teachers of English, 2nd ed., Nat. Council of Teachers of English, 1973. Annotated listings within subject categories and interest level groupings. May be used by children since it is carefully annotated for child appeal.

Africa: An Annotated List of Printed Materials Suitable for Children. ALA, Children's Services Division and the African-American Institute. Information Center on Children's Cultures, United States Committee for UNICEF, 1968. An evaluation of all in-print English language materials on Africa for children, arranged by countries.

African-Asian Reading Guide for Children and Young Adults, comp. by Jeanette Hotchkiss. Scarecrow. 1976. Divided by countries and by genre.

Aids to Choosing Books for Children, prepared by Ingeborg Boudreau. Children's Book Council, 1969. A selected, annotated bibliography of book lists and review media, designed to aid librarians, teachers, students of children's literature, and parents in book selection. Both general and specialized book lists are included as well as a list of general sources of information.

American Historical Fiction and Biography for Children and Young People, comp. by Jeanette Hotchkiss. Scarecrow, 1973. Annotations are arranged chronologically and by subject. Symbols are used for reading and interest levels.

American History, comp. by Bernard Titowsky. McKinley, 1964. Annotated selective listings.

Appraisal: Children's Science Books. Harvard Graduate School of Education, Cambridge, Mass. Published three times each year. Around fifty books reviewed in each issue, all rated on a five-point scale by both a librarian and a science specialist.

Asia: A Guide to Books for Children. The Asia Society, 1966. Asia is defined as all the countries from Afghanistan eastward to Japan. The guide is arranged by country and approximate grade levels are suggested in the annotated listings.

A Basic Book Collection for Elementary Grades. ALA, 1960. Suggested as a minimum collection, this is a helpful annotated guide to books in subject fields as well as to fiction and picture books.

A Basic Book Collection for High Schools, 7th ed. ALA, 1963. Includes paperbacks, magazines, and audiovisual aids.

A Basic Book Collection for Junior High Schools. ALA, 1960. Similar in pattern to the book for elementary grades.

Basic Books in the Mass Media, comp. by Eleanor Blum, rev. ed. Univ. of Ill. Pr., 1972. An annotated, selective book list covering book publishing, broadcasting, films, newspapers, magazines, and advertising. The bibliography is intended to provide sources for facts and figures, names, addresses, and other biographical information, and to suggest starting points for research.

Behavior Patterns in Children's Books: A Bibliography, comp. by Clara J. Kircher. Catholic Univ. of America Pr., 1966. The purpose of this book is the development of wholesome principles of conduct and the prevention of delinquency through the therapeutic use of books in which good character traits are embodied. The list is arranged by such categories as making friends, spiritual values, or boy-girl relationships rather than age, and is followed by a list of selected readings and a behavior index.

Best Books for Children. Bowker, 1959 to date. An annual catalog of 4000 titles annotated and arranged under preschool to grade 3; grades 4–6; grades 7 up; adult books for younger readers; and special subjects.

The Best in Children's Books: The University of Chicago Guide to Children's Literature, 1973–1978, comp. by Zena Sutherland. Univ. of Chicago Pr., 1980. Reviews chosen from the *Bulletin of the Center for Children's Books* are indexed by developmental values, types of literature, reading level, and curricular use as well as conventional indexes.

The Best of the Best: Die Besten der Besten, ed. by Walter Scherf. Bowker, 1971. A bibliography of children's books in fifty-seven languages. Annotations are not provided, but the lists are selective.

Bibliography of Books for Children, comp. by Bonnie Baron. Assoc. for Childhood Education International, 1977. Annotated list of books for children from preschool through elementary grades, grouped by subject or form in useful categories.

A Bicultural Heritage: Themes for the Exploration of Mexican and Mexican-American Culture in Books for Children and Adolescents, comp. by Isabel Schon. Scarecrow Press, 1978. Hoping to expose students to elements of Mexican and Mexican-American culture and to combat stereotypes, Schon has compiled this annotated bibliography of English fiction and non-fiction titles; recommended books are marked with a special notation.

The Black Experience and the School Curriculum: Teaching Materials for Grades K–12; An Annotated Bibliography, comp. by Katherine Baxter. Wellsprings Ecumenical Center, 1968. Annotated lists of books grouped by subject matter, about black history, social studies, biography, fiction, and poetry, with additional material on teachers' guides and audiovisual aids.

The Black Experience in Children's Books, prepared by Barbara Rollock, rev. ed. New York Public Library, 1974. An annotated bibliography, classified by age and subject mat-

---

1. See also the bibliographies accompanying the articles in Part 5.

ter about black life in America, in the Islands, in Africa, and in England.

Black Image: Education Copes With Color, ed. by Jean Grambs and John Carr. Wm. C. Brown, 1972. Short essays on the problems of the black image in children's books, with evaluations of instructional materials, texts, and some fiction.

Black Studies: A Bibliography, comp. by Leonard Irwin. McKinley, 1973. For young people and adults, annotations grouped under such headings as biographical material, African background, essays and anthologies, etc.

The Black World in Literature for Children: A Bibliography of Print and Non-Print Materials, comp. by Joyce White Mills. Atlanta Univ., 1975. Divided by broad age groups and subject areas, this is for children ages 3–13.

Book Bait: Detailed Notes on Adult Books Popular with Young People, ed. by Elinor Walker, 3rd ed. ALA, 1979. Revised from the earlier editions to add current titles, this volume describes adult books that young readers have enjoyed. A detailed plot summary, suggestions for book talks, and references to related titles are given for each book. Includes a subject index.

The Bookfinder: A Guide to Children's Literature About the Needs and Problems of Youth Aged 2–15, ed. by Sharon Dreyer. American Guidance Service, 1977. A split-page format allows indexes and text to be browsed independently in this critical assessment of fiction touching on upheavals in children's lives.

Books for Beginning Readers, prepared by Elizabeth Guilefoile, ill. by Norma Phillips. Nat. Council of Teachers of English, 1962. A useful bibliography of over 300 easy-reading books for beginners. The majority have been published to meet the need for entertainment and information.

Books for Children 1960–1965, as selected and reviewed by *The Booklist* and *Subscription Books Bulletin*. ALA, 1966. A compilation of reviews of recommended books, expressly for teachers and librarians. Reviews are grouped by subject matter and genre. The first of an annual compilation, now issued under the title *Books for Children, Preschool Through Junior High School*, with inclusive dates for each compilation.

Books for Friendship: A List of Books Recommended for Children, 4th ed. of *Books Are Bridges*. American Friends Service Committee and Anti-Defamation League of B'nai B'rith, 1968. Books of high literary quality selected to help boys and girls widen their friendships and follow the path of peace and brotherhood.

Books for the Chinese-American Child: A Selected List, comp. by Cecilia Mei-Chi Chen. Cooperative Children's Book Center, 1969. A carefully selected list of books, included for their honesty and literary quality.

Books for You: A Reading List for Senior High School Students, comp. by Nat. Council of Teachers of English, rev. ed. Washington Square Pr., 1971. An annotated bibliography divided by subject.

Books in American History: A Basic List for High Schools, comp. by John E. Wiltz. Indiana Univ. Pr., 1964. Chronological, annotated bibliography.

Books in Spanish for Children and Young Adults: An Annotated Guide, ed. by Isabel Schon. Scarecrow, 1978. Critical annotations describe Spanish-language titles.

Books on American Indians and Eskimos: A Selection Guide for Children and Young Adults, comp. by Mary Jo Lass-Woodfin. ALA, 1977. This guide grades the titles, both fiction and non-fiction, and summarizes their contents.

Books to Help Children Cope with Separation and Loss, by Joanne Bernstein. Bowker, 1977. An introductory discussion of bibliotherapy, with annotated book lists grouped by subject headings.

Building Bridges of Understanding, prepared by Charlotte Matthews Keating. Palo Verde, 1967. An annotated bibliography of books about blacks, Indians, Spanish-speaking ethnic groups, Chinese-Americans, Japanese-Americans, Jews, and other minority groups.

Building Bridges of Understanding Between Cultures, prepared by Charlotte Matthews Keating. Palo Verde, 1971. A companion volume to the title above, the annotations arranged by age level within each minority group.

Building Ethnic Collections: An Annotated Guide for School Media Centers and Public Libraries, by Lois Buttlar and Lubomyr Wynar. Libraries Unlimited, 1977. A selection of fiction, non-fiction, reference and audio-visual materials are discussed for over forty minority groups.

Bulletin of the Center for Children's Books. The Univ. of Chicago, Graduate Library School, Univ. of Chicago Pr. Published monthly except August. Ongoing review of new titles for children and young people, annotated according to whether the book is recommended, acceptable, marginal, not recommended, or for special collections or unusual readers only. The reviews are detailed, and grade levels and prices are given.

Canadian Books for Young People: Livres canadiens pour la jeunesse, comp. by Irma McDonough. Univ. of Toronto Pr., 1978. A revised and expanded (titles are now given for children up to the age of 14) version of *Canadian Books for Children*, 1976. Book lists are given in both French and English, arranged under subject headings.

Canadian Children's Literature: A Journal of Criticism and Review. Canadian Children's Press/Canadian Children's Literature Association. Includes articles, reviews, and bibliographies.

Children and Poetry: A Selective Annotated Bibliography, comp. by Virginia Haviland and William Jay Smith, 2nd ed., rev. Library of Congress, 1979. Enhanced with illustrations from recommended books, this is a selective guide to poetry, old and new, for use with children. Includes sections on rhymes, twentieth-century poetry, anthologies, and world poetry.

Children's Authors and Illustrators: An Index to Biographical Dictionaries, ed. by Adele Sarkissian, 2nd ed. Gale, 1978. A useful finding tool, collating references to biographical sources for information about specific children's authors and illustrators.

Children's Book Review Index, ed. by Gary Tarbert. Gale, 1976. Triannual publication indexing sources of reviews in over 200 periodicals.

Children's Books, comp. by Children's Book Section, U.S. Library of Congress. An annual bibliography, selective and annotated.

Children's Books: Awards and Prizes, comp. and ed. by the Children's Book Council, 1979. A compilation of honors awarded in the children's book field by organizations, schools, publishers, and newspapers. A brief description of each award is followed by a list of all the winners since it was first given.

Children's Books for $1.50 or Less. See *Good and Inexpensive Books for Children*.

Children's Books for Times of Stress: An Annotated Bibliography, comp. by Ruth Gillis. Indiana Univ. Pr., 1978. A selective listing of children's books, arranged by subject, which bear on stressful episodes in children's lives.

Children's Books in Print. Bowker, annual. An index to 35,000 books in print at time of publication, including such books as have become children's classics based on inclusion in publishers' catalogs. There are separate author, title, illustrator, and publisher indexes. Prices are given for trade and library bindings, and for paperback editions.

Children's Books of International Interest, ed. by Virginia Haviland, 2nd ed. ALA, 1978. A guide to the best children's books published in the U.S. which are of interest to people working with children in other countries.

Children's Books on Africa and Their Authors: An Annotated Bibliography, comp. by Nancy Schmidt. African Bibliography Series, Vol. 3. Africana Pub. Co., 1975. Full annotations, no age or reading level assigned. A supplement, also compiled by Schmidt, was issued by Africana in 1979.

Children's Books to Enrich the Social Studies for the Elementary Grades, comp. by Helen Huus. Nat. Council for the Social Studies, 1966. Excellent annotated bibliographies, topically arranged, cover world history and geography from ancient times to today.

Children's Books Too Good to Miss, comp. by May Hill Arbuthnot, Margaret Mary Clark, Harriet Geneva Long, and Ruth M. Hadlow, 7th ed. University Press Books, 1980. A select list of books suggested as the irreducible minimum, which every child should be exposed to. The books are grouped by ages.

The Children's Bookshelf: A Guide to Books for and About Children, prepared by the Child Study Assoc. of America, rev. ed. Bantam, 1974. Short articles on books and reading; annotated bibliography for different age groups and books for parents about children and family life.

Children's Catalog. Wilson, 1971. Annual supp. A selected, classified catalog of children's books, arranged with nonfiction first, classified by Dewey Decimal Classification, followed by fiction, short stories, and the easy books. Five-year cumulations and yearly supplements.

Children's Interracial Fiction: An Unselective Bibliography, comp. by Barbara Jean Glancy. American Federation of Teachers, 1969. Comprehensive annotated bibliography, accompanied by articles dealing with the black perspective and a survey-review of children's literature about black people.

Children's Literature Review, ed. by Ann Block and Carolyn Riley. Gale, 1976. A paragraph of information about the author introduces review excerpts relative to specific titles. Cumulative indexes in each volume.

Core Media Collection for Elementary Schools, by Lucy Gregor Brown. Bowker, 1978. A selection guide to nonprint items.

The Dobler World Directory of Youth Periodicals, comp. by Lavinia G. Dobler and Muriel Fuller. Schulte, 1966. A revised and expanded listing, a successor to the *Dobler International List of Periodicals for Boys and Girls.*

Doors to More Mature Reading, prepared by Elinor Walker, Donald W. Allyn, Alice E. Johnson, and Helen Lutton. ALA, 1964. Detailed notes on adult books for use with young people.

The Elementary School Library Collection: Phases 1-2-3, ed. by Mary V. Gaver. Bro-Dart, 1965. Annual supplements. Contains discussion of selection policy and classification principles and policy. Books, shown on reproductions of catalog cards, are classified according to Dewey Decimal System of Classification in the first section. Section 2 contains author-title and subject indexes.

European Historical Fiction and Biography, comp. by Jeanette Hotchkiss, 2nd ed. Scarecrow, 1972. Divided by country and, within that, by period, with brief annotations.

Fables from Incunabula to Modern Picture Books: A Selective Bibliography, comp. by Barbara Quinnan. The Library of Congress General Reference and Bibliography Division, Reference Department, 1966.

Fantasy for Children: An Annotated Checklist, by Ruth Nadelman Lynn. Bowker, 1979. A bibliographic guide to works of fantasy, divided by type and theme, incorporating references to review sources.

Fantasy Literature: A Core Collection and Reference Guide, by Marshall B. Tymn, Kenneth J. Zahorski, and Robert H. Boyer. Bowker, 1979. Includes a brief discussion of fantasy, an annotated bibliography of some 240 volumes recommended for a collection of high fantasy, and a section on research aids.

Fare for the Reluctant Reader, comp. by Anita E. Dunn, Mabel E. Jackman, and Bernice C. Bush, rev. ed. State Univ. of N.Y., 1952. Annotated bibliography to help teachers and librarians select books for reluctant readers from grades 7 through 12. Books are grouped by age and subject. There are chapters on developmental and remedial reading.

Folklore: An Annotated Bibliography and Index to Single Editions, comp. by Elsie Ziegler. Faxon, 1973. Particularly useful because it gives access to single editions.

Folklore for Children and Young People: A Critical and Descriptive Bibliography for Use in the Elementary and Intermediate School, comp. by Eloise Ramsey. Reprint of 1952 ed., Krause Reprints. Originally published by the American Folklore Society. Includes a section on literary uses.

Folklore of the American Indians: An Annotated Bibliography, comp. by Judith C. Ullom, ill. Library of Congress, 1969. Carefully selected items arranged by culture areas.

For Storytellers and Storytelling: Bibliographies, Materials and Resource Aids. ALA, 1968. Recommended materials on storytelling, including books, pamphlets, and multimedia aids.

4000 Books for Secondary School Libraries: A Basic List, comp. by the Library Committee of the Nat. Assoc. of Independent Schools. Bowker, 1968. Arranged by Dewey Decimal Classification; periodicals and recordings are also listed.

Gateways to Readable Books, comp. by Dorothy Withrow, Helen Carey, and Bertha Hirzel. Wilson, 1975. An annotated list of titles chosen for the reluctant adolescent reader.

Good and Inexpensive Books for Children, rev. ed. Assoc. for Childhood Education International, 1972. Annotated lists, primarily paperbacks, grouped by genre.

Good Books for Children: A Selection of Outstanding Children's Books Published 1950-65, ed. by Mary K. Eakin, 3rd ed. Univ. of Chicago Pr., 1966. The bibliography consists of graded reviews chosen from the *Bulletin of the Center for Children's Books.*

Good Reading for the Disadvantaged Reader: Multi-Ethnic Resources, by George Spache. Garrard, 1975. One-sentence annotations describe books and audio-visual materials suitable for use in the development of self-concept among seven minority groups, including the inner city child.

Good Reading for Poor Readers, comp. by George Spache, rev. ed. Garrard, 1974. Consists primarily of bibliographies: four chapters discuss children's interests and motives in reading, choosing and using books for children, and estimating readability.

Growing Point, published by Margery Fisher. Belmont, 1962 to date. Nine issues yearly, published in England, reviews books for parents, teachers, and librarians in the English-speaking world.

Guide to Children's Magazines, Newspapers, Reference Books, prepared by Judy Matthews and Lillian Drag. Assoc. for Childhood Education International, 1974. Revised guide to provide a quick index of available materials.

A Guide to Historical Fiction, comp. by Leonard B. Irwin. 10th ed. rev. McKinley, 1971. Annotated entries are chronologically arranged within geographical regions.

A Guide to Historical Reading: Non-Fiction, comp. by Leonard B. Irwin, 9th ed. McKinley, 1970. Annotated listing in the McKinley series.

A Guide to Non-Sexist Children's Books, comp. by Judith Adell and Hilary Klein. Academy Pr., 1976. An annotated bibliography is divided by grade groups: preschool to 3, 3–7, 7–12, and one for all ages.

Her Way: Biographies of Women for Young People, by Mary-Ellen Kulkin. ALA, 1976. Single and collective biographies of prominent women are graded and carefully annotated.

High Interest-Easy Reading for Junior and Senior High School Students, ed. by Marian White, rev. ed. NCTE, 1979. Brief annotations describe, but do not critique, high interest/low reading level titles; arrangement is by subject.

History in Children's Books: An Annotated Bibliography for Schools and Libraries, comp. by Zena Sutherland. McKinley, 1967. The fifth in a series of bibliographies for schools, libraries, and teachers.

The Horn Book Magazine. Horn Book. Published six times a year. A magazine about children's books, authors, illustrators, with a section for reviews.

How to Find Out About Children's Literature, comp. by Alec Ellis, 3rd ed., Pergamon, 1973. Bibliography of bibliographies as well as other useful listings of organizations and collections, both national and international.

I Can Read It Myself: Some Books for Independent Reading in the Primary Grades, prepared by Frieda M. Heller. Ohio State Univ., 1965. Annotated lists divided into three levels of competence.

In Review: Canadian Books for Children. Provincial Library Service, Ontario. Articles by and about authors are included in a journal devoted primarily to reviews of books written in French or English.

Independent Reading Grades One Through Three: An Annotated Bibliography with Reading Levels. Bro-Dart, 1975. Has cross-referenced subject headings and a reading level index.

Index to Short Biographies: For Elementary and Junior High Grades, comp. by Ellen Stanius. Scarecrow, 1971. Listed by subject and by author, with pages given. Collective biographies only.

An Index to Young Readers' Collective Biographies, comp. by Judith Silverman, 3rd ed. Bowker, 1979. Newly augmented to include listings for over seven thousand individuals, this volume indexes the contents of some 950 collective biographies. A subject index groups biographies by fields of activity and nationality.

Introducing Books: A Guide for the Middle Grades, comp. by John Gillespie and Diane Lembo. Bowker, 1970. Titles for reading guidance and book talks are grouped according to the developmental goals of childhood, and a subject index groups these same titles under their conventional headings.

Junior High School Library Catalog, ed. by Estelle A. Fidell and Gary L. Bogart, 3rd ed. Wilson, 1975. Annual supp. Part 1, the Classified Catalog, is arranged with nonfiction books first, classified according to Dewey Decimal Classification system. Fiction books follow and short stories are next. Part 2 is an author, title, subject, analytical index. Cumulated every five years, with yearly supplements.

Juniorplots: A Book Talk Manual for Teachers and Librarians, comp. by John Gillespie and Diane Lembo. Bowker, 1967. Thematic discussions of specific books grouped under eight categories of basic goals of adolescence.

The Kirkus Service. A bimonthly publication: reviews are done from galleys and appear early, but information on illustrations is not always available.

Language Arts. Nat. Council of Teachers of English. Issued monthly, September through May. Besides regular book reviews, this journal has articles on children's reading and related subjects.

Latin America: An Annotated List of Materials for Children, ed. by Anne Pellowski, selected by a committee of librarians, teachers, and Latin-American specialists in cooperation with the Center for Inter-American Relations. Information Center on Children's Cultures, United States Committee for UNICEF, 1969. Materials are arranged by country and age-graded.

A Layman's Guide to Negro History, ed. and comp. by Erwin A. Salk. McGraw, 1967. Comprehensive compilation of books and teaching aids, conveniently categorized, and listings of important dates and people in black history.

Let's Read Together: Books for Family Enjoyment, 3rd ed. Children's Services Division, ALA, and National Congress of Parents and Teachers. ALA, 1969. Arranged by age levels and annotated.

Literature by and About the American Indian: An Annotated Bibliography, for Junior and Senior High School Students, comp. by Anna Lee Stensland, 2nd ed. Nat. Council of Teachers of English, 1979. A divided bibliography with study guides and biographies of American Indian authors.

Magazines for School Libraries: A Brief Survey by Laura K. Martin. Univ. of Ky., 1967. This is a discussion rather than a listing of magazines useful to teachers and librarians, as well as students, covering such areas as selection of materials, general comment, family life, fine arts, etc.

Magazines Recommended for Use with Children, Grades K–12: A Comparative Survey of Six Basic Lists Compiled by Librarians and Educators, ed. by Sylvia Hart Wright, 2nd ed. Franklin Square-Mayfair Subscription Agency, 1969.

Mexico and Its Literature for Children and Adolescents, comp. by Isabel Schon. Arizona State Univ., 1977. The first annotated guide to Mexican children's books, this volume reflects the compiler's thorough familiarity with the field. Biographical information about authors precedes annotations of their work.

More Juniorplots: A Guide for Teachers and Librarians, comp. by John Gillespie. Bowker, 1977. A companion volume to the author's *Juniorplots,* listed above. Information about selected authors is included.

A Multimedia Approach to Children's Literature: A Selective List of Films, Filmstrips, and Recordings Based on Children's Books, comp. by Ellin Greene and Madalynne Schoenfeld. ALA, 1977. Selective information about book-related, nonprint materials, arranged by book title. Descriptive annotations are provided.

Negro Literature for High School Students, prepared by Barbara Dodds. Nat. Council of Teachers of English, 1968. A valuable reference guide offering a historical survey of black writers, an annotated list of works about blacks, annotated lists of novels for boys and girls, and biographies. both historical and modern, as well as suggested classroom uses of black literature. Extensive bibliography.

Notable Children's Books, 1940–1970. ALA, 1977. A reappraisal of ALA's Children's Services Division's annual Notable lists, from 1940 to 1970. Short descriptive annotations are given for each title.

Notes from a Different Drummer: A Guide to Juvenile Fiction Portraying the Handicapped, comp. by Barbara Baskin and Karen Harris. Bowker, 1977. This annotated guide to books that have handicapped characters is prefaced by an analysis of the treatment of the disabled in literature.

Patterns in Reading, prepared by Jean Carolyn Roos, 2nd ed. ALA, 1961. A useful selection of books for older children, youth, and young adults. The books are grouped around more than a hundred major reading interests and are well annotated and indexed. This is quite a valuable reference.

Periodicals for School Media Programs: A Guide to Magazines, Newspapers, Periodical Indexes, comp. by Selma Richardson, rev. ed. ALA, 1978. A buying guide to periodicals and newspapers for school library purchases. Entries are alphabetical, and each is accompanied by appropriate grade level, name and address of publisher, frequency of publication, and price. Also included are annotations describing the nature and scope of the publication and possible curricular use.

Previews: Non-Print Software & Hardware News & Reviews. Bowker. Monthly, September through May. Reviews divided (filmstrips, slides, kits, etc.) and articles included. Hardware reviews thorough.

Reading for Young People: The Great Plains, ed. by Mildred Laughlin. ALA, 1979. One in a series of annotated bibliographies collating fiction and non-fiction pertinent to the states in the regional designation. Other titles include *The Midwest,* ed. by Dorothy Hinman and Ruth Zimmerman (1979); *The Rocky Mountains,* ed. by Mildred Laughlin (1980); *The Middle Atlantic,* ed. by Arabelle Pennypacker (1980); and *The Southeast,* ed. by Dorothy Heald (1980).

Reading Ladders for Human Relations, ed. by Virginia Reid, rev. ed. Am. Council on Education, 1972. This enlarged and revised edition contains an introduction and bibliographies on the role of reading in developing children's self-knowledge and social awareness.

Red, White and Black: (and Brown and Yellow): Minorities in America, Harold H. Laskey, director. Combined Paperback Exhibit, 1970. Catalog of paperbacks on minority groups, with an order form for purchasing books or previewing films.

Reference Books for Elementary and Junior High School Libraries, comp. by Carolyn Sue Peterson. Scarecrow, 1970. A very useful annotated bibliography divided into general reference books (dictionaries, atlases, fact books, etc.) and those for subject areas.

School Library Journal. Bowker. A journal for librarians especially, it is published September through May, and in August. Approximately 1500 titles are reviewed, sometimes with dissenting opinions. There are also many articles on library services, books, and reading for children and young people.

Science Books: A Quarterly Review. Am. Assoc. for the Advancement of Science. Reviews around 100 science and mathematics books, elementary through college and beyond. Reviews are by specialists in the field.

Science for Youth, comp. by Hannah Logasa. McKinley, 1967. Annotated bibliography in the McKinley series.

Standard Catalog for High School Libraries. Annual supplements. Wilson. Part 1, the Classified Catalog, is arranged with nonfiction first, classified by Dewey Decimal System; fiction next; and then short stories. Each book is listed under one main entry where full information is given. Part 2 contains an author, title, subject, and analytical index of all the books in the catalog.

Starting Out Right: Choosing Books About Black People for Young Children, ed. by Bettye Lattimer. Wis. Dept of Public Instruction, 1972. A bibliography preceded by a discussion of the extent of integration in books for children.

Stories to Tell to Children, ed. by Sara C. Bryant. Carnegie Library of Pittsburgh, frequently revised. One of the outstanding bibliographies of folk and fairy literature available for the storyteller.

Subject and Title Index to Short Stories for Children. Subcommittee of the ALA Editorial Committee, 1955. Designed to assist librarians and teachers in locating stories on specific subjects. Approximate grades given.

Subject Guide to Children's Books in Print. Bowker, annual. A subject index to children's books in 7000 categories.

Subject Index to Books for Intermediate Grades, comp. by Mary K. Eakin, 3rd ed. ALA, 1963. An index of 1800 titles with emphasis on trade books.

Subject Index to Books for Primary Grades, comp. by Mary K. Eakin and Eleanor Merritt, 3rd ed. ALA, 1967. Approximately 1000 textbooks and trade books for primary grades are indexed under detailed subject headings useful for the classroom teacher and librarian.

Subject Index to Poetry for Children and Young People. ALA, 1957. Indicates grade level.

Translated Children's Books: Offered by Publishers in the U.S.A. Storybooks International, 1968. Annotated list of books, arranged alphabetically according to language of origin, with an author index and a title index.

Treasure for the Taking, prepared by Anne Thaxter Eaton. Viking, 1957. First published in 1946, this revised, annotated bibliography is arranged according to many types of children's books.

We Build Together: A Reader's Guide to Negro Life and Literature for Elementary and High School Use, ed. by Charlemae Rollins, 3rd ed. Nat. Council of Teachers of English, 1967. A selected, annotated bibliography of picture books, fiction, history, biography, poetry, folklore, music, science, and sports, with an introduction dealing with the criteria by which the books were selected.

World Culture, comp. by Hannah Logasa. McKinley, 1963. Arranged in subject categories.

World Historical Fiction Guide, comp. by Daniel McGarry and Sarah White, 2nd ed. Scarecrow, 1973. A selective, annotated list for junior and senior high school.

The World of Books for Children: A Parent's Guide, by Abby Campbell Hunt. Sovereign, 1979. A guide to recommended children's books; titles are arranged by subject within age level designations.

The World of Children's Literature, comp. by Anne Pellowski. Bowker, 1968. An annotated bibliography giving a picture of the development of children's literature in every country where it exists.

Your Reading: A Book List for Junior High Schools, ed. by Charles B. Willard and the Committee on the Junior High School Book List of the Nat. Council of Teachers of English, 5th ed. Walker, 1975. Annotated guide to almost 1300 books.

Appendix B: Adult References[1]

ABRAHAMS, ROGER, and GEORGE FOSS. *Anglo-American Folksong Style*. Prentice, 1968. Although many songs are included as examples, this is primarily an evaluation of the style, content, and form of folksong, and of the types of ballads and the changes in ballad style.

AFANASIEV, ALEXANDER N. *Russian Fairy Tales*, tr. by Norbert Guterman, ill. by A. Alexeieff. Pantheon, 1945. See the valuable "Folkloristic Commentary" by Roman Jakobson.

ALDERSON, BRIAN. *Looking at Picture Books 1973*. National Book League, Children's Book Council, 1974. Perceptive and knowledgeable comments on children's book illustration.

ALDISS, BRIAN. *The True History of Science Fiction*. Doubleday, 1973. On the origins of science fiction and its emergence as a genre in the 20th century.

ALMY, MILLIE. *Ways of Studying Children*. Bureau of Publications, Teachers College. Columbia University, 1969. Chapter 5 relates to the use of literature in studying children.

ALMY, MILLIE, E. CHITTENDEN, and PAULA MILLER. *Young Children's Thinking: Studies of Some Aspects of Piaget's Theory*. Teachers College Pr., 1966. An application of Piaget's developmental psychology to the field of education.

ALTICK, RICHARD D. *Lives and Letters: A History of Literary Biography in England and America*. Knopf, 1965. With liberal bibliographical notes for each chapter, the author discusses the achievement and influence of literary biographers from the seventeenth century to today. A thoroughly researched and comprehensive study.

AMERICAN COUNCIL ON EDUCATION. *Helping Teachers Understand Children*. Am. Council on Education, 1945. Report of a project designed to deepen understanding of children's growth and development by analyzing and identifying causes that underlie children's behavior.

ANDERSON, HAROLD, ed. *Creativity and Its Cultivation*. Harper, 1959. A compilation of outstanding research papers in the field of creativity. Carl Rogers's paper entitled "Toward a Theory of Creativity" presents his findings on psychological safety, which he considers essential to creative thinking.

ANDERSON, ROBERT, and HAROLD SHANE, eds. *As the Twig Is Bent: Readings in Early Childhood Education*. Houghton, 1971. A collection of articles, the majority devoted to the development of the preschool child.

ANDERSON, VERNA. *Reading and Young Children*. Macmillan, 1968. A survey of the approaches to the teaching of reading, the problems and the techniques of meeting them, and the use of materials with children.

APPLEBEE, ARTHUR. *The Child's Concept of Story: Ages Two to Seventeen*. Univ. of Chicago Press, 1978. Stories children tell and their responses to stories they hear are used to support this theory of a child's perception of storying.

AQUINO, JOHN. *Fantasy in Literature*. National Education Assoc., 1977. A teacher's handbook on curricular use of fantasy.

ARBUTHNOT, MAY HILL. *Children's Reading in the Home*, ill. Scott, Foresman, 1969. A description of a good home environment for reading followed by a discussion of books according to age range and type.

ARBUTHNOT, MAY HILL, and ZENA SUTHERLAND. *The Arbuthnot Anthology*, 4th ed. Scott, Foresman, 1976. A source book for children's literature classes as well as a book to be used with children, containing poetry, fantasy, and realism. Special sections are "Milestones in Children's Literature," "Illustrations in Children's Books," and "Guiding Literary Experience."

ARNOTT, ANN. *The Secret Country of C. S. Lewis*. Eerdmans, 1975. A concise biography suitable for both young and adult readers.

ARNSTEIN, FLORA. *Children Write Poetry: A Creative Approach*, 2nd ed. Stanford Univ. Pr., 1967. A teacher's careful record of her step-by-step procedures in conducting an experiment in creative writing with a group of elementary-school children, with discussions of qualities that mark authentic poetry.

The Art of Beatrix Potter, with an appreciation by Anne Carroll Moore. Warne, 1956. In a truly beautiful book, landscapes, still life, experimental drawings, and the tiny pictures for her children's classics are reproduced, giving new insight into the versatility of Beatrix Potter.

ARTLEY, A. STERL. "Oral Reading as a Communication Process." *The Reading Teacher*, 26 (October 1972): 46–51. Identifies classroom situations for oral interpretation and includes a description of teacher-guided interpretation.

ASBJÖRNSEN, PETER C., and JÖRGEN MOE. *Norwegian Folk Tales*, tr. by Pat Shaw Iversen and Carl Norman, ill. by Erik Werenskiold and Theodor Kittelson. Viking, 1961. Thirty-six folk tales in an excellent translation which reintroduces the original Asbjörnsen illustrators.

————. *Popular Tales from the Norse*, tr. by Sir George Webbe Dasent. Putnam, 1908. A long and rich introduction by the translator is particulary good on changes from myth to fairy tale.

ASHTON, JOHN. *Chap-Books of the Eighteenth Century*. London: Chatto, 1882. (Facsimile of the original: Singing Tree, 1968.) The author reproduces the stories and some of the pages and illustrations from the old chapbooks.

ASIMOV, ISAAC. *Words from the Myths*. Houghton, 1961. From the Greek myths come many word roots used in science and daily language. Asimov tells the legends briefly and explains origins of current usage.

ASSOCIATION OF HOSPITAL AND INSTITUTION LIBRARIES. *Bibliotherapy: Methods and Materials*. ALA, 1971. Discusses applications of reading as therapy, and provides a guide to children's books of potential usefulness in bibliotherapy.

[1] This list provides data and annotations for the Adult References in Chapters 1–16. Consult Appendix A for any reference not found here. For additional useful reading suggestions see the bibliographies accompanying the articles in Part 5.

AUSLANDER, JOSEPH, and FRANK ERNEST HILL. *The Winged Horse: The Story of Poets and Their Poetry.* Doubleday, 1927. Written for older children and young people, this is a thoroughly interesting book for teachers and parents as well. Fine references on ballads and epics.

BADER, BARBARA. *American Picturebooks from Noah's Ark to The Beast Within.* Macmillan, 1976. A critical and historical study.

BAIRD, BIL. *The Art of the Puppet,* ill. Macmillan. 1965. A fascinating and handsomely illustrated book "designed to tell people about puppets and how they differ from each other and how they are alike" by a man with "forty years of practice in a profession that has given me the greatest satisfaction."

BALDWIN, RUTH, comp. *One Hundred Nineteenth-Century Rhyming Alphabets in English.* Southern Ill. Univ. Pr., 1972. Reproductions, some in full color, of alphabets that vary in theme, tone, and degrees of difficulty or didacticism.

BAMMAN, HENRY A., MILDRED A. DAWSON, and ROBERT J. WHITEHEAD. *Oral Interpretation of Children's Literature,* 2nd ed. Brown, 1971. Includes recommended selections as well as guidelines for improving oral reading and oral interpretation.

BANDURA, ALBERT, and RICHARD H. WALTERS. *Social Learning and Personality Development.* Holt, 1963. The authors deal with the relationships between social learning and the environment, looking at the acquisition of behavior through observational learning.

BARBER, RICHARD. *A Companion to World Mythology.* Delacorte, 1980. Colorful illustrations based on original prototypes embellish this dictionary of world mythological personalities.

BARCHILON, JACQUES, and HENRY PETTIT. *The Authentic Mother Goose Fairy Tales and Nursery Rhymes.* Swallow Pr., 1960. Following a scholarly introduction to the history of Mother Goose and the Perrault fairy tales, there are facsimiles of the complete *Mother Goose's Melody,* and of the 1729 English translation of Perrault's *Tales.*

BARING-GOULD, WILLIAM and CECIL, eds. *The Annotated Mother Goose.* The complete text and illustrations in a fully annotated edition, ill. by Caldecott, Crane, Greenaway, Rackham, Parrish, and historical woodcuts. With chapter decorations by E. M. Simon. Potter, 1962. Mother Goose and other rhymes, ditties, and jingles of the nursery run side by side with columns of absorbing historical notes. This impressively large, beautiful book contains over 200 illustrations with a first-line index.

BARRY, FLORENCE V. *A Century of Children's Books.* Doran, 1923; reissued. Singing Tree, 1969. A readable account of early English books for children, with unusually good evaluations.

BAUGHMAN, ERNEST. *A Type and Motif Index of the Folktales of England and North America.* Indiana Univ. Folklore Series, No. 20, 1966. Gives extensive bibliographic references to the well-known folk-tale types.

BEADLE, MURIEL. *A Child's Mind; How Children Learn During the Critical Years from Birth to Age Five,* ill. Doubleday, 1970. A review, prepared for the lay person, of what had been learned in the preceding twenty-five years about the child's mind and development.

BECHTEL, LOUISE SEAMAN, ed. *Books in Search of Children.* Macmillan, 1969. Speeches and essays by a pioneering editor and critic.

BEHN, HARRY. *Chrysalis: Concerning Children and Poetry.* Harcourt, 1968. A children's poet reminisces and writes about children and poetry.

BERRY, THOMAS ELLIOTT, ed. *The Biographer's Craft.* Odyssey, 1967. A textbook with examples of the work of seventeen biographers from Plutarch to contemporary writers, with one-page analyses of the biographers' genres and output. Introductory essay and short additional-reading list.

BETT, HENRY. *The Games of Children; Their Origin and History.* Singing Tree, 1968. Intended for both the student of folklore and the general reader, this book explores the primitive, often religious origin of many of the games still played by children.

BETTELHEIM, BRUNO. *The Uses of Enchantment: Meaning and Importance of Fairy Tales.* Knopf, 1976. A defense of the genre and an analysis of some popular fairy tales.

The Bewick Collector. A descriptive catalog of the works of Thomas and John Bewick. . . . The whole described from the originals by Thomas Hugo. M.A., F.R.S.I., etc. London: Lovell Reeve, Vol. 1. 1866. Supp., 1868; reissued, Singing Tree, 1968.

BILLINGTON, ELIZABETH T., ed. *The Randolph Caldecott Treasury,* with an appreciation by Maurice Sendak. Warne, 1978. A compilaton of Caldecott's oeuvre, with meticulous reproductions of many original drawings.

BLACKBURN, HENRY. *Randolph Caldecott: A Personal Memoir of His Early Art Career,* ill. with reproductions and photographs. London: Sampson Low, 1886.

BLISHEN, EDWARD, ed. *The Thorny Paradise.* Kestrel, 1975. A collection of reflections by authors of children's books on diverse approaches to writing for children.

BLOUNT, MARGARET. *Animal Land: The Creatures of Children's Fiction.* Morrow, 1975. Discusses and analyzes types of animal stories.

BOLTON, HENRY CARRINGTON. *The Counting-Out Rhymes of Children: Their Antiquity, Origin, and Wide Distribution: A Study in Folk-Lore.* Singing Tree, 1969. Almost 900 rhymes in 18 languages, including Japanese, Hawaiian, Turkish, and the Penobscot dialect, as well as the more common European languages.

BOSTON, LUCY M. *Perverse and Foolish: A Memoir of Childhood and Youth.* Atheneum, 1979. Boston's very personal reminiscences of her youth up to the time of her marriage.

BOVA, BENJAMIN. *Through Eyes of Wonder: Science Fiction and Science.* Addison, 1975. An assessment of the contribution of science fiction to scientific knowledge, with some history of the development of the genre.

BOWEN, CATHERINE DRINKER. *Biography: The Craft and the Calling.* Little, 1968. Dealing with the planning, research, and techniques involved, the book analyzes four major biographies, with side excursions for further examples, and provides a good tool for writers in the field.

BRAND, OSCAR. *The Ballad Mongers: Rise of the Modern Folk Song.* Funk, 1962. An excellent survey of the interest in, and development of, the folk music of America.

BREDSDORFF, ELIAS. *Hans Christian Andersen: The Story of His Life and Work.* Scribner's, 1975. Incorporates Andersen's autobiographical writing and analyzes his stories.

BREWTON, JOHN E. and SARA W., comps. *Index to Children's Poetry.* Wilson, 1942. First supp., 1954; second supp., 1965; third supp., 1972. Helpful in finding poem sources. Indexed by author, title, subject, and first line. Thorough analysis of book contents, number of poems in a book, and grade placement.

BRIDGE, ETHEL B. "Hickory Dickory Dock: Prelude to Choral Speaking." *Elementary English* 49 (December 1972): 1169–70. Develops ideas for choral reading sessions.

BRIGGS, KATHARINE M. *A Dictionary of British Folk-Tales in the English Language.* Indiana Univ. Pr., 1970. Part A, Folk

Narratives, Vols. 1 and 2. Part B, Folk Legends, Vols, 1 and 2. Contains complete texts and summaries of all British tales in English with extensive comparative notes.

————. *An Encyclopedia of Fairies: Hobgoblins, Brownies, Bogies, and Other Supernatural Creatures.* Pantheon, 1977. Describes many varieties of fairy people, with references to their appearance in international folklore.

————. *The Personnel of Fairyland: A Short Account of the Fairy People of Great Britain for Those Who Tell Stories to Children.* Bentley, 1954. While this is a shorter treatment than the author's *Encyclopedia,* above, it remains a useful directory to the supernatural beings found in British lore.

BRODERICK, DOROTHY M. *Image of the Black in Children's Fiction.* Bowker, 1973. Limited only by the fact that later titles were chosen from headings assigned by *Children's Catalog,* thus excluding some books with major black characters, this is an incisive and perceptive analysis of issues and attitudes.

BROWN, JAMES W. *AV Instruction: Materials and Methods.* McGraw, 1959. A textbook for teacher-training sources in audiovisual instruction, with emphasis on interrelatedness of all teaching aids and the role of the instructor in the presentation of such material.

BRUNER, JEROME S. *Toward a Theory of Instruction.* Belknap Pr. of Harvard Univ., 1966. A collection of essays concerned with the relation between the growth and development of the child and the art of teaching.

BRUNVAND, JAN H. *The Study of American Folklore, an Introduction.* Norton, 1968. The best introductory textbook presently available, with excellent bibliographic references for each chapter.

BULFINCH, THOMAS. *Age of Fable: Or, Stories of Gods and Heroes,* introduction by Dudley Fitts, ill. by Joe Mugnaini. Heritage, 1958. This handsome edition of Bulfinch is almost completely devoted to the Greek and Roman myths, though it does include brief materials from the Norse, Celtic, and Hindu lore.

BUTLER, DOROTHY. *Babies Need Books.* Atheneum, 1980. Stresses the importance of books for young children, both for encouraging the love of reading and for the contribution to language arts skills.

————. *Cushla and Her Books.* Horn Book, 1980. An account of the role books played in the progress of a child with severe handicaps.

CADOGAN, MARY, and PATRICIA CRAIG. *You're a Brick, Angela: A New Look at Girls' Fiction from 1839–1975.* London: Gollancz, 1976. Stories for girls are examined as reflections of social history as well as for their place in literary history.

CAMERON, ELEANOR. *The Green and Burning Tree: On the Writing and Enjoyment of Children's Books.* Little, 1969. Critical essays by a writer for children, with a special emphasis on fantasy.

CARLSON, ATELIA, and GILBERT B. CROFF. *World Folk Tales: A Scribner Resource Collection.* Scribner's, 1980. Provides indexes of tale types, motifs, and parallel stories for each section.

CARLSON, RUTH KEARNEY. *Emerging Humanity: Multi-Ethnic Literature for Children and Adolescents.* Brown, 1972. Describes values of and criteria for multi-ethnic literature, suggests ways to use it. Separate chapters discuss black, American Indian, and Mexican-American books.

————. *Enrichment Ideas: Sparkling Fireflies.* Brown, 1970. For the elementary school classroom teacher, suggestions for dramatization, art projects, language games, and ways of using literature to enrich the curriculum. The suggestions for activities are accompanied by selected references for children and selected references for adults.

CARLTON, LESLIE, and ROBERT H. MOORE. *Reading, Self-Directive Dramatization and Self-Concept.* Merrill, 1968. Reports research results of studies dealing with self-directive dramatization. Chapters on selection of materials are also included.

CARROLL, LEWIS (pseud.). *The Annotated Alice: Alice's Adventures in Wonderland & Through the Looking Glass,* ill. by John Tenniel. With introduction and notes by Martin Gardner. Potter, 1960. Significant quotations from Carroll biographies and other sources are placed parallel to the story text. An enriching background source for students.

CATALDO, JOHN W. *Words and Calligraphy for Children.* Van Nostrand, 1969. Reproductions of paintings, drawings, and designs by children in an art workshop intended to give, through free expression, a familiarity with language symbols. Arranged by age groups.

CATTERSON, JANE H., ed. *Children and Literature.* International Reading Assoc., 1969. A selection of papers from the Association's annual convention that should help teachers, both elementary and high school, bring literature into the curriculum and provide positive literary experience.

CHALL, JEANNE. *Learning to Read: The Great Debate.* McGraw, 1967. The findings of a three-year study on teaching beginning reading with a sober discussion of conclusions and recommendations.

CHAMBERS, AIDAN. *Introducing Books to Children.* Horn Book, 1975. A presentation of the importance of children's literature and of how to introduce it to children.

————. *The Reluctant Reader.* Pergamon, 1969. A lively account by a Britisher of why young people are reluctant to read creative fiction, with suggestions for authors, teachers, publishers, and librarians. Bibliographies for reluctant readers in appendixes.

CHAMBERS, DEWEY W. *Children's Literature in the Curriculum.* Rand, 1971. A "plea" to make children's literature "an integral part of the elementary school's curriculum" and "an important factor in the lives of children." The three sections are "The Role of Literature in the Elementary Curriculum," "How Books Can Affect Children," and "Thoughts on Some Controversial Issues in Children's Literature."

————. *Literature for Children: Storytelling and Creative Drama.* Brown, 1970. Recommendations for organizing storytelling and creative drama sessions are accompanied by discussion of educational implications for those activities.

CHAMBERS, ROBERT. *Popular Rhymes of Scotland.* Singing Tree, 1969. First published in 1826, this work has been revised and expanded several times. The 1870 edition is reproduced in this volume.

CHILD, FRANCIS JAMES, ed. *English and Scottish Popular Ballads,* 5 vols. Houghton, 1882–1898. This is our most authoritative source for all English and Scottish traditional ballads. Many variants are given for each ballad, together with copious notes.

CHILD STUDY ASSOCIATION OF AMERICA. *Insights: A Selection of Creative Literature About Childhood.* Aronson, 1974. Excerpts and short stories about aspects of childhood.

Children's Literature Abstracts. Published quarterly by the Children's Library Section of the International Federation of Library Associations. An abstracting service that focuses primarily on articles in English-language journals.

Chosen for Children: An Account of the Books Which Have Been Awarded the Library Association Carnegie Medal, 1936–1965, rev. ed. London: The Library Assoc., 1967. A discussion of the prize-winning books for children by British authors, with excerpts, illustrations, biographical material, comments by and pictures of the authors.

CHUKOVSKY, KORNEI. *From Two to Five,* tr. and ed. by Miriam Morton. Univ. of Calif. Pr., 1965. A book on the language and comprehension of the very young child written by the dean of Russian children's writers, rich in its insights and observations.

CIANCIOLO, PATRICIA. *Illustrations in Children's Books,* 2nd ed. Brown, 1976. The book deals with art and design as areas of study in the elementary school: styles, techniques, appraisal of illustrations and their use in class. Up-to-date references by chapters, and with bibliography and index.

CIANCIOLO, PATRICIA, and the NATIONAL COUNCIL OF TEACHERS OF ENGLISH, PICTURE BOOK COMMITTEE, eds. *Picture Books for Children.* ALA, 1973. An annotated bibliography for children of all ages, this focuses on illustration rather than text.

CIARDI, JOHN, and MILLER WILLIAMS. *How Does a Poem Mean?* 2nd ed. Houghton, 1975. A college text for the study of poetry in general with an analysis of specific poems.

CLARK, ANN NOLAN. *Journey to the People,* with introduction by Annis Duff, ill. Viking, 1969. Essays about a lifelong experience with teaching Indian children: Zuni, Navajo, Pueblo, and other tribes of the Southwest, as well as the Dakota Sioux and the Indians of Guatemala and Peru.

CLEARY, FLORENCE. *Blueprints for Better Reading: School Programs for Promoting Skill and Interest in Reading.* Wilson, 1970. Offers both inspiration and ideas to teachers and librarians.

CLIFFORD, JAMES L. *From Puzzles to Portraits: Problems of a Literary Biographer.* Univ. of N. Car. Pr., 1970. An approach to biography writing that deals in anecdotal style with such problems as testing authenticity, the fictional method, the pursuit of vague footnotes, and the ethics of the biographer's selectivity.

————. ed. *Biography as an Art.* Oxford, 1962. A most useful collection of forty-seven essays of selected literary criticism by biographers, ranging from writers of the 16th to the mid-20th century, with an additional bibliography of about 150 modern books and articles.

COFFIN, TRISTRAM P. *The British Traditional Ballad in North America.* The American Folklore Society, Bibliographic and Special Series II (1950, 1963). Contains bibliographic listings for all the versions of the traditional (Child) ballads collected in North America.

COGER, LESLIE IRENE, and MELVIN R. WHITE. *Readers Theatre Handbook: A Dramatic Approach to Literature,* 2nd ed. Scott, Foresman, 1973. Provides sample scripts and suggestions for casting and rehearsing Readers Theatre productions.

COHEN, MONROE, ed. *Literature with Children.* Assoc. for Childhood Education International, 1972. A collection of articles.

COLBY, JEAN POINDEXTER. *Writing, Illustrating and Editing Children's Books,* ill. Hastings, 1967. A rewritten and enlarged edition of *The Children's Book Field,* this covers all phases of juvenile publishing and provides a wealth of practical data for authors and illustrators.

COLES, ROBERT. *Children of Crisis.* Atlantic, 1964. Based on the author's interviews with black and white people in the South, a long-term study of children, analyzing their drawings as well as their conversation.

COLES, ROBERT, and MARIA PIERS. *Wages of Neglect.* Quadrangle, 1969. An examination of the behavior of young children of the poor, their special hardships, and social and personal anxieties that determine their behavior.

COLLINGWOOD, STUART DODGSON. *The Life and Letters of Lewis Carroll (Rev. C. L. Dodgson).* Gale Library of Lives and Letters: British Writers Series. Singing Tree, 1967. The biography of Lewis Carroll, written by his nephew shortly after his death, is a primary source book of information about the public and private life of this children's writer.

COLUM, PADRAIC, ed. *A Treasury of Irish Folklore.* Crown, 1954. This book gives insight into Irish history and heroism as well as folklore.

COMENIUS, JOHN AMOS. *The Orbis Pictus of John Amos Comenius.* Singing Tree, 1968. The first children's picture book and the most widely known textbook of the 17th and 18th centuries, reproduced from an 1887 photographic copy of a 1728 London edition, this volume is of interest to educators and historians alike.

COMMIRE, ANNE. *Something About the Author: Facts and Pictures About Contemporary Authors and Illustrators of Books for Young People.* Vol. I. Gale, 1971. The inclusion of biographical information and lists of writings makes this reference series useful to adults.

————. *Yesterday's Authors of Books for Children.* Gale, 1977. Biographical information for some authors deceased before 1961. Discontinued after publication of two volumes; merged with Commire's *Something About the Author* series.

CONRAD, EDNA, and MARY VAN DYKE. *History on the Stage: Children Make Plays from Historical Novels,* ill. with photos. Van Nostrand, 1971. Approaches the making of plays as a teaching technique, from choosing and reading a book and improvising to developing a script, to performance. Can be used by children 11 to 14 as well as by adults.

COODY, BETTY. *Using Literature with Young Children.* Brown, 1973. A practical literature program for young children at home and in school.

COOK, ELIZABETH. *The Ordinary and the Fabulous: An Introduction to Myths, Legends, and Fairy Tales for Teachers and Storytellers.* Cambridge Univ. Pr., 1969. The author undertakes to show that an adult understanding of life is incomplete without an understanding of myths, legends, and fairy tales and that there are many ways of presenting them.

COUGHLAN, MARGARET, comp. *Folklore from Africa to the United States.* Library of Congress, 1976. A bibliography of African tales with annotations that emphasize sources and patterns of diffusion.

CRAVEN, PAUL R. *Biography.* Dickenson Pub. Co., 1968. An introductory textbook, organized under autobiography, journals, obituaries, personality sketches, and extracts from books such as Samuel L. Clemens's *Life on the Mississippi.*

CREIGHTON, HELEN, comp. *Songs and Ballads from Nova Scotia.* Dover, 1966. Includes Scottish and English ballads and folk songs of English and Scottish origin as well as songs native to North America.

CROSBY, MURIEL. *An Adventure in Human Relations.* Follett, 1965. Report of a three-year experimental project in schools in changing neighborhoods, with two main goals: improving the schools through developing appropriate curriculum and in-service teacher training, and upgrading family and community life through the development of indigenous leadership.

CROUCH, MARCUS. *The Nesbit Tradition: The Children's Novel 1945–1970.* Rowman and Littlefield, 1973. A major English critic of children's literature examines, by theme, genre, or setting, the work of contemporary writers of fiction, chiefly British and American.

————. *Treasure Seekers and Borrowers: Children's Books in Britain, 1900–1960.* London: The Library Assoc., 1962. Excellent brief appraisals of authors and books, chiefly British, published during the first sixty years of the twentieth century.

CULLINAN, BERNICE E. *Literature for Children: Its Discipline and Content.* Brown, 1971. For elementary classroom teachers, this book is intended to build effective courses in literature. Well constructed and researched with numerous references for each chapter.

CULLINAN, BERNICE, and CAROLYN CARMICHAEL, eds. *Literature and Young Children.* NCTE, 1977. Essays relating the education of young children to resources in children's literature, including audio-visual materials.

CURRELL, DAVID. *The Complete Book of Puppetry.* Plays, 1975. A comprehensive book on making and using every kind of puppet.

A Curriculum for English. The Nebraska Curriculum Development Center. Univ. of Nebraska Pr., 1966. This excellently worked-out curriculum covers the years of kindergarten through high school and also makes suggestions for the first year of college.

DARLING, RICHARD L. *The Rise of Children's Book Reviewing in America, 1865–1881.* Bowker, 1968. A scholarly and thorough examination of the publishing and reviewing of children's books, set in the historical context. Thirty-six periodicals are examined, including the most important literary periodicals of the time.

DARTON, F. J. H. *Children's Books in England: Five Centuries of Social Life,* 2nd ed. Cambridge Univ. Pr., 1958. A scholarly study of children's books, from the fables to Robert Louis Stevenson. Chapter VII is about John Newbery and the first English books for children.

DAVIS, MARY GOULD. *Randolph Caldecott 1846–1886: An Appreciation.* Lippincott, 1946. An evaluation of the great English artist's contribution to children's literature.

DeANGELI, MARGUERITE. *Butter at the Old Price.* Doubleday, 1971. A grande dame of the children's book world describes, in her autobiography, her long career as an author.

DEL REY, LESTER. *The World of Science Fiction 1926–1976: The History of a Subculture.* Ballantine, 1979. A literary history of the development of science fiction.

De MONTREVILLE, DORIS, and DONNA HILL, eds. *Third Book of Junior Authors.* Wilson, 1972. A companion volume to the Kunitz and Fuller titles cited below, recently supplemented by the *Fourth Book of Junior Authors and Illustrators* (Wilson, 1978), Doris De Montreville and Elizabeth Crawford, eds.

DENNISON, GEORGE. *The Lives of Children: The Story of the First Street School.* Random, 1969. A fascinating account of a free school working with twenty-three students, white, black, and Puerto Rican, all from low-income homes, half of them rejects from the public schools, with severe learning and behavior problems.

DEUTSCH, MARTIN, and others. *The Disadvantaged Child.* Basic, 1967. Selected papers on the social environment for learning, and on such factors as race, social class, and language in the education of the disadvantaged child.

DeVRIES, LEONARD. *Little Wide-Awake: An Anthology from Victorian Children's Books and Periodicals in the Collection of Anne and Fernand G. Renier,* ill. World, 1967. Interesting examples of what was read by children during the sixty years of Victoria's reign.

DeWITT, MARGUERITE E., and others. *Practical Methods in Choral Speaking.* Expression, 1936. A compilation of papers by American teachers covering methods from the primary grades through the university, with many practical suggestions.

DOMAN, GLENN. *How to Teach Your Baby to Read: The Gentle Revolution.* Random, 1964. Work with brain-injured children has led to more complete understanding of how all children learn and the development of a startling reading program.

DONELSON, KENNETH L., and ALLEEN PACE NILSEN. *Literature for Today's Young Adults.* Scott, Foresman, 1980. Provides an excellent balance among historical, practical, and literary approaches to books for the adolescent reader.

DORSON, RICHARD M. *American Folklore.* Univ. of Chicago Pr., 1959. A very readable general survey of prose forms of oral folklore in the United States. Devotes little attention to folksong.

————. *Buying the Wind, Regional Folklore in the United States.* Univ. of Chicago Pr., 1964. A good selection of authentic folklore texts with useful notes and introduction.

————. ed. *Folktales of the World.* Univ. of Chicago Pr. This most impressive series for the student of folklore has been published under the general editorship of Richard Dorson, a professor of history and director of the Folklore Institute at Indiana University. In each volume, his foreword is learned, informative, and beautifully written. The editor for each volume is a distinguished folklorist in his or her own right. The full notes, index of motifs, glossary, bibliography, and general index in each volume add to their usefulness for the scholar. Each book contains from fifty to one hundred tales; several titles are discussed in Chapter 7.

————. ed. *Folktales Told Around the World.* Univ. of Chicago Pr., 1975. Sources are cited for each tale; included are indexes by motif and type, notes on contributors, and a general index.

DOUGLAS, NORMAN. *London Street Games.* Singing Tree, 1968. Greatly expanded from an article published in *English Review* in 1913, this running account of English street life in the early part of the century captures the vocabulary and tone of the children Douglas collected from.

DOYLE, BRIAN, comp. and ed. *The Who's Who of Children's Literature,* ill. Schocken, 1969. Full and lively biographical sketches of authors and illustrators.

DREW, ELIZABETH, and GEORGE CONNOR. *Discovering Modern Poetry.* Holt, 1961. "There is no single 'meaning' to much poetry. Different interpretations are always possible.... Analysis is not destructive, it is creative." These are clues to the authors' approach to the interpretation of modern poetry. Modern authors are examined with an appreciation that should help the most skeptical to a better understanding of modern poetry.

DUFF, ANNIS. *"Bequest of Wings": A Family's Pleasures with Books.* Viking, 1944. A pleasant account of one family's use of books, pictures, and music.

————. *"Longer Flight": A Family Grows Up with Books.* Viking, 1955. Another pleasant, anecdotal account of a family and its reading, and some apt generalizations about what books mean to children and adolescents.

DURKIN, DOLORES. *Teaching Young Children to Read,* 2nd ed. Allyn, 1976. Techniques for teaching language skills and reading to children from preschool through third grade. Includes a discussion of reading readiness.

EASTMAN, MARY HUSE. *Index to Fairy Tales, Myths and Legends.* Faxon, 1926. First supp., 1937; second supp., 1952. Useful for locating various sources in which individual tales may be found. There are geographical and racial groupings and lists for storytellers. See entry for Ireland, Norma.

EASTMAN, MAX. *The Enjoyment of Poetry.* Scribner's, 1921, 1951. This book is an excellent introduction to the pleasures of poetry. Chapter I. "Poetic People," in which he gives his reasons for listing the child as one of the "poetic people," and Chapter V, "Practical Values of Poetry," should be noted.

ECKENSTEIN, LINA. *Comparative Studies in Nursery Rhymes.* London: Duckworth, 1906; reissued, Singing Tree, 1968. A study of the ancient folk origins of the Mother Goose verses and their European counterparts.

EDEN, HORATIA K. F. *Juliana Horatia Ewing and Her Books.* Gale

Library of Lives and Letters: British Writers Series. Singing Tree, 1969. The biography of Juliana Horatia Ewing (1841–1885), her letters, and a bibliography, compiled by the younger sister of this esteemed writer for children.

EGOFF, SHEILA. *The Republic of Childhood: A Critical Guide to Canadian Children's Literature in English.* Oxford, 1967. Creative writing for children by Canadian authors between the years of 1950 and 1965.

EGOFF, SHEILA, G. T. STUBBS, and L. F. ASHLEY, eds. *Only Connect: Readings on Children's Literature,* ill. Oxford, 1969. A compilation of essays by well-known, competent writers and critics covering literary criticism and history, standards, changing tastes, children's responses, writers and their writing, and illustration.

ELLIS, ALEC. *A History of Children's Reading and Literature.* Pergamon, 1968. History of schools, educational practice, and library development in England.

ELLIS, ANNE W. *The Family Story in the 1960's.* Archon Books & Clive Bingley, 1970. A survey, with comments on trends, on family stories, almost all of British origin, published during the decade. Good commentary and checklist.

ENGEN, RODNEY. *Kate Greenaway.* Harmony Books, Crown, 1976. A brief discussion of Greenaway's work is followed by pages of reproductions from original editions of her best-known books.

———. *Randolph Caldecott: Lord of the Nursery.* Oresko, 1976. A historical essay accompanies reproductions of Caldecott's illustrations for children's books and some of his drawings for newspapers and periodicals.

———. *Walter Crane as a Book Illustrator.* St. Martin's, 1975. A short essay places Crane in his historical and artistic context, and introduces reproductions of his work. Color plates are outstanding for their vividness.

ERIKSON, ERIK H. *Childhood and Society,* 2nd ed., rev. and enl. Norton, 1964. The noted psychoanalyst's summary of his studies of childhood, emphasizing the importance of early experiences in the development of adult attitudes and actions.

ERNEST, EDWARD, comp., assisted by PATRICIA TRACY LOWE. *The Kate Greenaway Treasury,* ill. World, 1967. A biography of Kate Greenaway, an evaluation of her art, a fine essay about her work by the late Anne Carroll Moore, and an introduction by Ruth Hill Viguers, make this rich collection the definitive study of a beloved children's book illustrator.

ESBENSEN, BARBARA JUSTER. *A Celebration of Bees: Helping Children Write Poetry.* Winston Press, 1975. An informally written guide by an experienced teacher.

EVERTTS, ELDONNA, ed. *Explorations in Children's Writing.* Nat. Council of Teachers of English, 1970. Papers growing out of a conference on teaching elementary English, in which teachers discuss experiences with children's writing.

EYRE, FRANK. *British Children's Books in the Twentieth Century.* Dutton, 1973. A revised edition of the 1952 title, *20th Century Children's Books,* this historical survey discusses trends and includes an extensive divided bibliography.

FADER, DANIEL N., and ELTON B. MCNEIL. *Hooked on Books: Program and Proof.* Putnam. 1968. A detailed description of a program to get bored and apathetic students to read, accompanied by a description of a research project evaluating the program.

FAVAT, F. ANDRÉ. *Child and Tale: The Origins of Interest.* NCTE, 1977. Report on research exploring the psychology of children's interest in fairy tales.

FEAVER, WILLIAM. *When We Were Young: Two Centuries of Children's Book Illustration.* Holt, 1977. Features a potpourri of illustrations from children's books over the past two hundred years, with a concise historical essay.

FEITELSON, DINA, ed. *Cross-Cultural Perspectives on Reading and Reading Research.* International Reading Association, 1978. Essays reflecting research in reading from an international perspective.

FELDMAN, EDMUND BURKE. *Becoming Human Through Art: Aesthetic Experience in the School,* ill. Prentice, 1970. An interdisciplinary approach to visual education, primarily for teachers and teachers of teachers.

FENNER, PHYLLIS. *The Proof of the Pudding.* Day, 1957. An entertaining discussion of many books children enjoy.

———. ed. *Something Shared: Children and Books.* Day, 1959. A spirited compilation from many authors interested in children and books offers genuine entertainment as well as inspiration.

FENWICK, SARA INNIS, ed. *A Critical Approach to Children's Literature.* Univ. of Chicago Pr., 1967. Collected papers from a conference on children's literature, representing a variety of aspects.

FIELD, CAROLYN W., ed., with VIRGINIA HAVILAND and ELIZABETH NESBITT, consultants. *Subject Collections in Children's Literature.* Bowker, 1969. Identifies and publicizes special collections of children's literature, especially for those interested in research.

FIELD, ELINOR WHITNEY, comp. *Horn Book Reflections: On Children's Books and Reading.* Selected from eighteen years of *The Horn Book Magazine*—1949–1966. Horn Book, 1969. Contributors are writers, illustrators, teachers, librarians, and parents.

FIELD, LOUISE F. *The Child and His Book: Some Account of the History and Progress of Children's Literature in England.* Singing Tree, 1968. An important scholarly work tracing the history of English books for children from before the Conquest to the 19th century, this book is also a social history of England.

FISHER, MARGERY. *Intent Upon Reading.* Watts, 1962. A refreshing and critical approach to children's books, both recent and standard selections. Though many of the titles are English publications, a great number are familiar to American readers.

———. *Matters of Fact: Aspects of Non-Fiction for Children.* T. Crowell, 1972. An excellent guide to evaluative criteria.

———. *Who's Who in Children's Books.* Holt, 1975. A guide to characters and personalities in children's literature; entries describe the character, the book or books in which the character appeared, and the way the author achieved a successful characterization.

FOLMSBEE, BEULAH. *A Little History of the Horn Book.* Horn Book, 1942. A tiny book, beautifully printed, with a history of hornbooks, in all their variations, both in England and New England.

FORD, PAUL LEICESTER, ed. *The New England Primer.* Dodd, 1897, 1962. The subtitle explains the content: "A history of its origin with a reprint of the unique copy of the earliest known first edition."

FORD, ROBERT. *Children's Rhymes, Children's Games, Children's Songs, Children's Stories: A Book for Bairns and Big Folk.* Singing Tree, 1968. The collection is a pioneer effort of the late 19th century to record the natural literature of the children of Scotland; it includes nursery and counting-out rhymes, rhyme games, songs and ballads, anecdotes, and stories.

FORDYCE, RACHEL. *Children's Theatre and Creative Dramatics: An Annotated Bibliography of Critical Works.* Hall, 1975. A most useful compilation of pertinent articles and books.

FOSTER, FLORENCE P., comp. *Literature and the Young Child.* N.J. Dept. of Education, 1967. Criteria for selecting books for young children, techniques for reading aloud and storytelling, and suggestions for stimulating interest.

FOX, GEOFF, ed. *Writers, Critics and Children.* Agathon, 1976. An anthology of provocative articles from the journal, *Children's Literature in Education.*

FRANK, JOSETTE. *Your Child's Reading Today,* rev. and updated. Doubleday, 1969. Sensible advice from a pioneer in the child study movement concerning a child's reading, given from the standpoint of the child's social-emotional development. Don't deprecate children's tastes, she advises, but capitalize on reading enjoyment.

FRASER, JAMES H., ed. *Society and Children's Literature.* David R. Godine, 1978. Collected papers from a 1976 symposium on the history of children's literature.

FRAZER, SIR JAMES GEORGE. *The Golden Bough: A Study in Magic and Religion,* 1 vol. abr. ed. Macmillan, 1922. First published in 1890, this is a monumental study (originally 13 volumes) in comparative folklore, magic, and religion.

FREEMAN, LA VERNE, and RUTH SUNDERLIN FREEMAN. *The Child and His Picture Book,* ill. Century House, 1967. A reissue of a pioneer study, updated with particular attention to methods for using picture books to help underprivileged preschoolers and kindergartners get a head start toward successful school adjustment.

FRIEDMAN, ALBERT B. *The Viking Book of Folk Ballads of the English Speaking World.* Viking, 1956. Contains many ballads, with useful notes.

FRYATT, NORMA R., ed. *A Horn Book Sampler.* Horn Book, 1959. Selected articles on authors, artists, and books that appeared in *The Horn Book Magazine* between 1924 and 1948 provide illuminating background to some of the most significant years in children's book publication.

FRYE, BURTON C., ed. *A St. Nicholas Anthology: The Early Years,* ill. Meredith, 1969. A selection from the years 1870 to 1905 of stories, articles, and poems, as well as illustrations which appeared in this most beloved of all children's magazines.

FULLER, MURIEL, ed. *More Junior Authors.* Wilson, 1963. Companion volume to *The Junior Book of Authors,* 1951, rev. ed. Contains biographical material on current juvenile authors and illustrators not included in that work. See also De Montreville and Kunitz entries.

Funk and Wagnalls Standard Dictionary of Folklore, Mythology and Legend, ed. by Maria Leach and Jerome Fried, 2 vols. Funk, 1949. Working with a staff of internationally known folklorists and anthropologists, the editors have compiled an invaluable source on national folklores, characters, and symbols in folklore and mythology.

FURTH, HANS G. *Piaget for Teachers.* Prentice, 1970. A clearly written discussion of Piaget's developmental theories as they relate to observation of children.

GERSONI-STAVN, DIANE, ed. *Sexism and Youth.* Bowker, 1974. An anthology of fifty previously published articles.

GESELL, ARNOLD, and FRANCES ILG. *Child Development: An Introduction to the Study of Human Growth.* Harper, 1949. This research study considers child growth in its broadest sense—intellectual, emotional, and social—from infancy through adolescence. Lucid style and revealing case histories make this a readable and essential book for parents and teachers.

GESELL, ARNOLD, and others. *The First Five Years of Life: A Guide to the Study of the Preschool Child.* Harper, 1940. Discusses the nature of mental growth, developmental changes, and such facets of growth as language development and personal-social behavior.

GILLESPIE, MARGARET C. *Literature for Children: History and Trends.* Brown, 1970. Covering time from the 15th century to the present, the book has chapters on fantasy, poetry, realism (catechisms, religion, manners, primers, etc.), and landmarks of publishing, with selected references and index. For elementary teachers.

GILLIES, EMILY. *Creative Dramatics for All Children.* ACEI, 1973. Includes suggestions for the use of creative drama in the classroom and means for involving handicapped children.

GLASSER, WILLIAM. *Schools Without Failure.* Harper, 1969. This book presents suggestions for making "involvement, relevance, and thinking realities in our schools . . . combined into a total program they can provide a foundation upon which to build the schools our children need."

GODDEN, RUMER. *Hans Christian Andersen: A Great Life in Brief.* Knopf, 1955. "Life itself is the most wonderful fairy tale." So wrote Andersen, and no one could have told his fairy tale more poignantly than Rumer Godden, the English novelist.

GOODRIDGE, JANET. *Creative Drama and Improvised Movement for Children.* Plays, 1971. Practical techniques, tested in schools and studios, for teaching creative drama and correlating it with other school subjects, such as English, physical education, music, and art.

GORUCH, RICHARD L. "Moral Education from a Psychological View of Man as an Ethical Being." *The Educational Forum* (January 1973): 173. Discusses the moral development of people from youth to adulthood, including Kohlberg's stages of moral development.

GOTTLIEB, GERALD. *Early Children's Books and Their Illustration.* Godine, 1975. Witty and erudite commentary accompanies beautiful reproductions of books in the collection of the Pierpont Morgan Library.

GREEN, PERCY B. *A History of Nursery Rhymes.* Singing Tree, 1968. Detailed explanations of children's games, potentially useful to kindergarten and nursery school teachers as well as parents.

GREEN, PETER. *Kenneth Grahame,* ill. with photos. World, 1959. This very welcome biography is authoritatively and perceptively written.

GREEN, ROGER LANCELYN. *Tellers of Tales,* enl. ed. E. Ward, 1953; reissued, Watts, 1965. This is a delightfully written discussion of English authors of children's books. Only twenty pages are devoted to modern writers.

GRIMM, JACOB and WILHELM. *Grimm's Fairy Tales,* tr. by Margaret Hunt, rev. by James Stern, ill. by Josef Scharl. Pantheon, 1944. The "Introduction" by Padraic Colum and "Folkloristic Commentary" by Joseph Campbell are important contributions.

GUERBER, HELENE A. *Myths of Greece and Rome.* American Bk., 1893; reissued, British Book Center, 1963. A standard reference, retelling and reinterpreting the myths.

GULLAN, MARJORIE. *The Speech Choir.* Harper, 1937. This is one of the most useful of all Gullan's books because it is both an anthology as well as a methods text. It contains American poetry as well as English ballads, with a detailed description of the presentation and development of each poem. Most of the poems are for upper-grade children and the high schools.

HALES, JOHN W., and FREDERICK J. FURNIVALL, assisted by FRANCIS J. CHILD. *Bishop Percy's Folio Manuscript.* London: Trübner, 1967. Here are the ballads that Bishop Percy found, together with the reproduction of an actual page of the manuscript with Percy's notes scribbled in the margin.

HALLIWELL-PHILLIPPS, JAMES O. *Popular Rhymes and Nursery Tales: A Sequel to the Nursery Rhymes of England.* Singing Tree, 1968. This mid-nineteenth-century book is a collection of material of interest to folklorists as well as teachers and librarians.

HALSEY, ROSALIE V. *Forgotten Books of the American Nursery: A History of the Development of the American Story-Book.* Singing Tree, 1969. A reissue of a book first published at the turn of the century, this volume traces the history of children's books in America from colonial days to the early part of the nineteenth century, with emphasis on the light children's books shed on the social history of the country.

HASKINS, JAMES. *Diary of a Harlem Schoolteacher.* Grove, 1969. A year's notes kept by a black teacher and author show starkly the educational deficiencies and social problems that affect Harlem children's learning.

HAVILAND, VIRGINIA. *Children's Literature: A Guide to Reference Sources,* ill. Library of Congress, 1966. The only reference tool of its kind in scope and coverage, this book offers bibliographic guidance to books available today and to the history of children's literature. First supplement, 1972. Second supplement, 1977.

———. ed. *Children and Literature: Views and Reviews.* Scott, Foresman, 1973. An anthology reprinting many classic essays and articles central to a study of children's literature.

HAVILAND, VIRGINIA, and MARGARET COUGHLAN, comps. *Yankee Doodle's Literary Sampler of Prose, Poetry, & Pictures.* T. Crowell, 1974. A sampling of writing and illustration drawn from the collection of the Library of Congress.

HAZARD, PAUL. *Books, Children and Men,* tr. by Marguerite Mitchell, 4th ed. Horn Book, 1960. A member of the French Academy and professor of comparative literature both in France and in the United States has written engagingly of the great children's books of many countries.

HEARN, MICHAEL. *The Annotated Wizard of Oz.* Potter, 1973. The text and original drawings for Baum's *The Wonderful Wizard of Oz* are reproduced, illuminated by notes describing the author's life, the history of the Oz books, and the social philosophy of Oz.

HEINS, PAUL, ed. *Crosscurrents of Criticism: Horn Book Essays 1968–1977.* Horn Book, 1977. A compilation of essays which appeared originally in *Horn Book.* treating diverse themes and trends in children's literature.

HELMS, RANDALL. *Tolkien's World.* Houghton, 1974. A discussion of the relevance of Tolkien's writings as mythic literature.

HENTOFF, NAT. *Does Anybody Give a Damn?* Knopf, 1977. A highly readable polemic on the failings of the American educational system.

———. *Our Children Are Dying.* Four Winds, 1967. An account of the problems and challenges of education, set in a public school in Harlem. Compare and contrast with John McPhee's *The Headmaster,* set in a private boys' boarding school.

HEWINS, CAROLINE M. *A Mid-Century Child and Her Books.* Singing Tree, 1969. The autobiography of a pioneer children's librarian who was also the author of many books on children's literature, this book provides a detailed picture of what life was like for a book-loving child in New England in the mid-nineteenth century.

HIGGINS, JAMES E. *Beyond Words: Mystical Fancy in Children's Literature.* Teachers College Pr., 1970. The author discusses the importance of mystical fantasy in the development of the child and its significance as a literary form, with special detailed analysis of the work of such great authors as George Macdonald, W. H. Hudson, Saint-Exupéry, Tolkien, and C. S. Lewis.

HILDICK, WALLACE. *Children and Fiction.* World, 1971. A critical study of the artistic and psychological factors involved in writing fiction for and about children, suggesting the application of high standards in examining children's literature both from the literary and the sociological point of view.

HILLYER, ROBERT. *In Pursuit of Poetry.* McGraw, 1960. A distinguished poet and winner of the Pulitzer Prize, Hillyer has written an entrancing introduction to the appreciation of poetry, old and modern, with unforgettable examples from some of the finest English poetry.

HODGART, M. J. C. *The Ballads.* Hutchinson's Universal Library, 1950. Useful general discussion of the traditional ballads, stressing the literary approach.

HOFFMAN, MIRIAM, and EVA SAMUELS, eds. *Authors and Illustrators of Children's Books: Writings on Their Lives and Works.* Bowker, 1972. A compilation of articles from magazines gives more depth than many of the briefer entries in other sources, although the coverage is not as broad.

HOLT, JOHN. *How Children Fail.* Pitman, 1964. An important book, based on records of classroom experience, dealing with the ways children meet or dodge the demands adults make on them, the interaction between fear and failure, the difference between what children are expected to know and what they really know, and finally how the schools fail to meet the real needs of children.

———. *How Children Learn.* Pitman, 1967. This book, written in journal form about the reactions of various children in games, experiments, reading, talking, and being involved in arts and math, throws light on using their minds effectively and on the relationship between encouragement and progress in learning.

———. *What Do I Do Monday?* Dutton, 1970. A school teacher's innovative observations on modern education and theories of the learning process, supported by ideas, exercises, and examples in several subjects.

HOPKINS, LEE BENNETT. *The Best of Book Bonanza.* Holt, 1980. Suggestions for the creative use of children's literature in conjunction with special occasions, seasons, and holidays.

———. *Books Are by People,* ill. Citation, 1969. Human interest interviews with 104 writers and illustrators for children, to be used with children to make their authors "come alive."

———. *Let Them Be Themselves.* Citation, 1969. Recommendations for enriching the language arts curriculum for all children, but especially the disadvantaged.

———. *More Books by More People.* Citation, 1974. Interviews with 65 children's authors give information about the author's work and his or her personal life.

HUBER, MIRIAM BLANTON. *Story and Verse for Children,* ill. Macmillan, 1965. With introductory chapters on the selection and history of children's books, followed by an anthology of poetry and prose, this book is intended primarily for teachers, librarians, and parents.

HUCK, CHARLOTTE S. *Children's Literature in the Elementary School,* 3rd ed., ill. Holt, 1976. A reorganized and updated revision of a well-known textbook.

HUDSON, DEREK. *Arthur Rackham: His Life and Work.* London: Heinemann, 1960, 1974. A biography that includes perceptive analysis of Rackham's art, with a fully annotated bibliography.

HUGHES, TED. *Poetry Is.* Doubleday, 1970. Based on a series of BBC talks, a discussion of poetry intended for young writers, but interesting for poetry readers as well.

HUNTER, MOLLIE. *Talent Is Not Enough.* Harper, 1976. A

thoughtful exploration of the responsibilities of writing for children. Included is an essay on historical fiction.

HÜRLIMANN, BETTINA. *Picture-Book World*, ed. and tr. by Brian Alderson, ill. World, 1969. Modern picture books for children from 24 countries, with introductory chapters on particular countries and with a bio-bibliographical supplement.

――――. *Seven Houses: My Life with Books*. T. Crowell, 1977. An autobiographical account of the author's lifelong involvement with international children's book publishing.

――――. *Three Centuries of Children's Books in Europe*, ed. and tr. by Brian Alderson, ill. World, 1968. A comparative study as well as a history which includes a survey of contemporary books for children in all of the countries of Europe.

HUTCHINS, MICHAEL, ed. *Yours Pictorially: Illustrated Letters of Randolph Caldecott*. Warne, 1977. Caldecott's chatty letters, with companion sketches, give insights into his life, his art, and the world in which he lived.

HUTT, S. J., and CORINNE, eds. *Early Human Development*. Oxford, 1973. A collection of studies on various aspects of early human behavior.

HYMES, JAMES LEE. *Understanding Your Child*. Prentice, 1952. This is a practical and entertaining discussion of child behavior and parent-child conflicts. It is built around these four major considerations: children grow, there is a plan to their growth, they want things out of life, and there is a reason for their behavior.

ILG, FRANCES L., and LOUISE BATES AMES. *Child Behavior*. Harper, 1955. Frances Ilg, M.D., and Louise Ames, Ph.D., give direct advice, based on their research at the Gesell Institute, to parents concerning problems of child behavior.

IRELAND, NORMA. *Index to Fairy Tales, 1949–1972: Including Folklore, Legends and Myths in Collections*. Faxon, 1973. A supplement to the Eastman indexes, which indexed fairy tales through 1948. A useful addition, this indexes material in collections, not single tales.

JACOBS, JOSEPH. See listings of his collections of English, Celtic, and Indian folk tales in the Chapter 7 bibliography. They contain significant introductions, and the notes in each appendix are treasures of folklore information.

JACOBS, LELAND B., ed. *Using Literature with Young Children*. Teachers College Pr., 1965. A collection of papers on providing good literature for young children, storytelling, reading aloud, poetry, choral speaking, dramatization, and relating literature to other school experiences.

JAN, ISABELLE. *On Children's Literature*. Schocken, 1974. Extended essays on the appeals of literature to children, focusing on the work of French and British authors. Translated from the French.

JENKINS, GLADYS GARDNER. *Helping Children Reach Their Potential*. Scott, Foresman, 1961. Describes how teachers have handled the particular emotional needs and problems of their pupils.

JENKINS, GLADYS GARDNER, HELEN S. SHACTER, and WILLIAM W. BAUER. *These Are Your Children*, 4th ed. Scott, Foresman, 1975. A series of case studies with charts of normal child development and the special needs of children at various ages, enlivened by photographs of children in problem situations or normal activities.

JOHNSON, DIANA L. *Fantastic Illustration and Design in Britain, 1850–1930*. Rhode Island School of Design, 1979. The catalog for an exhibition of the work of British illustrators, including Rackham, Crane, and Potter.

JOHNSON, EDNA, EVELYN SICKELS, and FRANCES CLARKE SAYERS. *Anthology of Children's Literature*, 4th ed. Houghton, 1970. The editors in this latest edition have attempted to hold to the long view, choosing from the present that which gives promise of lasting value and fitting it into the interstices of the proven past.

JOHNSON, FERNE. *Start Early for an Early Start*. ALA, 1976. An analysis of the role of literature and libraries in the child's development, stressing parental involvement.

JORDAN, ALICE M. *From Rollo to Tom Sawyer*. Horn Book, 1948. Here in beautiful format with decorations by Nora Unwin are twelve little essays on some of the most important nineteenth-century writers for children.

JOSEPH, STEPHEN M., ed. *The Me Nobody Knows: Children's Voices from the Ghetto*. Avon, 1969. Moving and revealing writing by children, mostly black and Puerto Rican, in the most impoverished city neighborhoods.

KAMM, ANTONY, and BOSWELL TAYLOR. *Books and the Teacher*. Univ. of London Pr., 1966. A handbook on the choice, requisition, and use of books. References are to British authors and publishers, and organizations listed are also exclusively British.

KARL, JEAN. *From Childhood to Childhood: Children's Books and Their Creators*. Day, 1970. An editor's views on children's books.

KELLOGG, RHODA, and SCOTT O'DELL. *The Psychology of Children's Art*, ill. Random, 1967. Selected examples from a collection of over a million pieces of children's art, accompanied by text explaining the developmental phases common to all children.

KIEFER, MONICA. *American Children Through Their Books, 1700–1835*. Univ. of Penn. Pr., 1948, 1970. The American child at the beginning of the 18th century was too insignificant for physicians to waste time on, the author tells us. She traces the child's developing place in the world through an examination of children's books.

KINGMAN, LEE, ed. *The Illustrator's Notebook*. Horn Book, 1978. A valuable collection of articles by and about children's book illustrators, drawn from the pages of *The Horn Book*.

――――, ed. *Newbery and Caldecott Medal Books: 1956–1965*. Horn Book, 1965. A biographical sketch of each author or illustrator, along with his or her acceptance paper and related material from *The Horn Book*.

――――, ed. *Newbery and Caldecott Medal Books: 1966–1975*. Horn Book, 1975. A companion volume to others in the series of acceptance speeches and articles taken from the magazine.

KINGMAN, LEE, JOANNA FOSTER, and RUTH GILES LONTOFT, comps. *Illustrators of Children's Books, 1957–1966*, ill. Horn Book, 1968. This volume, a supplement to *Illustrators of Children's Books, 1744–1945*, and *Illustrators of Children's Books, 1946–1956*, reviews the decade, offers biographies of active illustrators and a bibliography of their works.

KINGMAN, LEE, GRACE HOGARTH, and HARRIET QUIMBY. *Illustrators of Children's Books, 1967–1976*. Horn Book, 1978. Continues the Horn Book series on illustrators.

KINGSTON, CAROLYN. *The Tragic Mode in Children's Literature*. Teachers College Pr., 1974. Dicusses tragedy in realistic fiction for ages 8–12, using books published before 1970.

KIRK, GEOFFREY S. *Myth*. Univ. of Calif. Pr., 1970. Discusses the function of myth in various cultures.

KIRKPATRICK, DANIEL, ed. *Twentieth-Century Children's Writers*. St. Martin's, 1978. Biographical information, including lists of publications, for over six hundred English language authors of children's literature.

KITTREDGE, GEORGE LYMAN, ed. *English and Scottish Popular Ballads: Student's Cambridge Edition*, ed. by Helen Child Sargeant. Houghton, 1904. This is the invaluable one-volume edition of the Child collection. It contains the 305 ballads, a few variants of each, brief notes, and the excellent glossary giving the definitions and pronunciations of the difficult ballad words.

KLEMIN, DIANA. *The Art of Art for Children's Books,* ill. Potter, 1966. Examples and commentary on the work of sixty-four illustrators of children's books.

————. *The Illustrated Book: Its Art and Craft,* ill. Potter, 1970. A contemporary survey with examples and commentary on the work of seventy-four artists. A chapter on drawing for reproduction is included, which clarifies the process involved in printing.

KOCH, KENNETH. *Rose, Where Did You Get That Red?* Random, 1973. Koch explains his own successful approach to teaching adult poetry to children. Includes sample lessons and an anthology of poetry recommended for this use.

————. *Wishes, Lies, and Dreams: Teaching Children to Write Poetry,* ill. with photos. Random, 1971. Working with the children of P.S. 61 in New York City, the author, himself an outstanding poet, has developed ways of getting children to release their ideas and feelings into writing. The book is a collection of their poetry preceded and accompanied by his description of his teaching methods.

KOHL, HERBERT R. *The Open Classroom: A Practical Guide to a New Way of Teaching.* New York Review, 1969. Primarily addressed to public school teachers, this book is a "handbook for teachers who want to work in an open environment. . . . [and] is based upon the experience of teachers: their problems, failures, and frustrations, as well as their successes."

————. *Teaching the Unteachable: The Story of an Experiment in Children's Writing.* New York Review, 1967. An innovative approach to teaching in East Harlem, illustrated by examples of the children's writing.

————. *36 Children,* ill. by Robert George Jackson. New Am. Lib., 1967. The author's experiences in a sixth-grade Harlem classroom demonstrate the progress that children can make when a good teacher meets their needs.

KRAPPE, ALEXANDER HAGGERTY. *The Science of Folk-Lore.* Dial, 1930. This book covers various types of folk literature, evaluates theories of origin and content, and analyzes motives. Chapter IX, "The Popular Ballad," discusses the ballad as part of the great stream of folklore, related to the epic, the carol, and the folk tale, migrating even as they have.

KREIDER, BARBARA. *Children's Plays in Collections.* Scarecrow, 1972. An interalphabetized author, title, and subject listing. Plays are also listed by cast size; no listings are annotated.

KUJOTH, JEAN SPEALMAN. *Reading Interests of Children and Young Adults.* Scarecrow, 1970. A collection of research findings and observations by teachers, authors, and librarians on reading interests and how they are influenced. Divided by age groups.

KUNITZ, STANLEY J., and HOWARD HAYCRAFT, eds. *The Junior Book of Authors,* 2nd ed. Wilson, 1951. Biographical sketches of outstanding authors and illustrators of books for children. See also De Montreville and Fuller entries.

LAMME, LINDA LEONARD. "Song Picture Books—A Maturing Genre of Children's Literature," *Language Arts* 56 (April 1979): 400–407. Describes films and books of lullabies, animal songs, and folk songs and suggests means of involving young children with these song picture books. Useful print and non-print bibliographies.

LANDECK, BEATRICE. *Learn to Read: Read to Learn: Poetry and Prose from Afro-Rooted Sources.* McKay, 1975. Suggestions for broadening and enriching the approach to teaching reading, writing, and speech in the elementary school.

LANE, MARGARET. *The Magic Years of Beatrix Potter.* Warne, 1978. A close look at the most intensely creative period of Potter's life, before her marriage. During this time the majority of her books for Warne were published, and her talent probably reached its zenith.

————. *The Tale of Beatrix Potter: A Biography,* ill. Warne, 1968. Revised and updated, with new material from the secret code journals of Beatrix Potter.

LANES, SELMA G. *Down the Rabbit Hole: Adventures and Misadventures in the Realm of Children's Literature,* ill. Atheneum, 1971. A series of essays, by an editor of children's books, exploring the literary and artistic merits of a particular selection of books. A small bibliography of choice books is appended.

LANG, ANDREW, ed. *Perrault's Popular Tales.* London: Clarendon, 1888. A careful study of Perrault and the tales he edited.

LARKIN, DAVID, ed. *The Art of Nancy Ekholm Burkert.* Harper, 1977. An exquisite volume containing color reproductions of Burkert's work from children's books as well as some previously unpublished paintings, drawings and sculptures. An interpretive essay was written by Michael Danoff.

————, ed. *Once Upon a Time: Some Contemporary Illustrators of Fantasy.* Peacock/Bantam, 1976. The work of fifteen illustrators is pictured here in brilliant color; some pages fold out. The introductory essay suggests that the artist is "emerging as a true author in tales of fantasy where every picture tells a story."

LARRICK, NANCY. *A Parent's Guide to Children's Reading,* rev. and enl. 4th ed., ill. Doubleday, 1975. Sponsored by the National Book Committee, this is a comprehensive handbook for parents' use in developing reading interests from infancy on.

————. *A Teacher's Guide to Children's Books,* ill. Merrill, 1960. How to stimulate and develop reading interests in the elementary grades, accompanied by extensive bibliographies for the child and the teacher.

————, ed. *Somebody Turned on a Tap in These Kids.* Delacorte, 1971. A lively collection of articles on changing the attitudes and expectations of young people toward poetry, with liberal examples of what they like and what they write themselves.

LEACH, MacEDWARD. *Folk Ballads and Songs of the Lower Labrador Coast.* Ottawa: Queen's Printer and Controller of Stationery, 1965.

————, ed. *The Ballad Book.* Harper, 1955. Gives about 250 ballads, many in several variants. The major section is "Ballads of England and Scotland with American and Danish Variants." "American Ballads by Origin and Adoption" contains forty-five ballads. The headnotes to each ballad are useful and a general introduction gives a brief survey of ballad scholarship.

LEAR, EDWARD. *Lear in the Original: 110 Drawings for Limericks and Other Nonsense.* Kraus, 1975. Facsimile reproductions of Lear's drawings, some previously unpublished, with explanatory notes by Herman Liebert.

LENNON, FLORENCE BECKER. *Victoria Through the Looking-Glass.* Simon, 1945; reissued as *The Life of Lewis Carroll,* Collier Books, 1962, paperback. A fine biography of Lewis Carroll.

LEPMAN, JELLA. *A Bridge of Children's Books,* tr. by Edith McCormick. ALA, 1969. Fascinating autobiographical account of bringing books of all nations to the children of postwar Germany to replace their Nazi-oriented literature.

LEWIS, C. S. *Of Other Worlds: Essays and Stories,* ed. by Walter Hooper. Harcourt, 1966. A posthumous collection which includes essays on fantasy and science fiction, three unpublished short stories, and the first chapters of a novel.

LIEBERT, ROBERT, JOHN NEALE, and EMILY DAVIDSON. *The Early*

Window: Effects of Television on Children and Youth. Pergamon, 1973. A survey of studies done on content of programs and their effects on children.

LINDSTROM, MIRIAM. *Children's Art: A Study of Normal Development in Children's Modes of Visualization,* ill. Univ. of Calif. Pr., 1970. Illustrated study of stages of development in expression of visual imagery.

LINES, KATHLEEN, ed. *Walck Monographs.* Walck. Personal anecdotes and a pleasing style make these brief biographies and critical evaluations of internationally known authors invaluable to the teacher or student of children's literature. The series includes:
Louisa M. Alcott, Cornelia Meigs
J. M. Barrie, Roger Lancelyn Green
Lucy Boston, Jasper Rose
Lewis Carroll, Roger Lancelyn Green
Walter de la Mare, Leonard Clark
Eleanor Farjeon, Eileen H. Colwell
Kenneth Grahame, Eleanor Graham
Rudyard Kipling, Rosemary Sutcliff
Andrew Lang, Roger Lancelyn Green
C. S. Lewis, Roger Lancelyn Green
John Masefield, Margery Fisher
Mrs. Molesworth, Roger Lancelyn Green
Beatrix Potter, Marcus Crouch
Howard Pyle, Elizabeth Nesbitt
Arthur Ransome, Hugh Shelley
Ruth Sawyer, Virginia Haviland
Noel Streatfeild, Barbara Ker Wilson
Rosemary Sutcliff, Margaret Meek
Geoffrey Trease, Margaret Meek

LIVINGSTON, MYRA COHN. *When You Are Alone/It Keeps You Capone: An Approach to Creative Writing with Children.* Atheneum, 1973. An insightful discussion by a well-known children's poet.

LOMAX, JOHN A., ed. *Songs of the Cattle Trail and Cow Camp.* Duell, 1950.

LOMAX, JOHN A., and ALAN LOMAX, comps. *American Ballads and Folk Songs.* Macmillan, 1946.

————, eds. *Cowboy Songs and Other Frontier Ballads,* rev. and enl. Macmillan, 1948. The Lomax collections of our native ballads are of major importance as sources, not only because they were the first ones made, but also because they were gathered firsthand and the tunes were recorded on wax cylinders, on the spot, unedited.

LOWNDES, BETTY. *Movement and Creative Drama for Children.* Plays, 1971. A description of the movement and drama work carried on in an infants' school in North London with an emphasis on how both can be used to get children to communicate and to learn with enjoyment.

LUKENS, REBECCA. *A Critical Handbook of Children's Literature.* Scott, Foresman, 1976. A discussion of the criteria for, and elements of, imaginative literature for children.

LURIE, ALISON, and JUSTIN SCHILLER, eds. "Classics of Children's Literature 1621–1932," Garland. A series of photofacsimile editions of hard-to-find books. The 117 titles include books by Bunyan, Edgeworth, Grahame, Goodrich, Lang, Molesworth, and others.

LÜTHI, MAX. *Once Upon a Time: On the Nature of Fairy Tales.* Indiana Univ. Press, 1976. Uses familiar tales as examples in probing analyses of the form and content of fairy tales, their style, symbolism, and relationship to legend and primitive tales.

LYSTAD, MARY. *From Dr. Mather to Dr. Seuss: 200 Years of American Books for Children.* G. K. Hall, 1980. An exploration of social values expressed in American children's books since the colonial period. The author uses graphs to measure changes in social values and views of children, based on the sample of books evaluated.

MacCANN, DONNARAE, and OLGA RICHARD. *The Child's First Books.* Wilson, 1973. A discussion of the role of picture books in the history of children's literature.

MacCANN, DONNARAE, and GLORIA WOODWARD, eds. *The Black American in Books for Children: Readings in Racism.* Scarecrow, 1972. A broad selection of brief essays, with notes on contributors.

McGUFFEY, WILLIAM HOLMES. *Old Favorites from the McGuffey Readers,* ed. by Harvey C. Minnich. Singing Tree, 1969. Selections from all six of the readers are of special interest to students of educational and social history.

MacLEOD, ANNE SCOTT. *A Moral Tale: Children's Fiction and American Culture 1820–1860.* Archon, 1975. Explores the concepts and the concerns of a period of rapid change as reflected in the stories for children, especially what adults expected of children and wanted for them.

McPHEE, JOHN. *The Headmaster: Frank L. Boyden of Deerfield.* Farrar, 1966. An account of the problems and challenges of education, set in a private boys' boarding school. Compare with Nat Hentoff's *Our Children Are Dying,* set in a public school in Harlem.

MAHONY, BERTHA E., and ELINOR WHITNEY FIELD. eds. *Newbery Medal Books, 1922–1955.* Horn Book, 1955. Here in one handsome volume are brief biographies of Newbery authors along with their acceptance speeches. See also supplementary volumes by Kingman.

MAHONY, BERTHA E., LOUISE P. LATIMER, and BEULAH FOLMSBEE, comps. *Illustrators of Children's Books, 1744–1945.* Horn Book, 1947. A superb history of illustration in children's books considered as a part of the whole stream of art. Many pictures are reproduced from early books as well as from more recent ones. A major reference. See also supplementary volumes by Viguers and others and by Kingman and others.

MAHONY, BERTHA E., and ELINOR WHITNEY, comps. *Contemporary Illustrators of Children's Books.* Gale, 1978. Originally published in 1930. Includes a directory of children's illustrators with essays on trends in illustrating, as they were perceived in the first quarter of this century.

MAIER, HENRY W. *Three Theories of Child Development: The Contributions of Erik H. Erikson, Jean Piaget and Robert R. Sears, and Their Applications,* rev. ed. Harper, 1969. The expanded psychoanalytic theory of Erikson, Piaget's theories on the development of behavior, and those of Robert Sears are explicated and compared, and the last two chapters deal with how they can be used in working with children. A useful bibliography is appended.

MAY, JILL P. "Encouraging Children's Creative Oral Responses Through Nonnarrative Films," *Language Arts* 56 (March 1979): 244–50. Discusses the use of films to encourage response and to introduce children to some characteristics of literature such as theme and plot.

MAYERSON, CHARLOTTE LEON, ed. *Two Blocks Apart: Juan Gonzales and Peter Quinn,* ill. with photos by the Still Photography Workshop Harlem Youth Unlimited. Holt, 1965. Biographies, from tapes, of two boys in New York, living in the same neighborhood, going to the same school, sharing the same religion, one white middle class, the other Puerto Rican, members of two cultures separated by social and economic conditions.

MEACHAM, MARY. *Information Sources in Children's Literature.* Greenwood, 1978. A comprehensive guide to book selection tools, review sources, and reference aids.

MEEK, MARGARET, AIDAN WARLOW, and GRISELDA BARTON, eds. *The Cool Web: The Pattern of Children's Reading.* Atheneum, 1978. Deeply perceptive essays on the nature of the reading process, approaches to writing for children, perspectives on criticism, and suggested areas for further research.

MEEKER, ALICE M. *Enjoying Literature with Children.* Odyssey, 1969. A book for parents and teachers, with annotated bibliographies for the preschool years, for the culturally deprived, storytelling, poetry, choral speaking, holidays, and teachers' browsing. Though short, the book is full of practical suggestions for helping children enjoy books.

MEIGS, CORNELIA, ANNE EATON, ELIZABETH NESBITT, and RUTH HILL VIGUERS. *A Critical History of Children's Literature,* rev. ed. Macmillan, 1969. Three librarians and an author of children's books have surveyed the field from ancient to recent times. The evaluations of books, authors, illustrators, and trends make this a valuable reference.

MILLAR, SUSANNA. *The Psychology of Play.* Penguin, 1968. Chapter V, "Phantasy, Feeling, and Make-Believe Play."

MILLER, BERTHA MAHONY, and ELINOR WHITNEY FIELD, eds. *Caldecott Medal Books: 1938–1957.* Horn Book, 1957. Stories of artists who have won awards for the most distinguished picture book of each year, together with their acceptance speeches. An invaluable source for schools and libraries. See also supplementary volume by Kingman.

MOE, CHRISTIAN, and DARWIN REID PAYNE, eds. *Six New Plays for Children.* Southern Ill. Pr., 1971. This is an interesting collection of new plays for child audiences.

MONSON, DIANNE, and DAYANN MCCLENATHAN, eds. *Developing Active Readers: Ideas for Parents, Teachers, and Librarians.* IRA, 1979. Each chapter considers means of developing children's responses to literature, some focusing on the experiences of preschool children and others dealing with children on through early adolescence.

MONSON, DIANNE L., and BETTE J. PELTOLA, comps. *Research in Children's Literature: An Annotated Bibliography.* International Reading Association, 1976. Includes abstracts of over 170 doctoral studies and ERIC documents, along with citations to journal articles, monographs, and theses pertaining to children's literature.

MONTGOMERIE, NORAH. *To Read and to Tell,* ill. by Margery Gill. Arco Pub. Co., 1964. Fairy stories, folk tales, fables, and legends from many lands.

MOORE, ANNE CARROLL. *A Century of Kate Greenaway.* Warne, 1946. An appreciation of the artist and her distinctive contribution.

———. *My Roads to Childhood.* Doubleday, 1939. A distinguished librarian and critic of children's books comments on outstanding books up to the year 1938.

MOORE, VARDINE. *Pre-School Story Hour,* 2nd ed. Scarecrow, 1972. A discussion of the techniques, programming, and physical arrangements for the story hour, and a chapter on the needs and characteristics of the preschool child is followed by a subject-oriented bibliography and a chapter on games and rhythmic play.

MOORMAN, CHARLES. *Kings & Captains: Variations on a Heroic Theme.* Univ. Press of Kentucky, 1971. A fresh look at the classic hero tales of western civilization.

MORRIS, RONALD. *Success and Failure in Learning to Read,* rev. ed. Penguin, 1973. Various aspects of the reading process are examined. Introduction and appendixes are valuable commentaries in themselves.

MUIR, PERCY. *English Children's Books, 1600 to 1900.* Praeger, 1954, 1969. Muir acknowledges his indebtedness to the books of Darton and the Opies, but his work adds to both. There are excellent indexes and lavish illustrations from the books discussed.

MUNCH, PETER A. *Norse Mythology, Legends of Gods and Heroes,* rev. by Magnus Olsen, tr. by Sigurd B. Hustvedt. American-Scandinavian Foundation, 1926; reissued, Singing Tree, 1968. Authoritative and complete interpretation of sources.

MYRUS, DONALD. *Ballads, Blues, and the Big Beat.* Macmillan, 1966. A survey of the singers and the songs of today, with separate chapters on musical genres.

NICHOLSEN, MARGARET. *People in Books: A Selective Guide to Biographical Literature Arranged by Vocations and Other Fields of Reader Interest.* Wilson, 1969. Appended: an index by century and by country; an index to autobiographical books; and an index of persons about whom a book or part of a collective biography is included in the main section.

OLLILA, LLOYD O., ed. *The Kindergarten Child and Reading.* International Reading Association, 1977. Reports research appraising recent efforts to teach beginning reading skills at the kindergarten level.

OMOTOSO, SAM. "Storytelling: A Cherished Cultural Heritage in Nigeria," *Language Arts* 55 (September 1978): 724–27. Discusses the storytelling tradition in Nigeria and its benefits to children.

Once upon a time . . . , rev. ed. New York Library Assoc., 1964. Help for librarians with preschool hours, picture-book hours, and story hours. Suggested programs and bibliographies are included.

OPIE, IONA and PETER. *Children's Games in Street and Playground.* Oxford, 1969. This record of the games children play draws its authority from more than 10,000 children in England, Scotland, and Wales.

———. *The Lore and Language of Schoolchildren.* Oxford, 1959; Oxford paperbacks, 1967. "The curious lore passing between children about 6–14, which today holds in its spell some 7 million inhabitants" of Great Britain includes rhymes, riddles, childhood customs, and beliefs. Some can traced back for generations and others are current. "The present study is based on the contributions of some 5000 children attending 70 schools."

———, comps. *A Family Book of Nursery Rhymes,* ill. by Pauline Baynes. Oxford, 1964. In addition to the rhymes, this contains excellent notes on origins.

———, eds. *The Oxford Dictionary of Nursery Rhymes.* Oxford, 1951. This is the most exhaustive and scholarly study yet made of the origins of the nursery rhymes, their earliest recordings, and variations through the years. Copious illustrations from old plates add to its real interest.

The Original Mother Goose's Melody, As First Issued by John Newbery, of London, about A.D. 1760. Reproduced in Facsimile from the Edition as Reprinted by Isaiah Thomas of Worcester, Mass., about A.D. 1785, with Introductory Notes by William H. Whitmore. Singing Tree, 1969. Whitmore's introductory notes discuss the origin, development, and popularity of the Mother Goose rhymes in this reprint.

OVID. *The Metamorphoses,* tr. by Henry T. Riley. McKay, 1899. A literal prose translation of the Latin versions of the Greek myths and hero tales, with copious notes explaining their fable or allegorical significance.

PAINTER, HELEN W. *Poetry and Children.* International Reading Association, 1970. An explanatory guide to the use of poetry with children.

PERRAULT, CHARLES. *Perrault's Complete Fairy Tales,* tr. by A. E. Johnson and others, ill. by W. Heath Robinson. Dodd,

1961. The unabridged fairy tales of Perrault, together with tales by Mme. de Beaumont and Mme. d'Aulnoy.

Phaedrus: An International Journal of Children's Literature. Published three times a year by K. G. Saur. Articles and abstracts.

PIAGET, JEAN. *Language and Thought of the Child,* tr. by Marjorie Gabain. London: Routledge and Kegan Paul, 1932. Piaget describes his own observations of children's growth in language and thought.

PIAGET, JEAN, and BARBEL INHELDER. *The Psychology of the Child,* tr. from the French by Helen Weaver. Basic, 1969. A comprehensive summary of Piaget's child psychology, tracing the stages of cognitive development over the entire period of childhood, from infancy to adolescence.

PILGRIM, GENEVA HANNA, and MARIANNA McALLISTER. *Books, Young People, and Reading Guidance.* Harper, 1968. For use by teachers, librarians, and parents, and also as a college text. Emphasis is chiefly on contemporary books.

PINES, MAYA. *Revolution in Learning: The Years from Birth to Six.* Harper, 1967. A report on the growing number of research projects on increasing intellectual growth in childhood.

PITZ, HENRY C. *Howard Pyle: Writer, Illustrator, Founder of the Brandywine School.* Potter, 1975. A generously illustrated biography of Pyle, following his career as both an author and an artist.

———. *Illustrating Children's Books: History, Technique, Production.* Watson-Guptill, 1963. Detailed and authoritative, profusely illustrated, a book that is particularly useful for its lucid explanations of techniques of art reproduction and how the artist prepares his work.

———. *The Practice of American Book Illustration.* Watson-Guptill, 1947.

———, ed. *A Treasury of American Book Illustration.* Watson-Guptill, 1947. A distinguished artist discusses illustration as one of the seven lively arts. With many pictures from modern sources he proves his point. The second volume contains a good chapter on "Pictures for Childhood."

Plays, the Drama Magazine for Young People. Plays, Inc. 8 Arlington Street, Boston, Mass. 02116. This useful magazine is published monthly, October through May. Each issue, in addition to providing plays for lower grades, middle grades, and junior and senior high, always has a special feature—a dramatized classic, a radio play, or material for an assembly.

POST, ROBERT M. "Children's Readers Theatre," *Language Arts* 56 (March 1979): 262–67. Suggestions for adapting scenes from stories and for helping children develop characterization.

POUND, LOUISE, ed. *American Ballads and Songs.* Scribner's, 1922, 1969. A good collection of United States remnants of old ballads along with our native compositions. No music. Excellent introduction.

———. *Poetic Origins and the Ballad.* Macmillan, 1921; Russell and Russell, 1961. The author furnishes lively evidence against the communal origin of the ballad, besides adding ballad history.

POWER, EFFIE. *Bag O'Tales: A Source Book for Story-Tellers,* ill. by Corydon Bell. Dutton, 1969. Stories for little children, folk tales, myths, and tales of heroes and chivalry, with good lists of source material for the storyteller at the end of each section.

PURVES, ALAN C. "Research in the Teaching of Literature." *Elementary English* (April 1975): 463–66. Reports an analysis of responses made by children, grades 3 to 12, to literary selections.

———, ed. *How Porcupines Make Love: Notes on a Response-Centered Curriculum.* Xerox College Publications, 1972. A response-centered handbook of suggestions for guiding the literary experience.

PURVES, ALAN C., and RICHARD BEACH. *Literature and the Reader: Research in Response to Literature, Reading Interests, and the Teaching of Literature.* Nat. Council of Teachers of English, 1972. Each of the three areas is treated separately, with a discussion of the factors, instruments, and quality of studies that have been made, followed by a very extensive bibliography. The citations for Reading Interests run 34 pages, for example. A most useful survey.

PURVES, ALAN C., with VICTORIA RIPPERE. *Elements of Writing About a Literary Work: A Study of Response to Literature.* NCTE, 1968. A cataloguing of elements of literary response, classified as emotional, perception, interpretation, and evaluation responses.

QUAYLE, ERIC. *The Collector's Book of Children's Books,* photos by Gabriel Monro. Potter, 1971. Profusely illustrated with pictures of old books, a history of British and American children's books that is erudite and enthusiastic, emphasizing early books.

QUIMBY, HARRIET, CLARA JACKSON, and ROSEMARY WEBER. *Building a Children's Literature Collection.* Choice, 1975. *Choice* Bibliographic Essay Series, No. 3. This useful paperback consists of two parts: a suggested reference collection for academic libraries, consisting of guides and background reading for a children's literature collection, and a suggested basic collection of children's books.

RANK, OTTO. *The Myth of the Birth of the Hero: A Psychological Interpretation of Mythology,* tr. by F. Robbins and Smith Ely Jellife. Brunner/Mazel, 1952. A classic exposition of the connection between the form of myths and the unconscious emotions of the child. Studies the myths of the birth of the hero from Moses to Lohengrin, interpreting each myth in terms of the Oedipus complex.

READ, HERBERT. *This Way, Delight.* Pantheon, 1956. An excellent anthology, mentioned here because of its unusual introduction in which the author defines poetry and gives practical suggestions for writing it.

REES, DAVID. *The Marble in the Water.* Horn Book, 1980. A collection of essays on contemporary writers of fiction for children and young adults, by a British critic.

RIBNER, IRVING, and HARRY MORRIS. *Poetry: A Critical and Historical Introduction.* Scott, Foresman, 1962. Designed to help the beginning poetry reader read with greater understanding and appreciation.

RICHARD, OLGA. "The Visual Language of the Picture Book." *Wilson Library Bulletin,* December 1969. A discussion of criteria by which to evaluate picture book art.

RICHARDSON, ELWYN. *In the Early World.* Pantheon, 1969. Written by a New Zealand teacher, this is an exploration of the stimulation of activity and creativity, particularly with reference to appreciation of nature and particularly expressed in the children's writing. Good book on teaching; good book on children's expression of appreciation of the world around them.

ROBINSON, EVELYN ROSE. *Readings About Children's Literature.* McKay, 1966. Excerpts from books, magazines, journals, and newspapers providing an understanding of the child as a reader, criteria for book selection, and appropriate materials. Contributors are well-known writers, librarians, and teachers of children's literature.

ROSELLE, DANIEL. *Samuel Griswold Goodrich, Creator of Peter Parley: A Study of His Life and Work,* ill. State Univ. of N.Y., 1968. The Peter Parley books, now largely forgotten, entertained children in the first half of the 19th century with cautionary tales, instructive fables, and reports of strange lands.

ROSENBACH, ABRAHAM S. W. *Early American Children's Books with Bibliographical Descriptions of the Books in His Private Collection,* foreword by A. Edward Newton. Southworth Pr., Portland, Me., 1933; Dover (paperback), 1971. Facsimile pages and illustrations (many in color) of American children's books published between 1732 and 1836. Probably the greatest and most comprehensive book on juvenile Americana.

ROSENBLATT, LOUISE M. *Literature as Exploration,* rev. ed. Noble, 1969. A probing evaluation of the nature of the literary experience.

ROSS, ELINOR P. "Comparing Folk Tale Variants," *Language Arts* 56 (April 1979): 422–26. Suggestions for generating discussions that point out similarities and differences among folk-tale variants.

ROWE, MARY BUDD. "Reflections on Wait-time: Some Methodological Questions." *Journal of Research in Science Teaching* (1974): 263–79. Discusses research concerned with the effect of thinking time on children's ability to respond to questions about science concepts.

RUDDELL, ROBERT B. *Reading Language Instruction: Innovative Practices.* Prentice, 1974. A text about reading instruction which operates from a language development base and includes instruction in language arts, including literature.

RUDMAN, MASHA KABAKOW. *Children's Literature: An Issues Approach.* Heath, 1976. Extensive annotated book lists accompany discussions of recent themes (divorce, war, sex) in children's books.

SADKER, MYRA POLLACK and DAVID MILLER. *Now Upon a Time: A Contemporary View of Children's Literature.* Harper, 1977. A topical approach to children's literature: fiction and nonfiction are integrated and grouped by subject matter.

ST. JOHN, JUDITH. *The Osborne Collection of Early Children's Books 1566–1910: A Catalogue,* introduction by Edgar Osborne. Toronto Public Library, 1958; vol. 2, 1976. Descriptive notes on this world-famous collection, illustrated with many facsimiles. Fascinating background material for scholars and students of children's literature.

SALE, ROGER. *Fairy Tales and After: From Snow White to E.B. White.* Harvard Univ. Press, 1978. A highly personalized literary criticism, linking the development of fantasy in children's literature to fairy tales.

SALWAY, LANCE, ed. *A Peculiar Gift.* Penguin, 1976. (Kestrel Books) An anthology of essays on children's literature written by or about authors of the 19th century.

SANDBURG, CARL, ed. *The American Songbag.* Harcourt, 1927. While this collection borrows from others, Sandburg's illuminating notes make it a particularly useful and enjoyable volume.

SANDERS, THOMAS E. *The Discovery of Poetry.* Scott, Foresman, 1967. An introduction to the aesthetics of poetry, this book discusses how poetry is written and how it can be read in the same creative way.

SARAFINO, EDWARD P., and JAMES W. ARMSTRONG. *Child and Adolescent Development.* Scott, Foresman, 1980. Good basic coverage of child and adolescent development.

SAWYER, RUTH. *My Spain: A Storyteller's Year of Collecting.* Viking, 1967. Pleasant account of a journey through Spain in search of folk tales.

———. *The Way of the Storyteller.* Viking, 1942, 1962. Informally written in Ruth Sawyer's fine style, this is a contribution both to the art of storytelling and to the history of the old tales.

SAXTON, MARTHA. *Louisa May.* Houghton, 1977. A striking and original reinterpretation of Louisa May Alcott's life.

SAYERS, FRANCES CLARKE. *Summoned by Books: Essays and Speeches by Frances Clarke Sayers,* comp. by Marjeanne Jenson Blinn. Viking, 1965. Essays by an outstanding and influential children's librarian.

SCHOLES, ROBERT, and ERIC S. RABKIN. *Science Fiction: History, Science, Vision.* Oxford Univ. Press, 1977. A literary history of science fiction, with analyses of predominant themes.

SCHOOL LIBRARY JOURNAL/LIBRARY JOURNAL. *Issues in Children's Book Selection.* Bowker, 1973. A broad array of provocative writings on many aspects of book selection.

SCHWAB, GUSTAV. *Gods and Heroes,* tr. by Olga Marx and Ernst Morwitz, ill. with designs from Greek vases. Pantheon, 1946. This large, handsome book is not comprehensive, and the English translation from a German adaptation is not always satisfactory, but it is an excellent source nevertheless.

SCOTT, JOHN ANTHONY. *The Ballad of America: The History of the United States in Song and Story.* Grosset, 1966. Chronologically arranged, with musical notation and with substantial comment on the background for each selection.

SEBESTA, SAM LEATON. "The Neglected Art: Thought Questions." *Elementary English* (December 1967): 888–95. Describes the use of the point-of-view question and other questioning techniques.

SEBESTA, SAM L., and WILLIAM J. IVERSON. *Literature for Thursday's Child.* Science Research Associates, 1975. Intended primarily for the classroom teacher, this volume intermingles descriptions of genres in children's literature with suggestions for curricular applications.

SHAFTEL, FANNIE R., and GEORGE SHAFTEL. *Role-Playing for Social Values: Decision-Making in the Social Studies.* Prentice, 1967. Describes procedures for guiding role-playing experiences and includes stories developed for role-playing.

SHAPIRO, JON, ed. *Using Literature & Poetry Affectively.* International Reading Association, 1979. Essays exploring children's reactions to reading, and uses of literature and poetry to stimulate their interest.

SHARP, CECIL J., comp. *English Folk-Songs from the Southern Appalachians,* ed. by Maud Karpeles, rev. and enl., 2 vols. Oxford, 1953. A major contribution by an English collector and musician.

———. *Nursery Songs from the Appalachian Mountains,* 2 vols. London: Novello, 1921–1923. A collection that should be better known in our schools. Many selections for the youngest children.

SHAW, JOHN MACKAY. *Childhood in Poetry: A Catalogue,* with Biographical and Critical Annotations, of the Books of English and American Poets Comprising the Shaw Childhood in Poetry Collection in the Library of the Florida State University, with Lists of the Poems that Relate to Childhood, 5 vols. Gale, 1967. Although the price of this work makes it inaccessible to many individuals and small libraries, it is a comprehensive bibliographic guide to English-language children's poetry.

SHEDLOCK, MARIE. *Art of the Story-Teller,* 3rd ed., bibl. by Eulalie Steinmetz. Dover, 1951. Guidance in selection of material, techniques of storytelling, and useful bibliographies are included.

SIKS, GERALDINE BRAIN. *Creative Dramatics.* Harper, 1958. Various suggestions for encouraging children to use their imaginations in dramatization.

SILBERMAN, CHARLES E. *Crisis in the Classroom: The Remaking of American Education.* Random, 1970. Addressed to laymen and professionals alike, its four parts include: The Educating Society, What's Wrong with the Schools, How the Schools Should Be Changed, and The Education of Educators. A fascinating account based on a three-and-a-half-year study commissioned by the Carnegie Corporation of New York.

SINGER, DOROTHY G., and TRACEY A. REVENSON. *A Piaget Primer: How a Child Thinks.* International Universities Press, Inc., 1978. A lucid clarification of Piaget's theories of child development for the beginning student in psychology, enlivened by passages from children's literature.

SMITH, DORA V. *Fifty Years of Children's Books,* with an introduction by Muriel Crosby, ill. Nat. Council of Teachers of English, 1963. From Dora Smith's years of experience with children and books, she has selected and discussed significant titles which appeared between 1910 and 1959. Numerous illustrations are reproduced from the original books.

SMITH, IRENE. *A History of the Newbery and Caldecott Medals.* Viking, 1957. Excellent historical background material on two major annual awards for distinguished children's books in the United States.

SMITH, JAMES STEEL. *A Critical Approach to Children's Literature.* McGraw, 1967. A serious, careful analysis of children's books as creative literary works.

SMITH, LILLIAN. *The Unreluctant Years.* ALA, 1953; reissued, Viking, 1967. A Canadian librarian writes discerningly of children's literature from the standpoint of literary quality only.

SMITH, RUTH, ed. *The Tree of Life,* ill. by Boris Artzybasheff. Viking, 1942. A distinguished text for a comparative study of religious ideas. It is a compilation of the "testaments of beauty and faith from many lands." Excerpts from the expressions of religious ideals of the Navaho Indians, the Norse, Hindu, Buddhist, Confucian, and other religions (including the Hebrew and Christian) make up the content of the book, which is for adolescents or for adults to use with older children.

Some British Ballads, ill. by Arthur Rackham. Dodd, 1920. This is a superb edition for home and school.

SOUTHALL, IVAN. *A Journey of Discovery: On Writing for Children.* Macmillan, 1976. Six essays by Southall setting forth his perspective on children's literature and defending controversial aspects of his own books for children.

SPACHE, GEORGE D. *Parents and the Reading Program.* Garrard, 1965. Suggestions for a program to inform parents on what is involved in teaching pupils to read; a question-and-answer format is used.

SQUIRE, JAMES, ed. *Response to Literature: Dartmouth Seminar Paper No. 6.* NCTE, 1968. Selected papers from the Dartmouth conference discuss various aspects of children's experiences with literature.

————. *The Responses of Adolescents While Reading Four Short Stories.* NCTE, 1964. A report of research which elicited and classified the responses of adolescents to short stories.

STEWART, CHRISTINA. *The Taylors of Ongar: An Analytical Bio-Bibliography,* 2 vols. Garland, 1975. A superb source of information about the works of the prolific family that included Isaac, Jane, and Ann.

STEWIG, JOHN WARREN. *Read to Write: Using Children's Literature as a Springboard to Writing.* Hawthorn, 1975. A description of a writing program designed to help children improve their ability by becoming conscious of the nature of the writing process.

STEWIG, JOHN WARREN, and SAM L. SEBESTA, eds. *Using Literature in the Elementary Classroom.* NCTE, 1978. A collection of articles discussing means that elementary teachers may use to create interest in and understanding of literature.

STIRLING, MONICA. *The Wild Swan: The Life and Times of Hans Christian Andersen.* Harcourt, 1965. Thoroughly documented, a serious and mature study of Andersen's life and work.

STIRLING, NORA. *Who Wrote the Classics?* 2 vols., ill. Day, 1965, 1968. Short biographies of nineteen English and American writers.

STRICKLAND, RUTH G. *The Language Arts in the Elementary School,* 3rd ed., ill. Heath, 1969. Comprehensive treatment of all aspects of language development with three chapters on reading.

SUTHERLAND, ZENA. *The Arbuthnot Lectures 1970–1979.* ALA, 1980. The first ten years of a lecture series established by Scott, Foresman, with a brief biography of Mrs. Arbuthnot.

TANYZER, HAROLD, and JEAN KARL, eds. *Reading, Children's Books and Our Pluralistic Society.* International Reading Association, 1972. An array of essays on problems of prejudice in children's books, and the difficulties of providing literature for and about minorities in America.

TARG, WILLIAM, ed. *Bibliophile in the Nursery.* World, 1969. Articles by scholars, collectors, and authors have been combined into a delightful whole, highlighting developments in children's literature and the joys of collecting. Lavishly illustrated.

TATLOCK, JESSIE M. *Greek and Roman Mythology.* Appleton, 1917. Although intended for high-school study, this is a useful book for teachers. Tatlock retells the myths, gives excerpts from the "Homeric Hymn" and modern poetry, and presents some fine photographs of Greek sculpture.

Teaching Literature in Wisconsin. Wisconsin English Language Arts Curriculum Project. State of Wisconsin Department of Public Instruction, 1965. (Madison) A carefully developed approach to a literature curriculum for kindergarten through grade twelve.

Teaching Reading Through Children's Literature: Proceedings of the 1971 First Annual Reading Conference, June 21–22. Curriculum Research and Developmental Center, School of Education, Indiana State University, Terre Haute. Articles include "Role Playing in Children's Literature and Its Effect Upon the Affective Domain of Children's Thinking," "Teaching Reading Through the Use of Films and Children's Literature," and "Reading the Pictures in Children's Books."

TERRY, ANN. *Children's Poetry Preferences: A National Survey of Upper Elementary Grades.* Nat. Council of Teachers of English, 1974. Results of a survey in which students in over 500 classes participated.

THOMAS, KATHERINE ELWES. *The Real Personages of Mother Goose.* Lothrop, 1930. Scholarly research into the historical origins of the Mother Goose rhymes as political diatribes, religious philippics, and popular street songs.

THOMAS, R. MURRAY, and SHERWIN G. SWARTOUT. *Integrated Teaching Materials,* rev. ed. McKay, 1963. Designed to help teachers improve their skills in choosing, creating, and using audiovisual teaching materials, including reading sources, this book also presents specific classroom illustrations—both verbal and photographic—which add to its practicality.

THOMPSON, STITH. *The Folktale.* Dryden, 1946. A standard work in the field discusses the nature and forms of folk tales, traces their spread, analyzes types, describes the north American Indian folk tale in detail, and examines studies of folk tales.

————, comp. *One Hundred Favorite Folktales*. Indiana Univ. Pr., 1968. Tales chosen by a famous folklorist "as the result of more than a half century of almost daily familiarity with these tales." (p. xi)

THWAITE, MARY. *From Primer to Pleasure in Reading*, 2nd ed. London: The Library Assoc., 1972. A history of English children's books from the invention of printing to 1914, with some material on developments in other countries.

TOOZE, RUTH. *Storytelling*. Prentice, 1959. Extensive bibliographies add to the value of this helpful guide for storytellers.

TOWNSEND, JOHN ROWE. *A Sense of Story*. Longmans, 1971. An analysis of the work of nineteen writers of children's books, American, British, and Australian, with some notes by the authors on their own writing, and short biographical notes.

————. *A Sounding of Storytellers*. Lippincott, 1979. A companion volume to *A Sense of Story*, above, overlapping but also adding new material.

————. *Written for Children: An Outline of English Children's Literature*, rev. ed., ill. Lothrop, 1974. A short, selective survey of prose for British children from its beginnings to today.

TRAVERS, PAMELA L. *About the Sleeping Beauty*. McGraw, 1975. Six versions of the story are accompanied by an essay in which it is analyzed as a part of a discussion of fairy tales.

TREASE, GEOFFREY. *Tales Out of School: A Survey of Children's Fiction*, 2nd ed. Dufour, 1964. A highly personal, entertaining, critical survey of juvenile fiction.

TUCKER, NICHOLAS, ed. *Suitable for Children? Controversies in Children's Literature*. Univ. of California Press, 1976. A selection of excerpts, historic and contemporary, addressing various issues in children's literature.

TUER, ANDREW W. *Pages and Pictures from Forgotten Children's Books: Brought Together and Introduced to the Reader*, ill. Singing Tree, 1969. The introduction offers a description of the various methods used to illustrate children's books published in England in the 18th and 19th centuries: wood blocks, copper plates, and stone lithographs.

————. *Stories from Old-Fashioned Children's Books: Brought Together and Introduced to the Reader*. Singing Tree, 1968. A collection of old children's stories, by a nineteenth-century publisher.

TUROW, JOSEPH. *Getting Books to Children: An Exploration of Publisher-Market Relations*. ALA, 1978. A discussion of children's book publishing for the library and for mass markets, using a case study approach.

VANCE, LUCILLE, and ESTHER TRACEY. *Illustration Index*, 2nd ed. Scarecrow, 1966. A topical index to illustrations in periodicals such as *Life*, *National Geographic*, and *American Heritage*, ranging from abacus to Zurich.

VIGUERS, RUTH HILL. *Margin for Surprise: About Books, Children, and Librarians*. Little, 1964. Essays by a dedicated and enthusiastic children's librarian.

VIGUERS, RUTH HILL, MARCIA DALPHIN, and BERTHA MAHONY MILLER, comps. *Illustrators of Children's Books, 1946–1956*. Horn Book, 1958. An outstanding supplement to *Illustrators of Children's Books, 1744–1945*. Includes art trends, artists' biographies, and a wealth of illustrations from modern children's books.

Volsunga Saga: The Story of the Volsungs and Niblungs, with Certain Songs from the Elder Edda, tr. by Eirikr Magnusson and William Morris. London: Walter Scott, n.d. This prose translation of the difficult verse form of the *Elder Edda* is easy to read and is the basis for Morris's beautiful verse version of the saga. (In 1962, Collier Bks. published a paperback version using the Morris translation.)

WAGGONER, DIANA. *The Hills of Faraway: A Guide to Fantasy*. Atheneum, 1978. Types of literary fantasy are analyzed and compared in this imaginative exposition, which includes annotated book lists of fantastic literature.

WAGNER, JOSEPH A. *Children's Literature Through Storytelling*. Brown, 1970. Includes suggestions for preparing and using visual aids and puppets as well as guidelines for telling stories.

WALSH, FRANCES, ed. *That Eager Zest: First Discoveries in the Magic World of Books*. Lippincott, 1961. Almost 50 delightful verses and sketches about their own childhood reading experiences by such well-known writers as Carl Sandburg, James Thurber, Sherwood Anderson, and Lewis Mumford.

WARD, MARTHA E., and DOROTHY A. MARQUARDT. *Authors of Books for Young People*, 2nd ed. Scarecrow, 1971. Biographical sketches of authors.

————. *Illustrators of Books for Young People*. Scarecrow, 1970. Biographical information about 370 illustrators of books for children.

WARD, WINIFRED. *Playmaking with Children from Kindergarten Through Junior High School*, 2nd ed. Prentice, 1957. Procedures and suggested materials for developing extemporaneous drama.

WEISS, HARRY B. *A Book About Chapbooks: The People's Literature of Bygone Times*, ill. Singing Tree, 1969. A history of chapbooks, their printers, authors, and salesmen, with reproductions of woodcuts and title pages.

WELSH, CHARLES. *A Bookseller of the Last Century, Being some Account of the Life of John Newbery, and of the Books he published with a Notice of the later Newberys*. London: Griffith, Farran, 1885; reissued, Singing Tree, 1969. A readable history of Newbery, his famous bookshop, and his varied activities.

————, ed. *The Renowned History of Little Goody Two Shoes, Otherwise Called Mrs. Margery Two Shoes*, attributed to Oliver Goldsmith. Heath, 1930.

WHALLEY, JOYCE IRENE. *Cobwebs to Catch Flies: Illustrated Books for the Nursery and Schoolroom, 1700–1900*. Univ. of Calif. Pr., 1975. Profusely illustrated, a text that focuses on instructional works.

WHITE, DOROTHY MARY NEAL. *About Books for Children*. Oxford, 1947. Although the author selects predominantly British children's books, she also discusses many American publications.

————. *Books Before Five*, ill. by Joan Smith. Oxford, 1954. A New Zealand children's librarian's study of her two-year-old daughter's progression in the experience of books over three years, ranging over more than 100 books, from Adams's *First Things* to Tolkien's *The Hobbit*.

WHITE, VIRGINIA, and EMERITA SCHULTE. *Books About Children's Books: An Annotated Bibliography*. International Reading Association, 1979. The coverage and special features of books about children's literature are given detailed descriptions in this inclusive bibliography.

WHITEHEAD, ROBERT. *Children's Literature: Strategies of Teaching*. Prentice, 1968. Specific practices which help the teacher present an attractive and effective program in literature.

WILKIN, BINNIE TATE. *Survival Themes in Fiction for Children and Young People*. Scarecrow, 1978. Not only life-and-death themes, but also loneliness, fear, and related subjects are presented; an analysis of each topic is supplemented by annotated book lists.

WILLIAMS, SIDNEY H., and FALCONER MADAN. *The Lewis Carroll Handbook*, rev. and enl. by Roger Lancelyn Green. Oxford, 1962. A valuable and comprehensive bibliography of Lewis Carroll's own writings and what others have written about his life and works. Descriptive notes are comprehensive and scholarly.

WILSON, BARBARA KER. *Writing for Children: An English Editor and Author's Point of View.* Watts, 1960. Sound comment on writing fiction, nonfiction, and picture books.

WILSON, ROY R. *Teaching Children Language Arts.* Parker Pub. Co., 1970. Wilson says that the purpose of his book is to provide practical, imaginative ideas—specifics to try as well as ideas to stir the reader's thinking about "what needs to be done in the language arts classroom."

WINN, MARIE. *The Plug-In Drug: Television, Children and the Family.* Viking, 1977. Examines the effects of television-watching on children and their family relationships.

WINTLE, JUSTIN, and EMMA FISHER. *The Pied Pipers.* Paddington, 1975. Interviews in question-and-answer format with American and British writers of children's books.

WITUCKE, VIRGINIA. *Poetry in the Elementary School.* Brown, 1970. An illuminating treatment of strategies for generating interest in poetry, with generous references and un-hackneyed selections of examples, including audiovisual materials.

WOLSCH, ROBERT A. *Poetic Composition Through the Grades: A Language Sensitivity Program. Practical Suggestions for Teaching.* ed. by Alice Miel. Teachers College Pr., 1970. A teacher's handbook for teaching poetry writing in the elementary school.

WYNDHAM, LEE. *Writing for Children and Teen-Agers.* Writer's Digest, 1968. Practical, detailed advice presented in a lively style and covering all phases of writing children's books, marketing them, and seeing them through publication, by a woman who is herself a prolific writer for children.

Yale French Studies: The Child's Part. Yale Univ. Pr., 1969. A collection of essays exploring children's literature as a vast subspecies, attention to which can illuminate culture, society, literature itself.

YARDLEY, ALICE. *Young Children Thinking.* Citation, 1973. A British educator discusses the mental development of young children, giving suggestions for adding intellectual dimensions to the child's education.

YOLEN, JANE. *Writing Books for Children.* The Writer, Inc., 1973. Discusses genres and the children's book market as well as the literary, financial, and legal aspects of writing books.

Appendix C: Publishers and Their Addresses[1]

ABELARD. Abelard-Schuman, 666 Fifth Ave., New York, NY 10019

ABINGDON. Abingdon Pr., 201 Eighth Ave. S., Nashville, TN 37202

ABRAMS. Harry N. Abrams, Inc., 110 E. 59th St., New York, NY 10022

ACADEMIC. Academic Press, Inc., 111 Fifth Ave., New York, NY 10003

ADDISON. Addison-Wesley Pub. Co., Inc., Jacob Way, Reading, MA 01867

ALA. American Library Assoc., Pub. Dept., 50 E. Huron St., Chicago, IL 60611

ALLYN. Allyn & Bacon, Inc. 470 Atlantic Ave., Boston, MA 02210

AM. ASSOC. FOR THE ADVANCEMENT OF SCIENCE. 1776 Massachusetts Ave., N. W., Washington, D.C. 20036

AMERICAN BK. American Book Co., 450 W. 33rd St., New York, NY 10001

AM. COUNCIL ON EDUCATION. 1 Dupont Circle, N. W., Washington, D.C. 20036

AMERICAN HERITAGE. American Heritage Pub. Co., Inc., 1221 Ave. of the Americas, New York, NY 10020

APPLETON. Appleton-Century-Crofts, 440 Park Ave. S., New York, NY 10016

ARCHON. See Shoe String

ARIEL. Ariel Books. See Farrar

ARLINGTON. Arlington House Pubs., 165 Huguenot St., New Rochelle, NY 10801

ARONSON. Jason Aronson, Inc., 59 Fourth Ave., New York, NY 10003

ASSOC. FOR CHILDHOOD EDUCATION INTERNATIONAL. 3615 Wisconsin Ave. N. W., Washington, D.C. 20016

ASSOCIATION PR. Association Press, 291 Broadway, New York, NY 10007

ASTOR. Astor-Honor, Inc., 48 E. 43rd St., New York, NY 10017

ATHENEUM. Atheneum Pubs., 597 Fifth Ave., New York, NY 10017

ATHERTON. Lieber-Atherton, Inc., 1841 Broadway, New York, NY 10023

ATLANTIC. Atlantic Monthly Pr., 8 Arlington St., Boston, MA 02116

ATLANTIC/LITTLE. Atlantic Monthly Pr. in association with Little, Brown & Co.

AVON. Avon Books, 959 Eighth Ave., New York, NY 10019

BALLANTINE. Ballantine Books, Inc., 201 E. 50th St., New York, NY 10022

BANTAM. Bantam Books, Inc., 666 Fifth Ave., New York, NY 10019

BARNES. Barnes & Noble Books, 5th Ave. and 18th St., New York, NY 10003

BASIC. Basic Books, Inc., 10 E. 53rd St., New York, NY 10022

BEACON. Beacon Pr., 25 Beacon St., Boston, MA 02108

BEECHURST. Beechurst Pr. See A. S. Barnes

BEHRMAN. Behrman House, Inc., 1261 Broadway, New York, NY 10001

BOBBS. Bobbs-Merrill Co., Inc., 4300 W. 62nd St., Indianapolis, IN 46206

BOWKER. R. R. Bowker and Co., 1180 Ave. of the Americas, New York, NY 10036

BRADBURY. Bradbury Pr., Inc., 2 Overhill Rd., Scarsdale, NY 10583

BRO-DART. Bro-Dart Pub. Co., 1609 Memorial Ave., Williamsport, PA 17701

BROWN. William C. Brown Co., Publishers, 2460 Kerper Blvd., Dubuque, IA 52001

CAMBRIDGE UNIV. PR. 32 E. 57th St., New York, NY 10022

CANADIAN WOMEN'S EDUCATIONAL PRESS. Canadian Women's Educational Press, 280 Bloor St. West, Suite 305, Toronto, Ont., Canada

JONATHAN CAPE. Jonathan Cape, Ltd. 99 Main St., Salem, NH 03079

CAXTON. The Caxton Printers, Ltd., Caldwell, ID 83605

CHATHAM/VIKING. 15 Wilmot Lane, Riverside, CT 06878. Distributed by Viking

CHATTO. Chatto & Windus, Ltd., 99 Main St., Salem, NH 03079

CHELSEA. Chelsea House Publishers, 70 W. 40th St., New York, NY 10018

CHILD STUDY ASSOC. OF AM. Child Study Association of America/Wel Met Inc., 50 Madison Ave., New York, NY 10010

CHILD STUDY PR. The Child Study Press, 50 Madison Ave., New York, NY 10010

CHILDREN'S BOOK COUNCIL. Children's Book Council, Inc., 67 Irving Place, New York, NY 10003

CHILDRENS PR. Childrens Press, Inc., 1224 W. Van Buren, Chicago, IL 60607

CHILTON. Chilton Book Co., Chilton Way, Radnor, PA 19089

CITATION. Citation Press. Imprint of Scholastic Book Services, Div. of Scholastic Magazines, 906 Sylvan Ave., Englewood Cliffs, NJ 07632

COLLINS. William Collins Pubs., 200 Madison Ave., New York, NY 10016

COPP CLARK. The Copp Clark Pub. Co., 517 Wellington St. W., Toronto 135, Ont., Canada

COUNCIL ON INTERRACIAL BOOKS FOR CHILDREN, 1841 Broadway, New York, NY 10023

COWARD. Coward, McCann & Geoghegan, Inc., 200 Madison Ave., New York, NY 10016

COWLES. Henry Regnery Co., 180 N. Michigan Ave., Chicago, IL 60601

CRITERION. Criterion Books, Inc., 10 E. 53rd St., New York, NY 10022

CROWN. Crown Pubs., Inc., 1 Park Ave. South, New York, NY 10016

CROWELL-COLLIER. Crowell Collier and Macmillan, Inc., 866 Third Ave., New York, NY 10022

T. CROWELL. Thomas Y. Crowell Co., 10 E. 53rd St., New York, NY 10022

DANDELION. Dandelion Press, Inc., RFD 2, Box 118, Bedford, NY 10506

DAY. Thomas Y. Crowell Co., 10 E. 53rd St., New York, NY 10022

DELACORTE. Delacorte Pr. See Dell

---

1. For the address of any publisher not listed here consult the latest *Literary Market Place* or Bowker's *Books in Print*.

DELL. Dell Pub. Co., Inc., 1 Dag Hammarskjold Plaza, 245 E. 47th St., New York, NY 10017

DEVIN. Devin-Adair Co., 143 Sound Beach Ave., Old Greenwich, CT 06870

DIAL. The Dial Pr., Inc. See Dell

DODD. Dodd, Mead & Co., 79 Madison Ave., New York, NY 10016

DOUBLEDAY. Doubleday & Co., Inc., 245 Park Ave., New York, NY 10017

DOVER. Dover Pubns., Inc., 180 Varick St., New York, NY 10014

DRYDEN. Dryden Pr., 901 N. Elm, Hinsdale, IL 60521

DUELL. Duell, Sloan & Pearce. See Hawthorn

DUFOUR. Dufour Editions, Inc., Chester Springs, PA 19425

DUTTON. E. P. Dutton & Co., Inc., 201 Park Ave. S., New York, NY 10003

EERDMANS. William B. Eerdmans Pub. Co., 255 Jefferson Ave., S. E., Grand Rapids. MI 49502

ERIKSSON. Paul S. Eriksson, Inc., Pub., 119 W. 57th St., New York, NY 10019

EVANS. M. Evans & Co., Inc., 216 E. 49th St., New York, NY 10017

EXPRESSION. Expression Co., 155 Columbus Ave., Boston, MA 02116

FABER. Faber & Faber, Inc., 99 Main St., Salem, NH 03079

FARRAR. Farrar, Straus & Giroux, Inc., 10 Union Sq., W., New York, NY 10003

FAWCETT. Fawcett World Library, 1515 Broadway, New York, NY 10036

FAXON. F. W. Faxon Co., Inc., 15 Southwest Park, Westwood, MA 02090

FEMINIST PR. Feminist Pr., SUNY/College at Old Westbury, Box 334, Old Westbury, NY 11568

FERNHILL. Humanities Pr., Inc., Atlantic Highlands, NJ 07716

FLEET. Fleet Pr. Corp., 160 Fifth Ave., New York, NY 10010

FOLLETT. Follett Pub. Co., 1010 W. Washington Blvd., Chicago, IL 60606

FOUR WINDS. Four Winds Pr. See Scholastic

FREE PR. The Free Press, 866 Third Ave., New York, NY 10022

FUNK. Funk & Wagnalls, Inc., 53 E. 77th St., New York, NY 10021

GALE. Gale Research Co., Book Tower, Detroit, MI 48226

GARDEN CITY. See Doubleday

GARLAND. Garland Publishing, Inc., 10 E. 44th St., New York, NY 10017

GARRARD. Garrard Pub. Co., 107 Cherry St., New Canaan, CT 06840

GLENCOE. Glencoe, Inc., 8701 Wilshire Blvd., Beverly Hills, CA 90211

GODINE. Godine Press, Inc., 306 Dartmouth St., Boston, MA 02116

GOLDEN GATE. Golden Gate Junior Books, 1247½ North Vista St., Hollywood, CA 90046

GOLDEN PR. Golden Press, Inc., 850 Third Ave., New York, NY 10022

GREENWILLOW. Greenwillow Books, 105 Madison Ave., New York, NY 10016

GROSSET. Grosset & Dunlap, Inc., 51 Madison Ave., New York, NY 10010

GROVE. Grove Press, Inc., 53 E. 11th St., New York, NY 10003

HALE. E. M. Hale & Co., Inc., 20 Waterside Plaza, New York, NY 10010

HANOVER HOUSE. See Doubleday

HARCOURT. Harcourt Brace Jovanovich, Inc., 757 Third Ave., New York, NY 10017

HARPER. Harper & Row, Pubs., 10 E. 53rd St., New York, NY 10022

HARVEY. Harvey House, Inc., 20 Waterside Plaza, New York, NY 10010

HASTINGS. Hastings House Pubs., 10 E. 40th St., New York, NY 10016

HAWTHORN. Hawthorn Books, Inc., 70 Fifth Ave., New York, NY 10011

HEBREW PUB. CO. Hebrew Publishing Co., 80 Fifth Ave., New York, NY 10011

HILL. Hill & Wang, Inc., 19 Union Sq. W., New York, NY 10003

HOLIDAY. Holiday House, Inc., 18 E. 53rd St., New York, NY 10022

HOLT. Holt, Rinehart & Winston, Inc., 383 Madison Ave., New York, NY 10017

HORN BOOK. Horn Book, Inc., 585 Boylston St., Boston, MA 02116

HOUGHTON. Houghton Mifflin Co., 2 Park St., Boston, MA 02107

HOUGHTON/CLARION. Houghton Mifflin/Clarion Books, 52 Vanderbilt Ave., New York, NY 10017

HUBBARD. Hubbard Pr. See Rand

INDIANA UNIV. PR. Tenth and Morton Sts., Bloomington, IN 47401

INTERNATIONAL PUBLICATIONS SERVICE, 114 E. 32nd St., New York, NY 10016

JOSSEY-BASS. Jossey-Bass, Inc., Pubs., 615 Montgomery St., San Francisco, CA 54111

KNOPF. Alfred A. Knopf, Inc., 201 E. 50th St., New York, NY 10022

KNOW. KNOW, Inc., P.O. Box 86031, Pittsburgh, PA 15221

LERNER. Lerner Pubns. Co., 241 First Ave. N., Minneapolis, MN 55401

LIBRARY OF CONGRESS. Supt. of Documents, U.S. Govt. Printing Office, Washington, D.C. 20402

LIPPINCOTT. J. B. Lippincott Co., 521 Fifth Ave., New York, NY 10017

LITTLE. Little, Brown & Co., 34 Beacon St., Boston, MA 02106

LONGMANS. Longmans, Green & Co. See McKay

LOTHROP. Lothrop, Lee & Shepard Co., Inc., 105 Madison Ave., New York, NY 10016

LUCE. Robert B. Luce, Inc., 2000 N. St., N. W., Washington, D.C. 20036

McCALL. McCall Books, 230 Park Ave., New York, NY 10017

McGRAW. McGraw-Hill Book & Educational Services Group, 1221 Avenue of the Americas, New York, NY 10020

McKAY. David McKay Co., Inc., 750 Third Ave., New York, NY 10017

McKINLEY. 112 S. New Broadway, Brooklawn, NJ 08030

MACMILLAN. Macmillan Co., 866 Third Ave., New York, NY 10022

MACRAE. Macrae Smith Co., 225 S. 15th St., Philadelphia, PA 19102

MEREDITH. Meredith Pr. See Hawthorn

MERRILL. Charles E. Merrill Pub. Co., 1300 Alum Creek Dr., Columbus, OH 43216

MESSNER. Julian Messner, Inc. See Simon & Schuster

METHUEN. Methuen Pubns., 2330 Midland Ave., Agincourt, Ont. MIS 1P7, Canada

MILLER-BRODY. Miller-Brody Productions, Inc., 342 Madison Ave., New York, NY 10017

MORROW. William Morrow & Co., Inc., 105 Madison Ave., New York, NY 10016

NAT. COUNCIL FOR THE SOCIAL STUDIES. National Education Assoc., 1515 Wilson Blvd., Arlington, VA 22209

NAT. COUNCIL OF TEACHERS OF ENGLISH. 1111 Kenyon Rd., Urbana, IL 61820

NATURAL HISTORY PR., 501 Franklin Blvd., Garden City, NY 11530

NELSON. Elsevier/Nelson. See Dutton

NEW AM. LIB. New American Library, 1301 Avenue of the Americas, New York, NY 10019

NEW YORK LIBRARY ASSOC. P.O. Box 521, Woodside, NY 11377

NEW YORK PUBLIC LIBRARY. Room 50A, Fifth Ave. and 42nd St., New York, NY 10018

NOBLE. Noble & Noble Pubs., Inc., 1 Dag Hammarskjold Plaza, New York, NY 10017

NORTON. W. W. Norton & Co., 500 Fifth Avenue, New York, NY 10036

NORTON/GROSSET. W. W. Norton in association with Grosset & Dunlap

OBOLENSKY. See Astor-Honor

ODYSSEY. See Bobbs-Merrill

O'HARA. J. Philip O'Hara Inc., Pubs., 20 E. Huron St., Chicago, IL 60611

OUTERBRIDGE. Outerbridge & Lazard, 200 W. 82nd St., New York, NY 10023

OXFORD. Oxford Univ. Pr., 200 Madison Ave., New York, NY 10016

PANTHEON. Pantheon Books, 201 E. 50th St., New York, NY 10022

PANTHER. Panther House, Ltd., P.O. Box 3552, New York, NY 10017

PARENTS' MAGAZINE. Parents' Magazine Pr. See Scholastic

PARNASSUS. Parnassus Pr. See Houghton

PELHAM. Pelham Books, Ltd., 52 Bedford Square, London, England WC1B 3EF

PENGUIN. Penguin Books, Inc., 625 Madison Ave., New York, NY 10022

PERGAMON. Pergamon Pr., Inc., Maxwell House, Fairview Park, Elmsford, NY 10523

PHILLIPS. S. G. Phillips, Inc., 305 W. 86th St., New York, NY 10024

PHOENIX HOUSE. See Univ. of Chicago Pr.

PITMAN. Pitman Pub. Corp., 6 E. 43rd St., New York, NY 10017

PLATT. Platt & Munk, Inc., 1055 Bronx River Ave., Bronx, NY 10472

PLAYS. Plays, Inc., 8 Arlington St., Boston, MA 02116

POCKET BOOKS. See Simon & Schuster

POPULAR PR. Popular Library, 600 Third Ave., New York, NY 10016

POTTER. Clarkson N. Potter, Inc., 419 Park Ave. S., New York, NY 10016

PRAEGER. Praeger Pubs., Inc., 111 Fourth Ave., New York, NY 10003

PRENTICE. Prentice-Hall, Inc., Englewood Cliffs, NJ 07632

PRESS OF CASE WESTERN RESERVE UNIVERSITY. Quail Bldg., Cleveland, OH 44106

PUTNAM. G. P. Putnam's Sons, 200 Madison Ave., New York, NY 10016

QUADRANGLE. Quadrangle/The New York Times Book Co., 10 E. 53rd St., New York, NY 10022

RAINTREE. Raintree Childrens Books, 205 W. Highland Ave., Milwaukee, WI 55203

RAND. Rand McNally & Co., P.O. Box 7600, Chicago, IL 60680

RANDOM. Random House, Inc., 201 E. 50th St., New York, NY 10022

REILLY. Reilly & Lee Books, 114 W. Illinois St., Chicago, IL 60610

RITCHIE. The Ward Ritchie Pr., 474 S. Arroyo Pkwy., Pasadena, CA 91105

RONALD. The Ronald Press Co., 79 Madison Ave., New York, NY 10016

ROY. Roy Pubs., Inc., 30 E. 74th St., New York, NY 10021

ST. MARTIN'S. St. Martin's Pr., Inc., 175 Fifth Ave., New York, NY 10010

SAT. REVIEW. Saturday Review Pr., 201 Park Ave. S., New York, NY 10003

SCARECROW. The Scarecrow Pr., 52 Liberty St., Metuchen, NJ 08840

SCHOCKEN. Schocken Books, Inc., 200 Madison Ave., New York, NY 10016

SCHOLASTIC. Scholastic Book Services, 50 W. 44th St., New York, NY 10036

W. R. SCOTT. See Addison-Wesley

SCOTT/ADDISON. See Addison-Wesley

SCOTT, FORESMAN. Scott, Foresman and Co., 1900 E. Lake Ave., Glenview, IL 60025

SCRIBNER'S. Charles Scribner's Sons, 597 Fifth Ave., New York, NY 10017

SEABURY. Seabury Pr. See Houghton/Clarion

SHEED. Sheed & Ward, Inc., 6700 Squibb Rd., Mission, KS 66202

SHERBOURNE PR. Sherbourne Pr., 1640 La Cienega Blvd., Los Angeles, CA 90035

SIGNET. See New American Library

SIMON. Simon & Schuster, Inc., 630 Fifth Ave., New York, NY 10020

SINGING TREE. See Gale

SNIFFEN COURT. See Atheneum

SPRINGER. Springer Publishing Co., Inc., 200 Park Ave. S., New York, NY 10003

STANFORD UNIV. PR. Stanford, CA 94305

STEIN & DAY. 7 E. 48th St., New York, NY 10017

STEMMER. Stemmer House, 2627 Caves Rd., Owings Mills, MD 21117

STERLING. Sterling Pub. Co., 419 Park Ave. S., New York, NY 10016

STOKES. Frederick A. Stokes Co. See Lippincott

SWALLOW. The Swallow Press, Inc., 1139 S. Wabash Ave., Chicago, IL 60605

TAPLINGER. Taplinger Pub. Co., 200 Park Ave. S., New York, NY 10003

TEACHERS COLLEGE PR. Teachers College, Columbia Univ., 1234 Amsterdam Ave., New York, NY 10027

TIME-LIFE. Time-Life Books. Time-Life Bldg., Rockefeller Center, New York, NY 10020

TOWER. Tower Pubns., Inc., c/o Belmont-Tower Books, Inc., 185 Madison Ave., New York, NY 10016

TROUTMAN. Troutman Pr., Sharon, CT 06069

TUNDRA. Tundra Books of Northern New York, 18 Cornelia St., Box 1030, Plattsburgh, NY 12901

TUTTLE. Charles E. Tuttle Co., Inc., 28 S. Main St., Rutland, VT 05701

TWAYNE. Twayne Pubs., 70 Lincoln St., Boston, MA 02111

UNIV. OF CALIF. PR. 2223 Fulton St., Berkeley, CA 94720

UNIV. OF CHICAGO PR. 5801 Ellis Ave., Chicago, IL 60637

UNIV. OF PA. PR. 3933 Walnut St., Philadelphia, PA 19104

VANGUARD. Vanguard Pr., Inc., 424 Madison Ave., New York, NY 10017

VAN NOSTRAND. Van Nostrand Reinhold Co., 450 W. 33rd St., New York, NY 10001

VIKING. Viking Pr., Inc., 625 Madison Ave., New York, NY 10022

VINTAGE. See Random House

WALCK. Henry Z. Walck, Inc., 750 Third Ave., New York, NY 10017

WALKER. Walker & Co., 720 Fifth Ave., New York, NY 10019

WARNE. Frederick Warne & Co., Inc., 2 Park Ave., New York, NY 10016

WASHBURN. Ives Washburn, Inc. See McKay

WATSON-GUPTILL. Watson-Guptill Pubns. Div. of Billboard Pubns., Inc., 1 Astor Plaza, New York, NY 10036

WATTS. Franklin Watts, Inc., 730 Fifth Ave., New York, NY 10019

WESTMINSTER. The Westminster Pr., 902 Witherspoon Bldg., Philadelphia, PA 19107

WESTERN. Western Pub. Co., 1220 Mound Ave., Racine, WI 53404

WEYBRIGHT. Weybright and Talley, Inc. See McKay

WHITE. David White Co., 60 E. 55th St., New York, NY 10022

WHITMAN. Albert Whitman & Co., 560 W. Lake St., Chicago, IL 60606

WHITTLESEY. Whittlesey House. See McGraw-Hill

WILEY. John Wiley & Sons, Inc., 605 Third Ave., New York, NY 10016

WILSON. H. W. Wilson Co., 950 University Ave., Bronx, NY 10452

WINDMILL. Windmill Books, Inc., 201 Park Ave. S., New York, NY 10010

WORLD. World Publishing Co., 2080 W. 117th St., Cleveland, OH 44111

YOUNG SCOTT. Young Scott Books. See Addison-Wesley

Appendix D: Children's Book Awards[1]

The awards and prizes given in the children's book field by organizations, schools, publishers, and newspapers, in the United States and other countries, have grown to a sizable number.[1] The Newbery and Caldecott Medals and National Book Award for Children's Literature, all given annually, are the best-known United States awards, and the Hans Christian Andersen Medal, given biennially, the best-known international award. The International Reading Association Children's Book Award is the only award that singles out new authors. The National Council of Teachers of English Award for Excellence in Poetry for Children is the first children's book award given solely for poetry. The Laura Ingalls Wilder Award is given every five years in honor of Wilder. The Carnegie and Kate Greenaway Medals are major British awards for children's books, and the Canadian Library Awards are the most significant given in Canada. In most cases, the awards are given for books published during the preceding year.

Following are brief histories of these awards and listings of the winners and runners-up.

The Newbery Medal

Frederic G. Melcher, editor of *Publisher's Weekly Magazine,* donated and named this award as a tribute to John Newbery (1713–1767), the first English publisher of books for children. Beginning in 1922 and every year since, the Newbery Medal has been given by an awards committee of the Children's Services Division of the American Library Association to the author of the most distinguished contribution to literature for children published in the United States during the preceding year. The author must be a citizen or resident of the United States.

1922   *The Story of Mankind* by Hendrik Willem van Loon, Liveright
   Honor Books: *The Great Quest* by Charles Hawes, Little; *Cedric the Forester* by Bernard Marshall, Appleton; *The Old Tobacco Shop* by William Bowen, Macmillan; *The Golden Fleece and the Heroes Who Lived Before Achilles* by Padraic Colum, Macmillan; *Windy Hill* by Cornelia Meigs, Macmillan
1923   *The Voyages of Doctor Dolittle* by Hugh Lofting, Lippincott
   Honor Books: No record
1924   *The Dark Frigate* by Charles Hawes, Atlantic/Little
   Honor Books: No record
1925   *Tales from Silver Lands* by Charles Finger, Doubleday
   Honor Books: *Nicholas* by Anne Carroll Moore, Putnam; *Dream Coach* by Anne Parrish, Macmillan
1926   *Shen of the Sea* by Arthur Bowie Chrisman, Dutton
   Honor Book: *Voyagers* by Padraic Colum, Macmillan

1. *Children's Books: Awards and Prizes* (comp. and ed. by the Children's Book Council, 1979) is a complete compilation of honors awarded in the children's book field.

1927   *Smoky, The Cowhorse* by Will James, Scribner's
   Honor Books: No record
1928   *Gayneck, The Story of a Pigeon* by Dhan Gopal Mukerji, Dutton
   Honor Books: *The Wonder Smith and His Son* by Ella Young, Longmans; *Downright Dencey* by Caroline Snedeker, Doubleday
1929   *The Trumpeter of Krakow* by Eric P. Kelly, Macmillan
   Honor Books: *Pigtail of Ah Lee Ben Loo* by John Bennett, Longmans; *Millions of Cats* by Wanda Gág, Coward; *The Boy Who Was* by Grace Hallock, Dutton; *Clearing Weather* by Cornelia Meigs, Little; *Runaway Papoose* by Grace Moon, Doubleday; *Tod of the Fens* by Elinor Whitney, Macmillan
1930   *Hitty, Her First Hundred Years* by Rachel Field, Macmillan
   Honor Books: *Daughter of the Seine* by Jeanette Eaton, Harper; *Pran of Albania* by Elizabeth Miller, Doubleday; *Jumping-Off Place* by Marian Hurd McNeely, Longmans; *Tangle-Coated Horse and Other Tales* by Ella Young, Longmans; *Vaino* by Julia Davis Adams, Dutton; *Little Blacknose* by Hildegarde Swift, Harcourt
1931   *The Cat Who Went to Heaven* by Elizabeth Coatsworth, Macmillan
   Honor Books: *Floating Island* by Anne Parrish, Harper; *The Dark Star of Itza* by Alida Malkus, Harcourt; *Queer Person* by Ralph Hubbard, Doubleday; *Mountains are Free* by Julia Davis Adams, Dutton; *Spice and the Devil's Cave* by Agnes Hewes, Knopf; *Meggy Macintosh* by Elizabeth Janet Gray, Doubleday; *Garram the Hunter* by Herbert Best, Doubleday; *Ood-Le-Uk the Wanderer* by Alice Lide and Margaret Johansen, Little
1932   *Waterless Mountain* by Laura Adams Armer, Longmans
   Honor Books: *The Fairy Circus* by Dorothy P. Lathrop, Macmillan; *Calico Bush* by Rachel Field, Macmillan; *Boy of the South Seas* by Eunice Tietjens, Coward; *Out of the Flame* by Eloise Lownsbery, Longmans; *Jane's Island* by Marjorie Allee, Houghton; *Truce of the Wolf and Other Tales of Old Italy* by Mary Gould Davis, Harcourt
1933   *Young Fu of the Upper Yangtze* by Elizabeth Foreman Lewis, Winston
   Honor Books: *Swift Rivers* by Cornelia Meigs, Little; *The Railroad to Freedom* by Hildegarde Swift, Harcourt; *Children of the Soil* by Nora Burglon, Doubleday
1934   *Invincible Louisa* by Cornelia Meigs, Little
   Honor Books: *The Forgotten Daughter* by Caroline Snedeker, Doubleday; *Swords of Steel* by Elsie Singmaster, Houghton; *ABC Bunny* by Wanda Gág, Coward; *Winged Girl of Knossos* by Erik Berry, Appleton; *New Land* by Sarah Schmidt, McBride; *Big Tree of Bunlahy* by Padraic Colum, Macmillan; *Glory of the Seas* by Agnes Hewes, Knopf; *Apprentice of Florence* by Anne Kyle, Houghton

1935 *Dobry* by Monica Shannon, Viking
Honor Books: *Pageant of Chinese History* by Elizabeth Seeger, Longmans; *Davy Crockett* by Constance Rourke, Harcourt; *Day on Skates* by Hilda Van Stockum, Harper

1936 *Caddie Woodlawn* by Carol Brink, Macmillan
Honor Books: *Honk, The Moose* by Phil Stong, Dodd; *The Good Master* by Kate Seredy, Viking; *Young Walter Scott* by Elizabeth Janet Gray, Viking; *All Sail Set* by Armstrong Sperry, Winston

1937 *Roller Skates* by Ruth Sawyer, Viking
Honor Books: *Phebe Fairchild: Her Book* by Lois Lenski, Stokes; *Whistler's Van* by Idwal Jones, Viking; *Golden Basket* by Ludwig Bemelmans, Viking; *Winterbound* by Margery Bianco, Viking; *Audubon* by Constance Rourke, Harcourt; *The Codfish Musket* by Agnes Hewes, Doubleday

1938 *The White Stag* by Kate Seredy, Viking
Honor Books: *Pecos Bill* by James Cloyd Bowman, Little; *Bright Island* by Mabel Robinson, Random; *On the Banks of Plum Creek* by Laura Ingalls Wilder, Harper

1939 *Thimble Summer* by Elizabeth Enright, Rinehart
Honor Books: *Nino* by Valenti Angelo, Viking; *Mr. Popper's Penguins* by Richard and Florence Atwater, Little; *"Hello the Boat!"* by Phyllis Crawford, Holt; *Leader by Destiny: George Washington, Man and Patriot* by Jeanette Eaton, Harcourt; *Penn* by Elizabeth Janet Gray, Viking

1940 *Daniel Boone* by James Daugherty, Viking
Honor Books: *The Singing Tree* by Kate Seredy, Viking; *Runner of the Mountain Tops* by Mabel Robinson, Random; *By the Shores of Silver Lake* by Laura Ingalls Wilder, Harper; *Boy with a Pack* by Stephen W. Meader, Harcourt

1941 *Call It Courage* by Armstrong Sperry, Macmillan
Honor Books: *Blue Willow* by Doris Gates, Viking; *Young Mac of Fort Vancouver* by Mary Jane Carr, T. Crowell; *The Long Winter* by Laura Ingalls Wilder, Harper; *Nansen* by Anna Gertrude Hall, Viking

1942 *The Matchlock Gun* by Walter D. Edmonds, Dodd
Honor Books: *Little Town on the Prairie* by Laura Ingalls Wilder, Harper; *George Washington's World* by Genevieve Foster, Scribner's; *Indian Captive: The Story of Mary Jemison* by Lois Lenski, Lippincott; *Down Ryton Water* by Eva Roe Gaggin, Viking

1943 *Adam of the Road* by Elizabeth Janet Gray, Viking
Honor Books: *The Middle Moffat* by Eleanor Estes, Harcourt; *Have You Seen Tom Thumb?* by Mabel Leigh Hunt, Lippincott

1944 *Johnny Tremain* by Esther Forbes, Houghton
Honor Books: *These Happy Golden Years* by Laura Ingalls Wilder, Harper; *Fog Magic* by Julia Sauer, Viking; *Rufus M.* by Eleanor Estes, Harcourt; *Mountain Born* by Elizabeth Yates, Coward

1945 *Rabbit Hill* by Robert Lawson, Viking
Honor Books: *The Hundred Dresses* by Eleanor Estes, Harcourt; *The Silver Pencil* by Alice Dalgliesh, Scribner's; *Abraham Lincoln's World* by Genevieve Foster, Scribner's; *Lone Journey: The Life of Roger Williams* by Jeanette Eaton, Harcourt

1946 *Strawberry Girl* by Lois Lenski, Lippincott
Honor Books: *Justin Morgan Had a Horse* by Marguerite Henry, Rand; *The Moved-Outers* by Florence Crannell Means, Houghton; *Bhimsa, The Dancing Bear* by Christine Weston, Scribner's; *New Found World* by Katherine Shippen, Viking

1947 *Miss Hickory* by Carolyn Sherwin Bailey, Viking
Honor Books: *Wonderful Year* by Nancy Barnes, Messner; *Big Tree* by Mary and Conrad Buff, Viking; *The Heavenly Tenants* by William Maxwell, Harper; *The Avion My Uncle Flew* by Cyrus Fisher, Appleton; *The Hidden Treasure of Glaston* by Eleanore Jewett, Viking

1948 *The Twenty-one Balloons* by William Pène du Bois, Viking
Honor Books: *Pancakes-Paris* by Claire Huchet Bishop, Viking; *Li Lun, Lad of Courage* by Carolyn Treffinger, Abingdon; *The Quaint and Curious Quest of Johnny Longfoot* by Catherine Besterman, Bobbs; *The Cow-Tail Switch, and Other West African Stories* by Harold Courlander, Holt; *Misty of Chincoteague* by Marguerite Henry, Rand

1949 *King of the Wind* by Marguerite Henry, Rand
Honor Books: *Seabird* by Holling C. Holling, Houghton; *Daughter of the Mountains* by Louise Rankin, Viking; *My Father's Dragon* by Ruth S. Gannett, Random; *Story of the Negro* by Arna Bontemps, Knopf

1950 *The Door in the Wall* by Marguerite de Angeli, Doubleday
Honor Books: *Tree of Freedom* by Rebecca Caudill, Viking; *The Blue Cat of Castle Town* by Catherine Coblentz, Longmans; *Kildee House* by Rutherford Montgomery, Doubleday; *George Washington* by Genevieve Foster, Scribner's; *Song of the Pines* by Walter and Marion Havighurst, Winston

1951 *Amos Fortune, Free Man* by Elizabeth Yates, Aladdin
Honor Books: *Better Known as Johnny Appleseed* by Mabel Leigh Hunt, Lippincott; *Gandhi, Fighter Without a Sword* by Jeanette Eaton, Morrow; *Abraham Lincoln, Friend of the People* by Clara Ingram Judson, Follett; *The Story of Appleby Capple* by Anne Parrish, Harper

1952 *Ginger Pye* by Eleanor Estes, Harcourt
Honor Books: *Americans Before Columbus* by Elizabeth Baity, Viking; *Minn of the Mississippi* by Holling C. Holling, Houghton; *The Defender* by Nicholas Kalashnikoff, Scribner's; *The Light at Tern Rock* by Julia Sauer, Viking; *The Apple and the Arrow* by Mary and Conrad Buff, Houghton

1953 *Secret of the Andes* by Ann Nolan Clark, Viking
Honor Books: *Charlotte's Web* by E. B. White, Harper; *Moccasin Trail* by Eloise McGraw, Coward; *Red Sails to Capri* by Ann Weil, Viking; *The Bears on Hemlock Mountain* by Alice Dalgliesh, Scribner's; *Birthdays of Freedom*, Vol. 1 by Genevieve Foster, Scribner's

1954 *... and now Miguel* by Joseph Krumgold, T. Crowell
Honor Books: *All Alone* by Claire Huchet Bishop, Viking; *Shadrach* by Meindert DeJong, Harper; *Hurry Home Candy* by Meindert DeJong, Harper; *Theodore Roosevelt, Fighting Patriot* by Clara Ingram Judson, Follett; *Magic Maize* by Mary and Conrad Buff, Houghton

1955 *The Wheel on the School* by Meindert DeJong, Harper
Honor Books: *The Courage of Sarah Noble* by Alice Dalgliesh, Scribner's; *Banner in the Sky* by James Ullman, Lippincott

1956 *Carry on, Mr. Bowditch* by Jean Lee Latham, Houghton
Honor Books: *The Secret River* by Marjorie Kinnan Rawlings, Scribner's; *The Golden Name Day* by Jennie Lindquist, Harper; *Men, Microscopes, and Living Things* by Katherine Shippen, Viking

1957 *Miracles on Maple Hill* by Virginia Sorensen, Harcourt

Honor Books: *Old Yeller* by Fred Gipson, Harper; *The House of Sixty Fathers* by Meindert DeJong, Harper; *Mr. Justice Holmes* by Clara Ingram Judson, Follett; *The Corn Grows Ripe* by Dorothy Rhoads, Viking; *Black Fox of Lorne* by Marguerite de Angeli, Doubleday

1958 *Rifles for Watie* by Harold Keith, T. Crowell

Honor Books: *The Horsecatcher* by Mari Sandoz, Westminster; *Gone-Away Lake* by Elizabeth Enright, Harcourt; *The Great Wheel* by Robert Lawson, Viking; *Tom Paine, Freedom's Apostle* by Leo Gurko, T. Crowell

1959 *The Witch of Blackbird Pond* by Elizabeth George Speare, Houghton

Honor Books: *The Family Under the Bridge* by Natalie S. Carlson, Harper; *Along Came a Dog* by Meindert DeJong, Harper; *Chucaro: Wild Pony of the Pampa* by Francis Kalnay, Harcourt; *The Perilous Road* by William O. Steele, Harcourt

1960 *Onion John* by Joseph Krumgold, T. Crowell

Honor Books: *My Side of the Mountain* by Jean George, Dutton; *America Is Born* by Gerald W. Johnson, Morrow; *The Gammage Cup* by Carol Kendall, Harcourt

1961 *Island of the Blue Dolphins* by Scott O'Dell, Houghton

Honor Books: *America Moves Forward* by Gerald W. Johnson, Morrow; *Old Ramon* by Jack Schaefer, Houghton; *The Cricket in Times Square* by George Selden, Farrar

1962 *The Bronze Bow* by Elizabeth George Speare, Houghton

Honor Books: *Frontier Living* by Edwin Tunis, World; *The Golden Goblet* by Eloise McGraw, Coward; *Belling the Tiger* by Mary Stolz, Harper

1963 *A Wrinkle in Time* by Madeleine L'Engle, Farrar

Honor Books: *Thistle and Thyme* by Sorche Nic Leodhas, Holt; *Men of Athens* by Olivia Coolidge, Houghton

1964 *It's Like This, Cat* by Emily Cheney Neville, Harper

Honor Books: *Rascal* by Sterling North, Dutton; *The Loner* by Ester Wier, McKay

1965 *Shadow of a Bull* by Maia Wojciechowska, Atheneum

Honor Book: *Across Five Aprils* by Irene Hunt, Follett

1966 *I, Juan de Pareja* by Elizabeth Borten de Trevino, Farrar

Honor Books: *The Black Cauldron* by Lloyd Alexander, Holt; *The Animal Family* by Randall Jarrell, Pantheon; *The Noonday Friends* by Mary Stolz, Harper

1967 *Up a Road Slowly* by Irene Hunt, Follett

Honor Books: *The King's Fifth* by Scott O'Dell, Houghton; *Zlateh the Goat and Other Stories* by Isaac Bashevis Singer, Harper; *The Jazz Man* by Mary H. Weik, Atheneum

1968 *From the Mixed-Up Files of Mrs. Basil E. Frankweiler* by E. L. Konigsburg, Atheneum

Honor Books: *Jennifer, Hecate, Macbeth, William McKinley, and Me, Elizabeth* by E. L. Konigsburg, Atheneum; *The Black Pearl* by Scott O'Dell, Houghton; *The Fearsome Inn* by Isaac Bashevis Singer, Scribner's; *The Egypt Game* by Zilpha Keatley Snyder, Atheneum

1969 *The High King* by Lloyd Alexander, Holt

Honor Books: *To Be a Slave* by Julius Lester, Dial; *When Shlemiel Went to Warsaw and Other Stories* by Isaac Bashevis Singer, Farrar

1970 *Sounder* by William H. Armstrong, Harper

Honor Books: *Our Eddie* by Sulamith Ish-Kishor, Pantheon; *The Many Ways of Seeing: An Introduction to the Pleasures of Art* by Janet Gaylord Moore, World; *Journey Outside* by Mary Q. Steele, Viking

1971 *Summer of the Swans* by Betsy Byars, Viking

Honor Books: *Kneeknock Rise* by Natalie Babbitt, Farrar; *Enchantress from the Stars* by Sylvia Louise Engdahl, Atheneum; *Sing Down the Moon* by Scott O'Dell, Houghton

1972 *Mrs. Frisby and the Rats of NIMH* by Robert C. O'Brien, Atheneum

Honor Books: *Incident at Hawk's Hill* by Allan W. Eckert, Little; *The Planet of Junior Brown* by Virginia Hamilton, Macmillan; *The Tombs of Atuan* by Ursula K. Le Guin, Atheneum; *Annie and the Old One* by Miska Miles, Atlantic/Little; *The Headless Cupid* by Zilpha Keatley Snyder, Atheneum

1973 *Julie of the Wolves* by Jean George, Harper

Honor Books: *Frog and Toad Together* by Arnold Lobel, Harper; *The Upstairs Room* by Johanna Reiss, Crowell; *The Witches of Worm* by Zilpha Keatley Snyder, Atheneum

1974 *The Slave Dancer* by Paula Fox, Bradbury

Honor Book: *The Dark Is Rising* by Susan Cooper, Atheneum/McElderry

1975 *M. C. Higgins, the Great* by Virginia Hamilton, Macmillan

Honor Books: *Figgs & Phantoms* by Ellen Raskin, Dutton; *My Brother Sam Is Dead* by James Lincoln Collier & Christopher Collier, Four Winds; *The Perilous Gard* by Elizabeth Marie Pope, Houghton; *Philip Hall Likes Me. I Reckon Maybe* by Bette Greene, Dial

1976 *The Grey King* by Susan Cooper, Atheneum/McElderry

Honor Books: *The Hundred Penny Box* by Sharon Bell Mathis, Viking; *Dragonwings* by Lawrence Yep, Harper

1977 *Roll of Thunder, Hear My Cry* by Mildred D. Taylor, Dial

Honor Books: *Abel's Island* by William Steig, Farrar; *A String in the Harp* by Nancy Bond, McElderry/Atheneum

1978 *Bridge to Terabithia* by Katherine Paterson, Crowell

Honor Books: *Anpao: An American Indian Odyssey* by Jamake Highwater, Lippincott; *Ramona and Her Father* by Beverly Cleary, Morrow

1979 *The Westing Game* by Ellen Raskin, Dutton

Honor Book: *The Great Gilly Hopkins* by Katherine Paterson, Crowell

1980 *A Gathering of Days: A New England Girl's Journal, 1830–32* by Joan Blos, Scribner's

Honor Book: *The Road from Home: The Story of an Armenian Girl* by David Kherdian, Greenwillow

The Caldecott Medal

This award is named in honor of Randolph Caldecott (1846–1886), the English illustrator whose pictures still delight children. In 1937, Frederic G. Melcher, the American editor and publisher who had conceived the idea of the Newbery Medal some years earlier, proposed the establishment of a similar award for picture books, and since 1938 the Caldecott Medal has been awarded annually by an awards committee of the American Library Association's Children's Services Division to the illustrator of the most distinguished picture book for children published in the United States during the preceding year. The award is limited to residents or citizens of the United States.

In cases where only one name is given, the book was written and illustrated by the same person.

1938   *Animals of the Bible* by Helen Dean Fish, ill. by Dorothy P. Lathrop, Lippincott
Honor Books: *Seven Simeons* by Boris Artzybasheff, Viking; *Four and Twenty Blackbirds* by Helen Dean Fish, ill. by Robert Lawson, Stokes

1939   *Mei Li* by Thomas Handforth, Doubleday
Honor Books: *The Forest Pool* by Laura Adams Armer, Longmans; *Wee Gillis* by Munro Leaf, ill. by Robert Lawson, Viking; *Snow White and the Seven Dwarfs* by Wanda Gág, Coward; *Barkis* by Clare Newberry, Harper; *Andy and the Lion* by James Daugherty, Viking

1940   *Abraham Lincoln* by Ingri and Edgar Parin d'Aulaire, Doubleday
Honor Books: *Cock-A-Doodle Doo . . .* by Berta and Elmer Hader, Macmillan; *Madeline* by Ludwig Bemelmans, Viking; *The Ageless Story,* ill. by Lauren Ford, Dodd

1941   *They Were Strong and Good* by Robert Lawson, Viking
Honor Book: *April's Kittens* by Clare Newberry, Harper

1942   *Make Way for Ducklings* by Robert McCloskey, Viking
Honor Books: *An American ABC* by Maud and Miska Petersham, Macmillan; *In My Mother's House* by Ann Nolan Clark, ill. by Velino Herrera, Viking; *Paddle-to-the-Sea* by Holling C. Holling, Houghton; *Nothing at All* by Wanda Gág, Coward

1943   *The Little House* by Virginia Lee Burton, Houghton
Honor Books: *Dash and Dart* by Mary and Conrad Buff, Viking; *Marshmallow* by Clare Newberry, Harper

1944   *Many Moons* by James Thurber, ill. by Louis Slobodkin, Harcourt
Honor Books: *Small Rain: Verses from the Bible* selected by Jessie Orton Jones, ill. by Elizabeth Orton Jones, Viking; *Pierre Pigeon* by Lee Kingman, ill. by Arnold E. Bare, Houghton; *The Mighty Hunter* by Berta and Elmer Hader, Macmillan; *A Child's Good Night Book* by Margaret Wise Brown, ill. by Jean Charlot, W. R. Scott; *Good Luck Horse* by Chih-Yi Chan, ill. by Plao Chan, Whittlesey

1945   *Prayer for a Child* by Rachel Field, ill. by Elizabeth Orton Jones, Macmillan
Honor Books: *Mother Goose* ill. by Tasha Tudor, Walck; *In the Forest* by Marie Hall Ets, Viking; *Yonie Wondernose* by Marguerite de Angeli, Doubleday; *The Christmas Anna Angel* by Ruth Sawyer, ill. by Kate Seredy, Viking

1946   *The Rooster Crows . . .* (traditional Mother Goose) ill. by Maud and Miska Petersham, Macmillan
Honor Books: *Little Lost Lamb* by Golden MacDonald, ill. by Leonard Weisgard, Doubleday; *Sing Mother Goose* by Opal Wheeler, ill. by Marjorie Torrey, Dutton; *My Mother Is the Most Beautiful Woman in the World* by Becky Reyher, ill. by Ruth Gannett, Lothrop; *You Can Write Chinese* by Kurt Wiese, Viking

1947   *The Little Island* by Golden MacDonald, ill. by Leonard Weisgard, Doubleday
Honor Books: *Rain Drop Splash* by Alvin Tresselt, ill. by Leonard Weisgard, Lothrop; *Boats on the River* by Marjorie Flack, ill. by Jay Hyde Barnum, Viking; *Timothy Turtle* by Al Graham, ill. by Tony Palazzo, Viking; *Pedro, the Angel of Olvera Street* by Leo Politi, Scribner's; *Sing in Praise: A Collection of the Best Loved Hymns* by Opal Wheeler, ill. by Marjorie Torrey, Dutton

1948   *White Snow, Bright Snow* by Alvin Tresselt, ill. by Roger Duvoisin, Lothrop
Honor Books: *Stone Soup* by Marcia Brown, Scribner's; *McElligot's Pool* by Dr. Seuss, Random; *Bambino the Clown* by George Schreiber, Viking; *Roger and the Fox* by Lavinia Davis, ill. by Hildegard Woodward, Doubleday; *Song of Robin Hood* ed. by Anne Malcolmson, ill. by Virginia Lee Burton, Houghton

1949   *The Big Snow* by Berta and Elmer Hader, Macmillan
Honor Books: *Blueberries for Sal* by Robert McCloskey, Viking; *All Around the Town* by Phyllis McGinley, ill. by Helen Stone, Lippincott; *Juanita* by Leo Politi, Scribner's; *Fish in the Air* by Kurt Wiese, Viking

1950   *Song of the Swallows* by Leo Politi, Scribner's
Honor Books: *America's Ethan Allen* by Stewart Holbrook, ill. by Lynd Ward, Houghton; *The Wild Birthday Cake* by Lavinia Davis, ill. by Hildegard Woodward, Doubleday; *The Happy Day* by Ruth Krauss, ill. by Marc Simont, Harper; *Bartholomew and the Oobleck* by Dr. Seuss, Random; *Henry Fisherman* by Marcia Brown, Scribner's

1951   *The Egg Tree* by Katherine Milhous, Scribner's
Honor Books: *Dick Whittington and His Cat* by Marcia Brown, Scribner's; *The Two Reds* by Will, ill. by Nicolas Harcourt; *If I Ran the Zoo* by Dr. Seuss, Random; *The Most Wonderful Doll in the World* by Phyllis McGinley, ill. by Helen Stone, Lippincott; *T-Bone, the Baby Sitter* by Clare Newberry, Harper

1952   *Finders Keepers* by Will, ill. by Nicolas, Harcourt
Honor Books: *Mr. T. W. Anthony Woo* by Marie Hall Ets, Viking; *Skipper John's Cook* by Marcia Brown, Scribner's; *All Falling Down* by Gene Zion, ill. by Margaret Bloy Graham, Harper; *Bear Party* by William Pène du Bois, Viking; *Feather Mountain* by Elizabeth Olds, Houghton

1953   *The Biggest Bear* by Lynd Ward, Houghton
Honor Books: *Puss in Boots* by Charles Perrault, ill. and tr. by Marcia Brown, Scribner's; *One Morning in Maine* by Robert McCloskey, Viking; *Ape in a Cape* by Fritz Eichenberg, Harcourt; *The Storm Book* by Charlotte Zolotow, ill. by Margaret Bloy Graham, Harper; *Five Little Monkeys* by Juliet Kepes, Houghton

1954   *Madeline's Rescue* by Ludwig Bemelmans, Viking
Honor Books: *Journey Cake, Ho!* by Ruth Sawyer, ill. by Robert McCloskey, Viking; *When Will the World Be Mine?* by Miriam Schlein, ill. by Jean Charlot, W. R. Scott; *The Steadfast Tin Solider* by Hans Christian Andersen, ill. by Marcia Brown, Scribner's; *A Very Special House* by Ruth Krauss, ill. by Maurice Sendak, Harper; *Green Eyes* by A. Birnbaum, Capitol

1955   *Cinderella, or the Little Glass Slipper* by Charles Perrault, tr. and ill. by Marcia Brown, Scribner's
Honor Books: *Book of Nursery and Mother Goose Rhymes,* ill. by Marguerite de Angeli, Doubleday; *Wheel on the Chimney* by Margaret Wise Brown, ill. by Tibor Gergely, Lippincott; *The Thanksgiving Story* by Alice Dalgliesh, ill. by Helen Sewell, Scribner's

1956   *Frog Went A-Courtin'* ed. by John Langstaff, ill. by Feodor Rojankovsky, Harcourt
Honor Books: *Play with Me* by Marie Hall Ets, Viking; *Crow Boy* by Taro Yashima, Viking

1957   *A Tree Is Nice* by Janice May Udry, ill. by Marc Simont, Harper
Honor Books: *Mr. Penny's Race Horse* by Marie Hall Ets, Viking; *1 Is One* by Tasha Tudor, Walck; *Anatole* by Eve Titus, ill. by Paul Galdone, McGraw; *Gillespie and the Guards* by Benjamin Elkin, ill. by James Daugherty, Viking; *Lion* by William Pène du Bois, Viking

1958   *Time of Wonder* by Robert McCloskey, Viking
Honor Books: *Fly High, Fly Low* by Don Freeman, Viking; *Anatole and the Cat* by Eve Titus, ill. by Paul Galdone, McGraw

1959   *Chanticleer and the Fox* adapted from Chaucer and ill. by Barbara Cooney, T. Crowell
Honor Books: *The House That Jack Built* by Antonio Frasconi, Harcourt; *What Do You Say, Dear?* by Sesyle Joslin, ill. by Maurice Sendak, W. R. Scott; *Umbrella* by Taro Yashima, Viking

1960   *Nine Days to Christmas* by Marie Hall Ets and Aurora Labastida, ill. by Marie Hall Ets, Viking
Honor Books: *Houses from the Sea* by Alice E. Goudey, ill. by Adrienne Adams, Scribner's; *The Moon Jumpers* by Janice May Udry, ill. by Maurice Sendak, Harper

1961   *Baboushka and the Three Kings* by Ruth Robbins, ill. by Nicolas Sidjakov, Parnassus
Honor Book: *Inch by Inch* by Leo Lionni, Obolensky

1962   *Once a Mouse . . .* by Marcia Brown, Scribner's
Honor Books: *The Fox Went Out on a Chilly Night* by Peter Spier, Doubleday; *Little Bear's Visit* by Else Holmelund Minarik, ill. by Maurice Sendak, Harper; *The Day We Saw the Sun Come Up* by Alice E. Goudey, ill. by Adrienne Adams, Scribner's

1963   *The Snowy Day* by Ezra Jack Keats, Viking
Honor Books: *The Sun Is a Golden Earring* by Natalia M. Belting, ill. by Bernarda Bryson, Holt; *Mr. Rabbit and the Lovely Present* by Charlotte Zolotow, ill. by Maurice Sendak, Harper

1964   *Where the Wild Things Are* by Maurice Sendak, Harper
Honor Books: *Swimmy* by Leo Lionni, Pantheon; *All in the Morning Early* by Sorche Nic Leodhas, ill. by Evaline Ness, Holt; *Mother Goose and Nursery Rhymes* ill. by Philip Reed, Atheneum

1965   *May I Bring a Friend?* by Beatrice Schenk de Regniers, ill. by Beni Montresor, Atheneum
Honor Books: *Rain Makes Applesauce* by Julian Scheer, ill. by Marvin Bileck, Holiday; *The Wave* by Margaret Hodges, ill. by Blair Lent, Houghton; *A Pocketful of Cricket* by Rebecca Caudill, ill. by Evaline Ness, Holt

1966   *Always Room for One More* by Sorche Nic Leodhas, ill. by Nonny Hogrogian, Holt
Honor Books: *Hide and Seek Fog* by Alvin Tresselt, ill. by Roger Duvoisin, Lothrop; *Just Me* by Marie Hall Ets, Viking; *Tom Tit Tot* by Evaline Ness, Scribner's

1967   *Sam, Bangs & Moonshine* by Evaline Ness, Holt
Honor Book: *One Wide River to Cross* by Barbara Emberley, ill. by Ed Emberley, Prentice

1968   *Drummer Hoff* by Barbara Emberley, ill. by Ed Emberley, Prentice
Honor Books: *Frederick* by Leo Lionni, Pantheon; *Seashore Story* by Taro Yashima, Viking; *The Emperor and the Kite* by Jane Yolen, ill. by Ed Young, World

1969   *The Fool of the World and the Flying Ship* by Arthur Ransome, ill. by Uri Shulevitz, Farrar
Honor Book: *Why the Sun and the Moon Live in the Sky* by Elphinstone Dayrell, ill. by Blair Lent, Houghton

1970   *Sylvester and the Magic Pebble* by William Steig, Windmill
Honor Books: *Goggles!* by Ezra Jack Keats, Macmillan; *Alexander and the Wind-Up Mouse* by Leo Lionni, Pantheon; *Pop Corn & Ma Goodness* by Edna Mitchell Preston, ill. by Robert Andrew Parker, Viking; *Thy Friend, Obadiah* by Brinton Turkle, Viking; *The Judge* by Harve Zemach, ill. by Margot Zemach, Farrar

1971   *A Story—A Story* by Gail E. Haley, Atheneum
Honor Books: *The Angry Moon* by William Sleator, ill. by Blair Lent, Atlantic/Little; *Frog and Toad Are Friends* by Arnold Lobel, Harper; *In the Night Kitchen* by Maurice Sendak, Harper

1972   *One Fine Day* by Nonny Hogrogian, Macmillan
Honor Books: *If All the Seas Were One Sea* by Janina Domanska, Macmillan; *Moja Means One: Swahili Counting Book* by Muriel Feelings, ill. by Tom Feelings, Dial; *Hildilid's Night* by Cheli Duran Ryan, ill. by Arnold Lobel, Macmillan

1973   *The Funny Little Woman* retold by Arlene Mosel, ill. by Blair Lent, Dutton
Honor Books: *Anansi the Spider* adapted and ill. by Gerald McDermott, Holt; *Hosie's Alphabet* by Hosea, Tobias and Lisa Baskin, ill. by Leonard Baskin, Viking; *Snow-White and the Seven Dwarfs* translated by Randall Jarrell, ill. by Nancy Ekholm Burkert, Farrar; *When Clay Sings* by Byrd Baylor, ill. by Tom Bahti, Scribner's

1974   *Duffy and the Devil* by Harve Zemach, ill. by Margot Zemach, Farrar
Honor Books: *Three Jovial Huntsmen* by Susan Jeffers, Bradbury; *Cathedral: The Story of Its Construction* by David Macaulay, Houghton

1975   *Arrow to the Sun* adapted and ill. by Gerald McDermott, Viking
Honor Book: *Jambo Means Hello* by Muriel Feelings, ill. by Tom Feelings, Dial

1976   *Why Mosquitoes Buzz in People's Ears* retold by Verna Aardema, ill. by Leo and Diane Dillon, Dial
Honor Books: *The Desert Is Theirs* by Byrd Baylor, ill. by Peter Parnall, Scribner's; *Strega Nona* retold and ill. by Tomie de Paola, Prentice

1977   *Ashanti to Zulu: African Traditions* by Margaret Musgrove, ill. by Leo and Diane Dillon, Dial
Honor Books: *The Amazing Bone* by William Steig, Farrar; *The Contest* retold & ill. by Nonny Hogrogian, Greenwillow; *Fish for Supper* by M. B. Goffstein, Dial; *The Golem* by Beverly Brodsky McDermott, Lippincott; *Hawk, I'm Your Brother* by Byrd Baylor, ill. by Peter Parnall, Scribner's

1978   *Noah's Ark* ill. by Peter Spier, Doubleday
Honor Books: *Castle* by David Macaulay, Houghton; *It Could Always Be Worse* retold & ill. by Margot Zemach, Farrar

1979   *The Girl Who Loved Wild Horses* by Paul Goble, Bradbury
Honor Books: *Freight Train* by Donald Crews, Greenwillow; *The Way to Start a Day* by Byrd Baylor, ill. by Peter Parnall, Scribner's

1980   *Ox-Cart Man* by Donald Hall, ill. by Barbara Cooney, Viking
Honor Books: *Ben's Trumpet* by Rachel Isadora, Greenwillow; *The Garden of Abdul Gasazi* by Chris Van Allsburg, Houghton

The Laura Ingalls Wilder Award

This prize, administered by the Association for Library Service to Children, was first awarded in 1954. Since 1960 it has been given every five years to an author or illustrator whose books, published in the United States, have made a substantial and lasting contribution to children's literature.

1954   Laura Ingalls Wilder
1960   Clara Ingram Judson
1965   Ruth Sawyer
1970   E. B. White
1975   Beverly Cleary
1980   Theodor Geisel (Dr. Seuss)

The National Book Award

In March 1969, the National Book Awards included for the first time in its twenty-year history a prize for Children's Literature. The $1000 prize, contributed by the Children's Book Council and administered by the National Book Committee, is presented annually to a juvenile title that a panel of judges considers the most distinguished written by an American citizen and published in the United States in the preceding year.

1969   *Journey from Peppermint Street* by Meindert DeJong, Harper
1970   *A Day of Pleasure: Stories of a Boy Growing Up in Warsaw* by Isaac Bashevis Singer, Farrar
1971   *The Marvelous Misadventures of Sebastian* by Lloyd Alexander, Dutton
1972   *The Slightly Irregular Fire Engine* by Donald Barthelme, Farrar
1973   *The Farthest Shore* by Ursula K. Le Guin, Atheneum
1974   *The Court of the Stone Children* by Eleanor Cameron, Dutton
1975   *M. C. Higgins, The Great* by Virginia Hamilton, Macmillan
1976   *Bert Breen's Barn* by Walter D. Edmonds, Little

International Reading Association Children's Book Award

Given for the first time in 1975, this award is presented annually for a book, published in the preceding year, written by an author "who shows unusual promise in the children's book field." Sponsored by the Institute for Reading Research, the award is administered by the International Reading Association.

1975   *Transport 7-41-R* by T. Degens, Viking
1976   *Dragonwings* by Laurence Yep, Harper
1977   *A String in the Harp* by Nancy Bond, McElderry/Atheneum
1978   *A Summer to Die* by Lois Lowry, Houghton
1979   *Reserved for Mark Anthony Crowder* by Alison Smith, Dutton
1980   *Words by Heart* by Ouida Sebestyen, Atlantic/Little

National Council of Teachers of English Award for Excellence in Poetry for Children

First presented in the fall of 1977 by the National Council of Teachers of English, the award is given to a living American poet in recognition of his or her aggregate work.

1977   David McCord
1978   Aileen Fisher
1979   Karla Kuskin
1980   Myra Cohn Livingston

The Carnegie Medal

The Carnegie Medal, established in 1937, is awarded annually by the British Library Association to an outstanding children's book written in English and first published in the United Kingdom.

1936   *Pigeon Post* by Arthur Ransome, Cape
1937   *The Family from One End Street* by Eve Garnett, Muller
1938   *The Circus Is Coming* by Noel Streatfeild, Dent
1939   *Radium Woman* by Eleanor Doorly, Heinemann
1940   *Visitors from London* by Kitty Barne, Dent
1941   *We Couldn't Leave Dinah* by Mary Treadgold, Penguin
1942   *The Little Grey Men,* by B. B., Eyre & Spottiswoode
1943   No Award
1944   *The Wind on the Moon* by Eric Linklater, Macmillan
1945   No Award
1946   *The Little White Horse* by Elizabeth Goudge, Brockhampton Press
1947   *Collected Stories for Children* by Walter de la Mare, Faber
1948   *Sea Change* by Richard Armstrong, Dent
1949   *The Story of Your Home* by Agnes Allen, Transatlantic
1950   *The Lark on the Wing* by Elfrida Vipont Foulds, Oxford
1951   *The Wool-Pack* by Cynthia Harnett, Methuen
1952   *The Borrowers* by Mary Norton, Dent
1953   *A Valley Grows Up* by Edward Osmond, Oxford
1954   *Knight Crusader* by Ronald Welch, Oxford
1955   *The Little Bookroom* by Eleanor Farjeon, Oxford
1956   *The Last Battle* by C. S. Lewis, Bodley Head
1957   *A Grass Rope* by William Mayne, Oxford
1958   *Tom's Midnight Garden* by Philippa Pearce, Oxford
1959   *The Lantern Bearers* by Rosemary Sutcliff, Oxford
1960   *The Making of Man* by I. W. Cornwall, Phoenix
1961   *A Stranger at Green Knowe* by Lucy Boston, Faber
1962   *The Twelve and the Genii* by Pauline Clarke, Faber
1963   *Time of Trial* by Hester Burton, Oxford
1964   *Nordy Banks* by Sheena Porter, Oxford
1965   *The Grange at High Force* by Philip Turner, Oxford
1966   No Award
1967   *The Owl Service* by Alan Garner, Collins
1968   *The Moon in the Cloud* by Rosemary Harris, Faber
1969   *The Edge of the Cloud* by K. M. Peyton, Oxford
1970   *The God Beneath the Sea* by Leon Garfield and Edward Blishen, Kestrel
1971   *Josh* by Ivan Southall, Angus & Robertson
1972   *Watership Down* by Richard Adams, Rex Collings
1973   *The Ghost of Thomas Kempe* by Penelope Lively, Heinemann
1974   *The Stronghold* by Mollie Hunter, Hamilton

1975 *The Machine-Gunners* by Robert Westall, Macmillan
1976 *Thunder and Lightnings* by Jan Mark, Kestrel
1977 *The Turbulent Term of Tyke Tiler* by Gene Kemp, Faber
1978 *The Exeter Blitz* by David Rees, Hamish Hamilton

The Kate Greenaway Medal

This medal is awarded each year by the British Library Association for the most distinguished work in illustration of a children's book first published in the United Kingdom during the preceding year.

In cases where only one name is given, the book was written and illustrated by the same person.

1956 *Tim All Alone* by Edward Ardizzone, Oxford
1957 *Mrs. Easter and the Storks* by V. H. Drummond, Faber
1958 No Award
1959 *Kashtanka and a Bundle of Ballads* by William Stobbs, Oxford
1960 *Old Winkle and the Seagulls* by Elizabeth Rose, ill. by Gerald Rose, Faber
1961 *Mrs. Cockle's Cat* by Philippa Pearce, ill. by Antony Maitland, Kestrel
1962 *Brian Wildsmith's ABC* by Brian Wildsmith, Oxford
1963 *Borka* by John Burningham, Cape
1964 *Shakespeare's Theatre* by C. W. Hodges, Oxford
1965 *Three Poor Tailors* by Victor Ambrus, Hamilton
1966 *Mother Goose Treasury* by Raymond Briggs, Hamilton
1967 *Charlie, Charlotte & the Golden Canary* by Charles Keeping, Oxford
1968 *Dictionary of Chivalry* by Grant Uden, ill. by Pauline Baynes, Kestrel
1969 *The Quangle-Wangle's Hat* by Edward Lear, ill. by Helen Oxenbury, Heinemann; *Dragon of an Ordinary Family* by Margaret May Mahy, ill. by Helen Oxenbury, Heinemann
1970 *Mr. Gumpy's Outing* by John Burningham, Cape
1971 *The Kingdom Under the Sea* by Jan Pienkowski, Cape
1972 *The Woodcutter's Duck* by Krystyna Turska, Hamilton
1973 *Father Christmas* by Raymond Briggs, Hamilton
1974 *The Wind Blew* by Pat Hutchins, Bodley Head
1975 *Horses in Battle* by Victor Ambrus, Oxford; *Mishka* by Victor Ambrus, Oxford
1976 *The Post Office Cat* by Gail E. Haley, Bodley Head
1977 *Dogger* by Shirley Hughes, Bodley Head
1978 *Each Peach Pear Plum* by Janet and Allan Ahlberg, Kestrel

The Canadian Library Awards

This award, first presented in June 1947, was established by the Canadian Library Association. It is given annually to a children's book of outstanding literary merit, written by a Canadian citizen. Since 1954 a similar medal has also been awarded yearly to an outstanding children's book published in French.

1947 *Starbuck Valley Winter* by Roderick Haig-Brown, Collins
1948 *Kristli's Trees* by Mabel Dunham, Hale
1949 No Award
1950 *Franklin of the Arctic* by Richard S. Lambert, McClelland & Stewart
1951 No Award

1952 *The Sun Horse* by Catherine Anthony Clark, Macmillan of Canada
1953 No Award
1954 No English Award
Mgr. de Laval by Emile S. J. Gervais, Comité des Fondateurs de l'Eglise Canadienne
1955 No Awards
1956 *Train for Tiger Lily* by Louise Riley, Macmillan of Canada
No French Award
1957 *Glooskap's Country* by Cyrus Macmillan, Oxford
No French Award
1958 *Lost in the Barrens* by Farley Mowat, Little
Le Chevalier du Roi by Béatrice Clément, Les Editions de l'Atelier
1959 *The Dangerous Cove* by John F. Hayes, Copp Clark
Un Drôle de Petit Cheval by Hélène Flamme, Editions Lémèac
1960 *The Golden Phoenix* by Marius Barbeau and Michael Hornyansky, Walck
L'Eté Enchanté by Paule Daveluy, Les Editions de l'Atelier
1961 *The St. Lawrence* by William Toye, Oxford
Plantes Vagabondes by Marcelle Gauvreau, Centre de Psychologie et de Pédagogie
1962 No English Award
Les Iles du Roi Maha Maha II by Claude Aubry, Les Editions du Pélican
1963 *The Incredible Journey* by Sheila Burnford, Little
Drôle d'Automne by Paule Daveluy, Les Editions du Pélican
1964 *The Whale People* by Roderick Haig-Brown, William Collins of Canada
Feerie by Cécile Chabot, Librairie Beauchemin Ltée.
1965 *Tales of Nanabozho* by Dorothy Reid, Oxford
Le Loup de Noël by Claude Aubry, Centre de Psychologie de Montréal
1966 *Tikta'Liktak* by James Houston, Kestrel
Le Chêne des Tempêtes by Andrée Maillet-Hobden, Fides
The Double Knights by James McNeal, Walck
Le Wapiti by Monique Corriveau, Jeunesse
1967 *Raven's Cry* by Christie Harris, McClelland & Stewart
No French Award
1968 *The White Archer* by James Houston, Kestrel
Légendes Indiennes du Canada by Claude Mélancon, Editions du Jour
1969 *And Tomorrow the Stars* by Kay Hill, Dodd
No French Award
1970 *Sally Go Round the Sun* by Edith Fowke, McClelland & Stewart
Le Merveilleuse Histoire de la Naissance by Lionel Gendron, Les Editions de l'Homme
1971 *Cartier Discovers the St. Lawrence* by William Toye, Oxford University
La Surprise de Dame Chenille by Henriette Major, Centre de Psychologie de Montréal
1972 *Mary of Mile 18* by Ann Blades, Tundra
No French Award
1973 *The Marrow of the World* by Ruth Nichols, Macmillan of Canada
Le Petit Sapin Qui A Poussé Sur Une Étoile by Simone Bussières, Presses Laurentiennes
1974 *The Miraculous Hind* by Elizabeth Cleaver, Holt of Canada
No French Award
1975 *Alligator Pie* by Dennis Lee, Macmillan of Canada
No French Award

1976 *Jacob Two-Two Meets the Hooded Fang* by Mordecai Richler, Knopf
No French Award

1977 *Mouse Woman and the Vanished Princesses* by Christie Harris, McClelland & Stewart
No French Award

1978 *Garbage Delight* by Dennis Lee, Macmillan
No French Award

1979 *Hold Fast* by Kevin Major, Clarke, Irwin
No French Award

The Canadian Library Association has awarded the Amelia Frances Howard-Gibbon Medal annually since 1971 for outstanding illustrations in a children's book published in Canada. The illustrator must be a native or resident of Canada.

1971 *The Wind Has Wings*, ed. by Mary Alice Downie and Barbara Robertson, ill. by Elizabeth Cleaver, Oxford

1972 *A Child in Prison Camp* by Shizuye Takashima, Tundra

1973 *Au Dela du Soleil / Beyond the Sun* by Jacques de Roussan, Tundra

1974 *A Prairie Boy's Winter* by William Kurelek, Tundra

1975 *The Sleighs of My Childhood / Les Traineaux de Mon Enfance* by Carlos Italiano, Tundra

1976 *A Prairie Boy's Summer* by William Kurelek, Tundra

1977 *Down by Jim Long's Stage: Rhymes for Children and Young Fish* by Al Pittman, ill. by Pam Hall, Breakwater

1978 *The Loon's Necklace* by William Toye, ill. by Elizabeth Cleaver, Oxford

1979 *A Salmon for Simon* by Betty Waterton, ill. by Ann Blades, Douglas & McIntyre

The Hans Christian Andersen Award

This award was established in 1956 by the International Board on Books for Young People and is given every two years to one living author who, by his or her complete work, has made an important international contribution to children's literature. Since 1966 an artist's medal has also been given. Each national section of the International Board proposes one author and one illustrator as nominees and the final choice is made by a committee of five, each from a different country.

1956   Eleanor Farjeon (Great Britain)
1958   Astrid Lindgren (Sweden)
1960   Erich Kästner (Germany)
1962   Meindert DeJong (U.S.A.)
1964   René Guillot (France)
1966   Author: Tove Jansson (Finland)
       Illustrator: Alois Carigiet (Switzerland)
1968   Authors: James Krüss (Germany)
              Jose Maria Sanchez-Silva (Spain)
       Illustrator: Jiri Trnka (Czechoslovakia)
1970   Author: Gianni Rodari (Italy)
       Illustrator: Maurice Sendak (U.S.A.)
1972   Author: Scott O'Dell (U.S.A.)
       Illustrator: Ib Spang Olsen (Denmark)
1974   Author: Maria Gripe (Sweden)
       Illustrator: Farshid Mesghali (Iran)
1976   Author: Cecil Bødker (Denmark)
       Illustrator: Tatjana Mawrina (U.S.S.R.)
1978   Author: Paula Fox (U.S.A.)
       Illustrator: Svend Otto S. (Denmark)
1980   Author: Bohumil Riha (Czechoslovakia)
       Illustrator: Suekichi Akaba (Japan)

Appendix E: Pronunciation Guide

Symbols used in the pronunciation are as follows: a as in *hat;* ā as in *age;* ã as in *care;* ä as in *father;* e as in *let;* ē as in *see;* ėr as in *term;* i as in *pin;* ī as in *five;* o as in *hot;* ō as in *go;* ô as in *order, all;* oi as in *oil;* ou as in *house;* th as in *thin;* ŧ𝐡 as in *then;* u as in *cup;* u̇ as in *full;* ü as in *rule;* ū as in *use;* zh as in *measure;* ə as in the unaccented syllables of *about, taken, pencil, lemon, circus;* н as in the German *ach;* N as in the French *bon* (not pronounced, but shows that the vowel before it is nasal); œ as in the French *peu* and the German *könig* (pronounced by speaking ā with the lips rounded as for ō); Y as in the French *du* (pronounced by speaking ē with the lips rounded as for ü). All other symbols represent the consonant sounds that they commonly stand for in English spelling.

Aardema är′de mä
Abrashkin a brash′kin
Adoff ā′dof
Afanasiev ä fä nä′syif
Agle ā′gùl
Agra ä′grə
Aiken-drum ā kən drum
Aldis ôl′dis
Aleichem, Sholem ə lā′Həm, shō′ləm
Aliki ä lē′kī
Allingham al′ing əm
Almedingen al′mə ding′ən
Ambrus ôm′brùsh
Analdas ə näl′dəs
Anansi ə nan′si
Anckarsvärd äng′käs verd
Ankhsenpaaten anн′sen pät′en
Arawn ä ron′
Ardizzone är di zō′ni
Arora ə ro′rə
Arrietty är i e′tē
Artzybasheff är tsi ba′shif
Asbjörnsen äs′byėrn sen
Asimov as′im ov
Aucassin ō ka saN′
Averill ā′və ril
Ayars ārz
Baba Yaga bä′bə yä′gä
Babar bä′bär
Bacmeister bok′mī ster
Bandai ban dīj
Banneker ban′nə kėr
Barbauld bär′bôld
Barchilon, Jacques bär shē yoN′, zhäk
Basho bä shō

Baudouy, Michel-Aimé bô dü ē′, mē-shel-e mā′
Baumann bou′män
Behn bän
Beim bīm
Benary-Isbert, Margot ben är′ē-is′bért, mär′gō
Benét be nā′
Benezet ben′ ə zet′
Beowulf bā′ə wùlf
Berquin, Armand bėr kaN′, ar mäN′
Bertol bär′tôl
Beskow bes′kō
Bethune, Mary McLeod bə thūn′, mak loud′
Bevis bē′vis
Bewick bū′ik
Bidpai bid′pī
Binnorie bin′ə rē/bin′ô rē
Bishop, Claire Huchet œ shä′
Blegvad bleg′vad
Blos blōs
Blough blou
Bogosian bô gōz′yun
Bolognese bō lō nä′zē
Bontemps, Arna bôN tôN′, är′nə
Brinsmead, Hesba Fay hez′bə
Bryson brī′sən
Bubo bū′bō
Budulinek bu dū′lin ek
Bulla bùl′ə
Burchard bœr′ chärd
Cabeza de Vaca kä bā′thä dā vä′kä
Carigiet, Alois cä rē zhē ā′, al wä′
Caudill kô′dl
Cavanna kə van′ə
Cayuse kī ūs′
Chaga chä′gä
Chakoh chä′kō
Chincoteague ching′kə tēg
Christiansen, Reider kris′tyän sən, rēd ər
Chukovsky, Kornei chu kôf′ skē, kôr nā′
Chute, Marchette chüt, mär shet′
Chwast kwäst
Ciardi chär′dē
Cinderlad, Per, Paal, Espen sin′dər-läd, pär, pôl, es′pən
Coblentz kō′blents
Collodi kōl lô′dē
Colman, Hila hī′lä
Colum, Padraic kol′um, pä′drig
Comenius kə mē′ni us
Contes de Ma Mère l'Oye kôNt də mä mär lwä
Coombs kümz

Cormier kôr′ myä
Cowper kü′pèr
Credle crā′dəl
Cruikshank krùk′shangk
Cuchulain kü kü′lin
Dahl, Roald däl, rō′äl
Dalgliesh däl glēsh
D'Amelio da mēl′ē yō
D'Armancour där môN kür′
Dasent dā′sənt
d'Aulaire dō lär′
d'Aulnoy dōl nwä′
De Angeli də an′jel ē
De Beaumont, Madame Le Prince də bō môN′, ma dam′lə praNs′
De Brunhoff, Jean də brün′ôf, zhôN
De Gasztold, Carmen Bernos də gaz′tōl, bér′nōs
De Genlis, Madame də zhôN lē′, ma dam′
DeJong, Meindert də yung′, mīn′dèrt
De la Mare də la mär′
Demetrius of Phalerum də mē′tri us, fu lēr′əm
De Pareja dā pə rä′hä
De Regniers də rän′yā
DeRoin də roin′
Derleth dėr′leth
De Treviño dā trə vē′nyō
Deucher dü shä′
Deutsch, Babette doich, bab et′
Ditlabeng dit′lə beng
Dobry dō′brē
Dodge, Mary Mapes māps
Domanska, Janina dô män′skä, yä-nē′nä
Doob düb
Douty dü′tē
Du Bois, William Pène dy bwä, pen
Duvoisin dy vwä zaN′
Eckenstein, Lina ek′en stīn, lē′nä
Edda ed′ə
Eichenberg ī′ken bėrg
Engdahl əng′dôl
Epaminondas i pam i non′dəs
Farjeon fär′jun
Farquharson fär′kwėr sən
Feagles fē′gləs
Fenians fē ni ənz
Fflewddur Fflam flü′dœr flam
Figgis fig′is
Fiorello fē ō rel′ō
Fjeld fē el/fyel
Forberg, Ati ä′tē
Forten fôr′tən
Franchere frän′shär
Frascino frə shē′nō

639

Frasconi, Antonio frans kō'nē, än-tō'nyō
Frolov, Vadim frō'lof, vädim
Fyleman fīl'man
Gaer gär
Gaetano gä'ä tä nō
Gág gäg
Galdone gal dōn'
Galland, Antoine gə län', än twōn'
Gaudenzia gou den'tsya
Gautama Buddha gô'tə mə bú'də
Geisel gī'z'l
Gengi gən'jē
Gerda ger tə
Gidal gi dal'
Gilgamesh gil'gə mesh
Glubok glü'bok
Gobhai gō bī
Goff gof
Gottschalk, Fruma gät'shəlk, frü'mə
Goudey gou'dē
Gramatky gra mat'kē
Gripe grē̆pu
Gudbrand gúd'bränd
Guillot, René gē yō, rú nā'
Guion gī'ôn
Guiterman git'ér mən
Gurgi gœr'jē
Gwydion gwi'dē on
Gylfi gyl'fə
Haas häs
Hader hä'dér
Haida hī'du
Hakon hô'kən
Hallard Hal'lärd
Hanff hänf
Haugaard hou'gärd
Hautzig hout'zig
Hazard a zär'
Hazeltine häz'əl tīn'
Heinlein hīn'līn
Hepzibah hep'zi bah
Hesiod hē̆'si od
Heumann hoi'män
Heyerdahl, Thor hä'ér däl, túr
Heyward, Du Bose dú bōz'
Hidalgo y Costilla ēd häl'go ē kōs-te'yä
Hieatt hi'at
Hitopadesa hi tō pa dā'sha
Hoban hō'ban
Hofsinde hof'sin də
Hogrogian, Nonny hō grō'gē an, no'nē
Hokusai hō kú sī
Homily hom'i lē
Hosford hôs'fərd
Hyndman hīnd'man
Ignatow ig nä'tō
Ishi ē shē
Ish-Kishor, Sulamith ish'ki shor', su-lam'ith
Issa is'ə
Jahdu jä'dū
Jancsi yan'sē
Jansson, Tove yän'sən, tō'vä

Janosh yä'nōsh
Jarrell jar'rel
Jataka jä'tä kə
Jean-Claude zhôn klōd
Jeanne-Marie zhan'mä rē'
Jenness jen es'
Josian jō sī'ən
Kaa kä
Kahl käl
Karana kä rä'nä
Kästner, Erich kest'nər, ä'rik
Katia kä'tyə
Kaula kô lu
Kavaler ka'vúl ér
Kävik kä'vik
Kenofer ken'o fér
Kim Van Kieu kēm vən kyū
Kinder und Hausmärchen kin'dér únd hous'mär'hən
Kjelgaard kel'gärd
Konigsburg kō'nigs bérg
Krakatoa krak ə tō'ə
Kroeber krō'bər
Krush krush
Krylov kril ôf'
Kumin kew'min
Kuskin kus'kin
La Fontaine, Jean de lä fon ten', zhôn də
La Gallienne lə gal'yən
Lakshmi lok'shmē
Lalu la lü
Latham lä'thum
Lathrop lä'thrəp
Ledoux lə dy'
Le Guin le gwin'
Le Hibou et la Poussiquette lē bü' ä lä pü si ket'
Lexau lex ô
Liam lē'am
Liddell lid'əl
Liers lirs
Lindgren, Astrid lind grən, äs'trid
Lionni lē ō'nē
Lipkind lip'kind
Lippiza lip'it za
Llyn-Y-Fan hlin'ə van'
Lobel lō bel'
Lorenzini lô ren tsē'nē
Lueders lwē'dérs
Lurs lürz
McKuen mak kū'ən
Mafatu ma fa tu
Mahabharata mə hä'bä'rə tə
Mali mä'lē
Manolo män'ō lō
Mara mä rə
Mari, Iela and Enzo mä'rē, ī' la, en zō
Märchen mär'hən
Mary-Rousselière, Guy mä rē-rü se-li ä', gē
Massee ma'sē
Massignon mas ē nyôn'
Matthiesen math'i sən
Maui mou' ē
Maurois, André mô'rwä, än drä'

Mayne män
Megrimum me'grə məm
Mei Li mä lē
Melendy mə lən' dē
Miers mirz
Mikolaycak mīk ô lā' chək
Miklagard mik'la gärd
Milne miln
Minarik min'ə rik
Mirsky, Reba Paeff mér'skē, rē'bä paf
Mizamura, Kazue mi'zä mü rä, kä-zü'ä
Moe, Jörgen mō ə, yér'gən
Momolu mo'mō lü
Monjo mon'jō
Montresor, Beni mōn'trə sôr, bä'nē
Monvel, Boutet de mōn vel', bü tä' də
Moonta mün'tə
Mordvinoff mord'vin of
Mosel mō zəl'
Moskof mos'kof
Mowgli mou'glē
Mulready múl'red ē
Munari, Bruno mü nä'rē, brü'nō
Navarra na va'ra
Nefertiti ne fér tē'ti
Nibelungs/Niblungs nē'bə lüngz/nē'blüngz
Nic Leodhas, Sorche nic ly ōs', sôr'ä
Nicolette nē kô let'
Noguchi, Hideyo no gu'che, hē de yo
Nootka nút'kə
Okada Rokuo ō ka da, rō kú ō
Olatunji, Michael Babatunde o lä tün'jē, bä bä tün'dē
Orgel or'gel
Orisha ôr ē'sha
Ormondroyd ôr mond roid
Orphelines ôr fel ēnz'
Padre Porko pä'thre pôrk'ō
Palazzo pa lat'zō
Panchatantra pän chə tän'trə
Pandu pän'dü
Pantaloni pan tə lō'nē
Papashvily pa pash vē lē
Paracelsus par ə sel'səs
Pecos pā kəs
Pegeen pe gēn'
Pelle pel'lə
Perrault pe rō'
Petrides, Heidrun pə trē'dēz, hīd'drun
Petry pē'tri
Pettit pe tē'
Piatti, Celestino pyät'tē, chä läs tē'nō
Pibroch of Donnel Dhu pē'broh, don'nel dü
Picard, Barbara Leonie pi'kärd, lä'ō nē
Pincus pin'kəs
Planudes plə nü'dēz
Plasencia plä sen'thyä
Plouhinec plü'i nek
Podkayne pod kān
Politi pō lē'tē
Prelutsky pre lut'skē
Prishvin, Mikhail prēsh'vin, mē hä ēl'
Procyon prō'si on

Prydain pri dān′
Pulga púl′gä
Pwyll and Pyrderi pü′il, pru dā′rē
Quarles kwôrlz
Rabe rāb
Raman rä′mən
Ramayana rä mä′yə nə
Ranke räng′ke
Rasmussen, Knud räs′mus ən, nùd
Ravielli rav ē el′li
Repplier rep′lēr
Rey rā
Ripopet-Barabas rē′pō pā-bä′rä bä
Rocca, Guido rôk′kō, gwē dō
Roethke ret′kē
Rojankovsky rō jan kôf′skē
Rossetti rō set′ē
Rugh rü
Rukeyser rü′kī zér
Saba sä′bä
Sadko säd′kô
Saemund sā′múnd
Saint Exupéry, Antoine de
   san tāg zy pā rē, än twän′də
Sasek, Miroslav sä′sek, mī′rō släv
Savigny säv′in yē
Scheele shē′lē
Schoenherr shún′här
Schweitzer shvī′tsər
Seignobosc, Françoise sāngn′yō bosk,
   frän swäz′
Sellew se′lü
Selsam sel′səm
Sendak sen′dak
Seredy shär′ə dē
Serraillier sə räl′yā
Seuss süs
Shawneen shä nēn′
Shecter shek′tér
Sheftu shef′tü
Shimin, Symeon shi′min, sim′ē un
Shogomoc shō gō môk
Showalter shō′wäl tér
Shulevitz, Uri shü′lə vitz, ü′rē

Sidjakov sij′ə kof
Sigurdson si′gûth son
Singer, Isaac Bashevis bə shä′vis
Sita sē′tä
Slobodkin slō bod′kin
Slote slōt
Smolicheck smol′i chek
Snegourka snye gür′kä
Sojo, Toba sō jō, to bä
Sokol sō′kol
Sonneborn son′ne born
Soupault sü pō′
Southall south′ôl
Spier spēr
Spyri, Johanna shpē′rē, yō hän′ä
Stahl stäl
Steegmuller steg mul′ər
Steig stīg
Stolz stōlts
Strachey strä′chi
Streatfeild, Noel stret′feld, nō′əl
Sture-Vasa stür-vä sä
Sturluson, Snorri stür′le sôn, snôr′ā
Suba sü′bə
Sundiata sün dē ä′tä
Syme sīm
Tagore, Rabindranath tä′gōr, rä
   bēn′drä nät′
Taliesin tal ē ā′zin
Taran ta′ran
Tashjian täs jun
Tatsinda tat sin′dä
Tenniel ten′yel
Ter Haar, Jaap tér här, yop
Terzian ter′zian
Thorne-Thomsen, Gudrun thôrn-
   tom′sen, gü′drun
Thorvall, Kerstin tùr′väl, char′stin
Tistou tē stü′
Tituba ti′tū bä
Tlingit tling′git
Tolkien tōl′ken
Treece trēs
Tresselt tre′selt

Truro trúr′ō
Tunis tū′nis
Turska, Krystyna turs′kä, kris tē′na
Tutankhaten tüt änн ä′tən
Uchida, Yoshiko ü chē dä, yō shē kō
Udry ū′dri
Ullman úl′män
Undset, Sigrid ūn′set, si′grid
Ungerer, Tomi un′gœ rœr
Unnerstad un′nér stadt
Ushinsky ù shin′skē
Van Iterson, Siny vän ē′ter sôn, sē nē
Vasilisa va syē′le sa
Vedge vej
Viehmann vē′män
Viollet vē ō let′
Vivier viv ē ā′
Volsung vol′súng
Vulpes vul′pēz
Watie wä′tē
Wayah wā ä
Weisgard wīs′gärd
Weiss wīs
Whippety Stourie wip′ə tē stür′ē/
   stür′ē
Whuppie wúp′ē
Wibberley wi′bér lē
Wier wēr
Wiese vē′zə
Wild, Dortchen vilt, dôrt′shən
Wodehouse wúd′hous
Wojciechowska, Maia woi je hov′-
   ska, mä′ē ä
Wuorio, Eva-Lis wür yō, ā vä-lēs
Yashima, Taro yä′shi ma, tä′rō
Yonge yung
Yonie Wondernose yō nē wun′dər-
   nōz
Yorubaland yôr u′ba land
Yulya yü lyä
Zamani zä mä nē
Zemach zē′mak
Zhenya zhä′nyə
Zolotow zol′ə tou

Subject Index

Author, Illustrator, Title Index